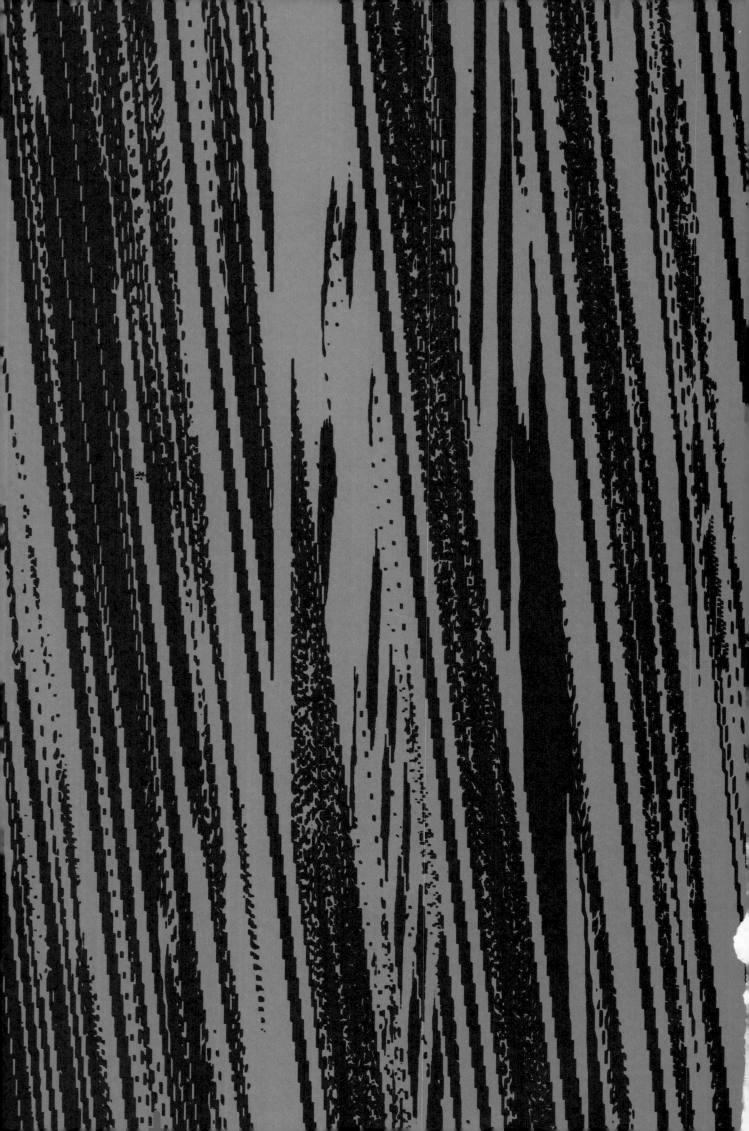

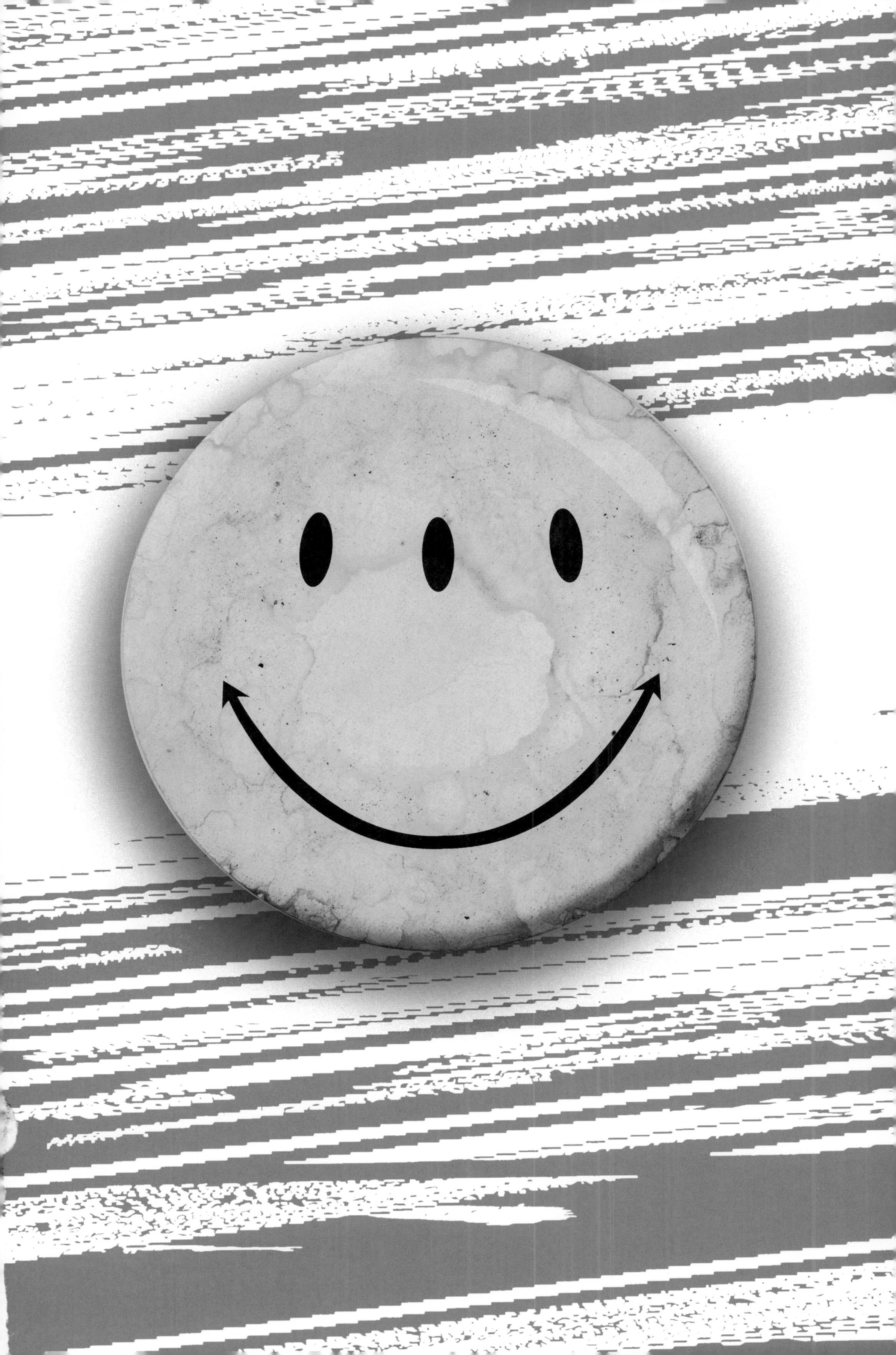

# ABSO
# TRANSMET

Written by Warren Ellis
Art by Darick Robert

with Keith Aiken  Jerome K. Moore  Kim
Coloring by Nathan Eyring  Lettering by
Slipcase Art by Darick Robertson and
Original Series Cover Art by Geof Darrow  Frank
TRANSMETROPOLITAN created by

# LUTE
# ROPOLITAN

son  Rodney Ramos

DeMulder  Ray Kryssing  Dick Giordano

Clem Robins

Nathan Eyring  Case Art by Geof Darrow

Quitely  Darick Robertson  Jae Lee  Dave Gibbons

Warren Ellis and Darick Robertson

# TRANSMETROPOLITAN

Stuart Moore  Axel Alonso  Shelly Roeberg........................................Editors – Original Series
Julie Rottenberg........................................Associate Editor – Original Series
Cliff Chiang  Jennifer Lee........................................Assistant Editors – Original Series
Scott Nybakken ........................................Editor
Robbin Brosterman........................................Design Director – Books
Louis Prandi........................................Publication Design

Shelly Bond........................................Executive Editor – Vertigo
Hank Kanalz........................................Senior VP – Vertigo & Integrated Publishing

Diane Nelson........................................President
Dan DiDio and Jim Lee........................................Co-Publishers
Geoff Johns........................................Chief Creative Officer
Amit Desai........................................Senior VP – Marketing & Franchise Management
Amy Genkins........................................Senior VP – Business & Legal Affairs
Nairi Gardiner........................................Senior VP – Finance
Jeff Boison........................................VP – Publishing Planning
Mark Chiarello........................................VP – Art Direction & Design
John Cunningham........................................VP – Marketing
Terri Cunningham........................................VP – Editorial Administration
Larry Ganem........................................VP – Talent Relations & Services
Alison Gill........................................Senior VP – Manufacturing & Operations
Jay Kogan........................................VP – Business & Legal Affairs, Publishing
Jack Mahan........................................VP – Business Affairs, Talent
Nick Napolitano........................................VP – Manufacturing Administration
Sue Pohja........................................VP – Book Sales
Fred Ruiz........................................VP – Manufacturing Operations
Courtney Simmons........................................Senior VP – Publicity
Bob Wayne........................................Senior VP – Sales

**ABSOLUTE TRANSMETROPOLITAN VOLUME ONE**

Published by DC Comics. Compilation Copyright © 2015 Warren Ellis and Darick Robertson. All Rights Reserved. Originally published in single magazine form in TRANSMETROPOLITAN 1-18, VERTIGO: WINTER'S EDGE 2, and TRANSMETROPOLITAN: I HATE IT HERE. Copyright © 1997, 1998, 1999, 2000 Warren Ellis and Darick Robertson. All Rights Reserved. All characters, their distinctive likenesses and related elements featured in this publication are trademarks of Warren Ellis and Darick Robertson. VERTIGO is a trademark of DC Comics. The stories, characters and incidents featured in this publication are entirely fictional. DC Comics does not read or accept unsolicited submissions of ideas, stories or artwork.

DC Comics
1700 Broadway, New York, NY 10019
A Warner Bros. Entertainment Company.
Printed by OGI, China. 5/18/15.
First Printing.
ISBN: 978-1-4012-5430-8.

Library of Congress Cataloging-in-Publication Data

Ellis, Warren, author.
  Absolute Transmetropolitan / Warren Ellis, Darick Robertson, Rodney Ramos.
    volumes cm
  Originally published in single magazine form in TRANSMETROPOLITAN 1-21
  ISBN 978-1-4012-5430-8 (v. 1 : hardback) 1.  Graphic novels. I. Robertson, Darick, illustrator. II. Ramos, Rodney illustrator. III. Title.
  PN6728.T68E36 2015
  741.5'973–dc23
                    2014049020

# TABLE OF CONTENTS (CONTINUED ON PAGE 5)

# TABLE OF CONTENTS (CONTINUED)

# UP A GODDAMN MOUNTAIN:
## TRANSMETROPOLITAN and the Future

Take that Moto out of your ear, unplug the router, and put down that Kindle Fire. We're going back to 1997 – a time before the iPad, before the Galaxy Note, before even the Handspring Treo. The very first Palm Pilots had just crawled up onto land, and the iMac was still a year off, a mere glimmer on the technological horizon.

You, with the Google Glasses: Lose 'em. *Now.*

In 1997 we had email, but most of our friends didn't. Nobody used cell phones except Scully, Mulder, and the girls from *Clueless*. The Web? Five garish sites that loaded ver-r-r-r-ry slowly. The fax machine was still the tool of choice for procrastinating comic artists, and I ran a weekly Vertigo chat on AOL that typically attracted fewer than a dozen people

– including, often, a young writer named Warren Ellis.

Comics were different too, back in the waning years of the 20th century. You couldn't buy them digitally, of course, and trade paperbacks, as a category, were less than a decade old. Most monthly series, even from adult-oriented imprints like Vertigo, were collected sporadically, long after publication of the monthly issues.

And the literary world still viewed comics along a spectrum from indifference to hostility. Sure, writers like Warren, Grant Morrison, and Neil Gaiman were on the radar of the science fiction community. But they were regarded with tolerant amusement, the way you might smile at a little brother who's decided to pursue performance art as a career. These guys were quirky and

interesting, yes; but they weren't *accepted* yet.

One reason: There are a lot of science fiction comics today – most notably the breakout hit *Saga* – but in 1997, there weren't. There were a lot of comics with science fiction *elements* in them, but very few comics had the rigor, the world building, the sense of wonder of the best science fiction.

Flash back a further 13 years to 1984, when a paperback called *Neuromancer* turned the science fiction prose community upside-down. William Gibson's novel defined an entire new subgenre called cyberpunk, characterized by urban grit, punk pro- tagonists, and a postmodern overload of imagery. Writers like Bruce Sterling, Pat Cadigan, Rudy Rucker, Richard

Kadrey, and others quickly followed suit, wrenching science fiction away from its twin paths of can-do engineering fables and literary experimentation into a whole new realm.

TRANSMETROPOLITAN was the first series to take the settings and sensibility of cyberpunk and weld them onto the newfound freedom of long-form creator-owned comics – like a mirrorshaded hacker in an abandoned building, jury-rigging a plug to connect his brain to cyberspace.

In TRANSMET, Warren explores the technology of the (then-)near-future by showing how ordinary people might adapt it to their own needs. Thus we have Makers, food- and goods-synthesizers fueled by "base blocks" bought by the wealthy, while the poor must scrounge garbage from the streets for raw material. The information-rich society that surrounds Spider is a powerful research tool, but it's only as good as the maniac using it.

And that maniac, that character, is the core of this book. Spider Jerusalem, a brilliant journalist with a massive problem hardwired into him: He hates the City, with its filth and injustice and constant sensory overload. But outside its walls, he cannot write.

Spider is violent, dangerous, often hostile to his friends. Yet he's also caring at unexpected moments. He's capable of showing kindness to a stray mutant cat, and generosity to a promising coworker. And then, in the next second, he's inducing bowel prolapse in the President, or screaming *"FUCKERS FUCKERS DIE FUCKPIGS DIE FUCKING BASTARDS!"* while mowing down assassins at his door.

Spider's voice is a constant presence in these stories, like the overlapping rhythms of the City itself. We're assaulted by his opinions, his columns, his drug-fueled rants to his "filthy assistants." From one early column: *"I can see a blatantly unarmed Transient man with half his face*

*hanging off, and three cops working him over anyway. One of them is groping his own erection."*

Spider spares no one, least of all his own audience. *"You must like it when people in authority they never earned lie to you."* And while he views himself as a champion of the powerless, he doesn't romanticize them: *"There's one hole in every revolution, large or small. And it's one word long – people."* All this serves his much-repeated mantra: *"The truth. No matter what."*

The first story in this volume, the three-part "Back on the Street," is a masterpiece of timing, character, and atmosphere. And that ending! After forcing the police to back down from a deliberately incited riot and securing his own victorious return to public life, Spider is ambushed from an unmarked car and savagely beaten. "You fuck with us ever again," the helmeted assailants warn him, "you go home in a bag." Darick Robertson's brilliant art oscillates here from sharp cruelty to a blurred, surreal impression of a fist, the only object present at that moment in Spider's world.

And here's the kicker: The beating doesn't intimidate Spider – it emboldens him. He knows now that he can provoke a reaction from the powerful, can sting the City's institutions and make them lash back. This isn't the end of Spider's defiance, his primal scream, his rage against an all-too-human machine. It's the beginning.

*[An aside – TRANSMET originally launched as part of the Helix line, a science fiction imprint that DC Comics and I started with more good intentions than good sense. The story of Helix is a saga in itself, including the heart-stopping week when I had to change the name from the original "Matrix" because of, ironically, a cyberpunk-inspired film in the works at Warner Bros. The point is: When Helix folded, TRANSMET was the sole title to transition over to the Vertigo imprint without missing a beat. Which shows that this comic, like Spider himself, is a survivor.]*

Another key element of TRANSMET is its treatment of social injustice, explored through the book's science fiction trappings. The Transients, humans who have infused their bodies with alien DNA, are part body-mod fetishists, part transgender activists. The twin plights of the homeless and the aged are explored through the Revivals, cryogenically frozen people from an earlier time, rebuilt and dumped out on the street in new bodies.

TRANSMET is also, in a very central way, about the act of writing. Warren walks us through Spider's return to his craft, dipping into his thoughts as he composes his first new column (from a strip club overlooking a riot). *"There's going to be Transient blood all over this place,"* he writes. *"And you know something? It's not their fault."* Then he pauses, chides himself: *"Too slow, too careful. The typewriter's a gun. Show 'em some steel."*

None of this would work, would carry the necessary weight, without Darick's flawless storytelling, his incredible eye for detail, and his gift for conveying human emotion. His cityscapes are packed to bursting with futuristic buildings and distinct characters. His faces draw you *into* the page, their expressions ranging from subtle emotion to hysterical caricature, mirroring Spider's mood swings. The Smiler is terrifying from his first appearance. Spider's assistants, Channon and Yelena, serve to ground the proceedings, providing a much-needed brake on their boss' amphetamine-paced mania.

Darick lived in Italy while working on some of these stories, and I remember him drawing on the local architecture to give the City an international feel. The downloading facility in "Boyfriend Is a Virus" is one example, as are the wildly disparate reservations of "Wild in the Country." Darick also takes every opportunity to push the limits of comics-page layout, as in the crazed-collage newspaper headlines on view in "Year of the Bastard."

As with many long-running serial comics, TRANSMET starts out very dense, introducing characters and throwing out new concepts with every issue. Then, gradually, it slows down, inviting the reader into a more deeply immersive experience. By the end of this volume, we feel less like a newly thawed Revival and more like a fellow traveler in Spider Jerusalem's City. We're acclimating, just as he is.

The title also takes a strong turn for the political. At the start of "Year of the Bastard" — issue #13, beginning the second year of the series — Spider is on call to cover a major election campaign, the likes of which had once made him a star. But Spider himself has changed. He's taking too many pills, dodging his editor's calls. Most disturbing of all, he's avoiding his work. He isn't writing.

## "Too slow, too careful. The typewriter's a gun. Show 'em some steel."

*"Two days in the whirlwind have left me shipwrecked and abandoned. Even the stuff I've been shooting in order to, Holmes-like, keep my interest in the world alive is failing me now. I've played the game like a good little whore, snarled and cursed on cue, done the work and banged out the columns."*

Perhaps the most acclaimed story in this volume is "Another Cold Morning." It uses science fiction tropes in the best way possible, as a lens through which to examine timeless social problems. And it does this through Spider's confident, compassionate voice — while hehimself barely appears on-panel.

Spider's camera-glasses may raise a shrug in modern readers; his use of landlines is an occasional anachronism. The giant wallscreen TV in his apartment doesn't look very futuristic anymore. Makers

are on the market as I write this, and soon they'll be more affordable and more useful. Writers like Alan Moore and Warren himself are now full-fledged members of the larger literary community.

But TRANSMET still speaks to us. And that's because the core of it — the character of Spider Jerusalem and his primal outrage against social injustice — remains as relevant today as it was in 1997. And it'll continue to endure, even when we're all swapping holoclips through our brain implants and uploading our consciousness to the Cloud. (Hopefully with stronger passwords.)

Another thing that hasn't changed is the implacable power of authority. In that regard, Spider is a true wish-fulfillment character — as much so as Superman, Iron Man, or the Hulk. He challenges the entrenched power structures, armed with no more than a laptop and, well, a few guns. He takes his beatings, and sometimes he causes more suffering than he prevents. But once in a while, maybe one time in four, he wins.

So climb down off the mountain and smell the City air. It's Spider's world, and yours, and mine too. If you give yourself over to it, if you let its grisly life flow into and through you, I think you'll find it a surprisingly human place to be. Spider's a man of his time, and of 1997, and of any time in which the people need a voice they can trust.

Though today, he probably wouldn't smoke so much.

**– Stuart Moore**
Whorehopper (reformed)
October 2014

*Stuart Moore's recent writing includes the Image Comics series EGOs and Disney's The Zodiac Legacy (with Stan Lee). As a comics editor, Moore served as one of the founders of the Vertigo imprint, where his titles included PREACHER, THE INVISIBLES, and TRANSMETROPOLITAN.*

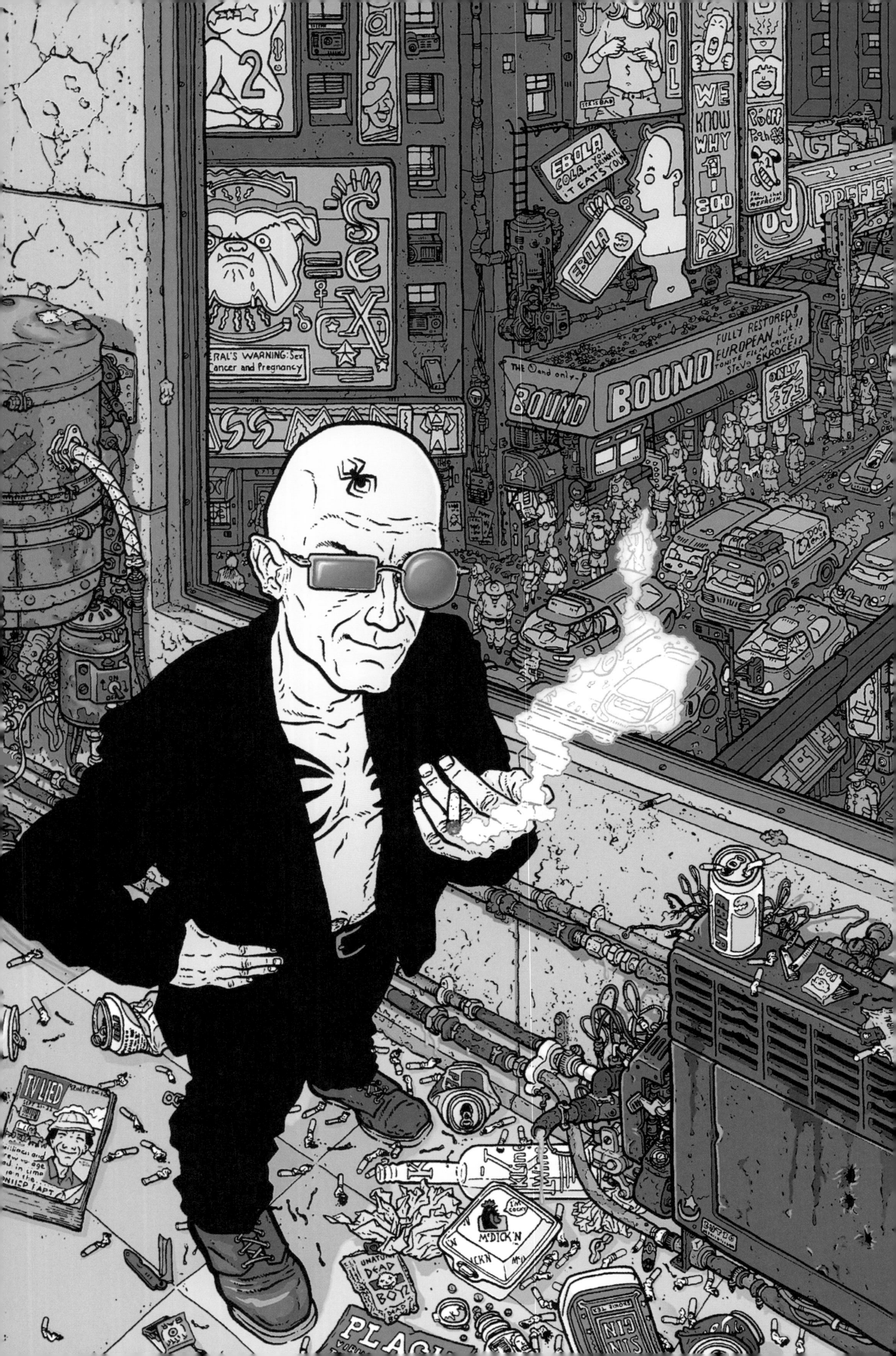

WE KNOW WHY 1 800 PSY
EBOLA COLA... YOU DRINK IT IT EATS YOU
EBOLA
ERAL'S WARNING: Sex
Cancer and Pregnancy
FULLY RESTORED!
EUROPEAN Cut!!
TONITE FILM CRITIC STEVE SKROCE!?
THE and only
BOUND
BOUND
ONLY $75
TV LIED
I'M COCKY
M'DICK'N
DEAD BOYZ
SIN GIN

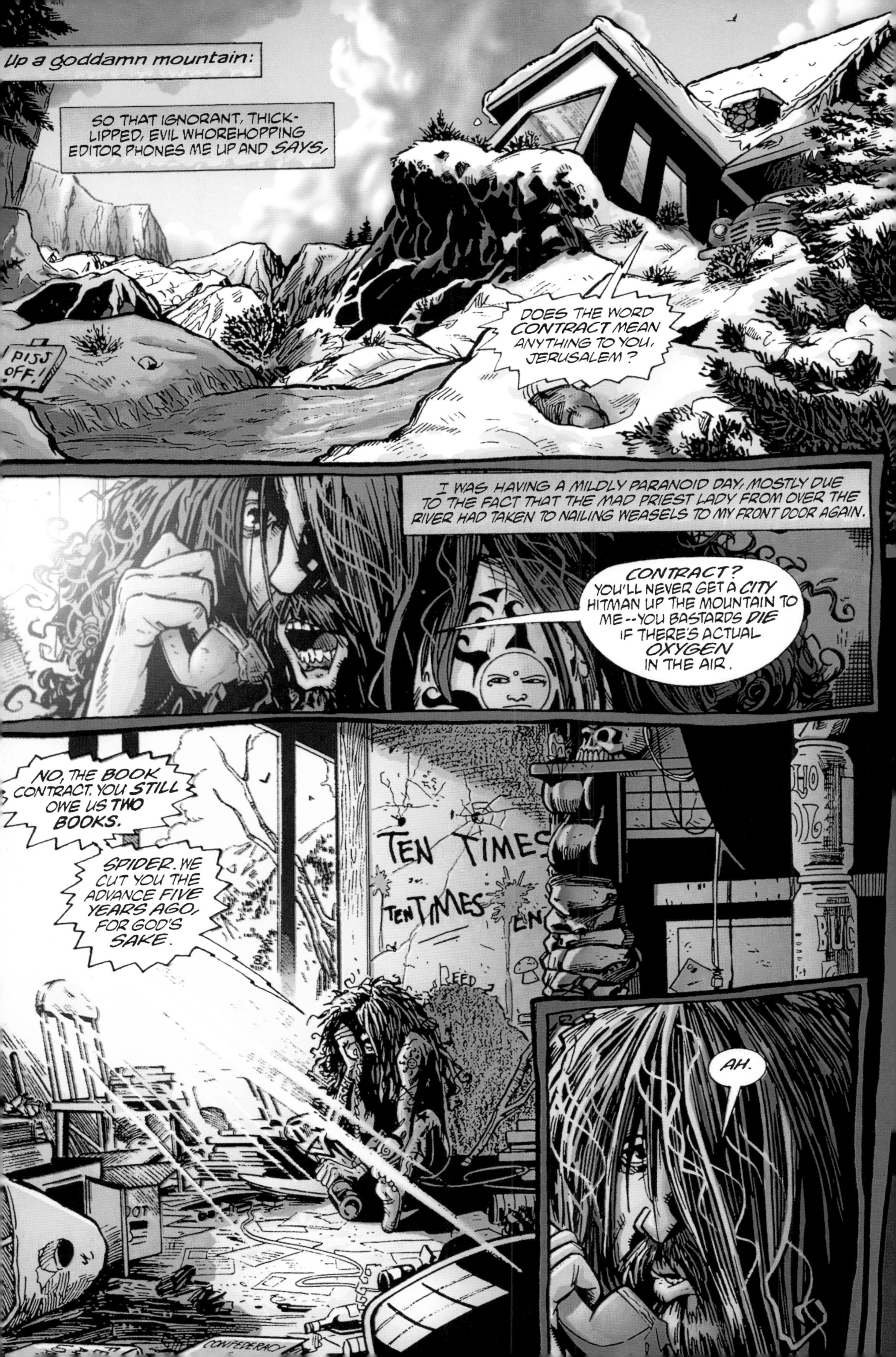

Up a goddamn mountain:
SO THAT IGNORANT, THICK-LIPPED, EVIL WHOREHOPPING EDITOR PHONES ME UP AND SAYS,
PISS OFF!
DOES THE WORD CONTRACT MEAN ANYTHING TO YOU, JERUSALEM?
I WAS HAVING A MILDLY PARANOID DAY, MOSTLY DUE TO THE FACT THAT THE MAD PRIEST LADY FROM OVER THE RIVER HAD TAKEN TO NAILING WEASELS TO MY FRONT DOOR AGAIN.
CONTRACT? YOU'LL NEVER GET A CITY HITMAN UP THE MOUNTAIN TO ME--YOU BASTARDS DIE IF THERE'S ACTUAL OXYGEN IN THE AIR.
NO, THE BOOK CONTRACT. YOU STILL OWE US TWO BOOKS.
SPIDER. WE CUT YOU THE ADVANCE FIVE YEARS AGO, FOR GOD'S SAKE.
TEN TIMES
TEN TIMES
AH.

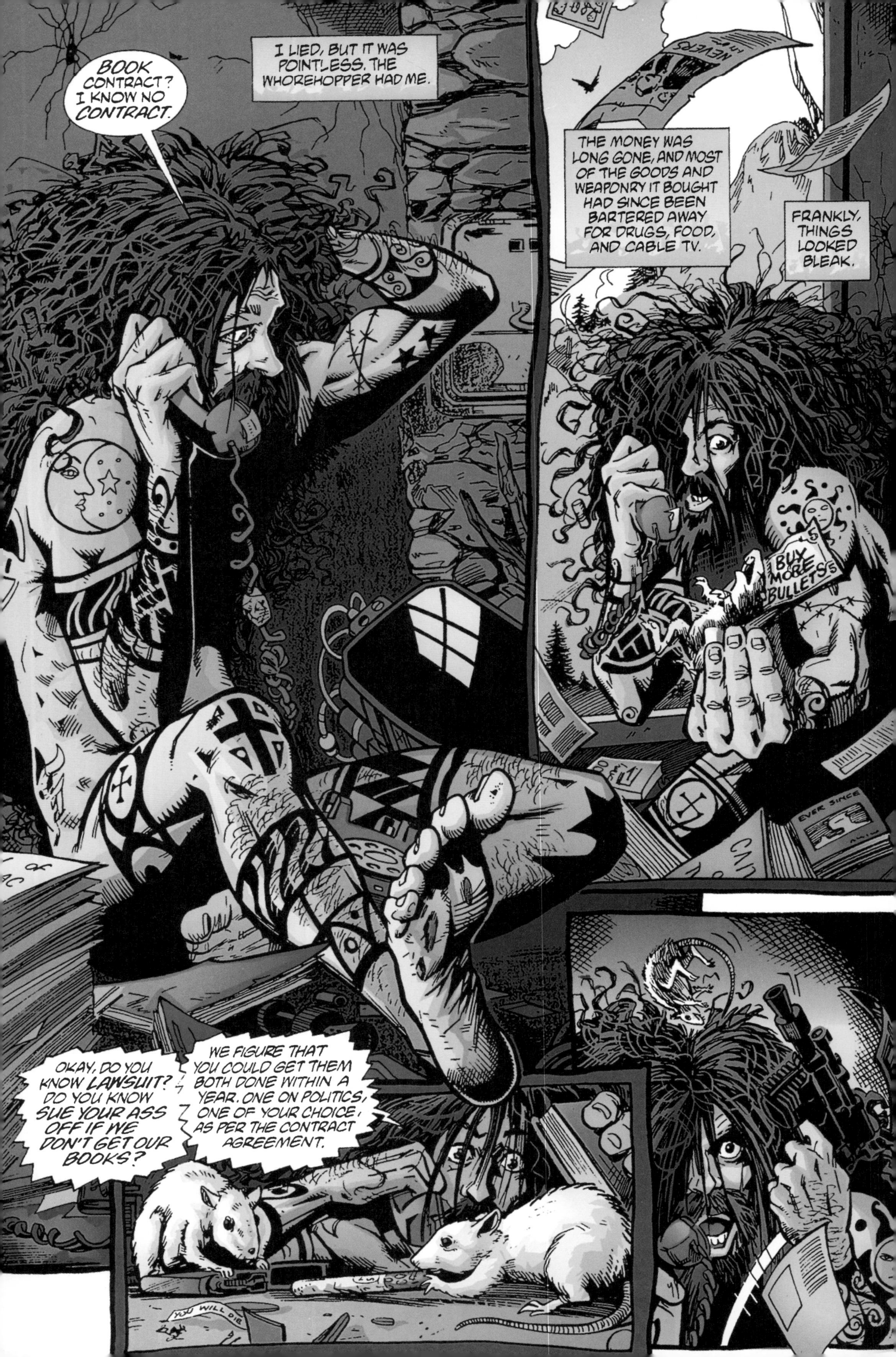
BOOK CONTRACT? I KNOW NO CONTRACT.
I LIED, BUT IT WAS POINTLESS. THE WHOREHOPPER HAD ME.
THE MONEY WAS LONG GONE, AND MOST OF THE GOODS AND WEAPONRY IT BOUGHT HAD SINCE BEEN BARTERED AWAY FOR DRUGS, FOOD, AND CABLE TV.
FRANKLY, THINGS LOOKED BLEAK.
BUY MORE BULLETS
EVER SINCE
OKAY, DO YOU KNOW LAWSUIT? DO YOU KNOW SUE YOUR ASS OFF IF WE DON'T GET OUR BOOKS?
WE FIGURE THAT YOU COULD GET THEM BOTH DONE WITHIN A YEAR. ONE ON POLITICS, ONE OF YOUR CHOICE, AS PER THE CONTRACT AGREEMENT.
YOU WILL DIE

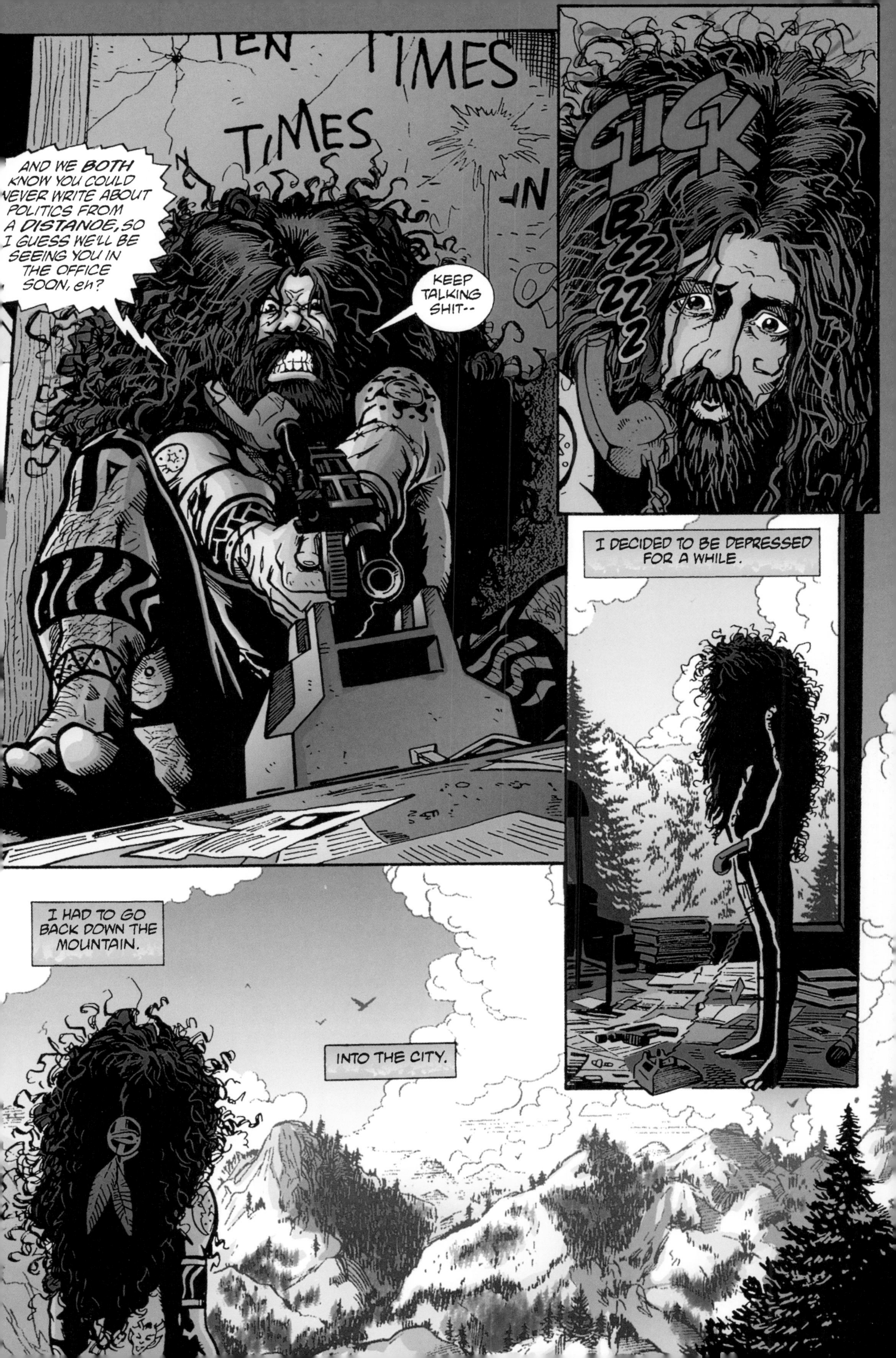
TEN TIMES
TIMES
AND WE BOTH KNOW YOU COULD NEVER WRITE ABOUT POLITICS FROM A DISTANCE, SO I GUESS WE'LL BE SEEING YOU IN THE OFFICE SOON, eh?
KEEP TALKING SHIT--
CLICK
BZZZZZ
I DECIDED TO BE DEPRESSED FOR A WHILE.
I HAD TO GO BACK DOWN THE MOUNTAIN.
INTO THE CITY.

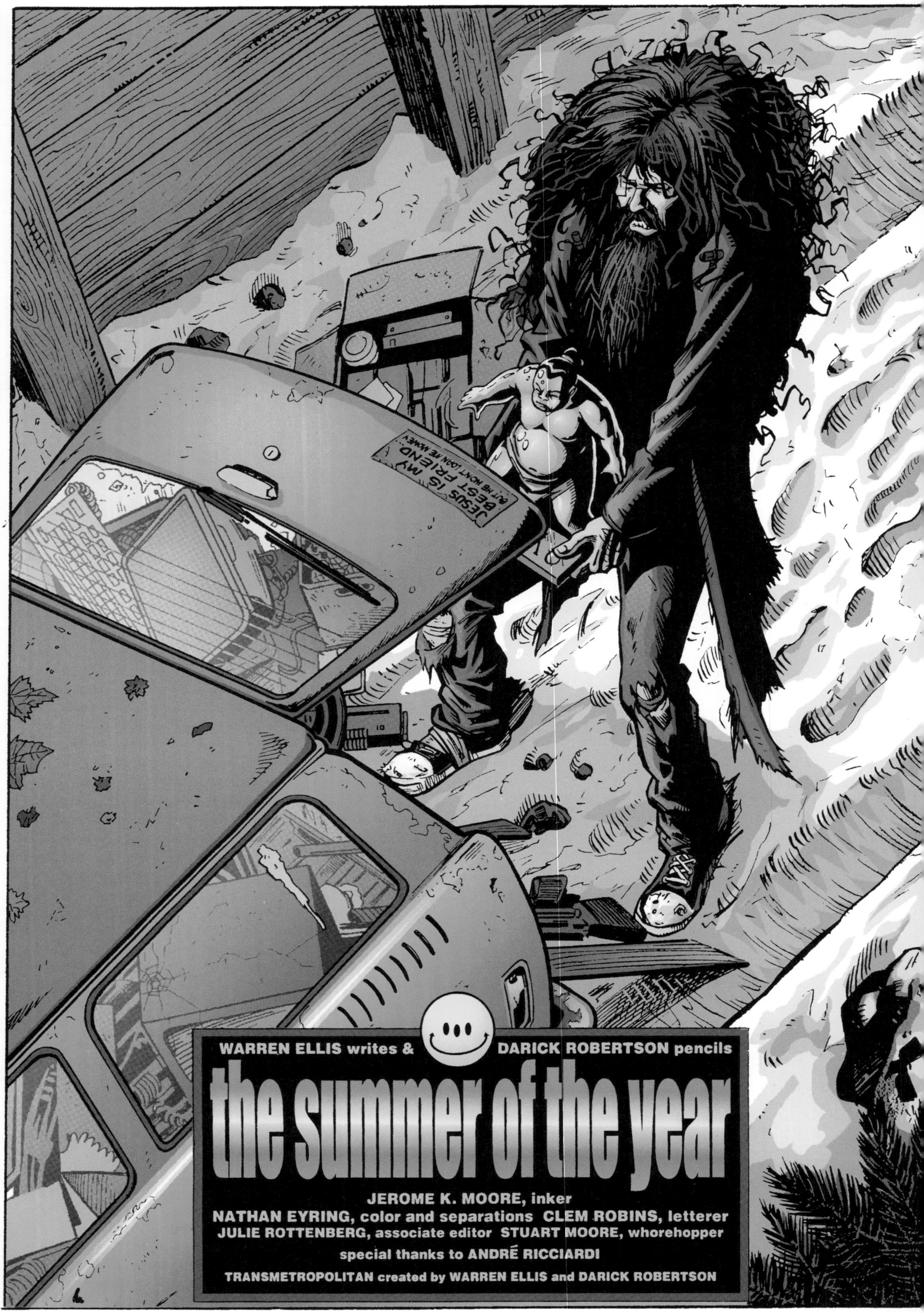
JESUS IS MY BEST FRIEND.
BUT HE WON'T LOAN ME MONEY.
WARREN ELLIS writes & DARICK ROBERTSON pencils
the summer of the year
JEROME K. MOORE, inker
NATHAN EYRING, color and separations CLEM ROBINS, letterer
JULIE ROTTENBERG, associate editor STUART MOORE, whorehopper
special thanks to ANDRÉ RICCIARDI
TRANSMETROPOLITAN created by WARREN ELLIS and DARICK ROBERTSON

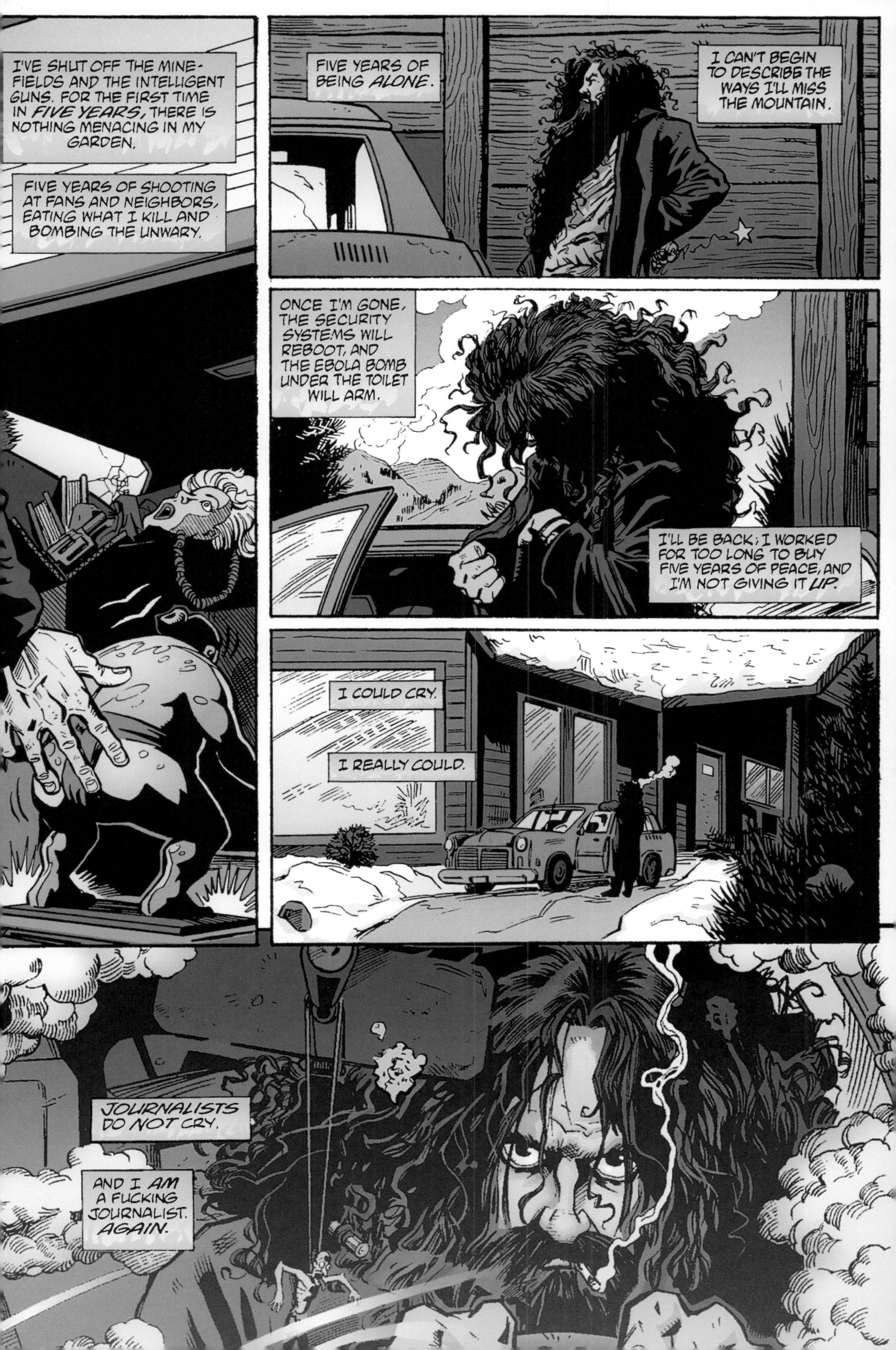

I'VE SHUT OFF THE MINE-FIELDS AND THE INTELLIGENT GUNS. FOR THE FIRST TIME IN FIVE YEARS, THERE IS NOTHING MENACING IN MY GARDEN.
FIVE YEARS OF SHOOTING AT FANS AND NEIGHBORS, EATING WHAT I KILL AND BOMBING THE UNWARY.
FIVE YEARS OF BEING ALONE.
I CAN'T BEGIN TO DESCRIBE THE WAYS I'LL MISS THE MOUNTAIN.
ONCE I'M GONE, THE SECURITY SYSTEMS WILL REBOOT, AND THE EBOLA BOMB UNDER THE TOILET WILL ARM.
I'LL BE BACK; I WORKED FOR TOO LONG TO BUY FIVE YEARS OF PEACE, AND I'M NOT GIVING IT UP.
I COULD CRY.
I REALLY COULD.
JOURNALISTS DO NOT CRY.
AND I AM A FUCKING JOURNALIST. AGAIN.

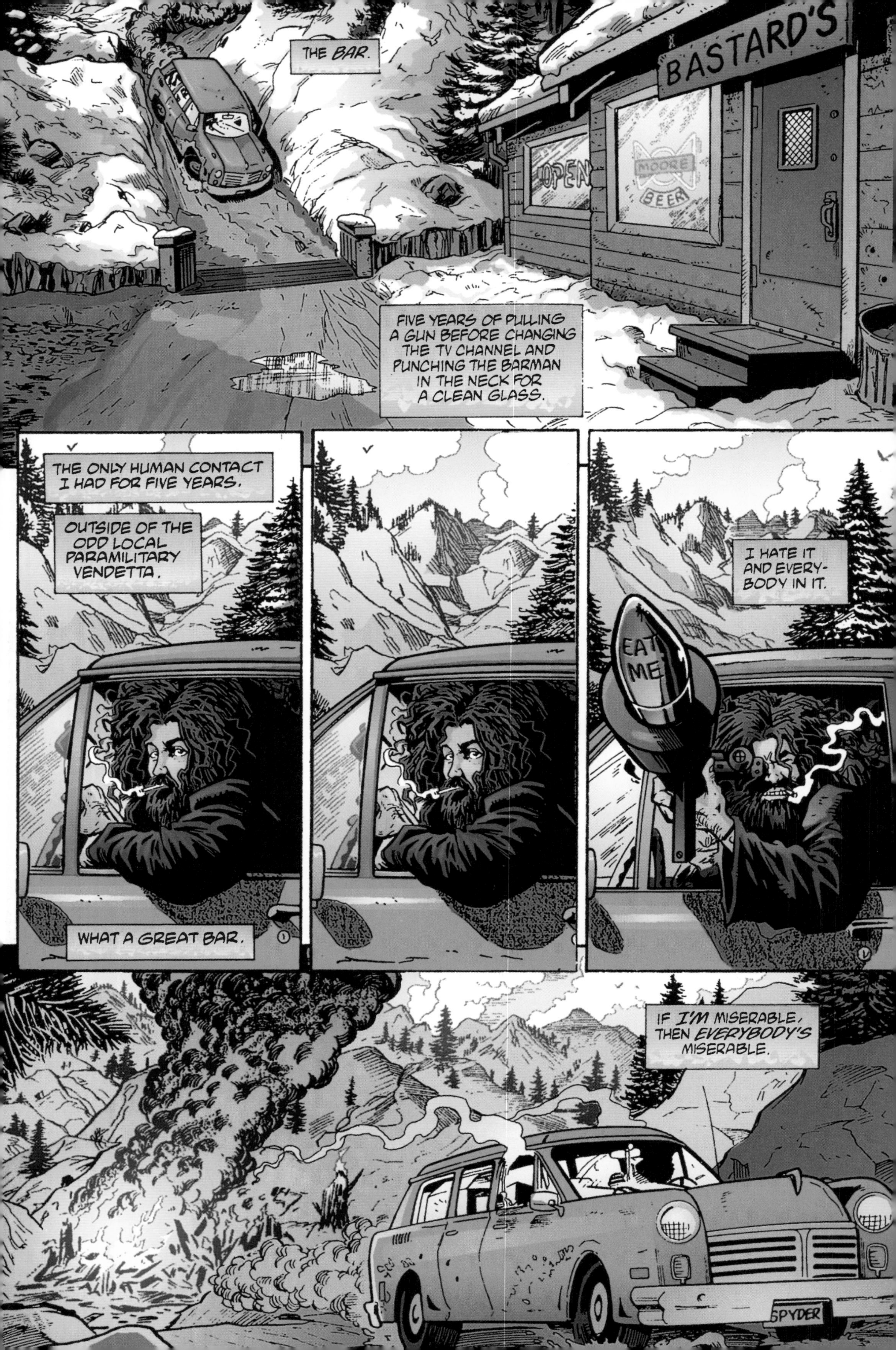

BASTARD'S
THE BAR.
OPEN
MOORE
BEER
FIVE YEARS OF PULLING A GUN BEFORE CHANGING THE TV CHANNEL AND PUNCHING THE BARMAN IN THE NECK FOR A CLEAN GLASS.
THE ONLY HUMAN CONTACT I HAD FOR FIVE YEARS.
OUTSIDE OF THE ODD LOCAL PARAMILITARY VENDETTA.
WHAT A GREAT BAR.
I HATE IT AND EVERYBODY IN IT.
EAT ME
IF I'M MISERABLE, THEN EVERYBODY'S MISERABLE.
SPYDER

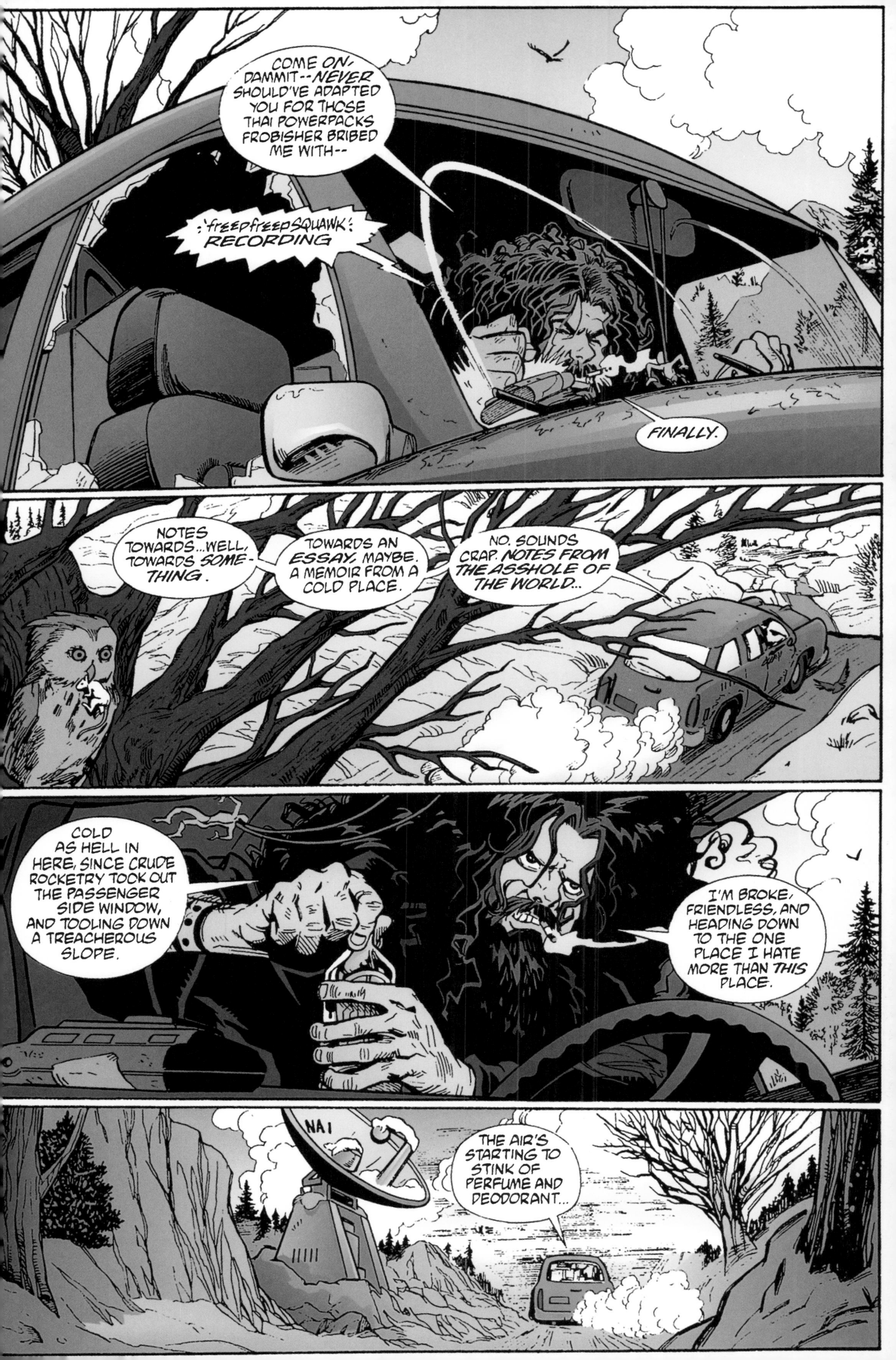
COME ON, DAMMIT--NEVER SHOULD'VE ADAPTED YOU FOR THOSE THAI POWERPACKS FROBISHER BRIBED ME WITH--
:freepfreepSQUAWK: RECORDING
FINALLY.
NOTES TOWARDS...WELL, TOWARDS SOME-THING.
TOWARDS AN ESSAY, MAYBE. A MEMOIR FROM A COLD PLACE.
NO. SOUNDS CRAP. NOTES FROM THE ASSHOLE OF THE WORLD...
COLD AS HELL IN HERE, SINCE CRUDE ROCKETRY TOOK OUT THE PASSENGER SIDE WINDOW, AND TOOLING DOWN A TREACHEROUS SLOPE.
I'M BROKE, FRIENDLESS, AND HEADING DOWN TO THE ONE PLACE I HATE MORE THAN THIS PLACE.
NA1
THE AIR'S STARTING TO STINK OF PERFUME AND DEODORANT...

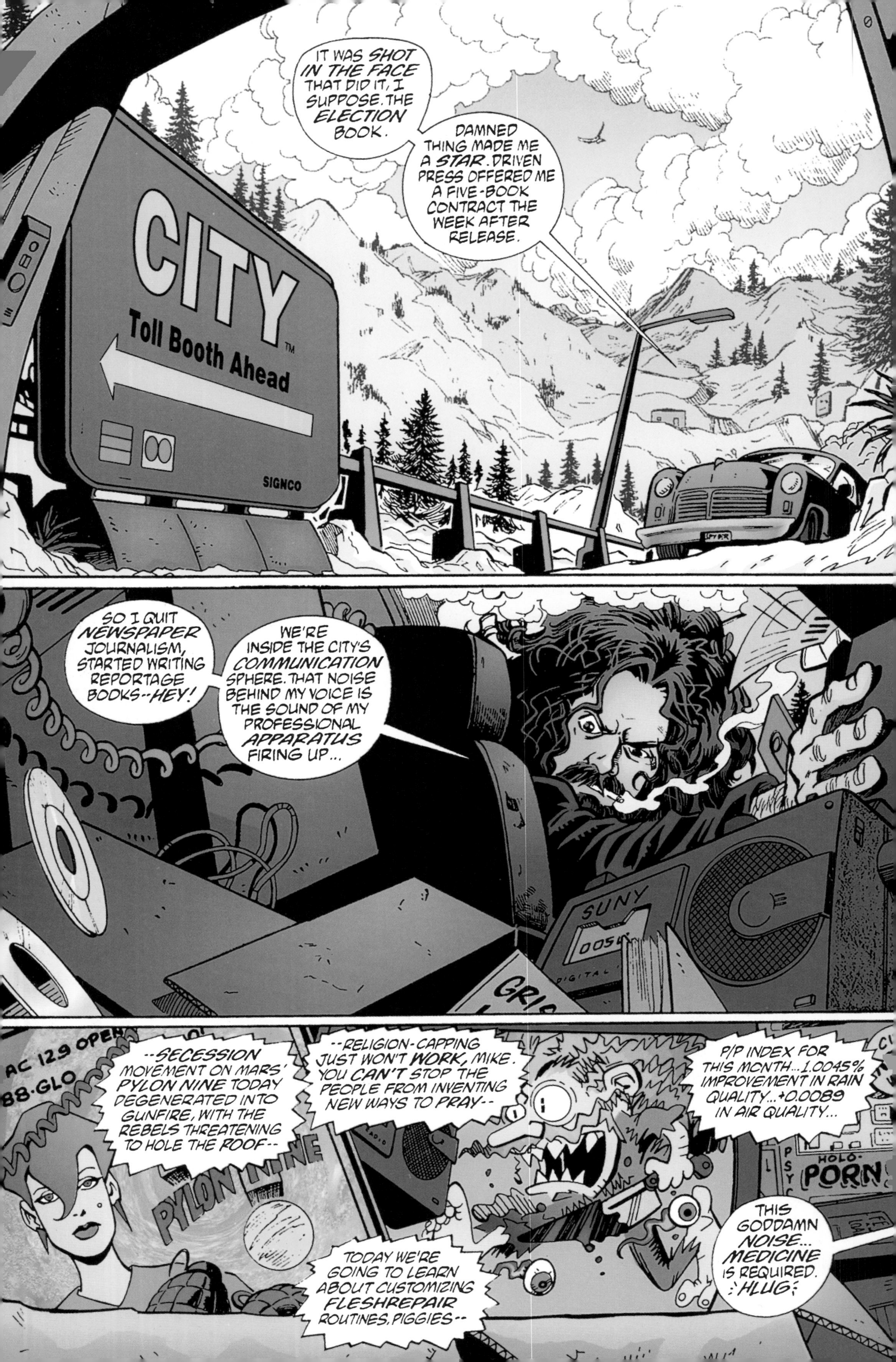
IT WAS SHOT IN THE FACE THAT DID IT, I SUPPOSE. THE ELECTION BOOK.
DAMNED THING MADE ME A STAR. DRIVEN PRESS OFFERED ME A FIVE-BOOK CONTRACT THE WEEK AFTER RELEASE.
CITY
Toll Booth Ahead
TM
SIGNCO
SO I QUIT NEWSPAPER JOURNALISM, STARTED WRITING REPORTAGE BOOKS--HEY!
WE'RE INSIDE THE CITY'S COMMUNICATION SPHERE. THAT NOISE BEHIND MY VOICE IS THE SOUND OF MY PROFESSIONAL APPARATUS FIRING UP...
SUNY
--SECESSION MOVEMENT ON MARS' PYLON NINE TODAY DEGENERATED INTO GUNFIRE, WITH THE REBELS THREATENING TO HOLE THE ROOF--
PYLON NINE
--RELIGION-CAPPING JUST WON'T WORK, MIKE. YOU CAN'T STOP THE PEOPLE FROM INVENTING NEW WAYS TO PRAY--
P/P INDEX FOR THIS MONTH... 1.0045% IMPROVEMENT IN RAIN QUALITY... +0.0089 IN AIR QUALITY...
HOLO-PORN
TODAY WE'RE GOING TO LEARN ABOUT CUSTOMIZING FLESHREPAIR ROUTINES, PIGGIES--
THIS GODDAMN NOISE... MEDICINE IS REQUIRED. HLUG

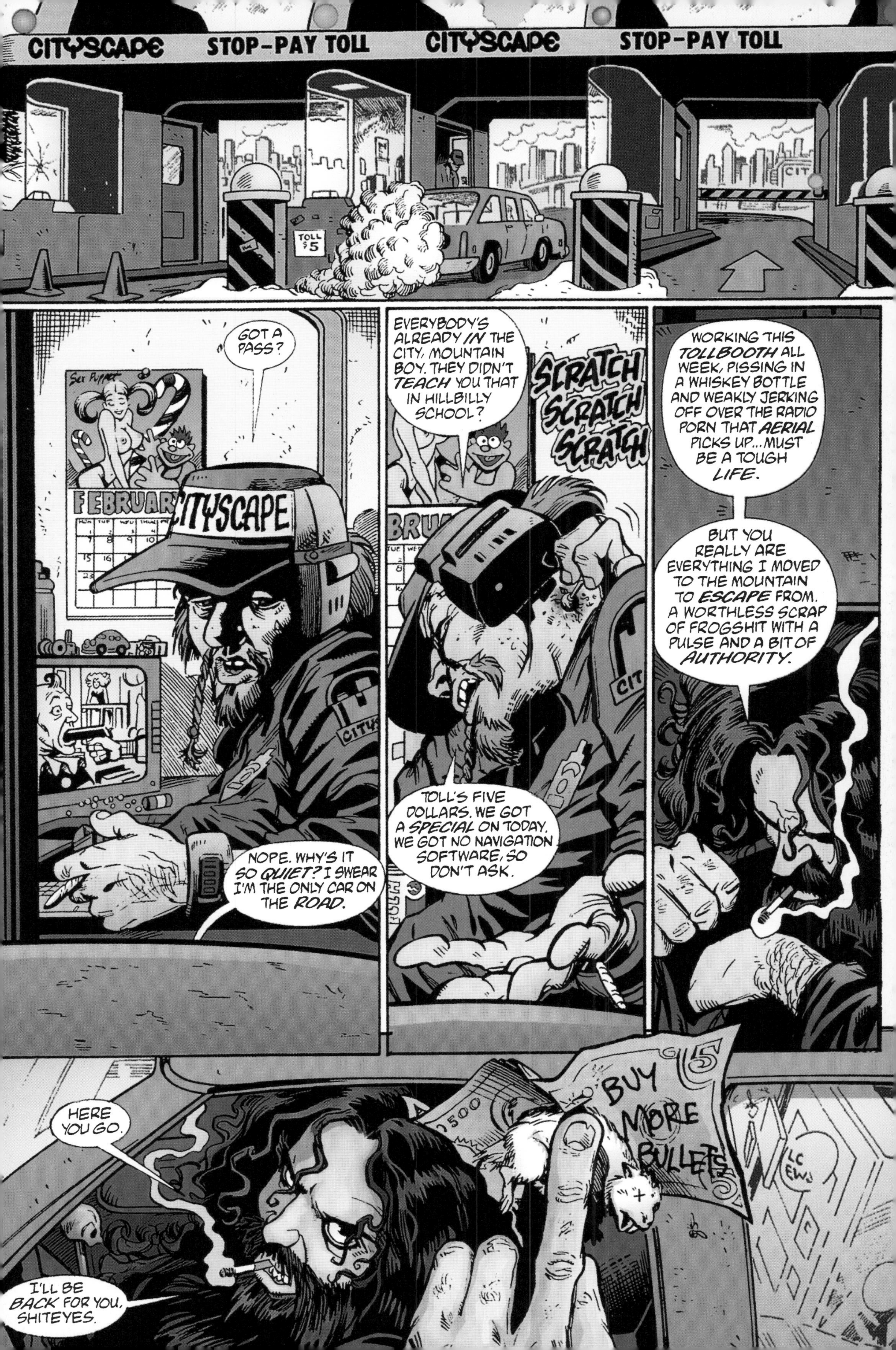
CITYSCAPE
STOP-PAY TOLL
CITYSCAPE
STOP-PAY TOLL
TOLL $5
GOT A PASS?
NOPE. WHY'S IT SO QUIET? I SWEAR I'M THE ONLY CAR ON THE ROAD.
EVERYBODY'S ALREADY IN THE CITY, MOUNTAIN BOY. THEY DIDN'T TEACH YOU THAT IN HILLBILLY SCHOOL?
SCRATCH SCRATCH SCRATCH
TOLL'S FIVE DOLLARS. WE GOT A SPECIAL ON TODAY. WE GOT NO NAVIGATION SOFTWARE, SO DON'T ASK.
WORKING THIS TOLLBOOTH ALL WEEK, PISSING IN A WHISKEY BOTTLE AND WEAKLY JERKING OFF OVER THE RADIO PORN THAT AERIAL PICKS UP... MUST BE A TOUGH LIFE.
BUT YOU REALLY ARE EVERYTHING I MOVED TO THE MOUNTAIN TO ESCAPE FROM. A WORTHLESS SCRAP OF FROGSHIT WITH A PULSE AND A BIT OF AUTHORITY.
HERE YOU GO.
BUY MORE BULLETS
I'LL BE BACK FOR YOU, SHITEYES.

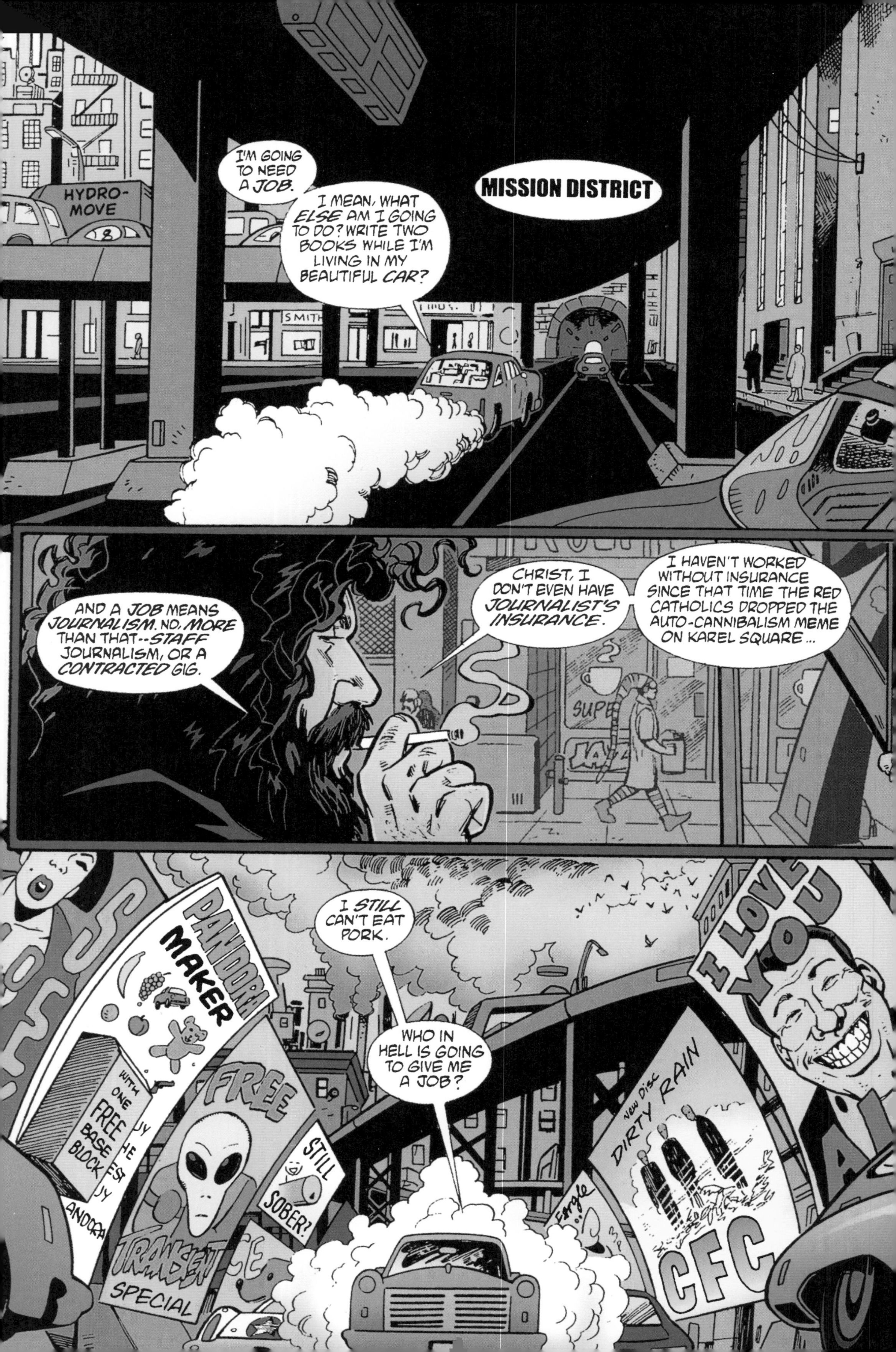
HYDRO-MOVE
SMITH
I'M GOING TO NEED A *JOB*.
I MEAN, WHAT *ELSE* AM I GOING TO DO? WRITE TWO BOOKS WHILE I'M LIVING IN MY BEAUTIFUL *CAR*?
MISSION DISTRICT
AND A *JOB* MEANS *JOURNALISM*. NO, *MORE* THAN THAT--*STAFF* JOURNALISM, OR A *CONTRACTED* GIG.
CHRIST, I DON'T EVEN HAVE *JOURNALIST'S INSURANCE*.
I HAVEN'T WORKED WITHOUT INSURANCE SINCE THAT TIME THE RED CATHOLICS DROPPED THE AUTO-CANNIBALISM MEME ON KAREL SQUARE ...
I *STILL* CAN'T EAT PORK.
WHO IN HELL IS GOING TO GIVE ME A JOB?
PANDORA MAKER
WITH ONE FREE BASE BLOCK
FREE
TRANSIENT SPECIAL
STILL SOBER?
I LOVE YOU
New Disc DIRTY RAIN
CFC

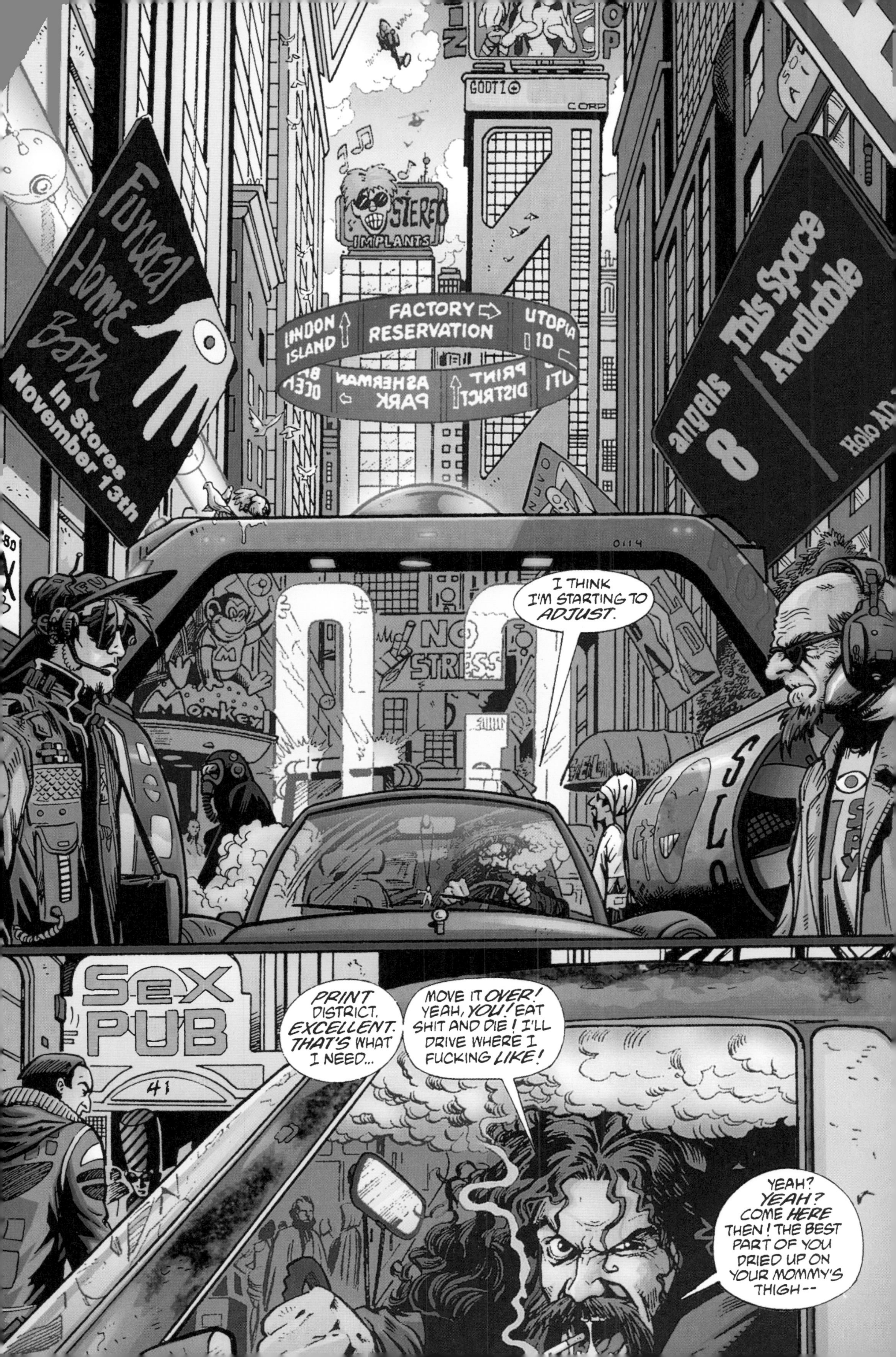

Funeral Home Bath In Stores November 13th
FACTORY RESERVATION
LONDON ISLAND
UTOPIA 10
ASHERMAN PARK
PRINT DISTRICT
STEREO IMPLANTS
This Space Available
angels 8
NO STRESS
I THINK I'M STARTING TO ADJUST.
SEX PUB
41
PRINT DISTRICT. EXCELLENT. THAT'S WHAT I NEED...
MOVE IT OVER! YEAH, YOU! EAT SHIT AND DIE! I'LL DRIVE WHERE I FUCKING LIKE!
YEAH? YEAH? COME HERE THEN! THE BEST PART OF YOU DRIED UP ON YOUR MOMMY'S THIGH--

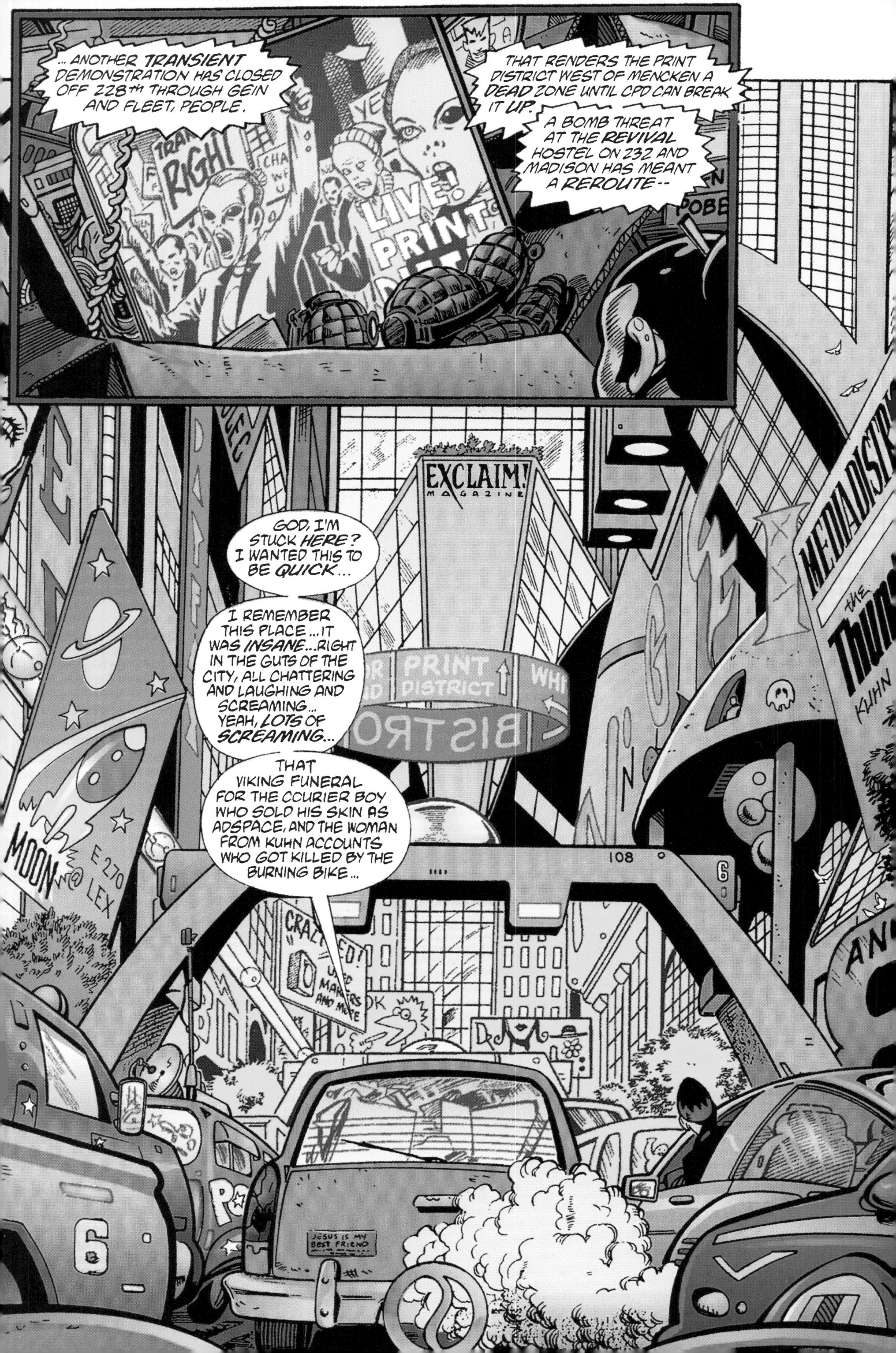
... ANOTHER TRANSIENT DEMONSTRATION HAS CLOSED OFF 228th THROUGH GEIN AND FLEET, PEOPLE.
THAT RENDERS THE PRINT DISTRICT WEST OF MENCKEN A DEAD ZONE UNTIL CPD CAN BREAK IT UP.
A BOMB THREAT AT THE REVIVAL HOSTEL ON 232 AND MADISON HAS MEANT A REROUTE--
LIVE! PRINT
EXCLAIM! MAGAZINE
GOD, I'M STUCK HERE? I WANTED THIS TO BE QUICK...
I REMEMBER THIS PLACE ...IT WAS INSANE...RIGHT IN THE GUTS OF THE CITY, ALL CHATTERING AND LAUGHING AND SCREAMING... YEAH, LOTS OF SCREAMING...
THAT VIKING FUNERAL FOR THE COURIER BOY WHO SOLD HIS SKIN AS ADSPACE, AND THE WOMAN FROM KUHN ACCOUNTS WHO GOT KILLED BY THE BURNING BIKE...
PRINT DISTRICT
BISTRO
MOON E-270 @ LEX
MEDIA DISTR
JESUS IS MY BEST FRIEND

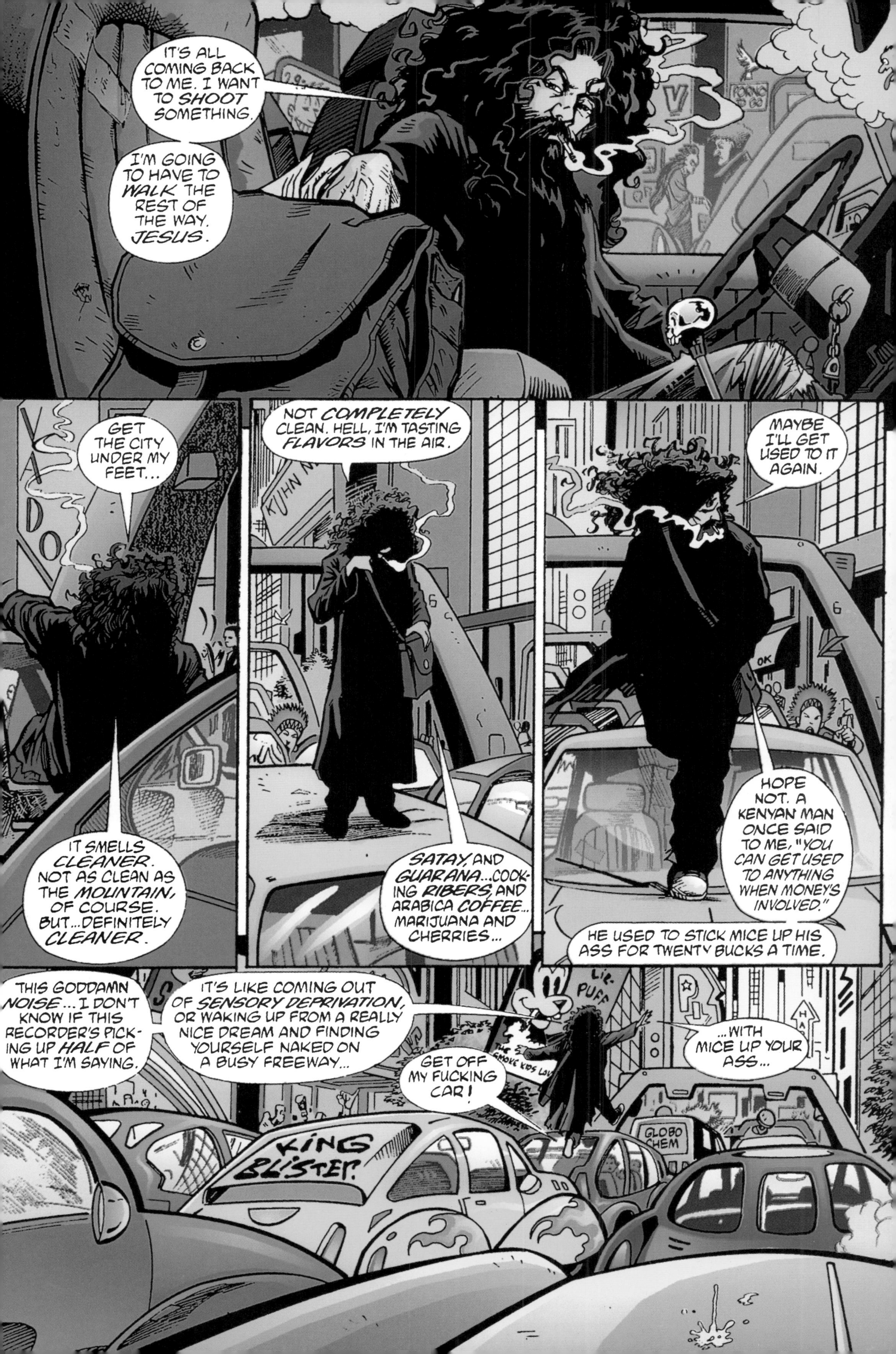
IT'S ALL COMING BACK TO ME. I WANT TO SHOOT SOMETHING.
I'M GOING TO HAVE TO WALK THE REST OF THE WAY. JESUS.
PORNO TO GO
GET THE CITY UNDER MY FEET...
IT SMELLS CLEANER. NOT AS CLEAN AS THE MOUNTAIN, OF COURSE. BUT...DEFINITELY CLEANER.
NOT COMPLETELY CLEAN. HELL, I'M TASTING FLAVORS IN THE AIR.
SATAY, AND GUARANA...COOKING RIBERS, AND ARABICA COFFEE... MARIJUANA AND CHERRIES...
MAYBE I'LL GET USED TO IT AGAIN.
HOPE NOT. A KENYAN MAN ONCE SAID TO ME, "YOU CAN GET USED TO ANYTHING WHEN MONEY'S INVOLVED."
HE USED TO STICK MICE UP HIS ASS FOR TWENTY BUCKS A TIME.
THIS GODDAMN NOISE... I DON'T KNOW IF THIS RECORDER'S PICKING UP HALF OF WHAT I'M SAYING.
IT'S LIKE COMING OUT OF SENSORY DEPRIVATION, OR WAKING UP FROM A REALLY NICE DREAM AND FINDING YOURSELF NAKED ON A BUSY FREEWAY...
GET OFF MY FUCKING CAR!
...WITH MICE UP YOUR ASS...
LIL PUFF
KING BLISTER
GLOBO CHEM

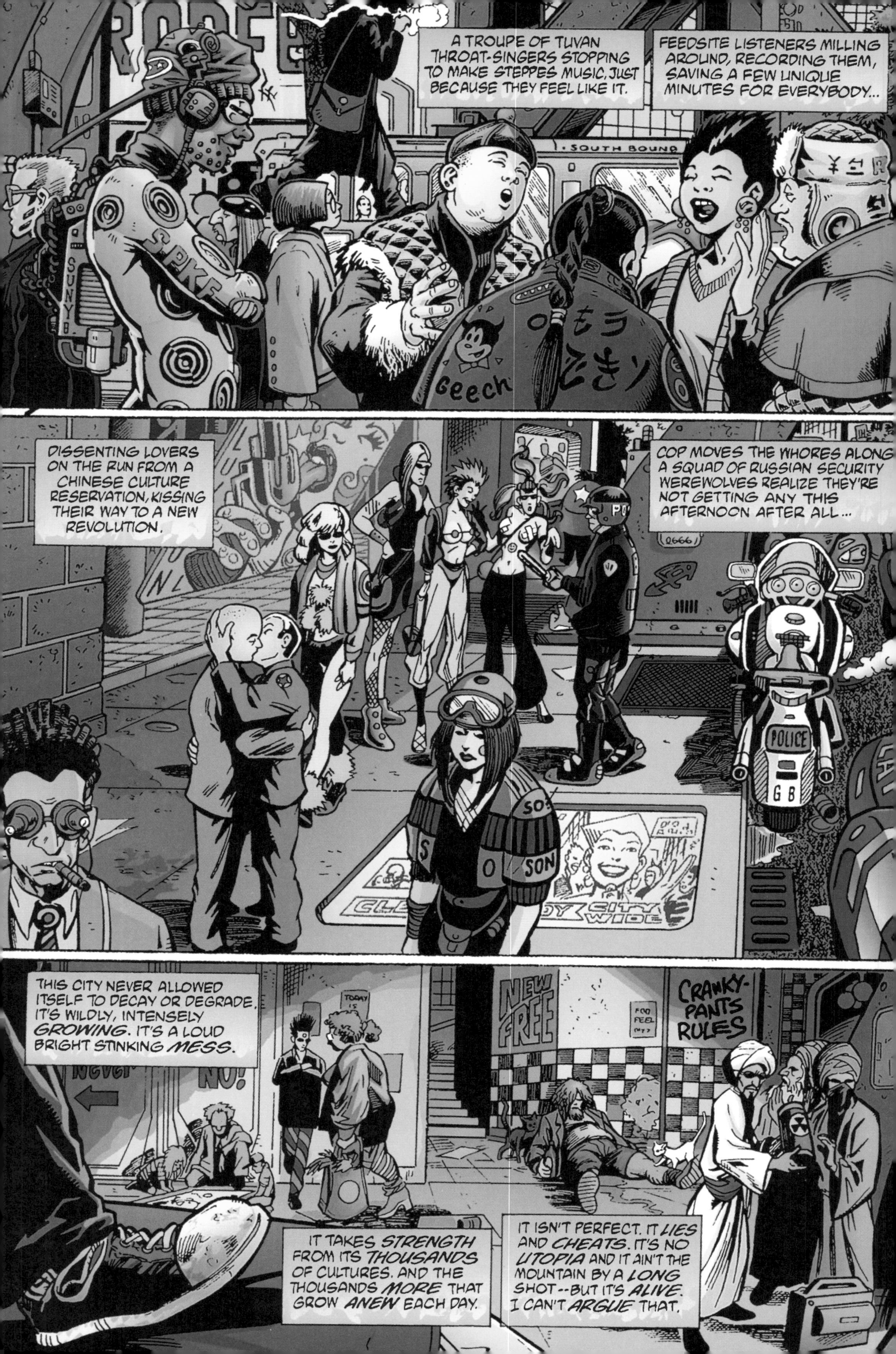
A TROUPE OF TUVAN THROAT-SINGERS STOPPING TO MAKE STEPPES MUSIC, JUST BECAUSE THEY FEEL LIKE IT.
FEEDSITE LISTENERS MILLING AROUND, RECORDING THEM, SAVING A FEW UNIQUE MINUTES FOR EVERYBODY...
SOUTH BOUND
Geech
DISSENTING LOVERS ON THE RUN FROM A CHINESE CULTURE RESERVATION, KISSING THEIR WAY TO A NEW REVOLUTION.
COP MOVES THE WHORES ALONG A SQUAD OF RUSSIAN SECURITY WEREWOLVES REALIZE THEY'RE NOT GETTING ANY THIS AFTERNOON AFTER ALL...
POLICE
GB
THIS CITY NEVER ALLOWED ITSELF TO DECAY OR DEGRADE. IT'S WILDLY, INTENSELY *GROWING*. IT'S A LOUD BRIGHT STINKING *MESS*.
NEW FREE
CRANKY-PANTS RULES
NO!
IT TAKES *STRENGTH* FROM ITS *THOUSANDS* OF CULTURES. AND THE THOUSANDS *MORE* THAT GROW *ANEW* EACH DAY.
IT ISN'T PERFECT. IT *LIES* AND *CHEATS*. IT'S NO *UTOPIA* AND IT AIN'T THE MOUNTAIN BY A *LONG* SHOT--BUT IT'S *ALIVE*. I CAN'T *ARGUE* THAT.

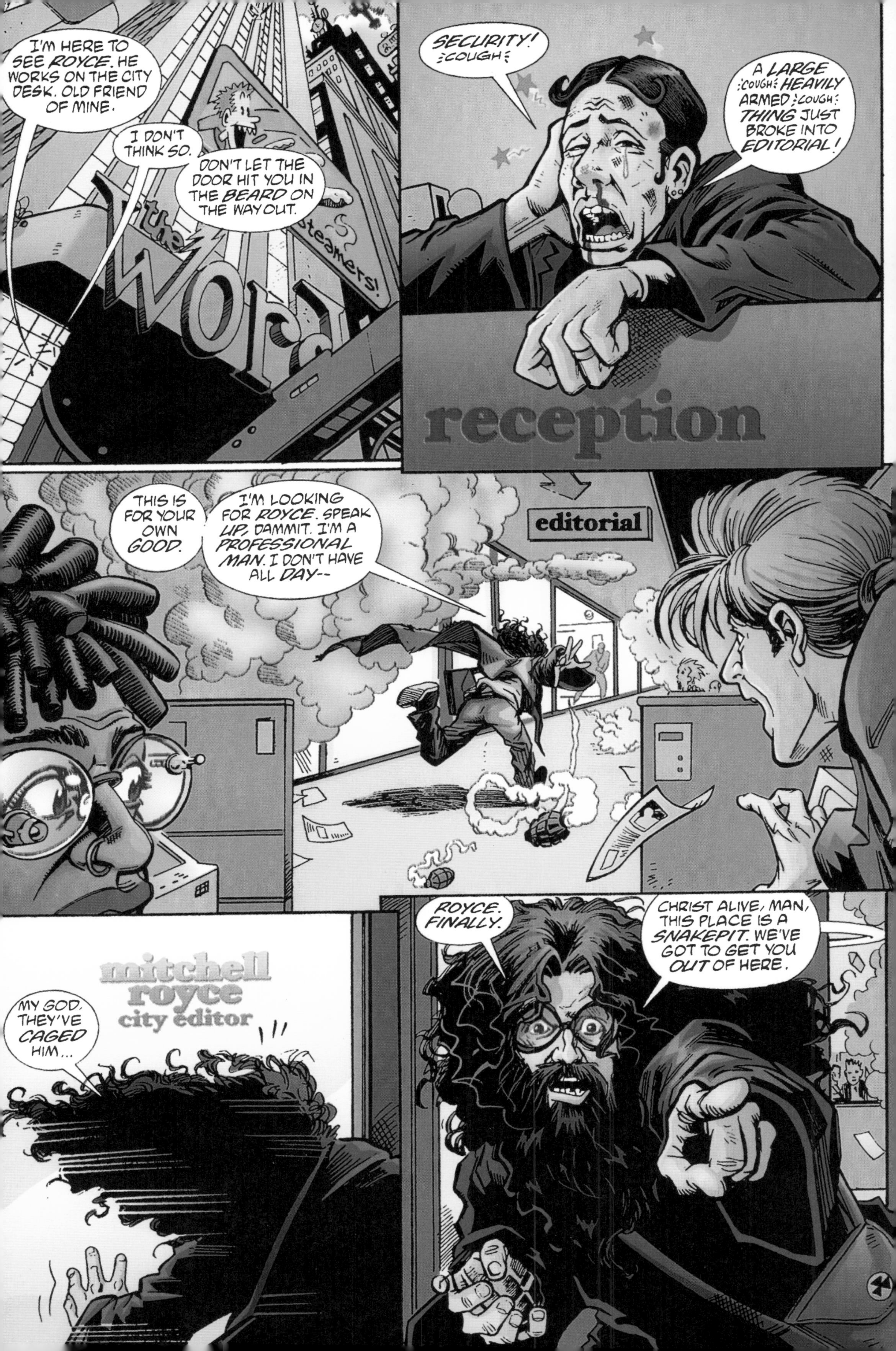
I'M HERE TO SEE ROYCE. HE WORKS ON THE CITY DESK. OLD FRIEND OF MINE.
I DON'T THINK SO.
DON'T LET THE DOOR HIT YOU IN THE BEARD ON THE WAY OUT.
the Word
steamers!
SECURITY! :COUGH:
A LARGE :COUGH: HEAVILY ARMED :COUGH: THING JUST BROKE INTO EDITORIAL!
reception
THIS IS FOR YOUR OWN GOOD.
I'M LOOKING FOR ROYCE. SPEAK UP, DAMMIT. I'M A PROFESSIONAL MAN. I DON'T HAVE ALL DAY--
editorial
mitchell royce city editor
MY GOD, THEY'VE CAGED HIM...
ROYCE. FINALLY.
CHRIST ALIVE, MAN, THIS PLACE IS A SNAKEPIT. WE'VE GOT TO GET YOU OUT OF HERE.

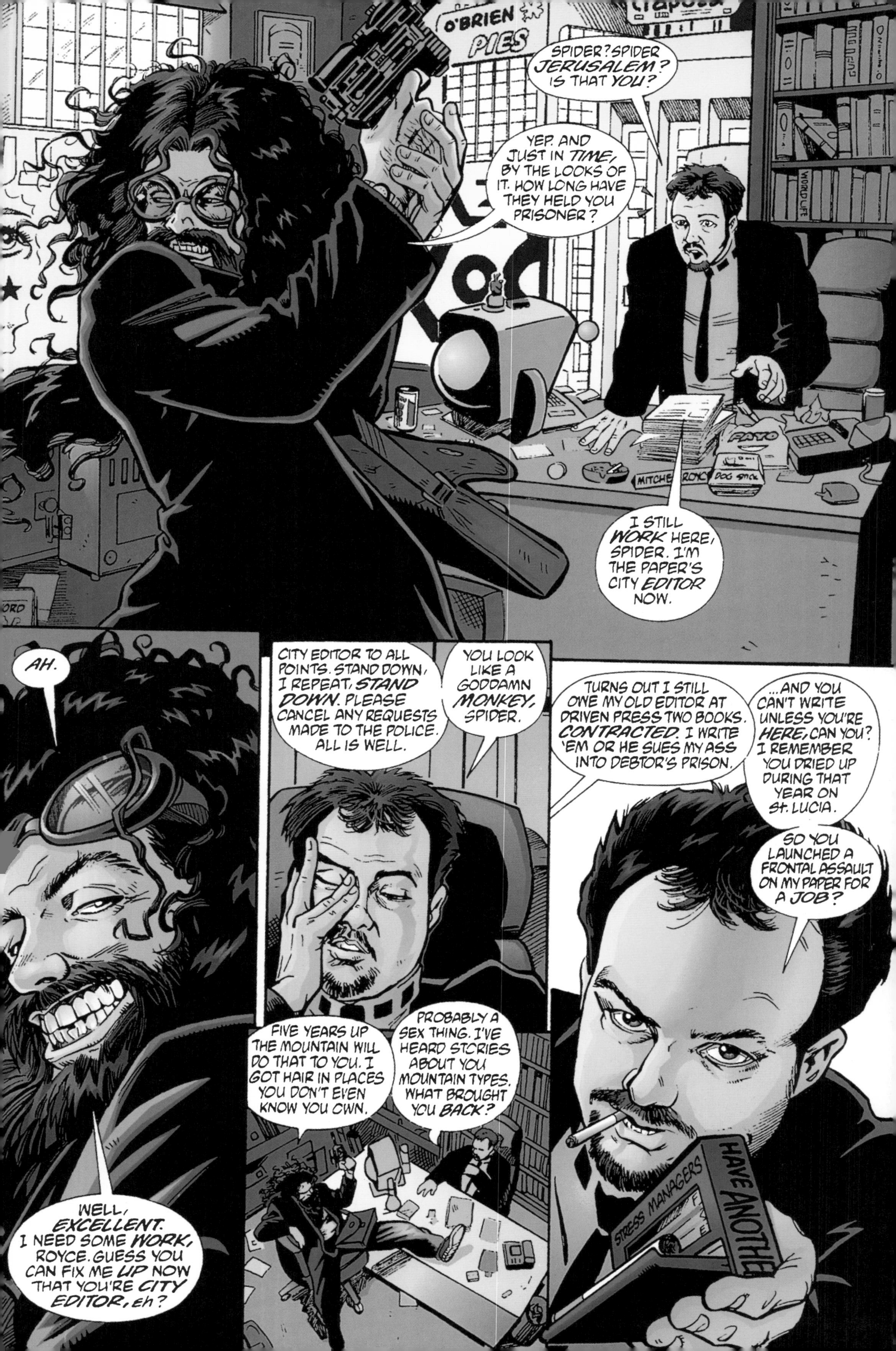
O'BRIEN
PIES
SPIDER? SPIDER JERUSALEM? IS THAT YOU?
YEP. AND JUST IN TIME, BY THE LOOKS OF IT. HOW LONG HAVE THEY HELD YOU PRISONER?
I STILL WORK HERE, SPIDER. I'M THE PAPER'S CITY EDITOR NOW.
AH.
WELL, EXCELLENT. I NEED SOME WORK, ROYCE. GUESS YOU CAN FIX ME UP NOW THAT YOU'RE CITY EDITOR, eh?
CITY EDITOR TO ALL POINTS. STAND DOWN, I REPEAT, STAND DOWN. PLEASE CANCEL ANY REQUESTS MADE TO THE POLICE. ALL IS WELL.
YOU LOOK LIKE A GODDAMN MONKEY, SPIDER.
FIVE YEARS UP THE MOUNTAIN WILL DO THAT TO YOU. I GOT HAIR IN PLACES YOU DON'T EVEN KNOW YOU OWN.
PROBABLY A SEX THING. I'VE HEARD STORIES ABOUT YOU MOUNTAIN TYPES. WHAT BROUGHT YOU BACK?
TURNS OUT I STILL OWE MY OLD EDITOR AT DRIVEN PRESS TWO BOOKS. CONTRACTED. I WRITE 'EM OR HE SUES MY ASS INTO DEBTOR'S PRISON.
...AND YOU CAN'T WRITE UNLESS YOU'RE HERE, CAN YOU? I REMEMBER YOU DRIED UP DURING THAT YEAR ON St. LUCIA.
SO YOU LAUNCHED A FRONTAL ASSAULT ON MY PAPER FOR A JOB?
STRESS MANAGERS
HAVE ANOTHE

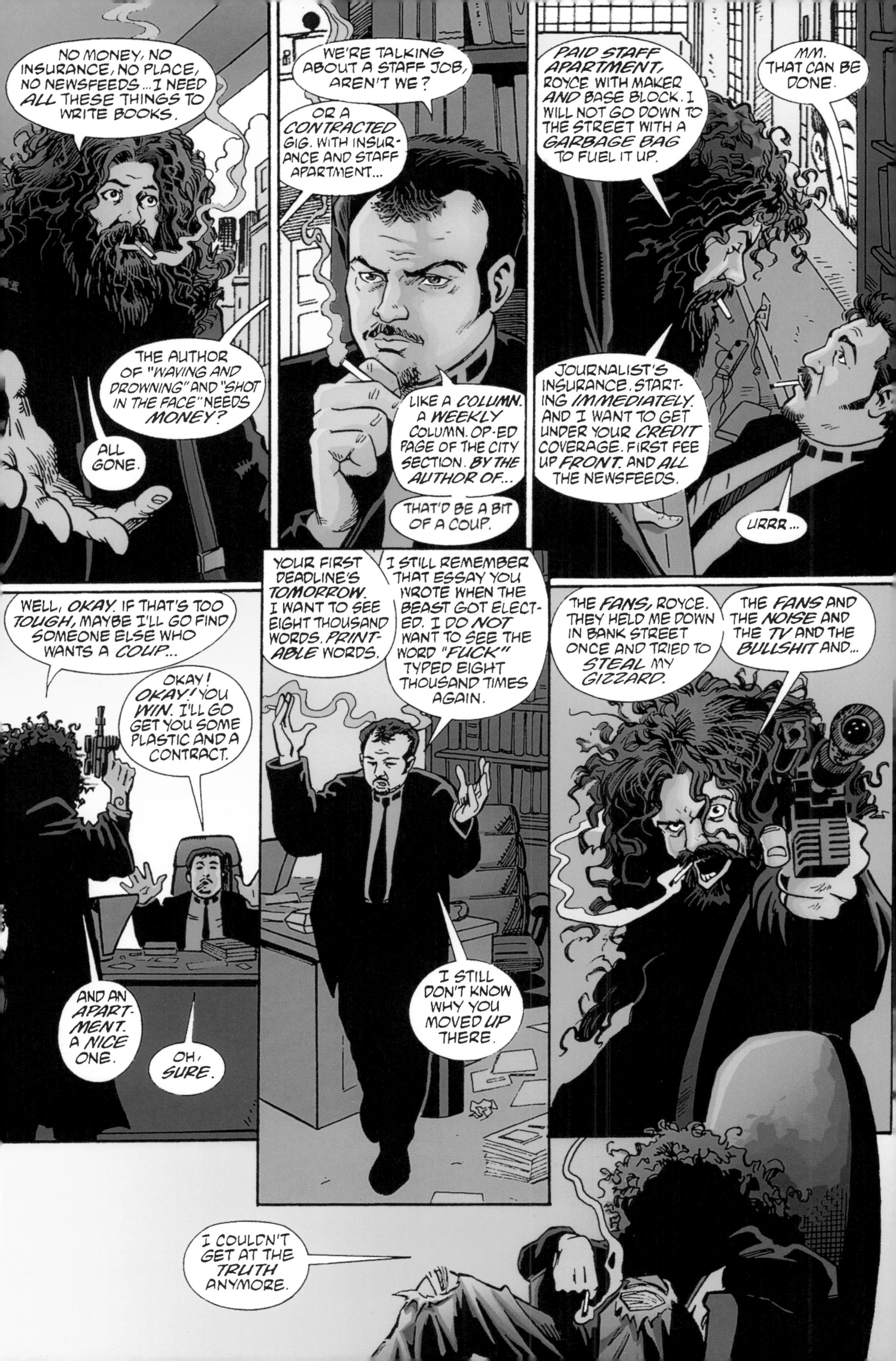
NO MONEY, NO INSURANCE, NO PLACE, NO NEWSFEEDS... I NEED ALL THESE THINGS TO WRITE BOOKS.
WE'RE TALKING ABOUT A STAFF JOB, AREN'T WE?
OR A CONTRACTED GIG. WITH INSURANCE AND STAFF APARTMENT...
PAID STAFF APARTMENT, ROYCE WITH MAKER AND BASE BLOCK. I WILL NOT GO DOWN TO THE STREET WITH A GARBAGE BAG TO FUEL IT UP.
MM. THAT CAN BE DONE.
THE AUTHOR OF "WAVING AND DROWNING" AND "SHOT IN THE FACE" NEEDS MONEY?
ALL GONE.
LIKE A COLUMN. A WEEKLY COLUMN. OP-ED PAGE OF THE CITY SECTION. BY THE AUTHOR OF...
THAT'D BE A BIT OF A COUP.
JOURNALIST'S INSURANCE. STARTING IMMEDIATELY. AND I WANT TO GET UNDER YOUR CREDIT COVERAGE. FIRST FEE UP FRONT. AND ALL THE NEWSFEEDS.
URRR...
WELL, OKAY. IF THAT'S TOO TOUGH, MAYBE I'LL GO FIND SOMEONE ELSE WHO WANTS A COUP...
OKAY! OKAY! YOU WIN. I'LL GO GET YOU SOME PLASTIC AND A CONTRACT.
AND AN APARTMENT. A NICE ONE.
OH, SURE.
YOUR FIRST DEADLINE'S TOMORROW. I WANT TO SEE EIGHT THOUSAND WORDS. PRINTABLE WORDS.
I STILL REMEMBER THAT ESSAY YOU WROTE WHEN THE BEAST GOT ELECTED. I DO NOT WANT TO SEE THE WORD "FUCK" TYPED EIGHT THOUSAND TIMES AGAIN.
I STILL DON'T KNOW WHY YOU MOVED UP THERE.
THE FANS, ROYCE. THEY HELD ME DOWN IN BANK STREET ONCE AND TRIED TO STEAL MY GIZZARD.
THE FANS AND THE NOISE AND THE TV AND THE BULLSHIT AND...
I COULDN'T GET AT THE TRUTH ANYMORE.

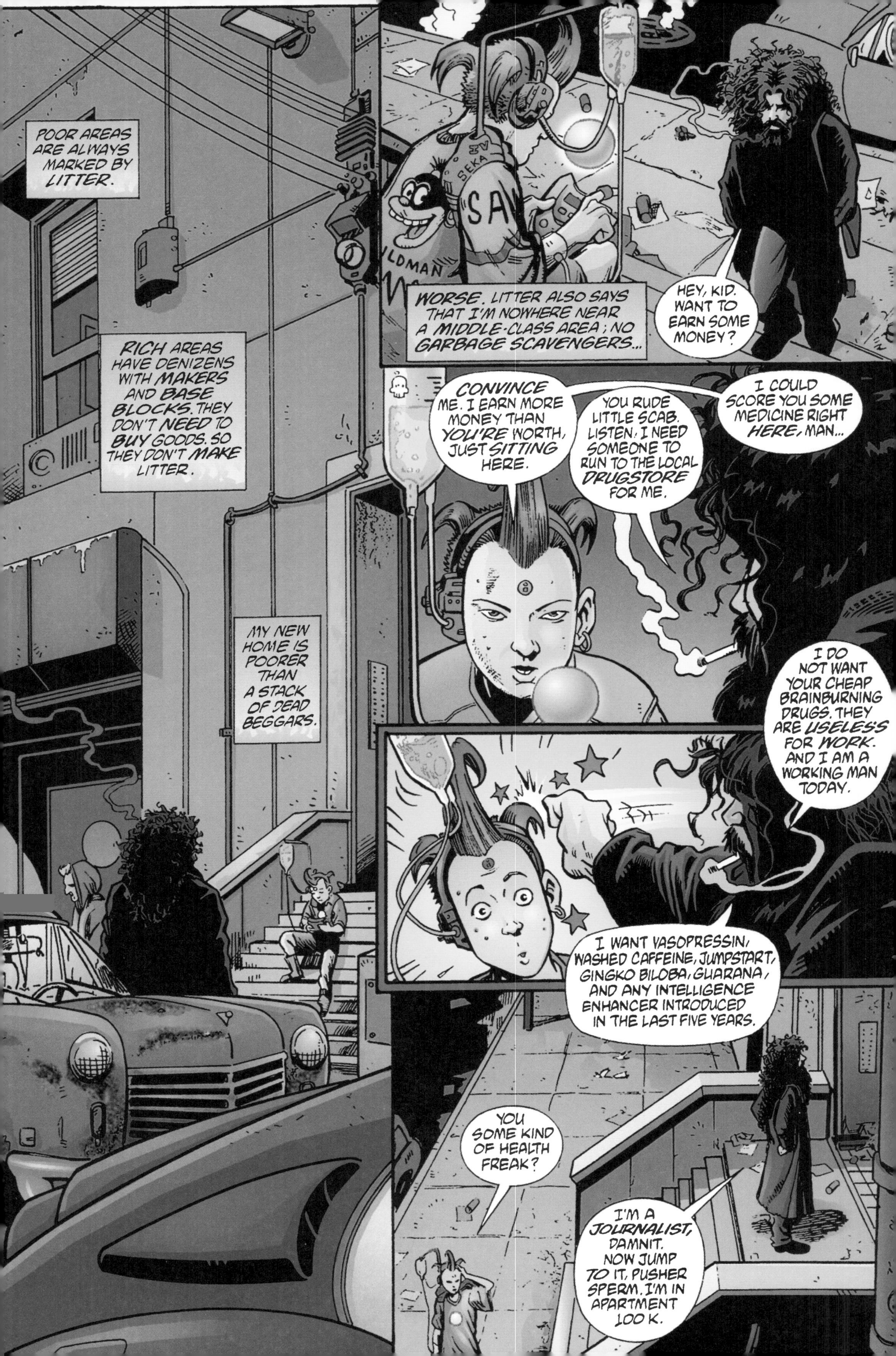
POOR AREAS ARE ALWAYS MARKED BY LITTER.
WORSE. LITTER ALSO SAYS THAT I'M NOWHERE NEAR A MIDDLE-CLASS AREA; NO GARBAGE SCAVENGERS...
HEY, KID. WANT TO EARN SOME MONEY?
RICH AREAS HAVE DENIZENS WITH MAKERS AND BASE BLOCKS. THEY DON'T NEED TO BUY GOODS. SO THEY DON'T MAKE LITTER.
I COULD SCORE YOU SOME MEDICINE RIGHT HERE, MAN...
CONVINCE ME. I EARN MORE MONEY THAN YOU'RE WORTH, JUST SITTING HERE.
YOU RUDE LITTLE SCAB. LISTEN. I NEED SOMEONE TO RUN TO THE LOCAL DRUGSTORE FOR ME.
MY NEW HOME IS POORER THAN A STACK OF DEAD BEGGARS.
I DO NOT WANT YOUR CHEAP BRAINBURNING DRUGS. THEY ARE USELESS FOR WORK. AND I AM A WORKING MAN TODAY.
I WANT VASOPRESSIN, WASHED CAFFEINE, JUMPSTART, GINGKO BILOBA, GUARANA, AND ANY INTELLIGENCE ENHANCER INTRODUCED IN THE LAST FIVE YEARS.
YOU SOME KIND OF HEALTH FREAK?
I'M A JOURNALIST, DAMNIT. NOW JUMP TO IT, PUSHER SPERM. I'M IN APARTMENT 100 K.

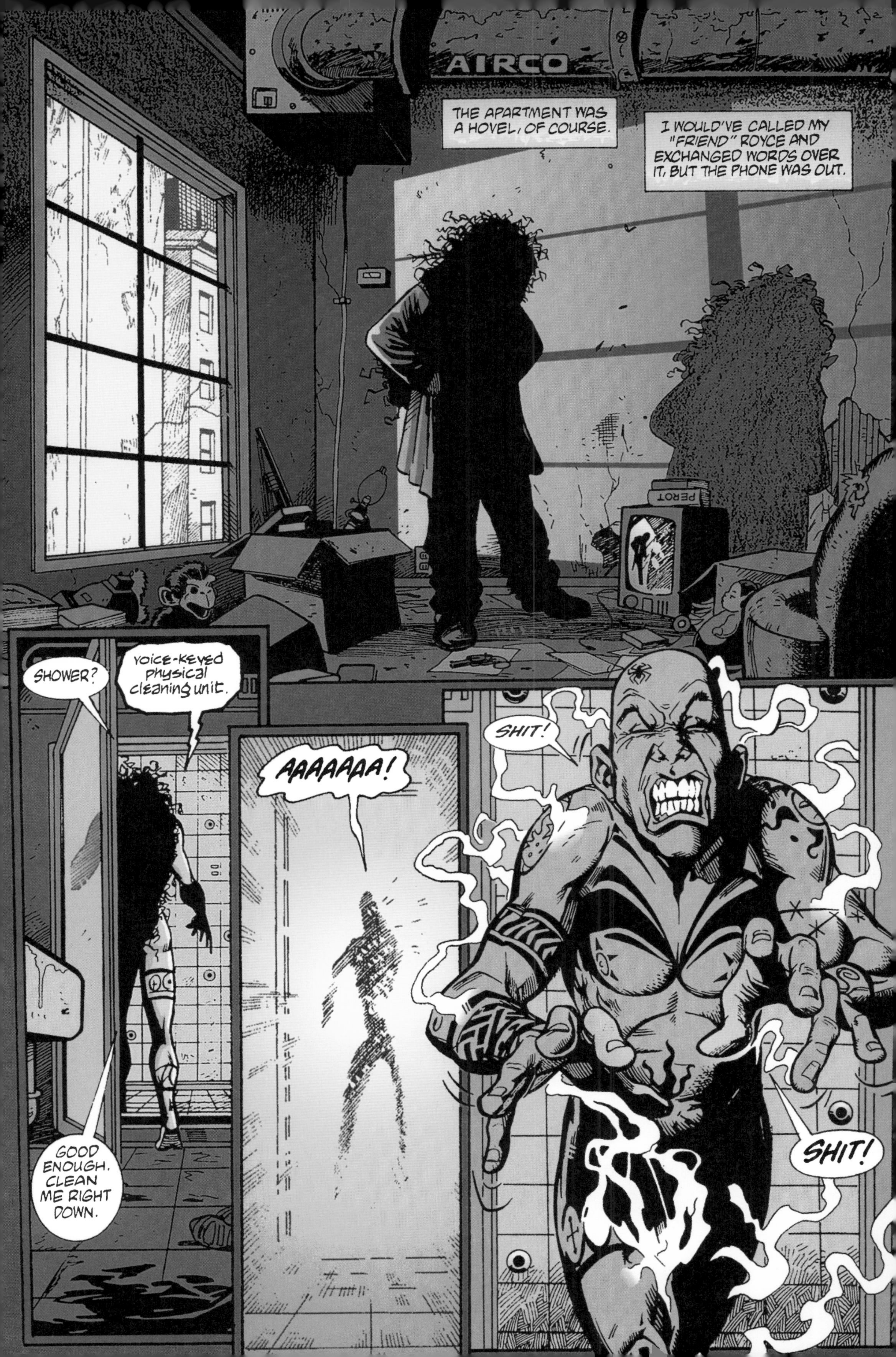
AIRCO
THE APARTMENT WAS A HOVEL, OF COURSE.
I WOULD'VE CALLED MY "FRIEND" ROYCE AND EXCHANGED WORDS OVER IT, BUT THE PHONE WAS OUT.
PEROT
SHOWER?
Voice-keyed physical cleaning unit.
GOOD ENOUGH. CLEAN ME RIGHT DOWN.
AAAAAAA!
SHIT!
SHIT!

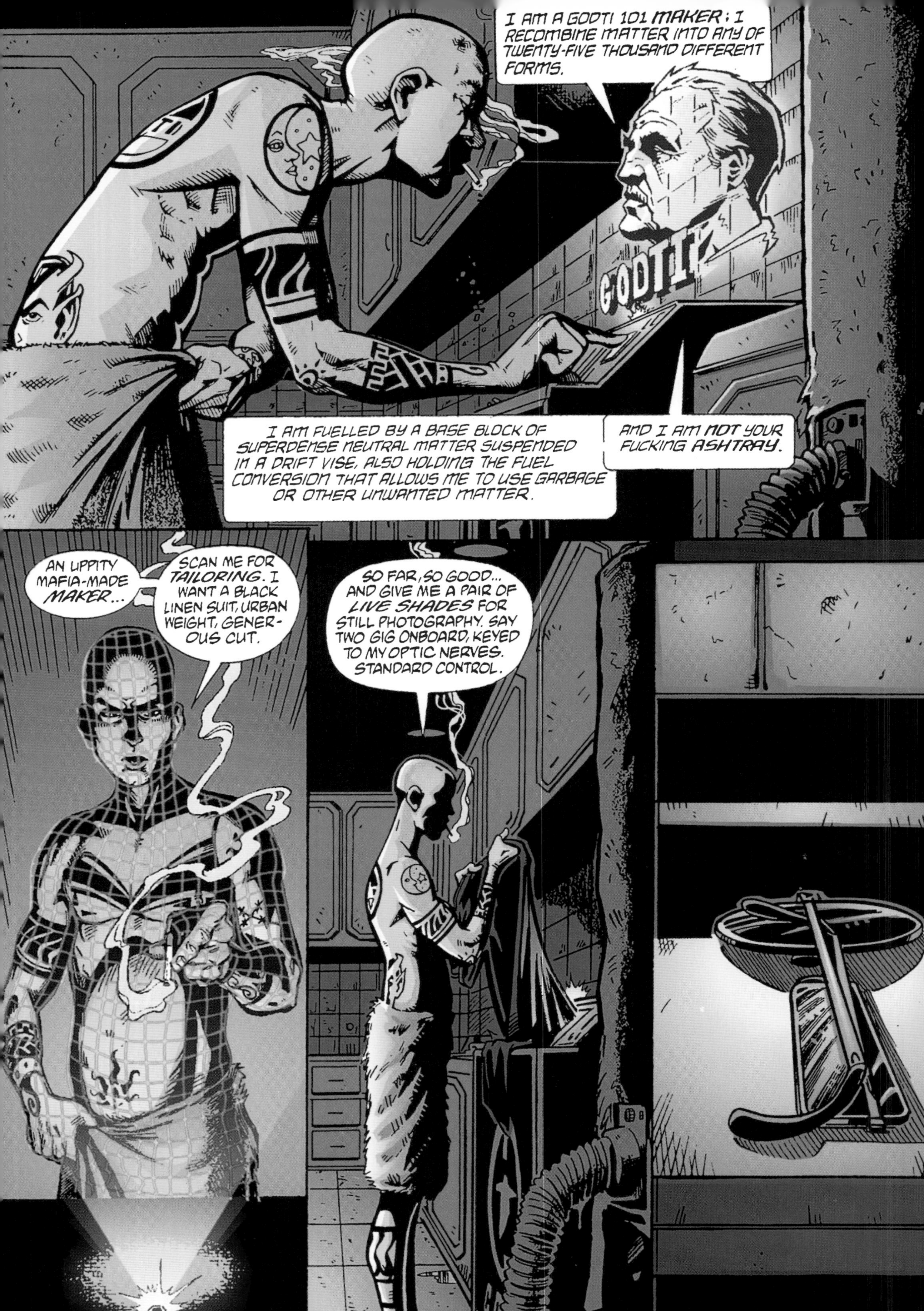
I AM A GODTI 101 MAKER; I RECOMBINE MATTER INTO ANY OF TWENTY-FIVE THOUSAND DIFFERENT FORMS.
GODTI
I AM FUELLED BY A BASE BLOCK OF SUPERDENSE NEUTRAL MATTER SUSPENDED IN A DRIFT VISE, ALSO HOLDING THE FUEL CONVERSION THAT ALLOWS ME TO USE GARBAGE OR OTHER UNWANTED MATTER.
AND I AM NOT YOUR FUCKING ASHTRAY.
AN UPPITY MAFIA-MADE MAKER...
SCAN ME FOR TAILORING. I WANT A BLACK LINEN SUIT, URBAN WEIGHT, GENEROUS CUT.
SO FAR, SO GOOD... AND GIVE ME A PAIR OF LIVE SHADES FOR STILL PHOTOGRAPHY. SAY TWO GIG ONBOARD, KEYED TO MY OPTIC NERVES. STANDARD CONTROL.

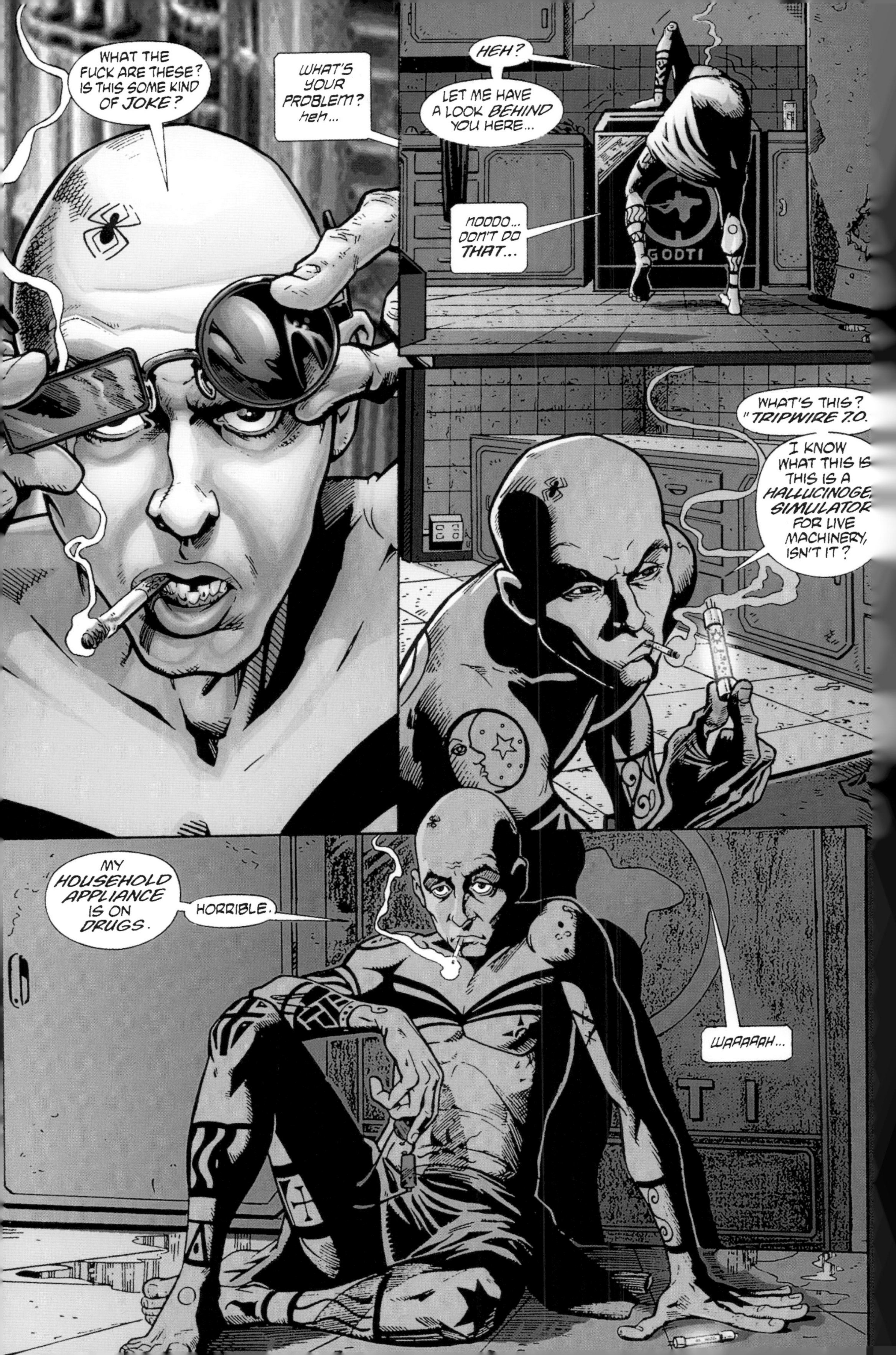
WHAT THE FUCK ARE THESE? IS THIS SOME KIND OF JOKE?
WHAT'S YOUR PROBLEM? heh...
HEH?
LET ME HAVE A LOOK BEHIND YOU HERE...
NOOOO... DON'T DO THAT...
WHAT'S THIS? "TRIPWIRE 7.0.
I KNOW WHAT THIS IS THIS IS A HALLUCINOGE SIMULATOR FOR LIVE MACHINERY, ISN'T IT?
MY HOUSEHOLD APPLIANCE IS ON DRUGS.
HORRIBLE.
WAAAAAH...

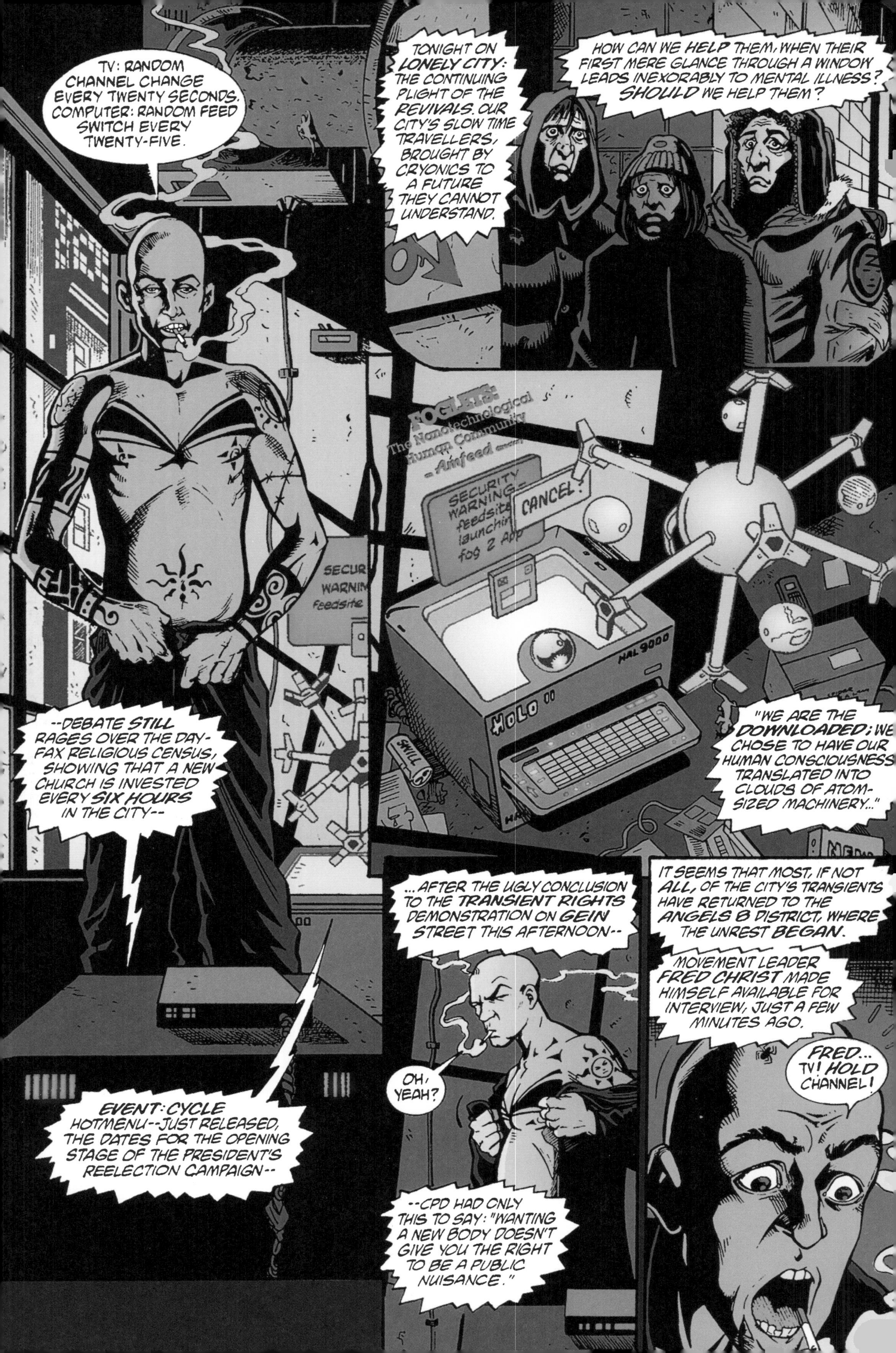
TV: RANDOM CHANNEL CHANGE EVERY TWENTY SECONDS. COMPUTER: RANDOM FEED SWITCH EVERY TWENTY-FIVE.
TONIGHT ON LONELY CITY: THE CONTINUING PLIGHT OF THE REVIVALS. OUR CITY'S SLOW TIME TRAVELLERS, BROUGHT BY CRYONICS TO A FUTURE THEY CANNOT UNDERSTAND.
HOW CAN WE HELP THEM, WHEN THEIR FIRST MERE GLANCE THROUGH A WINDOW LEADS INEXORABLY TO MENTAL ILLNESS? SHOULD WE HELP THEM?
FOGLETS: The Nanotechnological Human Community
SECURITY WARNING
CANCEL?
HAL 9000
HOLO II
--DEBATE STILL RAGES OVER THE DAY-FAX RELIGIOUS CENSUS, SHOWING THAT A NEW CHURCH IS INVESTED EVERY SIX HOURS IN THE CITY--
"WE ARE THE DOWNLOADED; WE CHOSE TO HAVE OUR HUMAN CONSCIOUSNESS TRANSLATED INTO CLOUDS OF ATOM-SIZED MACHINERY..."
...AFTER THE UGLY CONCLUSION TO THE TRANSIENT RIGHTS DEMONSTRATION ON GEIN STREET THIS AFTERNOON--
IT SEEMS THAT MOST, IF NOT ALL, OF THE CITY'S TRANSIENTS HAVE RETURNED TO THE ANGELS 8 DISTRICT, WHERE THE UNREST BEGAN.
MOVEMENT LEADER FRED CHRIST MADE HIMSELF AVAILABLE FOR INTERVIEW, JUST A FEW MINUTES AGO.
OH, YEAH?
FRED... TV! HOLD CHANNEL!
EVENT: CYCLE HOTMENU--JUST RELEASED, THE DATES FOR THE OPENING STAGE OF THE PRESIDENT'S REELECTION CAMPAIGN--
--CPD HAD ONLY THIS TO SAY: "WANTING A NEW BODY DOESN'T GIVE YOU THE RIGHT TO BE A PUBLIC NUISANCE."

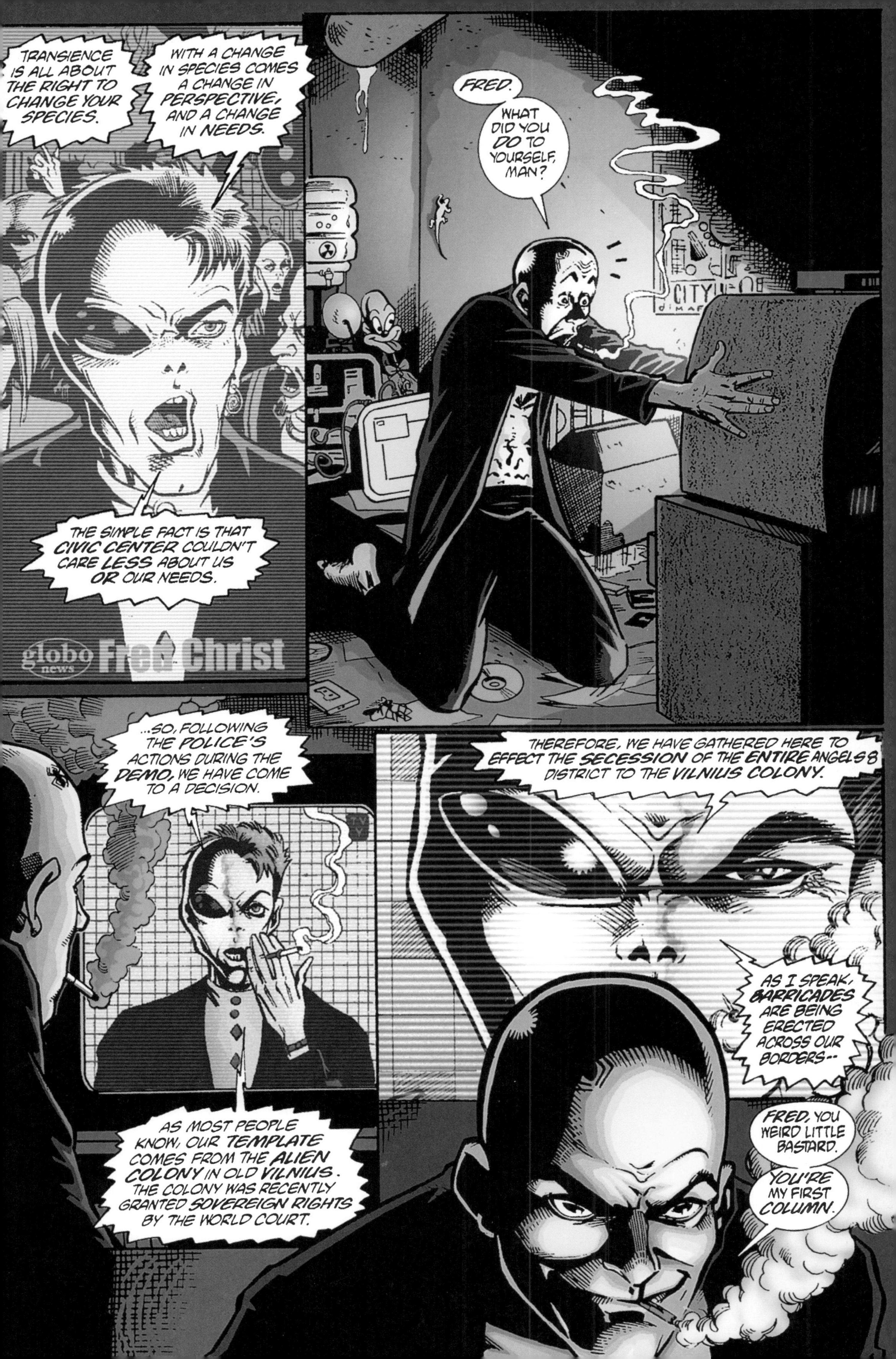
TRANSIENCE IS ALL ABOUT THE RIGHT TO CHANGE YOUR SPECIES.
WITH A CHANGE IN SPECIES COMES A CHANGE IN PERSPECTIVE, AND A CHANGE IN NEEDS.
THE SIMPLE FACT IS THAT CIVIC CENTER COULDN'T CARE LESS ABOUT US OR OUR NEEDS.
globo news Fred Christ
FRED.
WHAT DID YOU DO TO YOURSELF, MAN?
CITY
...SO, FOLLOWING THE POLICE'S ACTIONS DURING THE DEMO, WE HAVE COME TO A DECISION.
AS MOST PEOPLE KNOW, OUR TEMPLATE COMES FROM THE ALIEN COLONY IN OLD VILNIUS. THE COLONY WAS RECENTLY GRANTED SOVEREIGN RIGHTS BY THE WORLD COURT.
THEREFORE, WE HAVE GATHERED HERE TO EFFECT THE SECESSION OF THE ENTIRE ANGELS 8 DISTRICT TO THE VILNIUS COLONY.
AS I SPEAK, BARRICADES ARE BEING ERECTED ACROSS OUR BORDERS--
FRED, YOU WEIRD LITTLE BASTARD.
YOU'RE MY FIRST COLUMN.

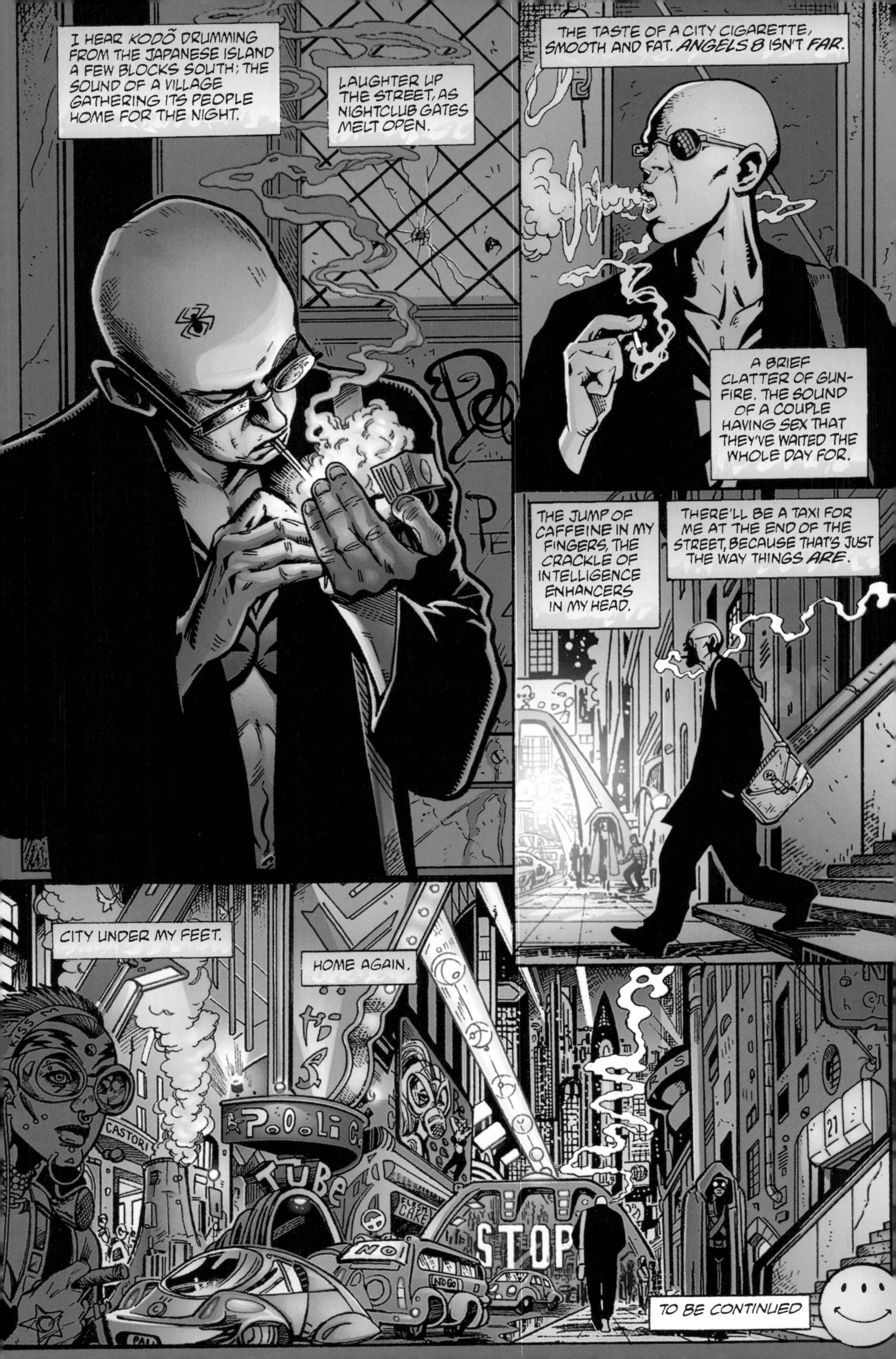
I HEAR KODÕ DRUMMING FROM THE JAPANESE ISLAND A FEW BLOCKS SOUTH; THE SOUND OF A VILLAGE GATHERING ITS PEOPLE HOME FOR THE NIGHT.
LAUGHTER UP THE STREET, AS NIGHTCLUB GATES MELT OPEN.
THE TASTE OF A CITY CIGARETTE, SMOOTH AND FAT. ANGELS 8 ISN'T FAR.
A BRIEF CLATTER OF GUN-FIRE. THE SOUND OF A COUPLE HAVING SEX THAT THEY'VE WAITED THE WHOLE DAY FOR.
THE JUMP OF CAFFEINE IN MY FINGERS, THE CRACKLE OF INTELLIGENCE ENHANCERS IN MY HEAD.
THERE'LL BE A TAXI FOR ME AT THE END OF THE STREET, BECAUSE THAT'S JUST THE WAY THINGS ARE.
CITY UNDER MY FEET.
HOME AGAIN.
P.O.Li.C.
TUBE
CASTORI
FLESH CAKE
STOP
21
TO BE CONTINUED

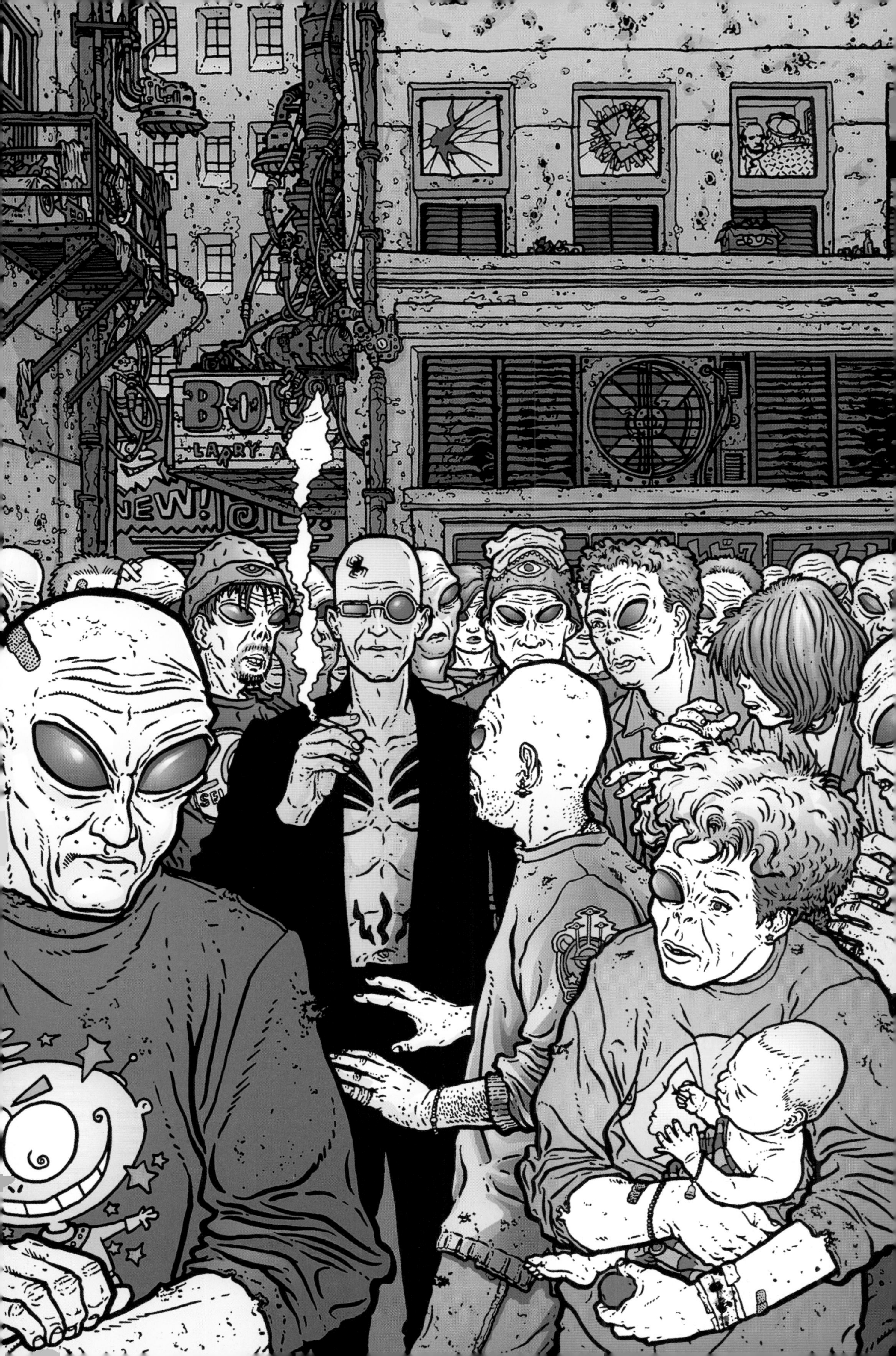
NEW!

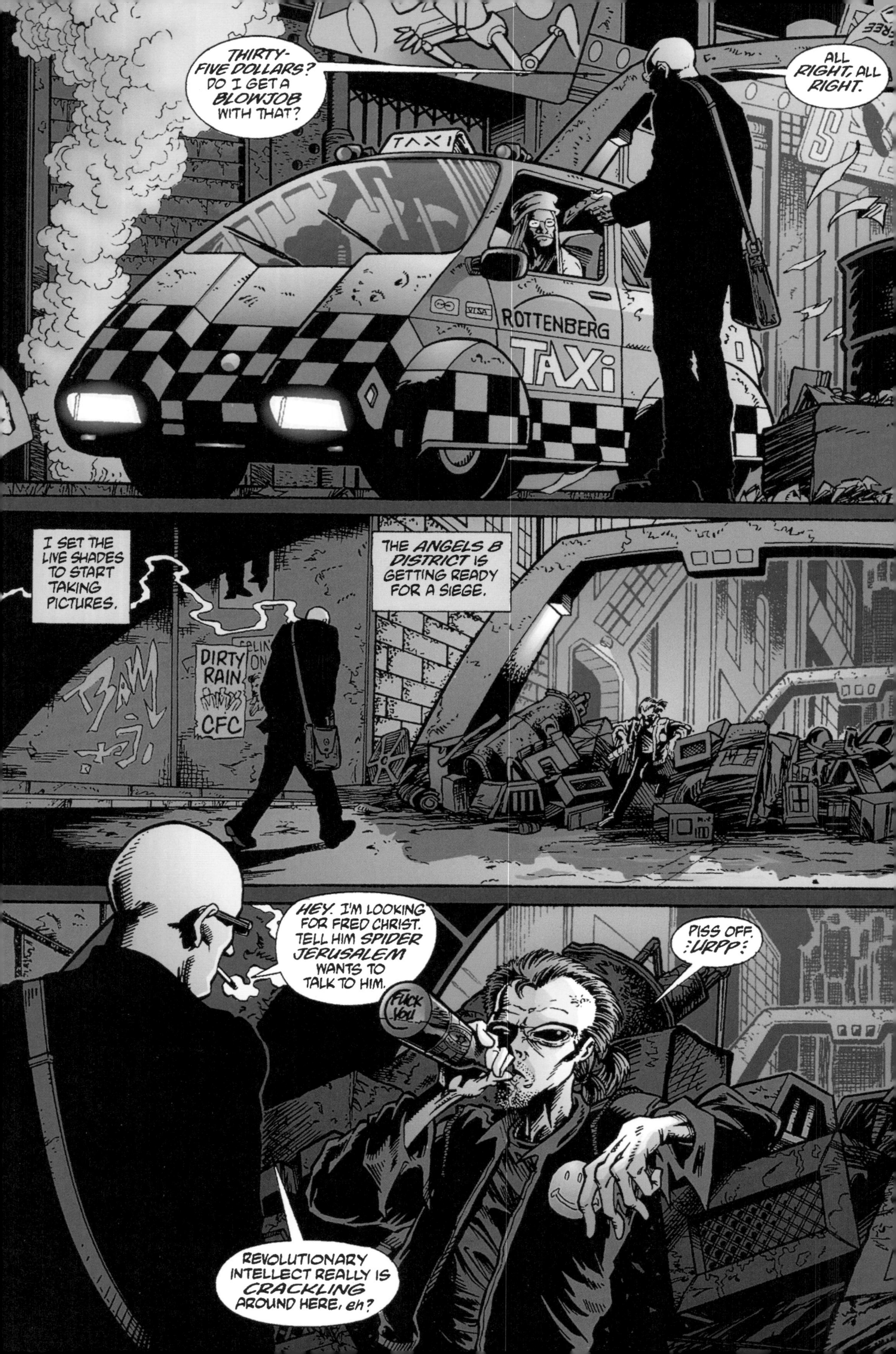
THIRTY-FIVE DOLLARS? DO I GET A BLOWJOB WITH THAT?
ALL RIGHT, ALL RIGHT.
TAXI
ROTTENBERG TAXi
I SET THE LIVE SHADES TO START TAKING PICTURES.
THE ANGELS 8 DISTRICT IS GETTING READY FOR A SIEGE.
DIRTY RAIN
CFC
HEY. I'M LOOKING FOR FRED CHRIST. TELL HIM SPIDER JERUSALEM WANTS TO TALK TO HIM.
PISS OFF. :URPP:
FUCK YOU
REVOLUTIONARY INTELLECT REALLY IS CRACKLING AROUND HERE, eh?

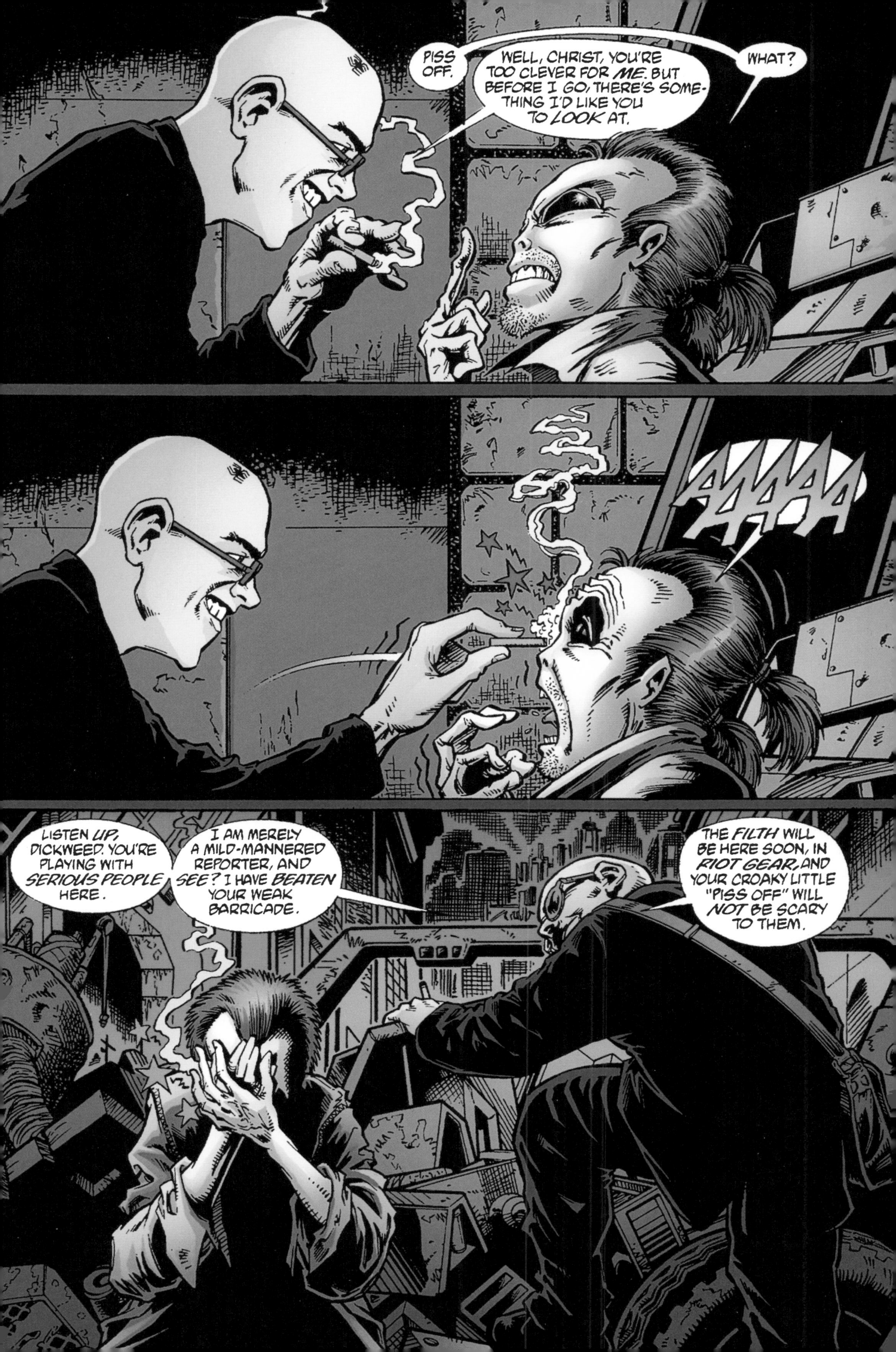
PISS OFF.
WELL, CHRIST, YOU'RE TOO CLEVER FOR ME. BUT BEFORE I GO, THERE'S SOMETHING I'D LIKE YOU TO LOOK AT.
WHAT?
AAAAA
LISTEN UP, DICKWEED. YOU'RE PLAYING WITH SERIOUS PEOPLE HERE.
I AM MERELY A MILD-MANNERED REPORTER, AND SEE? I HAVE BEATEN YOUR WEAK BARRICADE.
THE FILTH WILL BE HERE SOON, IN RIOT GEAR, AND YOUR CROAKY LITTLE "PISS OFF" WILL NOT BE SCARY TO THEM.

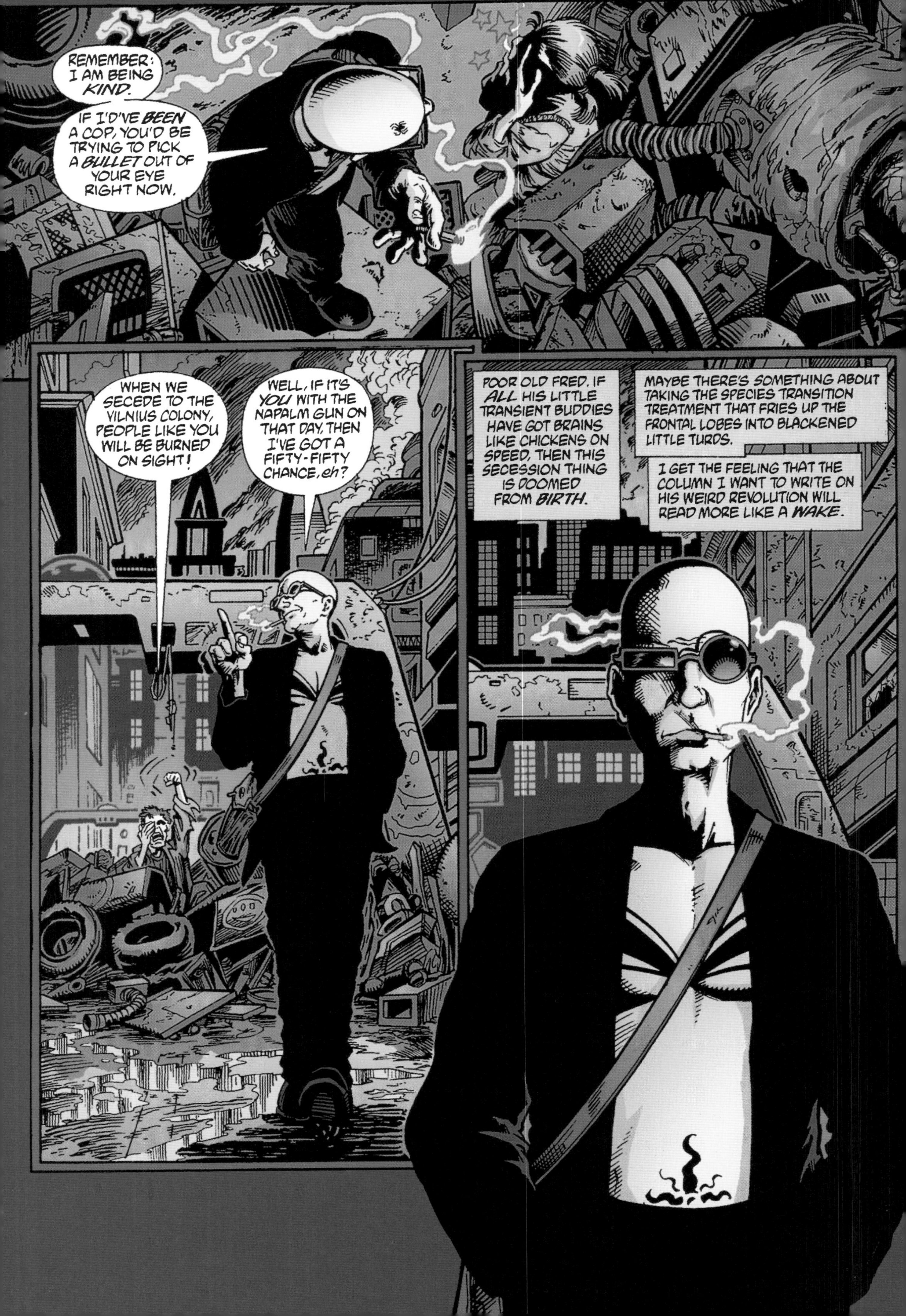
REMEMBER: I AM BEING KIND.
IF I'D'VE BEEN A COP, YOU'D BE TRYING TO PICK A BULLET OUT OF YOUR EYE RIGHT NOW.
WHEN WE SECEDE TO THE VILNIUS COLONY, PEOPLE LIKE YOU WILL BE BURNED ON SIGHT!
WELL, IF IT'S YOU WITH THE NAPALM GUN ON THAT DAY, THEN I'VE GOT A FIFTY-FIFTY CHANCE, eh?
POOR OLD FRED. IF ALL HIS LITTLE TRANSIENT BUDDIES HAVE GOT BRAINS LIKE CHICKENS ON SPEED, THEN THIS SECESSION THING IS DOOMED FROM BIRTH.
MAYBE THERE'S SOMETHING ABOUT TAKING THE SPECIES TRANSITION TREATMENT THAT FRIES UP THE FRONTAL LOBES INTO BLACKENED LITTLE TURDS.
I GET THE FEELING THAT THE COLUMN I WANT TO WRITE ON HIS WEIRD REVOLUTION WILL READ MORE LIKE A WAKE.

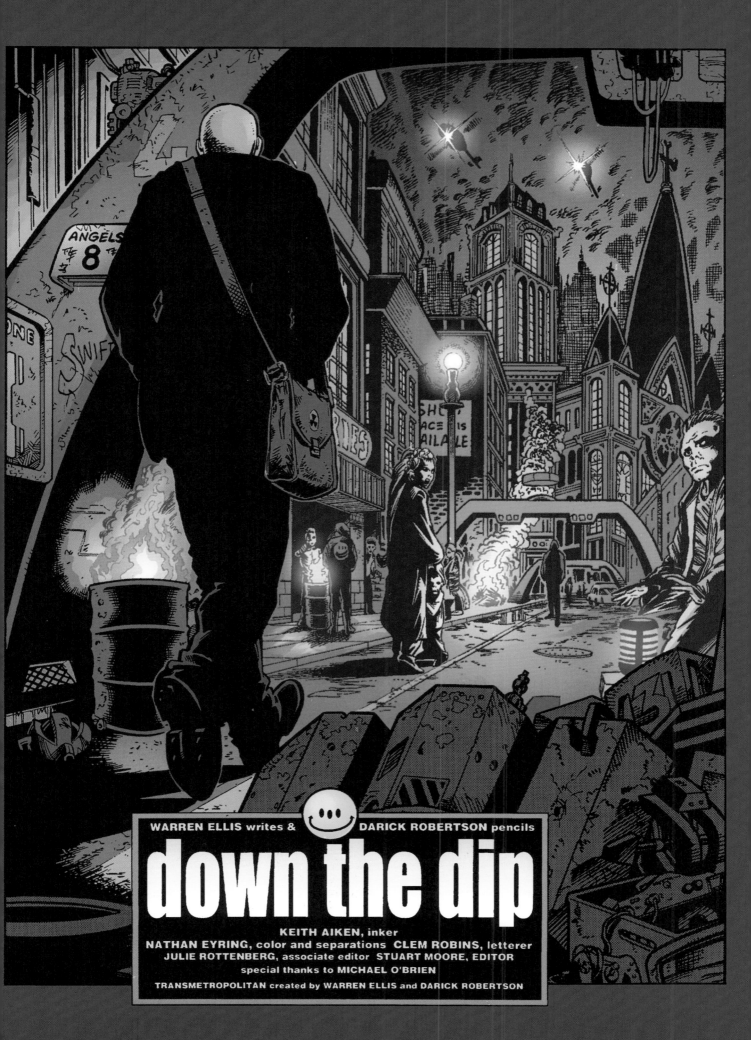

WARREN ELLIS writes & 😀 DARICK ROBERTSON pencils

# down the dip

KEITH AIKEN, inker
NATHAN EYRING, color and separations   CLEM ROBINS, letterer
JULIE ROTTENBERG, associate editor   STUART MOORE, EDITOR
special thanks to MICHAEL O'BRIEN

TRANSMETROPOLITAN created by WARREN ELLIS and DARICK ROBERTSON

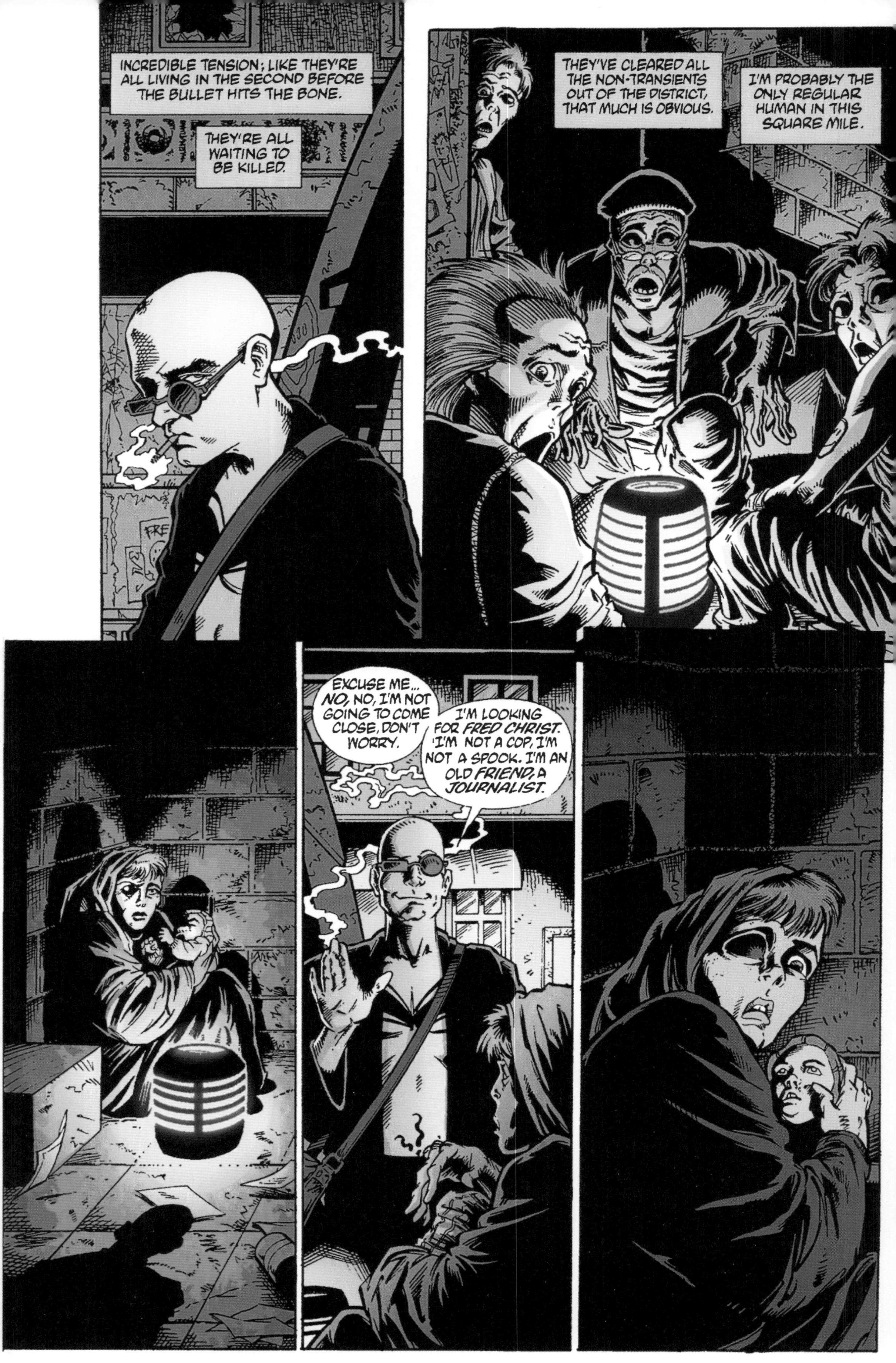
INCREDIBLE TENSION; LIKE THEY'RE ALL LIVING IN THE SECOND BEFORE THE BULLET HITS THE BONE.
THEY'RE ALL WAITING TO BE KILLED.
THEY'VE CLEARED ALL THE NON-TRANSIENTS OUT OF THE DISTRICT, THAT MUCH IS OBVIOUS.
I'M PROBABLY THE ONLY REGULAR HUMAN IN THIS SQUARE MILE.
EXCUSE ME... NO, NO, I'M NOT GOING TO COME CLOSE, DON'T WORRY.
I'M LOOKING FOR FRED CHRIST. I'M NOT A COP, I'M NOT A SPOOK. I'M AN OLD FRIEND, A JOURNALIST.

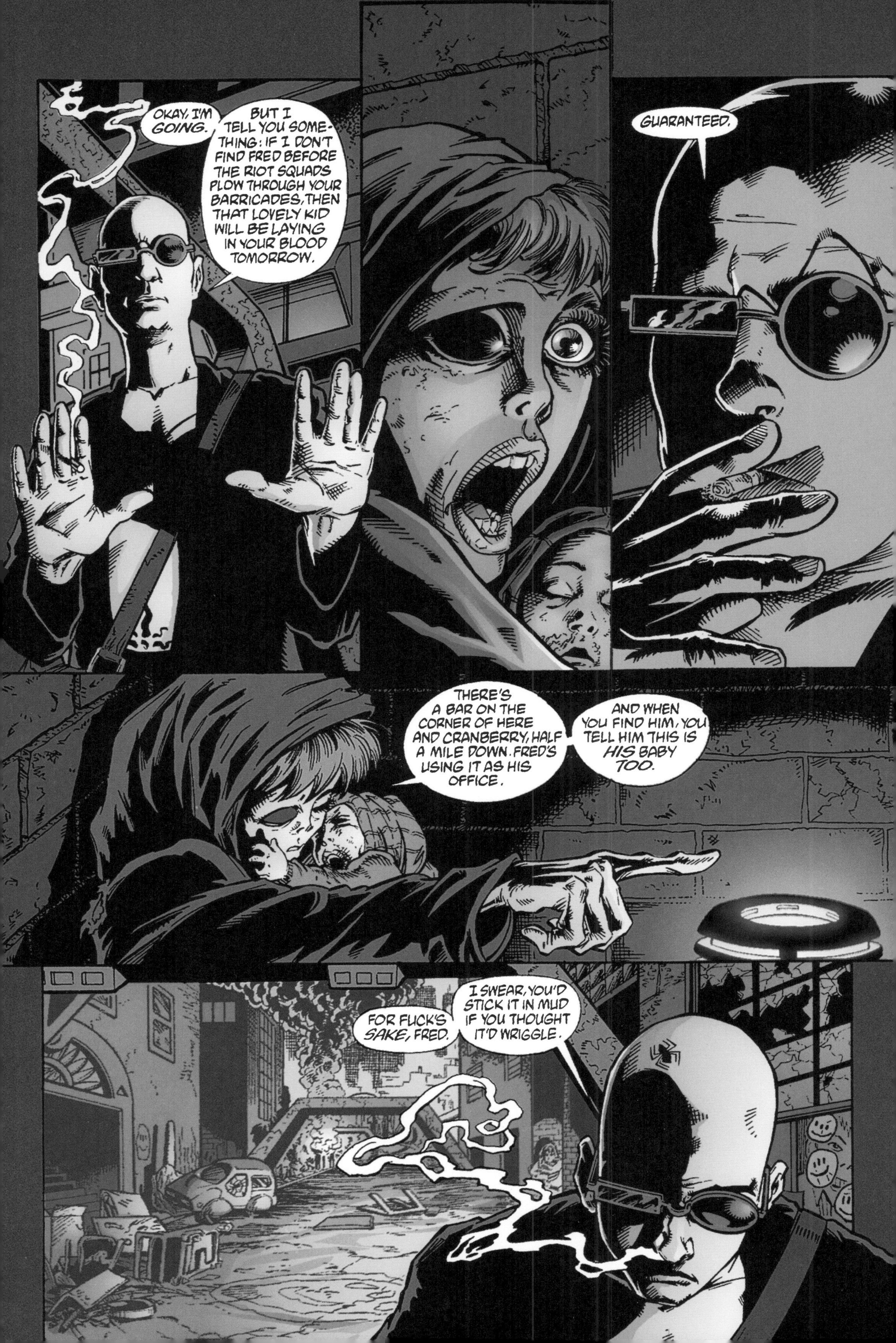
OKAY, I'M GOING.
BUT I TELL YOU SOMETHING: IF I DON'T FIND FRED BEFORE THE RIOT SQUADS PLOW THROUGH YOUR BARRICADES, THEN THAT LOVELY KID WILL BE LAYING IN YOUR BLOOD TOMORROW.
GUARANTEED.
THERE'S A BAR ON THE CORNER OF HERE AND CRANBERRY, HALF A MILE DOWN. FRED'S USING IT AS HIS OFFICE.
AND WHEN YOU FIND HIM, YOU TELL HIM THIS IS *HIS* BABY *TOO*.
FOR FUCK'S *SAKE*, FRED.
I SWEAR, YOU'D STICK IT IN MUD IF YOU THOUGHT IT'D WRIGGLE.

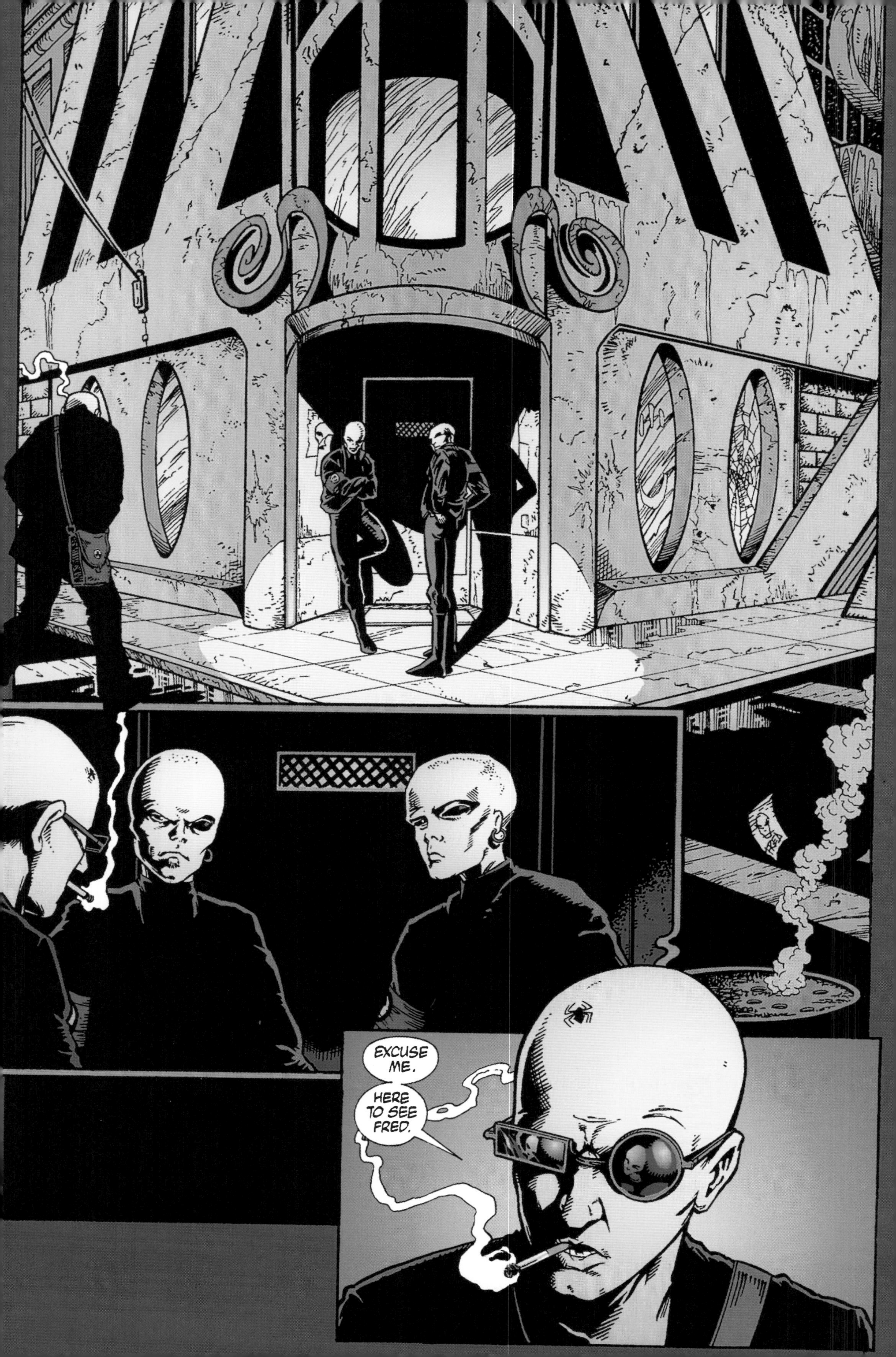
EXCUSE ME.
HERE TO SEE FRED.

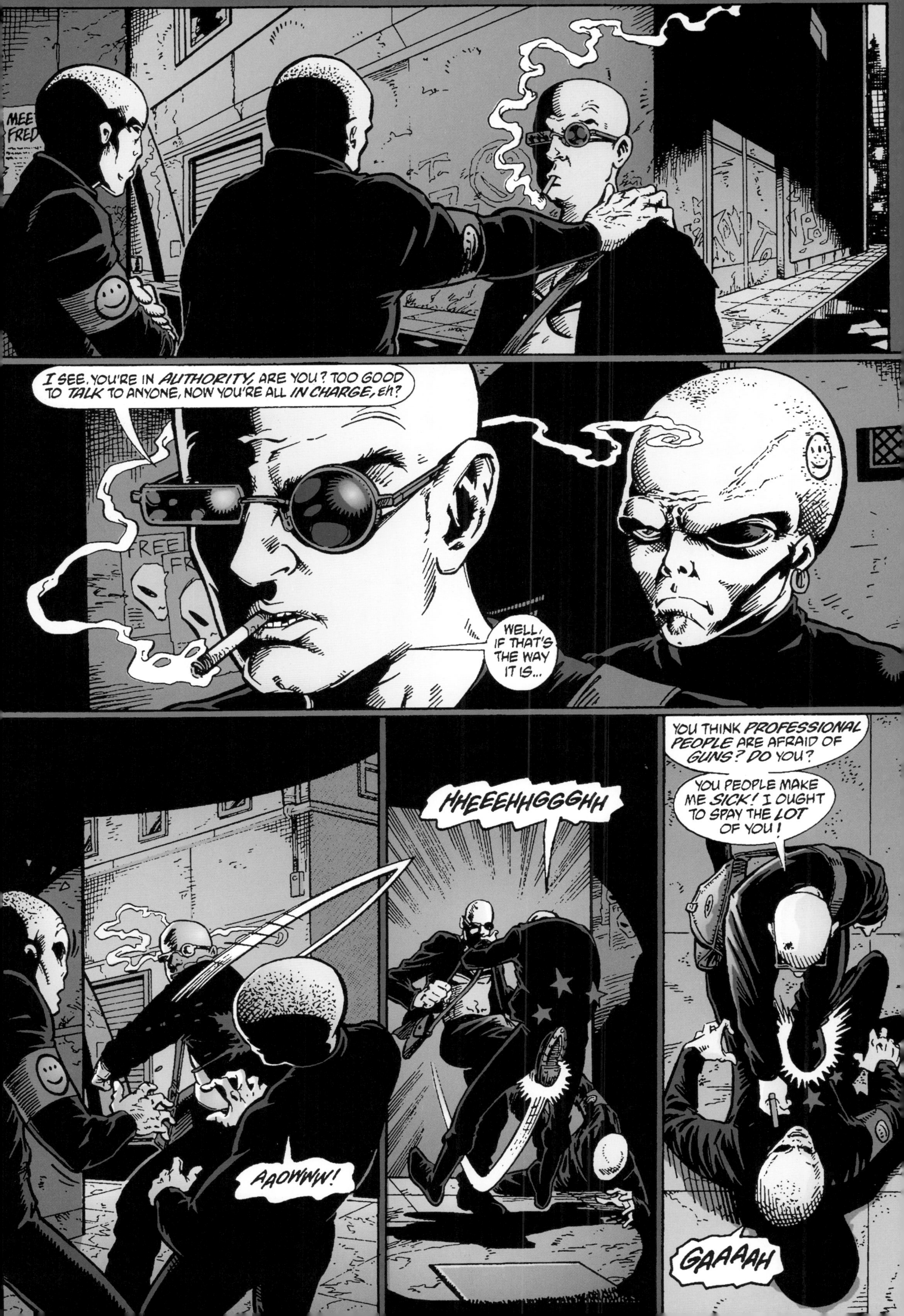

MEET FRED
I SEE. YOU'RE IN AUTHORITY, ARE YOU? TOO GOOD TO TALK TO ANYONE, NOW YOU'RE ALL IN CHARGE, eh?
FREE FR
WELL, IF THAT'S THE WAY IT IS...
AAOWWW!
HHEEEHHGGGHH
YOU THINK PROFESSIONAL PEOPLE ARE AFRAID OF GUNS? DO YOU?
YOU PEOPLE MAKE ME SICK! I OUGHT TO SPAY THE LOT OF YOU!
GAAAAH

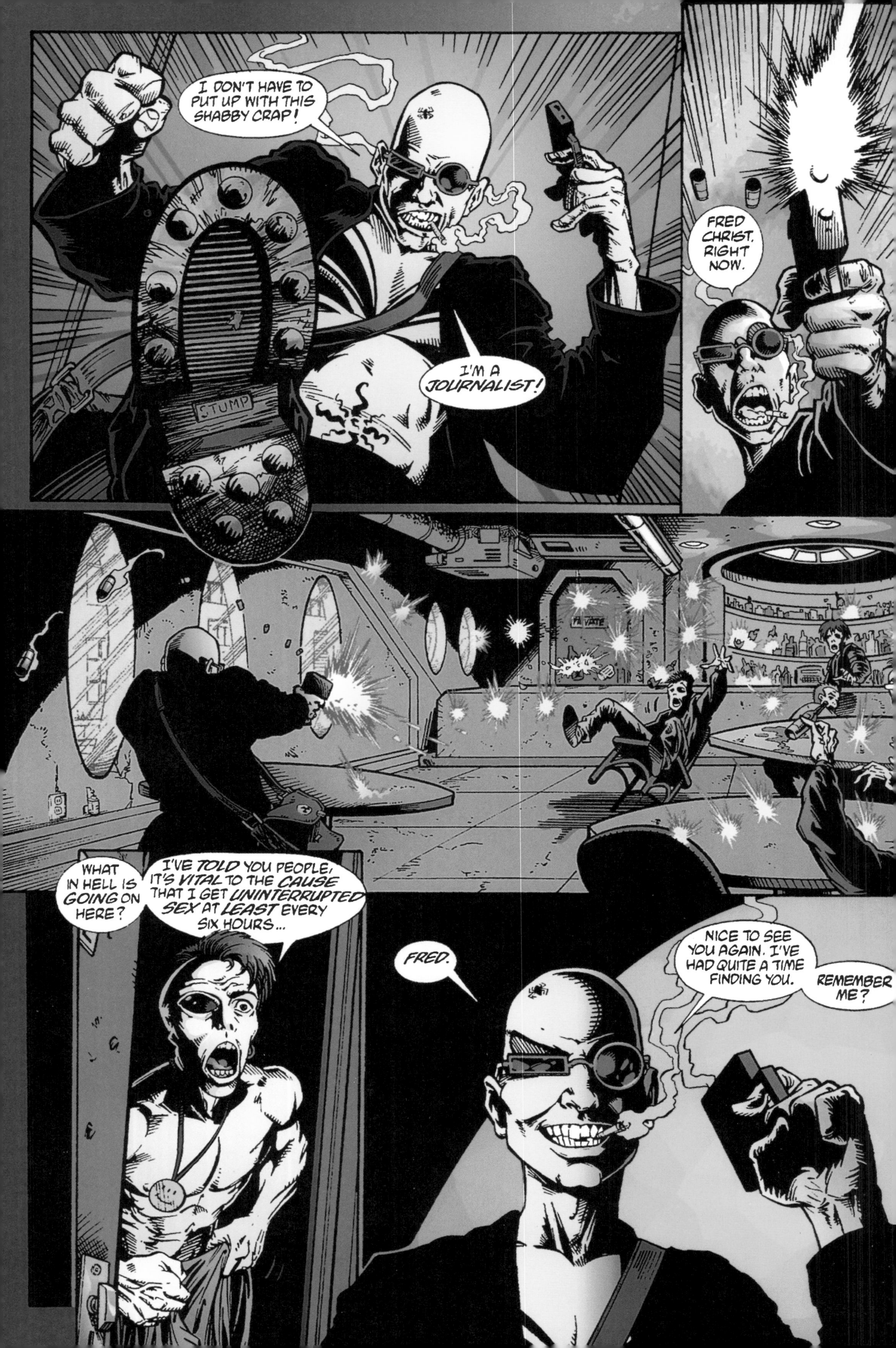

I DON'T HAVE TO PUT UP WITH THIS SHABBY CRAP!
STUMP
I'M A JOURNALIST!
FRED CHRIST. RIGHT NOW.
PRIVATE
WHAT IN HELL IS GOING ON HERE?
I'VE TOLD YOU PEOPLE, IT'S VITAL TO THE CAUSE THAT I GET UNINTERRUPTED SEX AT LEAST EVERY SIX HOURS...
FRED.
NICE TO SEE YOU AGAIN. I'VE HAD QUITE A TIME FINDING YOU.
REMEMBER ME?

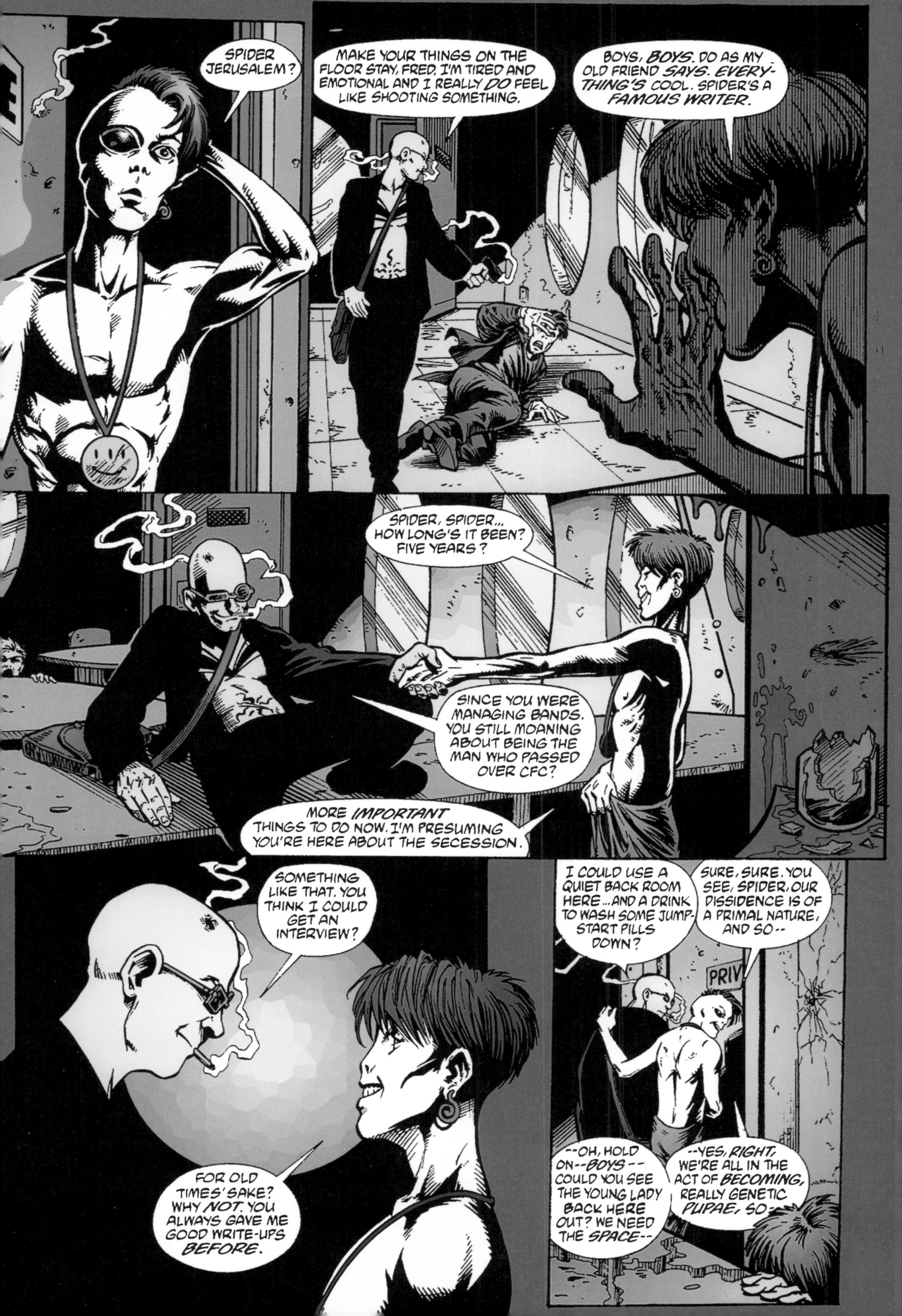
SPIDER JERUSALEM?
MAKE YOUR THINGS ON THE FLOOR STAY, FRED. I'M TIRED AND EMOTIONAL AND I REALLY *DO* FEEL LIKE SHOOTING SOMETHING.
BOYS, *BOYS*. DO AS MY OLD FRIEND *SAYS*. *EVERYTHING'S* COOL. SPIDER'S A *FAMOUS WRITER*.
SPIDER, SPIDER... HOW LONG'S IT BEEN? FIVE YEARS?
SINCE YOU WERE MANAGING BANDS. YOU STILL MOANING ABOUT BEING THE MAN WHO PASSED OVER CFC?
MORE *IMPORTANT* THINGS TO DO NOW. I'M PRESUMING YOU'RE HERE ABOUT THE SECESSION.
SOMETHING LIKE THAT. YOU THINK I COULD GET AN INTERVIEW?
FOR OLD TIMES' SAKE? WHY *NOT*. YOU ALWAYS GAVE ME GOOD WRITE-UPS *BEFORE*.
I COULD USE A QUIET BACK ROOM HERE... AND A DRINK TO WASH SOME JUMP-START PILLS DOWN?
SURE, SURE. YOU SEE, SPIDER, OUR DISSIDENCE IS OF A PRIMAL NATURE, AND SO--
PRIV
--OH, HOLD ON--*BOYS*-- COULD YOU SEE THE YOUNG LADY BACK HERE OUT? WE NEED THE *SPACE*--
--YES, *RIGHT*, WE'RE ALL IN THE ACT OF *BECOMING*, REALLY GENETIC *PUPAE*, SO--

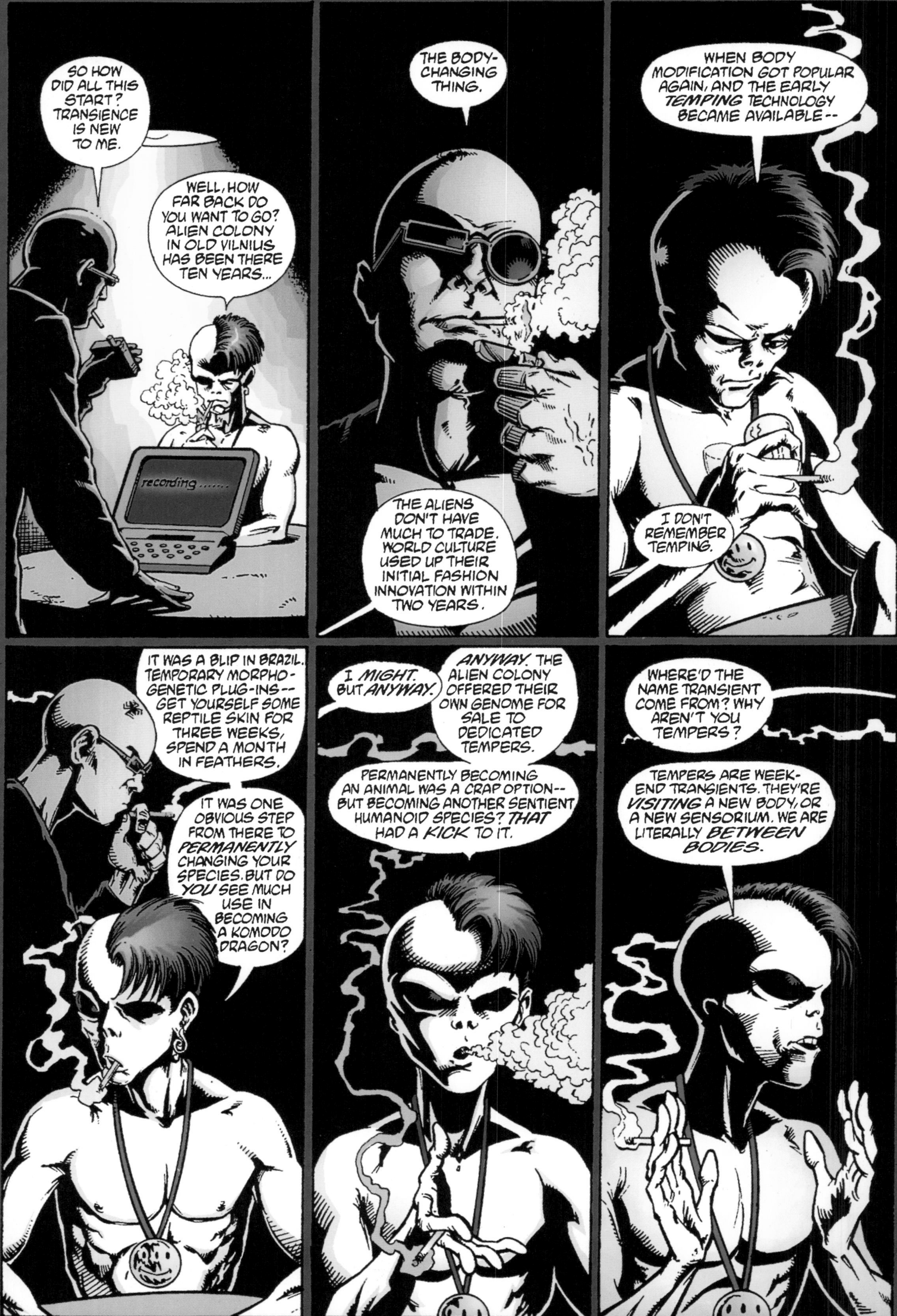
SO HOW DID ALL THIS START? TRANSIENCE IS NEW TO ME.
WELL, HOW FAR BACK DO YOU WANT TO GO? ALIEN COLONY IN OLD VILNIUS HAS BEEN THERE TEN YEARS...
recording.......
THE BODY-CHANGING THING.
THE ALIENS DON'T HAVE MUCH TO TRADE. WORLD CULTURE USED UP THEIR INITIAL FASHION INNOVATION WITHIN TWO YEARS.
WHEN BODY MODIFICATION GOT POPULAR AGAIN, AND THE EARLY TEMPING TECHNOLOGY BECAME AVAILABLE--
I DON'T REMEMBER TEMPING.
IT WAS A BLIP IN BRAZIL. TEMPORARY MORPHO-GENETIC PLUG-INS--GET YOURSELF SOME REPTILE SKIN FOR THREE WEEKS, SPEND A MONTH IN FEATHERS.
IT WAS ONE OBVIOUS STEP FROM THERE TO PERMANENTLY CHANGING YOUR SPECIES. BUT DO YOU SEE MUCH USE IN BECOMING A KOMODO DRAGON?
I MIGHT. BUT ANYWAY.
ANYWAY. THE ALIEN COLONY OFFERED THEIR OWN GENOME FOR SALE TO DEDICATED TEMPERS.
PERMANENTLY BECOMING AN ANIMAL WAS A CRAP OPTION--BUT BECOMING ANOTHER SENTIENT HUMANOID SPECIES? THAT HAD A KICK TO IT.
WHERE'D THE NAME TRANSIENT COME FROM? WHY AREN'T YOU TEMPERS?
TEMPERS ARE WEEK-END TRANSIENTS. THEY'RE VISITING A NEW BODY, OR A NEW SENSORIUM. WE ARE LITERALLY BETWEEN BODIES.

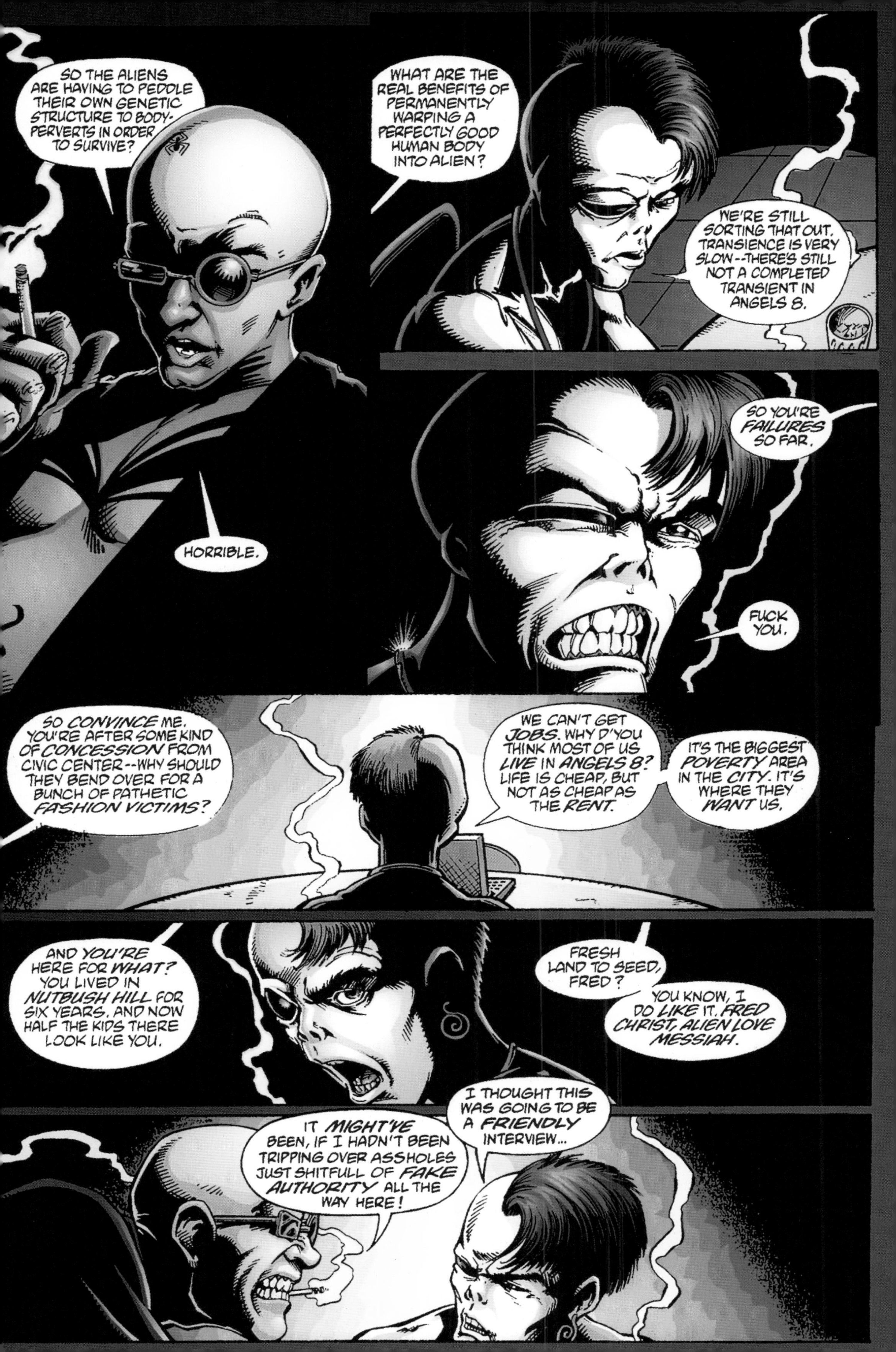
SO THE ALIENS ARE HAVING TO PEDDLE THEIR OWN GENETIC STRUCTURE TO BODY-PERVERTS IN ORDER TO SURVIVE?
HORRIBLE.
WHAT ARE THE REAL BENEFITS OF PERMANENTLY WARPING A PERFECTLY GOOD HUMAN BODY INTO ALIEN?
WE'RE STILL SORTING THAT OUT. TRANSIENCE IS VERY SLOW--THERE'S STILL NOT A COMPLETED TRANSIENT IN ANGELS 8.
SO YOU'RE FAILURES SO FAR.
FUCK YOU.
SO CONVINCE ME. YOU'RE AFTER SOME KIND OF CONCESSION FROM CIVIC CENTER--WHY SHOULD THEY BEND OVER FOR A BUNCH OF PATHETIC FASHION VICTIMS?
WE CAN'T GET JOBS. WHY D'YOU THINK MOST OF US LIVE IN ANGELS 8? LIFE IS CHEAP, BUT NOT AS CHEAP AS THE RENT.
IT'S THE BIGGEST POVERTY AREA IN THE CITY. IT'S WHERE THEY WANT US.
AND YOU'RE HERE FOR WHAT? YOU LIVED IN NUTBUSH HILL FOR SIX YEARS, AND NOW HALF THE KIDS THERE LOOK LIKE YOU.
FRESH LAND TO SEED, FRED?
YOU KNOW, I DO LIKE IT. FRED CHRIST, ALIEN LOVE MESSIAH.
I THOUGHT THIS WAS GOING TO BE A FRIENDLY INTERVIEW...
IT MIGHT'VE BEEN, IF I HADN'T BEEN TRIPPING OVER ASSHOLES JUST SHITFULL OF FAKE AUTHORITY ALL THE WAY HERE!

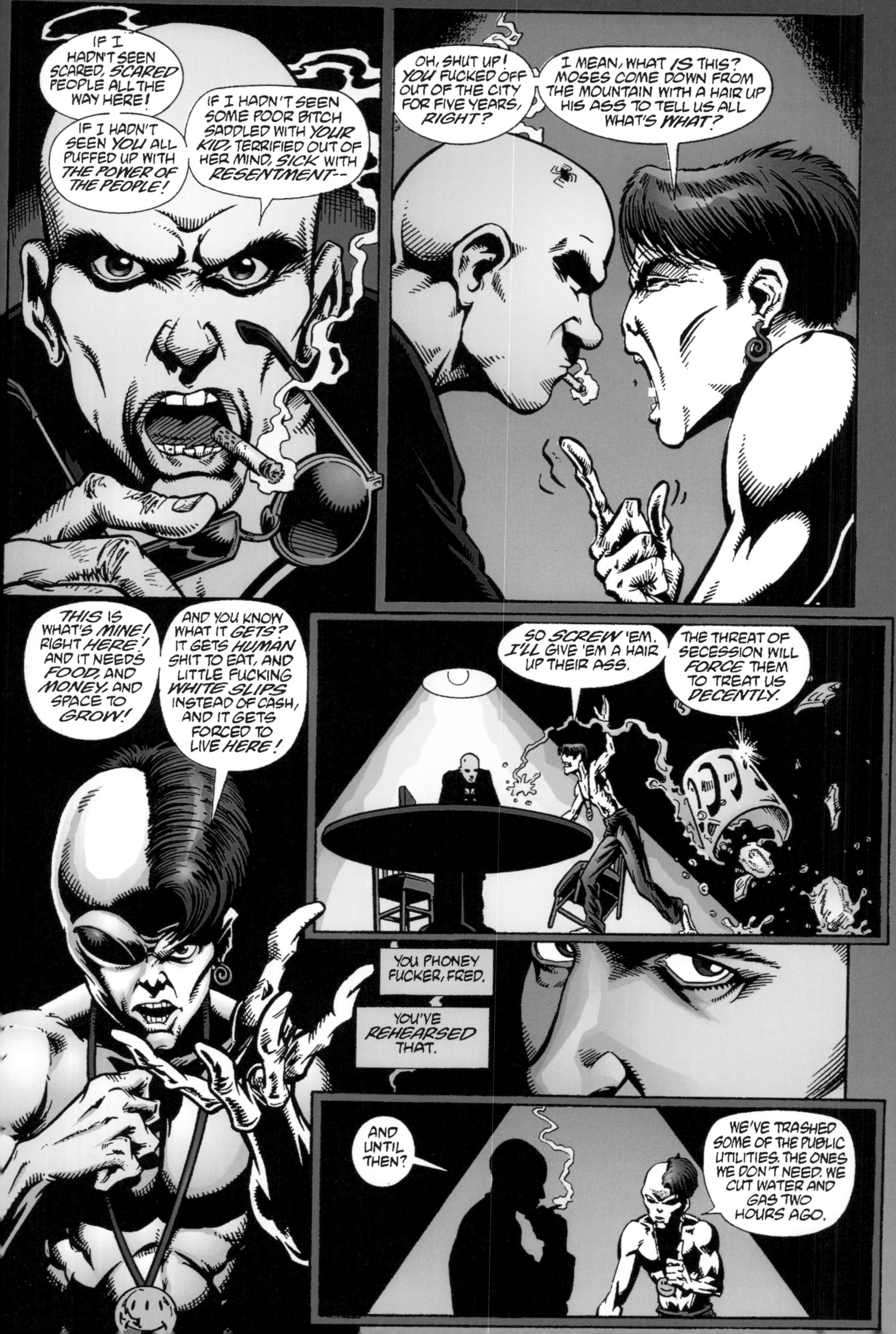
IF I HADN'T SEEN SCARED, SCARED PEOPLE ALL THE WAY HERE!
IF I HADN'T SEEN YOU ALL PUFFED UP WITH THE POWER OF THE PEOPLE!
IF I HADN'T SEEN SOME POOR BITCH SADDLED WITH YOUR KID, TERRIFIED OUT OF HER MIND, SICK WITH RESENTMENT--
OH, SHUT UP! YOU FUCKED OFF OUT OF THE CITY FOR FIVE YEARS, RIGHT?
I MEAN, WHAT IS THIS? MOSES COME DOWN FROM THE MOUNTAIN WITH A HAIR UP HIS ASS TO TELL US ALL WHAT'S WHAT?
THIS IS WHAT'S MINE! RIGHT HERE! AND IT NEEDS FOOD, AND MONEY, AND SPACE TO GROW!
AND YOU KNOW WHAT IT GETS? IT GETS HUMAN SHIT TO EAT, AND LITTLE FUCKING WHITE SLIPS INSTEAD OF CASH, AND IT GETS FORCED TO LIVE HERE!
SO SCREW 'EM. I'LL GIVE 'EM A HAIR UP THEIR ASS.
THE THREAT OF SECESSION WILL FORCE THEM TO TREAT US DECENTLY.
YOU PHONEY FUCKER, FRED.
YOU'VE REHEARSED THAT.
AND UNTIL THEN?
WE'VE TRASHED SOME OF THE PUBLIC UTILITIES. THE ONES WE DON'T NEED. WE CUT WATER AND GAS TWO HOURS AGO.

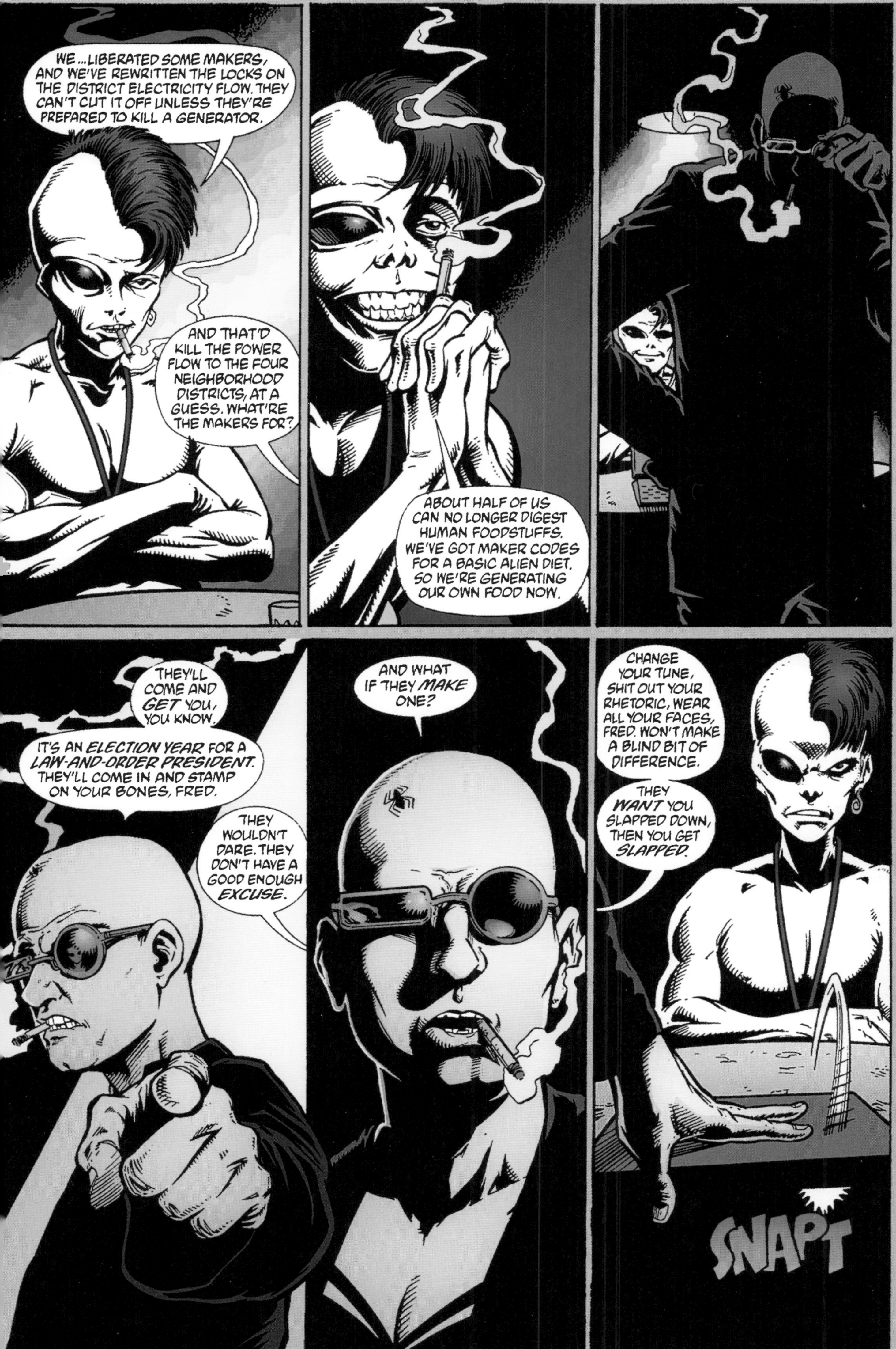
WE ...LIBERATED SOME MAKERS, AND WE'VE REWRITTEN THE LOCKS ON THE DISTRICT ELECTRICITY FLOW. THEY CAN'T CUT IT OFF UNLESS THEY'RE PREPARED TO KILL A GENERATOR.
AND THAT'D KILL THE POWER FLOW TO THE FOUR NEIGHBORHOOD DISTRICTS, AT A GUESS. WHAT'RE THE MAKERS FOR?
ABOUT HALF OF US CAN NO LONGER DIGEST HUMAN FOODSTUFFS. WE'VE GOT MAKER CODES FOR A BASIC ALIEN DIET, SO WE'RE GENERATING OUR OWN FOOD NOW.
THEY'LL COME AND *GET* YOU, YOU KNOW.
IT'S AN *ELECTION YEAR* FOR A *LAW-AND-ORDER PRESIDENT*. THEY'LL COME IN AND STAMP ON YOUR BONES, FRED.
THEY WOULDN'T DARE. THEY DON'T HAVE A GOOD ENOUGH *EXCUSE*.
AND WHAT IF THEY *MAKE* ONE?
CHANGE YOUR TUNE, SHIT OUT YOUR RHETORIC, WEAR ALL YOUR FACES, FRED. WON'T MAKE A BLIND BIT OF DIFFERENCE.
THEY *WANT* YOU SLAPPED DOWN, THEN YOU GET *SLAPPED*.
SNAPT

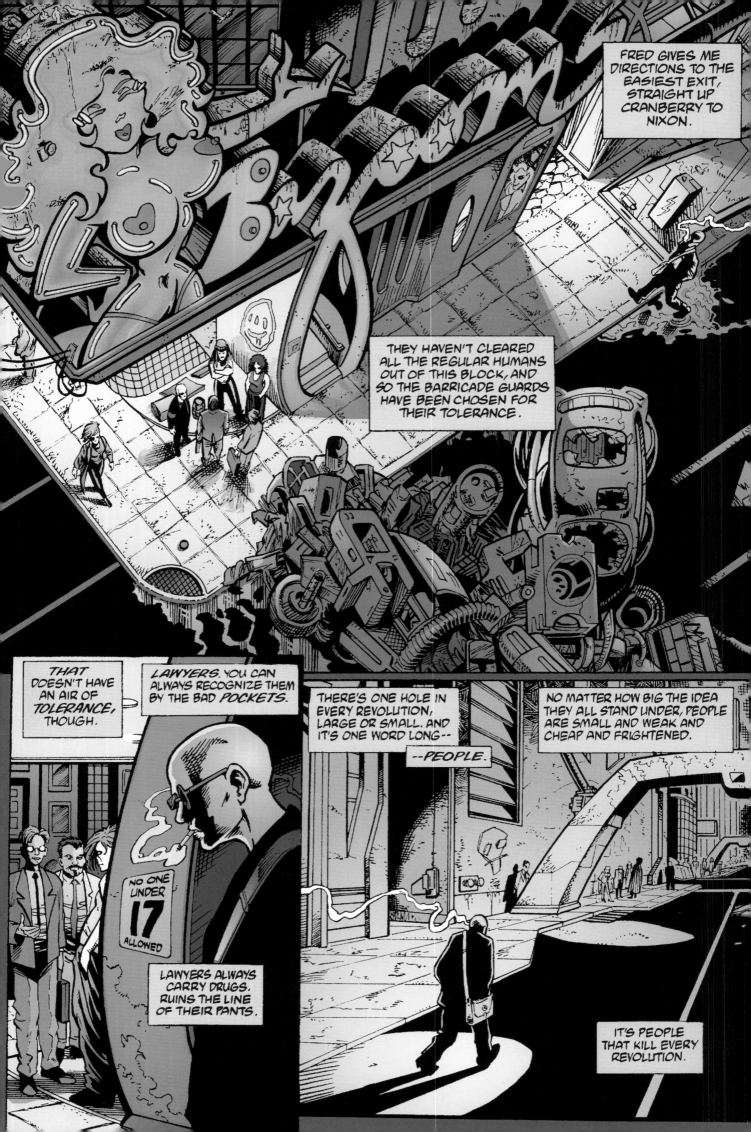

FRED GIVES ME DIRECTIONS TO THE EASIEST EXIT, STRAIGHT UP CRANBERRY TO NIXON.

THEY HAVEN'T CLEARED ALL THE REGULAR HUMANS OUT OF THIS BLOCK, AND SO THE BARRICADE GUARDS HAVE BEEN CHOSEN FOR THEIR TOLERANCE.

THAT DOESN'T HAVE AN AIR OF *TOLERANCE*, THOUGH.

*LAWYERS*. YOU CAN ALWAYS RECOGNIZE THEM BY THE BAD *POCKETS*.

THERE'S ONE HOLE IN EVERY REVOLUTION, LARGE OR SMALL. AND IT'S ONE WORD LONG--

--PEOPLE.

NO MATTER HOW BIG THE IDEA THEY ALL STAND UNDER, PEOPLE ARE SMALL AND WEAK AND CHEAP AND FRIGHTENED.

NO ONE UNDER 17 ALLOWED

LAWYERS ALWAYS CARRY DRUGS. RUINS THE LINE OF THEIR PANTS.

IT'S PEOPLE THAT KILL EVERY REVOLUTION.

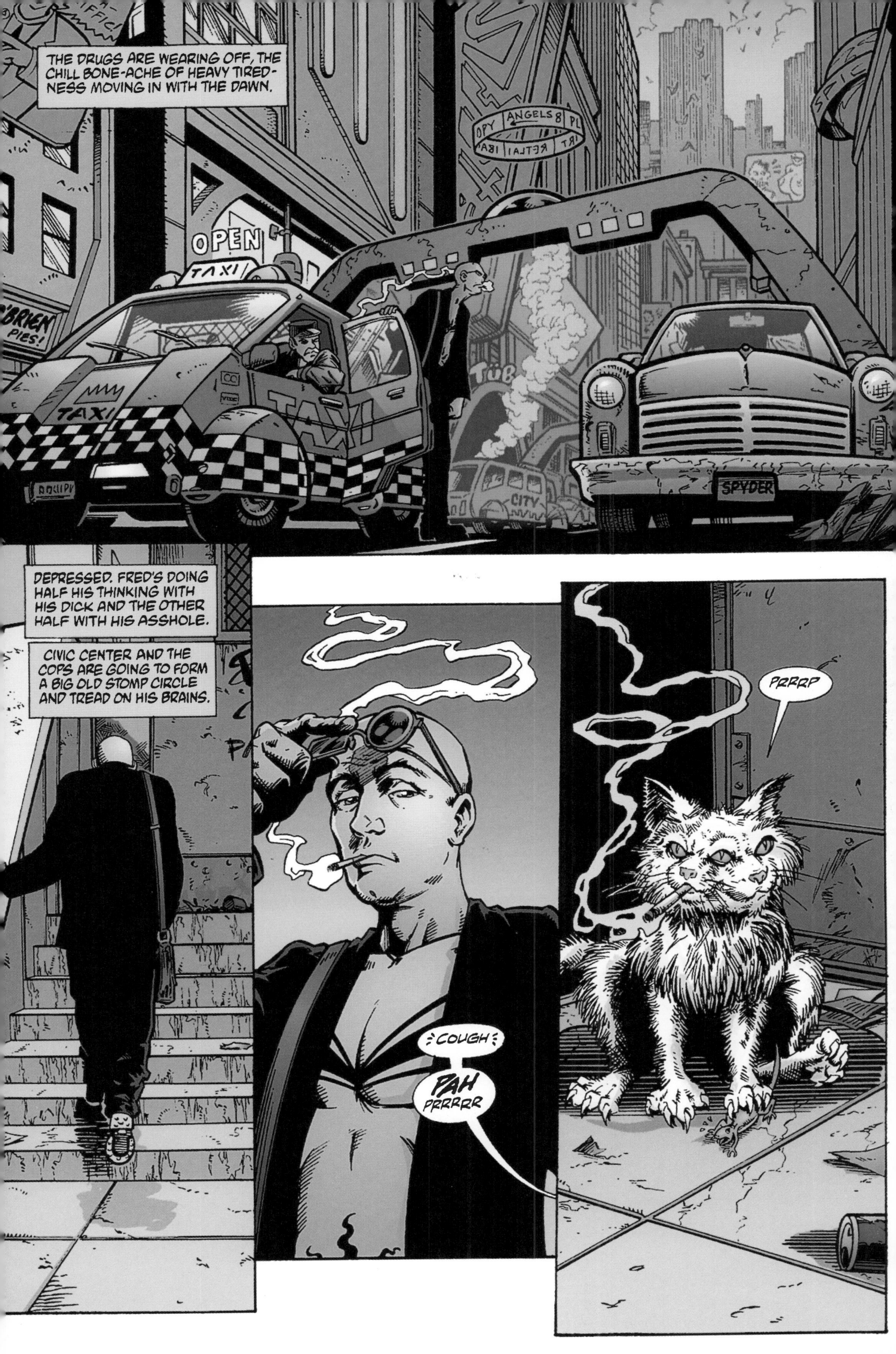

THE DRUGS ARE WEARING OFF, THE CHILL BONE-ACHE OF HEAVY TIRED-NESS MOVING IN WITH THE DAWN.
OPEN
TAXI
ANGELS 8
SPYDER
DEPRESSED. FRED'S DOING HALF HIS THINKING WITH HIS DICK AND THE OTHER HALF WITH HIS ASSHOLE.
CIVIC CENTER AND THE COPS ARE GOING TO FORM A BIG OLD STOMP CIRCLE AND TREAD ON HIS BRAINS.
PRRRP
COUGH
PAH PRRRRR

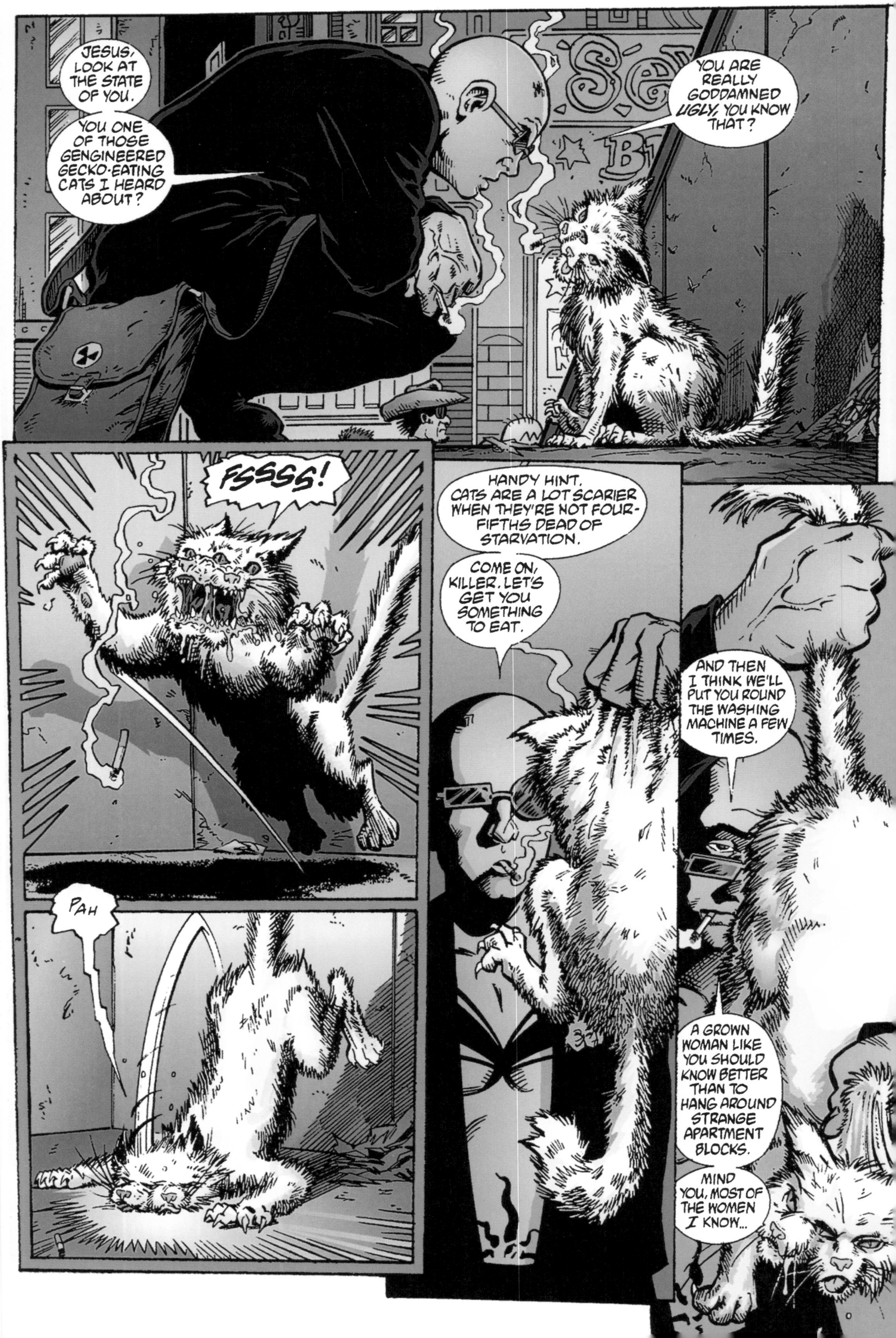
JESUS, LOOK AT THE STATE OF YOU.
YOU ONE OF THOSE GENGINEERED GECKO-EATING CATS I HEARD ABOUT?
YOU ARE REALLY GODDAMNED UGLY, YOU KNOW THAT?
FSSSS!
PAH
HANDY HINT. CATS ARE A LOT SCARIER WHEN THEY'RE NOT FOUR-FIFTHS DEAD OF STARVATION.
COME ON, KILLER. LET'S GET YOU SOMETHING TO EAT.
AND THEN I THINK WE'LL PUT YOU ROUND THE WASHING MACHINE A FEW TIMES.
A GROWN WOMAN LIKE YOU SHOULD KNOW BETTER THAN TO HANG AROUND STRANGE APARTMENT BLOCKS.
MIND YOU, MOST OF THE WOMEN I KNOW...

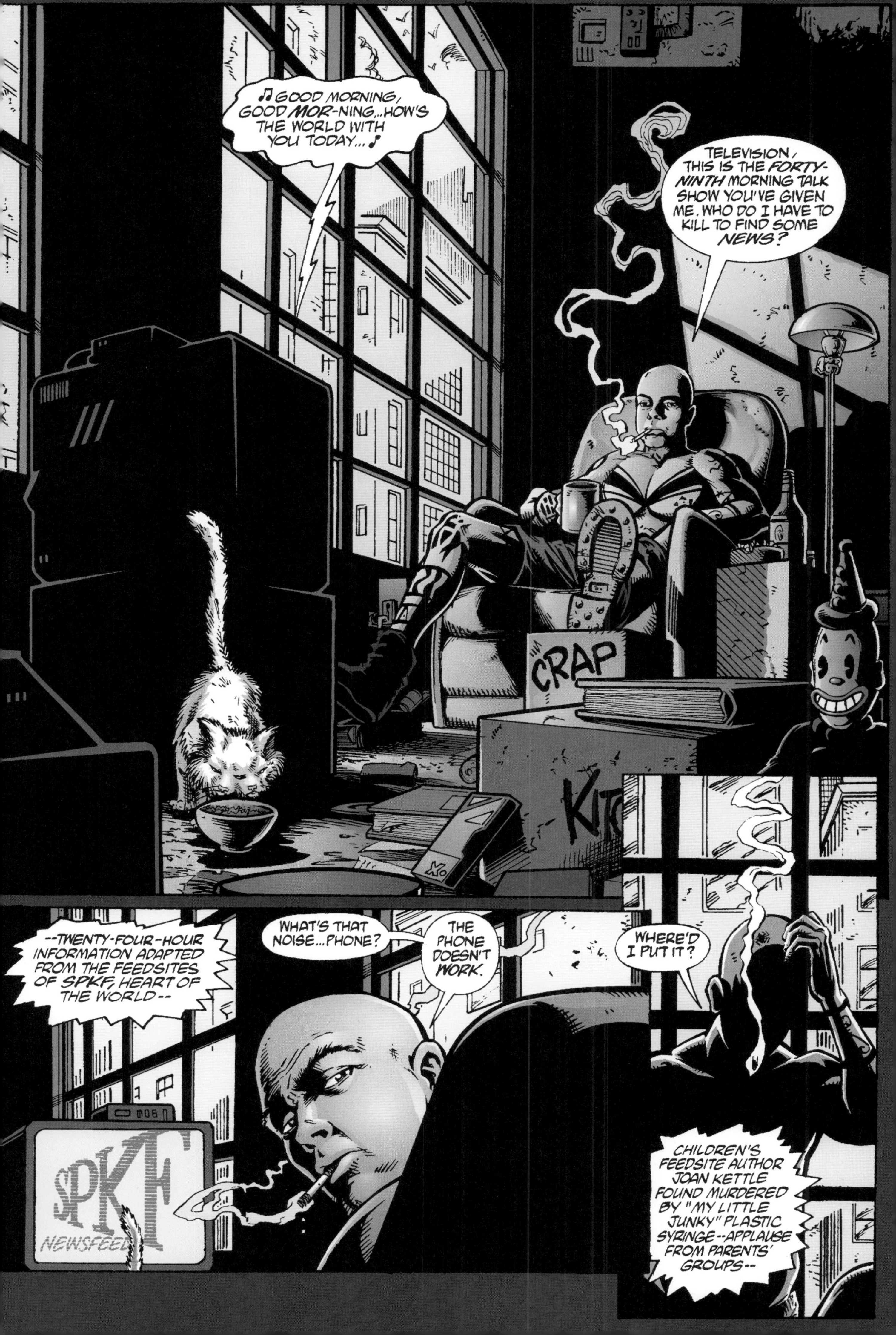
♫ GOOD MORNING, GOOD MOR-NING... HOW'S THE WORLD WITH YOU TODAY... ♪
TELEVISION, THIS IS THE FORTY-NINTH MORNING TALK SHOW YOU'VE GIVEN ME. WHO DO I HAVE TO KILL TO FIND SOME NEWS?
CRAP
--TWENTY-FOUR-HOUR INFORMATION ADAPTED FROM THE FEEDSITES OF SPKF, HEART OF THE WORLD--
WHAT'S THAT NOISE...PHONE?
THE PHONE DOESN'T WORK.
WHERE'D I PUT IT?
SPKF
NEWSFEED
CHILDREN'S FEEDSITE AUTHOR JOAN KETTLE FOUND MURDERED BY "MY LITTLE JUNKY" PLASTIC SYRINGE--APPLAUSE FROM PARENTS' GROUPS--

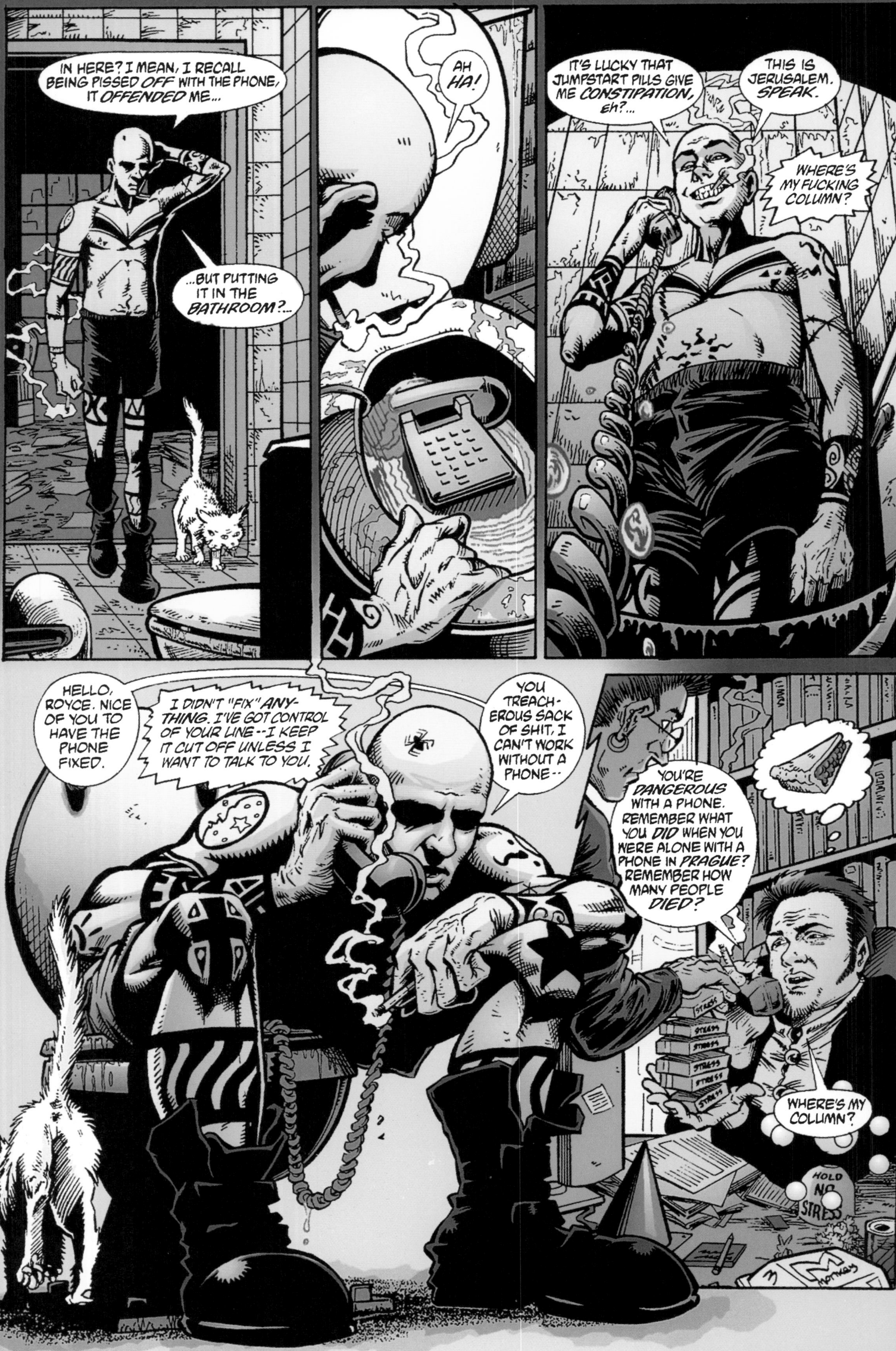
IN HERE? I MEAN, I RECALL BEING PISSED OFF WITH THE PHONE, IT OFFENDED ME...
...BUT PUTTING IT IN THE BATHROOM?...
AH HA!
IT'S LUCKY THAT JUMPSTART PILLS GIVE ME CONSTIPATION, eh?...
THIS IS JERUSALEM. SPEAK.
WHERE'S MY FUCKING COLUMN?
HELLO, ROYCE. NICE OF YOU TO HAVE THE PHONE FIXED.
I DIDN'T "FIX" ANYTHING. I'VE GOT CONTROL OF YOUR LINE--I KEEP IT CUT OFF UNLESS I WANT TO TALK TO YOU.
YOU TREACHEROUS SACK OF SHIT, I CAN'T WORK WITHOUT A PHONE--
YOU'RE DANGEROUS WITH A PHONE. REMEMBER WHAT YOU DID WHEN YOU WERE ALONE WITH A PHONE IN PRAGUE? REMEMBER HOW MANY PEOPLE DIED?
WHERE'S MY COLUMN?
HOLD NO STRESS

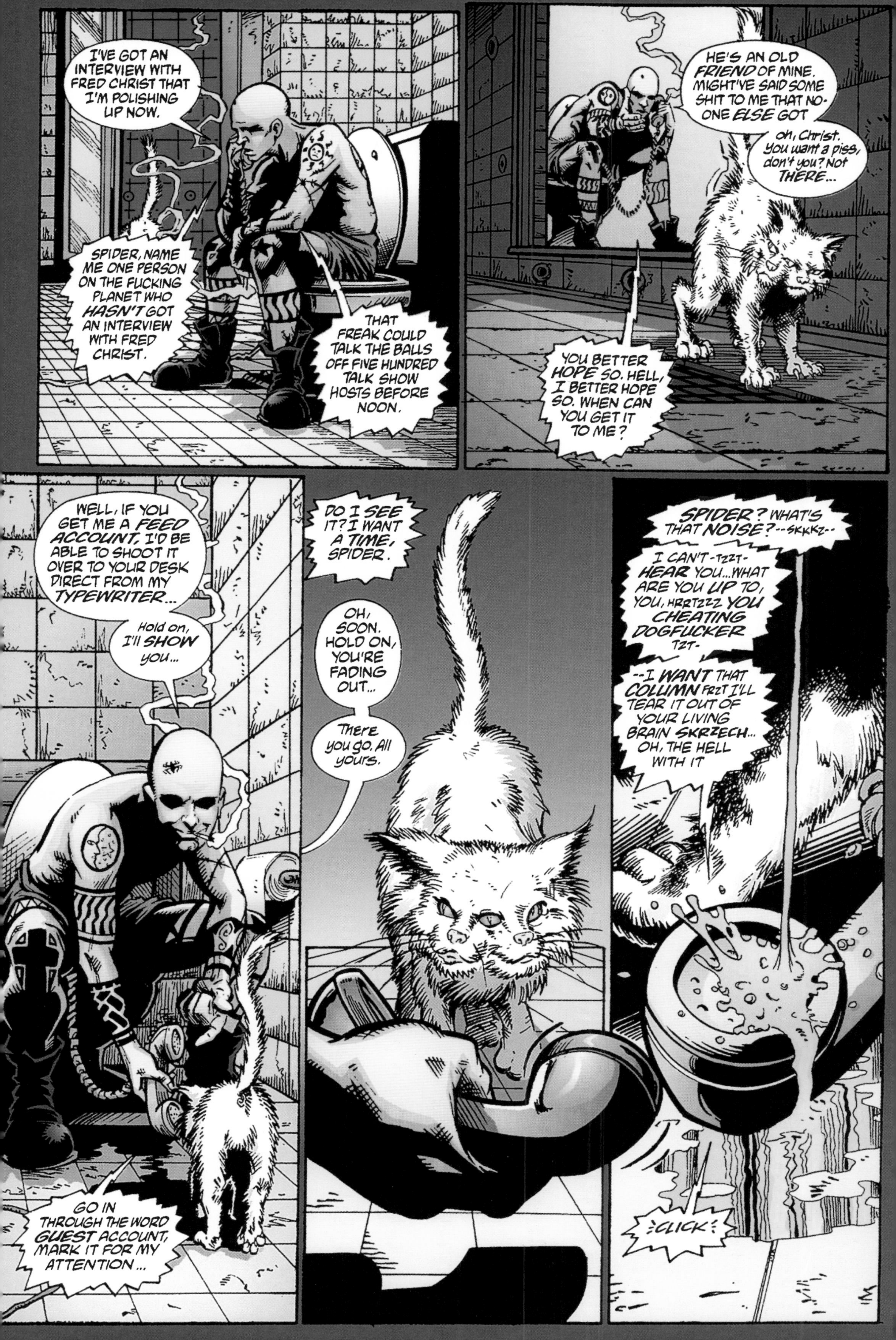
I'VE GOT AN INTERVIEW WITH FRED CHRIST THAT I'M POLISHING UP NOW.
SPIDER, NAME ME ONE PERSON ON THE FUCKING PLANET WHO HASN'T GOT AN INTERVIEW WITH FRED CHRIST.
THAT FREAK COULD TALK THE BALLS OFF FIVE HUNDRED TALK SHOW HOSTS BEFORE NOON.
HE'S AN OLD FRIEND OF MINE. MIGHT'VE SAID SOME SHIT TO ME THAT NO-ONE ELSE GOT
oh, Christ. You want a piss, don't you? Not THERE...
YOU BETTER HOPE SO. HELL, I BETTER HOPE SO. WHEN CAN YOU GET IT TO ME?
WELL, IF YOU GET ME A FEED ACCOUNT, I'D BE ABLE TO SHOOT IT OVER TO YOUR DESK DIRECT FROM MY TYPEWRITER...
Hold on, I'll SHOW you...
GO IN THROUGH THE WORD GUEST ACCOUNT, MARK IT FOR MY ATTENTION...
DO I SEE IT? I WANT A TIME, SPIDER.
OH, SOON. HOLD ON, YOU'RE FADING OUT...
There you go. All yours.
SPIDER? WHAT'S THAT NOISE? --SKKKZ--
I CAN'T -TZZT- HEAR YOU...WHAT ARE YOU UP TO, YOU, HRRTZZZ YOU CHEATING DOGFUCKER TZT-
--I WANT THAT COLUMN FRZT I'LL TEAR IT OUT OF YOUR LIVING BRAIN SKRZECH... OH, THE HELL WITH IT
CLICK

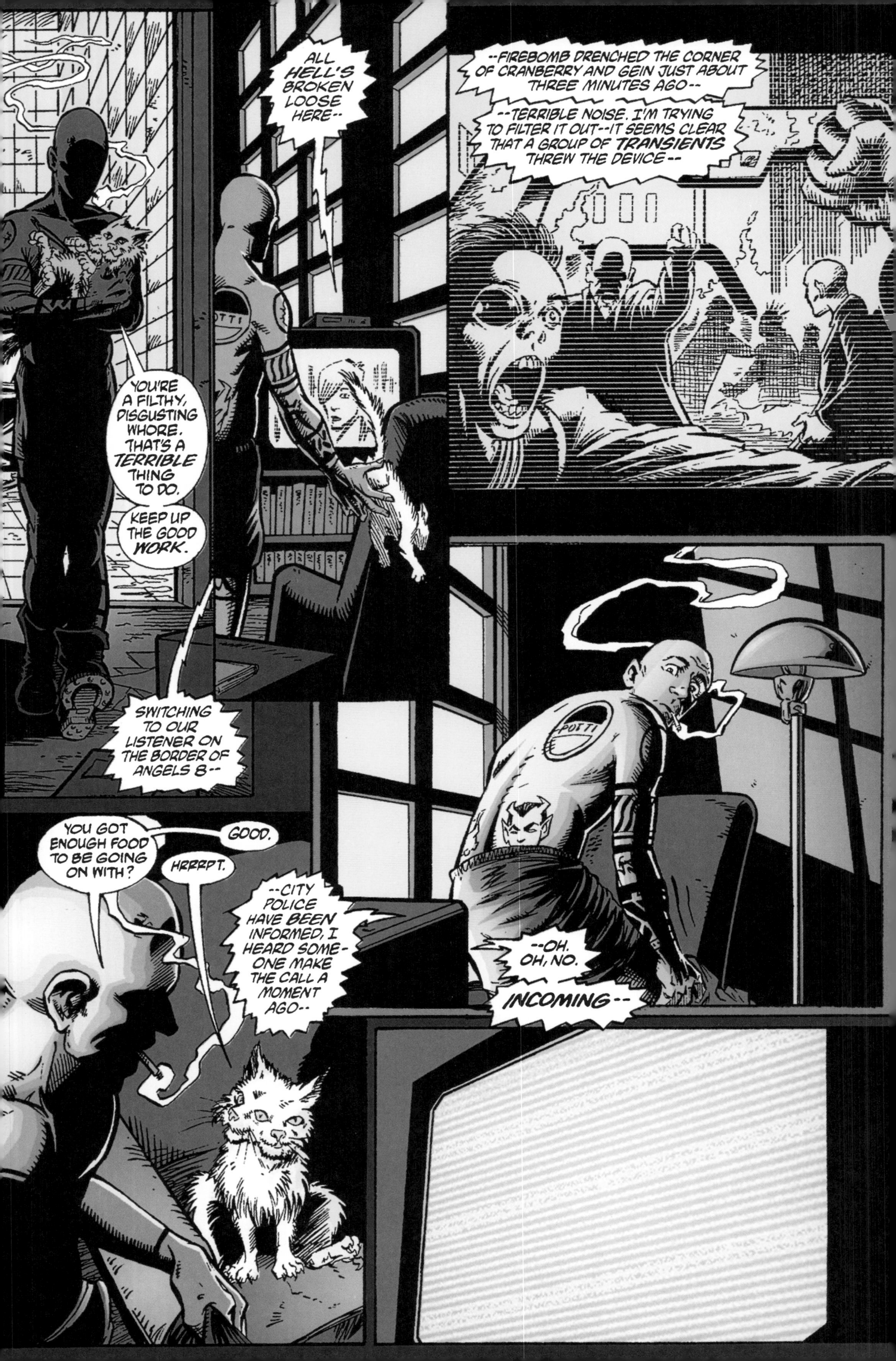
ALL HELL'S BROKEN LOOSE HERE--
YOU'RE A FILTHY, DISGUSTING WHORE. THAT'S A TERRIBLE THING TO DO.
KEEP UP THE GOOD WORK.
--FIREBOMB DRENCHED THE CORNER OF CRANBERRY AND GEIN JUST ABOUT THREE MINUTES AGO--
--TERRIBLE NOISE. I'M TRYING TO FILTER IT OUT--IT SEEMS CLEAR THAT A GROUP OF TRANSIENTS THREW THE DEVICE--
SWITCHING TO OUR LISTENER ON THE BORDER OF ANGELS 8--
POTTI
YOU GOT ENOUGH FOOD TO BE GOING ON WITH?
GOOD.
HRRRPT.
--CITY POLICE HAVE BEEN INFORMED, I HEARD SOME-ONE MAKE THE CALL A MOMENT AGO--
--OH. OH, NO.
INCOMING--

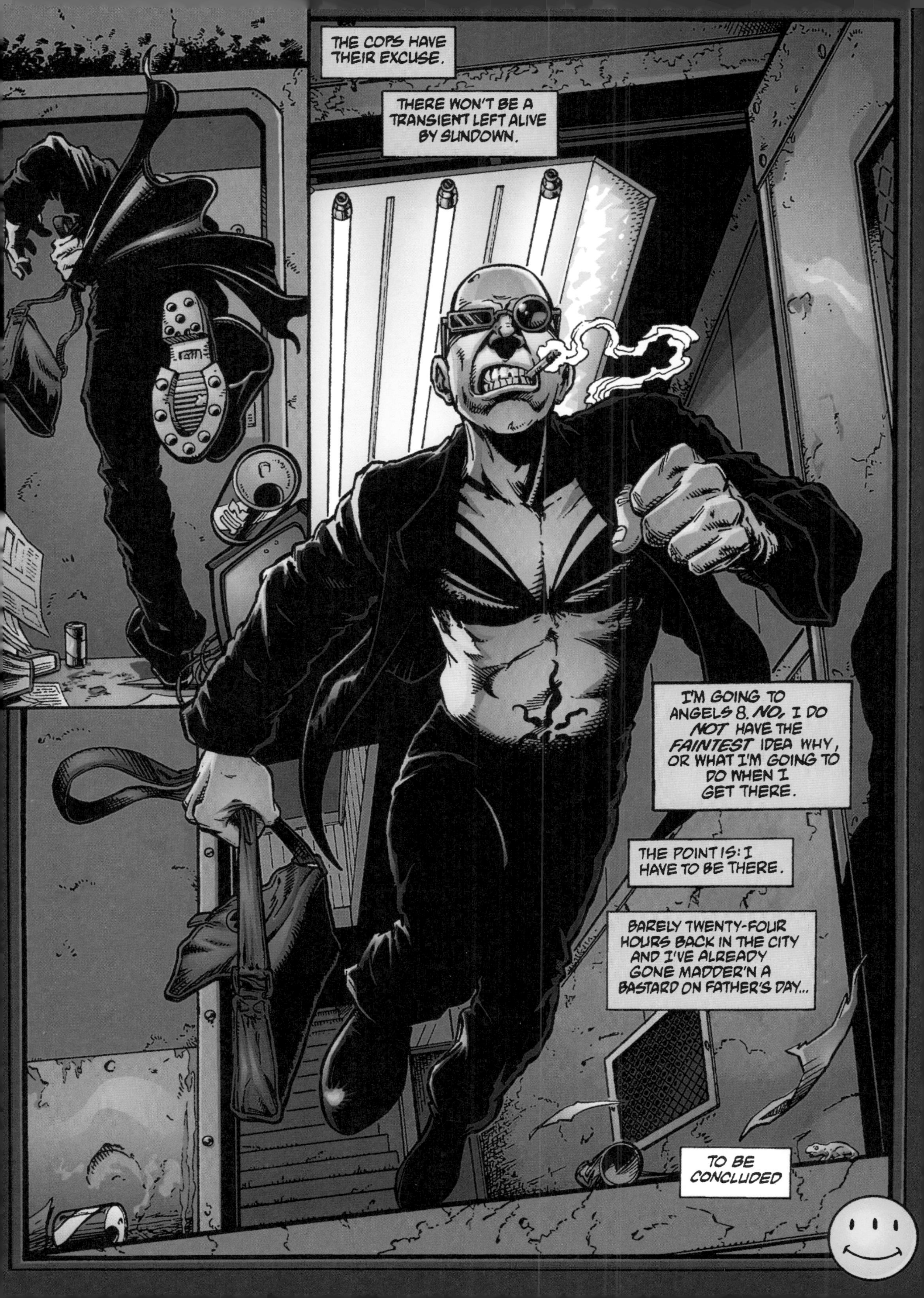
THE COPS HAVE THEIR EXCUSE.
THERE WON'T BE A TRANSIENT LEFT ALIVE BY SUNDOWN.
I'M GOING TO ANGELS 8. *NO,* I DO *NOT* HAVE THE *FAINTEST* IDEA WHY, OR WHAT I'M GOING TO DO WHEN I GET THERE.
THE POINT IS: I HAVE TO BE THERE.
BARELY TWENTY-FOUR HOURS BACK IN THE CITY AND I'VE ALREADY GONE MADDER'N A BASTARD ON FATHER'S DAY...
TO BE CONCLUDED

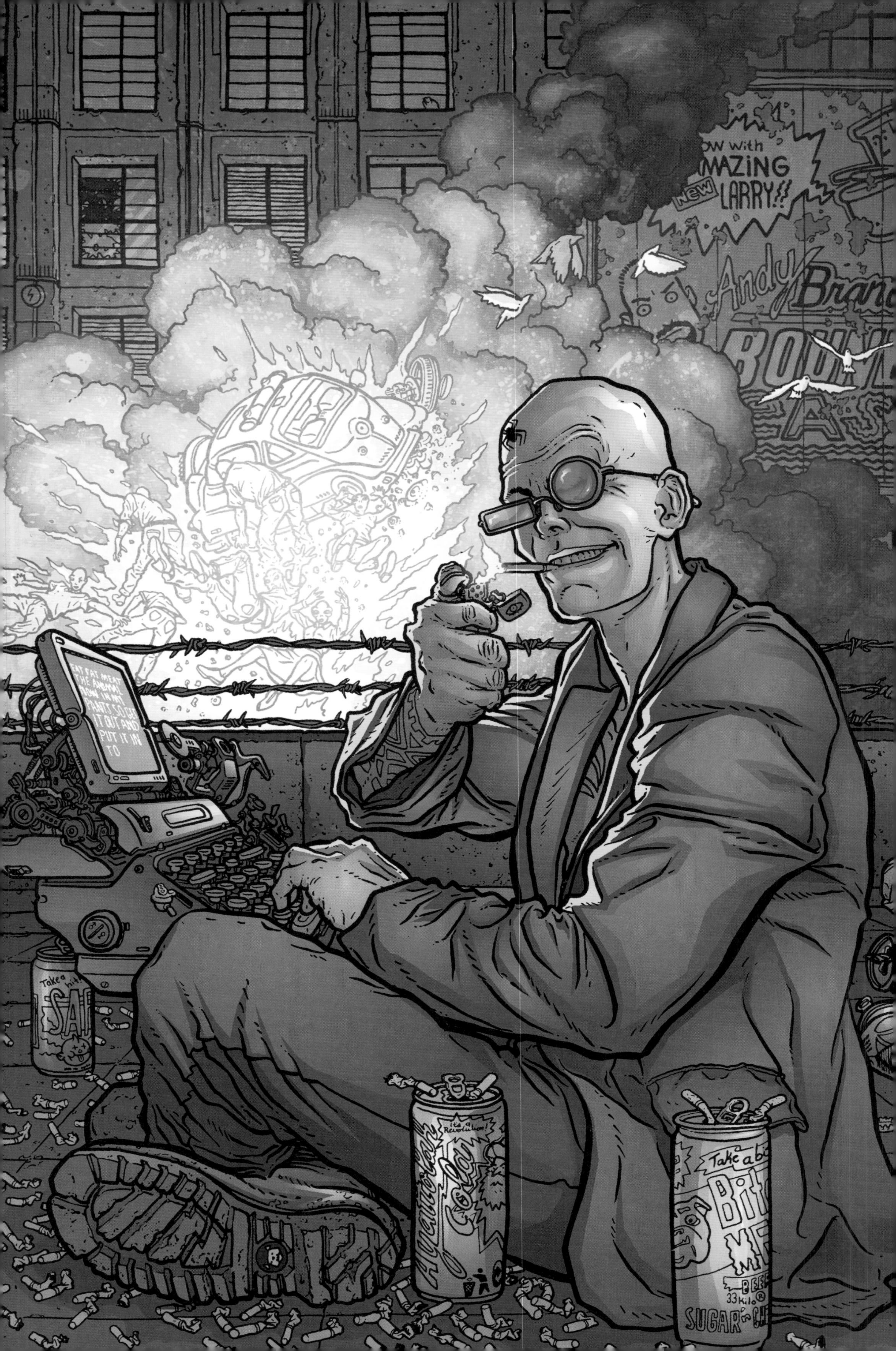

OW with
MAZING
New
LARRY!!
Andy
EAT FAT MEAT
THE ANIMAL
NOW IN ART
PARTS SO GET
IT OUT AND
PUT IT IN
TO
It's a Revolution!
Take a bi
33 Kilo

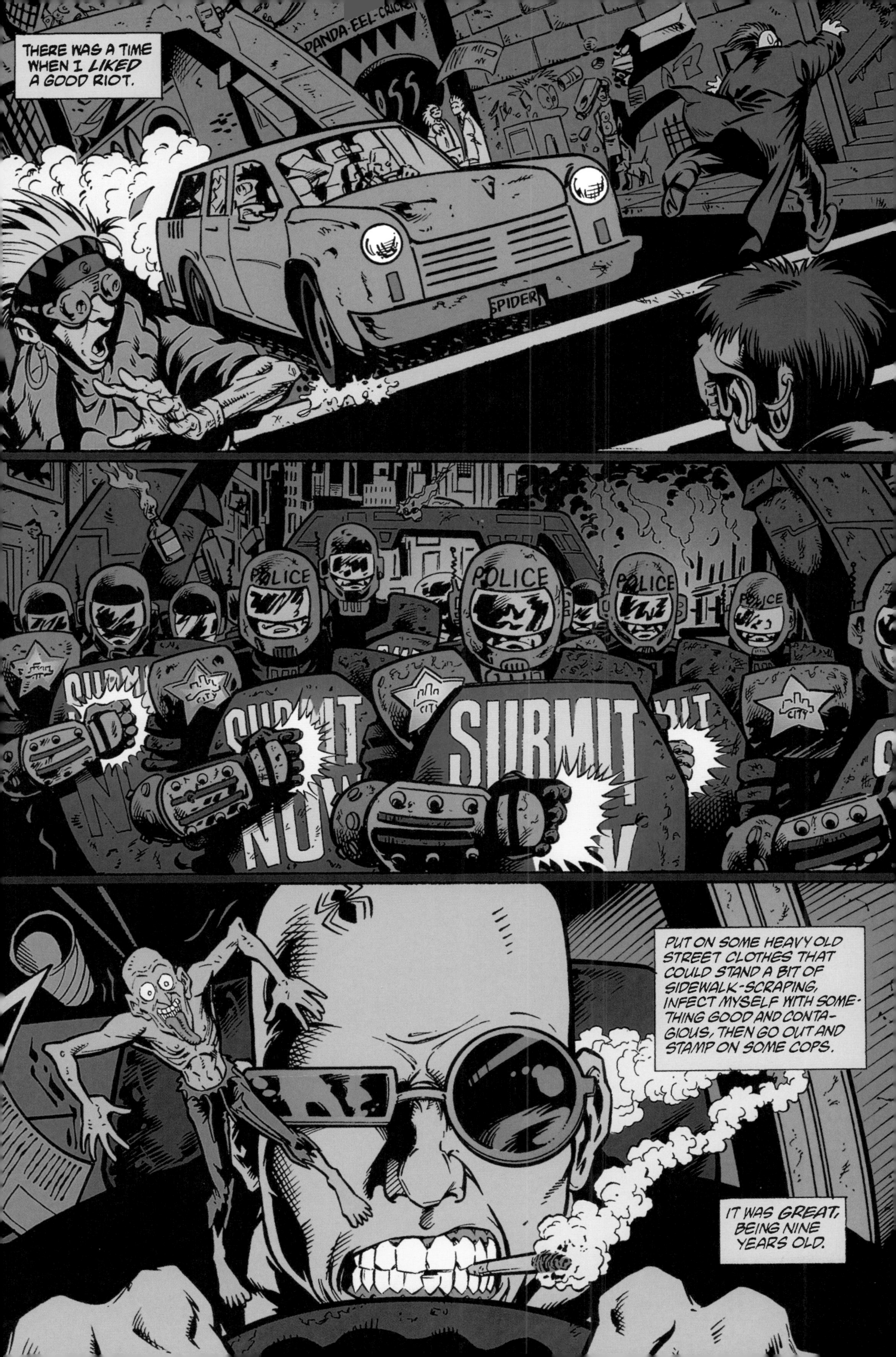
THERE WAS A TIME WHEN I LIKED A GOOD RIOT.
PANDA-EEL-CRICKET
SPIDER
POLICE
SUBMIT
NOW
CITY
PUT ON SOME HEAVY OLD STREET CLOTHES THAT COULD STAND A BIT OF SIDEWALK-SCRAPING, INFECT MYSELF WITH SOMETHING GOOD AND CONTAGIOUS, THEN GO OUT AND STAMP ON SOME COPS.
IT WAS GREAT, BEING NINE YEARS OLD.

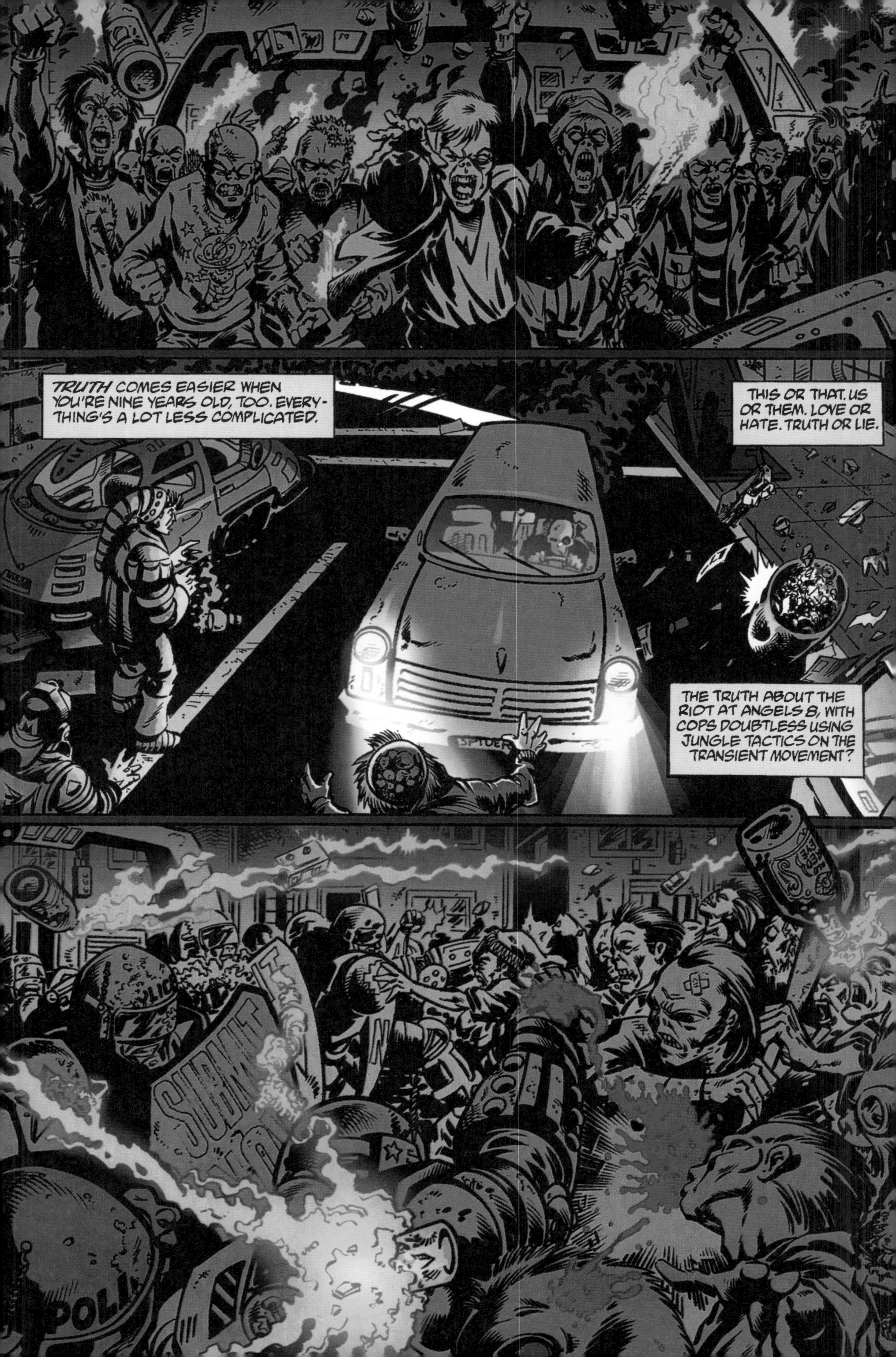
TRUTH COMES EASIER WHEN YOU'RE NINE YEARS OLD, TOO. EVERY-THING'S A LOT LESS COMPLICATED.
THIS OR THAT. US OR THEM. LOVE OR HATE. TRUTH OR LIE.
THE TRUTH ABOUT THE RIOT AT ANGELS 8, WITH COPS DOUBTLESS USING JUNGLE TACTICS ON THE TRANSIENT MOVEMENT?

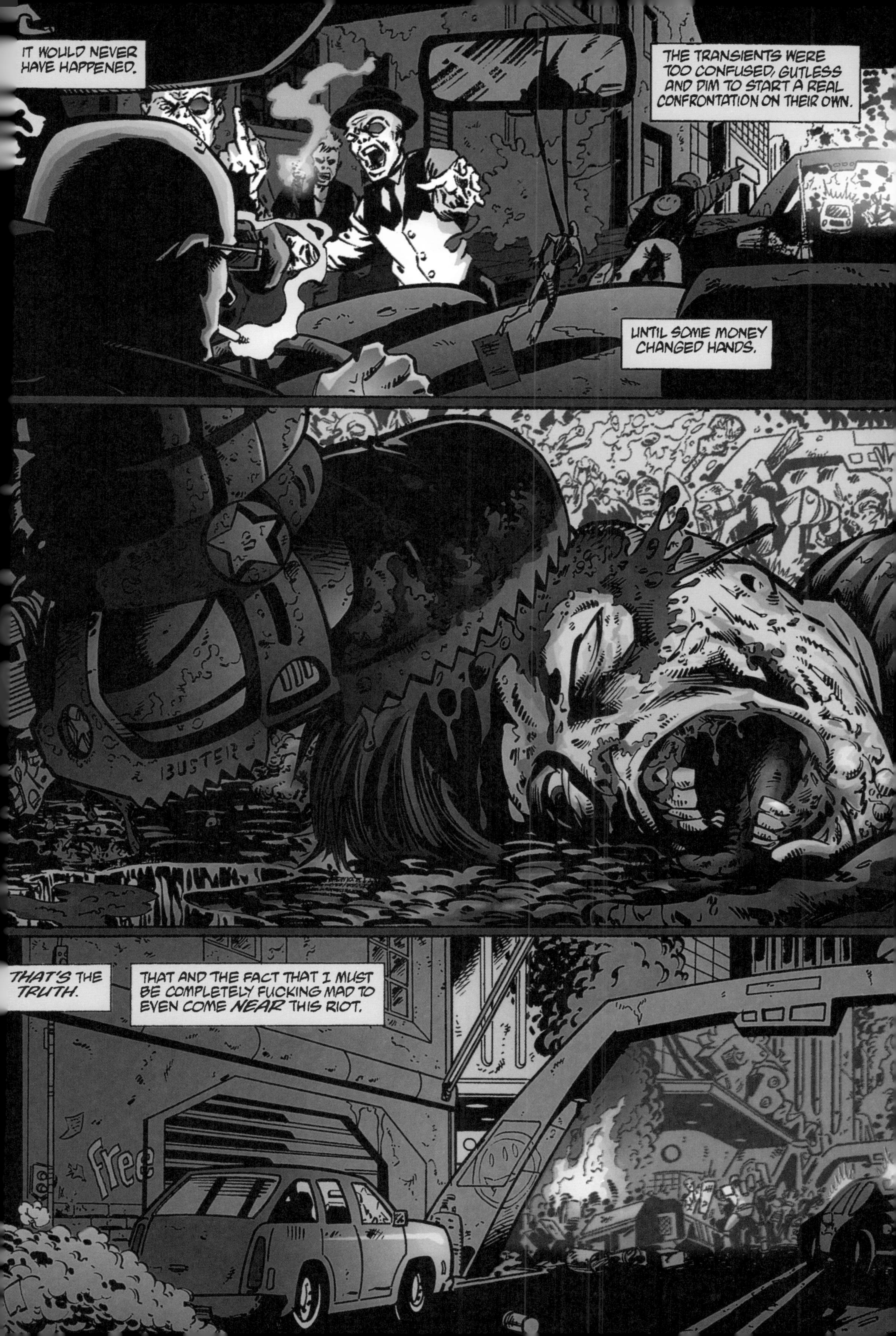
IT WOULD NEVER HAVE HAPPENED.
THE TRANSIENTS WERE TOO CONFUSED, GUTLESS AND DIM TO START A REAL CONFRONTATION ON THEIR OWN.
UNTIL SOME MONEY CHANGED HANDS.
BUSTER
THAT'S THE TRUTH.
THAT AND THE FACT THAT I MUST BE COMPLETELY FUCKING MAD TO EVEN COME NEAR THIS RIOT.
free

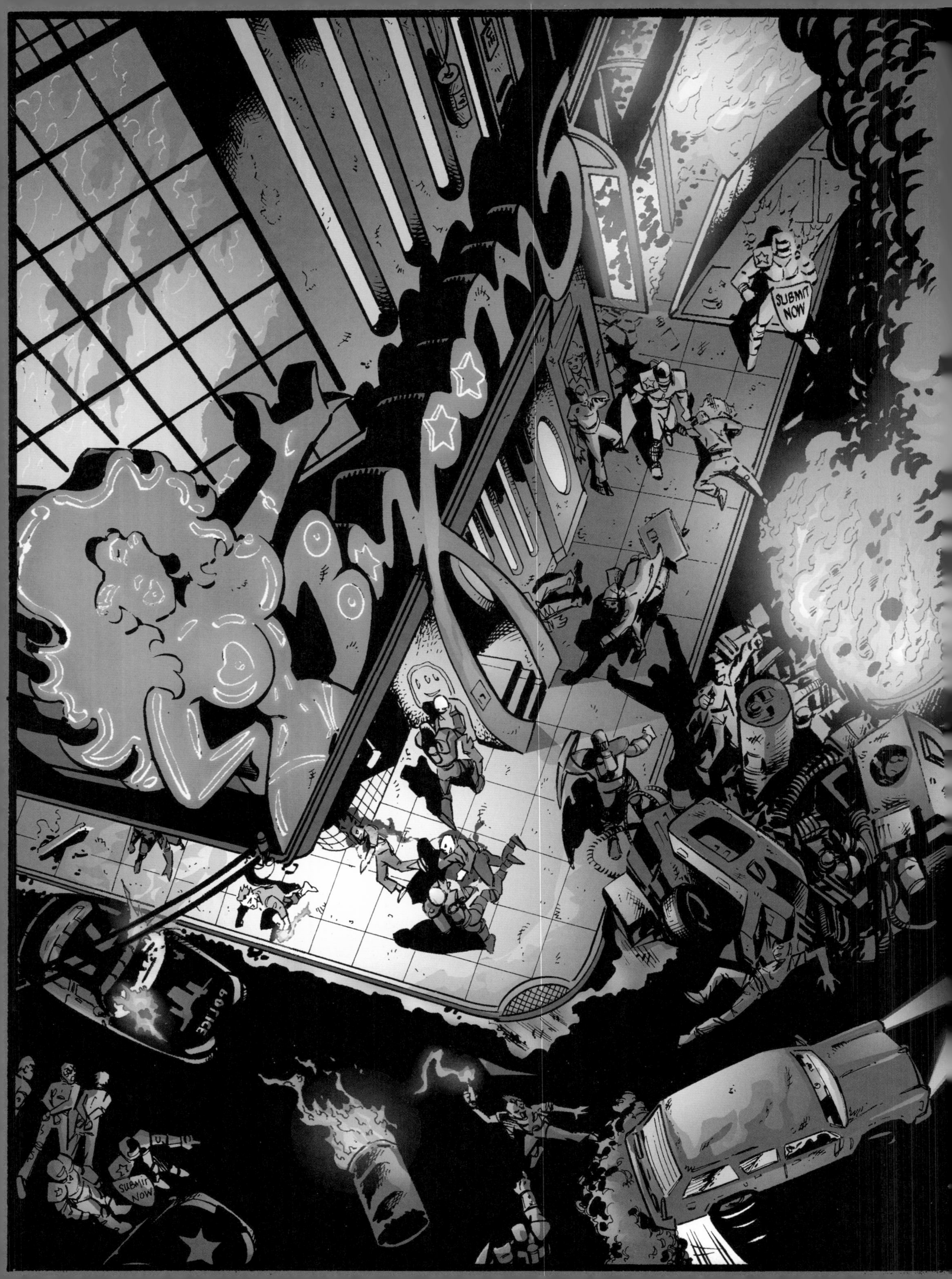
SUBMIT NOW
POLICE
SUBMIT NOW

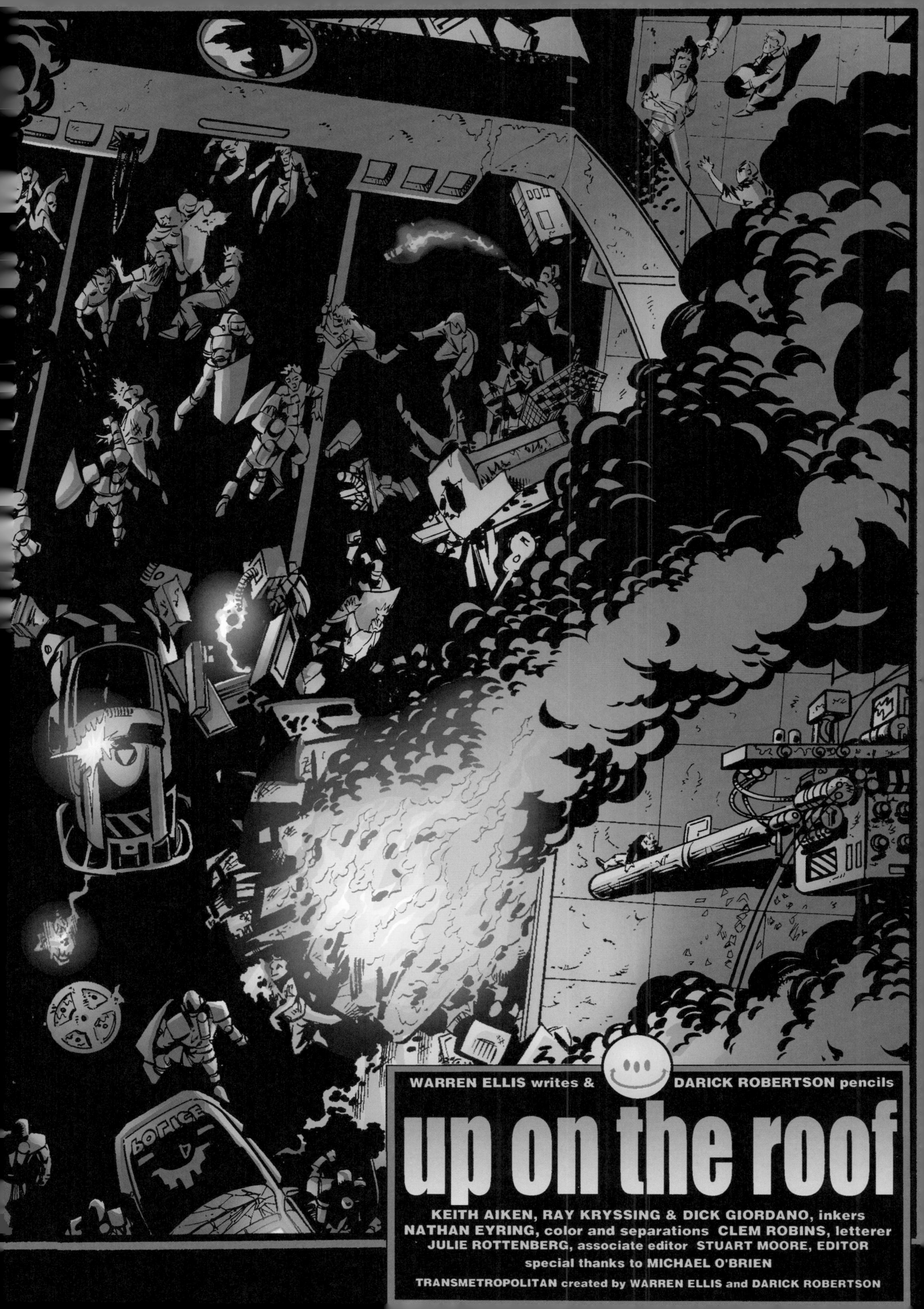
WARREN ELLIS writes & DARICK ROBERTSON pencils
up on the roof
KEITH AIKEN, RAY KRYSSING & DICK GIORDANO, inkers
NATHAN EYRING, color and separations CLEM ROBINS, letterer
JULIE ROTTENBERG, associate editor STUART MOORE, EDITOR
special thanks to MICHAEL O'BRIEN
TRANSMETROPOLITAN created by WARREN ELLIS and DARICK ROBERTSON

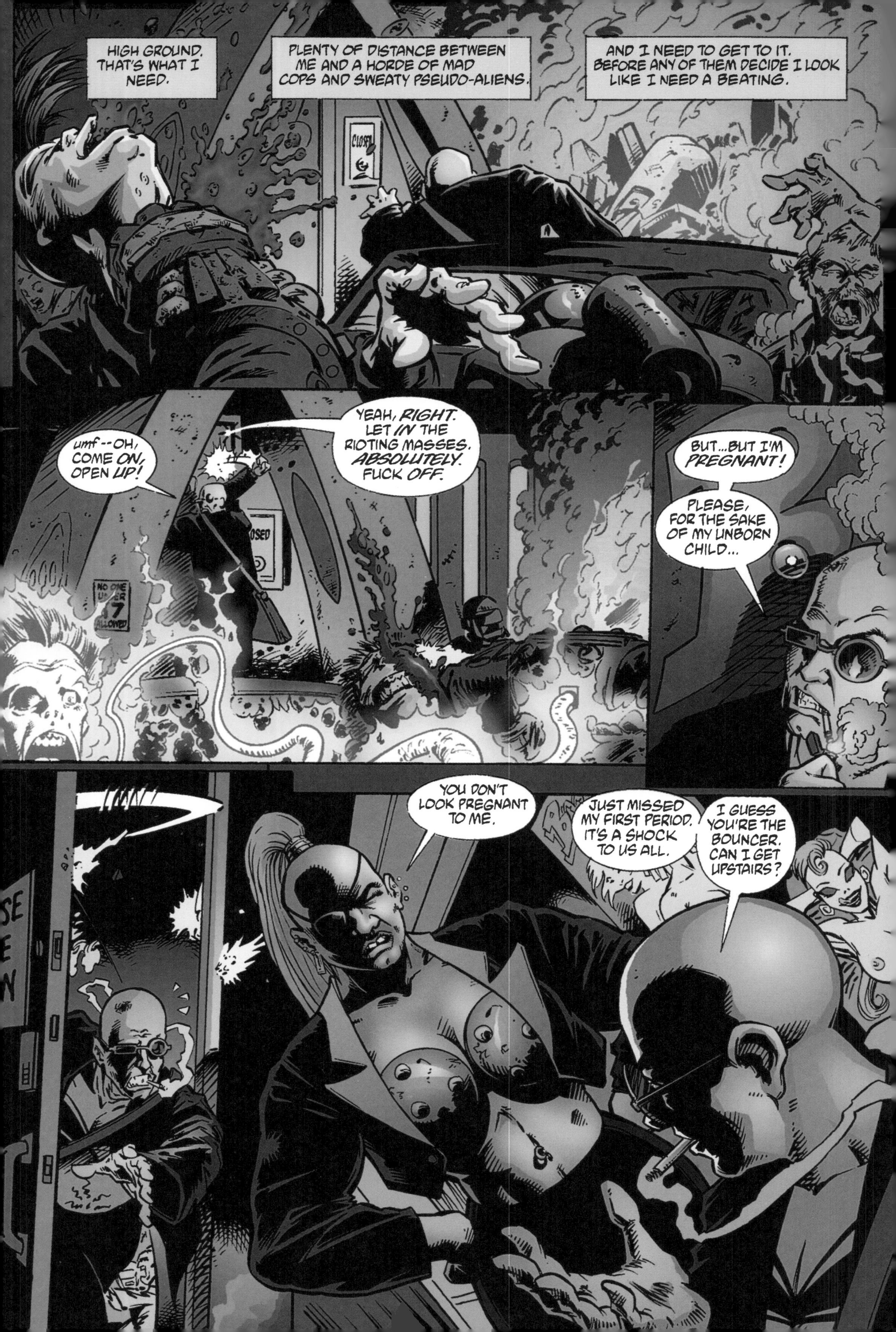
HIGH GROUND. THAT'S WHAT I NEED.
PLENTY OF DISTANCE BETWEEN ME AND A HORDE OF MAD COPS AND SWEATY PSEUDO-ALIENS.
AND I NEED TO GET TO IT. BEFORE ANY OF THEM DECIDE I LOOK LIKE I NEED A BEATING.
umf -- OH, COME ON, OPEN UP!
YEAH, RIGHT. LET IN THE RIOTING MASSES. ABSOLUTELY. FUCK OFF.
NO ONE UNDER 17 ALLOWED
BUT...BUT I'M PREGNANT!
PLEASE, FOR THE SAKE OF MY UNBORN CHILD...
YOU DON'T LOOK PREGNANT TO ME.
JUST MISSED MY FIRST PERIOD. IT'S A SHOCK TO US ALL.
I GUESS YOU'RE THE BOUNCER. CAN I GET UPSTAIRS?

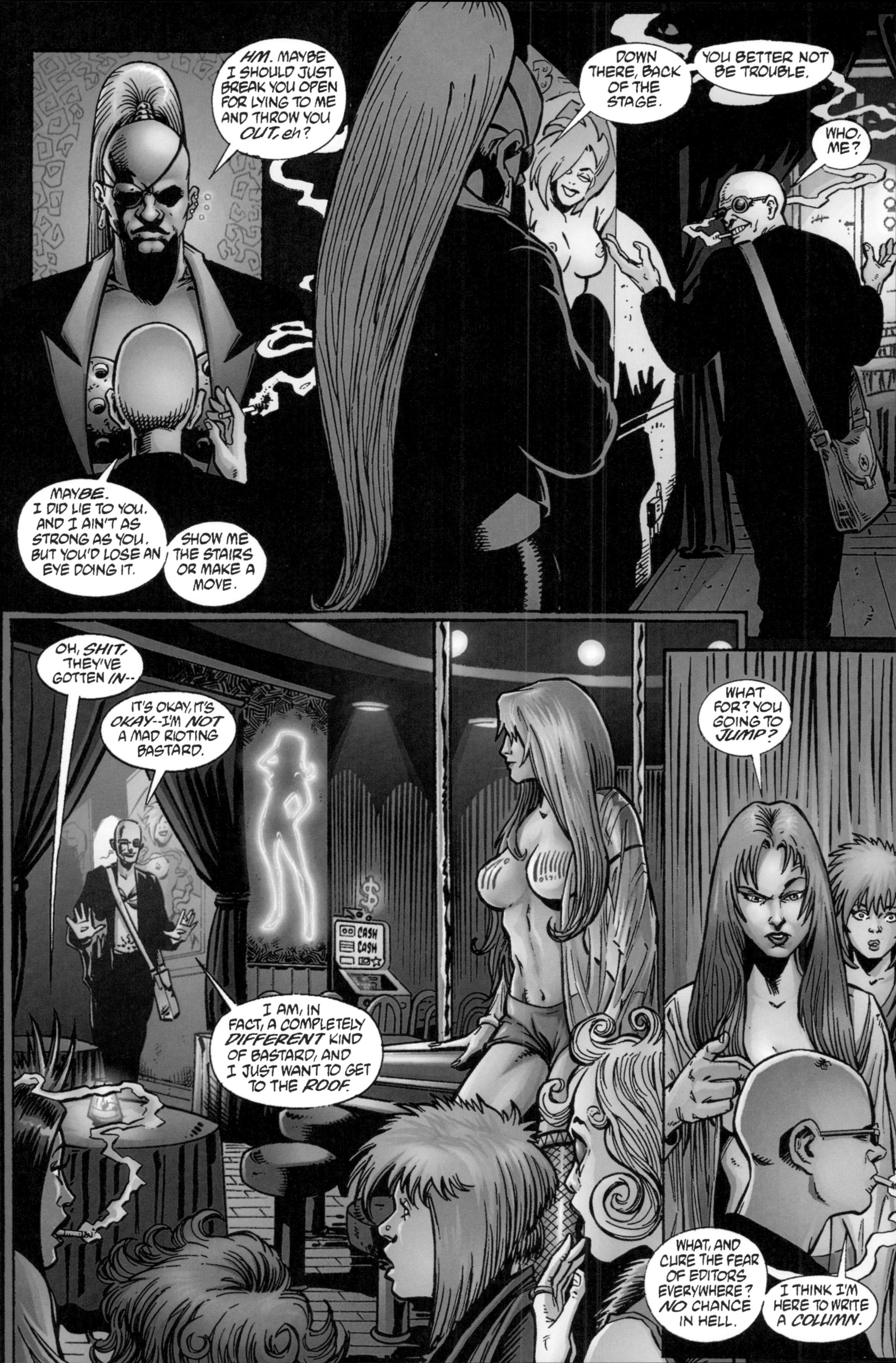
HM. MAYBE I SHOULD JUST BREAK YOU OPEN FOR LYING TO ME AND THROW YOU OUT, eh?
MAYBE. I DID LIE TO YOU. AND I AIN'T AS STRONG AS YOU. BUT YOU'D LOSE AN EYE DOING IT.
SHOW ME THE STAIRS OR MAKE A MOVE.
DOWN THERE, BACK OF THE STAGE.
YOU BETTER NOT BE TROUBLE.
WHO, ME?
OH, SHIT, THEY'VE GOTTEN IN--
IT'S OKAY, IT'S OKAY--I'M NOT A MAD RIOTING BASTARD.
I AM, IN FACT, A COMPLETELY DIFFERENT KIND OF BASTARD, AND I JUST WANT TO GET TO THE ROOF.
CASH
CASH
WHAT FOR? YOU GOING TO JUMP?
I THINK I'M HERE TO WRITE A COLUMN.
WHAT, AND CURE THE FEAR OF EDITORS EVERYWHERE? NO CHANCE IN HELL.

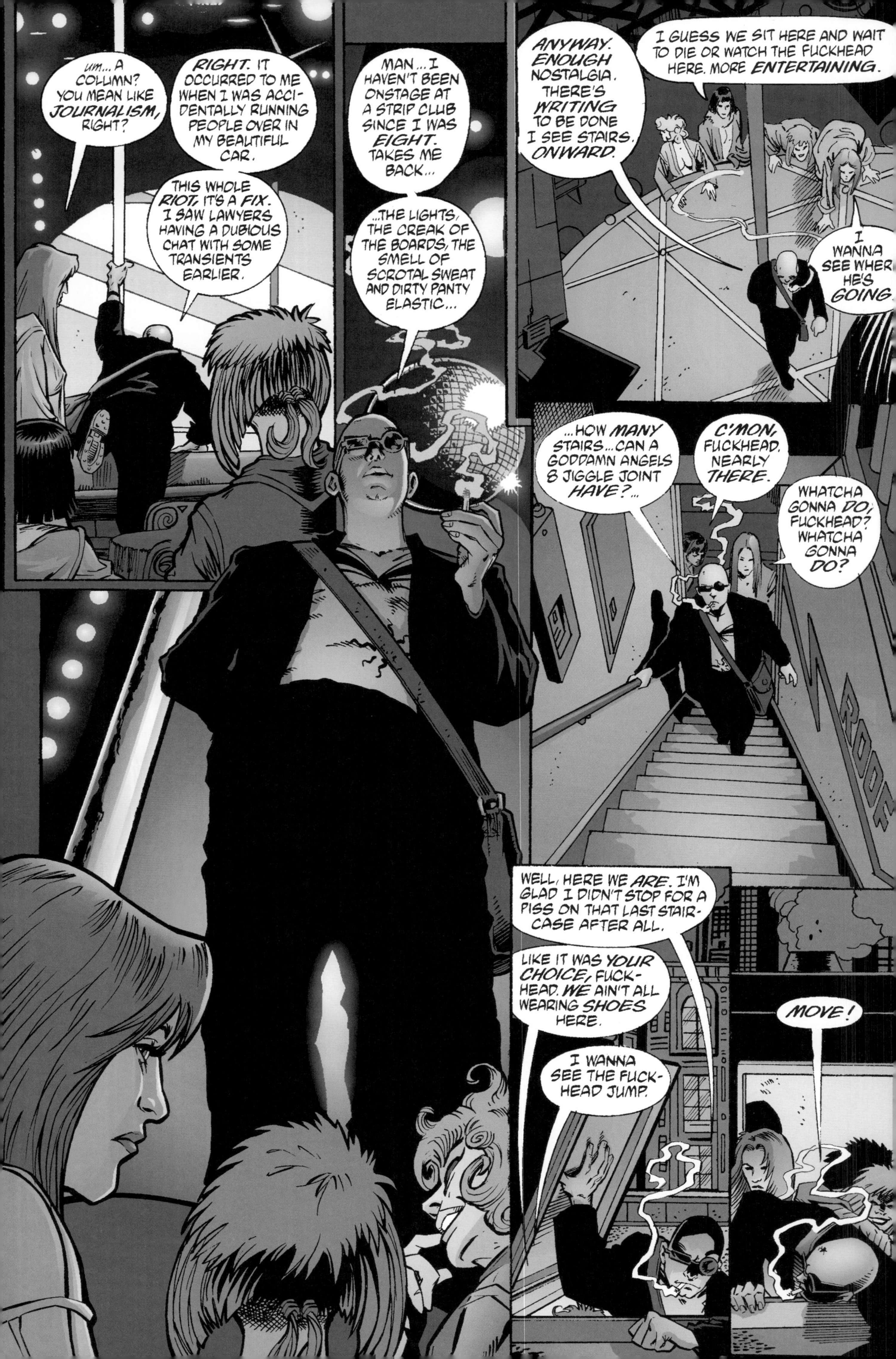
um... A COLUMN? YOU MEAN LIKE JOURNALISM, RIGHT?
RIGHT. IT OCCURRED TO ME WHEN I WAS ACCIDENTALLY RUNNING PEOPLE OVER IN MY BEAUTIFUL CAR.
THIS WHOLE RIOT, IT'S A FIX. I SAW LAWYERS HAVING A DUBIOUS CHAT WITH SOME TRANSIENTS EARLIER.
MAN... I HAVEN'T BEEN ONSTAGE AT A STRIP CLUB SINCE I WAS EIGHT. TAKES ME BACK...
...THE LIGHTS, THE CREAK OF THE BOARDS, THE SMELL OF SCROTAL SWEAT AND DIRTY PANTY ELASTIC...
ANYWAY. ENOUGH NOSTALGIA. THERE'S WRITING TO BE DONE. I SEE STAIRS. ONWARD.
I GUESS WE SIT HERE AND WAIT TO DIE OR WATCH THE FUCKHEAD HERE. MORE ENTERTAINING.
I WANNA SEE WHER HE'S GOING.
...HOW MANY STAIRS...CAN A GODDAMN ANGELS 8 JIGGLE JOINT HAVE?...
C'MON, FUCKHEAD. NEARLY THERE.
WHATCHA GONNA DO, FUCKHEAD? WHATCHA GONNA DO?
ROOF
WELL, HERE WE ARE. I'M GLAD I DIDN'T STOP FOR A PISS ON THAT LAST STAIRCASE AFTER ALL.
LIKE IT WAS YOUR CHOICE, FUCKHEAD. WE AIN'T ALL WEARING SHOES HERE.
I WANNA SEE THE FUCKHEAD JUMP.
MOVE!

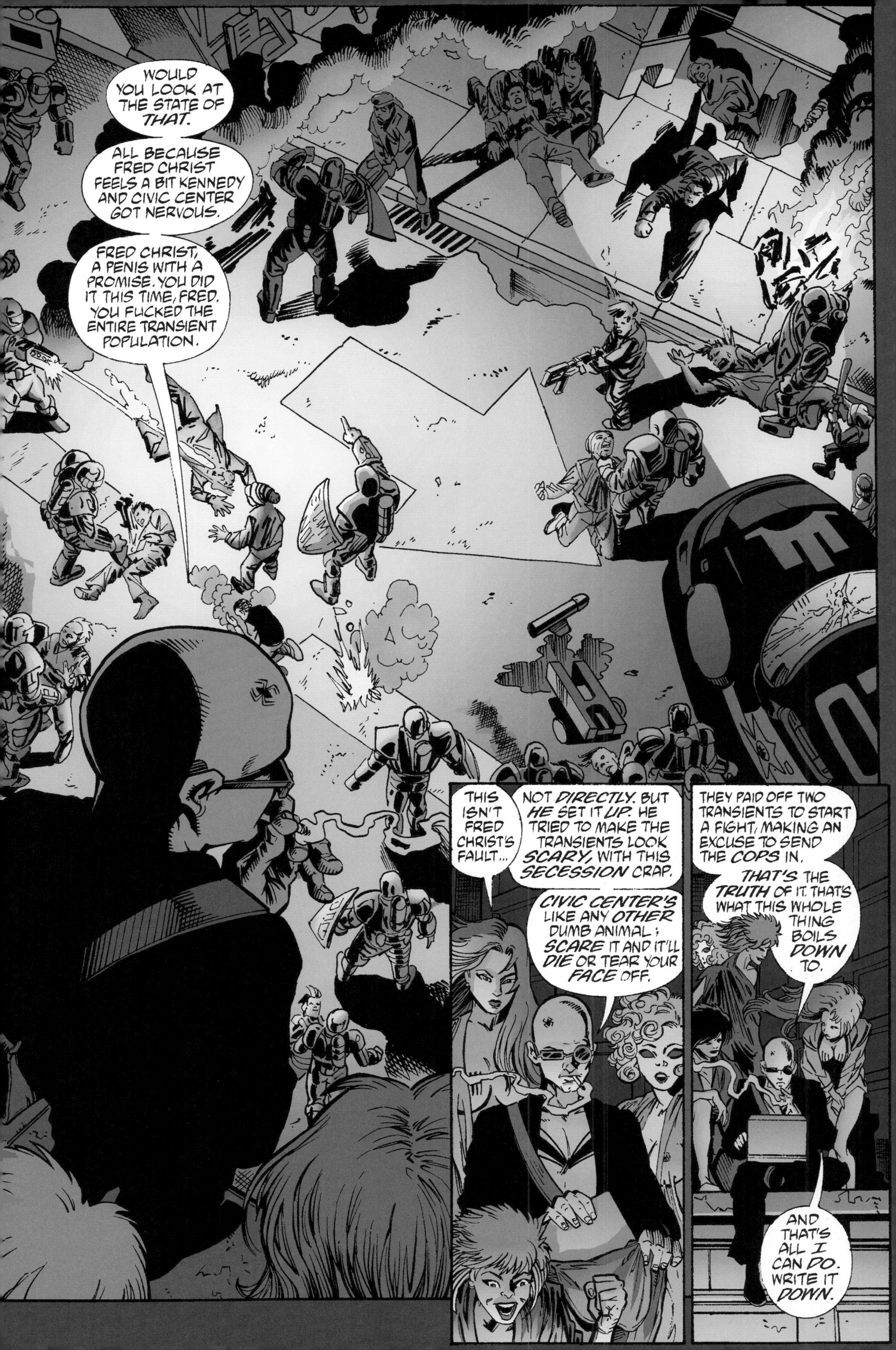
WOULD YOU LOOK AT THE STATE OF *THAT*.
ALL BECAUSE FRED CHRIST FEELS A BIT KENNEDY AND CIVIC CENTER GOT NERVOUS.
FRED CHRIST, A PENIS WITH A PROMISE. YOU DID IT THIS TIME, FRED. YOU FUCKED THE ENTIRE TRANSIENT POPULATION.
THIS ISN'T FRED CHRIST'S FAULT...
NOT *DIRECTLY*. BUT *HE* SET IT *UP*. HE TRIED TO MAKE THE TRANSIENTS LOOK *SCARY*, WITH THIS *SECESSION* CRAP.
*CIVIC CENTER'S* LIKE ANY *OTHER* DUMB ANIMAL ; *SCARE* IT AND IT'LL *DIE* OR TEAR YOUR *FACE* OFF.
THEY PAID OFF TWO TRANSIENTS TO START A FIGHT, MAKING AN EXCUSE TO SEND THE *COPS* IN.
*THAT'S* THE *TRUTH* OF IT. THAT'S WHAT THIS WHOLE THING BOILS *DOWN* TO.
AND THAT'S ALL *I* CAN *DO*. WRITE IT *DOWN*.

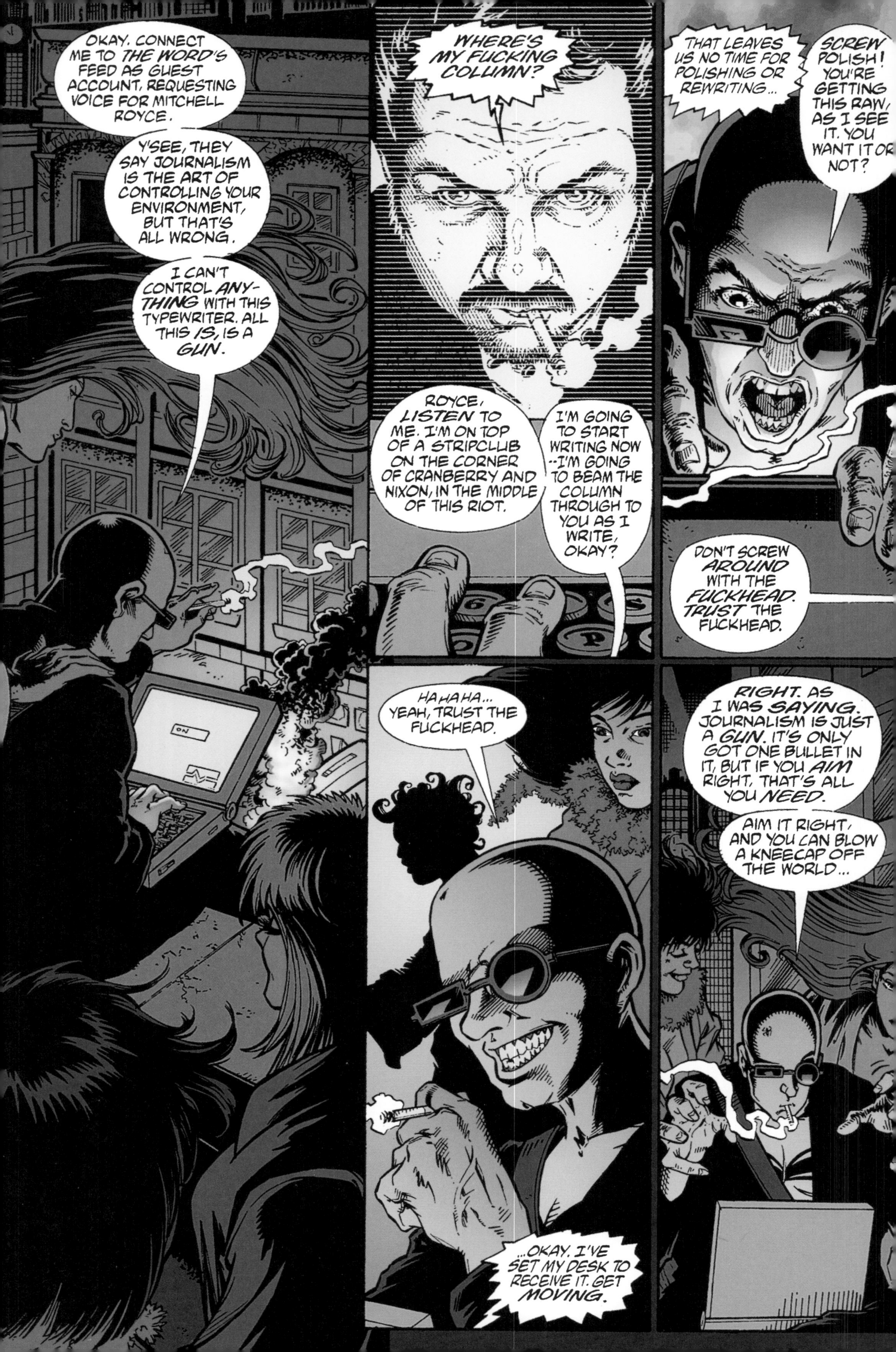
OKAY. CONNECT ME TO THE WORD'S FEED AS GUEST ACCOUNT, REQUESTING VOICE FOR MITCHELL ROYCE.
Y'SEE, THEY SAY JOURNALISM IS THE ART OF CONTROLLING YOUR ENVIRONMENT, BUT THAT'S ALL WRONG.
I CAN'T CONTROL ANYTHING WITH THIS TYPEWRITER. ALL THIS IS, IS A GUN.
WHERE'S MY FUCKING COLUMN?
ROYCE, LISTEN TO ME. I'M ON TOP OF A STRIPCLUB ON THE CORNER OF CRANBERRY AND NIXON, IN THE MIDDLE OF THIS RIOT.
I'M GOING TO START WRITING NOW --I'M GOING TO BEAM THE COLUMN THROUGH TO YOU AS I WRITE, OKAY?
THAT LEAVES US NO TIME FOR POLISHING OR REWRITING...
SCREW POLISH! YOU'RE GETTING THIS RAW, AS I SEE IT. YOU WANT IT OR NOT?
DON'T SCREW AROUND WITH THE FUCKHEAD. TRUST THE FUCKHEAD.
HAHAHA... YEAH, TRUST THE FUCKHEAD.
...OKAY. I'VE SET MY DESK TO RECEIVE IT. GET MOVING.
RIGHT. AS I WAS SAYING. JOURNALISM IS JUST A GUN. IT'S ONLY GOT ONE BULLET IN IT, BUT IF YOU AIM RIGHT, THAT'S ALL YOU NEED.
AIM IT RIGHT, AND YOU CAN BLOW A KNEECAP OFF THE WORLD...

I COULD NEVER WRITE UNLESS I WAS IN THE CITY.

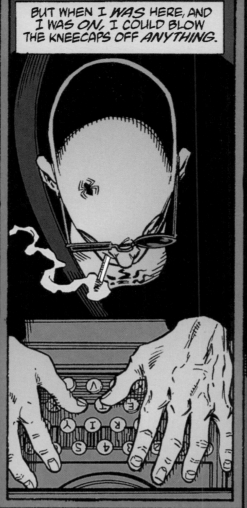

BUT WHEN I *WAS* HERE, AND I WAS *ON*, I COULD BLOW THE KNEECAPS OFF *ANYTHING*.

*I'M* NOT SCARED. I'M *NOT* SCARED. INDIRA, D'YOU KNOW HOW THE LIVE NEWSFEEDS ARE COVERING ANGELS 8?

THEY'RE HAVING SOME TROUBLE GETTING CLOSE. SOME PICTURES, NOT MUCH REPORTAGE.

mm. OKAY. GET ME A CONFERENCE CALL WITH THE CITY EDITOR AT *SPKF*. I THINK I HAVE SOMETHING TO *SELL* HER.

There's a jungle rhythm beating out below me; the sound of truncheons hammering on riot shields, police tradition when the streets get nasty.

I'm in Angels 8, above what will doubtless be called the Transient Riot. History's only written by the winners, after all, and if the cops want it called the Transient Riot, then that's how it'll be.

Because there's going to be Transient blood all over this place. And you know something?

It's not their fault.

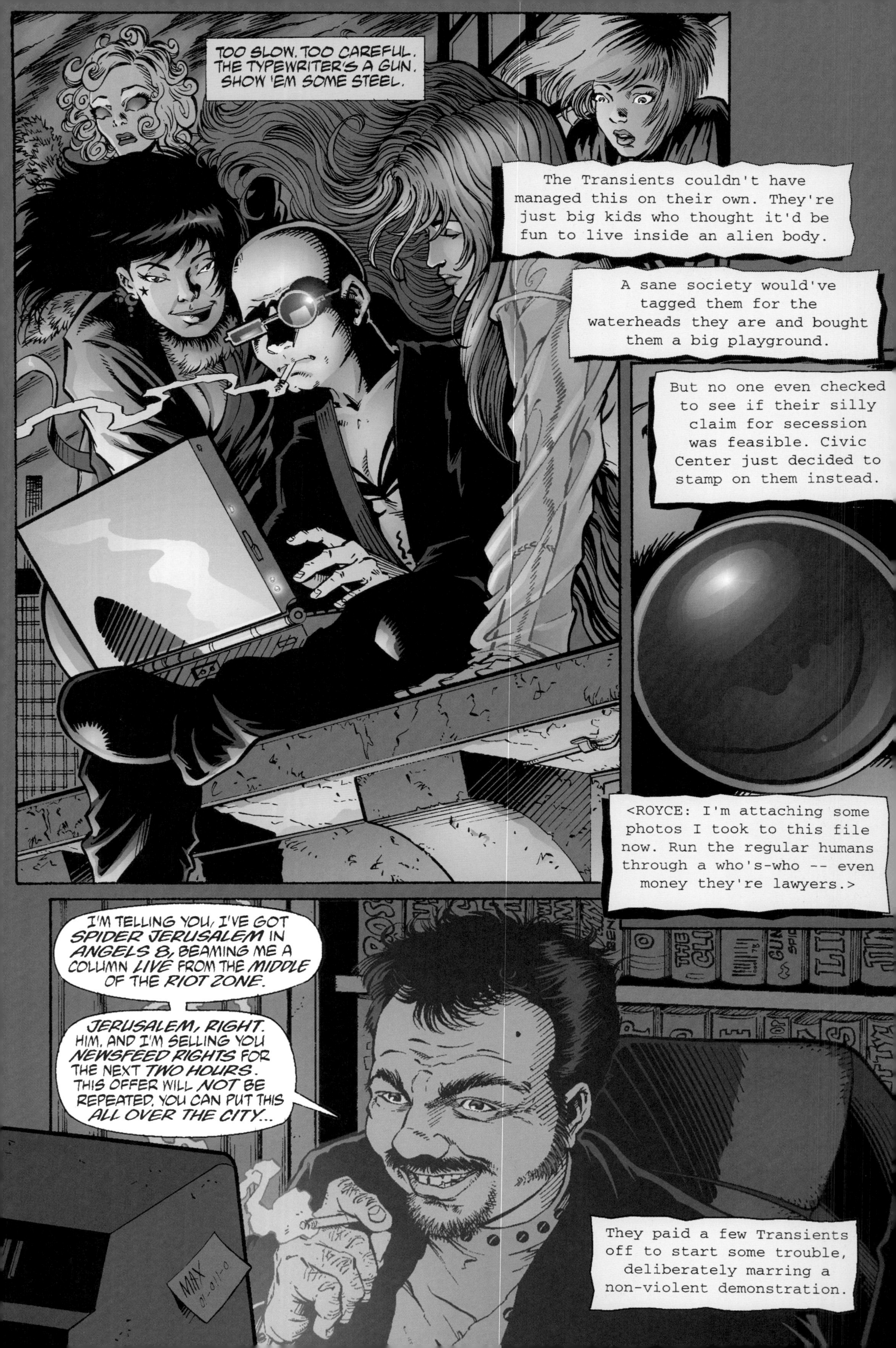
TOO SLOW. TOO CAREFUL. THE TYPEWRITER'S A GUN. SHOW 'EM SOME STEEL.
The Transients couldn't have managed this on their own. They're just big kids who thought it'd be fun to live inside an alien body.
A sane society would've tagged them for the waterheads they are and bought them a big playground.
But no one even checked to see if their silly claim for secession was feasible. Civic Center just decided to stamp on them instead.
<ROYCE: I'm attaching some photos I took to this file now. Run the regular humans through a who's-who -- even money they're lawyers.>
I'M TELLING YOU, I'VE GOT SPIDER JERUSALEM IN ANGELS 8, BEAMING ME A COLUMN LIVE FROM THE MIDDLE OF THE RIOT ZONE.
JERUSALEM, RIGHT. HIM. AND I'M SELLING YOU NEWSFEED RIGHTS FOR THE NEXT TWO HOURS. THIS OFFER WILL NOT BE REPEATED. YOU CAN PUT THIS ALL OVER THE CITY...
They paid a few Transients off to start some trouble, deliberately marring a non-violent demonstration.

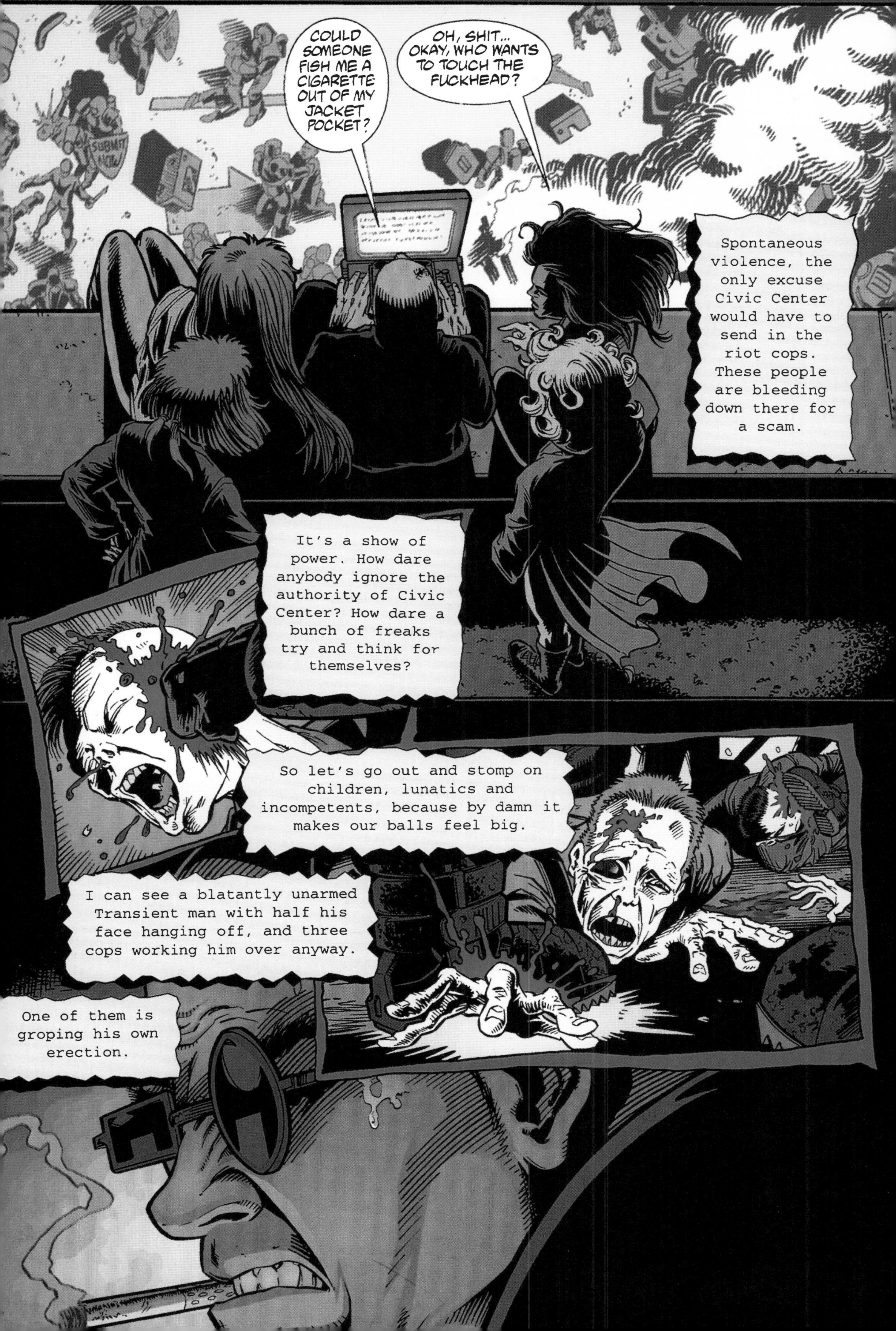
COULD SOMEONE FISH ME A CIGARETTE OUT OF MY JACKET POCKET?
OH, SHIT... OKAY, WHO WANTS TO TOUCH THE FUCKHEAD?
Spontaneous violence, the only excuse Civic Center would have to send in the riot cops. These people are bleeding down there for a scam.
It's a show of power. How dare anybody ignore the authority of Civic Center? How dare a bunch of freaks try and think for themselves?
So let's go out and stomp on children, lunatics and incompetents, because by damn it makes our balls feel big.
I can see a blatantly unarmed Transient man with half his face hanging off, and three cops working him over anyway.
One of them is groping his own erection.

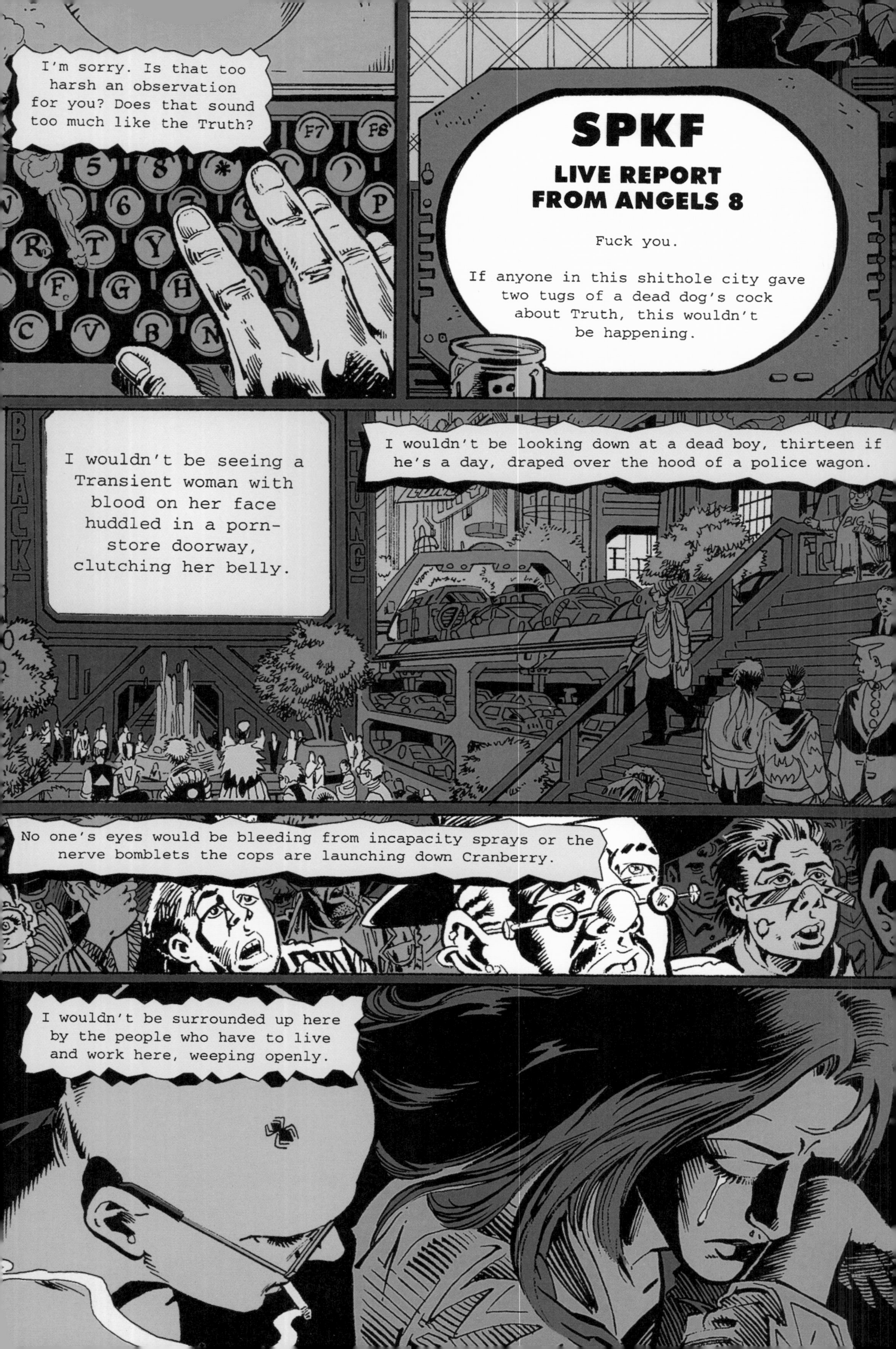
I'm sorry. Is that too harsh an observation for you? Does that sound too much like the Truth?
SPKF
LIVE REPORT FROM ANGELS 8
Fuck you.
If anyone in this shithole city gave two tugs of a dead dog's cock about Truth, this wouldn't be happening.
I wouldn't be seeing a Transient woman with blood on her face huddled in a porn-store doorway, clutching her belly.
I wouldn't be looking down at a dead boy, thirteen if he's a day, draped over the hood of a police wagon.
No one's eyes would be bleeding from incapacity sprays or the nerve bomblets the cops are launching down Cranberry.
I wouldn't be surrounded up here by the people who have to live and work here, weeping openly.

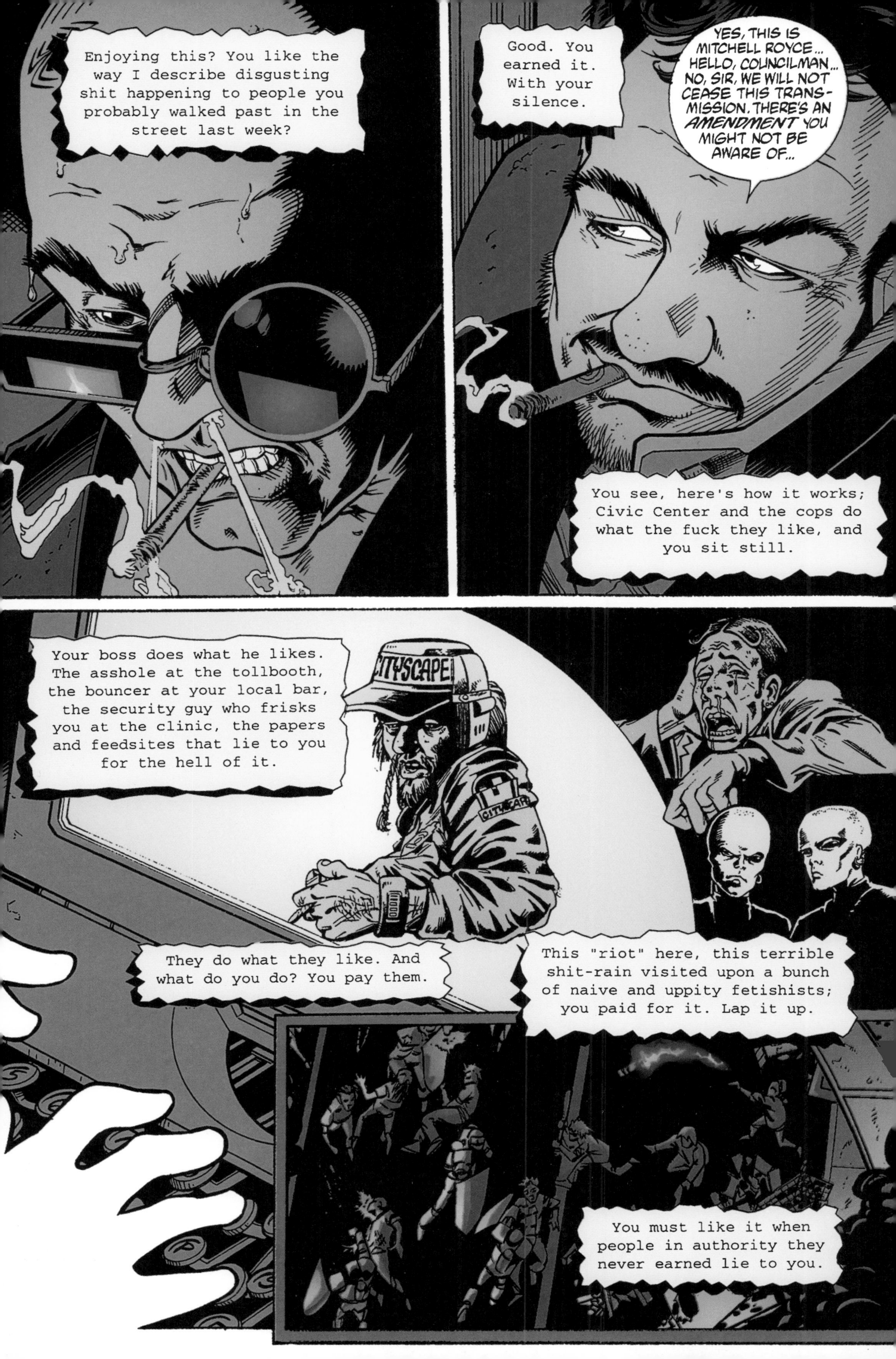
Enjoying this? You like the way I describe disgusting shit happening to people you probably walked past in the street last week?
Good. You earned it. With your silence.
YES, THIS IS MITCHELL ROYCE... HELLO, COUNCILMAN... NO, SIR, WE WILL NOT CEASE THIS TRANSMISSION. THERE'S AN *AMENDMENT* YOU MIGHT NOT BE AWARE OF...
You see, here's how it works; Civic Center and the cops do what the fuck they like, and you sit still.
Your boss does what he likes. The asshole at the tollbooth, the bouncer at your local bar, the security guy who frisks you at the clinic, the papers and feedsites that lie to you for the hell of it.
CITYSCAPE
They do what they like. And what do you do? You pay them.
This "riot" here, this terrible shit-rain visited upon a bunch of naive and uppity fetishists; you paid for it. Lap it up.
You must like it when people in authority they never earned lie to you.

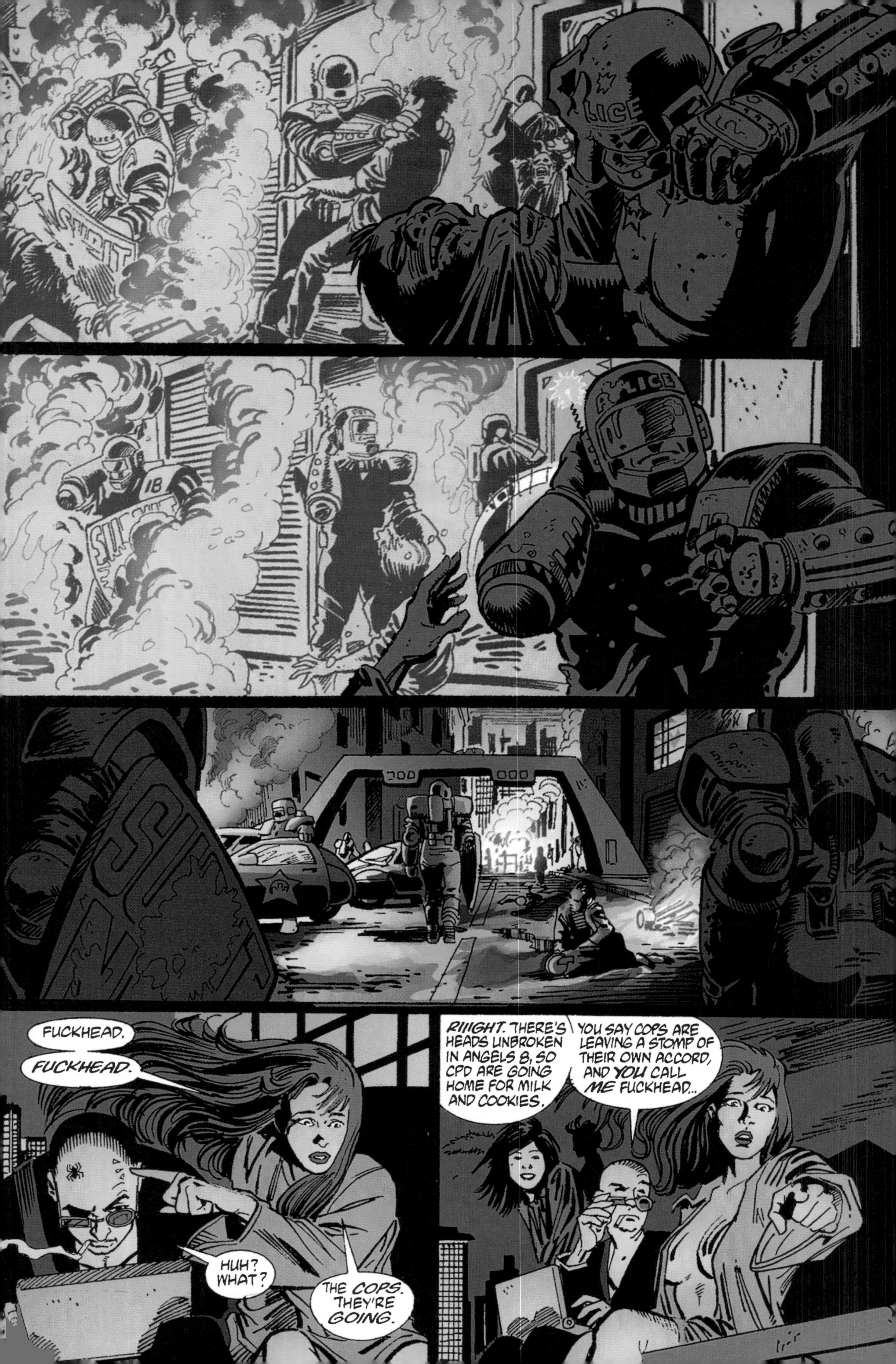
FUCKHEAD.
FUCKHEAD.
HUH? WHAT?
THE COPS. THEY'RE GOING.
RIIIGHT. THERE'S HEADS UNBROKEN IN ANGELS 8, SO CPD ARE GOING HOME FOR MILK AND COOKIES.
YOU SAY COPS ARE LEAVING A STOMP OF THEIR OWN ACCORD, AND YOU CALL ME FUCKHEAD...

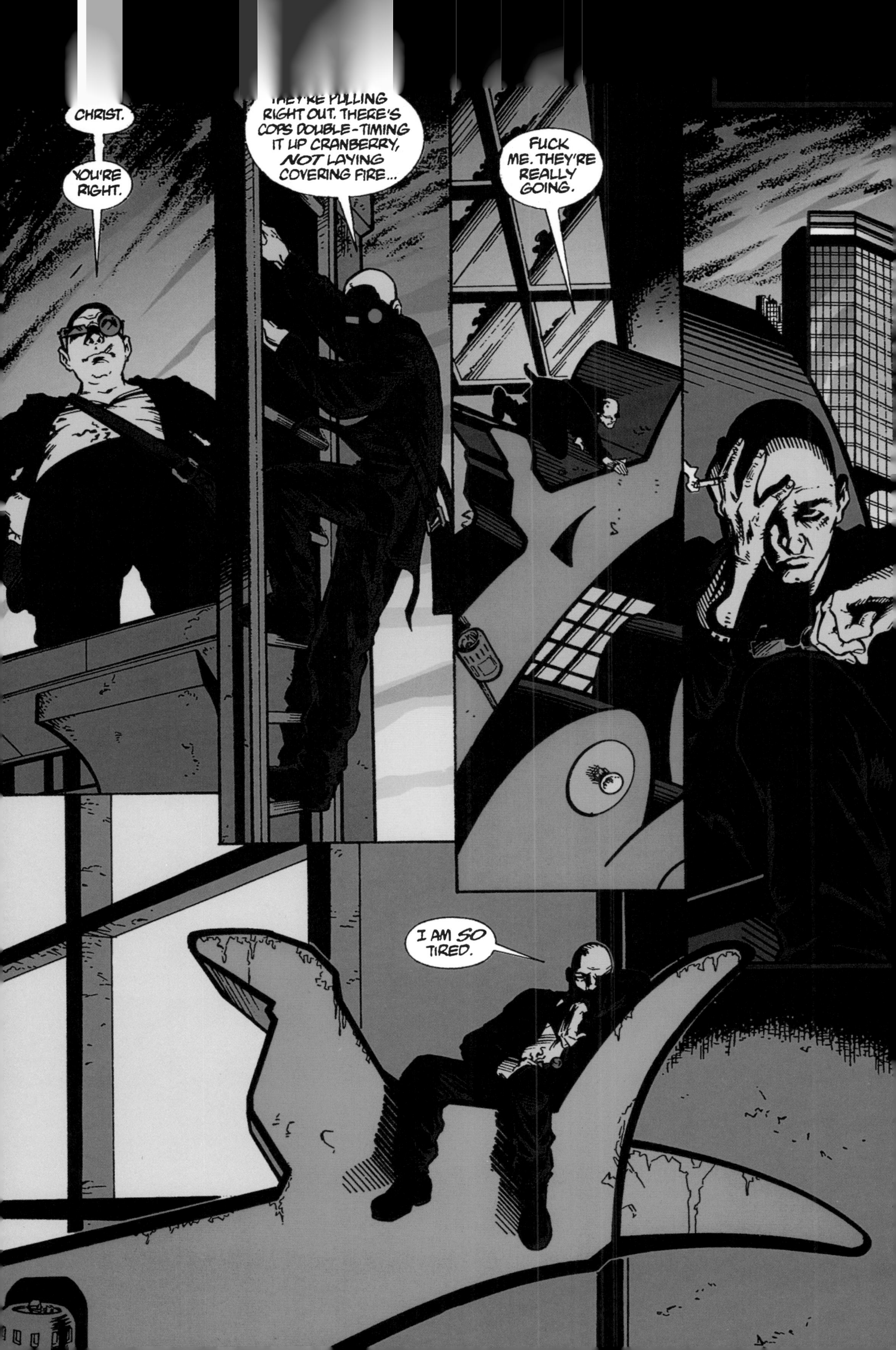
CHRIST.
YOU'RE RIGHT.
THEY'RE PULLING RIGHT OUT. THERE'S COPS DOUBLE-TIMING IT UP CRANBERRY, NOT LAYING COVERING FIRE...
FUCK ME. THEY'RE REALLY GOING.
I AM SO TIRED.

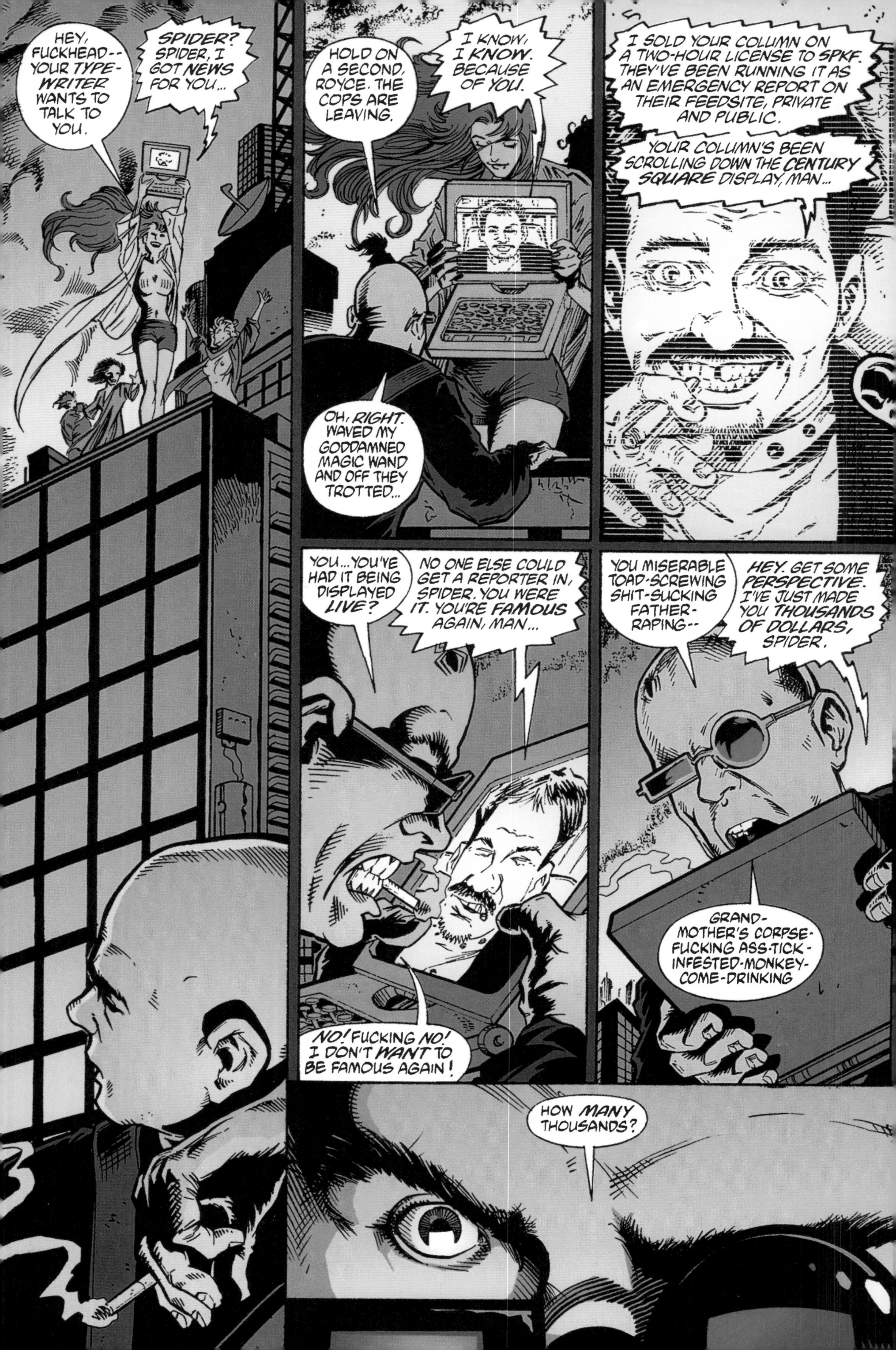
HEY, FUCKHEAD-- YOUR TYPE-WRITER WANTS TO TALK TO YOU.
SPIDER? SPIDER, I GOT NEWS FOR YOU...
HOLD ON A SECOND, ROYCE. THE COPS ARE LEAVING.
I KNOW, I KNOW. BECAUSE OF YOU.
OH, RIGHT. WAVED MY GODDAMNED MAGIC WAND AND OFF THEY TROTTED...
I SOLD YOUR COLUMN ON A TWO-HOUR LICENSE TO SPKF. THEY'VE BEEN RUNNING IT AS AN EMERGENCY REPORT ON THEIR FEEDSITE, PRIVATE AND PUBLIC.
YOUR COLUMN'S BEEN SCROLLING DOWN THE CENTURY SQUARE DISPLAY, MAN...
YOU...YOU'VE HAD IT BEING DISPLAYED LIVE?
NO ONE ELSE COULD GET A REPORTER IN, SPIDER. YOU WERE IT. YOU'RE FAMOUS AGAIN, MAN...
NO! FUCKING NO! I DON'T WANT TO BE FAMOUS AGAIN!
YOU MISERABLE TOAD-SCREWING SHIT-SUCKING FATHER-RAPING--
HEY. GET SOME PERSPECTIVE. I'VE JUST MADE YOU THOUSANDS OF DOLLARS, SPIDER.
GRAND-MOTHER'S CORPSE-FUCKING ASS-TICK-INFESTED-MONKEY-COME-DRINKING
HOW MANY THOUSANDS?

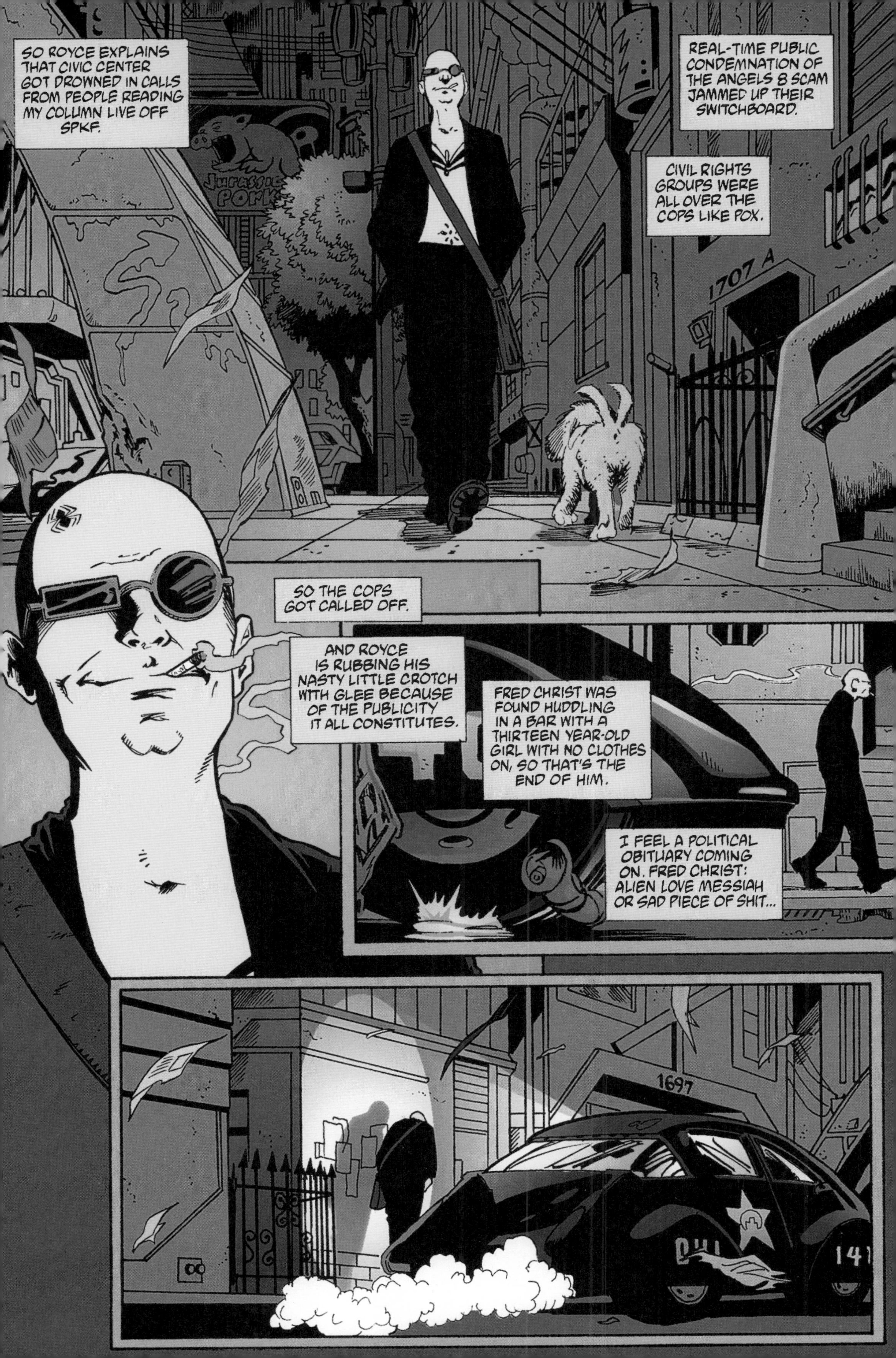

SO ROYCE EXPLAINS THAT CIVIC CENTER GOT DROWNED IN CALLS FROM PEOPLE READING MY COLUMN LIVE OFF SPKF.
REAL-TIME PUBLIC CONDEMNATION OF THE ANGELS 8 SCAM JAMMED UP THEIR SWITCHBOARD.
CIVIL RIGHTS GROUPS WERE ALL OVER THE COPS LIKE POX.
Jurassic Pork
1707 A
SO THE COPS GOT CALLED OFF.
AND ROYCE IS RUBBING HIS NASTY LITTLE CROTCH WITH GLEE BECAUSE OF THE PUBLICITY IT ALL CONSTITUTES.
FRED CHRIST WAS FOUND HUDDLING IN A BAR WITH A THIRTEEN YEAR-OLD GIRL WITH NO CLOTHES ON, SO THAT'S THE END OF HIM.
I FEEL A POLITICAL OBITUARY COMING ON. FRED CHRIST: ALIEN LOVE MESSIAH OR SAD PIECE OF SHIT...
1697
141

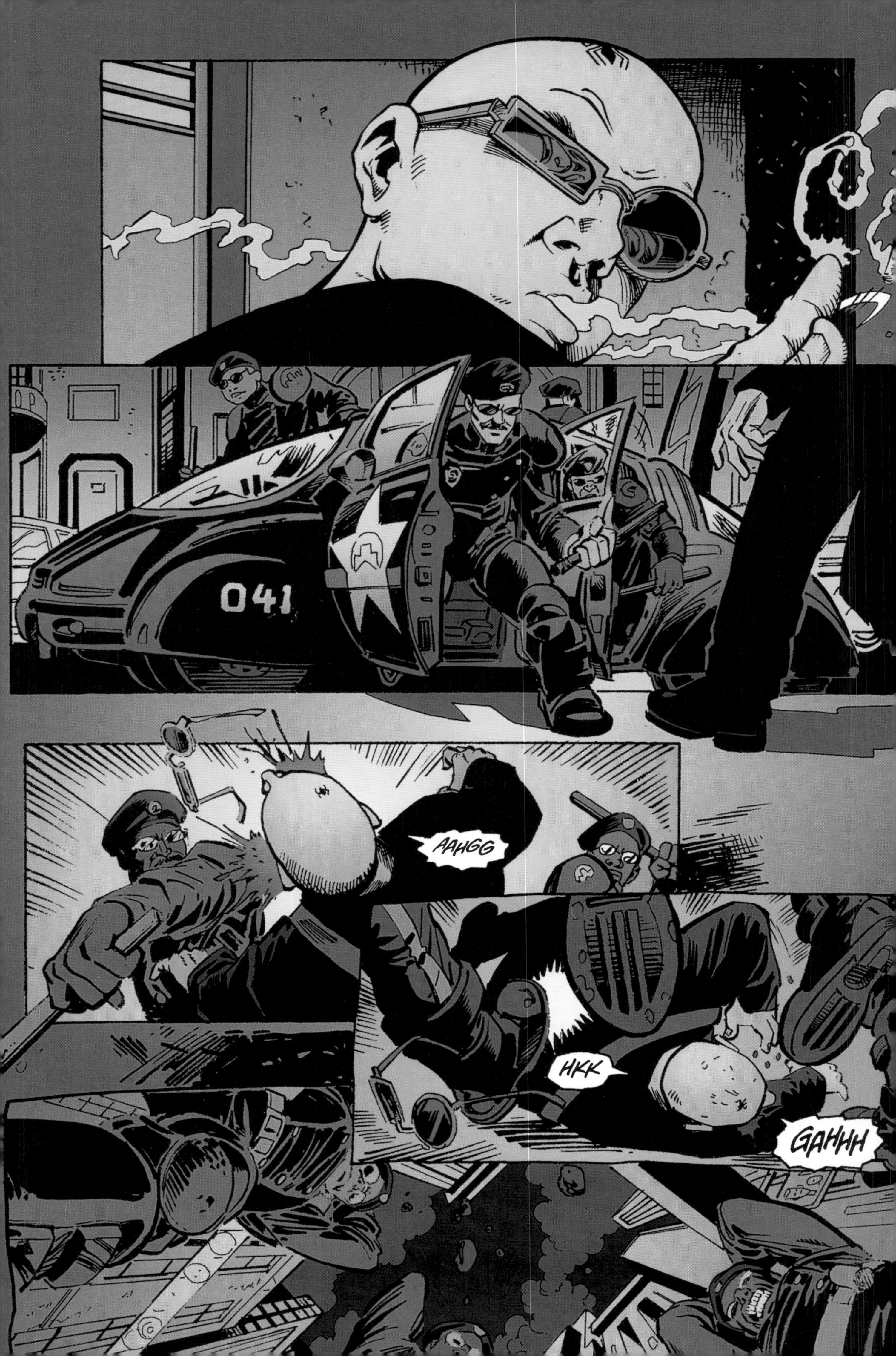
041
AAHGG
HKK
GAHHH

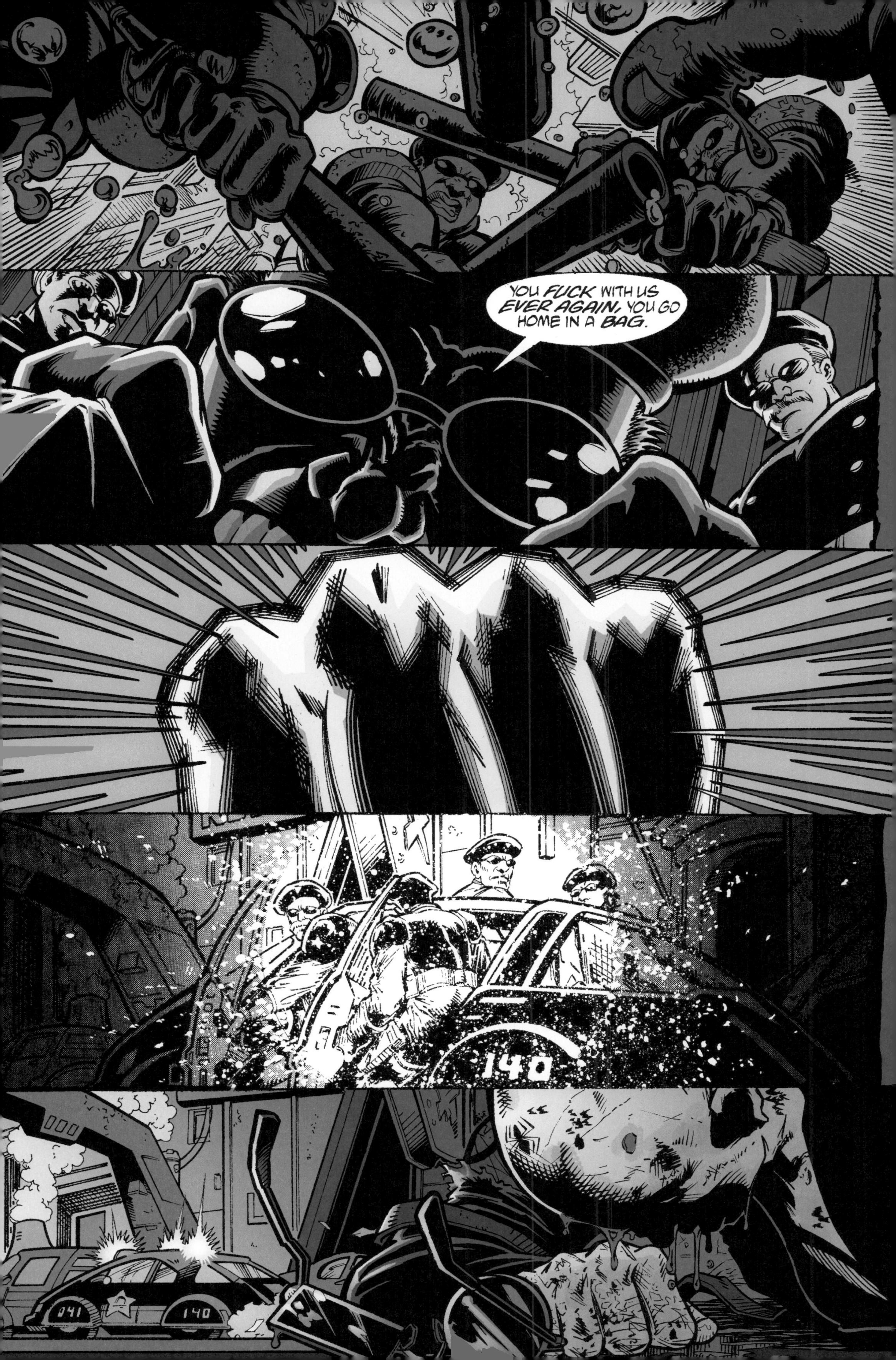

YOU FUCK WITH US EVER AGAIN, YOU GO HOME IN A BAG.
140
041
140

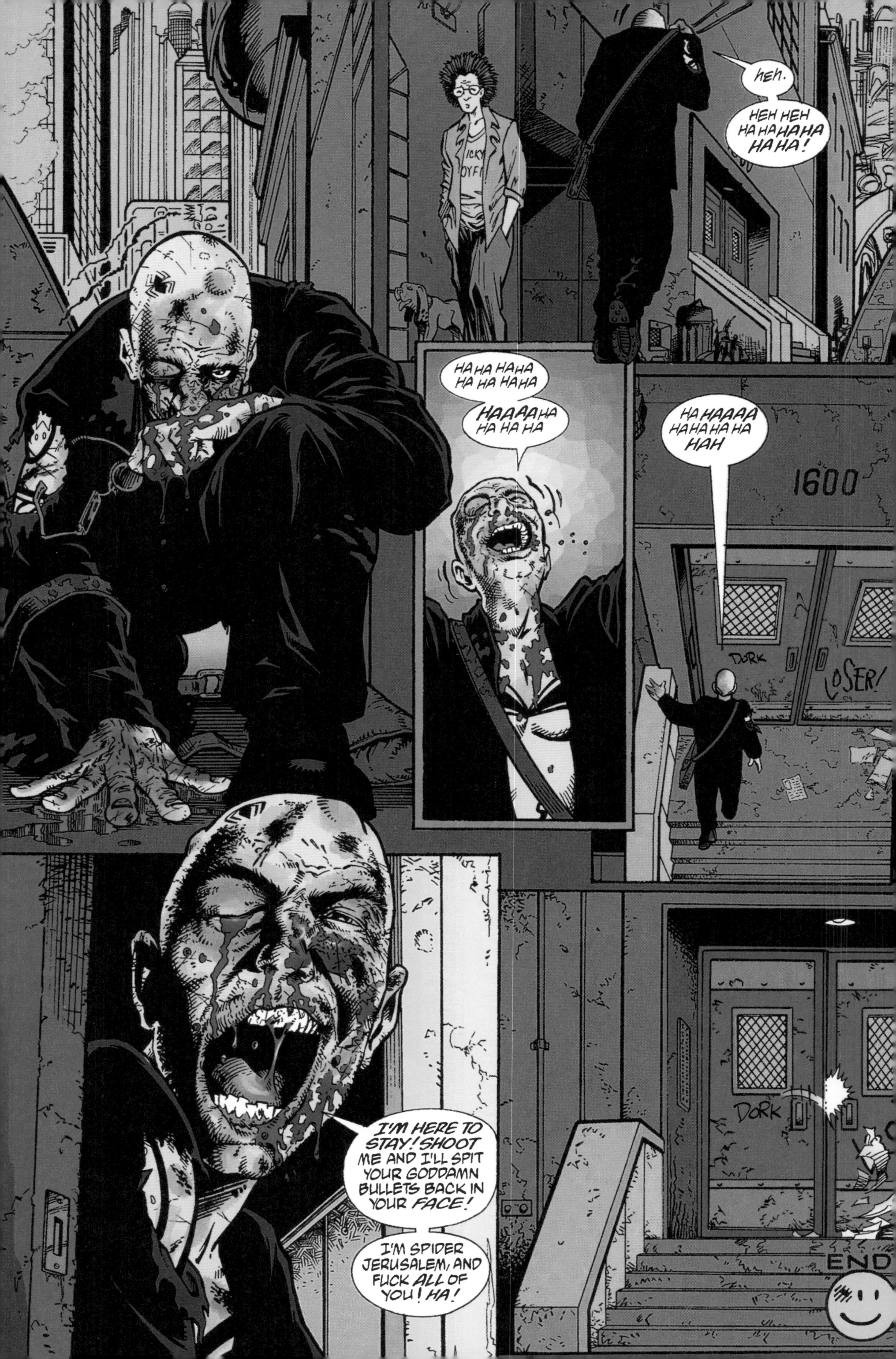
heh.
HEH HEH HA HA HAHA HA HA!
HA HA HAHA HA HA HA HA HA HA
HAAAA HA HA HA HA
HA HAAAA HA HA HA HA HA HAH
1600
DORK
LOSER!
I'M HERE TO STAY! SHOOT ME AND I'LL SPIT YOUR GODDAMN BULLETS BACK IN YOUR FACE!
I'M SPIDER JERUSALEM, AND FUCK ALL OF YOU! HA!
DORK
END

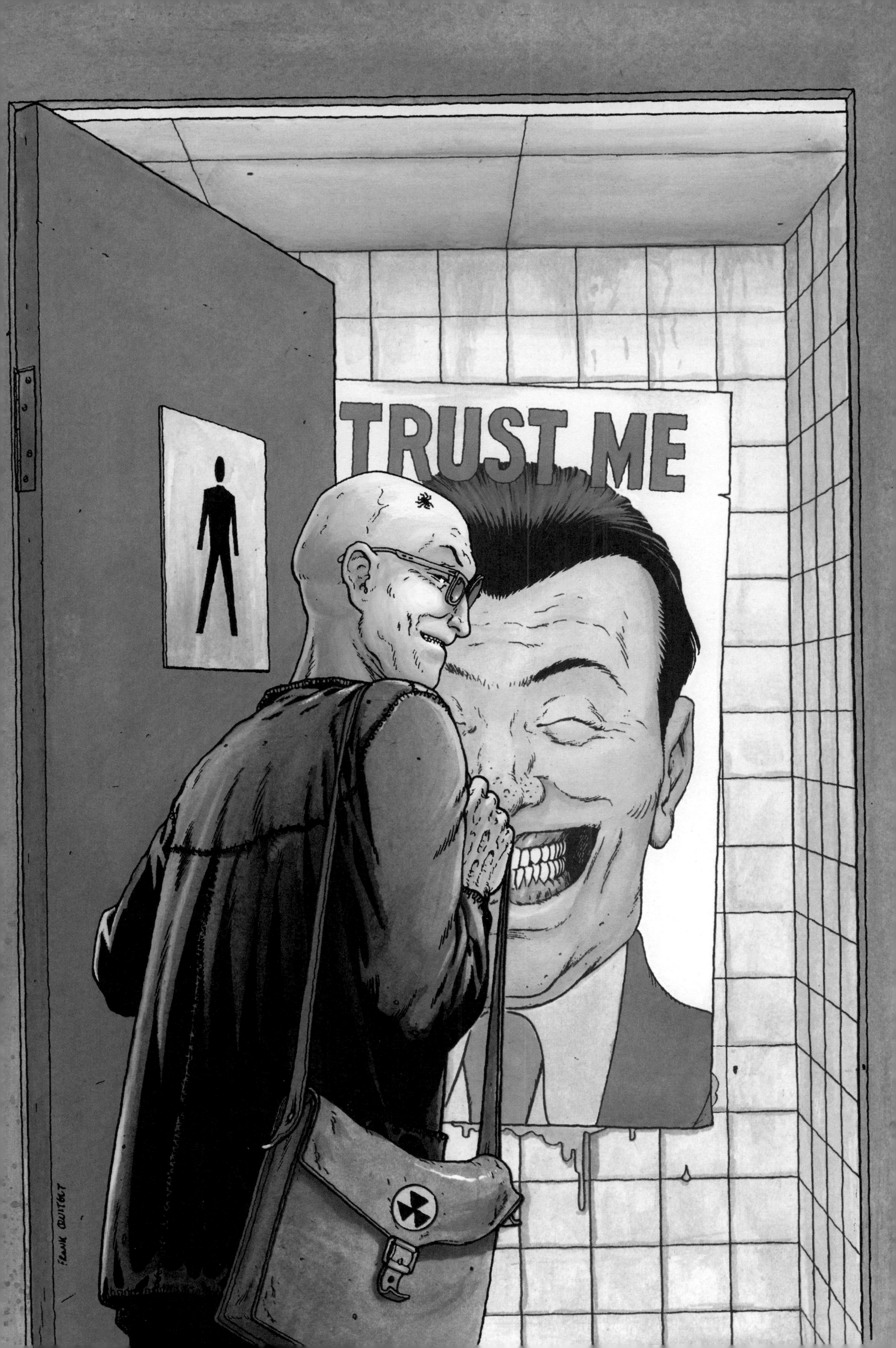
TRUST ME

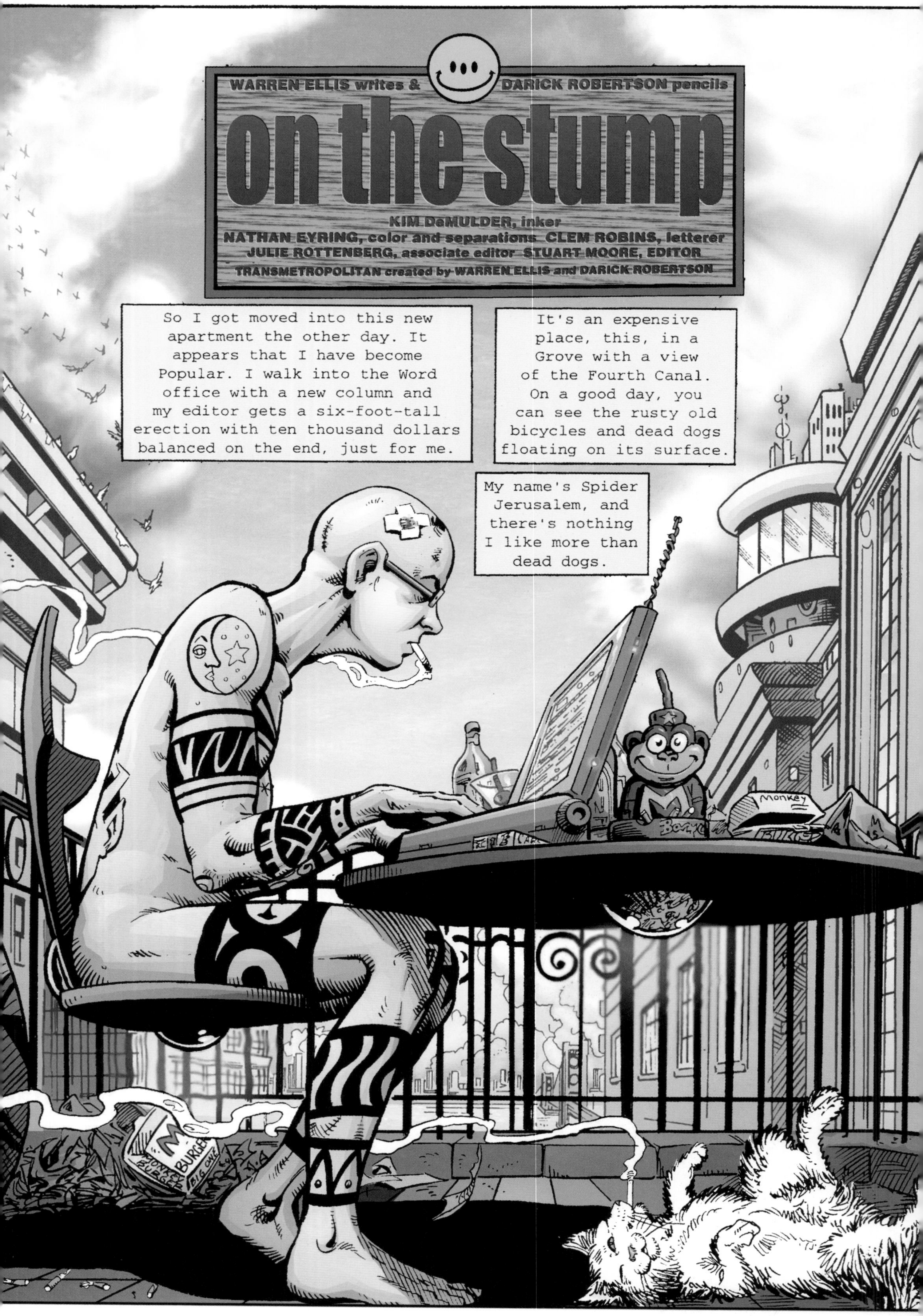
WARREN ELLIS writes & DARICK ROBERTSON pencils
on the stump
KIM DeMULDER, inker
NATHAN EYRING, color and separations CLEM ROBINS, letterer
JULIE ROTTENBERG, associate editor STUART MOORE, EDITOR
TRANSMETROPOLITAN created by WARREN ELLIS and DARICK ROBERTSON
So I got moved into this new apartment the other day. It appears that I have become Popular. I walk into the Word office with a new column and my editor gets a six-foot-tall erection with ten thousand dollars balanced on the end, just for me.
It's an expensive place, this, in a Grove with a view of the Fourth Canal. On a good day, you can see the rusty old bicycles and dead dogs floating on its surface.
My name's Spider Jerusalem, and there's nothing I like more than dead dogs.
Monkey
MONKEY BURGER BIG ONE

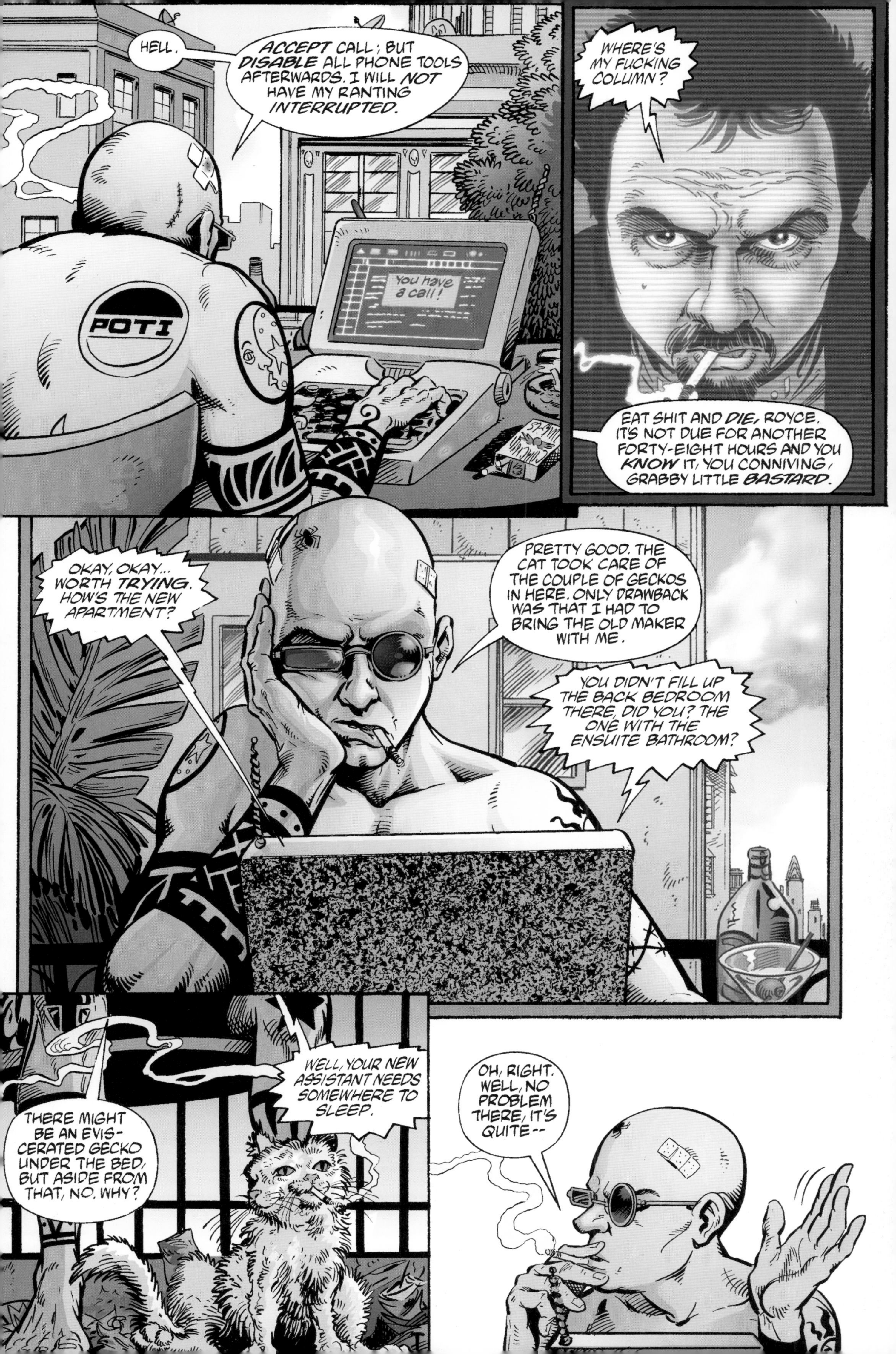
HELL.
ACCEPT CALL; BUT DISABLE ALL PHONE TOOLS AFTERWARDS. I WILL NOT HAVE MY RANTING INTERRUPTED.
You have a call!
POTI
WHERE'S MY FUCKING COLUMN?
EAT SHIT AND DIE, ROYCE. IT'S NOT DUE FOR ANOTHER FORTY-EIGHT HOURS AND YOU KNOW IT, YOU CONNIVING, GRABBY LITTLE BASTARD.
OKAY, OKAY... WORTH TRYING. HOW'S THE NEW APARTMENT?
PRETTY GOOD. THE CAT TOOK CARE OF THE COUPLE OF GECKOS IN HERE. ONLY DRAWBACK WAS THAT I HAD TO BRING THE OLD MAKER WITH ME.
YOU DIDN'T FILL UP THE BACK BEDROOM THERE, DID YOU? THE ONE WITH THE ENSUITE BATHROOM?
THERE MIGHT BE AN EVIS-CERATED GECKO UNDER THE BED, BUT ASIDE FROM THAT, NO. WHY?
WELL, YOUR NEW ASSISTANT NEEDS SOMEWHERE TO SLEEP.
OH, RIGHT. WELL, NO PROBLEM THERE, IT'S QUITE--

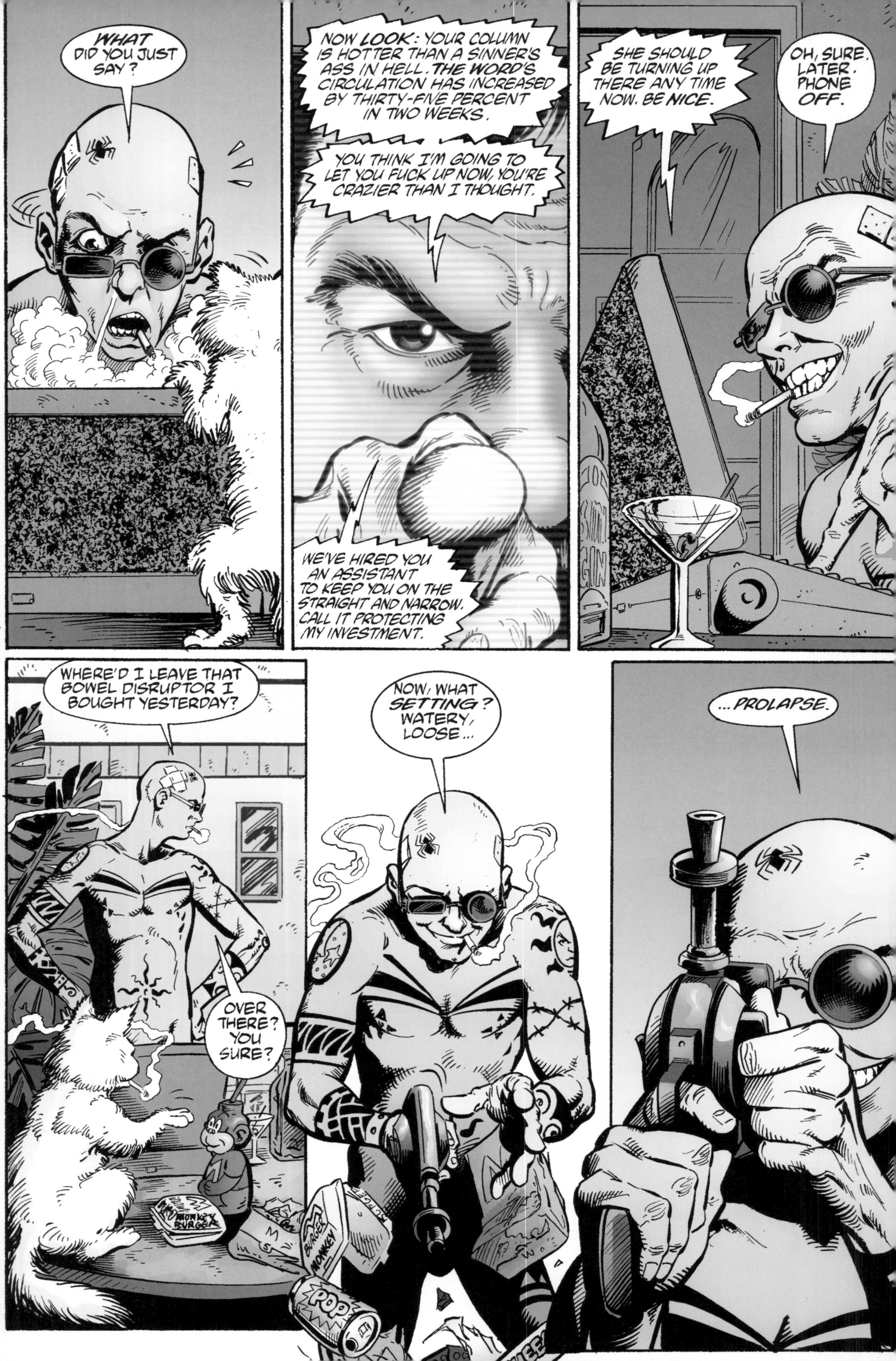
WHAT DID YOU JUST SAY?
NOW LOOK: YOUR COLUMN IS HOTTER THAN A SINNER'S ASS IN HELL. THE WORD'S CIRCULATION HAS INCREASED BY THIRTY-FIVE PERCENT IN TWO WEEKS.
YOU THINK I'M GOING TO LET YOU FUCK UP NOW, YOU'RE CRAZIER THAN I THOUGHT.
WE'VE HIRED YOU AN ASSISTANT TO KEEP YOU ON THE STRAIGHT AND NARROW. CALL IT PROTECTING MY INVESTMENT.
SHE SHOULD BE TURNING UP THERE ANY TIME NOW. BE NICE.
OH, SURE. LATER. PHONE OFF.
GIN
WHERE'D I LEAVE THAT BOWEL DISRUPTOR I BOUGHT YESTERDAY?
OVER THERE? YOU SURE?
MONKEY BURGER
NOW, WHAT SETTING? WATERY, LOOSE...
MONKEY BURGER
POP
...PROLAPSE.

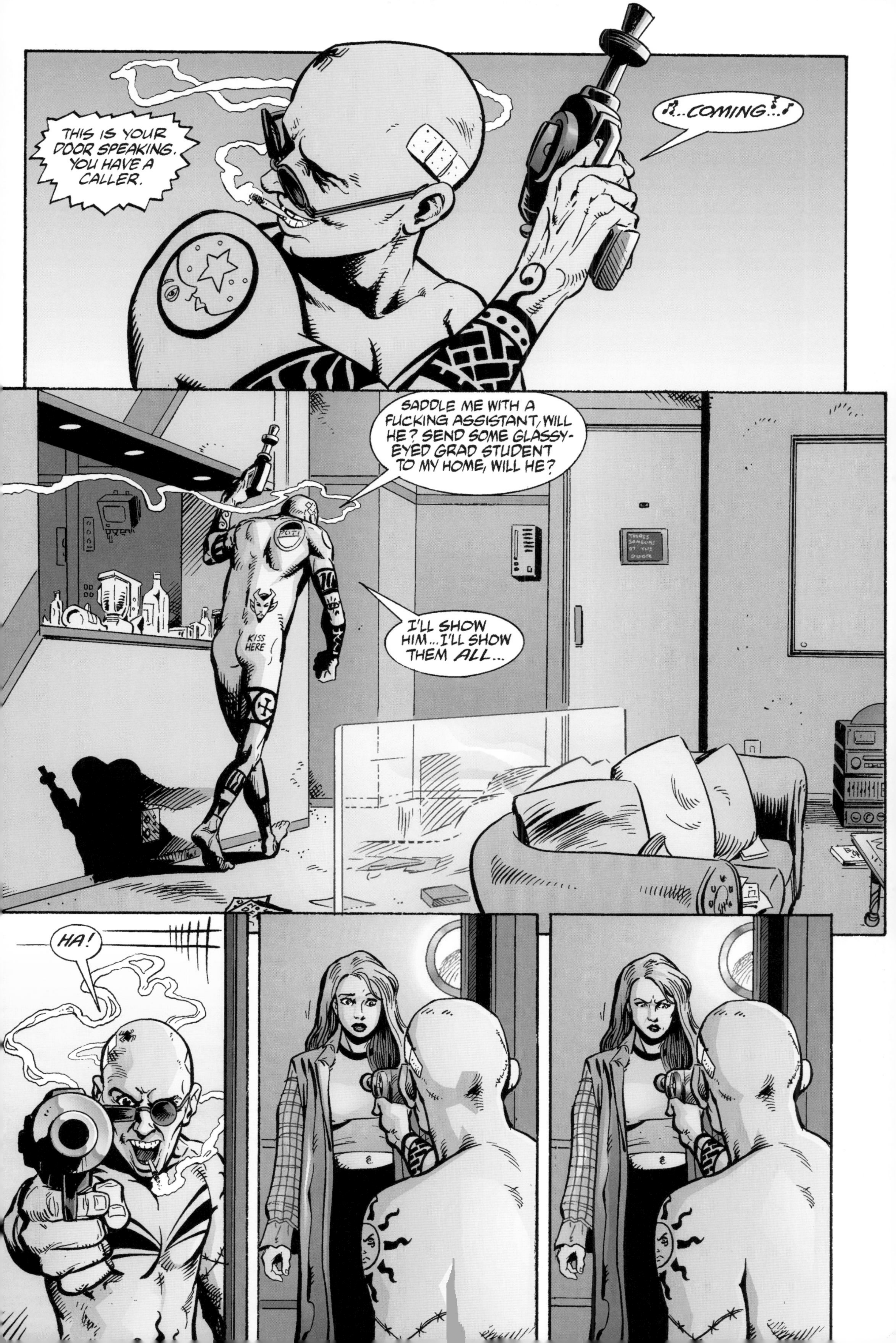
THIS IS YOUR DOOR SPEAKING. YOU HAVE A CALLER.
..COMING..
SADDLE ME WITH A FUCKING ASSISTANT, WILL HE? SEND SOME GLASSY-EYED GRAD STUDENT TO MY HOME, WILL HE?
KISS HERE
I'LL SHOW HIM...I'LL SHOW THEM ALL...
HA!

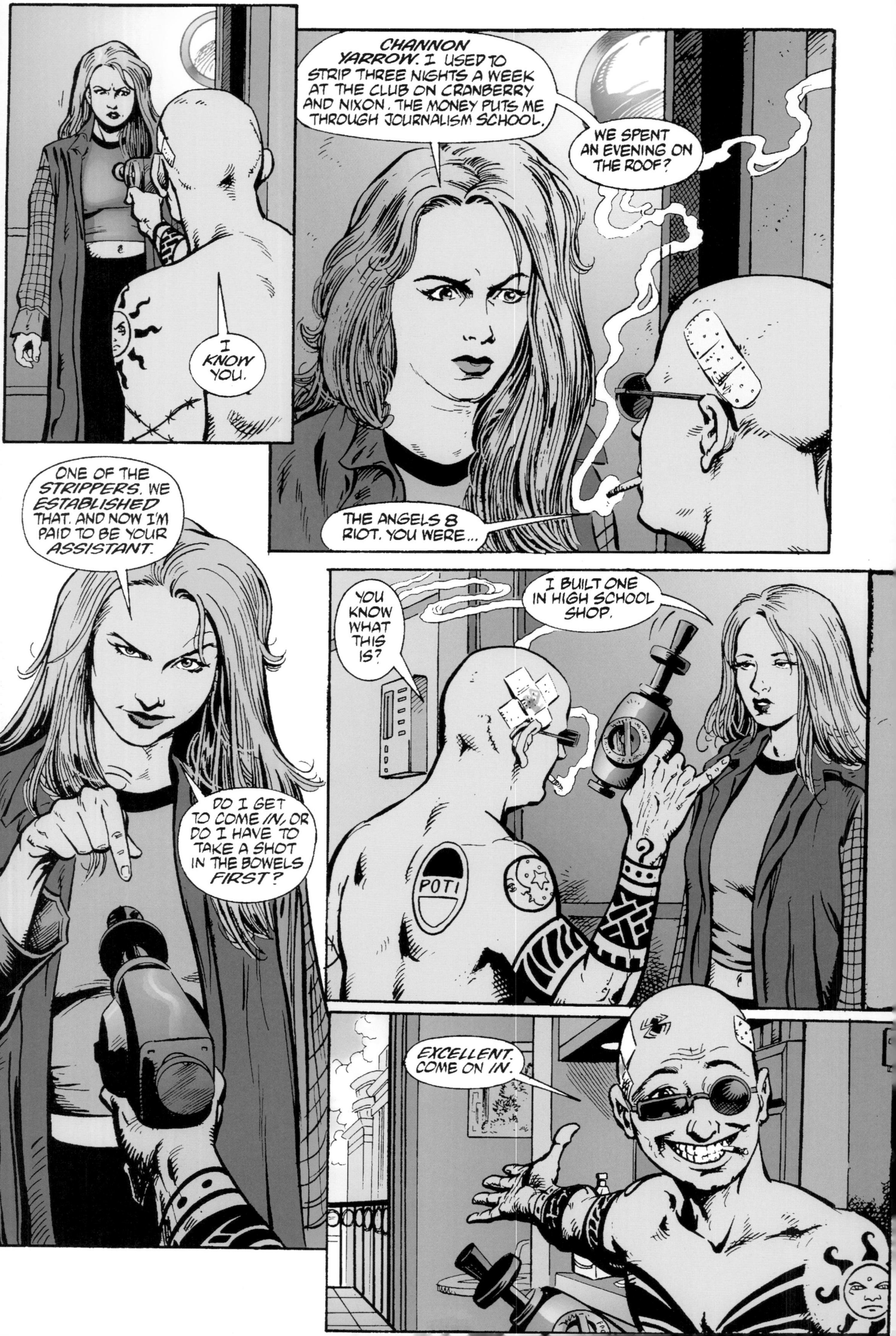
I KNOW YOU.
CHANNON YARROW. I USED TO STRIP THREE NIGHTS A WEEK AT THE CLUB ON CRANBERRY AND NIXON. THE MONEY PUTS ME THROUGH JOURNALISM SCHOOL.
WE SPENT AN EVENING ON THE ROOF?
THE ANGELS 8 RIOT. YOU WERE...
ONE OF THE STRIPPERS. WE ESTABLISHED THAT. AND NOW I'M PAID TO BE YOUR ASSISTANT.
DO I GET TO COME IN, OR DO I HAVE TO TAKE A SHOT IN THE BOWELS FIRST?
YOU KNOW WHAT THIS IS?
I BUILT ONE IN HIGH SCHOOL SHOP.
POTI
EXCELLENT. COME ON IN.

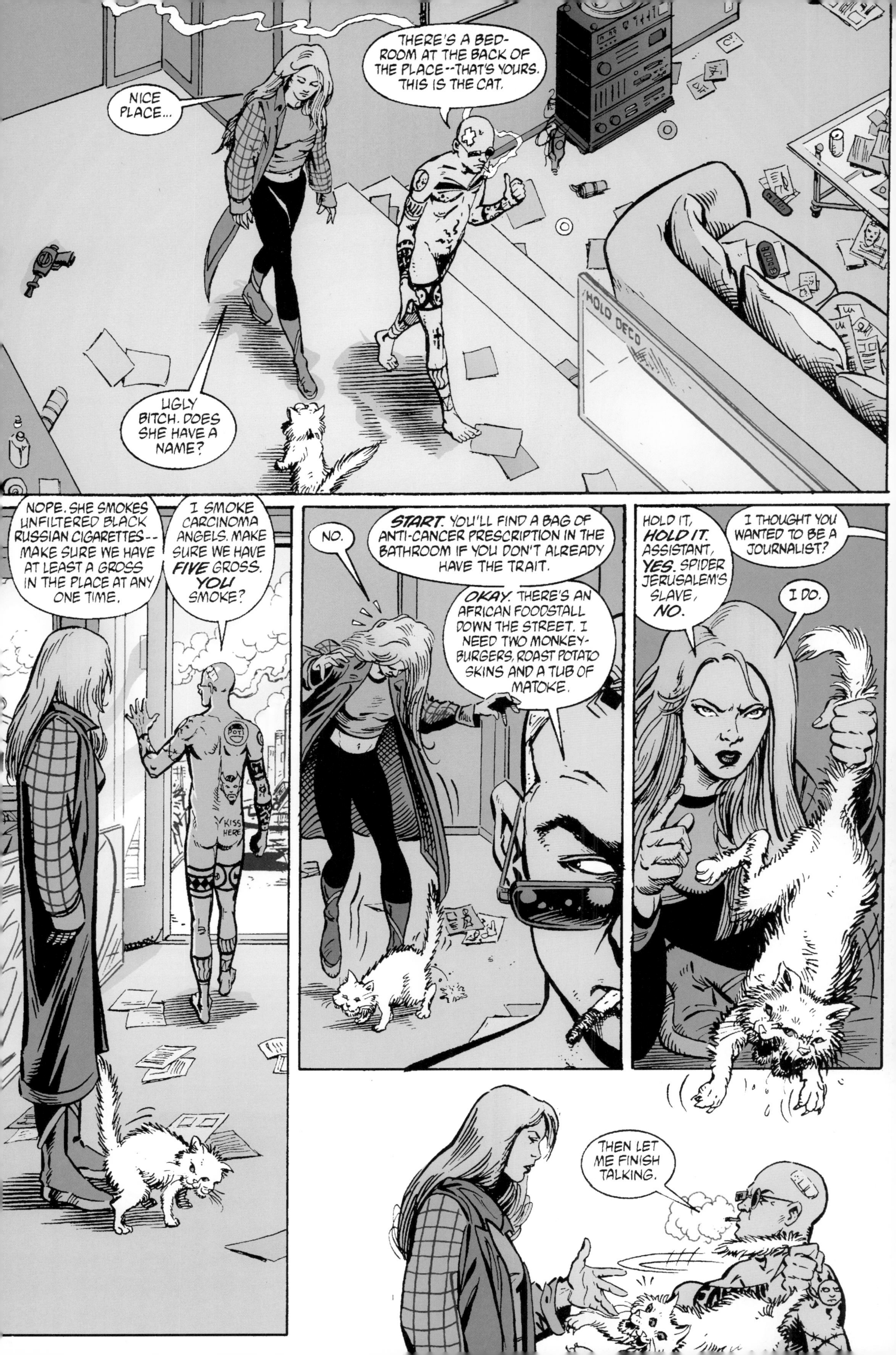
NICE PLACE...
THERE'S A BED-ROOM AT THE BACK OF THE PLACE--THAT'S YOURS. THIS IS THE CAT.
UGLY BITCH. DOES SHE HAVE A NAME?
HOLO DECO
NOPE. SHE SMOKES UNFILTERED BLACK RUSSIAN CIGARETTES-- MAKE SURE WE HAVE AT LEAST A GROSS IN THE PLACE AT ANY ONE TIME.
I SMOKE CARCINOMA ANGELS. MAKE SURE WE HAVE FIVE GROSS. YOU SMOKE?
KISS HERE
NO.
START. YOU'LL FIND A BAG OF ANTI-CANCER PRESCRIPTION IN THE BATHROOM IF YOU DON'T ALREADY HAVE THE TRAIT.
OKAY. THERE'S AN AFRICAN FOODSTALL DOWN THE STREET. I NEED TWO MONKEY-BURGERS, ROAST POTATO SKINS AND A TUB OF MATOKE.
HOLD IT, HOLD IT. ASSISTANT, YES. SPIDER JERUSALEM'S SLAVE, NO.
I THOUGHT YOU WANTED TO BE A JOURNALIST?
I DO.
THEN LET ME FINISH TALKING.

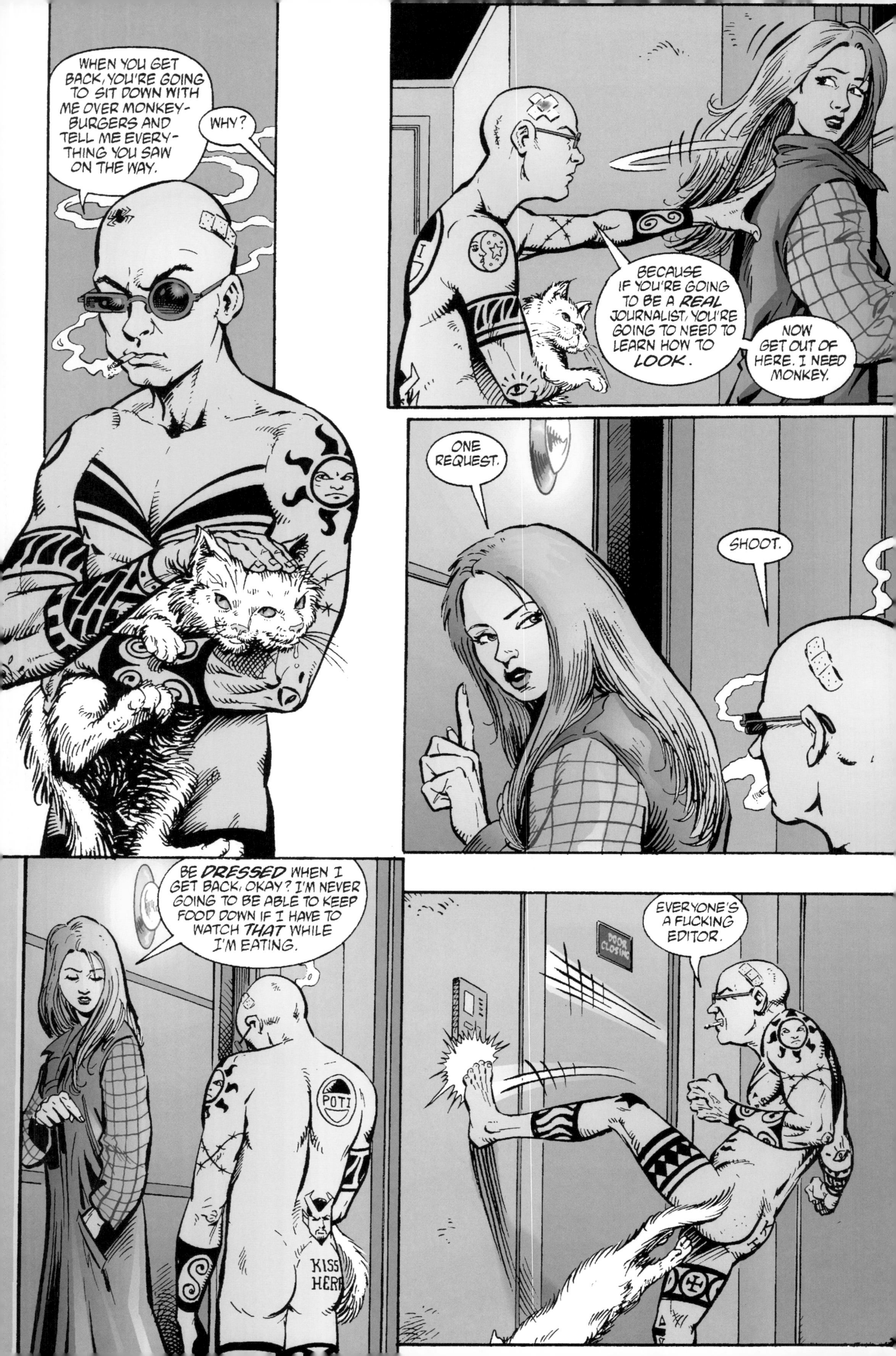
WHEN YOU GET BACK, YOU'RE GOING TO SIT DOWN WITH ME OVER MONKEY-BURGERS AND TELL ME EVERY-THING YOU SAW ON THE WAY.
WHY?
BECAUSE IF YOU'RE GOING TO BE A REAL JOURNALIST, YOU'RE GOING TO NEED TO LEARN HOW TO LOOK.
NOW GET OUT OF HERE. I NEED MONKEY.
ONE REQUEST.
SHOOT.
BE DRESSED WHEN I GET BACK, OKAY? I'M NEVER GOING TO BE ABLE TO KEEP FOOD DOWN IF I HAVE TO WATCH THAT WHILE I'M EATING.
KISS HERE
EVERYONE'S A FUCKING EDITOR.
DOOR CLOSING

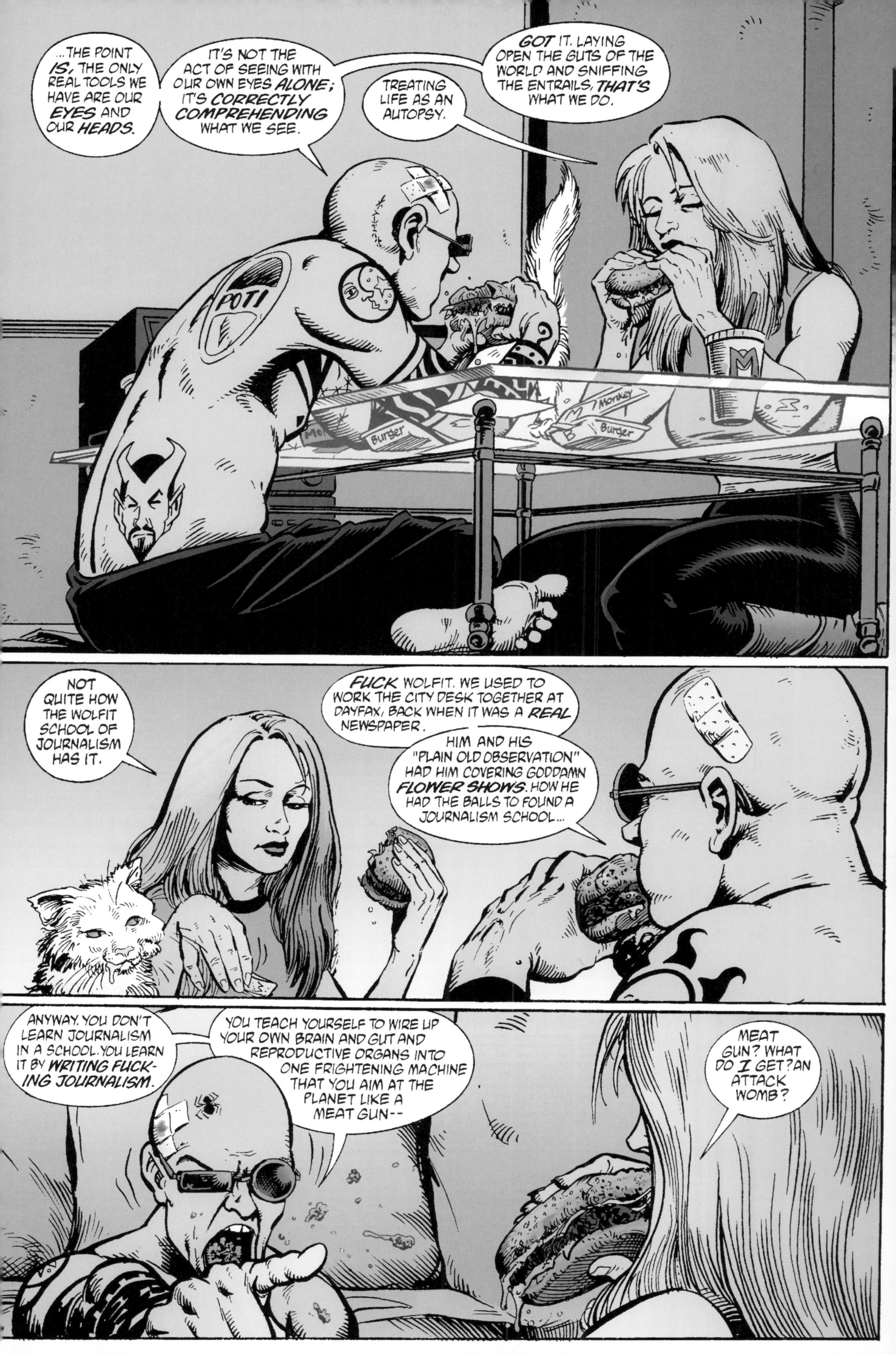
...THE POINT IS, THE ONLY REAL TOOLS WE HAVE ARE OUR EYES AND OUR HEADS.
IT'S NOT THE ACT OF SEEING WITH OUR OWN EYES ALONE; IT'S CORRECTLY COMPREHENDING WHAT WE SEE.
TREATING LIFE AS AN AUTOPSY.
GOT IT. LAYING OPEN THE GUTS OF THE WORLD AND SNIFFING THE ENTRAILS, THAT'S WHAT WE DO.
POTI
Monkey
Burger
Burger
NOT QUITE HOW THE WOLFIT SCHOOL OF JOURNALISM HAS IT.
FUCK WOLFIT. WE USED TO WORK THE CITY DESK TOGETHER AT DAYFAX, BACK WHEN IT WAS A REAL NEWSPAPER.
HIM AND HIS "PLAIN OLD OBSERVATION" HAD HIM COVERING GODDAMN FLOWER SHOWS. HOW HE HAD THE BALLS TO FOUND A JOURNALISM SCHOOL...
ANYWAY. YOU DON'T LEARN JOURNALISM IN A SCHOOL. YOU LEARN IT BY WRITING FUCKING JOURNALISM.
YOU TEACH YOURSELF TO WIRE UP YOUR OWN BRAIN AND GUT AND REPRODUCTIVE ORGANS INTO ONE FRIGHTENING MACHINE THAT YOU AIM AT THE PLANET LIKE A MEAT GUN--
MEAT GUN? WHAT DO I GET? AN ATTACK WOMB?

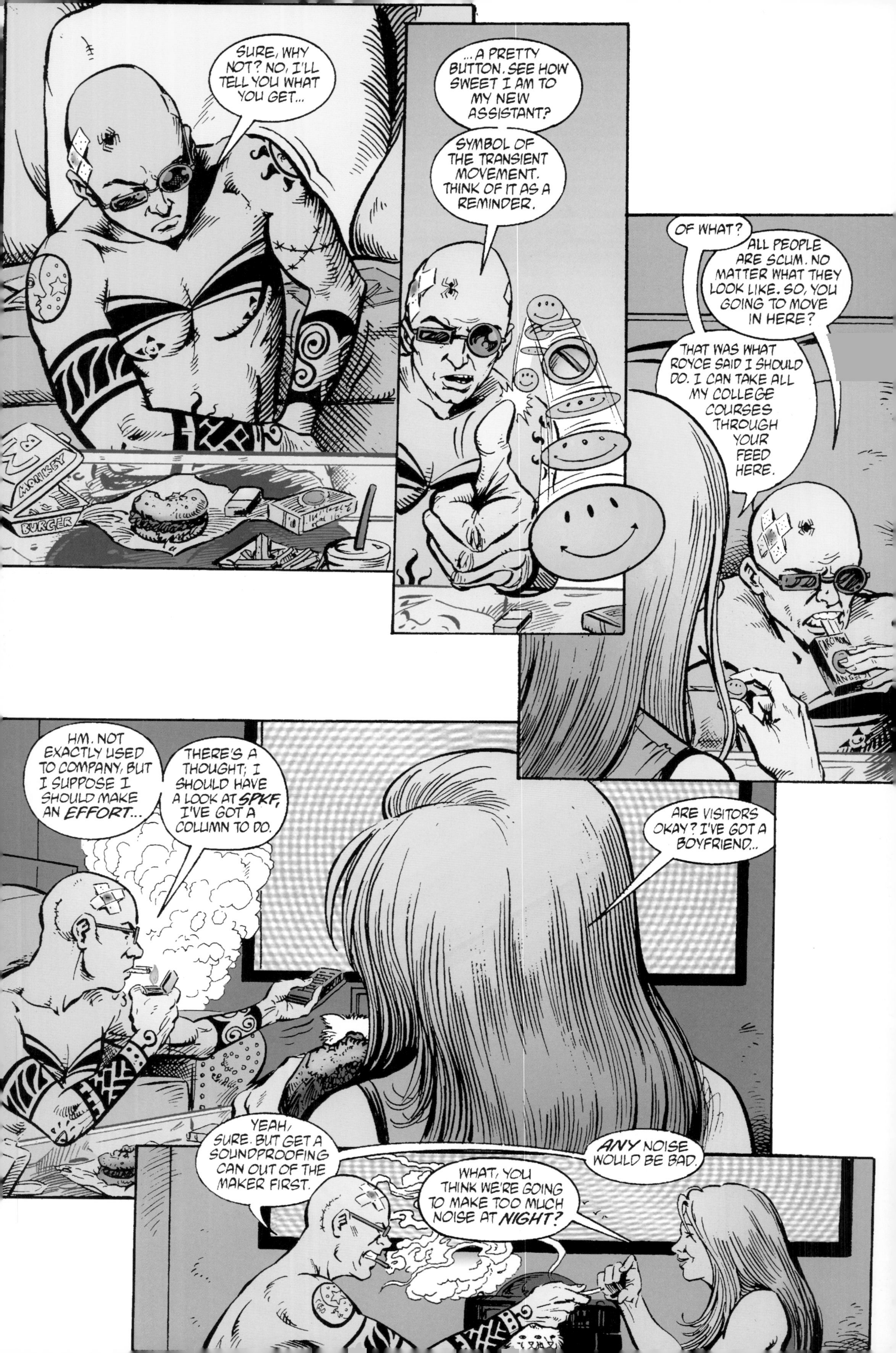
SURE, WHY NOT? NO, I'LL TELL YOU WHAT YOU GET...
...A PRETTY BUTTON. SEE HOW SWEET I AM TO MY NEW ASSISTANT?
SYMBOL OF THE TRANSIENT MOVEMENT. THINK OF IT AS A REMINDER.
OF WHAT?
ALL PEOPLE ARE SCUM. NO MATTER WHAT THEY LOOK LIKE. SO, YOU GOING TO MOVE IN HERE?
THAT WAS WHAT ROYCE SAID I SHOULD DO. I CAN TAKE ALL MY COLLEGE COURSES THROUGH YOUR FEED HERE.
HM. NOT EXACTLY USED TO COMPANY, BUT I SUPPOSE I SHOULD MAKE AN *EFFORT*...
THERE'S A THOUGHT; I SHOULD HAVE A LOOK AT *SPKF*, I'VE GOT A COLUMN TO DO.
ARE VISITORS OKAY? I'VE GOT A BOYFRIEND...
YEAH, SURE. BUT GET A SOUNDPROOFING CAN OUT OF THE MAKER FIRST.
*ANY* NOISE WOULD BE BAD.
WHAT, YOU THINK WE'RE GOING TO MAKE TOO MUCH NOISE AT *NIGHT*?
MONKEY
BURGER

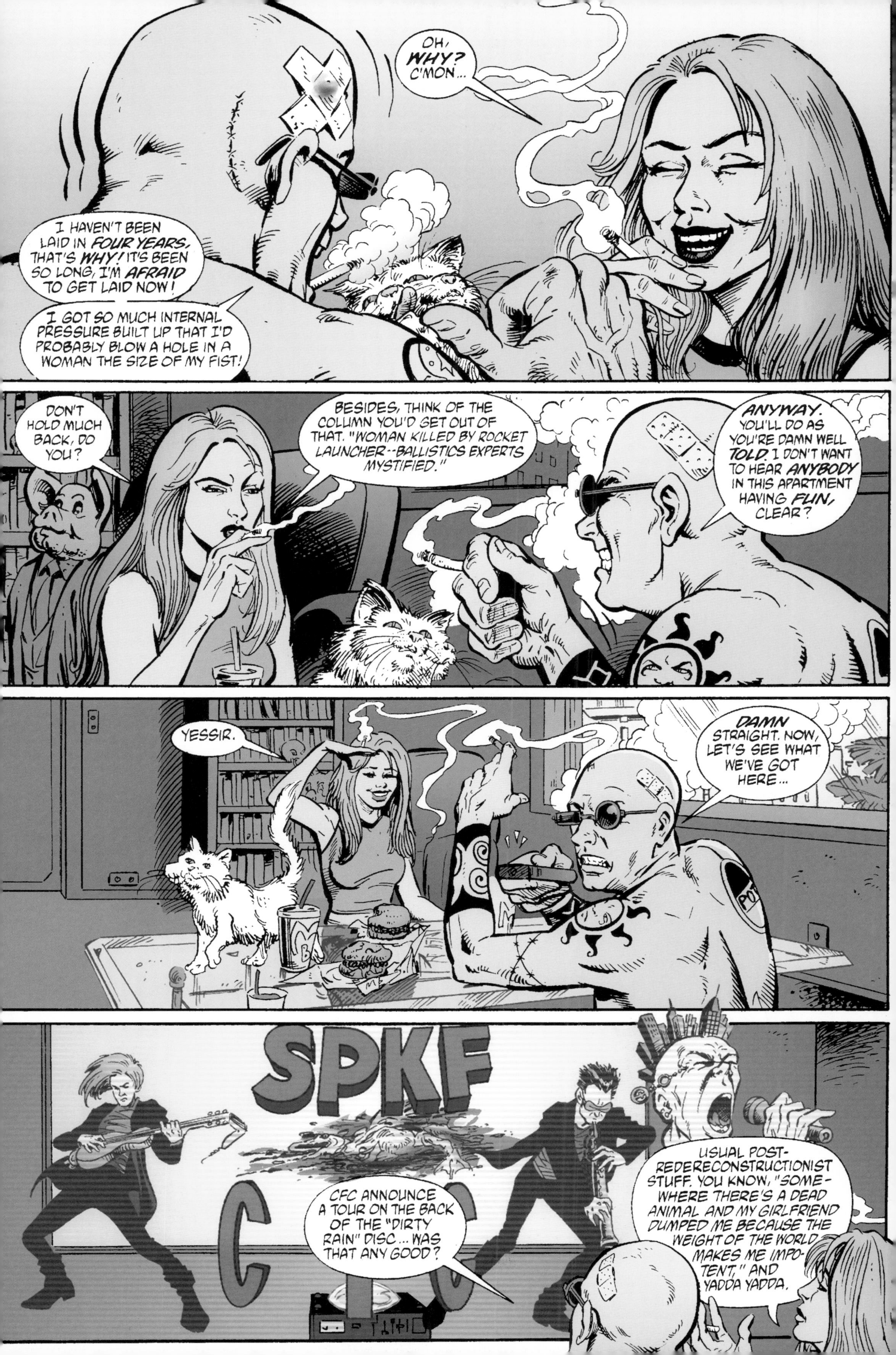
OH, WHY? C'MON...
I HAVEN'T BEEN LAID IN FOUR YEARS, THAT'S WHY! IT'S BEEN SO LONG, I'M AFRAID TO GET LAID NOW!
I GOT SO MUCH INTERNAL PRESSURE BUILT UP THAT I'D PROBABLY BLOW A HOLE IN A WOMAN THE SIZE OF MY FIST!
DON'T HOLD MUCH BACK, DO YOU?
BESIDES, THINK OF THE COLUMN YOU'D GET OUT OF THAT. "WOMAN KILLED BY ROCKET LAUNCHER--BALLISTICS EXPERTS MYSTIFIED."
ANYWAY. YOU'LL DO AS YOU'RE DAMN WELL TOLD. I DON'T WANT TO HEAR ANYBODY IN THIS APARTMENT HAVING FUN, CLEAR?
YESSIR.
DAMN STRAIGHT. NOW, LET'S SEE WHAT WE'VE GOT HERE...
SPKF
CFC ANNOUNCE A TOUR ON THE BACK OF THE "DIRTY RAIN" DISC... WAS THAT ANY GOOD?
USUAL POST-REDERECONSTRUCTIONIST STUFF. YOU KNOW, "SOME-WHERE THERE'S A DEAD ANIMAL AND MY GIRLFRIEND DUMPED ME BECAUSE THE WEIGHT OF THE WORLD MAKES ME IMPO-TENT," AND YADDA YADDA.

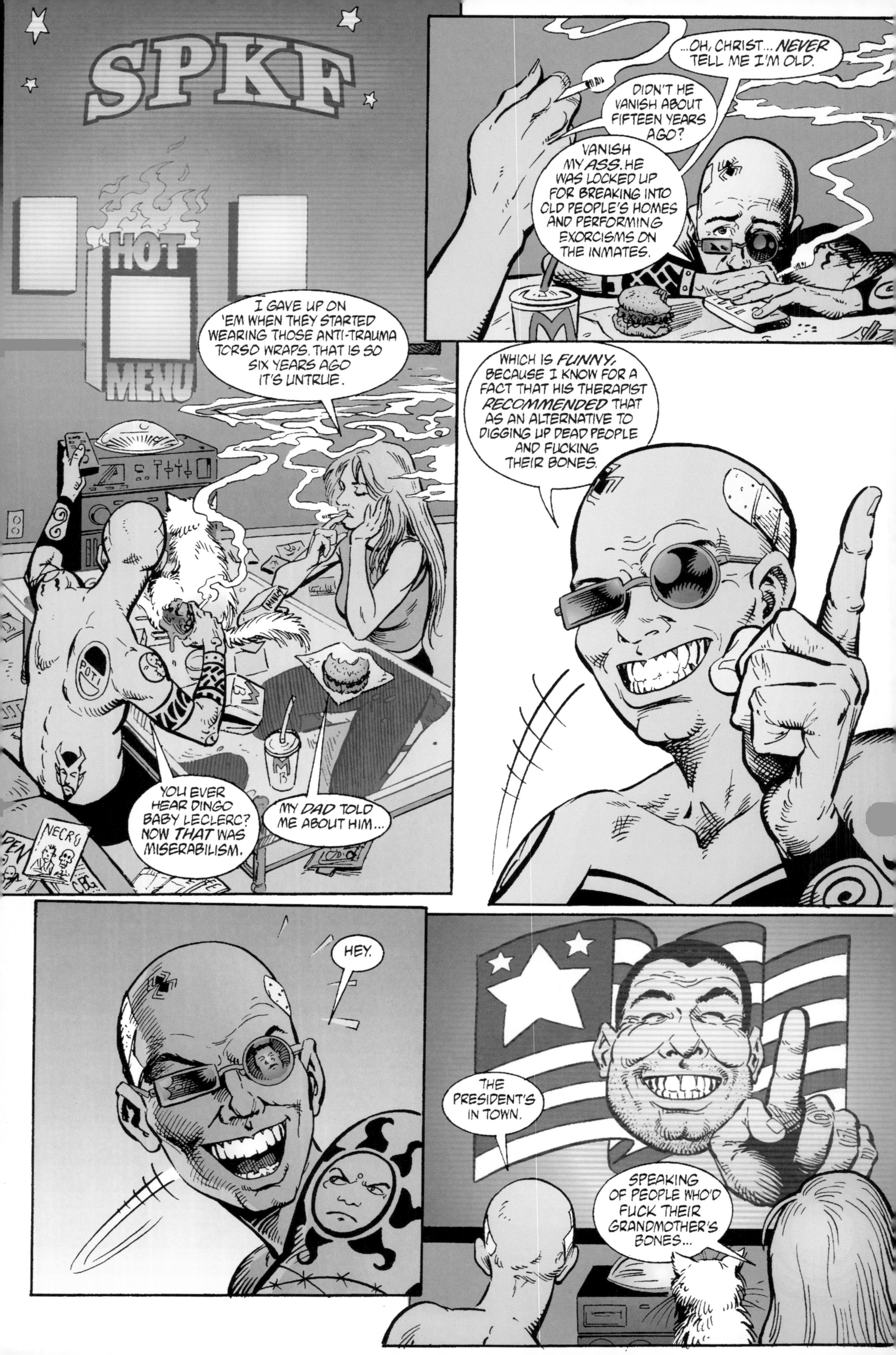
SPKF
HOT
MENU
...OH, CHRIST... NEVER TELL ME I'M OLD.
DIDN'T HE VANISH ABOUT FIFTEEN YEARS AGO?
VANISH MY ASS. HE WAS LOCKED UP FOR BREAKING INTO OLD PEOPLE'S HOMES AND PERFORMING EXORCISMS ON THE INMATES.
I GAVE UP ON 'EM WHEN THEY STARTED WEARING THOSE ANTI-TRAUMA TORSO WRAPS. THAT IS SO SIX YEARS AGO IT'S UNTRUE.
YOU EVER HEAR DINGO BABY LECLERC? NOW THAT WAS MISERABILISM.
MY DAD TOLD ME ABOUT HIM...
WHICH IS FUNNY, BECAUSE I KNOW FOR A FACT THAT HIS THERAPIST RECOMMENDED THAT AS AN ALTERNATIVE TO DIGGING UP DEAD PEOPLE AND FUCKING THEIR BONES.
HEY.
THE PRESIDENT'S IN TOWN.
SPEAKING OF PEOPLE WHO'D FUCK THEIR GRANDMOTHER'S BONES...

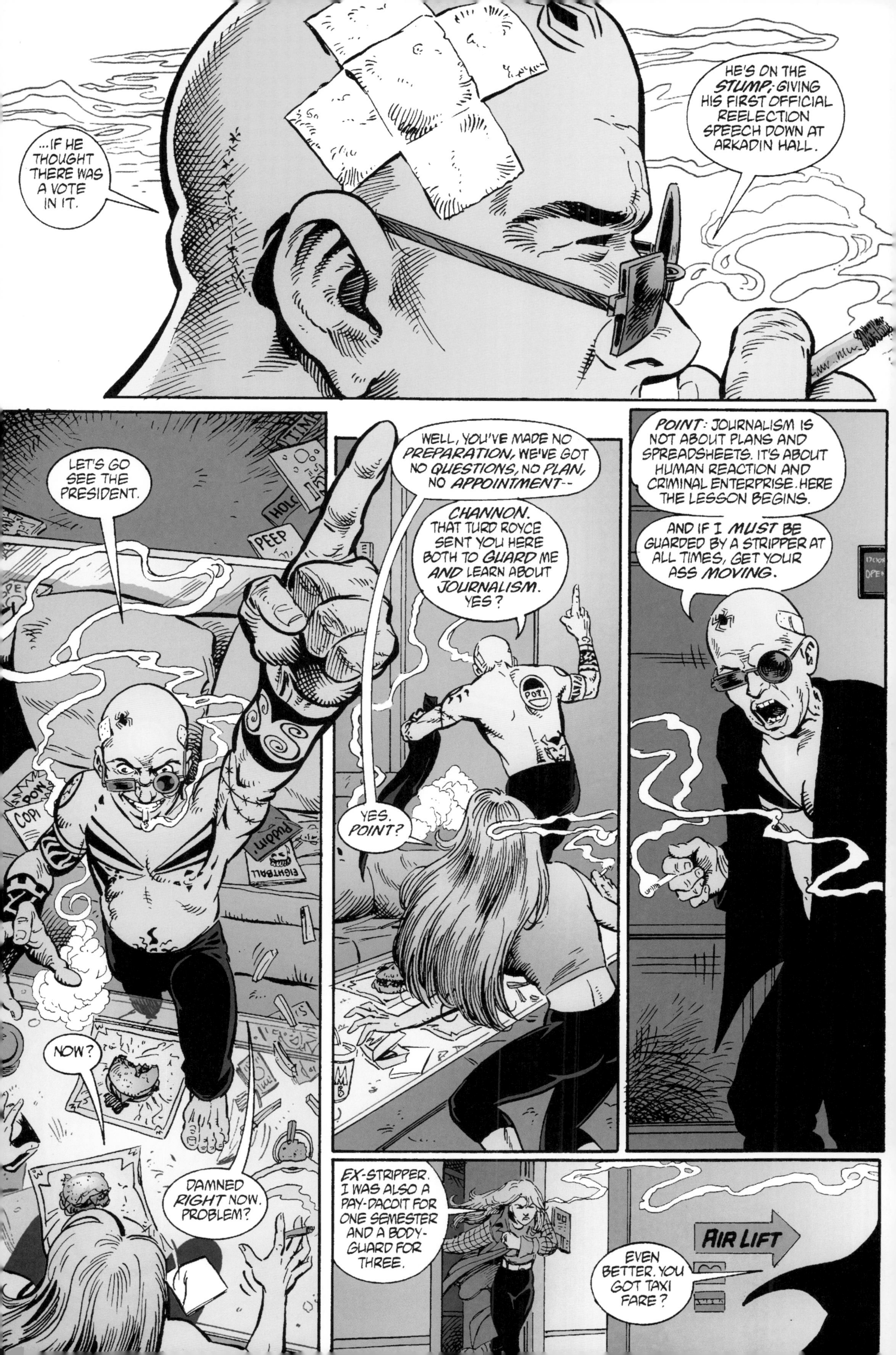
...IF HE THOUGHT THERE WAS A VOTE IN IT.
HE'S ON THE STUMP; GIVING HIS FIRST OFFICIAL REELECTION SPEECH DOWN AT ARKADIN HALL.
LET'S GO SEE THE PRESIDENT.
NOW?
DAMNED RIGHT NOW. PROBLEM?
WELL, YOU'VE MADE NO PREPARATION, WE'VE GOT NO QUESTIONS, NO PLAN, NO APPOINTMENT--
CHANNON. THAT TURD ROYCE SENT YOU HERE BOTH TO GUARD ME AND LEARN ABOUT JOURNALISM. YES?
YES. POINT?
POINT: JOURNALISM IS NOT ABOUT PLANS AND SPREADSHEETS. IT'S ABOUT HUMAN REACTION AND CRIMINAL ENTERPRISE. HERE THE LESSON BEGINS.
AND IF I MUST BE GUARDED BY A STRIPPER AT ALL TIMES, GET YOUR ASS MOVING.
EX-STRIPPER. I WAS ALSO A PAY-DACOIT FOR ONE SEMESTER AND A BODY-GUARD FOR THREE.
AIR LIFT
EVEN BETTER. YOU GOT TAXI FARE?

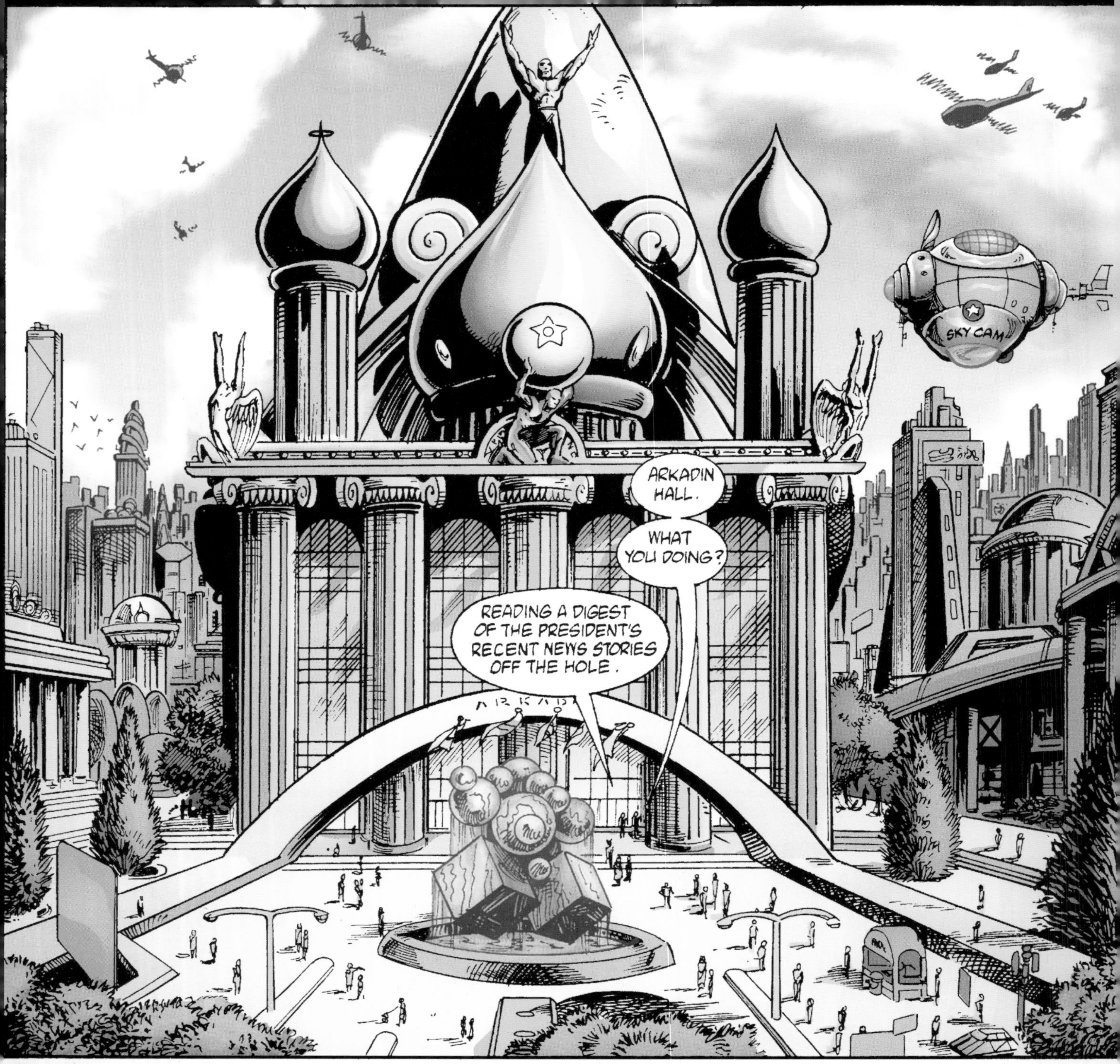
SKY CAM
ARKADIN HALL.
WHAT YOU DOING?
READING A DIGEST OF THE PRESIDENT'S RECENT NEWS STORIES OFF THE HOLE.

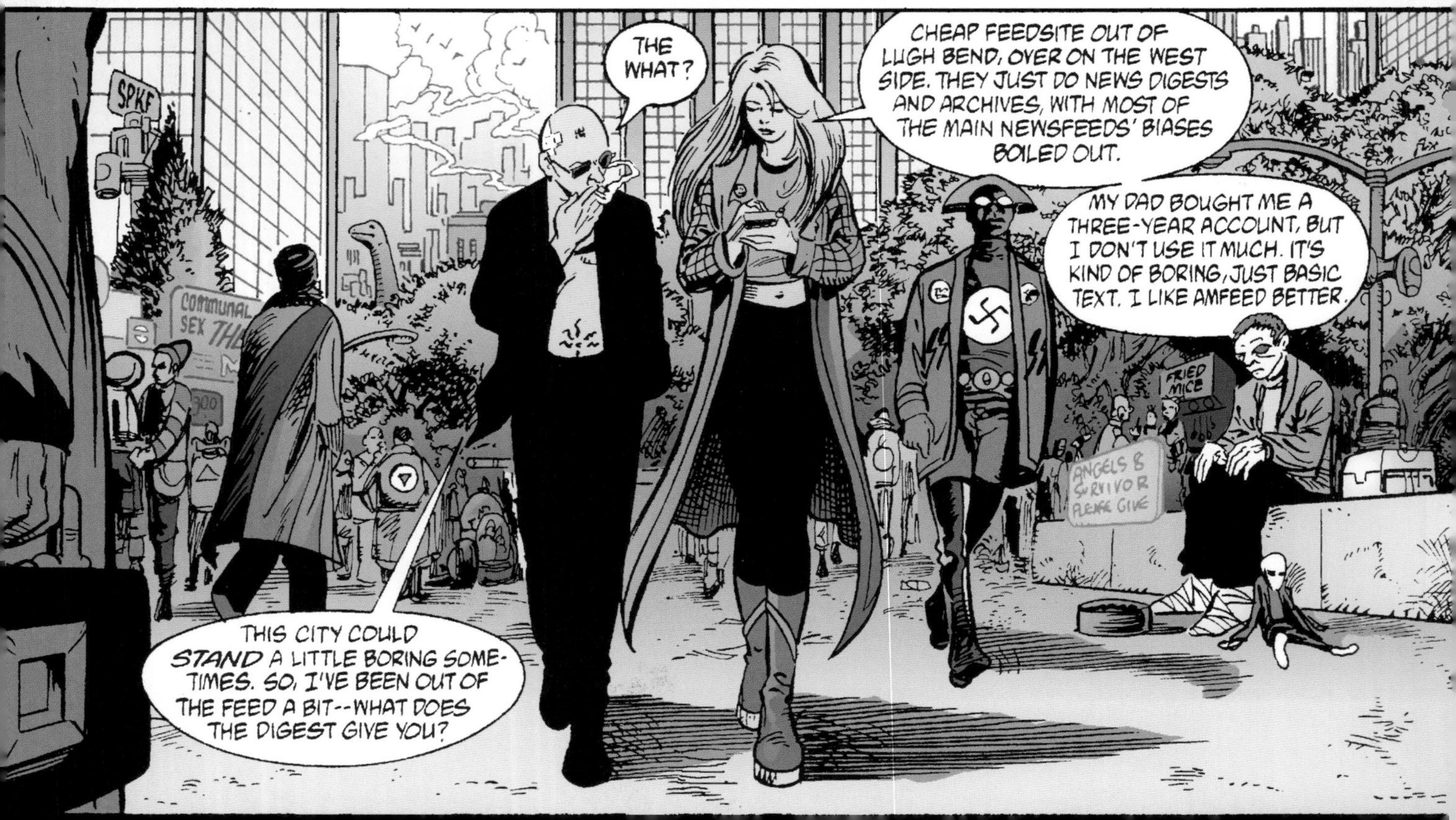
THE WHAT?
CHEAP FEEDSITE OUT OF LUGH BEND; OVER ON THE WEST SIDE. THEY JUST DO NEWS DIGESTS AND ARCHIVES, WITH MOST OF THE MAIN NEWSFEEDS' BIASES BOILED OUT.
MY DAD BOUGHT ME A THREE-YEAR ACCOUNT, BUT I DON'T USE IT MUCH. IT'S KIND OF BORING, JUST BASIC TEXT. I LIKE AMFEED BETTER.
THIS CITY COULD *STAND* A LITTLE BORING SOME-TIMES. SO, I'VE BEEN OUT OF THE FEED A BIT--WHAT DOES THE DIGEST GIVE YOU?
SPKF
COMMUNAL SEX
FRIED MICE
ANGELS 8 SURVIVOR PLEASE GIVE

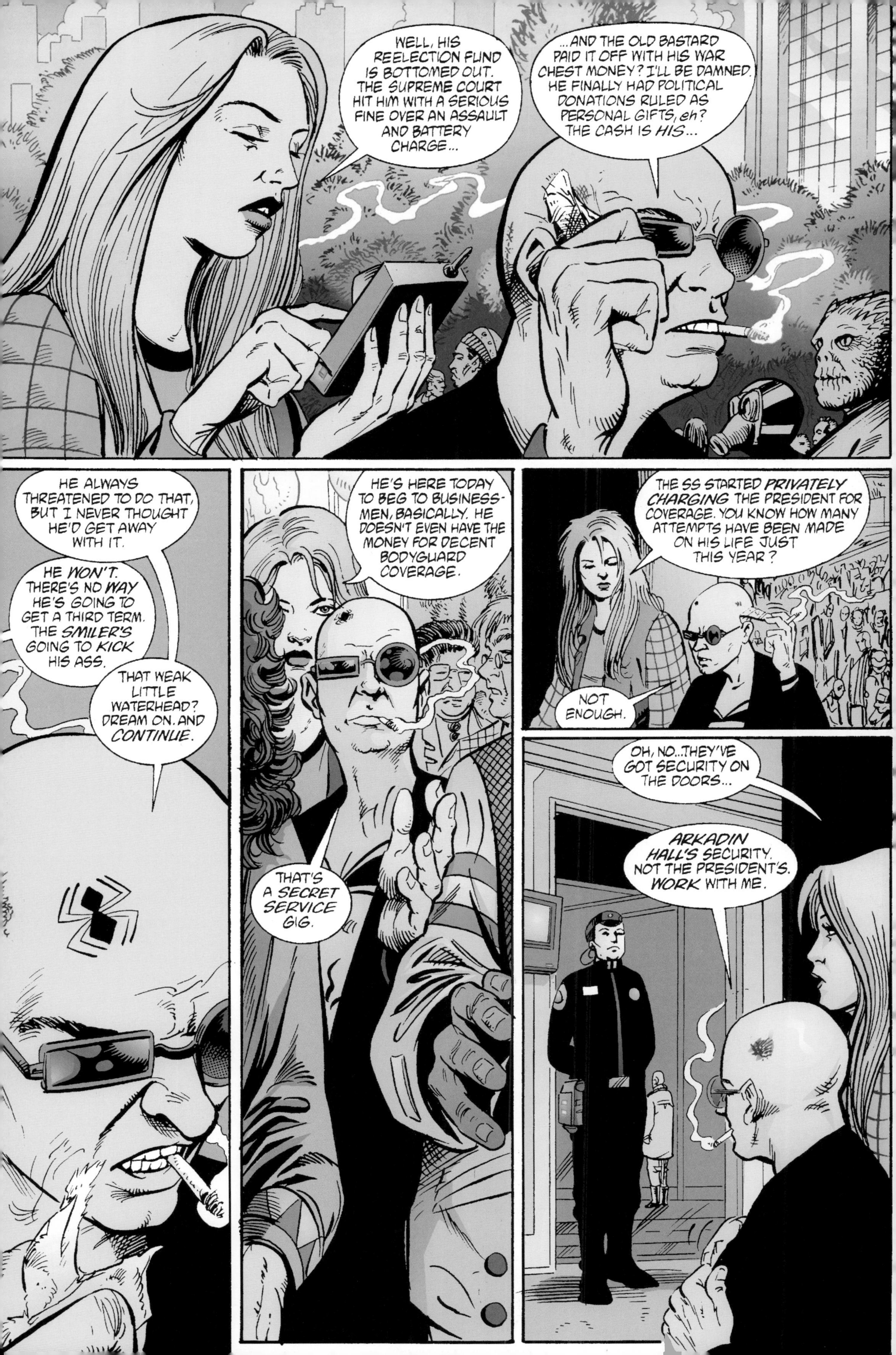
WELL, HIS REELECTION FUND IS BOTTOMED OUT. THE SUPREME COURT HIT HIM WITH A SERIOUS FINE OVER AN ASSAULT AND BATTERY CHARGE...
...AND THE OLD BASTARD PAID IT OFF WITH HIS WAR CHEST MONEY? I'LL BE DAMNED. HE FINALLY HAD POLITICAL DONATIONS RULED AS PERSONAL GIFTS, eh? THE CASH IS HIS...
HE ALWAYS THREATENED TO DO THAT, BUT I NEVER THOUGHT HE'D GET AWAY WITH IT.
HE WON'T. THERE'S NO WAY HE'S GOING TO GET A THIRD TERM. THE SMILER'S GOING TO KICK HIS ASS.
THAT WEAK LITTLE WATERHEAD? DREAM ON. AND CONTINUE.
HE'S HERE TODAY TO BEG TO BUSINESSMEN, BASICALLY. HE DOESN'T EVEN HAVE THE MONEY FOR DECENT BODYGUARD COVERAGE.
THAT'S A SECRET SERVICE GIG.
THE SS STARTED PRIVATELY CHARGING THE PRESIDENT FOR COVERAGE. YOU KNOW HOW MANY ATTEMPTS HAVE BEEN MADE ON HIS LIFE JUST THIS YEAR?
NOT ENOUGH.
OH, NO...THEY'VE GOT SECURITY ON THE DOORS...
ARKADIN HALL'S SECURITY. NOT THE PRESIDENT'S. WORK WITH ME.

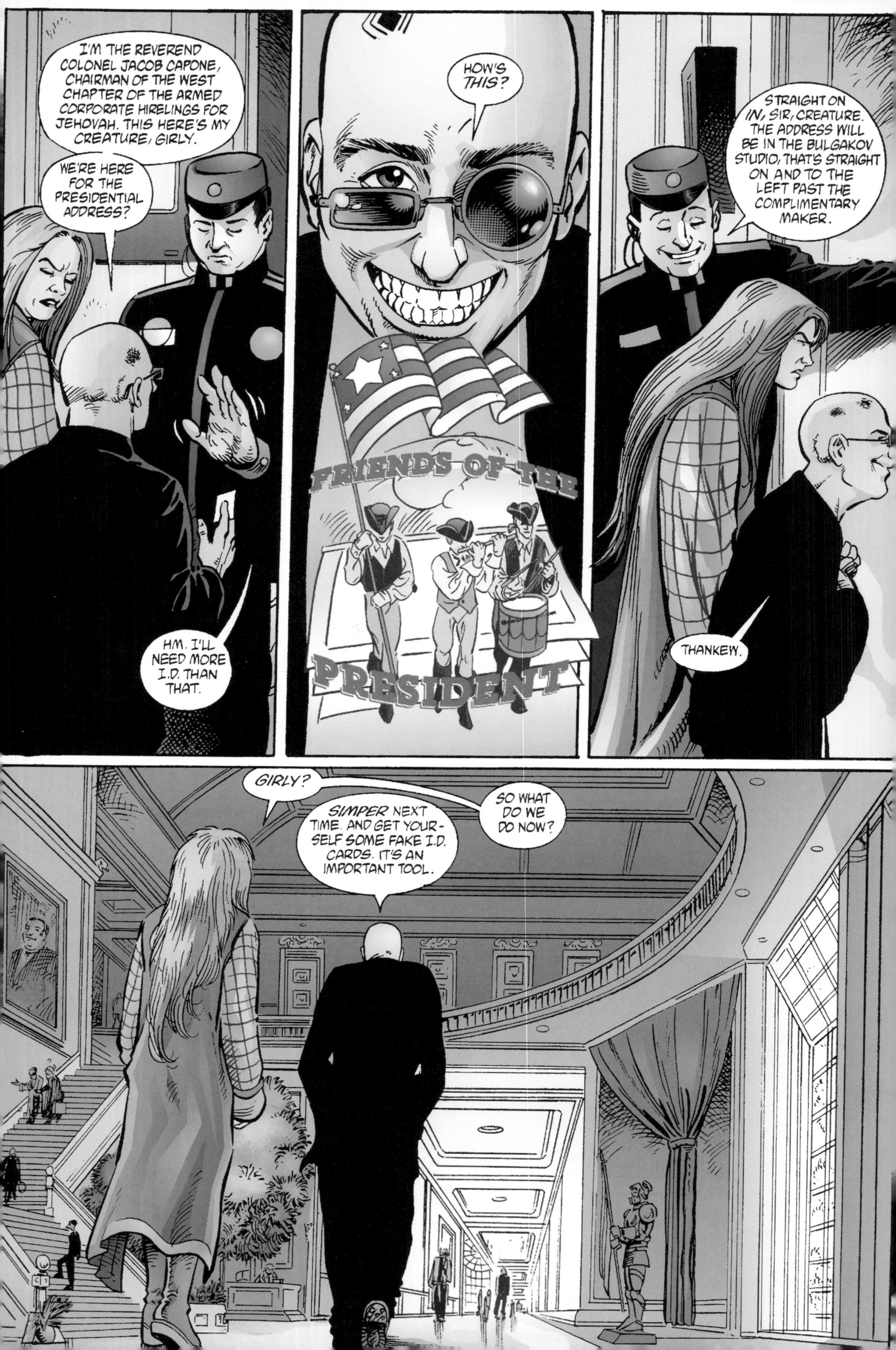
I'M THE REVEREND COLONEL JACOB CAPONE, CHAIRMAN OF THE WEST CHAPTER OF THE ARMED CORPORATE HIRELINGS FOR JEHOVAH. THIS HERE'S MY CREATURE, GIRLY.
WE'RE HERE FOR THE PRESIDENTIAL ADDRESS?
HM. I'LL NEED MORE I.D. THAN THAT.
HOW'S THIS?
FRIENDS OF THE PRESIDENT
STRAIGHT ON IN, SIR, CREATURE. THE ADDRESS WILL BE IN THE BULGAKOV STUDIO, THAT'S STRAIGHT ON AND TO THE LEFT PAST THE COMPLIMENTARY MAKER.
THANKEW.
GIRLY?
SIMPER NEXT TIME. AND GET YOURSELF SOME FAKE I.D. CARDS. IT'S AN IMPORTANT TOOL.
SO WHAT DO WE DO NOW?

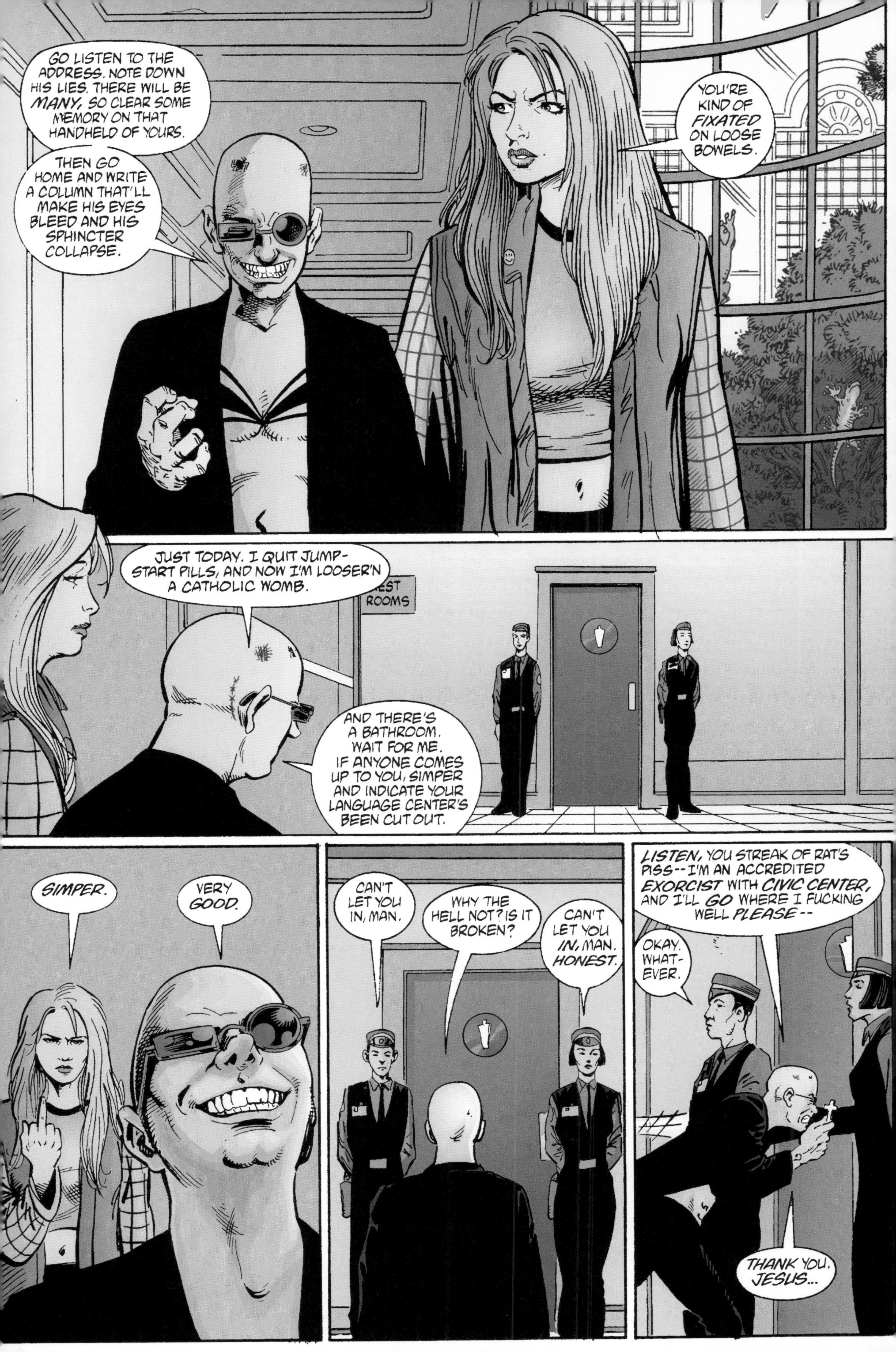
GO LISTEN TO THE ADDRESS. NOTE DOWN HIS LIES. THERE WILL BE *MANY,* SO CLEAR SOME MEMORY ON THAT HANDHELD OF YOURS.
THEN GO HOME AND WRITE A COLUMN THAT'LL MAKE HIS EYES BLEED AND HIS SPHINCTER COLLAPSE.
YOU'RE KIND OF *FIXATED* ON LOOSE BOWELS.
JUST TODAY. I QUIT JUMP-START PILLS, AND NOW I'M LOOSER'N A CATHOLIC WOMB.
REST ROOMS
AND THERE'S A BATHROOM. WAIT FOR ME. IF ANYONE COMES UP TO YOU, SIMPER AND INDICATE YOUR LANGUAGE CENTER'S BEEN CUT OUT.
*SIMPER.*
VERY *GOOD.*
CAN'T LET YOU IN, MAN.
WHY THE HELL NOT? IS IT BROKEN?
CAN'T LET YOU *IN,* MAN. *HONEST.*
*LISTEN,* YOU STREAK OF RAT'S PISS-- I'M AN ACCREDITED *EXORCIST* WITH *CIVIC CENTER,* AND I'LL *GO* WHERE I FUCKING WELL *PLEASE*--
OKAY. WHAT-EVER.
*THANK YOU. JESUS...*

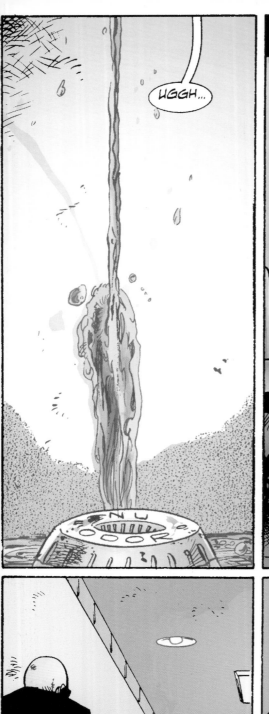

UGGH...

AAHHRR...
GODDAMN CHEAP AUSTRALIAN WHORES...

JERUSALEM.

MR. PRESIDENT.

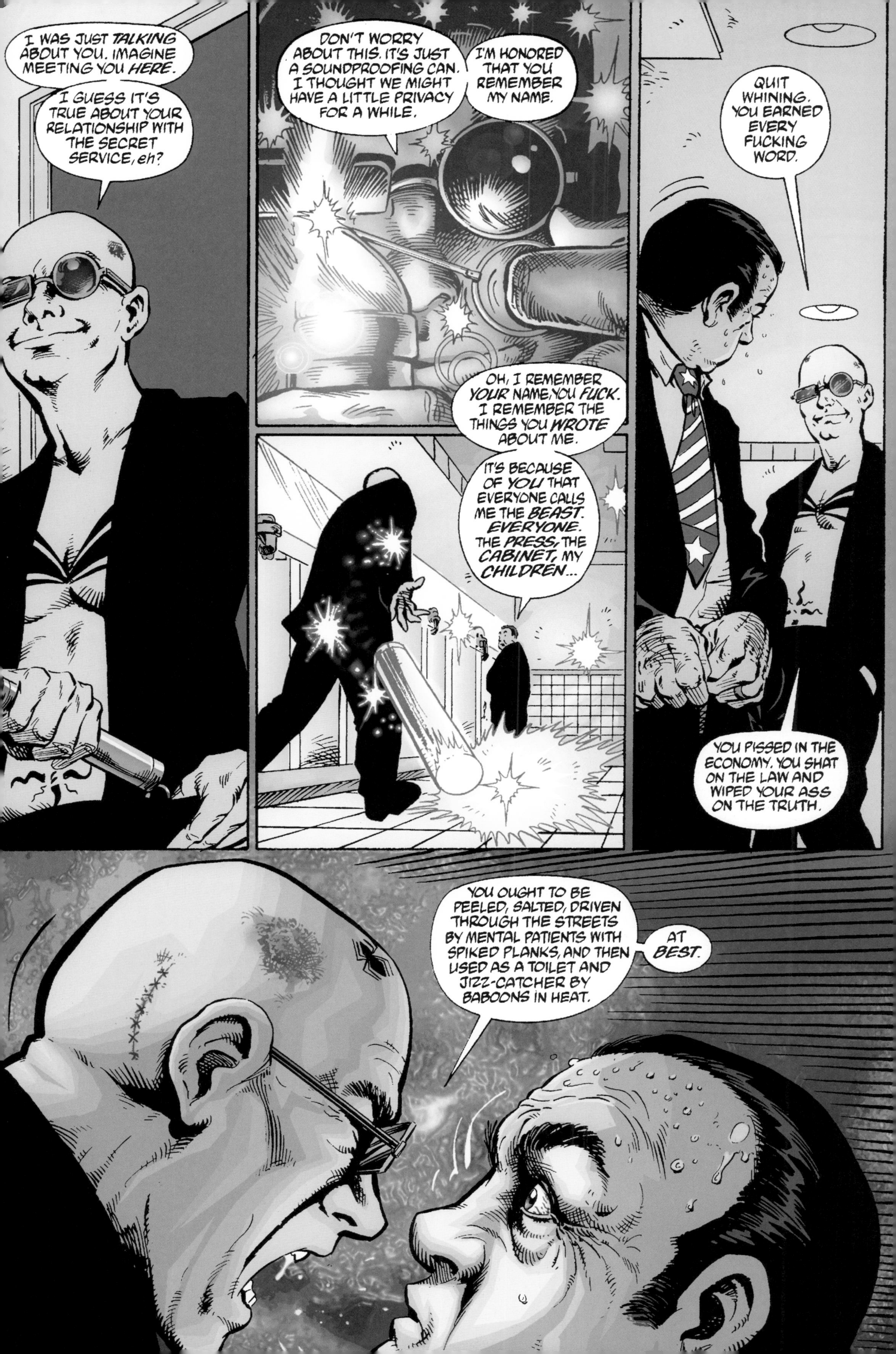
I WAS JUST TALKING ABOUT YOU. IMAGINE MEETING YOU HERE.
I GUESS IT'S TRUE ABOUT YOUR RELATIONSHIP WITH THE SECRET SERVICE, eh?
DON'T WORRY ABOUT THIS. IT'S JUST A SOUNDPROOFING CAN. I THOUGHT WE MIGHT HAVE A LITTLE PRIVACY FOR A WHILE.
I'M HONORED THAT YOU REMEMBER MY NAME.
OH, I REMEMBER YOUR NAME, YOU FUCK. I REMEMBER THE THINGS YOU WROTE ABOUT ME.
IT'S BECAUSE OF YOU THAT EVERYONE CALLS ME THE BEAST. EVERYONE. THE PRESS, THE CABINET, MY CHILDREN...
QUIT WHINING. YOU EARNED EVERY FUCKING WORD.
YOU PISSED IN THE ECONOMY. YOU SHAT ON THE LAW AND WIPED YOUR ASS ON THE TRUTH.
YOU OUGHT TO BE PEELED, SALTED, DRIVEN THROUGH THE STREETS BY MENTAL PATIENTS WITH SPIKED PLANKS, AND THEN USED AS A TOILET AND JIZZ-CATCHER BY BABOONS IN HEAT.
AT BEST.

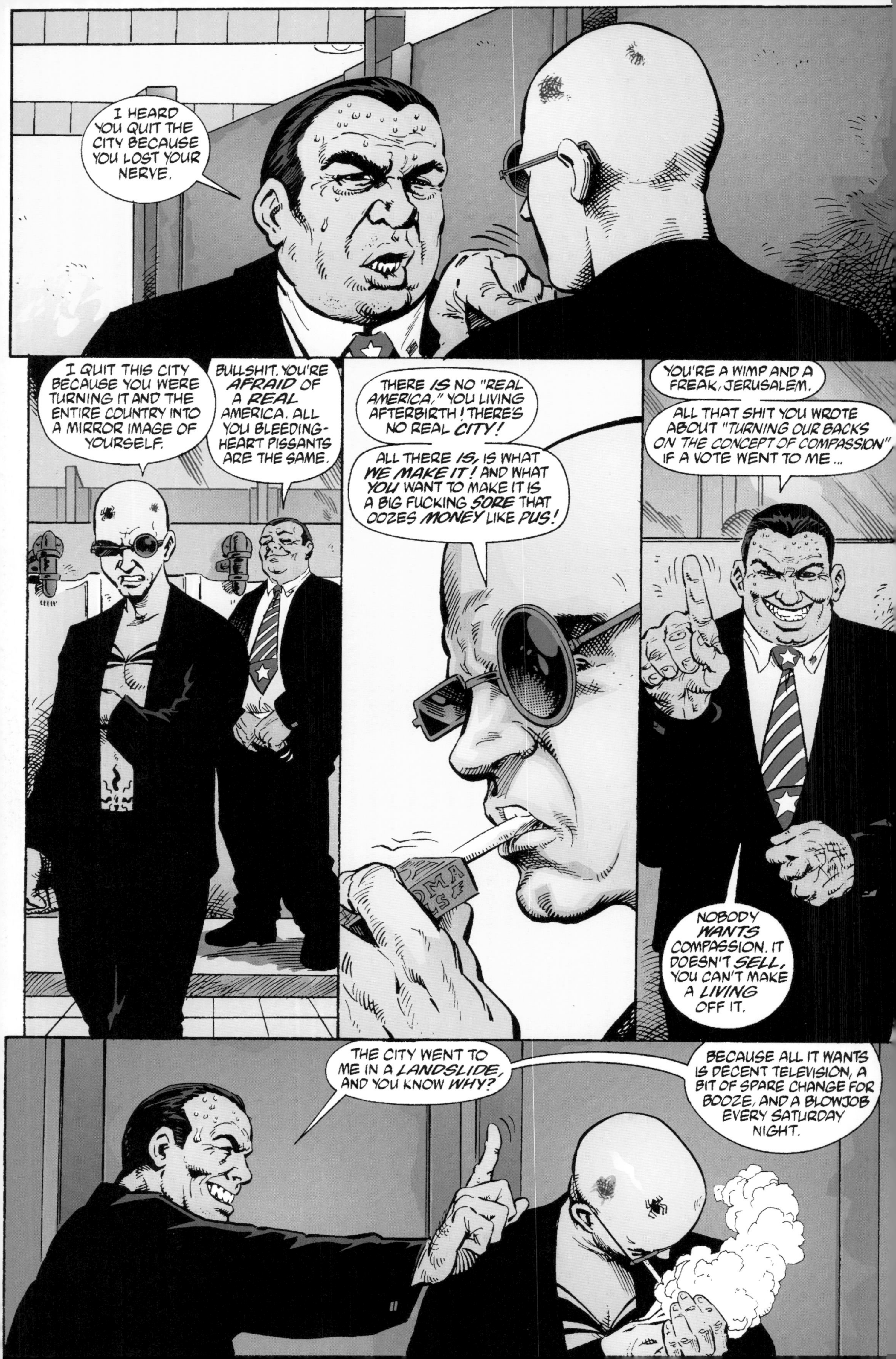
I HEARD YOU QUIT THE CITY BECAUSE YOU LOST YOUR NERVE.
I QUIT THIS CITY BECAUSE YOU WERE TURNING IT AND THE ENTIRE COUNTRY INTO A MIRROR IMAGE OF YOURSELF.
BULLSHIT. YOU'RE *AFRAID* OF A *REAL* AMERICA. ALL YOU BLEEDING-HEART PISSANTS ARE THE SAME.
THERE *IS* NO "REAL AMERICA," YOU LIVING AFTERBIRTH! THERE'S NO REAL *CITY*!
ALL THERE *IS*, IS WHAT *WE MAKE IT*! AND WHAT *YOU* WANT TO MAKE IT IS A BIG FUCKING *SORE* THAT OOZES *MONEY* LIKE *PUS*!
YOU'RE A WIMP AND A FREAK, JERUSALEM.
ALL THAT SHIT YOU WROTE ABOUT "*TURNING OUR BACKS ON THE CONCEPT OF COMPASSION*" IF A VOTE WENT TO ME...
NOBODY *WANTS* COMPASSION. IT DOESN'T *SELL*, YOU CAN'T MAKE A *LIVING* OFF IT.
THE CITY WENT TO ME IN A *LANDSLIDE*, AND YOU KNOW *WHY*?
BECAUSE ALL IT WANTS IS DECENT TELEVISION, A BIT OF SPARE CHANGE FOR BOOZE, AND A BLOWJOB EVERY SATURDAY NIGHT.

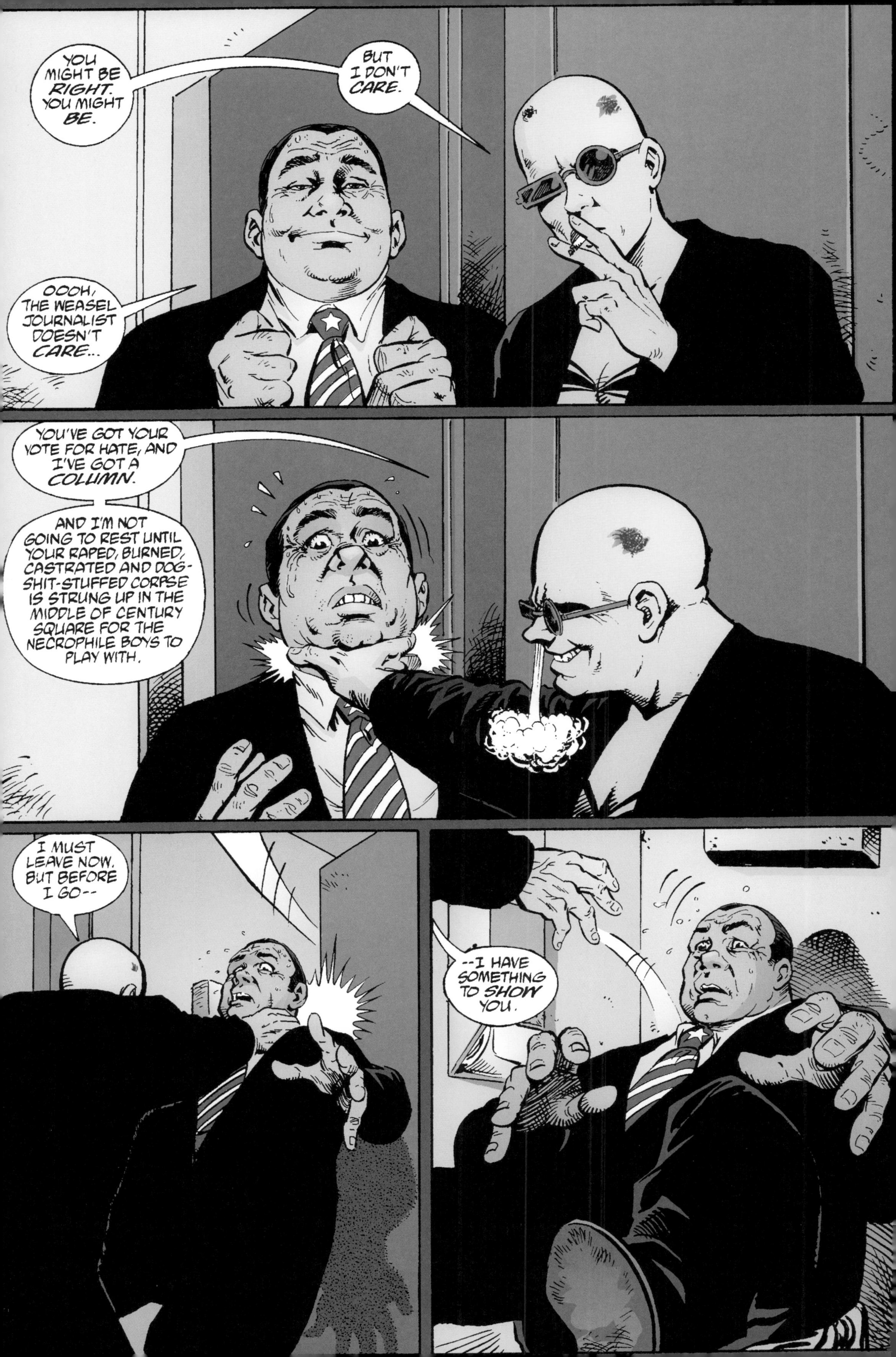
YOU MIGHT BE RIGHT. YOU MIGHT BE.
BUT I DON'T CARE.
OOOH, THE WEASEL JOURNALIST DOESN'T CARE...
YOU'VE GOT YOUR VOTE FOR HATE, AND I'VE GOT A COLUMN.
AND I'M NOT GOING TO REST UNTIL YOUR RAPED, BURNED, CASTRATED AND DOG-SHIT-STUFFED CORPSE IS STRUNG UP IN THE MIDDLE OF CENTURY SQUARE FOR THE NECROPHILE BOYS TO PLAY WITH.
I MUST LEAVE NOW. BUT BEFORE I GO--
--I HAVE SOMETHING TO SHOW YOU.

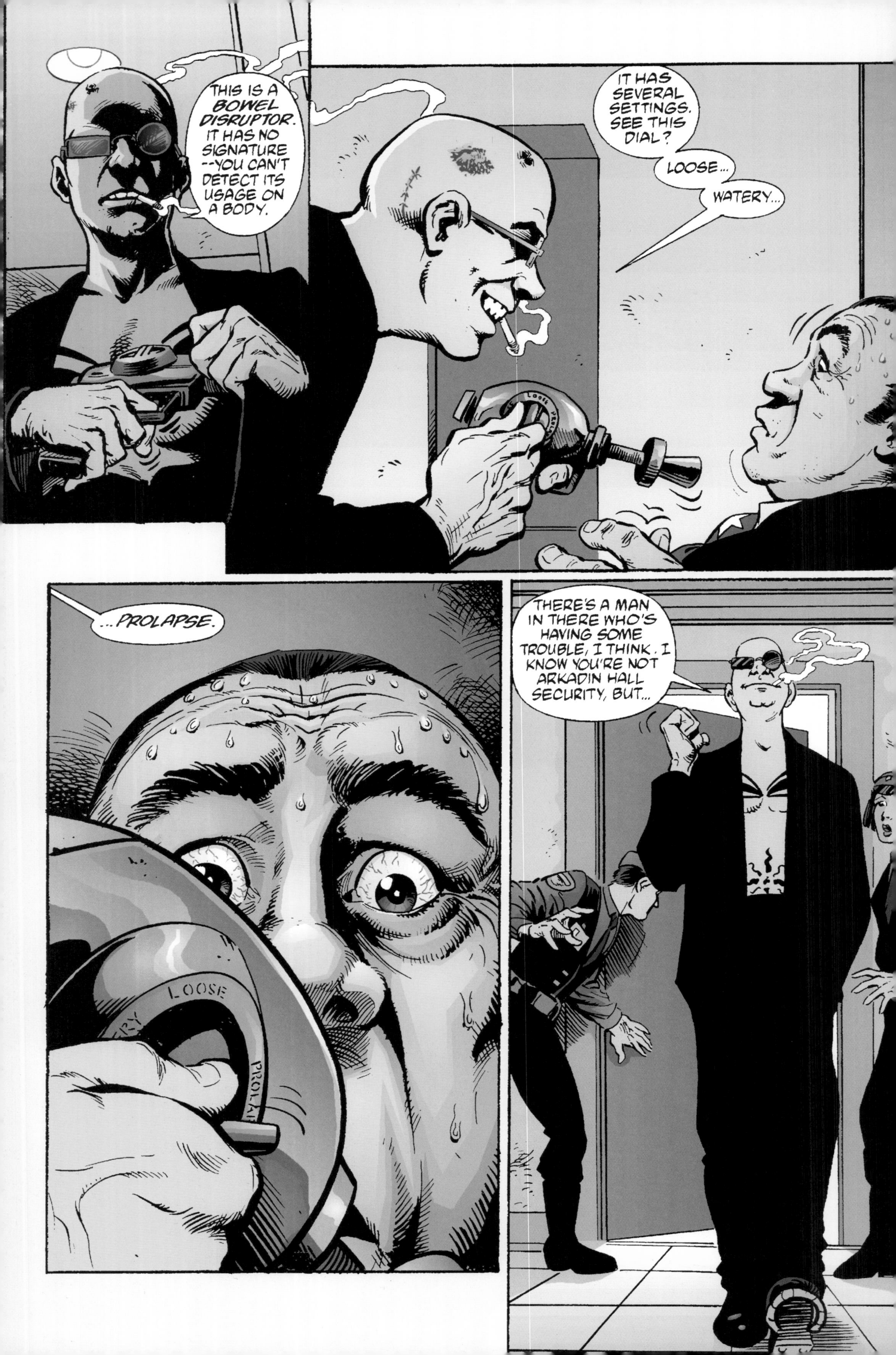
THIS IS A *BOWEL DISRUPTOR*. IT HAS NO SIGNATURE --YOU CAN'T DETECT ITS USAGE ON A BODY.
IT HAS SEVERAL SETTINGS. SEE THIS DIAL?
LOOSE...
WATERY...
...*PROLAPSE*.
LOOSE
THERE'S A MAN IN THERE WHO'S HAVING SOME TROUBLE, I THINK. I KNOW YOU'RE NOT ARKADIN HALL SECURITY, BUT...

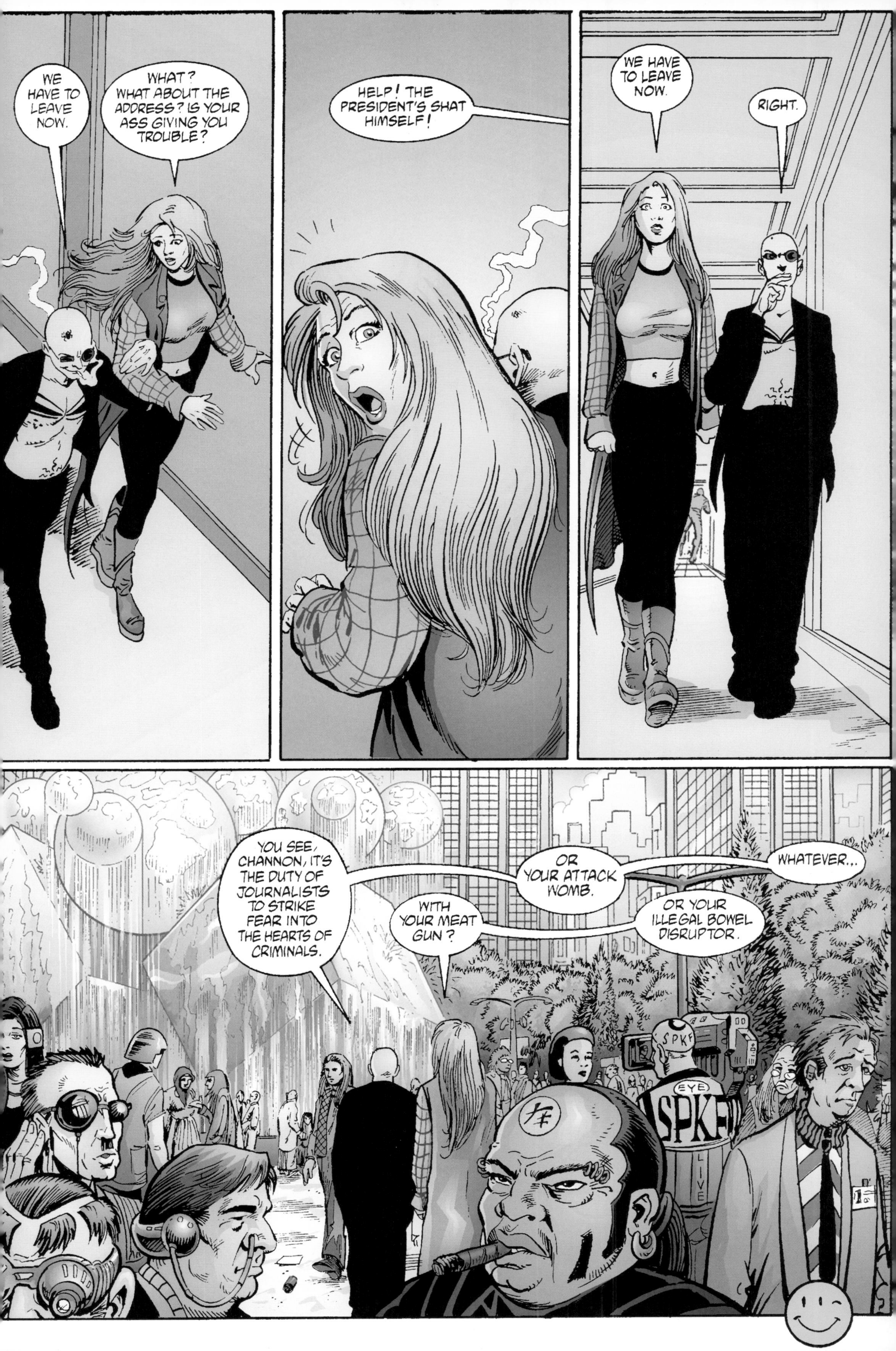
WE HAVE TO LEAVE NOW.
WHAT? WHAT ABOUT THE ADDRESS? IS YOUR ASS GIVING YOU TROUBLE?
HELP! THE PRESIDENT'S SHAT HIMSELF!
WE HAVE TO LEAVE NOW.
RIGHT.
YOU SEE, CHANNON, IT'S THE DUTY OF JOURNALISTS TO STRIKE FEAR INTO THE HEARTS OF CRIMINALS.
WITH YOUR MEAT GUN?
OR YOUR ATTACK WOMB.
OR YOUR ILLEGAL BOWEL DISRUPTOR.
WHATEVER...
SPKF
EYE
SPKF
LIVE

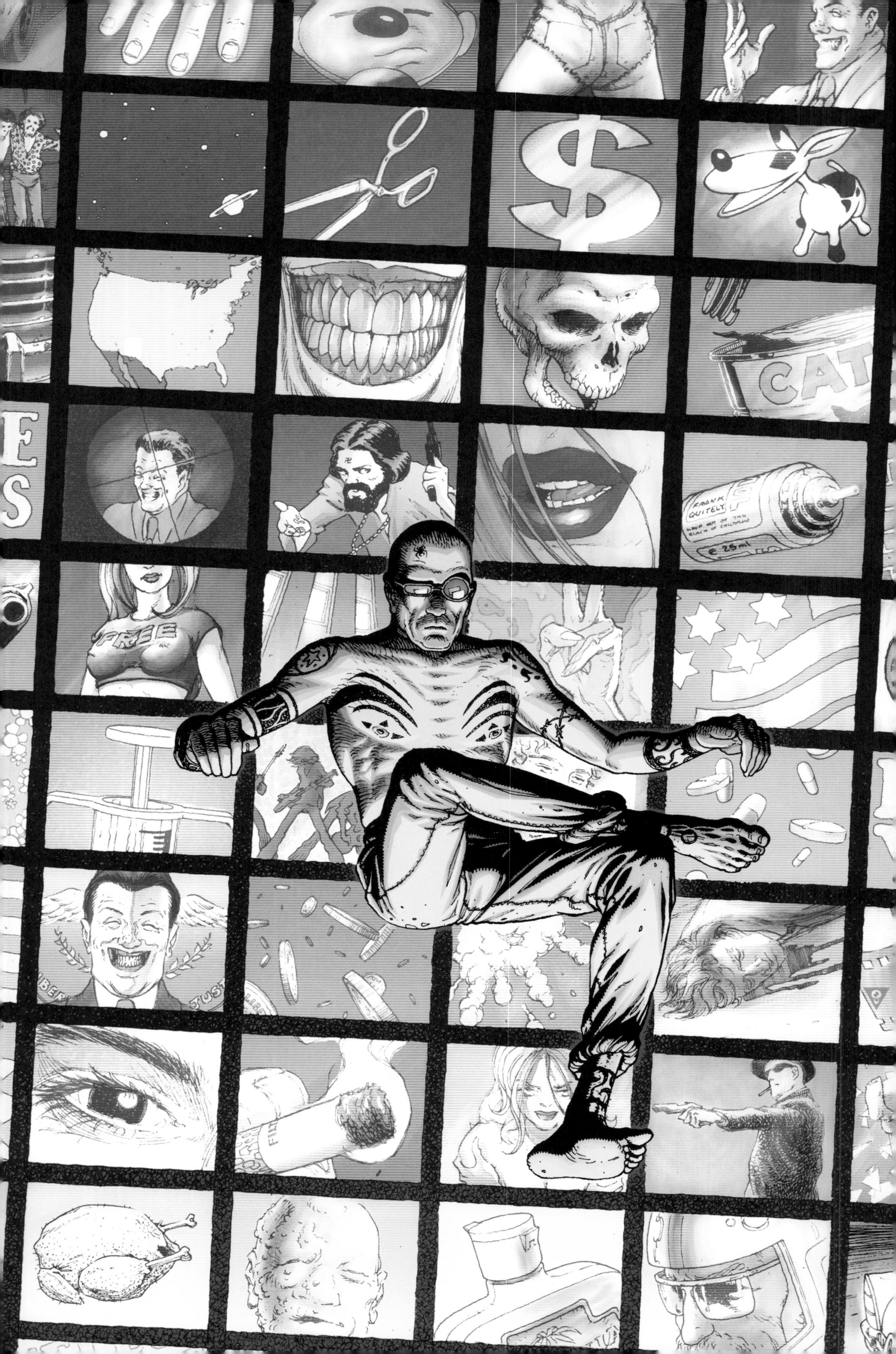
FREE
FRANK QUITELY

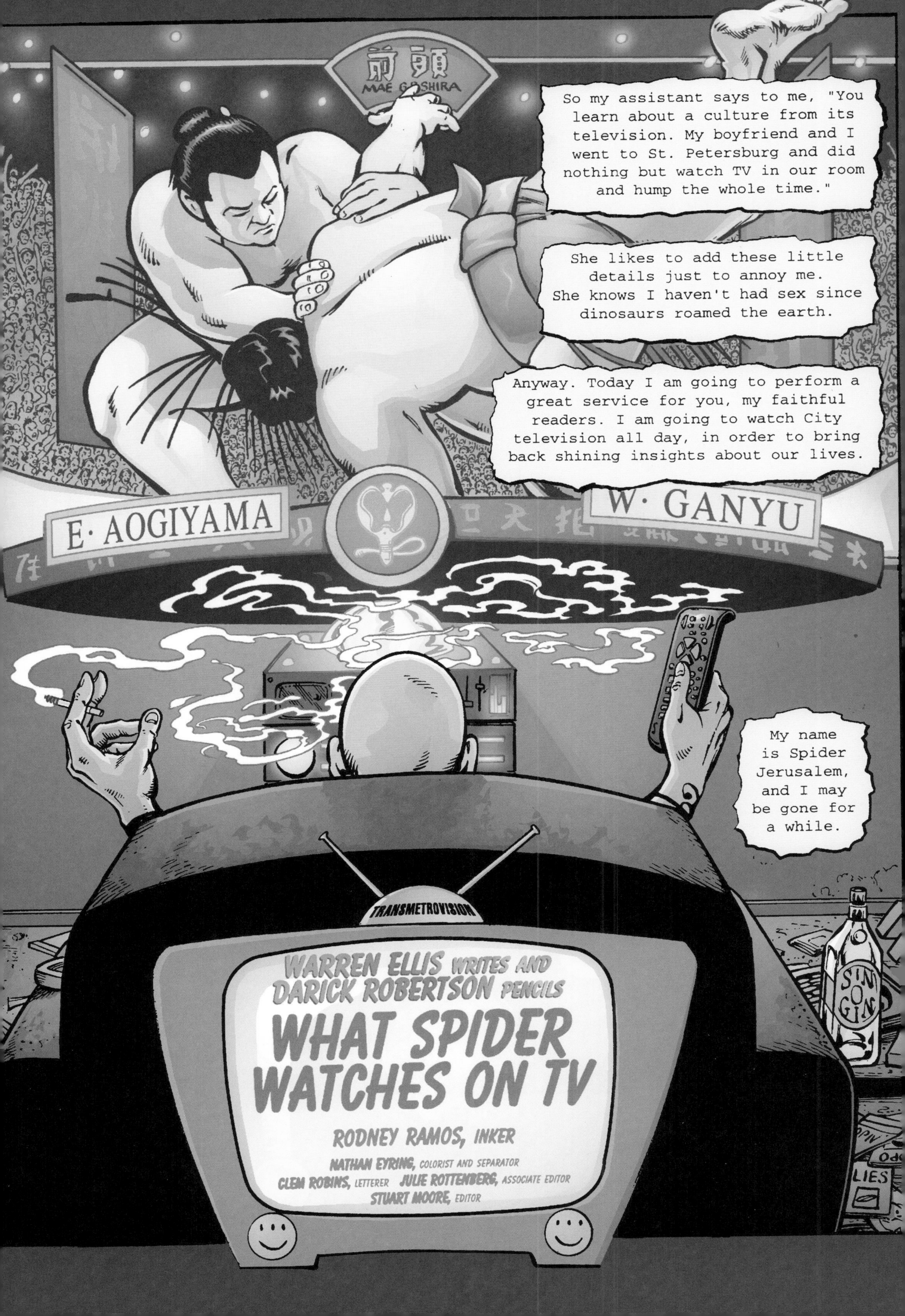

前頭
MAE GASHIRA
So my assistant says to me, "You learn about a culture from its television. My boyfriend and I went to St. Petersburg and did nothing but watch TV in our room and hump the whole time."
She likes to add these little details just to annoy me. She knows I haven't had sex since dinosaurs roamed the earth.
Anyway. Today I am going to perform a great service for you, my faithful readers. I am going to watch City television all day, in order to bring back shining insights about our lives.
E·AOGIYAMA
W·GANYU
My name is Spider Jerusalem, and I may be gone for a while.
TRANSMETROVISION
WARREN ELLIS WRITES AND DARICK ROBERTSON PENCILS
WHAT SPIDER WATCHES ON TV
RODNEY RAMOS, INKER
NATHAN EYRING, COLORIST AND SEPARATOR
CLEM ROBINS, LETTERER JULIE ROTTENBERG, ASSOCIATE EDITOR
STUART MOORE, EDITOR
SIN OGIN
LIES

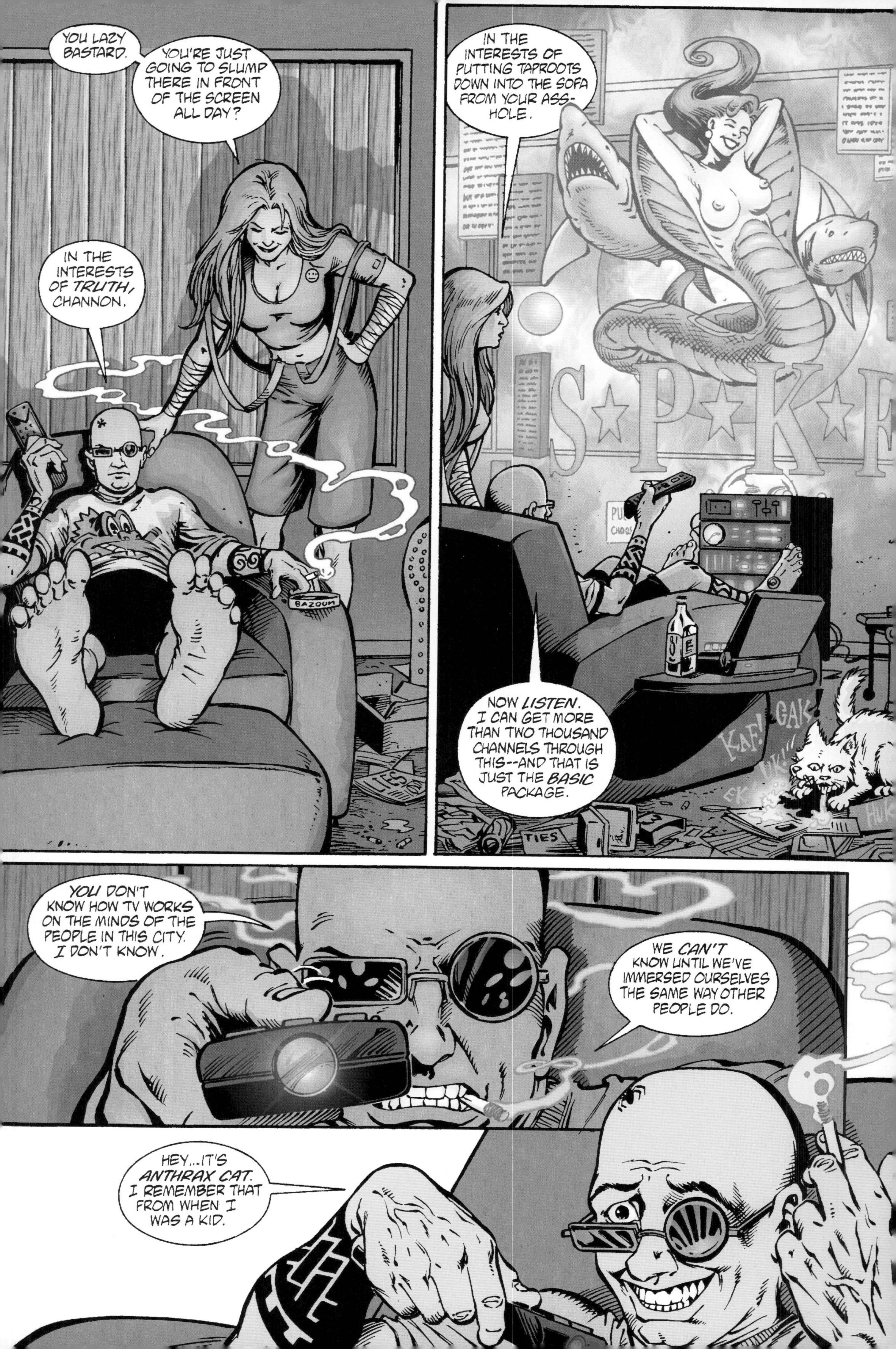
YOU LAZY BASTARD.
YOU'RE JUST GOING TO SLUMP THERE IN FRONT OF THE SCREEN ALL DAY?
IN THE INTERESTS OF *TRUTH*, CHANNON.
BAZOUM
IN THE INTERESTS OF PUTTING TAPROOTS DOWN INTO THE SOFA FROM YOUR ASS-HOLE.
S★P★K★F
NOW *LISTEN*. I CAN GET MORE THAN TWO THOUSAND CHANNELS THROUGH THIS--AND THAT IS JUST THE *BASIC* PACKAGE.
KAF!
GAK!
UK!
EK!
HUK
TIES
*YOU* DON'T KNOW HOW TV WORKS ON THE MINDS OF THE PEOPLE IN THIS CITY. *I* DON'T KNOW.
WE *CAN'T* KNOW UNTIL WE'VE IMMERSED OURSELVES THE SAME WAY OTHER PEOPLE DO.
HEY...IT'S *ANTHRAX CAT*. I REMEMBER THAT FROM WHEN I WAS A KID.

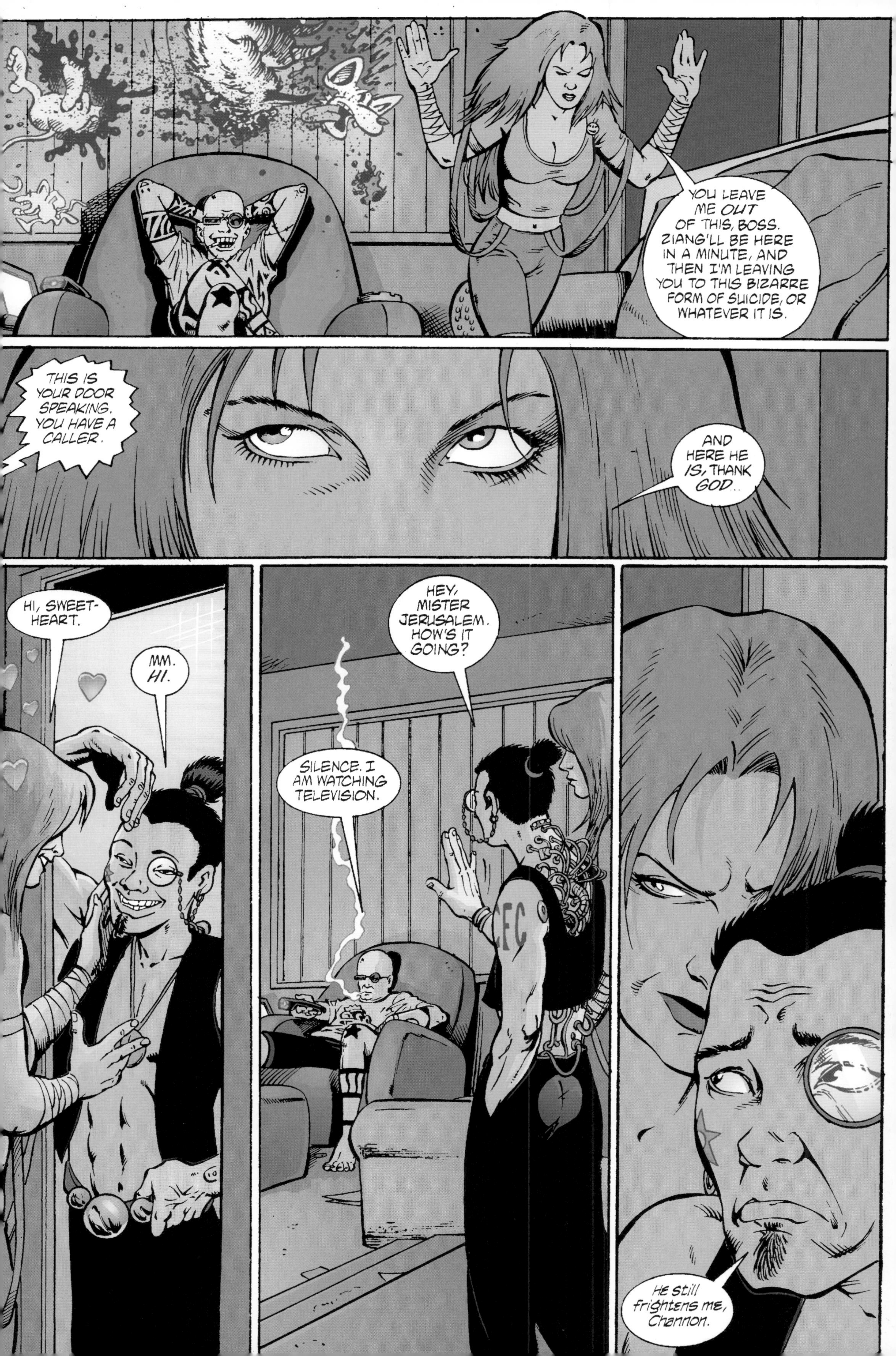
YOU LEAVE ME OUT OF THIS, BOSS. ZIANG'LL BE HERE IN A MINUTE, AND THEN I'M LEAVING YOU TO THIS BIZARRE FORM OF SUICIDE, OR WHATEVER IT IS.
THIS IS YOUR DOOR SPEAKING. YOU HAVE A CALLER.
AND HERE HE IS, THANK GOD...
HI, SWEET-HEART.
MM. HI.
HEY, MISTER JERUSALEM. HOW'S IT GOING?
SILENCE. I AM WATCHING TELEVISION.
He still frightens me, Channon.

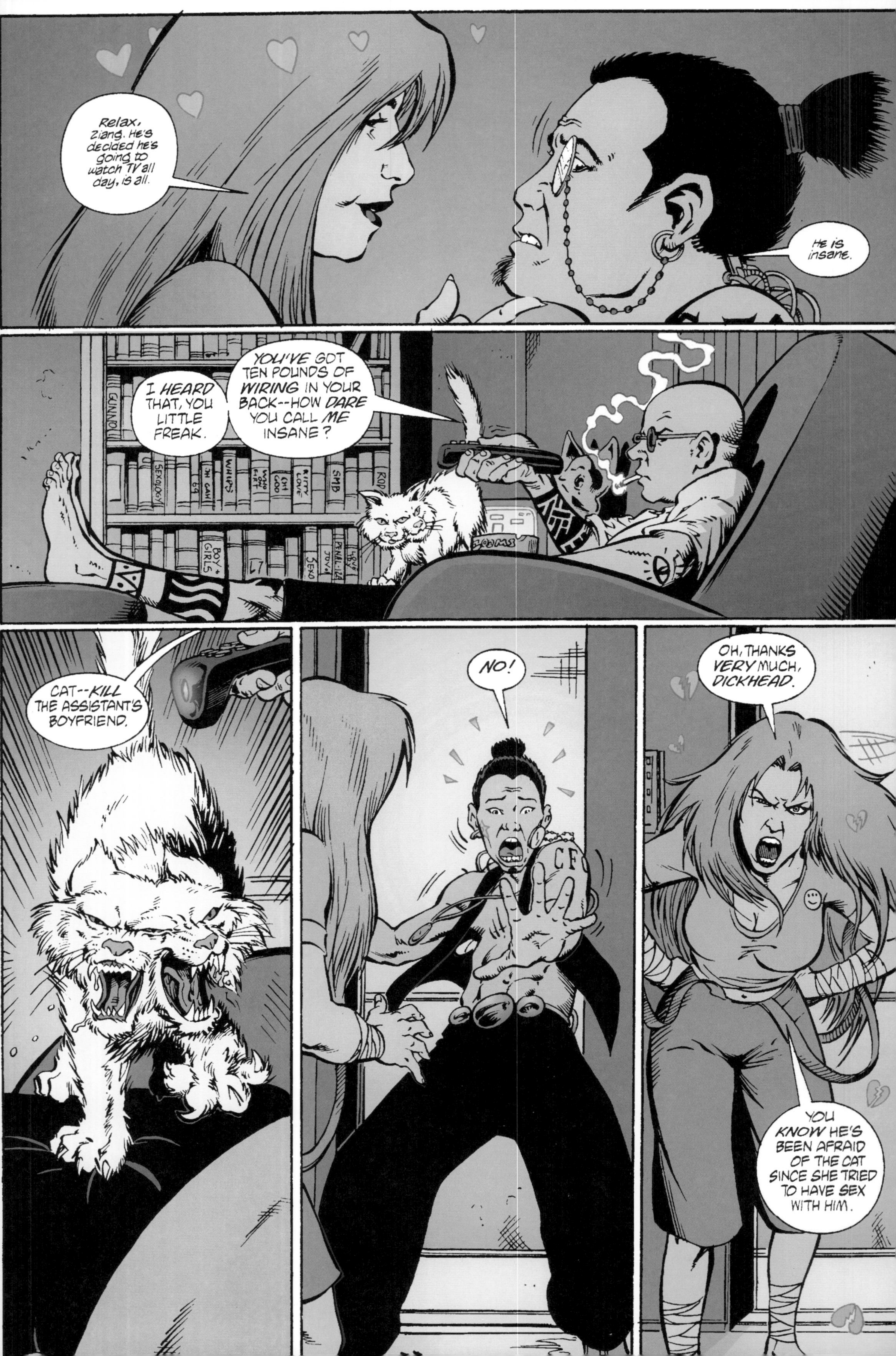
Relax, Ziang. He's decided he's going to watch TV all day, is all.
He is insane.
I HEARD THAT, YOU LITTLE FREAK.
YOU'VE GOT TEN POUNDS OF WIRING IN YOUR BACK--HOW DARE YOU CALL ME INSANE?
CAT--KILL THE ASSISTANT'S BOYFRIEND.
NO!
OH, THANKS VERY MUCH, DICKHEAD.
YOU KNOW HE'S BEEN AFRAID OF THE CAT SINCE SHE TRIED TO HAVE SEX WITH HIM.

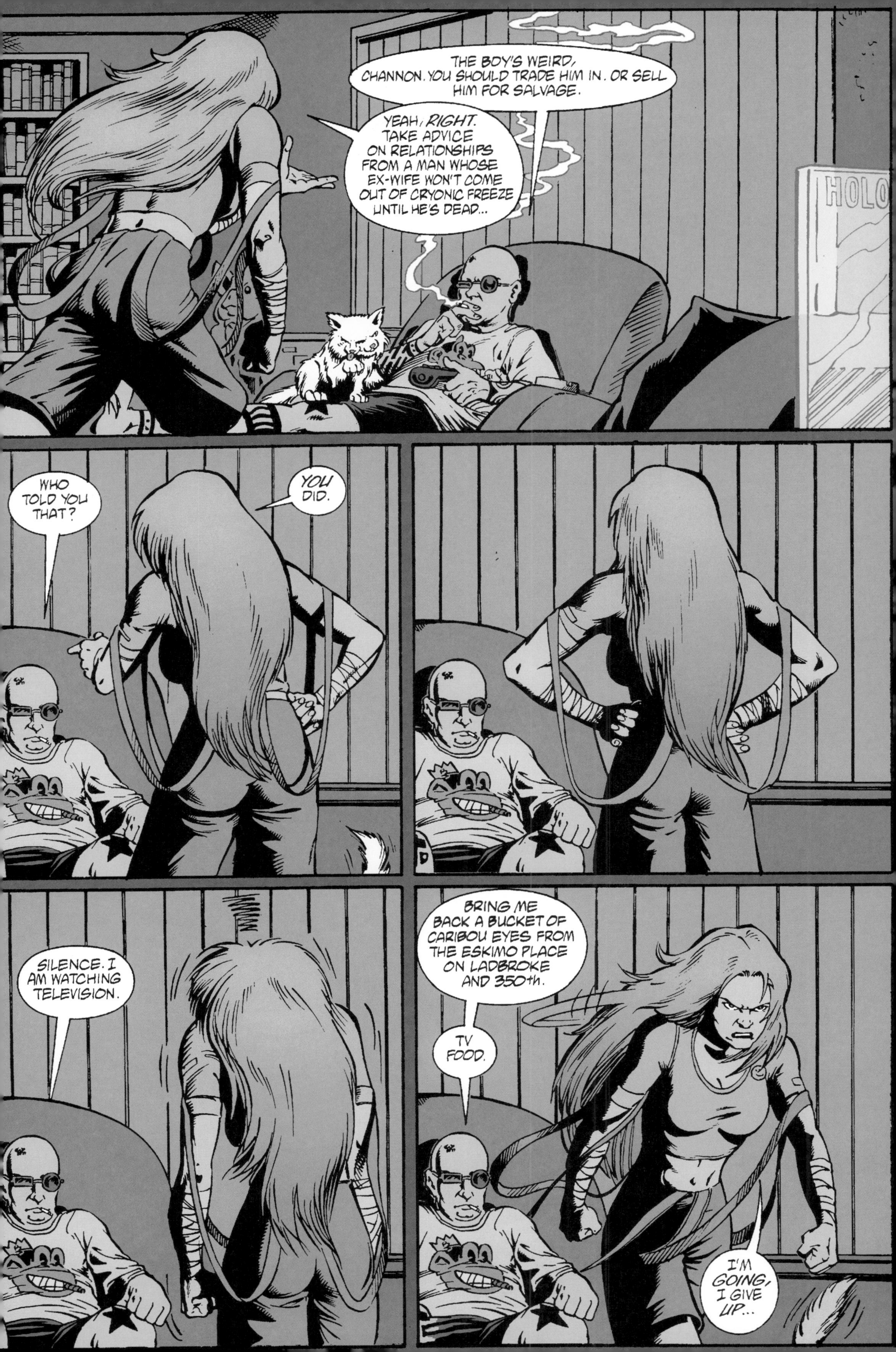
THE BOY'S WEIRD, CHANNON. YOU SHOULD TRADE HIM IN. OR SELL HIM FOR SALVAGE.
YEAH, *RIGHT*. TAKE ADVICE ON RELATIONSHIPS FROM A MAN WHOSE EX-WIFE WON'T COME OUT OF CRYONIC FREEZE UNTIL HE'S DEAD...
HOLO
WHO TOLD YOU THAT?
*YOU* DID.
SILENCE. I AM WATCHING TELEVISION.
BRING ME BACK A BUCKET OF CARIBOU EYES FROM THE ESKIMO PLACE ON LADBROKE AND 350th.
TV FOOD.
I'M *GOING*, I GIVE *UP*...

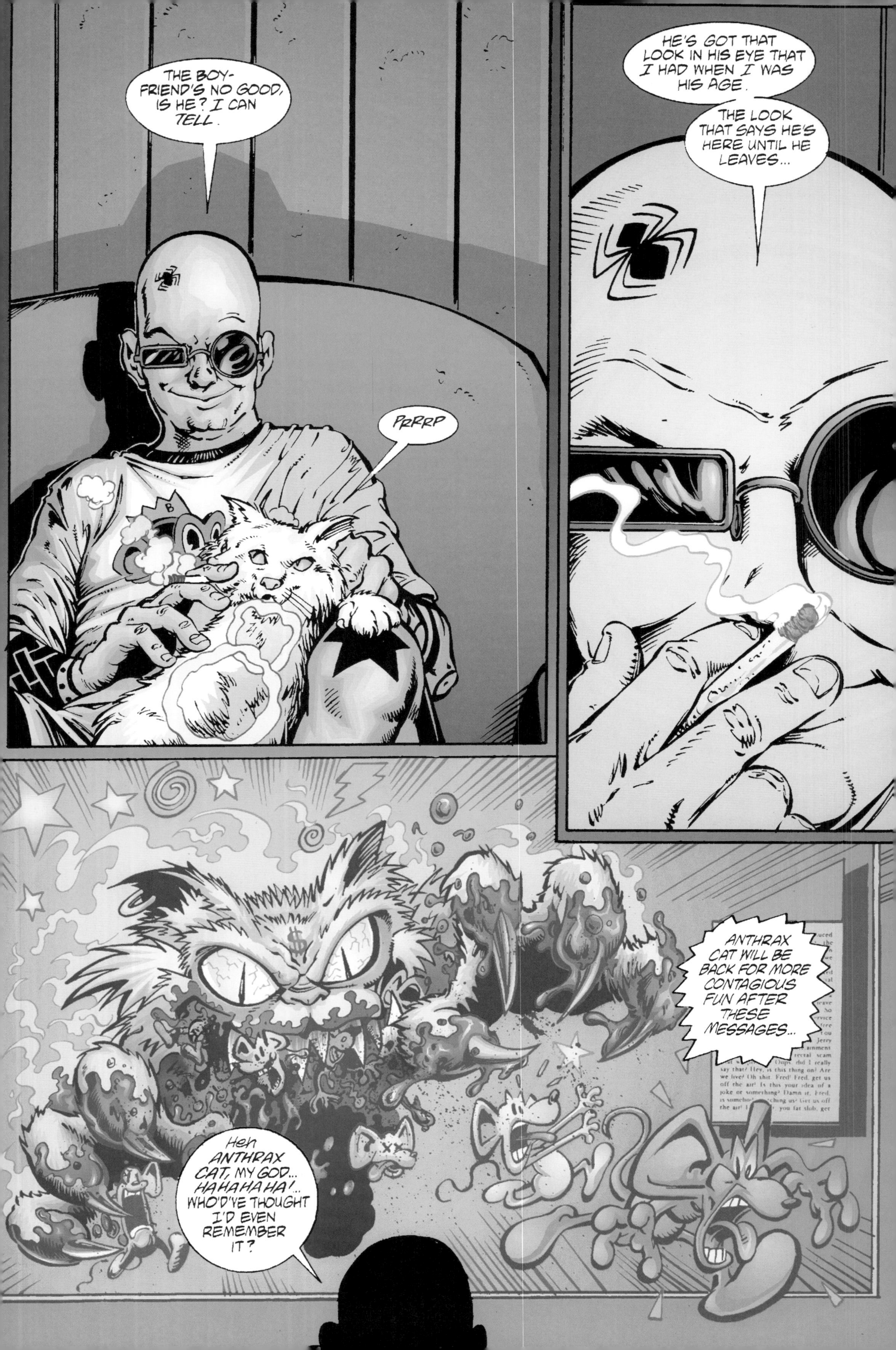
THE BOY-FRIEND'S NO GOOD, IS HE? I CAN TELL.
PRRRP
HE'S GOT THAT LOOK IN HIS EYE THAT I HAD WHEN I WAS HIS AGE.
THE LOOK THAT SAYS HE'S HERE UNTIL HE LEAVES...
ANTHRAX CAT WILL BE BACK FOR MORE CONTAGIOUS FUN AFTER THESE MESSAGES...
Heh ANTHRAX CAT, MY GOD... HAHAHAHA!... WHO'D'VE THOUGHT I'D EVEN REMEMBER IT?

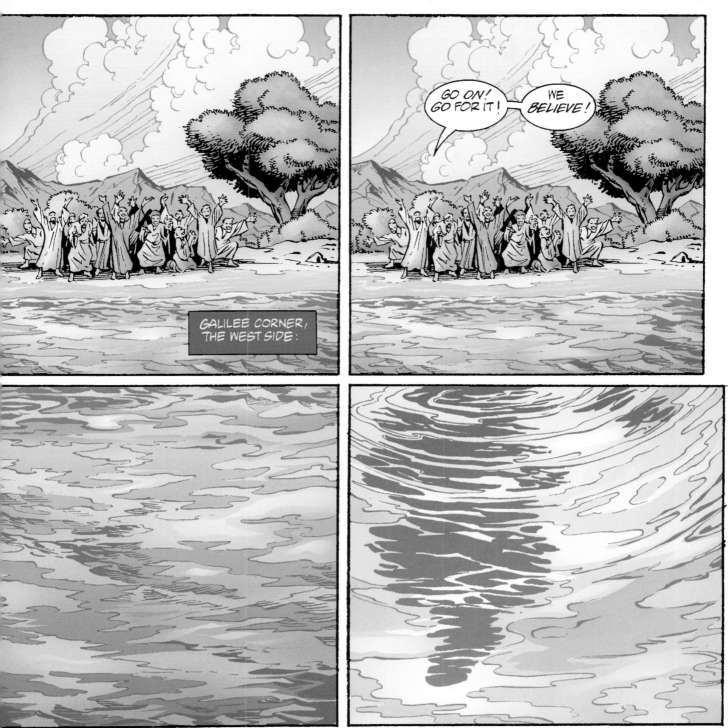

GALILEE CORNER, THE WEST SIDE:

GO ON! GO FOR IT!

WE BELIEVE!

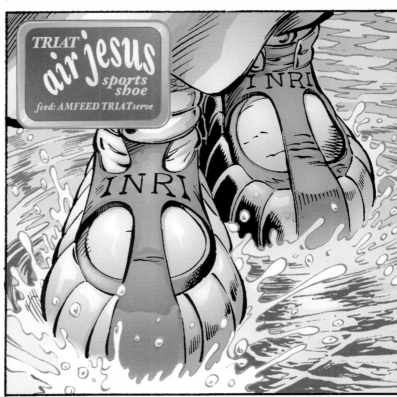

TRIAT air jesus sports shoe

feed: AMFEED TRIATserve

INRI

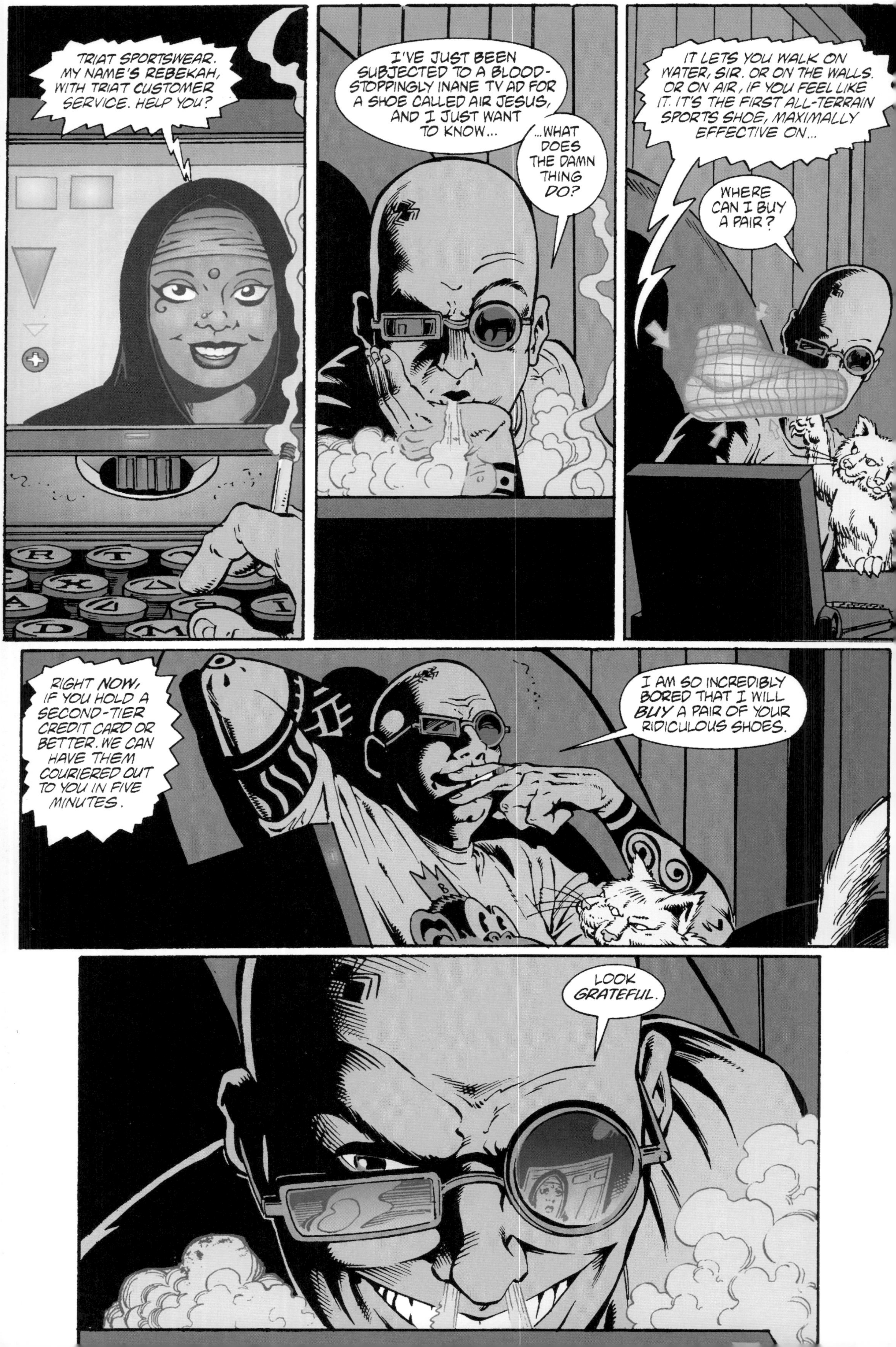

TRIAT SPORTSWEAR. MY NAME'S REBEKAH, WITH TRIAT CUSTOMER SERVICE. HELP YOU?
I'VE JUST BEEN SUBJECTED TO A BLOOD-STOPPINGLY INANE TV AD FOR A SHOE CALLED AIR JESUS, AND I JUST WANT TO KNOW...
...WHAT DOES THE DAMN THING DO?
IT LETS YOU WALK ON WATER, SIR. OR ON THE WALLS. OR ON AIR, IF YOU FEEL LIKE IT. IT'S THE FIRST ALL-TERRAIN SPORTS SHOE, MAXIMALLY EFFECTIVE ON...
WHERE CAN I BUY A PAIR?
RIGHT NOW, IF YOU HOLD A SECOND-TIER CREDIT CARD OR BETTER. WE CAN HAVE THEM COURIERED OUT TO YOU IN FIVE MINUTES.
I AM SO INCREDIBLY BORED THAT I WILL BUY A PAIR OF YOUR RIDICULOUS SHOES.
LOOK GRATEFUL.

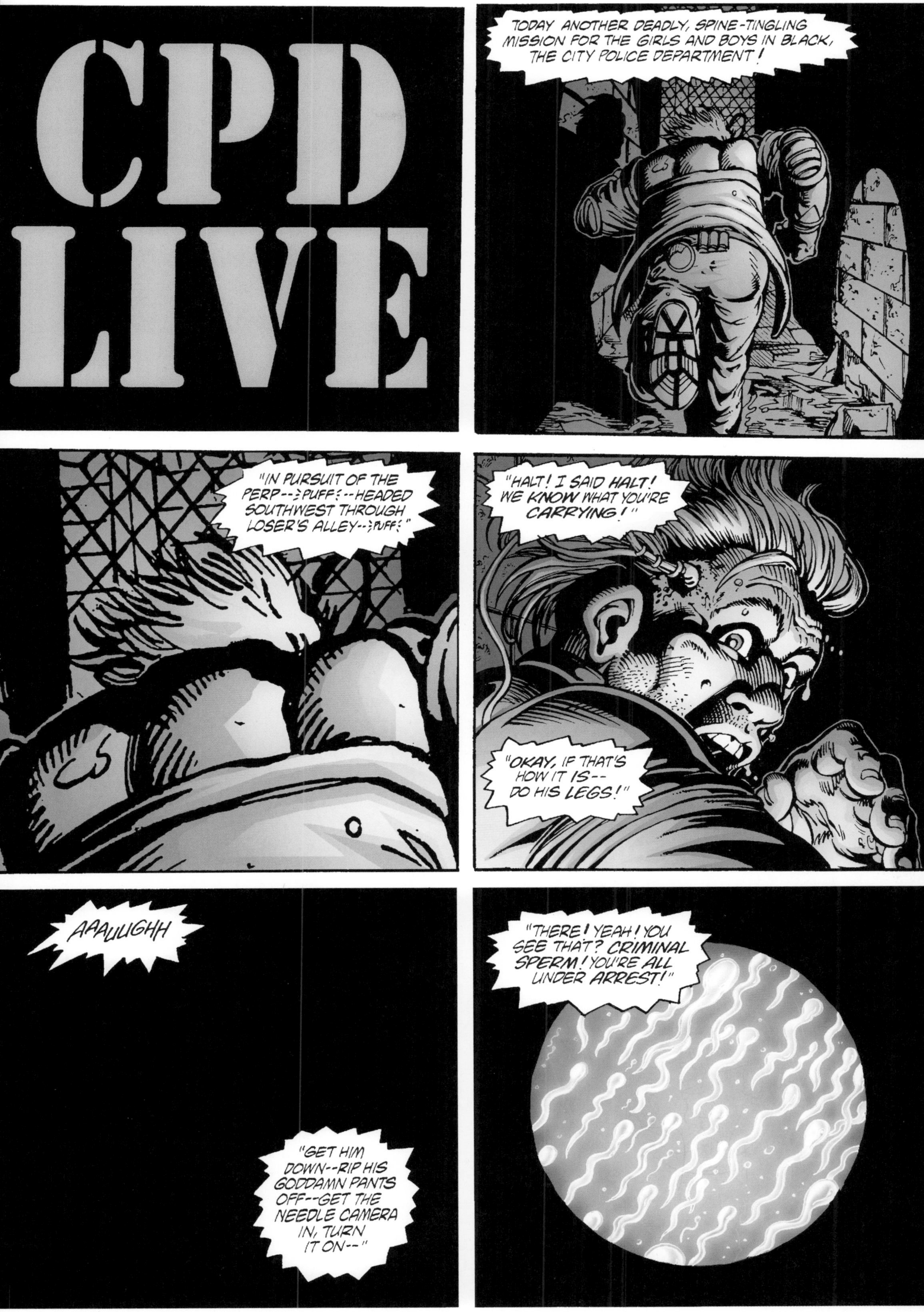
CPD LIVE
TODAY ANOTHER DEADLY, SPINE-TINGLING MISSION FOR THE GIRLS AND BOYS IN BLACK, THE CITY POLICE DEPARTMENT!
"IN PURSUIT OF THE PERP--PUFF--HEADED SOUTHWEST THROUGH LOSER'S ALLEY--PUFF"
"HALT! I SAID HALT! WE KNOW WHAT YOU'RE CARRYING!"
"OKAY, IF THAT'S HOW IT IS-- DO HIS LEGS!"
AAAUUGHH
"GET HIM DOWN--RIP HIS GODDAMN PANTS OFF--GET THE NEEDLE CAMERA IN, TURN IT ON--"
"THERE! YEAH! YOU SEE THAT? CRIMINAL SPERM! YOU'RE ALL UNDER ARREST!"

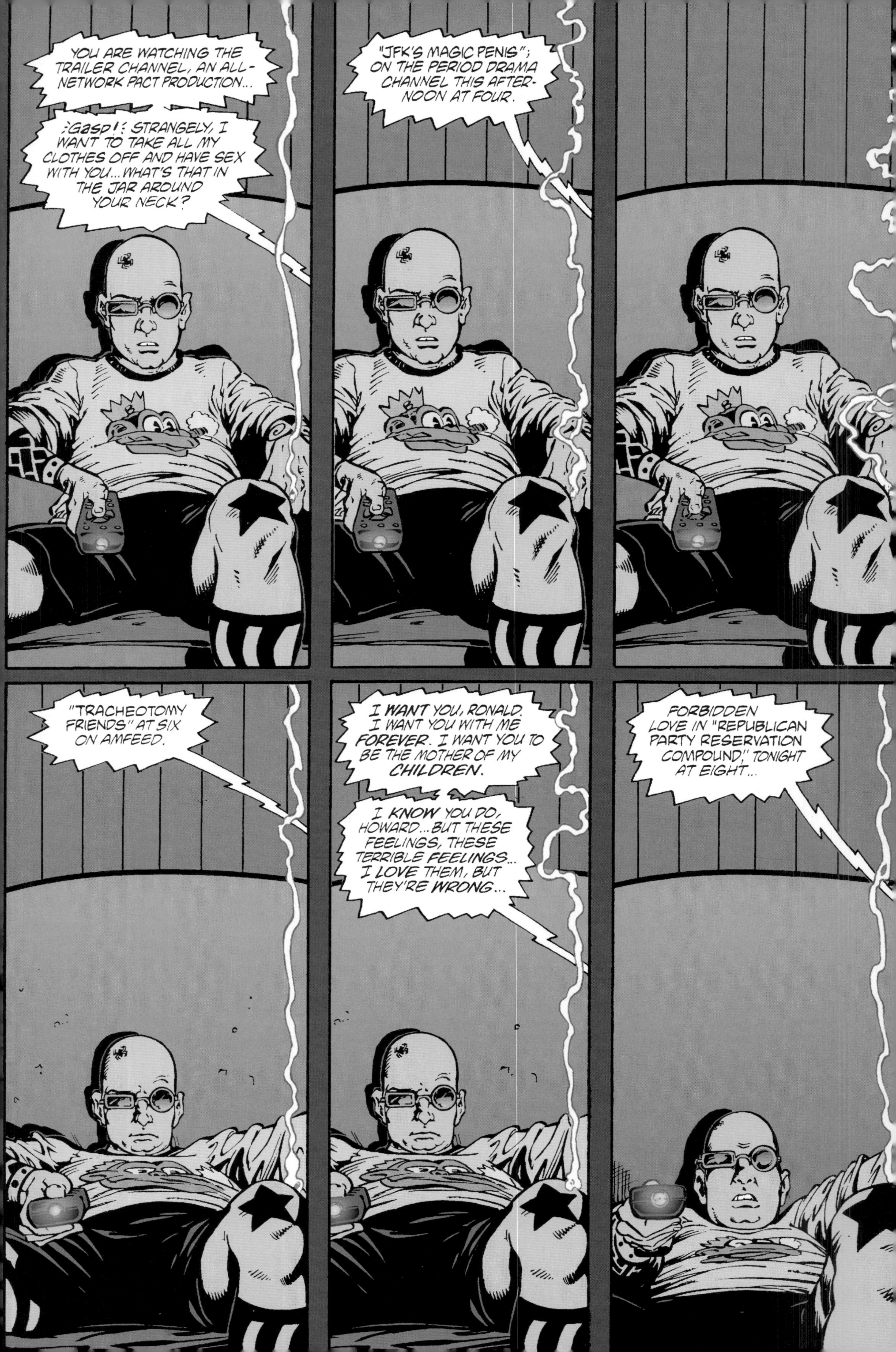
YOU ARE WATCHING THE TRAILER CHANNEL, AN ALL-NETWORK PACT PRODUCTION...
:Gasp!: STRANGELY, I WANT TO TAKE ALL MY CLOTHES OFF AND HAVE SEX WITH YOU... WHAT'S THAT IN THE JAR AROUND YOUR NECK?
"JFK'S MAGIC PENIS"; ON THE PERIOD DRAMA CHANNEL THIS AFTERNOON AT FOUR.
"TRACHEOTOMY FRIENDS" AT SIX ON AMFEED.
I WANT YOU, RONALD. I WANT YOU WITH ME FOREVER. I WANT YOU TO BE THE MOTHER OF MY CHILDREN.
I KNOW YOU DO, HOWARD... BUT THESE FEELINGS, THESE TERRIBLE FEELINGS... I LOVE THEM, BUT THEY'RE WRONG...
FORBIDDEN LOVE IN "REPUBLICAN PARTY RESERVATION COMPOUND," TONIGHT AT EIGHT...

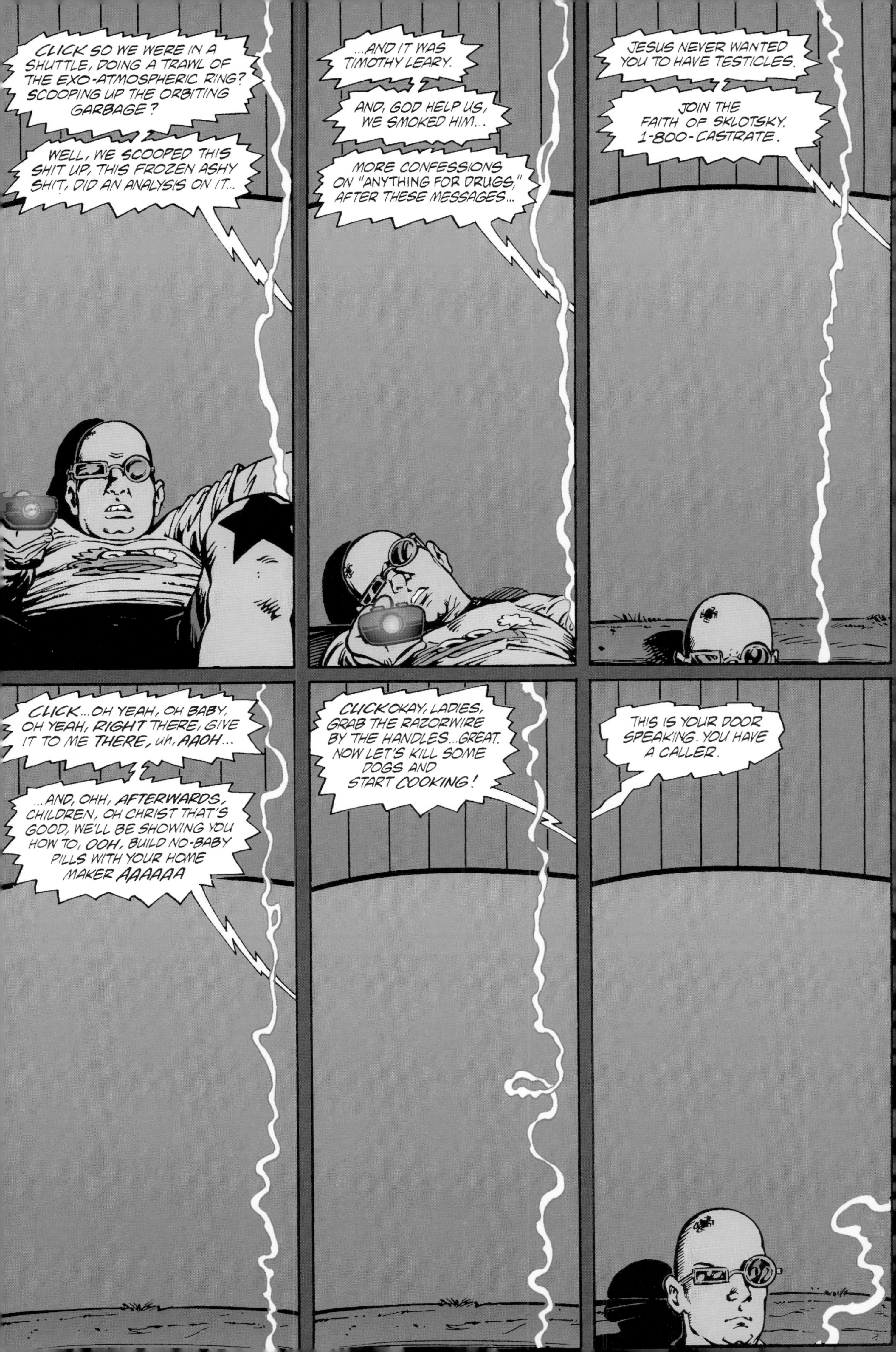
CLICK SO WE WERE IN A SHUTTLE, DOING A TRAWL OF THE EXO-ATMOSPHERIC RING? SCOOPING UP THE ORBITING GARBAGE?
WELL, WE SCOOPED THIS SHIT UP, THIS FROZEN ASHY SHIT, DID AN ANALYSIS ON IT...
...AND IT WAS TIMOTHY LEARY.
AND, GOD HELP US, WE SMOKED HIM...
MORE CONFESSIONS ON "ANYTHING FOR DRUGS," AFTER THESE MESSAGES...
JESUS NEVER WANTED YOU TO HAVE TESTICLES.
JOIN THE FAITH OF SKLOTSKY. 1-800-CASTRATE.
CLICK...OH YEAH, OH BABY, OH YEAH, RIGHT THERE, GIVE IT TO ME THERE, uh, AAOH...
...AND, OHH, AFTERWARDS, CHILDREN, OH CHRIST THAT'S GOOD, WE'LL BE SHOWING YOU HOW TO, OOH, BUILD NO-BABY PILLS WITH YOUR HOME MAKER AAAAAA
CLICK OKAY, LADIES, GRAB THE RAZORWIRE BY THE HANDLES...GREAT. NOW LET'S KILL SOME DOGS AND START COOKING!
THIS IS YOUR DOOR SPEAKING. YOU HAVE A CALLER.

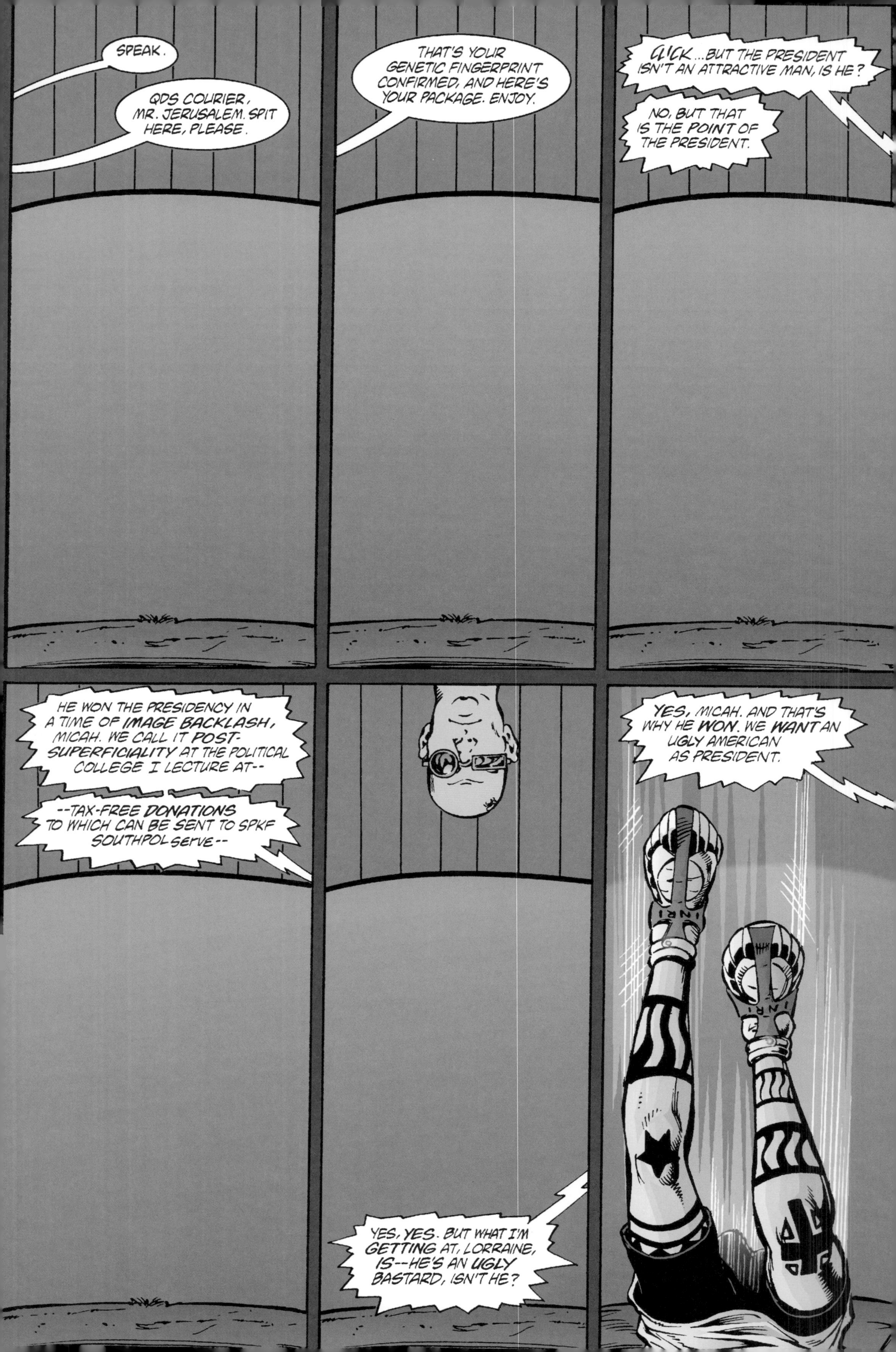
SPEAK.
QDS COURIER, MR. JERUSALEM. SPIT HERE, PLEASE.
THAT'S YOUR GENETIC FINGERPRINT CONFIRMED, AND HERE'S YOUR PACKAGE. ENJOY.
CLICK ...BUT THE PRESIDENT ISN'T AN ATTRACTIVE MAN, IS HE?
NO, BUT THAT IS THE POINT OF THE PRESIDENT.
HE WON THE PRESIDENCY IN A TIME OF IMAGE BACKLASH, MICAH. WE CALL IT POST-SUPERFICIALITY AT THE POLITICAL COLLEGE I LECTURE AT--
--TAX-FREE DONATIONS TO WHICH CAN BE SENT TO SPKF SOUTHPOL serve--
YES, YES. BUT WHAT I'M GETTING AT, LORRAINE, IS--HE'S AN UGLY BASTARD, ISN'T HE?
YES, MICAH. AND THAT'S WHY HE WON. WE WANT AN UGLY AMERICAN AS PRESIDENT.

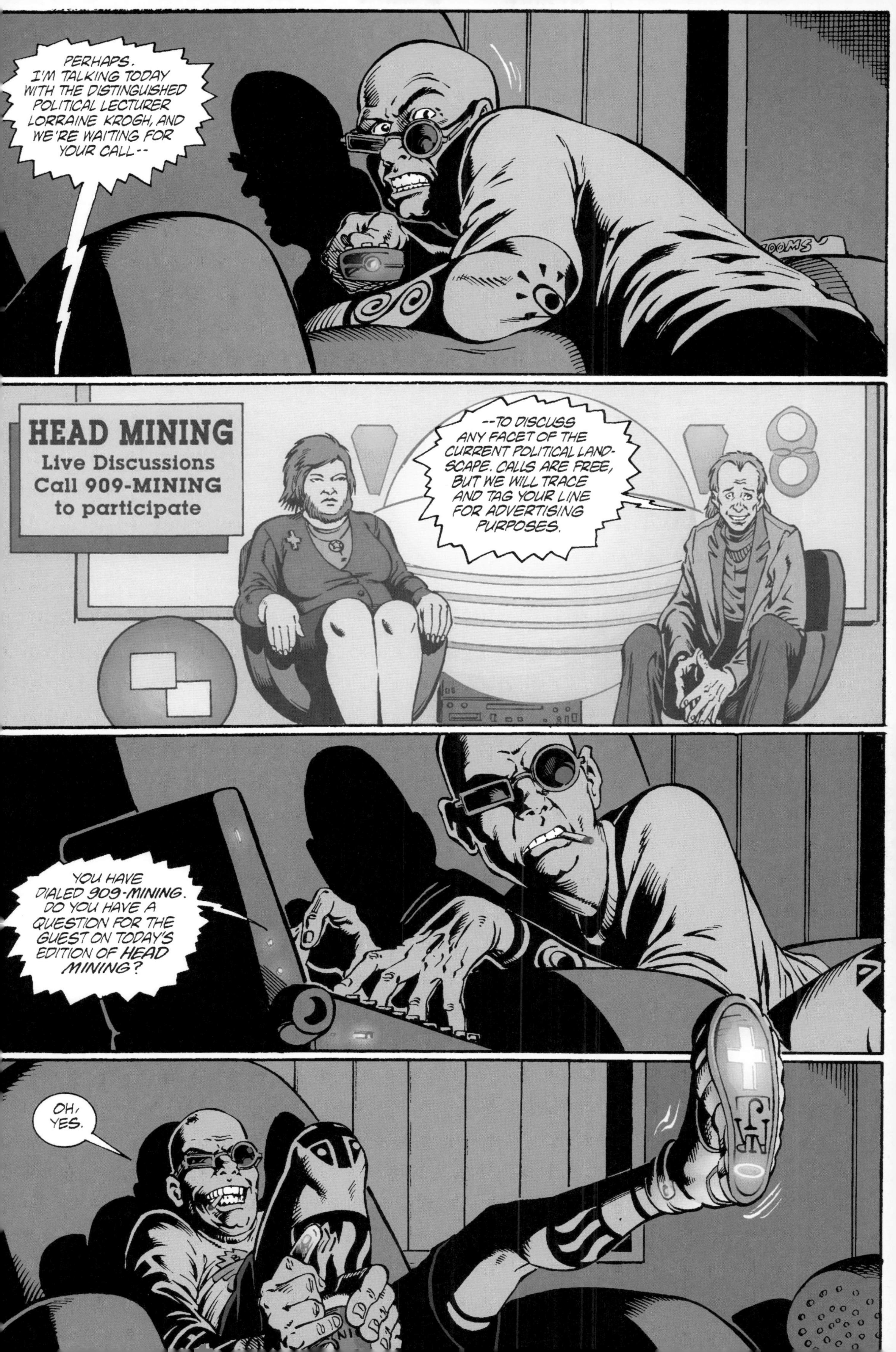
PERHAPS. I'M TALKING TODAY WITH THE DISTINGUISHED POLITICAL LECTURER LORRAINE KROGH, AND WE'RE WAITING FOR YOUR CALL--
HEAD MINING
Live Discussions
Call 909-MINING
to participate
--TO DISCUSS ANY FACET OF THE CURRENT POLITICAL LAND-SCAPE. CALLS ARE FREE, BUT WE WILL TRACE AND TAG YOUR LINE FOR ADVERTISING PURPOSES.
YOU HAVE DIALED 909-MINING. DO YOU HAVE A QUESTION FOR THE GUEST ON TODAY'S EDITION OF HEAD MINING?
OH, YES.

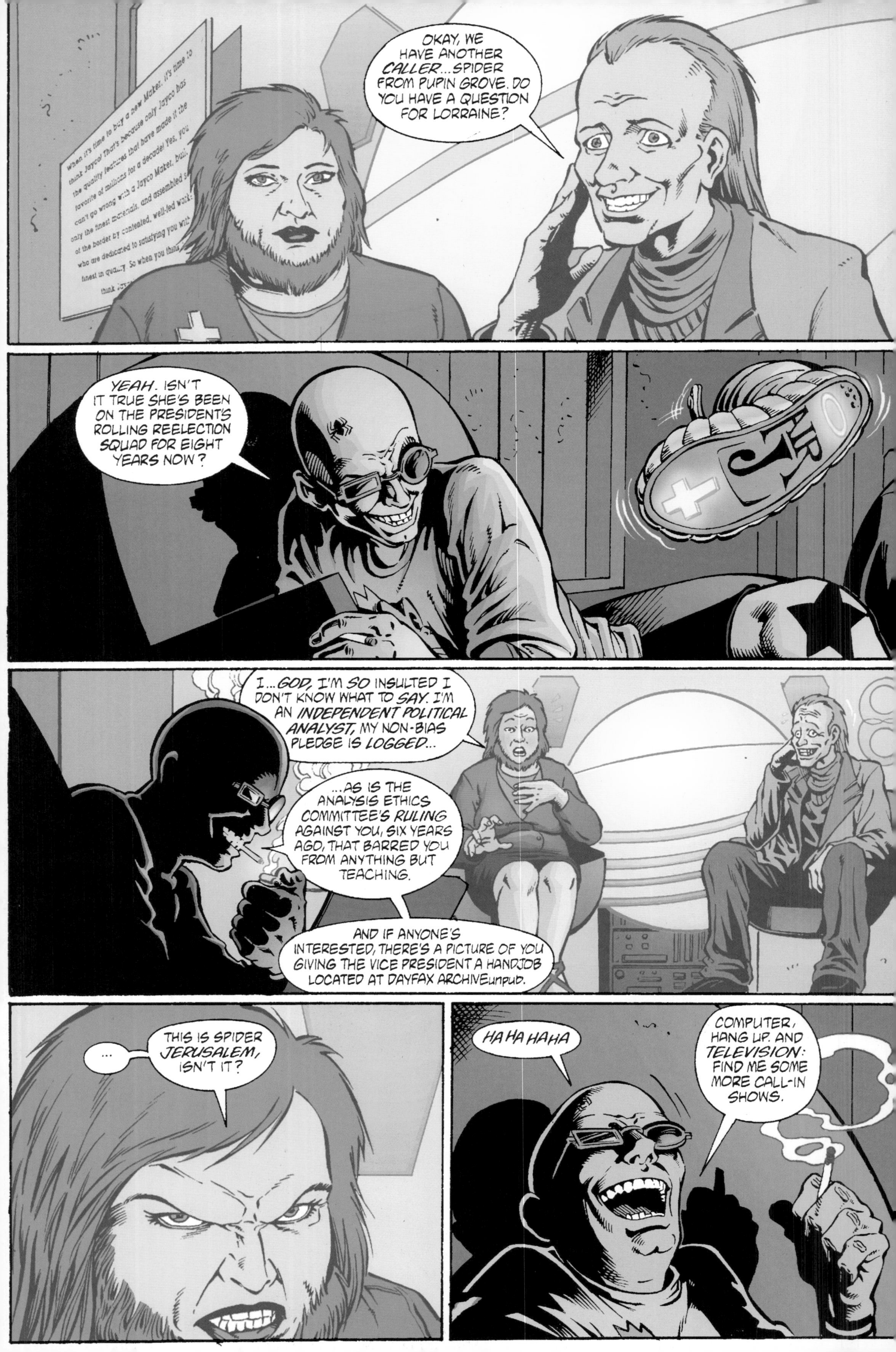
OKAY, WE HAVE ANOTHER CALLER...SPIDER FROM PUPIN GROVE. DO YOU HAVE A QUESTION FOR LORRAINE?
YEAH. ISN'T IT TRUE SHE'S BEEN ON THE PRESIDENT'S ROLLING REELECTION SQUAD FOR EIGHT YEARS NOW?
AIR J
I...GOD, I'M SO INSULTED I DON'T KNOW WHAT TO SAY. I'M AN INDEPENDENT POLITICAL ANALYST, MY NON-BIAS PLEDGE IS LOGGED...
...AS IS THE ANALYSIS ETHICS COMMITTEE'S RULING AGAINST YOU, SIX YEARS AGO, THAT BARRED YOU FROM ANYTHING BUT TEACHING.
AND IF ANYONE'S INTERESTED, THERE'S A PICTURE OF YOU GIVING THE VICE PRESIDENT A HANDJOB LOCATED AT DAYFAX ARCHIVEunpub.
...
THIS IS SPIDER JERUSALEM, ISN'T IT?
HA HA HA HA
COMPUTER, HANG UP. AND TELEVISION: FIND ME SOME MORE CALL-IN SHOWS.

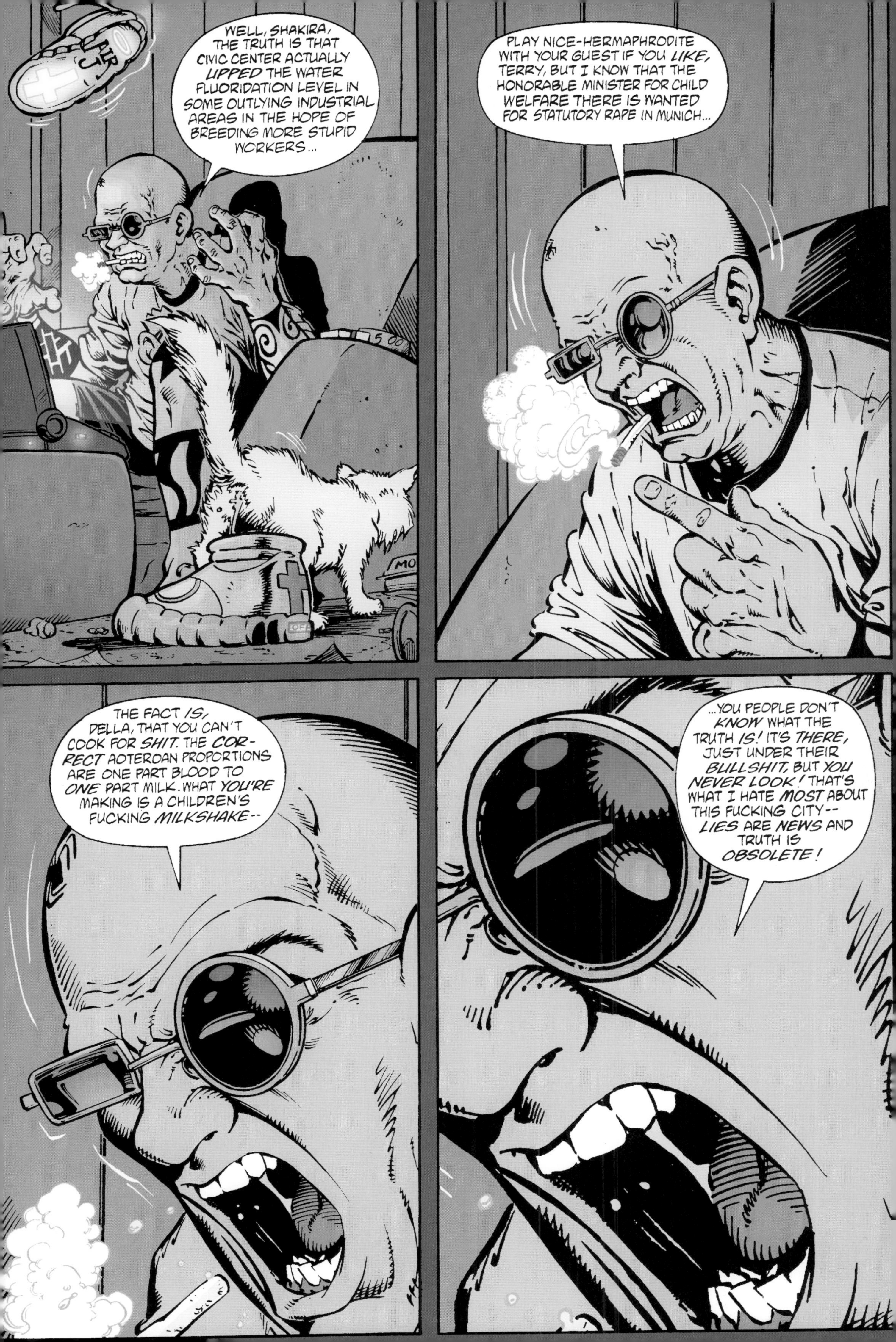
WELL, SHAKIRA, THE TRUTH IS THAT CIVIC CENTER ACTUALLY UPPED THE WATER FLUORIDATION LEVEL IN SOME OUTLYING INDUSTRIAL AREAS IN THE HOPE OF BREEDING MORE STUPID WORKERS...
PLAY NICE-HERMAPHRODITE WITH YOUR GUEST IF YOU LIKE, TERRY, BUT I KNOW THAT THE HONORABLE MINISTER FOR CHILD WELFARE THERE IS WANTED FOR STATUTORY RAPE IN MUNICH...
THE FACT IS, DELLA, THAT YOU CAN'T COOK FOR SHIT. THE COR-RECT AOTEROAN PROPORTIONS ARE ONE PART BLOOD TO ONE PART MILK. WHAT YOU'RE MAKING IS A CHILDREN'S FUCKING MILKSHAKE--
...YOU PEOPLE DON'T KNOW WHAT THE TRUTH IS! IT'S THERE, JUST UNDER THEIR BULLSHIT, BUT YOU NEVER LOOK! THAT'S WHAT I HATE MOST ABOUT THIS FUCKING CITY-- LIES ARE NEWS AND TRUTH IS OBSOLETE!

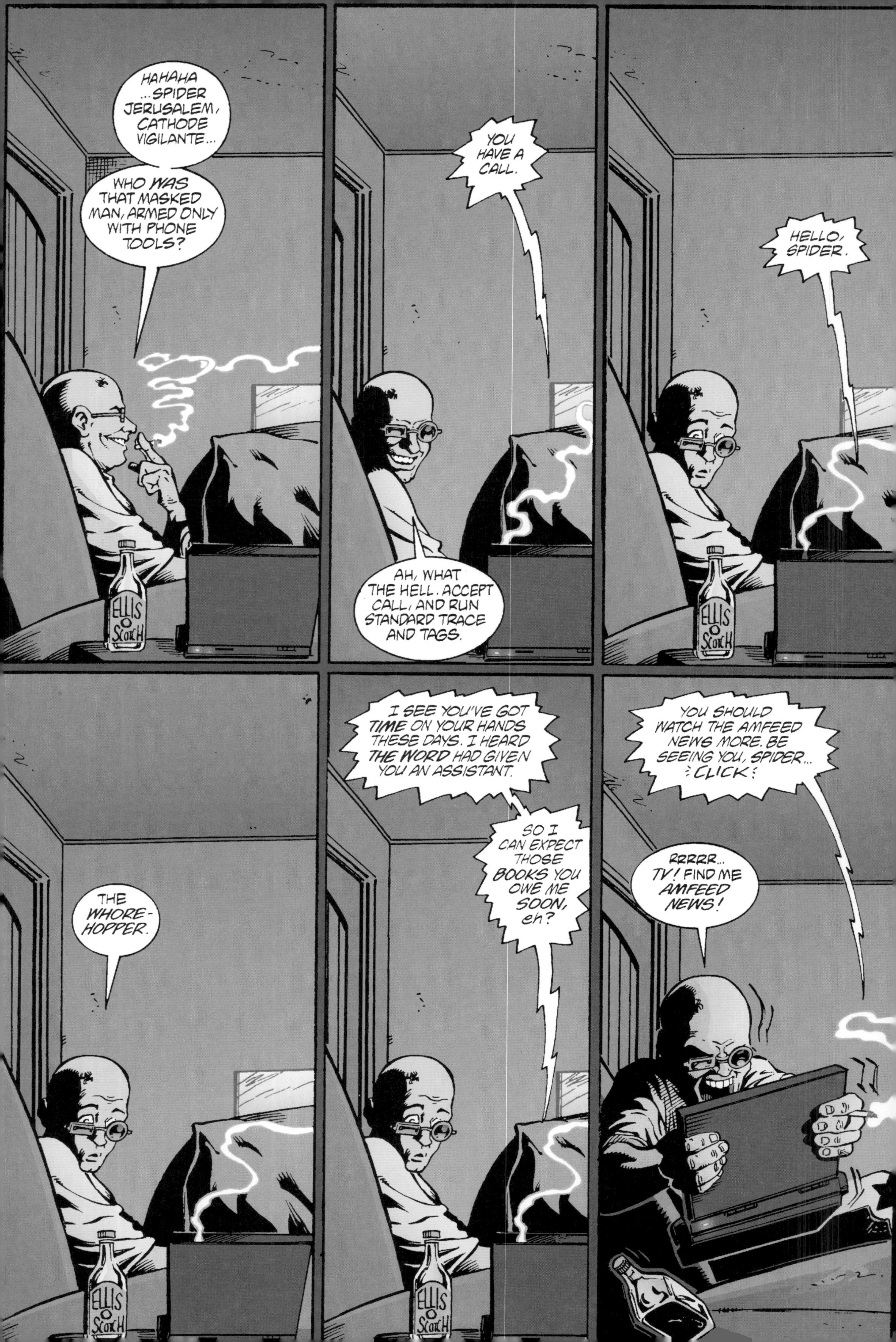
HAHAHA ...SPIDER JERUSALEM, CATHODE VIGILANTE...
WHO WAS THAT MASKED MAN, ARMED ONLY WITH PHONE TOOLS?
YOU HAVE A CALL.
AH, WHAT THE HELL. ACCEPT CALL, AND RUN STANDARD TRACE AND TAGS.
HELLO, SPIDER.
ELLIS SCOTCH
THE WHORE-HOPPER.
I SEE YOU'VE GOT TIME ON YOUR HANDS THESE DAYS. I HEARD THE WORD HAD GIVEN YOU AN ASSISTANT.
SO I CAN EXPECT THOSE BOOKS YOU OWE ME SOON, eh?
YOU SHOULD WATCH THE AMFEED NEWS MORE. BE SEEING YOU, SPIDER... CLICK
RRRRR... TV! FIND ME AMFEED NEWS!

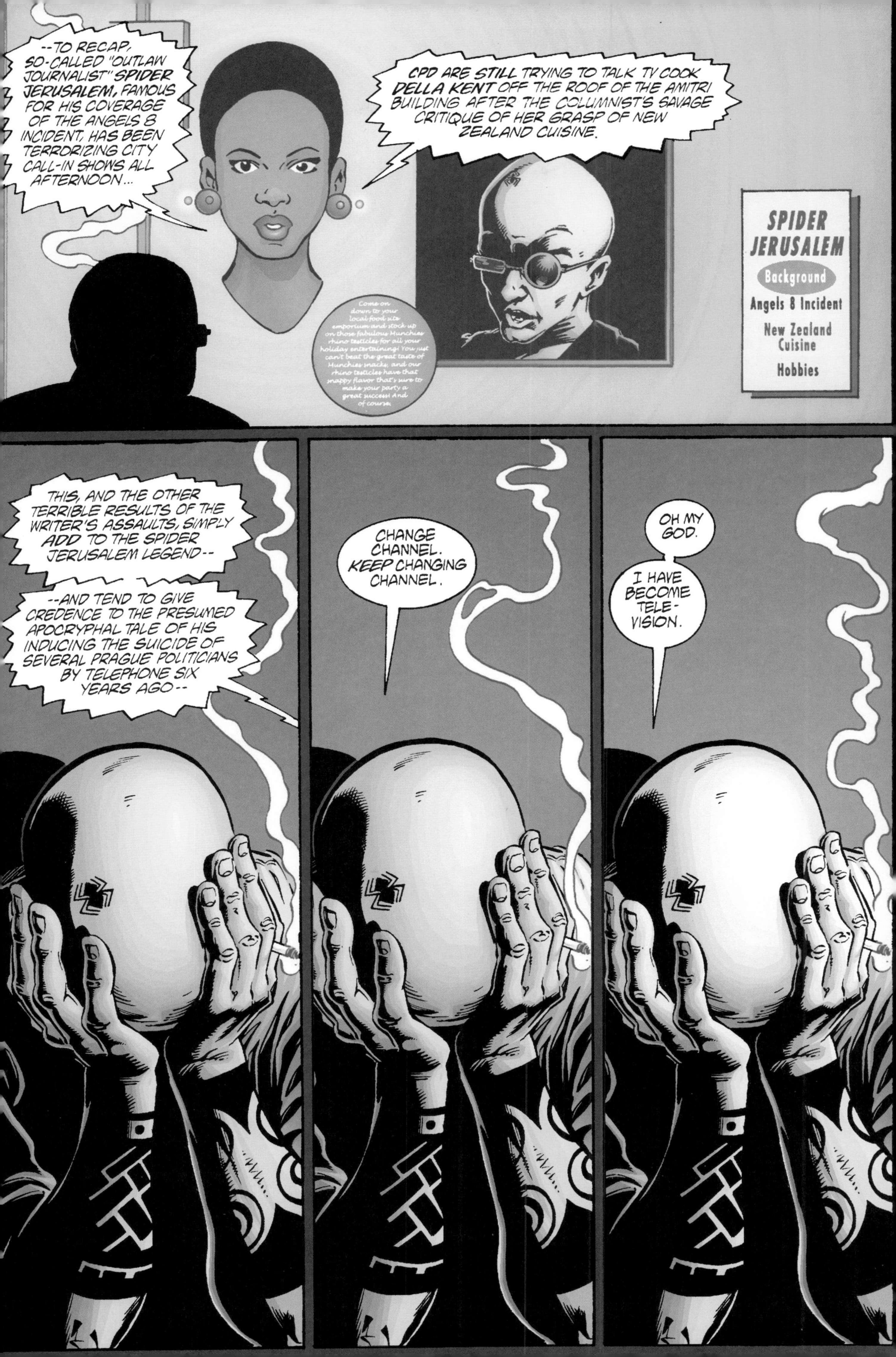
--TO RECAP, SO-CALLED "OUTLAW JOURNALIST" SPIDER JERUSALEM, FAMOUS FOR HIS COVERAGE OF THE ANGELS 8 INCIDENT, HAS BEEN TERRORIZING CITY CALL-IN SHOWS ALL AFTERNOON...
CPD ARE STILL TRYING TO TALK TV COOK DELLA KENT OFF THE ROOF OF THE AMITRI BUILDING AFTER THE COLUMNIST'S SAVAGE CRITIQUE OF HER GRASP OF NEW ZEALAND CUISINE.
Come on down to your local food site emporium and stock up on those fabulous Munchies rhino testicles for all your holiday entertaining! You just can't beat the great taste of Munchies snacks, and our rhino testicles have that snappy flavor that's sure to make your party a great success! And of course,
SPIDER JERUSALEM
Background
Angels 8 Incident
New Zealand Cuisine
Hobbies
THIS, AND THE OTHER TERRIBLE RESULTS OF THE WRITER'S ASSAULTS, SIMPLY ADD TO THE SPIDER JERUSALEM LEGEND--
--AND TEND TO GIVE CREDENCE TO THE PRESUMED APOCRYPHAL TALE OF HIS INDUCING THE SUICIDE OF SEVERAL PRAGUE POLITICIANS BY TELEPHONE SIX YEARS AGO--
CHANGE CHANNEL. KEEP CHANGING CHANNEL.
OH MY GOD.
I HAVE BECOME TELE-VISION.

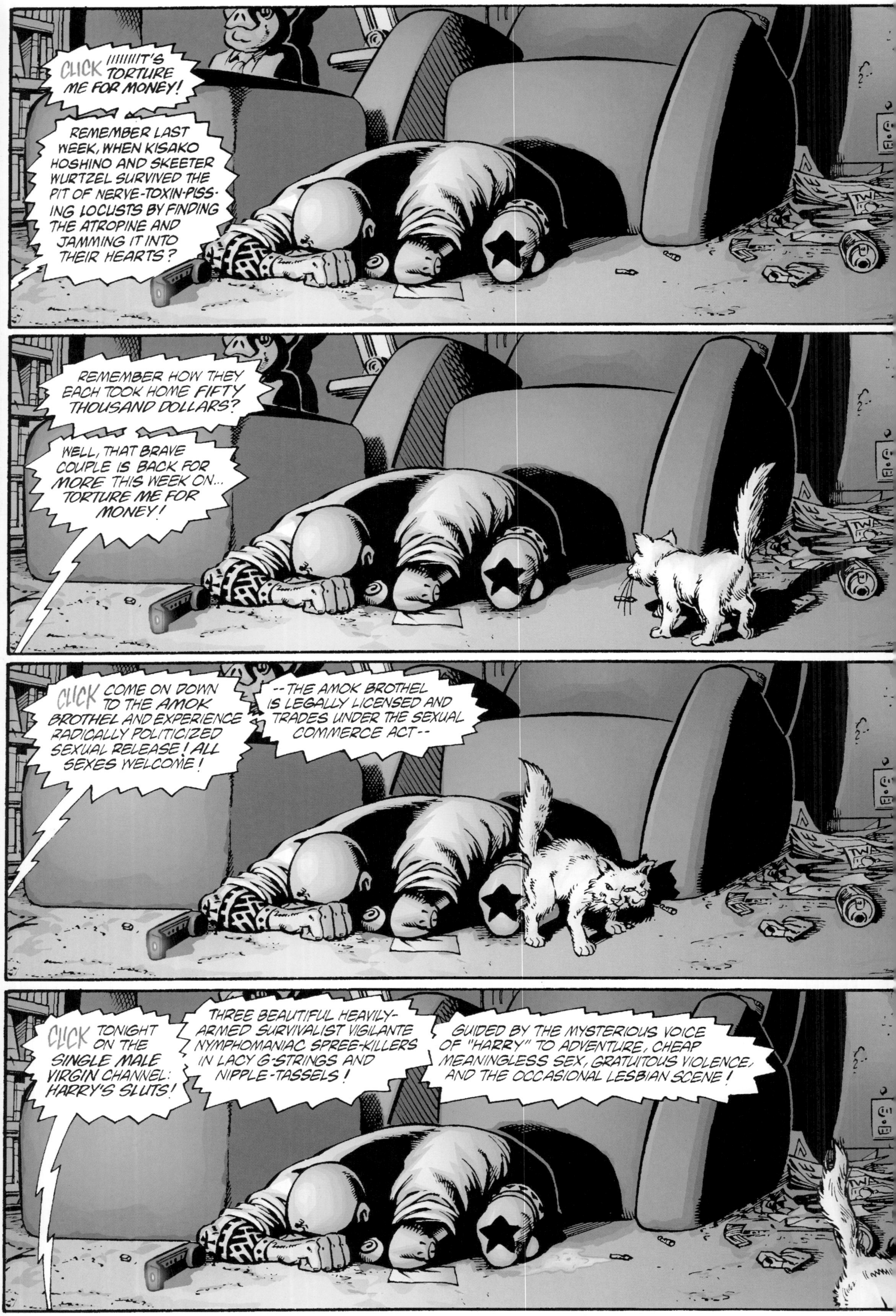

CLICK !!!!!!!IT'S TORTURE ME FOR MONEY!
REMEMBER LAST WEEK, WHEN KISAKO HOSHINO AND SKEETER WURTZEL SURVIVED THE PIT OF NERVE-TOXIN-PISSING LOCUSTS BY FINDING THE ATROPINE AND JAMMING IT INTO THEIR HEARTS?
REMEMBER HOW THEY EACH TOOK HOME FIFTY THOUSAND DOLLARS?
WELL, THAT BRAVE COUPLE IS BACK FOR MORE THIS WEEK ON... TORTURE ME FOR MONEY!
CLICK COME ON DOWN TO THE AMOK BROTHEL AND EXPERIENCE RADICALLY POLITICIZED SEXUAL RELEASE! ALL SEXES WELCOME!
--THE AMOK BROTHEL IS LEGALLY LICENSED AND TRADES UNDER THE SEXUAL COMMERCE ACT--
CLICK TONIGHT ON THE SINGLE MALE VIRGIN CHANNEL: HARRY'S SLUTS!
THREE BEAUTIFUL HEAVILY-ARMED SURVIVALIST VIGILANTE NYMPHOMANIAC SPREE-KILLERS IN LACY G-STRINGS AND NIPPLE-TASSELS!
GUIDED BY THE MYSTERIOUS VOICE OF "HARRY" TO ADVENTURE, CHEAP MEANINGLESS SEX, GRATUITOUS VIOLENCE, AND THE OCCASIONAL LESBIAN SCENE!

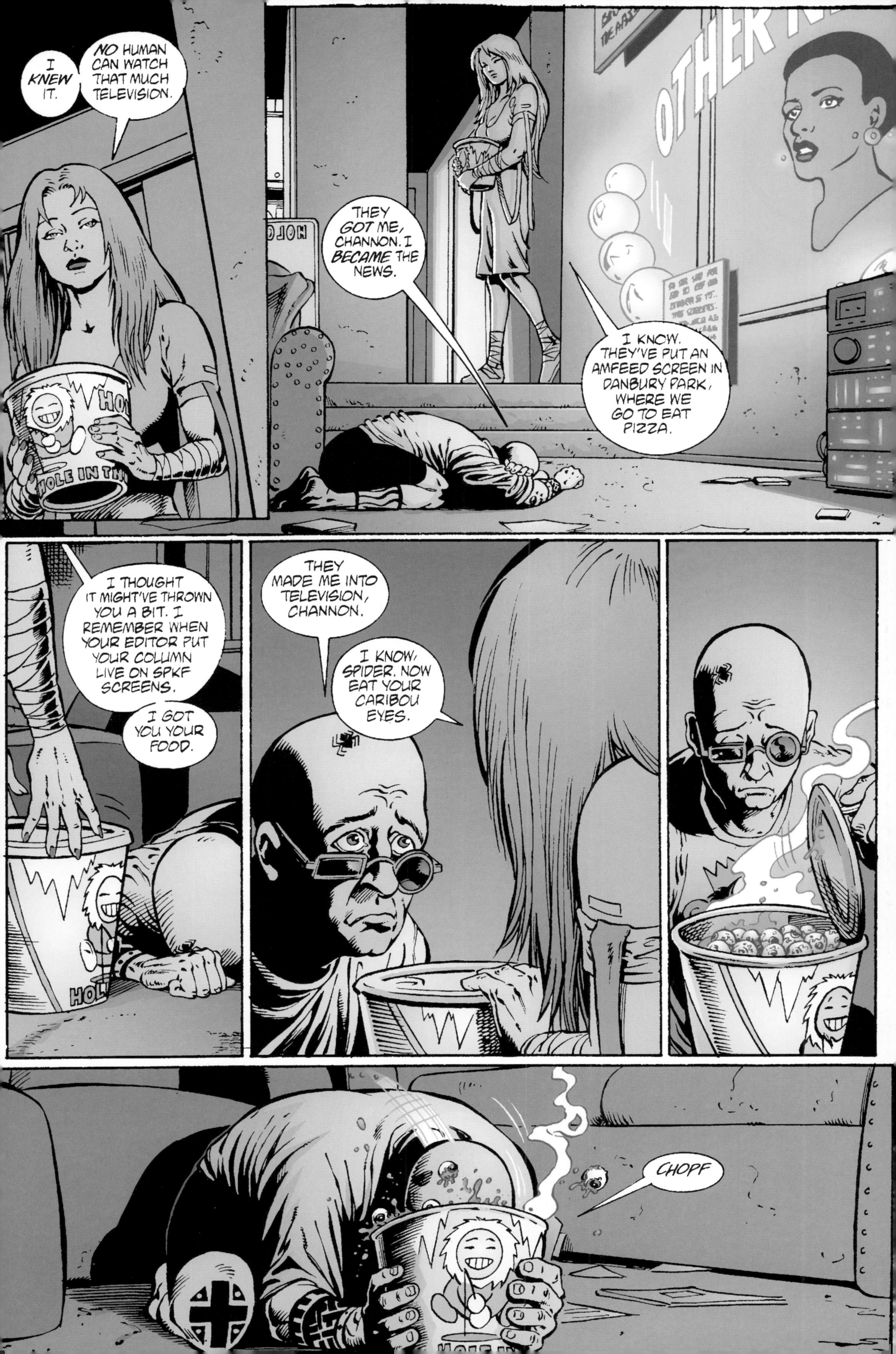
I KNEW IT.
NO HUMAN CAN WATCH THAT MUCH TELEVISION.
THEY GOT ME, CHANNON. I BECAME THE NEWS.
I KNOW. THEY'VE PUT AN AMFEED SCREEN IN DANBURY PARK, WHERE WE GO TO EAT PIZZA.
I THOUGHT IT MIGHT'VE THROWN YOU A BIT. I REMEMBER WHEN YOUR EDITOR PUT YOUR COLUMN LIVE ON SPKF SCREENS.
I GOT YOU YOUR FOOD.
THEY MADE ME INTO TELEVISION, CHANNON.
I KNOW, SPIDER. NOW EAT YOUR CARIBOU EYES.
CHOPF

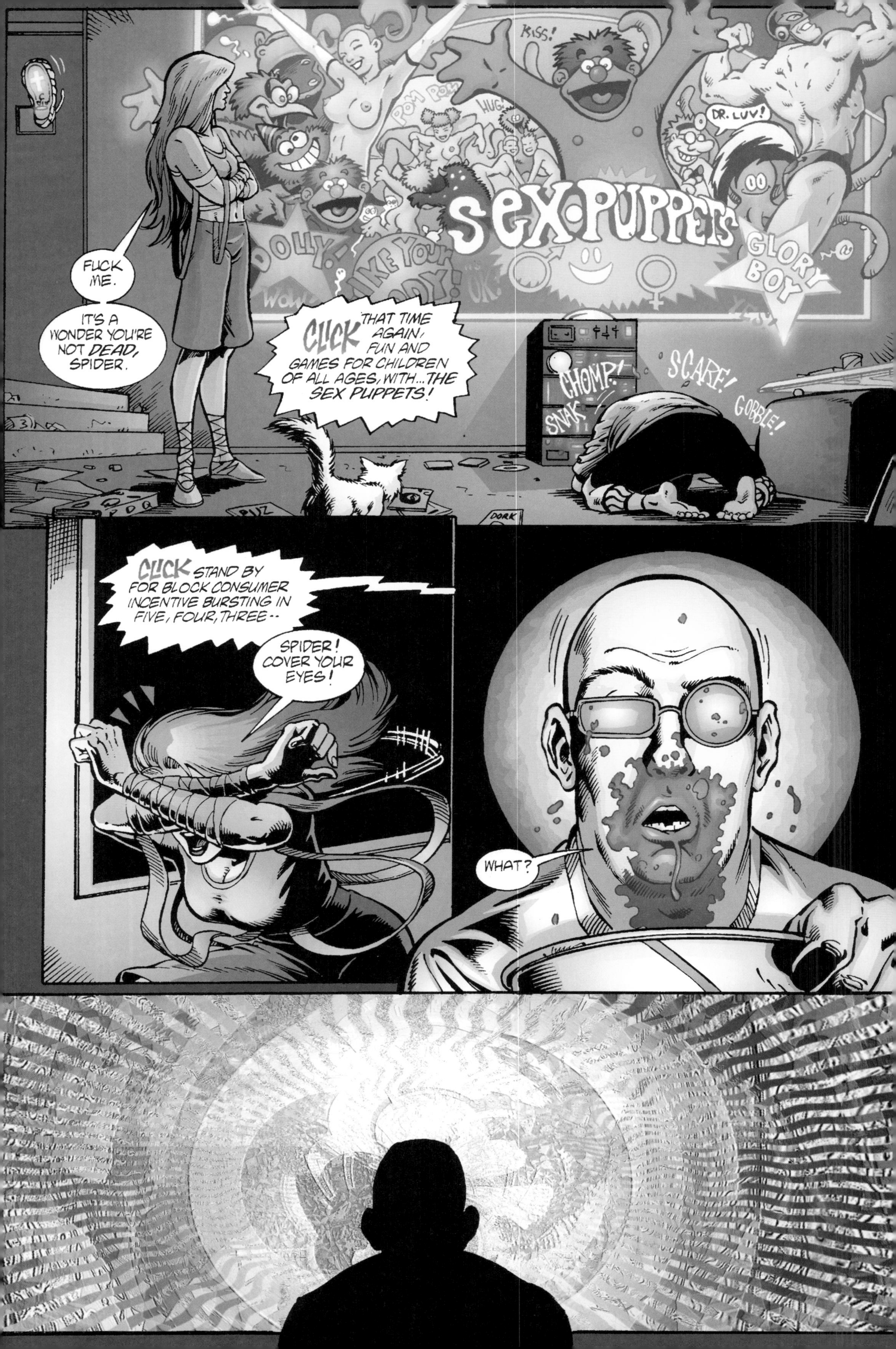
KISS!
HUG!
POM POM
DR. LUV!
SEX-PUPPETS
DOLLY
LIKE YOUR BODY!
IT'S OK!
GLORY BOY
FUCK ME.
IT'S A WONDER YOU'RE NOT DEAD, SPIDER.
CLICK THAT TIME AGAIN, FUN AND GAMES FOR CHILDREN OF ALL AGES, WITH... THE SEX PUPPETS!
CHOMP!
SNAK
SCARF!
GOBBLE!
DORK
CLICK STAND BY FOR BLOCK CONSUMER INCENTIVE BURSTING IN FIVE, FOUR, THREE--
SPIDER! COVER YOUR EYES!
WHAT?

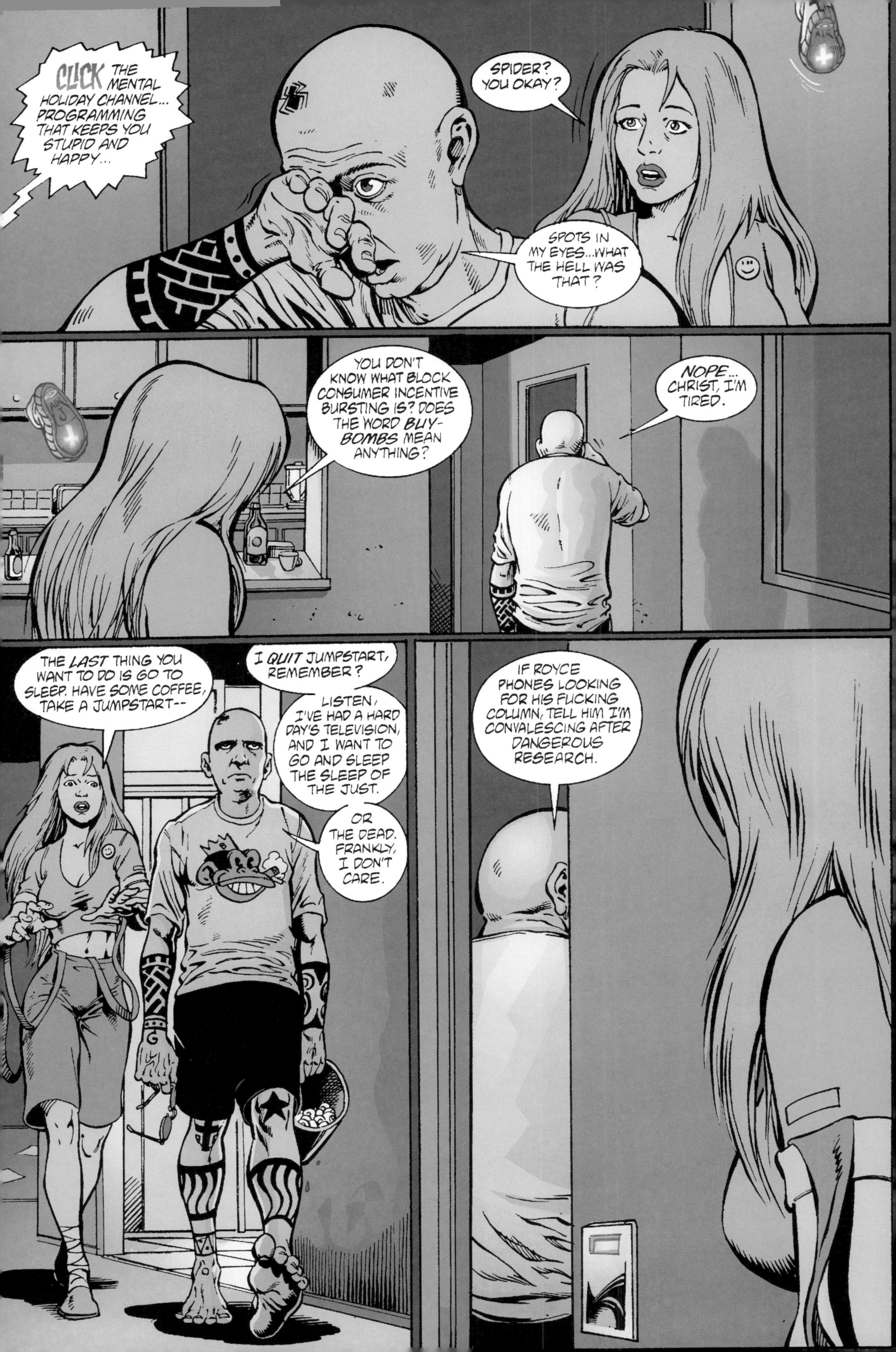
CLICK THE MENTAL HOLIDAY CHANNEL... PROGRAMMING THAT KEEPS YOU STUPID AND HAPPY...
SPIDER? YOU OKAY?
SPOTS IN MY EYES...WHAT THE HELL WAS THAT?
YOU DON'T KNOW WHAT BLOCK CONSUMER INCENTIVE BURSTING IS? DOES THE WORD BUY-BOMBS MEAN ANYTHING?
NOPE... CHRIST, I'M TIRED.
THE LAST THING YOU WANT TO DO IS GO TO SLEEP. HAVE SOME COFFEE, TAKE A JUMPSTART--
I QUIT JUMPSTART, REMEMBER?
LISTEN, I'VE HAD A HARD DAY'S TELEVISION, AND I WANT TO GO AND SLEEP THE SLEEP OF THE JUST.
OR THE DEAD. FRANKLY, I DON'T CARE.
IF ROYCE PHONES LOOKING FOR HIS FUCKING COLUMN, TELL HIM I'M CONVALESCING AFTER DANGEROUS RESEARCH.

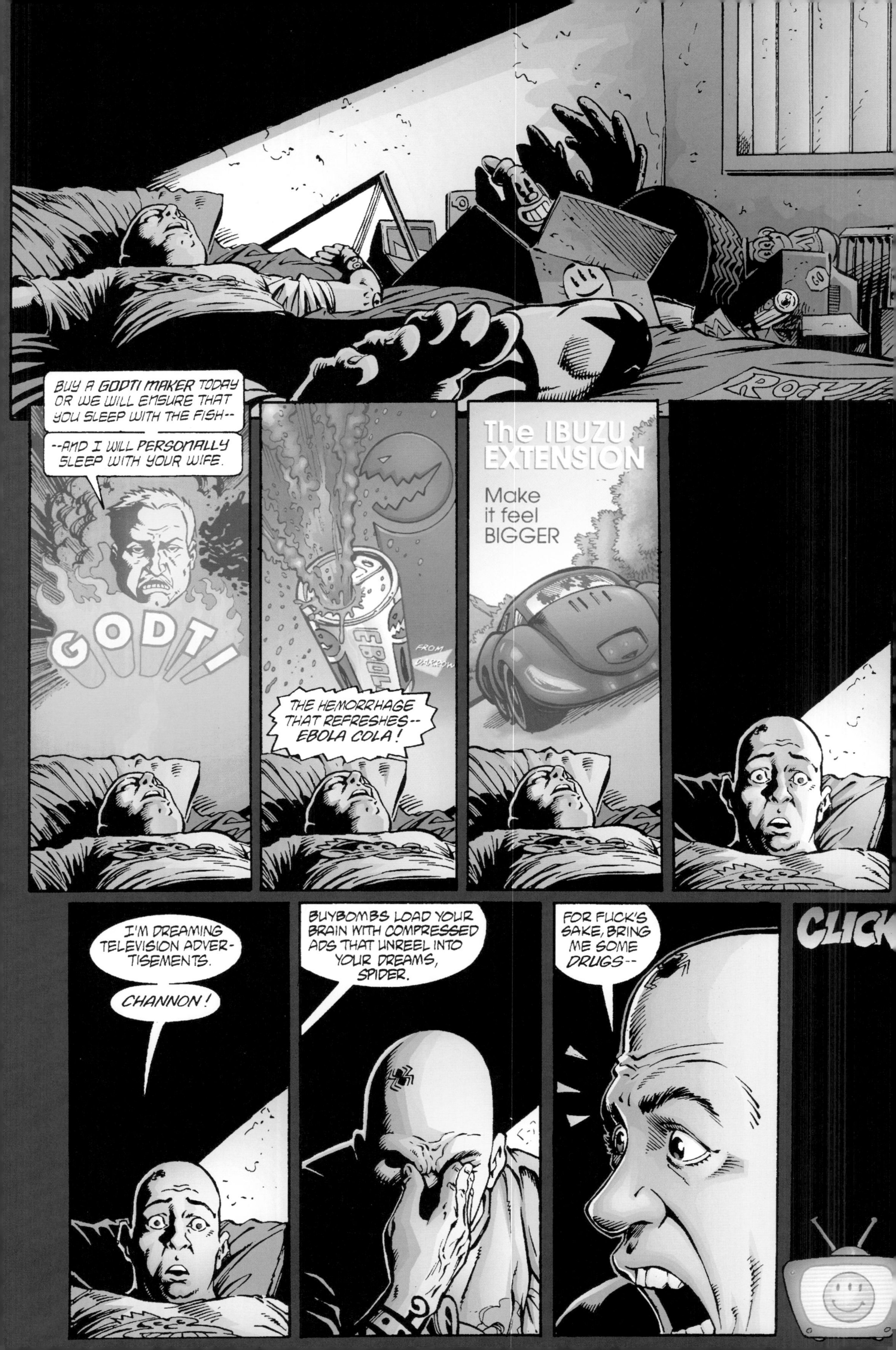
ROCK
BUY A GODTI MAKER TODAY OR WE WILL ENSURE THAT YOU SLEEP WITH THE FISH--
--AND I WILL PERSONALLY SLEEP WITH YOUR WIFE.
GODTI
FROM DARROW
EBOL
THE HEMORRHAGE THAT REFRESHES-- EBOLA COLA!
The IBUZU EXTENSION
Make it feel BIGGER
I'M DREAMING TELEVISION ADVERTISEMENTS.
CHANNON!
BUYBOMBS LOAD YOUR BRAIN WITH COMPRESSED ADS THAT UNREEL INTO YOUR DREAMS, SPIDER.
FOR FUCK'S SAKE, BRING ME SOME DRUGS--
CLICK

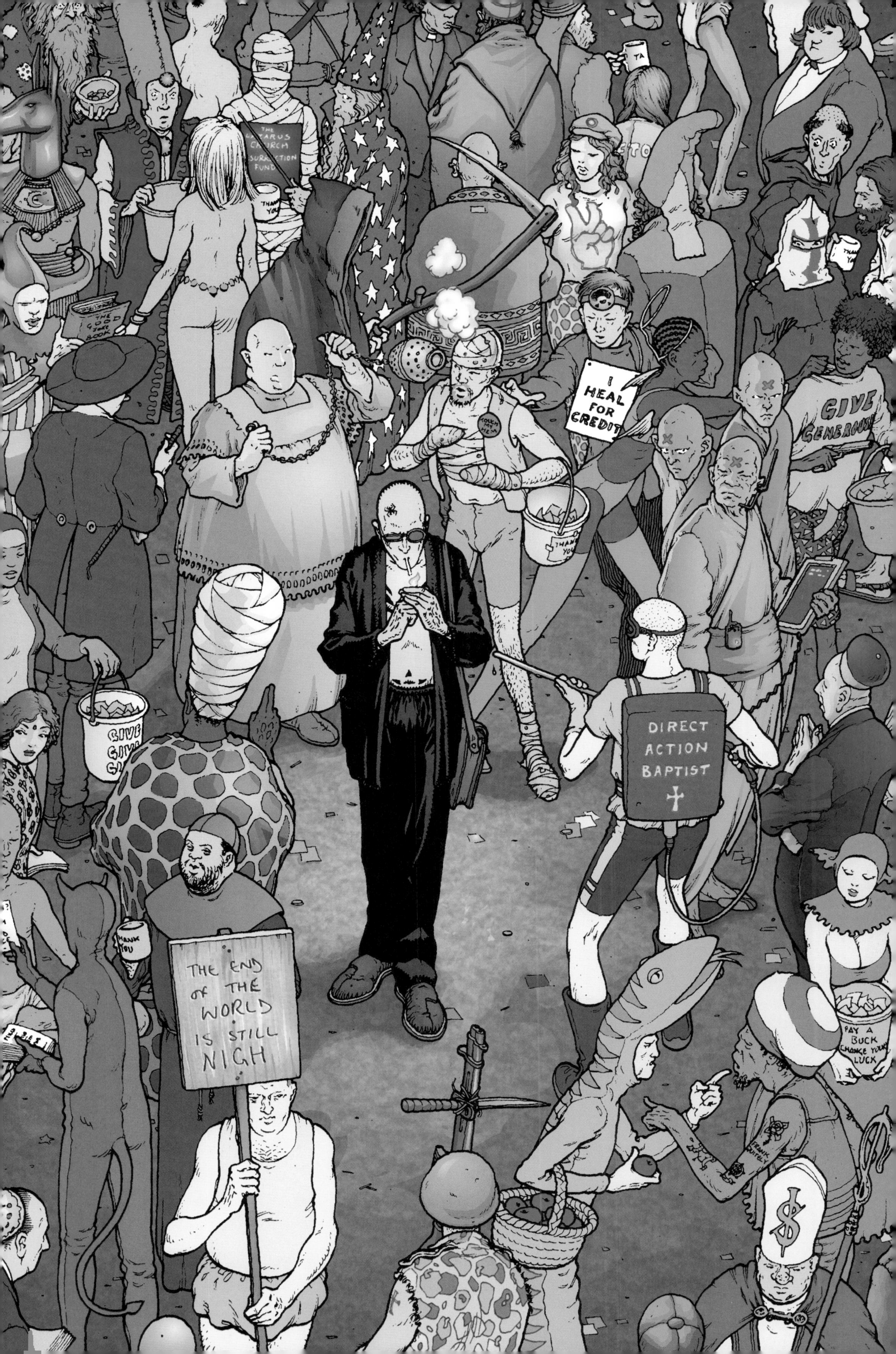
I HEAL FOR CREDIT
DIRECT ACTION BAPTIST
THE END OF THE WORLD IS STILL NIGH
PAY A BUCK CHANGE YOUR LUCK

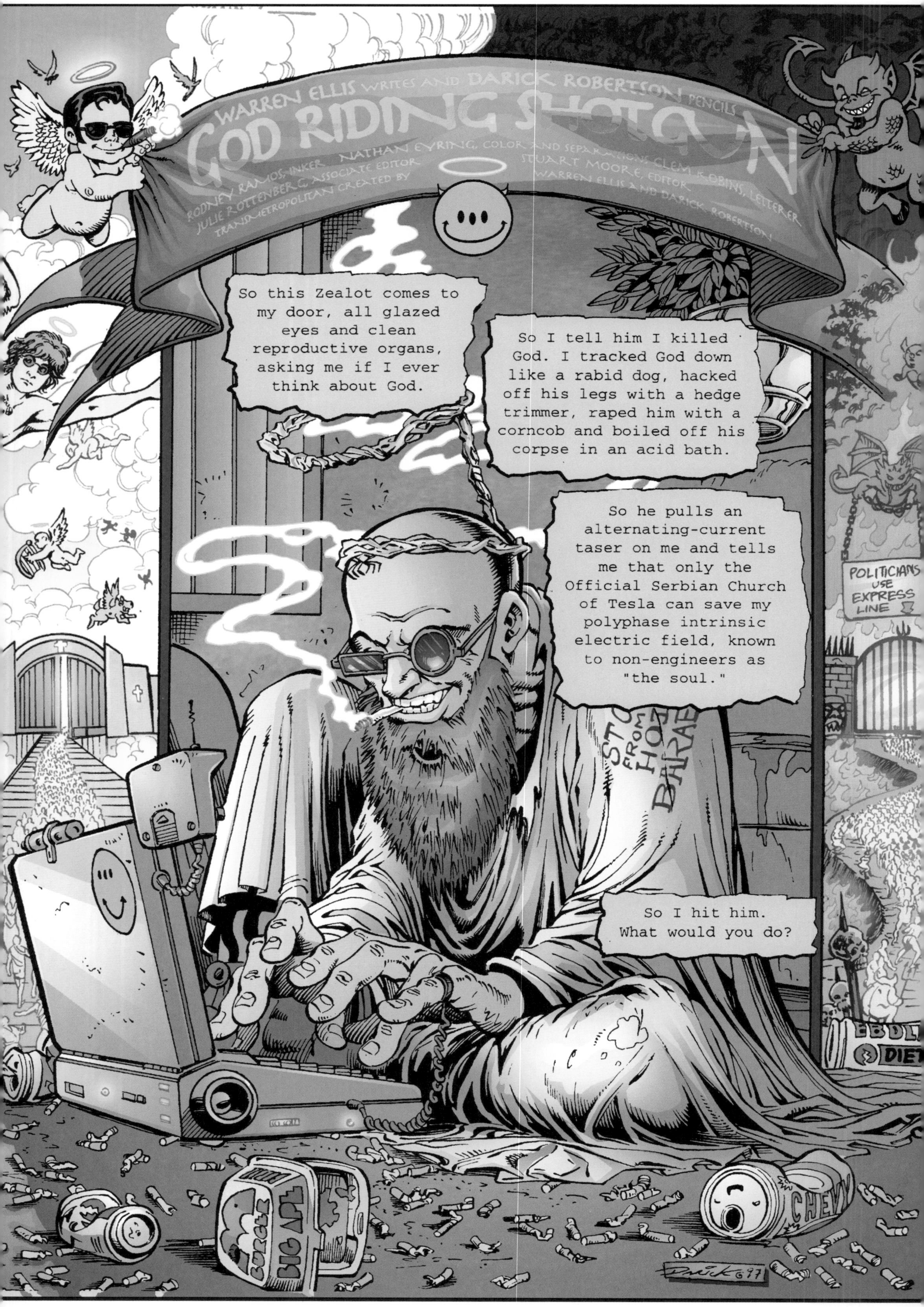
WARREN ELLIS WRITES AND DARICK ROBERTSON PENCILS
GOD RIDING SHOTGUN
RODNEY RAMOS, INKER NATHAN EYRING, COLOR AND SEPARATIONS CLEM ROBINS, LETTERER
JULIE ROTTENBERG, ASSOCIATE EDITOR STUART MOORE, EDITOR
TRANSMETROPOLITAN CREATED BY WARREN ELLIS AND DARICK ROBERTSON
So this Zealot comes to my door, all glazed eyes and clean reproductive organs, asking me if I ever think about God.
So I tell him I killed God. I tracked God down like a rabid dog, hacked off his legs with a hedge trimmer, raped him with a corncob and boiled off his corpse in an acid bath.
So he pulls an alternating-current taser on me and tells me that only the Official Serbian Church of Tesla can save my polyphase intrinsic electric field, known to non-engineers as "the soul."
POLITICIANS USE EXPRESS LINE
So I hit him. What would you do?
BIG APE
BURGER
CHEVY

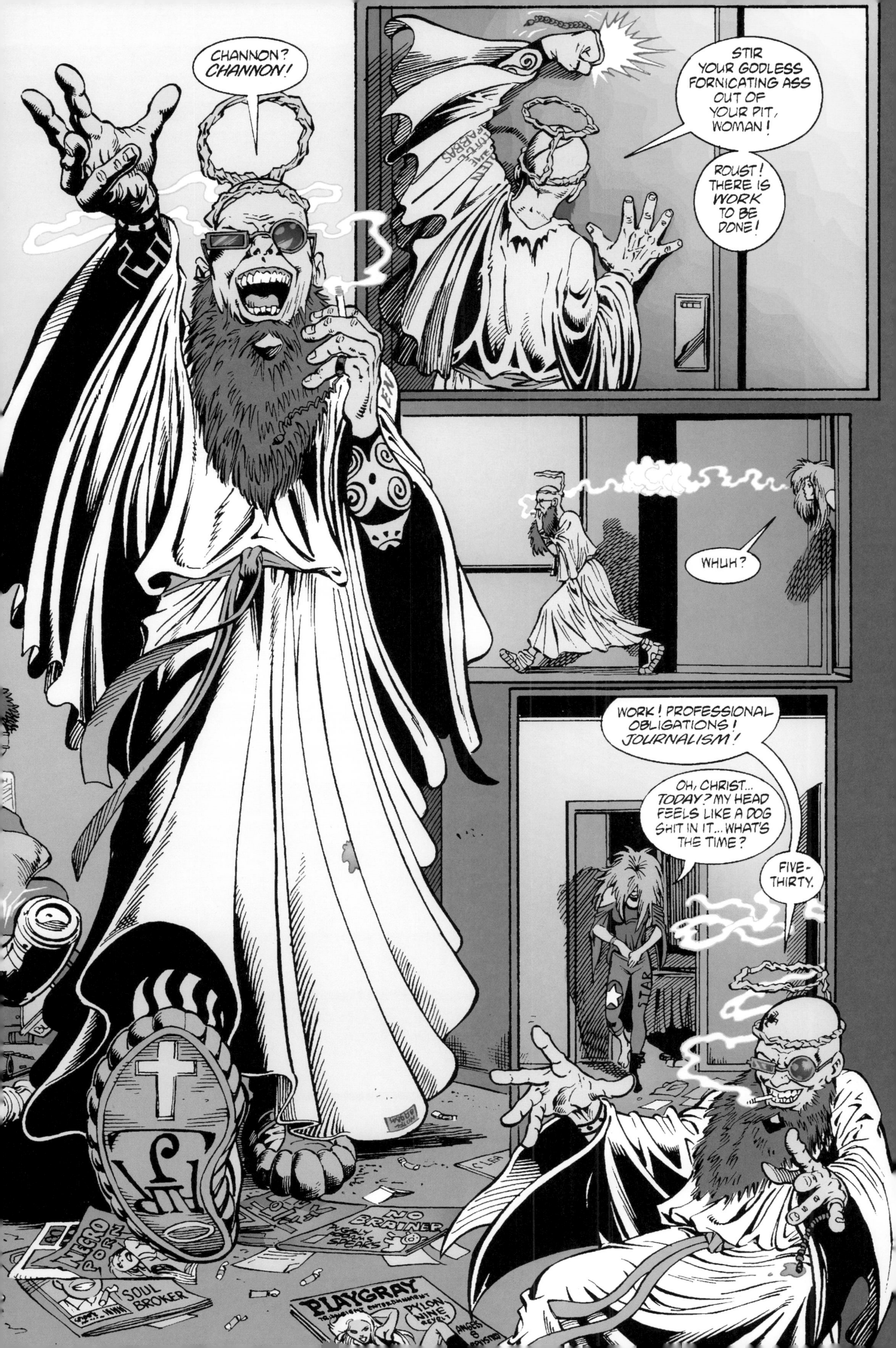
CHANNON? CHANNON!
STIR YOUR GODLESS FORNICATING ASS OUT OF YOUR PIT, WOMAN!
ROUST! THERE IS WORK TO BE DONE!
WHUH?
WORK! PROFESSIONAL OBLIGATIONS! JOURNALISM!
OH, CHRIST... TODAY? MY HEAD FEELS LIKE A DOG SHIT IN IT... WHAT'S THE TIME?
FIVE-THIRTY.
NEGRO PORN
SOUL BROKER
NO BRAINER
PLAYGRAY
PYLON NINE

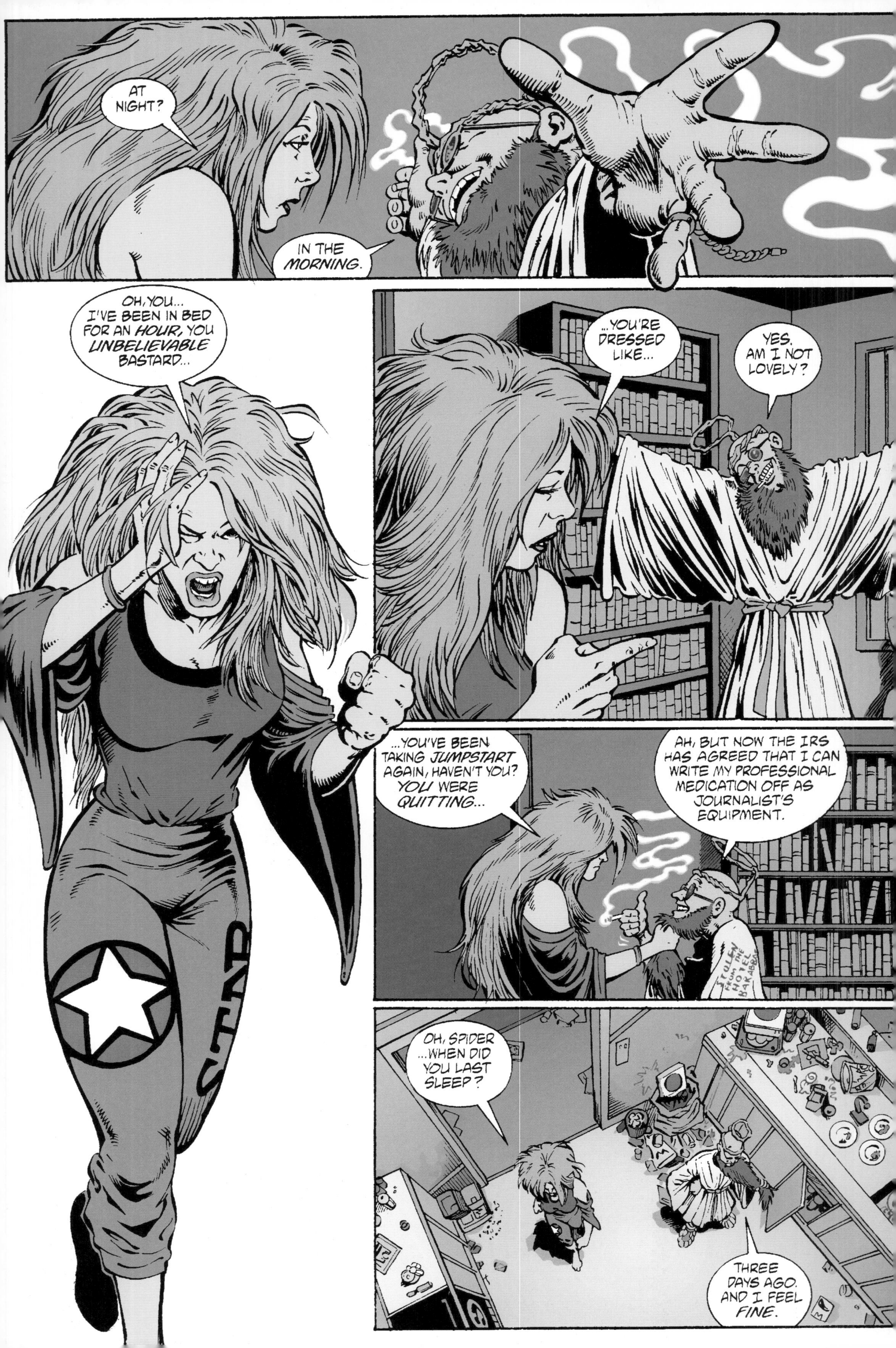
AT NIGHT?
IN THE *MORNING*.
OH, YOU... I'VE BEEN IN BED FOR AN *HOUR*, YOU *UNBELIEVABLE* BASTARD...
...YOU'RE DRESSED LIKE...
YES. AM I NOT LOVELY?
...YOU'VE BEEN TAKING *JUMPSTART* AGAIN, HAVEN'T YOU? *YOU* WERE *QUITTING*...
AH, BUT NOW THE IRS HAS AGREED THAT I CAN WRITE MY PROFESSIONAL MEDICATION OFF AS JOURNALIST'S EQUIPMENT.
OH, SPIDER ...WHEN DID YOU LAST SLEEP?
THREE DAYS AGO. AND I FEEL *FINE*.

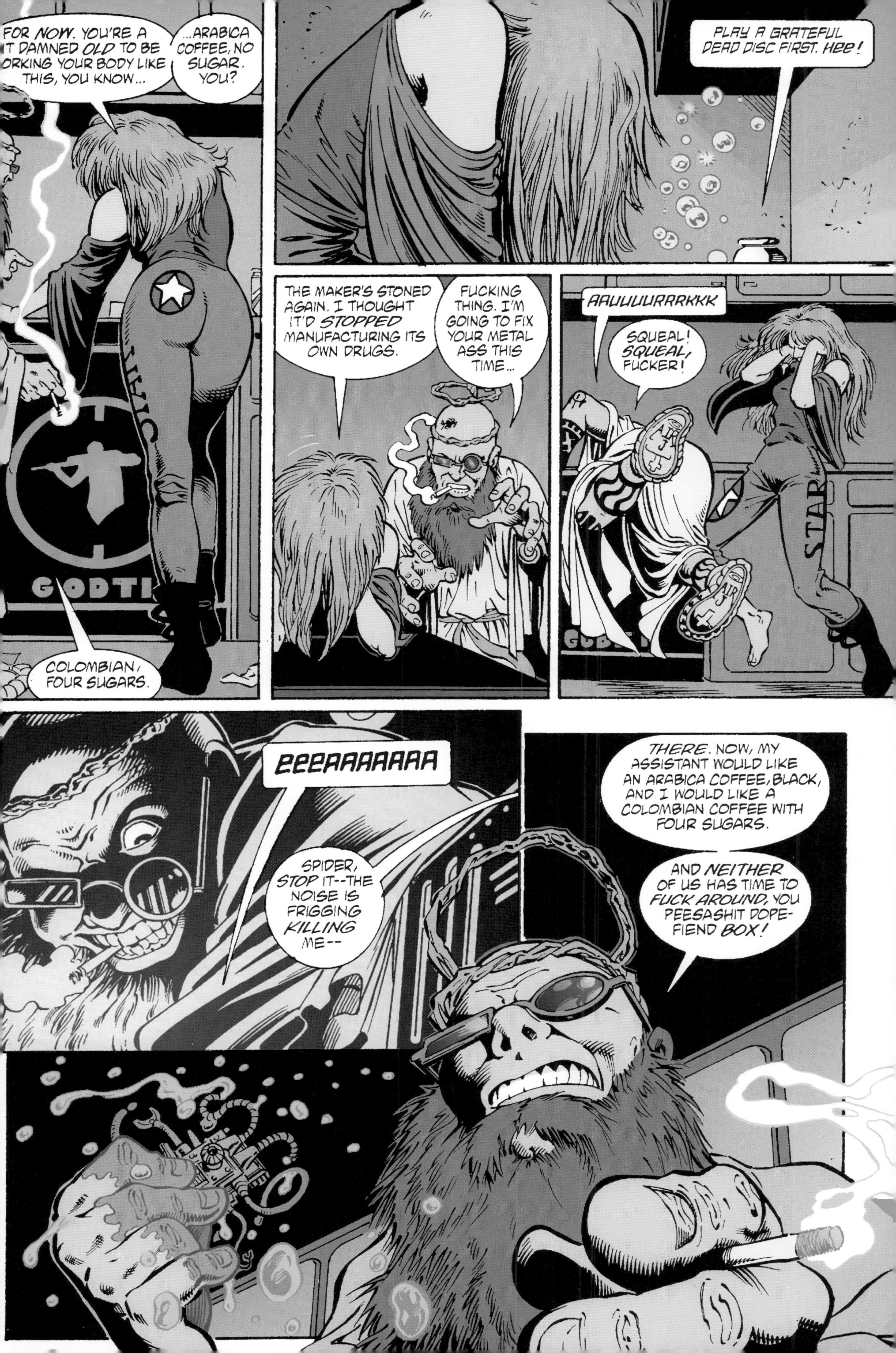
FOR NOW. YOU'RE A BIT DAMNED OLD TO BE WORKING YOUR BODY LIKE THIS, YOU KNOW...
...ARABICA COFFEE, NO SUGAR. YOU?
COLOMBIAN, FOUR SUGARS.
GODTI
PLAY A GRATEFUL DEAD DISC FIRST. HEE!
THE MAKER'S STONED AGAIN. I THOUGHT IT'D STOPPED MANUFACTURING ITS OWN DRUGS.
FUCKING THING. I'M GOING TO FIX YOUR METAL ASS THIS TIME...
AAUUUURARKKK
SQUEAL! SQUEAL, FUCKER!
STAR
EEEAAAAAAAA
SPIDER, STOP IT--THE NOISE IS FRIGGING KILLING ME--
THERE. NOW, MY ASSISTANT WOULD LIKE AN ARABICA COFFEE, BLACK, AND I WOULD LIKE A COLOMBIAN COFFEE WITH FOUR SUGARS.
AND NEITHER OF US HAS TIME TO FUCK AROUND, YOU PEESASHIT DOPE-FIEND BOX!

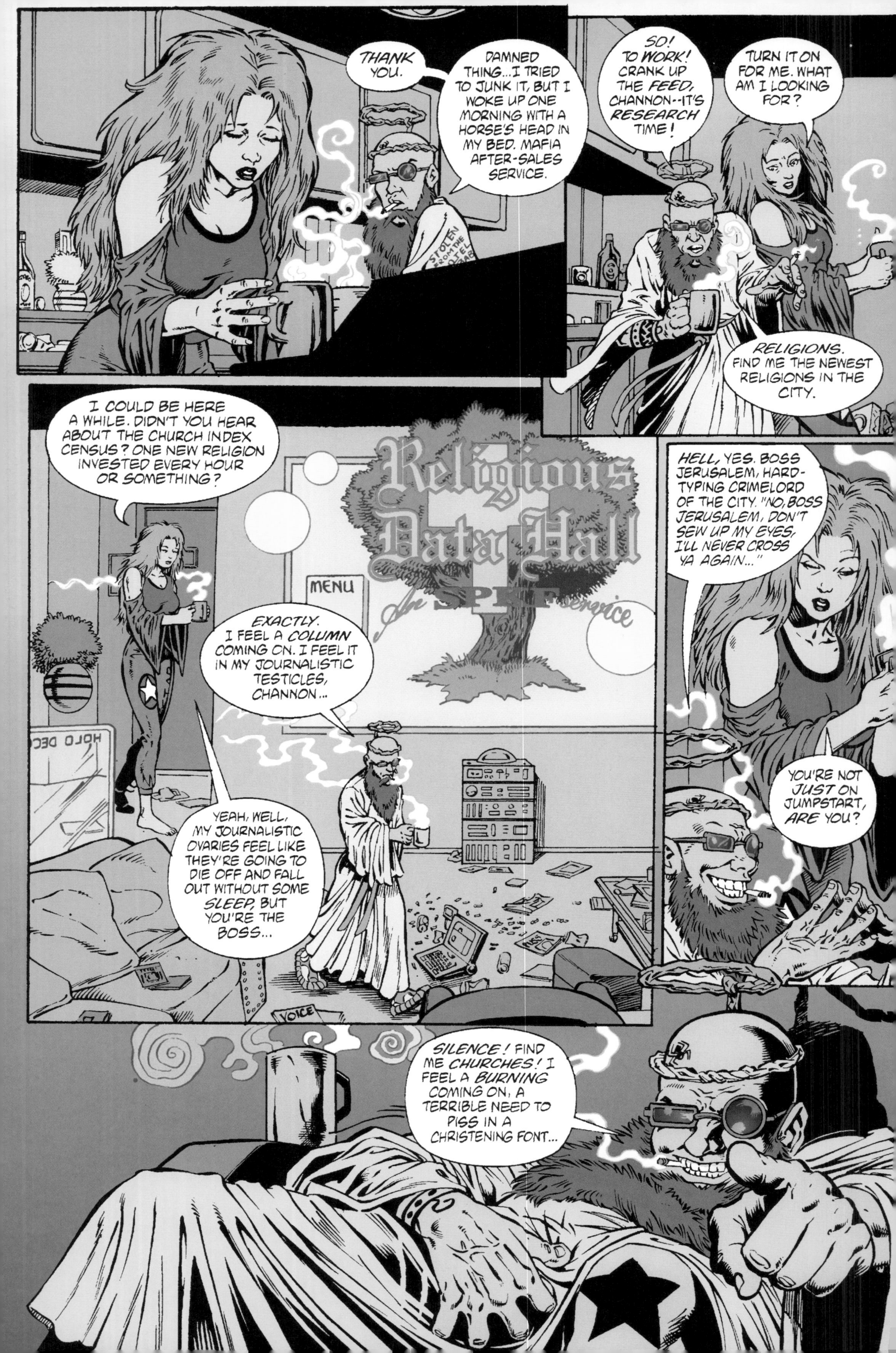
THANK YOU.
DAMNED THING...I TRIED TO JUNK IT, BUT I WOKE UP ONE MORNING WITH A HORSE'S HEAD IN MY BED. MAFIA AFTER-SALES SERVICE.
STOLEN FROM THE HOTEL
SO! TO WORK! CRANK UP THE FEED, CHANNON--IT'S RESEARCH TIME!
TURN IT ON FOR ME. WHAT AM I LOOKING FOR?
RELIGIONS. FIND ME THE NEWEST RELIGIONS IN THE CITY.
I COULD BE HERE A WHILE. DIDN'T YOU HEAR ABOUT THE CHURCH INDEX CENSUS? ONE NEW RELIGION INVESTED EVERY HOUR OR SOMETHING?
Religious Data Hall
MENU
EXACTLY. I FEEL A COLUMN COMING ON. I FEEL IT IN MY JOURNALISTIC TESTICLES, CHANNON...
YEAH, WELL, MY JOURNALISTIC OVARIES FEEL LIKE THEY'RE GOING TO DIE OFF AND FALL OUT WITHOUT SOME SLEEP, BUT YOU'RE THE BOSS...
VOICE
HELL, YES. BOSS JERUSALEM, HARD-TYPING CRIMELORD OF THE CITY. "NO, BOSS JERUSALEM, DON'T SEW UP MY EYES, I'LL NEVER CROSS YA AGAIN..."
YOU'RE NOT JUST ON JUMPSTART, ARE YOU?
SILENCE! FIND ME CHURCHES! I FEEL A BURNING COMING ON, A TERRIBLE NEED TO PISS IN A CHRISTENING FONT...

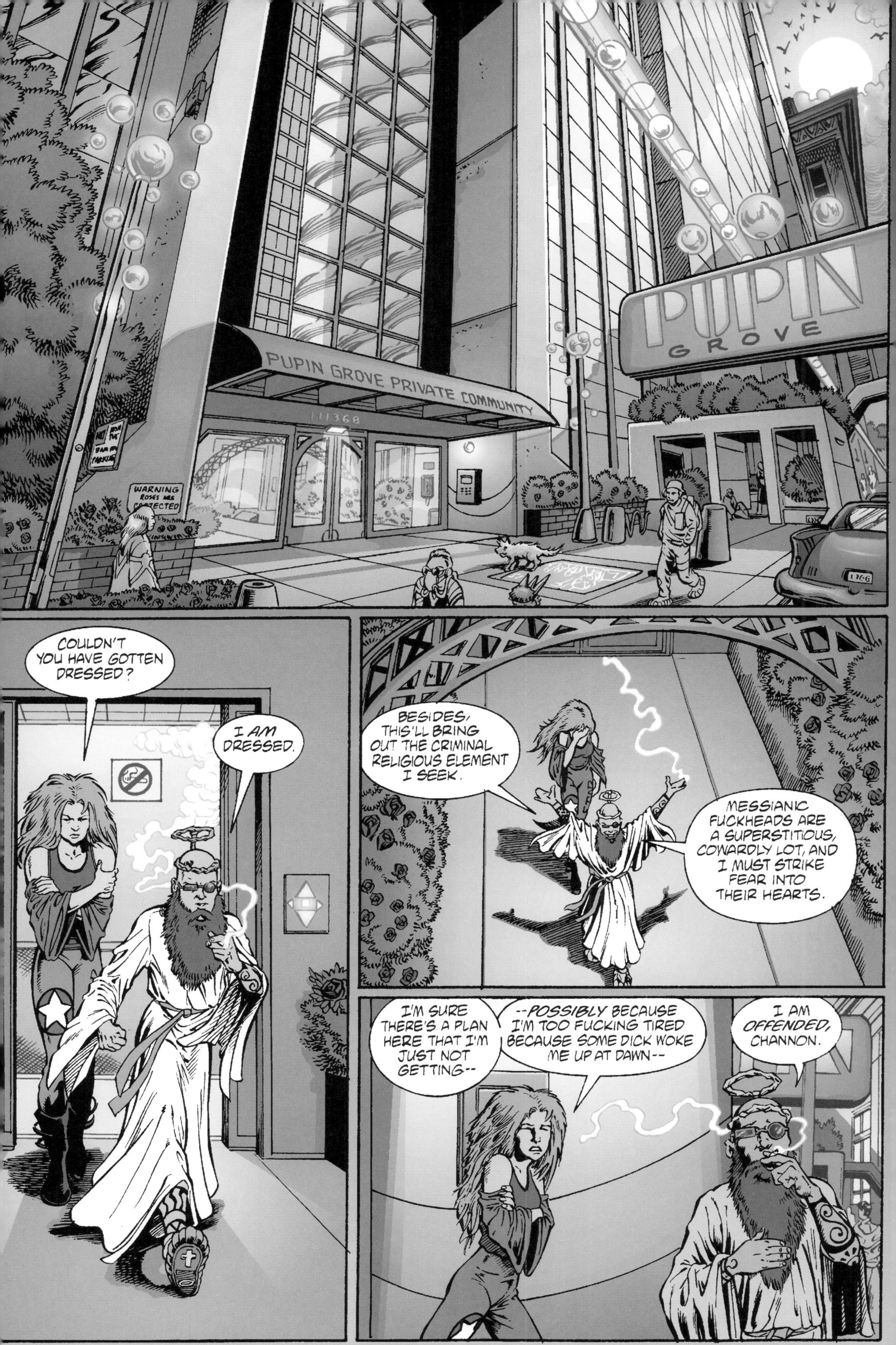

PUPIN GROVE PRIVATE COMMUNITY
111368
PUPIN GROVE
WARNING ROSES ARE PROTECTED
COULDN'T YOU HAVE GOTTEN DRESSED?
I AM DRESSED.
BESIDES, THIS'LL BRING OUT THE CRIMINAL RELIGIOUS ELEMENT I SEEK.
MESSIANIC FUCKHEADS ARE A SUPERSTITIOUS, COWARDLY LOT, AND I MUST STRIKE FEAR INTO THEIR HEARTS.
I'M SURE THERE'S A PLAN HERE THAT I'M JUST NOT GETTING--
--POSSIBLY BECAUSE I'M TOO FUCKING TIRED BECAUSE SOME DICK WOKE ME UP AT DAWN--
I AM OFFENDED, CHANNON.

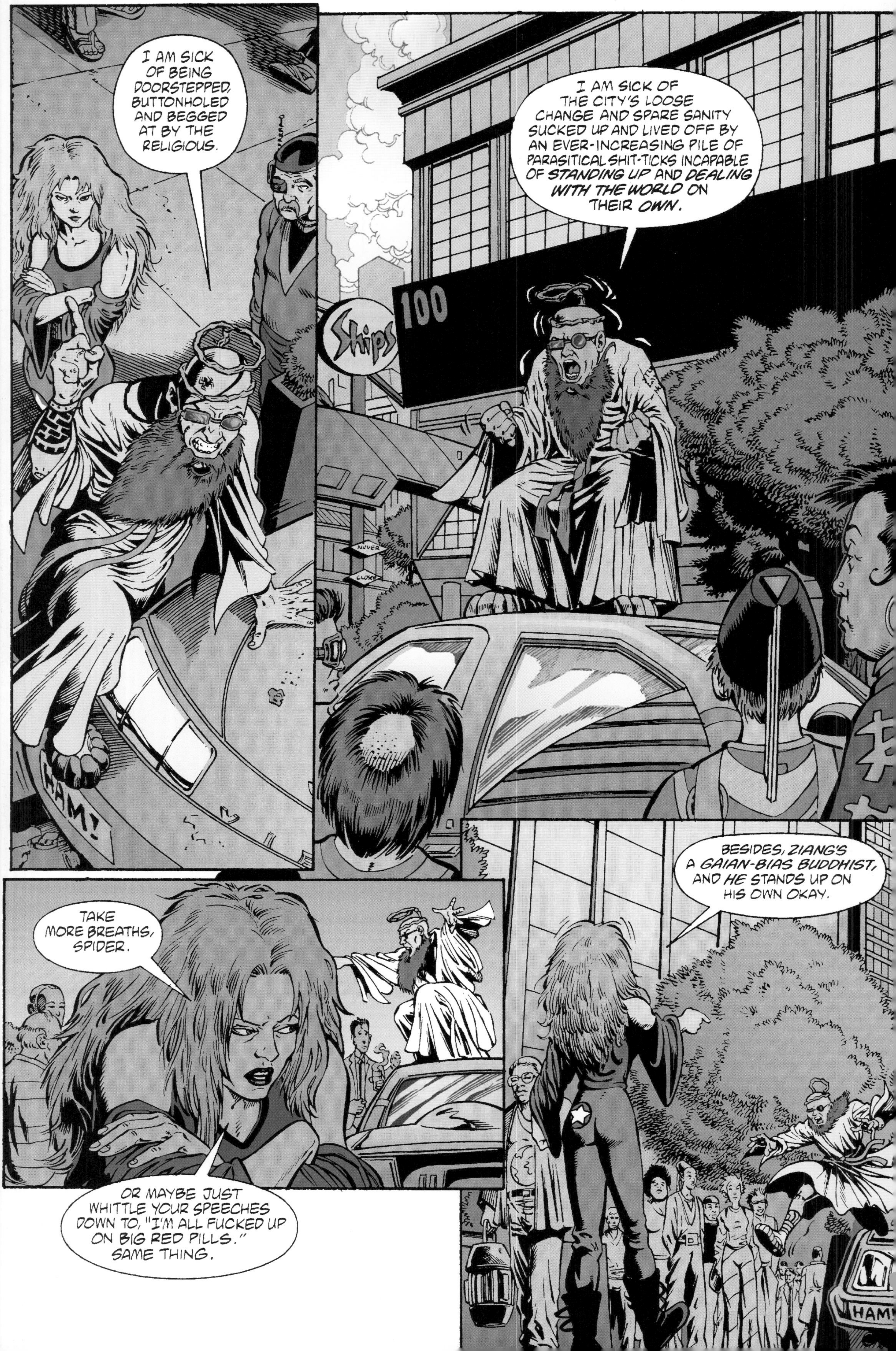
I AM SICK OF BEING DOORSTEPPED, BUTTONHOLED AND BEGGED AT BY THE RELIGIOUS.
I AM SICK OF THE CITY'S LOOSE CHANGE AND SPARE SANITY SUCKED UP AND LIVED OFF BY AN EVER-INCREASING PILE OF PARASITICAL SHIT-TICKS INCAPABLE OF STANDING UP AND DEALING WITH THE WORLD ON THEIR OWN.
100
Ships
HAM!
TAKE MORE BREATHS, SPIDER.
OR MAYBE JUST WHITTLE YOUR SPEECHES DOWN TO, "I'M ALL FUCKED UP ON BIG RED PILLS." SAME THING.
BESIDES, ZIANG'S A GAIAN-BIAS BUDDHIST, AND HE STANDS UP ON HIS OWN OKAY.

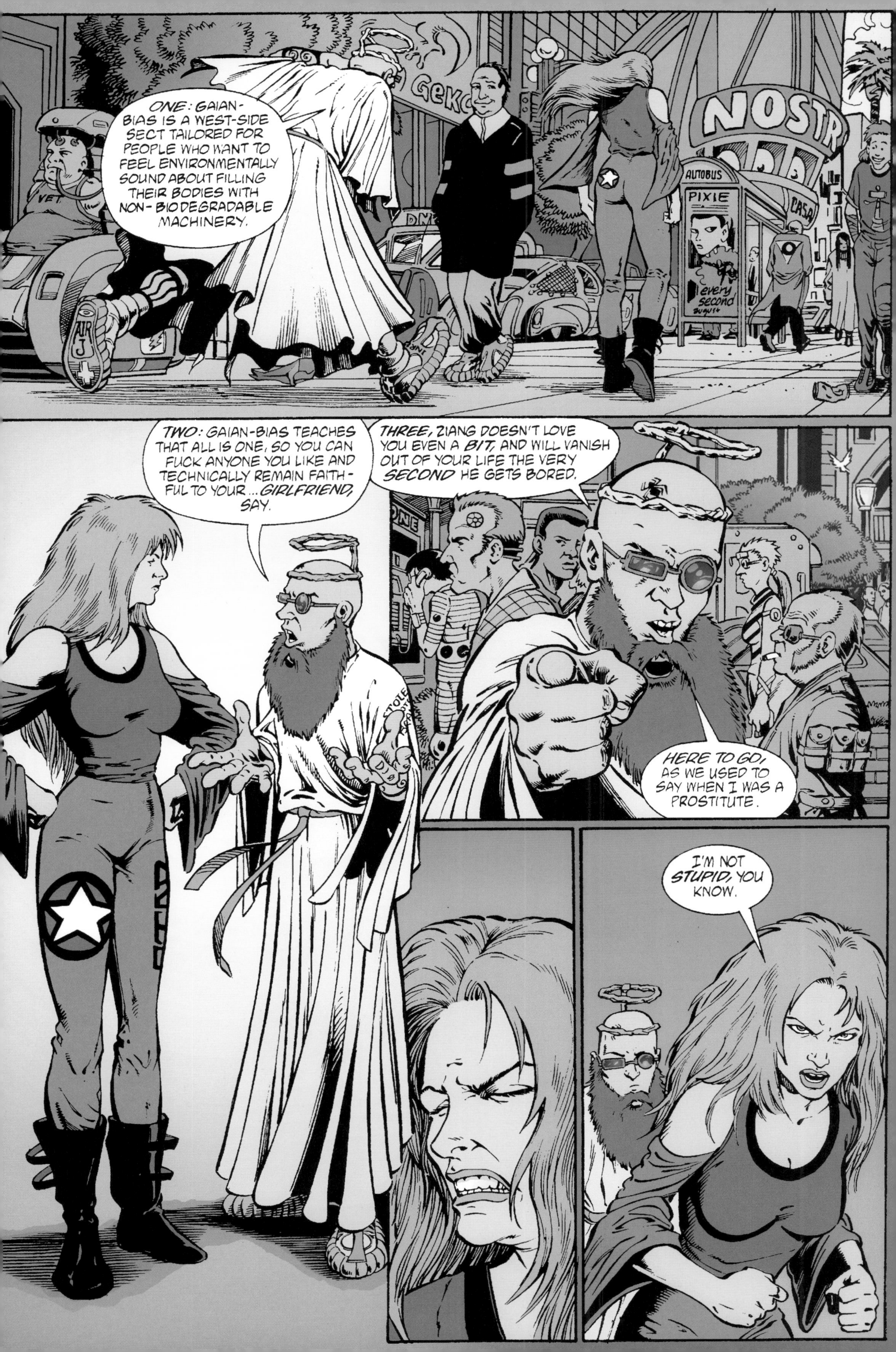

Gekc
NOSTR
AUTOBUS
PIXIE
every second
CASA
VET
AIR J
ONE: GAIAN-BIAS IS A WEST-SIDE SECT TAILORED FOR PEOPLE WHO WANT TO FEEL ENVIRONMENTALLY SOUND ABOUT FILLING THEIR BODIES WITH NON-BIODEGRADABLE MACHINERY.
TWO: GAIAN-BIAS TEACHES THAT ALL IS ONE, SO YOU CAN FUCK ANYONE YOU LIKE AND TECHNICALLY REMAIN FAITH-FUL TO YOUR ...GIRLFRIEND, SAY.
THREE, ZIANG DOESN'T LOVE YOU EVEN A BIT, AND WILL VANISH OUT OF YOUR LIFE THE VERY SECOND HE GETS BORED.
HERE TO GO, AS WE USED TO SAY WHEN I WAS A PROSTITUTE.
I'M NOT STUPID, YOU KNOW.

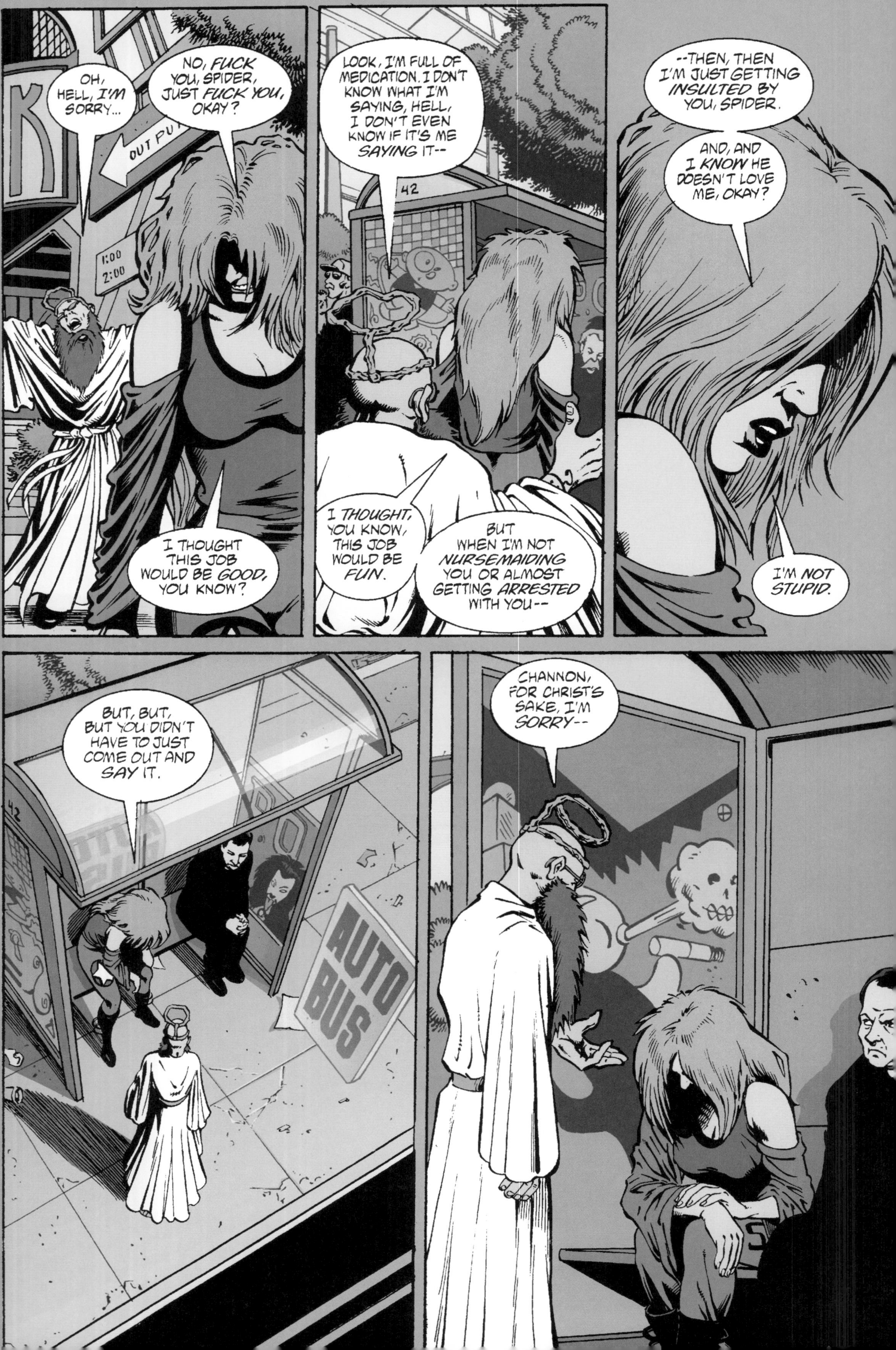
OH, HELL, I'M SORRY...
NO, FUCK YOU, SPIDER, JUST FUCK YOU, OKAY?
OUT PU
1:00
2:00
I THOUGHT THIS JOB WOULD BE GOOD, YOU KNOW?
LOOK, I'M FULL OF MEDICATION. I DON'T KNOW WHAT I'M SAYING, HELL, I DON'T EVEN KNOW IF IT'S ME SAYING IT--
42
I THOUGHT, YOU KNOW, THIS JOB WOULD BE FUN.
BUT WHEN I'M NOT NURSEMAIDING YOU OR ALMOST GETTING ARRESTED WITH YOU--
--THEN, THEN I'M JUST GETTING INSULTED BY YOU, SPIDER.
AND, AND I KNOW HE DOESN'T LOVE ME, OKAY?
I'M NOT STUPID.
BUT, BUT, BUT YOU DIDN'T HAVE TO JUST COME OUT AND SAY IT.
42
AUTO BUS
CHANNON, FOR CHRIST'S SAKE, I'M SORRY--

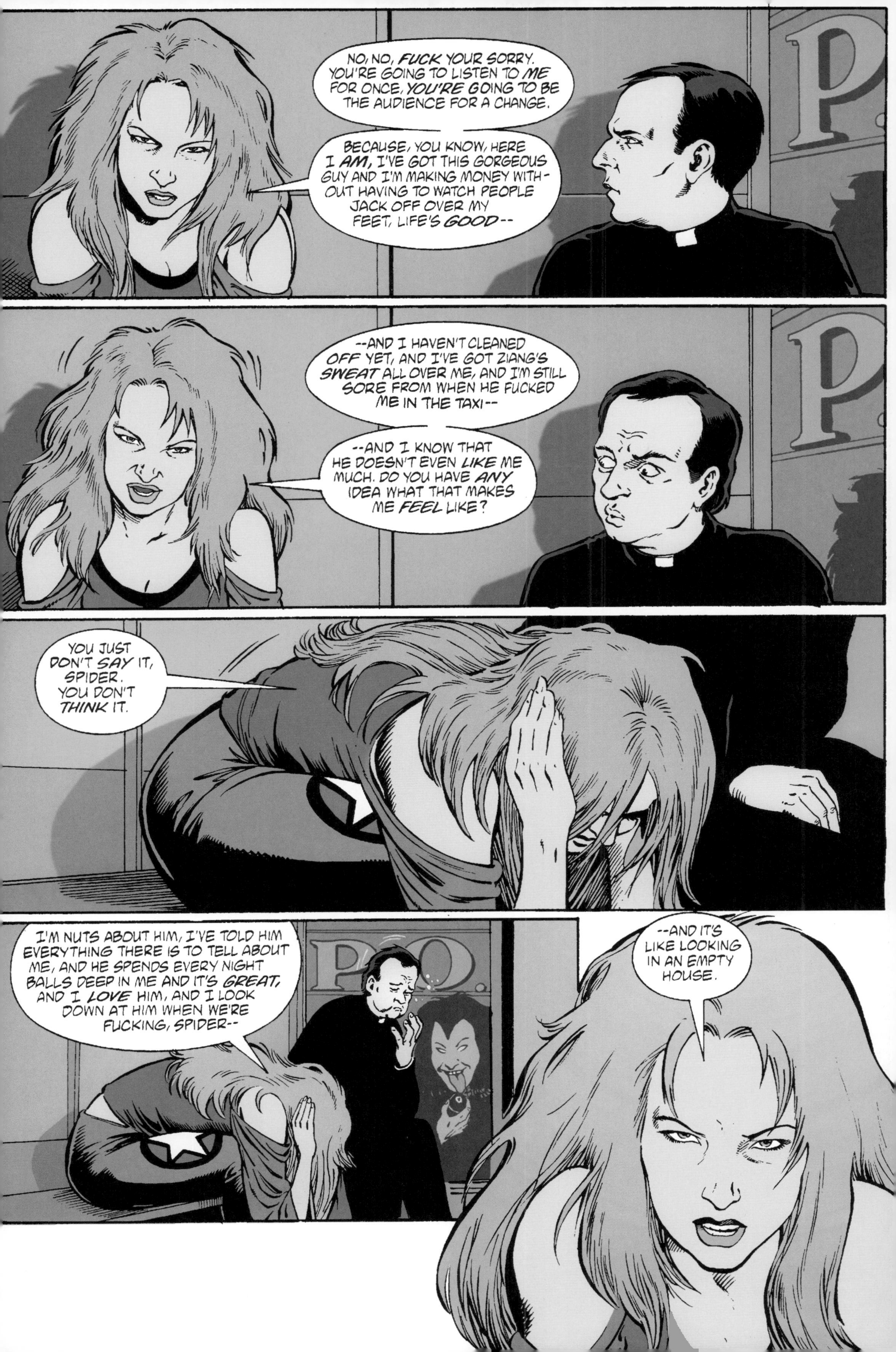
NO, NO, FUCK YOUR SORRY. YOU'RE GOING TO LISTEN TO ME FOR ONCE, YOU'RE GOING TO BE THE AUDIENCE FOR A CHANGE.
BECAUSE, YOU KNOW, HERE I AM, I'VE GOT THIS GORGEOUS GUY AND I'M MAKING MONEY WITH-OUT HAVING TO WATCH PEOPLE JACK OFF OVER MY FEET, LIFE'S GOOD--
--AND I HAVEN'T CLEANED OFF YET, AND I'VE GOT ZIANG'S SWEAT ALL OVER ME, AND I'M STILL SORE FROM WHEN HE FUCKED ME IN THE TAXI--
--AND I KNOW THAT HE DOESN'T EVEN LIKE ME MUCH. DO YOU HAVE ANY IDEA WHAT THAT MAKES ME FEEL LIKE?
YOU JUST DON'T SAY IT, SPIDER. YOU DON'T THINK IT.
I'M NUTS ABOUT HIM, I'VE TOLD HIM EVERYTHING THERE IS TO TELL ABOUT ME, AND HE SPENDS EVERY NIGHT BALLS DEEP IN ME AND IT'S GREAT, AND I LOVE HIM, AND I LOOK DOWN AT HIM WHEN WE'RE FUCKING, SPIDER--
--AND IT'S LIKE LOOKING IN AN EMPTY HOUSE.

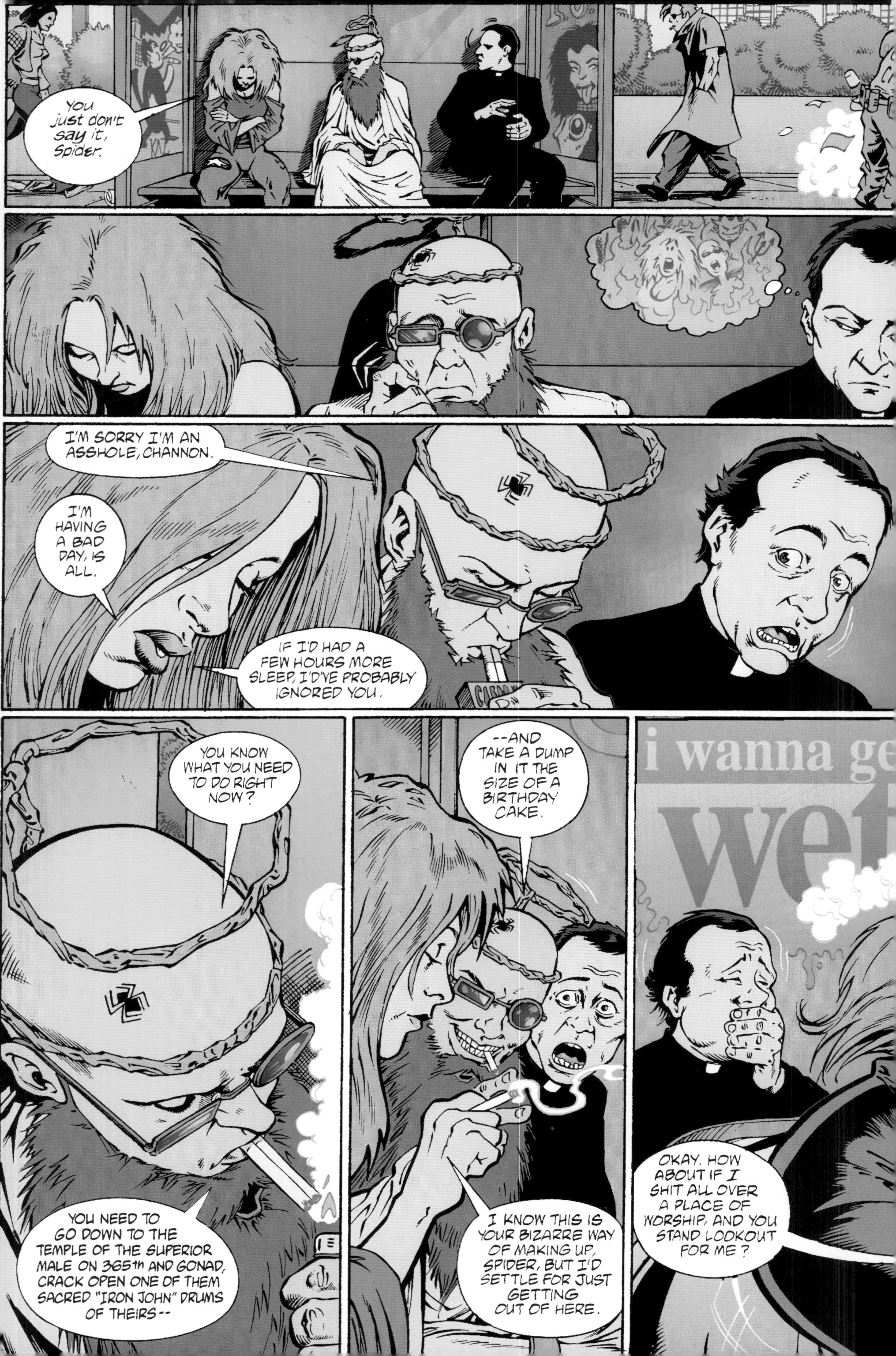
You just don't say it, Spider.
I'M SORRY I'M AN ASSHOLE, CHANNON.
I'M HAVING A BAD DAY, IS ALL.
IF I'D HAD A FEW HOURS MORE SLEEP, I'D'VE PROBABLY IGNORED YOU.
YOU KNOW WHAT YOU NEED TO DO RIGHT NOW?
YOU NEED TO GO DOWN TO THE TEMPLE OF THE SUPERIOR MALE ON 365th AND GONAD, CRACK OPEN ONE OF THEM SACRED "IRON JOHN" DRUMS OF THEIRS--
--AND TAKE A DUMP IN IT THE SIZE OF A BIRTHDAY CAKE.
I KNOW THIS IS YOUR BIZARRE WAY OF MAKING UP, SPIDER, BUT I'D SETTLE FOR JUST GETTING OUT OF HERE.
i wanna ge
wet
OKAY. HOW ABOUT IF I SHIT ALL OVER A PLACE OF WORSHIP, AND YOU STAND LOOKOUT FOR ME?

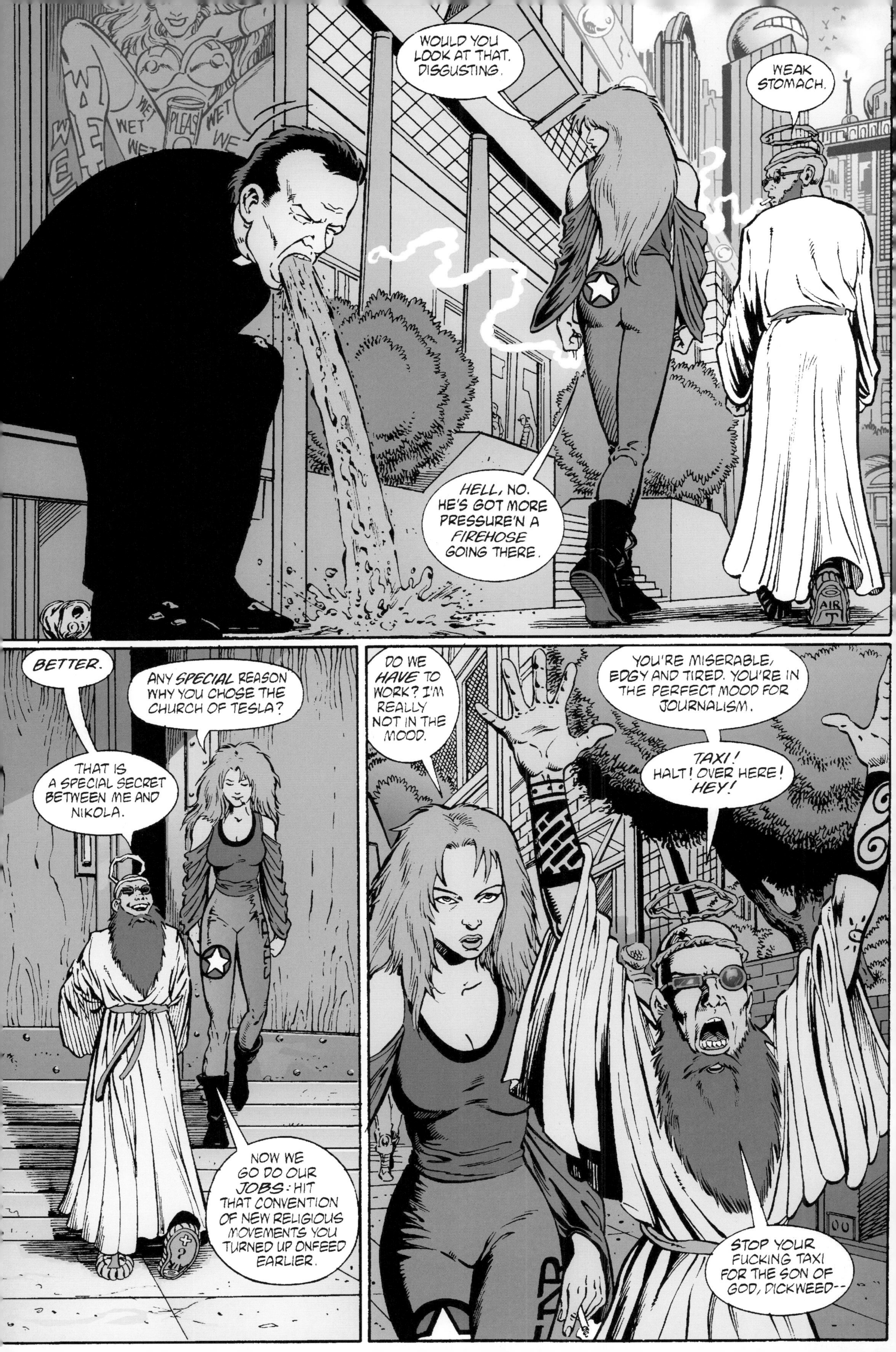
WOULD YOU LOOK AT THAT. DISGUSTING.
WEAK STOMACH.
HELL, NO. HE'S GOT MORE PRESSURE'N A FIREHOSE GOING THERE.
BETTER.
ANY SPECIAL REASON WHY YOU CHOSE THE CHURCH OF TESLA?
THAT IS A SPECIAL SECRET BETWEEN ME AND NIKOLA.
NOW WE GO DO OUR JOBS: HIT THAT CONVENTION OF NEW RELIGIOUS MOVEMENTS YOU TURNED UP ONFEED EARLIER.
DO WE HAVE TO WORK? I'M REALLY NOT IN THE MOOD.
YOU'RE MISERABLE, EDGY AND TIRED. YOU'RE IN THE PERFECT MOOD FOR JOURNALISM.
TAXI! HALT! OVER HERE! HEY!
STOP YOUR FUCKING TAXI FOR THE SON OF GOD, DICKWEED--

the little baby jesus is watching you all
PLANETLAR
Convert Here
We were grown by alien love gardeners
FUCK THE HOLY GUT WOUND OF ST. MARC
AT BOOTH #7474
FRZBE cometh!
Meet her at Booth
THOR NEEDS VIRGINS.
god loves guns. and so should you.
ERZULIE GE-ROUGE WEEPS FOR US
JESUS
The Truth is encoded in "The Nanny" reruns.
Watch The History Channel
The Beautician and the Beast
Do you want to eat Peyotl and Human Flesh on the path to Spiritual Fulfillment? Or just for the hell of it? Join the Ancient Cult of Anaszasi

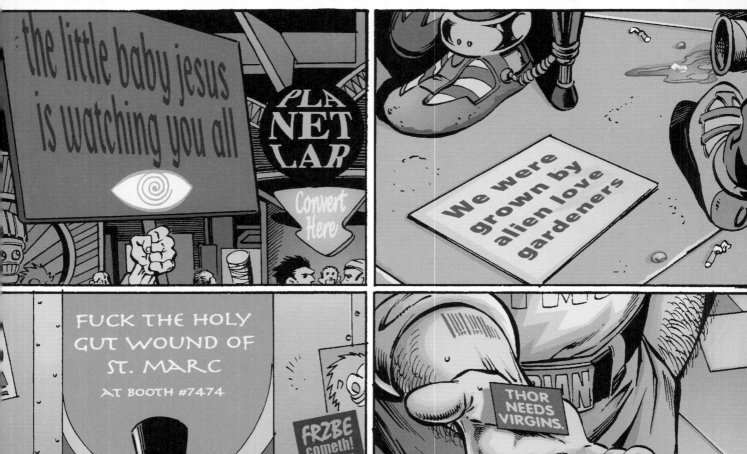

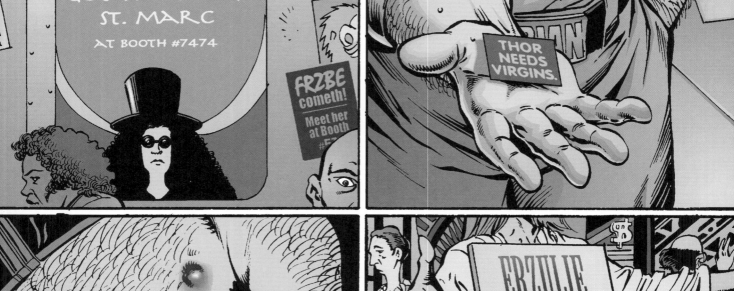

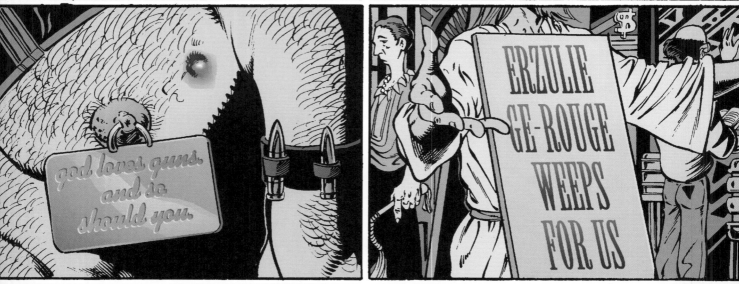

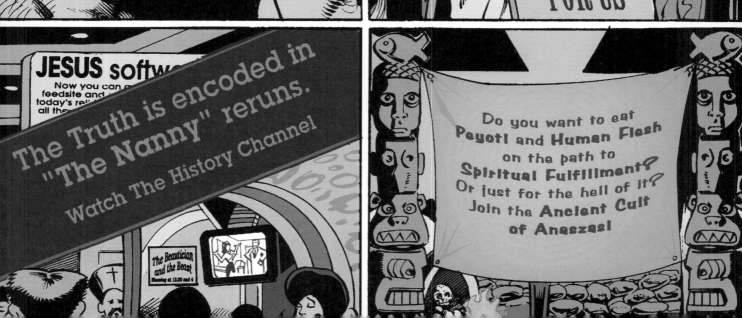

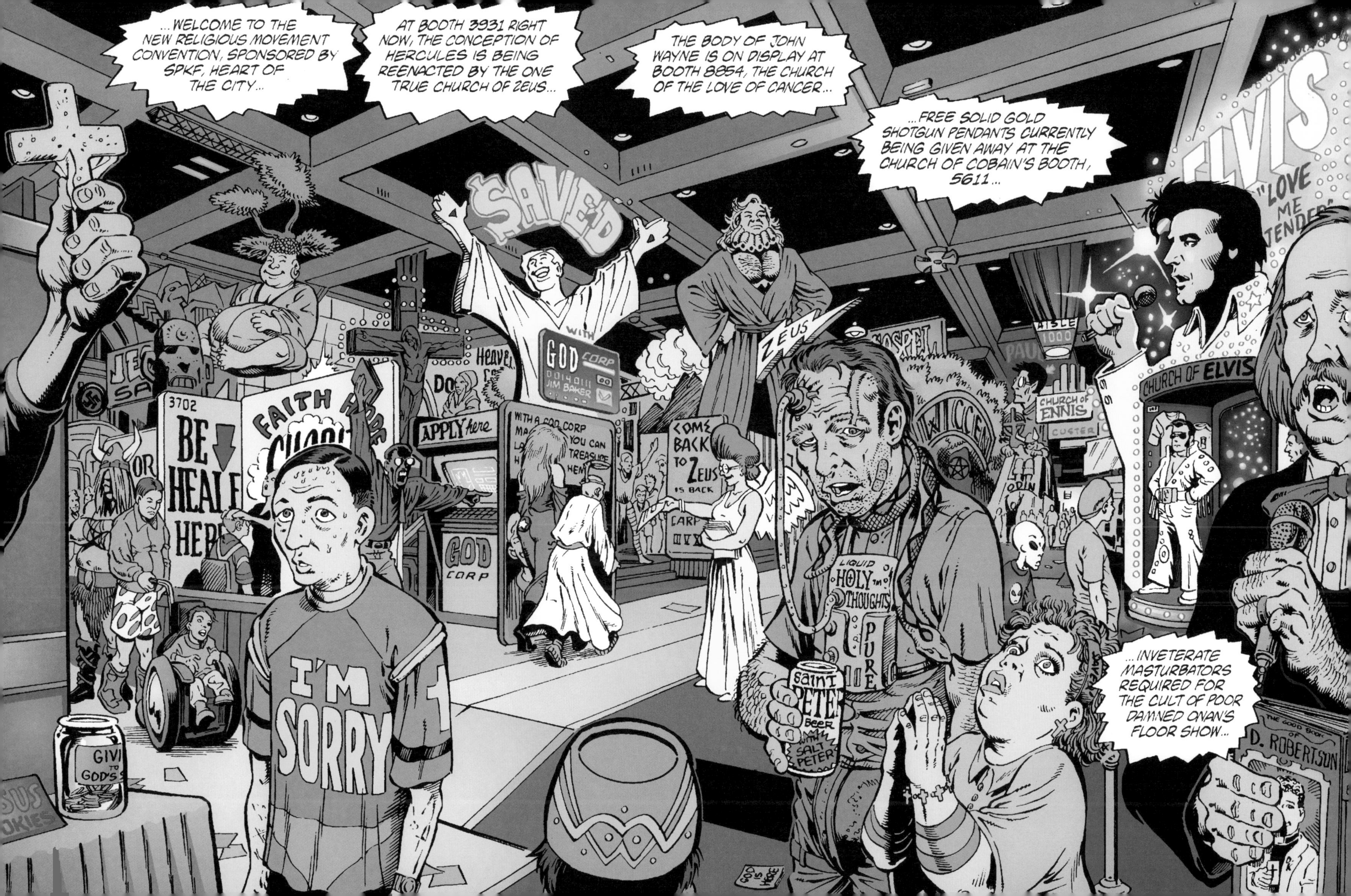
...WELCOME TO THE NEW RELIGIOUS MOVEMENT CONVENTION, SPONSORED BY SPKF, HEART OF THE CITY...
AT BOOTH 3931 RIGHT NOW, THE CONCEPTION OF HERCULES IS BEING REENACTED BY THE ONE TRUE CHURCH OF ZEUS...
THE BODY OF JOHN WAYNE IS ON DISPLAY AT BOOTH 8854, THE CHURCH OF THE LOVE OF CANCER...
...FREE SOLID GOLD SHOTGUN PENDANTS CURRENTLY BEING GIVEN AWAY AT THE CHURCH OF COBAIN'S BOOTH, 5611...
...INVETERATE MASTURBATORS REQUIRED FOR THE CULT OF POOR DAMNED ONAN'S FLOOR SHOW...
SAVED
WITH GOD CORP
JIM BAKER
ZEUS
ELVIS
"LOVE ME TENDER"
CHURCH OF ELVIS
AISLE 1000
CHURCH OF ENNIS
CUSTER
GOSPEL
3702
BE HEALE HERE
FAITH
APPLY here
WITH A GOD CORP
YOU CAN TREASURE
COME BACK TO ZEUS IS BACK
GOD CORP
LIQUID HOLY THOUGHTS
PURE
SAINT PETER BEER WITH SALT PETER
I'M SORRY
GIVE TO GOD'S
GOD IS HERE
THE GOOD BOOK OF D. ROBERTSON

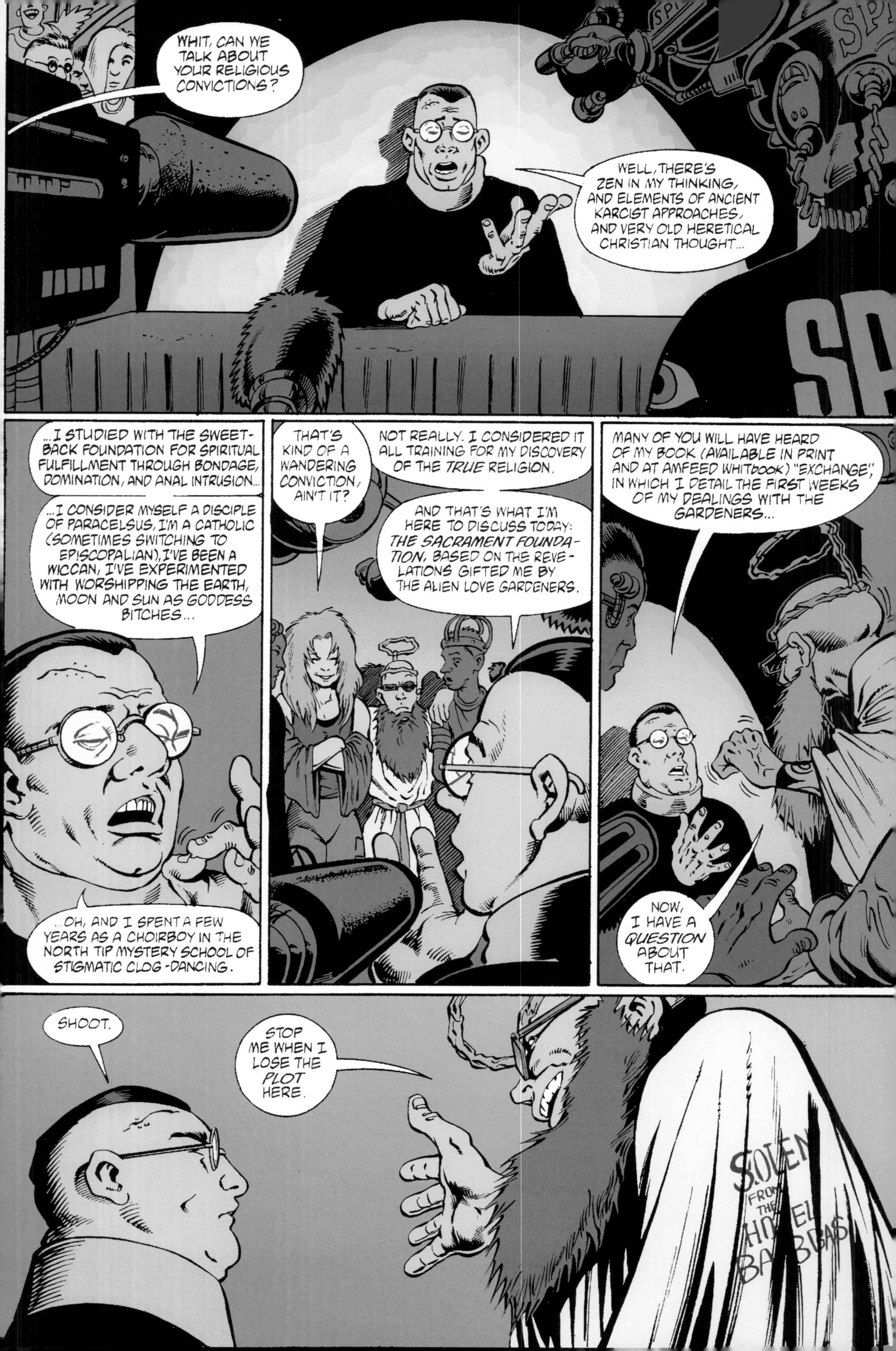
WHIT, CAN WE TALK ABOUT YOUR RELIGIOUS CONVICTIONS?
WELL, THERE'S ZEN IN MY THINKING, AND ELEMENTS OF ANCIENT KARCIST APPROACHES, AND VERY OLD HERETICAL CHRISTIAN THOUGHT...
...I STUDIED WITH THE SWEET-BACK FOUNDATION FOR SPIRITUAL FULFILLMENT THROUGH BONDAGE, DOMINATION, AND ANAL INTRUSION...
...I CONSIDER MYSELF A DISCIPLE OF PARACELSUS, I'M A CATHOLIC (SOMETIMES SWITCHING TO EPISCOPALIAN), I'VE BEEN A WICCAN, I'VE EXPERIMENTED WITH WORSHIPPING THE EARTH, MOON AND SUN AS GODDESS BITCHES...
...OH, AND I SPENT A FEW YEARS AS A CHOIRBOY IN THE NORTH TIP MYSTERY SCHOOL OF STIGMATIC CLOG-DANCING.
THAT'S KIND OF A WANDERING CONVICTION, AIN'T IT?
NOT REALLY. I CONSIDERED IT ALL TRAINING FOR MY DISCOVERY OF THE TRUE RELIGION.
AND THAT'S WHAT I'M HERE TO DISCUSS TODAY: THE SACRAMENT FOUNDATION, BASED ON THE REVELATIONS GIFTED ME BY THE ALIEN LOVE GARDENERS.
MANY OF YOU WILL HAVE HEARD OF MY BOOK (AVAILABLE IN PRINT AND AT AMFEED WHITbook) "EXCHANGE", IN WHICH I DETAIL THE FIRST WEEKS OF MY DEALINGS WITH THE GARDENERS...
NOW, I HAVE A QUESTION ABOUT THAT.
SHOOT.
STOP ME WHEN I LOSE THE PLOT HERE.

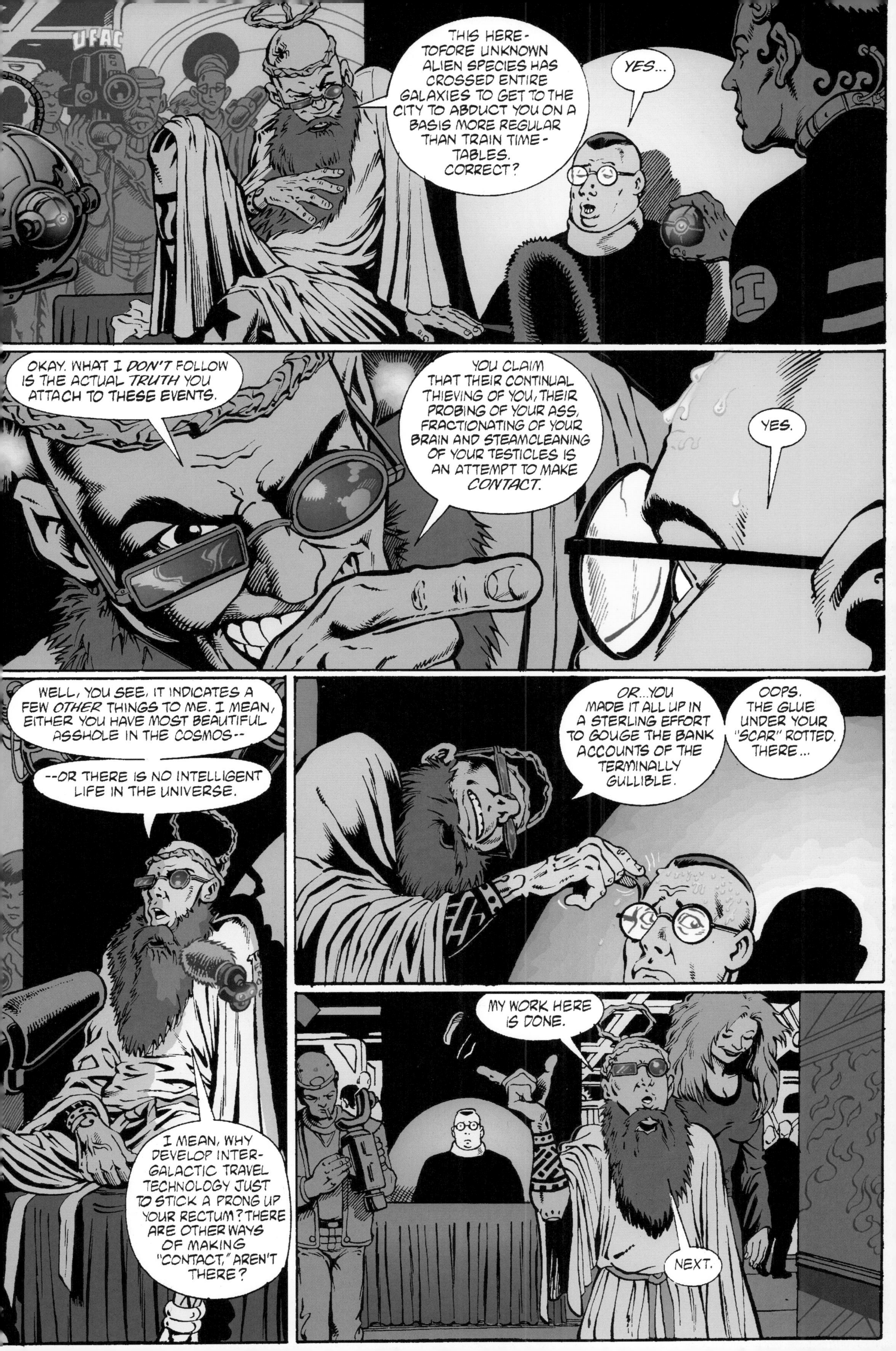
THIS HERE-TOFORE UNKNOWN ALIEN SPECIES HAS CROSSED ENTIRE GALAXIES TO GET TO THE CITY TO ABDUCT YOU ON A BASIS MORE REGULAR THAN TRAIN TIME-TABLES. CORRECT?
YES...
OKAY. WHAT I *DON'T* FOLLOW IS THE ACTUAL *TRUTH* YOU ATTACH TO THESE EVENTS.
YOU CLAIM THAT THEIR CONTINUAL THIEVING OF YOU, THEIR PROBING OF YOUR ASS, FRACTIONATING OF YOUR BRAIN AND STEAMCLEANING OF YOUR TESTICLES IS AN ATTEMPT TO MAKE *CONTACT*.
YES.
WELL, YOU SEE, IT INDICATES A FEW *OTHER* THINGS TO ME. I MEAN, EITHER YOU HAVE MOST BEAUTIFUL ASSHOLE IN THE COSMOS--
--OR THERE IS NO INTELLIGENT LIFE IN THE UNIVERSE.
I MEAN, WHY DEVELOP INTER-GALACTIC TRAVEL TECHNOLOGY JUST TO STICK A PRONG UP YOUR RECTUM? THERE ARE OTHER WAYS OF MAKING "CONTACT," AREN'T THERE?
*OR*...YOU MADE IT ALL UP IN A STERLING EFFORT TO GOUGE THE BANK ACCOUNTS OF THE TERMINALLY GULLIBLE.
OOPS. THE GLUE UNDER YOUR "SCAR" ROTTED. THERE...
MY WORK HERE IS DONE.
NEXT.

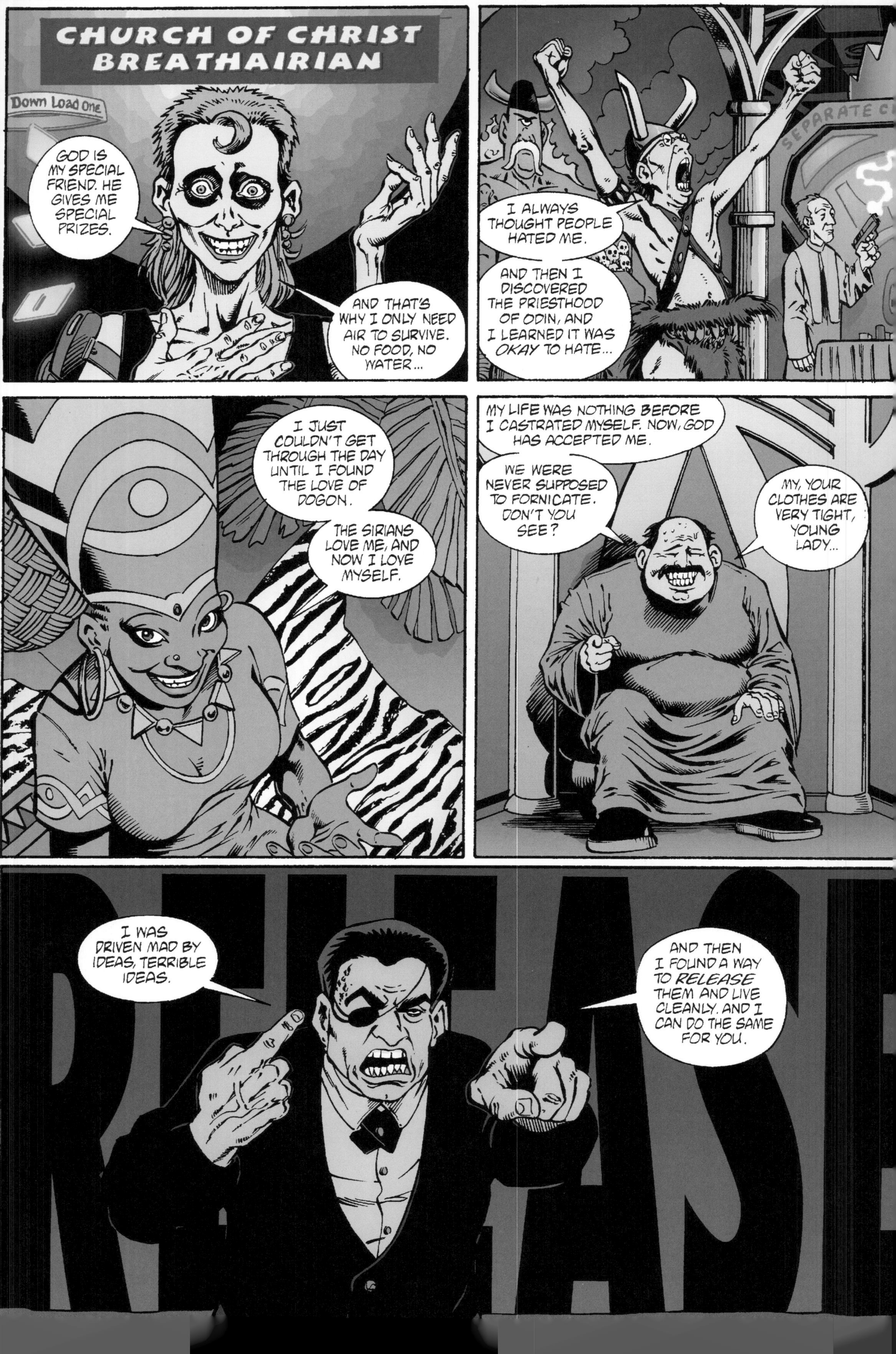
CHURCH OF CHRIST BREATHAIRIAN
Down Load One
GOD IS MY SPECIAL FRIEND. HE GIVES ME SPECIAL PRIZES.
AND THAT'S WHY I ONLY NEED AIR TO SURVIVE. NO FOOD, NO WATER...
I ALWAYS THOUGHT PEOPLE HATED ME.
AND THEN I DISCOVERED THE PRIESTHOOD OF ODIN, AND I LEARNED IT WAS OKAY TO HATE...
I JUST COULDN'T GET THROUGH THE DAY UNTIL I FOUND THE LOVE OF DOGON.
THE SIRIANS LOVE ME, AND NOW I LOVE MYSELF.
MY LIFE WAS NOTHING BEFORE I CASTRATED MYSELF. NOW, GOD HAS ACCEPTED ME.
WE WERE NEVER SUPPOSED TO FORNICATE. DON'T YOU SEE?
MY, YOUR CLOTHES ARE VERY TIGHT, YOUNG LADY...
I WAS DRIVEN MAD BY IDEAS, TERRIBLE IDEAS.
AND THEN I FOUND A WAY TO RELEASE THEM AND LIVE CLEANLY. AND I CAN DO THE SAME FOR YOU.

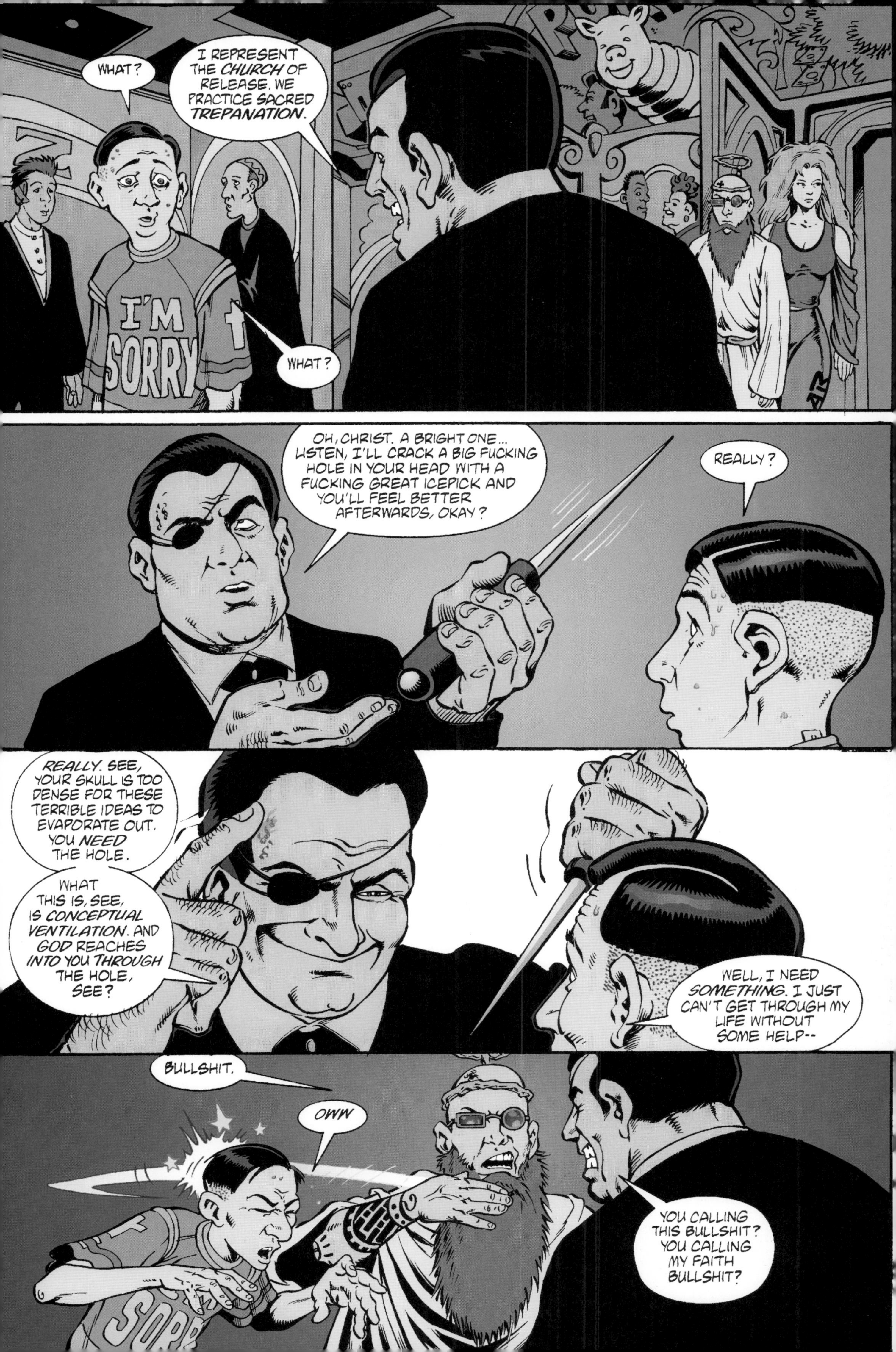
WHAT?
I REPRESENT THE CHURCH OF RELEASE. WE PRACTICE SACRED TREPANATION.
WHAT?
I'M SORRY
OH, CHRIST. A BRIGHT ONE... LISTEN, I'LL CRACK A BIG FUCKING HOLE IN YOUR HEAD WITH A FUCKING GREAT ICEPICK AND YOU'LL FEEL BETTER AFTERWARDS, OKAY?
REALLY?
REALLY. SEE, YOUR SKULL IS TOO DENSE FOR THESE TERRIBLE IDEAS TO EVAPORATE OUT. YOU NEED THE HOLE.
WHAT THIS IS, SEE, IS CONCEPTUAL VENTILATION. AND GOD REACHES INTO YOU THROUGH THE HOLE, SEE?
WELL, I NEED SOMETHING. I JUST CAN'T GET THROUGH MY LIFE WITHOUT SOME HELP--
BULLSHIT.
OWW
YOU CALLING THIS BULLSHIT? YOU CALLING MY FAITH BULLSHIT?

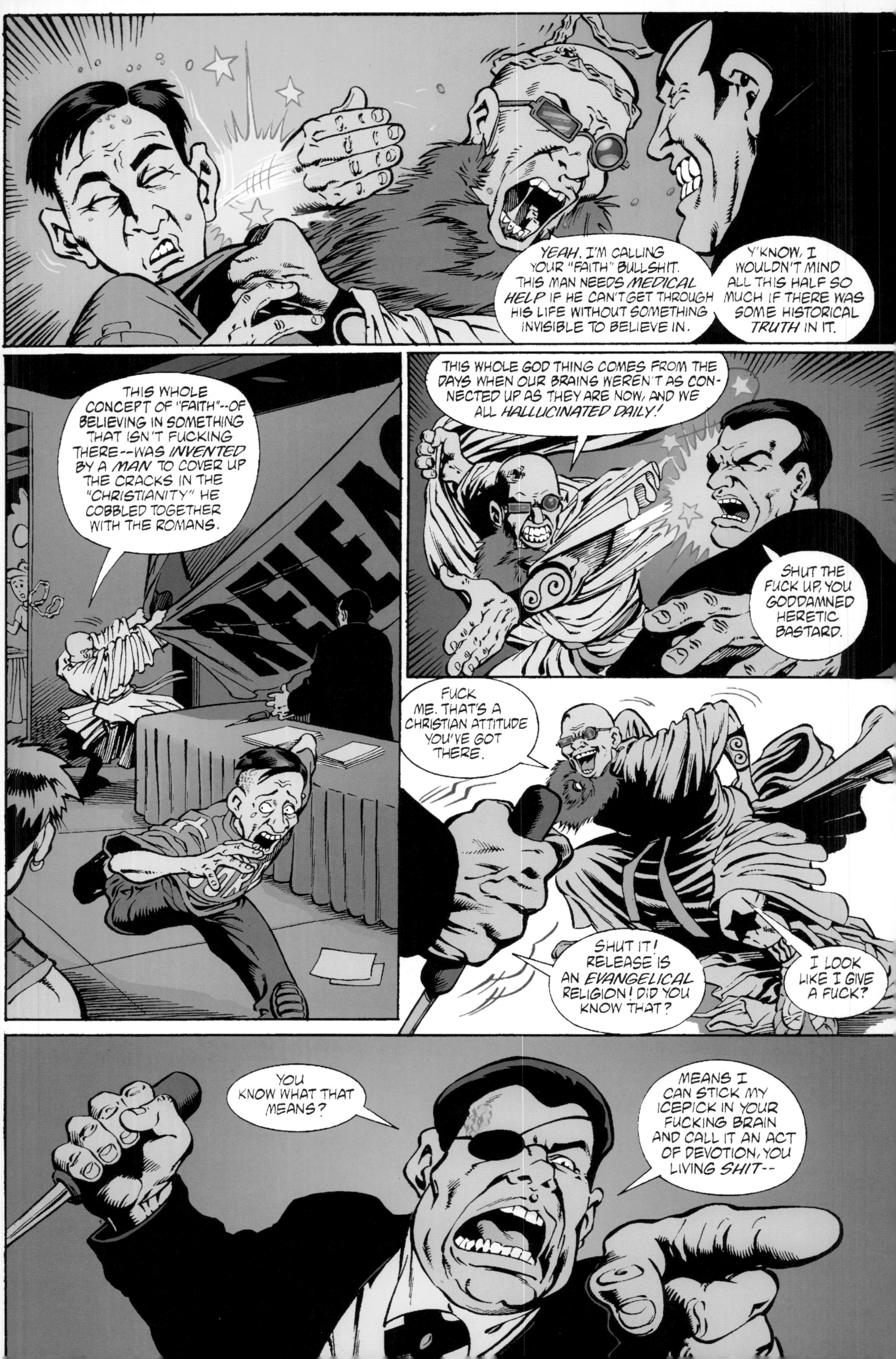
YEAH. I'M CALLING YOUR "FAITH" BULLSHIT. THIS MAN NEEDS MEDICAL HELP IF HE CAN'T GET THROUGH HIS LIFE WITHOUT SOMETHING INVISIBLE TO BELIEVE IN.
Y'KNOW, I WOULDN'T MIND ALL THIS HALF SO MUCH IF THERE WAS SOME HISTORICAL TRUTH IN IT.
THIS WHOLE CONCEPT OF "FAITH"--OF BELIEVING IN SOMETHING THAT ISN'T FUCKING THERE--WAS INVENTED BY A MAN TO COVER UP THE CRACKS IN THE "CHRISTIANITY" HE COBBLED TOGETHER WITH THE ROMANS.
THIS WHOLE GOD THING COMES FROM THE DAYS WHEN OUR BRAINS WEREN'T AS CONNECTED UP AS THEY ARE NOW, AND WE ALL HALLUCINATED DAILY!
SHUT THE FUCK UP, YOU GODDAMNED HERETIC BASTARD.
FUCK ME. THAT'S A CHRISTIAN ATTITUDE YOU'VE GOT THERE.
SHUT IT! RELEASE IS AN EVANGELICAL RELIGION! DID YOU KNOW THAT?
I LOOK LIKE I GIVE A FUCK?
YOU KNOW WHAT THAT MEANS?
MEANS I CAN STICK MY ICEPICK IN YOUR FUCKING BRAIN AND CALL IT AN ACT OF DEVOTION, YOU LIVING SHIT--

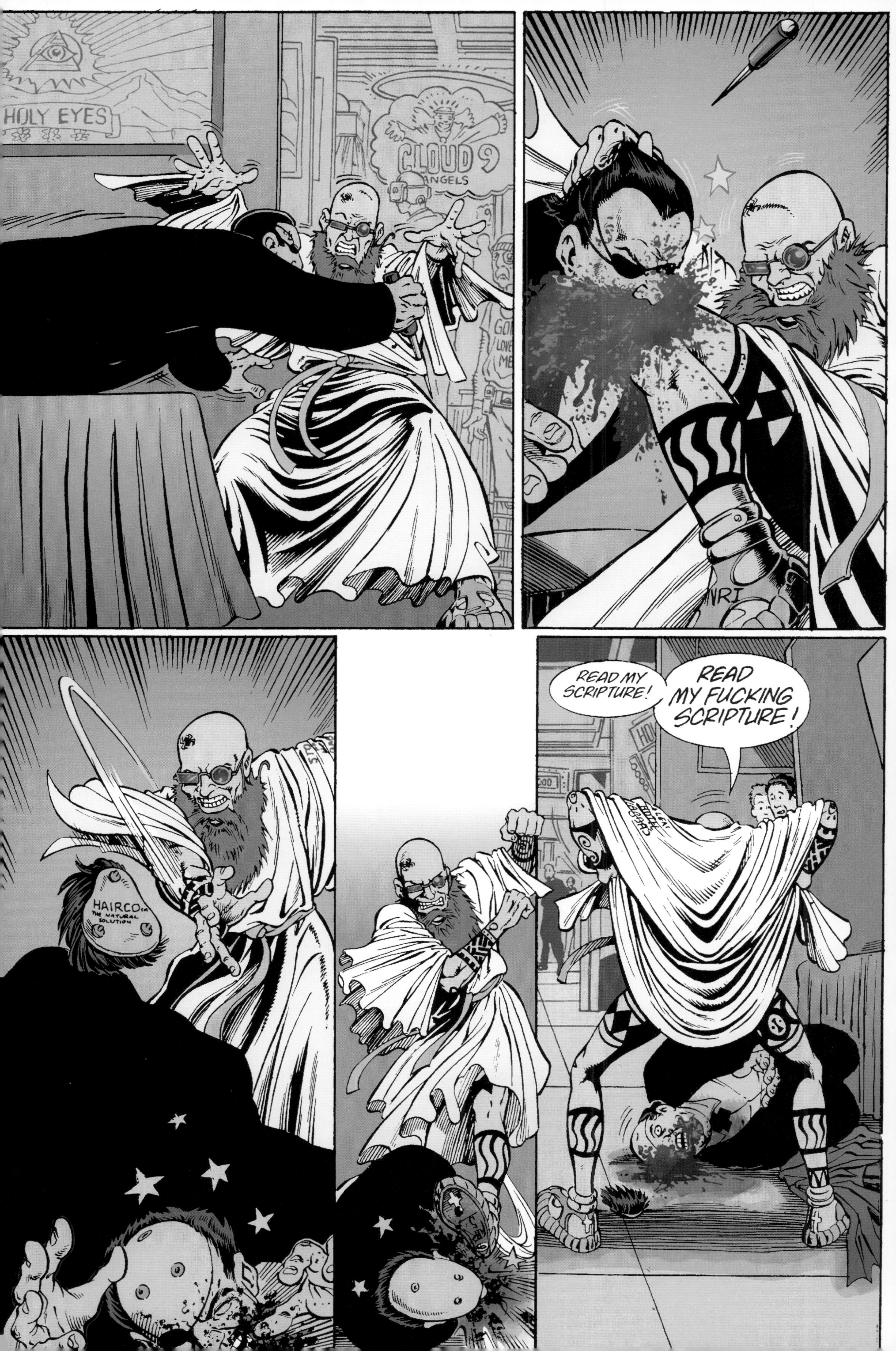
HOLY EYES
CLOUD 9
ANGELS
GOD LOVES ME
INRI
HAIRCO
THE NATURAL SOLUTION
READ MY SCRIPTURE!
READ MY FUCKING SCRIPTURE!

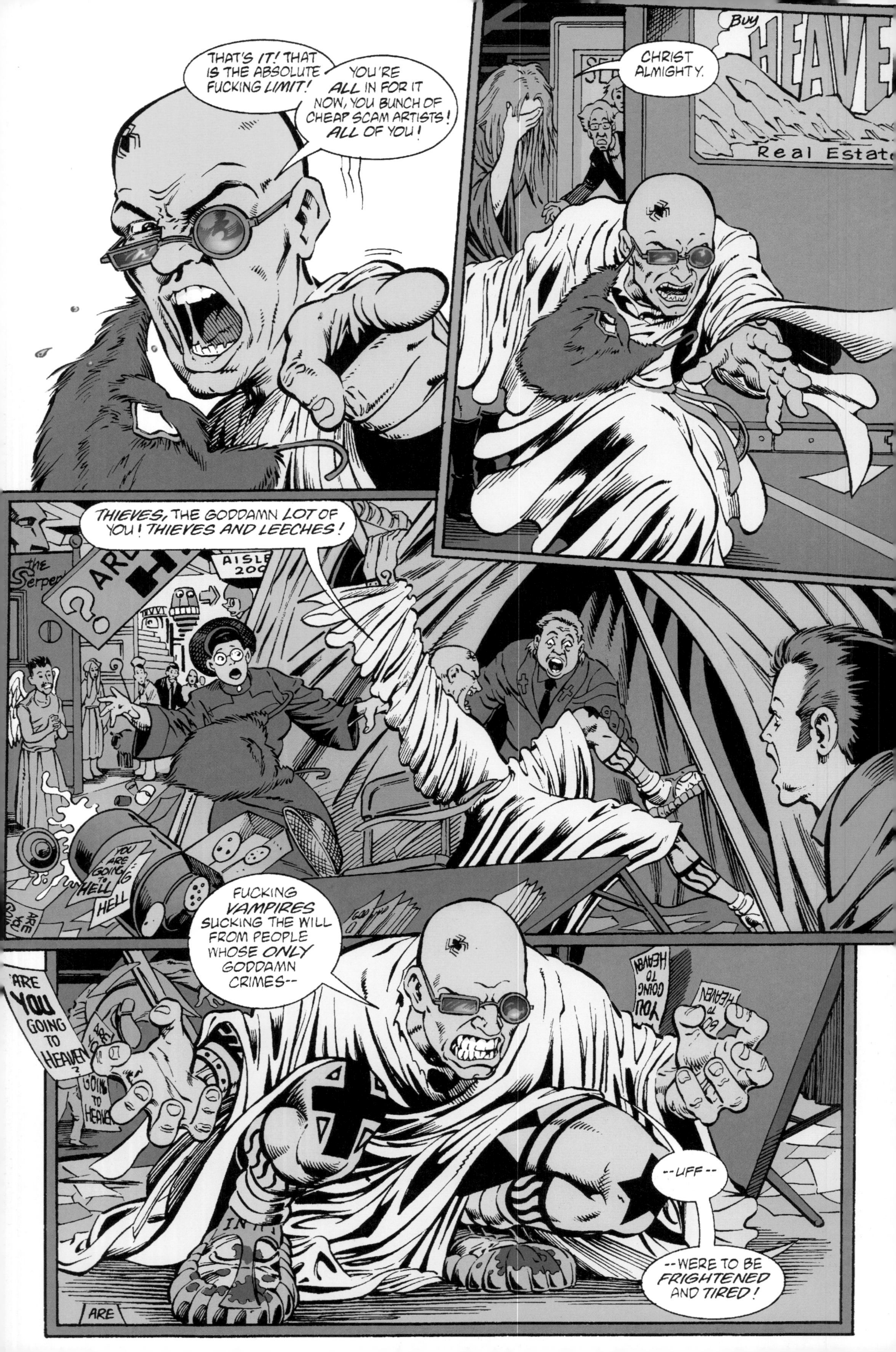
THAT'S IT! THAT IS THE ABSOLUTE FUCKING LIMIT!
YOU'RE ALL IN FOR IT NOW, YOU BUNCH OF CHEAP SCAM ARTISTS! ALL OF YOU!
Buy
HEAVE
Real Estate
CHRIST ALMIGHTY.
THIEVES, THE GODDAMN LOT OF YOU! THIEVES AND LEECHES!
AISLE 200
the Serpent
YOU ARE GOING TO HELL
HELL
FUCKING VAMPIRES SUCKING THE WILL FROM PEOPLE WHOSE ONLY GODDAMN CRIMES--
ARE YOU GOING TO HEAVEN?
YOU GOING TO HEAVEN
GOING TO HEAVEN
--UFF--
--WERE TO BE FRIGHTENED AND TIRED!
ARE

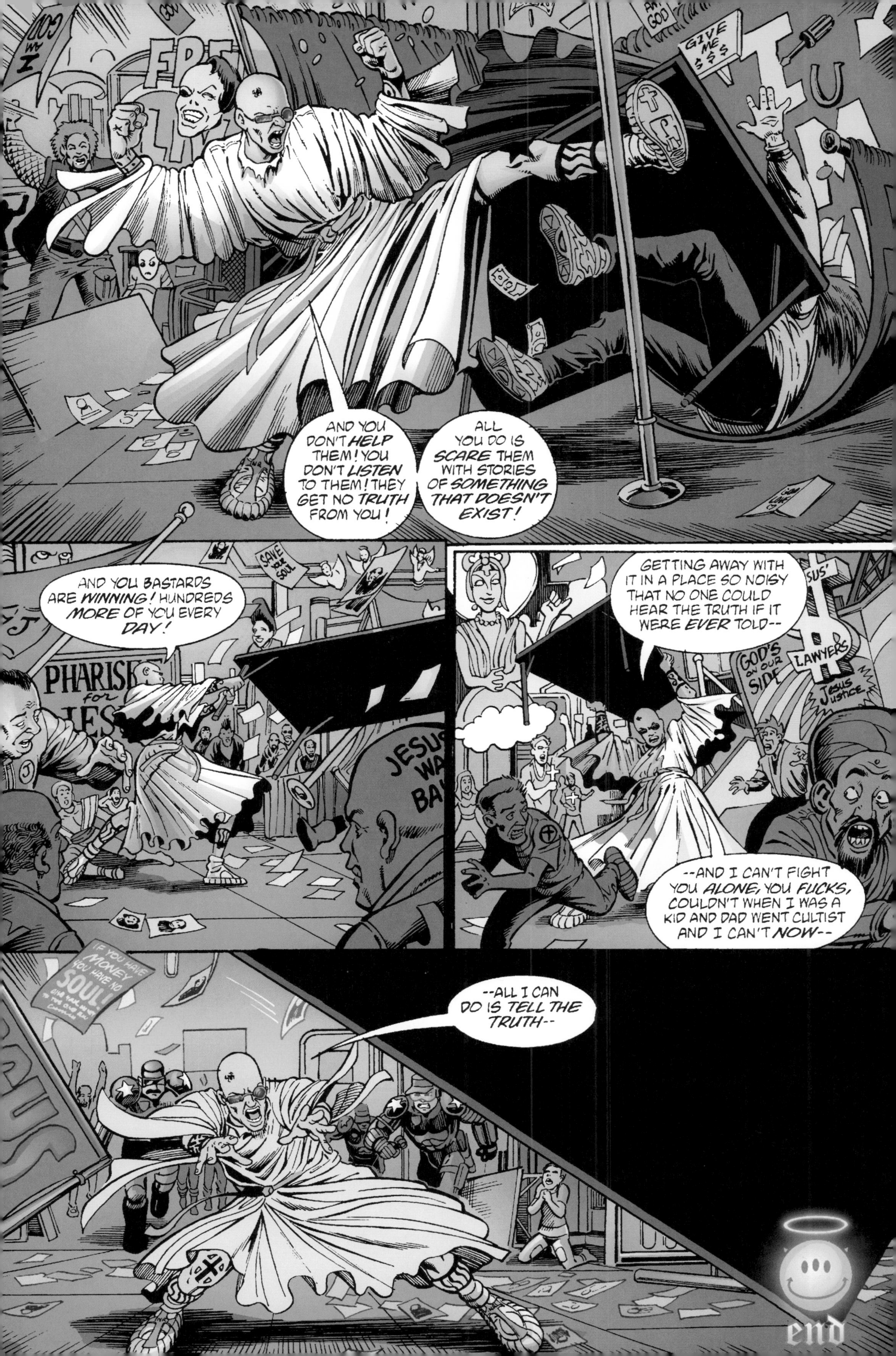
GIVE ME $$$
AND YOU DON'T HELP THEM! YOU DON'T LISTEN TO THEM! THEY GET NO TRUTH FROM YOU!
ALL YOU DO IS SCARE THEM WITH STORIES OF SOMETHING THAT DOESN'T EXIST!
SAVE YOUR SOUL
AND YOU BASTARDS ARE WINNING! HUNDREDS MORE OF YOU EVERY DAY!
GETTING AWAY WITH IT IN A PLACE SO NOISY THAT NO ONE COULD HEAR THE TRUTH IF IT WERE EVER TOLD--
GOD'S ON OUR SIDE
LAWYERS
Jesus Justice
--AND I CAN'T FIGHT YOU ALONE, YOU FUCKS, COULDN'T WHEN I WAS A KID AND DAD WENT CULTIST AND I CAN'T NOW--
IF YOU HAVE MONEY YOU HAVE NO SOUL!
--ALL I CAN DO IS TELL THE TRUTH--
end

by **Spider Jerusalem** [author of "waving and drown-

# I HATE IT HERE

—Yesterday, here in the middle of the City, I saw a wolf turn into a Russian ex-gymnast and hand over a business card that read YOUR OWN PERSONAL TRANSHUMAN SECURITY WHORE! STERILIZED INNARDS! ACCEPTS ALL CREDIT CARDS to a large man who wore trained attack cancers on his face and possessed seventy-five indentured Komodo Dragons instead of legs. And they had sex. Right in front of me. And six of the Komodo Dragons spat napalm on my new shoes.

Now listen. I'm told I'm a FAMOUS JOURNALIST these days. I'm told the five years I spent away from the City have vanished like the name of the guy you picked up last night, and that it's like I never left. (I was driven away, let me remind you, by things like Sickness, Hate and The Death of Truth.)

So why do I have to put up with this shabby crap on my front doorstep? Now my beautiful new apartment stinks of wet fur and burning dragon spit, and I think one of the cancers mated with the doormat. It keeps cursing at me in a thick Mexican accent. I may have to have it shot.

If you loved me, you'd all kill yourselves today.

— SPIDER JERUSALEM

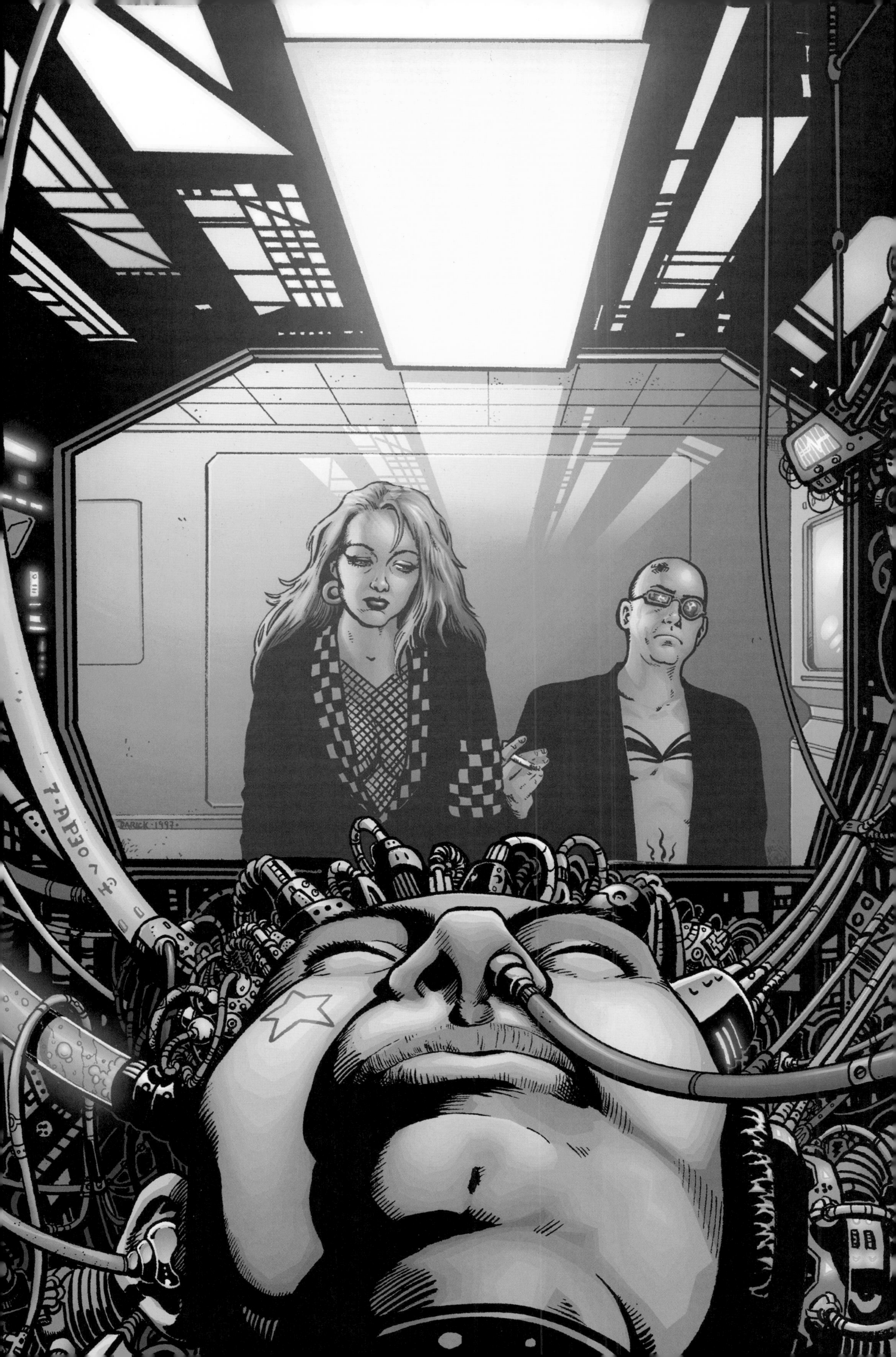
DARICK·1997·

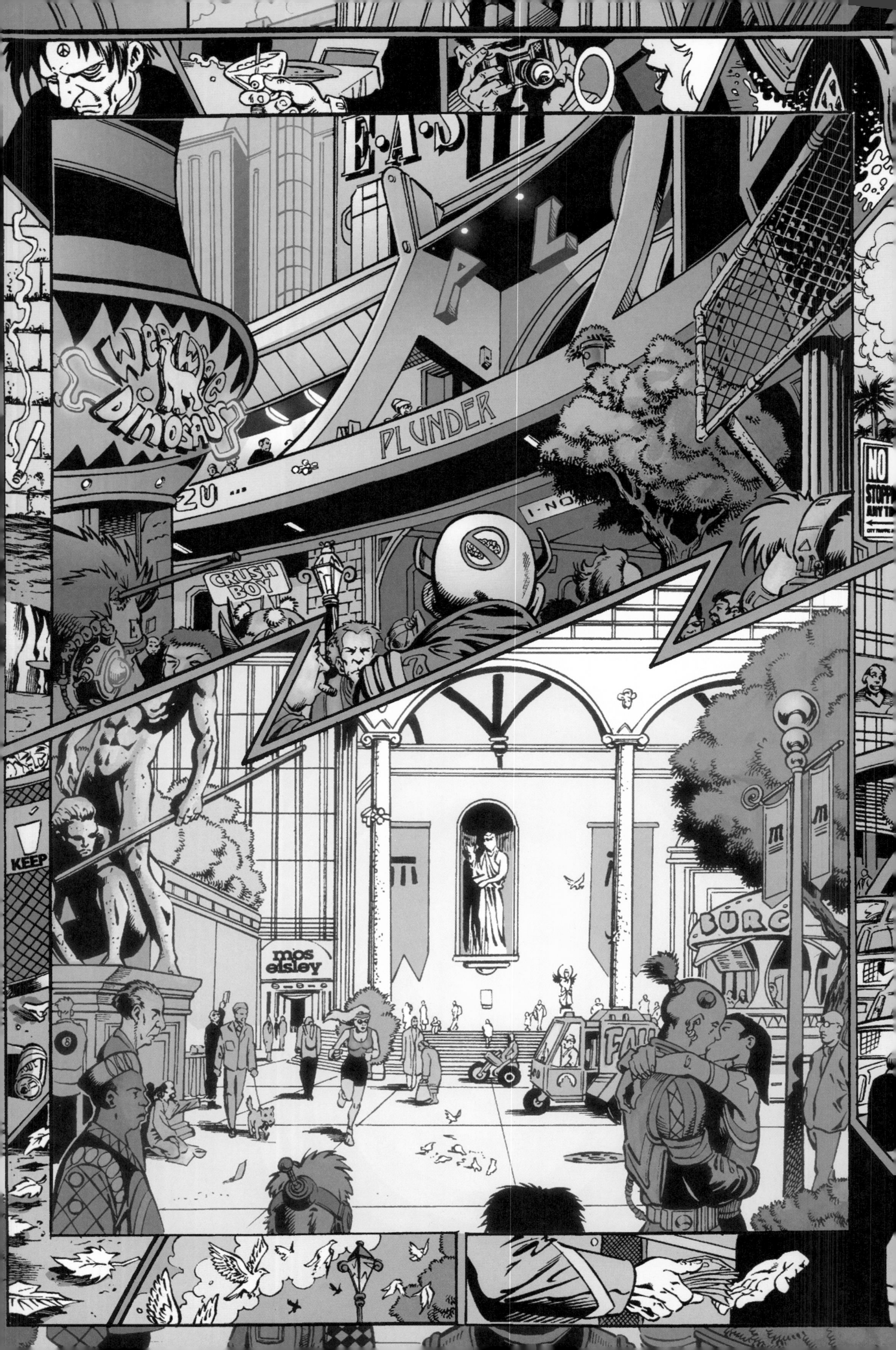

E-A-S
P
L
We Like Dinosaurs
PLUNDER
ZU
I-NO
CRUSH BOY
NO STOPPING ANY TIME
KEEP
mos eisley
BURG
FAL

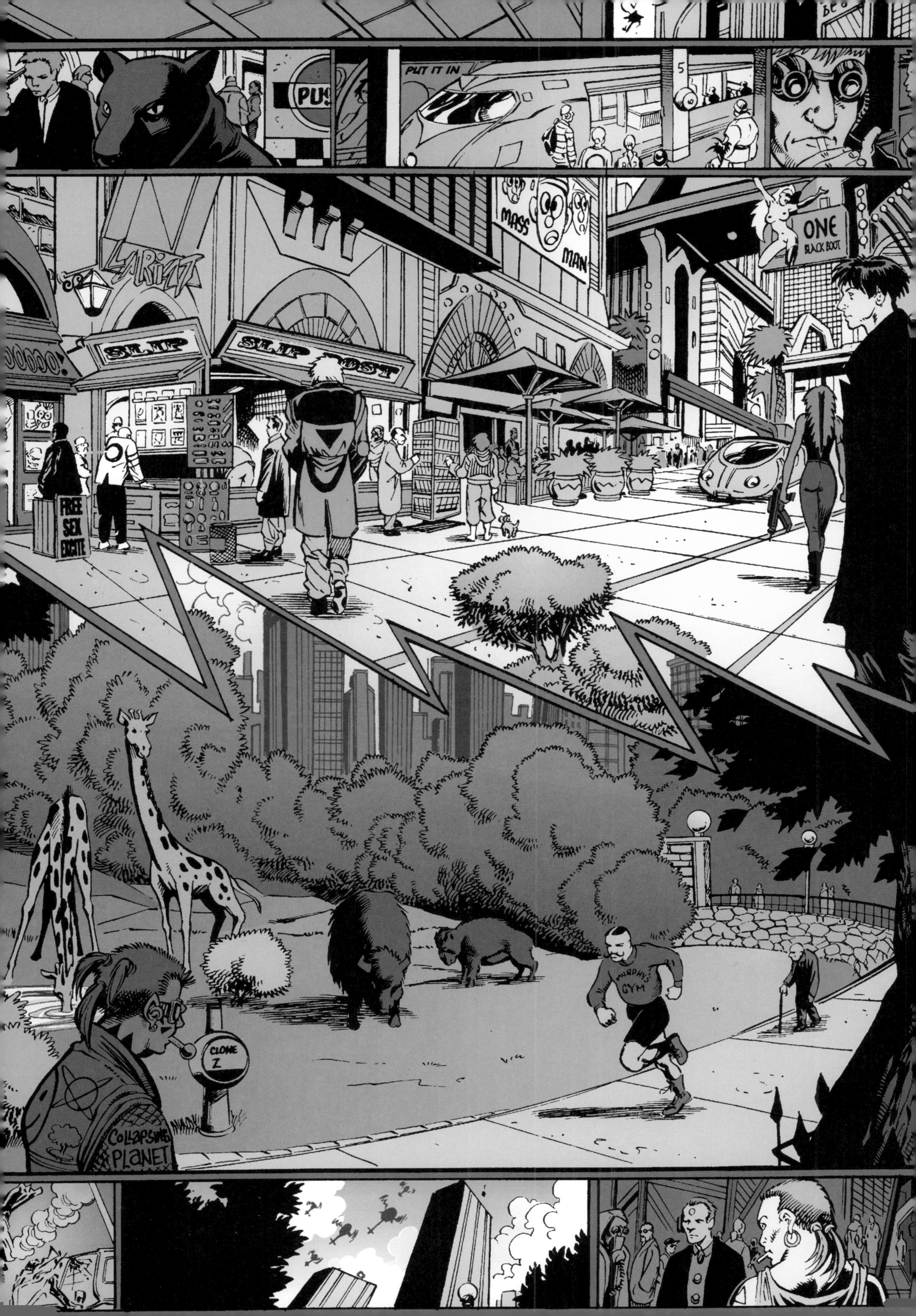

PUS
PUT IT IN
5
MASS
MAN
ONE
BLACK BOOT
SLIP
SLIP POST
FREE
SEX
EXCITE
CLONE
Z
MURPHY'S
GYM
COLLAPSING
PLANET

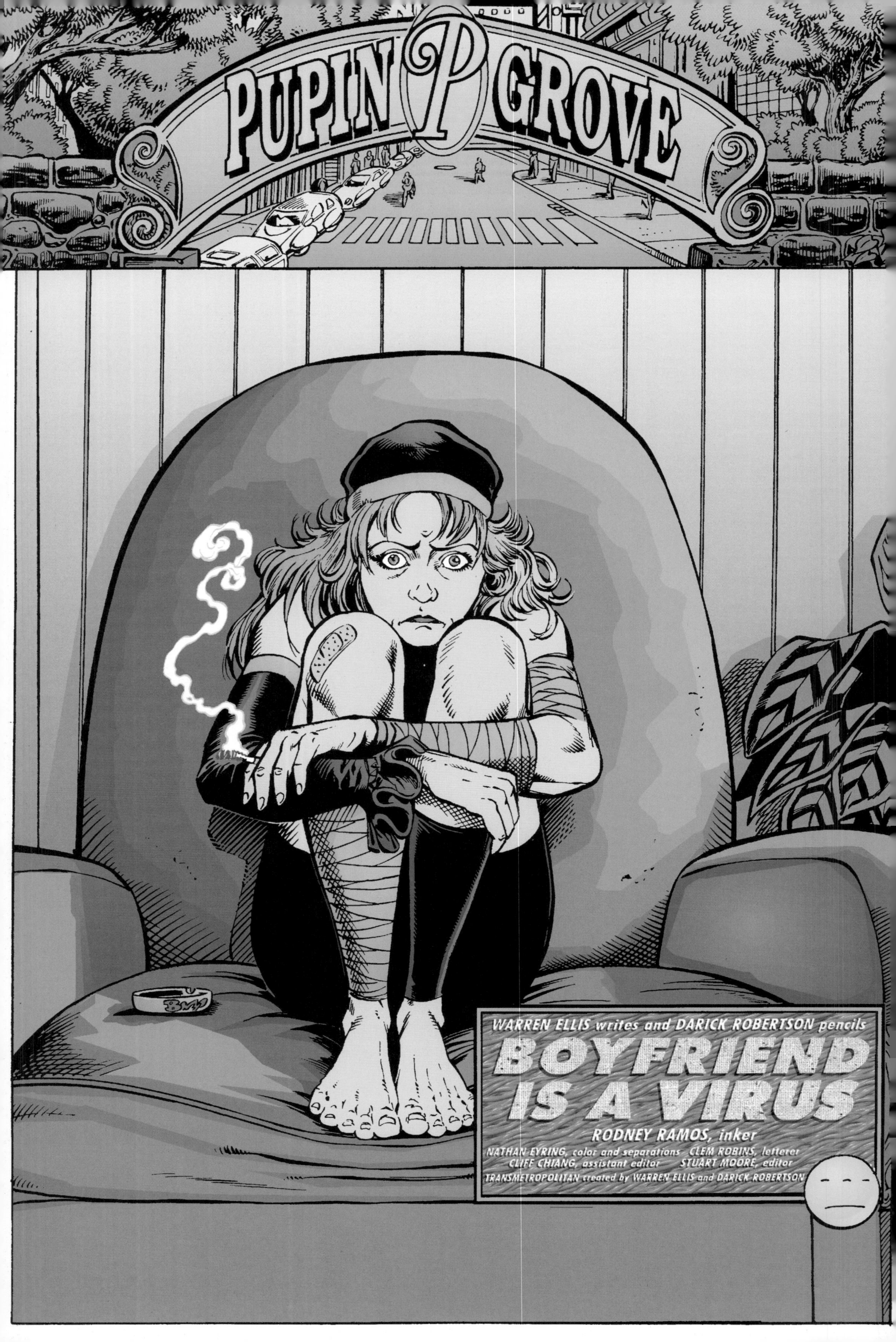
PUPIN P GROVE
WARREN ELLIS writes and DARICK ROBERTSON pencils
BOYFRIEND IS A VIRUS
RODNEY RAMOS, inker
NATHAN EYRING, color and separations CLEM ROBINS, letterer
CLIFF CHIANG, assistant editor STUART MOORE, editor
TRANSMETROPOLITAN created by WARREN ELLIS and DARICK ROBERTSON

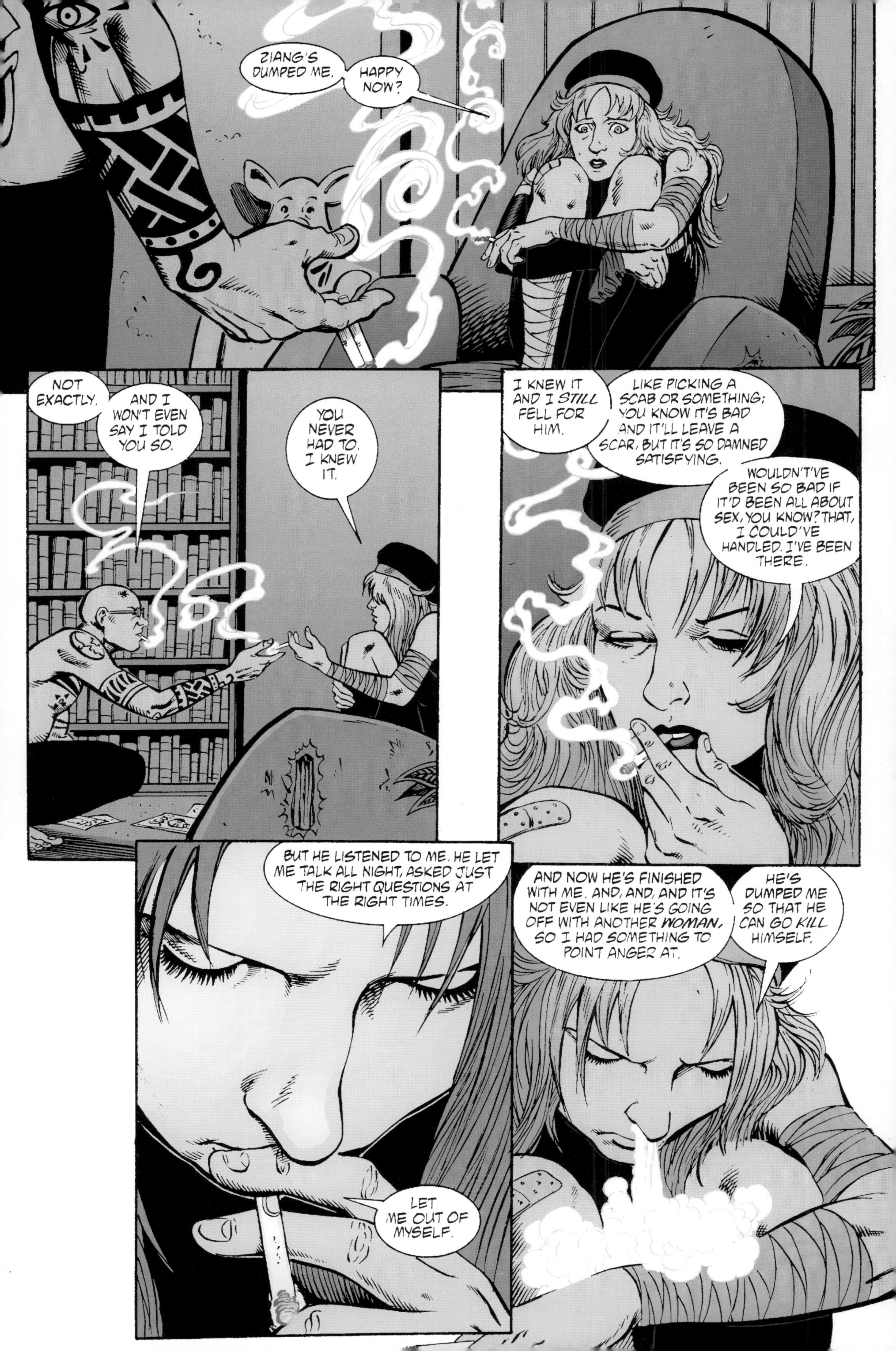
ZIANG'S DUMPED ME.
HAPPY NOW?
NOT EXACTLY.
AND I WON'T EVEN SAY I TOLD YOU SO.
YOU NEVER HAD TO. I KNEW IT.
I KNEW IT AND I STILL FELL FOR HIM.
LIKE PICKING A SCAB OR SOMETHING; YOU KNOW IT'S BAD AND IT'LL LEAVE A SCAR, BUT IT'S SO DAMNED SATISFYING.
WOULDN'T'VE BEEN SO BAD IF IT'D BEEN ALL ABOUT SEX, YOU KNOW? THAT, I COULD'VE HANDLED. I'VE BEEN THERE.
BUT HE LISTENED TO ME. HE LET ME TALK ALL NIGHT, ASKED JUST THE RIGHT QUESTIONS AT THE RIGHT TIMES.
LET ME OUT OF MYSELF.
AND NOW HE'S FINISHED WITH ME. AND, AND, AND IT'S NOT EVEN LIKE HE'S GOING OFF WITH ANOTHER WOMAN, SO I HAD SOMETHING TO POINT ANGER AT.
HE'S DUMPED ME SO THAT HE CAN GO KILL HIMSELF.

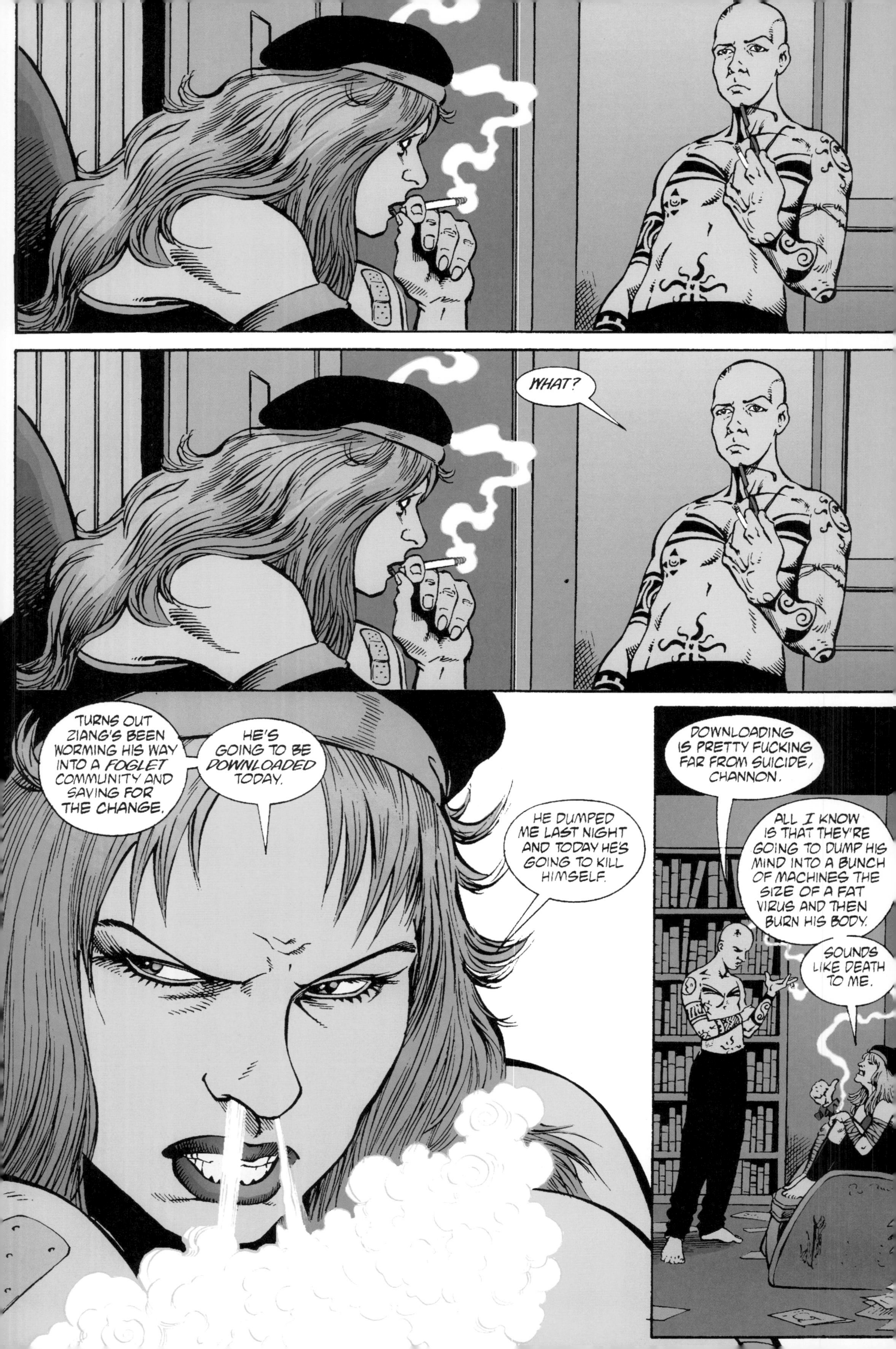
WHAT?
TURNS OUT ZIANG'S BEEN WORMING HIS WAY INTO A *FOGLET* COMMUNITY AND SAVING FOR THE CHANGE.
HE'S GOING TO BE *DOWNLOADED* TODAY.
HE DUMPED ME LAST NIGHT AND TODAY HE'S GOING TO KILL HIMSELF.
DOWNLOADING IS PRETTY FUCKING FAR FROM SUICIDE, CHANNON.
ALL *I* KNOW IS THAT THEY'RE GOING TO DUMP HIS MIND INTO A BUNCH OF MACHINES THE SIZE OF A FAT VIRUS AND THEN BURN HIS BODY.
SOUNDS LIKE DEATH TO ME.

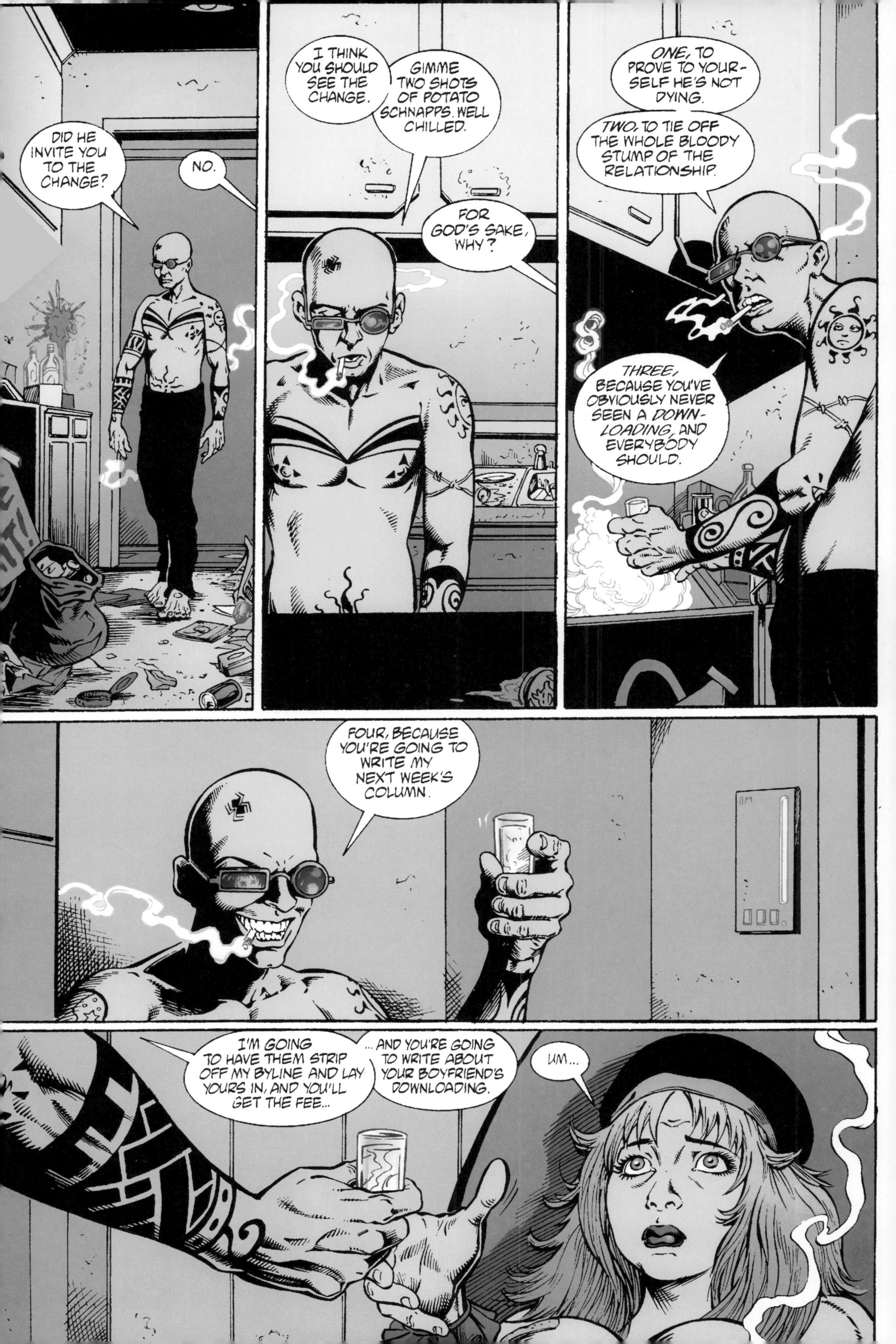
DID HE INVITE YOU TO THE CHANGE?
NO.
I THINK YOU SHOULD SEE THE CHANGE.
GIMME TWO SHOTS OF POTATO SCHNAPPS. WELL CHILLED.
FOR GOD'S SAKE, WHY?
ONE, TO PROVE TO YOURSELF HE'S NOT DYING.
TWO, TO TIE OFF THE WHOLE BLOODY STUMP OF THE RELATIONSHIP.
THREE, BECAUSE YOU'VE OBVIOUSLY NEVER SEEN A DOWNLOADING, AND EVERYBODY SHOULD.
FOUR, BECAUSE YOU'RE GOING TO WRITE MY NEXT WEEK'S COLUMN.
I'M GOING TO HAVE THEM STRIP OFF MY BYLINE AND LAY YOURS IN, AND YOU'LL GET THE FEE...
...AND YOU'RE GOING TO WRITE ABOUT YOUR BOYFRIEND'S DOWNLOADING.
UM...

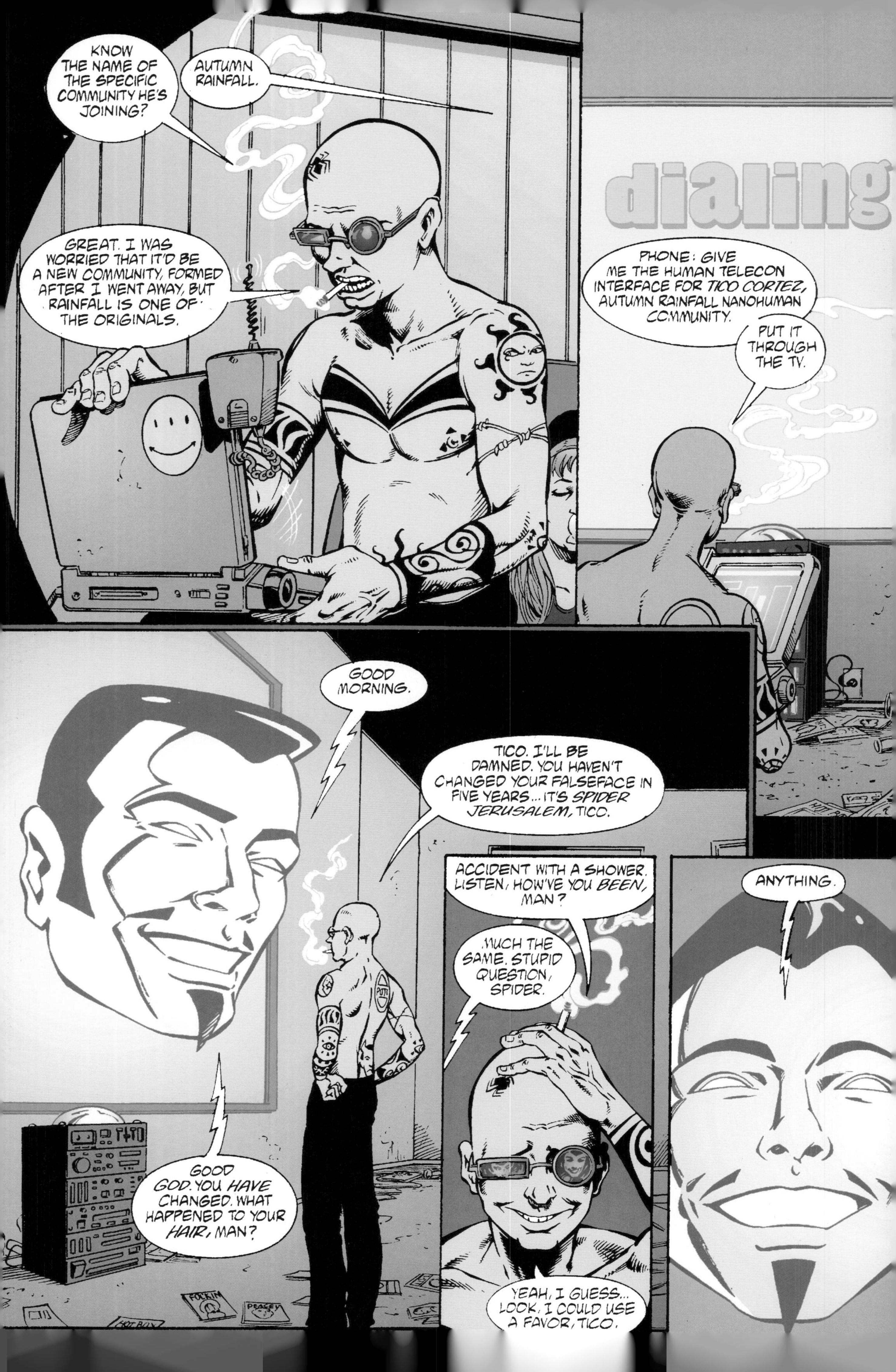
KNOW THE NAME OF THE SPECIFIC COMMUNITY HE'S JOINING?
AUTUMN RAINFALL.
GREAT. I WAS WORRIED THAT IT'D BE A NEW COMMUNITY, FORMED AFTER I WENT AWAY, BUT RAINFALL IS ONE OF THE ORIGINALS.
dialing
PHONE: GIVE ME THE HUMAN TELECON INTERFACE FOR TICO CORTEZ, AUTUMN RAINFALL NANOHUMAN COMMUNITY.
PUT IT THROUGH THE TV.
GOOD MORNING.
TICO. I'LL BE DAMNED. YOU HAVEN'T CHANGED YOUR FALSEFACE IN FIVE YEARS... IT'S SPIDER JERUSALEM, TICO.
GOOD GOD. YOU HAVE CHANGED. WHAT HAPPENED TO YOUR HAIR, MAN?
ACCIDENT WITH A SHOWER. LISTEN, HOW'VE YOU BEEN, MAN?
MUCH THE SAME. STUPID QUESTION, SPIDER.
YEAH, I GUESS... LOOK, I COULD USE A FAVOR, TICO.
ANYTHING.

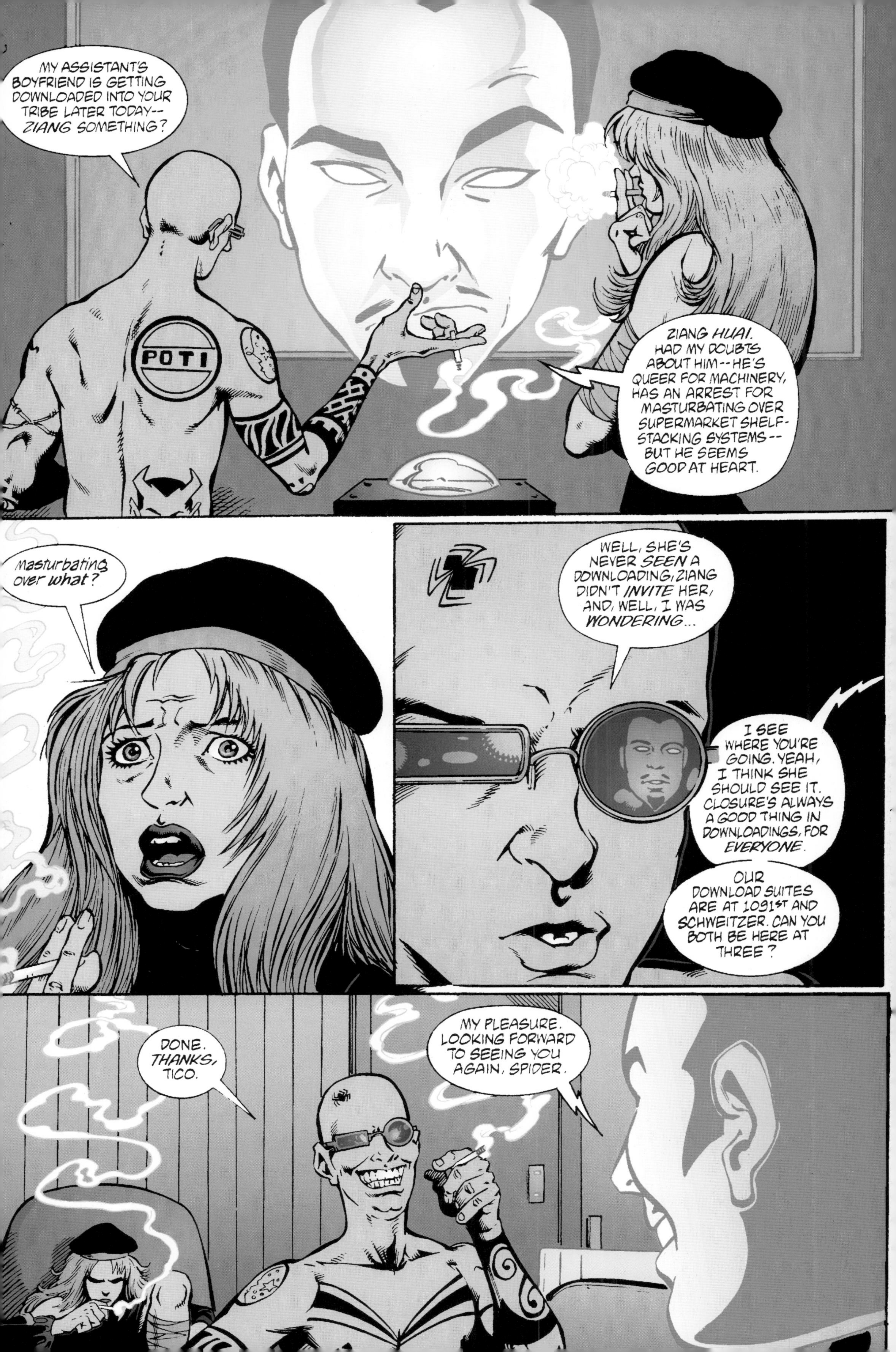
MY ASSISTANT'S BOYFRIEND IS GETTING DOWNLOADED INTO YOUR TRIBE LATER TODAY-- ZIANG SOMETHING?
ZIANG HUAI. HAD MY DOUBTS ABOUT HIM--HE'S QUEER FOR MACHINERY, HAS AN ARREST FOR MASTURBATING OVER SUPERMARKET SHELF-STACKING SYSTEMS--BUT HE SEEMS GOOD AT HEART.
POTI
Masturbating over what?
WELL, SHE'S NEVER SEEN A DOWNLOADING, ZIANG DIDN'T INVITE HER, AND, WELL, I WAS WONDERING...
I SEE WHERE YOU'RE GOING. YEAH, I THINK SHE SHOULD SEE IT. CLOSURE'S ALWAYS A GOOD THING IN DOWNLOADINGS, FOR EVERYONE.
OUR DOWNLOAD SUITES ARE AT 1091ST AND SCHWEITZER. CAN YOU BOTH BE HERE AT THREE?
DONE. THANKS, TICO.
MY PLEASURE. LOOKING FORWARD TO SEEING YOU AGAIN, SPIDER.

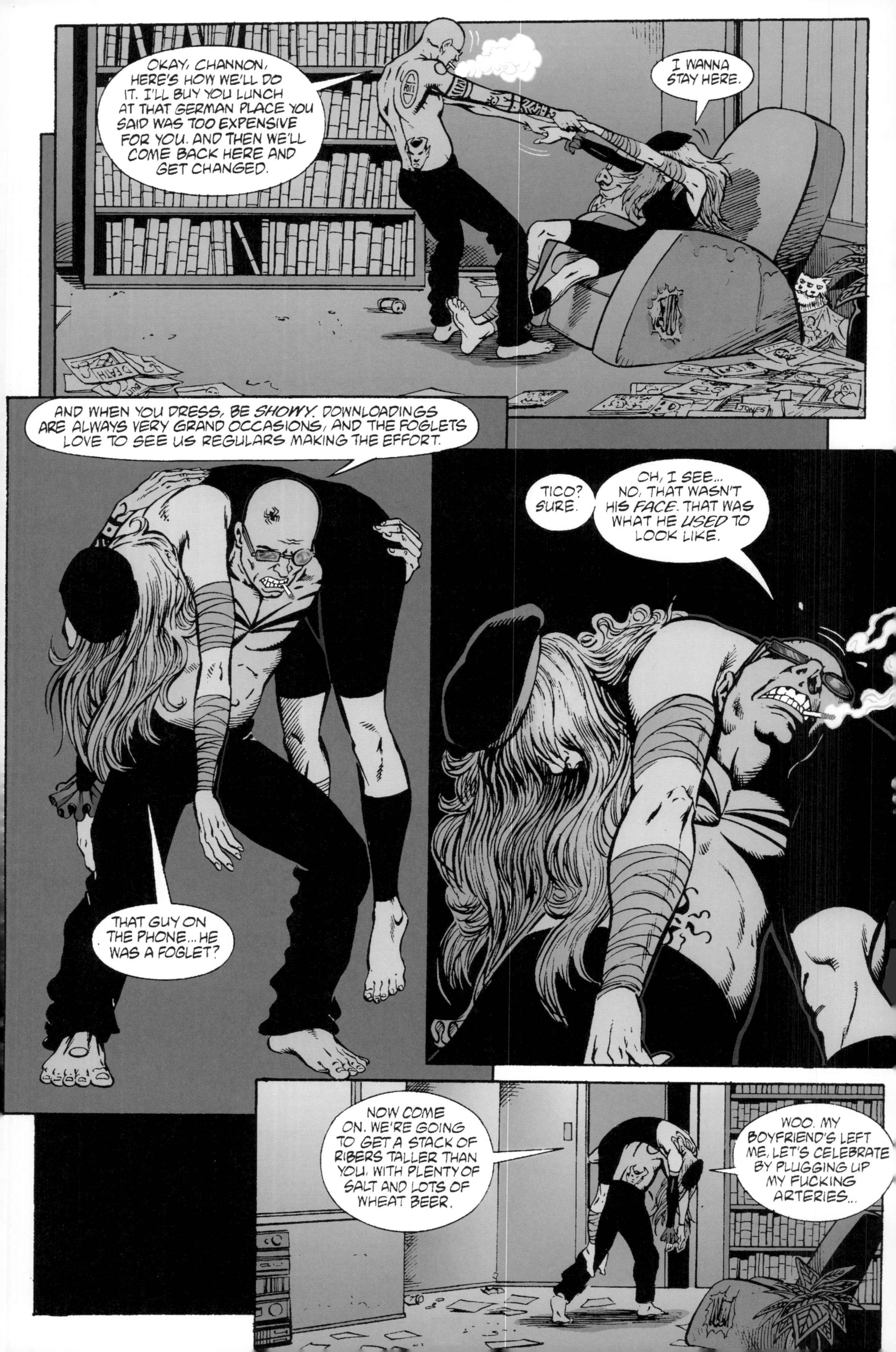
OKAY, CHANNON, HERE'S HOW WE'LL DO IT. I'LL BUY YOU LUNCH AT THAT GERMAN PLACE YOU SAID WAS TOO EXPENSIVE FOR YOU. AND THEN WE'LL COME BACK HERE AND GET CHANGED.
I WANNA STAY HERE.
AND WHEN YOU DRESS, BE *SHOWY*. DOWNLOADINGS ARE ALWAYS VERY GRAND OCCASIONS, AND THE FOGLETS LOVE TO SEE US REGULARS MAKING THE EFFORT.
THAT GUY ON THE PHONE... HE WAS A FOGLET?
TICO? SURE.
OH, I SEE... NO, THAT WASN'T HIS *FACE*. THAT WAS WHAT HE *USED* TO LOOK LIKE.
NOW COME ON. WE'RE GOING TO GET A STACK OF RIBERS TALLER THAN YOU, WITH PLENTY OF SALT AND LOTS OF WHEAT BEER.
WOO. MY BOYFRIEND'S LEFT ME, LET'S CELEBRATE BY PLUGGING UP MY FUCKING ARTERIES...

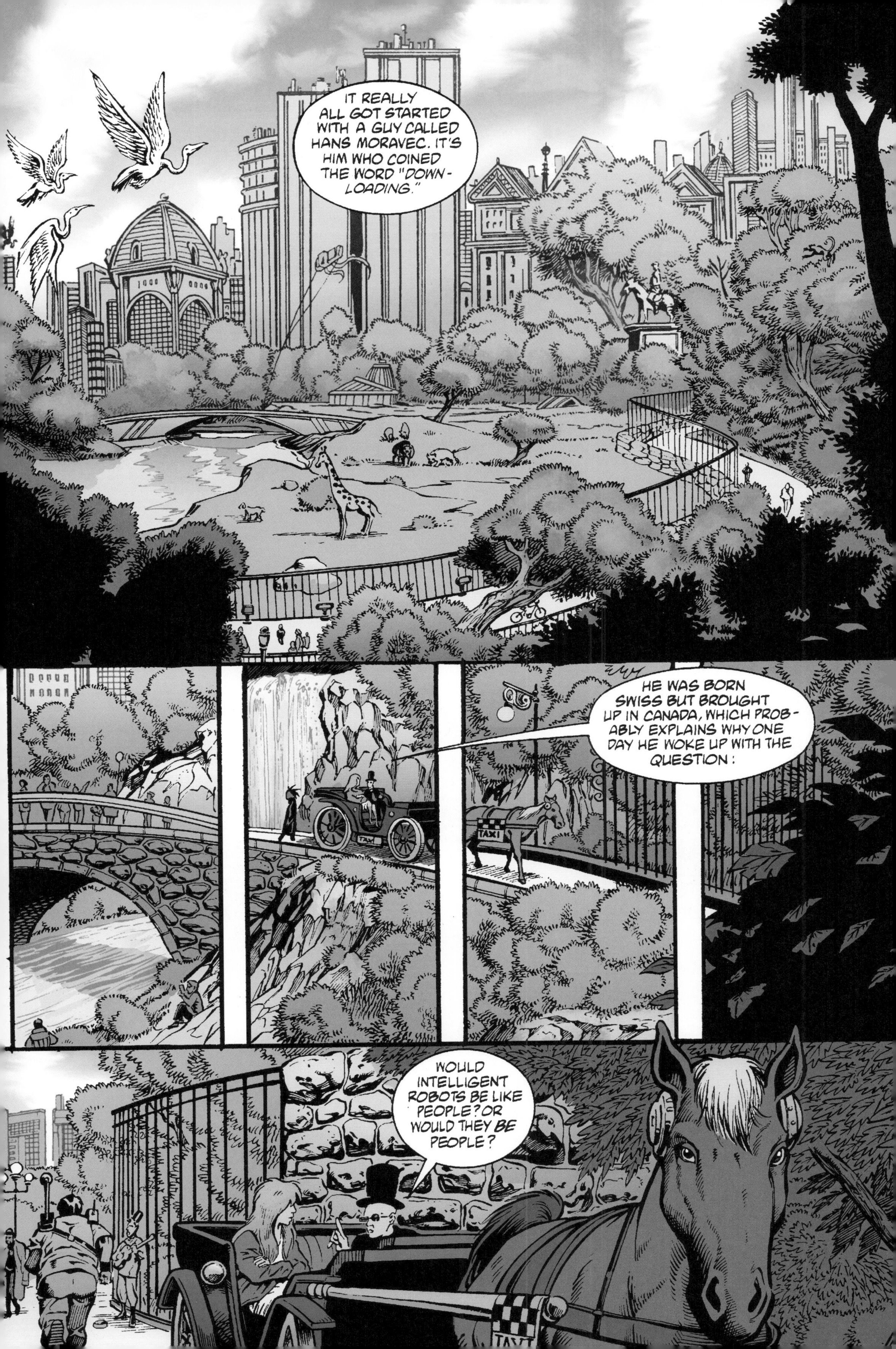
IT REALLY ALL GOT STARTED WITH A GUY CALLED HANS MORAVEC. IT'S HIM WHO COINED THE WORD "DOWN-LOADING."
HE WAS BORN SWISS BUT BROUGHT UP IN CANADA, WHICH PROB-ABLY EXPLAINS WHY ONE DAY HE WOKE UP WITH THE QUESTION:
TAXI
WOULD INTELLIGENT ROBOTS BE LIKE PEOPLE? OR WOULD THEY *BE* PEOPLE?

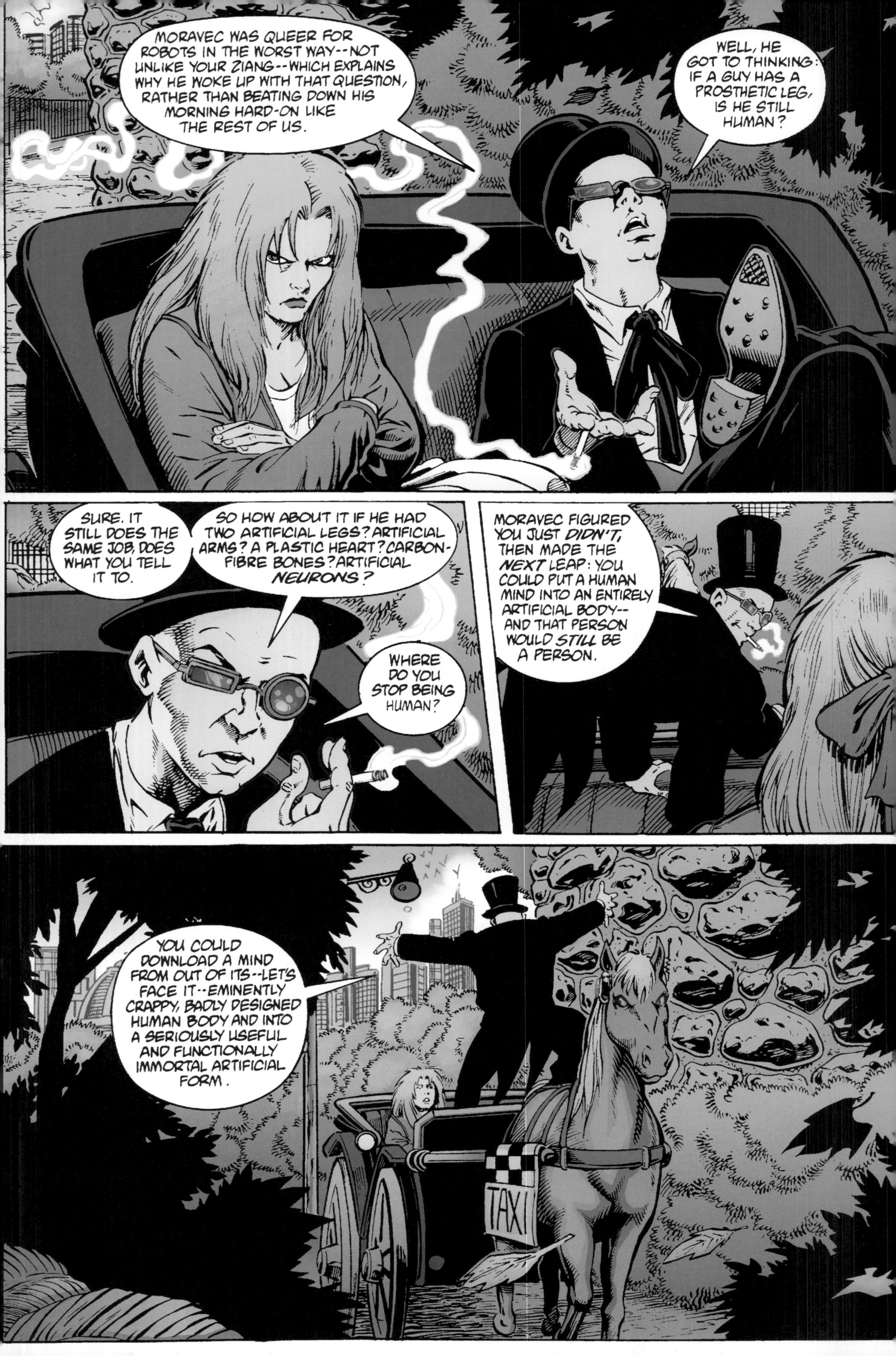
MORAVEC WAS QUEER FOR ROBOTS IN THE WORST WAY--NOT UNLIKE YOUR ZIANG--WHICH EXPLAINS WHY HE WOKE UP WITH THAT QUESTION, RATHER THAN BEATING DOWN HIS MORNING HARD-ON LIKE THE REST OF US.
WELL, HE GOT TO THINKING: IF A GUY HAS A PROSTHETIC LEG, IS HE STILL HUMAN?
SURE. IT STILL DOES THE SAME JOB, DOES WHAT YOU TELL IT TO.
SO HOW ABOUT IT IF HE HAD TWO ARTIFICIAL LEGS? ARTIFICIAL ARMS? A PLASTIC HEART? CARBON-FIBRE BONES? ARTIFICIAL NEURONS?
WHERE DO YOU STOP BEING HUMAN?
MORAVEC FIGURED YOU JUST DIDN'T, THEN MADE THE NEXT LEAP: YOU COULD PUT A HUMAN MIND INTO AN ENTIRELY ARTIFICIAL BODY--AND THAT PERSON WOULD STILL BE A PERSON.
YOU COULD DOWNLOAD A MIND FROM OUT OF ITS--LET'S FACE IT--EMINENTLY CRAPPY, BADLY DESIGNED HUMAN BODY AND INTO A SERIOUSLY USEFUL AND FUNCTIONALLY IMMORTAL ARTIFICIAL FORM.
TAXI

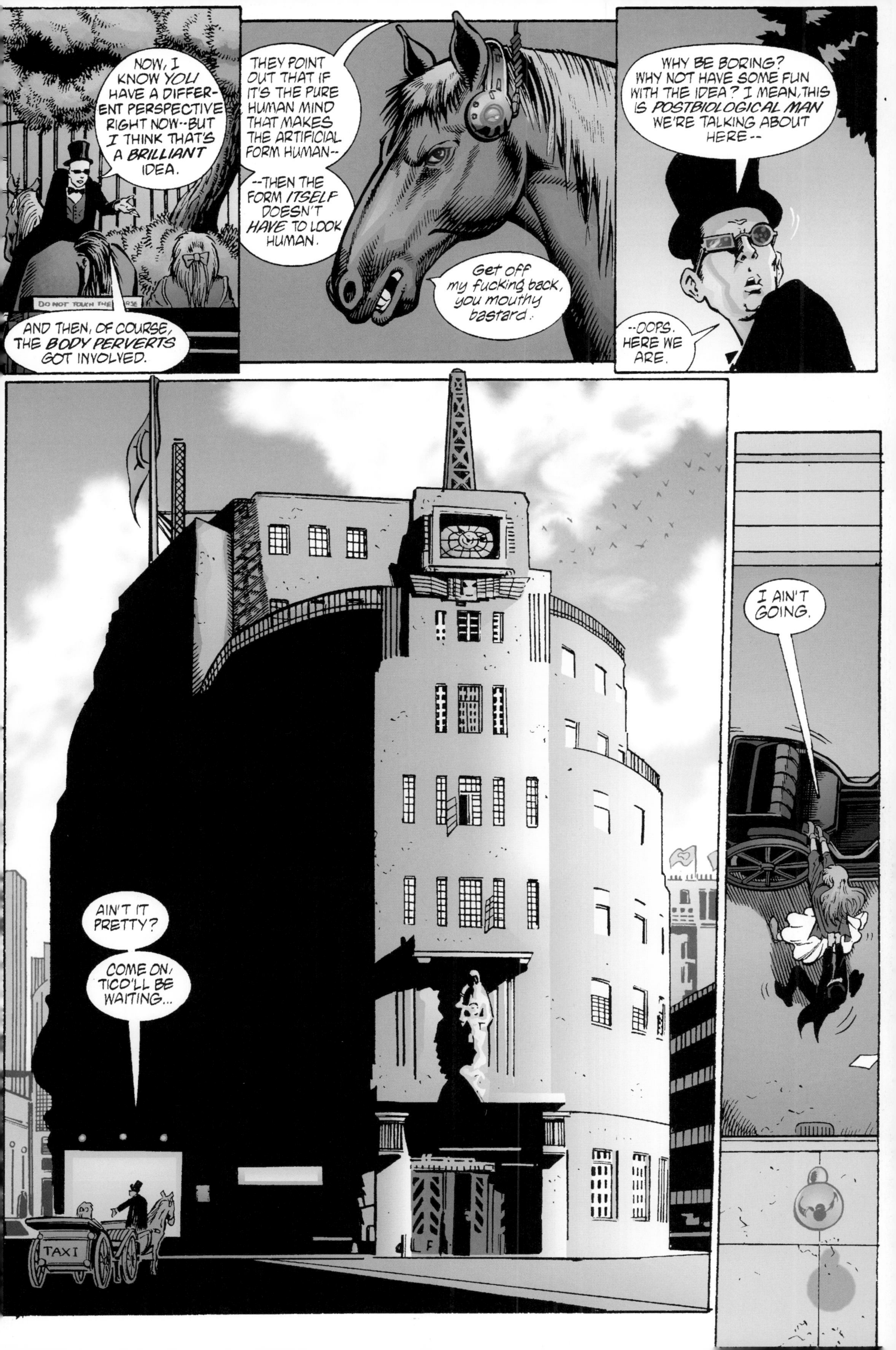
NOW, I KNOW *YOU* HAVE A DIFFERENT PERSPECTIVE RIGHT NOW--BUT *I* THINK THAT'S A ***BRILLIANT*** IDEA.
AND THEN, OF COURSE, THE ***BODY PERVERTS*** GOT INVOLVED.
THEY POINT OUT THAT IF IT'S THE PURE HUMAN MIND THAT MAKES THE ARTIFICIAL FORM HUMAN--
--THEN THE FORM *ITSELF* DOESN'T *HAVE* TO LOOK HUMAN.
*Get off my fucking back, you mouthy bastard.*
WHY BE BORING? WHY NOT HAVE SOME FUN WITH THE IDEA? I MEAN, THIS IS ***POSTBIOLOGICAL MAN*** WE'RE TALKING ABOUT HERE--
--OOPS. HERE WE ARE.
AIN'T IT PRETTY?
COME ON, TICO'LL BE WAITING...
TAXI
I AIN'T GOING.

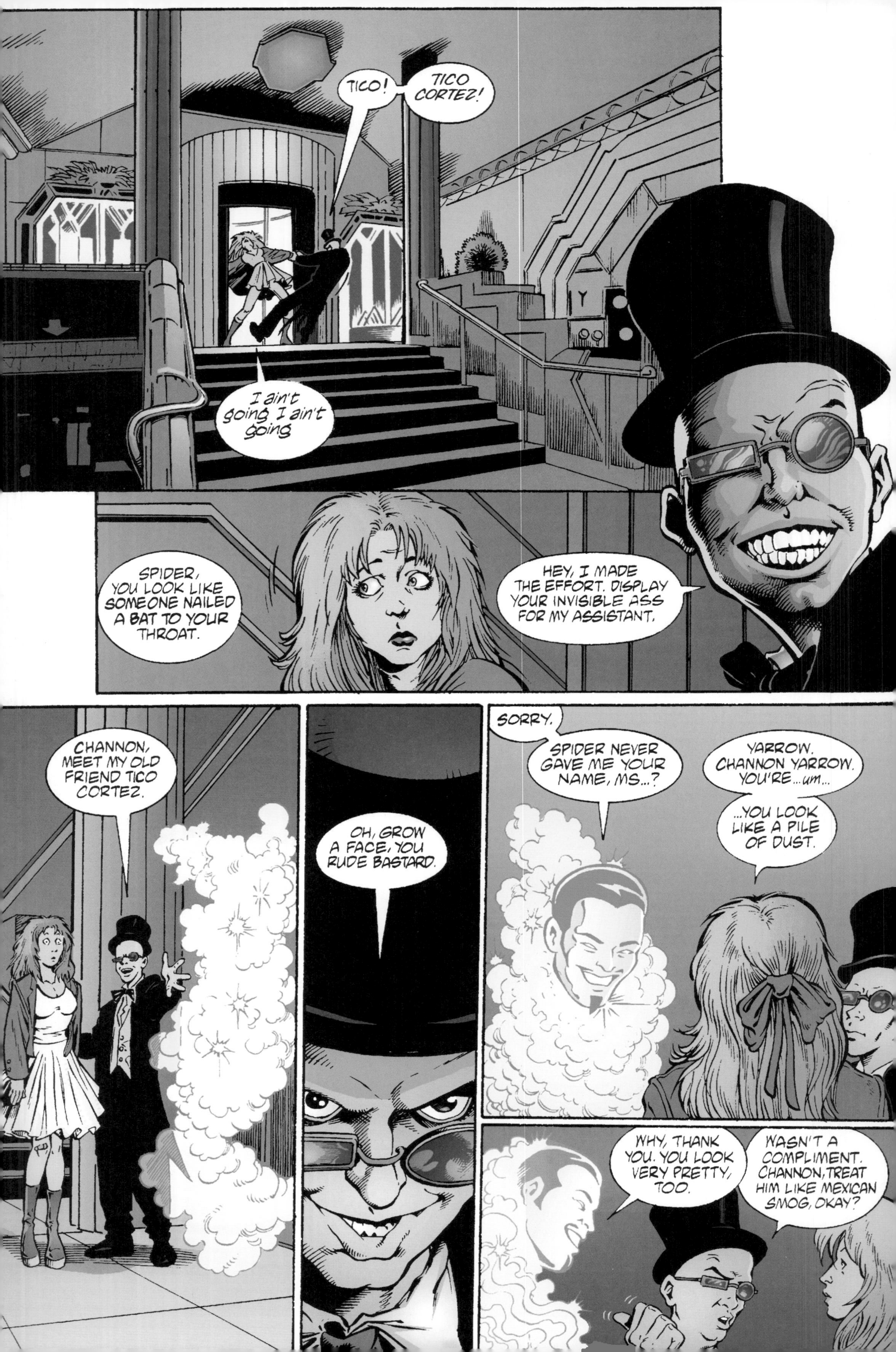
TICO!
TICO CORTEZ!
I ain't going I ain't going
SPIDER, YOU LOOK LIKE SOMEONE NAILED A BAT TO YOUR THROAT.
HEY, I MADE THE EFFORT. DISPLAY YOUR INVISIBLE ASS FOR MY ASSISTANT.
CHANNON, MEET MY OLD FRIEND TICO CORTEZ.
OH, GROW A FACE, YOU RUDE BASTARD.
SORRY.
SPIDER NEVER GAVE ME YOUR NAME, MS...?
YARROW. CHANNON YARROW. YOU'RE...um...
...YOU LOOK LIKE A PILE OF DUST.
WHY, THANK YOU. YOU LOOK VERY PRETTY, TOO.
WASN'T A COMPLIMENT. CHANNON, TREAT HIM LIKE MEXICAN SMOG, OKAY?

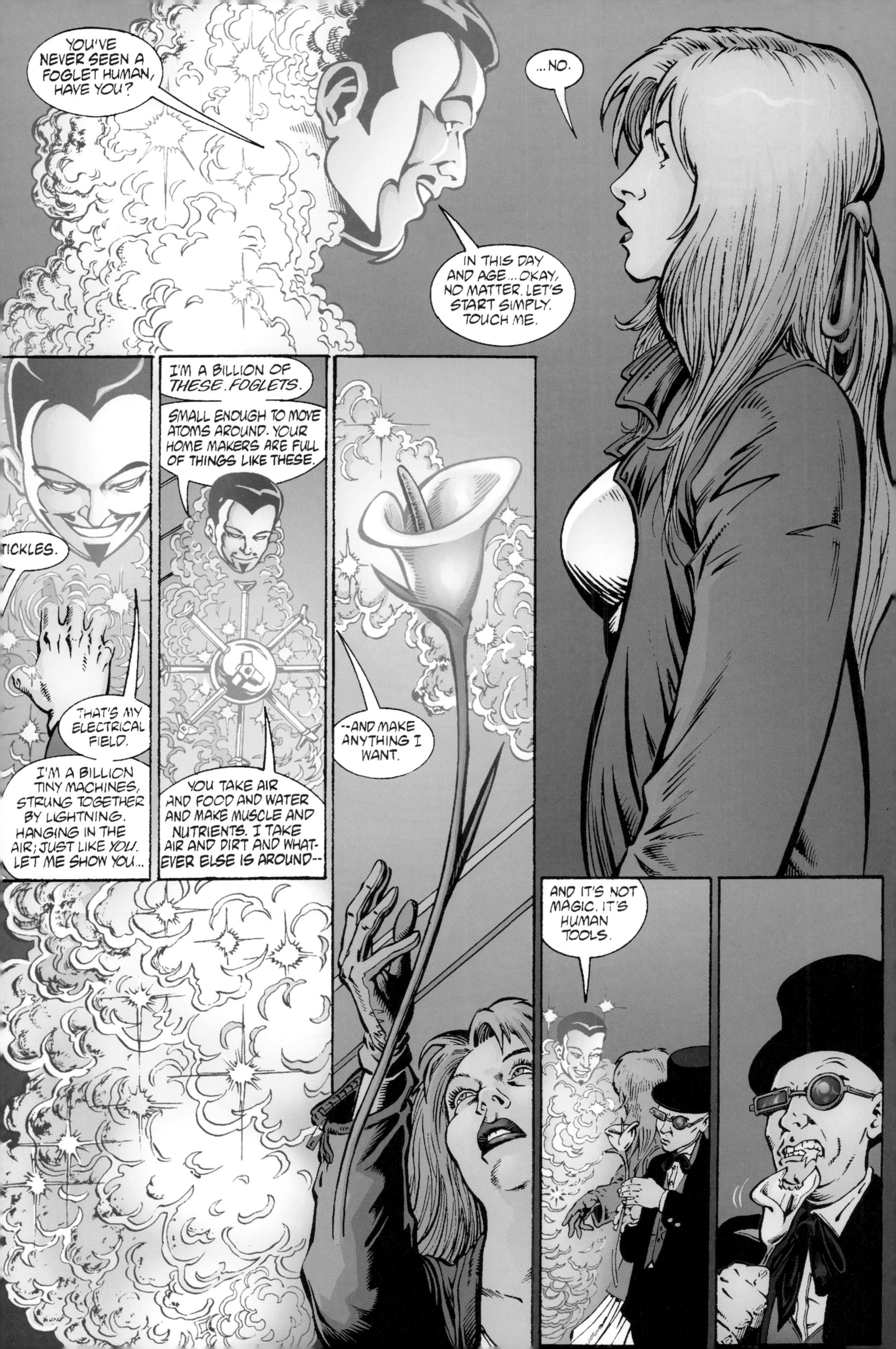
YOU'VE NEVER SEEN A FOGLET HUMAN, HAVE YOU?
...NO.
IN THIS DAY AND AGE... OKAY, NO MATTER. LET'S START SIMPLY. TOUCH ME.
TICKLES.
THAT'S MY ELECTRICAL FIELD.
I'M A BILLION TINY MACHINES, STRUNG TOGETHER BY LIGHTNING. HANGING IN THE AIR; JUST LIKE YOU. LET ME SHOW YOU...
I'M A BILLION OF THESE. FOGLETS.
SMALL ENOUGH TO MOVE ATOMS AROUND. YOUR HOME MAKERS ARE FULL OF THINGS LIKE THESE.
YOU TAKE AIR AND FOOD AND WATER AND MAKE MUSCLE AND NUTRIENTS. I TAKE AIR AND DIRT AND WHATEVER ELSE IS AROUND--
--AND MAKE ANYTHING I WANT.
AND IT'S NOT MAGIC. IT'S HUMAN TOOLS.

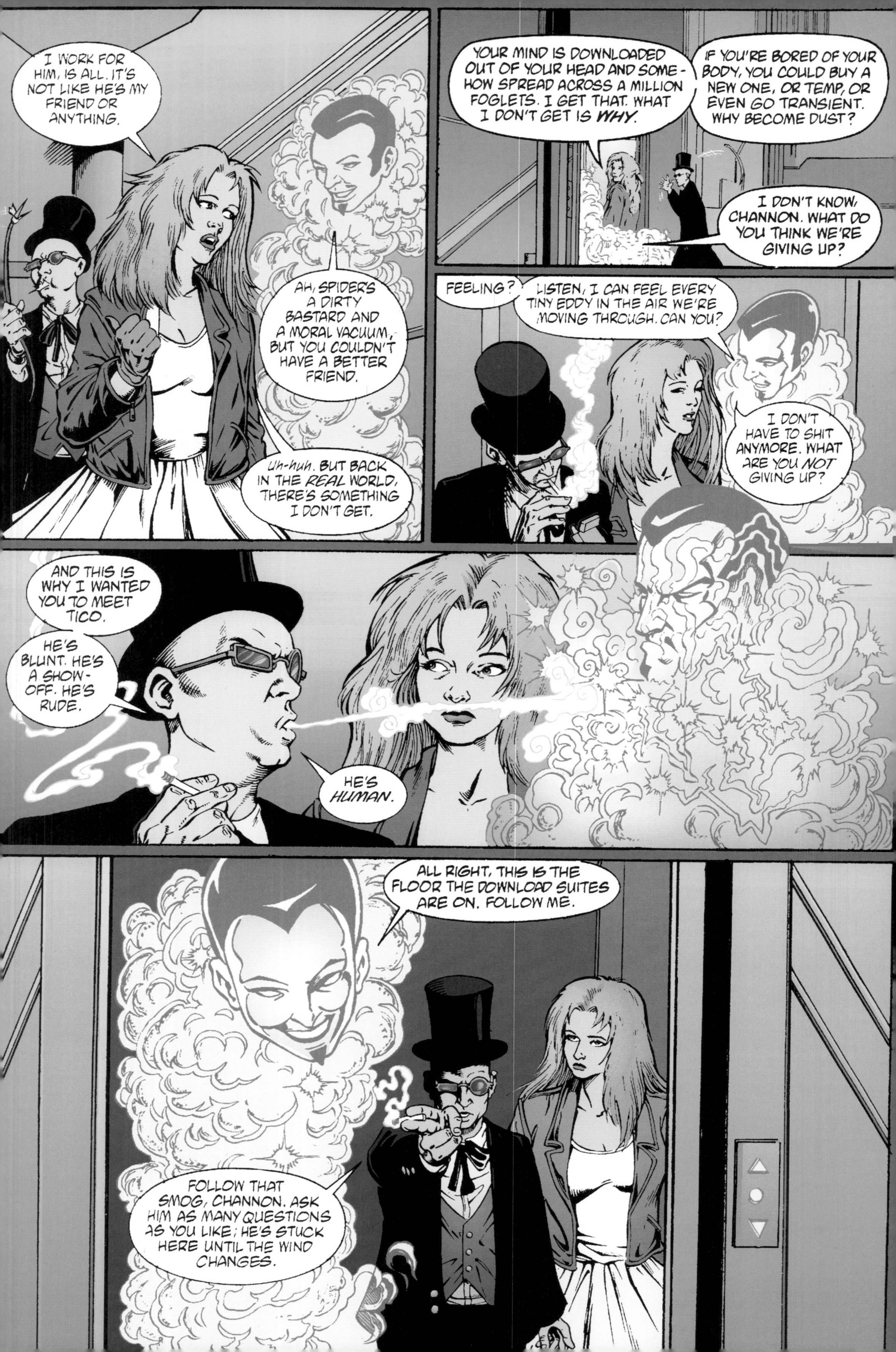
I WORK FOR HIM, IS ALL. IT'S NOT LIKE HE'S MY FRIEND OR ANYTHING.
AH, SPIDER'S A DIRTY BASTARD AND A MORAL VACUUM, BUT YOU COULDN'T HAVE A BETTER FRIEND.
UH-HUH. BUT BACK IN THE REAL WORLD, THERE'S SOMETHING I DON'T GET.
YOUR MIND IS DOWNLOADED OUT OF YOUR HEAD AND SOME-HOW SPREAD ACROSS A MILLION FOGLETS. I GET THAT. WHAT I DON'T GET IS WHY.
IF YOU'RE BORED OF YOUR BODY, YOU COULD BUY A NEW ONE, OR TEMP, OR EVEN GO TRANSIENT. WHY BECOME DUST?
I DON'T KNOW, CHANNON. WHAT DO YOU THINK WE'RE GIVING UP?
FEELING?
LISTEN, I CAN FEEL EVERY TINY EDDY IN THE AIR WE'RE MOVING THROUGH. CAN YOU?
I DON'T HAVE TO SHIT ANYMORE. WHAT ARE YOU NOT GIVING UP?
AND THIS IS WHY I WANTED YOU TO MEET TICO.
HE'S BLUNT. HE'S A SHOW-OFF. HE'S RUDE.
HE'S HUMAN.
ALL RIGHT, THIS IS THE FLOOR THE DOWNLOAD SUITES ARE ON. FOLLOW ME.
FOLLOW THAT SMOG, CHANNON. ASK HIM AS MANY QUESTIONS AS YOU LIKE; HE'S STUCK HERE UNTIL THE WIND CHANGES.

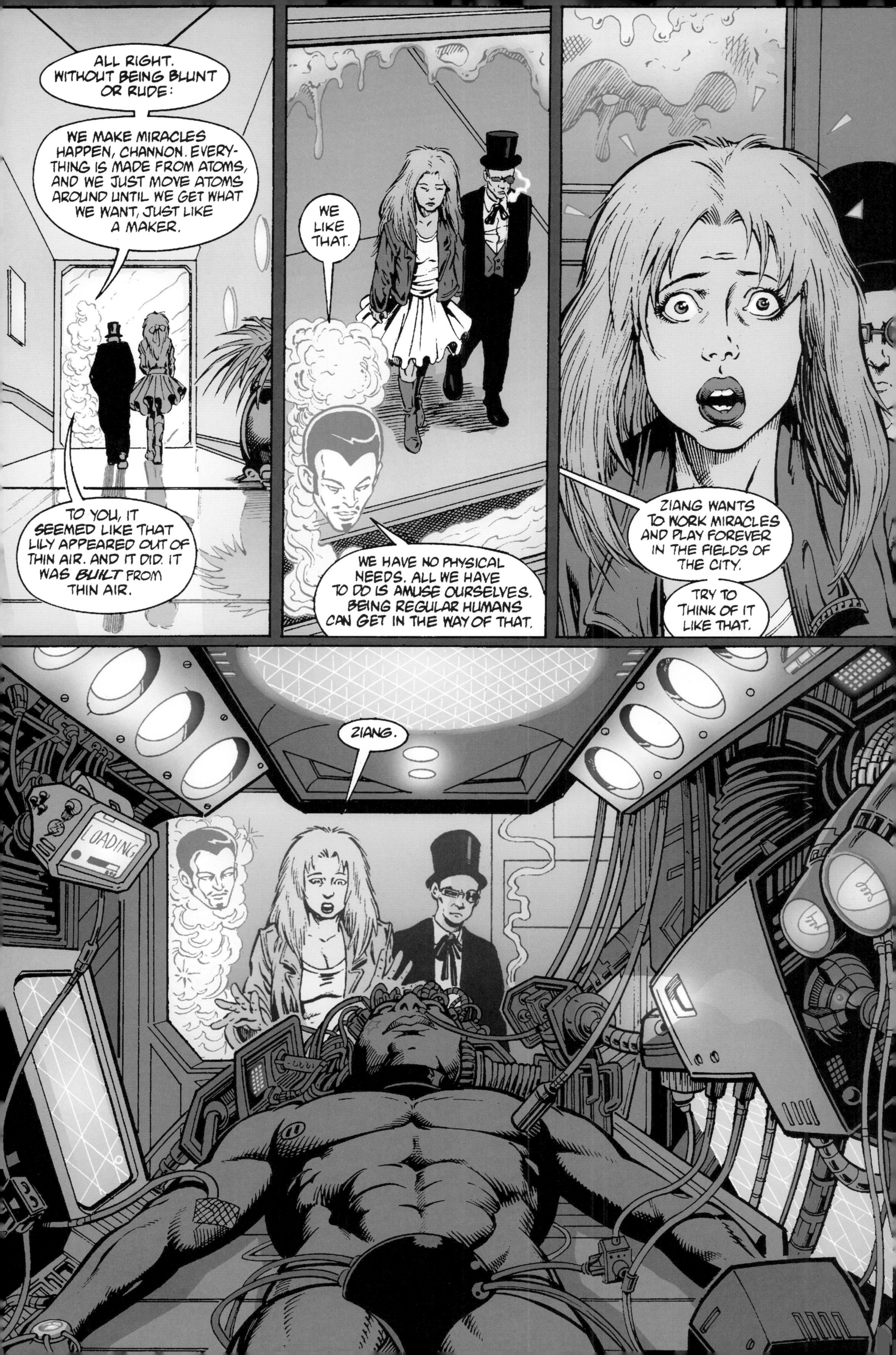
ALL RIGHT. WITHOUT BEING BLUNT OR RUDE:
WE MAKE MIRACLES HAPPEN, CHANNON. EVERYTHING IS MADE FROM ATOMS, AND WE JUST MOVE ATOMS AROUND UNTIL WE GET WHAT WE WANT, JUST LIKE A MAKER.
TO YOU, IT SEEMED LIKE THAT LILY APPEARED OUT OF THIN AIR. AND IT DID. IT WAS BUILT FROM THIN AIR.
WE LIKE THAT.
WE HAVE NO PHYSICAL NEEDS. ALL WE HAVE TO DO IS AMUSE OURSELVES. BEING REGULAR HUMANS CAN GET IN THE WAY OF THAT.
ZIANG WANTS TO WORK MIRACLES AND PLAY FOREVER IN THE FIELDS OF THE CITY.
TRY TO THINK OF IT LIKE THAT.
ZIANG.
LOADING

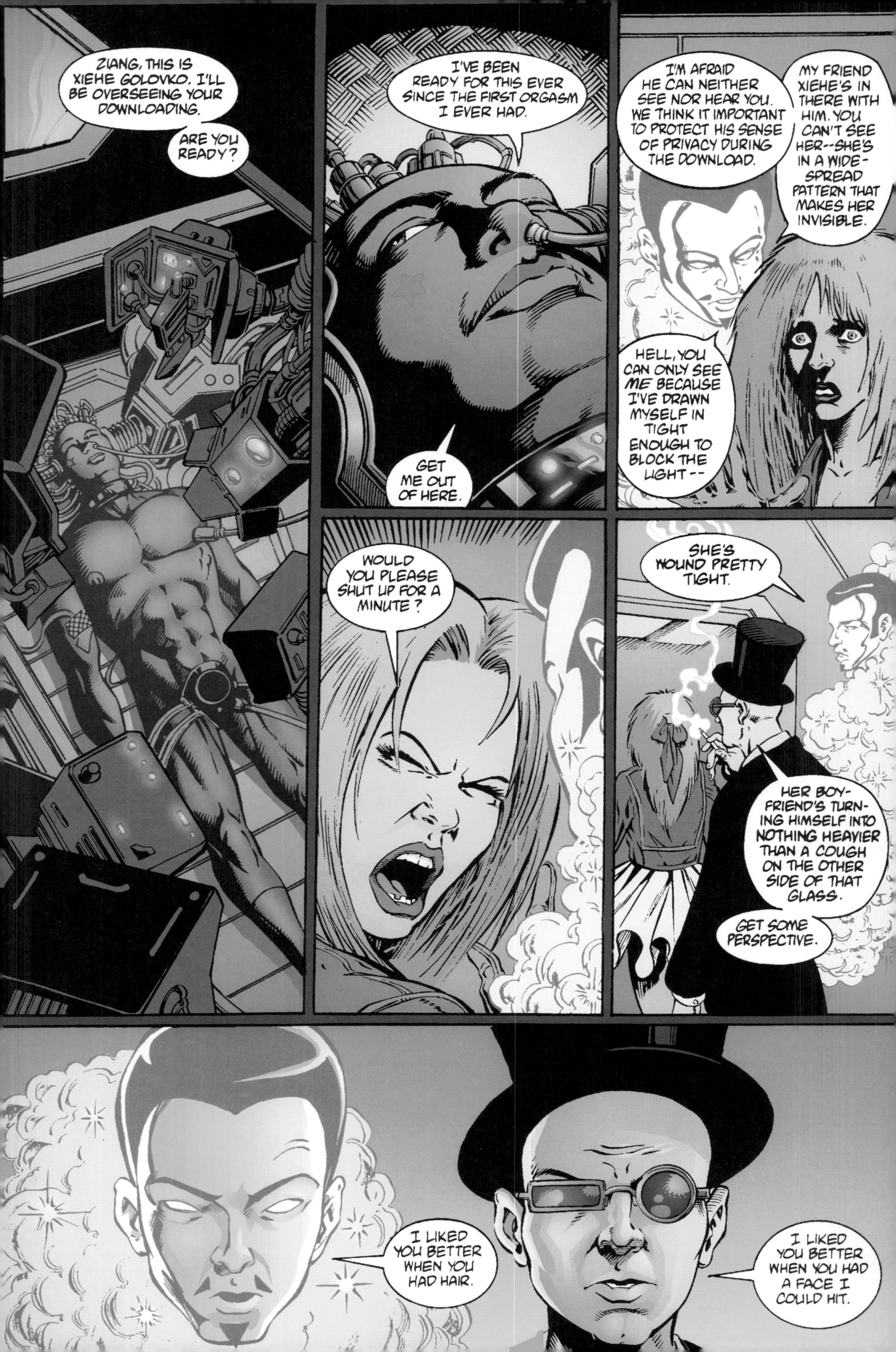
ZIANG, THIS IS XIEHE GOLOVKO. I'LL BE OVERSEEING YOUR DOWNLOADING.
ARE YOU READY?
I'VE BEEN READY FOR THIS EVER SINCE THE FIRST ORGASM I EVER HAD.
GET ME OUT OF HERE.
I'M AFRAID HE CAN NEITHER SEE NOR HEAR YOU. WE THINK IT IMPORTANT TO PROTECT HIS SENSE OF PRIVACY DURING THE DOWNLOAD.
MY FRIEND XIEHE'S IN THERE WITH HIM. YOU CAN'T SEE HER--SHE'S IN A WIDE-SPREAD PATTERN THAT MAKES HER INVISIBLE.
HELL, YOU CAN ONLY SEE ME BECAUSE I'VE DRAWN MYSELF IN TIGHT ENOUGH TO BLOCK THE LIGHT--
WOULD YOU PLEASE SHUT UP FOR A MINUTE?
SHE'S WOUND PRETTY TIGHT.
HER BOY-FRIEND'S TURNING HIMSELF INTO NOTHING HEAVIER THAN A COUGH ON THE OTHER SIDE OF THAT GLASS.
GET SOME PERSPECTIVE.
I LIKED YOU BETTER WHEN YOU HAD HAIR.
I LIKED YOU BETTER WHEN YOU HAD A FACE I COULD HIT.

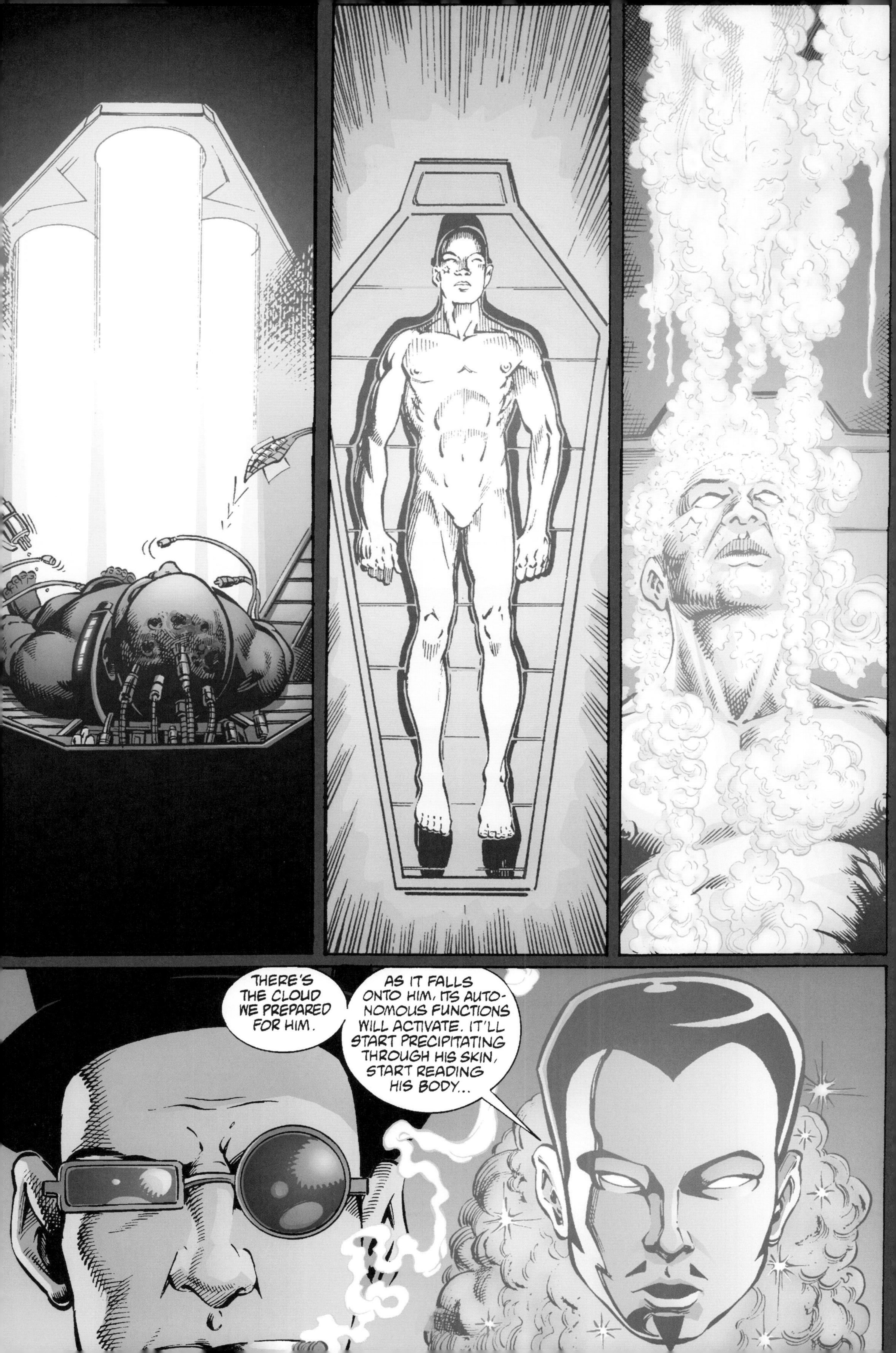
THERE'S THE CLOUD WE PREPARED FOR HIM.
AS IT FALLS ONTO HIM, ITS AUTO-NOMOUS FUNCTIONS WILL ACTIVATE. IT'LL START PRECIPITATING THROUGH HIS SKIN, START READING HIS BODY...

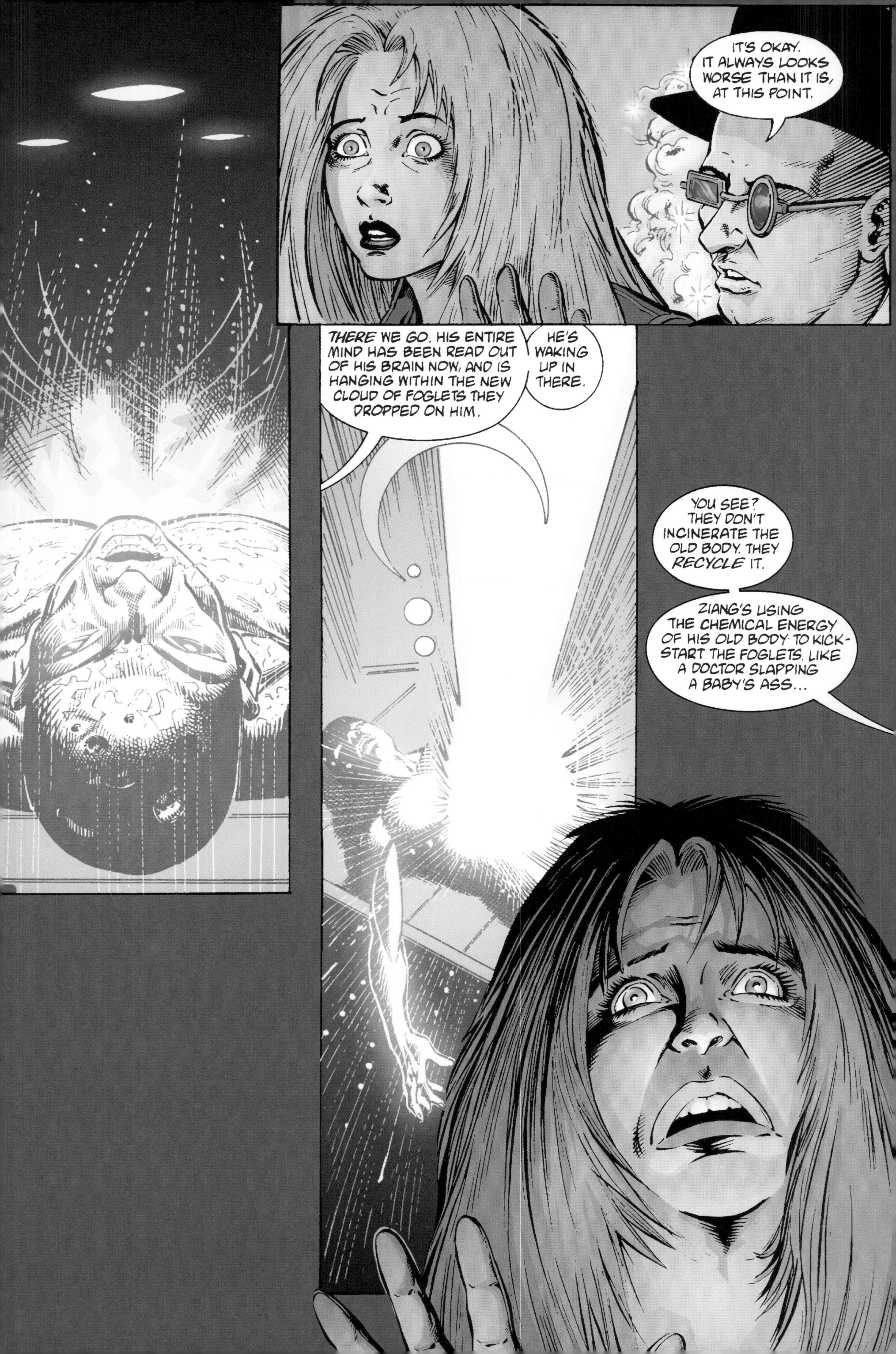
IT'S OKAY. IT ALWAYS LOOKS WORSE THAN IT IS, AT THIS POINT.
THERE WE GO. HIS ENTIRE MIND HAS BEEN READ OUT OF HIS BRAIN NOW, AND IS HANGING WITHIN THE NEW CLOUD OF FOGLETS THEY DROPPED ON HIM.
HE'S WAKING UP IN THERE.
YOU SEE? THEY DON'T INCINERATE THE OLD BODY. THEY RECYCLE IT.
ZIANG'S USING THE CHEMICAL ENERGY OF HIS OLD BODY TO KICK-START THE FOGLETS. LIKE A DOCTOR SLAPPING A BABY'S ASS...

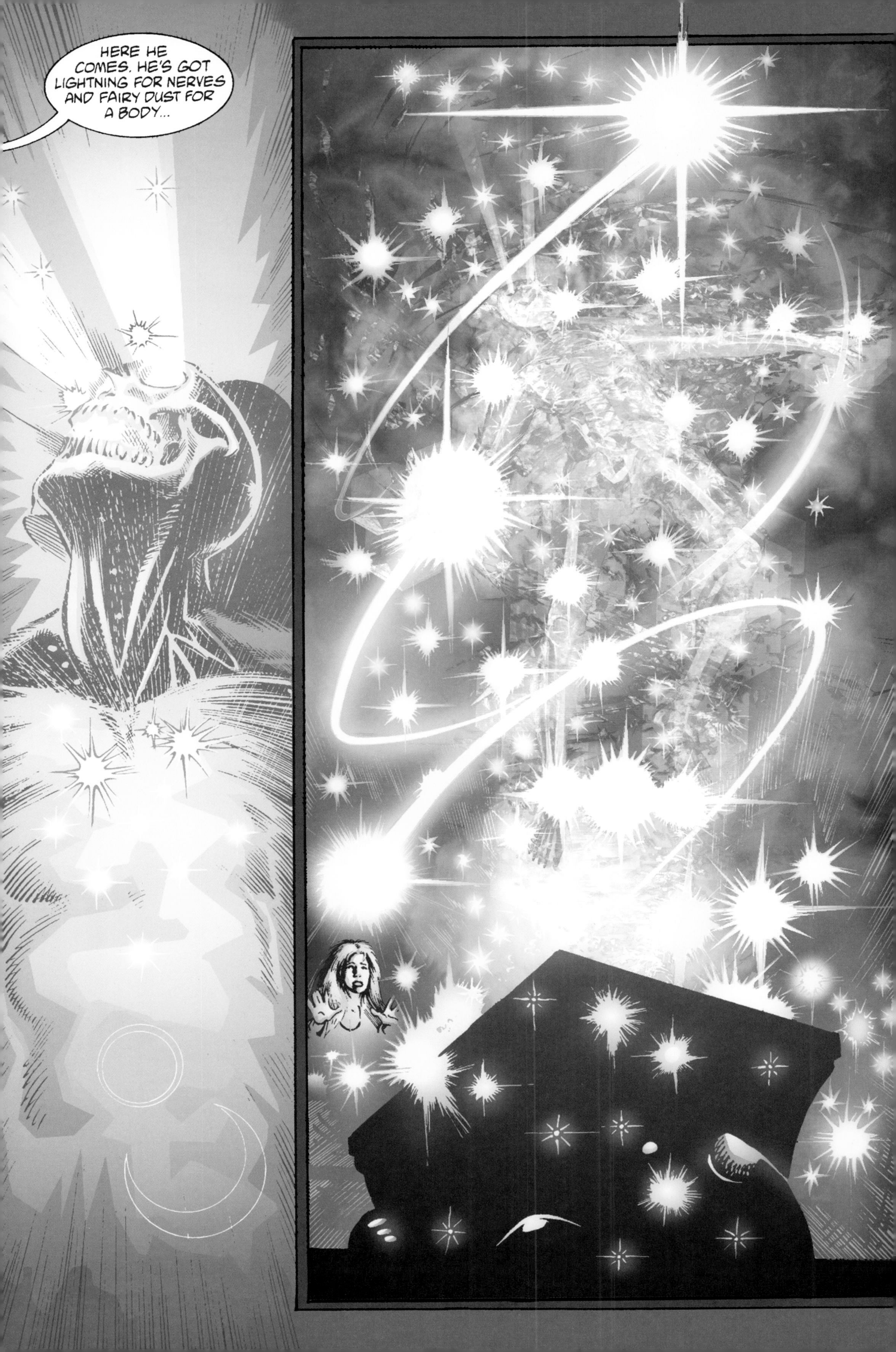
HERE HE COMES. HE'S GOT LIGHTNING FOR NERVES AND FAIRY DUST FOR A BODY...

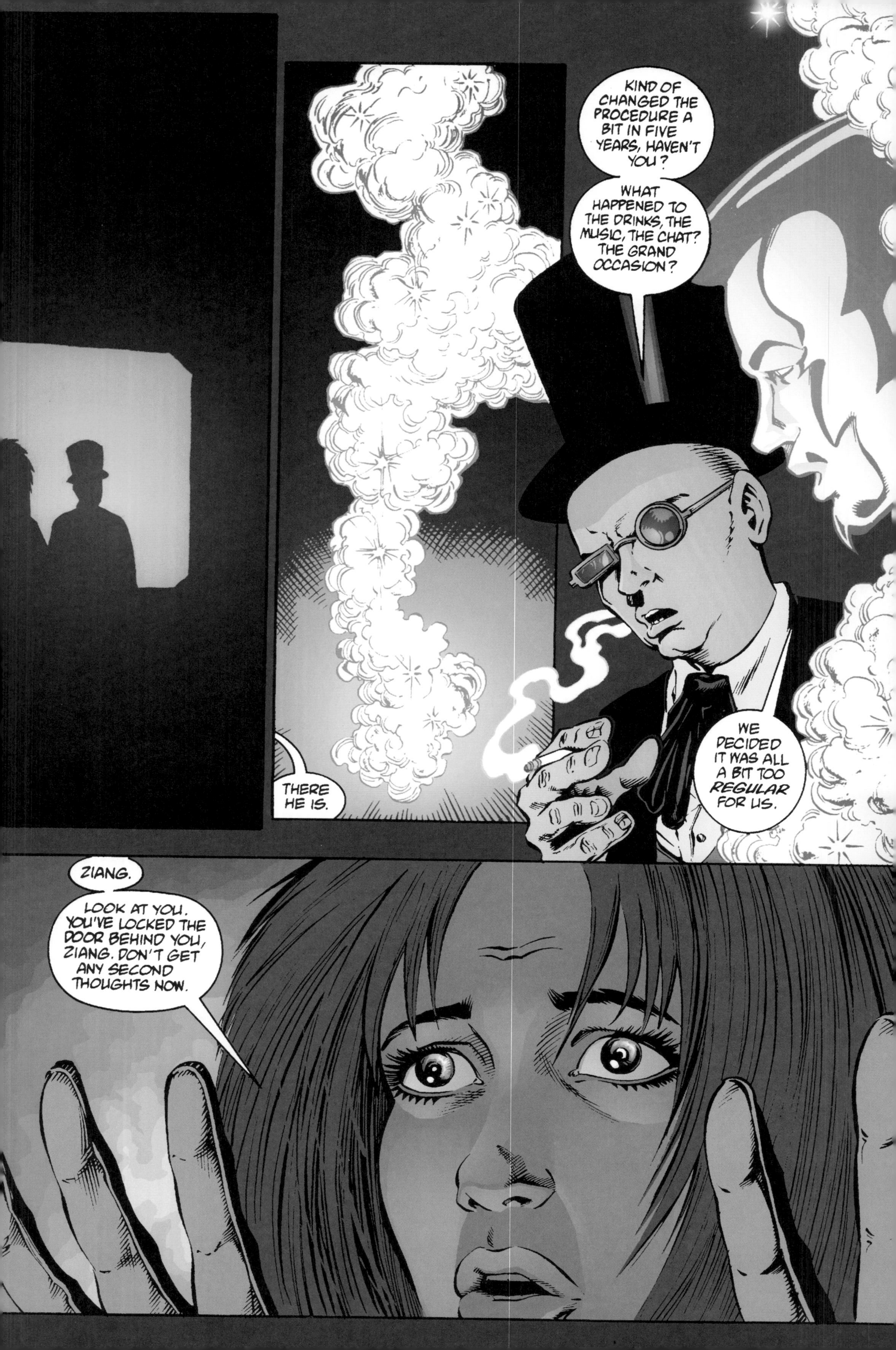
KIND OF CHANGED THE PROCEDURE A BIT IN FIVE YEARS, HAVEN'T YOU?
WHAT HAPPENED TO THE DRINKS, THE MUSIC, THE CHAT? THE GRAND OCCASION?
THERE HE IS.
WE DECIDED IT WAS ALL A BIT TOO *REGULAR* FOR US.
ZIANG.
LOOK AT YOU. YOU'VE LOCKED THE DOOR BEHIND YOU, ZIANG. DON'T GET ANY SECOND THOUGHTS NOW.

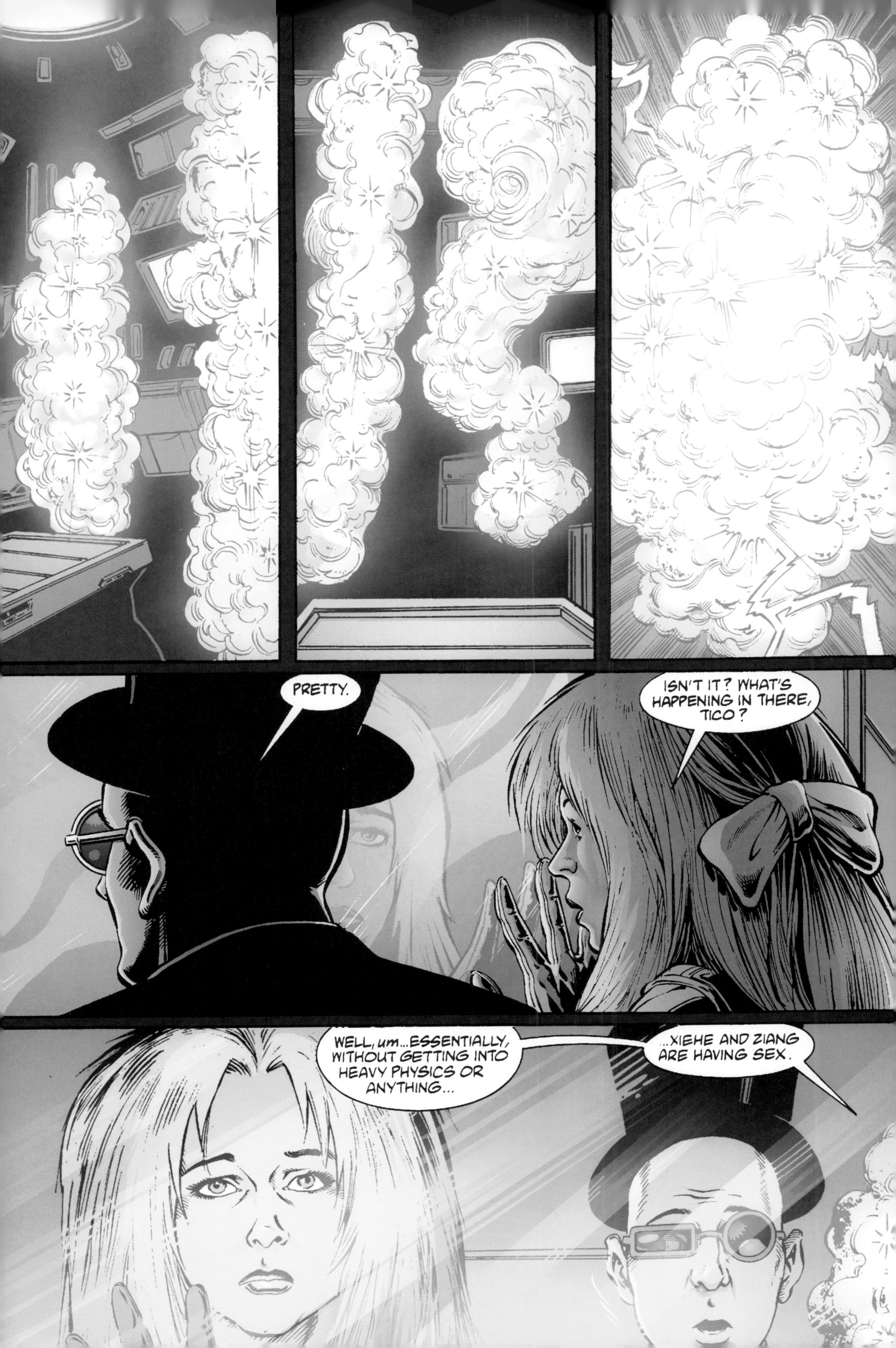
PRETTY.
ISN'T IT? WHAT'S HAPPENING IN THERE, TICO?
WELL, um...ESSENTIALLY, WITHOUT GETTING INTO HEAVY PHYSICS OR ANYTHING...
...XIEHE AND ZIANG ARE HAVING SEX.

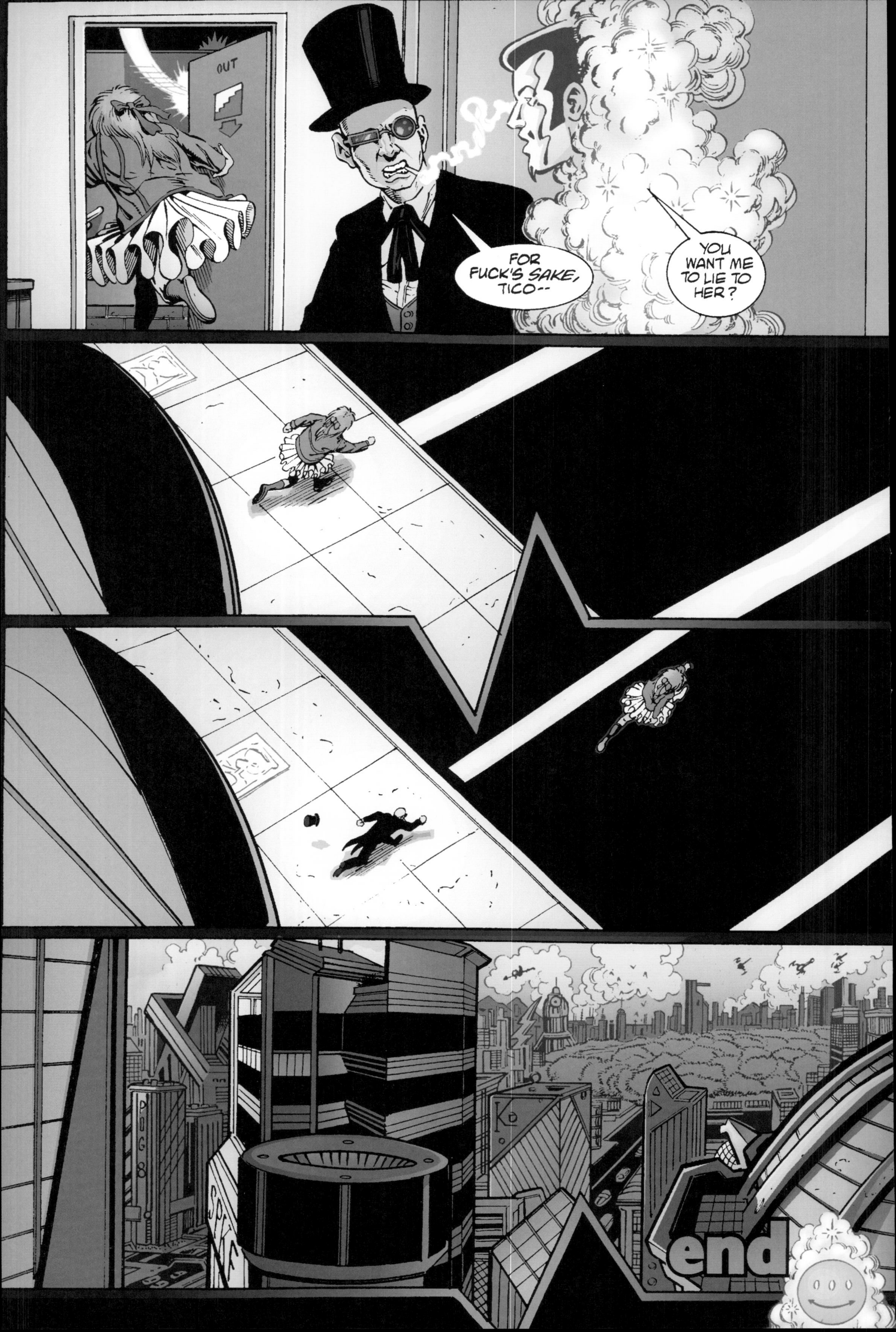
OUT
FOR FUCK'S SAKE, TICO--
YOU WANT ME TO LIE TO HER?
end

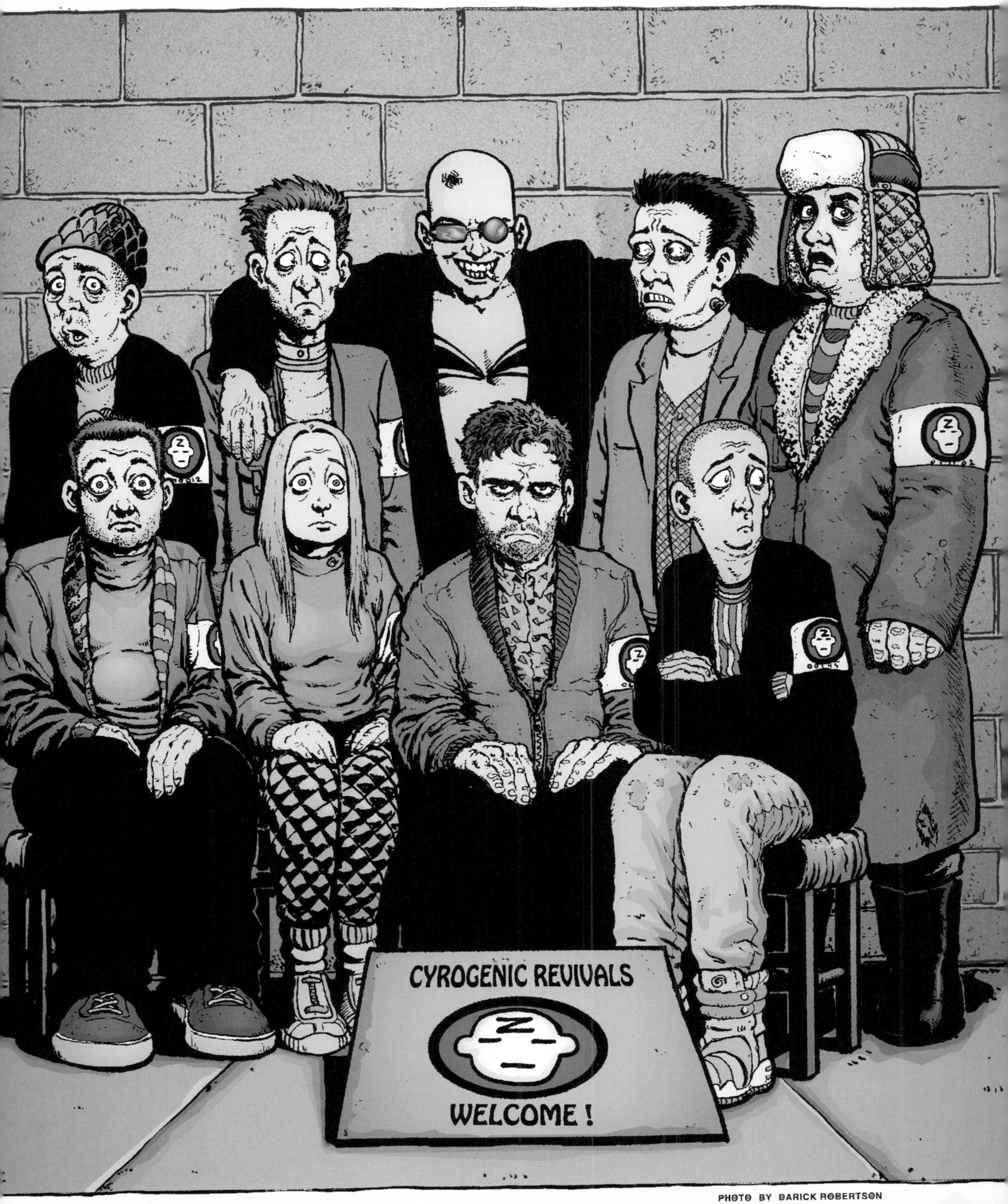
CYROGENIC REVIVALS
WELCOME !

PHOTO BY DARICK ROBERTSON

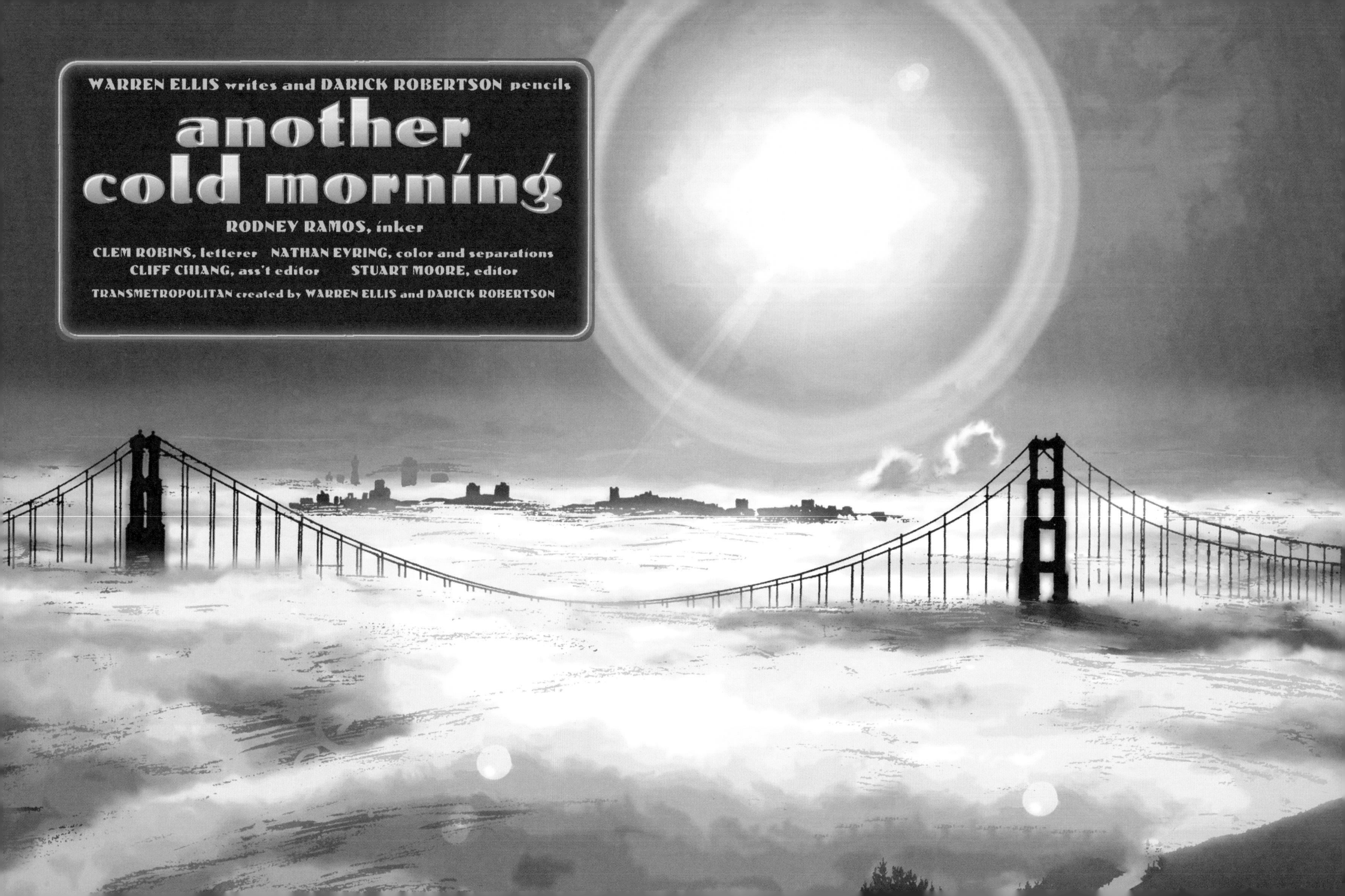
WARREN ELLIS writes and DARICK ROBERTSON pencils
another cold morning
RODNEY RAMOS, inker
CLEM ROBINS, letterer NATHAN EYRING, color and separations
CLIFF CHIANG, ass't editor STUART MOORE, editor
TRANSMETROPOLITAN created by WARREN ELLIS and DARICK ROBERTSON

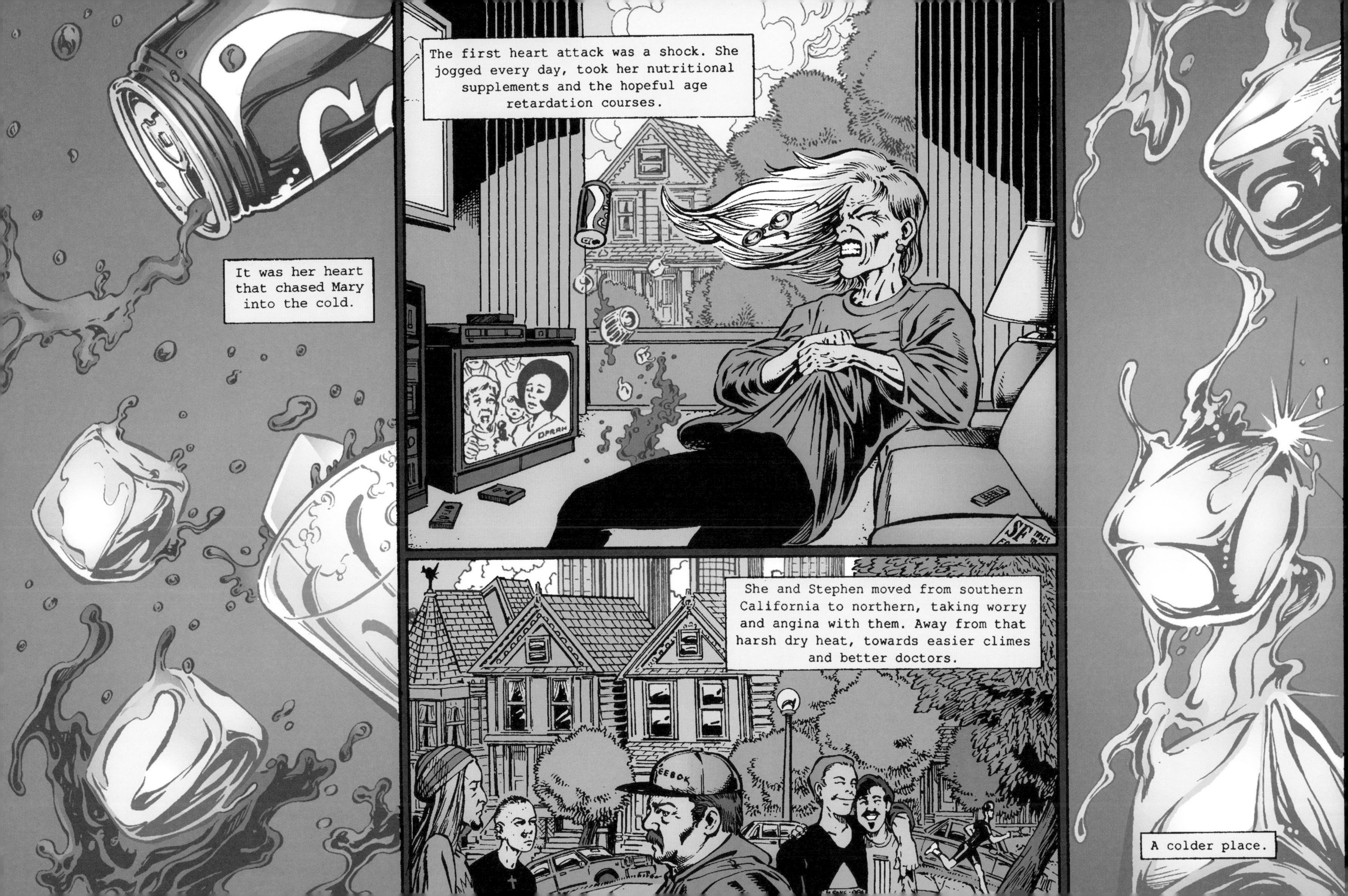
It was her heart that chased Mary into the cold.
The first heart attack was a shock. She jogged every day, took her nutritional supplements and the hopeful age retardation courses.
OPRAH
She and Stephen moved from southern California to northern, taking worry and angina with them. Away from that harsh dry heat, towards easier climes and better doctors.
A colder place.

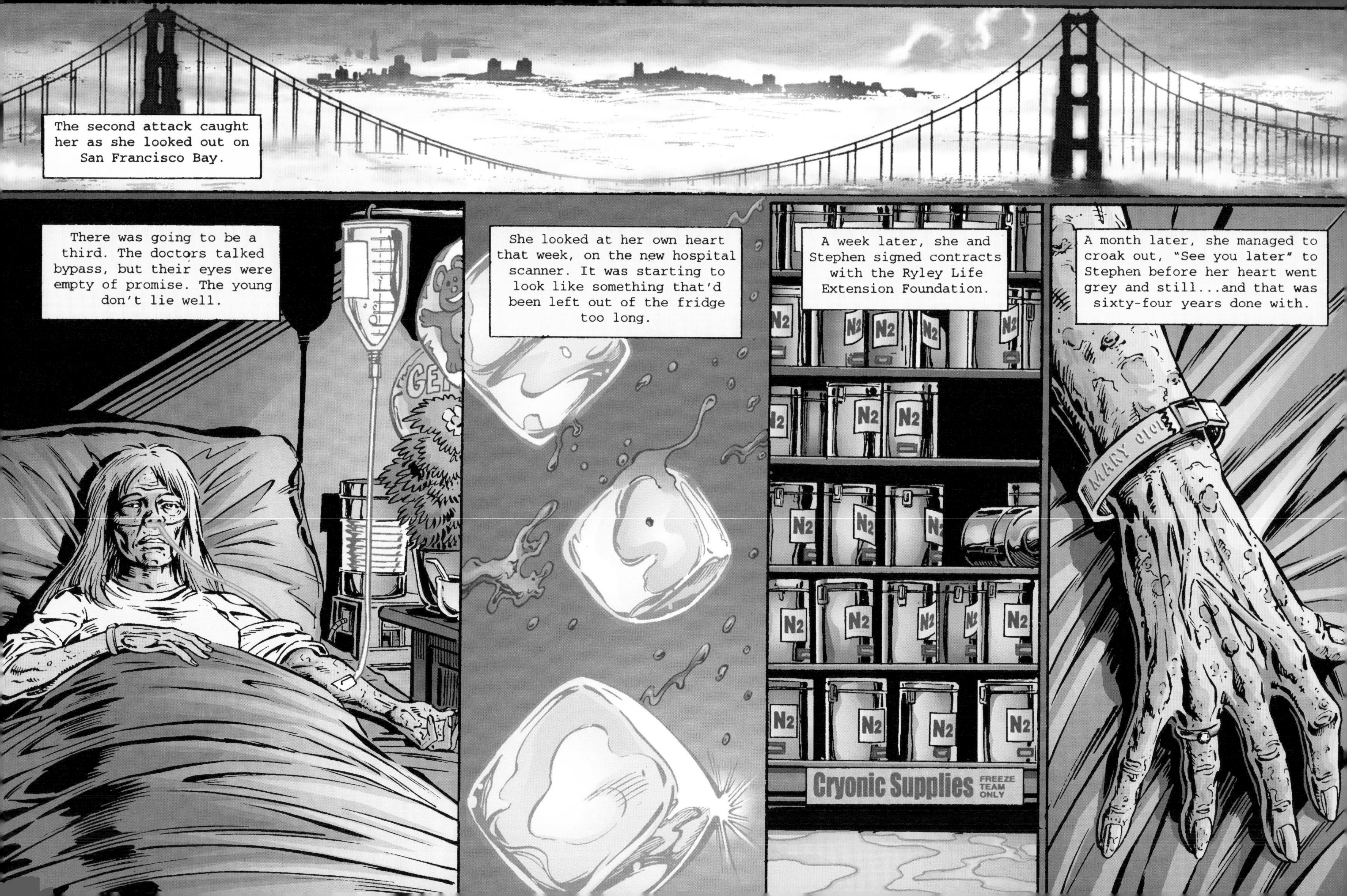
The second attack caught her as she looked out on San Francisco Bay.
There was going to be a third. The doctors talked bypass, but their eyes were empty of promise. The young don't lie well.
She looked at her own heart that week, on the new hospital scanner. It was starting to look like something that'd been left out of the fridge too long.
A week later, she and Stephen signed contracts with the Ryley Life Extension Foundation.
N2
Cryonic Supplies
FREEZE TEAM ONLY
A month later, she managed to croak out, "See you later" to Stephen before her heart went grey and still...and that was sixty-four years done with.
MARY

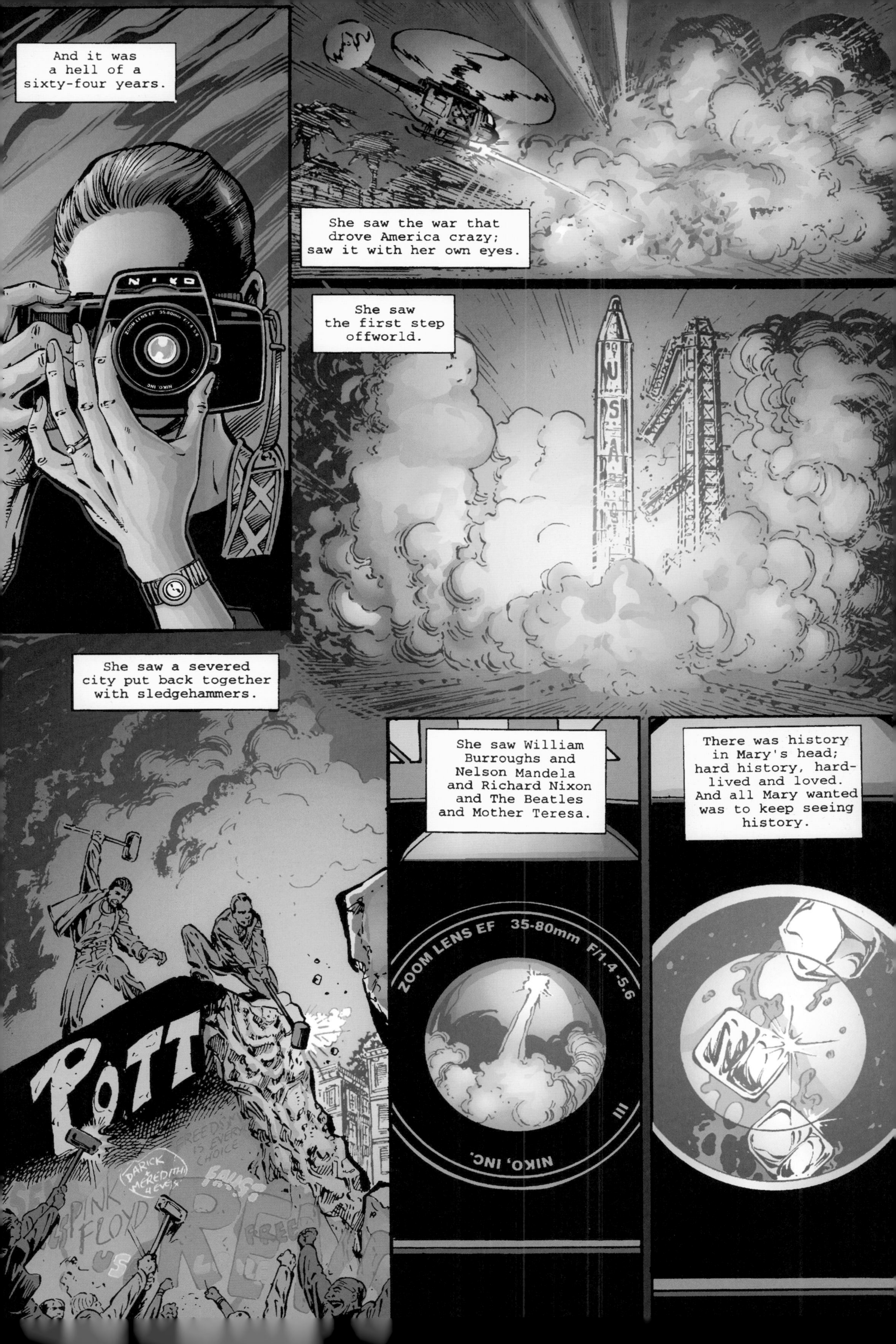
And it was a hell of a sixty-four years.
She saw the war that drove America crazy; saw it with her own eyes.
She saw the first step offworld.
NUSA
She saw a severed city put back together with sledgehammers.
POTT
FREEDOM IS EVERY CHOICE
DARICK + MEREDITH 4EVER
PINK FLOYD
She saw William Burroughs and Nelson Mandela and Richard Nixon and The Beatles and Mother Teresa.
ZOOM LENS EF 35-80mm F/1.4-5.6
NIKO, INC.
There was history in Mary's head; hard history, hard-lived and loved. And all Mary wanted was to keep seeing history.

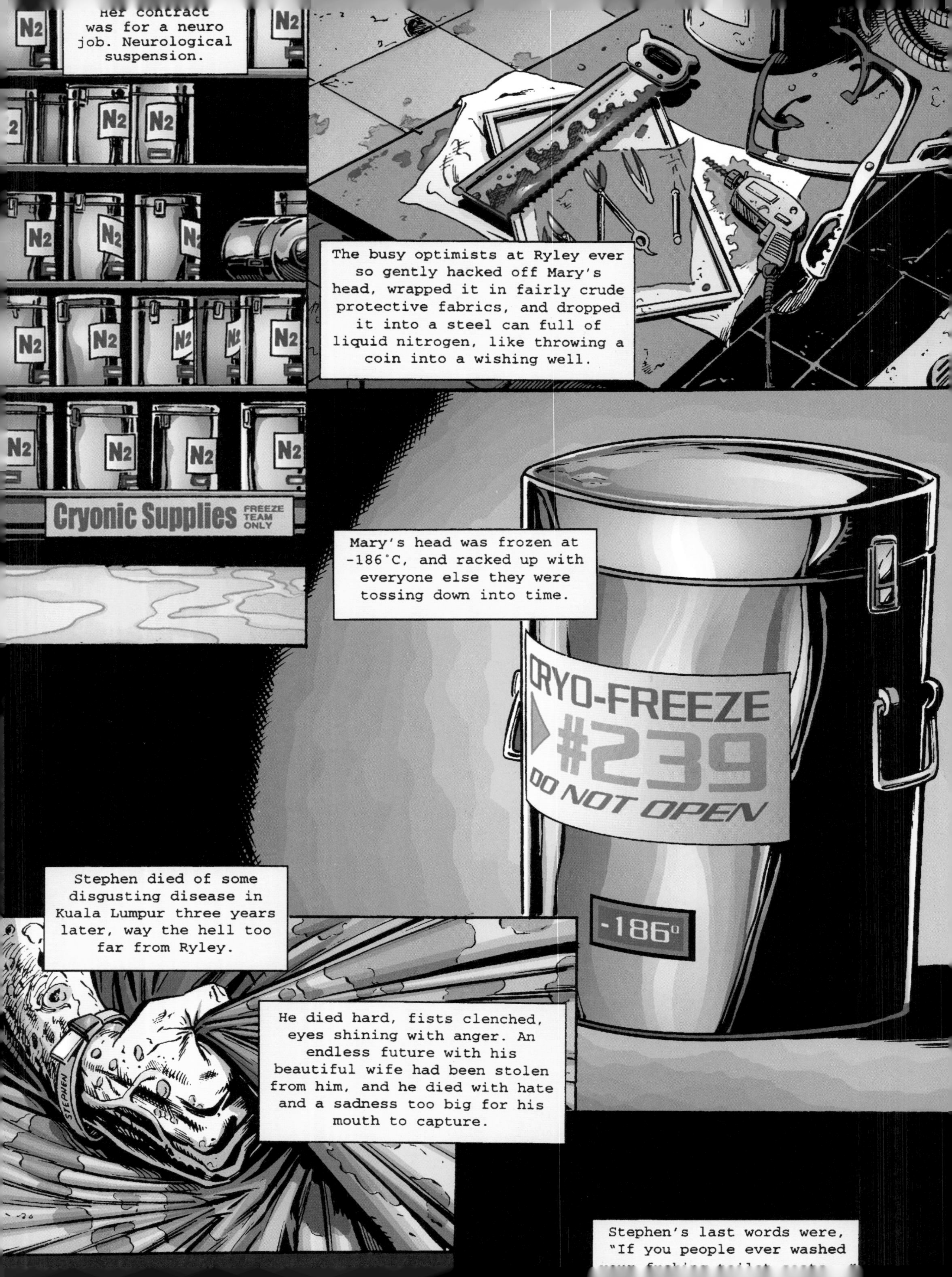
Her contract was for a neuro job. Neurological suspension.
N2
Cryonic Supplies
FREEZE TEAM ONLY
The busy optimists at Ryley ever so gently hacked off Mary's head, wrapped it in fairly crude protective fabrics, and dropped it into a steel can full of liquid nitrogen, like throwing a coin into a wishing well.
Mary's head was frozen at -186°C, and racked up with everyone else they were tossing down into time.
CRYO-FREEZE #239 DO NOT OPEN
-186°
Stephen died of some disgusting disease in Kuala Lumpur three years later, way the hell too far from Ryley.
He died hard, fists clenched, eyes shining with anger. An endless future with his beautiful wife had been stolen from him, and he died with hate and a sadness too big for his mouth to capture.
STEPHEN
Stephen's last words were, "If you people ever washed

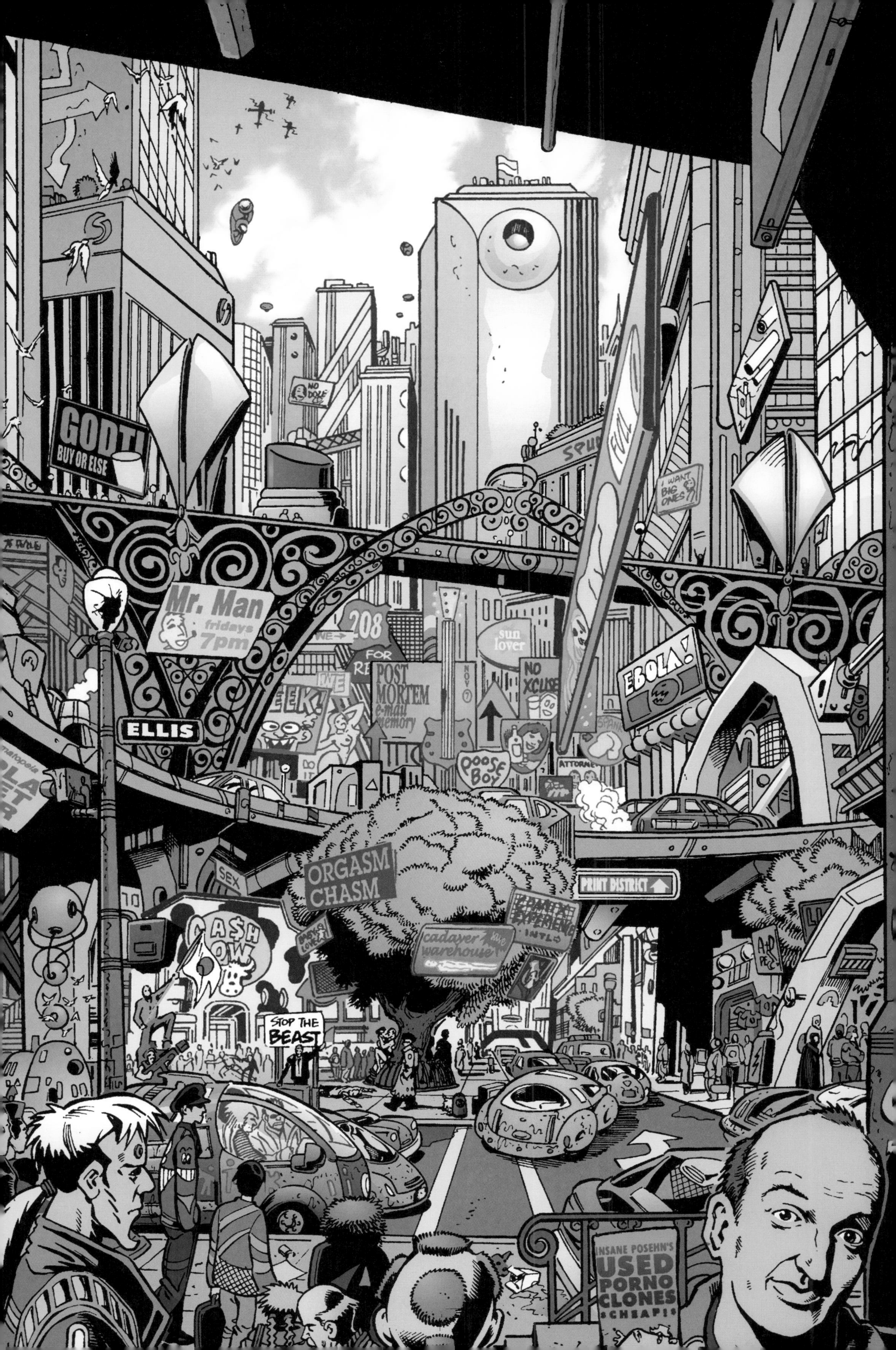
GODT!
BUY OR ELSE
NO DOLE
SPUD
FULL
I WANT BIG ONES
Mr. Man
fridays
7pm
208
FOR RE
sun lover
POST MORTEM
e-mail memory
NO XCUSE
EEK!
EBOLA!
ELLIS
POOSE BOY
ATTORNEY
SEX
ORGASM CHASM
PRINT DISTRICT
cadaver warehouse
CA$H COW
STOP THE BEAST
INSANE POSEHN'S
USED PORNO CLONES
CHEAP!!

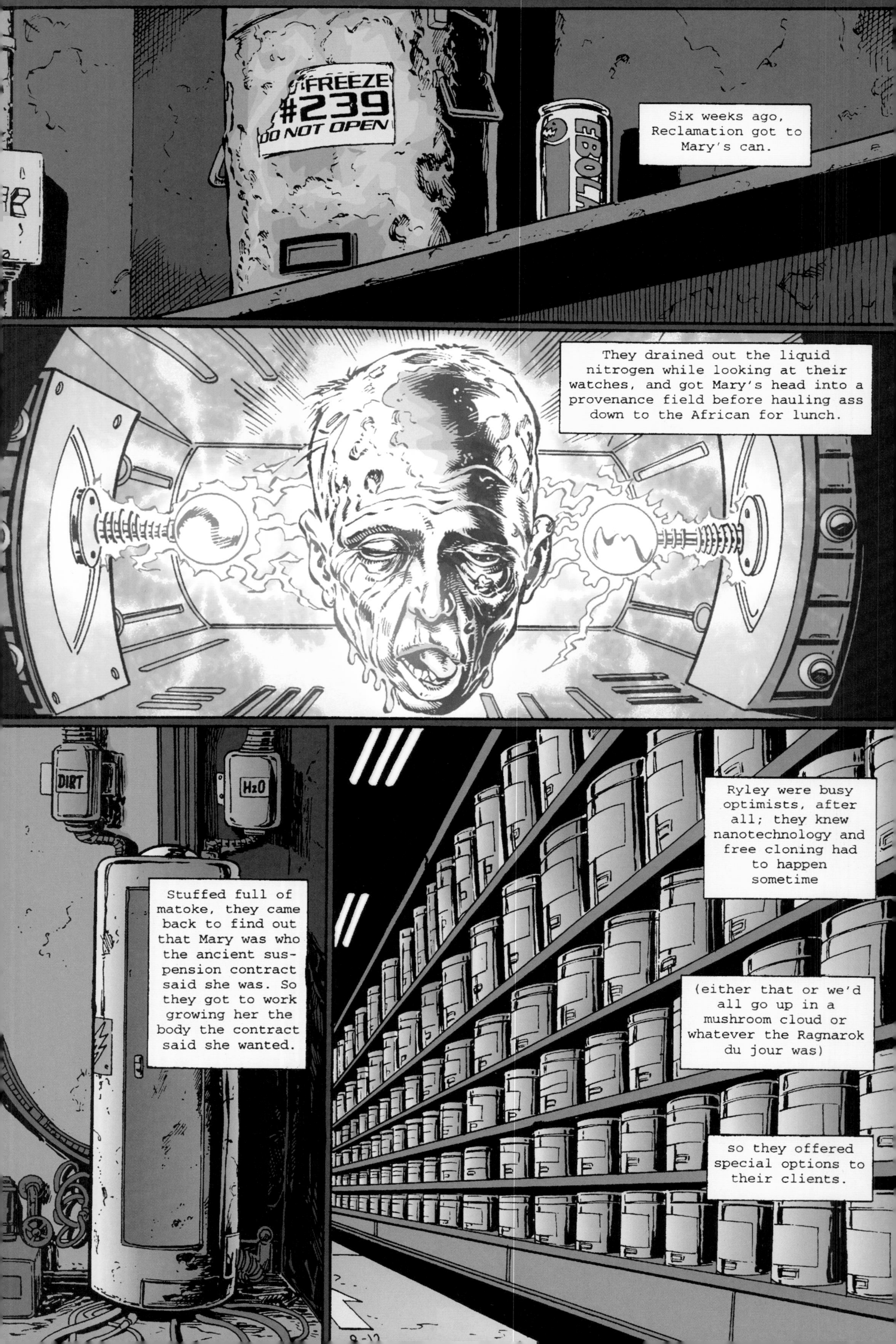

FREEZE
#239
DO NOT OPEN
EBOLA
Six weeks ago, Reclamation got to Mary's can.
They drained out the liquid nitrogen while looking at their watches, and got Mary's head into a provenance field before hauling ass down to the African for lunch.
DIRT
H2O
Stuffed full of matoke, they came back to find out that Mary was who the ancient suspension contract said she was. So they got to work growing her the body the contract said she wanted.
Ryley were busy optimists, after all; they knew nanotechnology and free cloning had to happen sometime
(either that or we'd all go up in a mushroom cloud or whatever the Ragnarok du jour was)
so they offered special options to their clients.

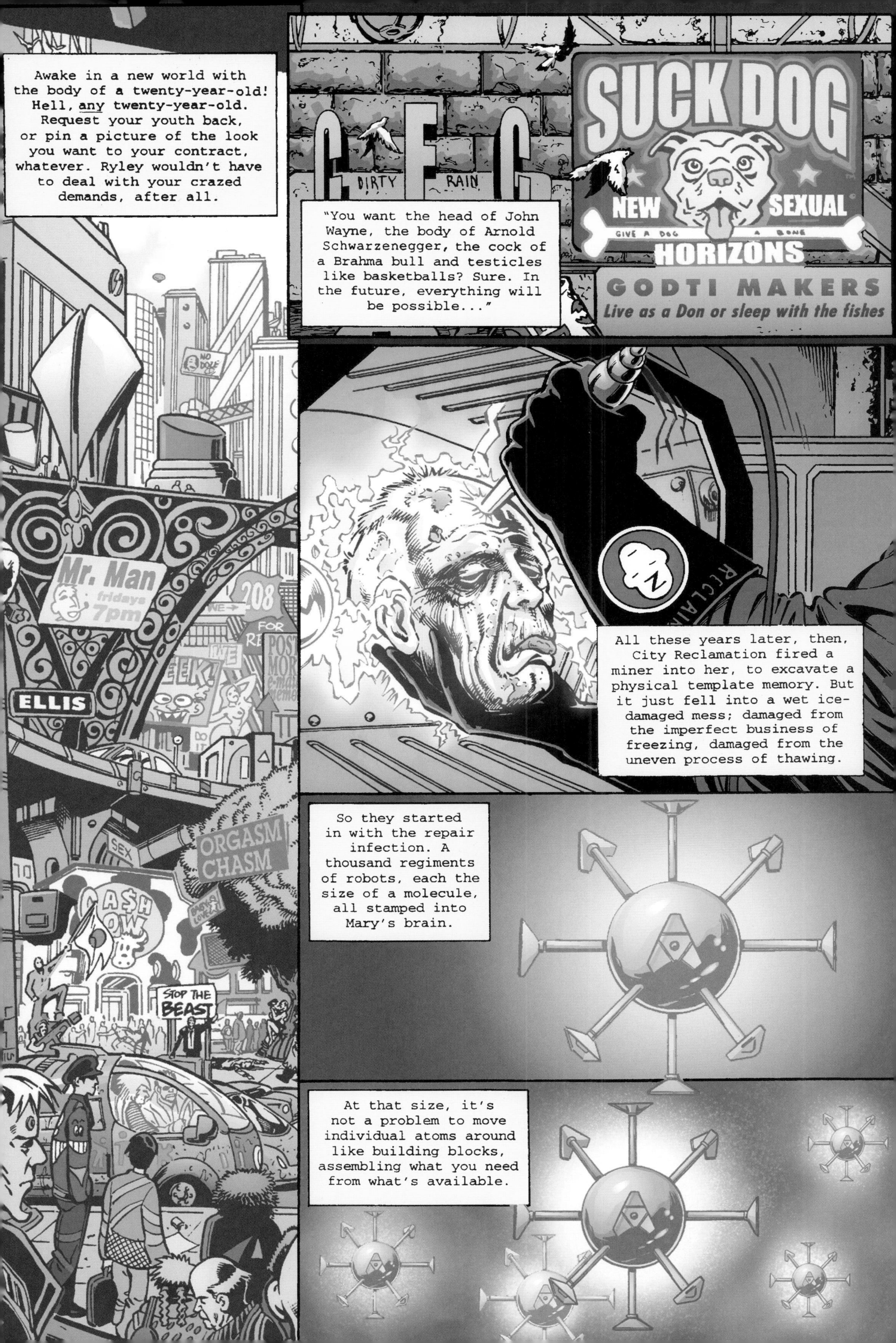

Awake in a new world with the body of a twenty-year-old! Hell, any twenty-year-old. Request your youth back, or pin a picture of the look you want to your contract, whatever. Ryley wouldn't have to deal with your crazed demands, after all.
C F C
DIRTY
RAIN
"You want the head of John Wayne, the body of Arnold Schwarzenegger, the cock of a Brahma bull and testicles like basketballs? Sure. In the future, everything will be possible..."
SUCK DOG
NEW
SEXUAL
GIVE A DOG A BONE
HORIZONS
GODTI MAKERS
Live as a Don or sleep with the fishes
Mr. Man
fridays
7pm
208
ELLIS
ORGASM CHASM
SEX
STOP THE BEAST
All these years later, then, City Reclamation fired a miner into her, to excavate a physical template memory. But it just fell into a wet ice-damaged mess; damaged from the imperfect business of freezing, damaged from the uneven process of thawing.
So they started in with the repair infection. A thousand regiments of robots, each the size of a molecule, all stamped into Mary's brain.
At that size, it's not a problem to move individual atoms around like building blocks, assembling what you need from what's available.

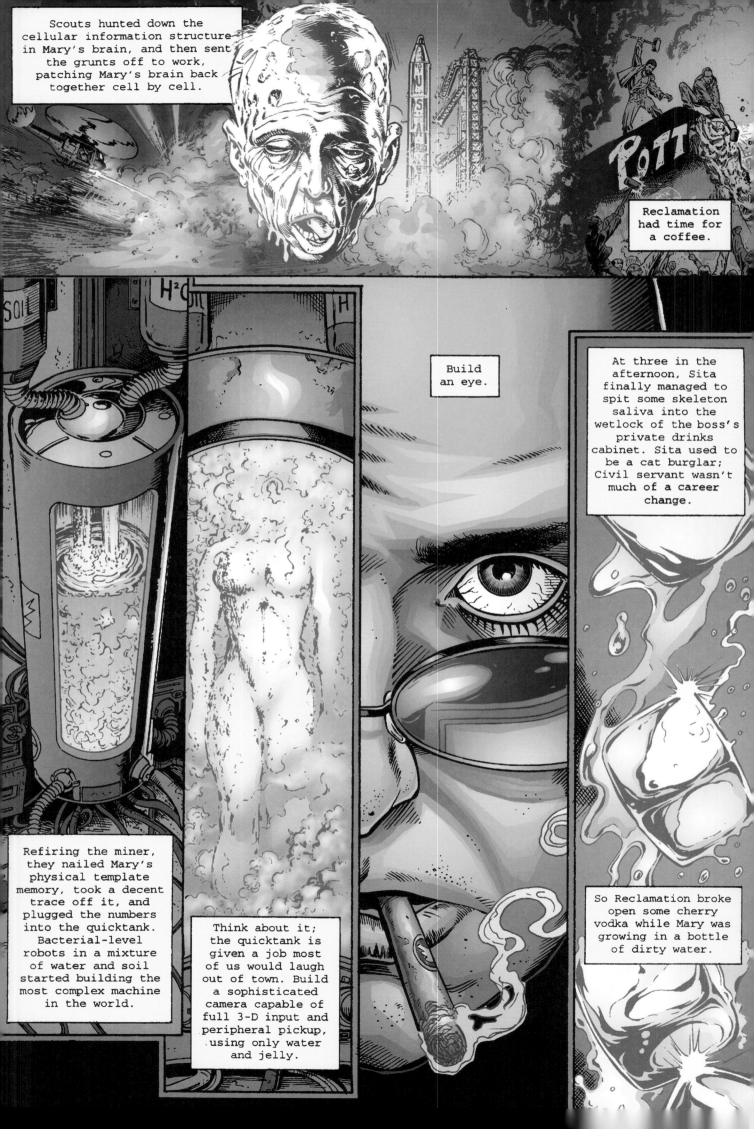

Scouts hunted down the cellular information structure in Mary's brain, and then sent the grunts off to work, patching Mary's brain back together cell by cell.

Reclamation had time for a coffee.

Build an eye.

At three in the afternoon, Sita finally managed to spit some skeleton saliva into the wetlock of the boss's private drinks cabinet. Sita used to be a cat burglar; Civil servant wasn't much of a career change.

Refiring the miner, they nailed Mary's physical template memory, took a decent trace off it, and plugged the numbers into the quicktank. Bacterial-level robots in a mixture of water and soil started building the most complex machine in the world.

Think about it; the quicktank is given a job most of us would laugh out of town. Build a sophisticated camera capable of full 3-D input and peripheral pickup, using only water and jelly.

So Reclamation broke open some cherry vodka while Mary was growing in a bottle of dirty water.

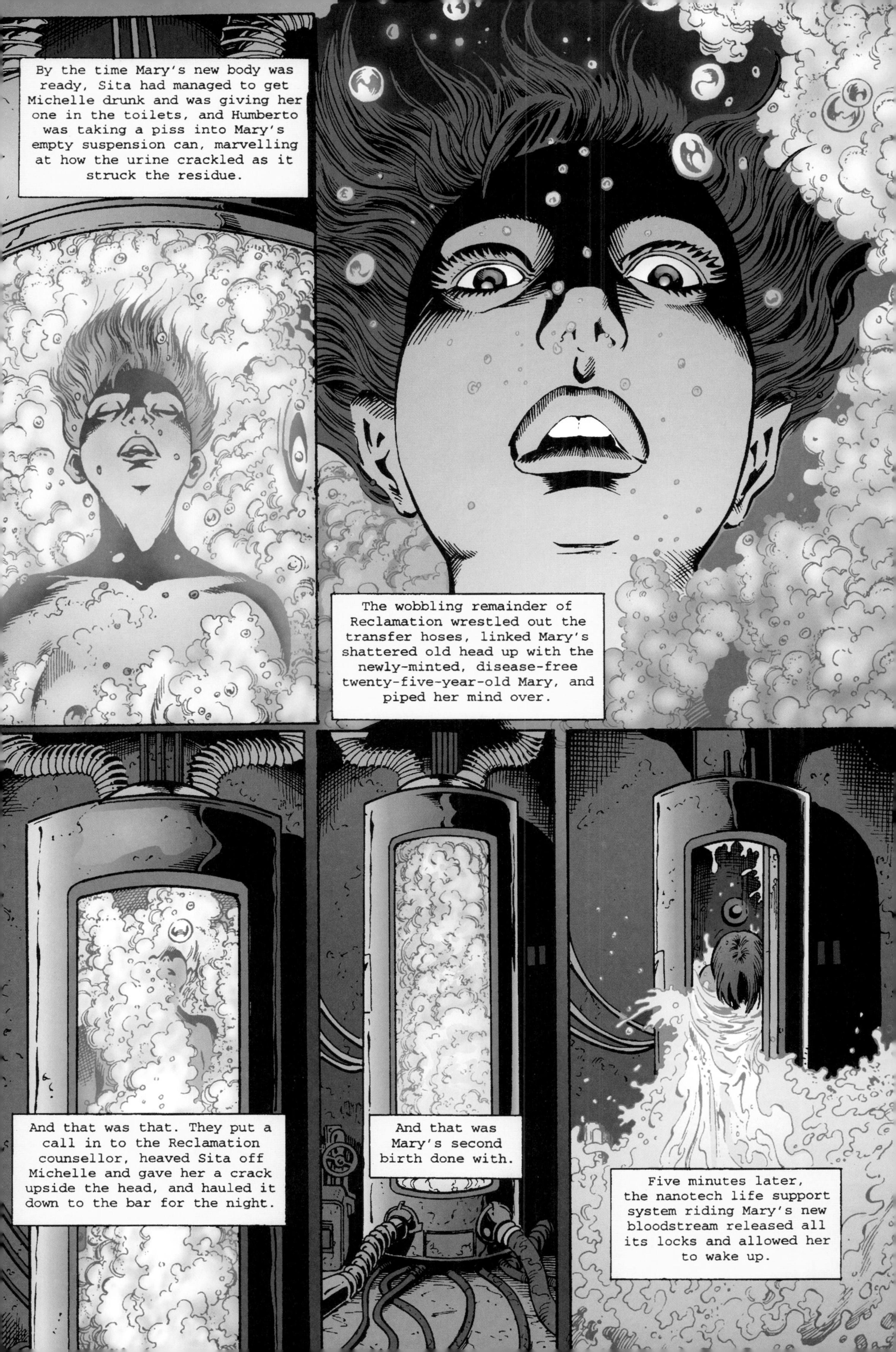
By the time Mary's new body was ready, Sita had managed to get Michelle drunk and was giving her one in the toilets, and Humberto was taking a piss into Mary's empty suspension can, marvelling at how the urine crackled as it struck the residue.
The wobbling remainder of Reclamation wrestled out the transfer hoses, linked Mary's shattered old head up with the newly-minted, disease-free twenty-five-year-old Mary, and piped her mind over.
And that was that. They put a call in to the Reclamation counsellor, heaved Sita off Michelle and gave her a crack upside the head, and hauled it down to the bar for the night.
And that was Mary's second birth done with.
Five minutes later, the nanotech life support system riding Mary's new bloodstream released all its locks and allowed her to wake up.

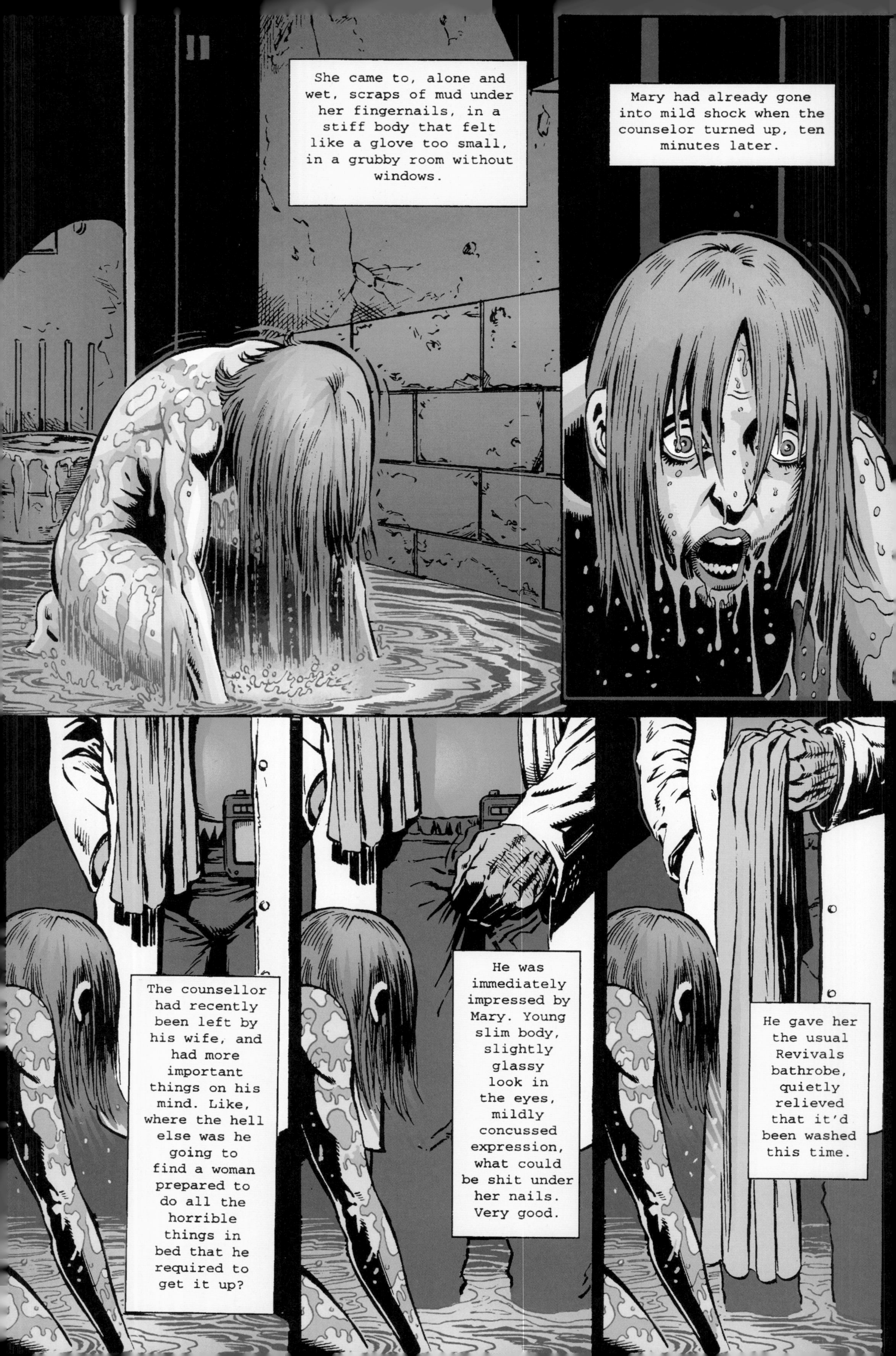

She came to, alone and wet, scraps of mud under her fingernails, in a stiff body that felt like a glove too small, in a grubby room without windows.
Mary had already gone into mild shock when the counselor turned up, ten minutes later.
The counsellor had recently been left by his wife, and had more important things on his mind. Like, where the hell else was he going to find a woman prepared to do all the horrible things in bed that he required to get it up?
He was immediately impressed by Mary. Young slim body, slightly glassy look in the eyes, mildly concussed expression, what could be shit under her nails. Very good.
He gave her the usual Revivals bathrobe, quietly relieved that it'd been washed this time.

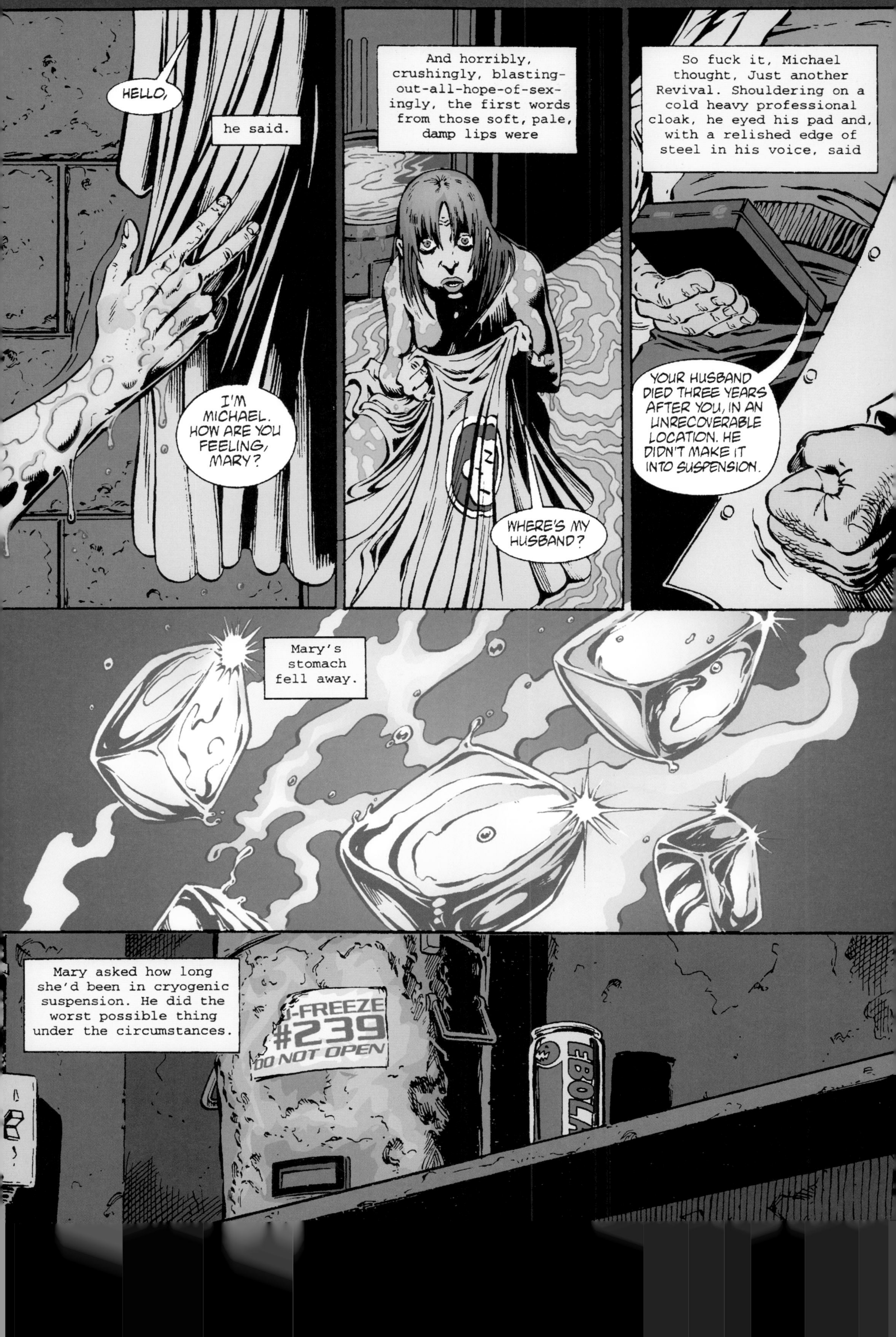
HELLO,
he said.
I'M MICHAEL. HOW ARE YOU FEELING, MARY?
And horribly, crushingly, blasting-out-all-hope-of-sex-ingly, the first words from those soft, pale, damp lips were
WHERE'S MY HUSBAND?
So fuck it, Michael thought, Just another Revival. Shouldering on a cold heavy professional cloak, he eyed his pad and, with a relished edge of steel in his voice, said
YOUR HUSBAND DIED THREE YEARS AFTER YOU, IN AN UNRECOVERABLE LOCATION. HE DIDN'T MAKE IT INTO SUSPENSION.
Mary's stomach fell away.
Mary asked how long she'd been in cryogenic suspension. He did the worst possible thing under the circumstances.
-FREEZE
#239
DO NOT OPEN
EBOLA

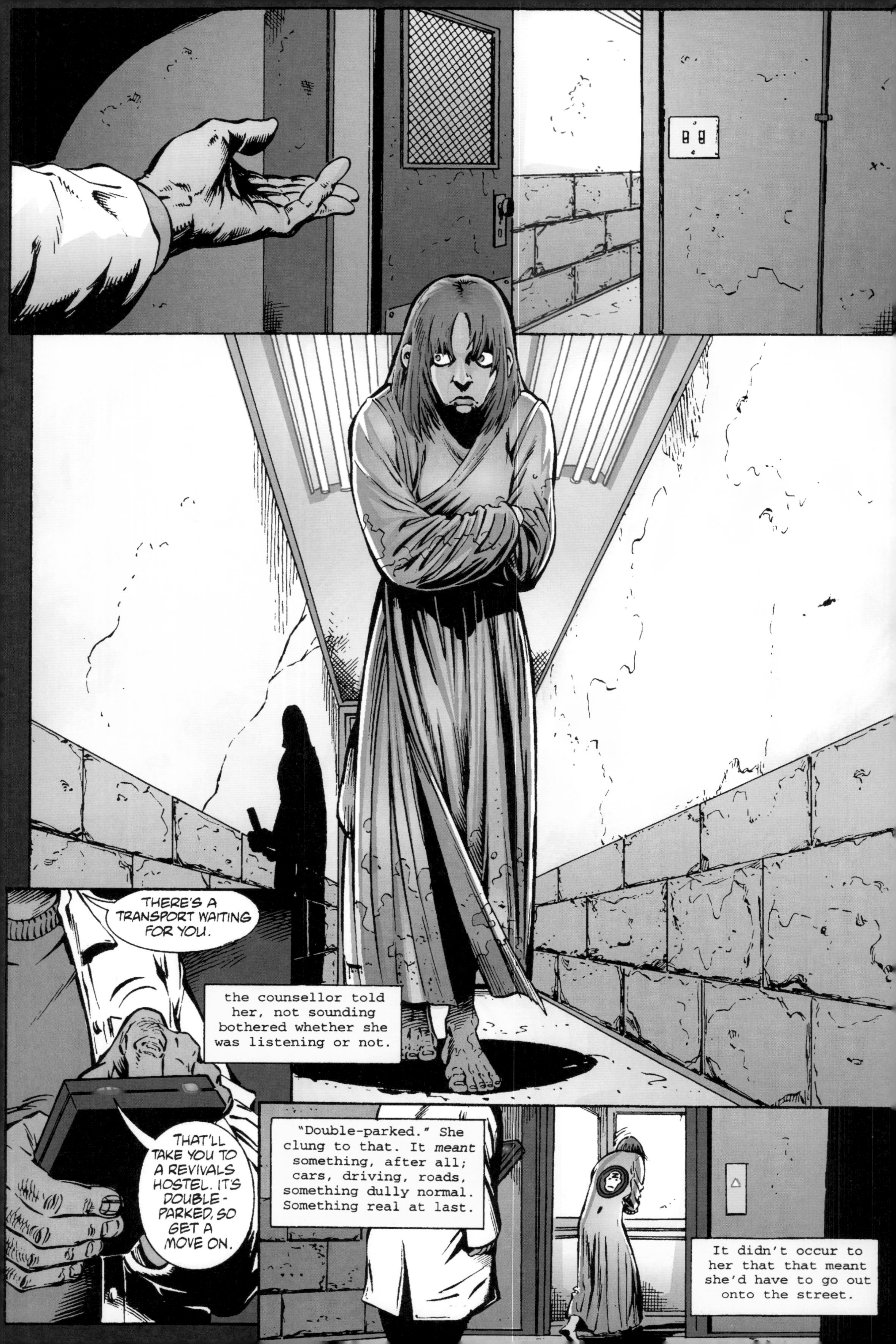
THERE'S A TRANSPORT WAITING FOR YOU.
the counsellor told her, not sounding bothered whether she was listening or not.
THAT'LL TAKE YOU TO A REVIVALS HOSTEL. IT'S DOUBLE-PARKED, SO GET A MOVE ON.
"Double-parked." She clung to that. It *meant* something, after all; cars, driving, roads, something dully normal. Something real at last.
It didn't occur to her that that meant she'd have to go out onto the street.

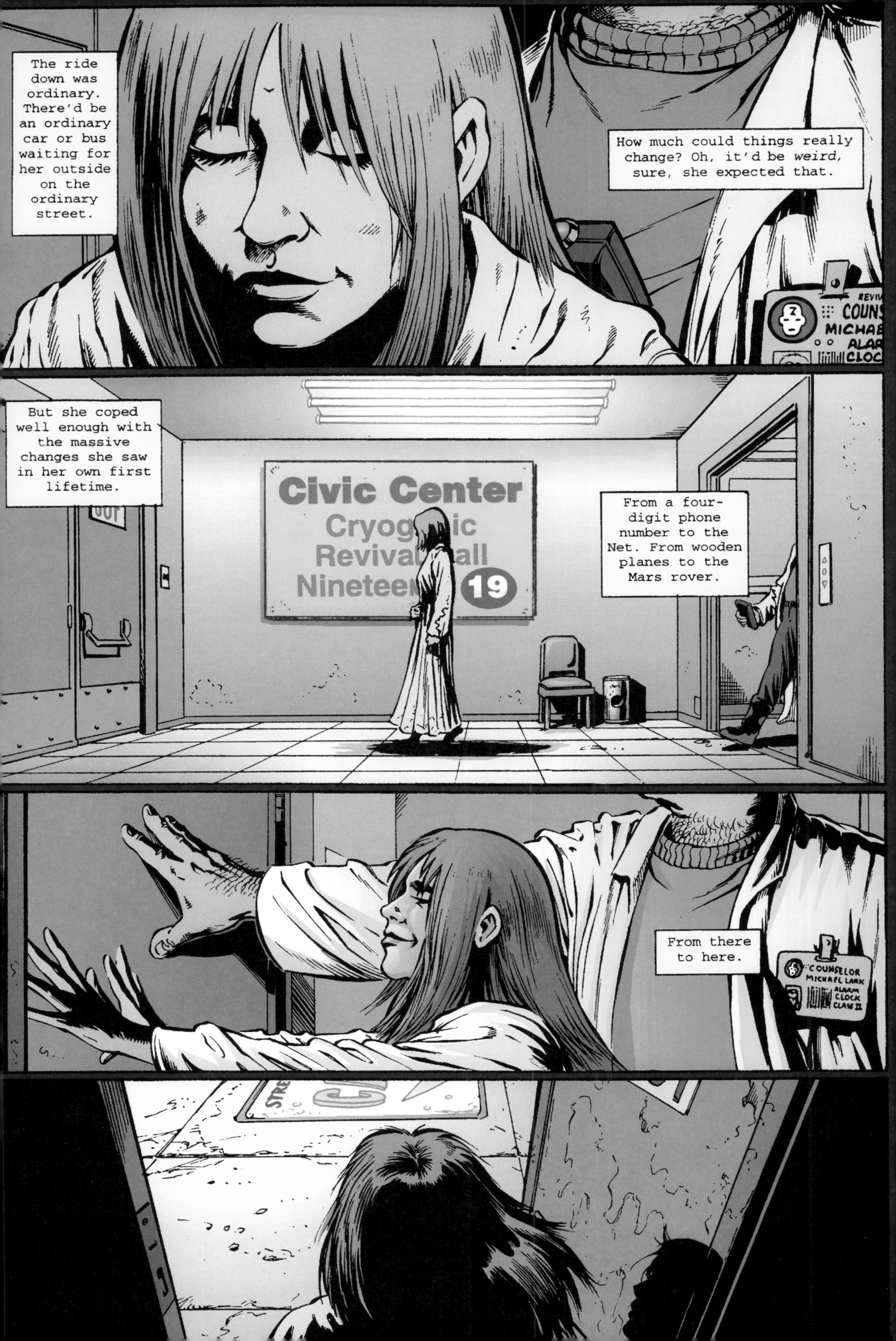

The ride down was ordinary. There'd be an ordinary car or bus waiting for her outside on the ordinary street.
How much could things really change? Oh, it'd be *weird*, sure, she expected that.
But she coped well enough with the massive changes she saw in her own first lifetime.
Civic Center
19
From a four-digit phone number to the Net. From wooden planes to the Mars rover.
From there to here.
COUNSELOR MICHAEL LARK ALARM CLOCK CLASS II

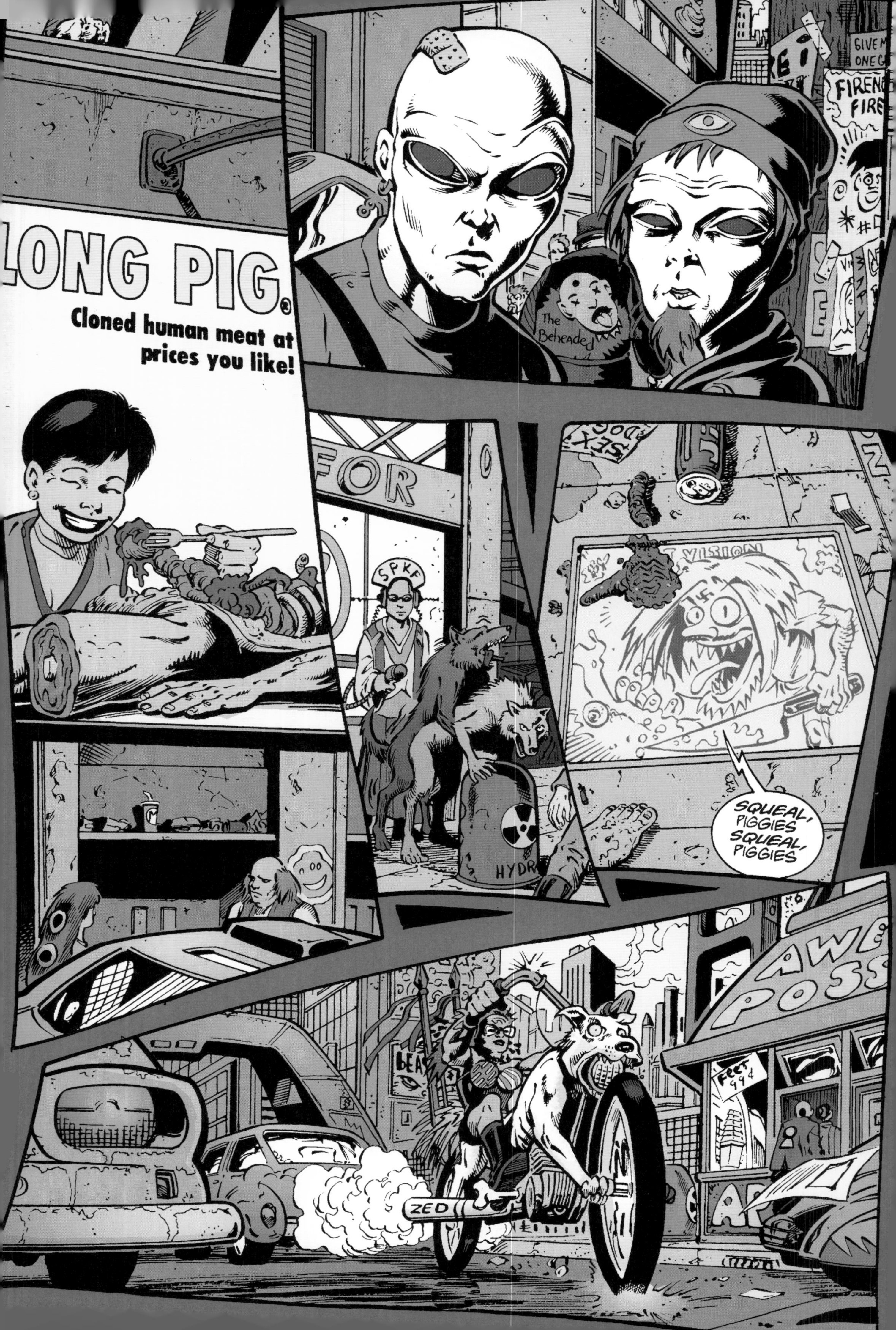
LONG PIG®
Cloned human meat at prices you like!
The Beheaded
FOR
SPKF
SEX DOG
VISION
SQUEAL, PIGGIES SQUEAL, PIGGIES
HYDR
ZED

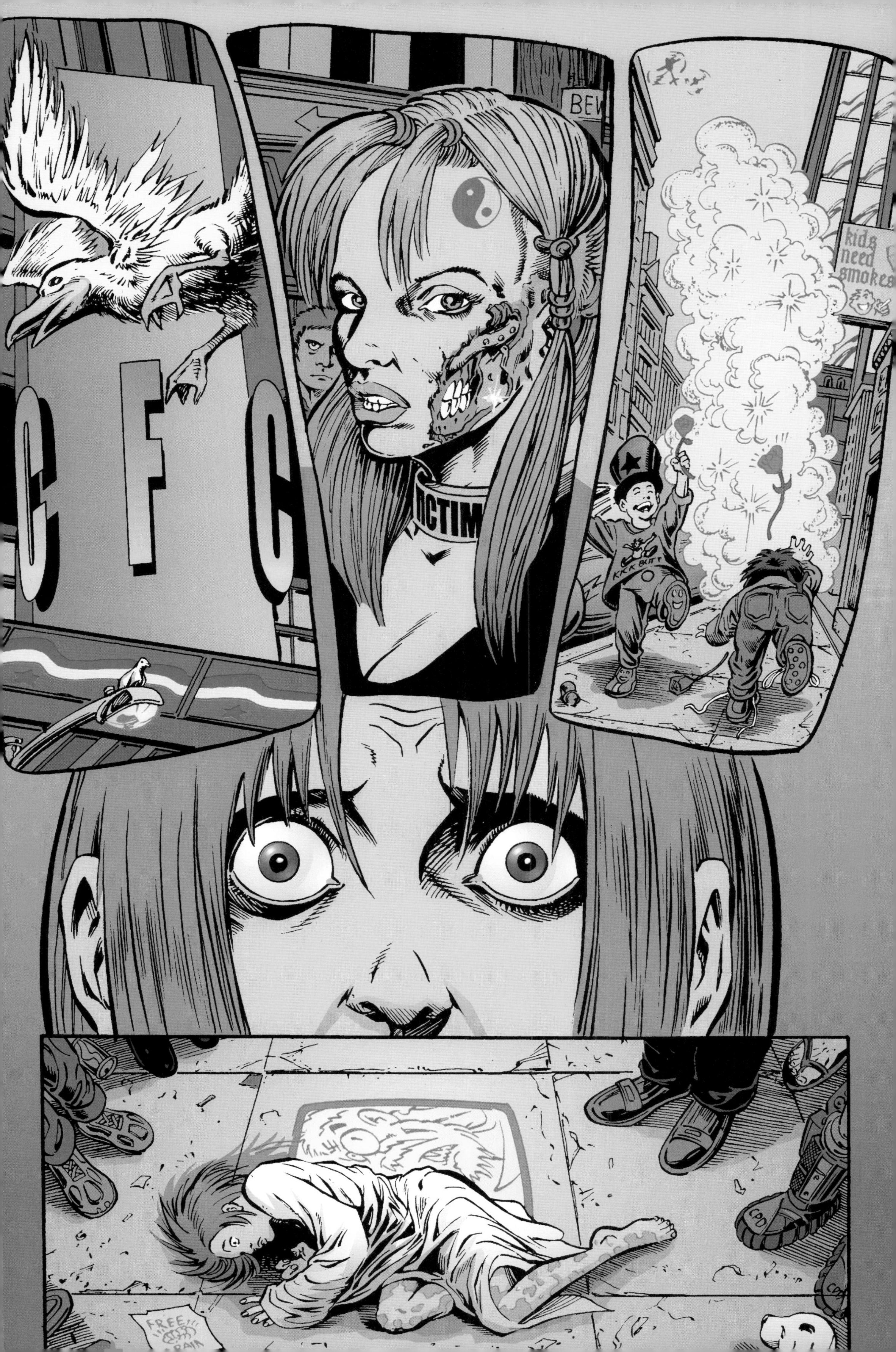
CFC
BEW
kids need smokes
KKK BUTT
CPD

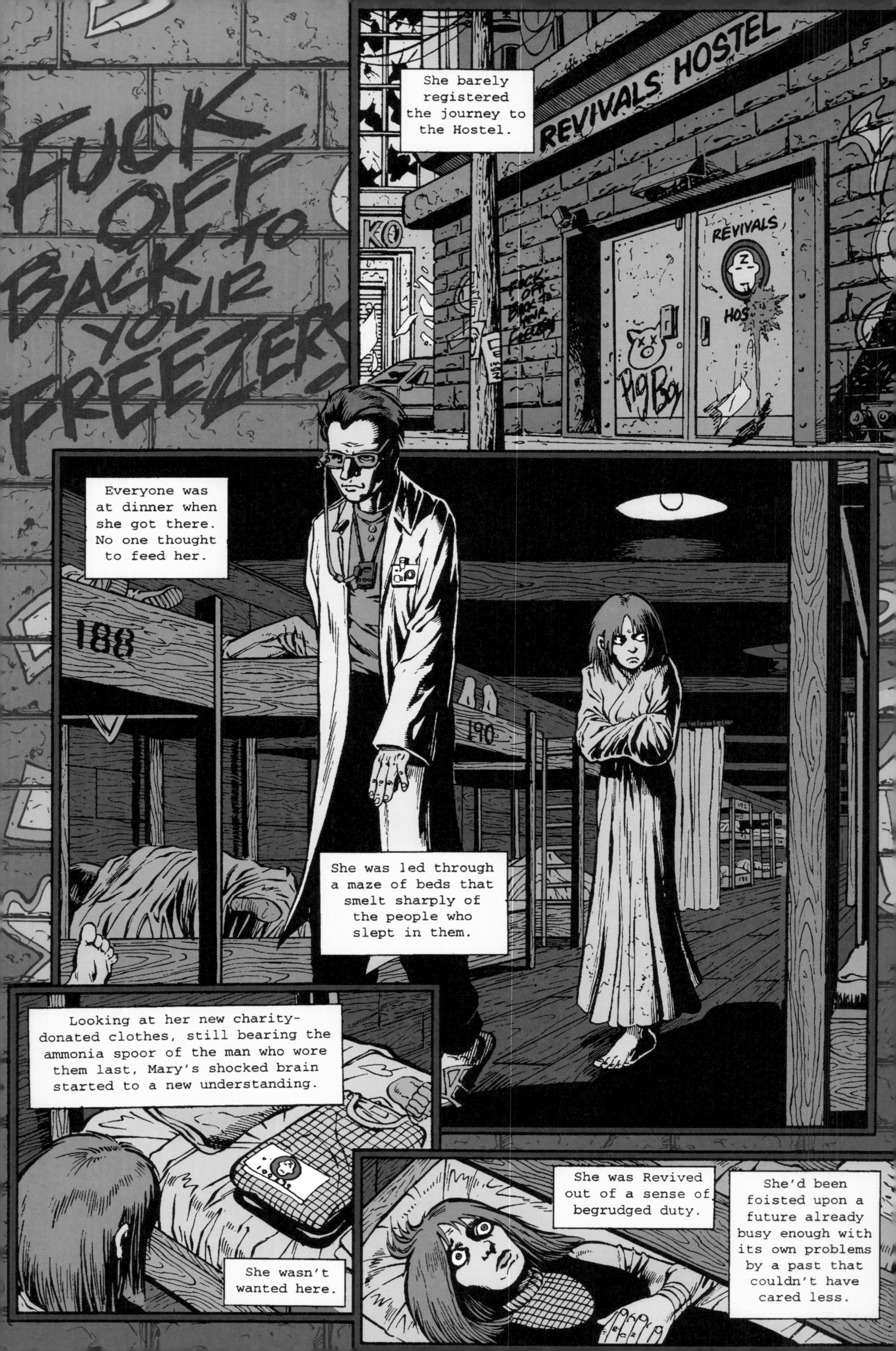
FUCK OFF BACK TO YOUR FREEZERS
She barely registered the journey to the Hostel.
REVIVALS HOSTEL
REVIVALS
HOS
Pig Boy
Everyone was at dinner when she got there. No one thought to feed her.
188
190
She was led through a maze of beds that smelt sharply of the people who slept in them.
Looking at her new charity-donated clothes, still bearing the ammonia spoor of the man who wore them last, Mary's shocked brain started to a new understanding.
She wasn't wanted here.
She was Revived out of a sense of begrudged duty.
She'd been foisted upon a future already busy enough with its own problems by a past that couldn't have cared less.

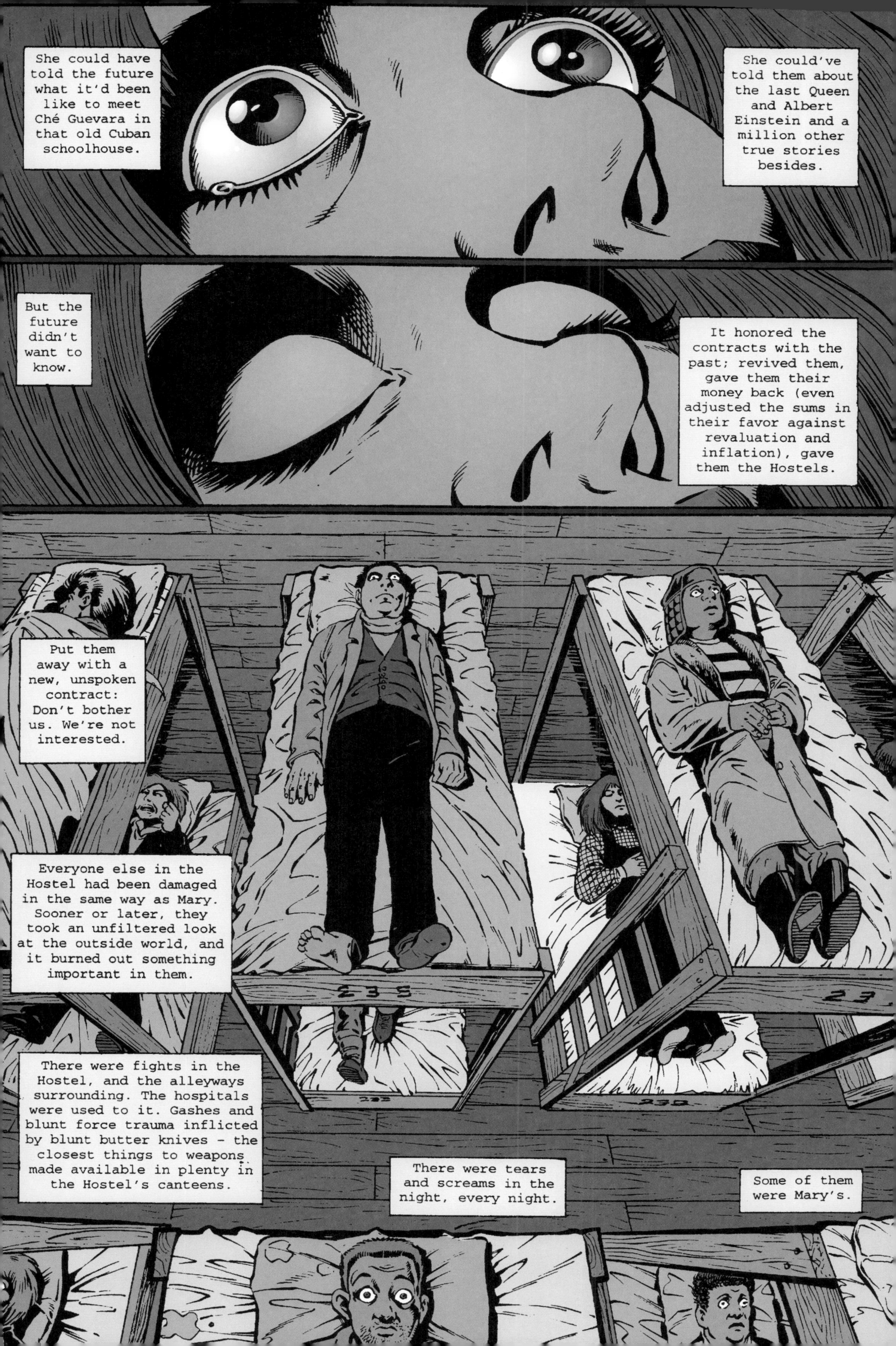
She could have told the future what it'd been like to meet Ché Guevara in that old Cuban schoolhouse.
She could've told them about the last Queen and Albert Einstein and a million other true stories besides.
But the future didn't want to know.
It honored the contracts with the past; revived them, gave them their money back (even adjusted the sums in their favor against revaluation and inflation), gave them the Hostels.
Put them away with a new, unspoken contract: Don't bother us. We're not interested.
Everyone else in the Hostel had been damaged in the same way as Mary. Sooner or later, they took an unfiltered look at the outside world, and it burned out something important in them.
There were fights in the Hostel, and the alleyways surrounding. The hospitals were used to it. Gashes and blunt force trauma inflicted by blunt butter knives - the closest things to weapons made available in plenty in the Hostel's canteens.
There were tears and screams in the night, every night.
Some of them were Mary's.

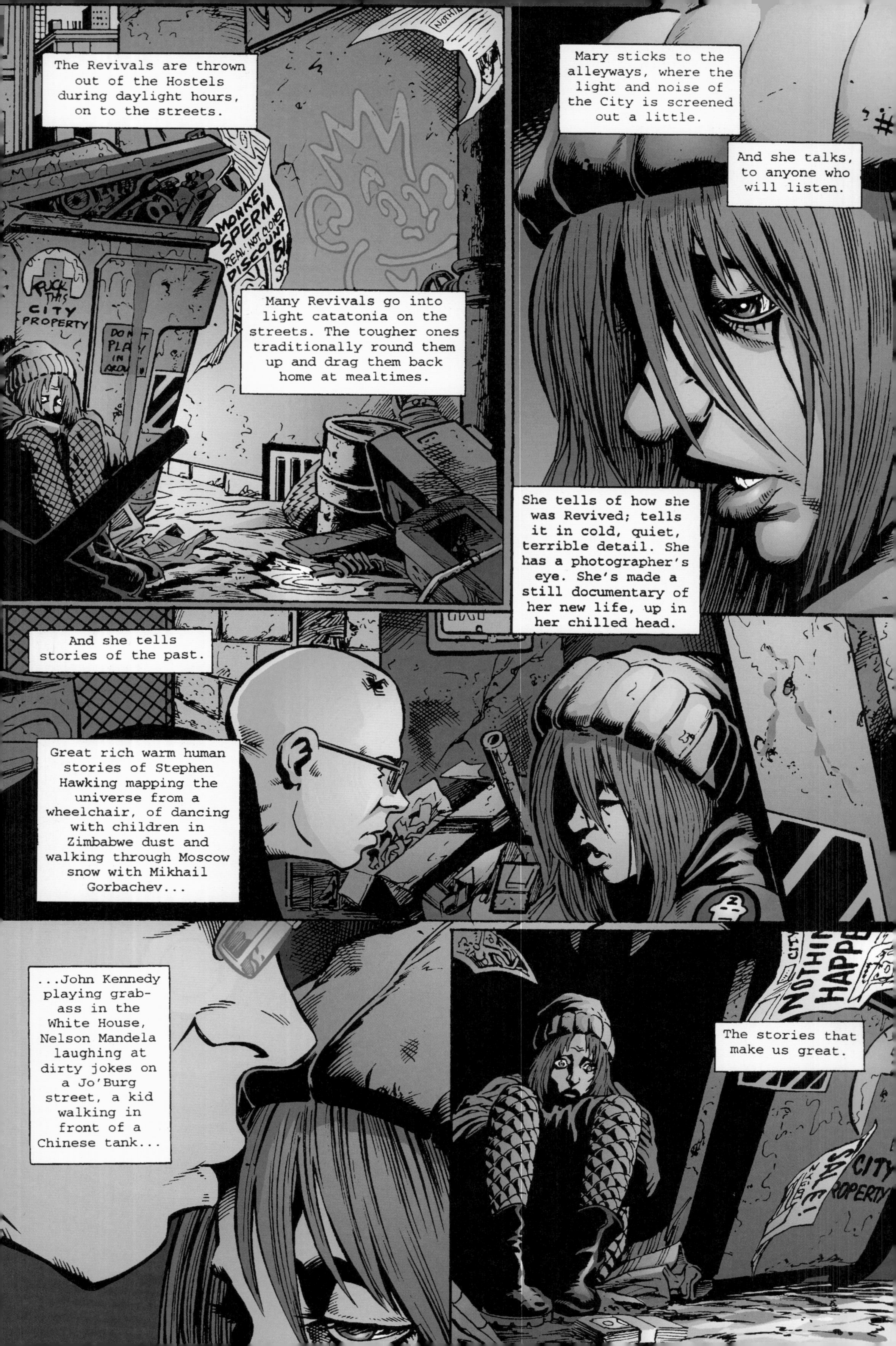
The Revivals are thrown out of the Hostels during daylight hours, on to the streets.
MONKEY SPERM REAL! NOT CLONED DISCOUNT
FUCK THIS CITY PROPERTY
Many Revivals go into light catatonia on the streets. The tougher ones traditionally round them up and drag them back home at mealtimes.
Mary sticks to the alleyways, where the light and noise of the City is screened out a little.
And she talks, to anyone who will listen.
She tells of how she was Revived; tells it in cold, quiet, terrible detail. She has a photographer's eye. She's made a still documentary of her new life, up in her chilled head.
And she tells stories of the past.
Great rich warm human stories of Stephen Hawking mapping the universe from a wheelchair, of dancing with children in Zimbabwe dust and walking through Moscow snow with Mikhail Gorbachev...
...John Kennedy playing grab-ass in the White House, Nelson Mandela laughing at dirty jokes on a Jo'Burg street, a kid walking in front of a Chinese tank...
The stories that make us great.

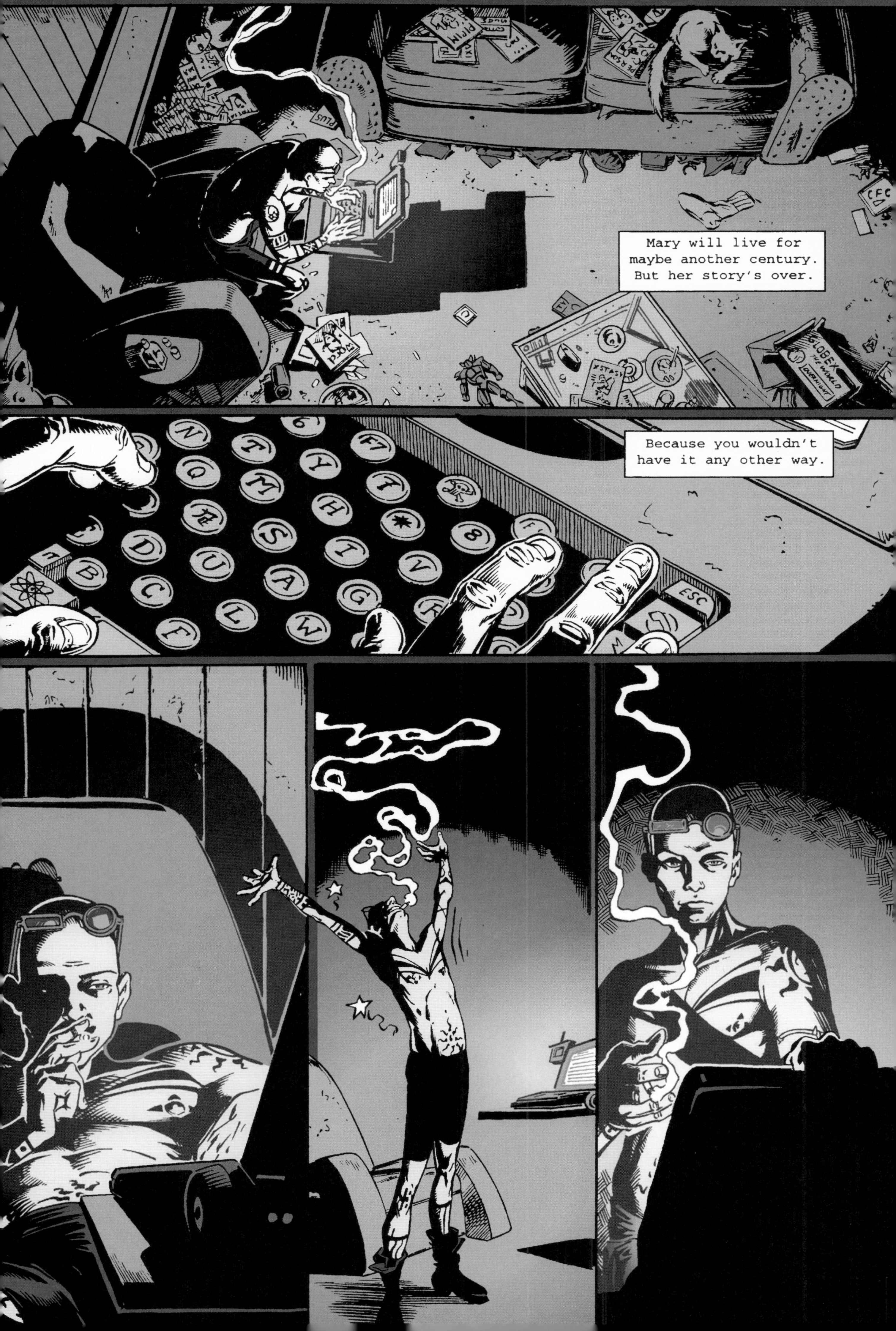
Mary will live for maybe another century. But her story's over.
Because you wouldn't have it any other way.

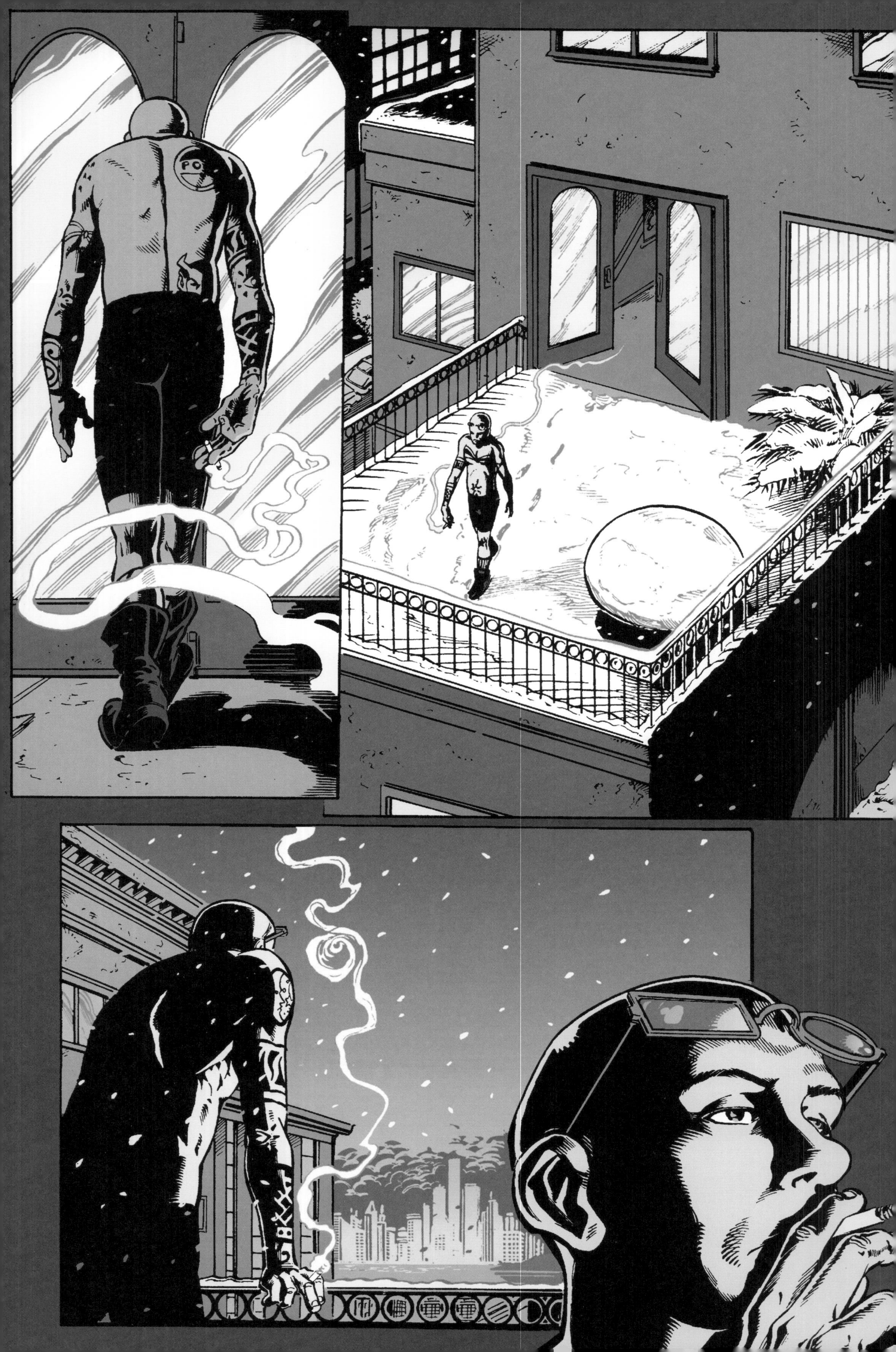

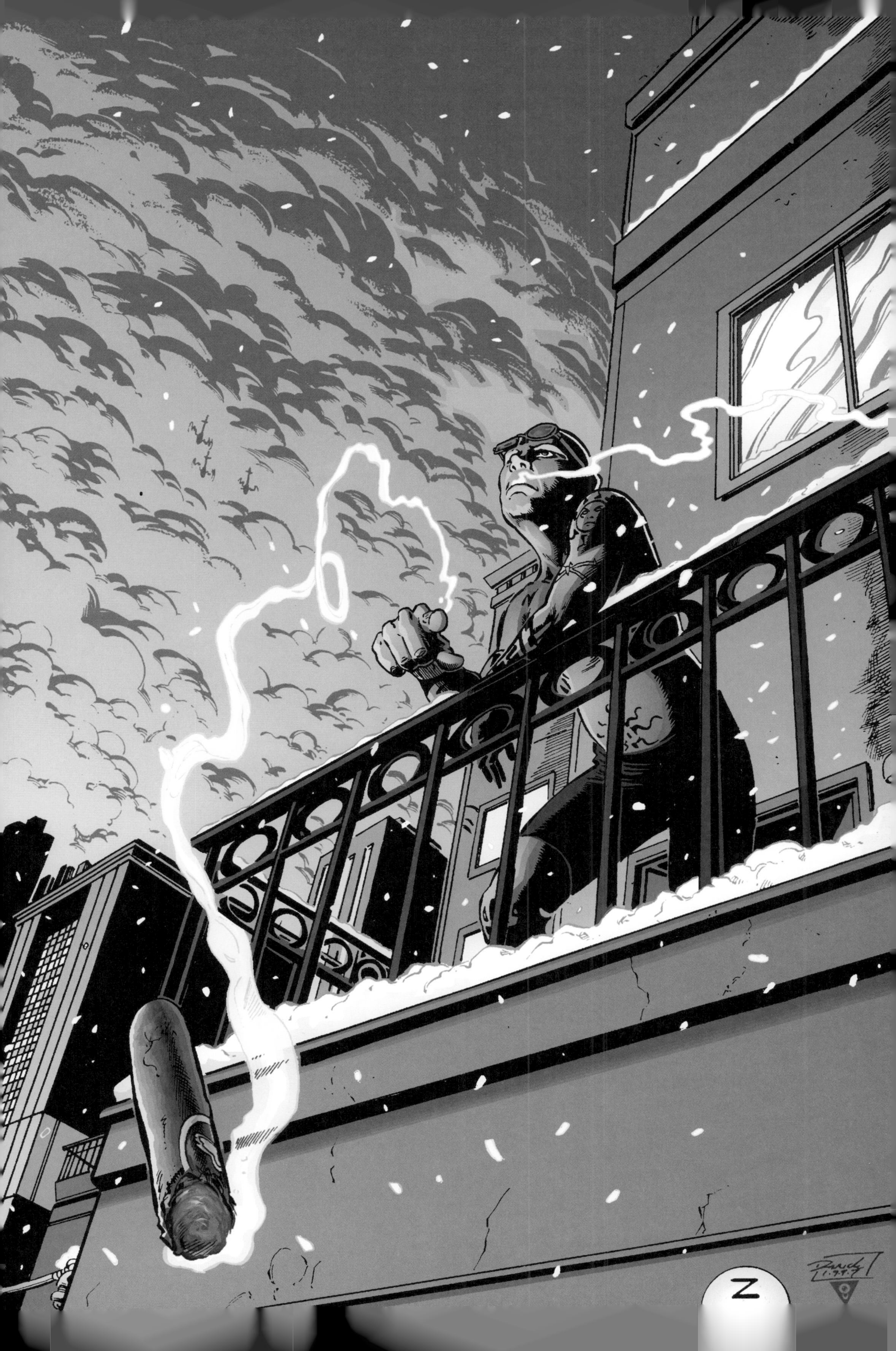

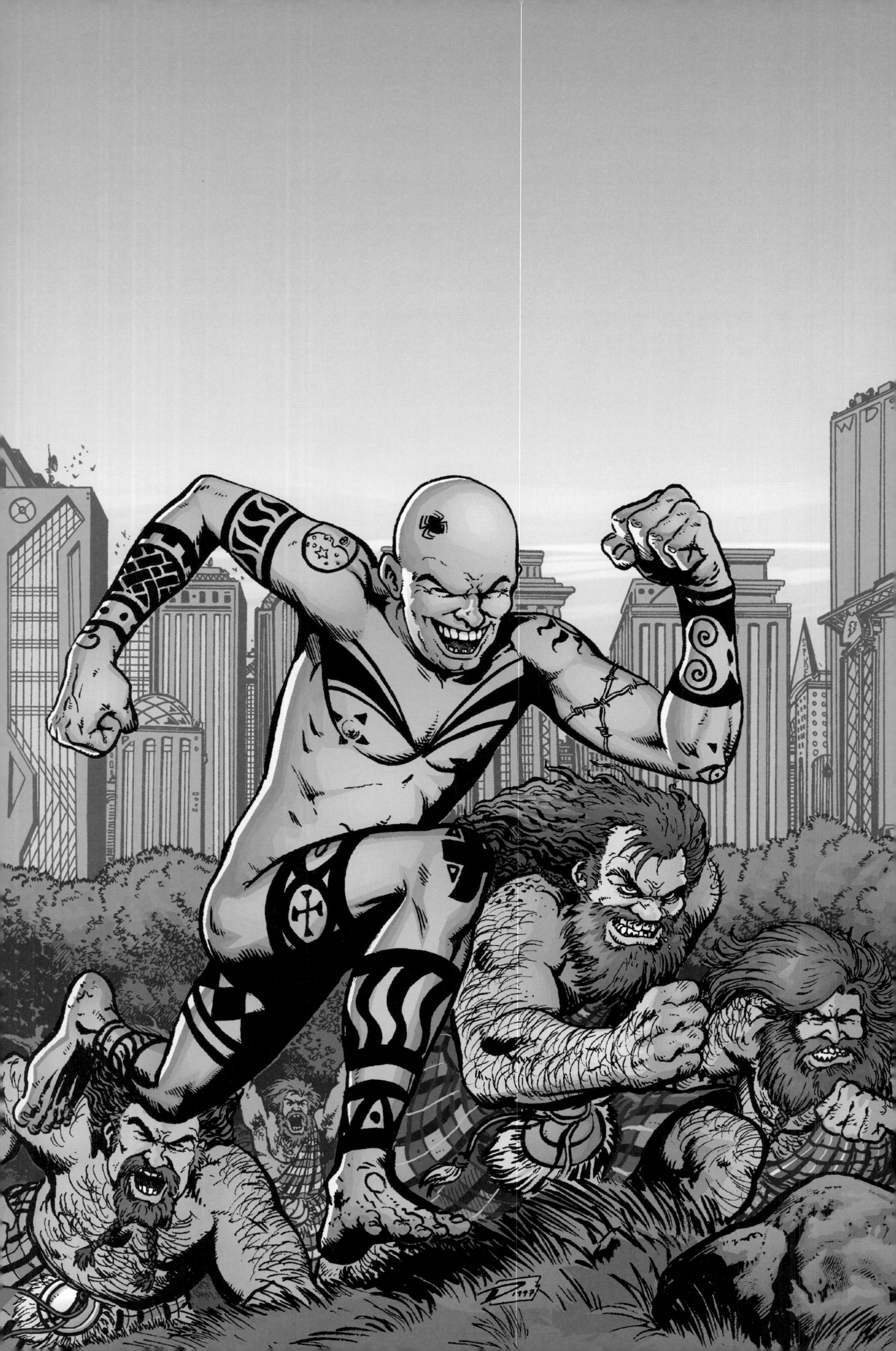

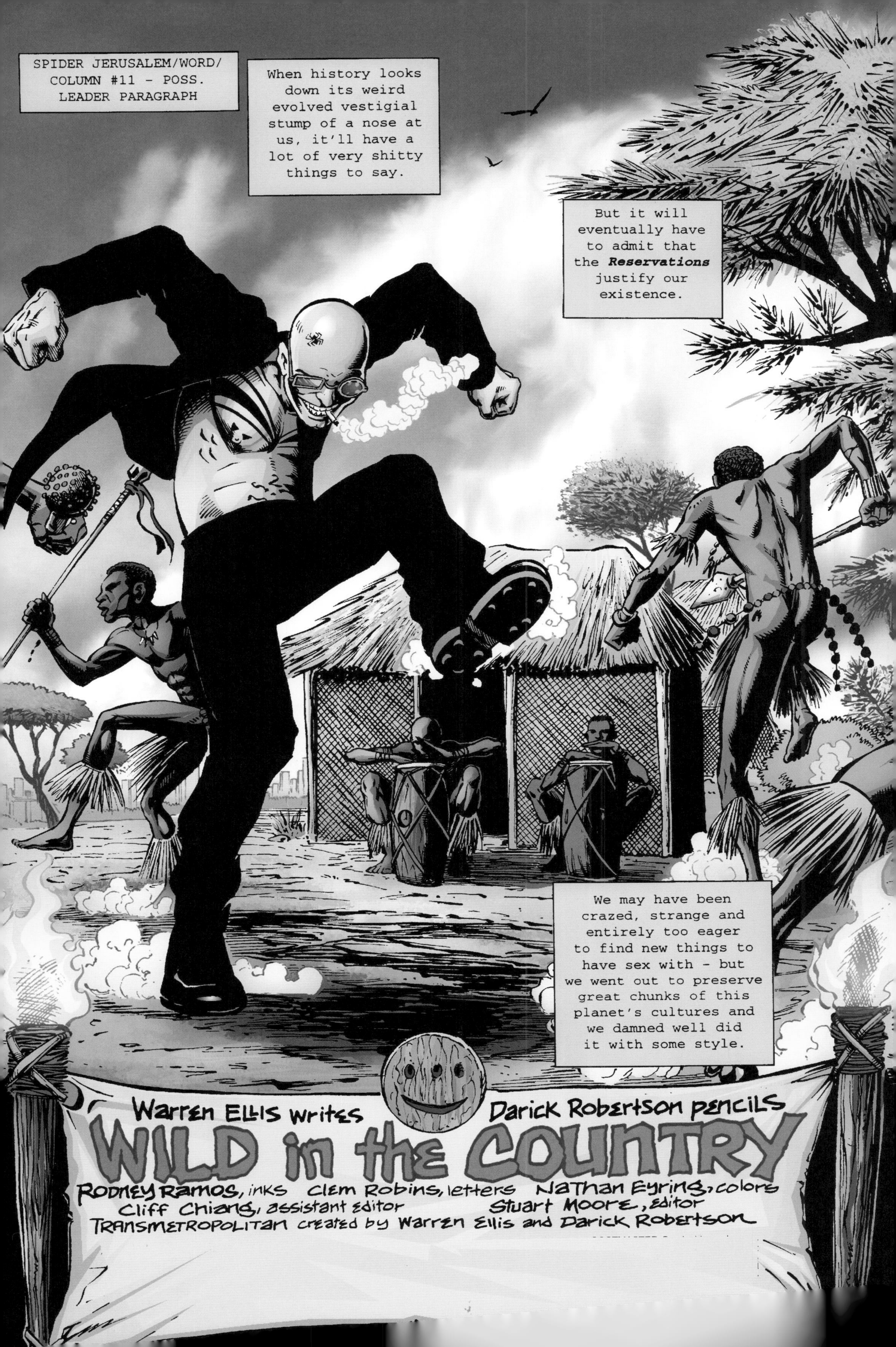
SPIDER JERUSALEM/WORD/ COLUMN #11 - POSS. LEADER PARAGRAPH
When history looks down its weird evolved vestigial stump of a nose at us, it'll have a lot of very shitty things to say.
But it will eventually have to admit that the *Reservations* justify our existence.
We may have been crazed, strange and entirely too eager to find new things to have sex with - but we went out to preserve great chunks of this planet's cultures and we damned well did it with some style.
Warren Ellis writes
Darick Robertson pencils
WILD in the COUNTRY
Rodney Ramos, inks
Clem Robins, letters
Nathan Eyring, colors
Cliff Chiang, assistant editor
Stuart Moore, editor
TRANSMETROPOLITAN created by Warren Ellis and Darick Robertson

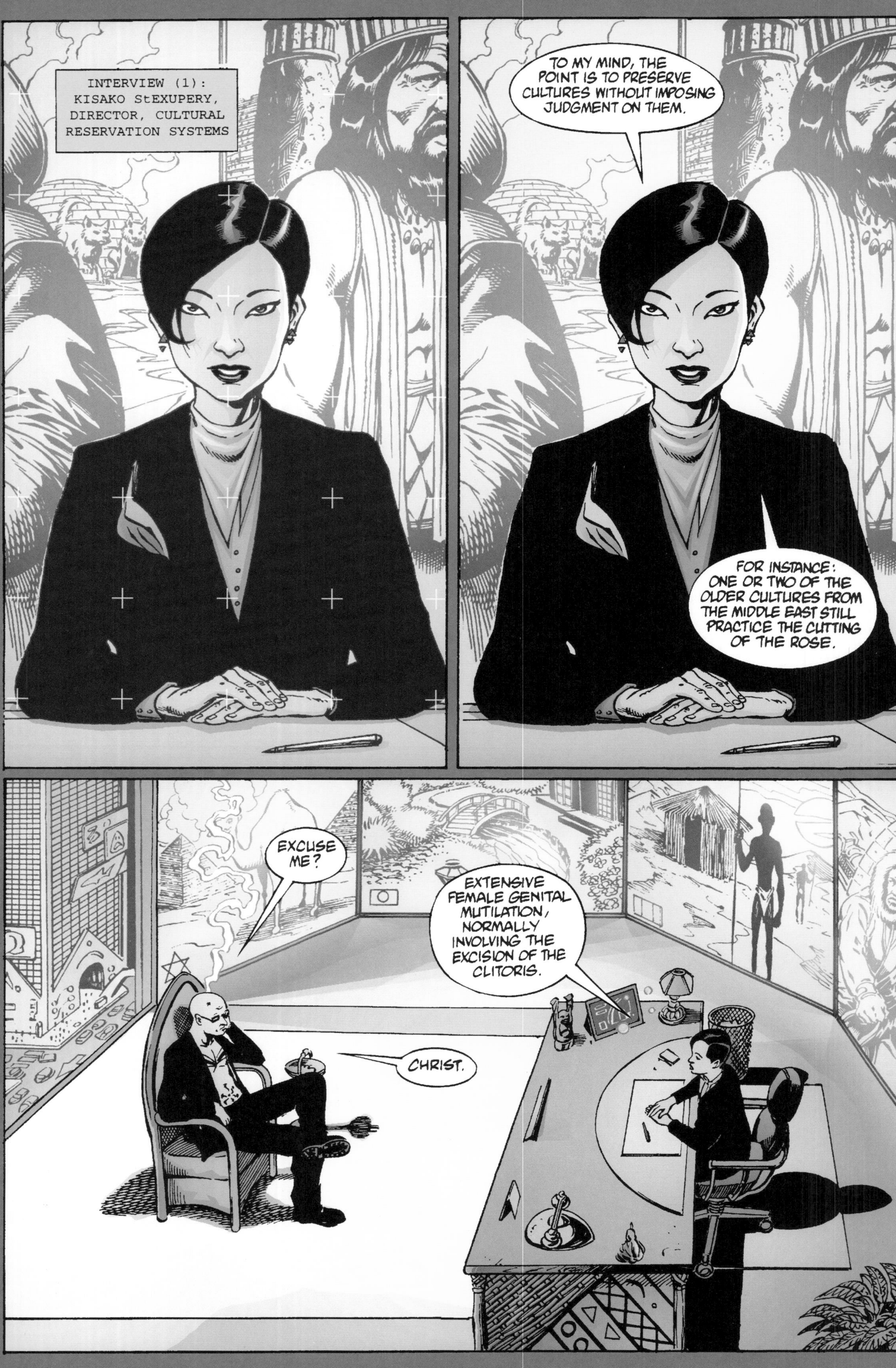
INTERVIEW (1): KISAKO StEXUPERY, DIRECTOR, CULTURAL RESERVATION SYSTEMS
TO MY MIND, THE POINT IS TO PRESERVE CULTURES WITHOUT IMPOSING JUDGMENT ON THEM.
FOR INSTANCE: ONE OR TWO OF THE OLDER CULTURES FROM THE MIDDLE EAST STILL PRACTICE THE CUTTING OF THE ROSE.
EXCUSE ME?
EXTENSIVE FEMALE GENITAL MUTILATION, NORMALLY INVOLVING THE EXCISION OF THE CLITORIS.
CHRIST.

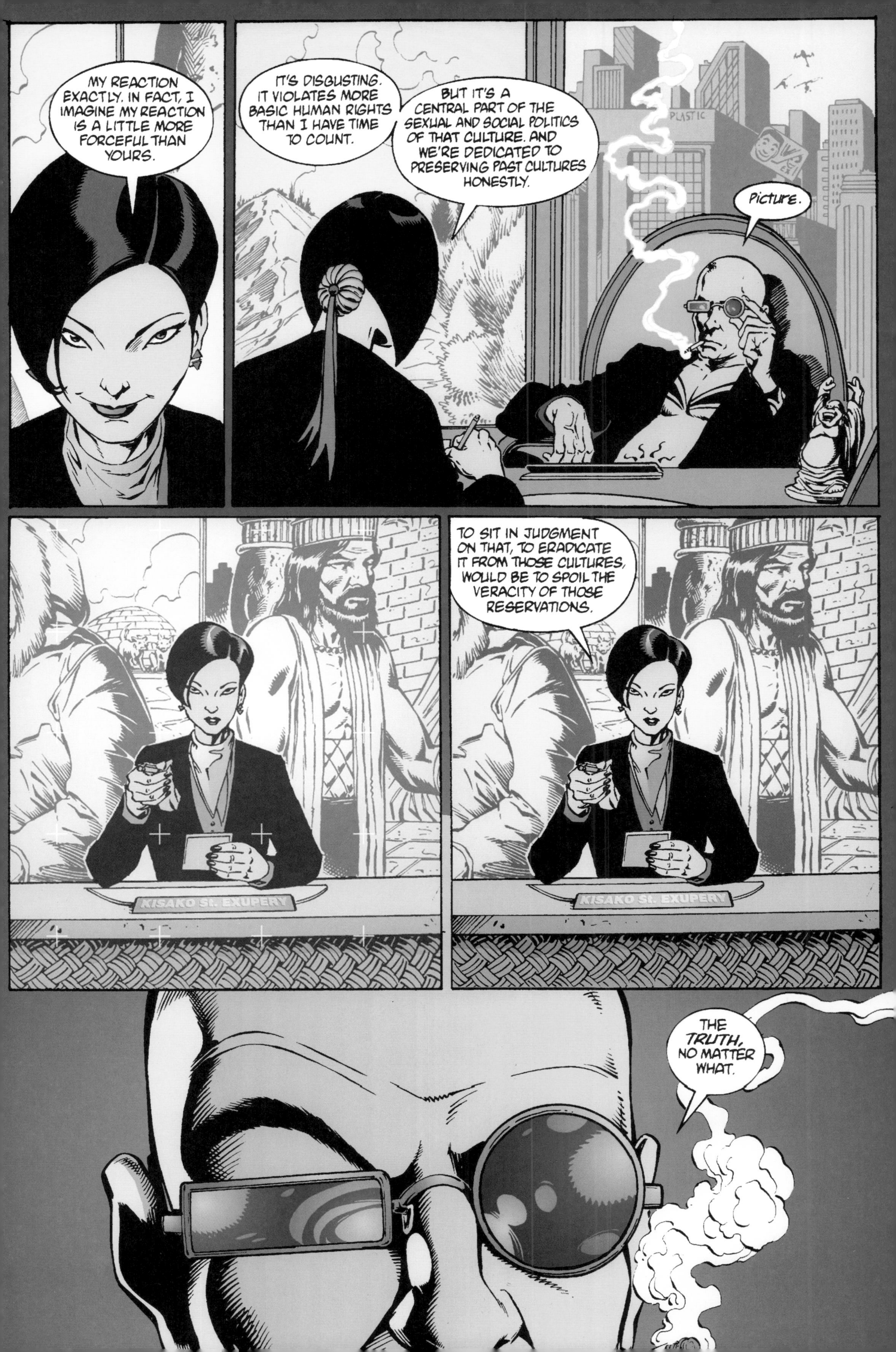
MY REACTION EXACTLY. IN FACT, I IMAGINE MY REACTION IS A LITTLE MORE FORCEFUL THAN YOURS.
IT'S DISGUSTING. IT VIOLATES MORE BASIC HUMAN RIGHTS THAN I HAVE TIME TO COUNT.
BUT IT'S A CENTRAL PART OF THE SEXUAL AND SOCIAL POLITICS OF THAT CULTURE. AND WE'RE DEDICATED TO PRESERVING PAST CULTURES HONESTLY.
PLASTIC
Picture.
KISAKO St. EXUPERY
TO SIT IN JUDGMENT ON THAT, TO ERADICATE IT FROM THOSE CULTURES, WOULD BE TO SPOIL THE VERACITY OF THOSE RESERVATIONS.
KISAKO St. EXUPERY
THE TRUTH, NO MATTER WHAT.

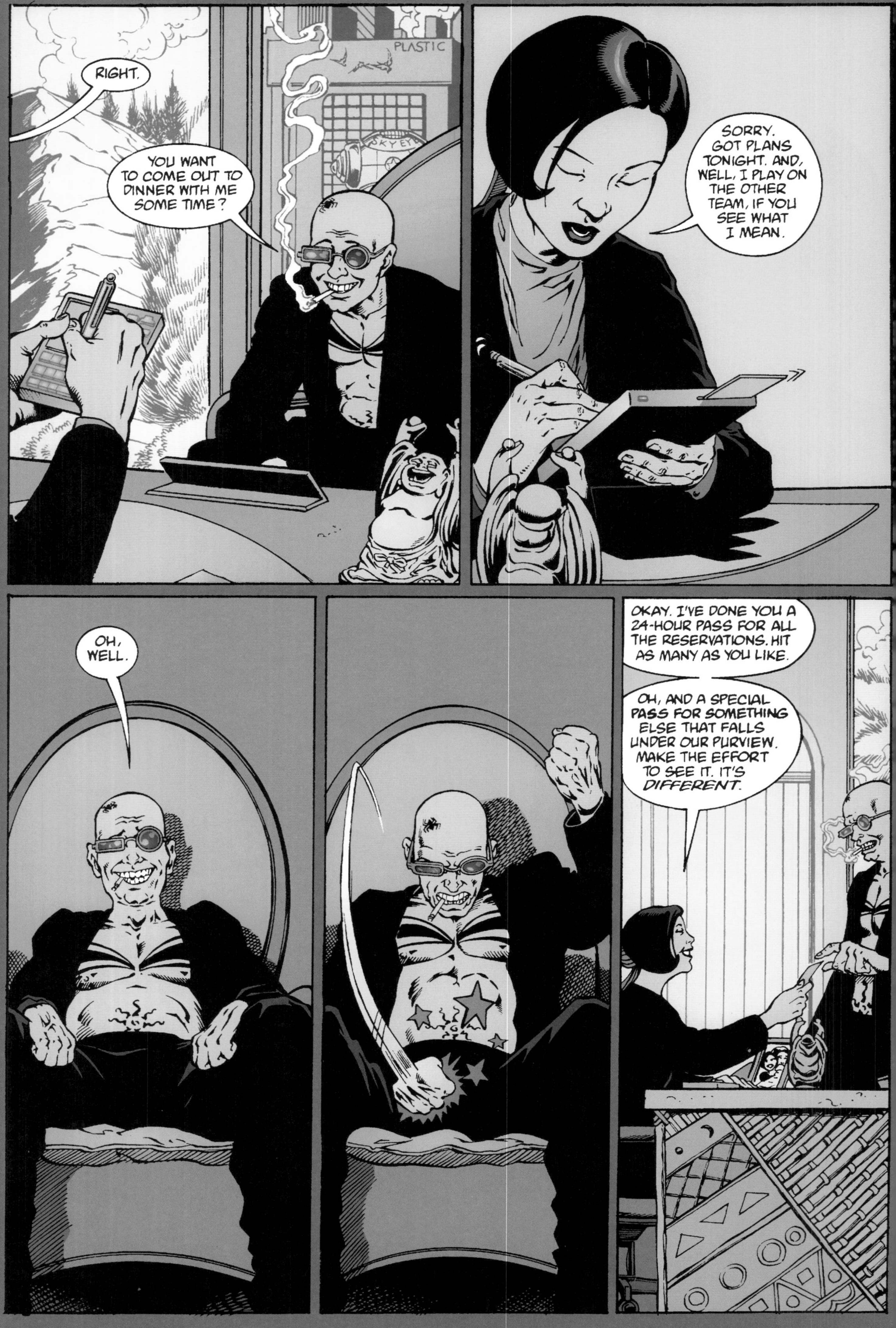
RIGHT.
YOU WANT TO COME OUT TO DINNER WITH ME SOME TIME?
PLASTIC
SORRY. GOT PLANS TONIGHT. AND, WELL, I PLAY ON THE OTHER TEAM, IF YOU SEE WHAT I MEAN.
OH, WELL.
OKAY. I'VE DONE YOU A 24-HOUR PASS FOR ALL THE RESERVATIONS. HIT AS MANY AS YOU LIKE.
OH, AND A SPECIAL PASS FOR SOMETHING ELSE THAT FALLS UNDER OUR PURVIEW. MAKE THE EFFORT TO SEE IT. IT'S *DIFFERENT*.

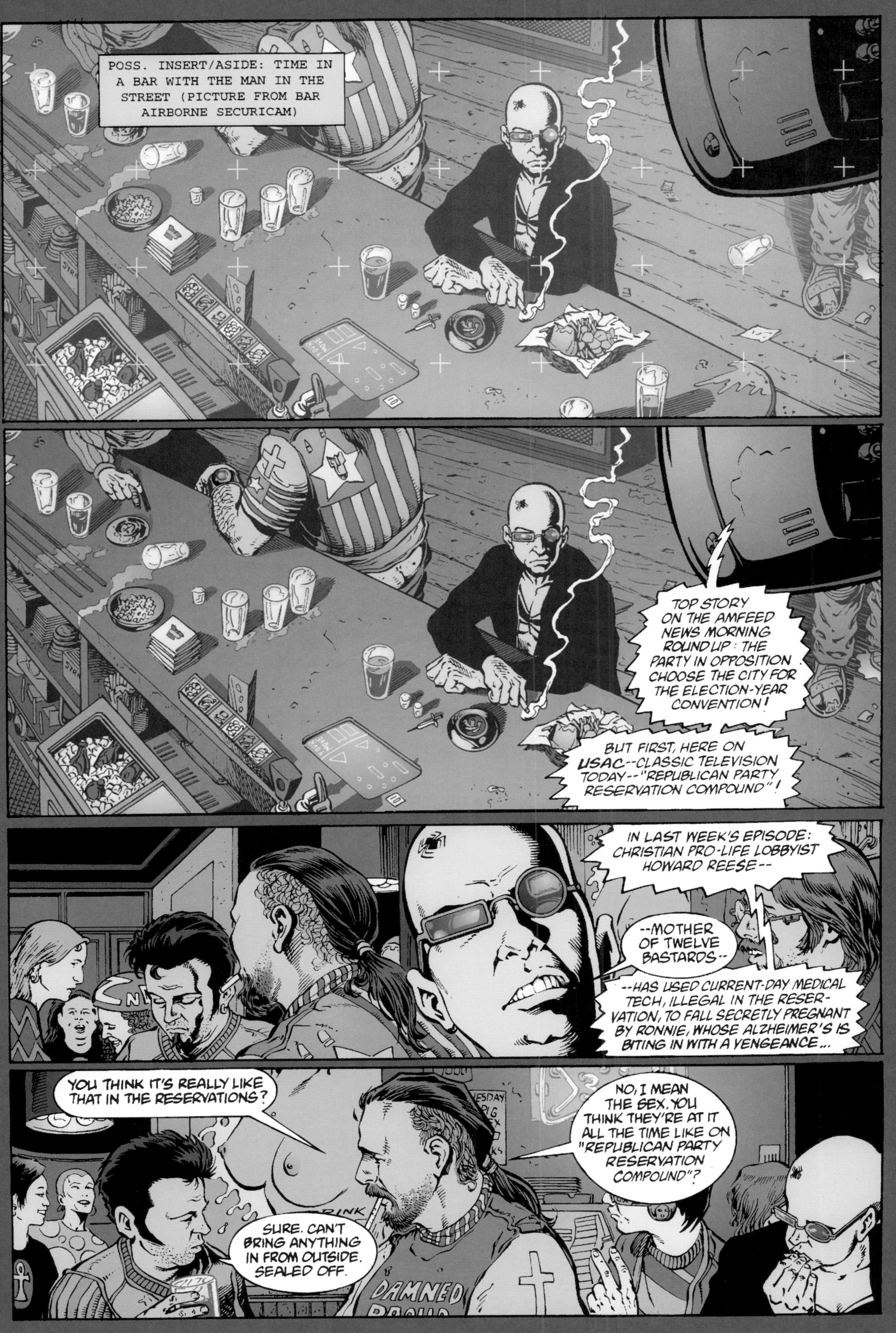
POSS. INSERT/ASIDE: TIME IN A BAR WITH THE MAN IN THE STREET (PICTURE FROM BAR AIRBORNE SECURICAM)
TOP STORY ON THE AMFEED NEWS MORNING ROUNDUP: THE PARTY IN OPPOSITION CHOOSE THE CITY FOR THE ELECTION-YEAR CONVENTION!
BUT FIRST, HERE ON USAC--CLASSIC TELEVISION TODAY--"REPUBLICAN PARTY RESERVATION COMPOUND"!
IN LAST WEEK'S EPISODE: CHRISTIAN PRO-LIFE LOBBYIST HOWARD REESE--
--MOTHER OF TWELVE BASTARDS--
--HAS USED CURRENT-DAY MEDICAL TECH, ILLEGAL IN THE RESERVATION, TO FALL SECRETLY PREGNANT BY RONNIE, WHOSE ALZHEIMER'S IS BITING IN WITH A VENGEANCE...
YOU THINK IT'S REALLY LIKE THAT IN THE RESERVATIONS?
SURE. CAN'T BRING ANYTHING IN FROM OUTSIDE. SEALED OFF.
NO, I MEAN THE SEX. YOU THINK THEY'RE AT IT ALL THE TIME LIKE ON "REPUBLICAN PARTY RESERVATION COMPOUND"?
DAMNED

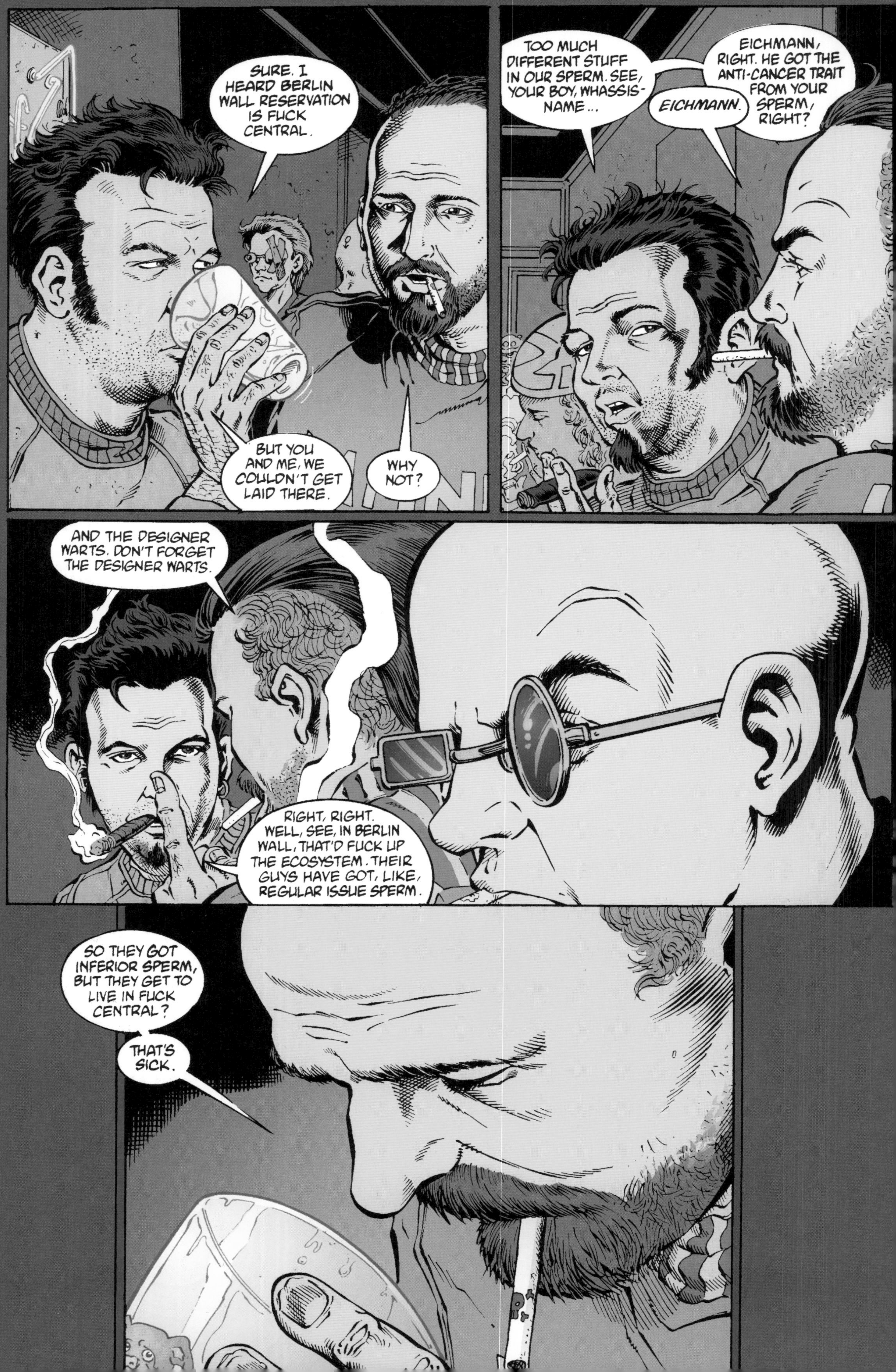
SURE. I HEARD BERLIN WALL RESERVATION IS FUCK CENTRAL.
BUT YOU AND ME, WE COULDN'T GET LAID THERE.
WHY NOT?
TOO MUCH DIFFERENT STUFF IN OUR SPERM. SEE, YOUR BOY, WHASSIS-NAME...
EICHMANN.
EICHMANN, RIGHT. HE GOT THE ANTI-CANCER TRAIT FROM YOUR SPERM, RIGHT?
AND THE DESIGNER WARTS. DON'T FORGET THE DESIGNER WARTS.
RIGHT, RIGHT. WELL, SEE, IN BERLIN WALL, THAT'D FUCK UP THE ECOSYSTEM. THEIR GUYS HAVE GOT, LIKE, REGULAR ISSUE SPERM.
SO THEY GOT INFERIOR SPERM, BUT THEY GET TO LIVE IN FUCK CENTRAL?
THAT'S SICK.

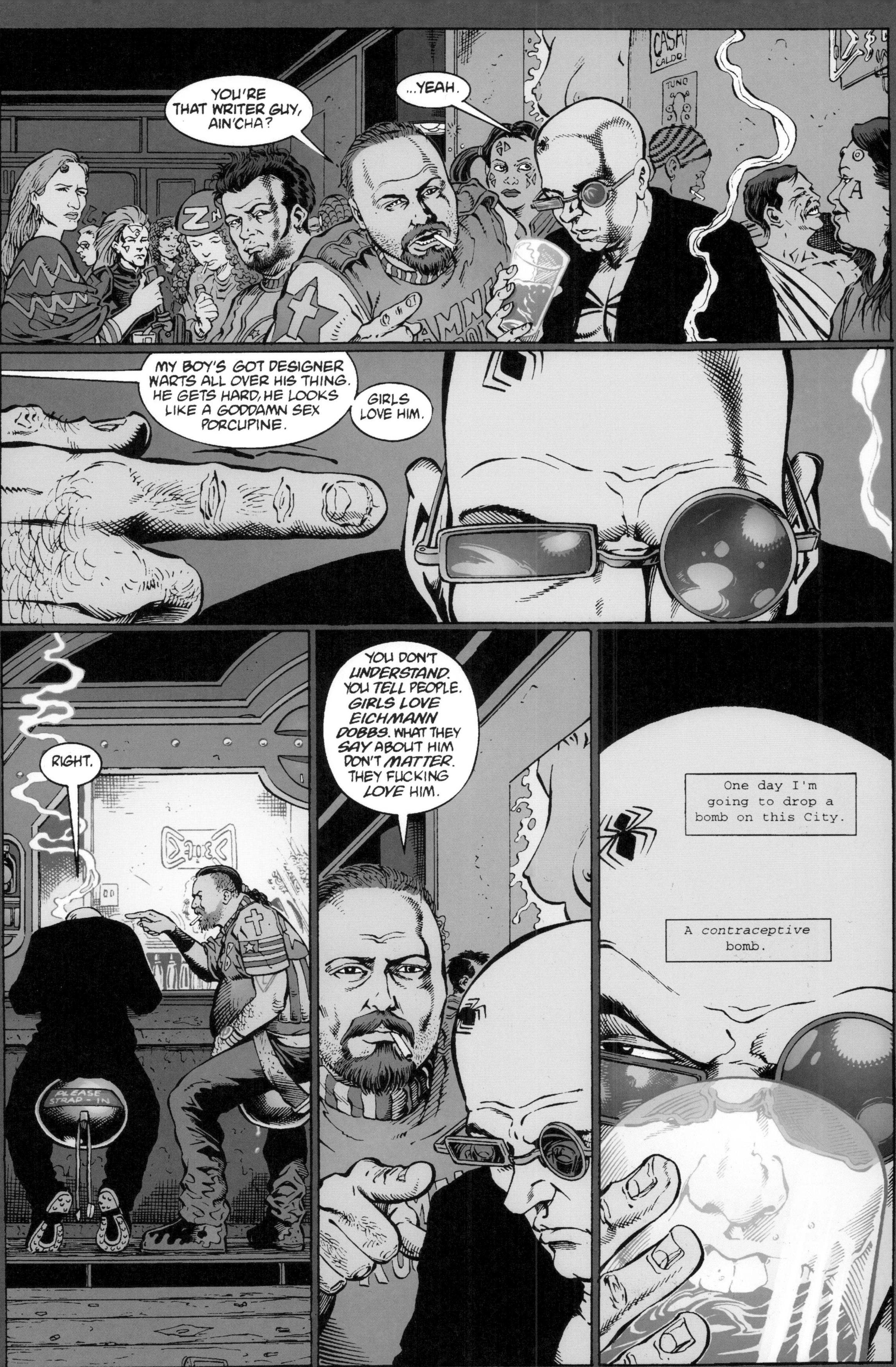

YOU'RE THAT WRITER GUY, AIN'CHA?
...YEAH.
CASA CALDO
MY BOY'S GOT DESIGNER WARTS ALL OVER HIS THING. HE GETS HARD, HE LOOKS LIKE A GODDAMN SEX PORCUPINE.
GIRLS LOVE HIM.
RIGHT.
PLEASE STRAP-IN
YOU DON'T UNDERSTAND. YOU TELL PEOPLE. GIRLS LOVE EICHMANN DOBBS. WHAT THEY SAY ABOUT HIM DON'T MATTER. THEY FUCKING LOVE HIM.
One day I'm going to drop a bomb on this City.
A contraceptive bomb.

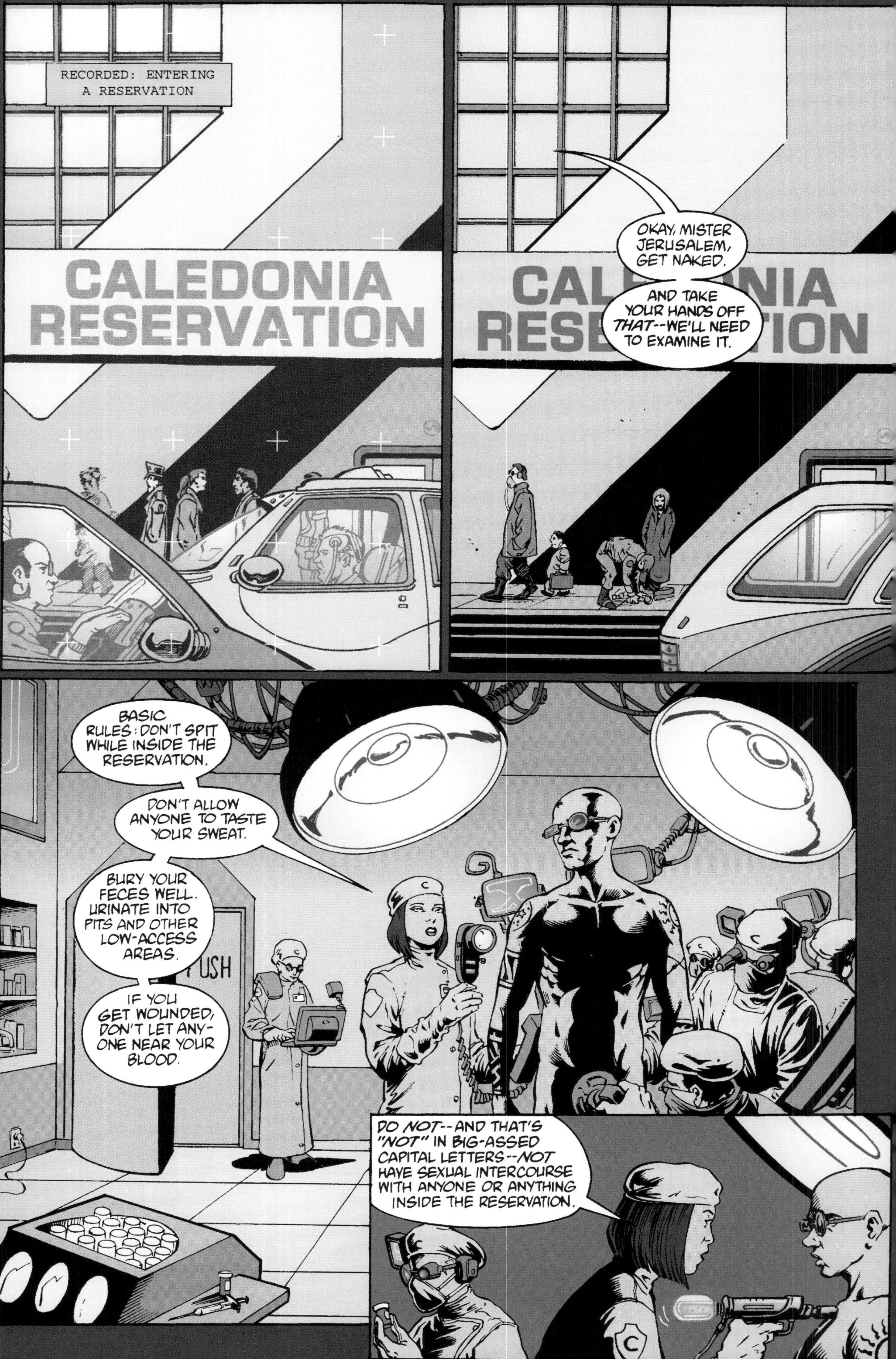
RECORDED: ENTERING A RESERVATION
CALEDONIA RESERVATION
OKAY, MISTER JERUSALEM, GET NAKED.
AND TAKE YOUR HANDS OFF THAT--WE'LL NEED TO EXAMINE IT.
BASIC RULES: DON'T SPIT WHILE INSIDE THE RESERVATION.
DON'T ALLOW ANYONE TO TASTE YOUR SWEAT.
BURY YOUR FECES WELL. URINATE INTO PITS AND OTHER LOW-ACCESS AREAS.
IF YOU GET WOUNDED, DON'T LET ANYONE NEAR YOUR BLOOD.
PUSH
DO NOT--AND THAT'S "NOT" IN BIG-ASSED CAPITAL LETTERS--NOT HAVE SEXUAL INTERCOURSE WITH ANYONE OR ANYTHING INSIDE THE RESERVATION.

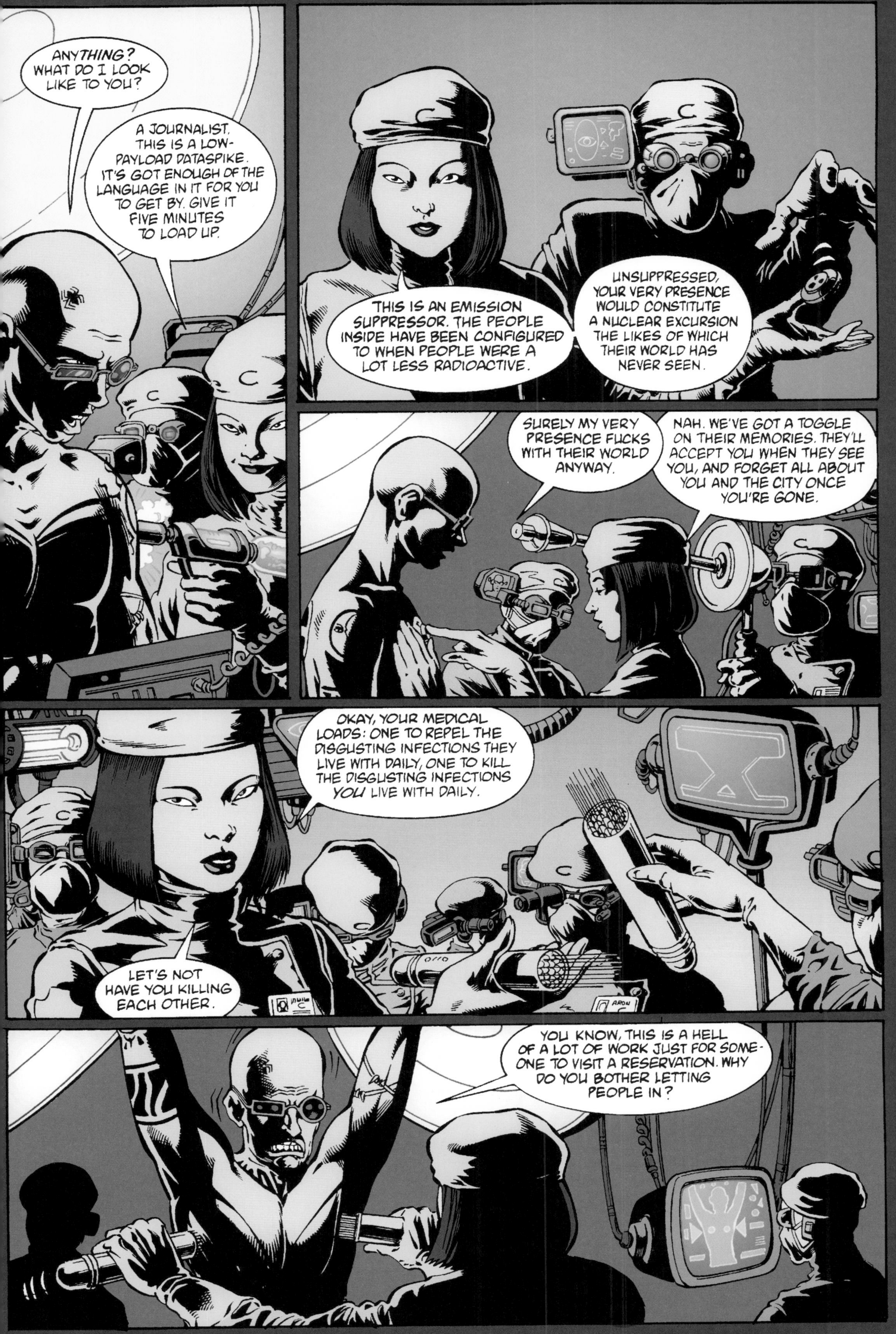
ANYTHING? WHAT DO I LOOK LIKE TO YOU?
A JOURNALIST. THIS IS A LOW-PAYLOAD DATASPIKE. IT'S GOT ENOUGH OF THE LANGUAGE IN IT FOR YOU TO GET BY. GIVE IT FIVE MINUTES TO LOAD UP.
THIS IS AN EMISSION SUPPRESSOR. THE PEOPLE INSIDE HAVE BEEN CONFIGURED TO WHEN PEOPLE WERE A LOT LESS RADIOACTIVE.
UNSUPPRESSED, YOUR VERY PRESENCE WOULD CONSTITUTE A NUCLEAR EXCURSION THE LIKES OF WHICH THEIR WORLD HAS NEVER SEEN.
SURELY MY VERY PRESENCE FUCKS WITH THEIR WORLD ANYWAY.
NAH. WE'VE GOT A TOGGLE ON THEIR MEMORIES. THEY'LL ACCEPT YOU WHEN THEY SEE YOU, AND FORGET ALL ABOUT YOU AND THE CITY ONCE YOU'RE GONE.
OKAY, YOUR MEDICAL LOADS: ONE TO REPEL THE DISGUSTING INFECTIONS THEY LIVE WITH DAILY, ONE TO KILL THE DISGUSTING INFECTIONS YOU LIVE WITH DAILY.
LET'S NOT HAVE YOU KILLING EACH OTHER.
YOU KNOW, THIS IS A HELL OF A LOT OF WORK JUST FOR SOME-ONE TO VISIT A RESERVATION. WHY DO YOU BOTHER LETTING PEOPLE IN?

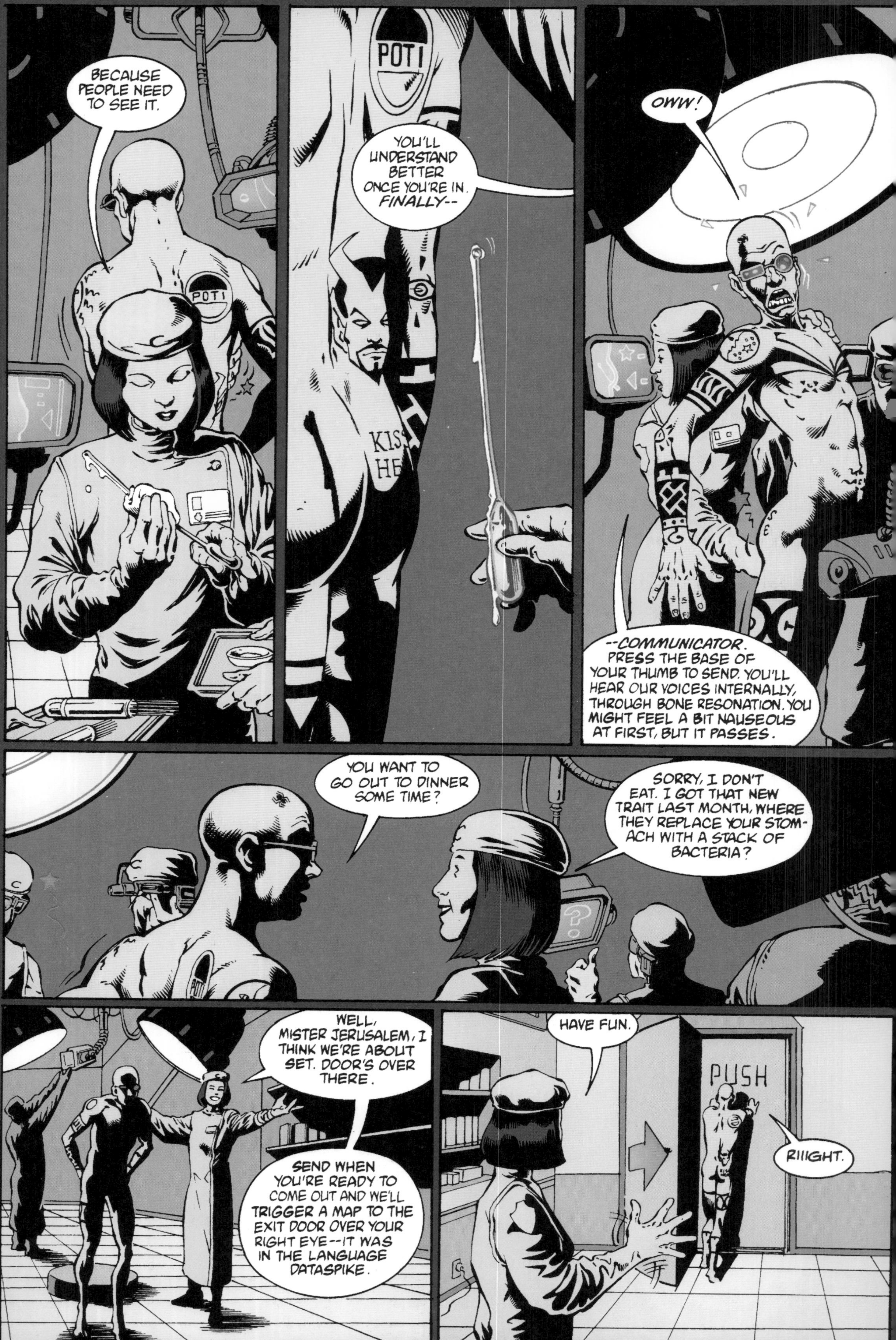
BECAUSE PEOPLE NEED TO SEE IT.
POTI
YOU'LL UNDERSTAND BETTER ONCE YOU'RE IN. FINALLY--
KISS HE
OWW!
--COMMUNICATOR. PRESS THE BASE OF YOUR THUMB TO SEND. YOU'LL HEAR OUR VOICES INTERNALLY, THROUGH BONE RESONATION. YOU MIGHT FEEL A BIT NAUSEOUS AT FIRST, BUT IT PASSES.
YOU WANT TO GO OUT TO DINNER SOME TIME?
SORRY, I DON'T EAT. I GOT THAT NEW TRAIT LAST MONTH, WHERE THEY REPLACE YOUR STOMACH WITH A STACK OF BACTERIA?
WELL, MISTER JERUSALEM, I THINK WE'RE ABOUT SET. DOOR'S OVER THERE.
SEND WHEN YOU'RE READY TO COME OUT AND WE'LL TRIGGER A MAP TO THE EXIT DOOR OVER YOUR RIGHT EYE--IT WAS IN THE LANGUAGE DATASPIKE.
HAVE FUN.
PUSH
RIIIGHT.

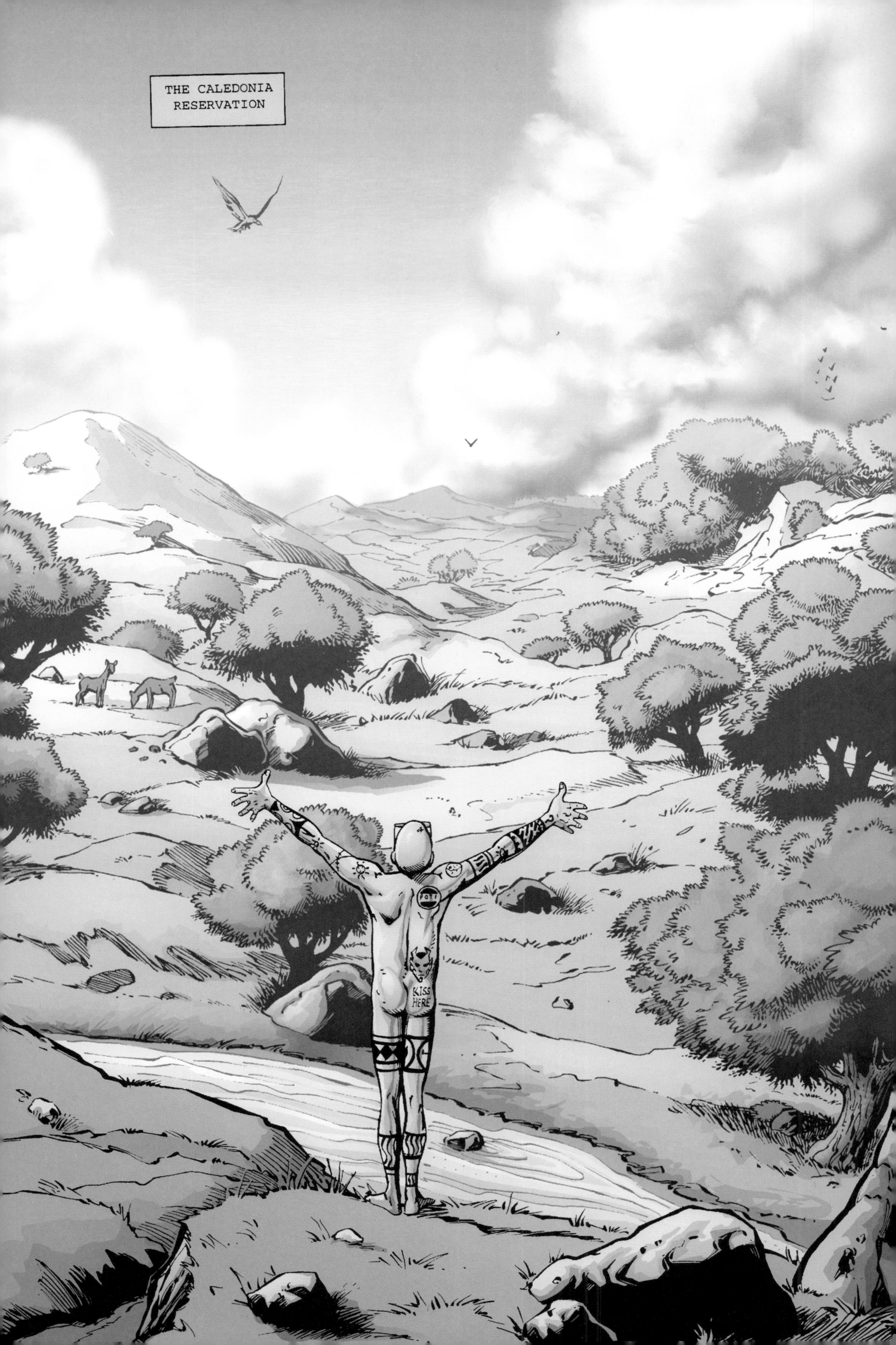
THE CALEDONIA RESERVATION
KISS HERE

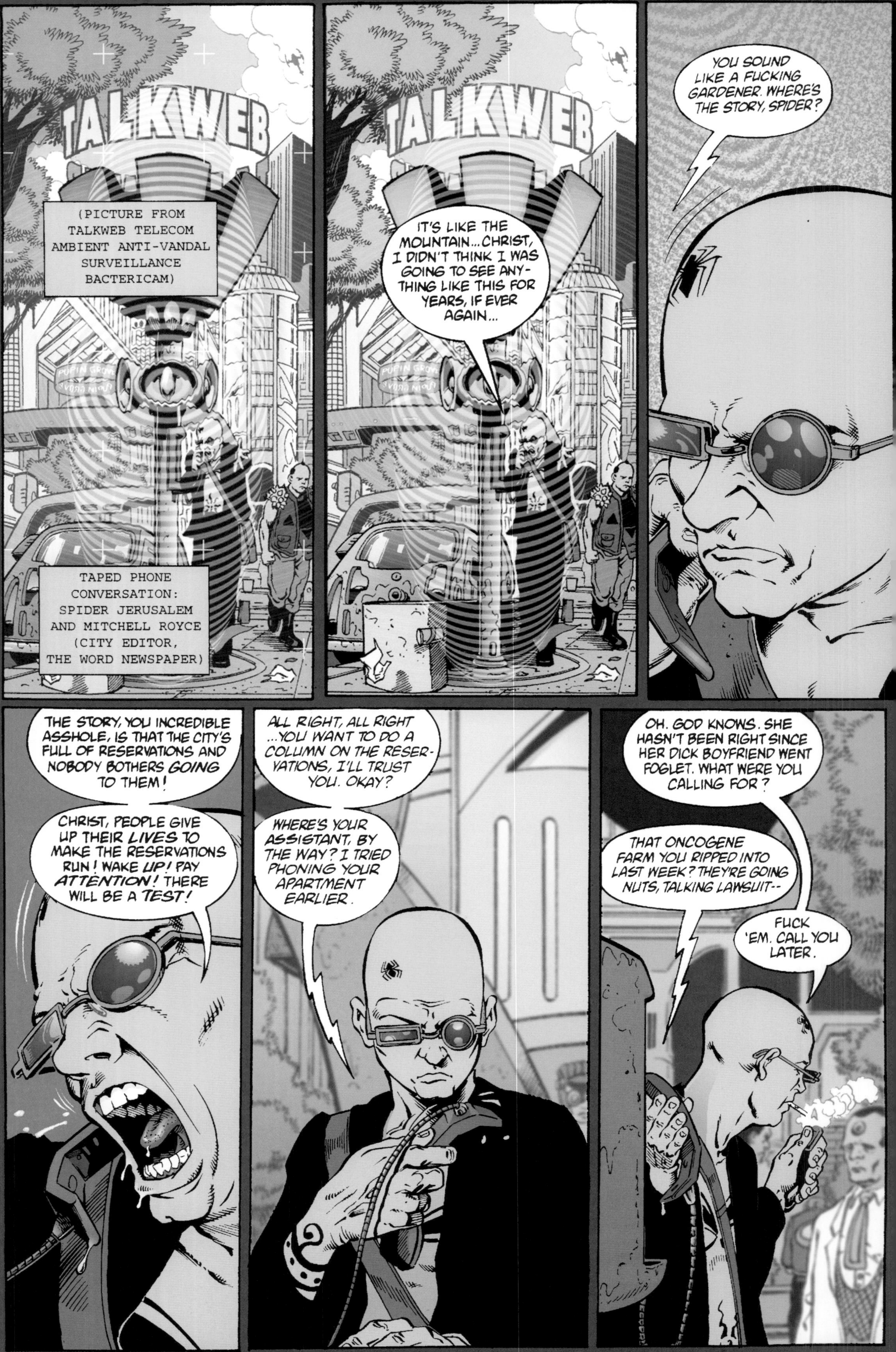

TALKWEB
(PICTURE FROM TALKWEB TELECOM AMBIENT ANTI-VANDAL SURVEILLANCE BACTERICAM)
TAPED PHONE CONVERSATION: SPIDER JERUSALEM AND MITCHELL ROYCE (CITY EDITOR, THE WORD NEWSPAPER)
TALKWEB
IT'S LIKE THE MOUNTAIN... CHRIST, I DIDN'T THINK I WAS GOING TO SEE ANYTHING LIKE THIS FOR YEARS, IF EVER AGAIN...
YOU SOUND LIKE A FUCKING GARDENER. WHERE'S THE STORY, SPIDER?
THE STORY, YOU INCREDIBLE ASSHOLE, IS THAT THE CITY'S FULL OF RESERVATIONS AND NOBODY BOTHERS GOING TO THEM!
CHRIST, PEOPLE GIVE UP THEIR LIVES TO MAKE THE RESERVATIONS RUN! WAKE UP! PAY ATTENTION! THERE WILL BE A TEST!
ALL RIGHT, ALL RIGHT ...YOU WANT TO DO A COLUMN ON THE RESERVATIONS, I'LL TRUST YOU. OKAY?
WHERE'S YOUR ASSISTANT, BY THE WAY? I TRIED PHONING YOUR APARTMENT EARLIER.
OH. GOD KNOWS. SHE HASN'T BEEN RIGHT SINCE HER DICK BOYFRIEND WENT FOGLET. WHAT WERE YOU CALLING FOR?
THAT ONCOGENE FARM YOU RIPPED INTO LAST WEEK? THEY'RE GOING NUTS, TALKING LAWSUIT--
FUCK 'EM. CALL YOU LATER.

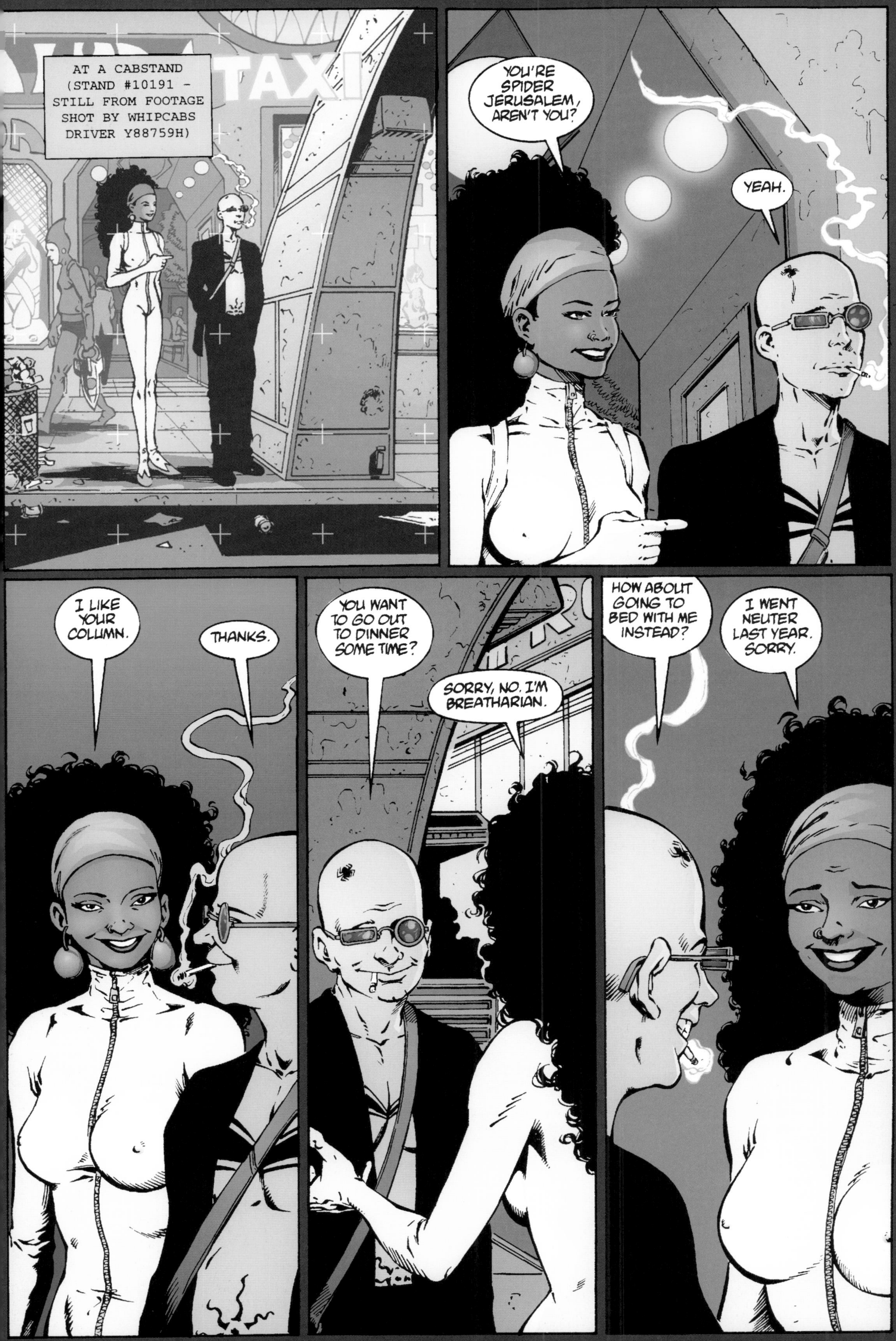
AT A CABSTAND (STAND #10191 - STILL FROM FOOTAGE SHOT BY WHIPCABS DRIVER Y88759H)
TAXI
YOU'RE SPIDER JERUSALEM, AREN'T YOU?
YEAH.
I LIKE YOUR COLUMN.
THANKS.
YOU WANT TO GO OUT TO DINNER SOME TIME?
SORRY, NO. I'M BREATHARIAN.
HOW ABOUT GOING TO BED WITH ME INSTEAD?
I WENT NEUTER LAST YEAR. SORRY.

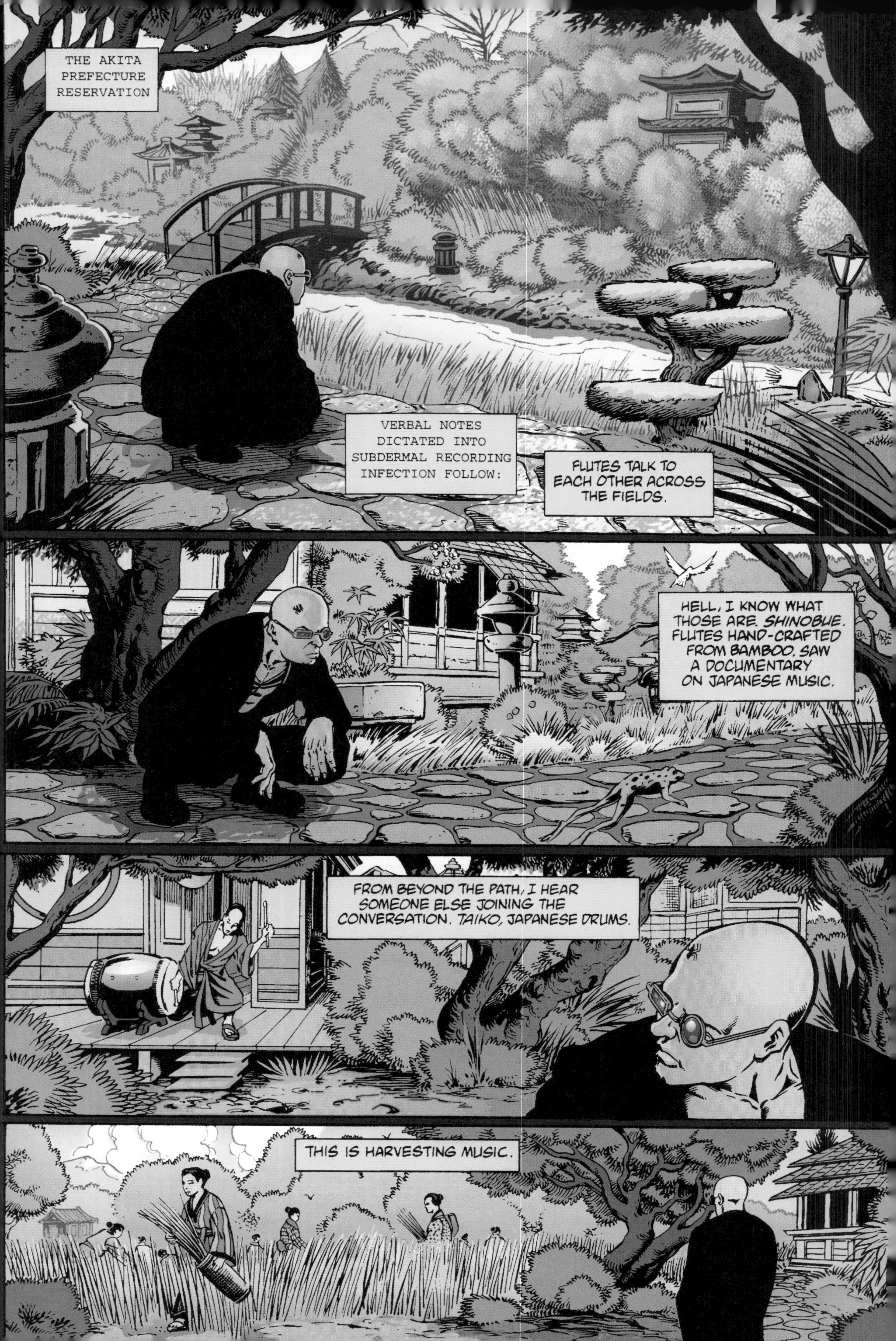
THE AKITA PREFECTURE RESERVATION
VERBAL NOTES DICTATED INTO SUBDERMAL RECORDING INFECTION FOLLOW:
FLUTES TALK TO EACH OTHER ACROSS THE FIELDS.
HELL, I KNOW WHAT THOSE ARE. SHINOBUE. FLUTES HAND-CRAFTED FROM BAMBOO. SAW A DOCUMENTARY ON JAPANESE MUSIC.
FROM BEYOND THE PATH, I HEAR SOMEONE ELSE JOINING THE CONVERSATION. TAIKO, JAPANESE DRUMS.
THIS IS HARVESTING MUSIC.

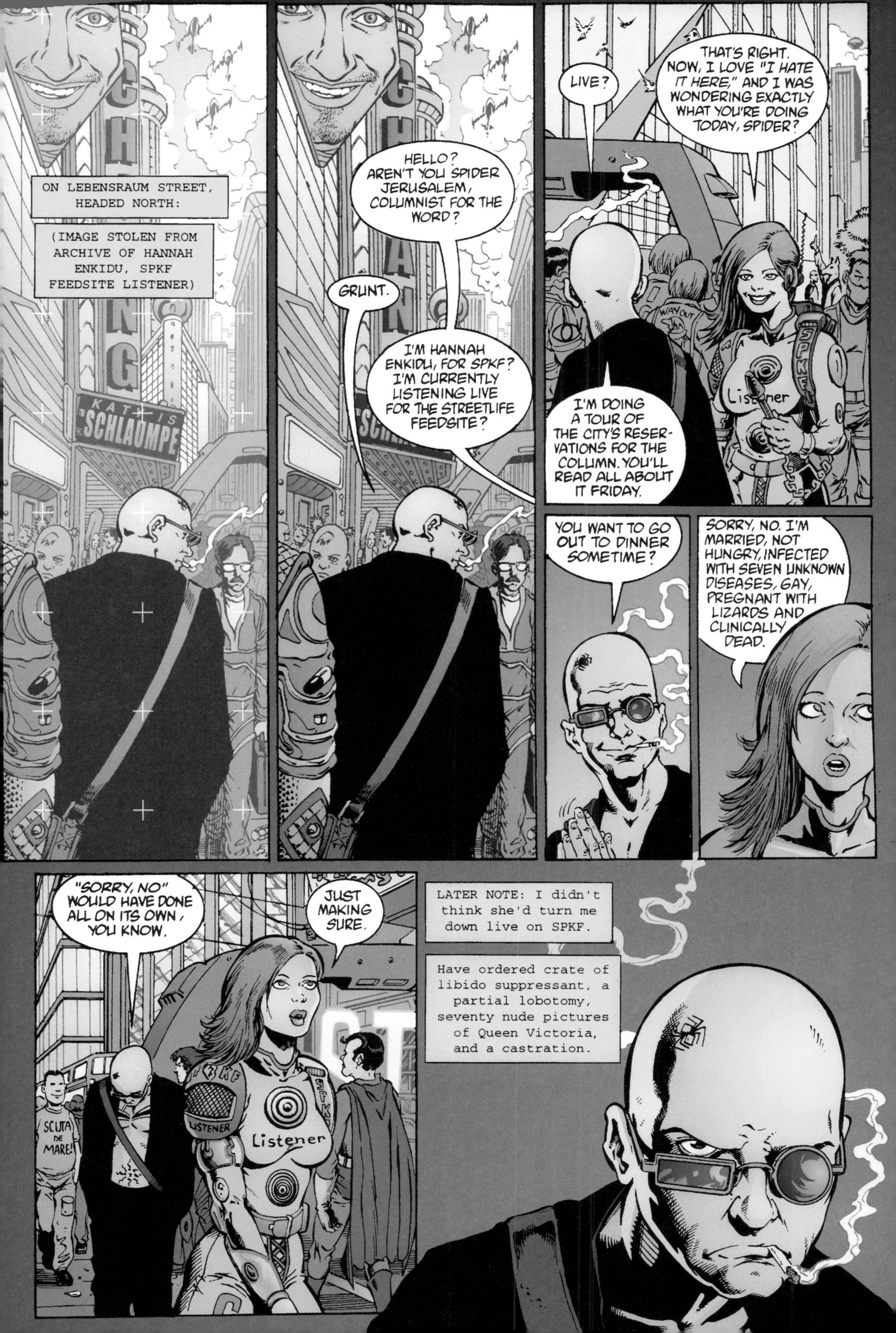
ON LEBENSRAUM STREET, HEADED NORTH:
(IMAGE STOLEN FROM ARCHIVE OF HANNAH ENKIDU, SPKF FEEDSITE LISTENER)
SCHLAUMPE
HELLO? AREN'T YOU SPIDER JERUSALEM, COLUMNIST FOR THE WORD?
GRUNT.
I'M HANNAH ENKIDU, FOR SPKF? I'M CURRENTLY LISTENING LIVE FOR THE STREETLIFE FEEDSITE?
LIVE?
THAT'S RIGHT. NOW, I LOVE "I HATE IT HERE," AND I WAS WONDERING EXACTLY WHAT YOU'RE DOING TODAY, SPIDER?
I'M DOING A TOUR OF THE CITY'S RESERVATIONS FOR THE COLUMN. YOU'LL READ ALL ABOUT IT FRIDAY.
Listener
YOU WANT TO GO OUT TO DINNER SOMETIME?
SORRY, NO. I'M MARRIED, NOT HUNGRY, INFECTED WITH SEVEN UNKNOWN DISEASES, GAY, PREGNANT WITH LIZARDS AND CLINICALLY DEAD.
"SORRY, NO" WOULD HAVE DONE ALL ON ITS OWN, YOU KNOW.
JUST MAKING SURE.
SCUTA DE MARE!
LISTENER
Listener
LATER NOTE: I didn't think she'd turn me down live on SPKF.
Have ordered crate of libido suppressant, a partial lobotomy, seventy nude pictures of Queen Victoria, and a castration.

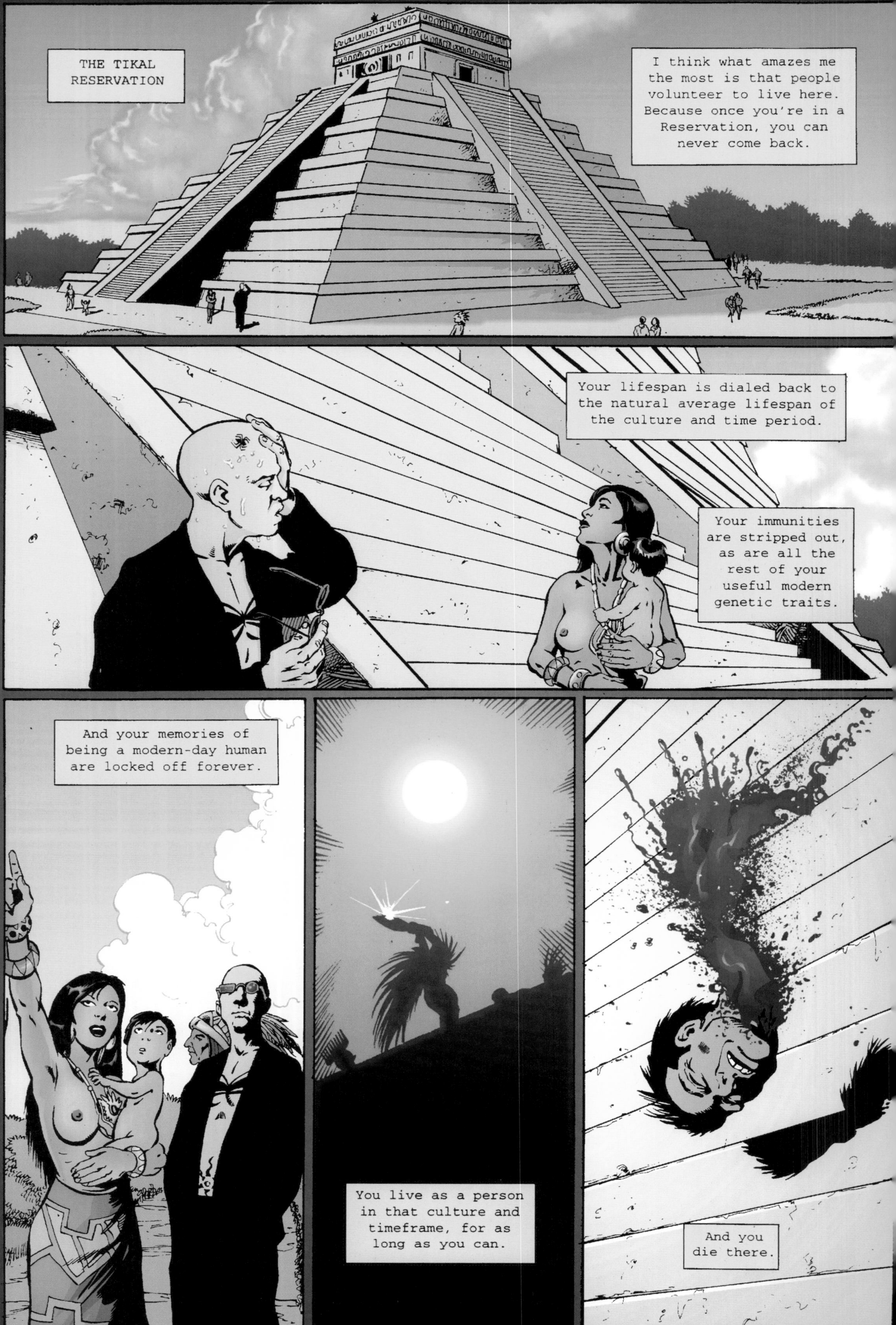
THE TIKAL RESERVATION
I think what amazes me the most is that people volunteer to live here. Because once you're in a Reservation, you can never come back.
Your lifespan is dialed back to the natural average lifespan of the culture and time period.
Your immunities are stripped out, as are all the rest of your useful modern genetic traits.
And your memories of being a modern-day human are locked off forever.
You live as a person in that culture and timeframe, for as long as you can.
And you die there.

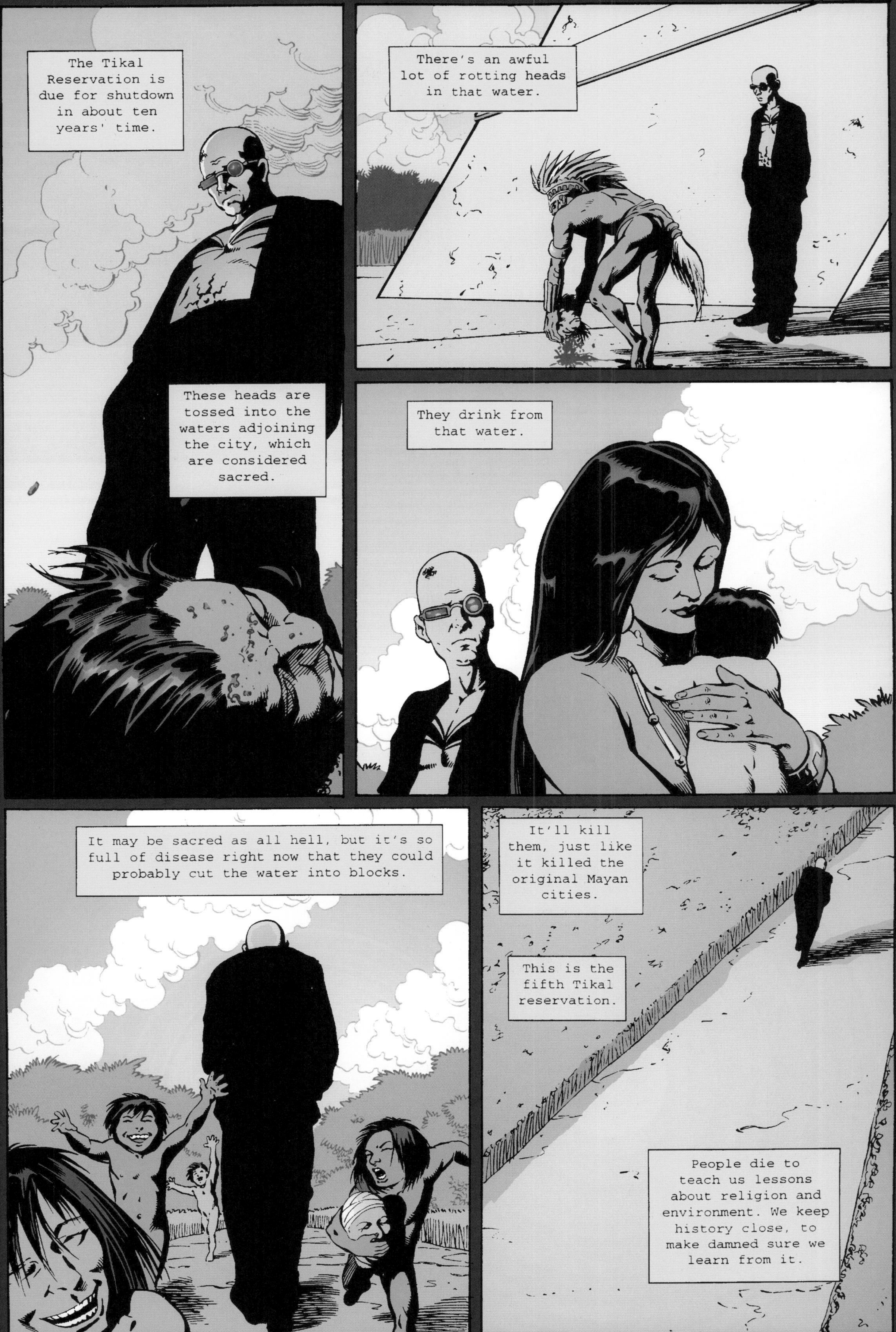
The Tikal Reservation is due for shutdown in about ten years' time.
These heads are tossed into the waters adjoining the city, which are considered sacred.
There's an awful lot of rotting heads in that water.
They drink from that water.
It may be sacred as all hell, but it's so full of disease right now that they could probably cut the water into blocks.
It'll kill them, just like it killed the original Mayan cities.
This is the fifth Tikal reservation.
People die to teach us lessons about religion and environment. We keep history close, to make damned sure we learn from it.

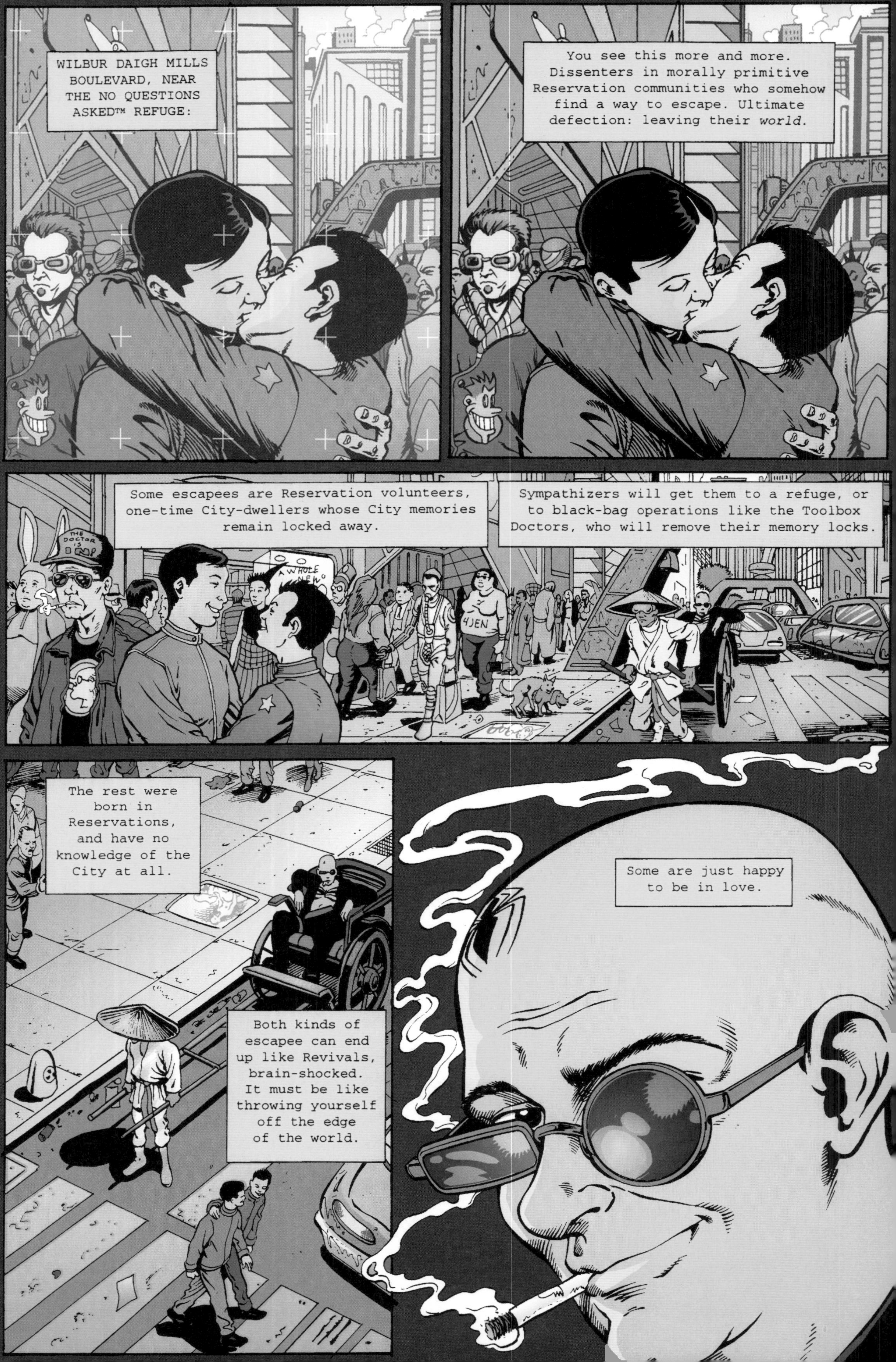
WILBUR DAIGH MILLS BOULEVARD, NEAR THE NO QUESTIONS ASKED™ REFUGE:
You see this more and more. Dissenters in morally primitive Reservation communities who somehow find a way to escape. Ultimate defection: leaving their *world*.
Some escapees are Reservation volunteers, one-time City-dwellers whose City memories remain locked away.
Sympathizers will get them to a refuge, or to black-bag operations like the Toolbox Doctors, who will remove their memory locks.
4JEN
The rest were born in Reservations, and have no knowledge of the City at all.
Both kinds of escapee can end up like Revivals, brain-shocked. It must be like throwing yourself off the edge of the world.
Some are just happy to be in love.

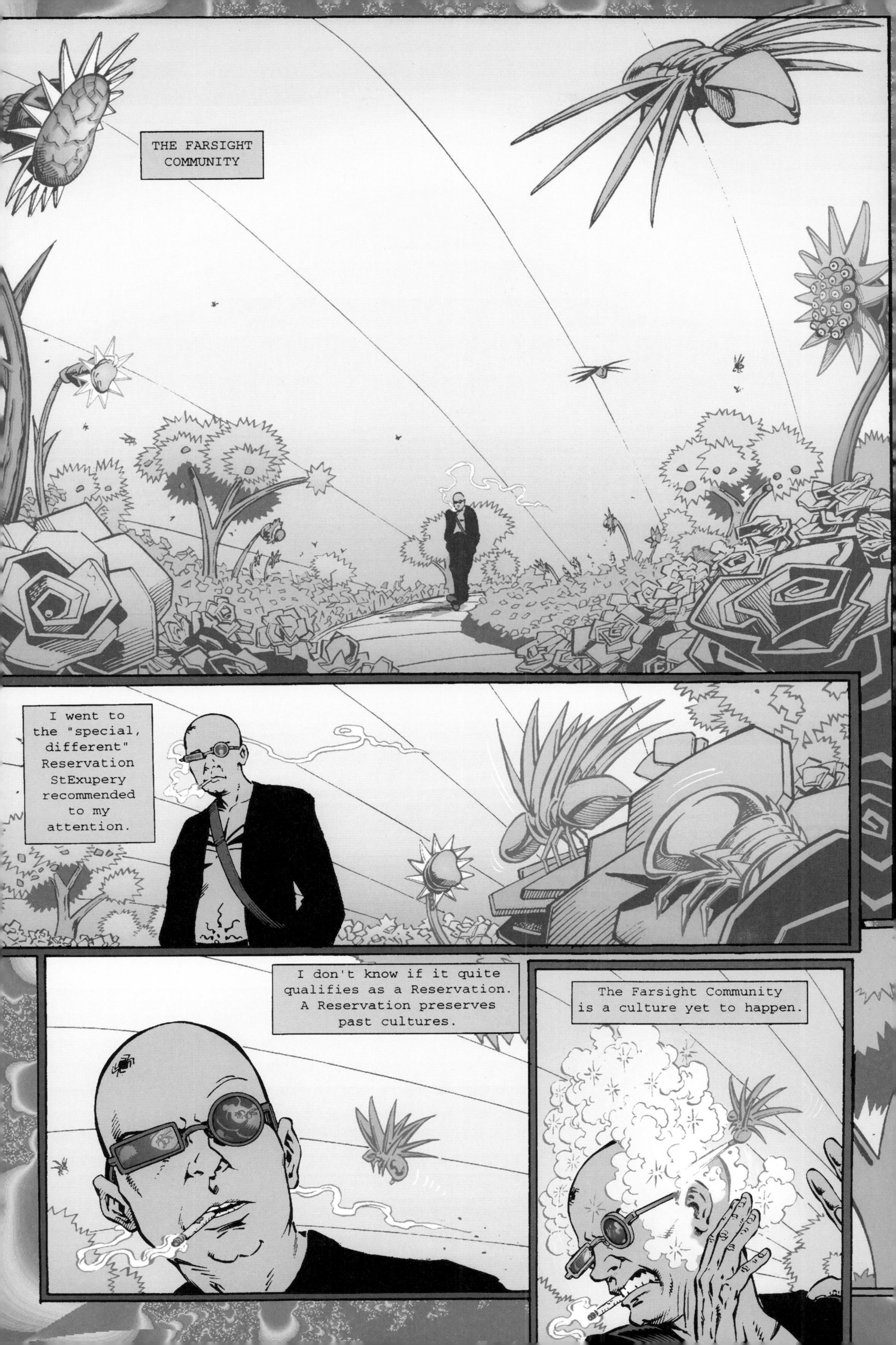
THE FARSIGHT COMMUNITY
I went to the "special, different" Reservation StExupery recommended to my attention.
I don't know if it quite qualifies as a Reservation. A Reservation preserves past cultures.
The Farsight Community is a culture yet to happen.

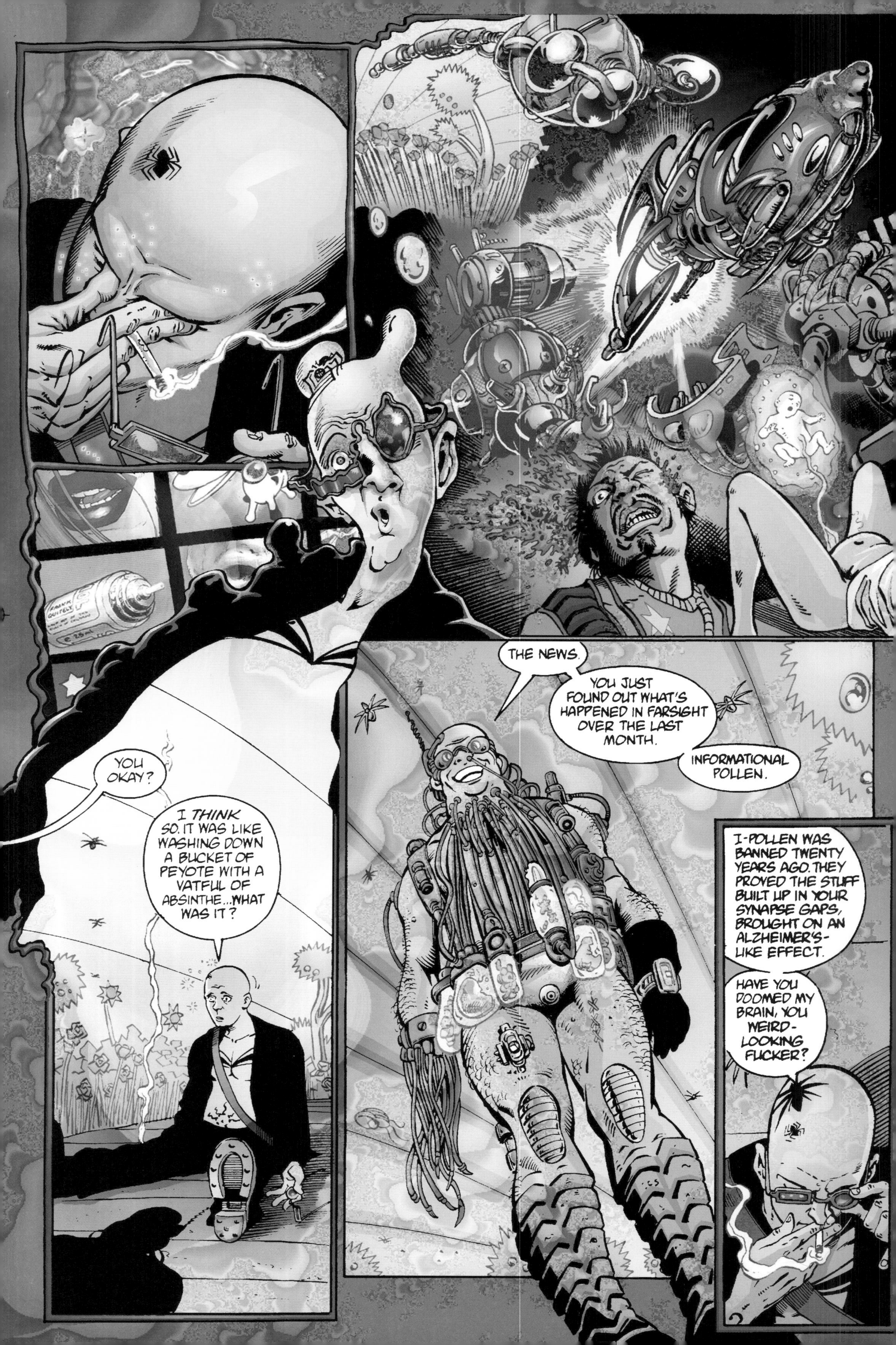
FRANK QUITELY
YOU OKAY?
I *THINK* SO. IT WAS LIKE WASHING DOWN A BUCKET OF PEYOTE WITH A VATFUL OF ABSINTHE...WHAT WAS IT?
THE NEWS.
YOU JUST FOUND OUT WHAT'S HAPPENED IN FARSIGHT OVER THE LAST MONTH.
INFORMATIONAL POLLEN.
I-POLLEN WAS BANNED TWENTY YEARS AGO. THEY PROVED THE STUFF BUILT UP IN YOUR SYNAPSE GAPS, BROUGHT ON AN ALZHEIMER'S-LIKE EFFECT.
HAVE YOU DOOMED MY BRAIN, YOU WEIRD-LOOKING FUCKER?

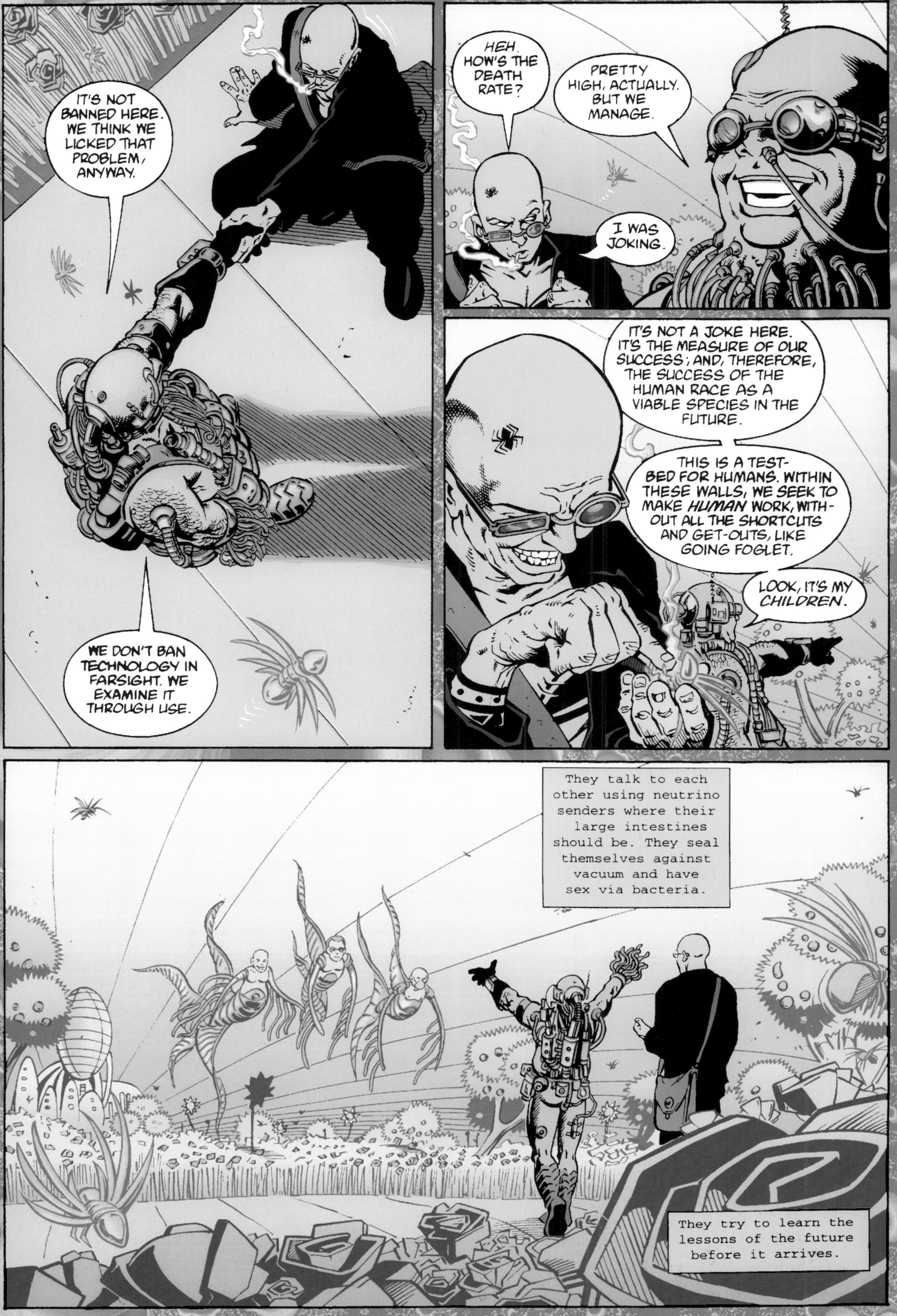
IT'S NOT BANNED HERE. WE THINK WE LICKED THAT PROBLEM, ANYWAY.
WE DON'T BAN TECHNOLOGY IN FARSIGHT. WE EXAMINE IT THROUGH USE.
HEH. HOW'S THE DEATH RATE?
PRETTY HIGH, ACTUALLY. BUT WE MANAGE.
I WAS JOKING.
IT'S NOT A JOKE HERE. IT'S THE MEASURE OF OUR SUCCESS; AND, THEREFORE, THE SUCCESS OF THE HUMAN RACE AS A VIABLE SPECIES IN THE FUTURE.
THIS IS A TEST-BED FOR HUMANS. WITHIN THESE WALLS, WE SEEK TO MAKE HUMAN WORK, WITHOUT ALL THE SHORTCUTS AND GET-OUTS, LIKE GOING FOGLET.
LOOK, IT'S MY CHILDREN.
They talk to each other using neutrino senders where their large intestines should be. They seal themselves against vacuum and have sex via bacteria.
They try to learn the lessons of the future before it arrives.

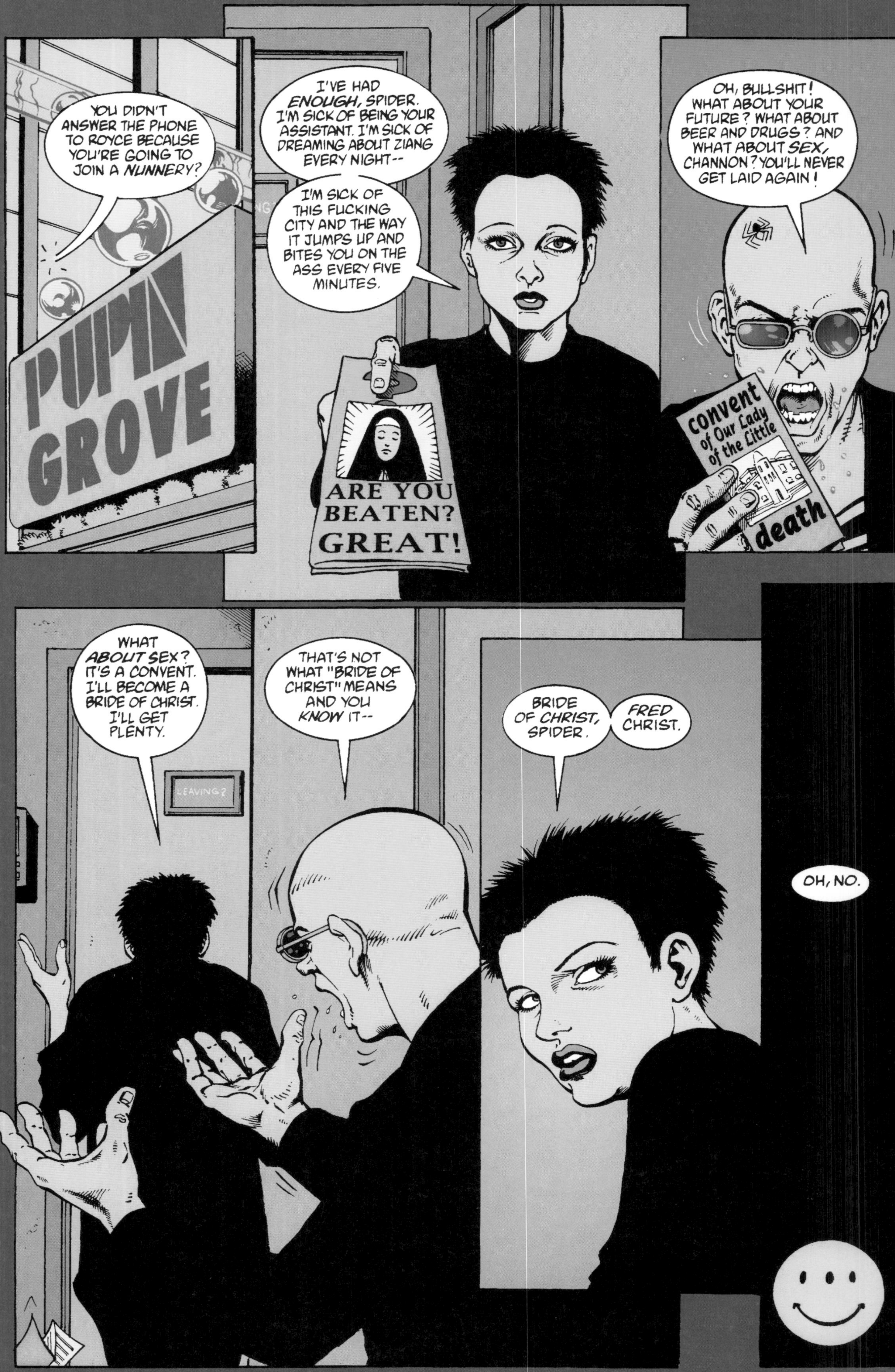
YOU DIDN'T ANSWER THE PHONE TO ROYCE BECAUSE YOU'RE GOING TO JOIN A NUNNERY?
PUPIN GROVE
I'VE HAD ENOUGH, SPIDER. I'M SICK OF BEING YOUR ASSISTANT. I'M SICK OF DREAMING ABOUT ZIANG EVERY NIGHT--
I'M SICK OF THIS FUCKING CITY AND THE WAY IT JUMPS UP AND BITES YOU ON THE ASS EVERY FIVE MINUTES.
ARE YOU BEATEN? GREAT!
OH, BULLSHIT! WHAT ABOUT YOUR FUTURE? WHAT ABOUT BEER AND DRUGS? AND WHAT ABOUT SEX, CHANNON? YOU'LL NEVER GET LAID AGAIN!
convent of Our Lady of the Little
death
WHAT ABOUT SEX? IT'S A CONVENT. I'LL BECOME A BRIDE OF CHRIST. I'LL GET PLENTY.
LEAVING?
THAT'S NOT WHAT "BRIDE OF CHRIST" MEANS AND YOU KNOW IT--
BRIDE OF CHRIST, SPIDER.
FRED CHRIST.
OH, NO.

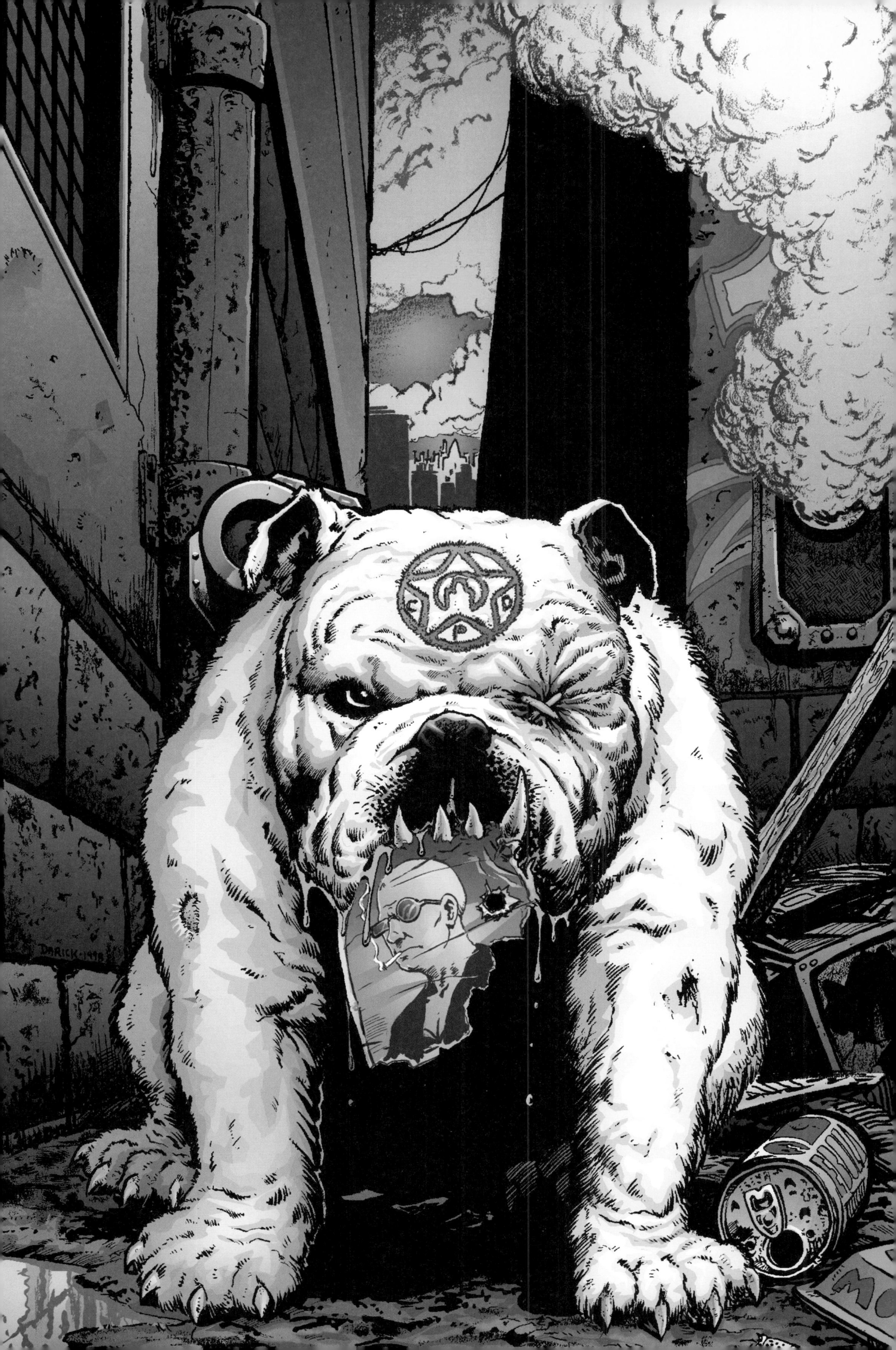
DARICK·1998

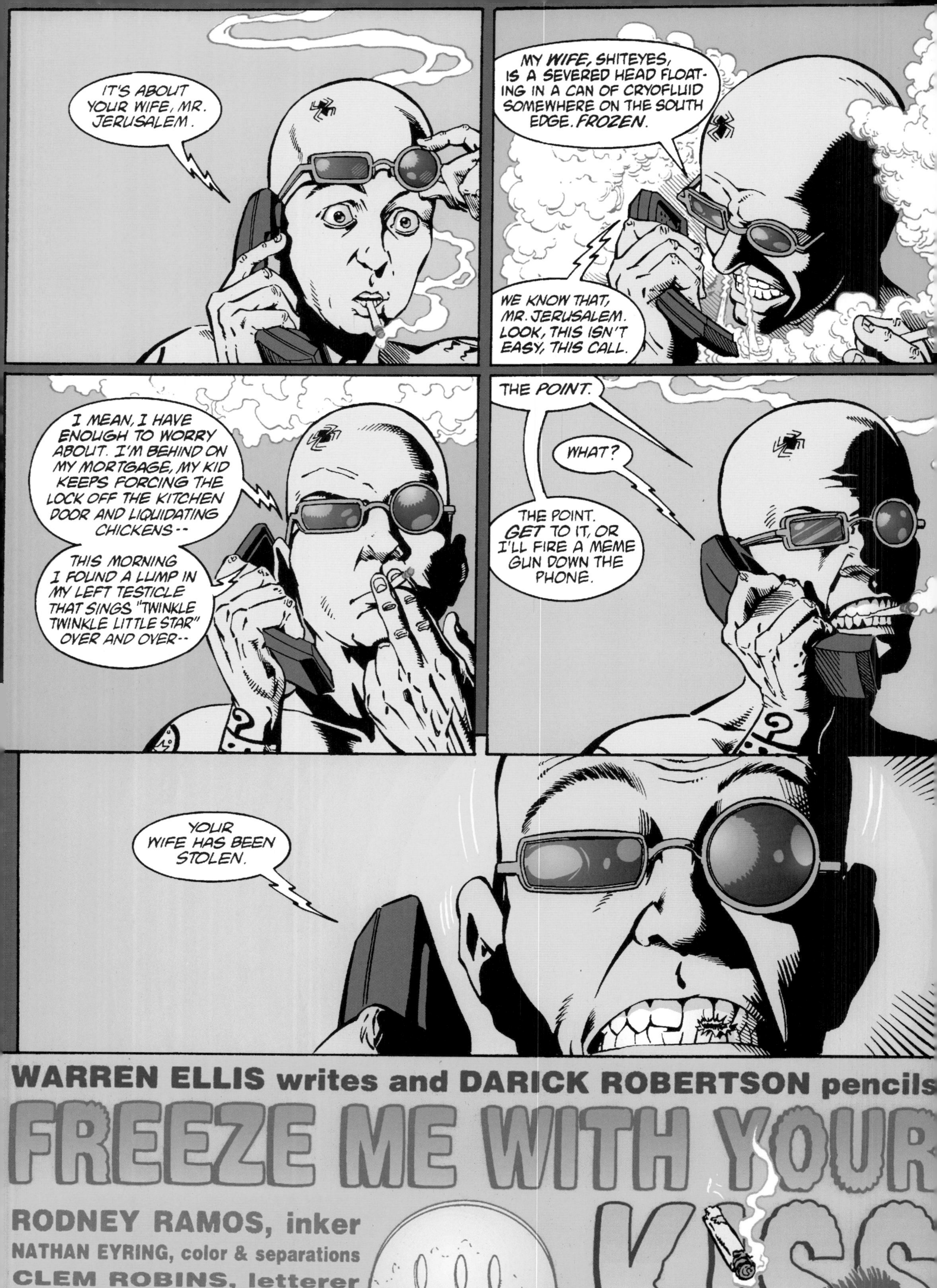
IT'S ABOUT YOUR WIFE, MR. JERUSALEM.
MY WIFE, SHITEYES, IS A SEVERED HEAD FLOATING IN A CAN OF CRYOFLUID SOMEWHERE ON THE SOUTH EDGE. FROZEN.
WE KNOW THAT, MR. JERUSALEM. LOOK, THIS ISN'T EASY, THIS CALL.
I MEAN, I HAVE ENOUGH TO WORRY ABOUT. I'M BEHIND ON MY MORTGAGE, MY KID KEEPS FORCING THE LOCK OFF THE KITCHEN DOOR AND LIQUIDATING CHICKENS--
THIS MORNING I FOUND A LUMP IN MY LEFT TESTICLE THAT SINGS "TWINKLE TWINKLE LITTLE STAR" OVER AND OVER--
THE POINT.
WHAT?
THE POINT. GET TO IT, OR I'LL FIRE A MEME GUN DOWN THE PHONE.
YOUR WIFE HAS BEEN STOLEN.

**WARREN ELLIS writes and DARICK ROBERTSON pencils**

# FREEZE ME WITH YOUR KISS

**RODNEY RAMOS, inker**
**NATHAN EYRING, color & separations**
**CLEM ROBINS, letterer**
**CLIFF CHIANG, assistant editor**
**STUART MOORE, editor**
**TRANSMETROPOLITAN CREATED BY WARREN ELLIS & DARICK ROBERTSON**

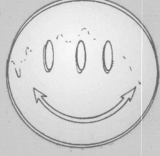

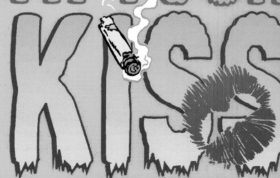

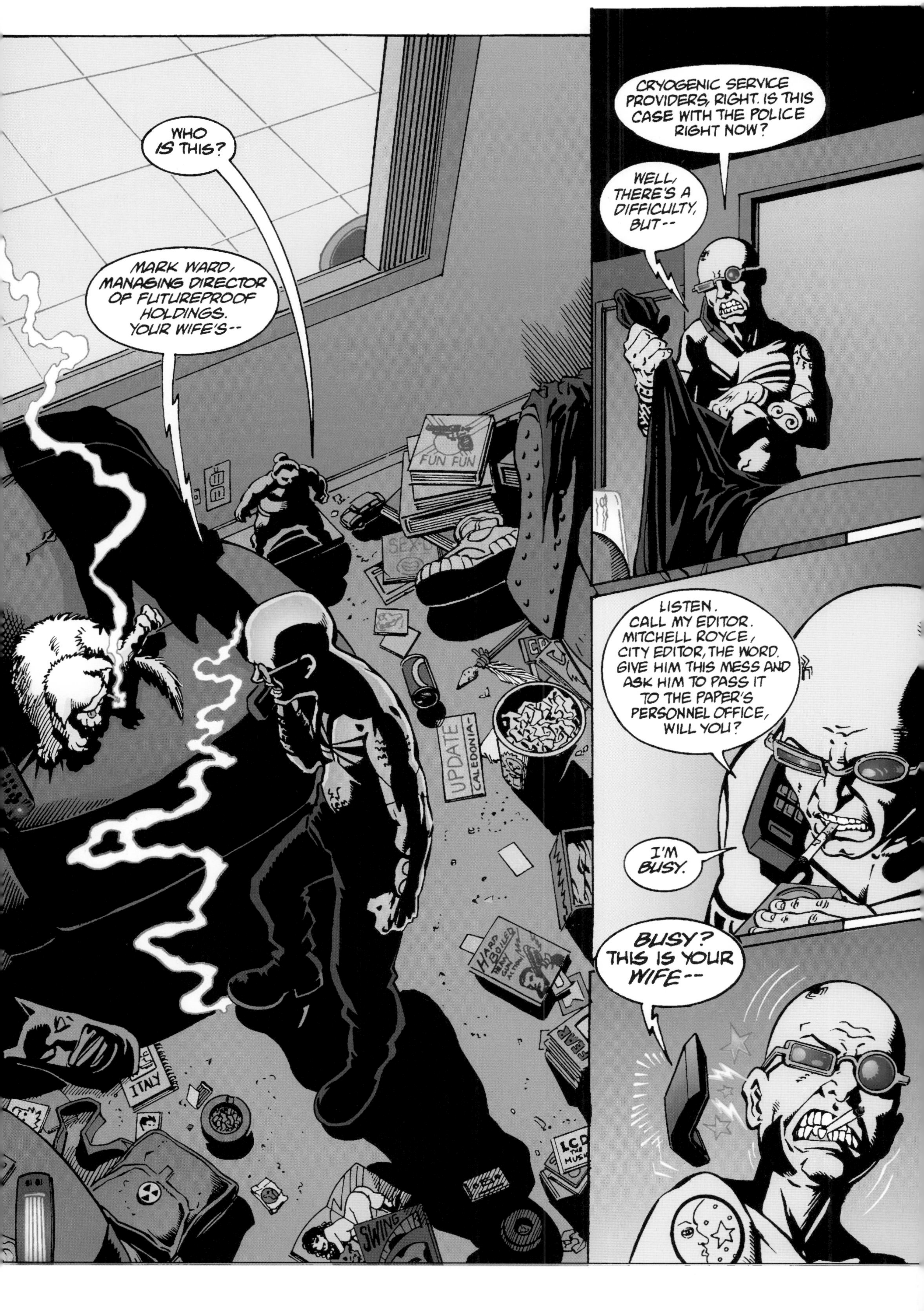
WHO IS THIS?
MARK WARD, MANAGING DIRECTOR OF FUTUREPROOF HOLDINGS. YOUR WIFE'S--
FUN FUN
UPDATE
CALEDONIA
HARD BOILED
ITALY
SWING
CRYOGENIC SERVICE PROVIDERS, RIGHT. IS THIS CASE WITH THE POLICE RIGHT NOW?
WELL, THERE'S A DIFFICULTY, BUT--
LISTEN. CALL MY EDITOR. MITCHELL ROYCE, CITY EDITOR, THE WORD. GIVE HIM THIS MESS AND ASK HIM TO PASS IT TO THE PAPER'S PERSONNEL OFFICE, WILL YOU?
I'M BUSY.
BUSY? THIS IS YOUR WIFE--

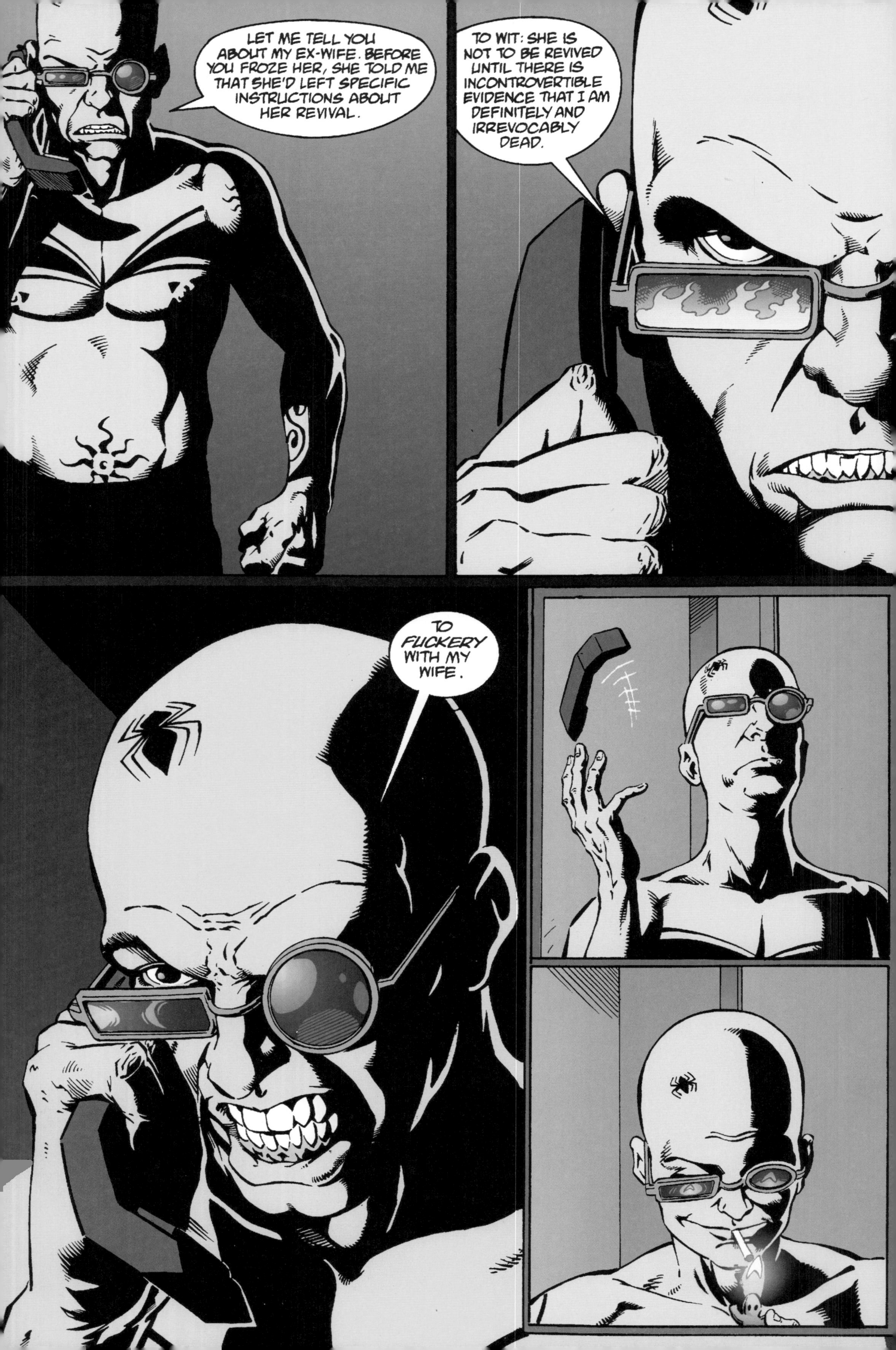
LET ME TELL YOU ABOUT MY EX-WIFE. BEFORE YOU FROZE HER, SHE TOLD ME THAT SHE'D LEFT SPECIFIC INSTRUCTIONS ABOUT HER REVIVAL.
TO WIT: SHE IS NOT TO BE REVIVED UNTIL THERE IS INCONTROVERTIBLE EVIDENCE THAT I AM DEFINITELY AND IRREVOCABLY DEAD.
TO FUCKERY WITH MY WIFE.

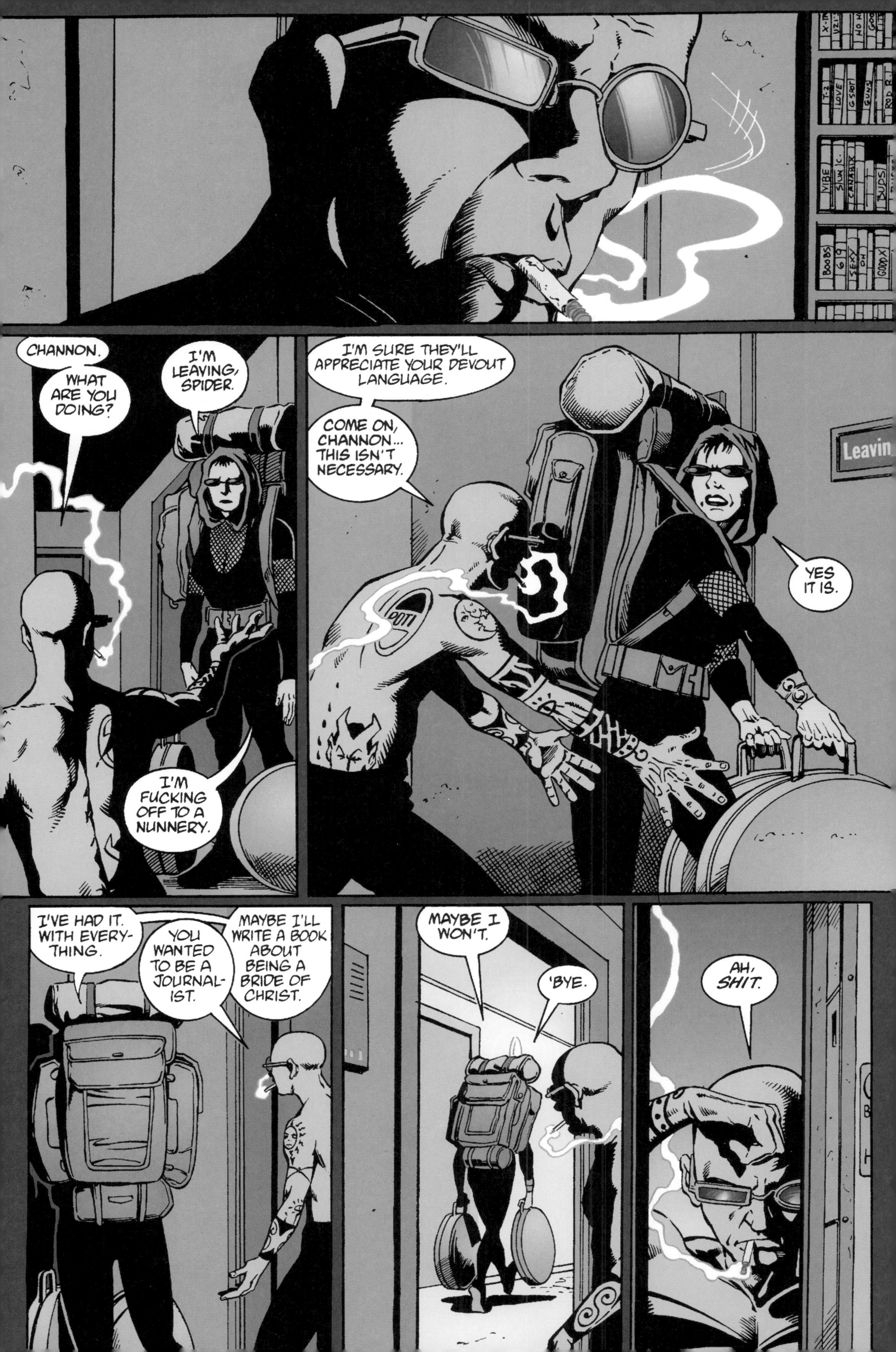

X-M
UZI
HO HO
GOOD
T-2
LOVE
G-SPOT
GUNS
ROD R
VIBE
SLUT
CANABIX
BUDS
BOOBS
69
SEXY
OH
GOOD X
CHANNON.
WHAT ARE YOU DOING?
I'M LEAVING, SPIDER.
I'M FUCKING OFF TO A NUNNERY.
I'M SURE THEY'LL APPRECIATE YOUR DEVOUT LANGUAGE.
COME ON, CHANNON... THIS ISN'T NECESSARY.
Leavin
YES IT IS.
I'VE HAD IT. WITH EVERYTHING.
YOU WANTED TO BE A JOURNALIST.
MAYBE I'LL WRITE A BOOK ABOUT BEING A BRIDE OF CHRIST.
MAYBE I WON'T.
'BYE.
AH, SHIT.

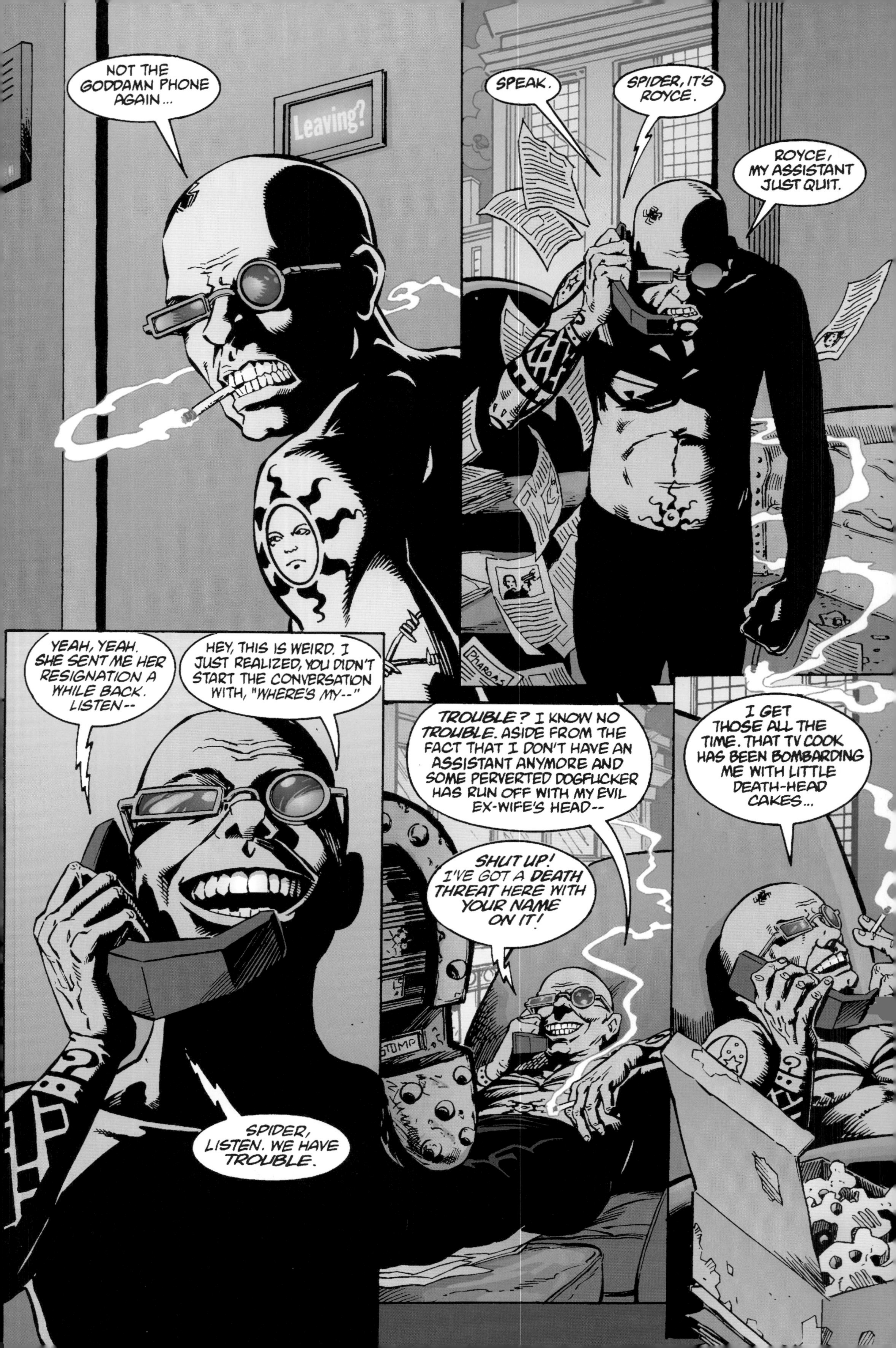

NOT THE GODDAMN PHONE AGAIN...
Leaving?
SPEAK.
SPIDER, IT'S ROYCE.
ROYCE, MY ASSISTANT JUST QUIT.
YEAH, YEAH. SHE SENT ME HER RESIGNATION A WHILE BACK. LISTEN--
HEY, THIS IS WEIRD. I JUST REALIZED, YOU DIDN'T START THE CONVERSATION WITH, "WHERE'S MY--"
SPIDER, LISTEN. WE HAVE TROUBLE.
TROUBLE? I KNOW NO TROUBLE. ASIDE FROM THE FACT THAT I DON'T HAVE AN ASSISTANT ANYMORE AND SOME PERVERTED DOGFLICKER HAS RUN OFF WITH MY EVIL EX-WIFE'S HEAD--
SHUT UP! I'VE GOT A DEATH THREAT HERE WITH YOUR NAME ON IT!
I GET THOSE ALL THE TIME. THAT TV COOK HAS BEEN BOMBARDING ME WITH LITTLE DEATH-HEAD CAKES...

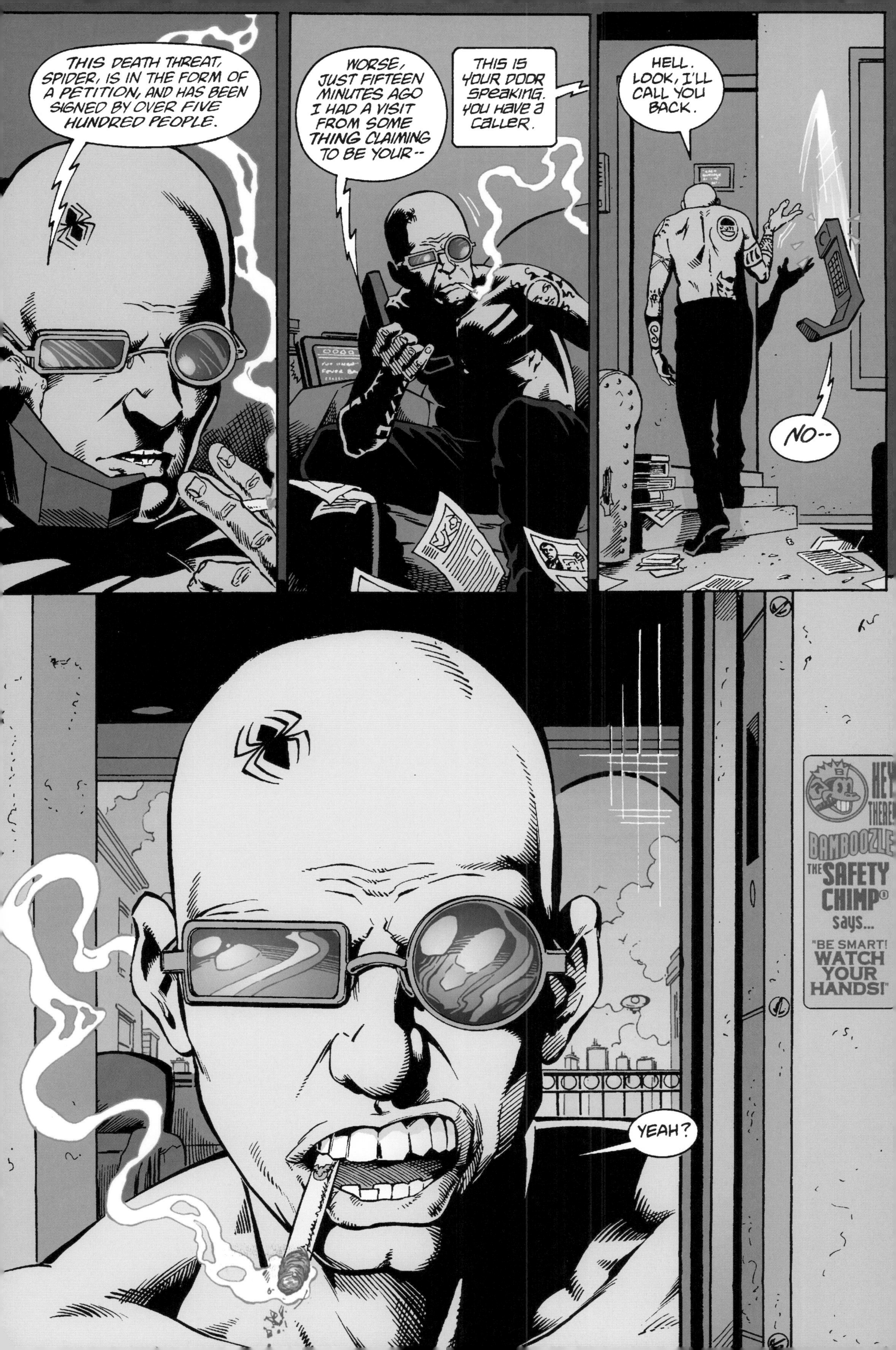
THIS DEATH THREAT, SPIDER, IS IN THE FORM OF A PETITION, AND HAS BEEN SIGNED BY OVER FIVE HUNDRED PEOPLE.
WORSE, JUST FIFTEEN MINUTES AGO I HAD A VISIT FROM SOME THING CLAIMING TO BE YOUR--
THIS IS YOUR DOOR SPEAKING. YOU HAVE A CALLER.
HELL. LOOK, I'LL CALL YOU BACK.
NO--
HEY THERE! BAMBOOZLE THE SAFETY CHIMP® says... "BE SMART! WATCH YOUR HANDS!"
YEAH?

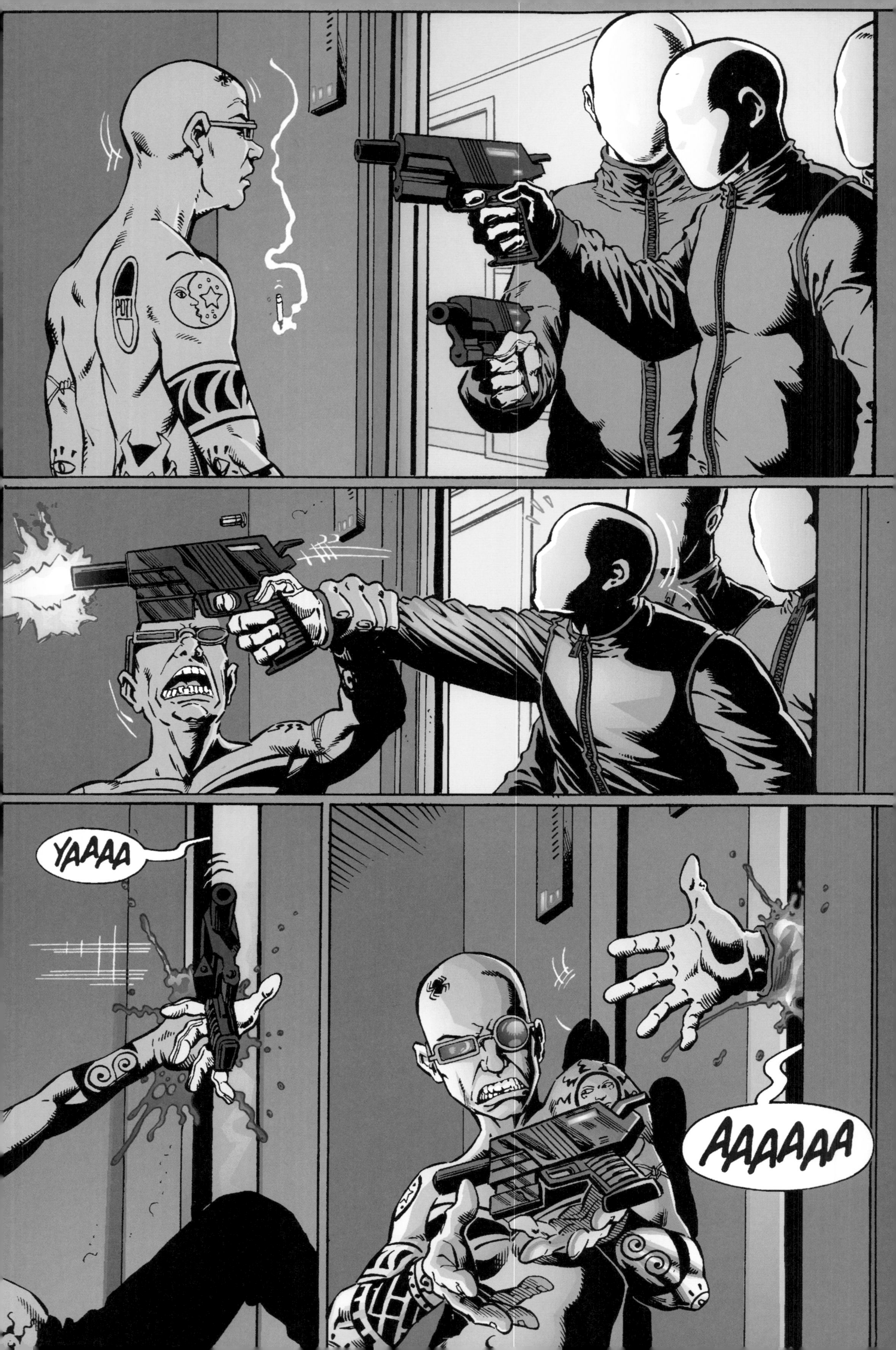
POTI
YAAAA
AAAAAA

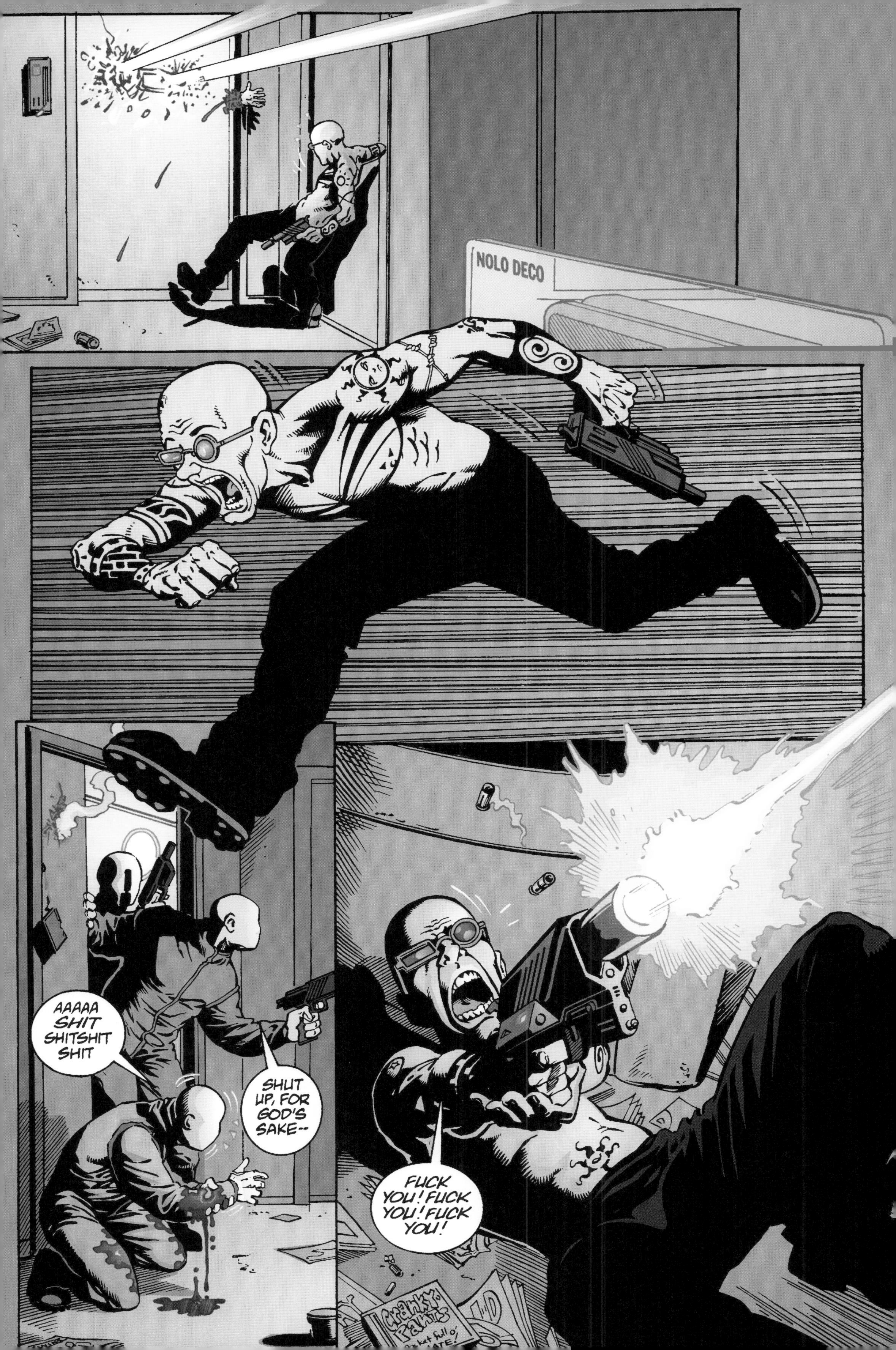
NOLO DECO
AAAAA SHIT SHITSHIT SHIT
SHUT UP, FOR GOD'S SAKE--
FUCK YOU! FUCK YOU! FUCK YOU!
Cranky Pants

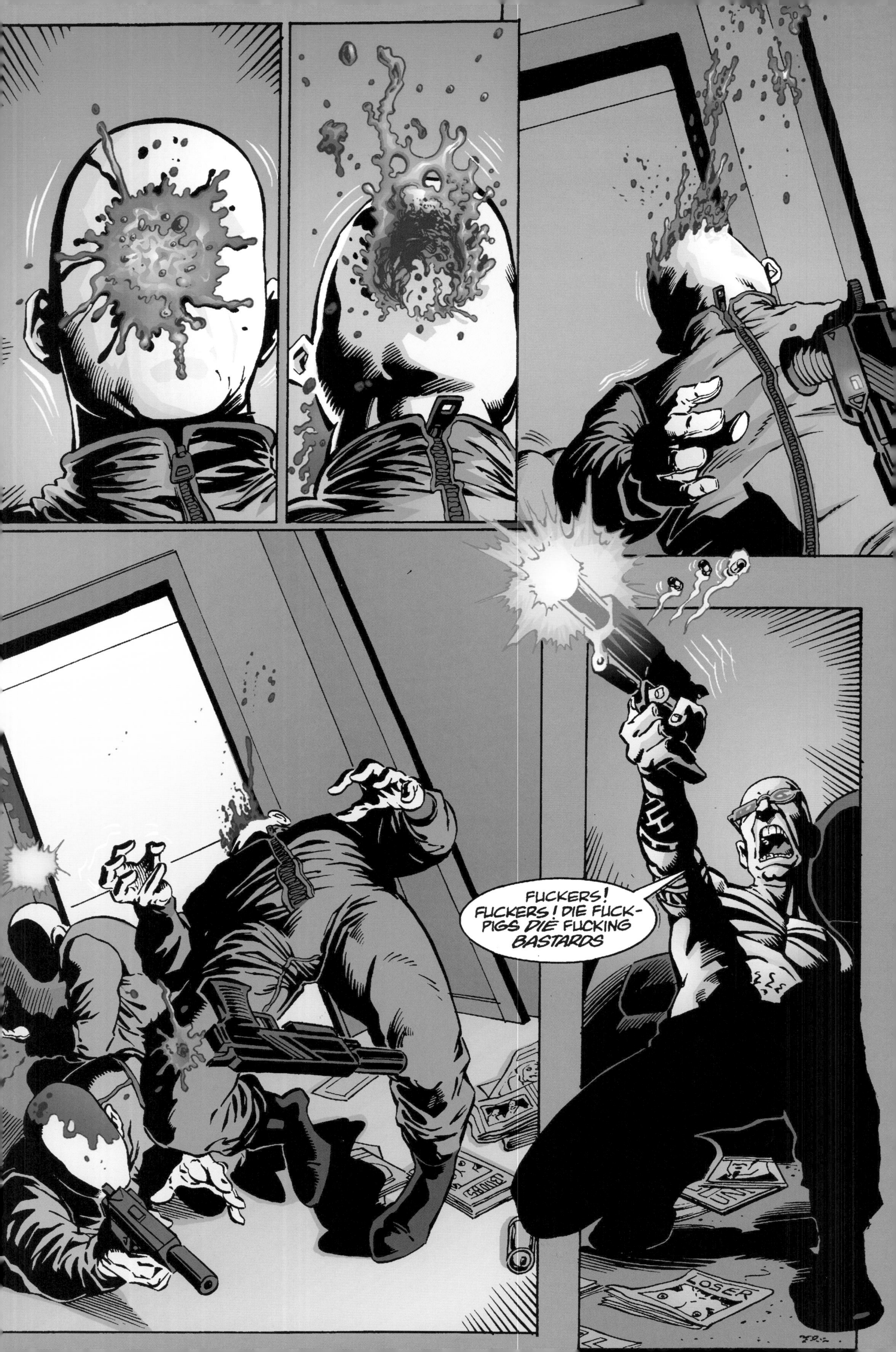
FUCKERS! FUCKERS! DIE FUCK-PIGS DIE FUCKING BASTARDS
LOSER

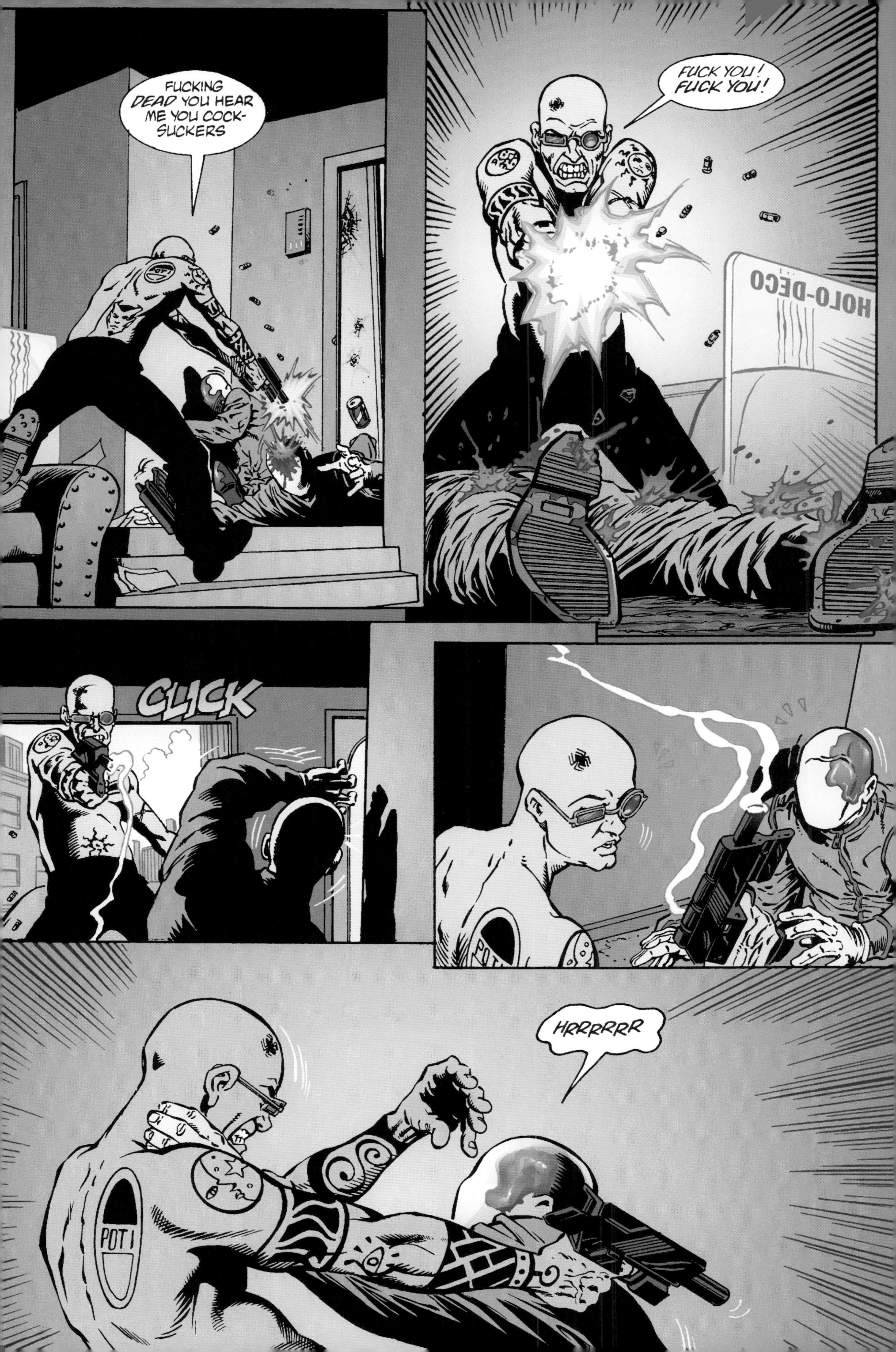
FUCKING DEAD YOU HEAR ME YOU COCK-SUCKERS
FUCK YOU! FUCK YOU!
HOLO-DECO
CLICK
HRRRRRR

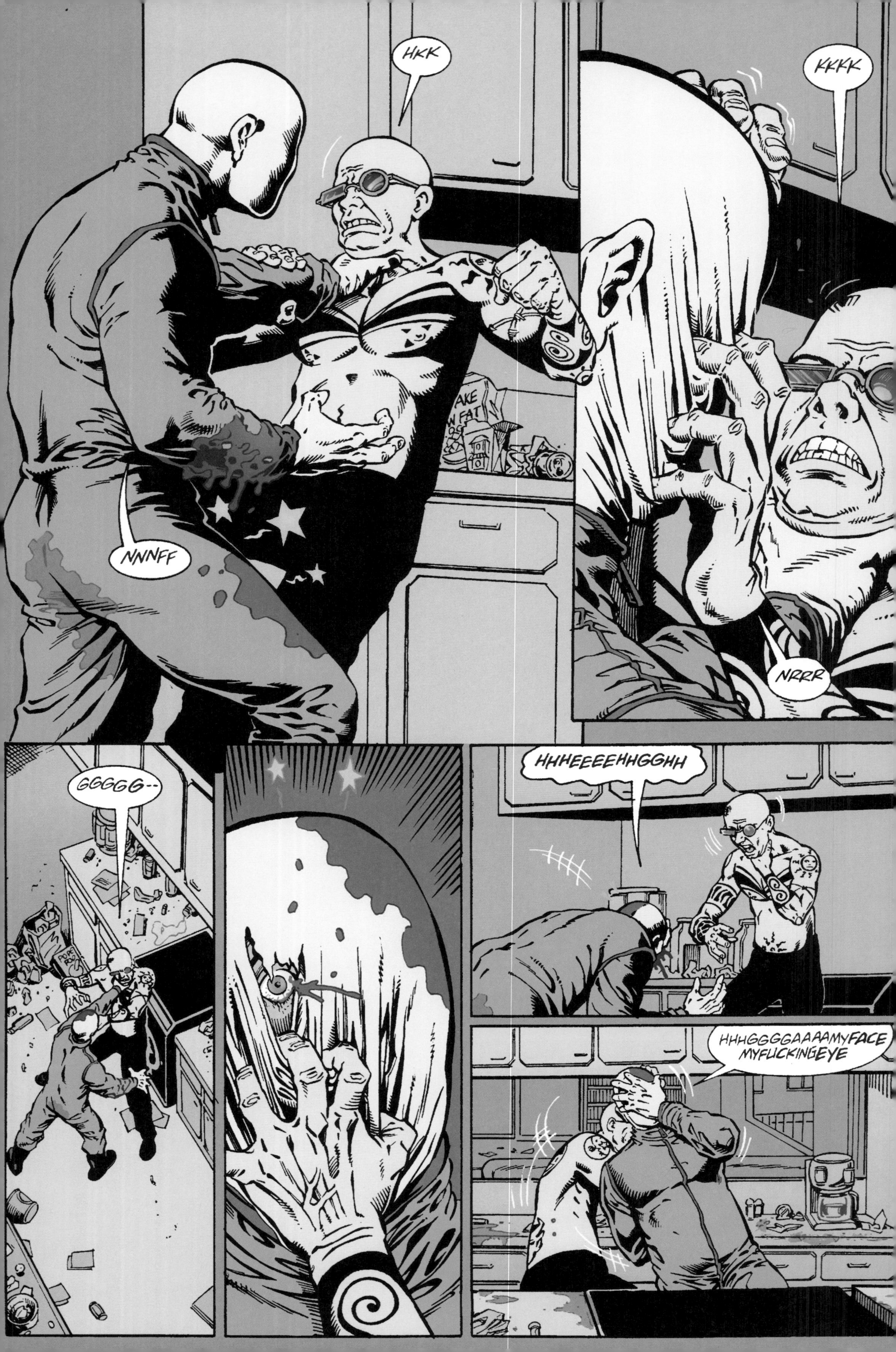
HKK
NNNFF
KKKK
NRRR
GGGGG--
HHHEEEEHHGGHH
HHHGGGGAAAAMYFACE
MYFUCKINGEYE

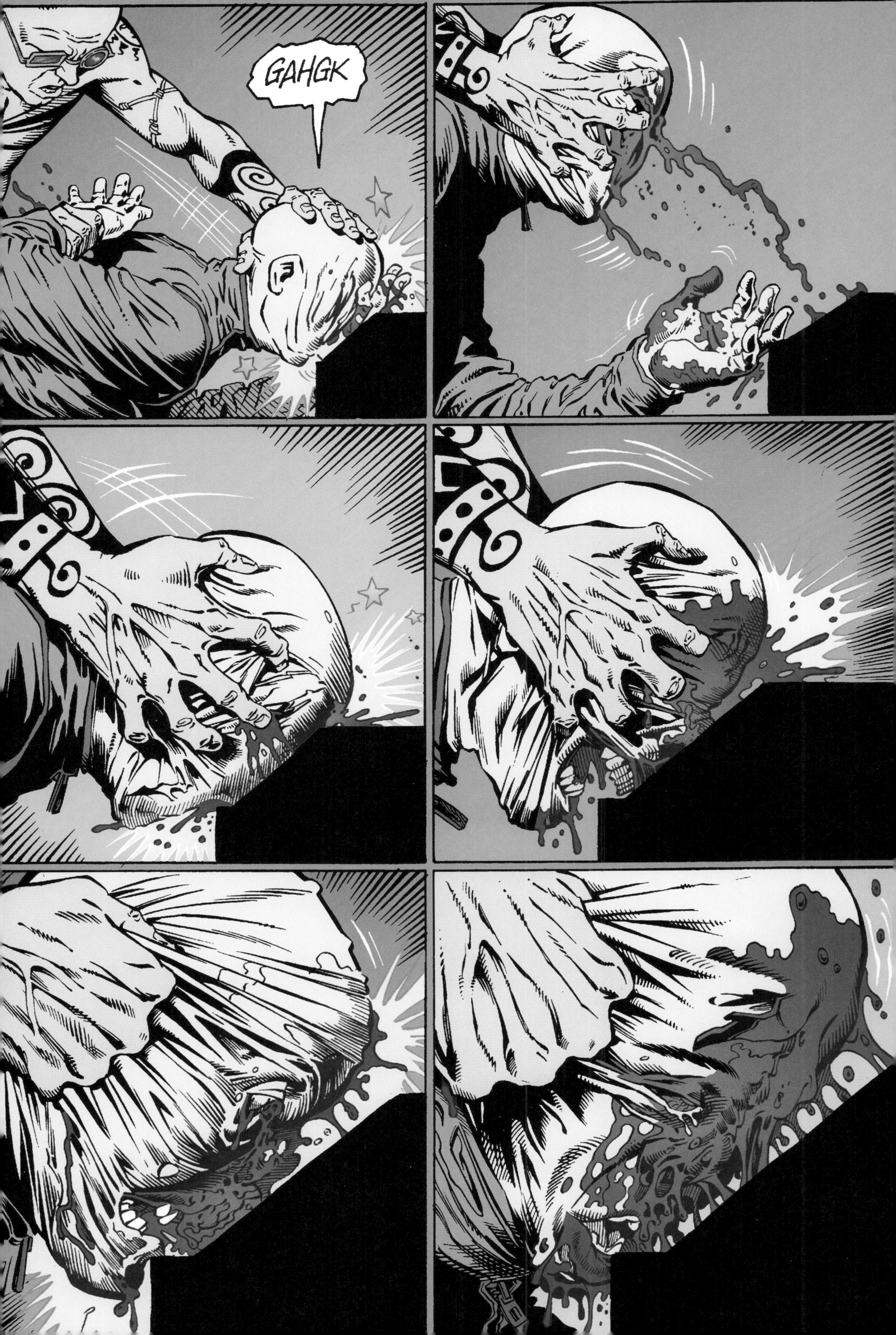
GAHGK

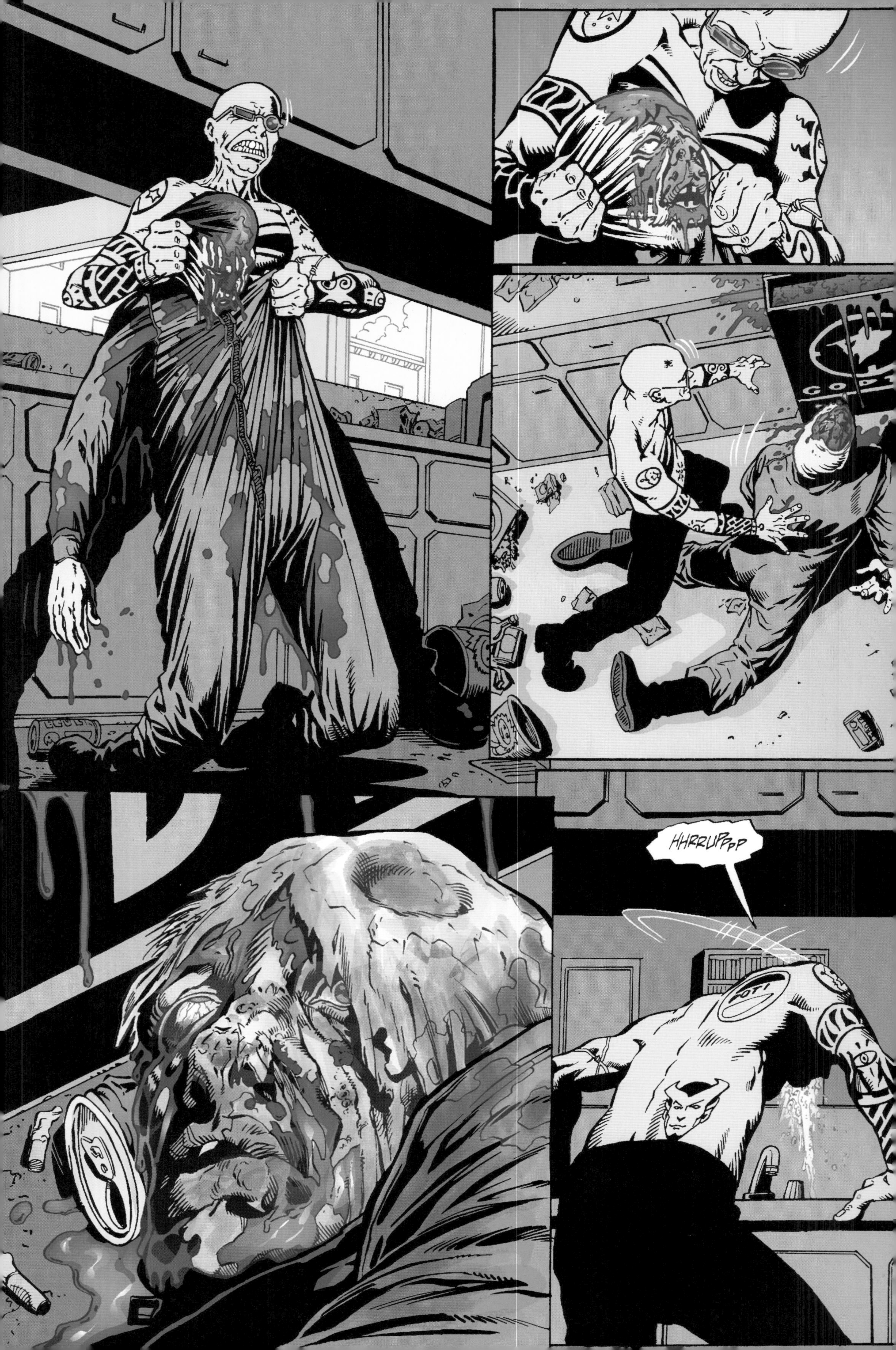
HHRRUPPPP

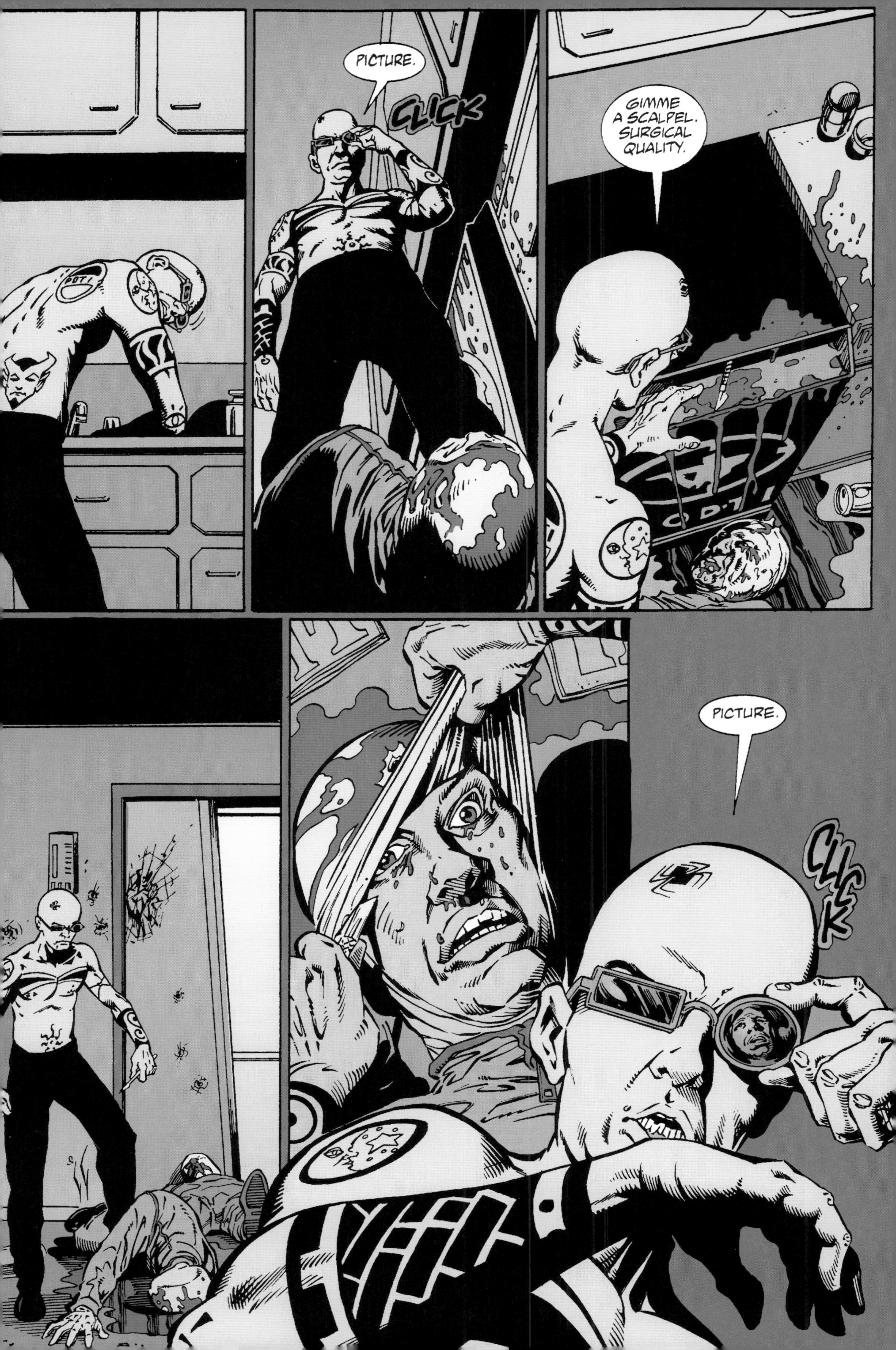
PICTURE.
CLICK
GIMME A SCALPEL. SURGICAL QUALITY.
PICTURE.
CLICK

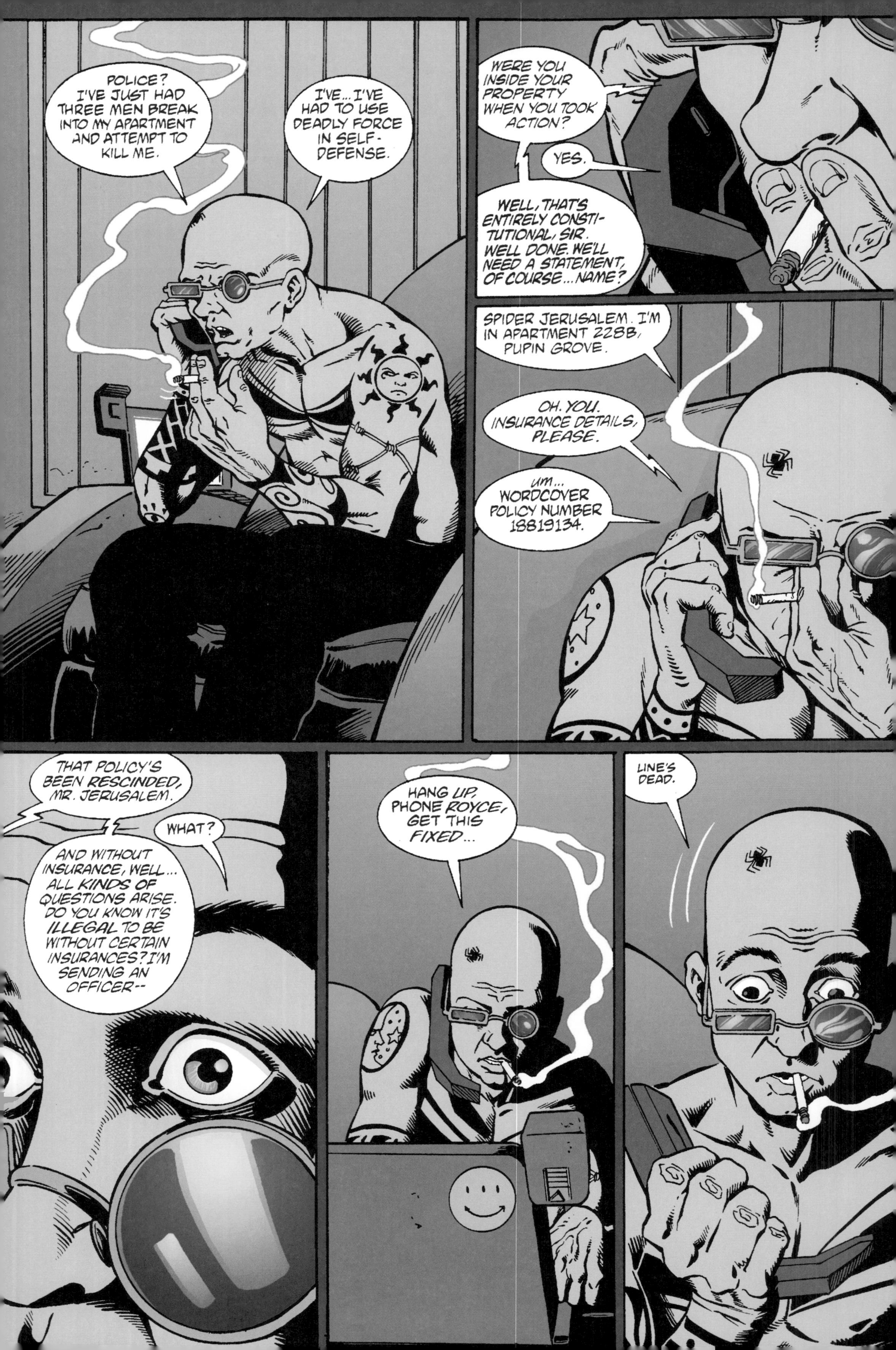
POLICE? I'VE JUST HAD THREE MEN BREAK INTO MY APARTMENT AND ATTEMPT TO KILL ME.
I'VE... I'VE HAD TO USE DEADLY FORCE IN SELF-DEFENSE.
WERE YOU INSIDE YOUR PROPERTY WHEN YOU TOOK ACTION?
YES.
WELL, THAT'S ENTIRELY CONSTITUTIONAL, SIR. WELL DONE. WE'LL NEED A STATEMENT, OF COURSE... NAME?
SPIDER JERUSALEM. I'M IN APARTMENT 228B, PUPIN GROVE.
OH. YOU. INSURANCE DETAILS, PLEASE.
UM... WORDCOVER POLICY NUMBER 18819134.
THAT POLICY'S BEEN RESCINDED, MR. JERUSALEM.
WHAT?
AND WITHOUT INSURANCE, WELL... ALL KINDS OF QUESTIONS ARISE. DO YOU KNOW IT'S ILLEGAL TO BE WITHOUT CERTAIN INSURANCES? I'M SENDING AN OFFICER--
HANG UP, PHONE ROYCE, GET THIS FIXED...
LINE'S DEAD.

# "THE POLICE DOG"

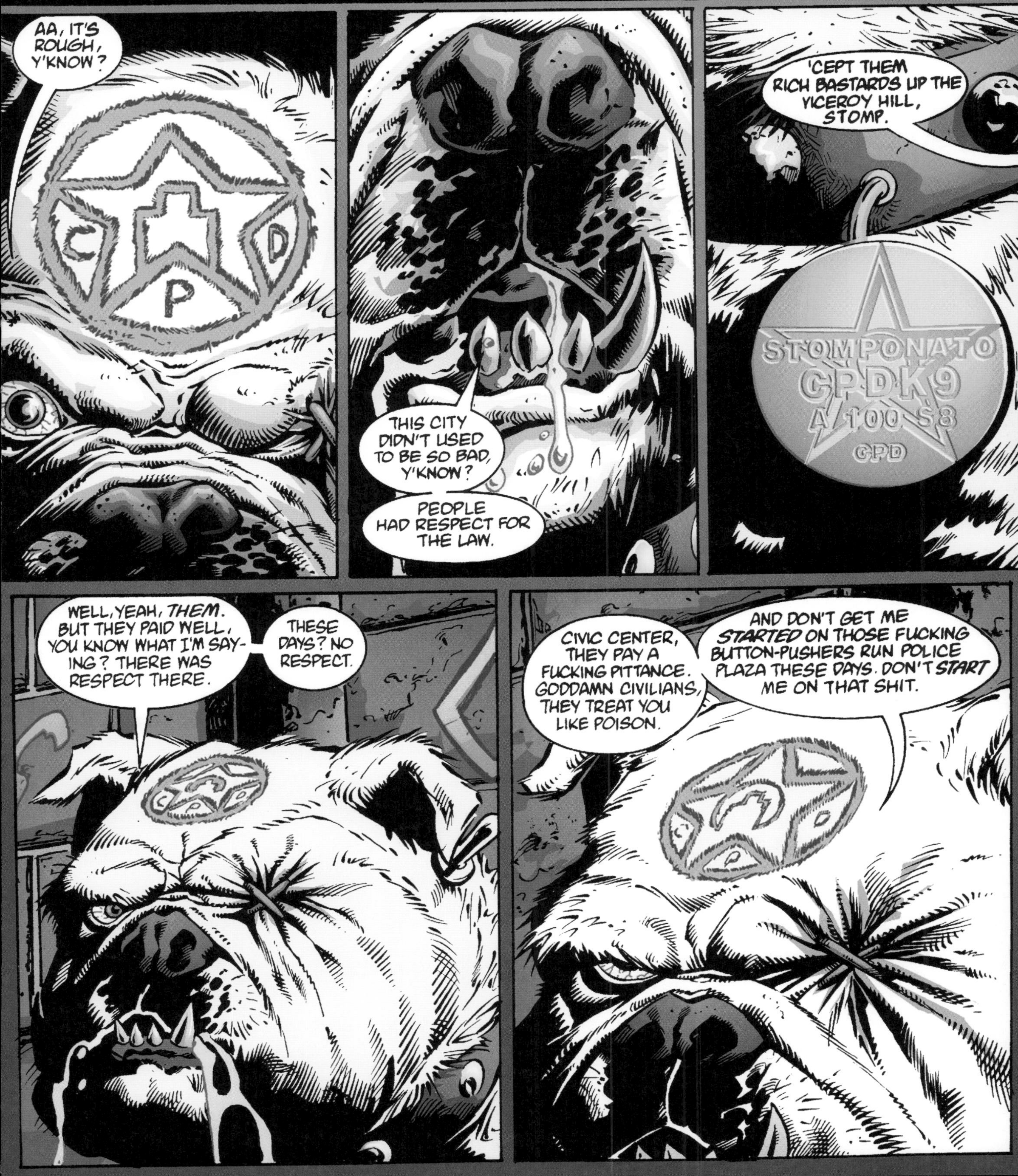
AA, IT'S ROUGH, Y'KNOW?
THIS CITY DIDN'T USED TO BE SO BAD, Y'KNOW?
PEOPLE HAD RESPECT FOR THE LAW.
'CEPT THEM RICH BASTARDS UP THE VICEROY HILL, STOMP.
STOMPONATO
CPDK9
A 100 S8
CPD
WELL, YEAH, *THEM*. BUT THEY PAID WELL, YOU KNOW WHAT I'M SAYING? THERE WAS RESPECT THERE.
THESE DAYS? NO RESPECT.
CIVIC CENTER, THEY PAY A FUCKING PITTANCE. GODDAMN CIVILIANS, THEY TREAT YOU LIKE POISON.
AND DON'T GET ME *STARTED* ON THOSE FUCKING BUTTON-PUSHERS RUN POLICE PLAZA THESE DAYS. DON'T *START* ME ON THAT SHIT.

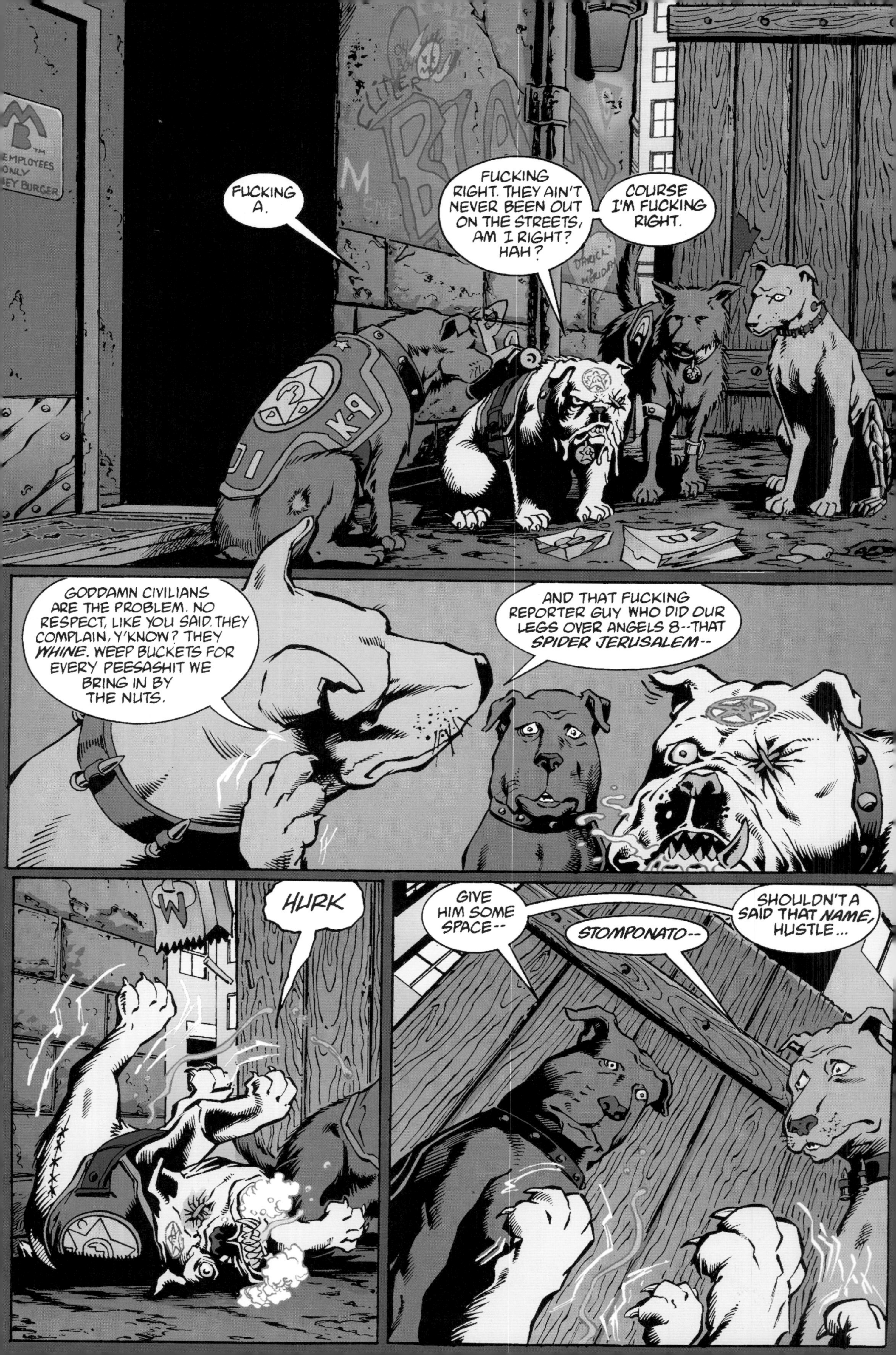

EMPLOYEES ONLY
FUCKING A.
FUCKING RIGHT. THEY AIN'T NEVER BEEN OUT ON THE STREETS, AM I RIGHT? HAH?
COURSE I'M FUCKING RIGHT.
K-9
GODDAMN CIVILIANS ARE THE PROBLEM. NO RESPECT, LIKE YOU SAID. THEY COMPLAIN, Y'KNOW? THEY *WHINE*. WEEP BUCKETS FOR EVERY PEESASHIT WE BRING IN BY THE NUTS.
AND THAT FUCKING REPORTER GUY WHO DID OUR LEGS OVER ANGELS 8--THAT *SPIDER JERUSALEM*--
HURK
GIVE HIM SOME SPACE--
STOMPONATO--
SHOULDN'T A SAID THAT *NAME*, HUSTLE...

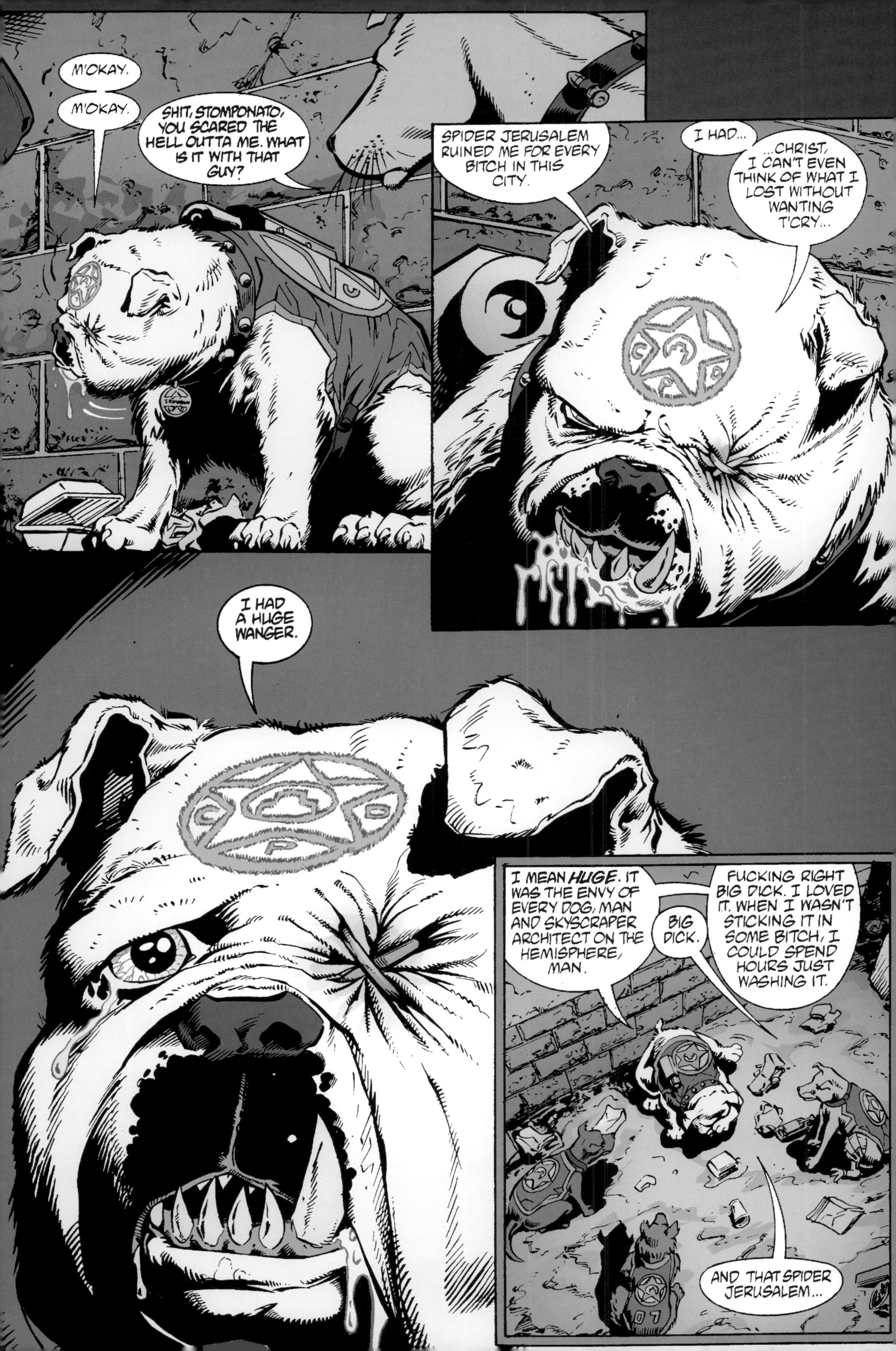
M'OKAY.
M'OKAY.
SHIT, STOMPONATO, YOU SCARED THE HELL OUTTA ME. WHAT IS IT WITH THAT GUY?
SPIDER JERUSALEM RUINED ME FOR EVERY BITCH IN THIS CITY.
I HAD...
...CHRIST, I CAN'T EVEN THINK OF WHAT I LOST WITHOUT WANTING T'CRY...
I HAD A HUGE WANGER.
I MEAN HUGE. IT WAS THE ENVY OF EVERY DOG, MAN AND SKYSCRAPER ARCHITECT ON THE HEMISPHERE, MAN.
BIG DICK.
FUCKING RIGHT BIG DICK. I LOVED IT. WHEN I WASN'T STICKING IT IN SOME BITCH, I COULD SPEND HOURS JUST WASHING IT.
AND THAT SPIDER JERUSALEM...

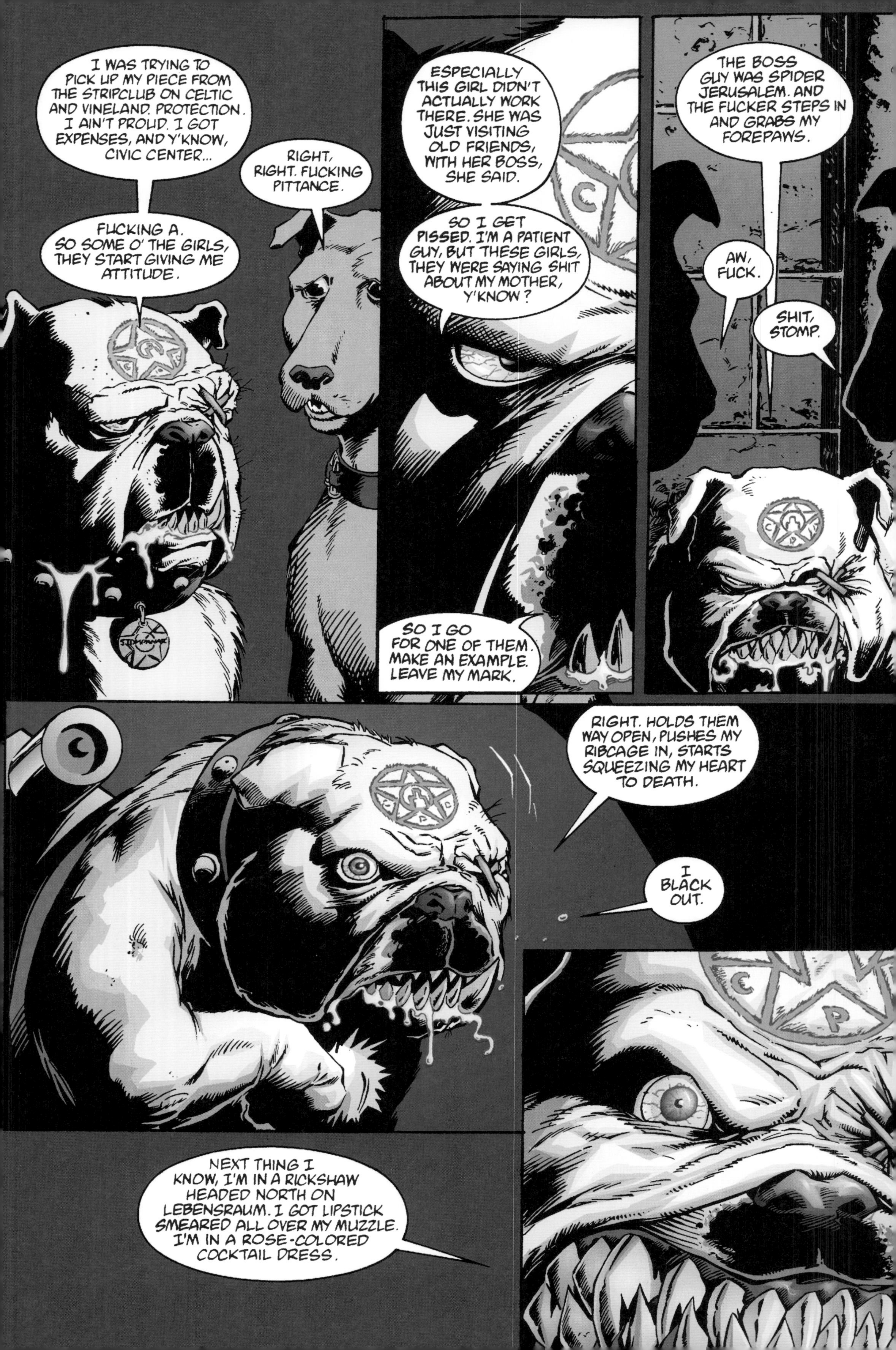
I WAS TRYING TO PICK UP MY PIECE FROM THE STRIPCLUB ON CELTIC AND VINELAND. PROTECTION. I AIN'T PROUD. I GOT EXPENSES, AND Y'KNOW, CIVIC CENTER...
RIGHT, RIGHT. FUCKING PITTANCE.
FUCKING A. SO SOME O' THE GIRLS, THEY START GIVING ME ATTITUDE.
ESPECIALLY THIS GIRL DIDN'T ACTUALLY WORK THERE. SHE WAS JUST VISITING OLD FRIENDS, WITH HER BOSS, SHE SAID.
SO I GET PISSED. I'M A PATIENT GUY, BUT THESE GIRLS, THEY WERE SAYING SHIT ABOUT MY MOTHER, Y'KNOW?
SO I GO FOR ONE OF THEM. MAKE AN EXAMPLE. LEAVE MY MARK.
THE BOSS GUY WAS SPIDER JERUSALEM. AND THE FUCKER STEPS IN AND GRABS MY FOREPAWS.
AW, FUCK.
SHIT, STOMP.
RIGHT. HOLDS THEM WAY OPEN, PUSHES MY RIBCAGE IN, STARTS SQUEEZING MY HEART TO DEATH.
I BLACK OUT.
NEXT THING I KNOW, I'M IN A RICKSHAW HEADED NORTH ON LEBENSRAUM. I GOT LIPSTICK SMEARED ALL OVER MY MUZZLE. I'M IN A ROSE-COLORED COCKTAIL DRESS.

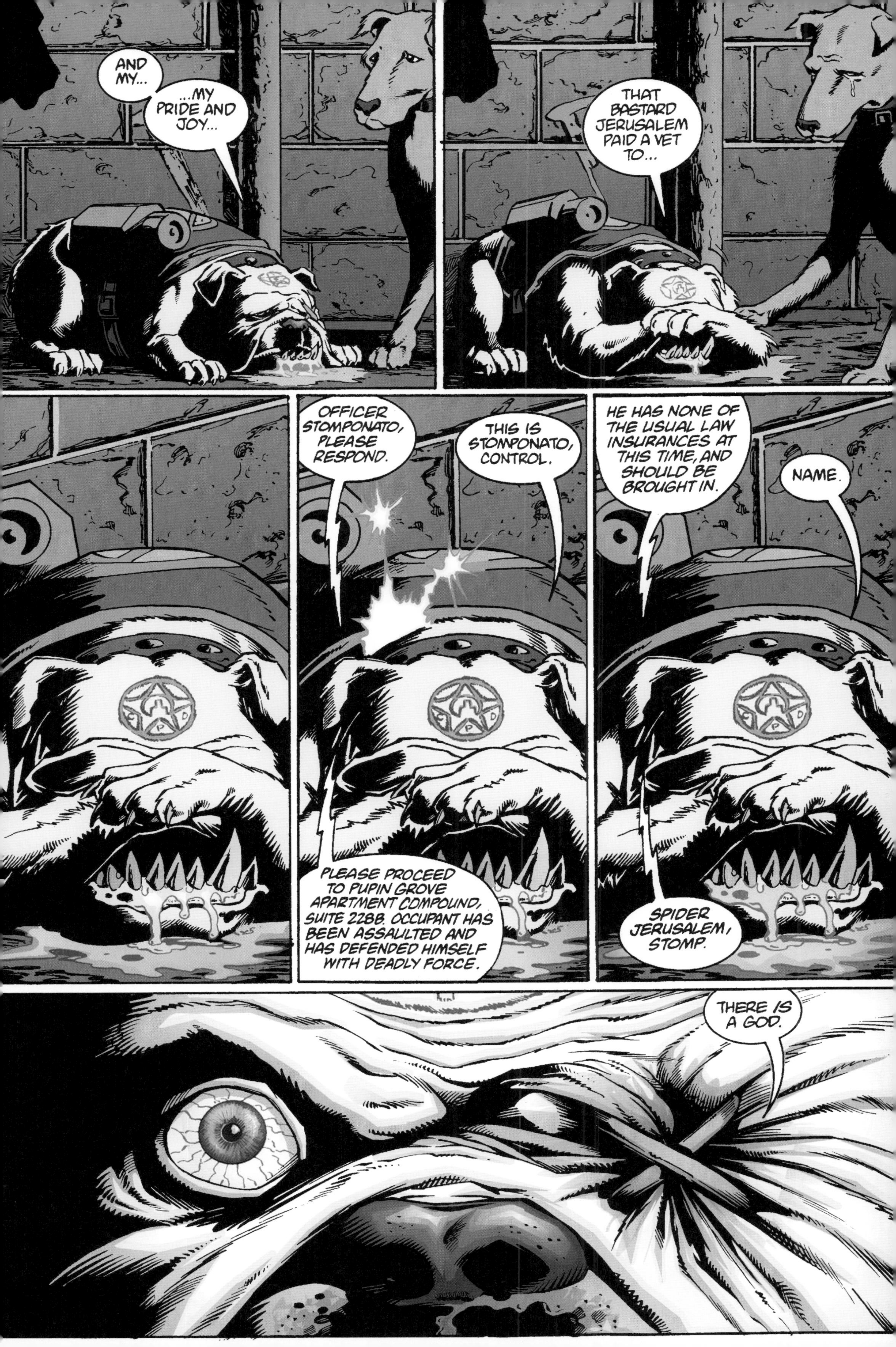
AND MY...
...MY PRIDE AND JOY...
THAT BASTARD JERUSALEM PAID A VET TO...
OFFICER STOMPONATO, PLEASE RESPOND.
THIS IS STOMPONATO, CONTROL.
PLEASE PROCEED TO PUPIN GROVE APARTMENT COMPOUND, SUITE 228B. OCCUPANT HAS BEEN ASSAULTED AND HAS DEFENDED HIMSELF WITH DEADLY FORCE.
HE HAS NONE OF THE USUAL LAW INSURANCES AT THIS TIME, AND SHOULD BE BROUGHT IN.
NAME.
SPIDER JERUSALEM, STOMP.
THERE IS A GOD.

# THE GREAT ESCAPE

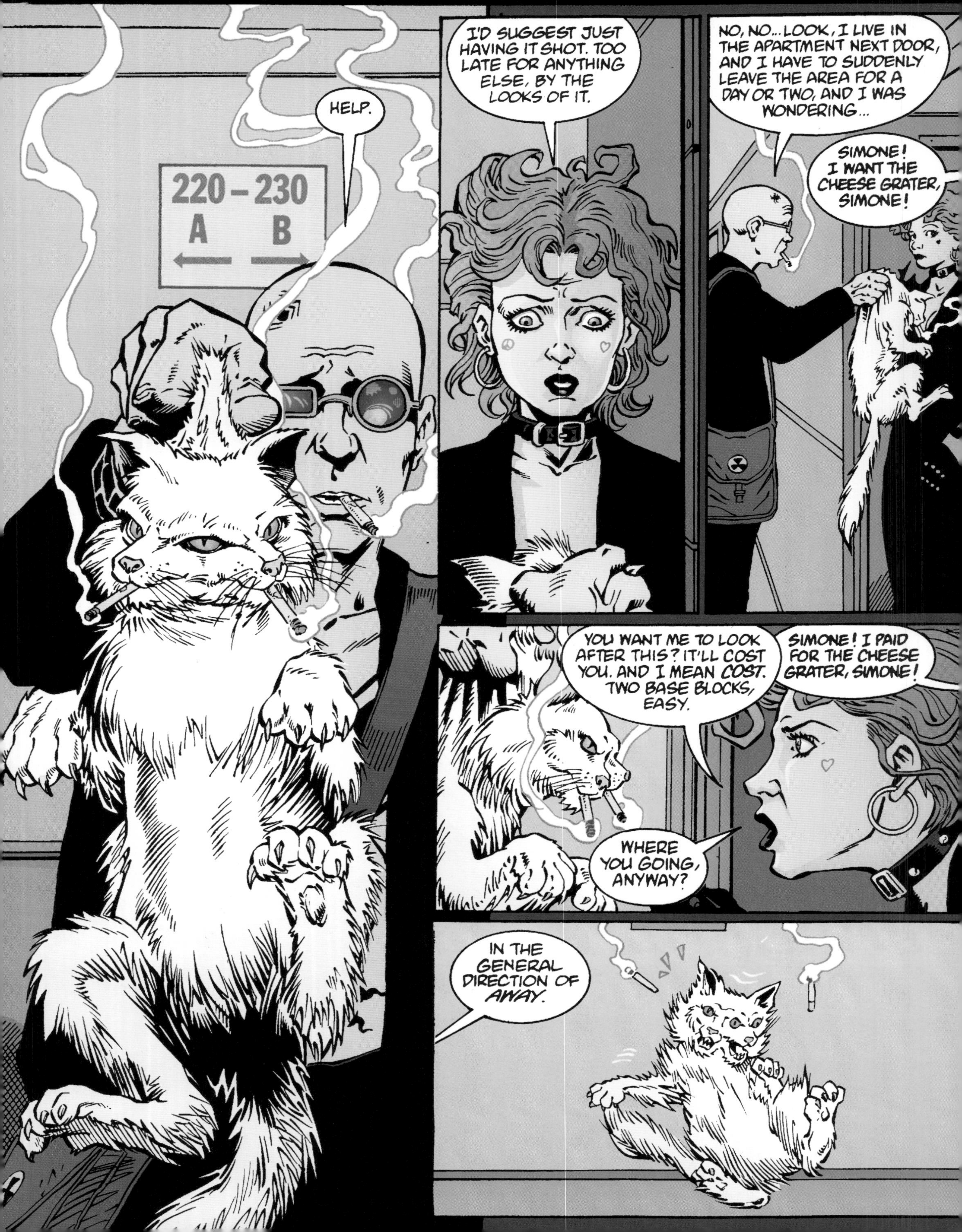

220 – 230
A B
HELP.
I'D SUGGEST JUST HAVING IT SHOT. TOO LATE FOR ANYTHING ELSE, BY THE LOOKS OF IT.
NO, NO... LOOK, I LIVE IN THE APARTMENT NEXT DOOR, AND I HAVE TO SUDDENLY LEAVE THE AREA FOR A DAY OR TWO, AND I WAS WONDERING...
SIMONE! I WANT THE CHEESE GRATER, SIMONE!
YOU WANT ME TO LOOK AFTER THIS? IT'LL COST YOU. AND I MEAN COST. TWO BASE BLOCKS, EASY.
SIMONE! I PAID FOR THE CHEESE GRATER, SIMONE!
WHERE YOU GOING, ANYWAY?
IN THE GENERAL DIRECTION OF AWAY.

# WILD OATS

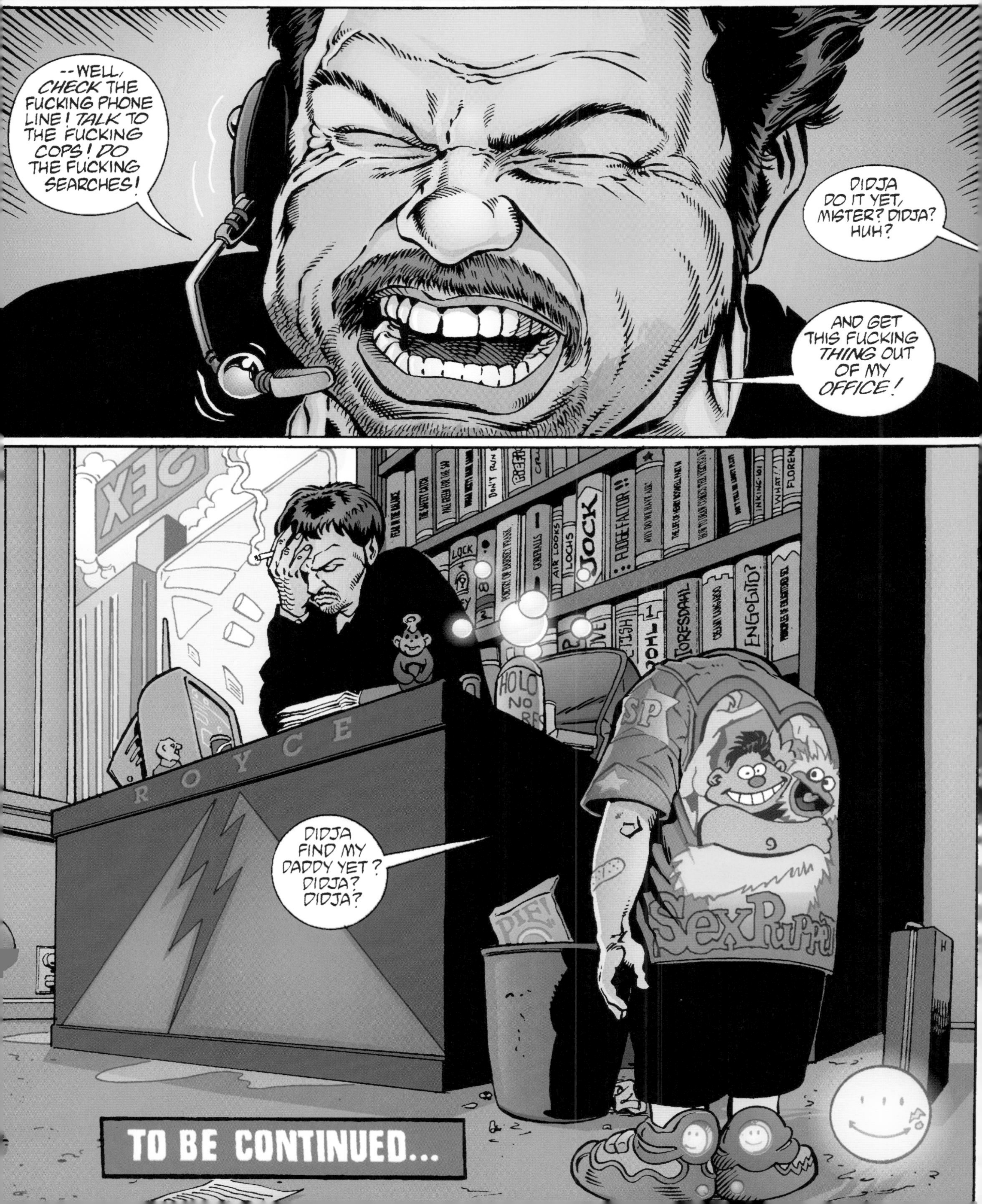
--WELL, CHECK THE FUCKING PHONE LINE! TALK TO THE FUCKING COPS! DO THE FUCKING SEARCHES!
DIDJA DO IT YET, MISTER? DIDJA? HUH?
AND GET THIS FUCKING THING OUT OF MY OFFICE!
SEX
JOCK
ROYCE
DIDJA FIND MY DADDY YET? DIDJA? DIDJA?
TO BE CONTINUED...

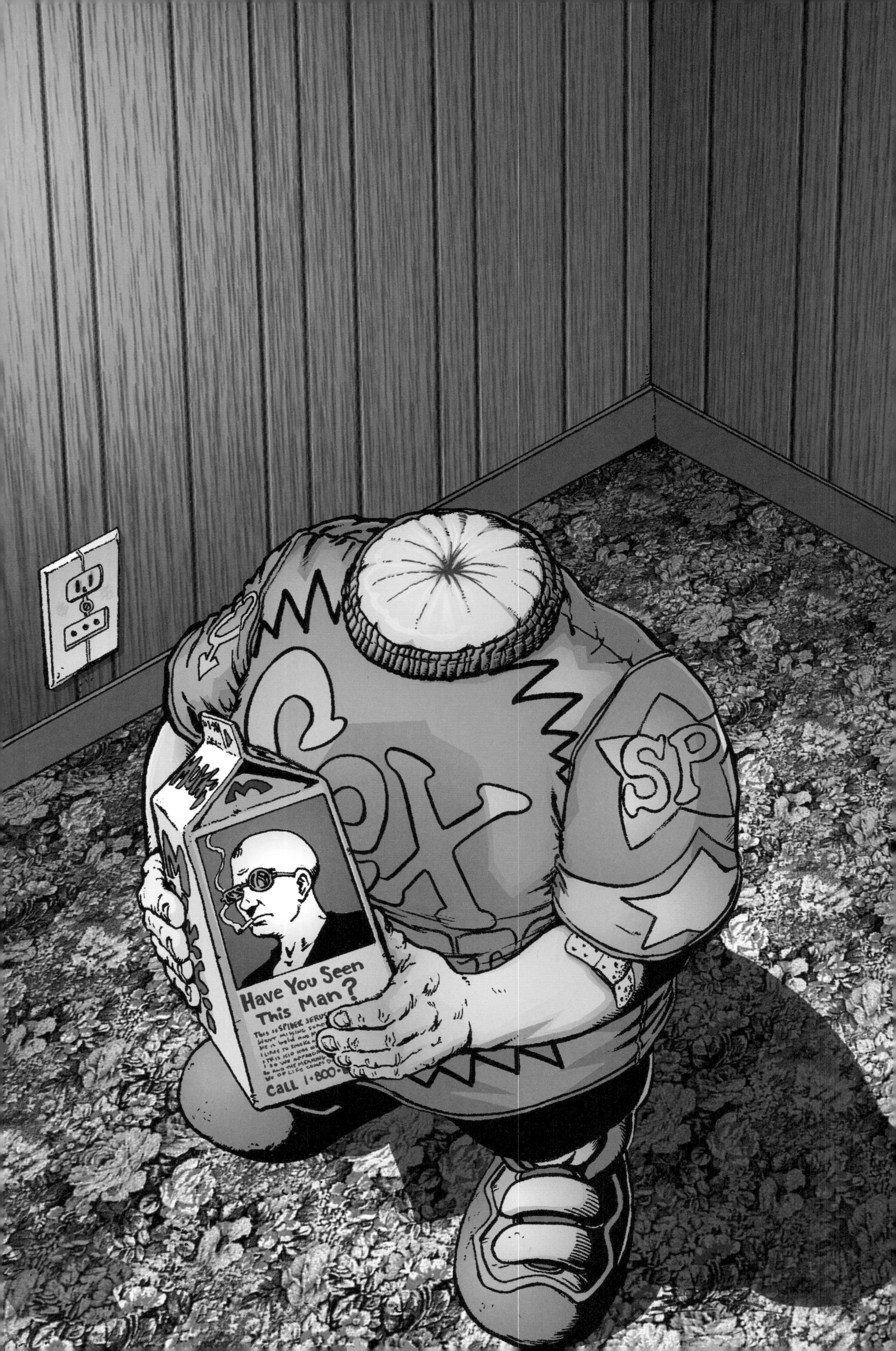
Have You Seen This Man?
CALL 1·800·
SP

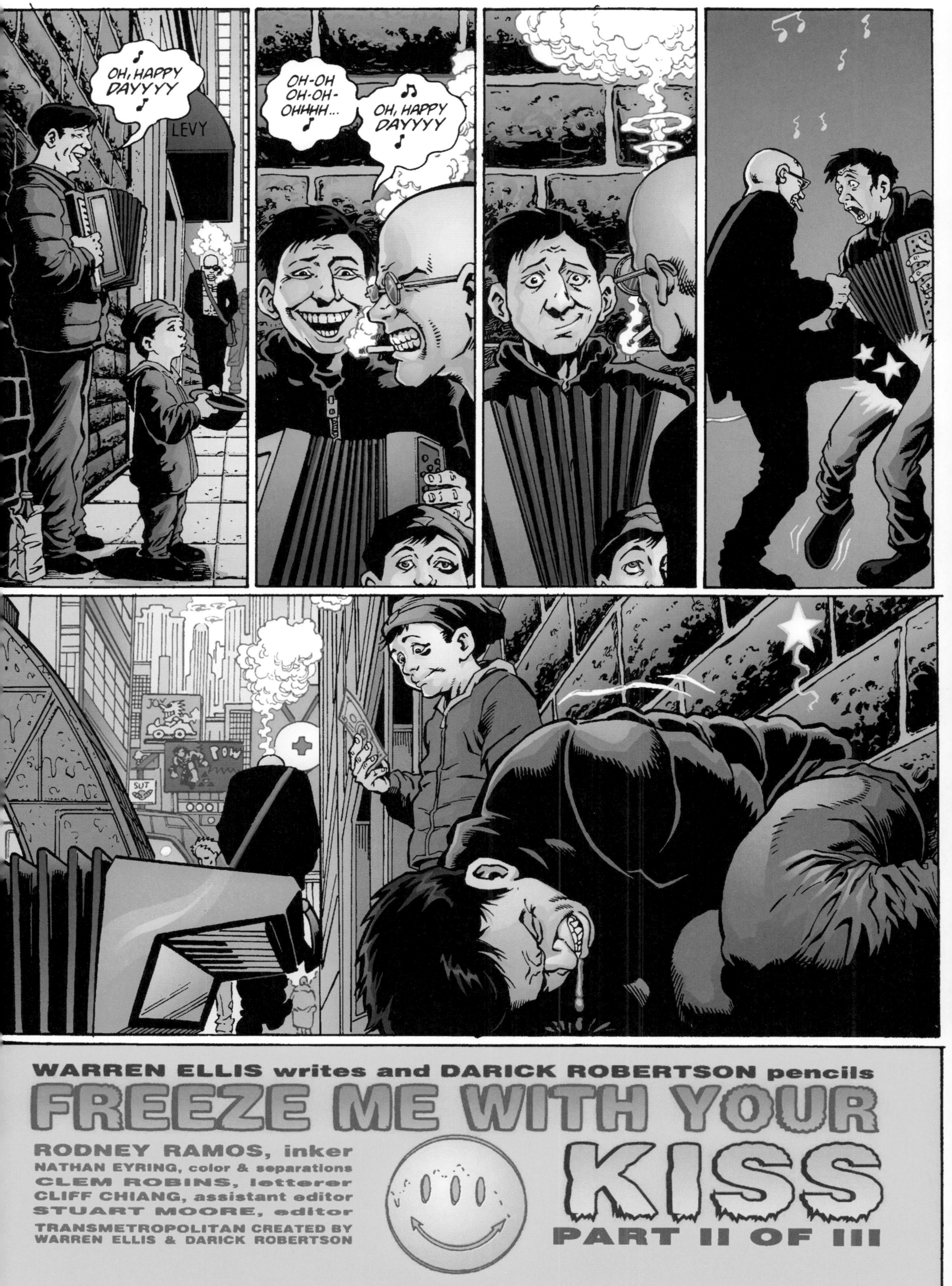
OH, HAPPY DAYYYY
LEVY
OH-OH OH-OH- OHHHH...
OH, HAPPY DAYYYY
JOY
POW
SUT

**WARREN ELLIS writes and DARICK ROBERTSON pencils**

# FREEZE ME WITH YOUR KISS

## PART II OF III

RODNEY RAMOS, inker
NATHAN EYRING, color & separations
CLEM ROBINS, letterer
CLIFF CHIANG, assistant editor
STUART MOORE, editor
TRANSMETROPOLITAN CREATED BY WARREN ELLIS & DARICK ROBERTSON

# the last time this happened...

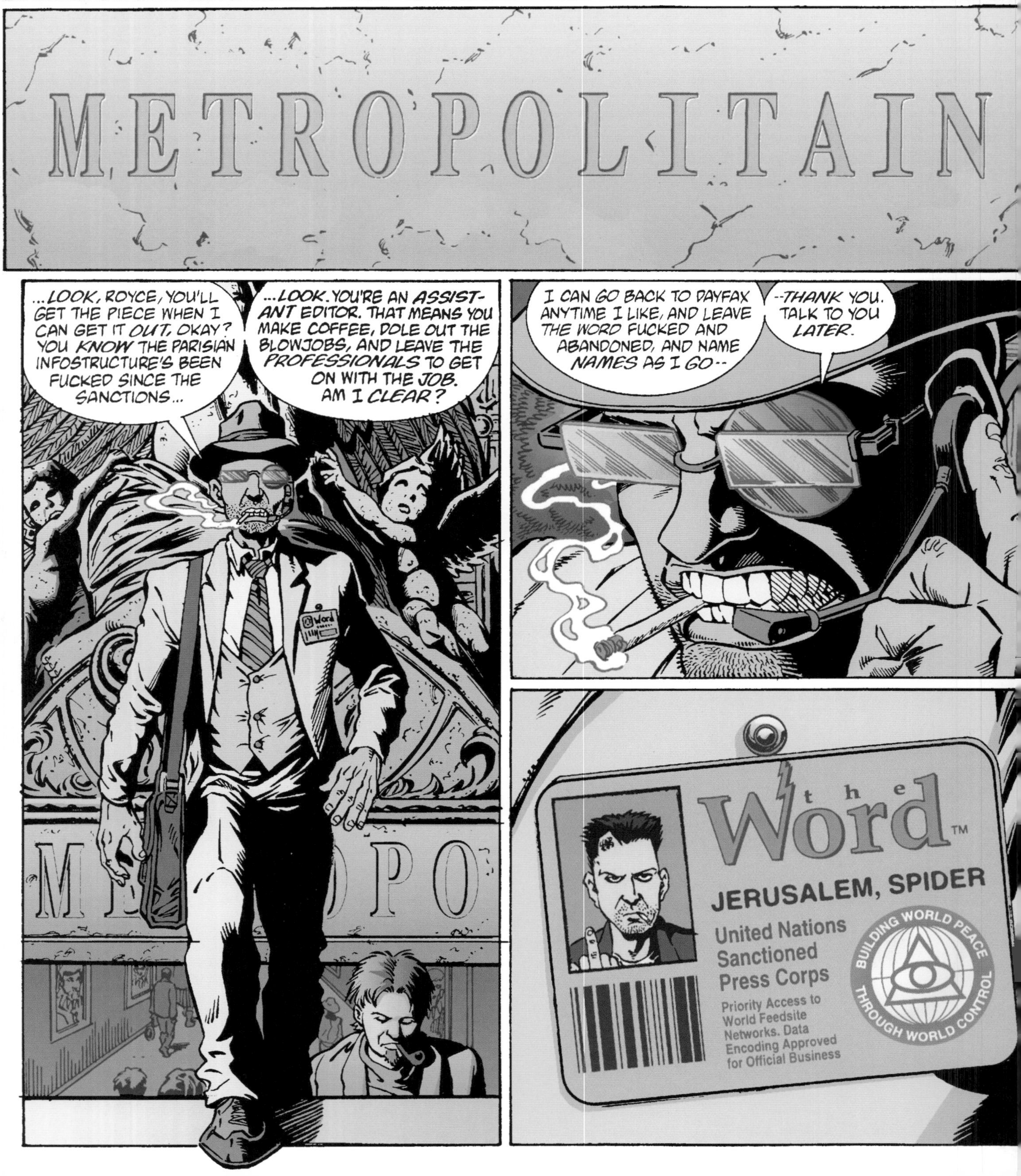
METROPOLITAIN
...LOOK, ROYCE, YOU'LL GET THE PIECE WHEN I CAN GET IT OUT, OKAY? YOU KNOW THE PARISIAN INFOSTRUCTURE'S BEEN FUCKED SINCE THE SANCTIONS...
...LOOK. YOU'RE AN ASSISTANT EDITOR. THAT MEANS YOU MAKE COFFEE, DOLE OUT THE BLOWJOBS, AND LEAVE THE PROFESSIONALS TO GET ON WITH THE JOB. AM I CLEAR?
I CAN GO BACK TO DAYFAX ANYTIME I LIKE, AND LEAVE THE WORD FUCKED AND ABANDONED, AND NAME NAMES AS I GO--
--THANK YOU. TALK TO YOU LATER.
the Word™
JERUSALEM, SPIDER
United Nations Sanctioned Press Corps
Priority Access to World Feedsite Networks. Data Encoding Approved for Official Business
BUILDING WORLD PEACE THROUGH WORLD CONTROL

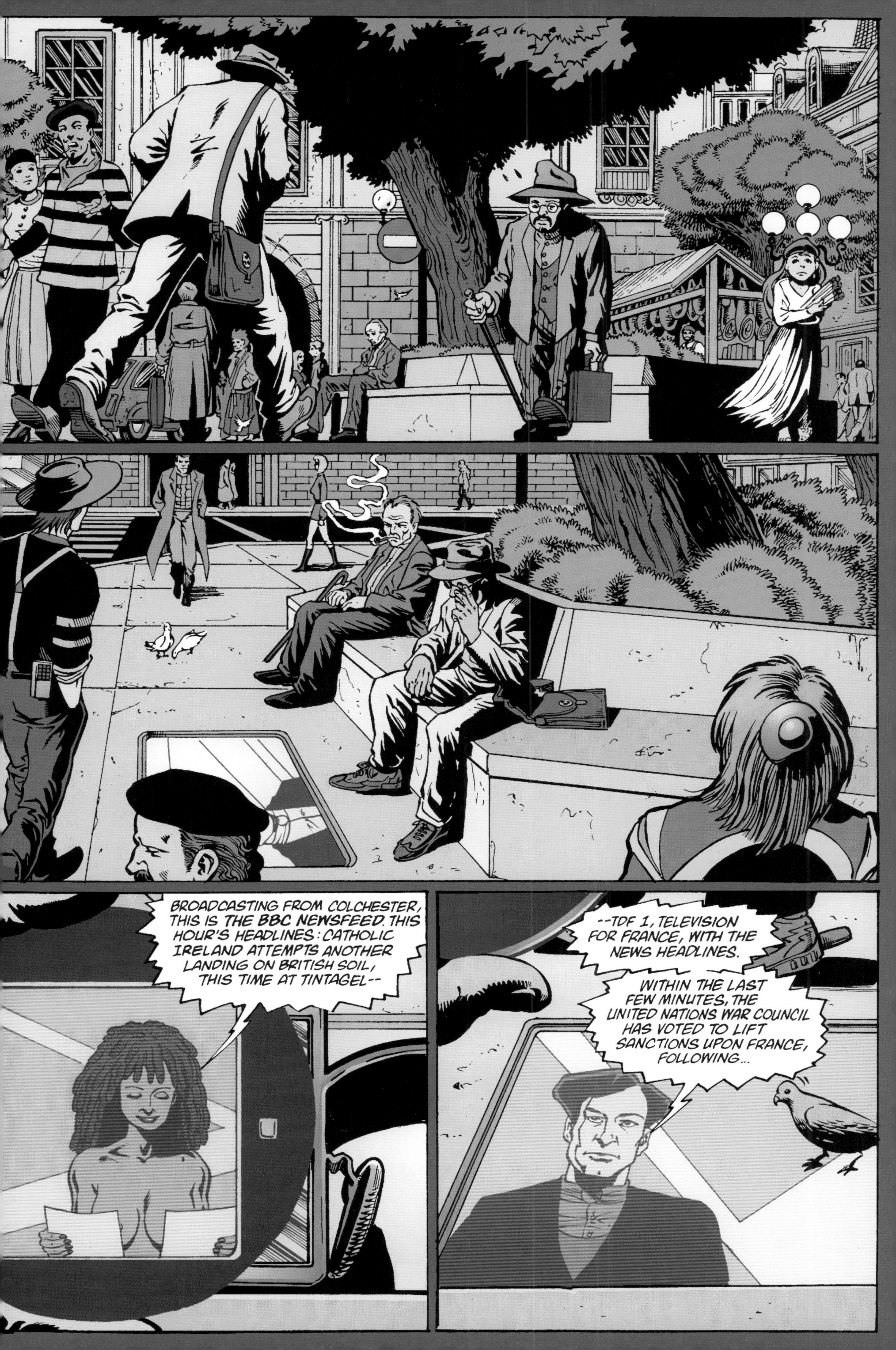
BROADCASTING FROM COLCHESTER, THIS IS THE BBC NEWSFEED. THIS HOUR'S HEADLINES: CATHOLIC IRELAND ATTEMPTS ANOTHER LANDING ON BRITISH SOIL, THIS TIME AT TINTAGEL--
--TDF 1, TELEVISION FOR FRANCE, WITH THE NEWS HEADLINES.
WITHIN THE LAST FEW MINUTES, THE UNITED NATIONS WAR COUNCIL HAS VOTED TO LIFT SANCTIONS UPON FRANCE, FOLLOWING...

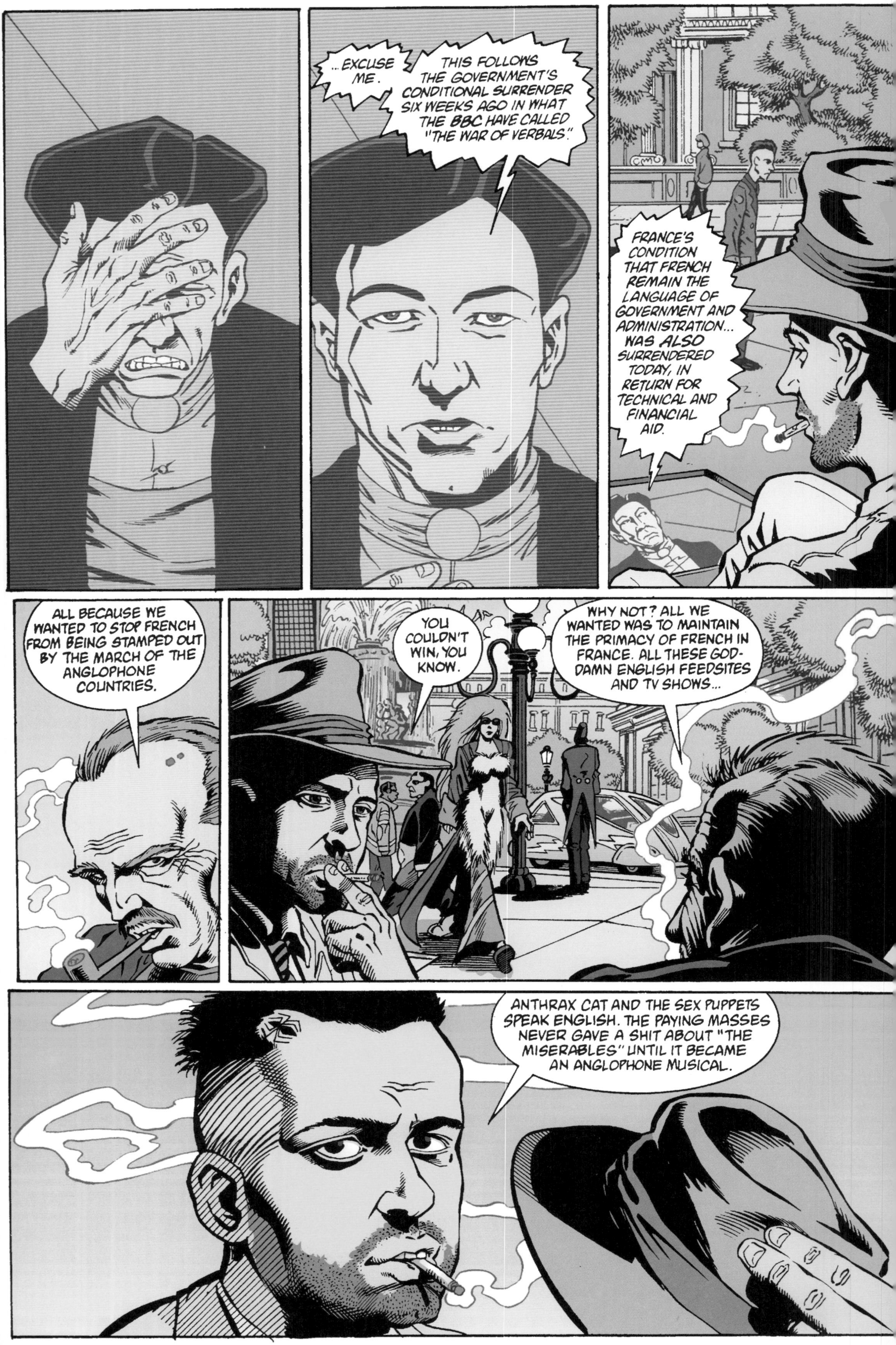

...EXCUSE ME.
THIS FOLLOWS THE GOVERNMENT'S CONDITIONAL SURRENDER SIX WEEKS AGO IN WHAT THE BBC HAVE CALLED "THE WAR OF VERBALS."
FRANCE'S CONDITION THAT FRENCH REMAIN THE LANGUAGE OF GOVERNMENT AND ADMINISTRATION... WAS ALSO SURRENDERED TODAY, IN RETURN FOR TECHNICAL AND FINANCIAL AID.
ALL BECAUSE WE WANTED TO STOP FRENCH FROM BEING STAMPED OUT BY THE MARCH OF THE ANGLOPHONE COUNTRIES.
YOU COULDN'T WIN, YOU KNOW.
WHY NOT? ALL WE WANTED WAS TO MAINTAIN THE PRIMACY OF FRENCH IN FRANCE. ALL THESE GOD-DAMN ENGLISH FEEDSITES AND TV SHOWS...
ANTHRAX CAT AND THE SEX PUPPETS SPEAK ENGLISH. THE PAYING MASSES NEVER GAVE A SHIT ABOUT "THE MISERABLES" UNTIL IT BECAME AN ANGLOPHONE MUSICAL.

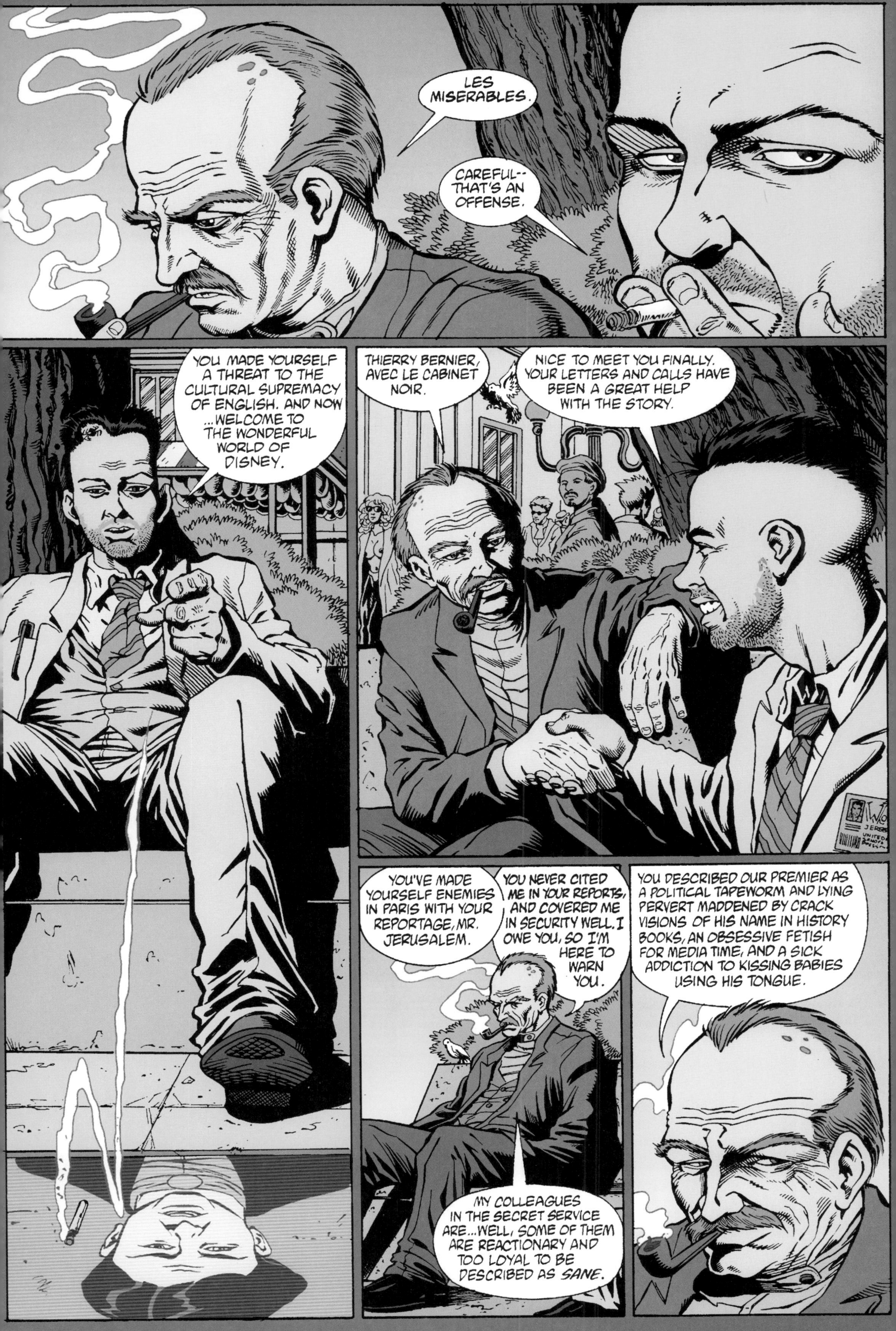
LES MISERABLES.
CAREFUL-- THAT'S AN OFFENSE.
YOU MADE YOURSELF A THREAT TO THE CULTURAL SUPREMACY OF ENGLISH. AND NOW ...WELCOME TO THE WONDERFUL WORLD OF DISNEY.
THIERRY BERNIER, AVEC LE CABINET NOIR.
NICE TO MEET YOU FINALLY. YOUR LETTERS AND CALLS HAVE BEEN A GREAT HELP WITH THE STORY.
YOU'VE MADE YOURSELF ENEMIES IN PARIS WITH YOUR REPORTAGE, MR. JERUSALEM.
YOU NEVER CITED ME IN YOUR REPORTS, AND COVERED ME IN SECURITY WELL. I OWE YOU, SO I'M HERE TO WARN YOU.
MY COLLEAGUES IN THE SECRET SERVICE ARE...WELL, SOME OF THEM ARE REACTIONARY AND TOO LOYAL TO BE DESCRIBED AS SANE.
YOU DESCRIBED OUR PREMIER AS A POLITICAL TAPEWORM AND LYING PERVERT MADDENED BY CRACK VISIONS OF HIS NAME IN HISTORY BOOKS, AN OBSESSIVE FETISH FOR MEDIA TIME, AND A SICK ADDICTION TO KISSING BABIES USING HIS TONGUE.

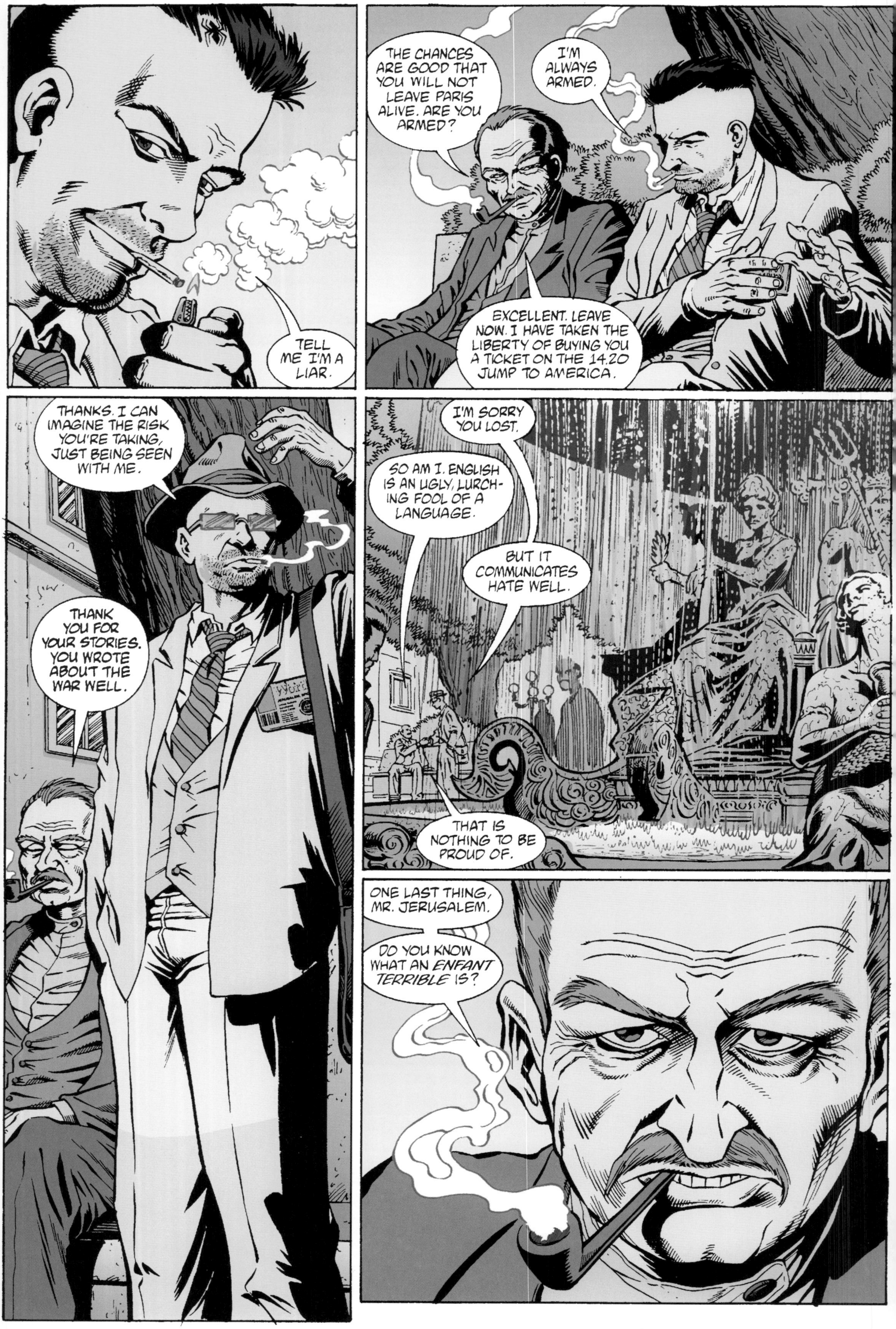
TELL ME I'M A LIAR.
THE CHANCES ARE GOOD THAT YOU WILL NOT LEAVE PARIS ALIVE. ARE YOU ARMED?
I'M ALWAYS ARMED.
EXCELLENT. LEAVE NOW. I HAVE TAKEN THE LIBERTY OF BUYING YOU A TICKET ON THE 14.20 JUMP TO AMERICA.
THANKS. I CAN IMAGINE THE RISK YOU'RE TAKING, JUST BEING SEEN WITH ME.
THANK YOU FOR YOUR STORIES. YOU WROTE ABOUT THE WAR WELL.
I'M SORRY YOU LOST.
SO AM I. ENGLISH IS AN UGLY, LURCHING FOOL OF A LANGUAGE.
BUT IT COMMUNICATES HATE WELL.
THAT IS NOTHING TO BE PROUD OF.
ONE LAST THING, MR. JERUSALEM.
DO YOU KNOW WHAT AN *ENFANT TERRIBLE* IS?

# Blood Hound

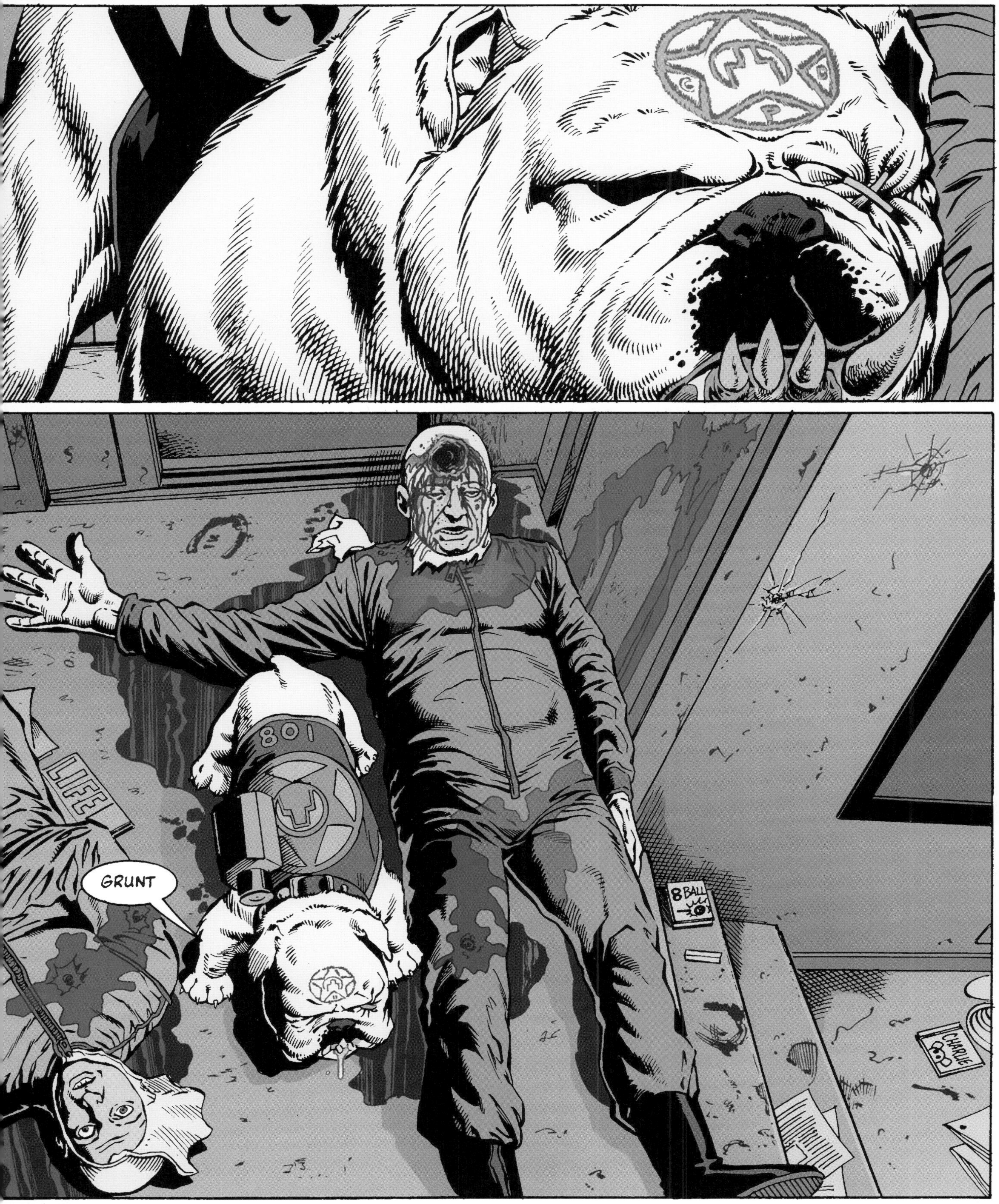
801
LIFE
GRUNT
8 BALL
CHARLIE

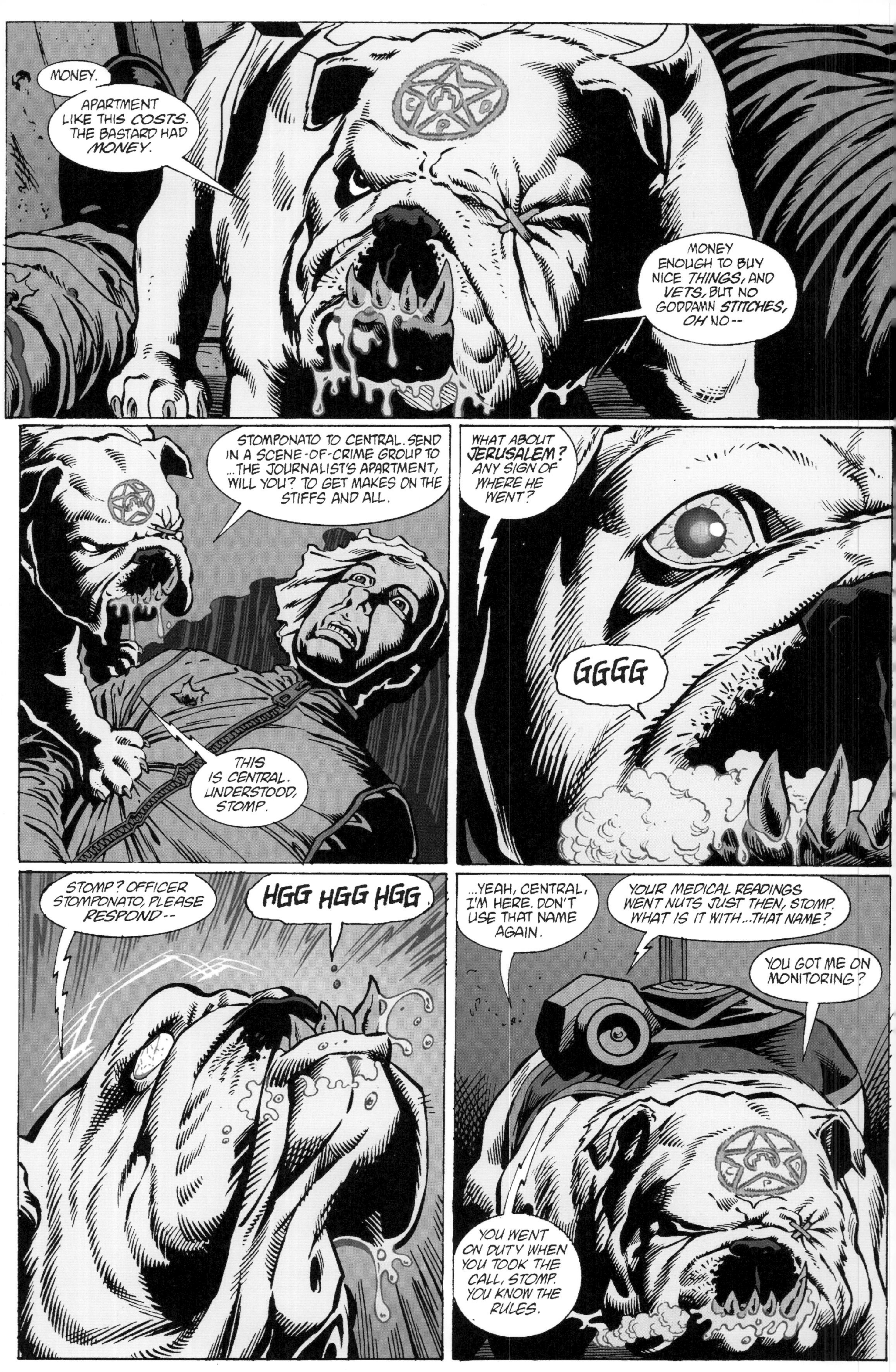
MONEY.
APARTMENT LIKE THIS COSTS. THE BASTARD HAD MONEY.
MONEY ENOUGH TO BUY NICE THINGS, AND VETS, BUT NO GODDAMN STITCHES, OH NO--
STOMPONATO TO CENTRAL. SEND IN A SCENE-OF-CRIME GROUP TO ...THE JOURNALIST'S APARTMENT, WILL YOU? TO GET MAKES ON THE STIFFS AND ALL.
THIS IS CENTRAL. UNDERSTOOD, STOMP.
WHAT ABOUT JERUSALEM? ANY SIGN OF WHERE HE WENT?
GGGG
STOMP? OFFICER STOMPONATO, PLEASE RESPOND--
HGG HGG HGG
...YEAH, CENTRAL, I'M HERE. DON'T USE THAT NAME AGAIN.
YOUR MEDICAL READINGS WENT NUTS JUST THEN, STOMP. WHAT IS IT WITH...THAT NAME?
YOU GOT ME ON MONITORING?
YOU WENT ON DUTY WHEN YOU TOOK THE CALL, STOMP. YOU KNOW THE RULES.

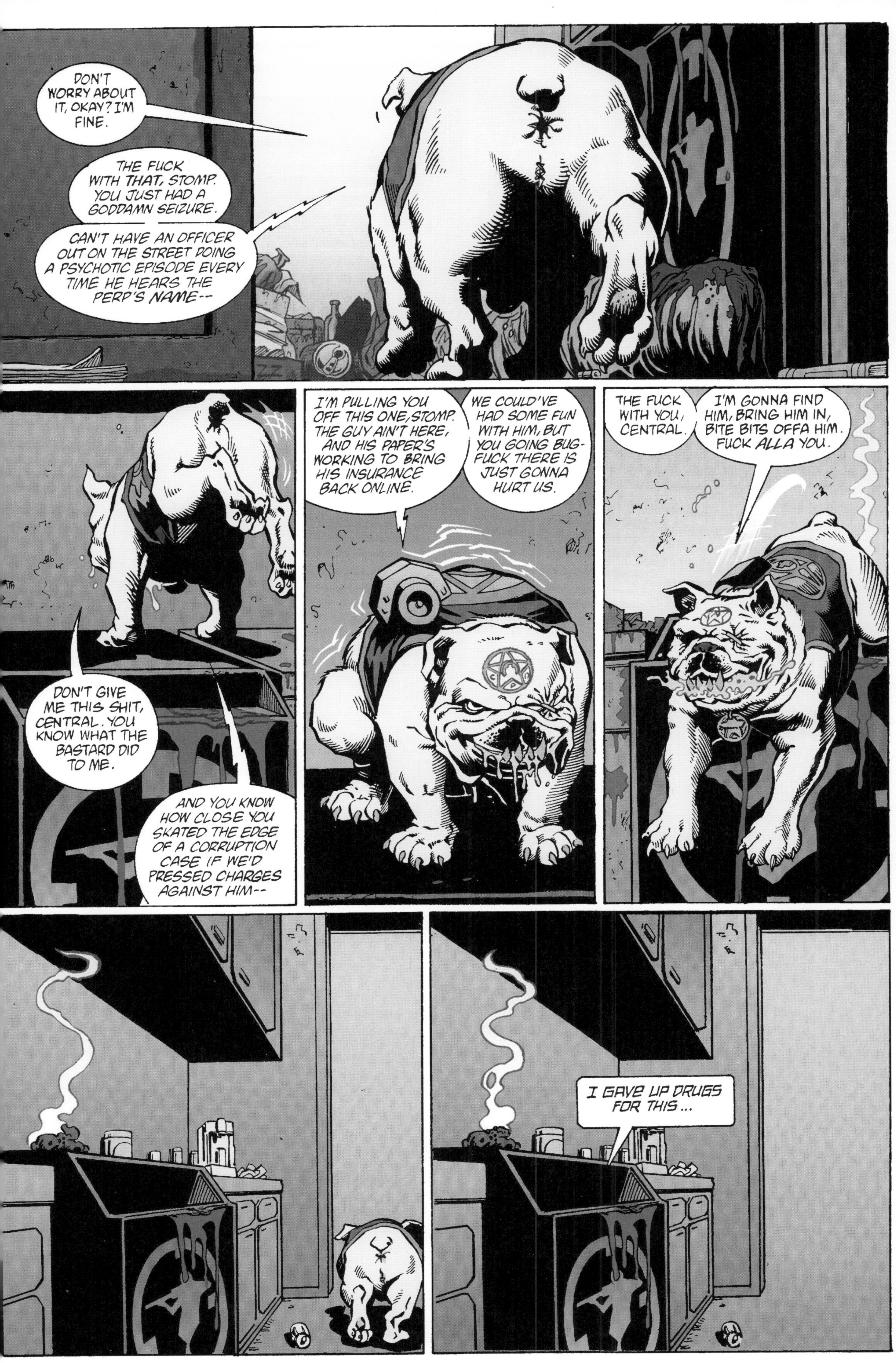
DON'T WORRY ABOUT IT, OKAY? I'M FINE.
THE FUCK WITH THAT, STOMP. YOU JUST HAD A GODDAMN SEIZURE.
CAN'T HAVE AN OFFICER OUT ON THE STREET DOING A PSYCHOTIC EPISODE EVERY TIME HE HEARS THE PERP'S NAME--
DON'T GIVE ME THIS SHIT, CENTRAL. YOU KNOW WHAT THE BASTARD DID TO ME.
AND YOU KNOW HOW CLOSE YOU SKATED THE EDGE OF A CORRUPTION CASE IF WE'D PRESSED CHARGES AGAINST HIM--
I'M PULLING YOU OFF THIS ONE, STOMP. THE GUY AIN'T HERE, AND HIS PAPER'S WORKING TO BRING HIS INSURANCE BACK ONLINE.
WE COULD'VE HAD SOME FUN WITH HIM, BUT YOU GOING BUG-FUCK THERE IS JUST GONNA HURT US.
THE FUCK WITH YOU, CENTRAL.
I'M GONNA FIND HIM, BRING HIM IN, BITE BITS OFFA HIM. FUCK ALLA YOU.
I GAVE UP DRUGS FOR THIS ...

# Lost at Home

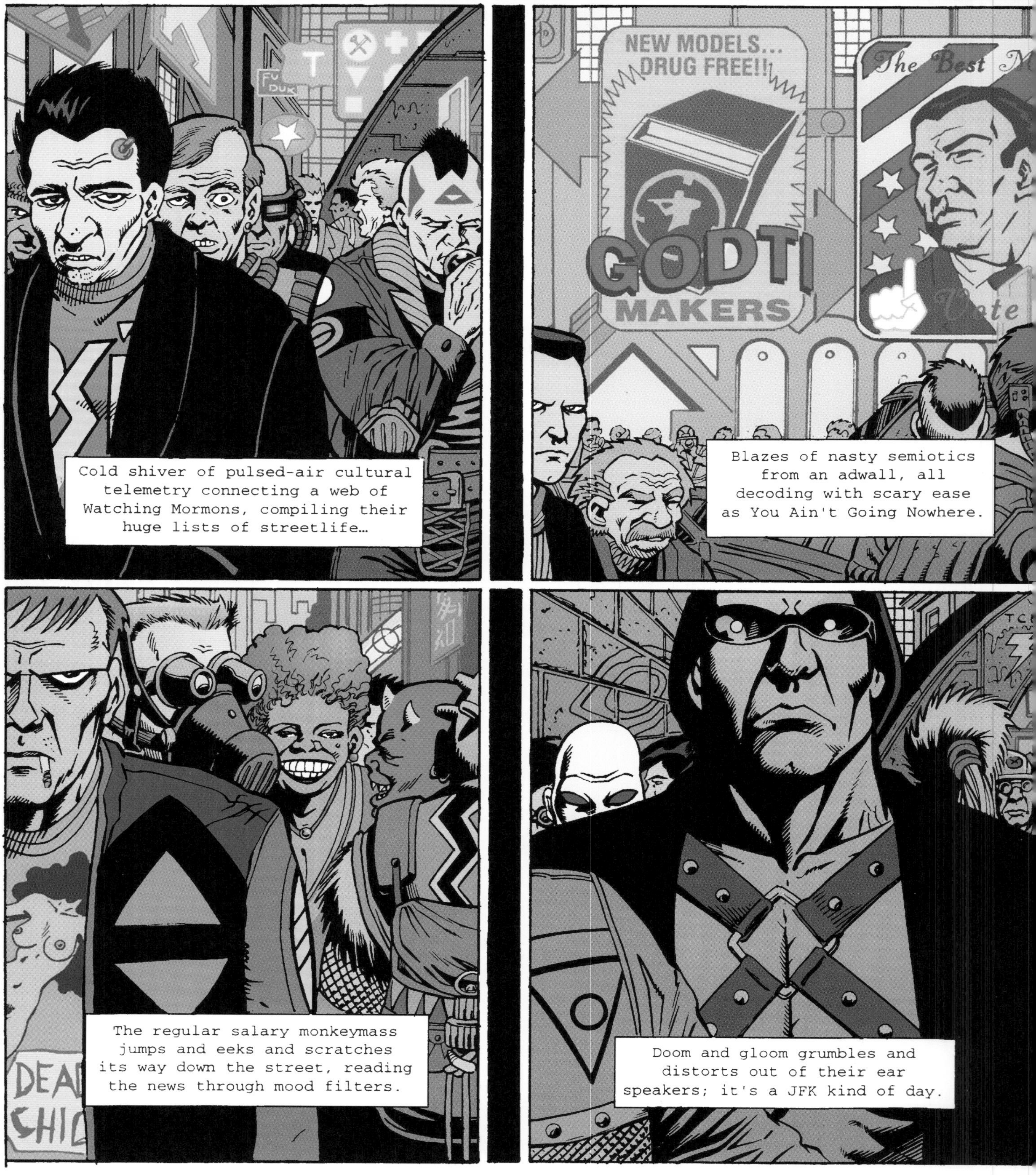
Cold shiver of pulsed-air cultural telemetry connecting a web of Watching Mormons, compiling their huge lists of streetlife...
NEW MODELS... DRUG FREE!!
GODTI
MAKERS
Blazes of nasty semiotics from an adwall, all decoding with scary ease as You Ain't Going Nowhere.
The regular salary monkeymass jumps and eeks and scratches its way down the street, reading the news through mood filters.
Doom and gloom grumbles and distorts out of their ear speakers; it's a JFK kind of day.

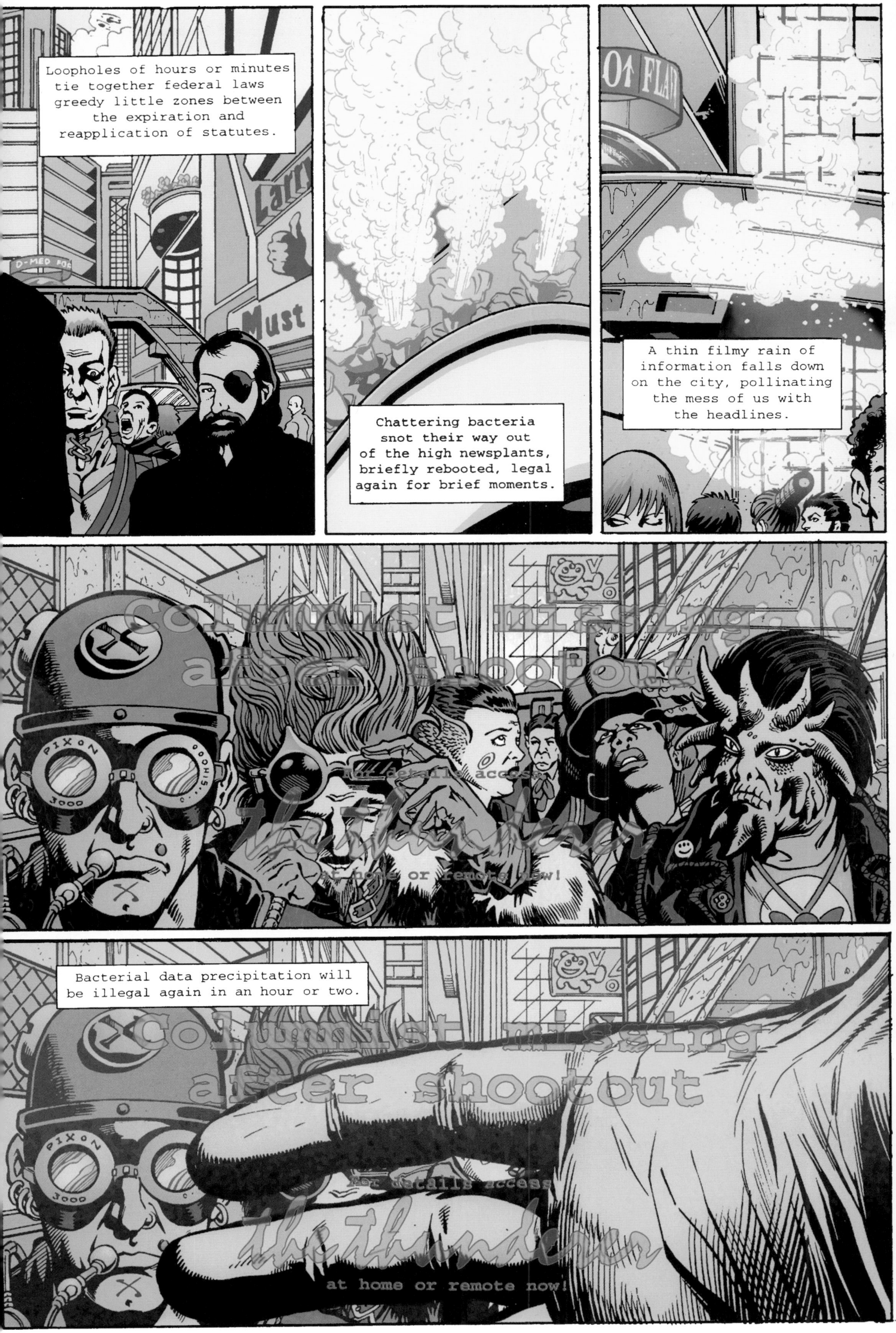
Loopholes of hours or minutes tie together federal laws greedy little zones between the expiration and reapplication of statutes.
Larry
Must
Chattering bacteria snot their way out of the high newsplants, briefly rebooted, legal again for brief moments.
A thin filmy rain of information falls down on the city, pollinating the mess of us with the headlines.
Columnist missing after shootout
For details access
thethunderer
at home or remote now!
PIXON 3000
Bacterial data precipitation will be illegal again in an hour or two.
Columnist missing after shootout
For details access
thethunderer
at home or remote now!

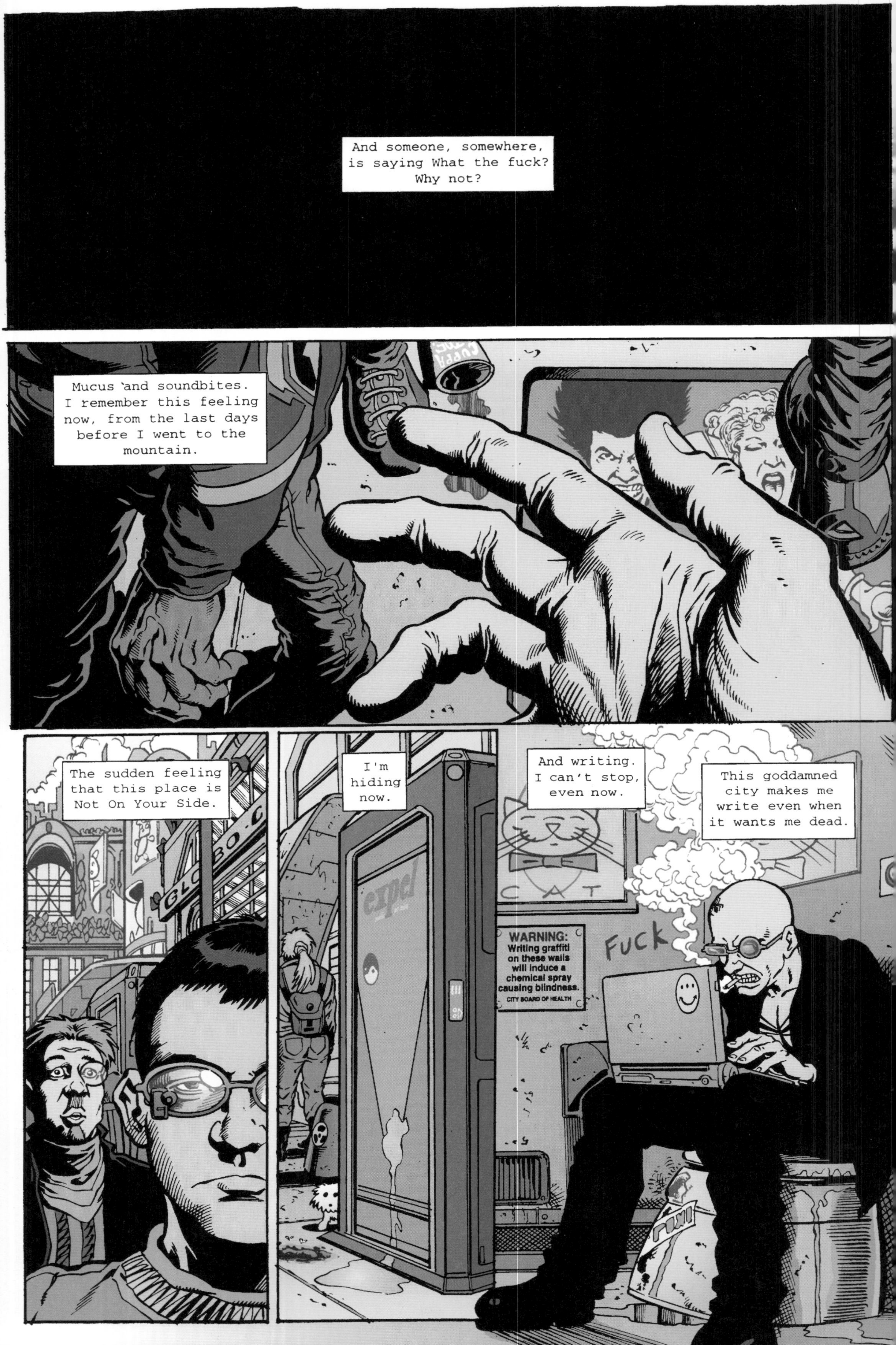
And someone, somewhere, is saying What the fuck? Why not?
Mucus and soundbites. I remember this feeling now, from the last days before I went to the mountain.
The sudden feeling that this place is Not On Your Side.
I'm hiding now.
And writing. I can't stop, even now.
This goddamned city makes me write even when it wants me dead.
expel
CAT
WARNING:
Writing graffiti on these walls will induce a chemical spray causing blindness.
CITY BOARD OF HEALTH
FUCK

# A VOYAGE ROUND MY FATHER

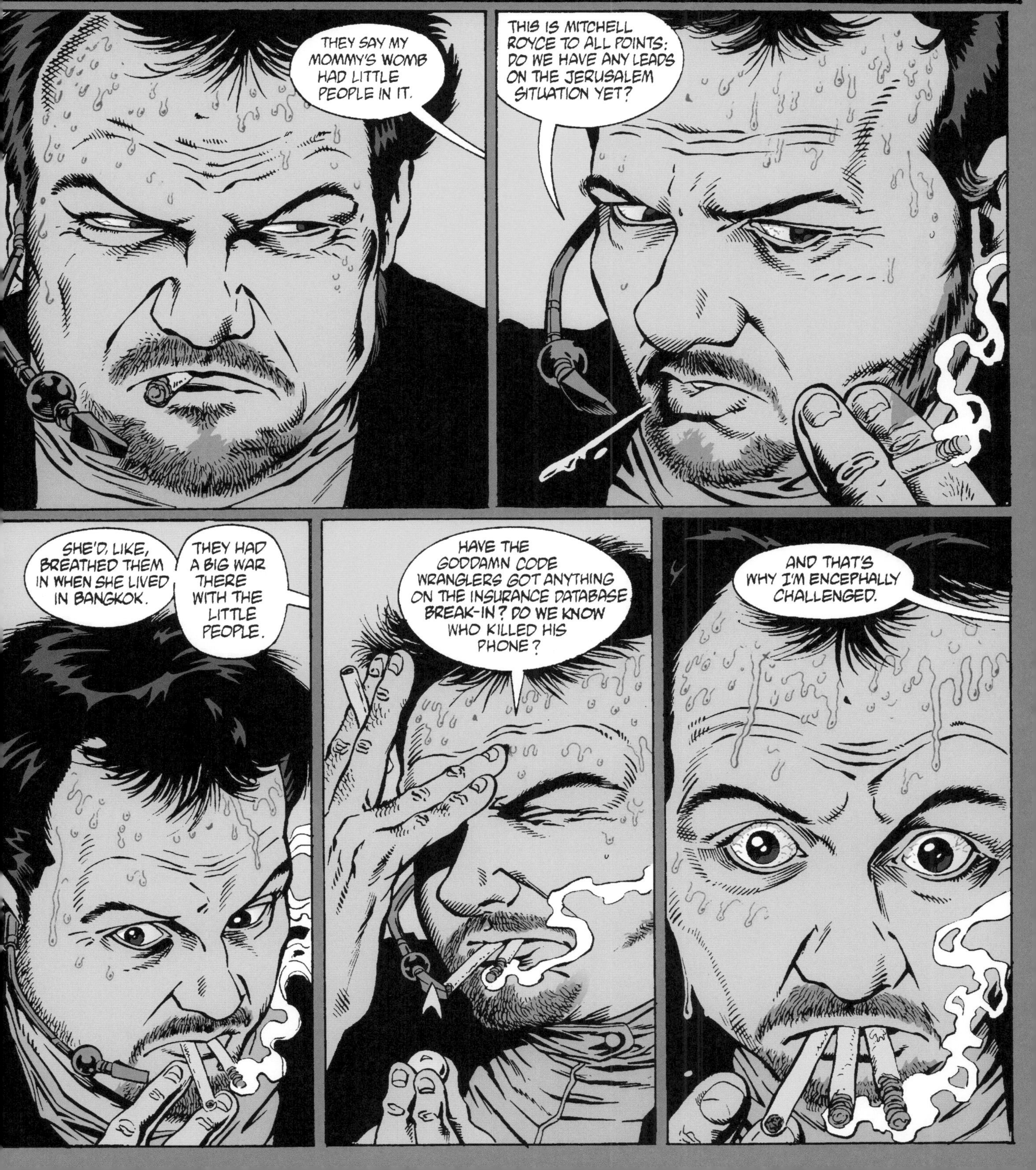

THEY SAY MY MOMMY'S WOMB HAD LITTLE PEOPLE IN IT.
THIS IS MITCHELL ROYCE TO ALL POINTS: DO WE HAVE ANY LEADS ON THE JERUSALEM SITUATION YET?
SHE'D, LIKE, BREATHED THEM IN WHEN SHE LIVED IN BANGKOK.
THEY HAD A BIG WAR THERE WITH THE LITTLE PEOPLE.
HAVE THE GODDAMN CODE WRANGLERS GOT ANYTHING ON THE INSURANCE DATABASE BREAK-IN? DO WE KNOW WHO KILLED HIS PHONE?
AND THAT'S WHY I'M ENCEPHALLY CHALLENGED.

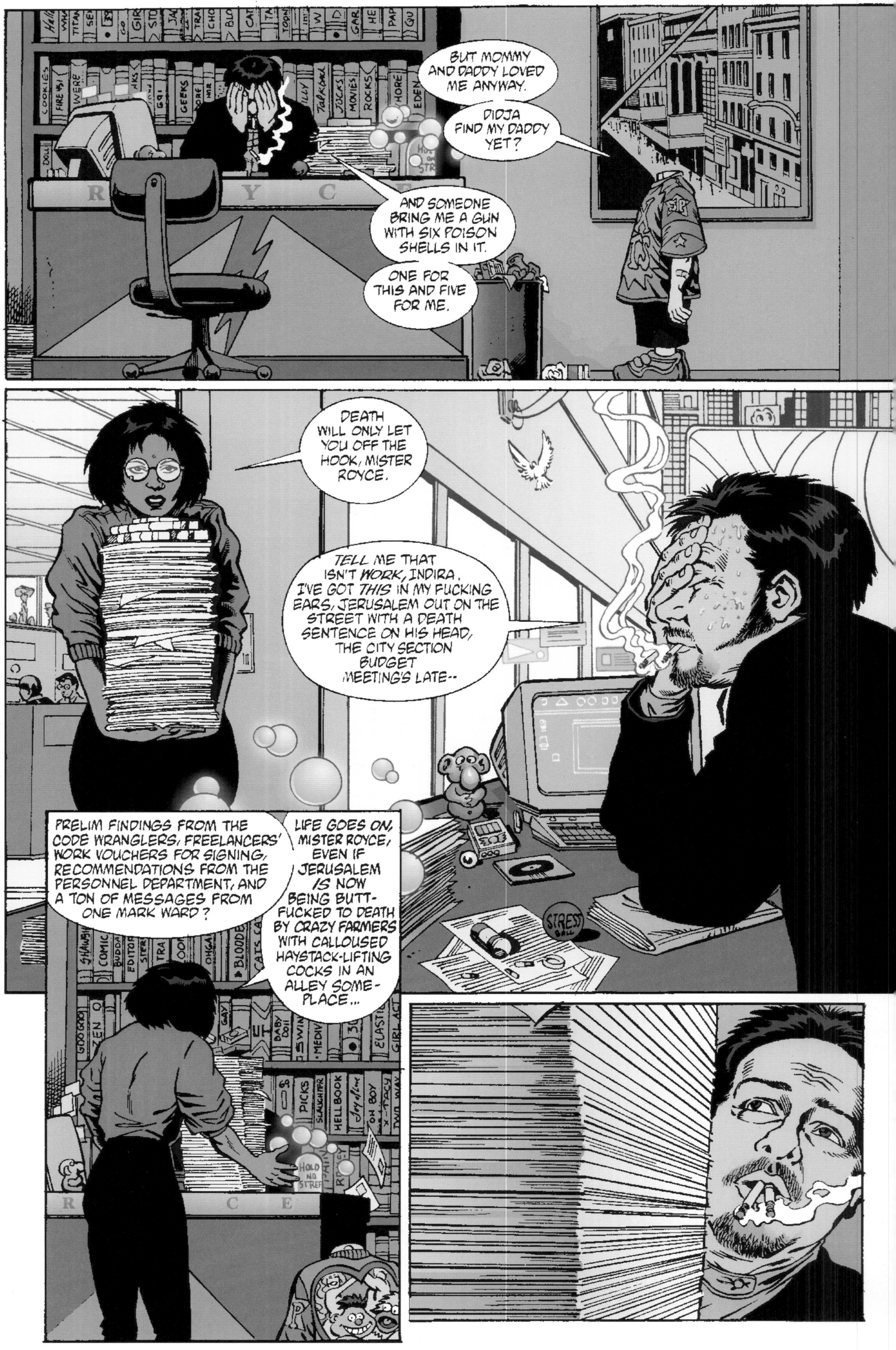

BUT MOMMY AND DADDY LOVED ME ANYWAY.
DIDJA FIND MY DADDY YET?
AND SOMEONE BRING ME A GUN WITH SIX POISON SHELLS IN IT.
ONE FOR THIS AND FIVE FOR ME.
DEATH WILL ONLY LET YOU OFF THE HOOK, MISTER ROYCE.
TELL ME THAT ISN'T WORK, INDIRA. I'VE GOT THIS IN MY FUCKING EARS, JERUSALEM OUT ON THE STREET WITH A DEATH SENTENCE ON HIS HEAD, THE CITY SECTION BUDGET MEETING'S LATE--
PRELIM FINDINGS FROM THE CODE WRANGLERS, FREELANCERS' WORK VOUCHERS FOR SIGNING, RECOMMENDATIONS FROM THE PERSONNEL DEPARTMENT, AND A TON OF MESSAGES FROM ONE MARK WARD?
LIFE GOES ON, MISTER ROYCE, EVEN IF JERUSALEM IS NOW BEING BUTT-FUCKED TO DEATH BY CRAZY FARMERS WITH CALLOUSED HAYSTACK-LIFTING COCKS IN AN ALLEY SOME-PLACE...
STRESS BALL

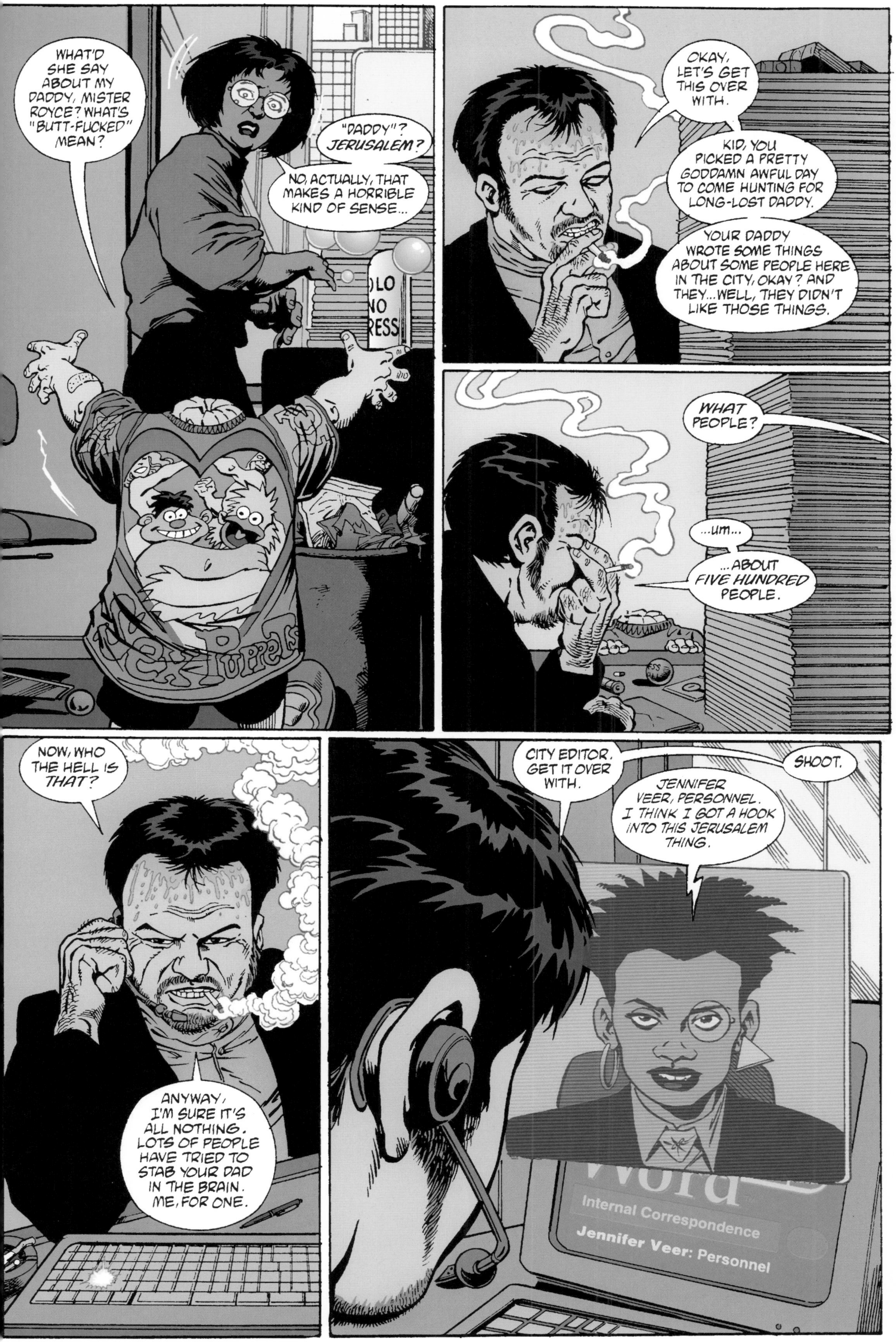
WHAT'D SHE SAY ABOUT MY DADDY, MISTER ROYCE? WHAT'S "BUTT-FUCKED" MEAN?
"DADDY"? JERUSALEM?
NO, ACTUALLY, THAT MAKES A HORRIBLE KIND OF SENSE...
OKAY, LET'S GET THIS OVER WITH.
KID, YOU PICKED A PRETTY GODDAMN AWFUL DAY TO COME HUNTING FOR LONG-LOST DADDY.
YOUR DADDY WROTE SOME THINGS ABOUT SOME PEOPLE HERE IN THE CITY, OKAY? AND THEY...WELL, THEY DIDN'T LIKE THOSE THINGS.
WHAT PEOPLE?
...um...
...ABOUT FIVE HUNDRED PEOPLE.
NOW, WHO THE HELL IS THAT?
ANYWAY, I'M SURE IT'S ALL NOTHING. LOTS OF PEOPLE HAVE TRIED TO STAB YOUR DAD IN THE BRAIN. ME, FOR ONE.
CITY EDITOR. GET IT OVER WITH.
SHOOT.
JENNIFER VEER, PERSONNEL. I THINK I GOT A HOOK INTO THIS JERUSALEM THING.
Word
Internal Correspondence
Jennifer Veer: Personnel

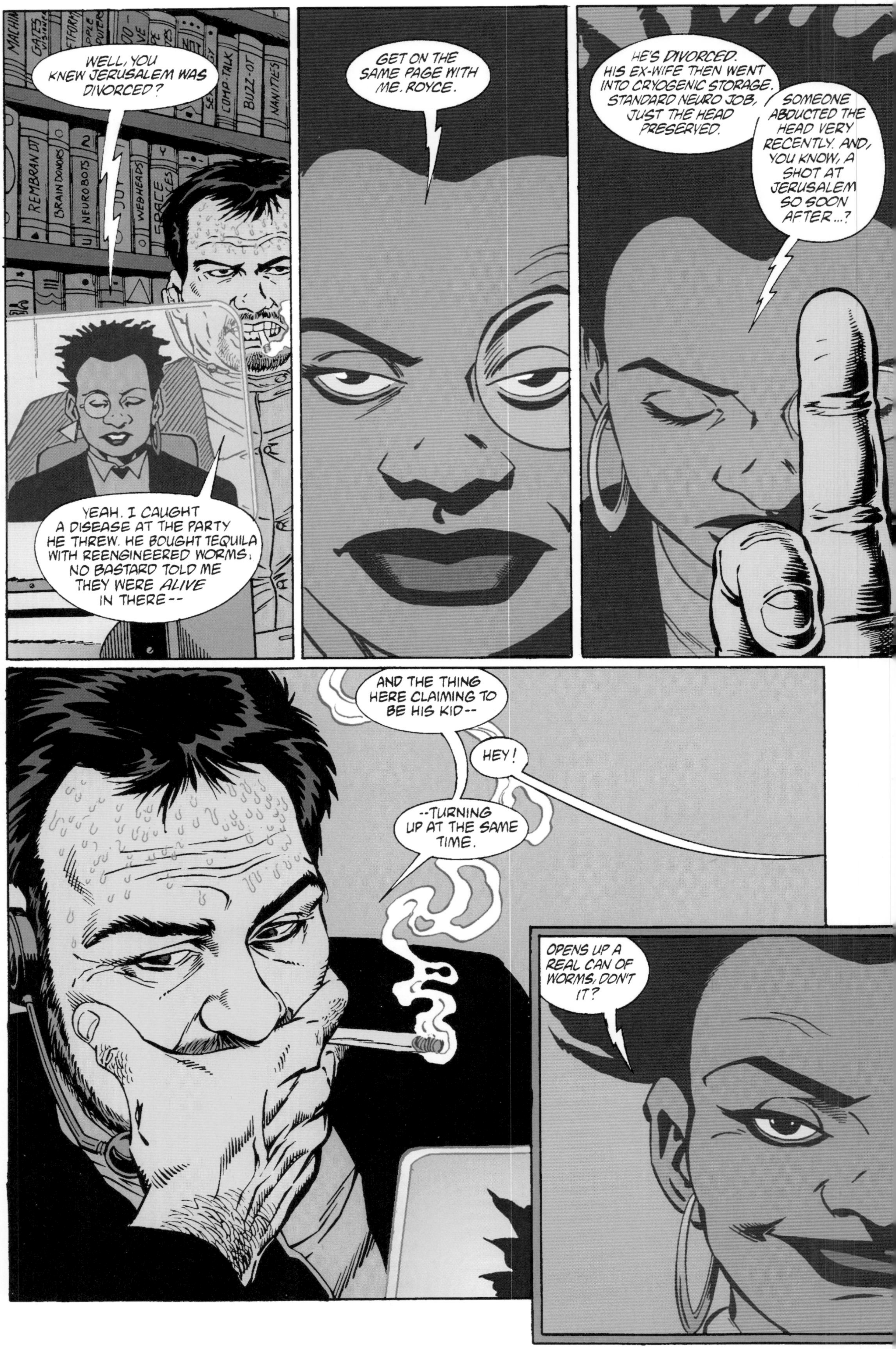
WELL, YOU KNEW JERUSALEM WAS DIVORCED?
YEAH. I CAUGHT A DISEASE AT THE PARTY HE THREW. HE BOUGHT TEQUILA WITH REENGINEERED WORMS; NO BASTARD TOLD ME THEY WERE *ALIVE* IN THERE--
GET ON THE SAME PAGE WITH ME, ROYCE.
HE'S *DIVORCED*. HIS EX-WIFE THEN WENT INTO CRYOGENIC STORAGE. STANDARD NEURO JOB, JUST THE HEAD PRESERVED.
SOMEONE ABDUCTED THE HEAD VERY RECENTLY. AND, YOU KNOW, A SHOT AT JERUSALEM SO SOON AFTER...?
AND THE THING HERE CLAIMING TO BE HIS KID--
HEY!
--TURNING UP AT THE SAME TIME.
OPENS UP A REAL CAN OF WORMS, DON'T IT?

# home is where the heart is...

LAST GODDAMN CREDIT CARD... PLEASE LET THIS WORK...

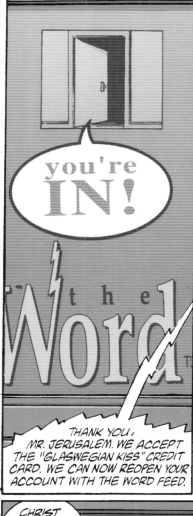

you're IN!

the Word™

THANK YOU, MR. JERUSALEM. WE ACCEPT THE "GLASWEGIAN KISS" CREDIT CARD. WE CAN NOW REOPEN YOUR ACCOUNT WITH THE WORD FEED.

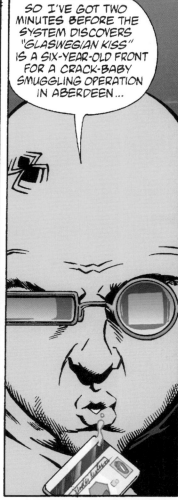

SO I'VE GOT TWO MINUTES BEFORE THE SYSTEM DISCOVERS "GLASWEGIAN KISS" IS A SIX-YEAR-OLD FRONT FOR A CRACK-BABY SMUGGLING OPERATION IN ABERDEEN...

GET ME MITCHELL ROYCE, CITY EDITOR, NOW. ABSOLUTE PRIORITY.

CHRIST ALMIGHTY, WON'T ANY-ONE LEAVE ME ALONE, WHO IS THIS --

WELCOME TO the Word™

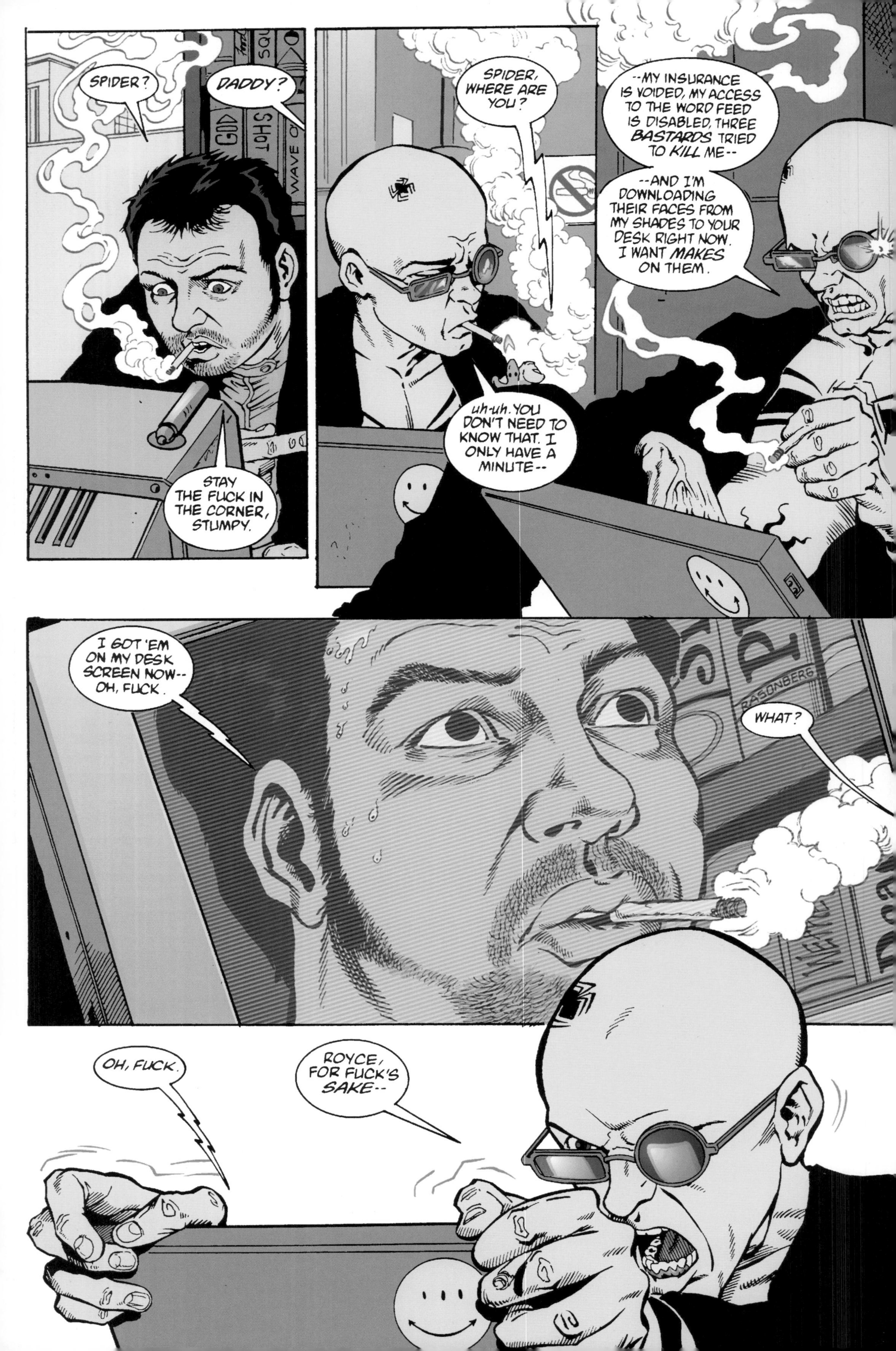
SPIDER?
DADDY?
STAY THE FUCK IN THE CORNER, STUMPY.
SPIDER, WHERE ARE YOU?
uh-uh. YOU DON'T NEED TO KNOW THAT. I ONLY HAVE A MINUTE--
--MY INSURANCE IS VOIDED, MY ACCESS TO THE WORD FEED IS DISABLED, THREE BASTARDS TRIED TO KILL ME--
--AND I'M DOWNLOADING THEIR FACES FROM MY SHADES TO YOUR DESK RIGHT NOW. I WANT MAKES ON THEM.
I GOT 'EM ON MY DESK SCREEN NOW-- OH, FUCK.
WHAT?
OH, FUCK.
ROYCE, FOR FUCK'S SAKE--

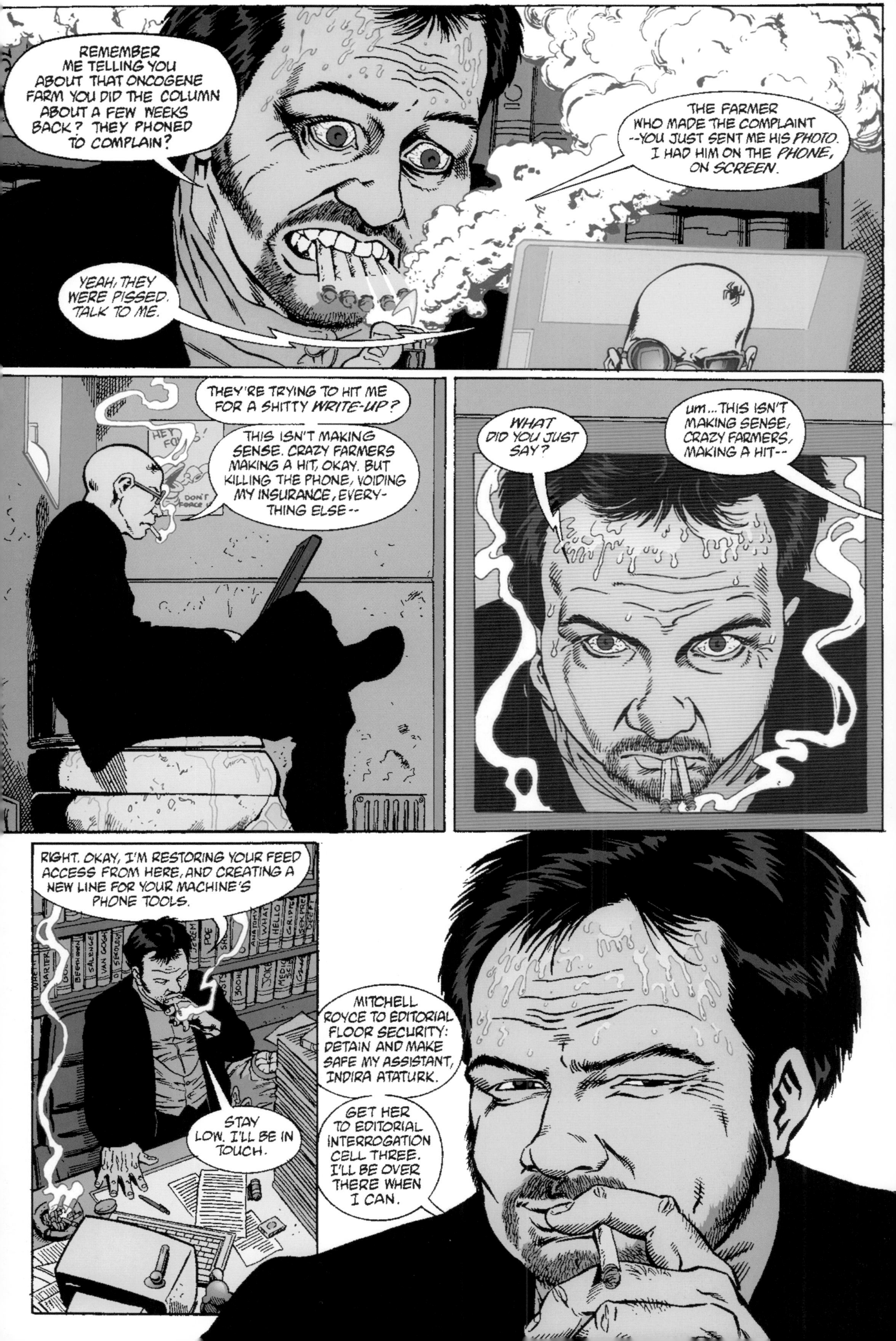
REMEMBER ME TELLING YOU ABOUT THAT ONCOGENE FARM YOU DID THE COLUMN ABOUT A FEW WEEKS BACK? THEY PHONED TO COMPLAIN?
YEAH, THEY WERE PISSED. TALK TO ME.
THE FARMER WHO MADE THE COMPLAINT --YOU JUST SENT ME HIS PHOTO. I HAD HIM ON THE PHONE, ON SCREEN.
THEY'RE TRYING TO HIT ME FOR A SHITTY WRITE-UP?
THIS ISN'T MAKING SENSE. CRAZY FARMERS MAKING A HIT, OKAY. BUT KILLING THE PHONE, VOIDING MY INSURANCE, EVERYTHING ELSE--
WHAT DID YOU JUST SAY?
um...THIS ISN'T MAKING SENSE, CRAZY FARMERS, MAKING A HIT--
RIGHT. OKAY, I'M RESTORING YOUR FEED ACCESS FROM HERE, AND CREATING A NEW LINE FOR YOUR MACHINE'S PHONE TOOLS.
STAY LOW. I'LL BE IN TOUCH.
MITCHELL ROYCE TO EDITORIAL FLOOR SECURITY: DETAIN AND MAKE SAFE MY ASSISTANT, INDIRA ATATURK.
GET HER TO EDITORIAL INTERROGATION CELL THREE. I'LL BE OVER THERE WHEN I CAN.

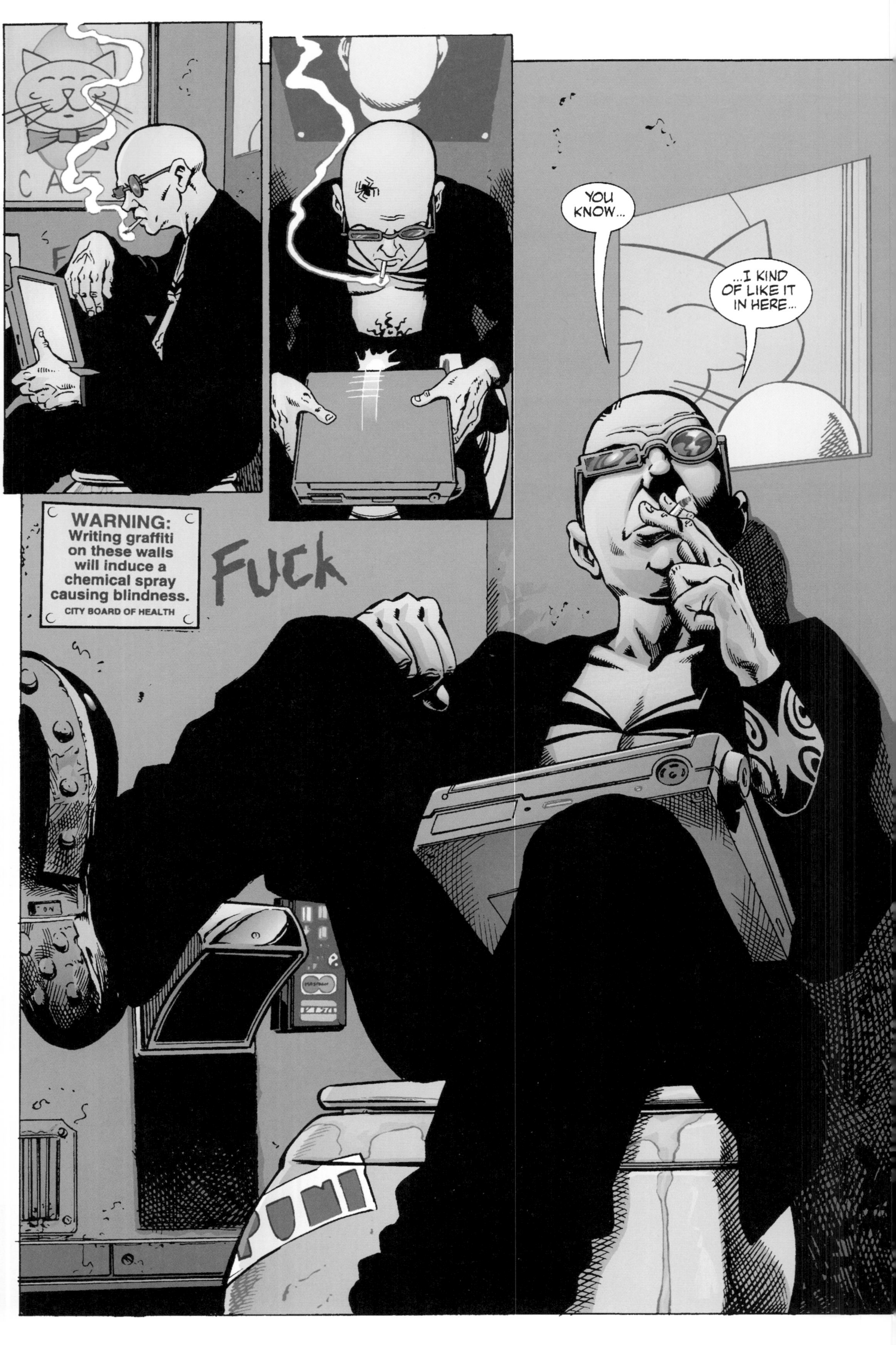
WARNING:
Writing graffiti on these walls will induce a chemical spray causing blindness.
CITY BOARD OF HEALTH
FUCK
YOU KNOW...
...I KIND OF LIKE IT IN HERE...

# MITCHELL ROYCE, TWO-FISTED EDITOR

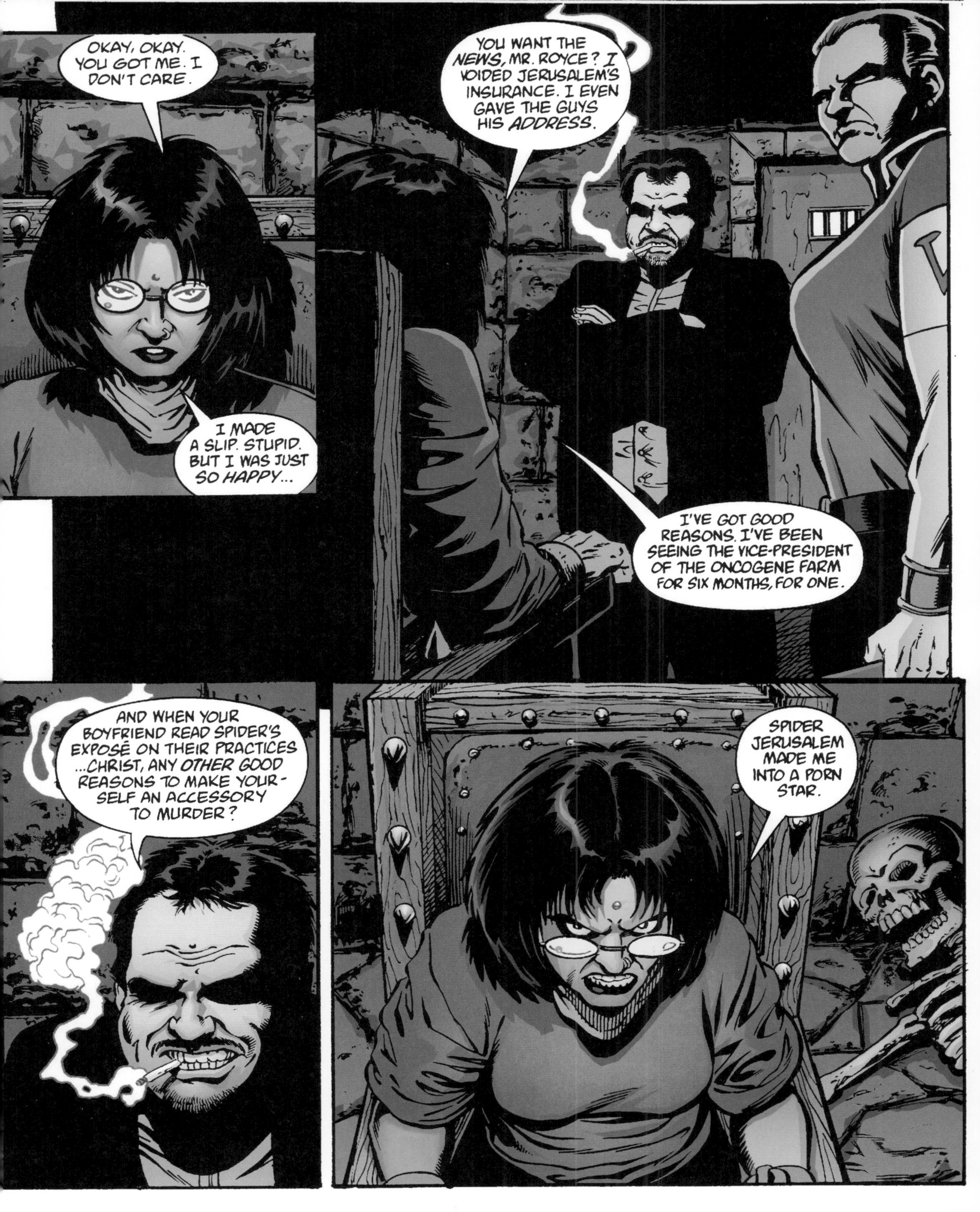
OKAY, OKAY. YOU GOT ME. I DON'T CARE.
I MADE A SLIP. STUPID. BUT I WAS JUST SO HAPPY...
YOU WANT THE NEWS, MR. ROYCE? I VOIDED JERUSALEM'S INSURANCE. I EVEN GAVE THE GUYS HIS ADDRESS.
I'VE GOT GOOD REASONS. I'VE BEEN SEEING THE VICE-PRESIDENT OF THE ONCOGENE FARM FOR SIX MONTHS, FOR ONE.
AND WHEN YOUR BOYFRIEND READ SPIDER'S EXPOSÉ ON THEIR PRACTICES ...CHRIST, ANY OTHER GOOD REASONS TO MAKE YOUR-SELF AN ACCESSORY TO MURDER?
SPIDER JERUSALEM MADE ME INTO A PORN STAR.

# Nowhere is Safe

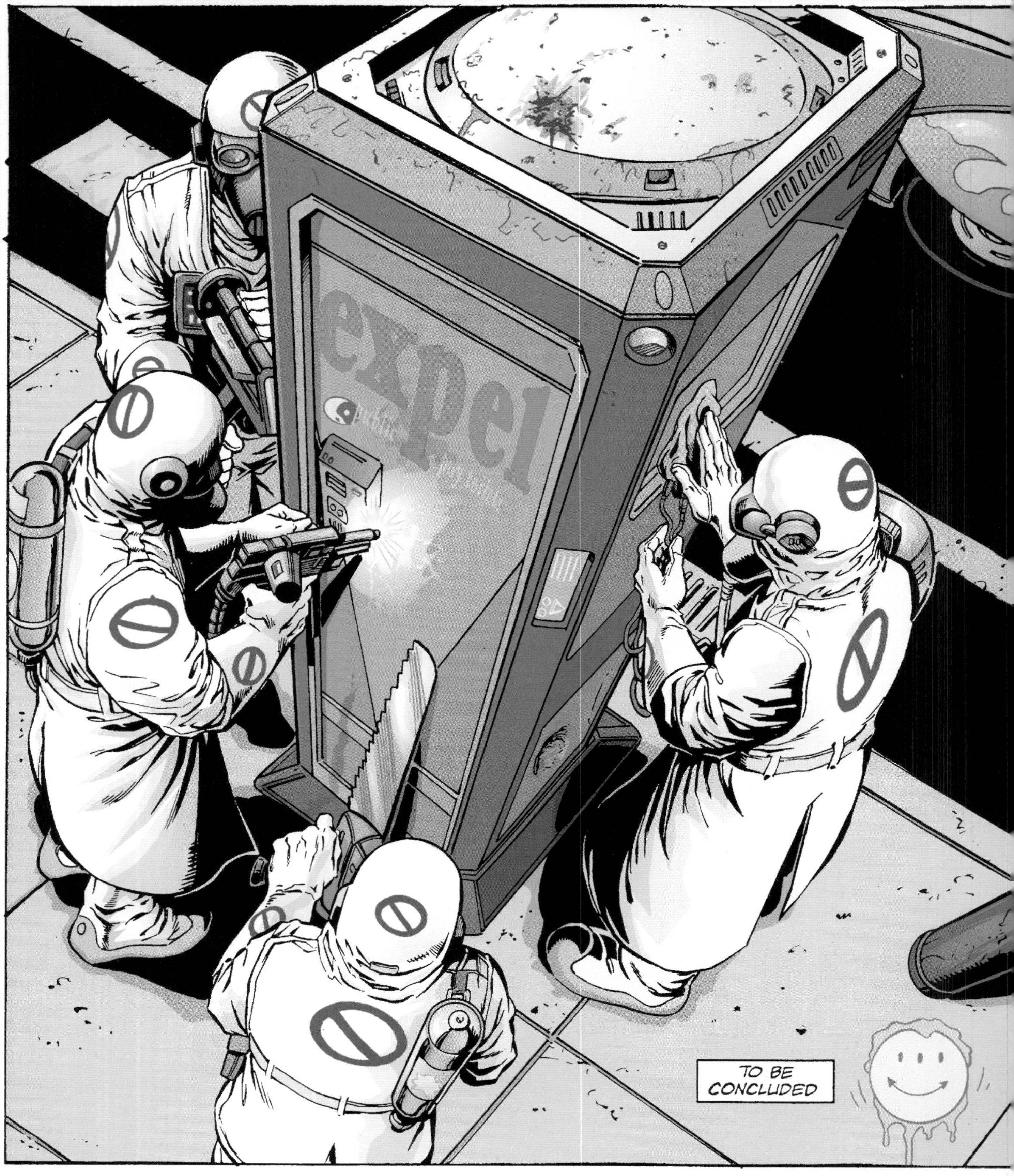
expel
public
pay toilets
TO BE CONCLUDED

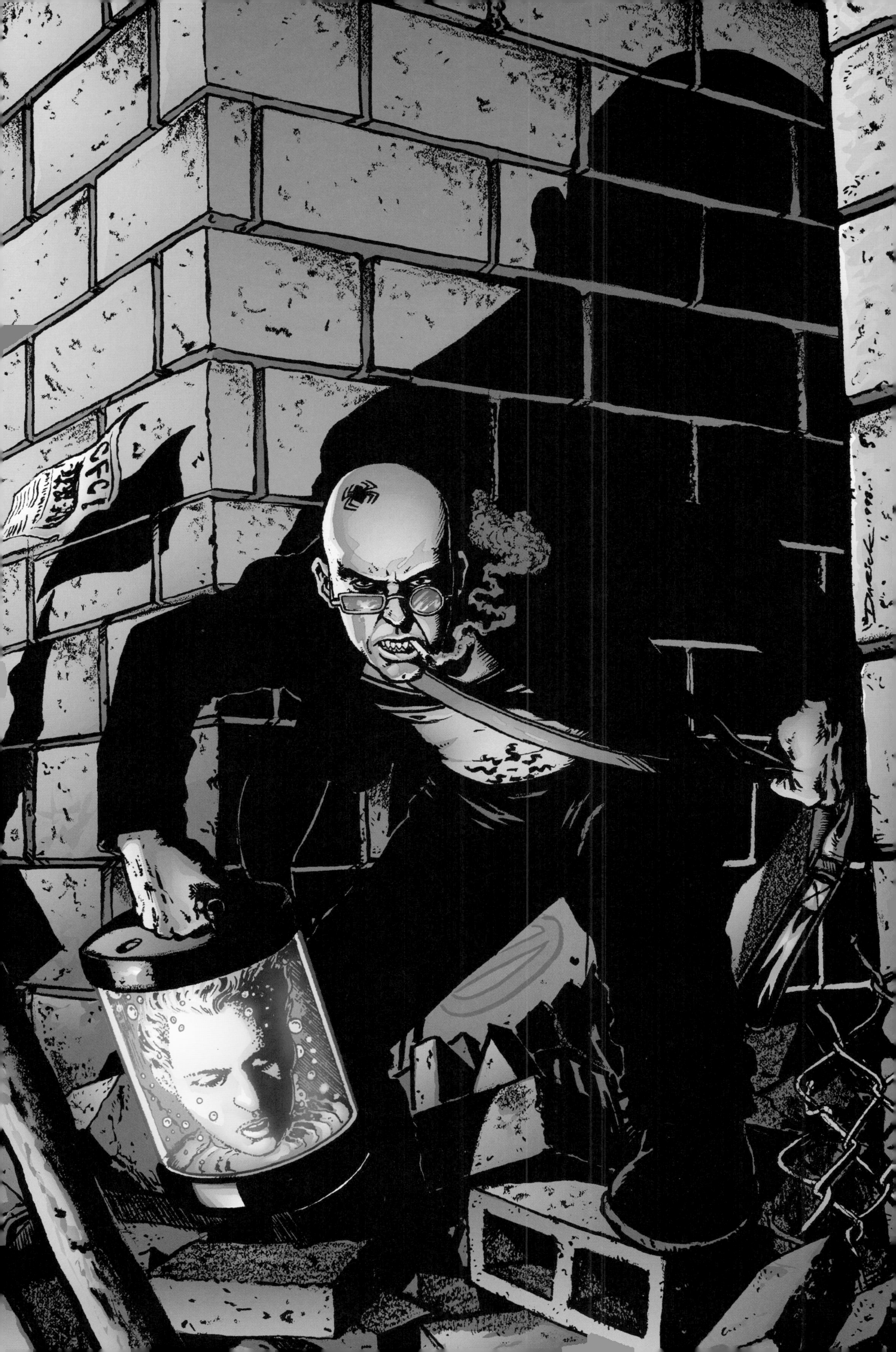
CFC!

expel
public pay toilets
expel
public pay toilets
expel
public pay toilets
expel
public pay toilets
CAN I NOT EVEN HAVE A GOOD HARD *SHIT* IN PEACE ANY MORE?

**WARREN ELLIS writes and DARICK ROBERTSON pencils**

# FREEZE ME WITH YOUR KISS

## PART III OF III

**RODNEY RAMOS, inker**
**NATHAN EYRING, color & separations**
**CLEM ROBINS, letterer**
**CLIFF CHIANG, assistant editor**
**STUART MOORE, editor**

**TRANSMETROPOLITAN CREATED BY WARREN ELLIS & DARICK ROBERTSON**

# True Confessions

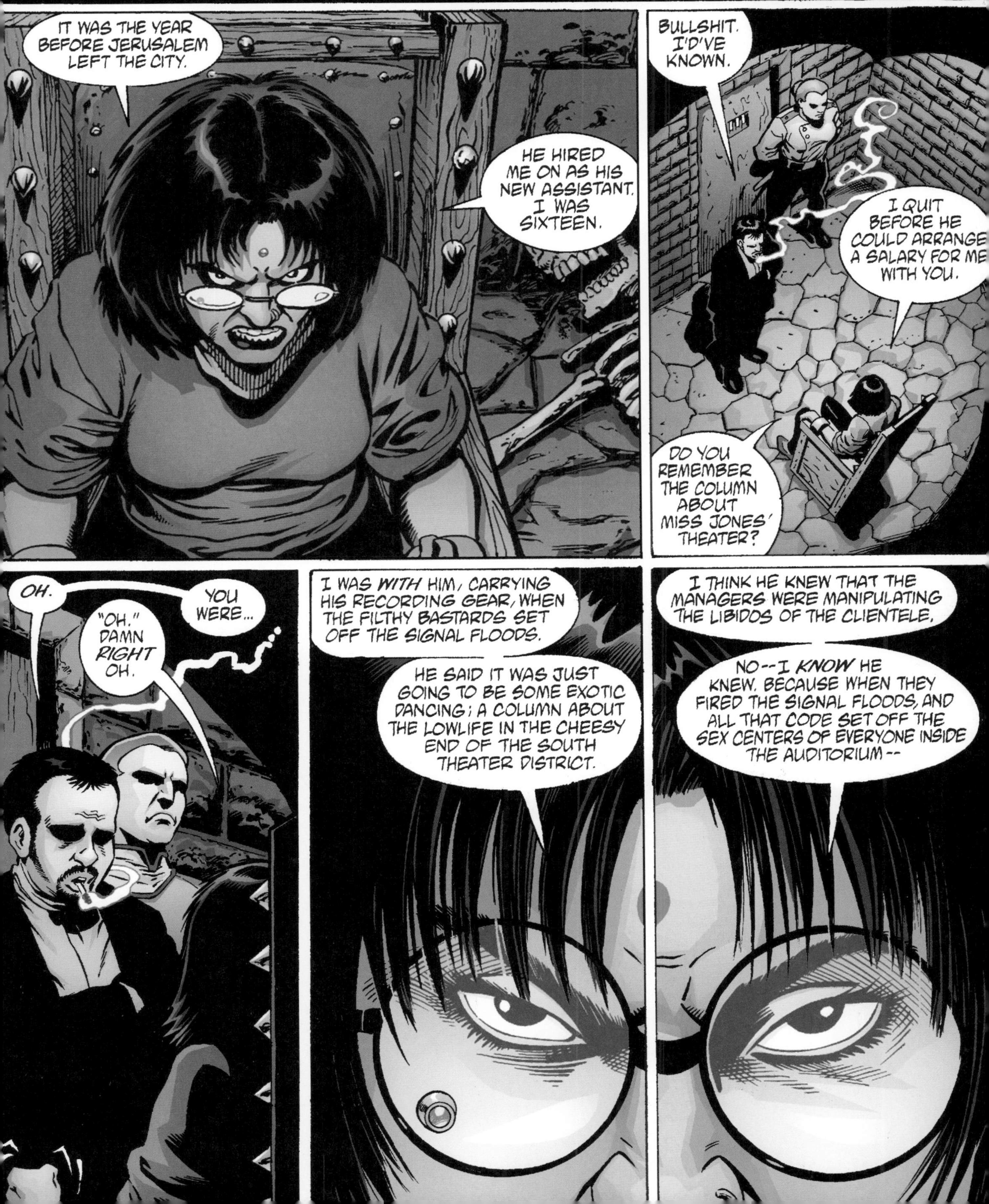
IT WAS THE YEAR BEFORE JERUSALEM LEFT THE CITY.
HE HIRED ME ON AS HIS NEW ASSISTANT. I WAS SIXTEEN.
BULLSHIT. I'D'VE KNOWN.
I QUIT BEFORE HE COULD ARRANGE A SALARY FOR ME WITH YOU.
DO YOU REMEMBER THE COLUMN ABOUT MISS JONES' THEATER?
OH.
YOU WERE...
"OH." DAMN *RIGHT* OH.
I WAS *WITH* HIM, CARRYING HIS RECORDING GEAR, WHEN THE FILTHY BASTARDS SET OFF THE SIGNAL FLOODS.
HE SAID IT WAS JUST GOING TO BE SOME EXOTIC DANCING; A COLUMN ABOUT THE LOWLIFE IN THE CHEESY END OF THE SOUTH THEATER DISTRICT.
I THINK HE KNEW THAT THE MANAGERS WERE MANIPULATING THE LIBIDOS OF THE CLIENTELE.
NO--I *KNOW* HE KNEW. BECAUSE WHEN THEY FIRED THE SIGNAL FLOODS, AND ALL THAT CODE SET OFF THE SEX CENTERS OF EVERYONE INSIDE THE AUDITORIUM--

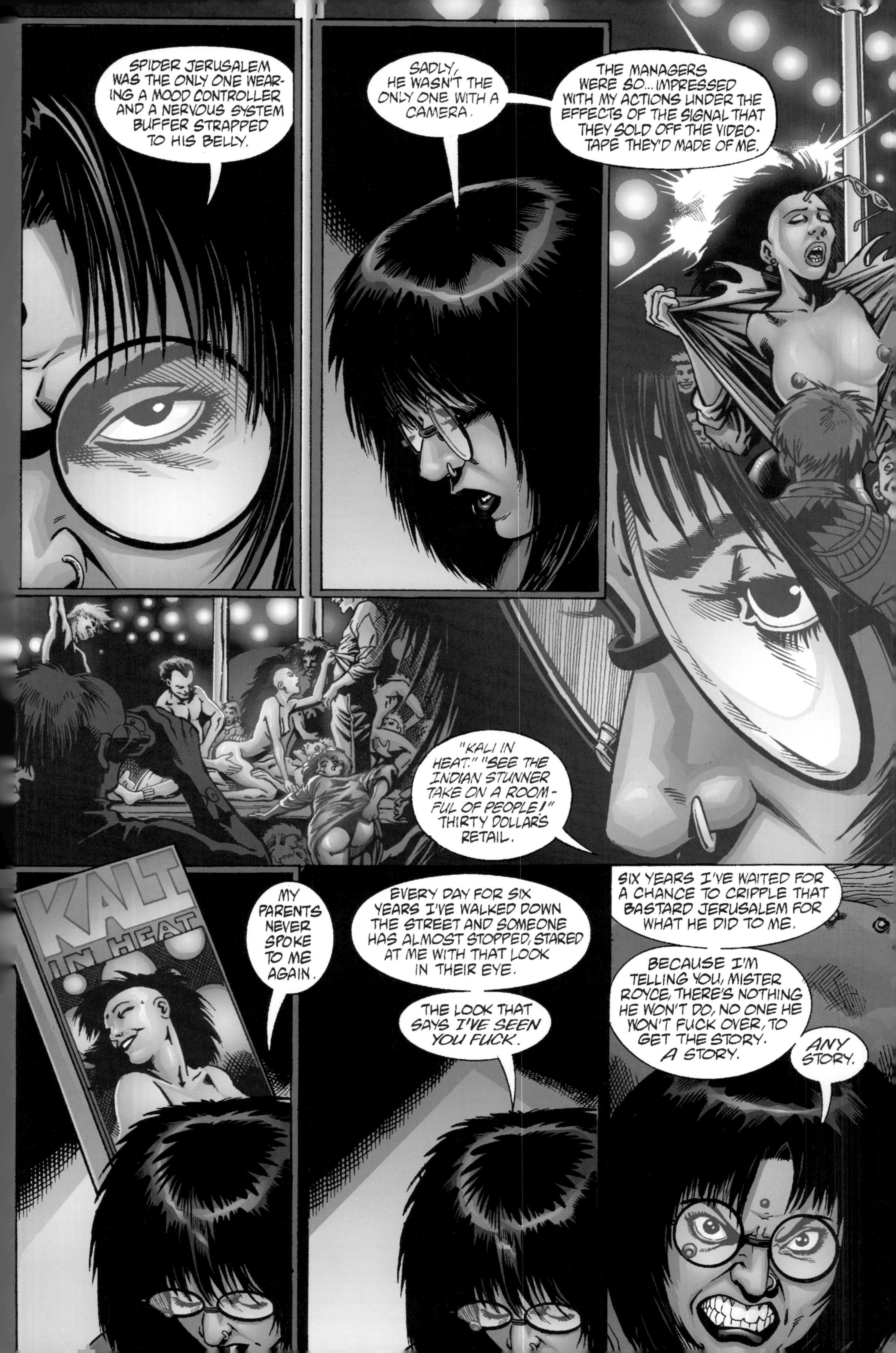
SPIDER JERUSALEM WAS THE ONLY ONE WEARING A MOOD CONTROLLER AND A NERVOUS SYSTEM BUFFER STRAPPED TO HIS BELLY.
SADLY, HE WASN'T THE ONLY ONE WITH A CAMERA.
THE MANAGERS WERE SO... IMPRESSED WITH MY ACTIONS UNDER THE EFFECTS OF THE SIGNAL THAT THEY SOLD OFF THE VIDEOTAPE THEY'D MADE OF ME.
"KALI IN HEAT." "SEE THE INDIAN STUNNER TAKE ON A ROOMFUL OF PEOPLE!" THIRTY DOLLARS RETAIL.
KALI IN HEAT
MY PARENTS NEVER SPOKE TO ME AGAIN.
EVERY DAY FOR SIX YEARS I'VE WALKED DOWN THE STREET AND SOMEONE HAS ALMOST STOPPED, STARED AT ME WITH THAT LOOK IN THEIR EYE.
THE LOOK THAT SAYS *I'VE SEEN YOU FUCK*.
SIX YEARS I'VE WAITED FOR A CHANCE TO CRIPPLE THAT BASTARD JERUSALEM FOR WHAT HE DID TO ME.
BECAUSE I'M TELLING YOU, MISTER ROYCE, THERE'S NOTHING HE WON'T DO, NO ONE HE WON'T FUCK OVER, TO GET THE STORY. *A* STORY.
*ANY* STORY.

# BAD DOGGIE

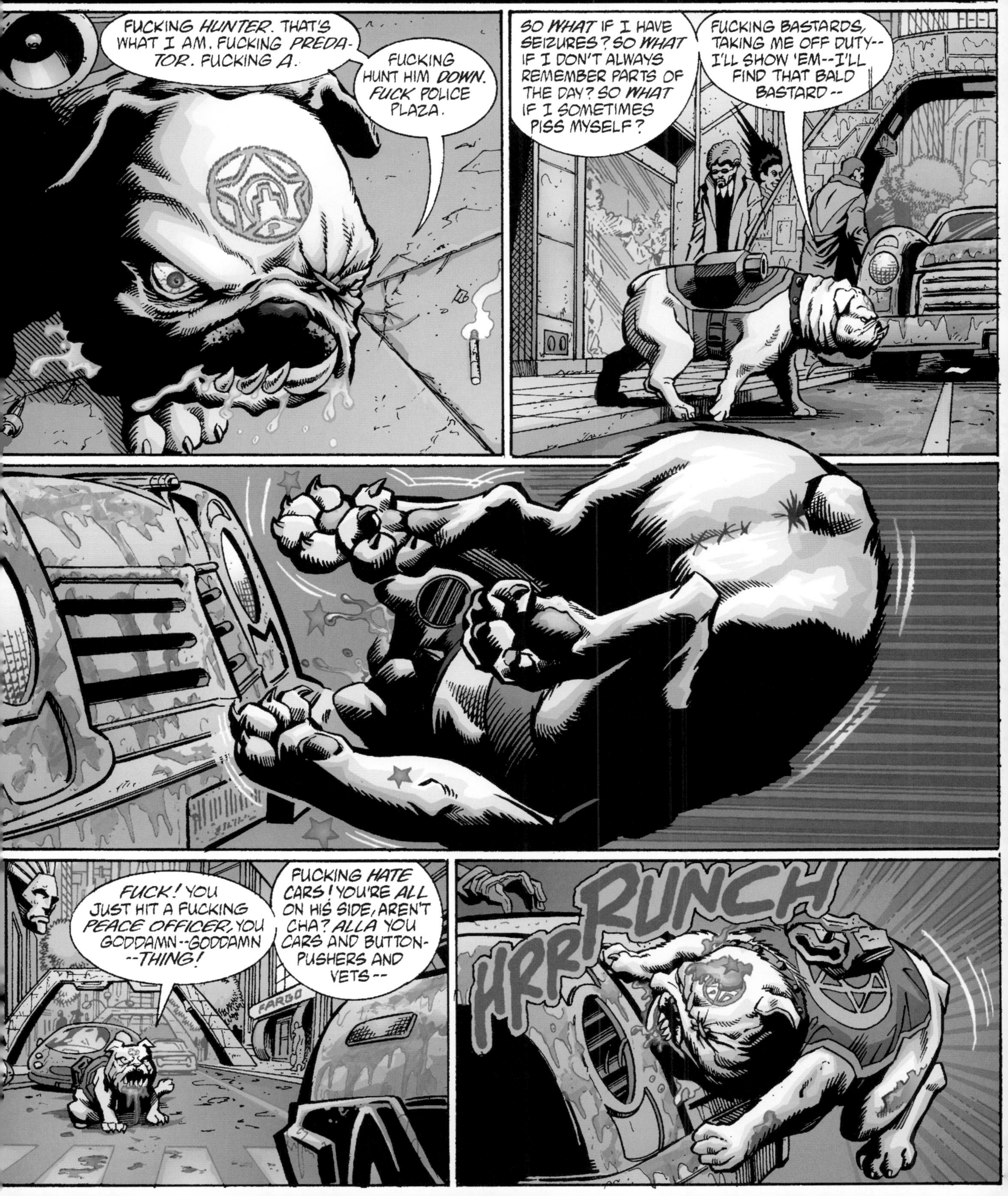

FUCKING HUNTER. THAT'S WHAT I AM. FUCKING PREDA-TOR. FUCKING A.
FUCKING HUNT HIM DOWN. FUCK POLICE PLAZA.
SO WHAT IF I HAVE SEIZURES? SO WHAT IF I DON'T ALWAYS REMEMBER PARTS OF THE DAY? SO WHAT IF I SOMETIMES PISS MYSELF?
FUCKING BASTARDS, TAKING ME OFF DUTY-- I'LL SHOW 'EM--I'LL FIND THAT BALD BASTARD--
FUCK! YOU JUST HIT A FUCKING PEACE OFFICER, YOU GODDAMN--GODDAMN --THING!
FUCKING HATE CARS! YOU'RE ALL ON HIS SIDE, AREN'T CHA? ALLA YOU CARS AND BUTTON-PUSHERS AND VETS--
FARGO
HRRRUNCH

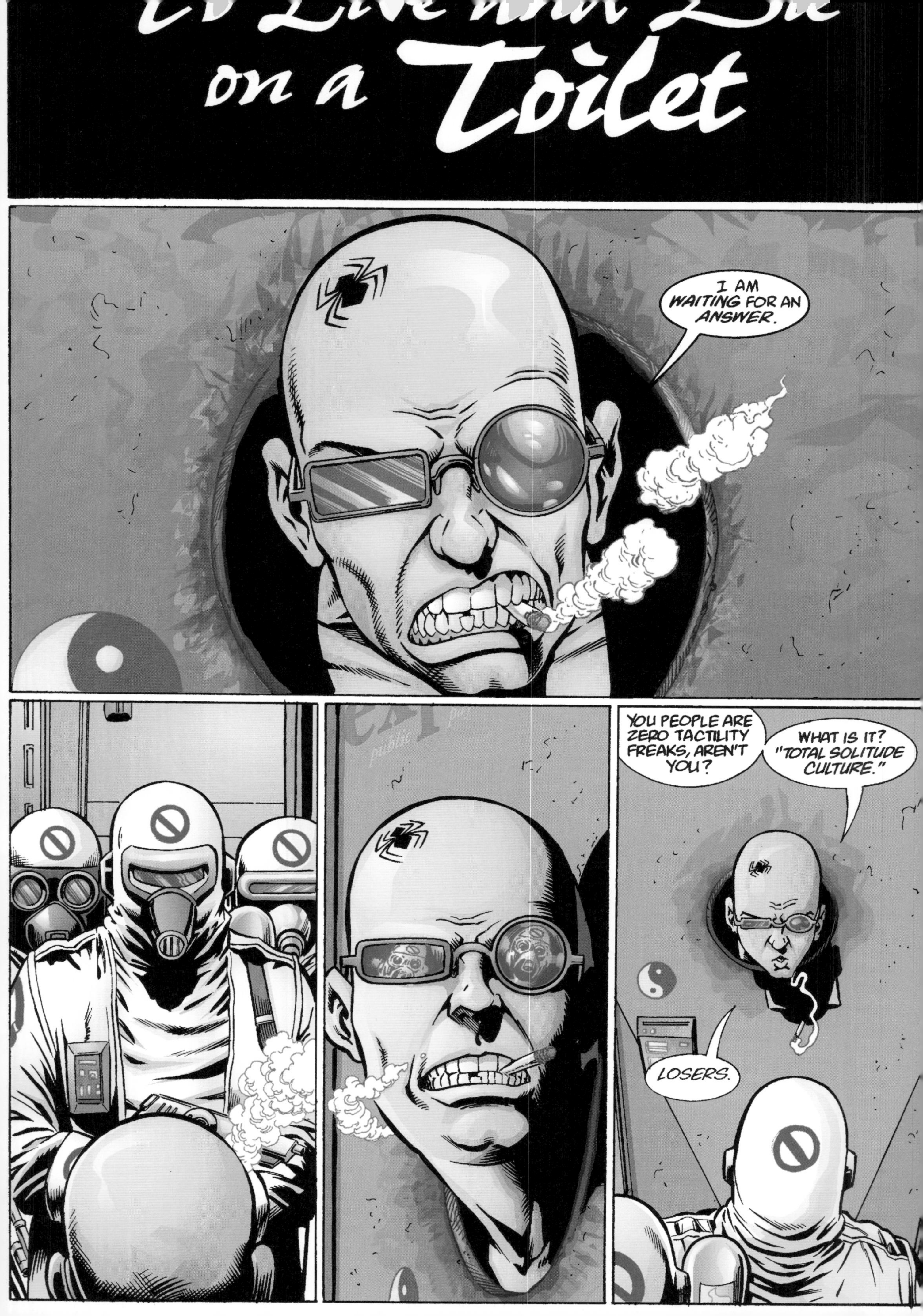
on a Toilet
I AM WAITING FOR AN ANSWER.
YOU PEOPLE ARE ZERO TACTILITY FREAKS, AREN'T YOU?
WHAT IS IT? "TOTAL SOLITUDE CULTURE."
LOSERS.

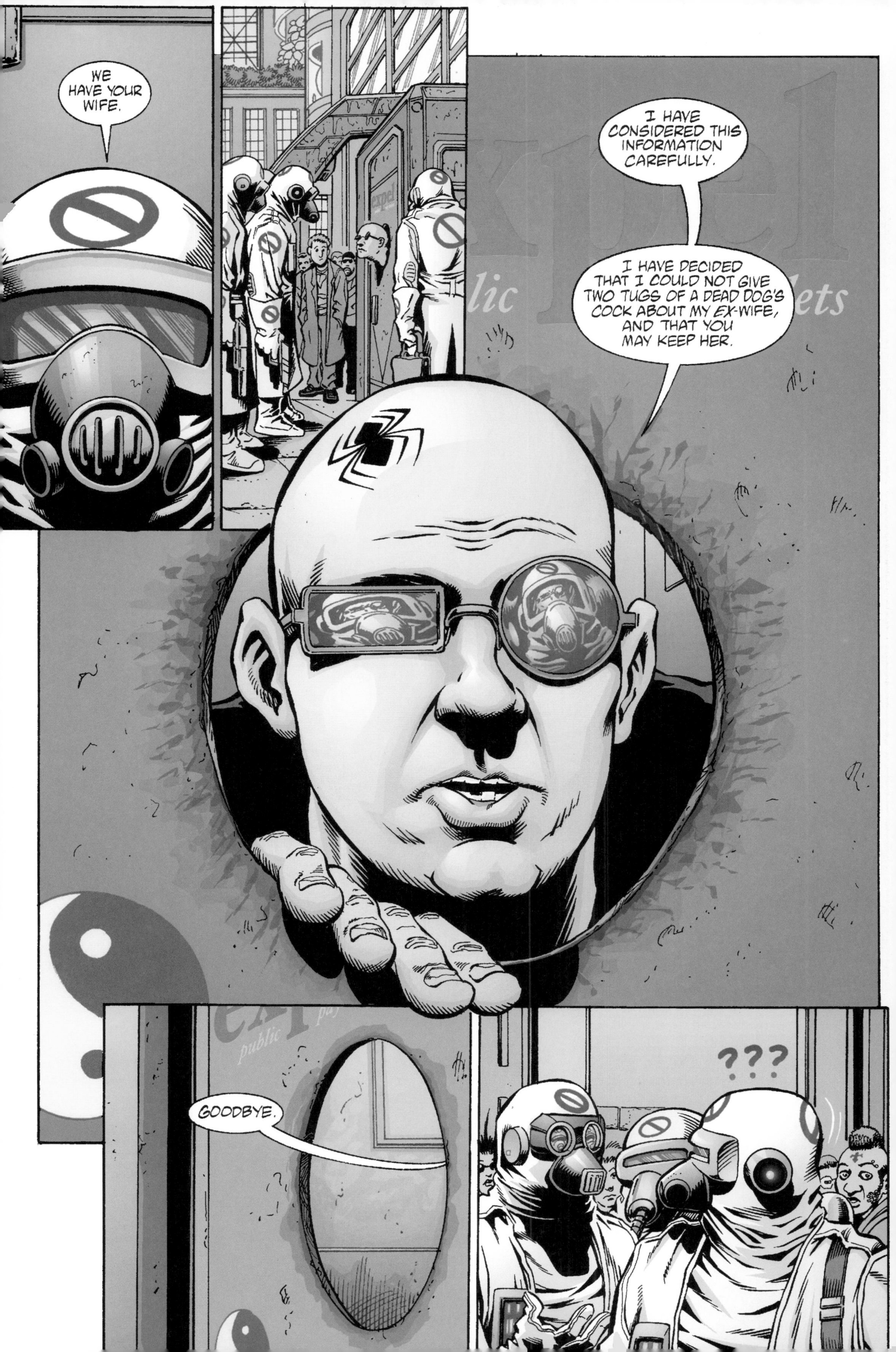
WE HAVE YOUR WIFE.
I HAVE CONSIDERED THIS INFORMATION CAREFULLY.
I HAVE DECIDED THAT I COULD NOT GIVE TWO TUGS OF A DEAD DOG'S COCK ABOUT MY EX-WIFE, AND THAT YOU MAY KEEP HER.
GOODBYE.
???

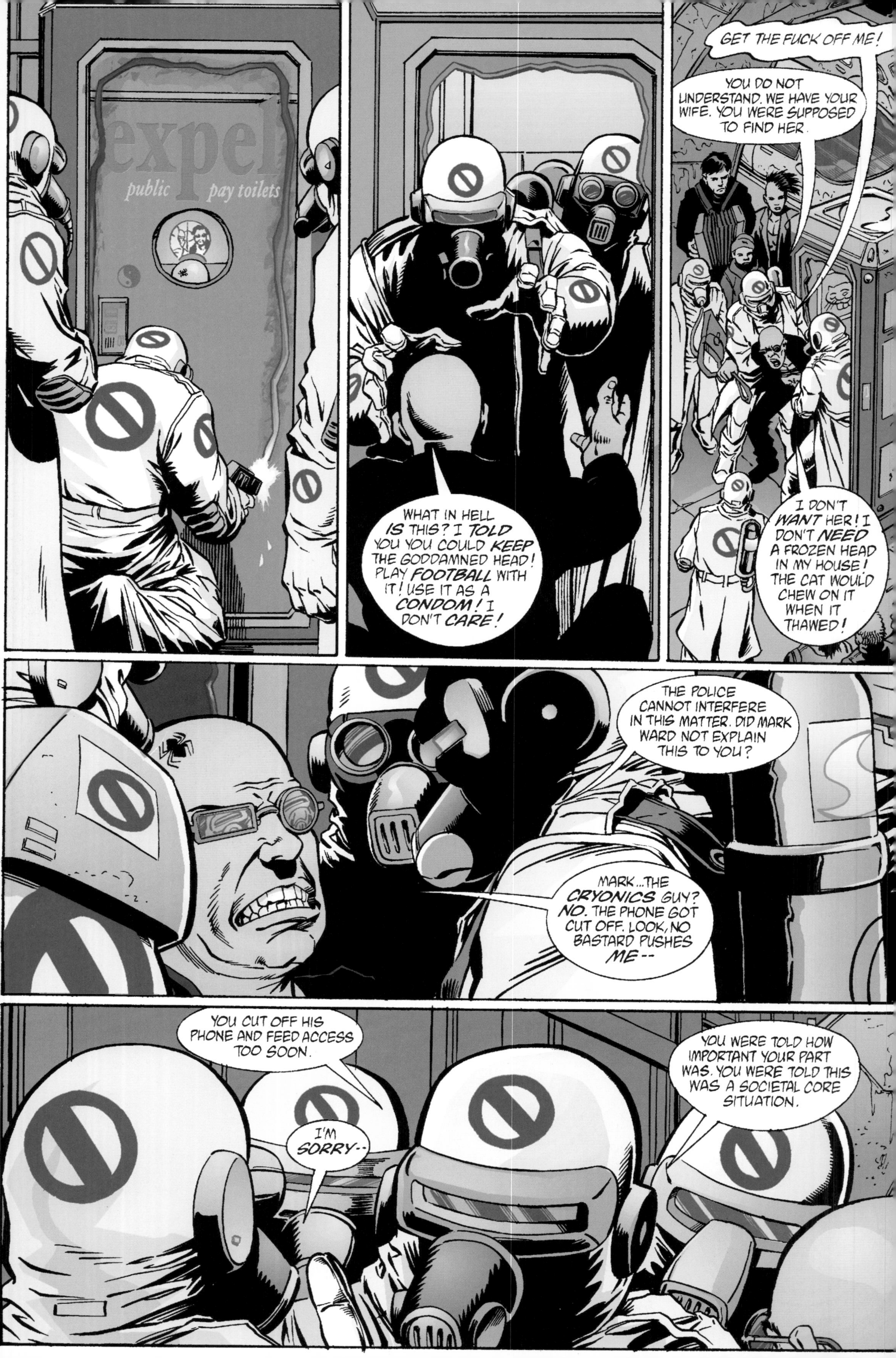
expel
public pay toilets
WHAT IN HELL IS THIS? I TOLD YOU YOU COULD KEEP THE GODDAMNED HEAD! PLAY FOOTBALL WITH IT! USE IT AS A CONDOM! I DON'T CARE!
GET THE FUCK OFF ME!
YOU DO NOT UNDERSTAND. WE HAVE YOUR WIFE. YOU WERE SUPPOSED TO FIND HER.
I DON'T WANT HER! I DON'T NEED A FROZEN HEAD IN MY HOUSE! THE CAT WOULD CHEW ON IT WHEN IT THAWED!
THE POLICE CANNOT INTERFERE IN THIS MATTER. DID MARK WARD NOT EXPLAIN THIS TO YOU?
MARK...THE CRYONICS GUY? NO. THE PHONE GOT CUT OFF. LOOK, NO BASTARD PUSHES ME--
YOU CUT OFF HIS PHONE AND FEED ACCESS TOO SOON.
I'M SORRY--
YOU WERE TOLD HOW IMPORTANT YOUR PART WAS. YOU WERE TOLD THIS WAS A SOCIETAL CORE SITUATION.

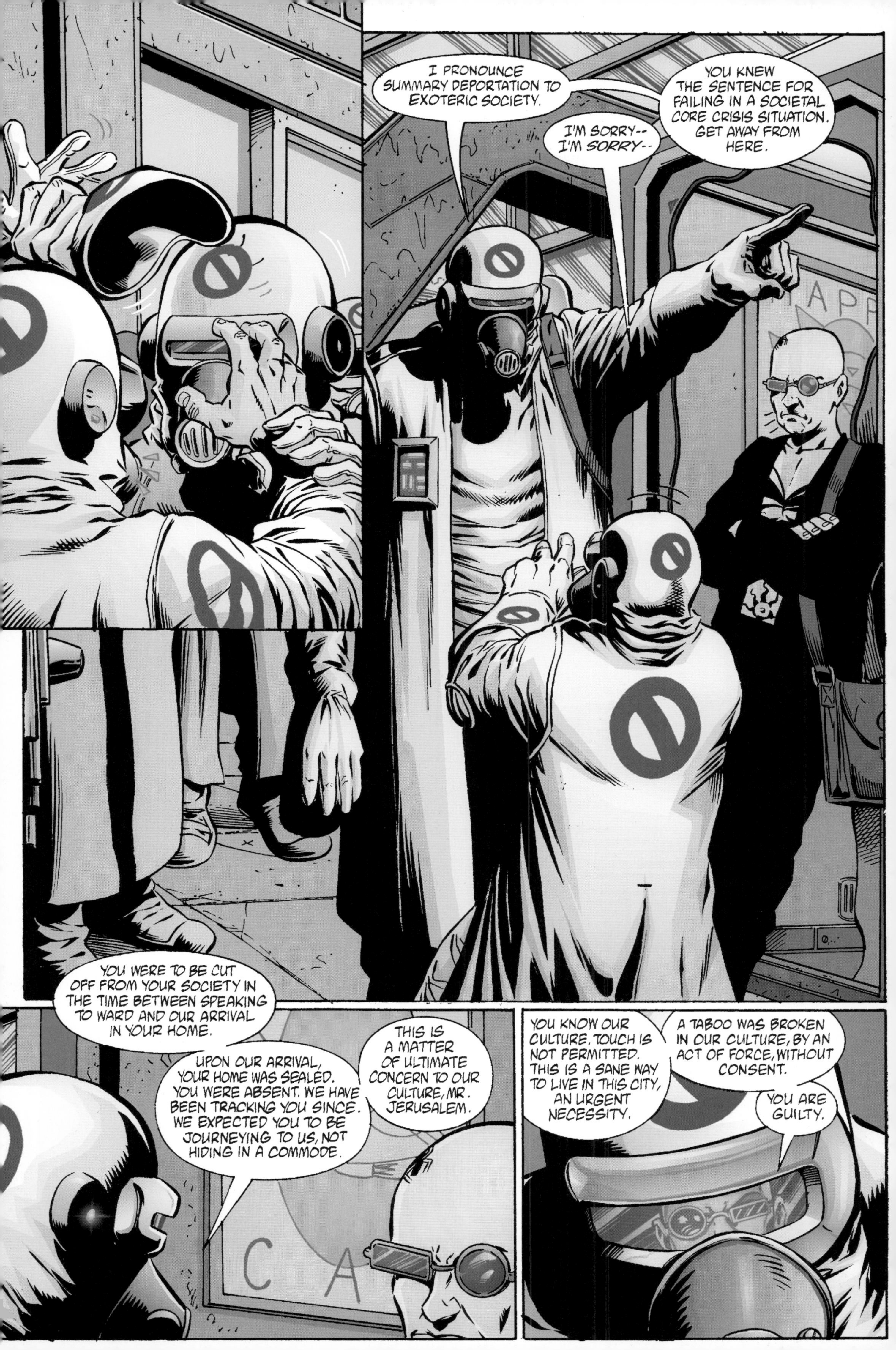
I PRONOUNCE SUMMARY DEPORTATION TO EXOTERIC SOCIETY.
YOU KNEW THE SENTENCE FOR FAILING IN A SOCIETAL CORE CRISIS SITUATION. GET AWAY FROM HERE.
I'M SORRY-- I'M SORRY--
YOU WERE TO BE CUT OFF FROM YOUR SOCIETY IN THE TIME BETWEEN SPEAKING TO WARD AND OUR ARRIVAL IN YOUR HOME.
UPON OUR ARRIVAL, YOUR HOME WAS SEALED. YOU WERE ABSENT. WE HAVE BEEN TRACKING YOU SINCE. WE EXPECTED YOU TO BE JOURNEYING TO US, NOT HIDING IN A COMMODE.
THIS IS A MATTER OF ULTIMATE CONCERN TO OUR CULTURE, MR. JERUSALEM.
YOU KNOW OUR CULTURE. TOUCH IS NOT PERMITTED. THIS IS A SANE WAY TO LIVE IN THIS CITY, AN URGENT NECESSITY.
A TABOO WAS BROKEN IN OUR CULTURE, BY AN ACT OF FORCE, WITHOUT CONSENT.
YOU ARE GUILTY.

# "TRUTH, JUSTICE, ALL THAT"

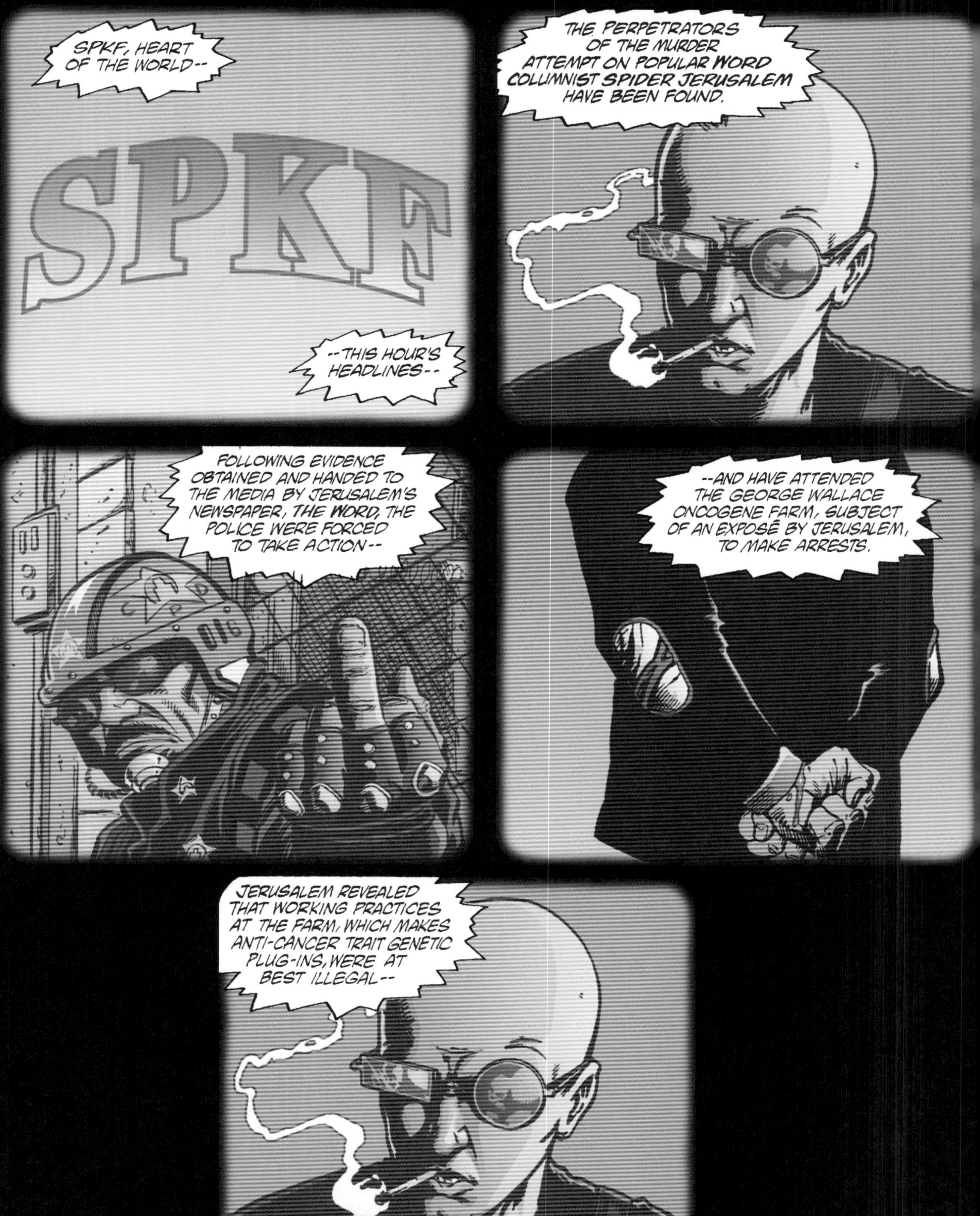
SPKF, HEART OF THE WORLD--
SPKF
--THIS HOUR'S HEADLINES--
THE PERPETRATORS OF THE MURDER ATTEMPT ON POPULAR WORD COLUMNIST SPIDER JERUSALEM HAVE BEEN FOUND.
FOLLOWING EVIDENCE OBTAINED AND HANDED TO THE MEDIA BY JERUSALEM'S NEWSPAPER, THE WORD, THE POLICE WERE FORCED TO TAKE ACTION--
--AND HAVE ATTENDED THE GEORGE WALLACE ONCOGENE FARM, SUBJECT OF AN EXPOSÉ BY JERUSALEM, TO MAKE ARRESTS.
JERUSALEM REVEALED THAT WORKING PRACTICES AT THE FARM, WHICH MAKES ANTI-CANCER TRAIT GENETIC PLUG-INS, WERE AT BEST ILLEGAL--

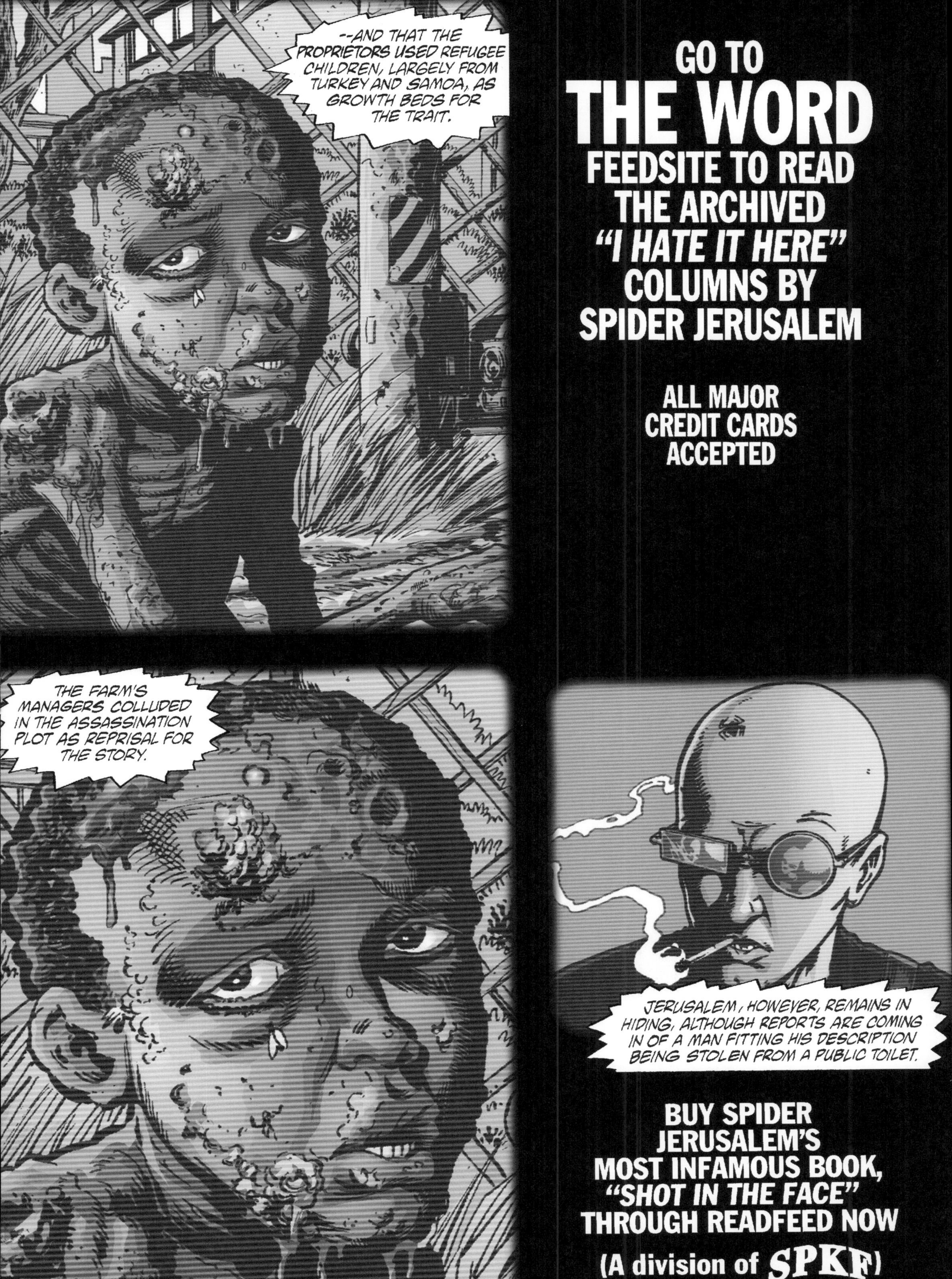
--AND THAT THE PROPRIETORS USED REFUGEE CHILDREN, LARGELY FROM TURKEY AND SAMOA, AS GROWTH BEDS FOR THE TRAIT.
GO TO THE WORD FEEDSITE TO READ THE ARCHIVED "I HATE IT HERE" COLUMNS BY SPIDER JERUSALEM
ALL MAJOR CREDIT CARDS ACCEPTED
THE FARM'S MANAGERS COLLUDED IN THE ASSASSINATION PLOT AS REPRISAL FOR THE STORY.
JERUSALEM, HOWEVER, REMAINS IN HIDING, ALTHOUGH REPORTS ARE COMING IN OF A MAN FITTING HIS DESCRIPTION BEING STOLEN FROM A PUBLIC TOILET.
BUY SPIDER JERUSALEM'S MOST INFAMOUS BOOK, "SHOT IN THE FACE" THROUGH READFEED NOW
(A division of SPKF)

# THE TRUTH ABOUT CATS AND DOGS

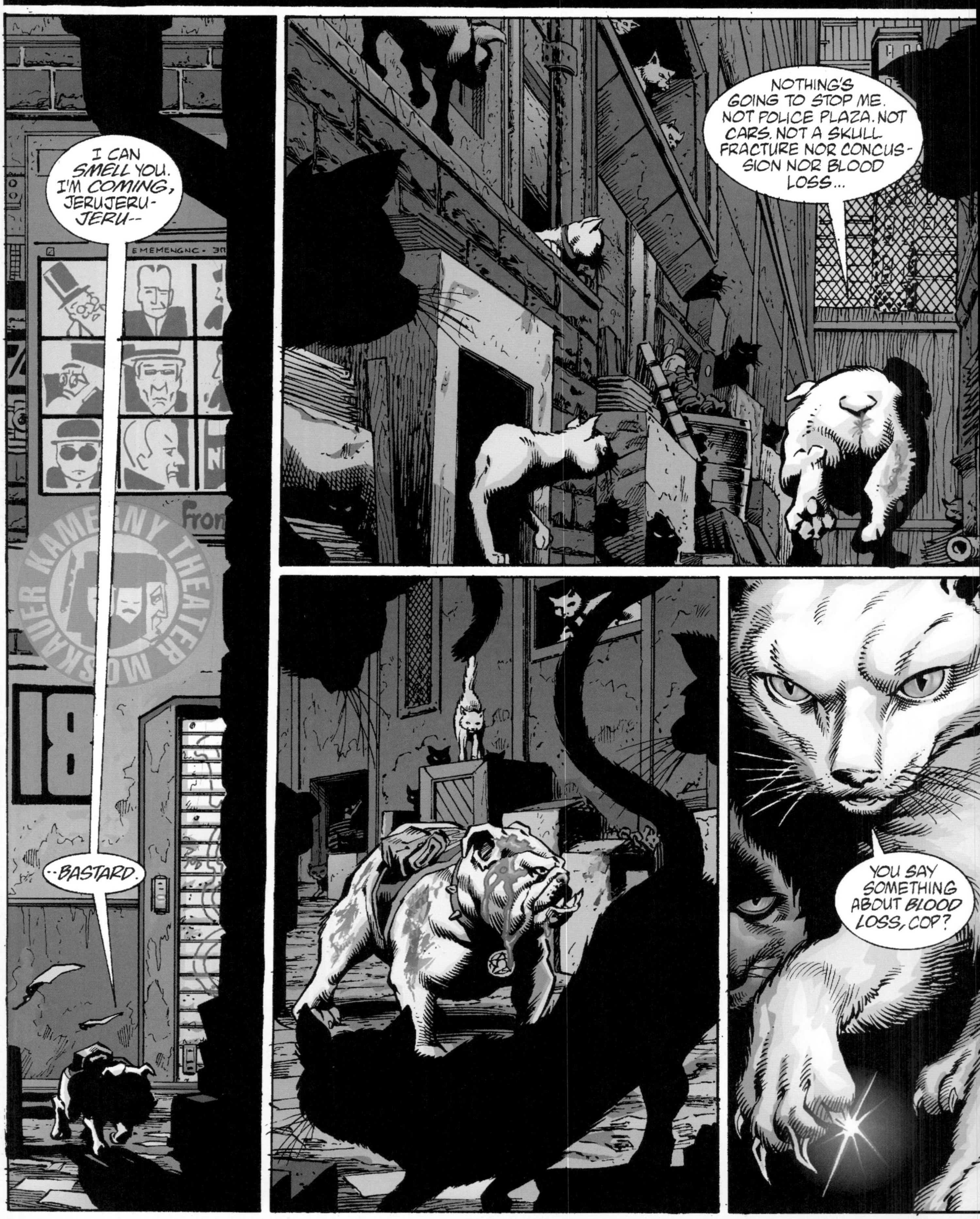

I CAN SMELL YOU. I'M COMING, JERUJERU-JERU--
MOSKAUER KAMERNY THEATER
--BASTARD.
NOTHING'S GOING TO STOP ME. NOT POLICE PLAZA. NOT CARS. NOT A SKULL FRACTURE NOR CONCUSSION NOR BLOOD LOSS...
YOU SAY SOMETHING ABOUT BLOOD LOSS, COP?

# on the waterfront

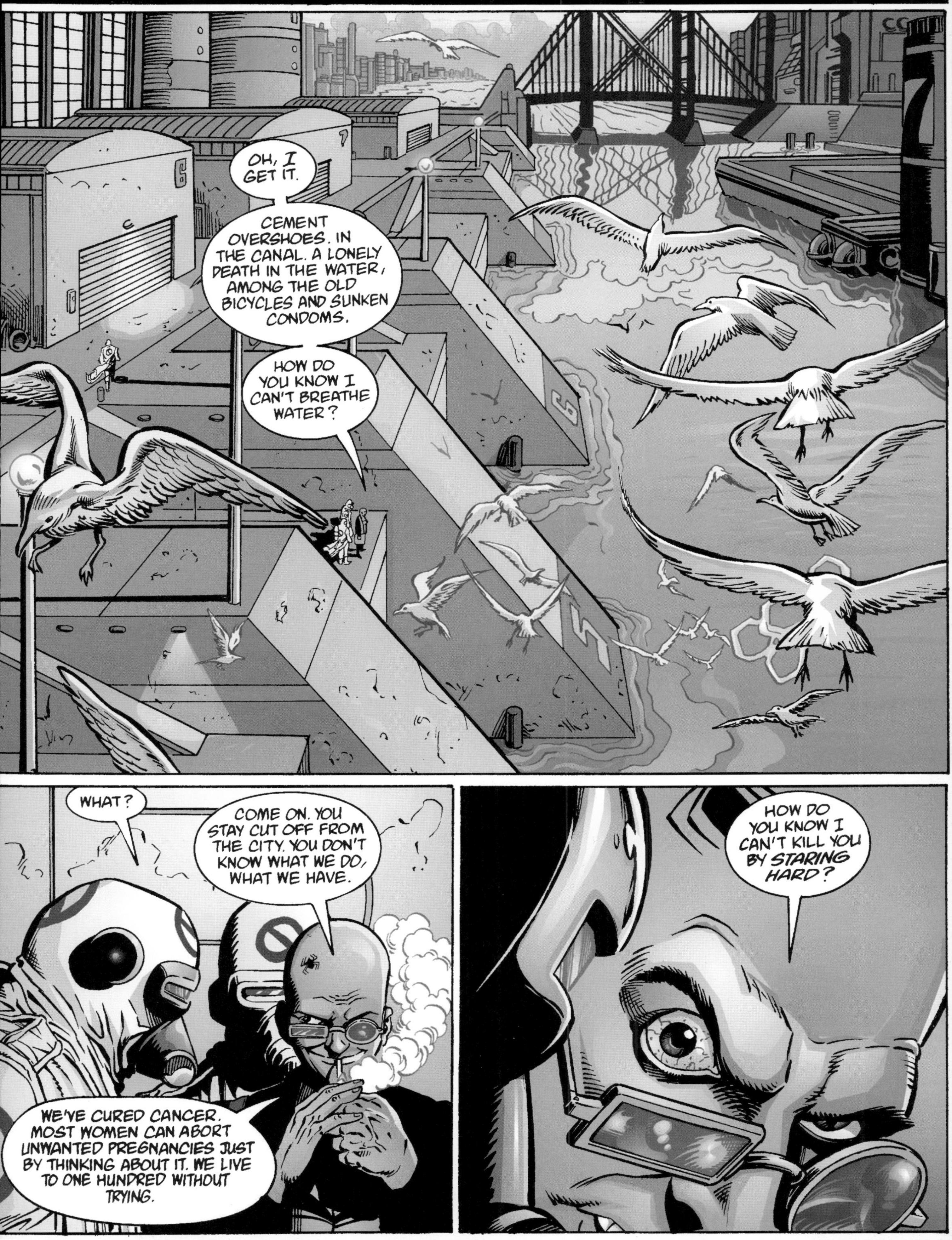
OH, I GET IT.
CEMENT OVERSHOES. IN THE CANAL. A LONELY DEATH IN THE WATER, AMONG THE OLD BICYCLES AND SUNKEN CONDOMS.
HOW DO YOU KNOW I CAN'T BREATHE WATER?
WHAT?
COME ON. YOU STAY CUT OFF FROM THE CITY. YOU DON'T KNOW WHAT WE DO, WHAT WE HAVE.
WE'VE CURED CANCER. MOST WOMEN CAN ABORT UNWANTED PREGNANCIES JUST BY THINKING ABOUT IT. WE LIVE TO ONE HUNDRED WITHOUT TRYING.
HOW DO YOU KNOW I CAN'T KILL YOU BY STARING HARD?

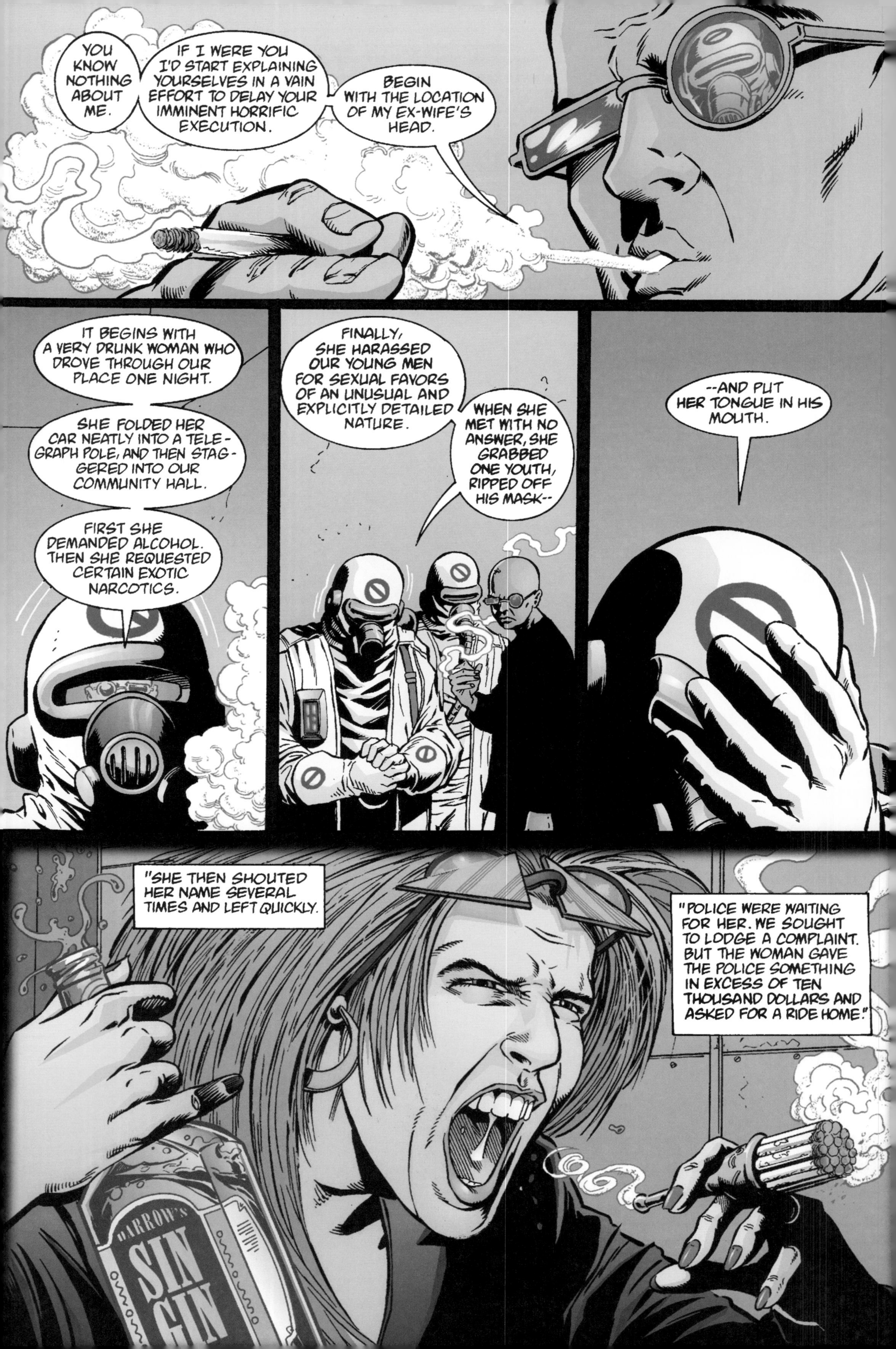
YOU KNOW NOTHING ABOUT ME.
IF I WERE YOU I'D START EXPLAINING YOURSELVES IN A VAIN EFFORT TO DELAY YOUR IMMINENT HORRIFIC EXECUTION.
BEGIN WITH THE LOCATION OF MY EX-WIFE'S HEAD.
IT BEGINS WITH A VERY DRUNK WOMAN WHO DROVE THROUGH OUR PLACE ONE NIGHT.
SHE FOLDED HER CAR NEATLY INTO A TELEGRAPH POLE, AND THEN STAGGERED INTO OUR COMMUNITY HALL.
FIRST SHE DEMANDED ALCOHOL. THEN SHE REQUESTED CERTAIN EXOTIC NARCOTICS.
FINALLY, SHE HARASSED OUR YOUNG MEN FOR SEXUAL FAVORS OF AN UNUSUAL AND EXPLICITLY DETAILED NATURE.
WHEN SHE MET WITH NO ANSWER, SHE GRABBED ONE YOUTH, RIPPED OFF HIS MASK--
--AND PUT HER TONGUE IN HIS MOUTH.
"SHE THEN SHOUTED HER NAME SEVERAL TIMES AND LEFT QUICKLY.
"POLICE WERE WAITING FOR HER. WE SOUGHT TO LODGE A COMPLAINT. BUT THE WOMAN GAVE THE POLICE SOMETHING IN EXCESS OF TEN THOUSAND DOLLARS AND ASKED FOR A RIDE HOME."
DARROW'S SIN GIN

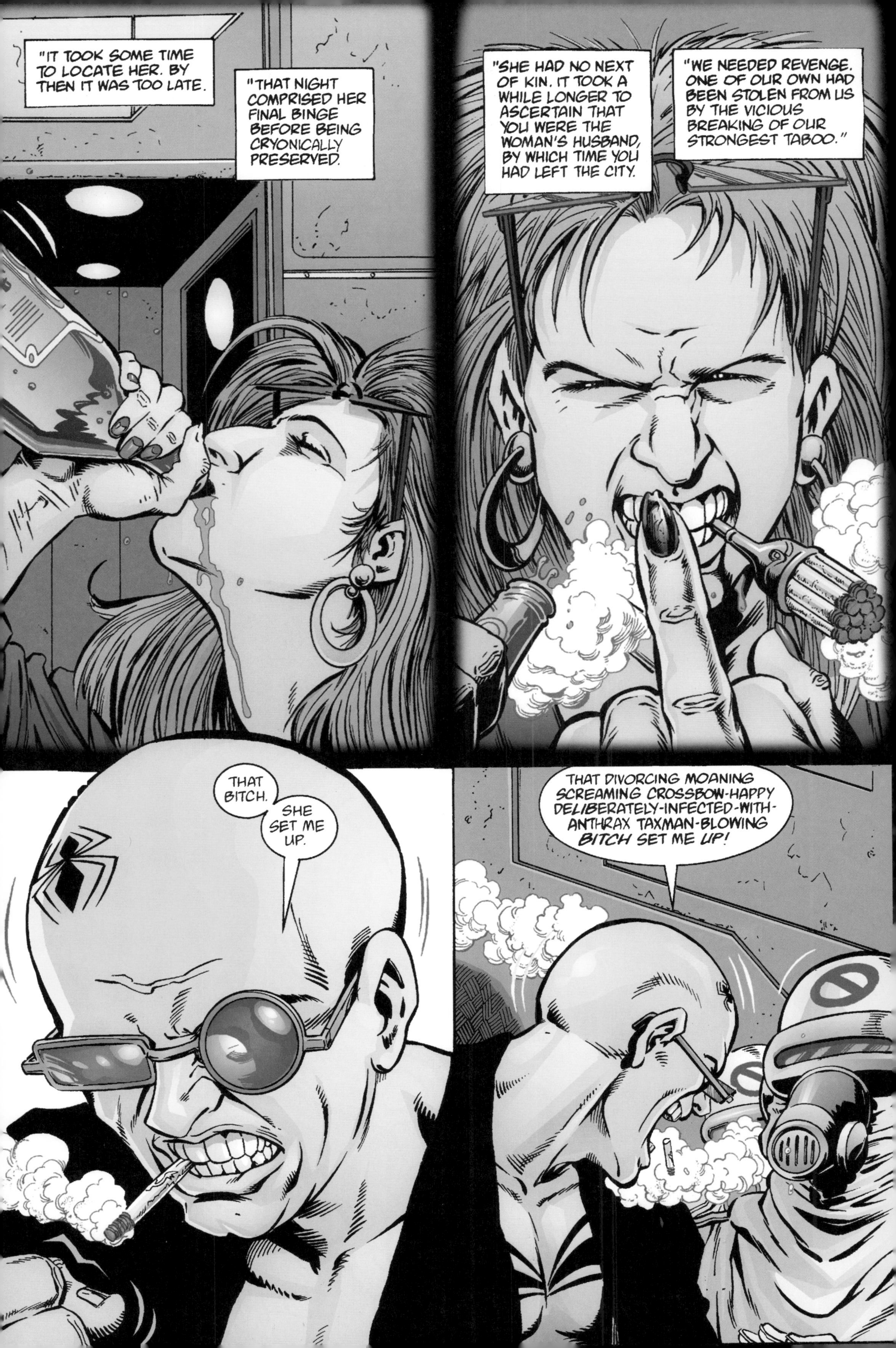
"IT TOOK SOME TIME TO LOCATE HER. BY THEN IT WAS TOO LATE.
"THAT NIGHT COMPRISED HER FINAL BINGE BEFORE BEING CRYONICALLY PRESERVED.
"SHE HAD NO NEXT OF KIN. IT TOOK A WHILE LONGER TO ASCERTAIN THAT YOU WERE THE WOMAN'S HUSBAND, BY WHICH TIME YOU HAD LEFT THE CITY.
"WE NEEDED REVENGE. ONE OF OUR OWN HAD BEEN STOLEN FROM US BY THE VICIOUS BREAKING OF OUR STRONGEST TABOO."
THAT BITCH.
SHE SET ME UP.
THAT DIVORCING MOANING SCREAMING CROSSBOW-HAPPY DELIBERATELY-INFECTED-WITH-ANTHRAX TAXMAN-BLOWING BITCH SET ME UP!

# God/Dog

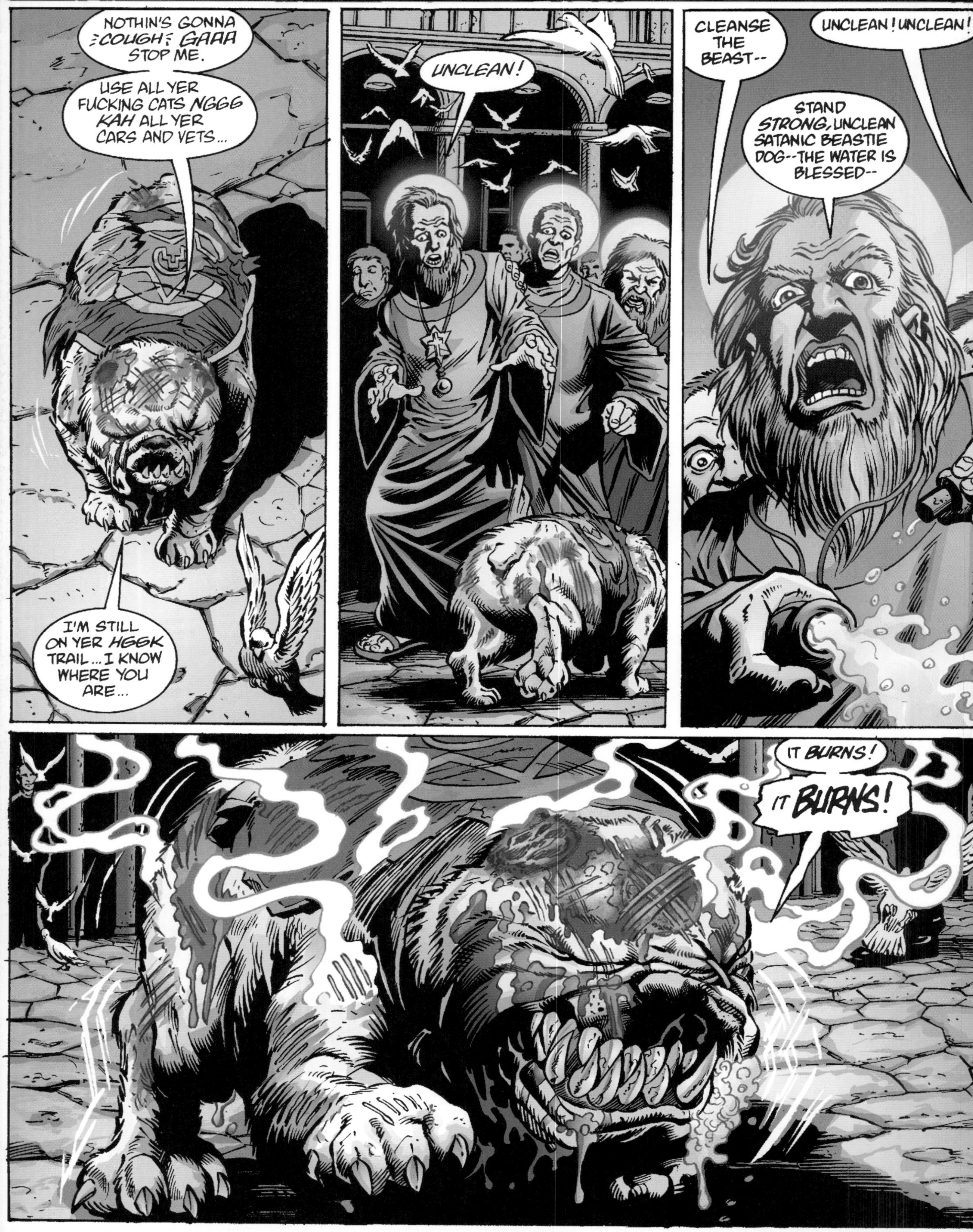
NOTHIN'S GONNA
COUGH GAAA
STOP ME.
USE ALL YER FUCKING CATS NGGG KAH ALL YER CARS AND VETS...
I'M STILL ON YER HGGK TRAIL... I KNOW WHERE YOU ARE...
UNCLEAN!
CLEANSE THE BEAST--
UNCLEAN! UNCLEAN!
STAND STRONG, UNCLEAN SATANIC BEASTIE DOG--THE WATER IS BLESSED--
IT BURNS!
IT BURNS!

# spider explains it all

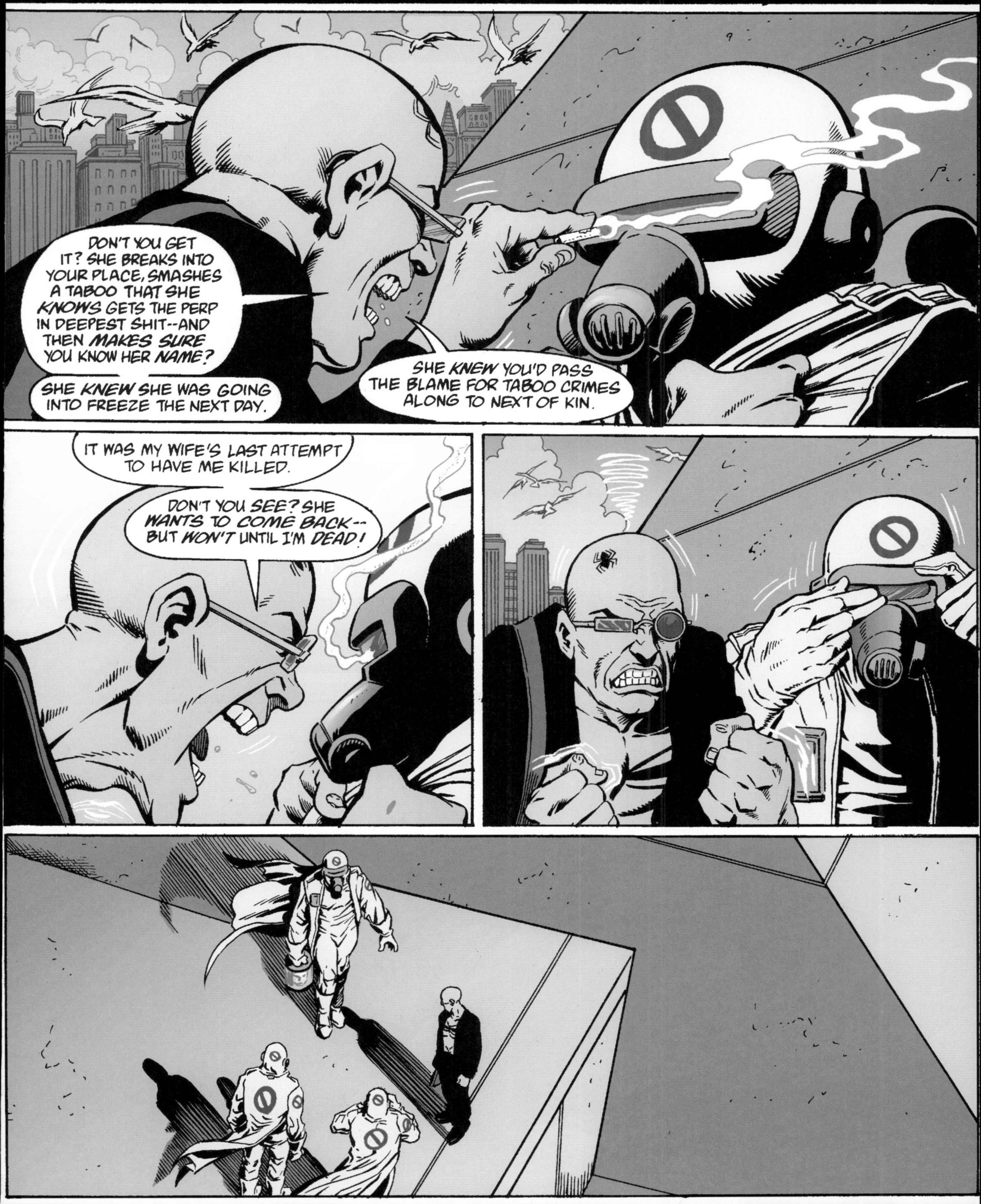
DON'T YOU GET IT? SHE BREAKS INTO YOUR PLACE, SMASHES A TABOO THAT SHE KNOWS GETS THE PERP IN DEEPEST SHIT--AND THEN MAKES SURE YOU KNOW HER NAME?
SHE KNEW SHE WAS GOING INTO FREEZE THE NEXT DAY.
SHE KNEW YOU'D PASS THE BLAME FOR TABOO CRIMES ALONG TO NEXT OF KIN.
IT WAS MY WIFE'S LAST ATTEMPT TO HAVE ME KILLED.
DON'T YOU SEE? SHE WANTS TO COME BACK-- BUT WON'T UNTIL I'M DEAD!

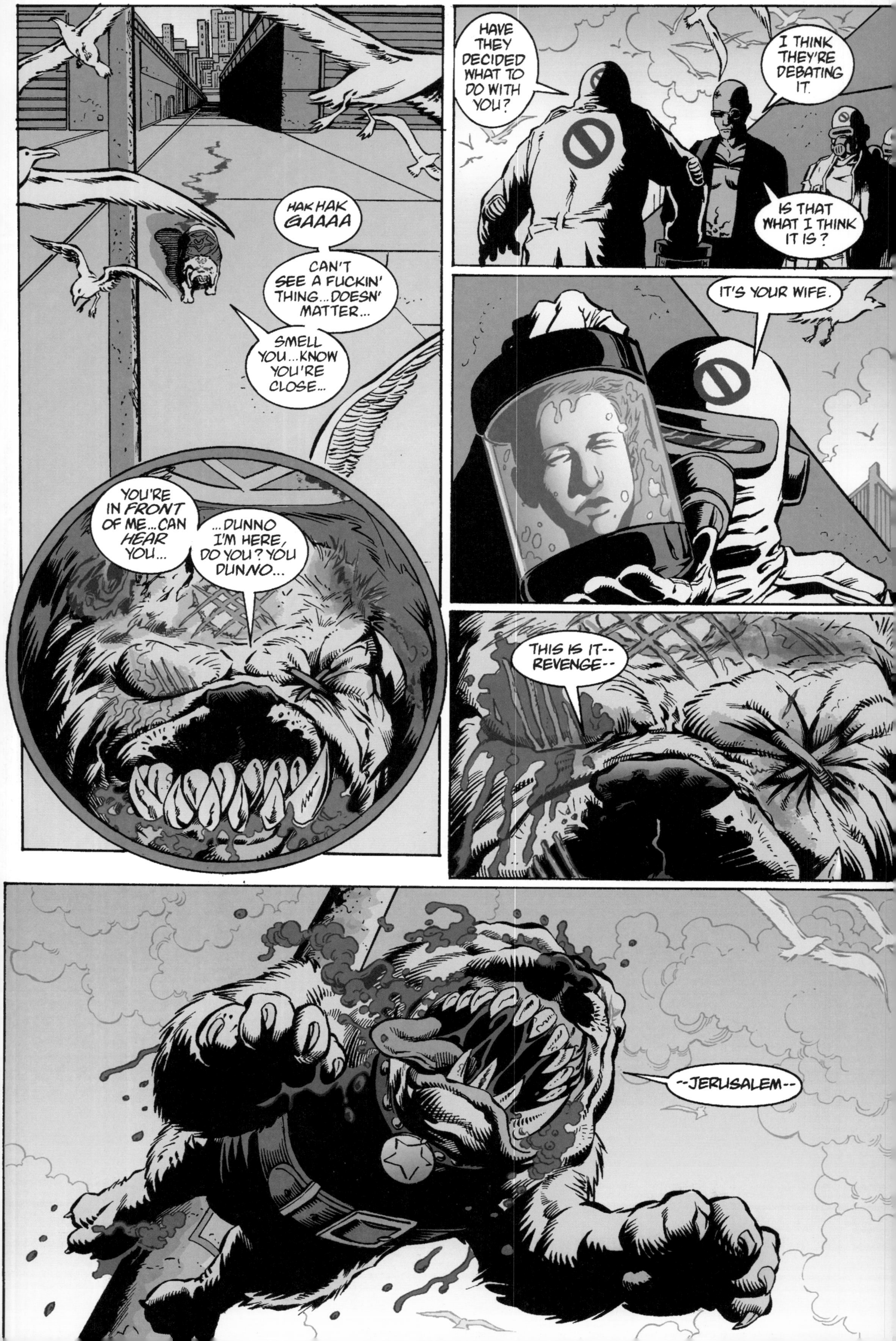
HAK HAK GAAAA
CAN'T SEE A FUCKIN' THING... DOESN' MATTER...
SMELL YOU... KNOW YOU'RE CLOSE...
YOU'RE IN FRONT OF ME... CAN HEAR YOU...
...DUNNO I'M HERE, DO YOU? YOU DUNNO...
HAVE THEY DECIDED WHAT TO DO WITH YOU?
I THINK THEY'RE DEBATING IT.
IS THAT WHAT I THINK IT IS?
IT'S YOUR WIFE.
THIS IS IT-- REVENGE--
--JERUSALEM--

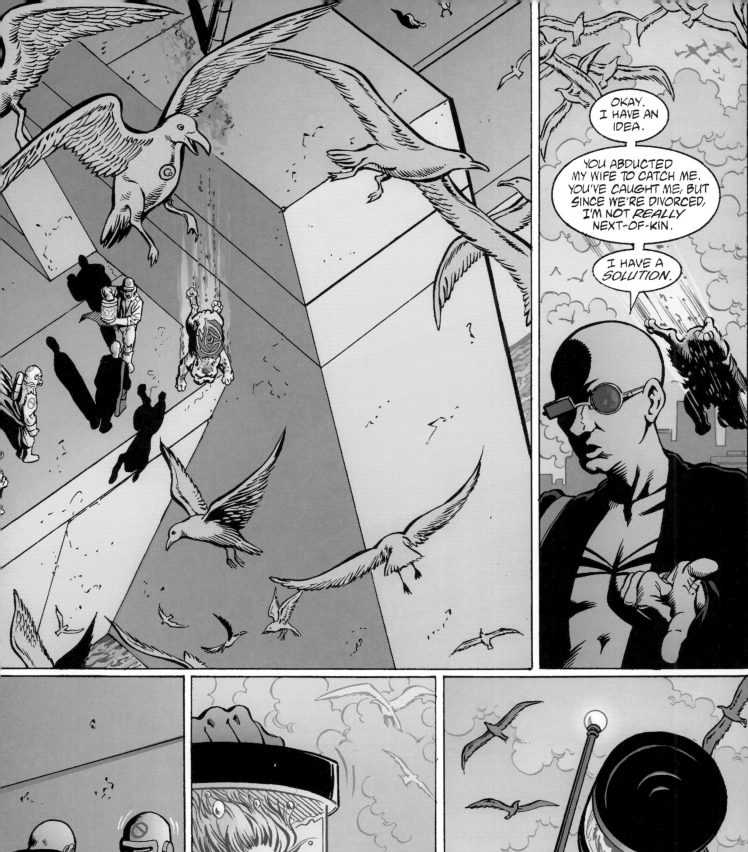

OKAY. I HAVE AN IDEA.

YOU ABDUCTED MY WIFE TO CATCH ME. YOU'VE CAUGHT ME, BUT SINCE WE'RE DIVORCED, I'M NOT *REALLY* NEXT-OF-KIN.

I HAVE A *SOLUTION.*

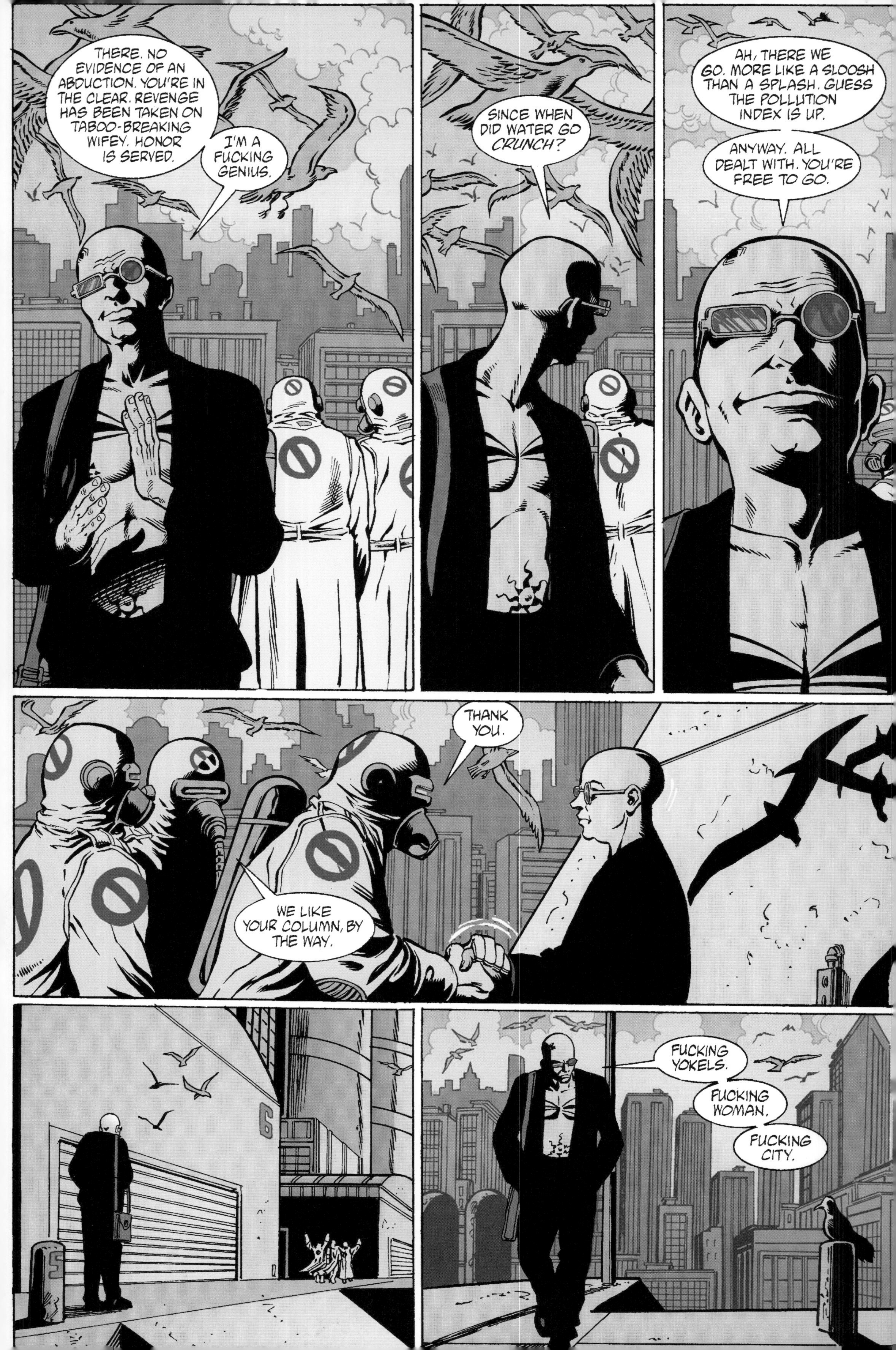
THERE. NO EVIDENCE OF AN ABDUCTION. YOU'RE IN THE CLEAR. REVENGE HAS BEEN TAKEN ON TABOO-BREAKING WIFEY. HONOR IS SERVED.
I'M A FUCKING GENIUS.
SINCE WHEN DID WATER GO *CRUNCH?*
AH, THERE WE GO. MORE LIKE A SLOOSH THAN A SPLASH. GUESS THE POLLUTION INDEX IS UP.
ANYWAY. ALL DEALT WITH. YOU'RE FREE TO GO.
THANK YOU.
WE LIKE YOUR COLUMN, BY THE WAY.
FUCKING YOKELS.
FUCKING WOMAN.
FUCKING CITY.

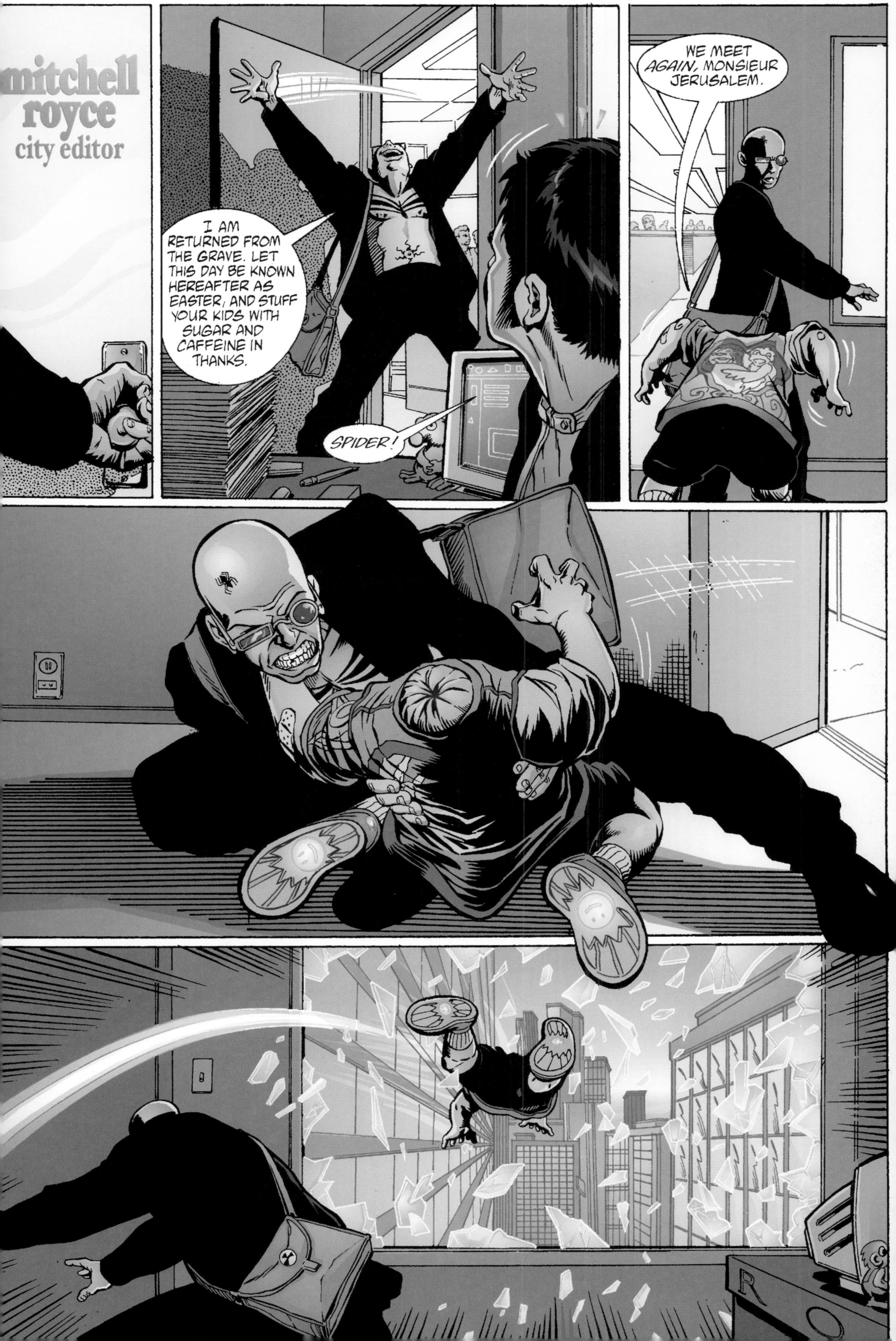
mitchell royce city editor
I AM RETURNED FROM THE GRAVE. LET THIS DAY BE KNOWN HEREAFTER AS EASTER, AND STUFF YOUR KIDS WITH SUGAR AND CAFFEINE IN THANKS.
SPIDER!
WE MEET AGAIN, MONSIEUR JERUSALEM.

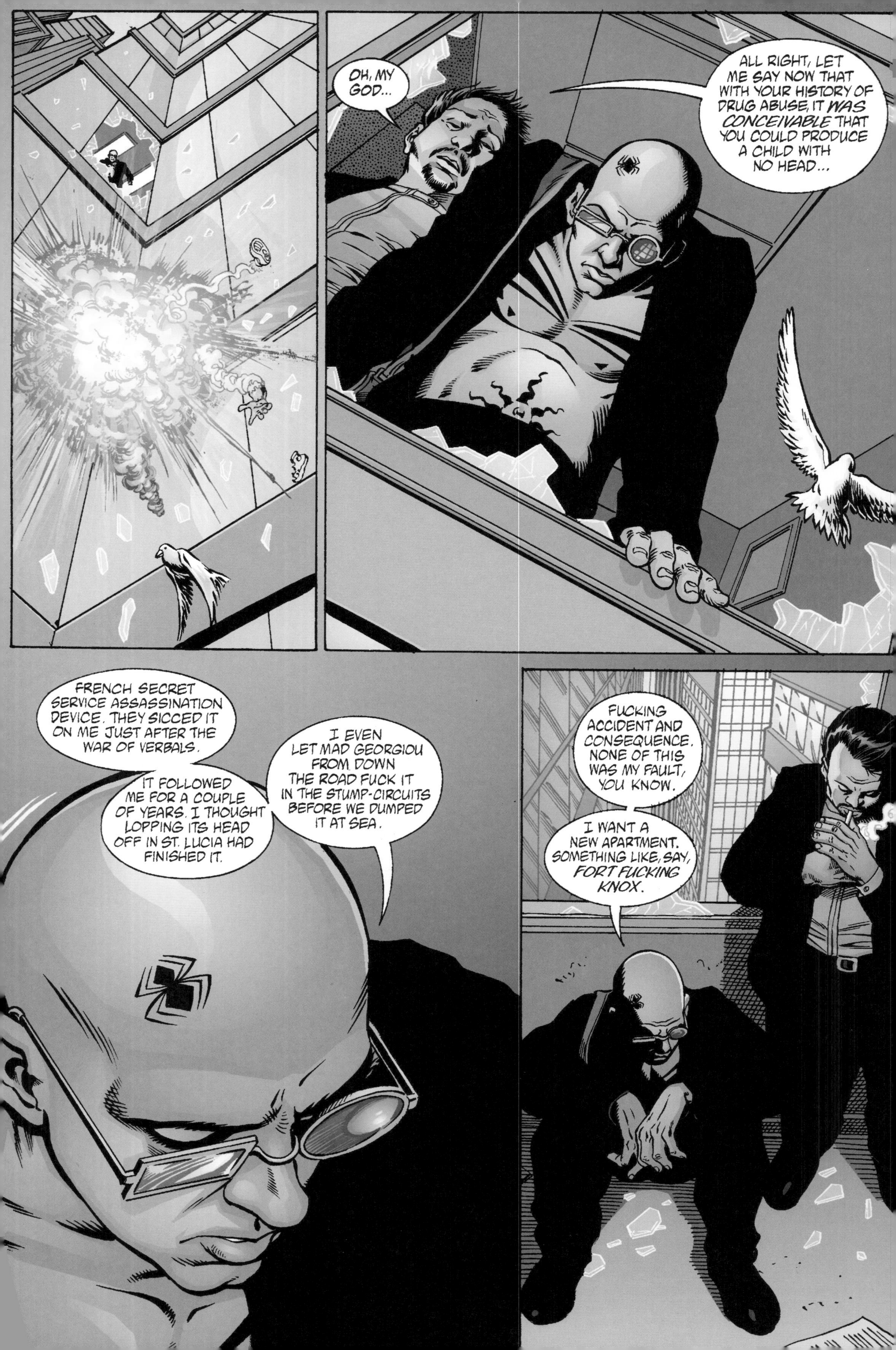
OH, MY GOD...
ALL RIGHT, LET ME SAY NOW THAT WITH YOUR HISTORY OF DRUG ABUSE, IT *WAS CONCEIVABLE* THAT YOU COULD PRODUCE A CHILD WITH NO HEAD...
FRENCH SECRET SERVICE ASSASSINATION DEVICE. THEY SICCED IT ON ME JUST AFTER THE WAR OF VERBALS.
IT FOLLOWED ME FOR A COUPLE OF YEARS. I THOUGHT LOPPING ITS HEAD OFF IN ST. LUCIA HAD FINISHED IT.
I EVEN LET MAD GEORGIOU FROM DOWN THE ROAD FUCK IT IN THE STUMP-CIRCUITS BEFORE WE DUMPED IT AT SEA.
FUCKING ACCIDENT AND CONSEQUENCE. NONE OF THIS WAS MY FAULT, YOU KNOW.
I WANT A NEW APARTMENT. SOMETHING LIKE, SAY, *FORT FUCKING KNOX*.

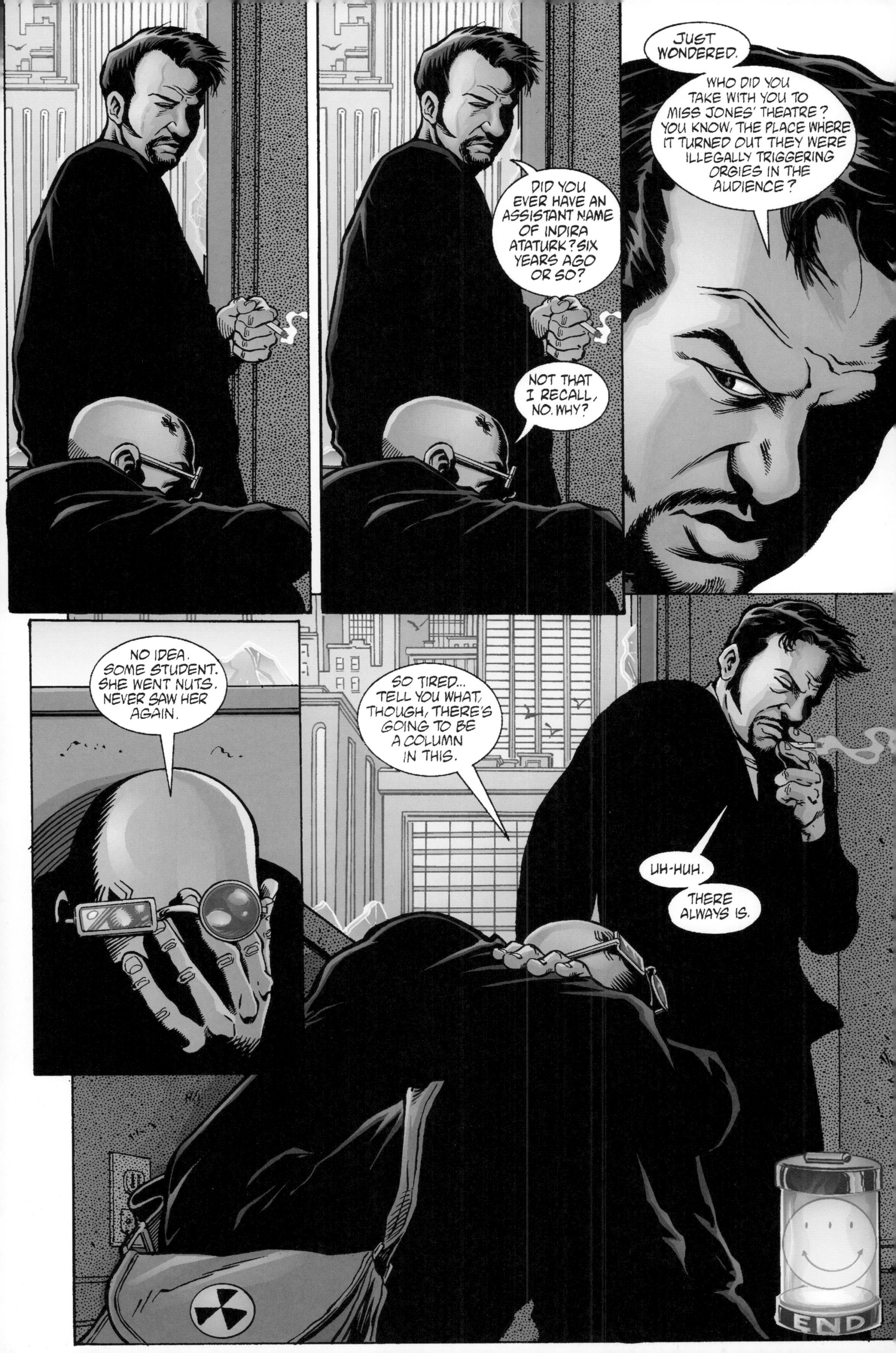
DID YOU EVER HAVE AN ASSISTANT NAME OF INDIRA ATATURK? SIX YEARS AGO OR SO?
NOT THAT I RECALL, NO. WHY?
JUST WONDERED.
WHO DID YOU TAKE WITH YOU TO MISS JONES' THEATRE? YOU KNOW, THE PLACE WHERE IT TURNED OUT THEY WERE ILLEGALLY TRIGGERING ORGIES IN THE AUDIENCE?
NO IDEA. SOME STUDENT. SHE WENT NUTS. NEVER SAW HER AGAIN.
SO TIRED... TELL YOU WHAT, THOUGH, THERE'S GOING TO BE A COLUMN IN THIS.
UH-HUH.
THERE ALWAYS IS.
END

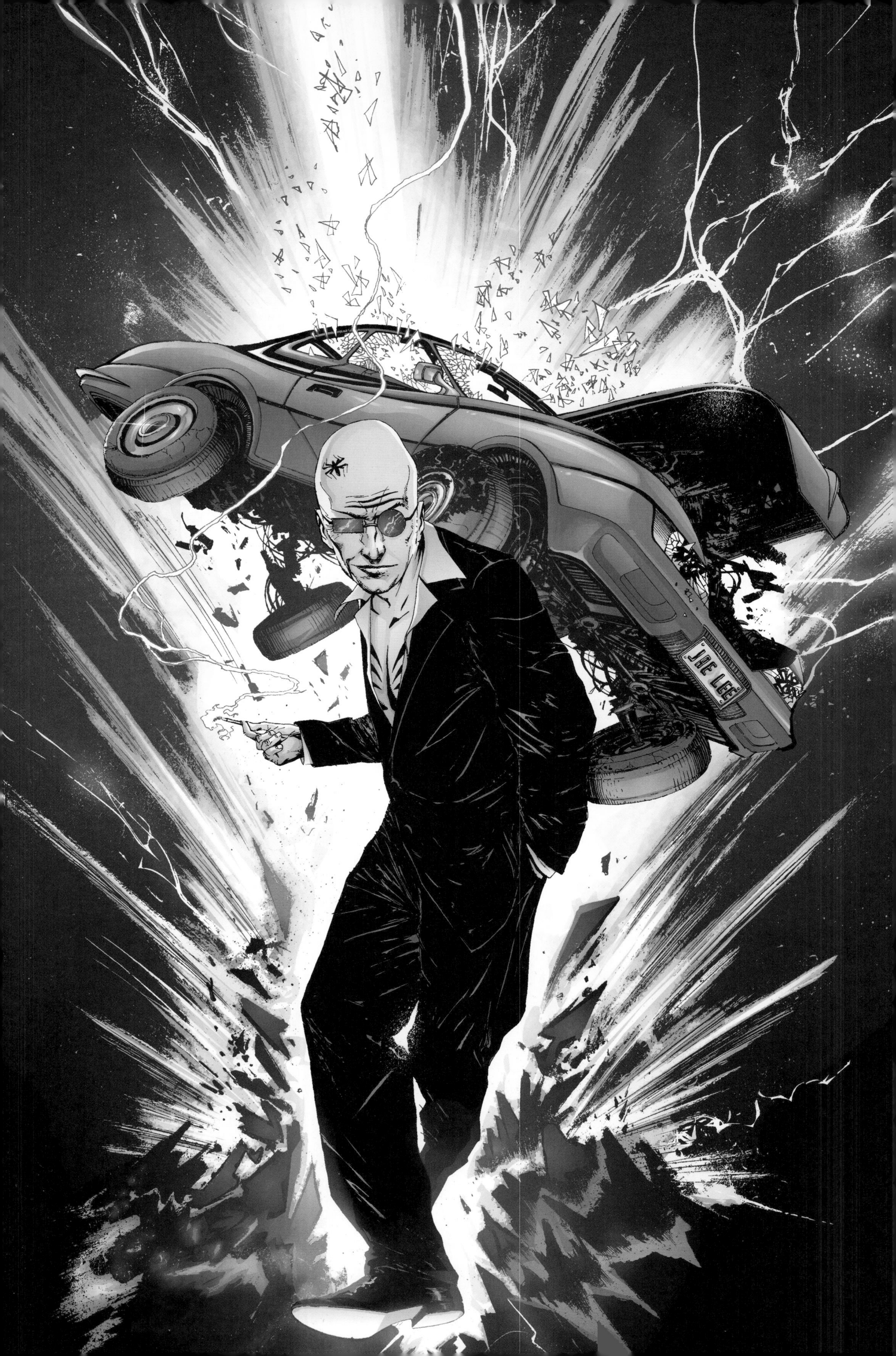
JAE LEE

WARREN ELLIS writes & DARICK ROBERTSON pencils

# year of the bastard

clem robins, letterer nathan eyring, color & separations RODNEY RAMOS, inker cliff chiang, ass't ed. stuart moore, editor

TRANSMETROPOLITAN created by WARREN ELLIS and DARICK ROBERTSON

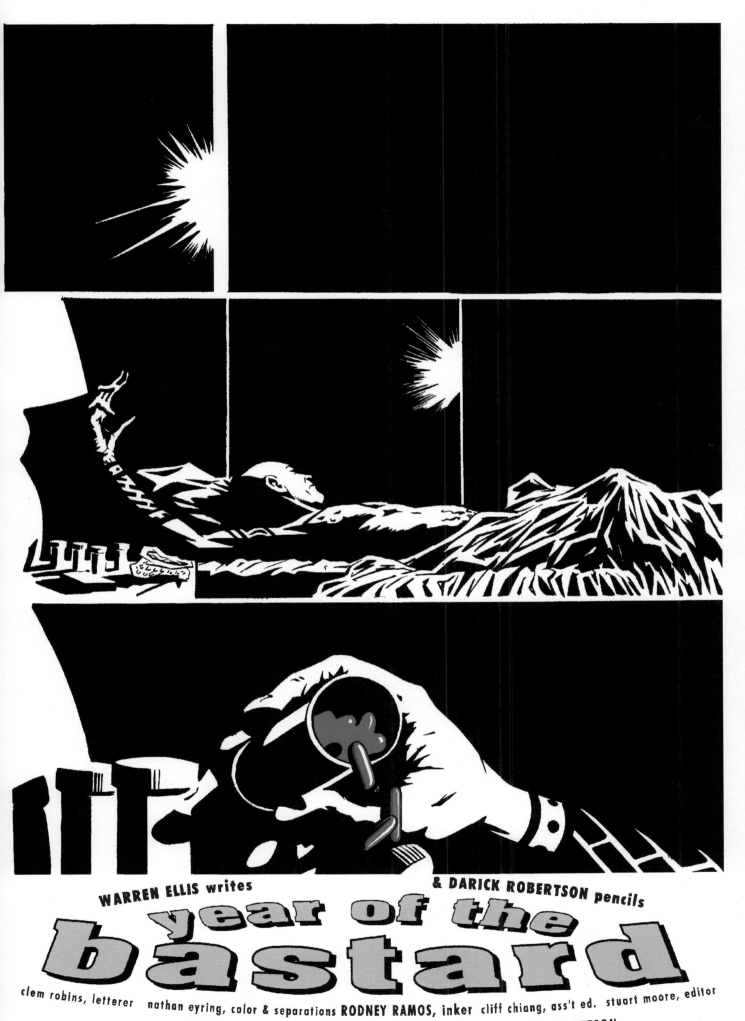

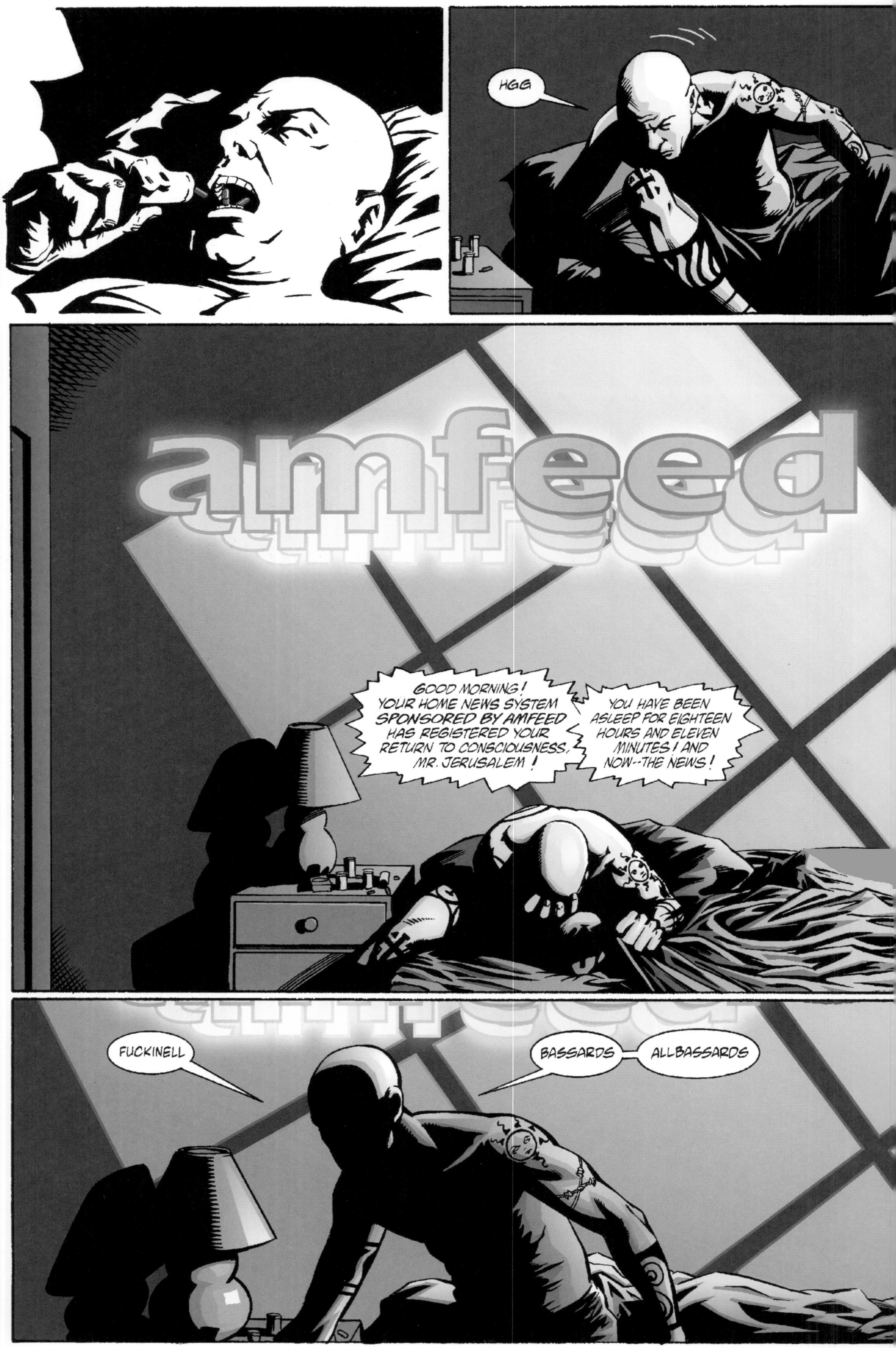
HGG
amfeed
GOOD MORNING! YOUR HOME NEWS SYSTEM SPONSORED BY AMFEED HAS REGISTERED YOUR RETURN TO CONSCIOUSNESS, MR. JERUSALEM!
YOU HAVE BEEN ASLEEP FOR EIGHTEEN HOURS AND ELEVEN MINUTES! AND NOW--THE NEWS!
FUCKINELL
BASSARDS
ALLBASSARDS

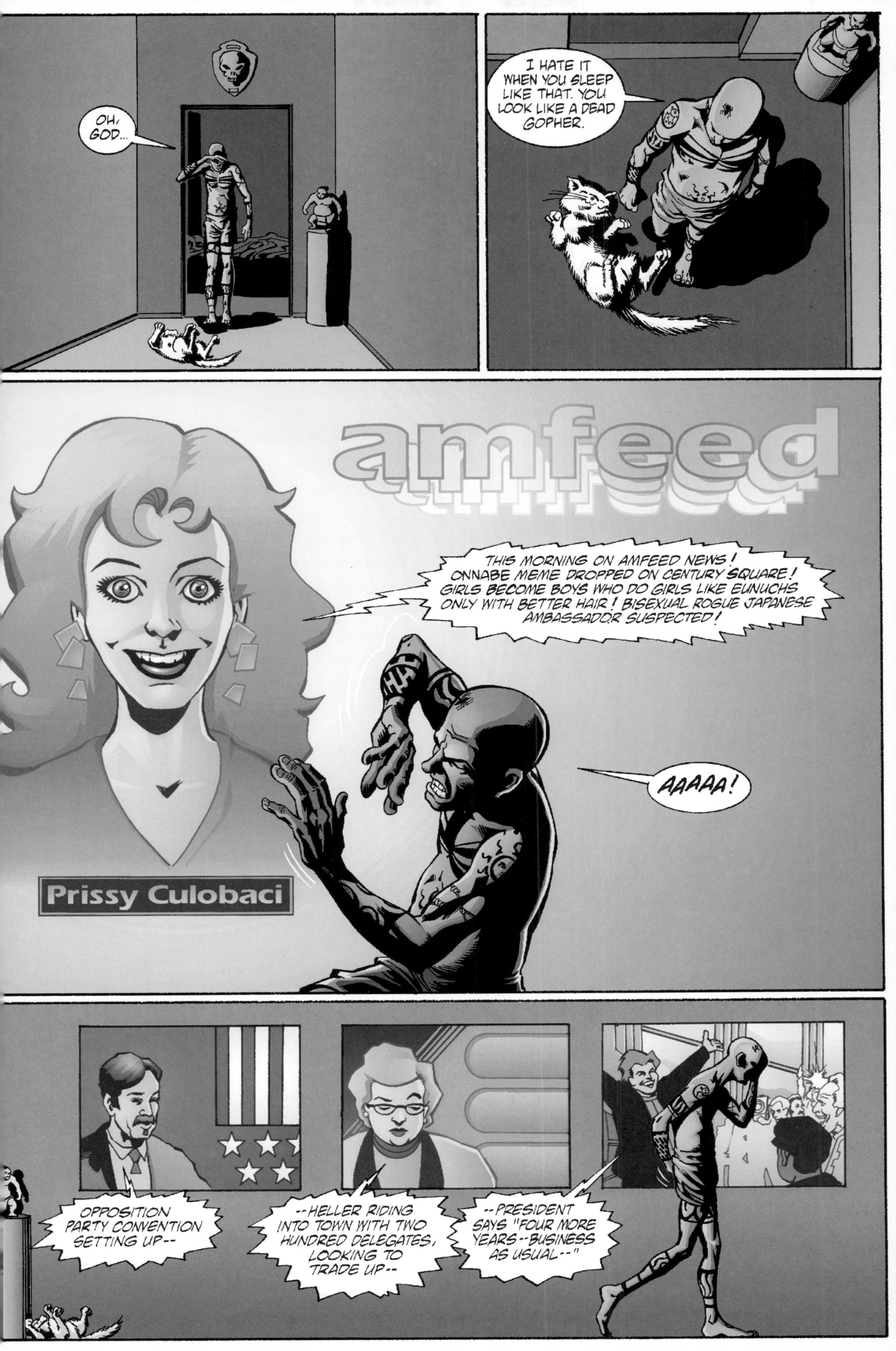
OH, GOD...
I HATE IT WHEN YOU SLEEP LIKE THAT. YOU LOOK LIKE A DEAD GOPHER.
amfeed
THIS MORNING ON AMFEED NEWS! ONNABE MEME DROPPED ON CENTURY SQUARE! GIRLS BECOME BOYS WHO DO GIRLS LIKE EUNUCHS ONLY WITH BETTER HAIR! BISEXUAL ROGUE JAPANESE AMBASSADOR SUSPECTED!
Prissy Culobaci
AAAAA!
OPPOSITION PARTY CONVENTION SETTING UP--
--HELLER RIDING INTO TOWN WITH TWO HUNDRED DELEGATES, LOOKING TO TRADE UP--
--PRESIDENT SAYS "FOUR MORE YEARS--BUSINESS AS USUAL--"

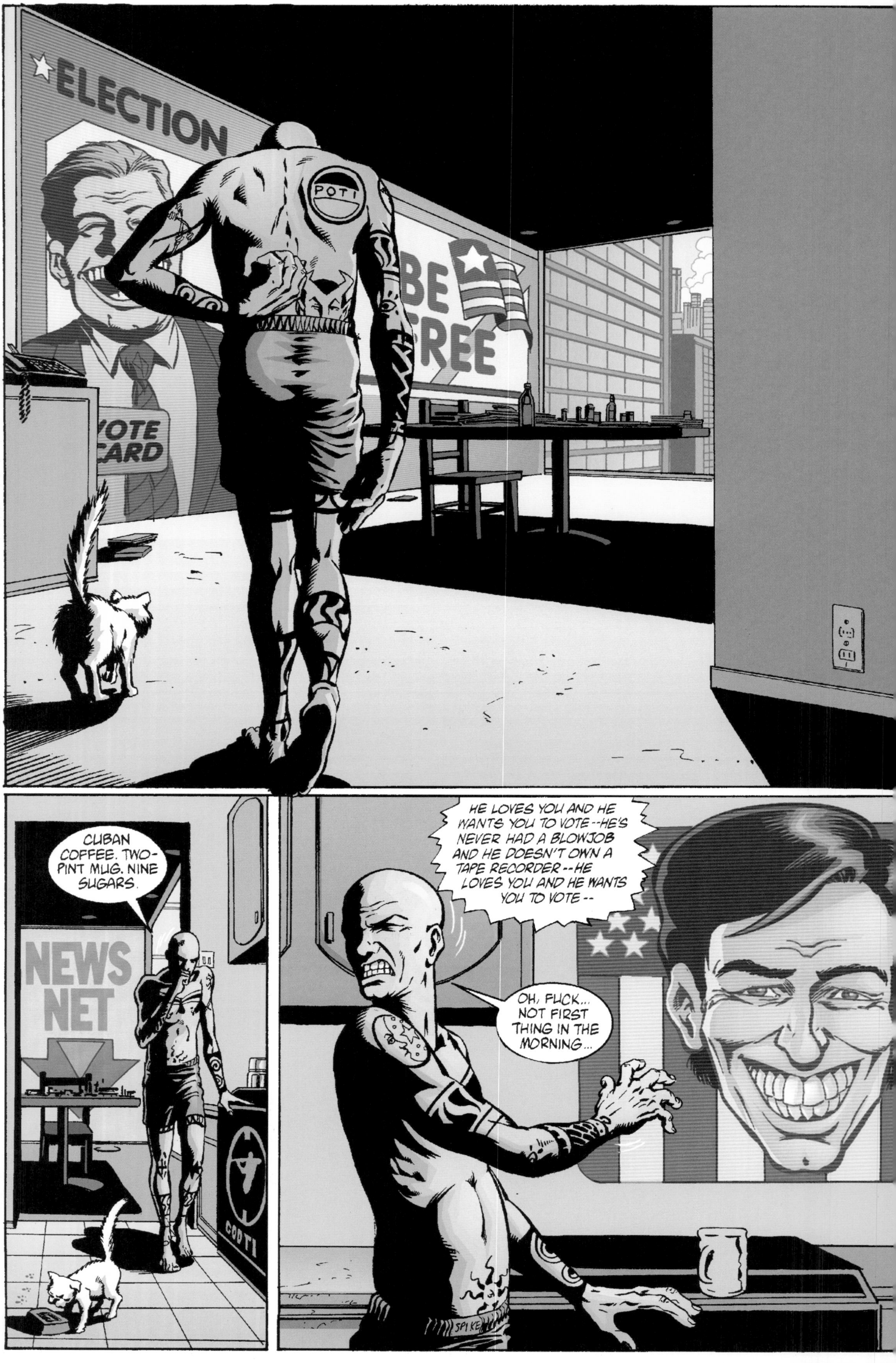
ELECTION
POTI
BE FREE
VOTE CARD
CUBAN COFFEE. TWO-PINT MUG. NINE SUGARS.
NEWS NET
HE LOVES YOU AND HE WANTS YOU TO VOTE--HE'S NEVER HAD A BLOWJOB AND HE DOESN'T OWN A TAPE RECORDER--HE LOVES YOU AND HE WANTS YOU TO VOTE--
OH, FUCK... NOT FIRST THING IN THE MORNING...
SPIKE

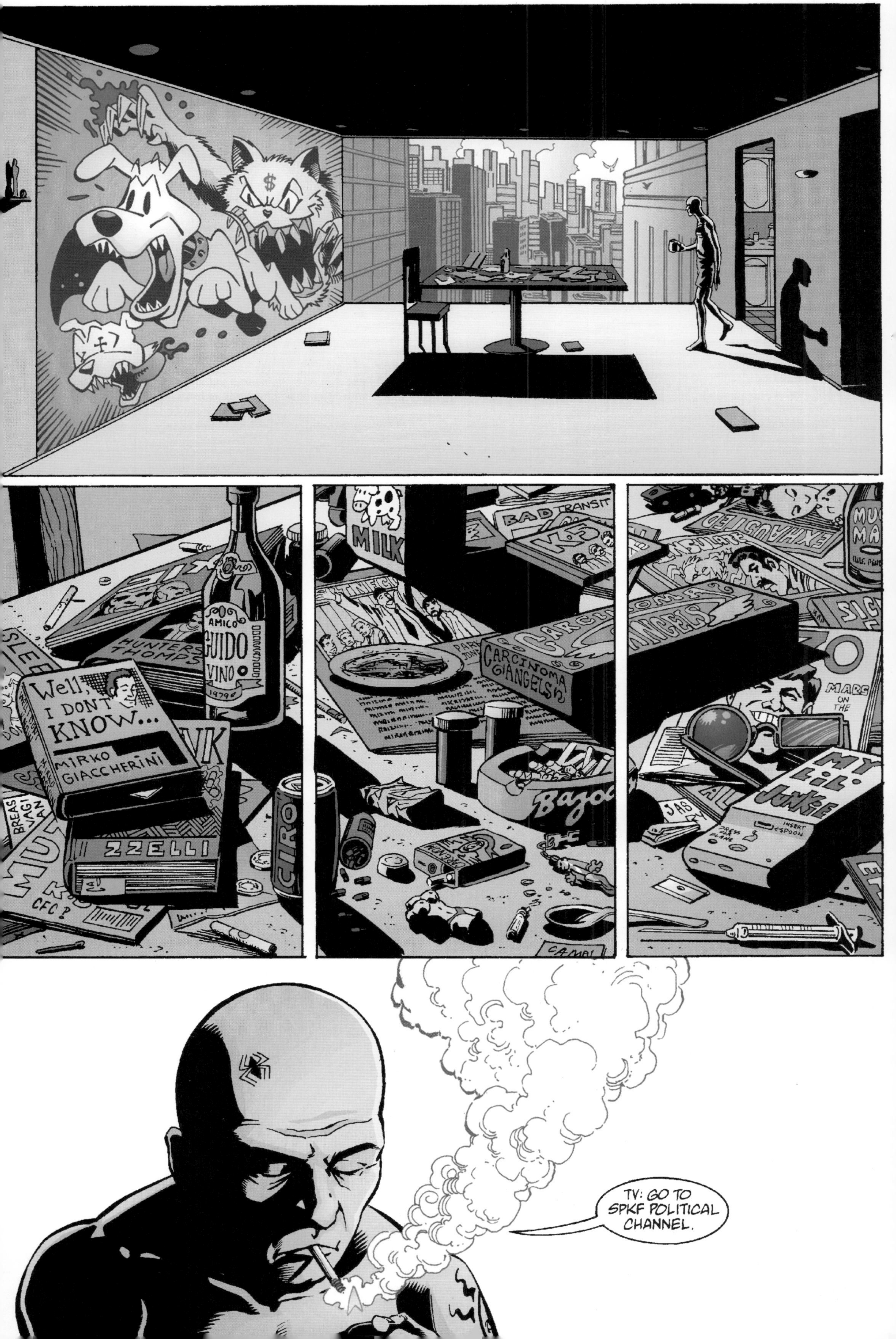

HUNTERS THOMPS
AMICO GUIDO VINO
Well, I DON'T KNOW...
MIRKO GIACCHERINI
ZZELLI
CIRO
MILK
BAD TRANSIT
CARCINOMA ANGELS
CARCINOMA ANGELS
EXHAUSTED
MY LIL JUNKIE
TV: GO TO SPKF POLITICAL CHANNEL.

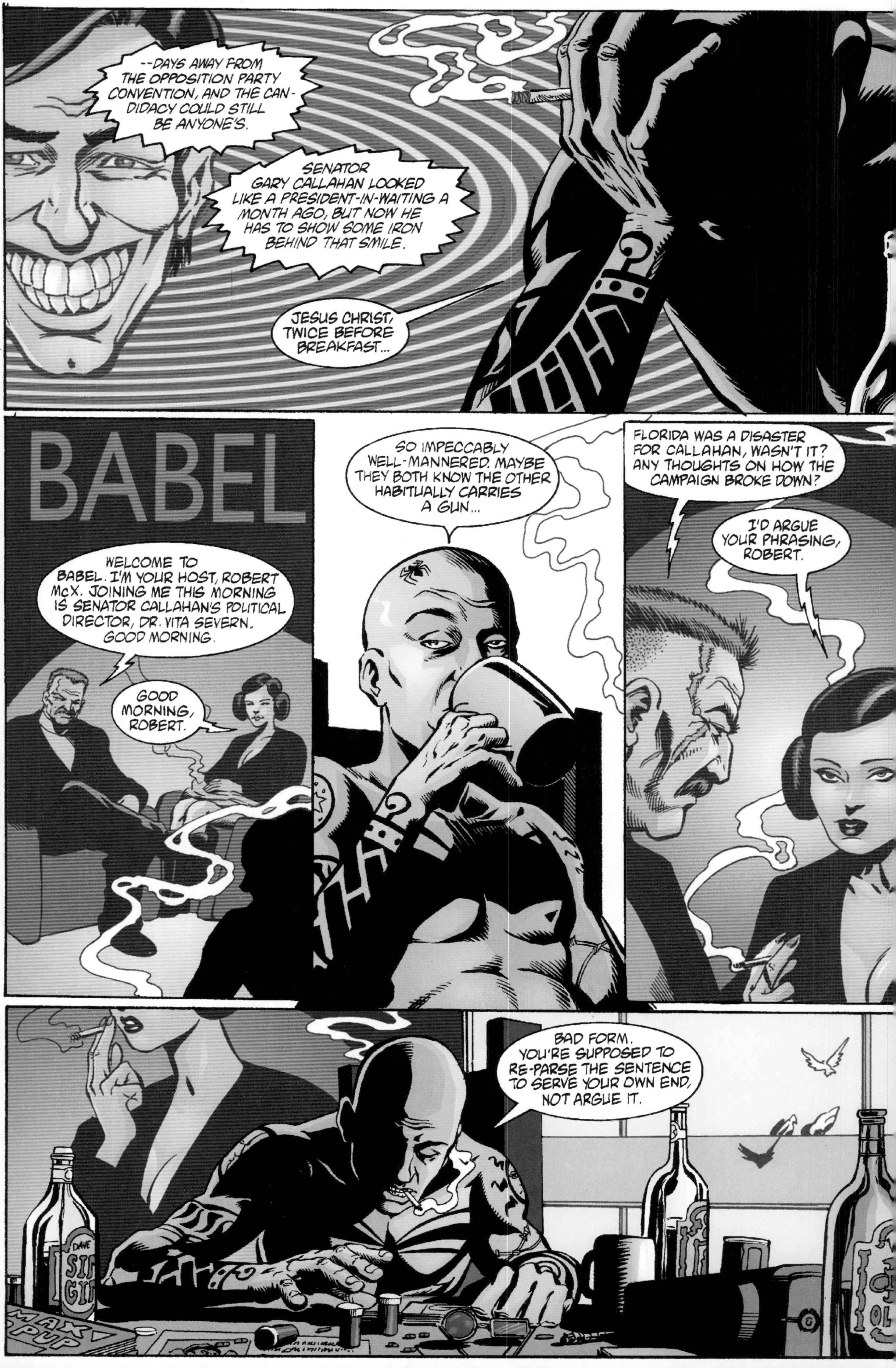
--DAYS AWAY FROM THE OPPOSITION PARTY CONVENTION, AND THE CANDIDACY COULD STILL BE ANYONE'S.
SENATOR GARY CALLAHAN LOOKED LIKE A PRESIDENT-IN-WAITING A MONTH AGO, BUT NOW HE HAS TO SHOW SOME IRON BEHIND THAT SMILE.
JESUS CHRIST, TWICE BEFORE BREAKFAST...
BABEL
WELCOME TO BABEL. I'M YOUR HOST, ROBERT McX. JOINING ME THIS MORNING IS SENATOR CALLAHAN'S POLITICAL DIRECTOR, DR. VITA SEVERN. GOOD MORNING.
GOOD MORNING, ROBERT.
SO IMPECCABLY WELL-MANNERED. MAYBE THEY BOTH KNOW THE OTHER HABITUALLY CARRIES A GUN...
FLORIDA WAS A DISASTER FOR CALLAHAN, WASN'T IT? ANY THOUGHTS ON HOW THE CAMPAIGN BROKE DOWN?
I'D ARGUE YOUR PHRASING, ROBERT.
BAD FORM. YOU'RE SUPPOSED TO RE-PARSE THE SENTENCE TO SERVE YOUR OWN END, NOT ARGUE IT.

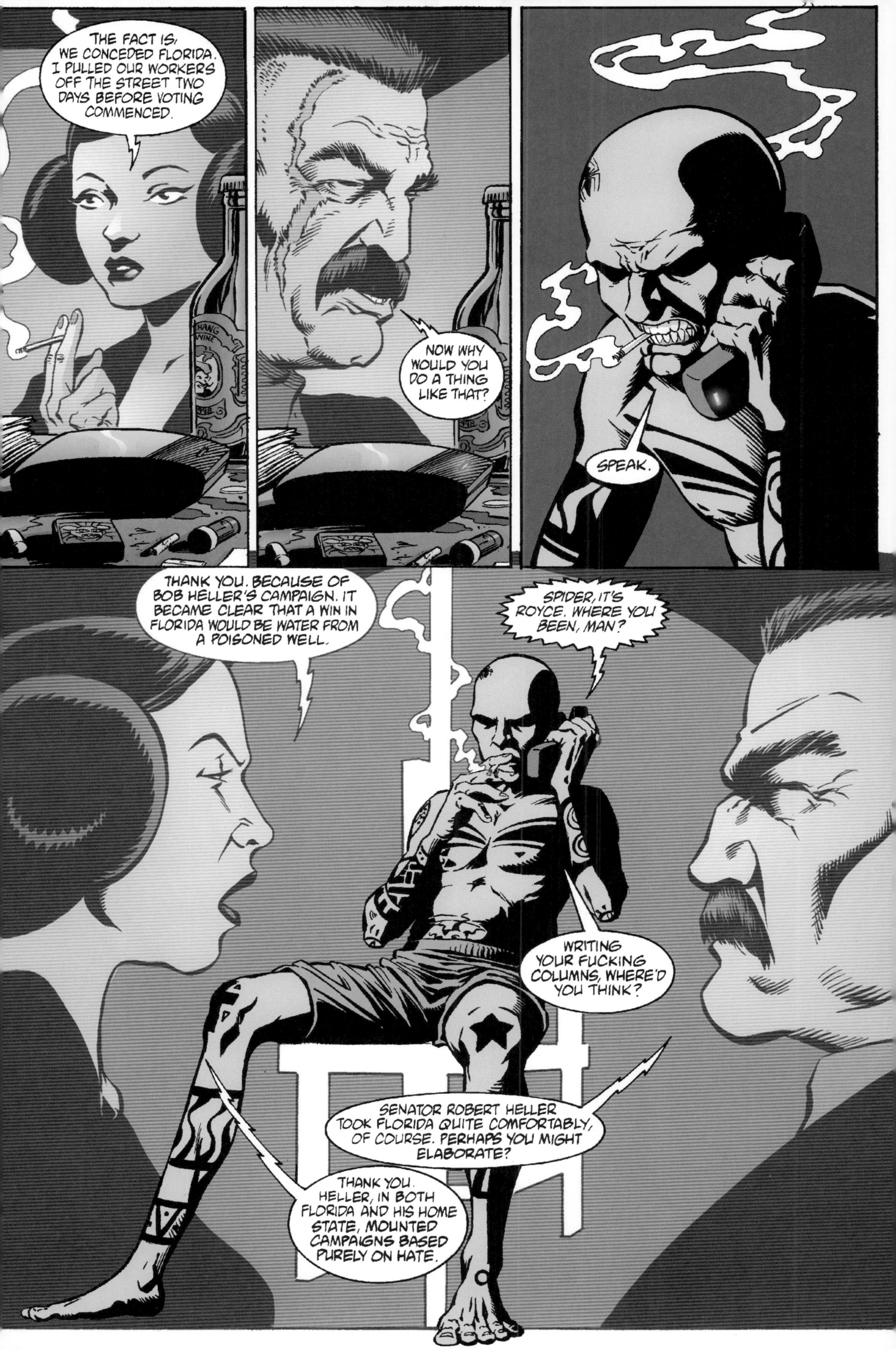
THE FACT IS, WE CONCEDED FLORIDA. I PULLED OUR WORKERS OFF THE STREET TWO DAYS BEFORE VOTING COMMENCED.
NOW WHY WOULD YOU DO A THING LIKE THAT?
SPEAK.
THANK YOU. BECAUSE OF BOB HELLER'S CAMPAIGN, IT BECAME CLEAR THAT A WIN IN FLORIDA WOULD BE WATER FROM A POISONED WELL.
SPIDER, IT'S ROYCE. WHERE YOU BEEN, MAN?
WRITING YOUR FUCKING COLUMNS, WHERE'D YOU THINK?
SENATOR ROBERT HELLER TOOK FLORIDA QUITE COMFORTABLY, OF COURSE. PERHAPS YOU MIGHT ELABORATE?
THANK YOU. HELLER, IN BOTH FLORIDA AND HIS HOME STATE, MOUNTED CAMPAIGNS BASED PURELY ON HATE.

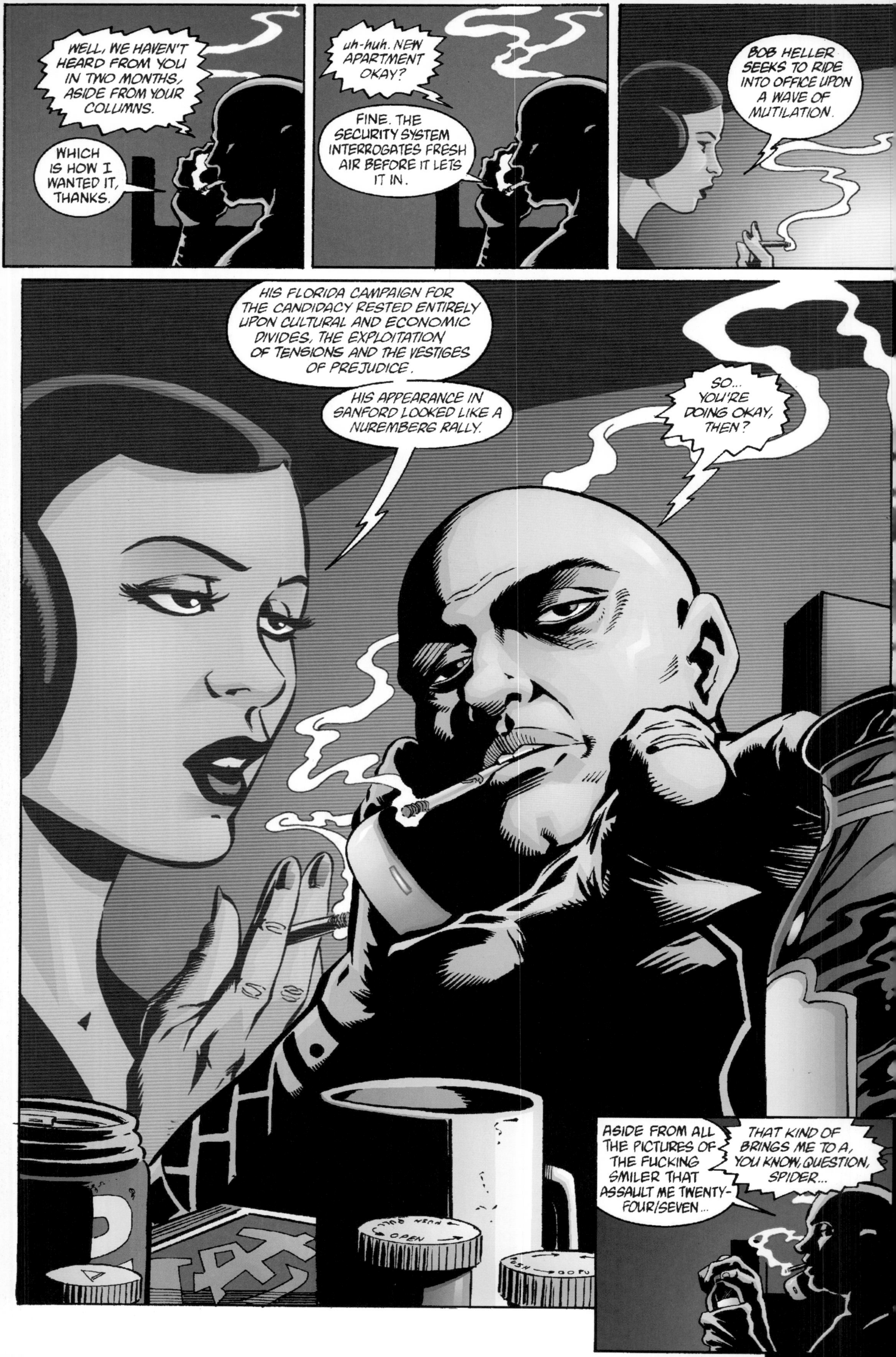
WELL, WE HAVEN'T HEARD FROM YOU IN TWO MONTHS, ASIDE FROM YOUR COLUMNS.
WHICH IS HOW I WANTED IT, THANKS.
uh-huh. NEW APARTMENT OKAY?
FINE. THE SECURITY SYSTEM INTERROGATES FRESH AIR BEFORE IT LETS IT IN.
BOB HELLER SEEKS TO RIDE INTO OFFICE UPON A WAVE OF MUTILATION.
HIS FLORIDA CAMPAIGN FOR THE CANDIDACY RESTED ENTIRELY UPON CULTURAL AND ECONOMIC DIVIDES, THE EXPLOITATION OF TENSIONS AND THE VESTIGES OF PREJUDICE.
HIS APPEARANCE IN SANFORD LOOKED LIKE A NUREMBERG RALLY.
SO... YOU'RE DOING OKAY, THEN?
ASIDE FROM ALL THE PICTURES OF THE FUCKING SMILER THAT ASSAULT ME TWENTY-FOUR/SEVEN...
THAT KIND OF BRINGS ME TO A, YOU KNOW, QUESTION, SPIDER...
OPEN

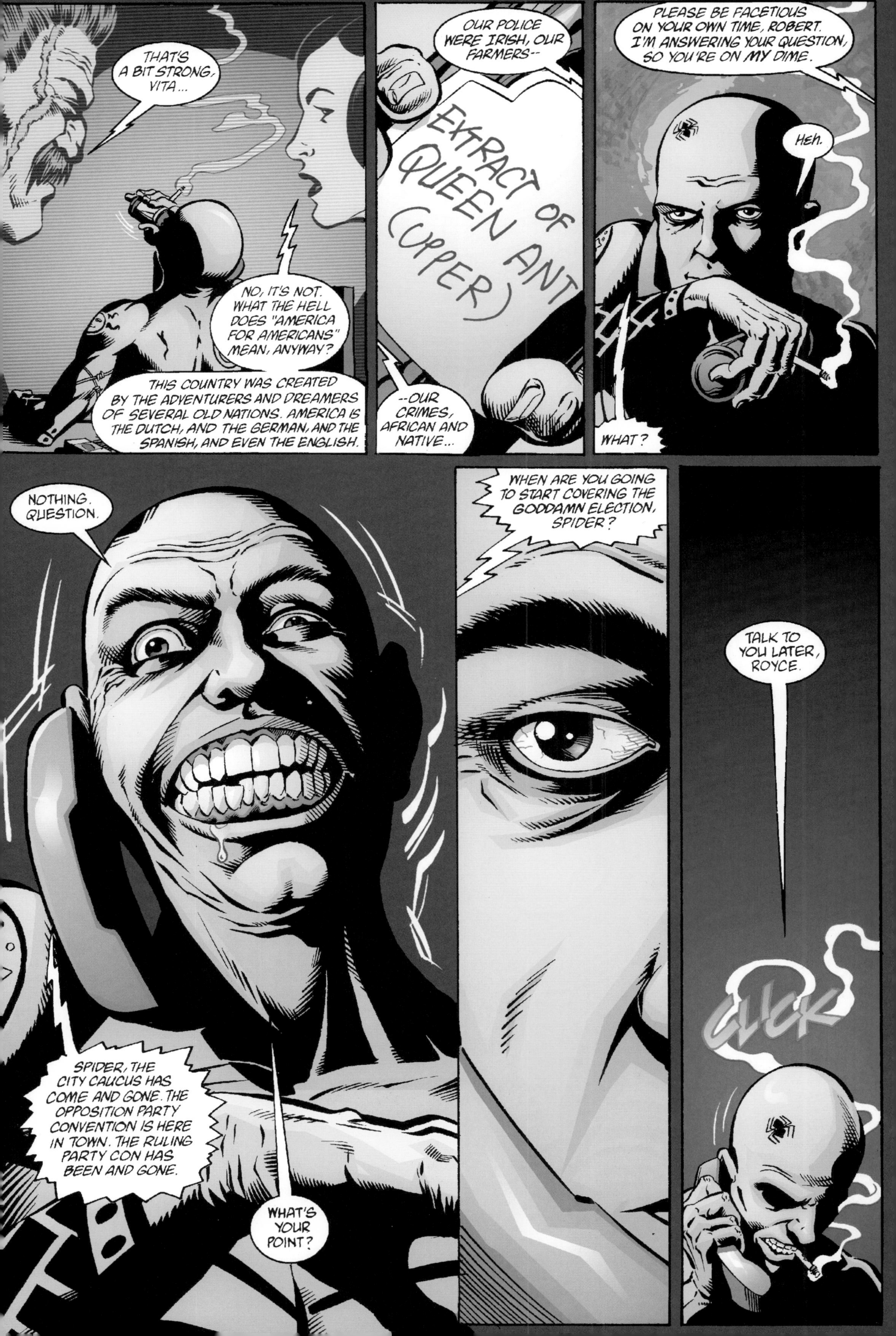
THAT'S A BIT STRONG, VITA...
NO, IT'S NOT. WHAT THE HELL DOES "AMERICA FOR AMERICANS" MEAN, ANYWAY?
THIS COUNTRY WAS CREATED BY THE ADVENTURERS AND DREAMERS OF SEVERAL OLD NATIONS. AMERICA IS THE DUTCH, AND THE GERMAN, AND THE SPANISH, AND EVEN THE ENGLISH.
OUR POLICE WERE IRISH, OUR FARMERS--
EXTRACT OF QUEEN ANT (UPPER)
--OUR CRIMES, AFRICAN AND NATIVE...
PLEASE BE FACETIOUS ON YOUR OWN TIME, ROBERT. I'M ANSWERING YOUR QUESTION, SO YOU'RE ON MY DIME.
Heh.
WHAT?
NOTHING. QUESTION.
SPIDER, THE CITY CAUCUS HAS COME AND GONE. THE OPPOSITION PARTY CONVENTION IS HERE IN TOWN. THE RULING PARTY CON HAS BEEN AND GONE.
WHAT'S YOUR POINT?
WHEN ARE YOU GOING TO START COVERING THE GODDAMN ELECTION, SPIDER?
TALK TO YOU LATER, ROYCE.
CLICK

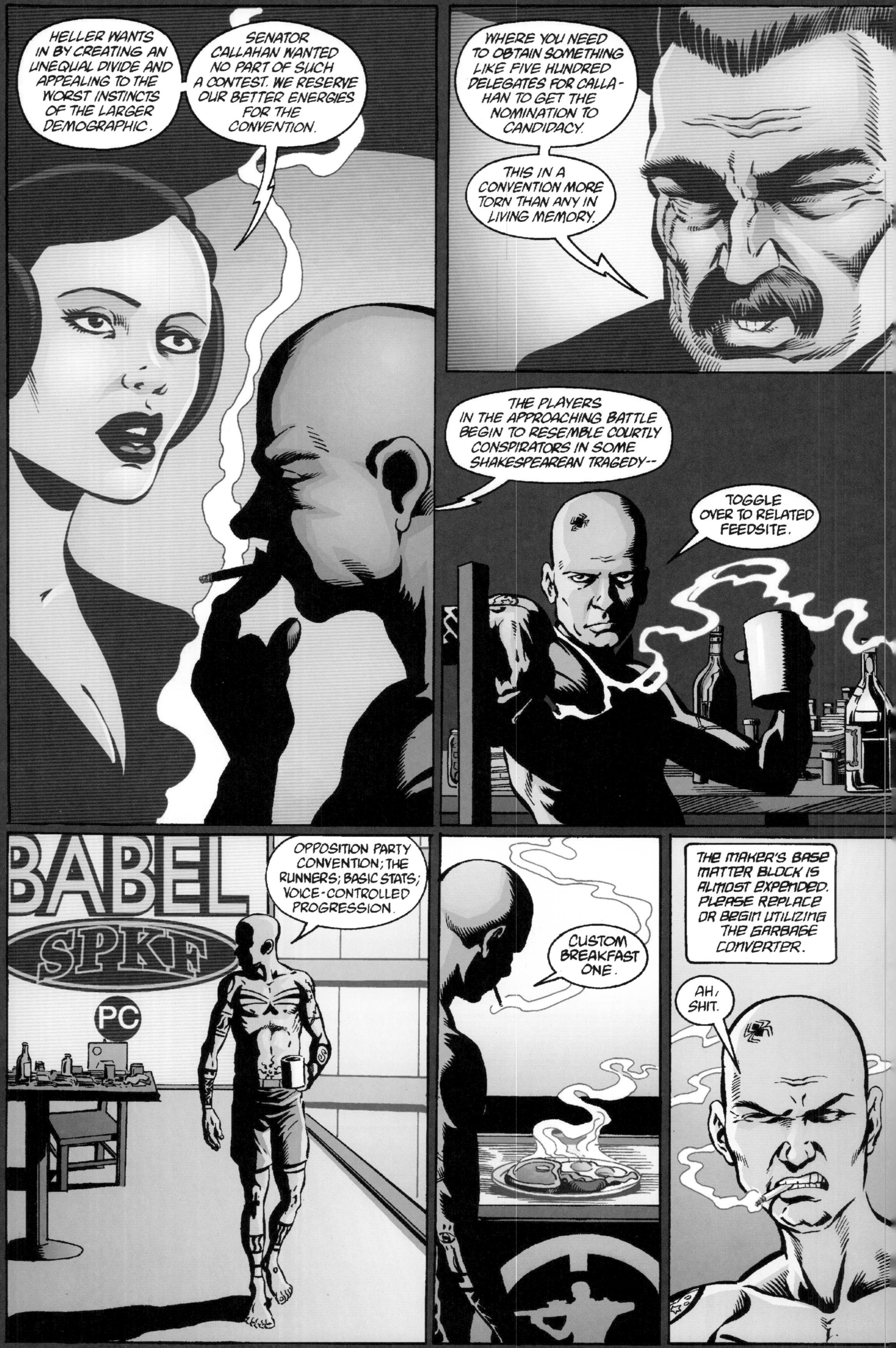
HELLER WANTS IN BY CREATING AN UNEQUAL DIVIDE AND APPEALING TO THE WORST INSTINCTS OF THE LARGER DEMOGRAPHIC.
SENATOR CALLAHAN WANTED NO PART OF SUCH A CONTEST. WE RESERVE OUR BETTER ENERGIES FOR THE CONVENTION.
WHERE YOU NEED TO OBTAIN SOMETHING LIKE FIVE HUNDRED DELEGATES FOR CALLA-HAN TO GET THE NOMINATION TO CANDIDACY.
THIS IN A CONVENTION MORE TORN THAN ANY IN LIVING MEMORY.
THE PLAYERS IN THE APPROACHING BATTLE BEGIN TO RESEMBLE COURTLY CONSPIRATORS IN SOME SHAKESPEAREAN TRAGEDY--
TOGGLE OVER TO RELATED FEEDSITE.
BABEL
SPKF
PC
OPPOSITION PARTY CONVENTION; THE RUNNERS; BASIC STATS; VOICE-CONTROLLED PROGRESSION.
CUSTOM BREAKFAST ONE.
THE MAKER'S BASE MATTER BLOCK IS ALMOST EXPENDED. PLEASE REPLACE OR BEGIN UTILIZING THE GARBAGE CONVERTER.
AH, SHIT.

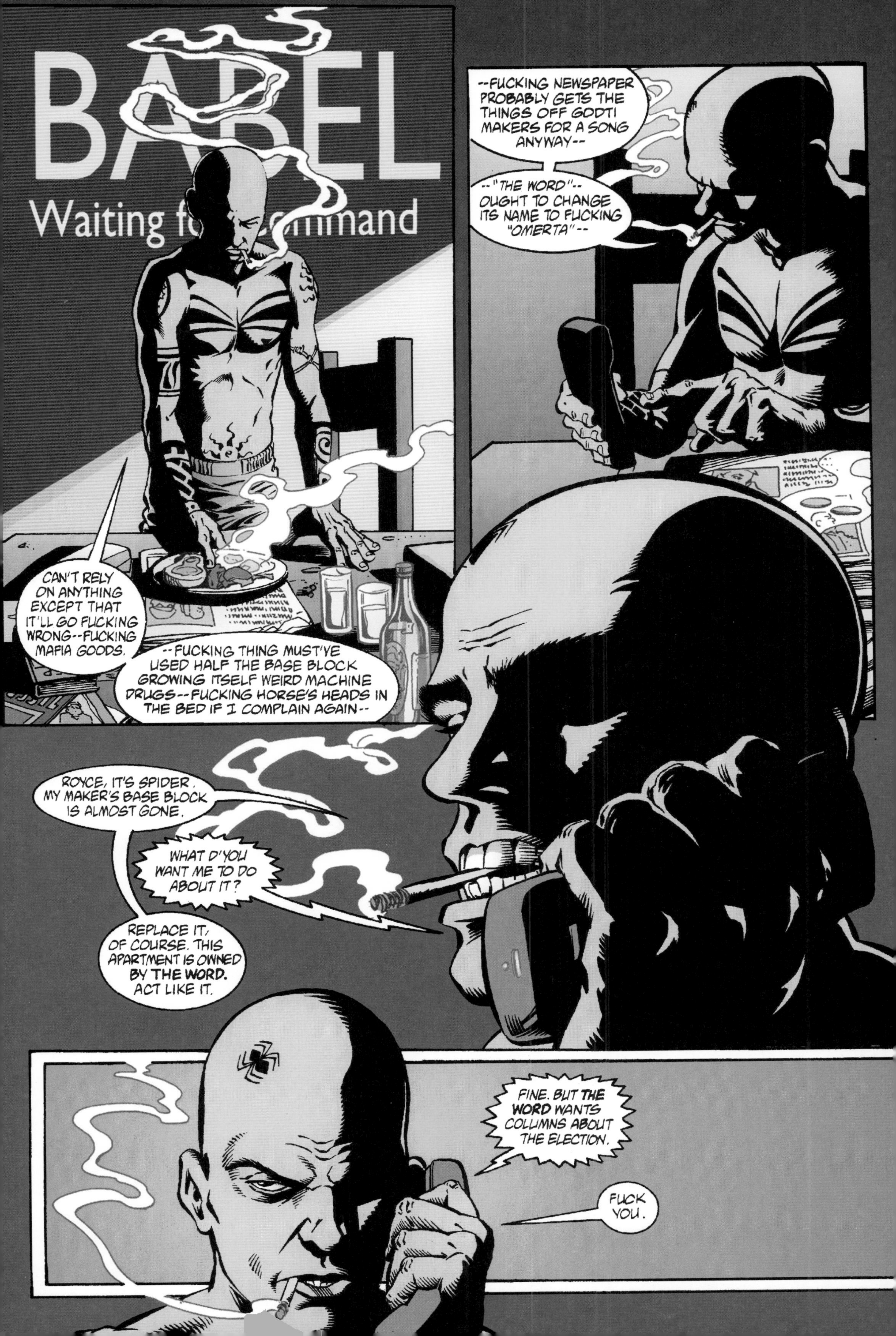
BABEL
Waiting for Command
CAN'T RELY ON ANYTHING EXCEPT THAT IT'LL GO FUCKING WRONG--FUCKING MAFIA GOODS.
--FUCKING THING MUST'VE USED HALF THE BASE BLOCK GROWING ITSELF WEIRD MACHINE DRUGS--FUCKING HORSE'S HEADS IN THE BED IF I COMPLAIN AGAIN--
--FUCKING NEWSPAPER PROBABLY GETS THE THINGS OFF GODTI MAKERS FOR A SONG ANYWAY--
--"THE WORD"--OUGHT TO CHANGE ITS NAME TO FUCKING "OMERTA"--
ROYCE, IT'S SPIDER. MY MAKER'S BASE BLOCK IS ALMOST GONE.
WHAT D'YOU WANT ME TO DO ABOUT IT?
REPLACE IT, OF COURSE. THIS APARTMENT IS OWNED BY THE WORD. ACT LIKE IT.
FINE. BUT THE WORD WANTS COLUMNS ABOUT THE ELECTION.
FUCK YOU.

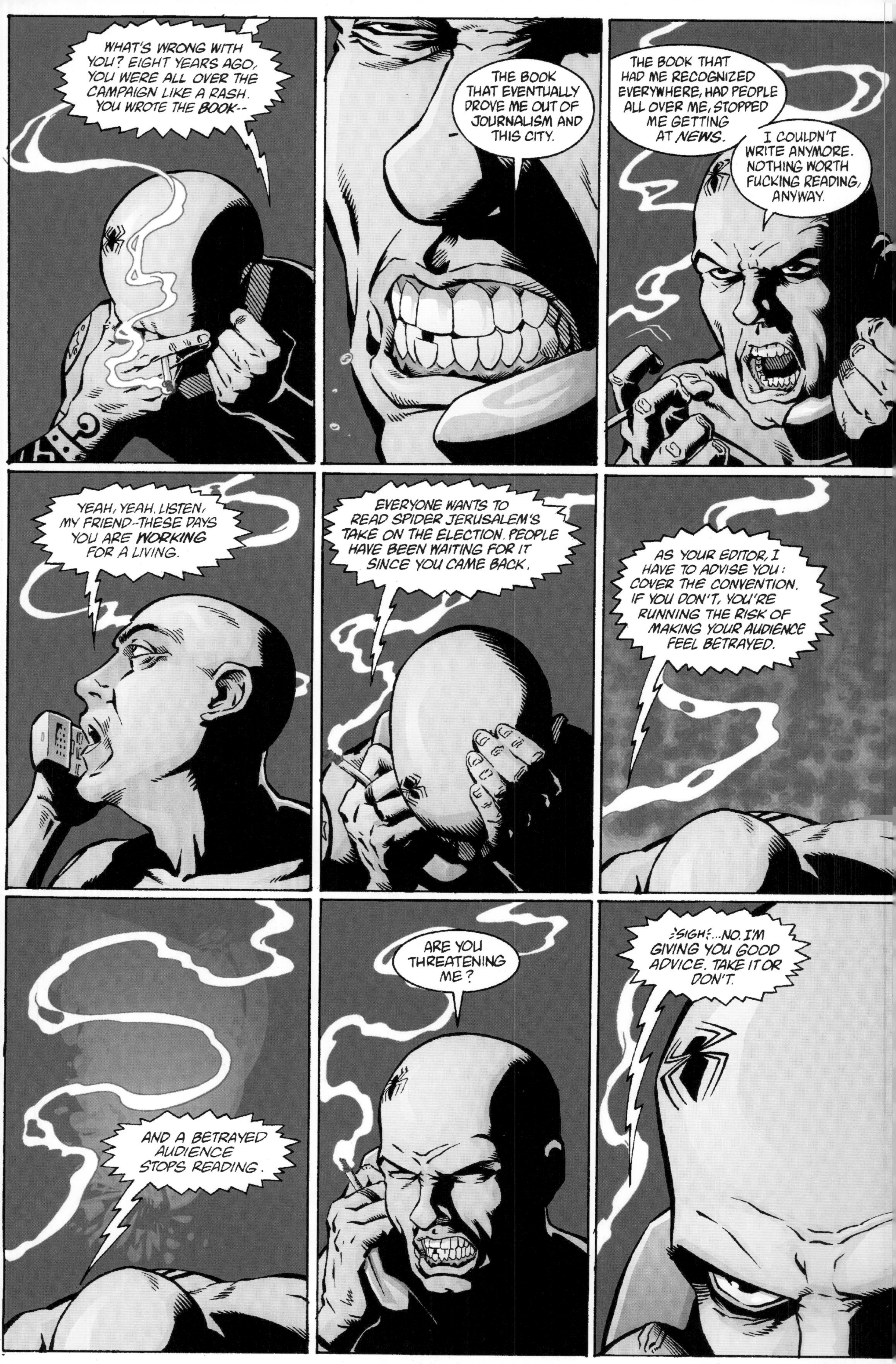
WHAT'S WRONG WITH YOU? EIGHT YEARS AGO, YOU WERE ALL OVER THE CAMPAIGN LIKE A RASH. YOU WROTE THE BOOK--
THE BOOK THAT EVENTUALLY DROVE ME OUT OF JOURNALISM AND THIS CITY.
THE BOOK THAT HAD ME RECOGNIZED EVERYWHERE, HAD PEOPLE ALL OVER ME, STOPPED ME GETTING AT NEWS.
I COULDN'T WRITE ANYMORE. NOTHING WORTH FUCKING READING, ANYWAY.
YEAH, YEAH. LISTEN, MY FRIEND--THESE DAYS YOU ARE WORKING FOR A LIVING.
EVERYONE WANTS TO READ SPIDER JERUSALEM'S TAKE ON THE ELECTION. PEOPLE HAVE BEEN WAITING FOR IT SINCE YOU CAME BACK.
AS YOUR EDITOR, I HAVE TO ADVISE YOU: COVER THE CONVENTION. IF YOU DON'T, YOU'RE RUNNING THE RISK OF MAKING YOUR AUDIENCE FEEL BETRAYED.
AND A BETRAYED AUDIENCE STOPS READING.
ARE YOU THREATENING ME?
:SIGH:...NO. I'M GIVING YOU GOOD ADVICE. TAKE IT OR DON'T.

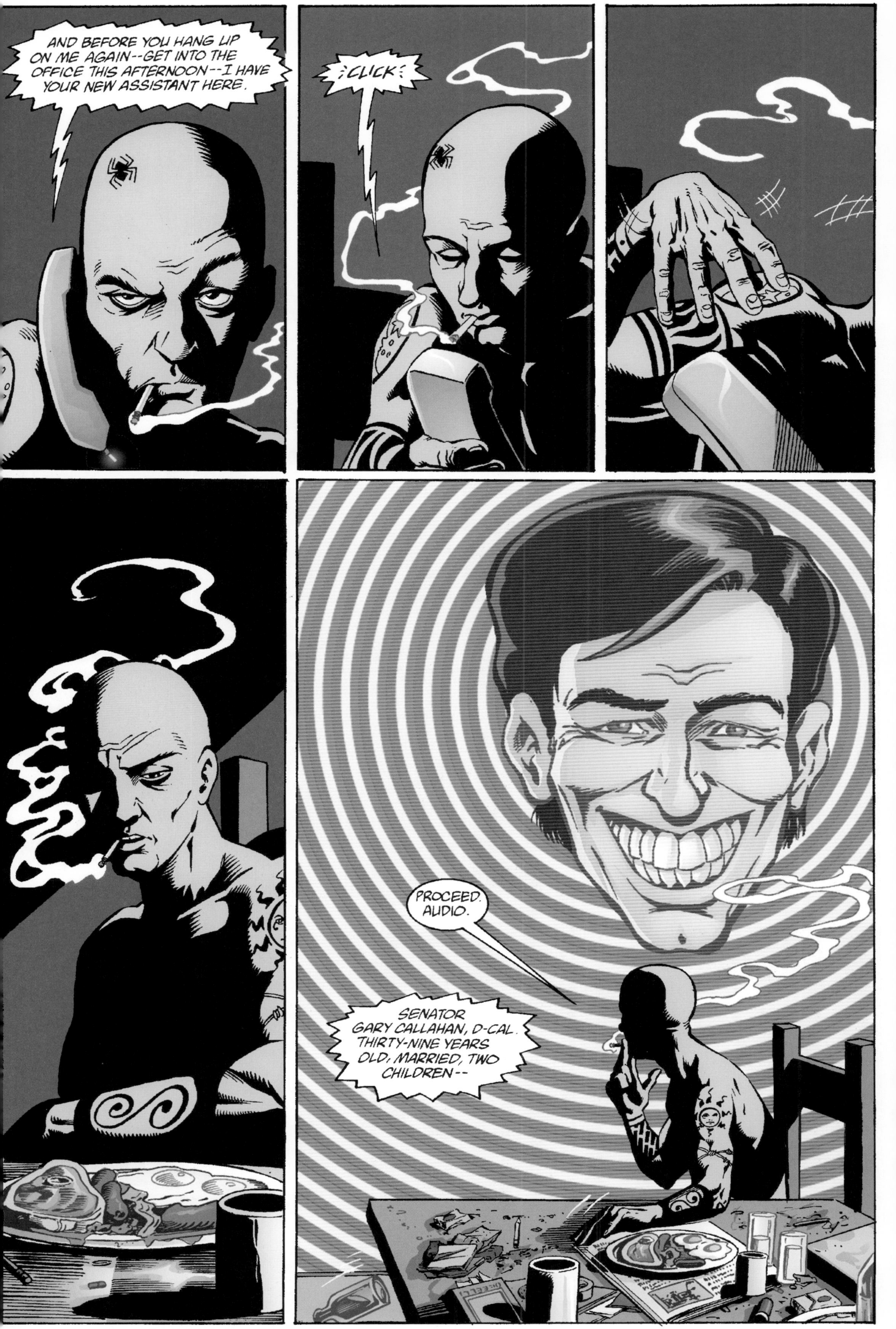
AND BEFORE YOU HANG UP ON ME AGAIN--GET INTO THE OFFICE THIS AFTERNOON--I HAVE YOUR NEW ASSISTANT HERE.
CLICK
PROCEED. AUDIO.
SENATOR GARY CALLAHAN, D-CAL. THIRTY-NINE YEARS OLD, MARRIED, TWO CHILDREN--

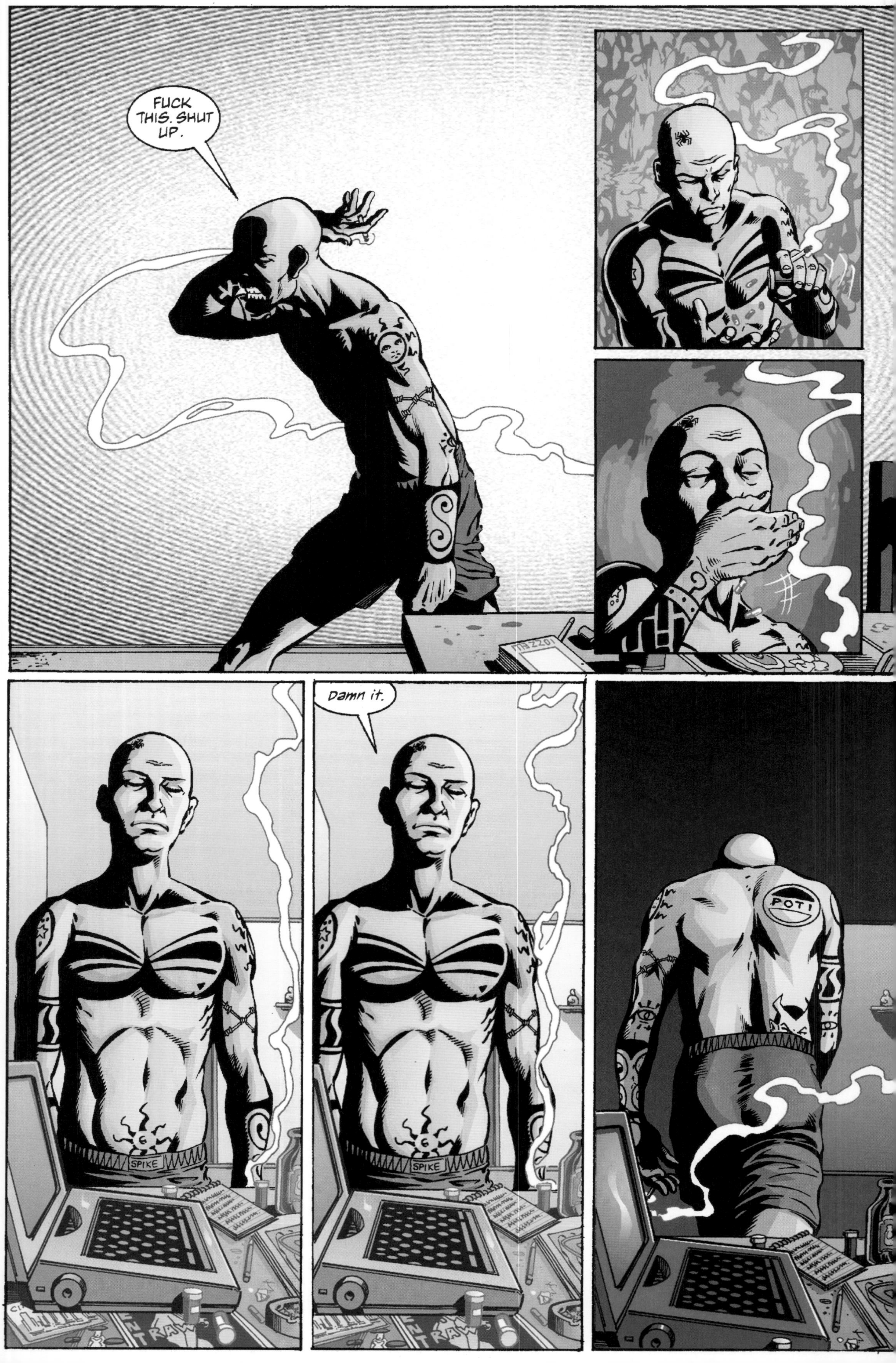

FUCK THIS. SHUT UP.
Damn it.

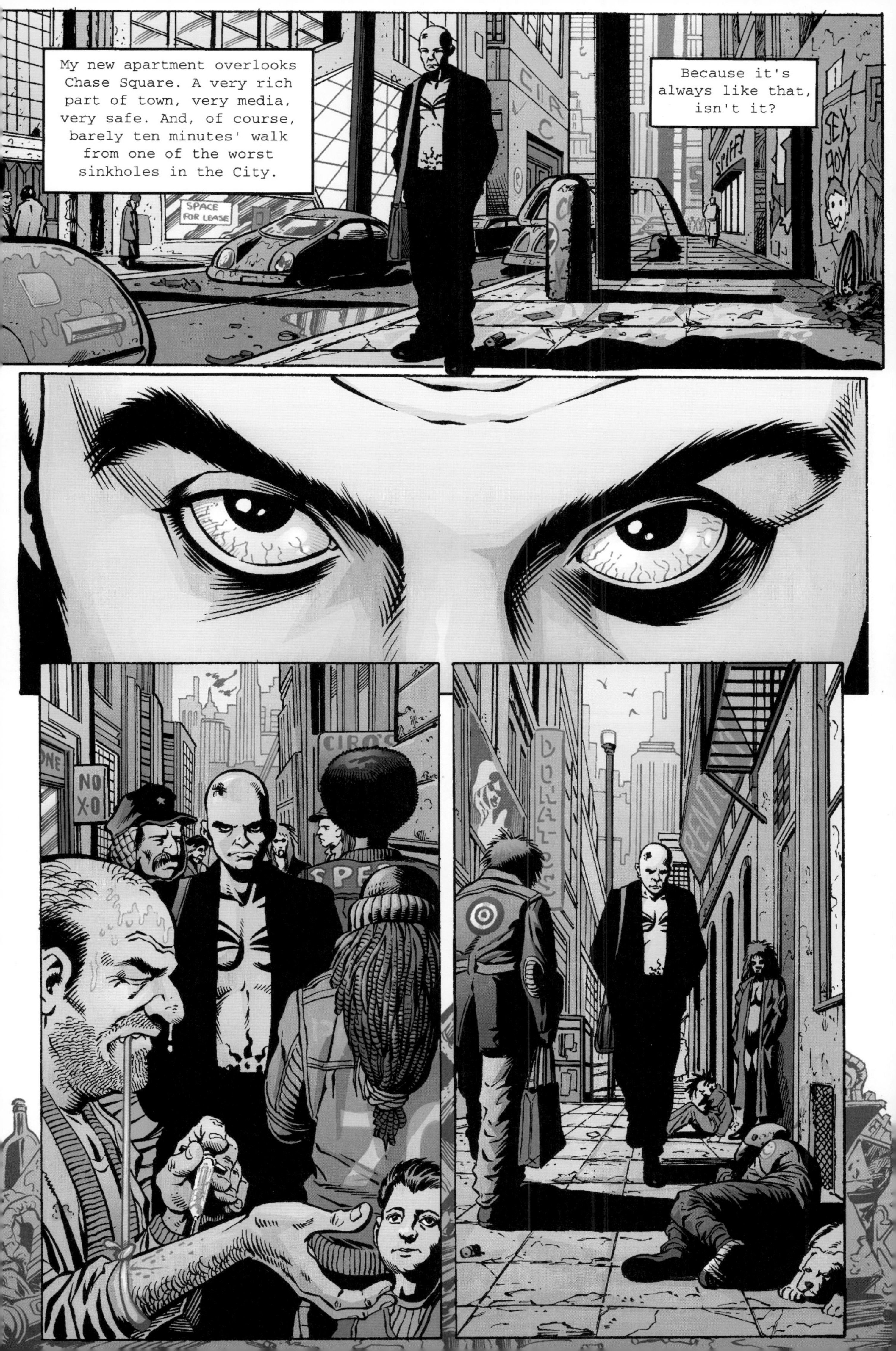

My new apartment overlooks Chase Square. A very rich part of town, very media, very safe. And, of course, barely ten minutes' walk from one of the worst sinkholes in the City.
Because it's always like that, isn't it?
SPACE FOR LEASE
SEX BOY
SPIFFY
CIRO'S
NO X-O

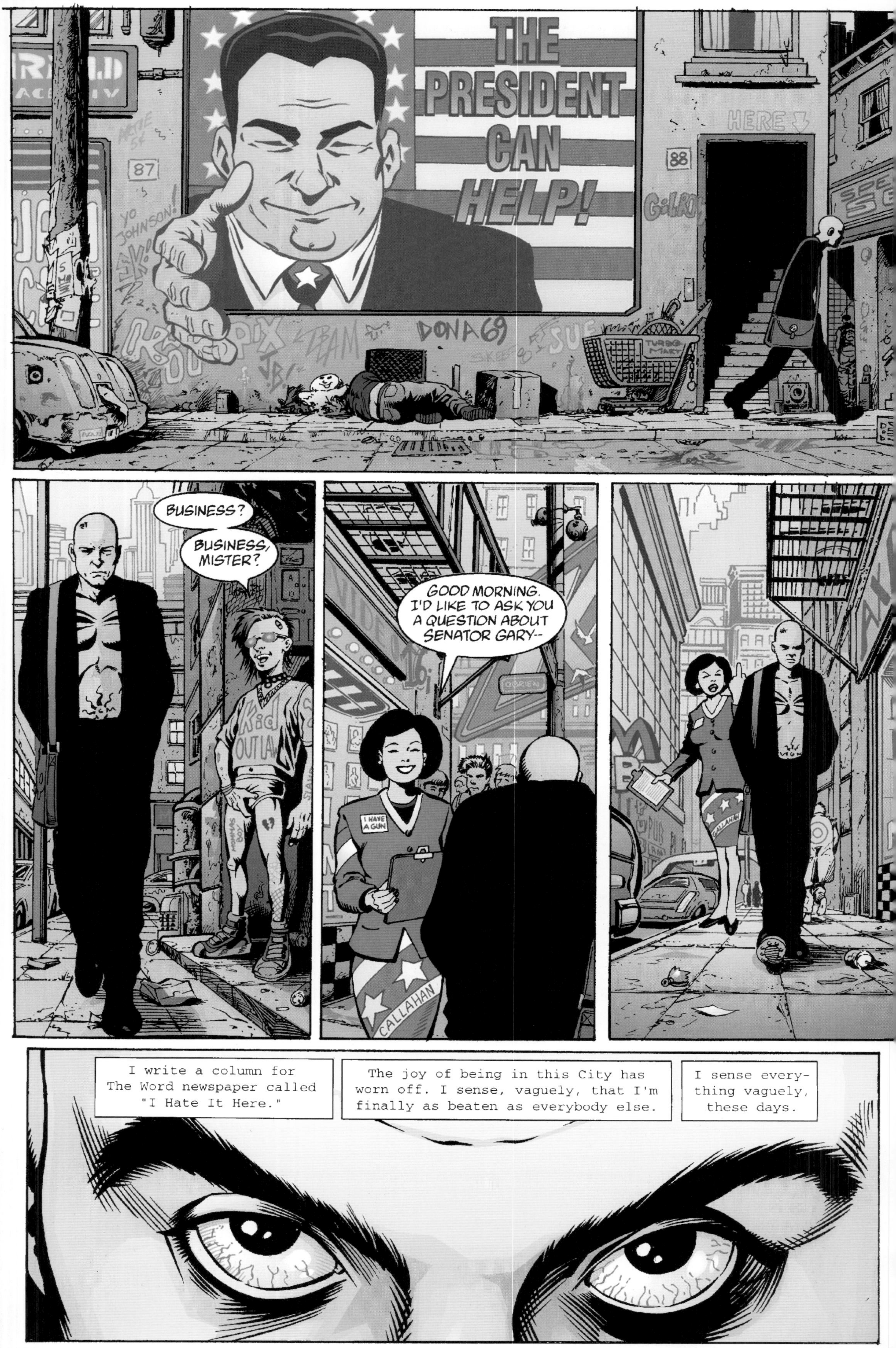
THE PRESIDENT CAN HELP!
HERE
BUSINESS?
BUSINESS, MISTER?
GOOD MORNING. I'D LIKE TO ASK YOU A QUESTION ABOUT SENATOR GARY--
I HAVE A GUN
CALLAHAN
I write a column for The Word newspaper called "I Hate It Here."
The joy of being in this City has worn off. I sense, vaguely, that I'm finally as beaten as everybody else.
I sense everything vaguely, these days.

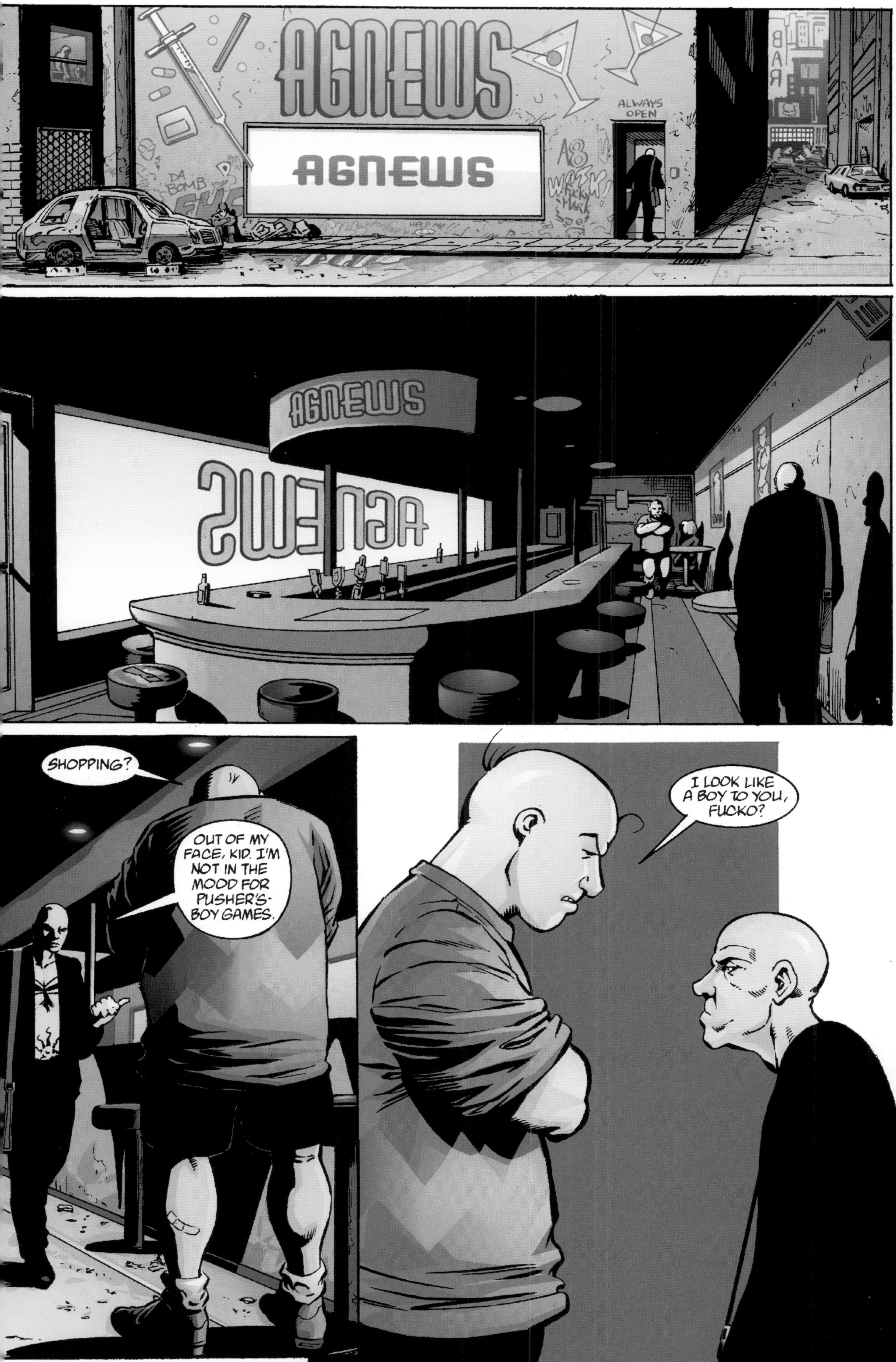
AGNEWS
AGNEWS
ALWAYS OPEN
BAR
DA BOMB
HELP ME!!
AGNEWS
AGNEWS
SHOPPING?
OUT OF MY FACE, KID. I'M NOT IN THE MOOD FOR PUSHER'S-BOY GAMES.
I LOOK LIKE A BOY TO YOU, FUCKO?

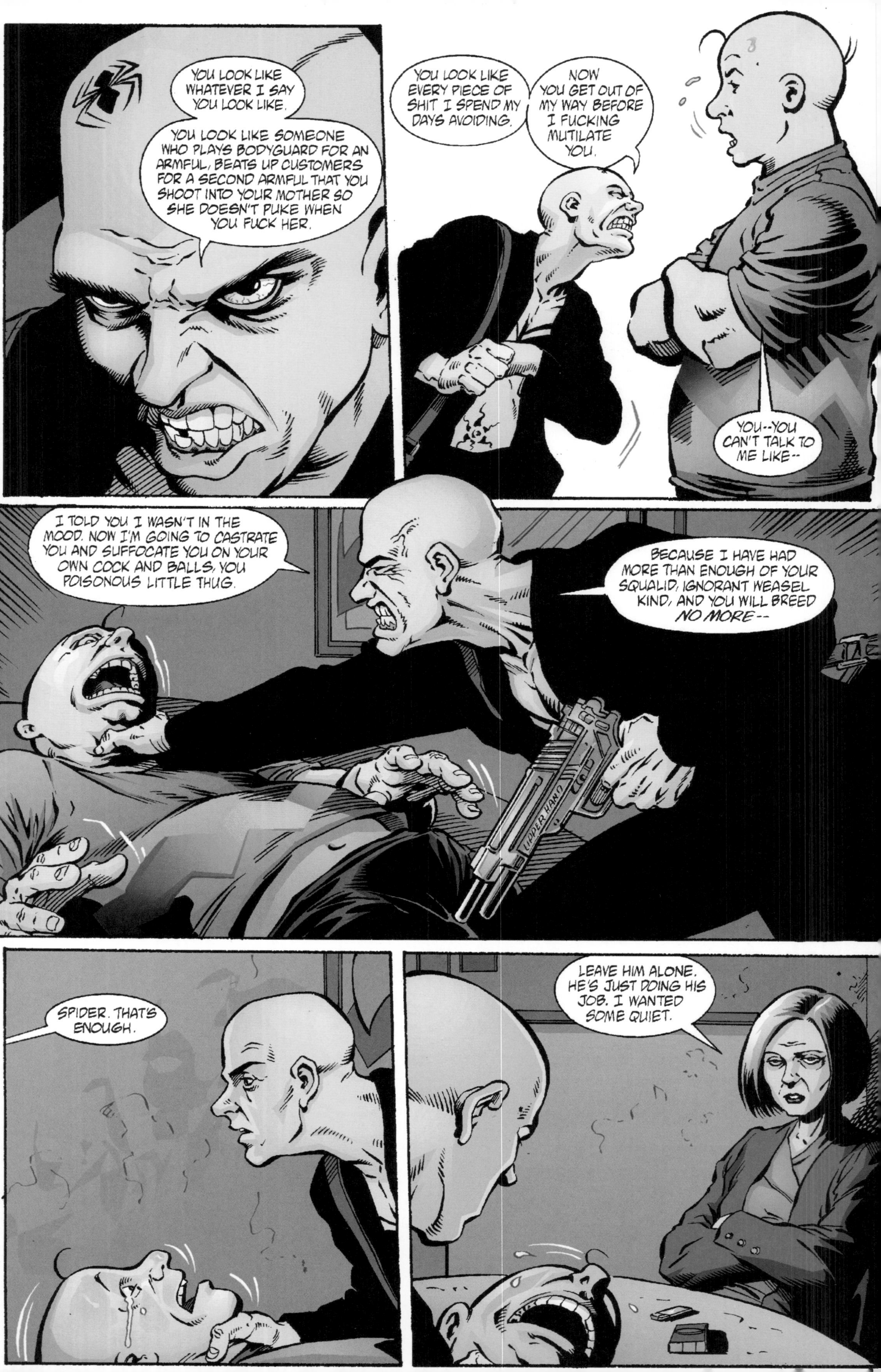
YOU LOOK LIKE WHATEVER I SAY YOU LOOK LIKE.
YOU LOOK LIKE SOMEONE WHO PLAYS BODYGUARD FOR AN ARMFUL, BEATS UP CUSTOMERS FOR A SECOND ARMFUL THAT YOU SHOOT INTO YOUR MOTHER SO SHE DOESN'T PUKE WHEN YOU FUCK HER.
YOU LOOK LIKE EVERY PIECE OF SHIT I SPEND MY DAYS AVOIDING.
NOW YOU GET OUT OF MY WAY BEFORE I FUCKING MUTILATE YOU.
YOU--YOU CAN'T TALK TO ME LIKE--
I TOLD YOU I WASN'T IN THE MOOD. NOW I'M GOING TO CASTRATE YOU AND SUFFOCATE YOU ON YOUR OWN COCK AND BALLS, YOU POISONOUS LITTLE THUG.
BECAUSE I HAVE HAD MORE THAN ENOUGH OF YOUR SQUALID, IGNORANT WEASEL KIND, AND YOU WILL BREED *NO MORE*--
UPPER HAND
SPIDER. THAT'S ENOUGH.
LEAVE HIM ALONE. HE'S JUST DOING HIS JOB. I WANTED SOME QUIET.

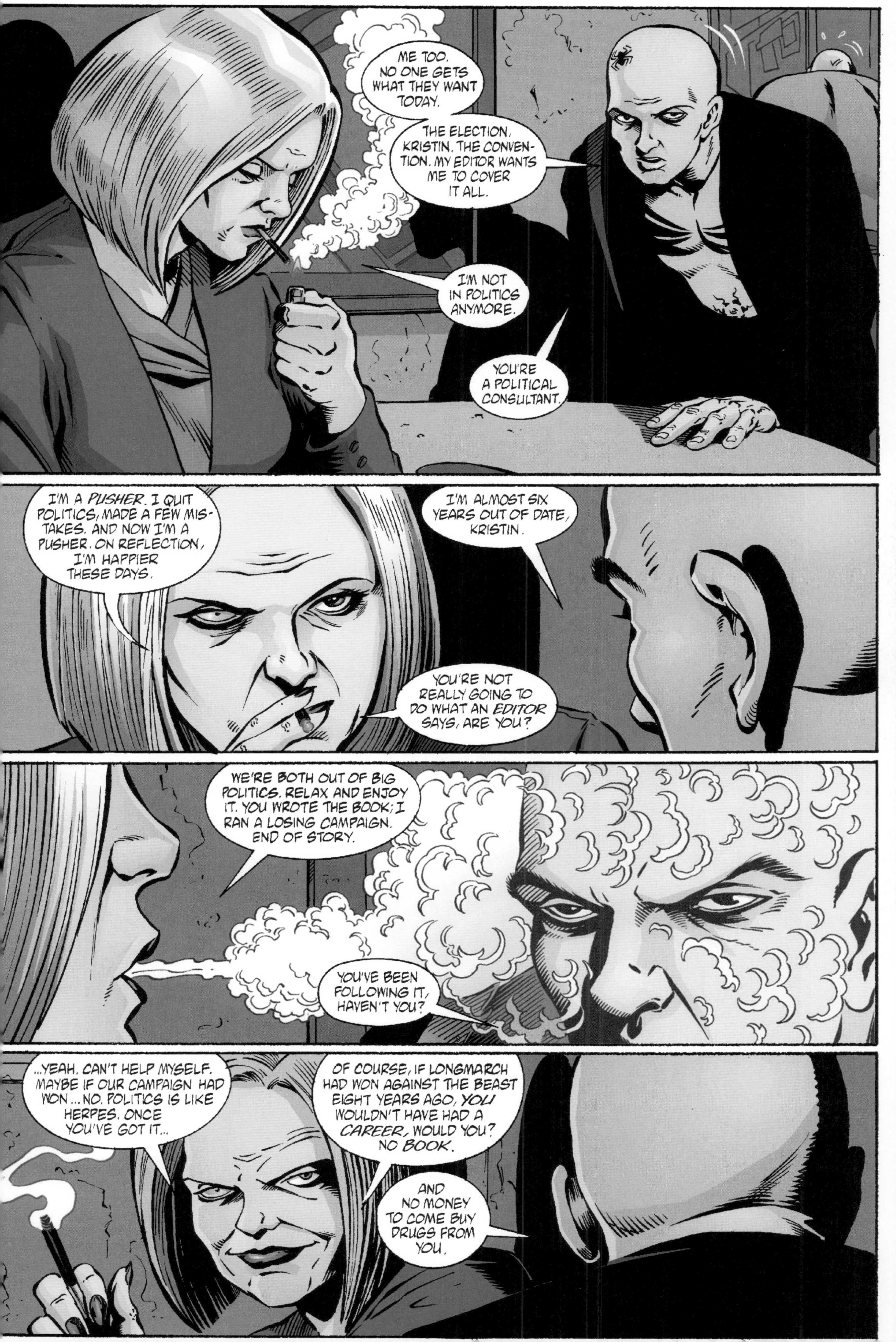
ME TOO. NO ONE GETS WHAT THEY WANT TODAY.
THE ELECTION, KRISTIN. THE CONVENTION. MY EDITOR WANTS ME TO COVER IT ALL.
I'M NOT IN POLITICS ANYMORE.
YOU'RE A POLITICAL CONSULTANT.
I'M A *PUSHER*. I QUIT POLITICS, MADE A FEW MISTAKES. AND NOW I'M A PUSHER. ON REFLECTION, I'M HAPPIER THESE DAYS.
I'M ALMOST SIX YEARS OUT OF DATE, KRISTIN.
YOU'RE NOT REALLY GOING TO DO WHAT AN *EDITOR* SAYS, ARE YOU?
WE'RE BOTH OUT OF BIG POLITICS. RELAX AND ENJOY IT. YOU WROTE THE BOOK; I RAN A LOSING CAMPAIGN. END OF STORY.
YOU'VE BEEN FOLLOWING IT, HAVEN'T YOU?
...YEAH. CAN'T HELP MYSELF. MAYBE IF OUR CAMPAIGN HAD WON ... NO. POLITICS IS LIKE HERPES. ONCE YOU'VE GOT IT...
OF COURSE, IF LONGMARCH HAD WON AGAINST THE BEAST EIGHT YEARS AGO, *YOU* WOULDN'T HAVE HAD A *CAREER*, WOULD YOU? NO *BOOK*.
AND NO MONEY TO COME BUY DRUGS FROM YOU.

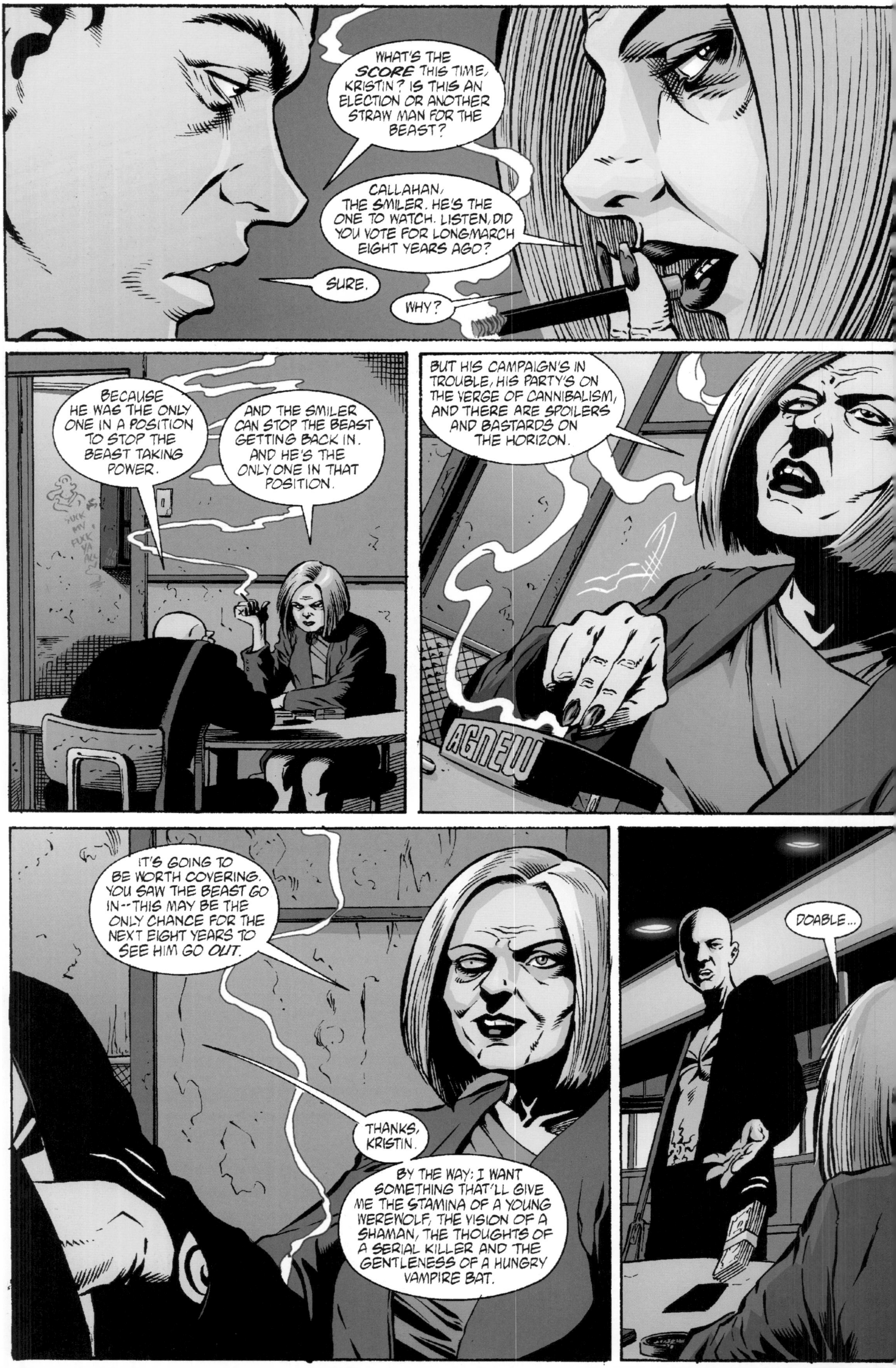
WHAT'S THE SCORE THIS TIME, KRISTIN? IS THIS AN ELECTION OR ANOTHER STRAW MAN FOR THE BEAST?
CALLAHAN, THE SMILER. HE'S THE ONE TO WATCH. LISTEN, DID YOU VOTE FOR LONGMARCH EIGHT YEARS AGO?
SURE.
WHY?
BECAUSE HE WAS THE ONLY ONE IN A POSITION TO STOP THE BEAST TAKING POWER.
AND THE SMILER CAN STOP THE BEAST GETTING BACK IN. AND HE'S THE ONLY ONE IN THAT POSITION.
BUT HIS CAMPAIGN'S IN TROUBLE, HIS PARTY'S ON THE VERGE OF CANNIBALISM, AND THERE ARE SPOILERS AND BASTARDS ON THE HORIZON.
AGNEW
IT'S GOING TO BE WORTH COVERING. YOU SAW THE BEAST GO IN--THIS MAY BE THE ONLY CHANCE FOR THE NEXT EIGHT YEARS TO SEE HIM GO OUT.
THANKS, KRISTIN.
BY THE WAY: I WANT SOMETHING THAT'LL GIVE ME THE STAMINA OF A YOUNG WEREWOLF, THE VISION OF A SHAMAN, THE THOUGHTS OF A SERIAL KILLER AND THE GENTLENESS OF A HUNGRY VAMPIRE BAT.
DOABLE...

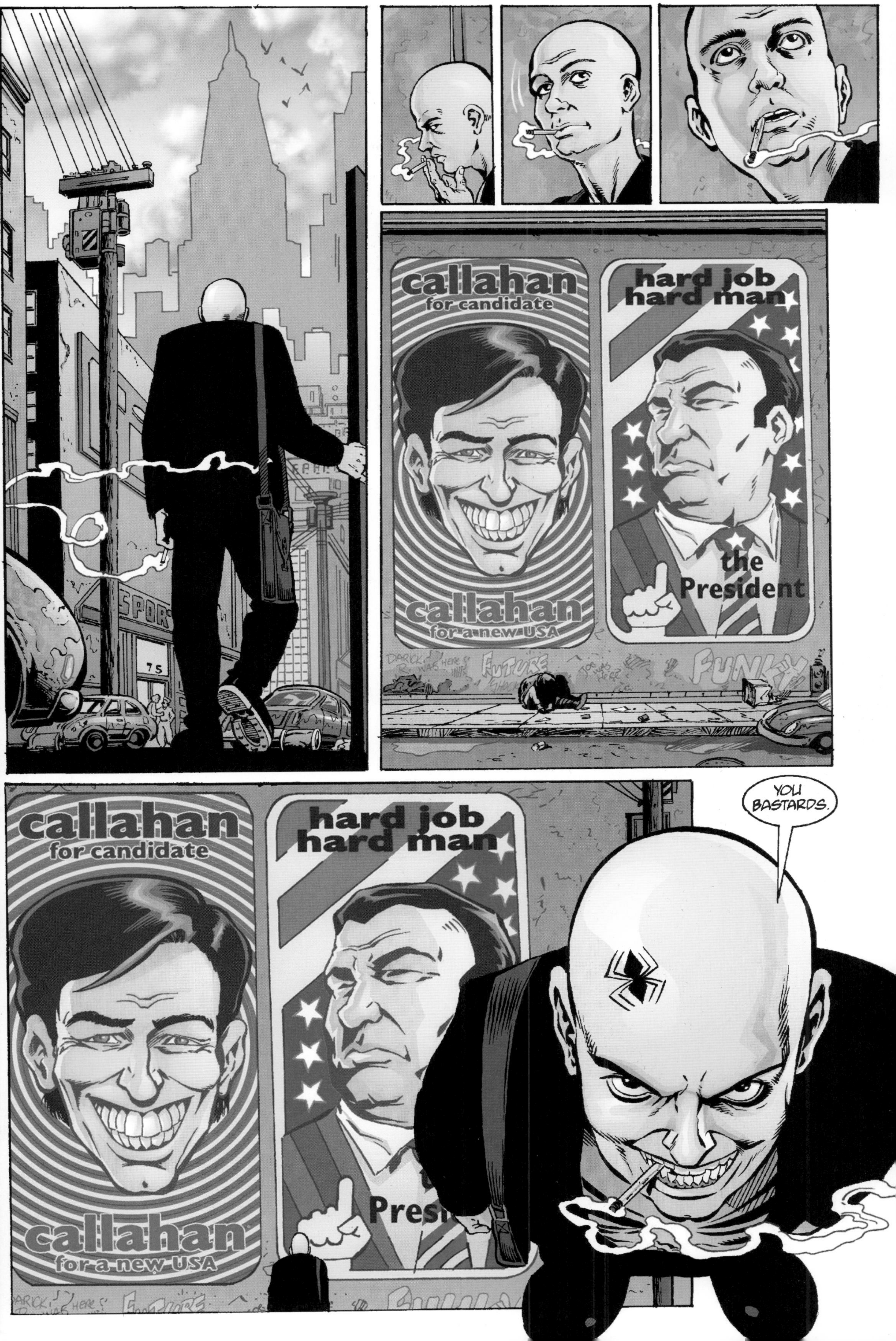
callahan
for candidate
callahan
for a new USA
hard job
hard man
the
President
DARICK R. WAS HERE
FUTURE SHOCK
JOE WAS HERE
FUNKY
YOU BASTARDS.

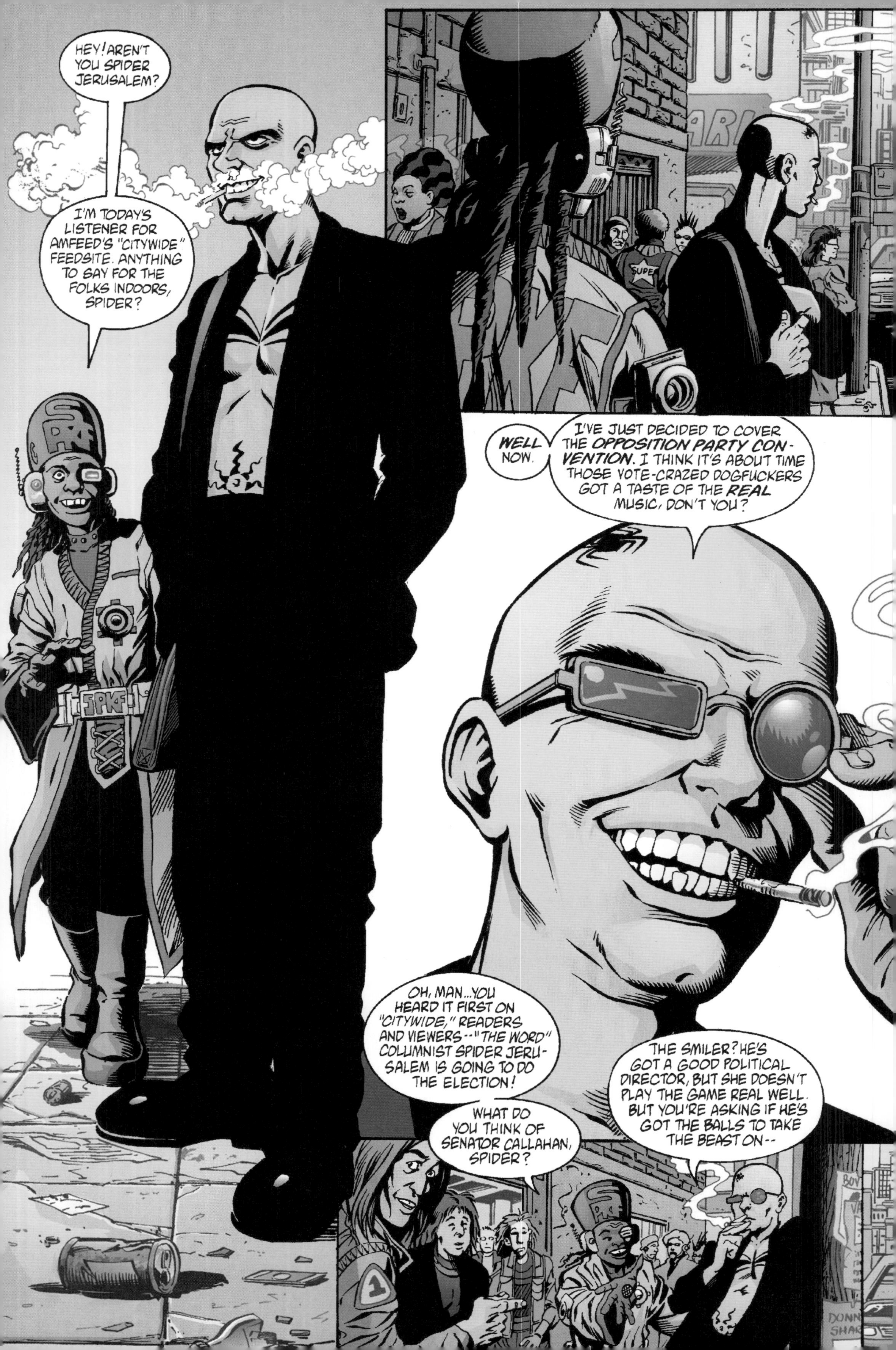
HEY! AREN'T YOU SPIDER JERUSALEM?
I'M TODAY'S LISTENER FOR AMFEED'S "CITYWIDE" FEEDSITE. ANYTHING TO SAY FOR THE FOLKS INDOORS, SPIDER?
WELL NOW.
I'VE JUST DECIDED TO COVER THE OPPOSITION PARTY CONVENTION. I THINK IT'S ABOUT TIME THOSE VOTE-CRAZED DOGFUCKERS GOT A TASTE OF THE REAL MUSIC, DON'T YOU?
OH, MAN...YOU HEARD IT FIRST ON "CITYWIDE," READERS AND VIEWERS--"THE WORD" COLUMNIST SPIDER JERUSALEM IS GOING TO DO THE ELECTION!
WHAT DO YOU THINK OF SENATOR CALLAHAN, SPIDER?
THE SMILER? HE'S GOT A GOOD POLITICAL DIRECTOR, BUT SHE DOESN'T PLAY THE GAME REAL WELL. BUT YOU'RE ASKING IF HE'S GOT THE BALLS TO TAKE THE BEAST ON--

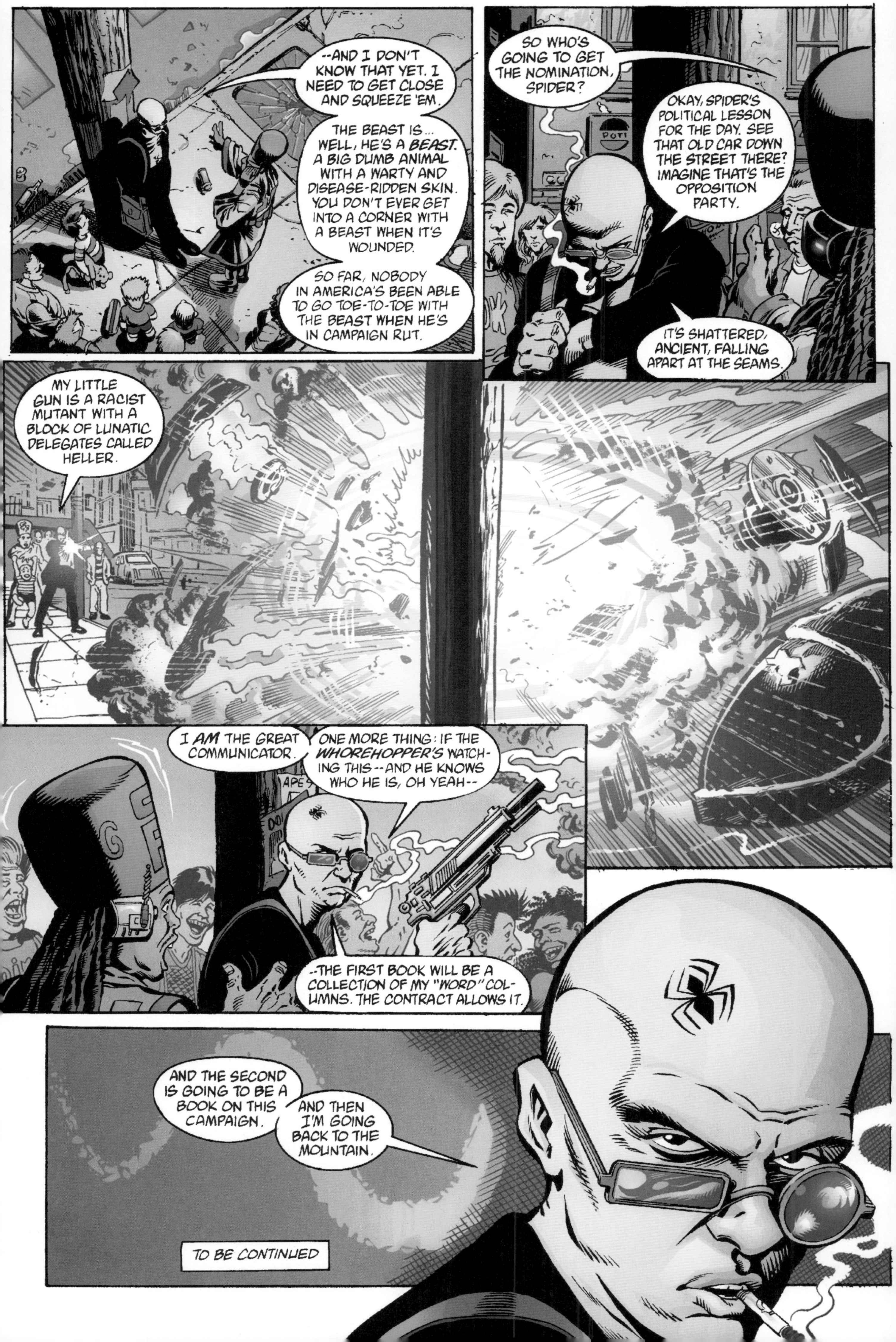
--AND I DON'T KNOW THAT YET. I NEED TO GET CLOSE AND SQUEEZE 'EM.
THE BEAST IS... WELL, HE'S A BEAST. A BIG DUMB ANIMAL WITH A WARTY AND DISEASE-RIDDEN SKIN. YOU DON'T EVER GET INTO A CORNER WITH A BEAST WHEN IT'S WOUNDED.
SO FAR, NOBODY IN AMERICA'S BEEN ABLE TO GO TOE-TO-TOE WITH THE BEAST WHEN HE'S IN CAMPAIGN RUT.
SO WHO'S GOING TO GET THE NOMINATION, SPIDER?
OKAY, SPIDER'S POLITICAL LESSON FOR THE DAY. SEE THAT OLD CAR DOWN THE STREET THERE? IMAGINE THAT'S THE OPPOSITION PARTY.
IT'S SHATTERED, ANCIENT, FALLING APART AT THE SEAMS.
MY LITTLE GUN IS A RACIST MUTANT WITH A BLOCK OF LUNATIC DELEGATES CALLED HELLER.
I AM THE GREAT COMMUNICATOR.
ONE MORE THING: IF THE WHOREHOPPER'S WATCHING THIS--AND HE KNOWS WHO HE IS, OH YEAH--
--THE FIRST BOOK WILL BE A COLLECTION OF MY "WORD" COLUMNS. THE CONTRACT ALLOWS IT.
AND THE SECOND IS GOING TO BE A BOOK ON THIS CAMPAIGN.
AND THEN I'M GOING BACK TO THE MOUNTAIN.
TO BE CONTINUED

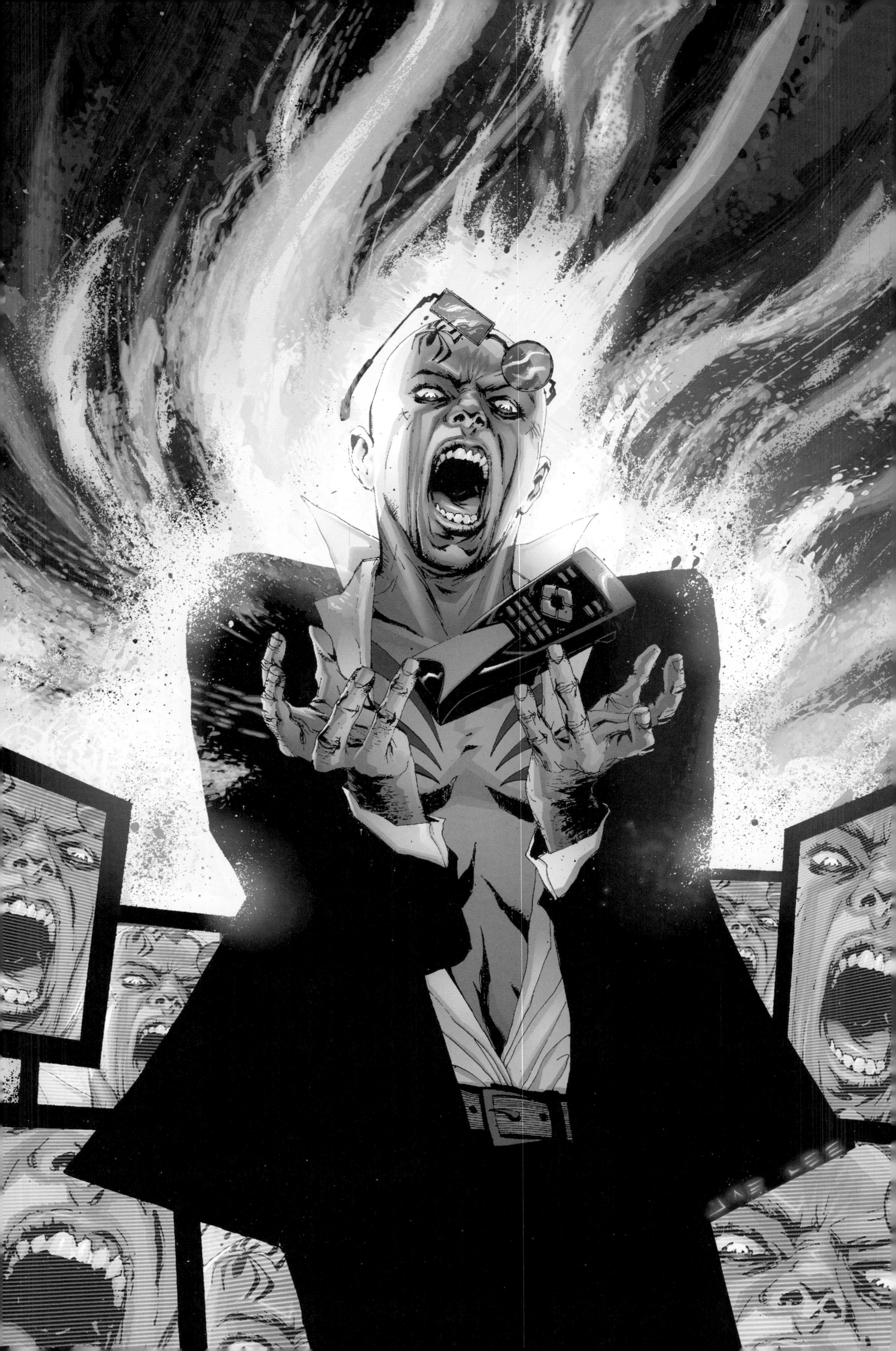

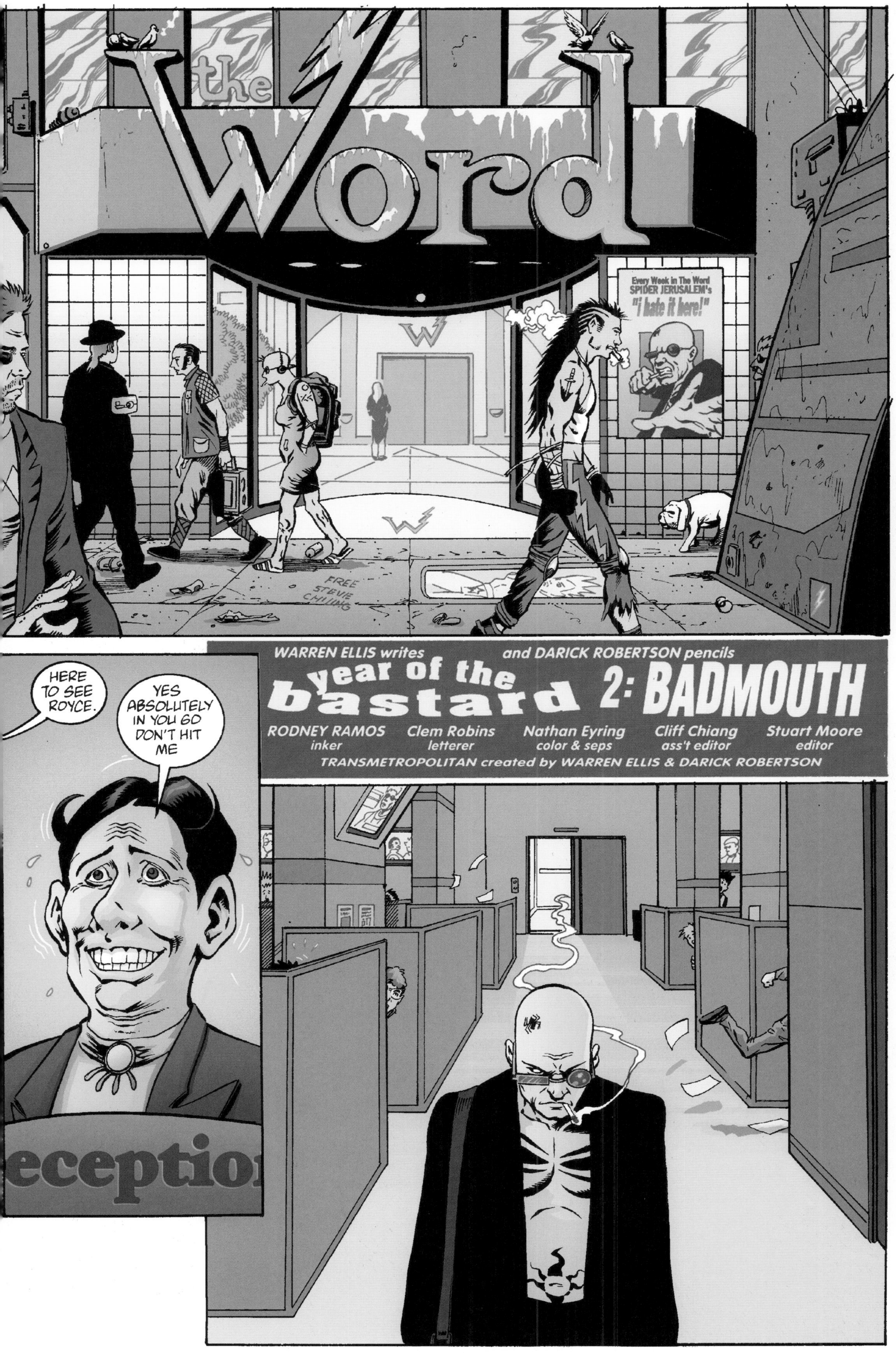
the Word
Every Week in The Word
SPIDER JERUSALEM's
"i hate it here!"
FREE STEVE CHIUNG
WARREN ELLIS writes and DARICK ROBERTSON pencils
year of the bastard 2: BADMOUTH
RODNEY RAMOS inker
Clem Robins letterer
Nathan Eyring color & seps
Cliff Chiang ass't editor
Stuart Moore editor
TRANSMETROPOLITAN created by WARREN ELLIS & DARICK ROBERTSON
HERE TO SEE ROYCE.
YES ABSOLUTELY IN YOU GO DON'T HIT ME

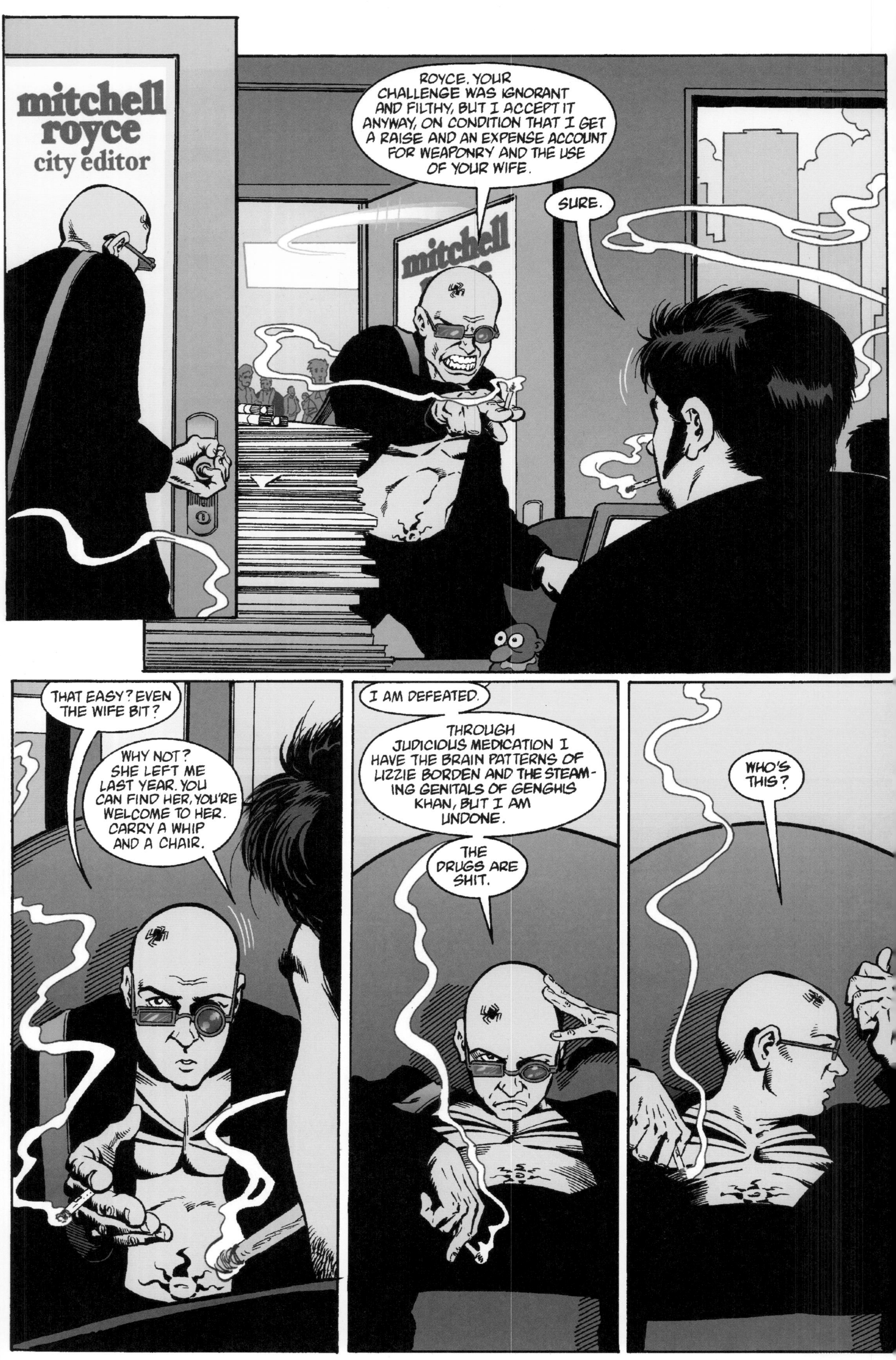
mitchell royce city editor
ROYCE. YOUR CHALLENGE WAS IGNORANT AND FILTHY, BUT I ACCEPT IT ANYWAY, ON CONDITION THAT I GET A RAISE AND AN EXPENSE ACCOUNT FOR WEAPONRY AND THE USE OF YOUR WIFE.
SURE.
THAT EASY? EVEN THE WIFE BIT?
WHY NOT? SHE LEFT ME LAST YEAR. YOU CAN FIND HER, YOU'RE WELCOME TO HER. CARRY A WHIP AND A CHAIR.
I AM DEFEATED.
THROUGH JUDICIOUS MEDICATION I HAVE THE BRAIN PATTERNS OF LIZZIE BORDEN AND THE STEAMING GENITALS OF GENGHIS KHAN, BUT I AM UNDONE.
THE DRUGS ARE SHIT.
WHO'S THIS?

THIS IS YELENA ROSSINI.

SHE'S YOUR NEW ASSISTANT.

LIKE FUCK SHE IS--

SHE IS ALSO MY NIECE, SO BEHAVE YOURSELF AND PLAY NICE, OR I'LL KNOW.

NIECE?

YOU-- YOU--

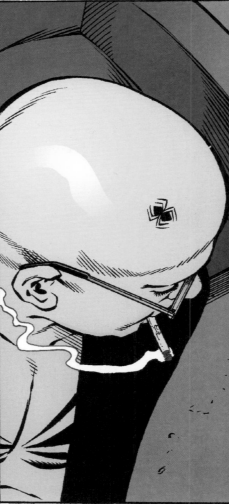

ALL RIGHT. YOU MEET ME OUTSIDE MEANY HALL TOMORROW AT 8 AM. BRING RECORDING GEAR AND A BIG KITBAG FOR MY PROFESSIONAL EQUIPMENT.

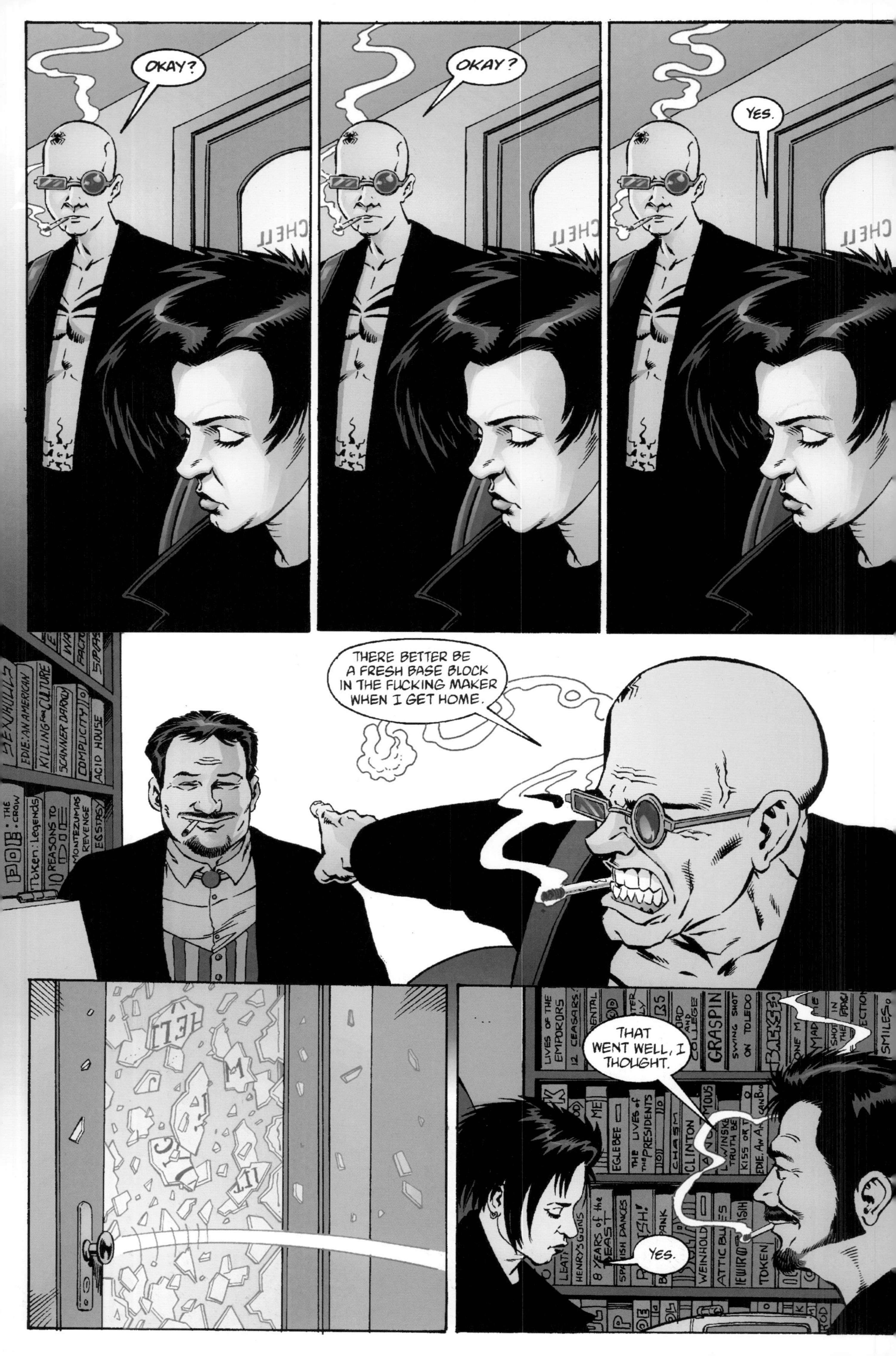
OKAY?
OKAY?
YES.
THERE BETTER BE A FRESH BASE BLOCK IN THE FUCKING MAKER WHEN I GET HOME.
THAT WENT WELL, I THOUGHT.
YES.

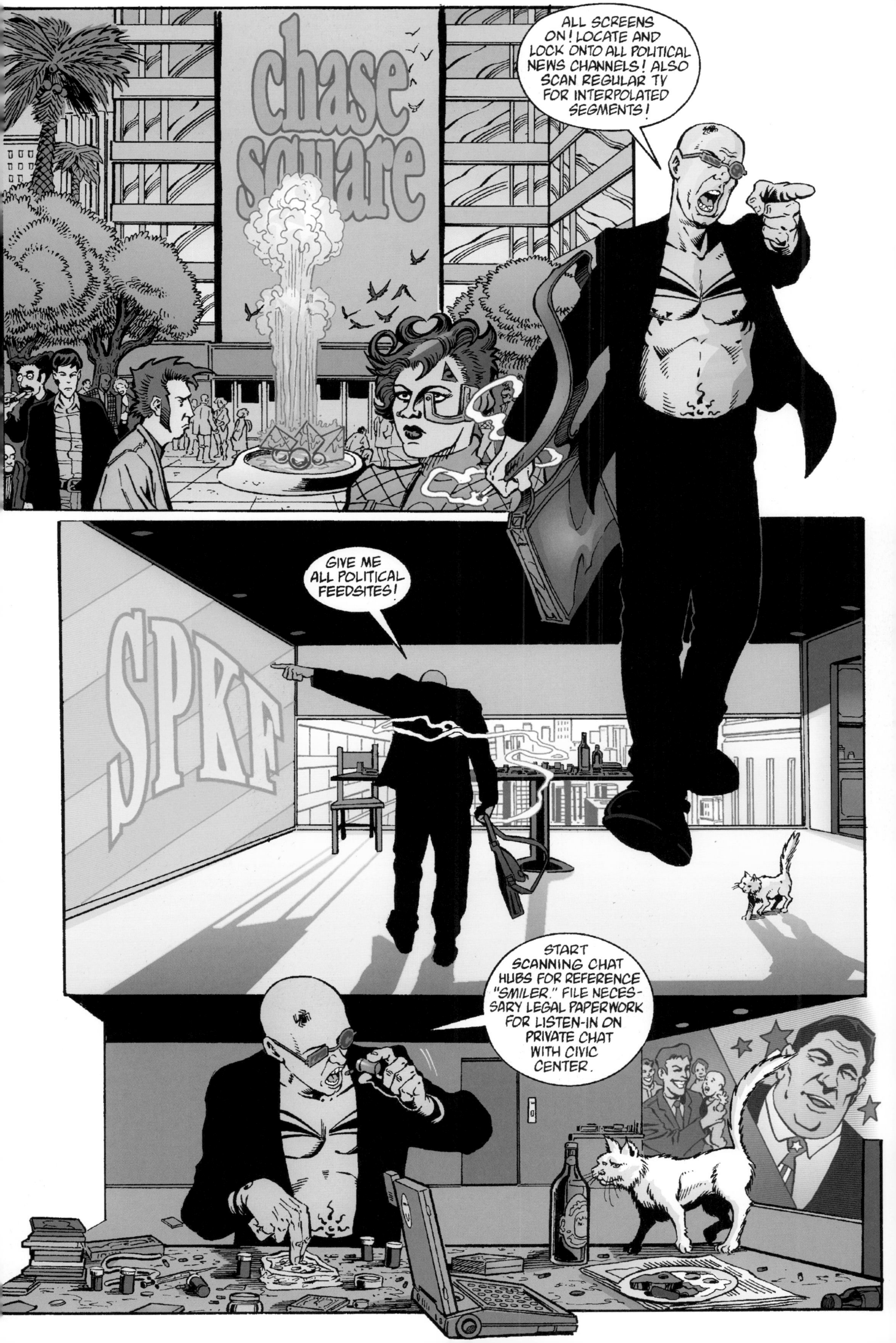
chase square
ALL SCREENS ON! LOCATE AND LOCK ONTO ALL POLITICAL NEWS CHANNELS! ALSO SCAN REGULAR TV FOR INTERPOLATED SEGMENTS!
SPKF
GIVE ME ALL POLITICAL FEEDSITES!
START SCANNING CHAT HUBS FOR REFERENCE "SMILER." FILE NECES-SARY LEGAL PAPERWORK FOR LISTEN-IN ON PRIVATE CHAT WITH CIVIC CENTER.

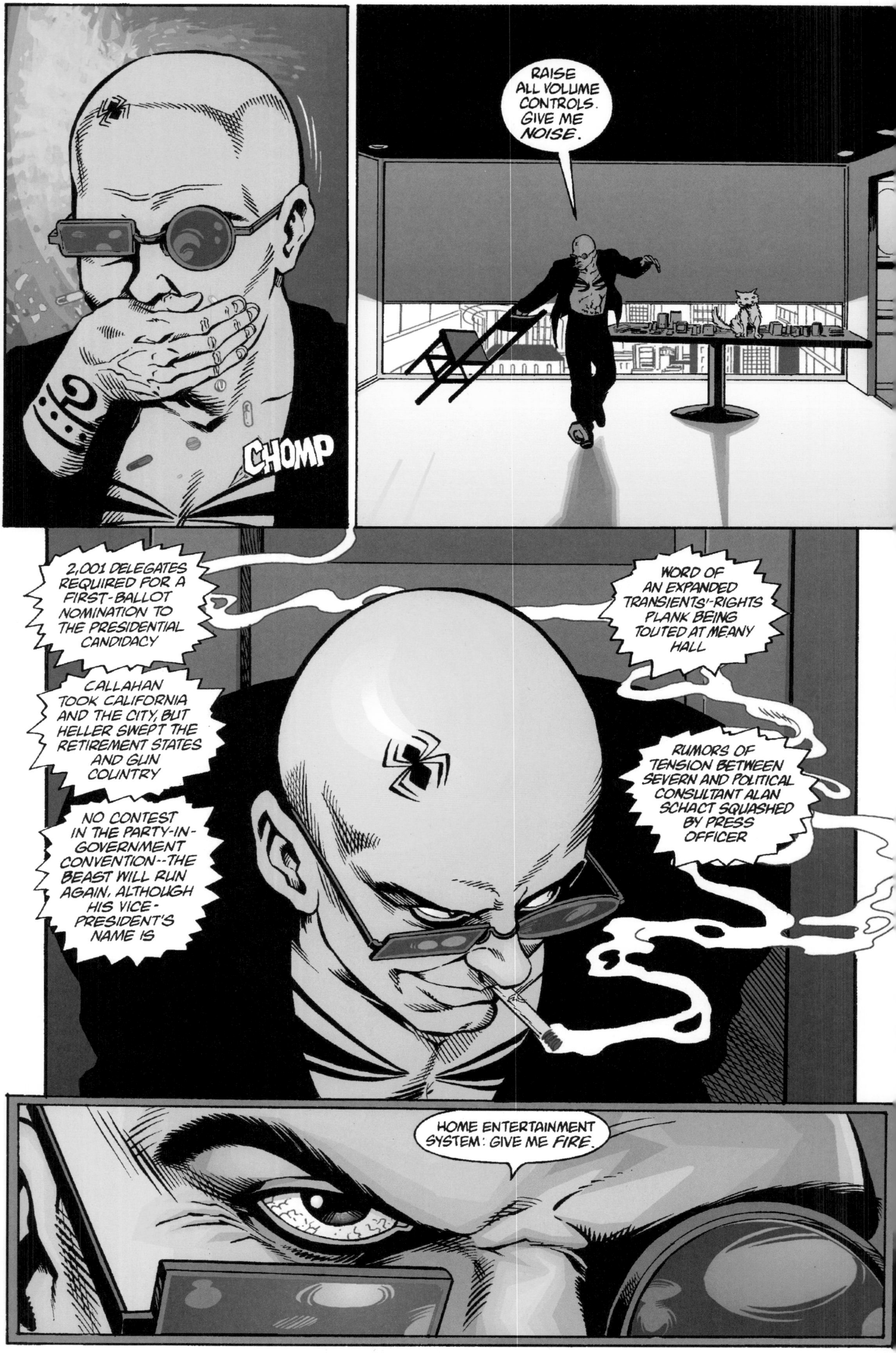
CHOMP
RAISE ALL VOLUME CONTROLS. GIVE ME NOISE.
2,001 DELEGATES REQUIRED FOR A FIRST-BALLOT NOMINATION TO THE PRESIDENTIAL CANDIDACY
CALLAHAN TOOK CALIFORNIA AND THE CITY, BUT HELLER SWEPT THE RETIREMENT STATES AND GUN COUNTRY
NO CONTEST IN THE PARTY-IN-GOVERNMENT CONVENTION--THE BEAST WILL RUN AGAIN, ALTHOUGH HIS VICE-PRESIDENT'S NAME IS
WORD OF AN EXPANDED TRANSIENTS'-RIGHTS PLANK BEING TOUTED AT MEANY HALL
RUMORS OF TENSION BETWEEN SEVERN AND POLITICAL CONSULTANT ALAN SCHACT SQUASHED BY PRESS OFFICER
HOME ENTERTAINMENT SYSTEM: GIVE ME FIRE.

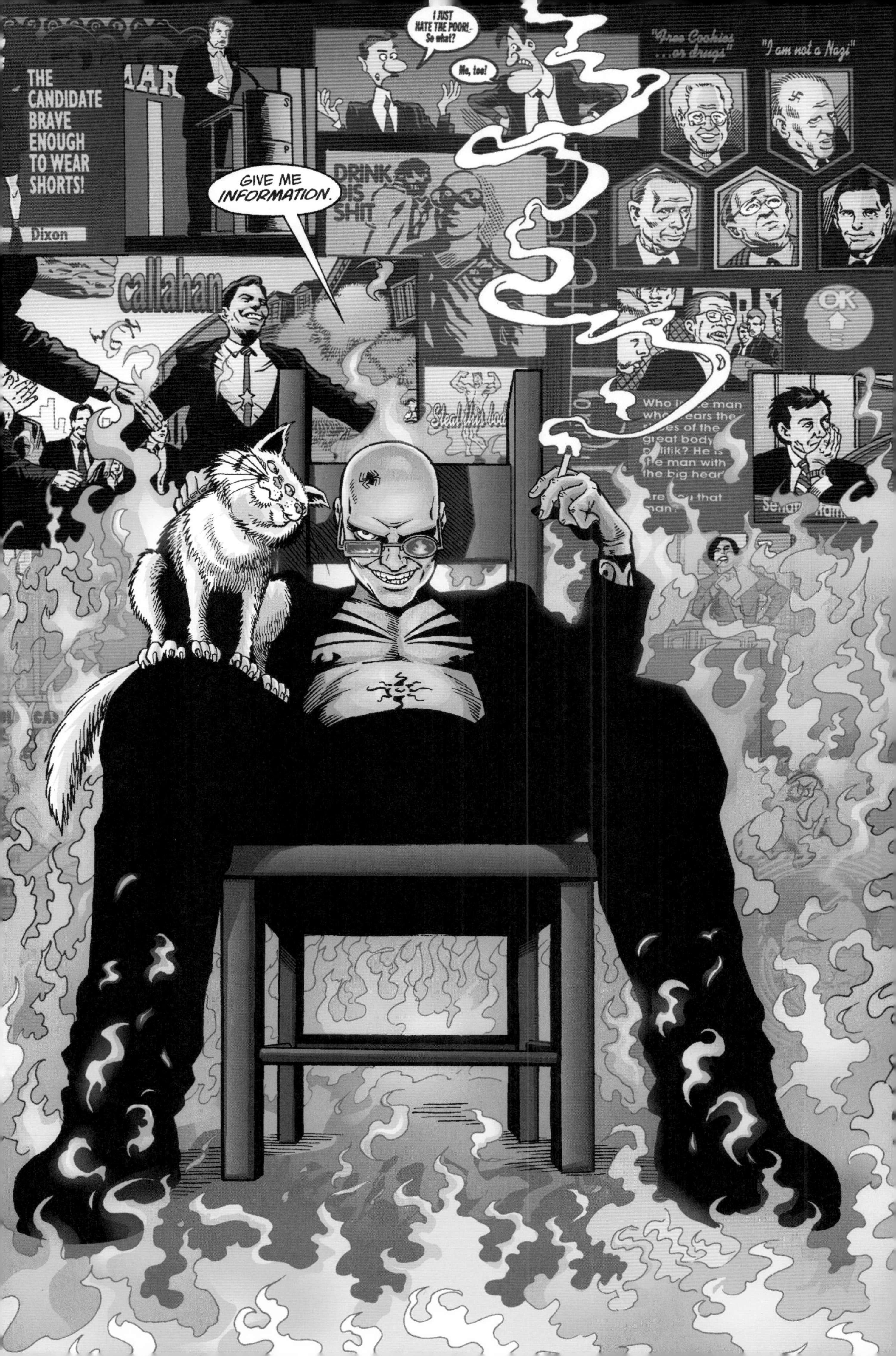
THE CANDIDATE BRAVE ENOUGH TO WEAR SHORTS!
Dixon
I JUST HATE THE POOR!- So what?
Me, too!
"Free Cookies ...or drugs"
"I am not a Nazi"
GIVE ME INFORMATION.
DRINK DIS SHIT
callahan
OK

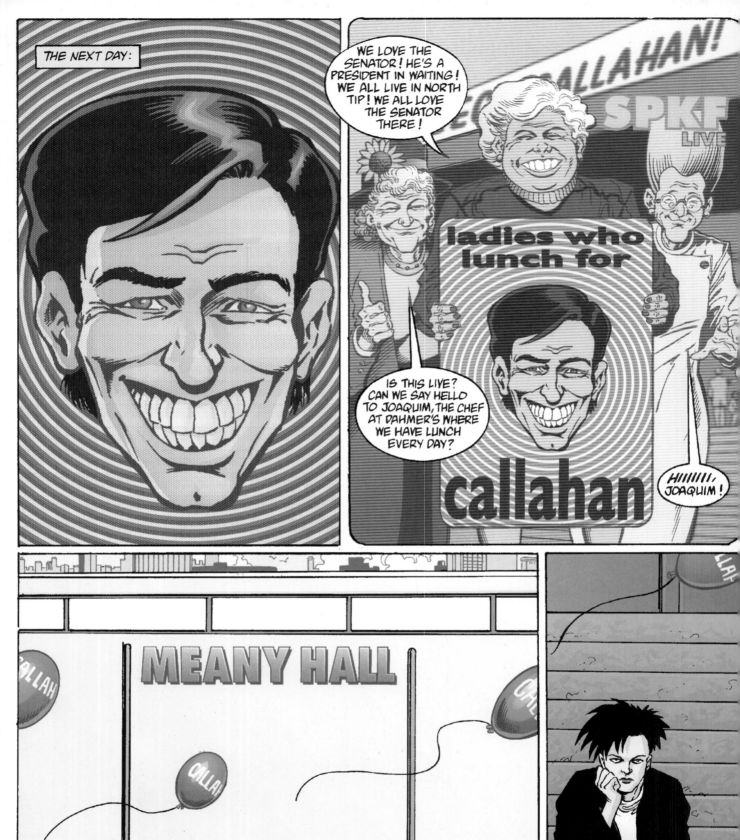

THE NEXT DAY:

WE LOVE THE SENATOR! HE'S A PRESIDENT IN WAITING! WE ALL LIVE IN NORTH TIP! WE ALL LOVE THE SENATOR THERE!

IS THIS LIVE? CAN WE SAY HELLO TO JOAQUIM, THE CHEF AT DAHMER'S WHERE WE HAVE LUNCH EVERY DAY?

HIIIIIIII, JOAQUIM!

ladies who lunch for callahan

MEANY HALL

ELECT CALLAHAN!

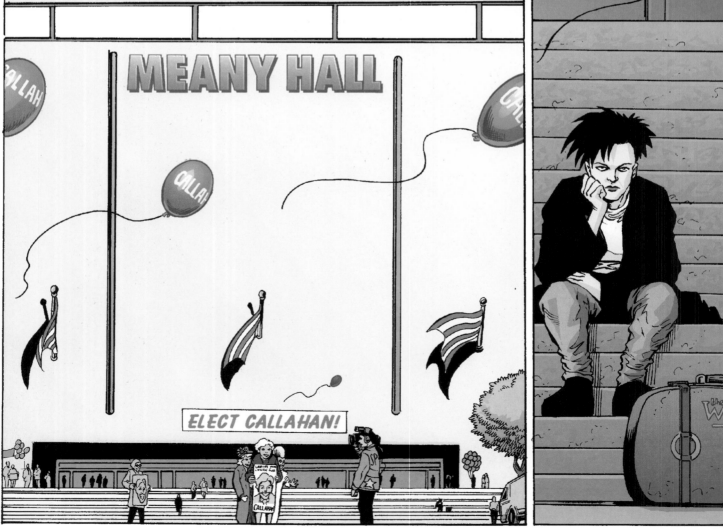

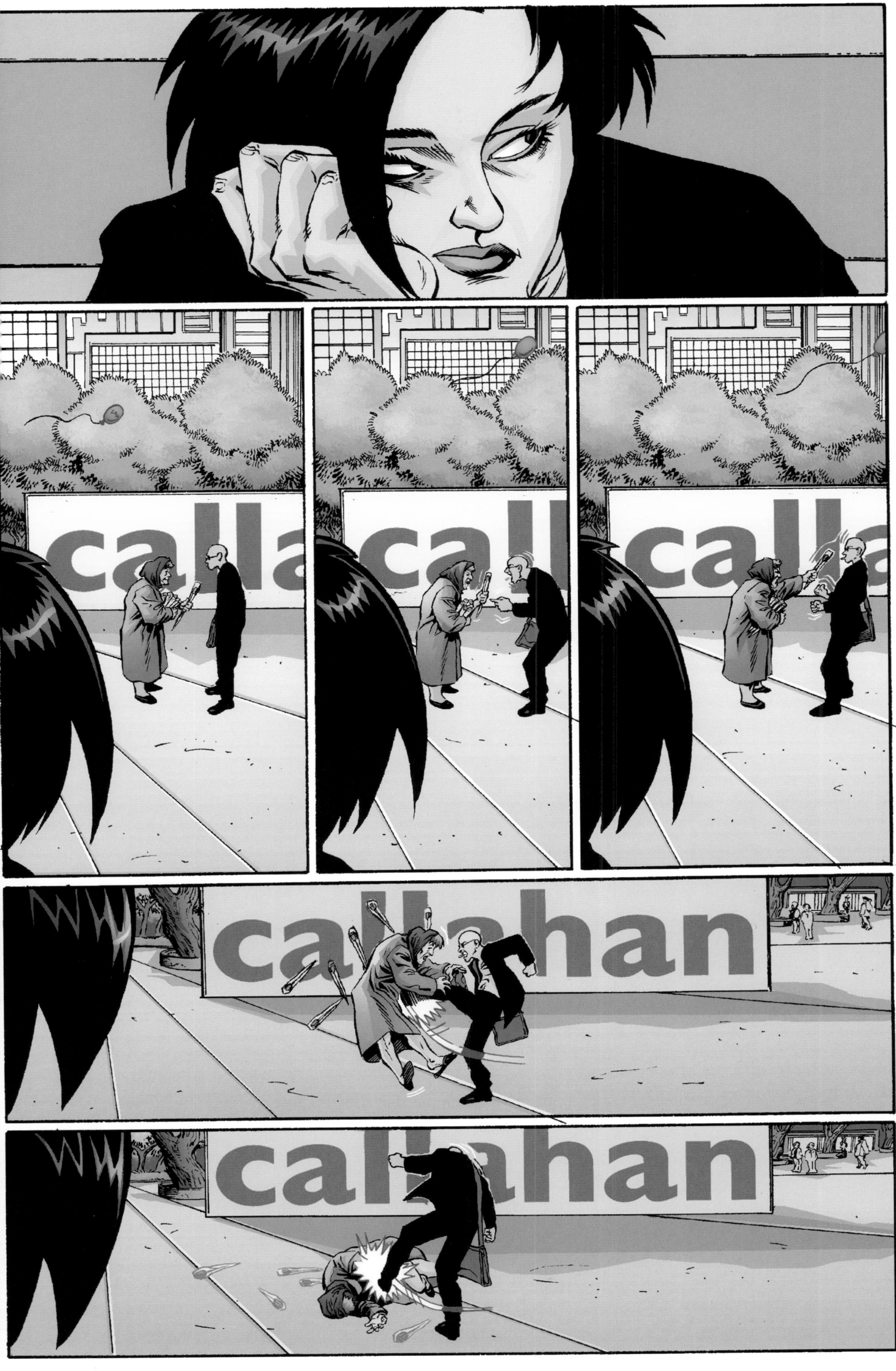
calla
call
calla
callahan
callahan

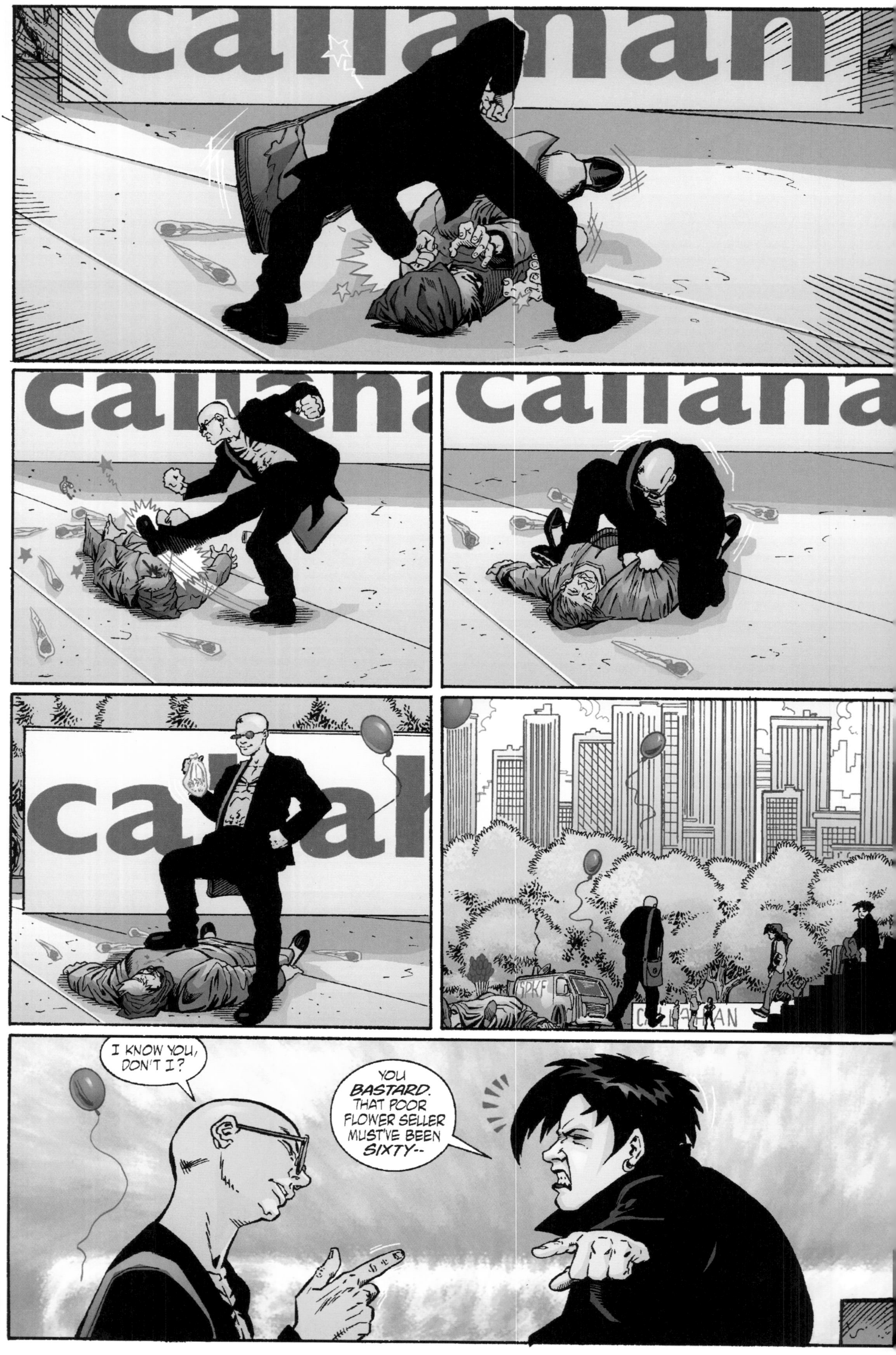
callahan
I KNOW YOU, DON'T I?
YOU *BASTARD*. THAT POOR FLOWER SELLER MUST'VE BEEN *SIXTY*--

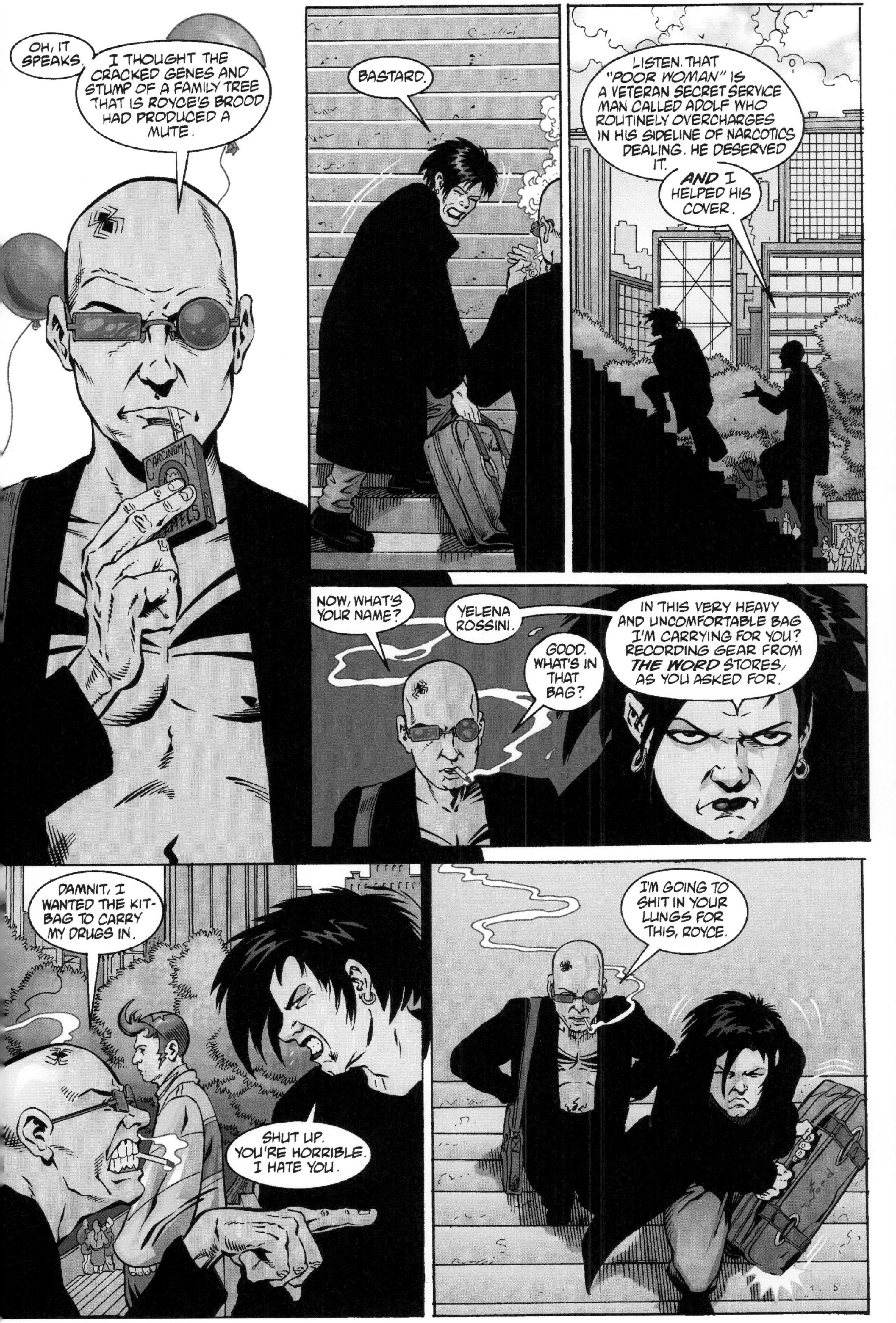
OH, IT SPEAKS.
I THOUGHT THE CRACKED GENES AND STUMP OF A FAMILY TREE THAT IS ROYCE'S BROOD HAD PRODUCED A MUTE.
CARCINUMA
BASTARD.
LISTEN. THAT "POOR WOMAN" IS A VETERAN SECRET SERVICE MAN CALLED ADOLF WHO ROUTINELY OVERCHARGES IN HIS SIDELINE OF NARCOTICS DEALING. HE DESERVED IT.
AND I HELPED HIS COVER.
NOW, WHAT'S YOUR NAME?
YELENA ROSSINI.
GOOD. WHAT'S IN THAT BAG?
IN THIS VERY HEAVY AND UNCOMFORTABLE BAG I'M CARRYING FOR YOU? RECORDING GEAR FROM THE WORD STORES, AS YOU ASKED FOR.
DAMNIT, I WANTED THE KIT-BAG TO CARRY MY DRUGS IN.
SHUT UP. YOU'RE HORRIBLE. I HATE YOU.
I'M GOING TO SHIT IN YOUR LUNGS FOR THIS, ROYCE.

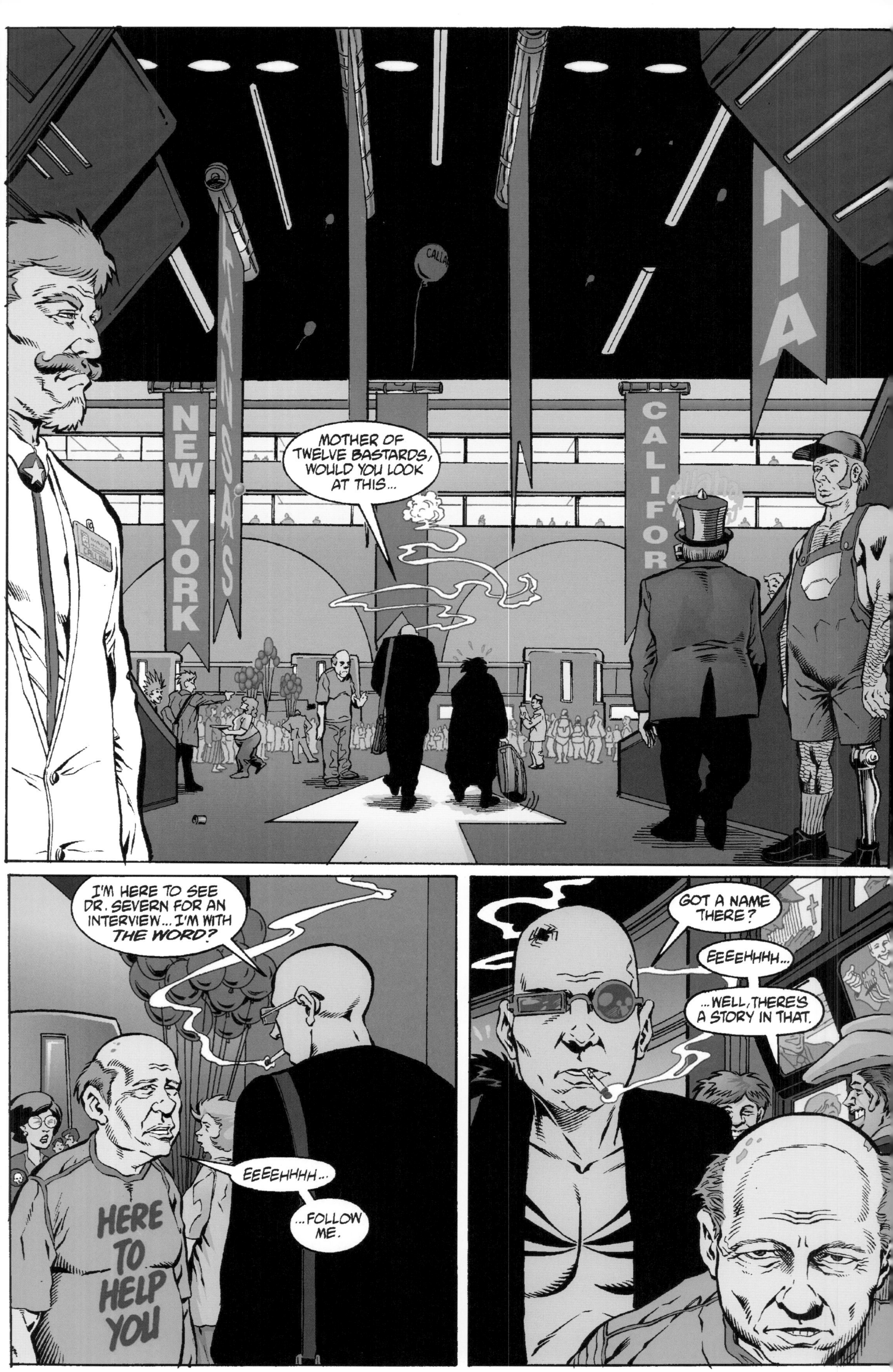
NEW YORK
KANSAS
CALIFOR
NIA
MOTHER OF TWELVE BASTARDS, WOULD YOU LOOK AT THIS...
I'M HERE TO SEE DR. SEVERN FOR AN INTERVIEW... I'M WITH THE WORD?
EEEEHHHH...
...FOLLOW ME.
HERE TO HELP YOU
GOT A NAME THERE?
EEEEHHHH...
...WELL, THERE'S A STORY IN THAT.

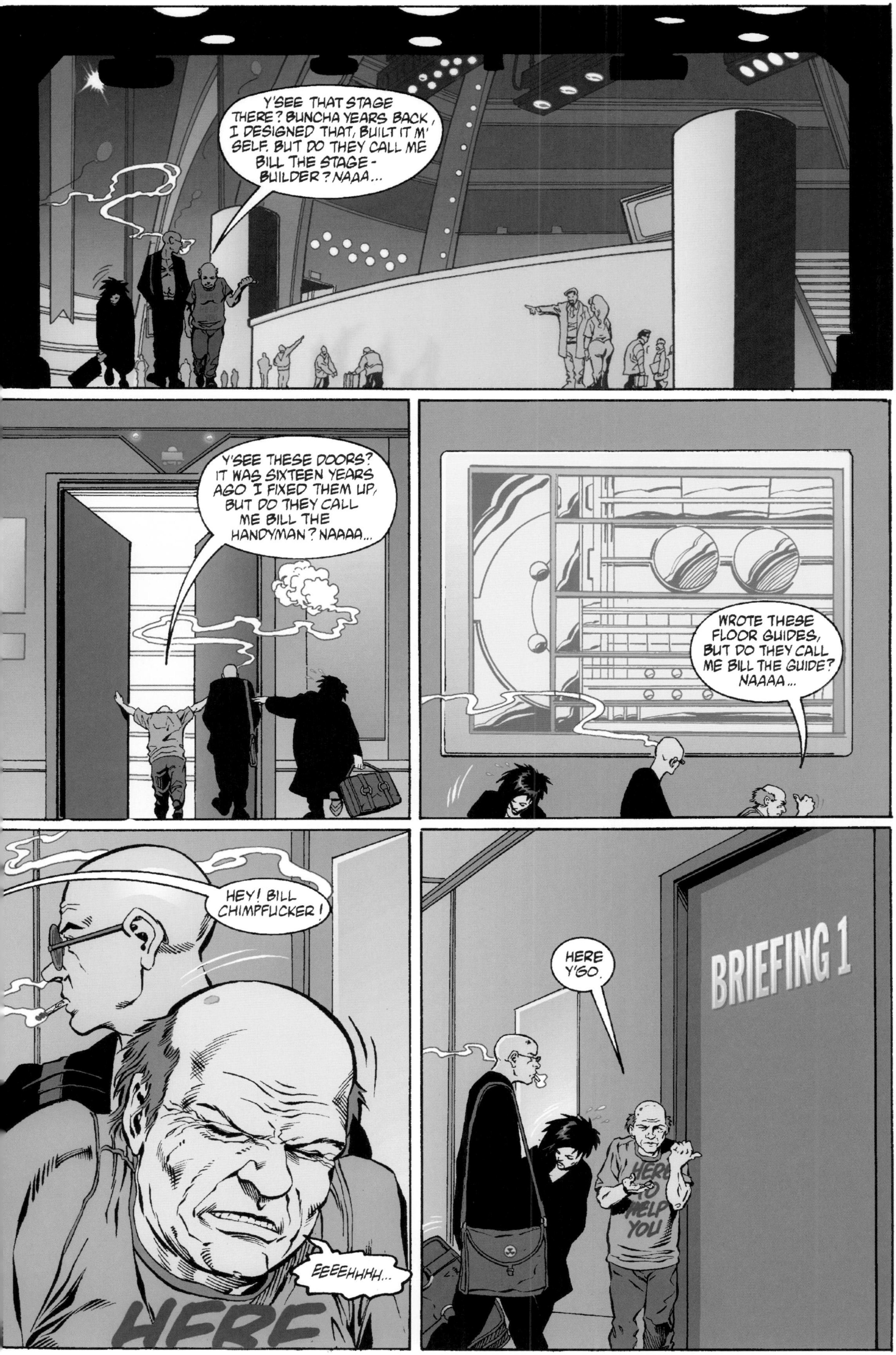
Y'SEE THAT STAGE THERE? BUNCHA YEARS BACK, I DESIGNED THAT, BUILT IT M' SELF. BUT DO THEY CALL ME BILL THE STAGE-BUILDER? NAAA...
Y'SEE THESE DOORS? IT WAS SIXTEEN YEARS AGO I FIXED THEM UP, BUT DO THEY CALL ME BILL THE HANDYMAN? NAAAA...
WROTE THESE FLOOR GUIDES, BUT DO THEY CALL ME BILL THE GUIDE? NAAAA...
HEY! BILL CHIMPFUCKER!
EEEEHHHH...
HERE
HERE Y'GO.
BRIEFING 1
HERE TO HELP YOU

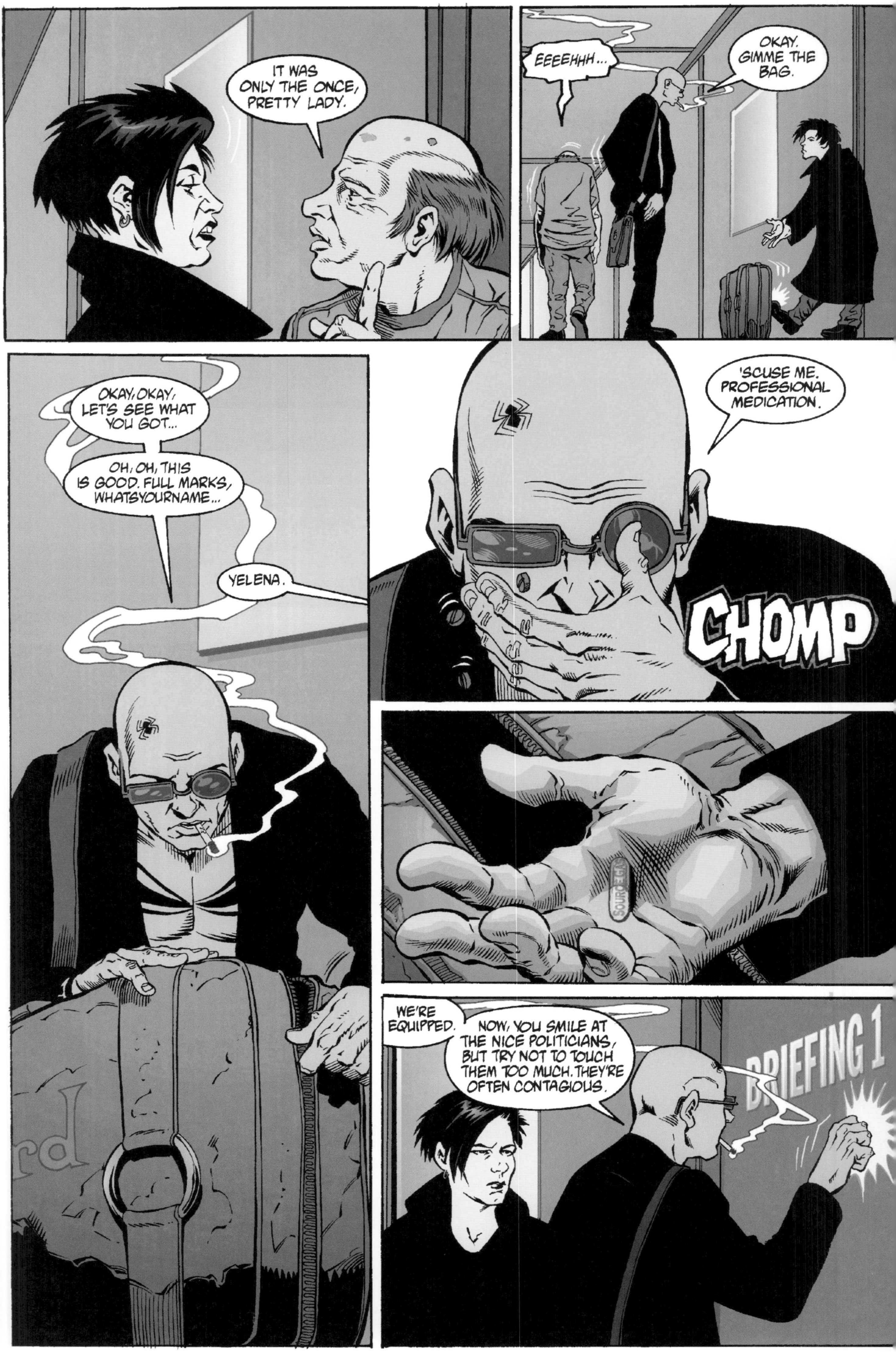
IT WAS ONLY THE ONCE, PRETTY LADY.
EEEEHHH...
OKAY. GIMME THE BAG.
OKAY, OKAY, LET'S SEE WHAT YOU GOT...
OH, OH, THIS IS GOOD. FULL MARKS, WHATSYOURNAME...
YELENA.
'SCUSE ME. PROFESSIONAL MEDICATION.
CHOMP
WE'RE EQUIPPED.
NOW, YOU SMILE AT THE NICE POLITICIANS, BUT TRY NOT TO TOUCH THEM TOO MUCH. THEY'RE OFTEN CONTAGIOUS.
BRIEFING 1

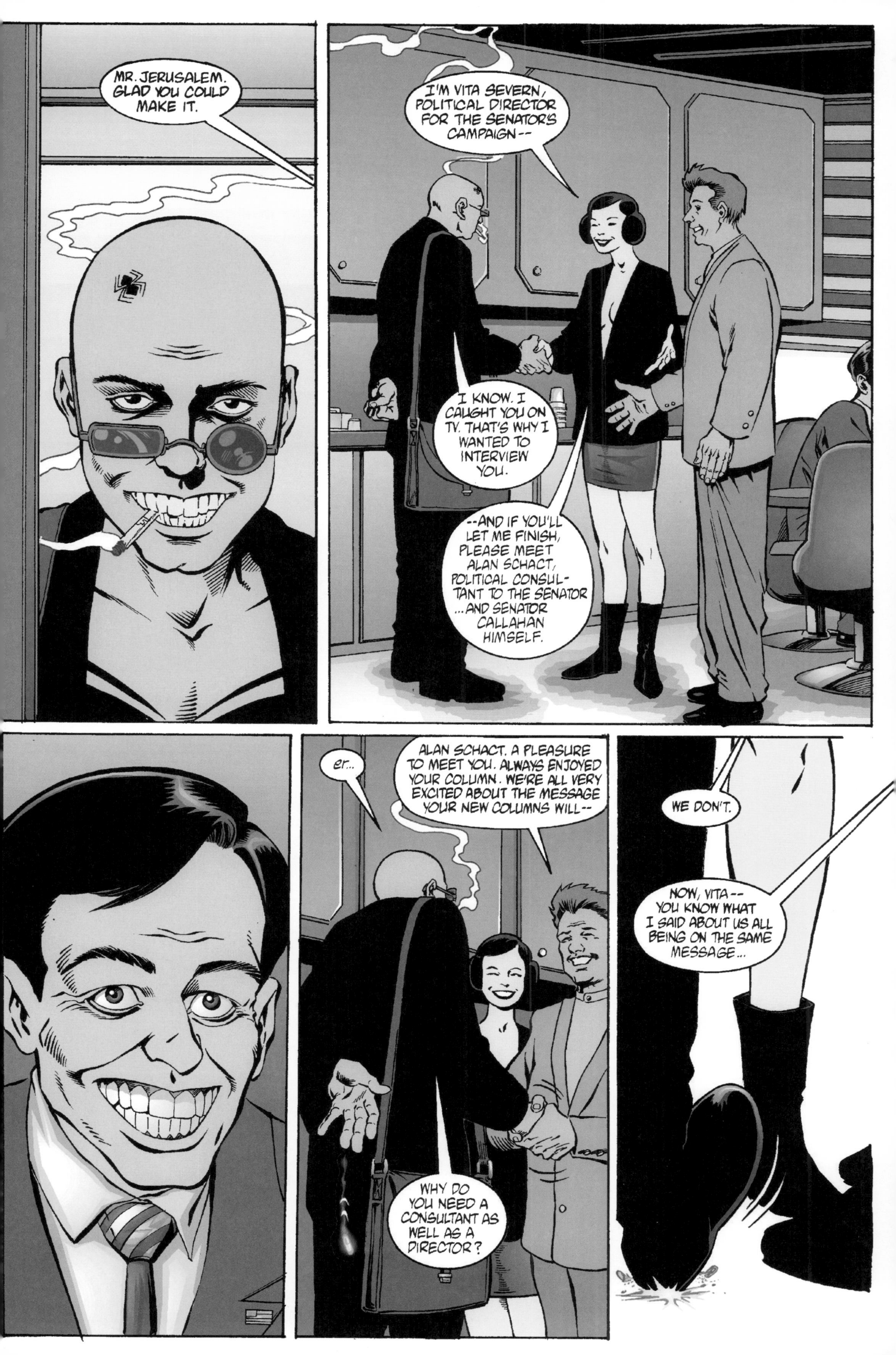
MR. JERUSALEM. GLAD YOU COULD MAKE IT.
I'M VITA SEVERN, POLITICAL DIRECTOR FOR THE SENATOR'S CAMPAIGN--
I KNOW. I CAUGHT YOU ON TV. THAT'S WHY I WANTED TO INTERVIEW YOU.
--AND IF YOU'LL LET ME FINISH, PLEASE MEET ALAN SCHACT, POLITICAL CONSUL-TANT TO THE SENATOR ...AND SENATOR CALLAHAN HIMSELF.
er..
ALAN SCHACT. A PLEASURE TO MEET YOU. ALWAYS ENJOYED YOUR COLUMN. WE'RE ALL VERY EXCITED ABOUT THE MESSAGE YOUR NEW COLUMNS WILL--
WHY DO YOU NEED A CONSULTANT AS WELL AS A DIRECTOR?
WE DON'T.
NOW, VITA-- YOU KNOW WHAT I SAID ABOUT US ALL BEING ON THE SAME MESSAGE...

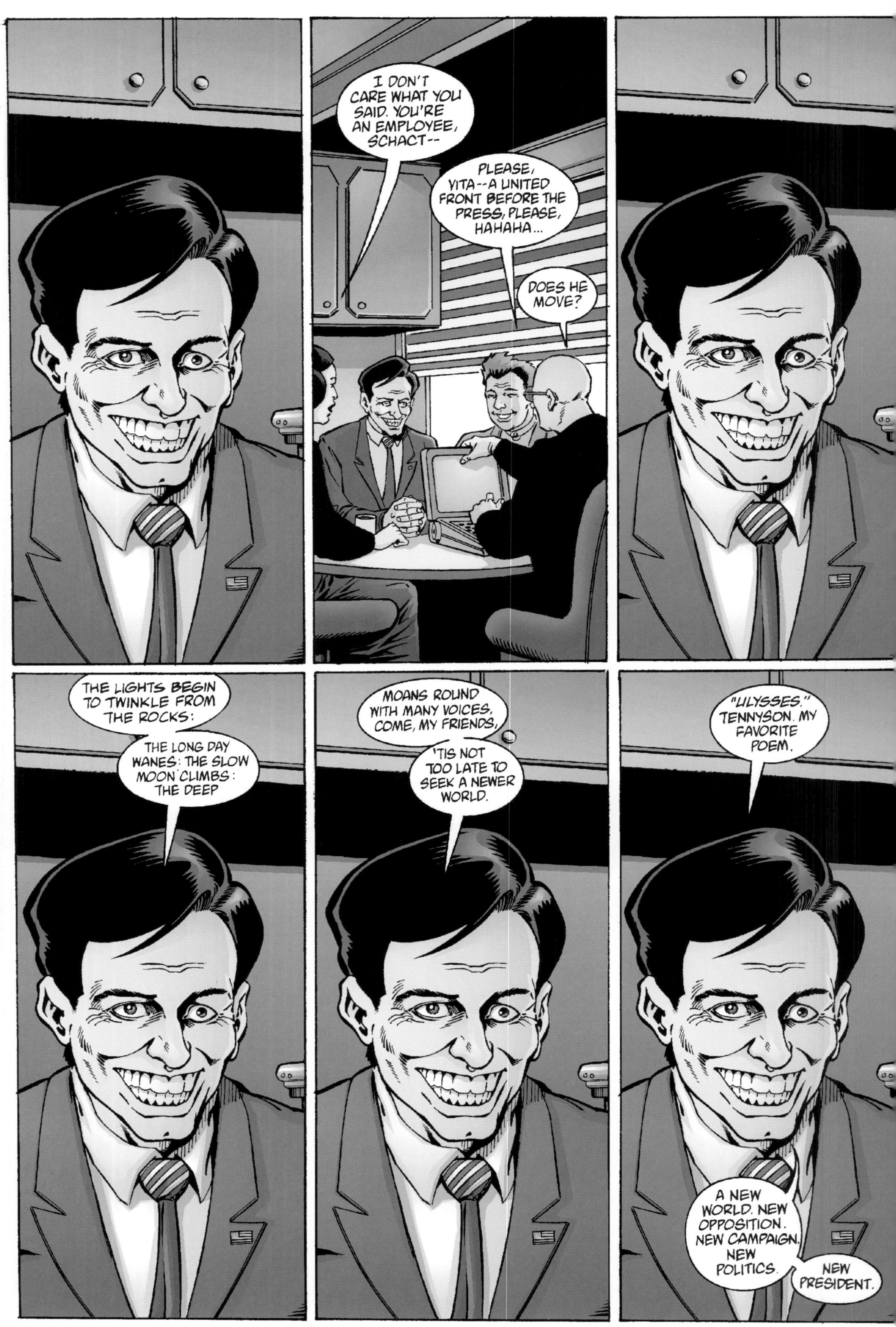
I DON'T CARE WHAT YOU SAID. YOU'RE AN EMPLOYEE, SCHACT--
PLEASE, YITA--A UNITED FRONT BEFORE THE PRESS, PLEASE, HAHAHA...
DOES HE MOVE?
THE LIGHTS BEGIN TO TWINKLE FROM THE ROCKS:
THE LONG DAY WANES: THE SLOW MOON CLIMBS: THE DEEP
MOANS ROUND WITH MANY VOICES. COME, MY FRIENDS,
'TIS NOT TOO LATE TO SEEK A NEWER WORLD.
"ULYSSES." TENNYSON. MY FAVORITE POEM.
A NEW WORLD. NEW OPPOSITION. NEW CAMPAIGN. NEW POLITICS.
NEW PRESIDENT.

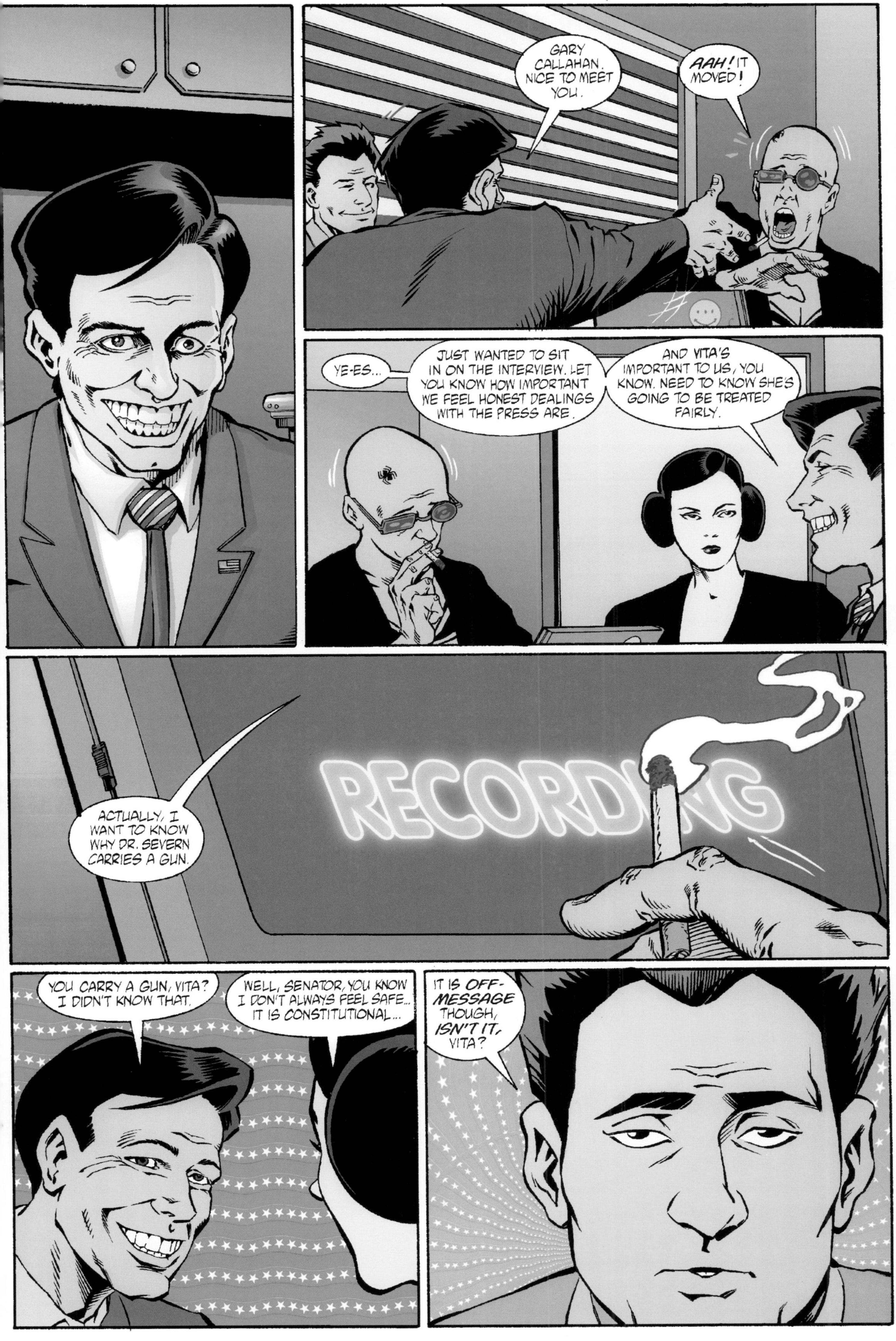
GARY CALLAHAN. NICE TO MEET YOU.
AAH! IT MOVED!
YE-ES...
JUST WANTED TO SIT IN ON THE INTERVIEW. LET YOU KNOW HOW IMPORTANT WE FEEL HONEST DEALINGS WITH THE PRESS ARE.
AND VITA'S IMPORTANT TO US, YOU KNOW. NEED TO KNOW SHE'S GOING TO BE TREATED FAIRLY.
RECORDING
ACTUALLY, I WANT TO KNOW WHY DR. SEVERN CARRIES A GUN.
YOU CARRY A GUN, VITA? I DIDN'T KNOW THAT.
WELL, SENATOR, YOU KNOW I DON'T ALWAYS FEEL SAFE... IT IS CONSTITUTIONAL...
IT IS OFF-MESSAGE THOUGH, ISN'T IT, VITA?

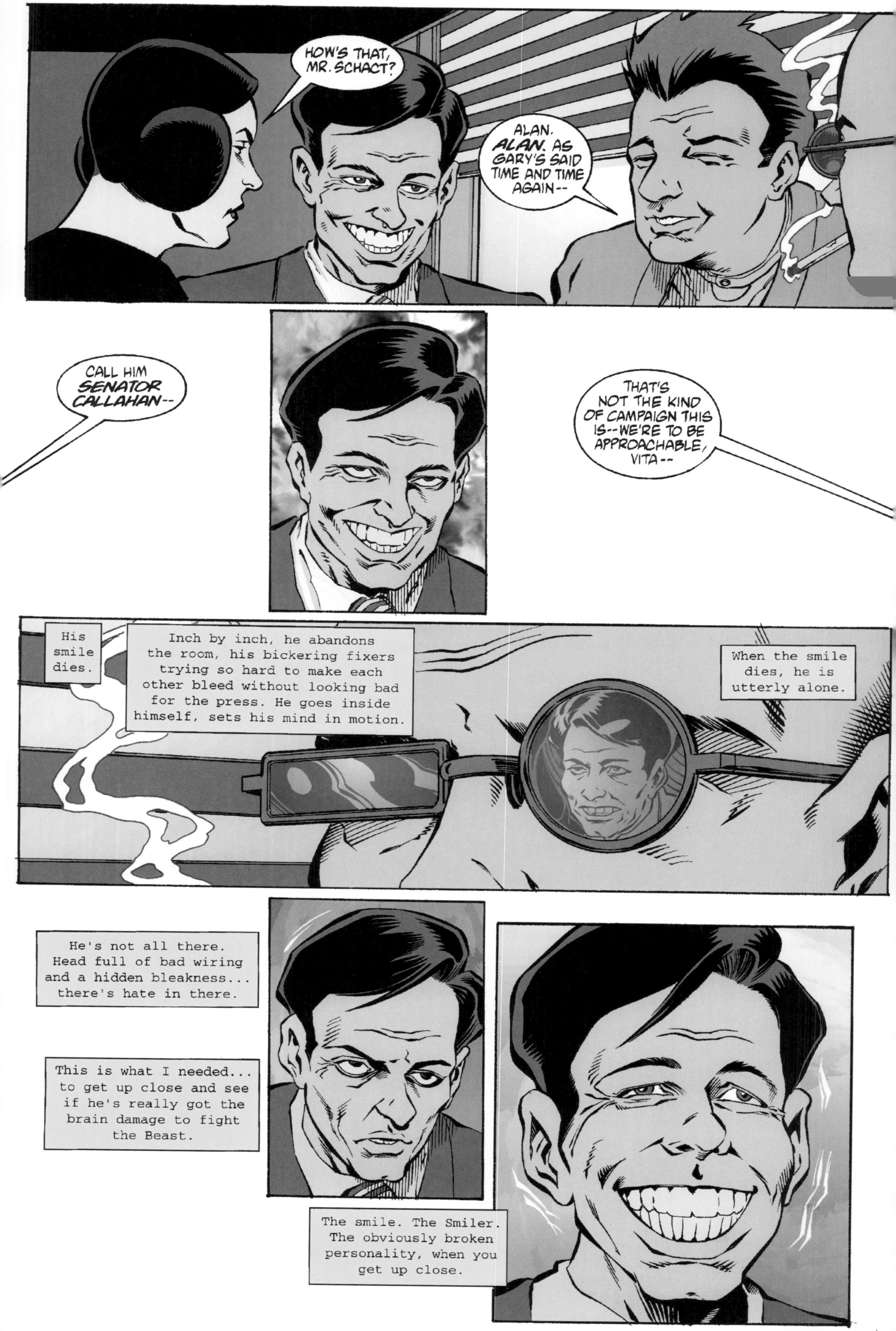
HOW'S THAT, MR. SCHACT?
ALAN. ALAN. AS GARY'S SAID TIME AND TIME AGAIN--
CALL HIM SENATOR CALLAHAN--
THAT'S NOT THE KIND OF CAMPAIGN THIS IS--WE'RE TO BE APPROACHABLE, VITA--
His smile dies.
Inch by inch, he abandons the room, his bickering fixers trying so hard to make each other bleed without looking bad for the press. He goes inside himself, sets his mind in motion.
When the smile dies, he is utterly alone.
He's not all there. Head full of bad wiring and a hidden bleakness... there's hate in there.
This is what I needed... to get up close and see if he's really got the brain damage to fight the Beast.
The smile. The Smiler. The obviously broken personality, when you get up close.

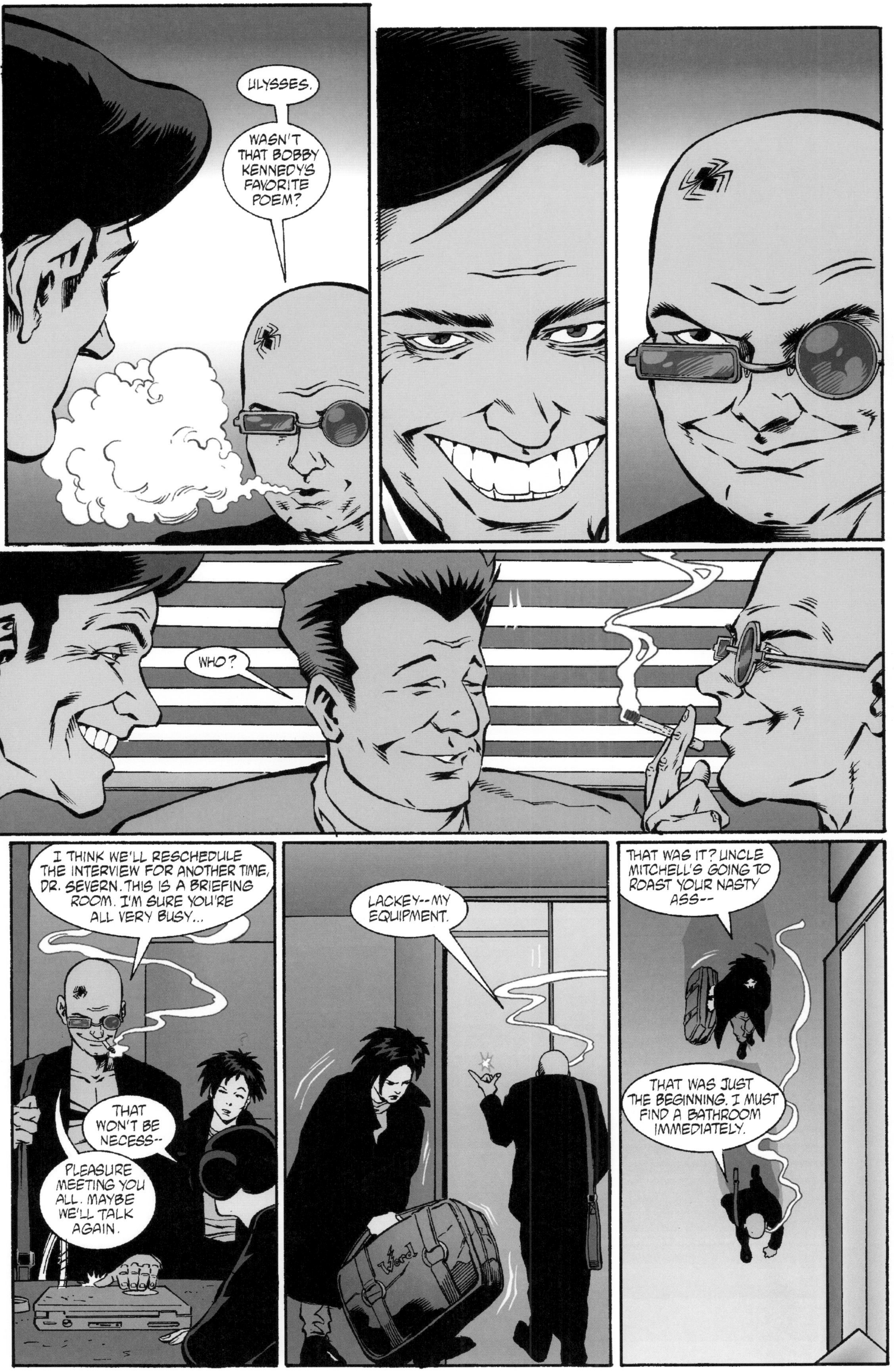
ULYSSES.
WASN'T THAT BOBBY KENNEDY'S FAVORITE POEM?
WHO?
I THINK WE'LL RESCHEDULE THE INTERVIEW FOR ANOTHER TIME, DR. SEVERN. THIS IS A BRIEFING ROOM. I'M SURE YOU'RE ALL VERY BUSY...
THAT WON'T BE NECESS--
PLEASURE MEETING YOU ALL. MAYBE WE'LL TALK AGAIN.
LACKEY--MY EQUIPMENT.
THAT WAS IT? UNCLE MITCHELL'S GOING TO ROAST YOUR NASTY ASS--
THAT WAS JUST THE BEGINNING. I MUST FIND A BATHROOM IMMEDIATELY.

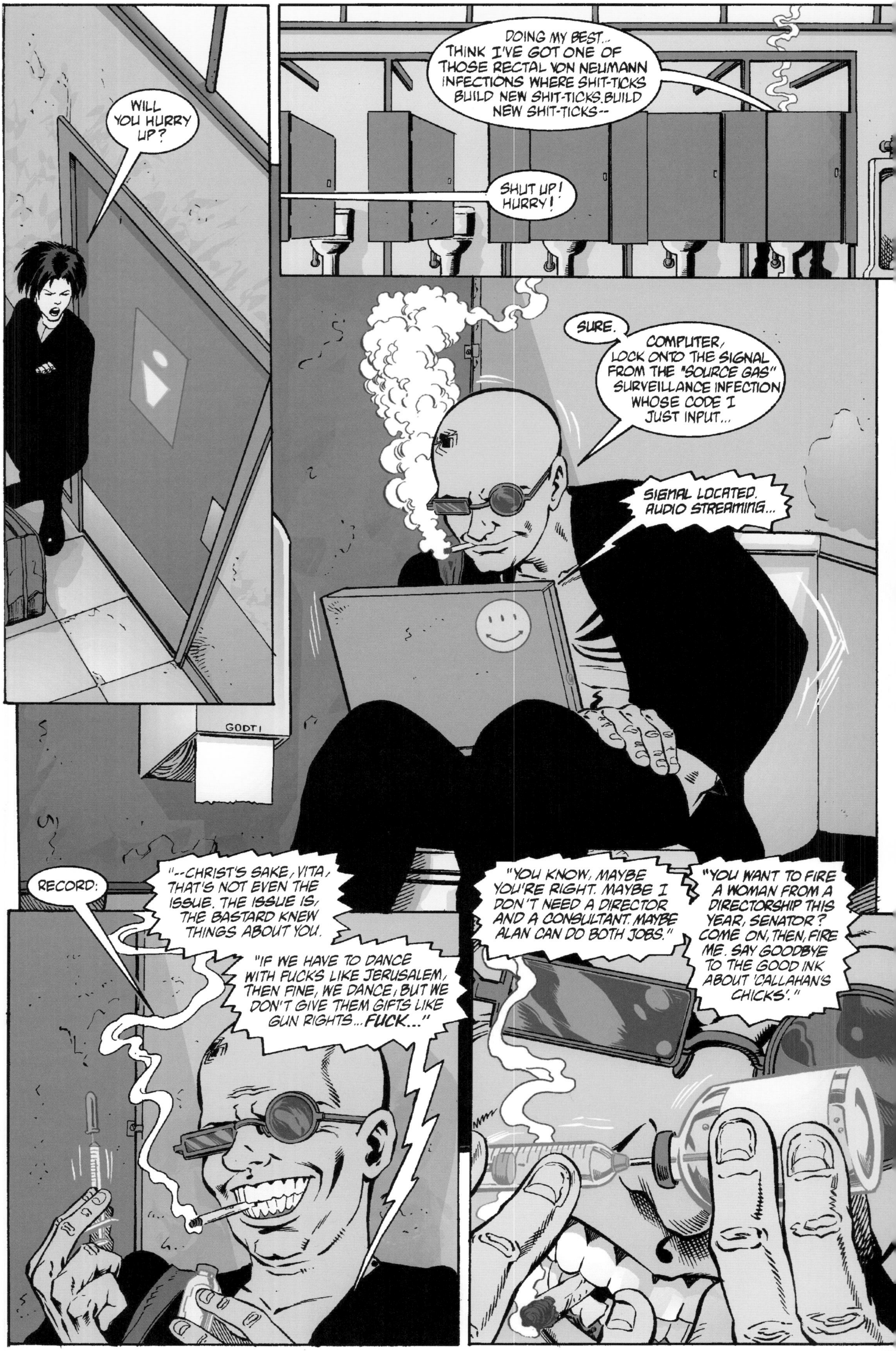
WILL YOU HURRY UP?
DOING MY BEST... THINK I'VE GOT ONE OF THOSE RECTAL VON NEUMANN INFECTIONS WHERE SHIT-TICKS BUILD NEW SHIT-TICKS. BUILD NEW SHIT-TICKS--
SHUT UP! HURRY!
SURE.
COMPUTER, LOCK ONTO THE SIGNAL FROM THE "SOURCE GAS" SURVEILLANCE INFECTION WHOSE CODE I JUST INPUT...
SIGNAL LOCATED. AUDIO STREAMING...
GODTI
RECORD:
"--CHRIST'S SAKE, VITA, THAT'S NOT EVEN THE ISSUE. THE ISSUE IS, THE BASTARD KNEW THINGS ABOUT YOU.
"IF WE HAVE TO DANCE WITH FUCKS LIKE JERUSALEM, THEN FINE, WE DANCE, BUT WE DON'T GIVE THEM GIFTS LIKE GUN RIGHTS... FUCK..."
"YOU KNOW, MAYBE YOU'RE RIGHT. MAYBE I DON'T NEED A DIRECTOR AND A CONSULTANT. MAYBE ALAN CAN DO BOTH JOBS."
"YOU WANT TO FIRE A WOMAN FROM A DIRECTORSHIP THIS YEAR, SENATOR? COME ON, THEN, FIRE ME. SAY GOODBYE TO THE GOOD INK ABOUT 'CALLAHAN'S CHICKS'."

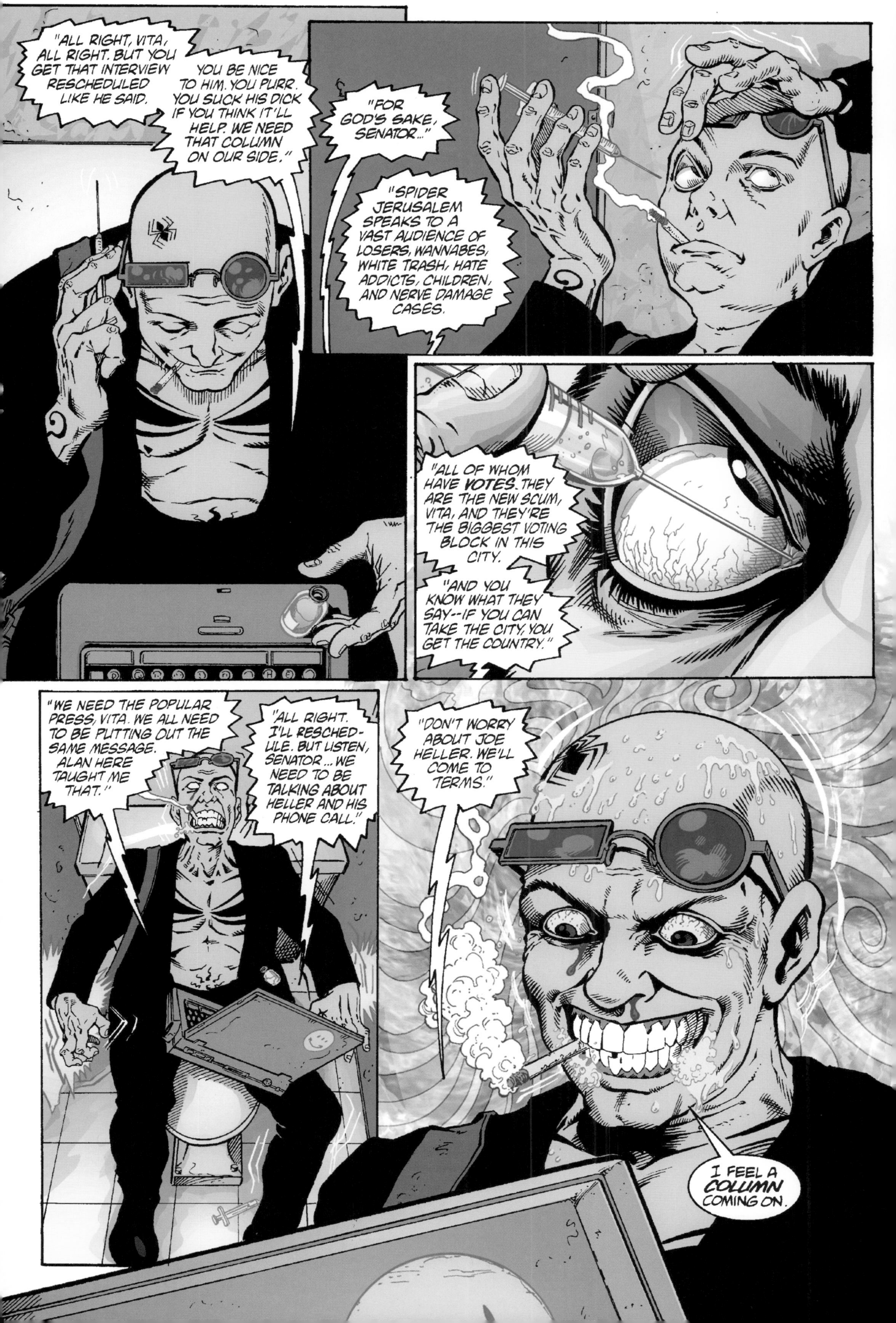
"ALL RIGHT, VITA, ALL RIGHT. BUT YOU GET THAT INTERVIEW RESCHEDULED LIKE HE SAID.
YOU BE NICE TO HIM. YOU PURR. YOU SUCK HIS DICK IF YOU THINK IT'LL HELP. WE NEED THAT COLUMN ON OUR SIDE."
"FOR GOD'S SAKE, SENATOR..."
"SPIDER JERUSALEM SPEAKS TO A VAST AUDIENCE OF LOSERS, WANNABES, WHITE TRASH, HATE ADDICTS, CHILDREN, AND NERVE DAMAGE CASES.
"ALL OF WHOM HAVE VOTES. THEY ARE THE NEW SCUM, VITA, AND THEY'RE THE BIGGEST VOTING BLOCK IN THIS CITY.
"AND YOU KNOW WHAT THEY SAY--IF YOU CAN TAKE THE CITY, YOU GET THE COUNTRY."
"WE NEED THE POPULAR PRESS, VITA. WE ALL NEED TO BE PUTTING OUT THE SAME MESSAGE. ALAN HERE TAUGHT ME THAT."
"ALL RIGHT. I'LL RESCHEDULE. BUT LISTEN, SENATOR ... WE NEED TO BE TALKING ABOUT HELLER AND HIS PHONE CALL."
"DON'T WORRY ABOUT JOE HELLER. WE'LL COME TO TERMS."
I FEEL A COLUMN COMING ON.

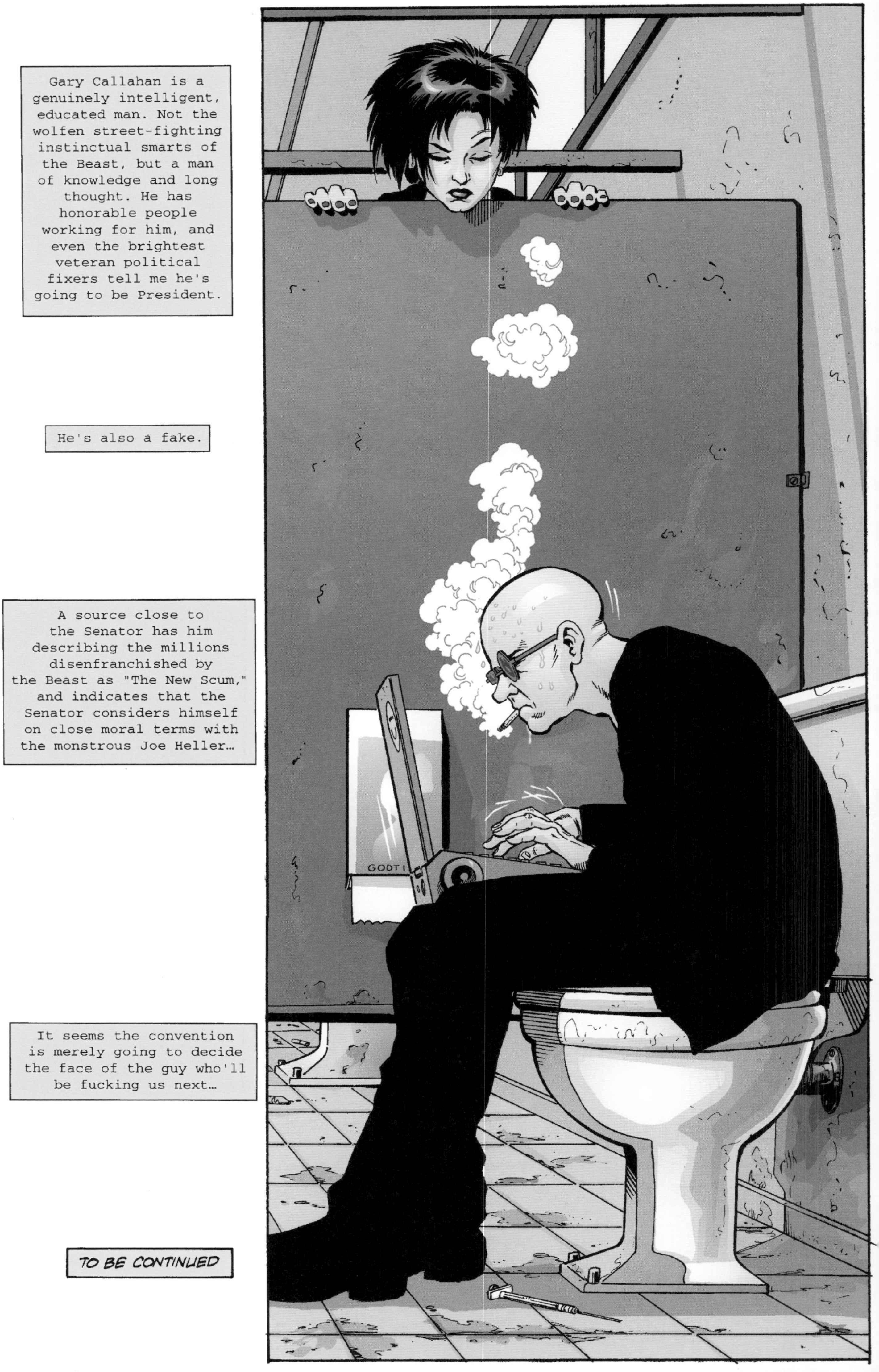
Gary Callahan is a genuinely intelligent, educated man. Not the wolfen street-fighting instinctual smarts of the Beast, but a man of knowledge and long thought. He has honorable people working for him, and even the brightest veteran political fixers tell me he's going to be President.
He's also a fake.
A source close to the Senator has him describing the millions disenfranchised by the Beast as "The New Scum," and indicates that the Senator considers himself on close moral terms with the monstrous Joe Heller...
It seems the convention is merely going to decide the face of the guy who'll be fucking us next...
TO BE CONTINUED

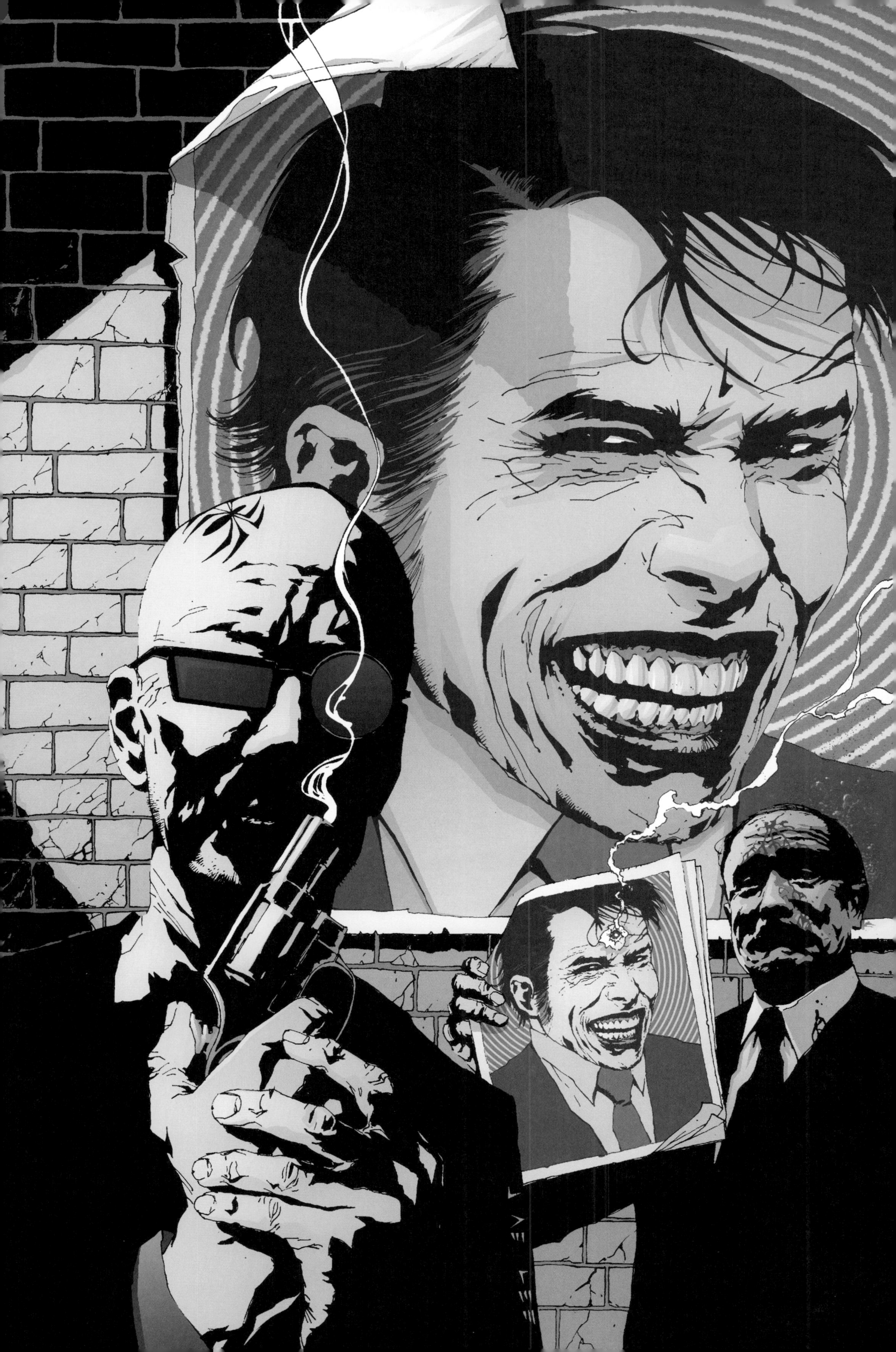

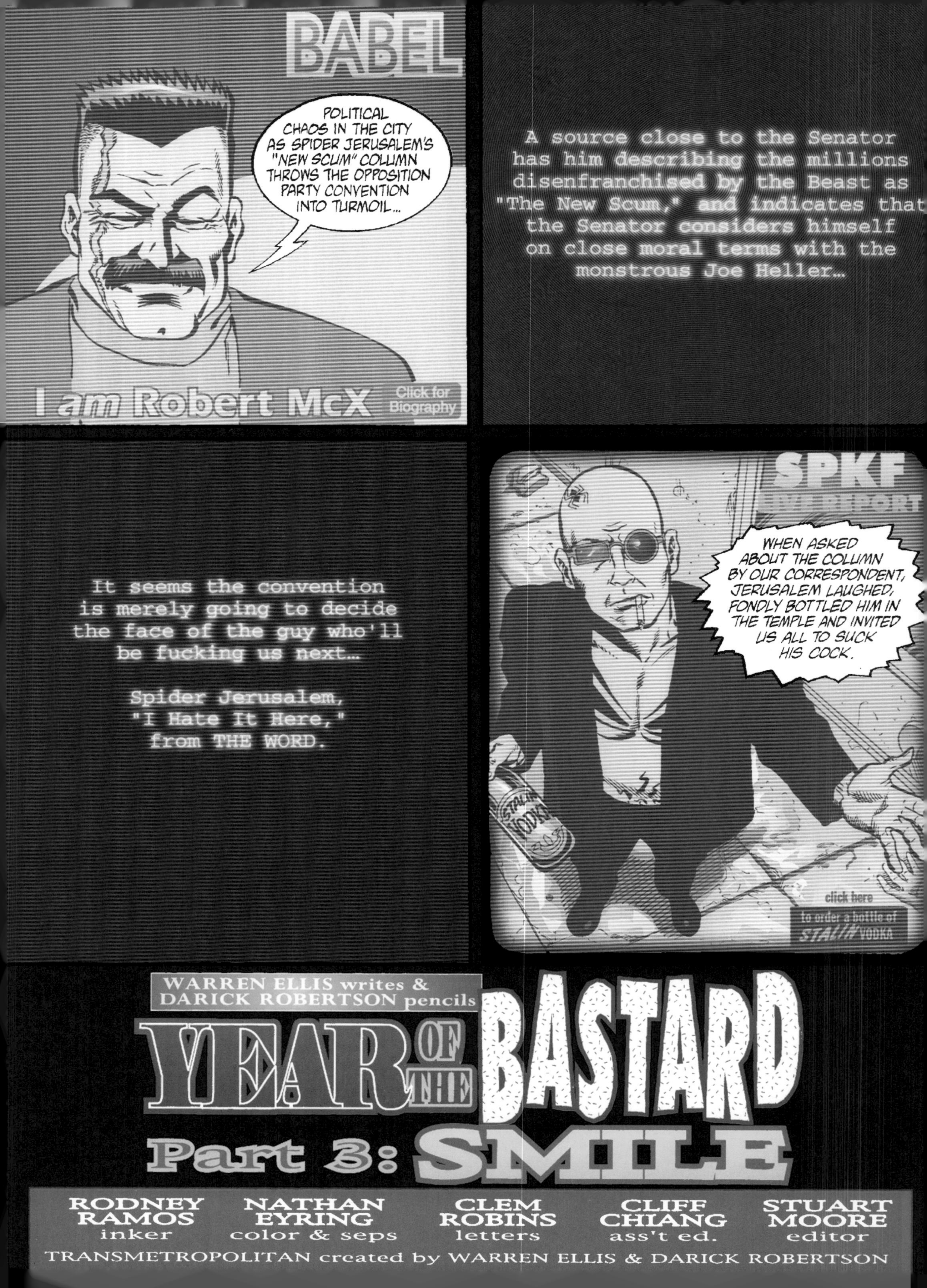
BABEL
POLITICAL CHAOS IN THE CITY AS SPIDER JERUSALEM'S "NEW SCUM" COLUMN THROWS THE OPPOSITION PARTY CONVENTION INTO TURMOIL...
I am Robert McX
Click for Biography
A source close to the Senator has him describing the millions disenfranchised by the Beast as "The New Scum," and indicates that the Senator considers himself on close moral terms with the monstrous Joe Heller...
It seems the convention is merely going to decide the face of the guy who'll be fucking us next...
Spider Jerusalem, "I Hate It Here," from THE WORD.
SPKF
LIVE REPORT
WHEN ASKED ABOUT THE COLUMN BY OUR CORRESPONDENT, JERUSALEM LAUGHED, FONDLY BOTTLED HIM IN THE TEMPLE AND INVITED US ALL TO SUCK HIS COCK.
click here
to order a bottle of STALIN VODKA
WARREN ELLIS writes & DARICK ROBERTSON pencils
YEAR OF THE BASTARD
Part 3: SMILE
RODNEY RAMOS inker
NATHAN EYRING color & seps
CLEM ROBINS letters
CLIFF CHIANG ass't ed.
STUART MOORE editor
TRANSMETROPOLITAN created by WARREN ELLIS & DARICK ROBERTSON

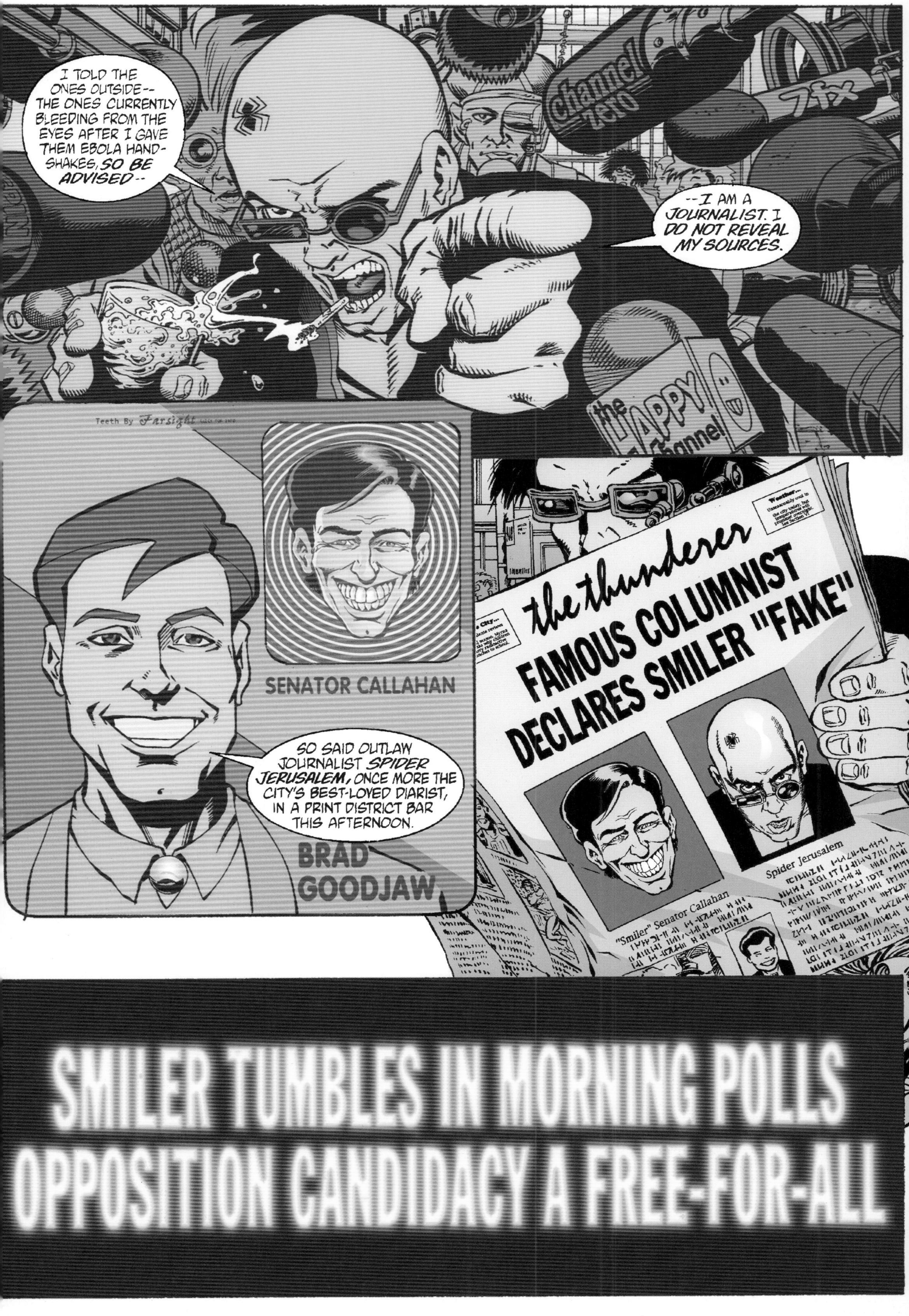

I TOLD THE ONES OUTSIDE-- THE ONES CURRENTLY BLEEDING FROM THE EYES AFTER I GAVE THEM EBOLA HAND-SHAKES, SO BE ADVISED--
--I AM A JOURNALIST. I DO NOT REVEAL MY SOURCES.
channel zero
Teeth By Farsight
SENATOR CALLAHAN
SO SAID OUTLAW JOURNALIST SPIDER JERUSALEM, ONCE MORE THE CITY'S BEST-LOVED DIARIST, IN A PRINT DISTRICT BAR THIS AFTERNOON.
BRAD GOODJAW
the thunderer
FAMOUS COLUMNIST DECLARES SMILER "FAKE"
"Smiler" Senator Callahan
Spider Jerusalem
SMILER TUMBLES IN MORNING POLLS
OPPOSITION CANDIDACY A FREE-FOR-ALL

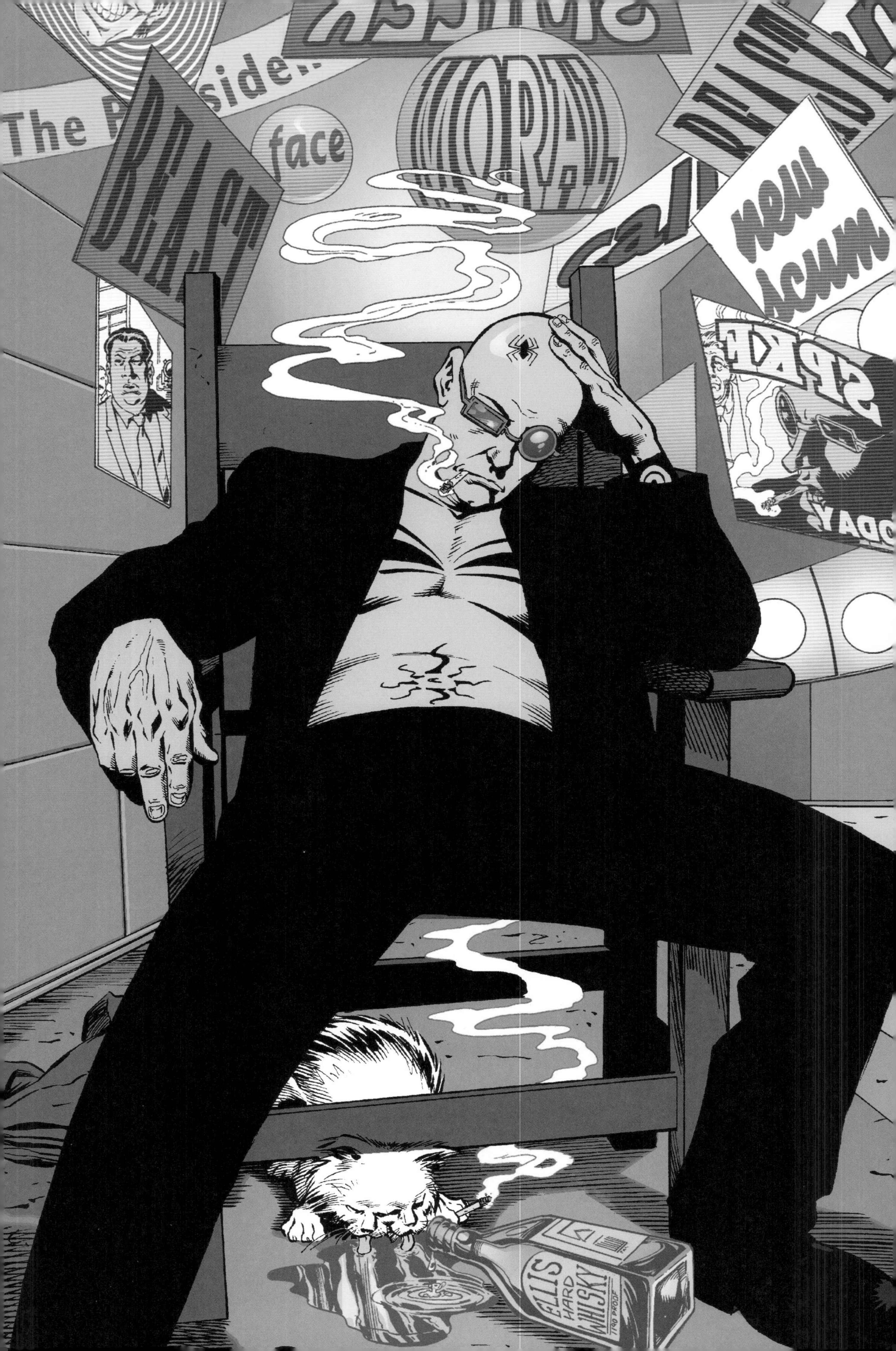
The
side...
BEAST
face
new
ELLIS
HARD
WHISKY

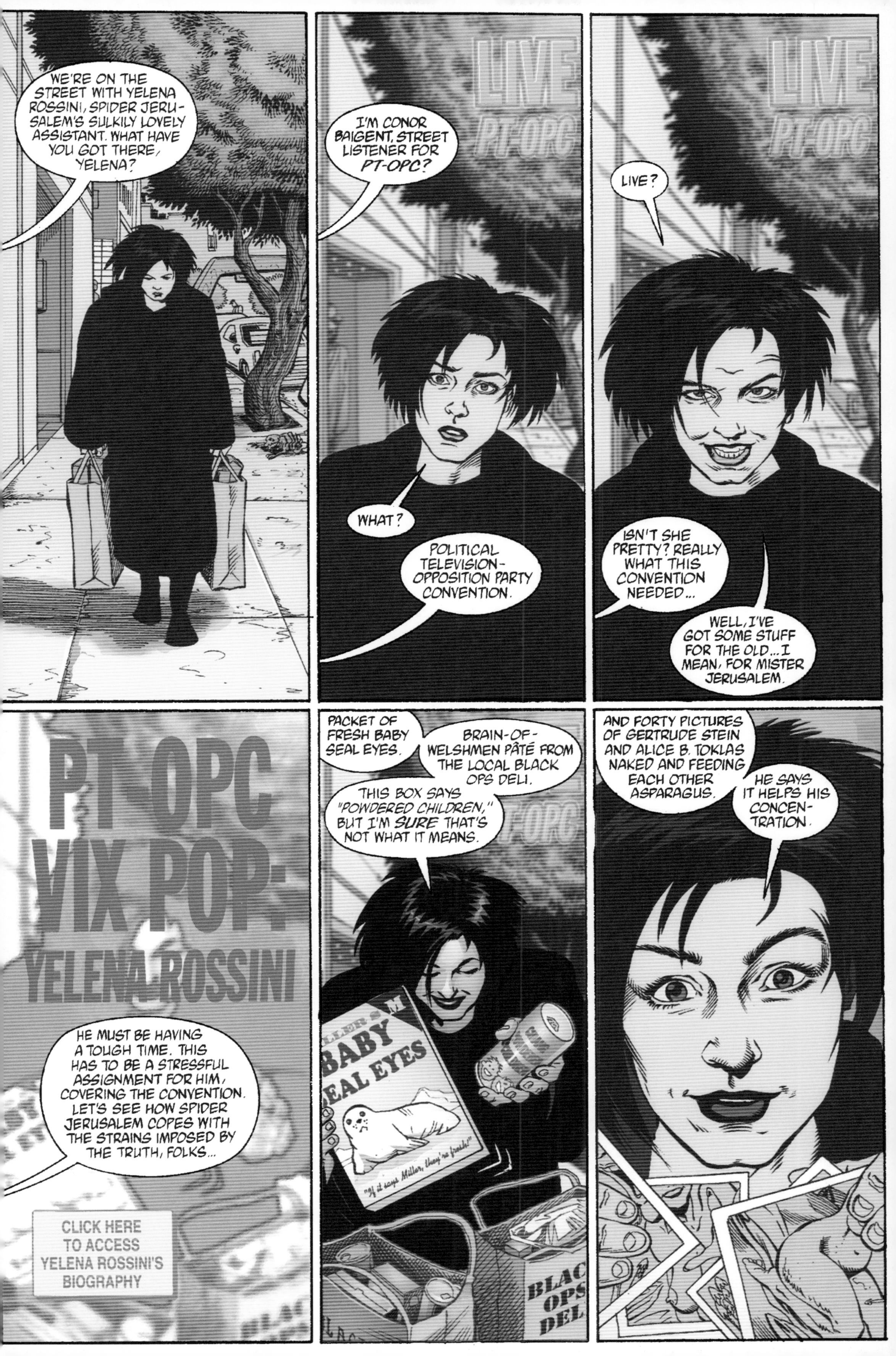
WE'RE ON THE STREET WITH YELENA ROSSINI, SPIDER JERUSALEM'S SULKILY LOVELY ASSISTANT. WHAT HAVE YOU GOT THERE, YELENA?
LIVE
PT-OPC
I'M CONOR BAIGENT, STREET LISTENER FOR *PT-OPC*?
WHAT?
POLITICAL TELEVISION-OPPOSITION PARTY CONVENTION.
LIVE?
ISN'T SHE PRETTY? REALLY WHAT THIS CONVENTION NEEDED...
WELL, I'VE GOT SOME STUFF FOR THE OLD... I MEAN, FOR MISTER JERUSALEM.
PT-OPC VIX POP: YELENA ROSSINI
HE MUST BE HAVING A TOUGH TIME. THIS HAS TO BE A STRESSFUL ASSIGNMENT FOR HIM, COVERING THE CONVENTION. LET'S SEE HOW SPIDER JERUSALEM COPES WITH THE STRAINS IMPOSED BY THE TRUTH, FOLKS...
CLICK HERE TO ACCESS YELENA ROSSINI'S BIOGRAPHY
PACKET OF FRESH BABY SEAL EYES.
BRAIN-OF-WELSHMEN PÂTÉ FROM THE LOCAL BLACK OPS DELI.
THIS BOX SAYS "POWDERED CHILDREN," BUT I'M *SURE* THAT'S NOT WHAT IT MEANS.
BABY
EAL EYES
"If it says Miller, they're fresh!"
AND FORTY PICTURES OF GERTRUDE STEIN AND ALICE B. TOKLAS NAKED AND FEEDING EACH OTHER ASPARAGUS.
HE SAYS IT HELPS HIS CONCENTRATION.

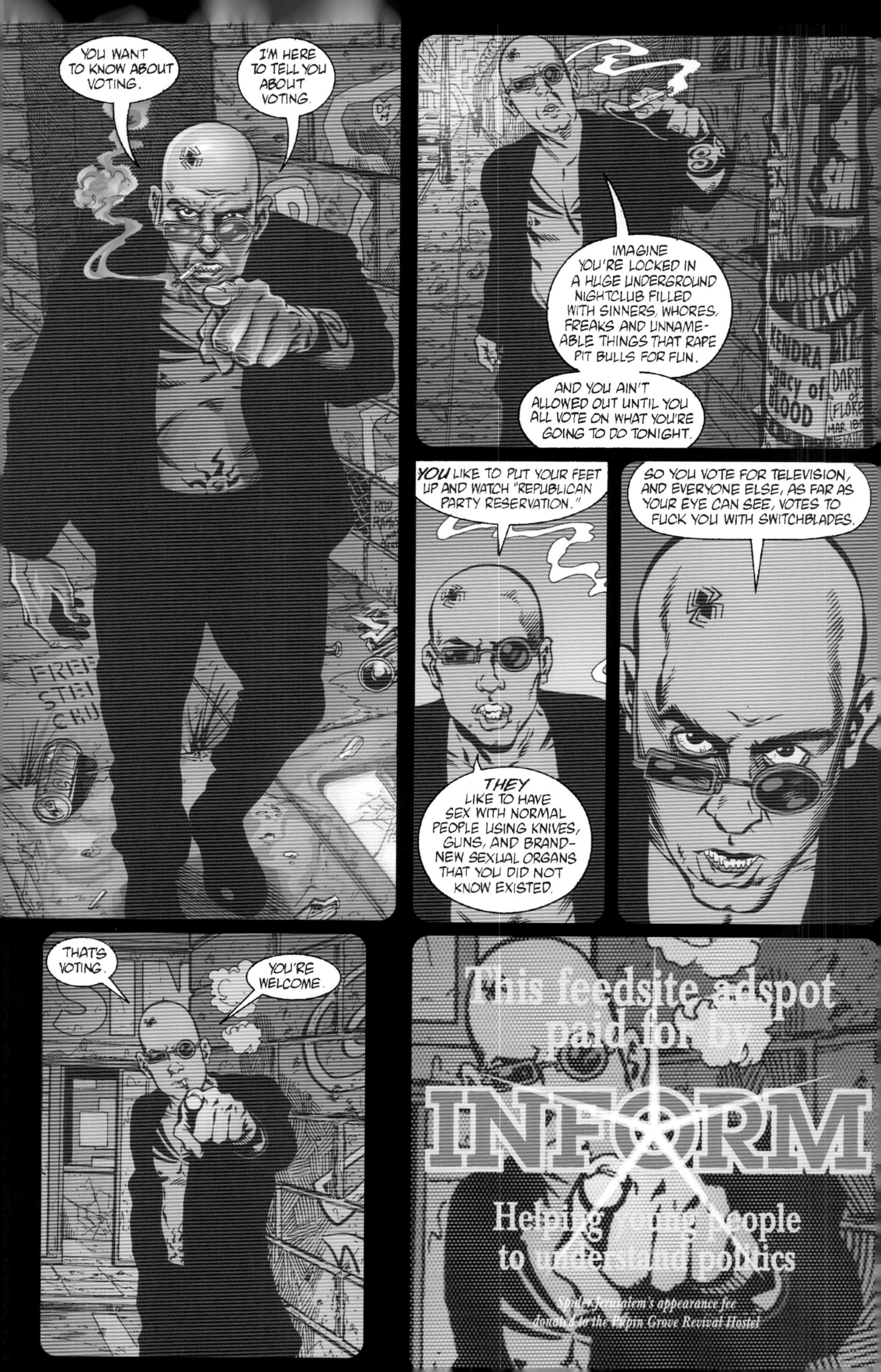
YOU WANT TO KNOW ABOUT VOTING.
I'M HERE TO TELL YOU ABOUT VOTING.
IMAGINE YOU'RE LOCKED IN A HUGE UNDERGROUND NIGHTCLUB FILLED WITH SINNERS, WHORES, FREAKS AND UNNAME-ABLE THINGS THAT RAPE PIT BULLS FOR FUN.
AND YOU AIN'T ALLOWED OUT UNTIL YOU ALL VOTE ON WHAT YOU'RE GOING TO DO TONIGHT.
YOU LIKE TO PUT YOUR FEET UP AND WATCH "REPUBLICAN PARTY RESERVATION."
THEY LIKE TO HAVE SEX WITH NORMAL PEOPLE USING KNIVES, GUNS, AND BRAND-NEW SEXUAL ORGANS THAT YOU DID NOT KNOW EXISTED.
SO YOU VOTE FOR TELEVISION, AND EVERYONE ELSE, AS FAR AS YOUR EYE CAN SEE, VOTES TO FUCK YOU WITH SWITCHBLADES.
THAT'S VOTING.
YOU'RE WELCOME.
This feedsite adspot paid for by
INFORM
Helping young people to understand politics
Spider Jerusalem's appearance fee donated to the Pipin Grove Revival Hostel

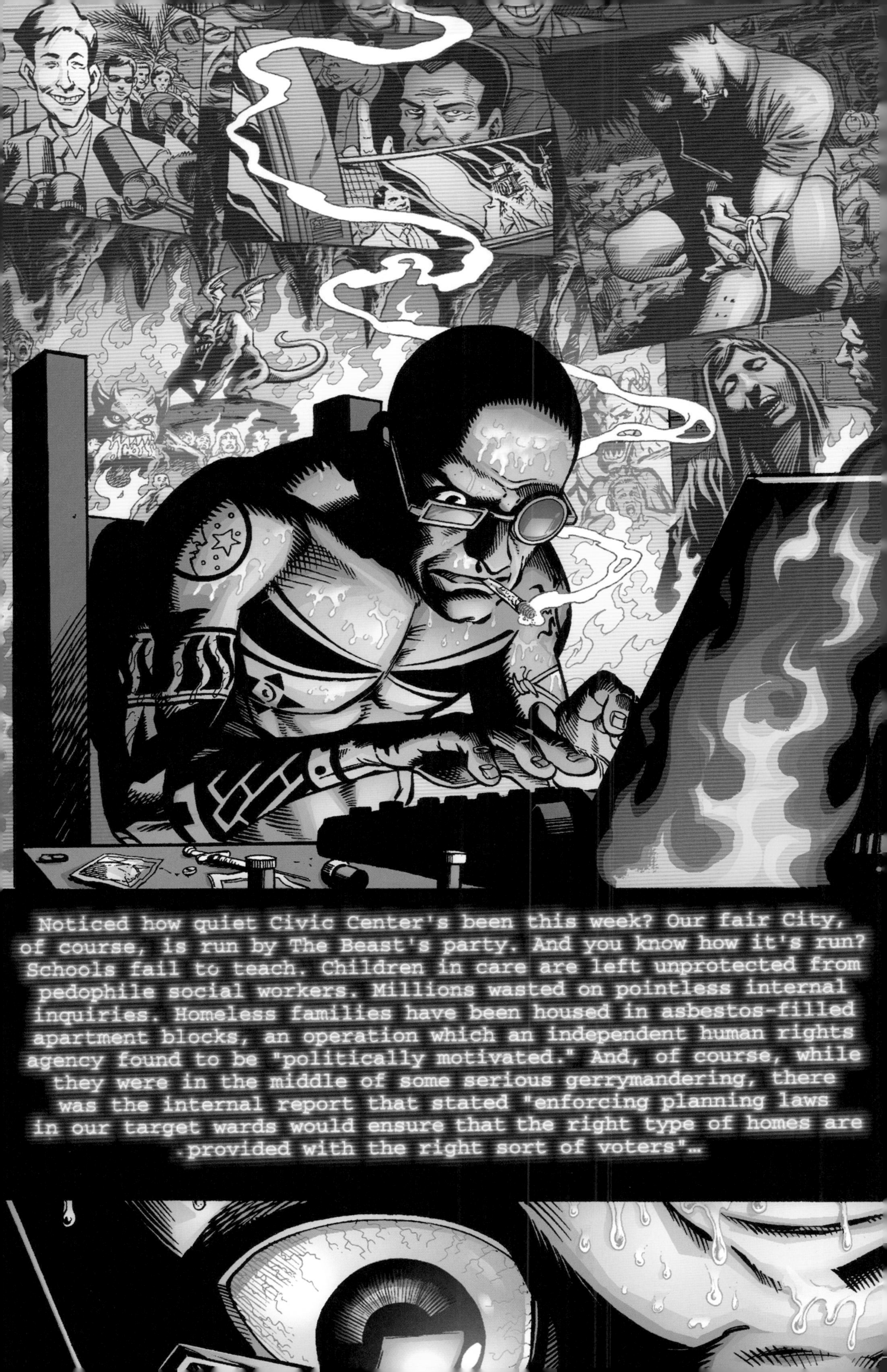
Noticed how quiet Civic Center's been this week? Our fair City, of course, is run by The Beast's party. And you know how it's run? Schools fail to teach. Children in care are left unprotected from pedophile social workers. Millions wasted on pointless internal inquiries. Homeless families have been housed in asbestos-filled apartment blocks, an operation which an independent human rights agency found to be "politically motivated." And, of course, while they were in the middle of some serious gerrymandering, there was the internal report that stated "enforcing planning laws in our target wards would ensure that the right type of homes are provided with the right sort of voters"...

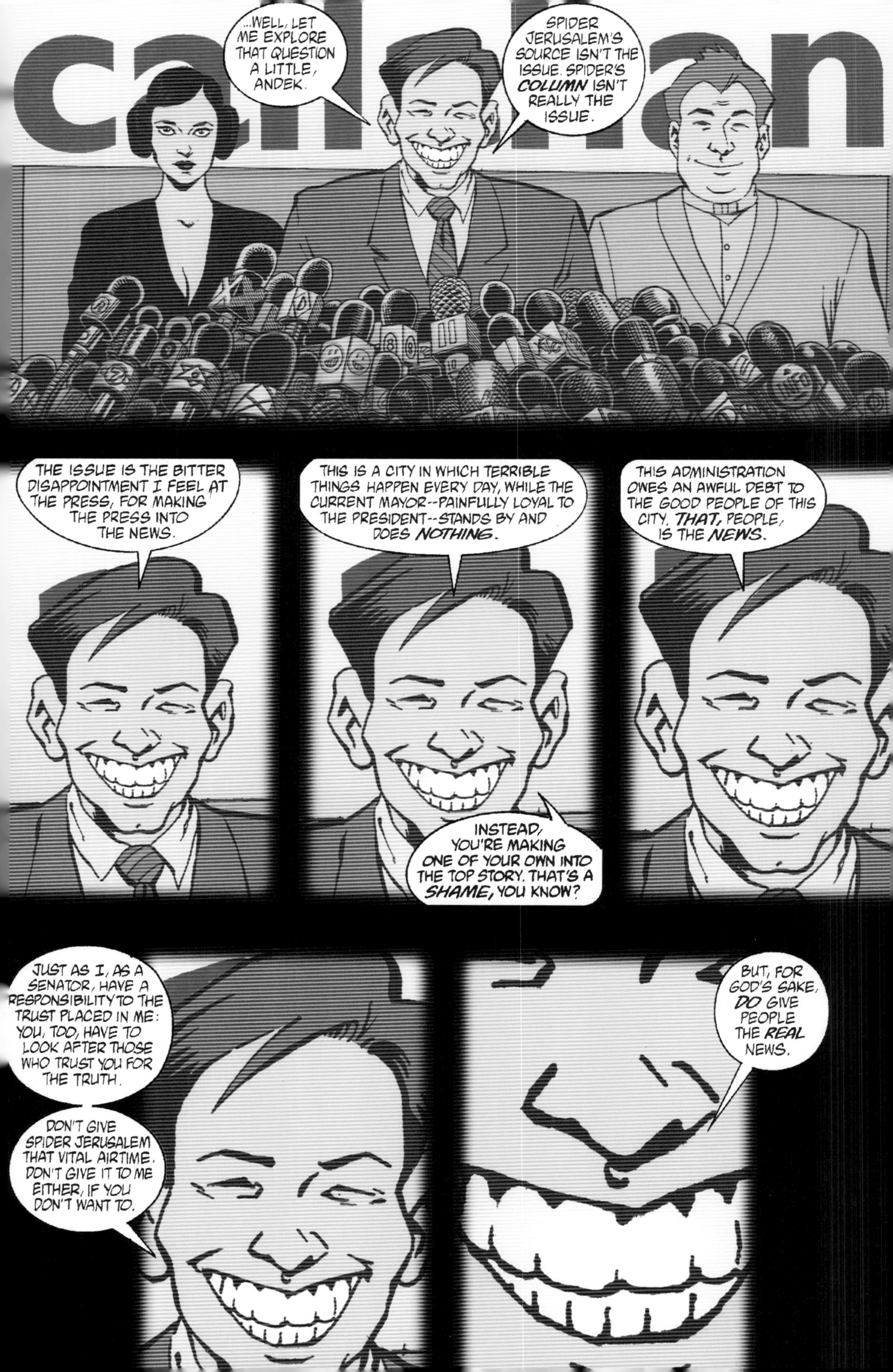
...WELL, LET ME EXPLORE THAT QUESTION A LITTLE, ANDEK.
SPIDER JERUSALEM'S SOURCE ISN'T THE ISSUE. SPIDER'S COLUMN ISN'T REALLY THE ISSUE.
THE ISSUE IS THE BITTER DISAPPOINTMENT I FEEL AT THE PRESS, FOR MAKING THE PRESS INTO THE NEWS.
THIS IS A CITY IN WHICH TERRIBLE THINGS HAPPEN EVERY DAY, WHILE THE CURRENT MAYOR--PAINFULLY LOYAL TO THE PRESIDENT--STANDS BY AND DOES NOTHING.
INSTEAD, YOU'RE MAKING ONE OF YOUR OWN INTO THE TOP STORY. THAT'S A SHAME, YOU KNOW?
THIS ADMINISTRATION OWES AN AWFUL DEBT TO THE GOOD PEOPLE OF THIS CITY. THAT, PEOPLE, IS THE NEWS.
JUST AS I, AS A SENATOR, HAVE A RESPONSIBILITY TO THE TRUST PLACED IN ME: YOU, TOO, HAVE TO LOOK AFTER THOSE WHO TRUST YOU FOR THE TRUTH.
DON'T GIVE SPIDER JERUSALEM THAT VITAL AIRTIME. DON'T GIVE IT TO ME EITHER, IF YOU DON'T WANT TO.
BUT, FOR GOD'S SAKE, DO GIVE PEOPLE THE REAL NEWS.

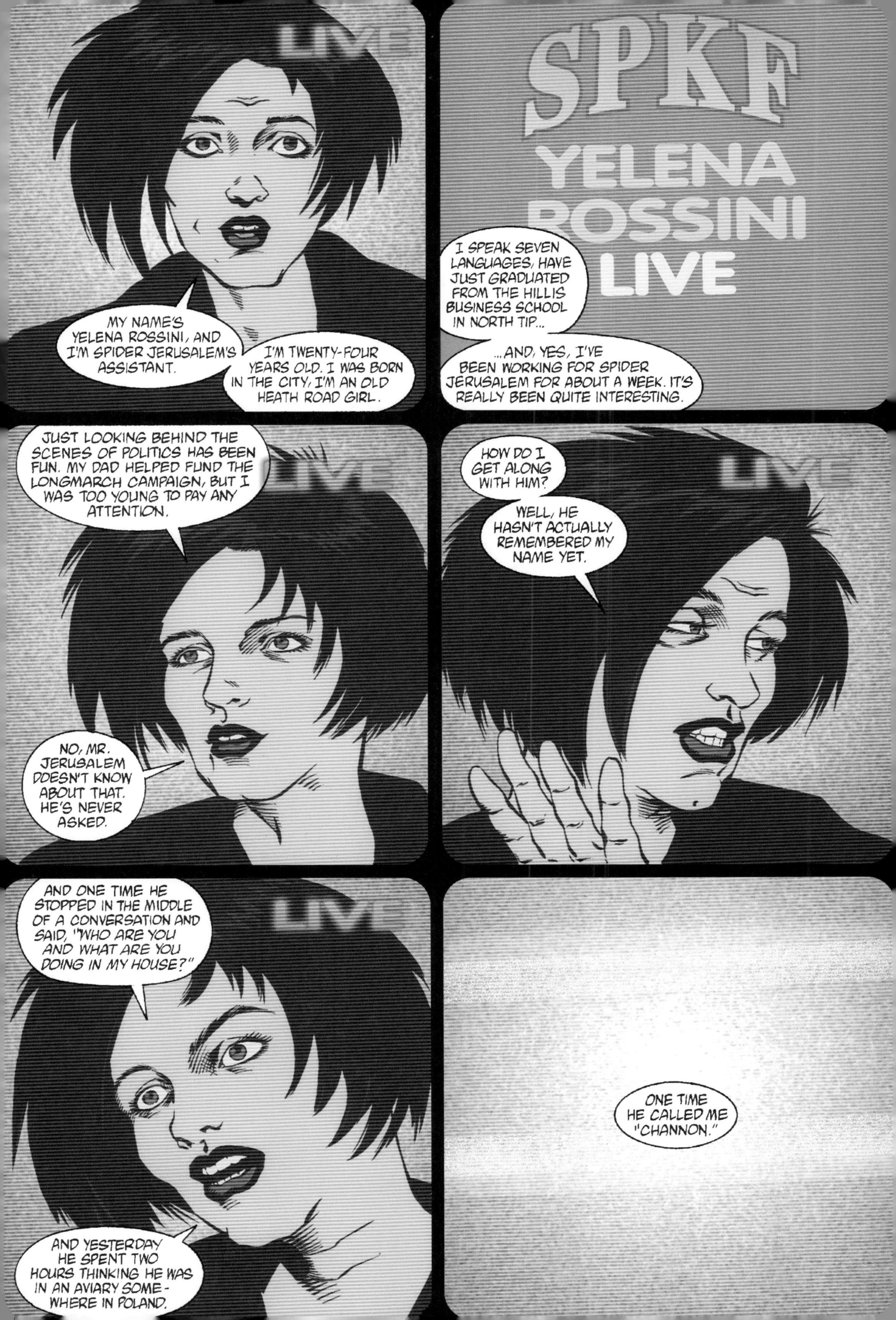
LIVE
MY NAME'S YELENA ROSSINI, AND I'M SPIDER JERUSALEM'S ASSISTANT.
I'M TWENTY-FOUR YEARS OLD. I WAS BORN IN THE CITY; I'M AN OLD HEATH ROAD GIRL.
SPKF
YELENA ROSSINI
LIVE
I SPEAK SEVEN LANGUAGES, HAVE JUST GRADUATED FROM THE HILLIS BUSINESS SCHOOL IN NORTH TIP...
...AND, YES, I'VE BEEN WORKING FOR SPIDER JERUSALEM FOR ABOUT A WEEK. IT'S REALLY BEEN QUITE INTERESTING.
JUST LOOKING BEHIND THE SCENES OF POLITICS HAS BEEN FUN. MY DAD HELPED FUND THE LONGMARCH CAMPAIGN, BUT I WAS TOO YOUNG TO PAY ANY ATTENTION.
NO, MR. JERUSALEM DOESN'T KNOW ABOUT THAT. HE'S NEVER ASKED.
HOW DO I GET ALONG WITH HIM?
WELL, HE HASN'T ACTUALLY REMEMBERED MY NAME YET.
AND ONE TIME HE STOPPED IN THE MIDDLE OF A CONVERSATION AND SAID, "WHO ARE YOU AND WHAT ARE YOU DOING IN MY HOUSE?"
AND YESTERDAY HE SPENT TWO HOURS THINKING HE WAS IN AN AVIARY SOME-WHERE IN POLAND.
ONE TIME HE CALLED ME "CHANNON."

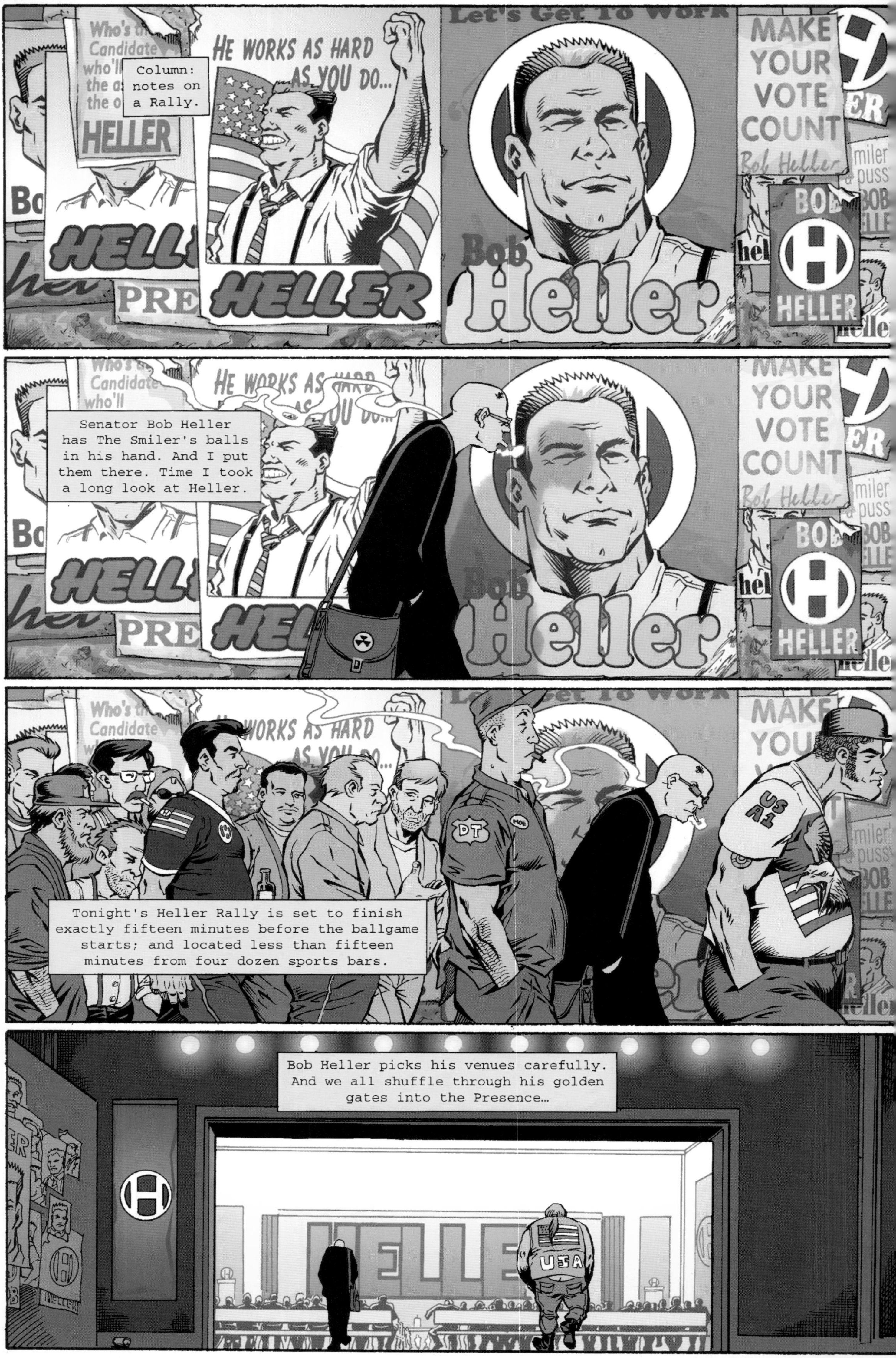
Column: notes on a Rally.
HE WORKS AS HARD AS YOU DO...
HELLER
Let's Get To Work
Bob Heller
MAKE YOUR VOTE COUNT
Bob Heller
BOB HELLER
Senator Bob Heller has The Smiler's balls in his hand. And I put them there. Time I took a long look at Heller.
Tonight's Heller Rally is set to finish exactly fifteen minutes before the ballgame starts; and located less than fifteen minutes from four dozen sports bars.
Bob Heller picks his venues carefully. And we all shuffle through his golden gates into the Presence…

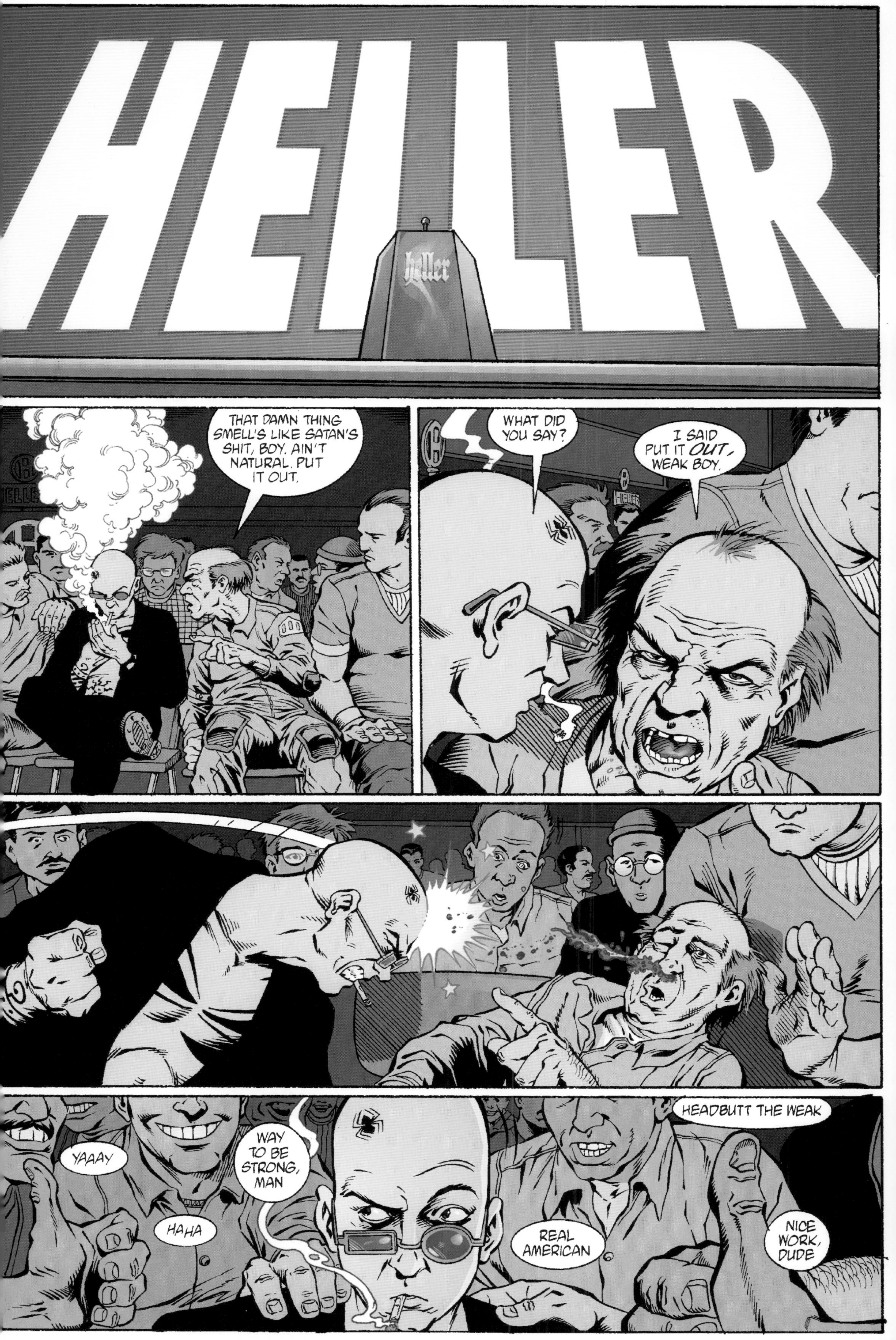
HELLER
heller
THAT DAMN THING SMELL'S LIKE SATAN'S SHIT, BOY. AIN'T NATURAL. PUT IT OUT.
WHAT DID YOU SAY?
I SAID PUT IT OUT, WEAK BOY.
HEADBUTT THE WEAK
YAAAY
WAY TO BE STRONG, MAN
HAHA
REAL AMERICAN
NICE WORK, DUDE

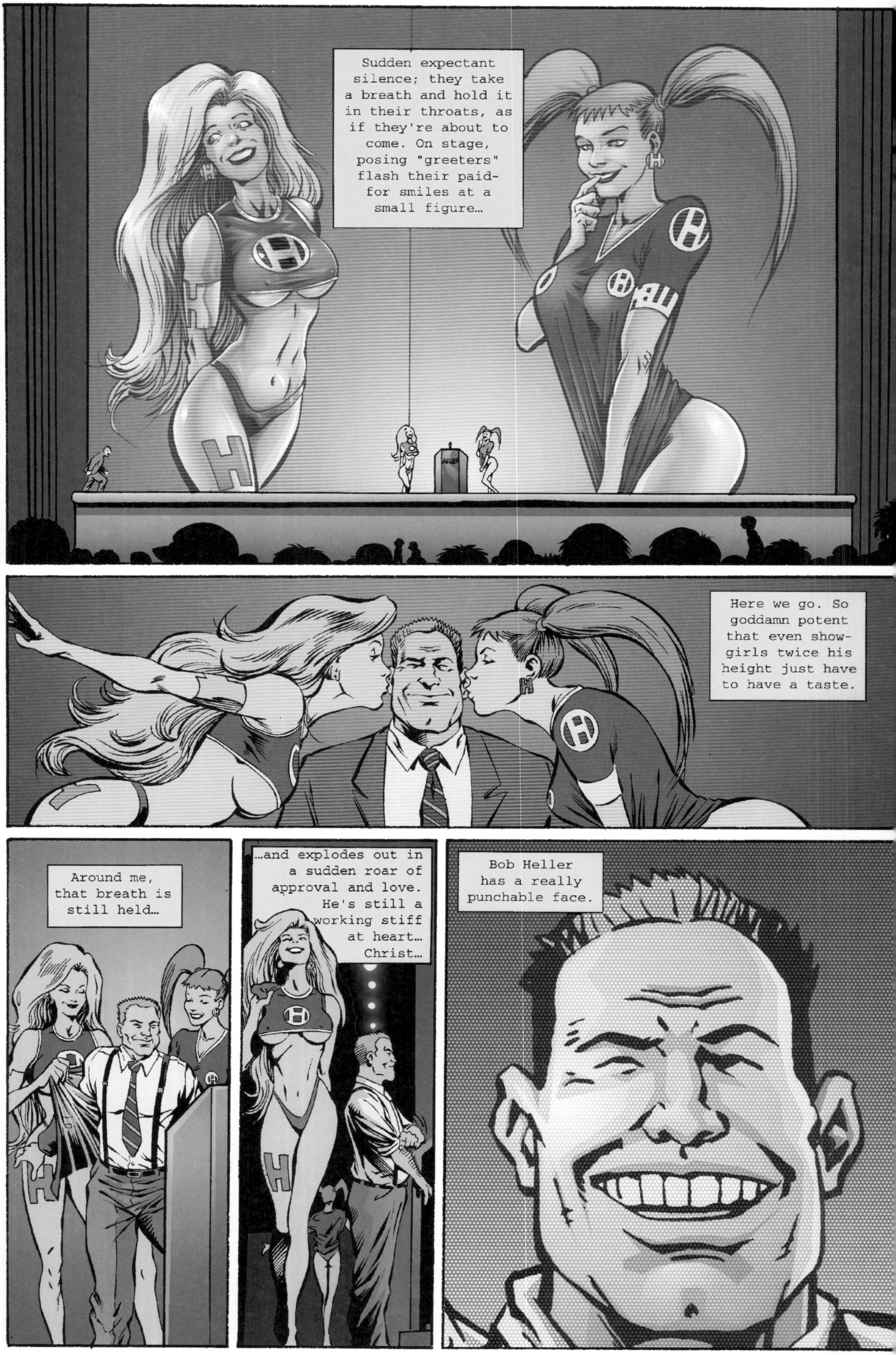

Sudden expectant silence; they take a breath and hold it in their throats, as if they're about to come. On stage, posing "greeters" flash their paid-for smiles at a small figure…
Here we go. So goddamn potent that even show-girls twice his height just have to have a taste.
Around me, that breath is still held…
…and explodes out in a sudden roar of approval and love. He's still a working stiff at heart… Christ…
Bob Heller has a really punchable face.

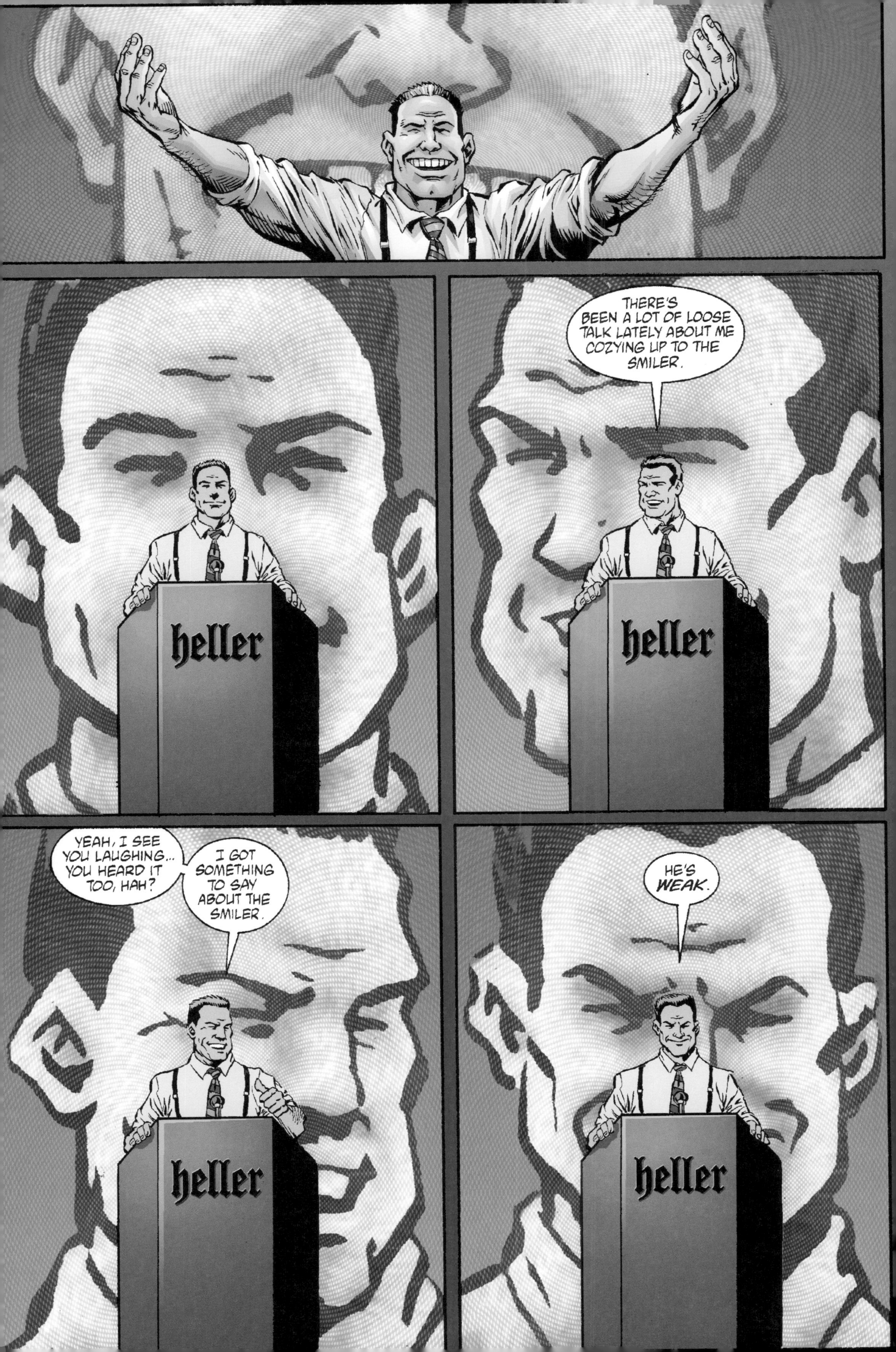
THERE'S BEEN A LOT OF LOOSE TALK LATELY ABOUT ME COZYING UP TO THE SMILER.
heller
YEAH, I SEE YOU LAUGHING... YOU HEARD IT TOO, HAH?
I GOT SOMETHING TO SAY ABOUT THE SMILER.
HE'S WEAK.

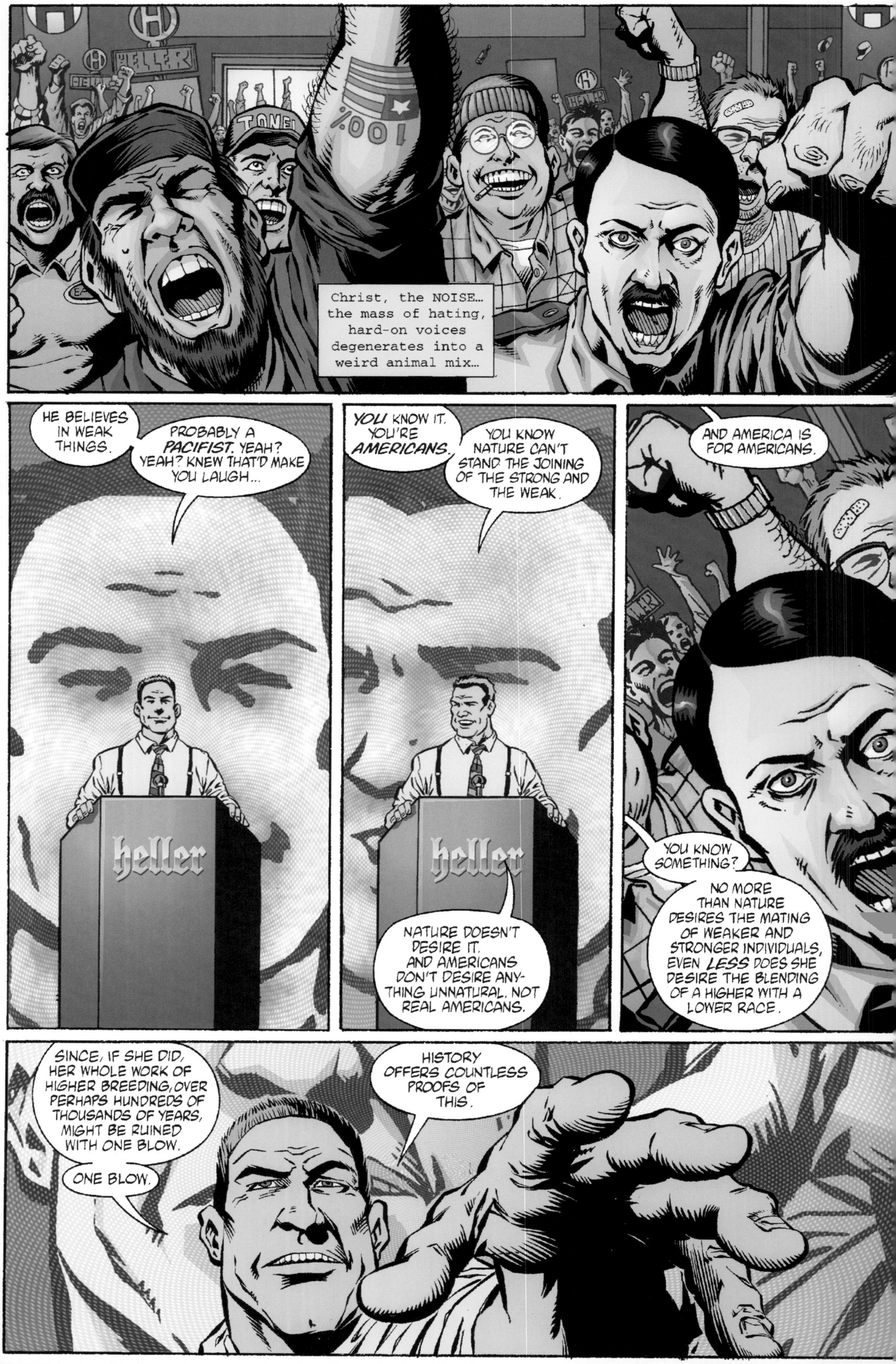
HELLER
HELLER
TONE
100%
HELLER
Christ, the NOISE... the mass of hating, hard-on voices degenerates into a weird animal mix...
HE BELIEVES IN WEAK THINGS.
PROBABLY A PACIFIST. YEAH? YEAH? KNEW THAT'D MAKE YOU LAUGH...
heller
YOU KNOW IT. YOU'RE AMERICANS.
YOU KNOW NATURE CAN'T STAND THE JOINING OF THE STRONG AND THE WEAK.
heller
NATURE DOESN'T DESIRE IT. AND AMERICANS DON'T DESIRE ANYTHING UNNATURAL. NOT REAL AMERICANS.
AND AMERICA IS FOR AMERICANS.
YOU KNOW SOMETHING?
NO MORE THAN NATURE DESIRES THE MATING OF WEAKER AND STRONGER INDIVIDUALS, EVEN LESS DOES SHE DESIRE THE BLENDING OF A HIGHER WITH A LOWER RACE.
SINCE, IF SHE DID, HER WHOLE WORK OF HIGHER BREEDING, OVER PERHAPS HUNDREDS OF THOUSANDS OF YEARS, MIGHT BE RUINED WITH ONE BLOW.
ONE BLOW.
HISTORY OFFERS COUNTLESS PROOFS OF THIS.

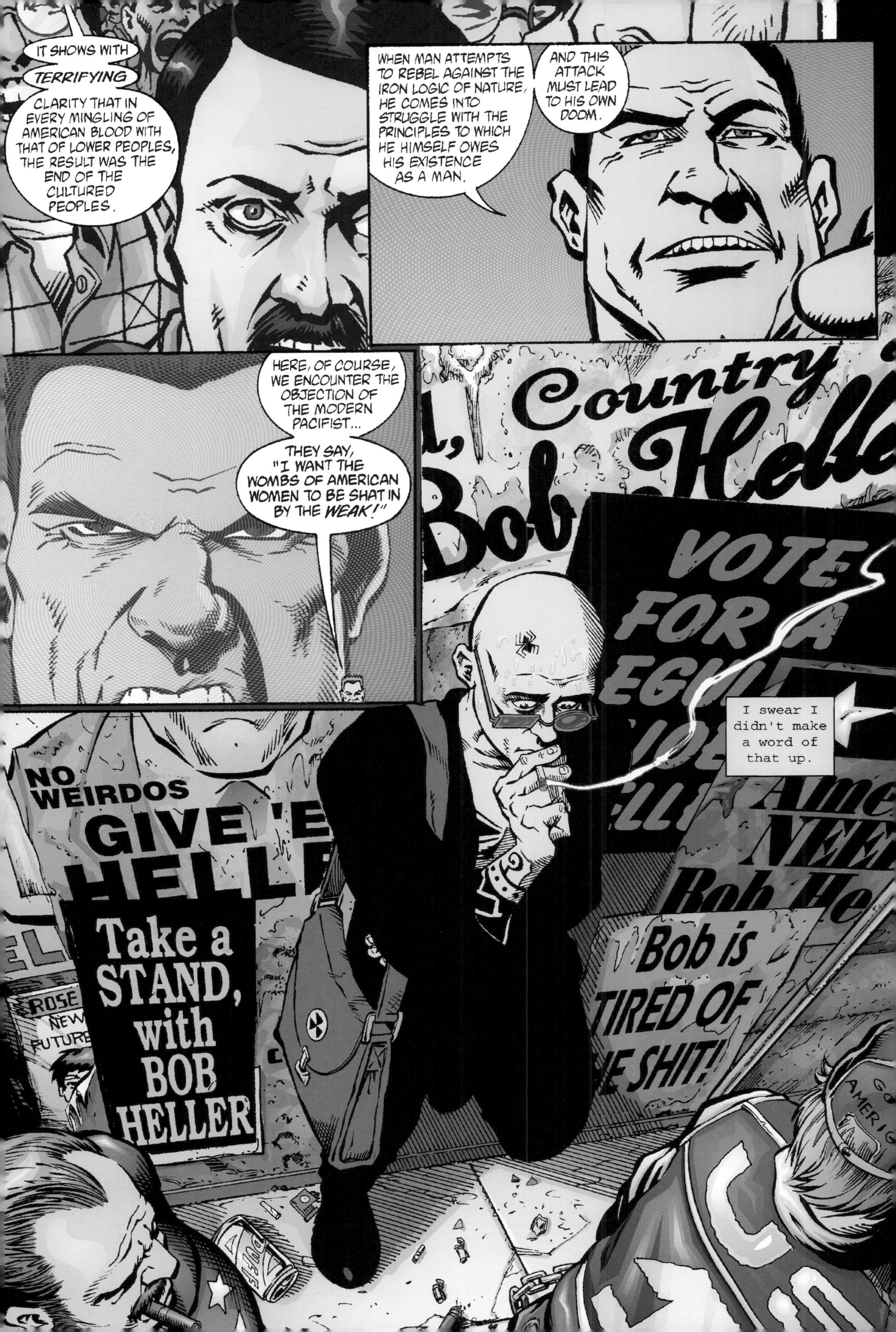

IT SHOWS WITH TERRIFYING CLARITY THAT IN EVERY MINGLING OF AMERICAN BLOOD WITH THAT OF LOWER PEOPLES, THE RESULT WAS THE END OF THE CULTURED PEOPLES.
WHEN MAN ATTEMPTS TO REBEL AGAINST THE IRON LOGIC OF NATURE, HE COMES INTO STRUGGLE WITH THE PRINCIPLES TO WHICH HE HIMSELF OWES HIS EXISTENCE AS A MAN.
AND THIS ATTACK MUST LEAD TO HIS OWN DOOM.
HERE, OF COURSE, WE ENCOUNTER THE OBJECTION OF THE MODERN PACIFIST...
THEY SAY, "I WANT THE WOMBS OF AMERICAN WOMEN TO BE SHAT IN BY THE WEAK!"
Country
Bob
VOTE FOR A
I swear I didn't make a word of that up.
NO WEIRDOS
GIVE 'E
Take a STAND, with BOB HELLER
Bob is TIRED OF

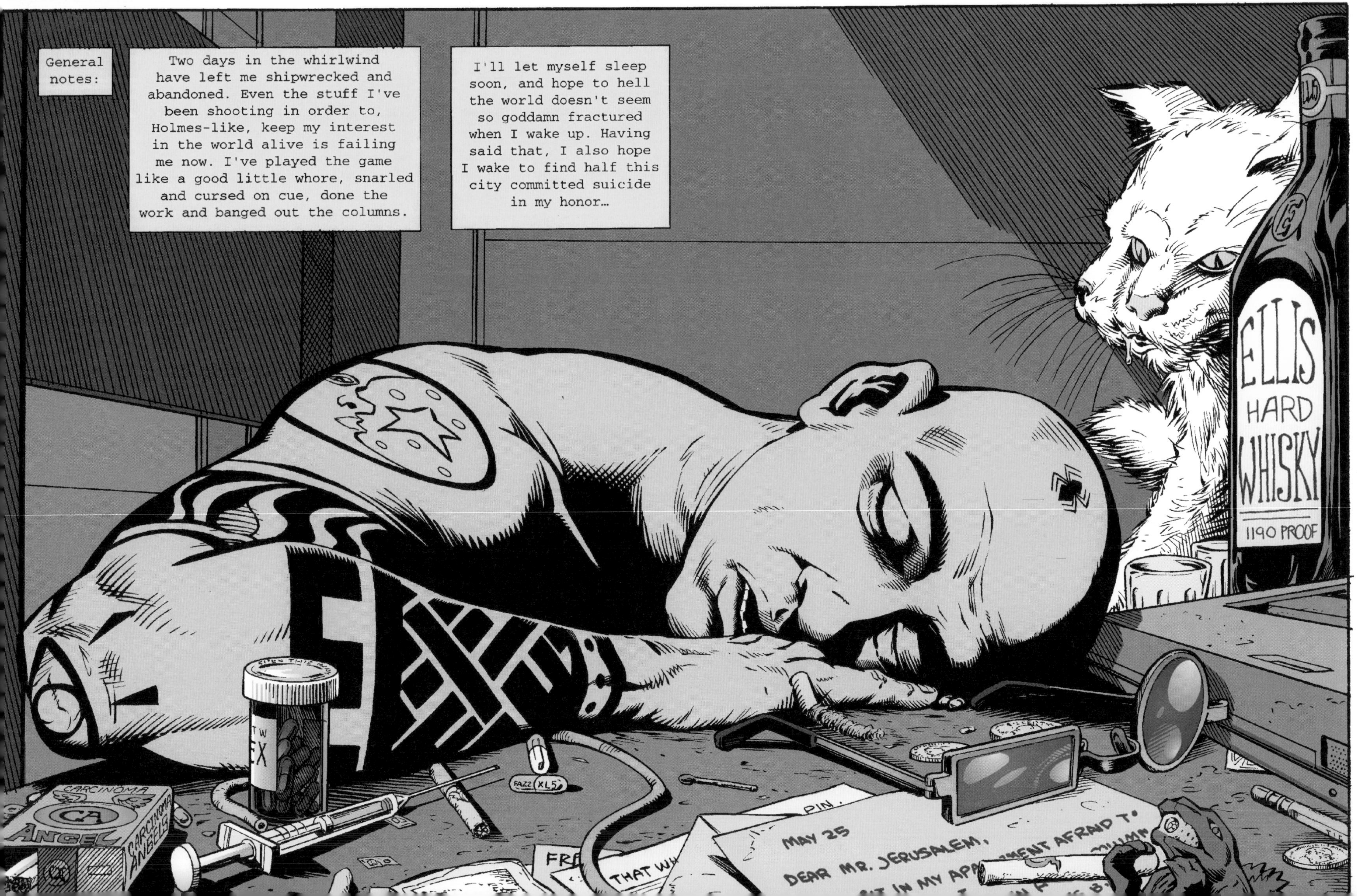

General notes:
Two days in the whirlwind have left me shipwrecked and abandoned. Even the stuff I've been shooting in order to, Holmes-like, keep my interest in the world alive is failing me now. I've played the game like a good little whore, snarled and cursed on cue, done the work and banged out the columns.
I'll let myself sleep soon, and hope to hell the world doesn't seem so goddamn fractured when I wake up. Having said that, I also hope I wake to find half this city committed suicide in my honor…
ELLIS HARD WHISKY
1190 PROOF
CARCINOMA
CA
ANGEL
CARCINOMA ANGELS
FAZZ XL5
PIN.
MAY 25
DEAR MR. JERUSALEM,

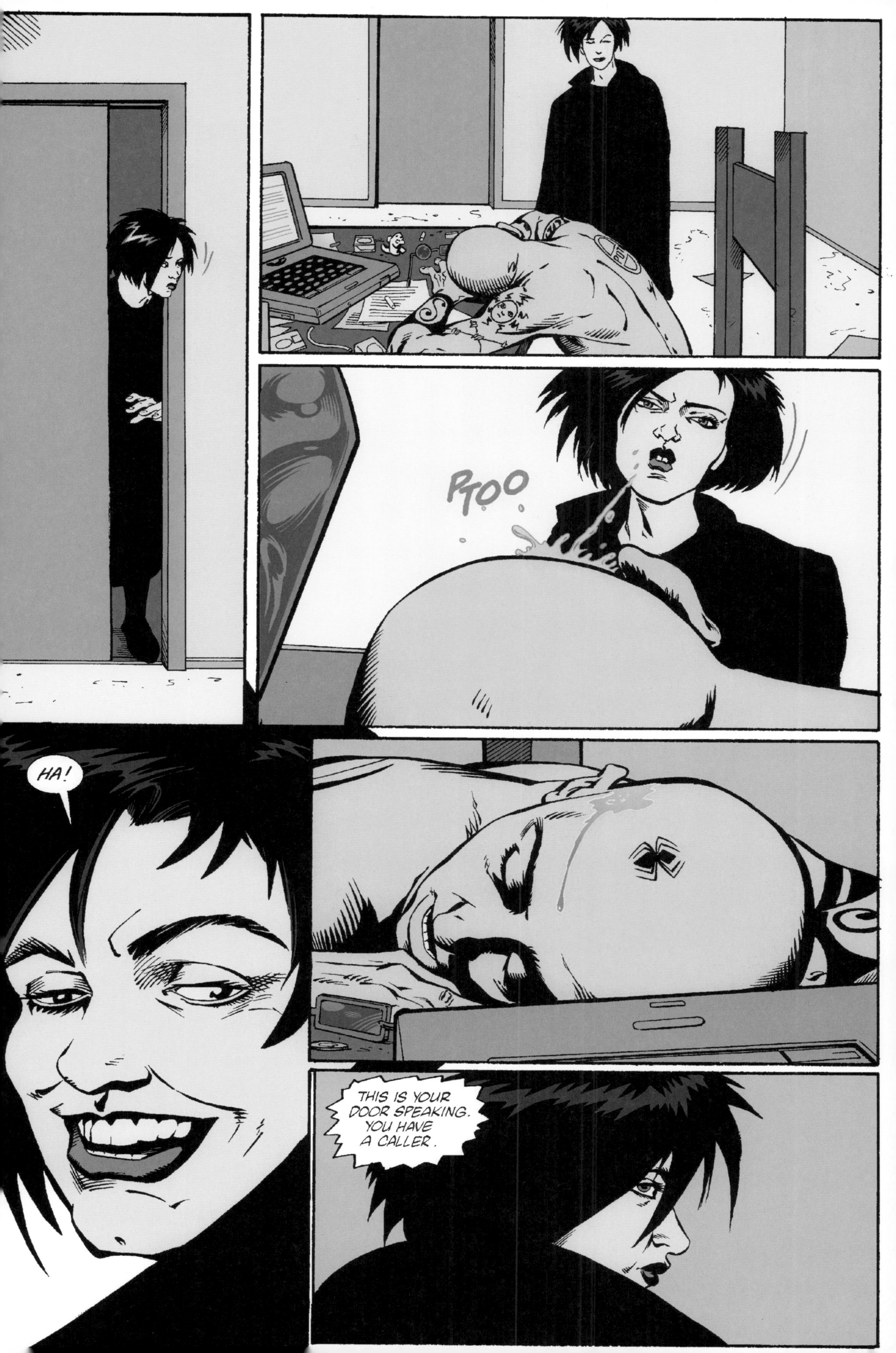
PTOO
HA!
THIS IS YOUR DOOR SPEAKING. YOU HAVE A CALLER.

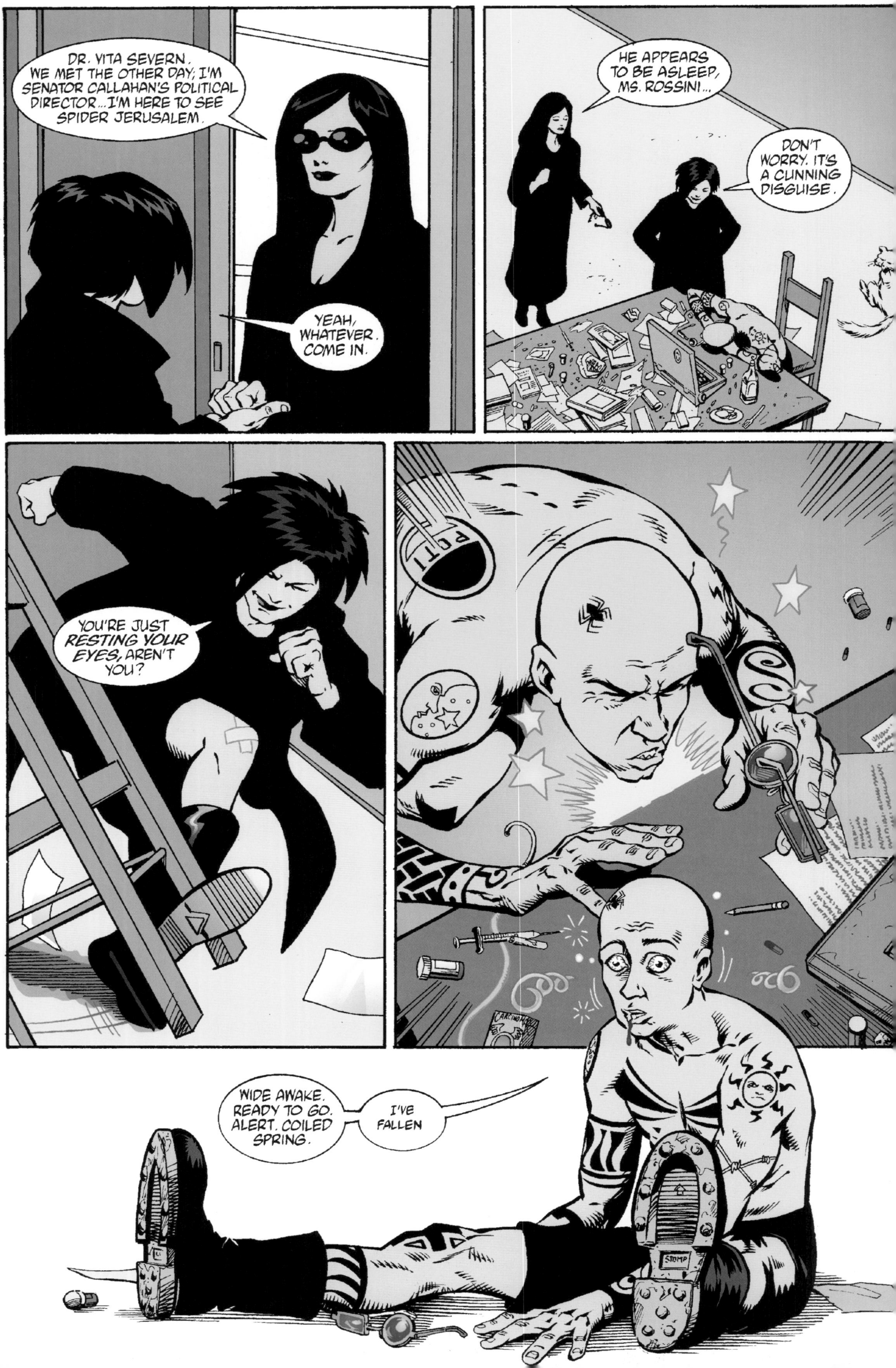
DR. VITA SEVERN. WE MET THE OTHER DAY; I'M SENATOR CALLAHAN'S POLITICAL DIRECTOR... I'M HERE TO SEE SPIDER JERUSALEM.
YEAH, WHATEVER. COME IN.
HE APPEARS TO BE ASLEEP, MS. ROSSINI...
DON'T WORRY. IT'S A CUNNING DISGUISE.
YOU'RE JUST RESTING YOUR EYES, AREN'T YOU?
PCT
WIDE AWAKE. READY TO GO. ALERT. COILED SPRING.
I'VE FALLEN
STOMP

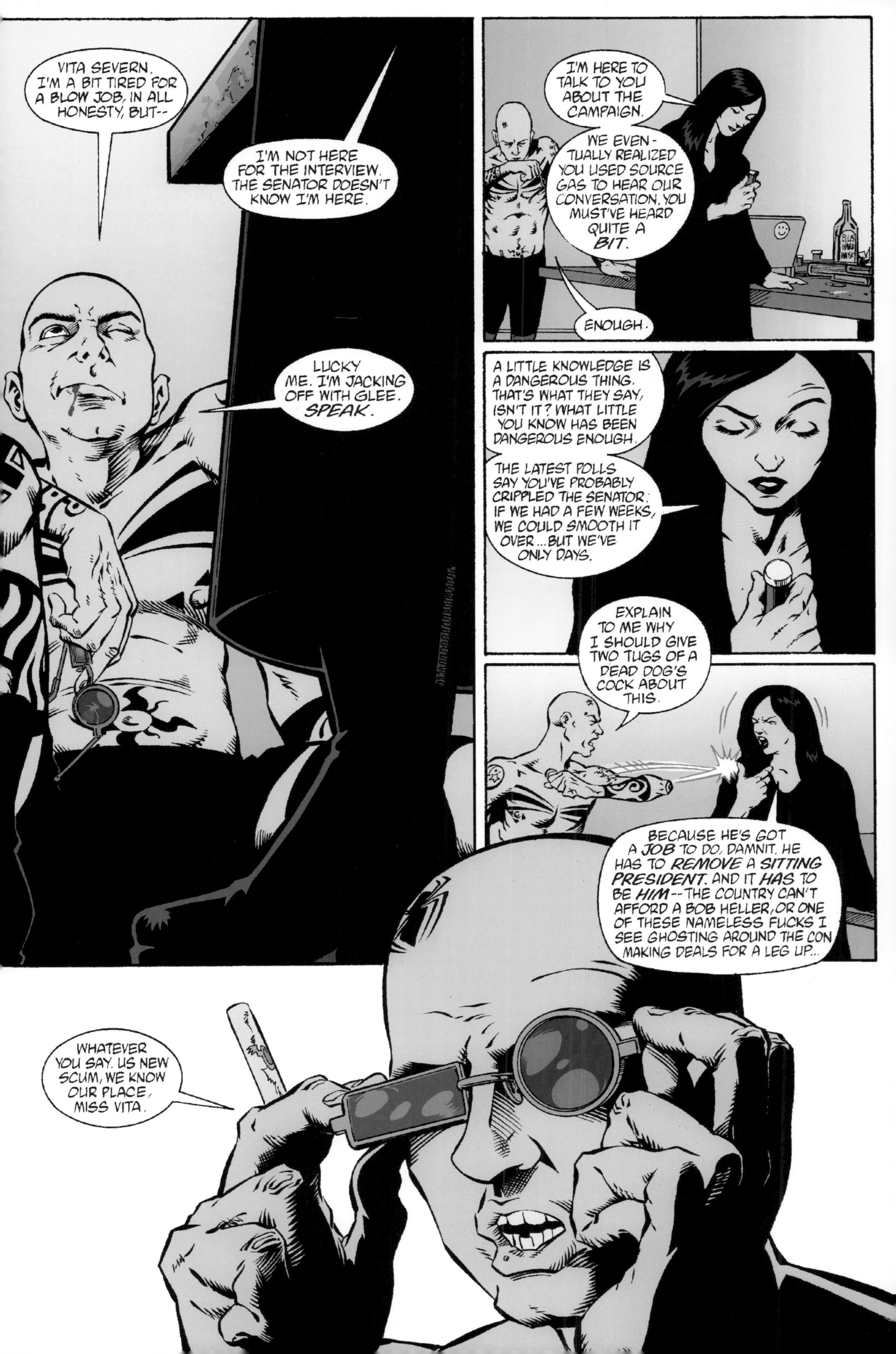
VITA SEVERN. I'M A BIT TIRED FOR A BLOW JOB, IN ALL HONESTY, BUT--
I'M NOT HERE FOR THE INTERVIEW. THE SENATOR DOESN'T KNOW I'M HERE.
LUCKY ME. I'M JACKING OFF WITH GLEE. SPEAK.
I'M HERE TO TALK TO YOU ABOUT THE CAMPAIGN.
WE EVENTUALLY REALIZED YOU USED SOURCE GAS TO HEAR OUR CONVERSATION. YOU MUST'VE HEARD QUITE A BIT.
ENOUGH.
A LITTLE KNOWLEDGE IS A DANGEROUS THING. THAT'S WHAT THEY SAY, ISN'T IT? WHAT LITTLE YOU KNOW HAS BEEN DANGEROUS ENOUGH.
THE LATEST POLLS SAY YOU'VE PROBABLY CRIPPLED THE SENATOR. IF WE HAD A FEW WEEKS, WE COULD SMOOTH IT OVER...BUT WE'VE ONLY DAYS.
EXPLAIN TO ME WHY I SHOULD GIVE TWO TUGS OF A DEAD DOG'S COCK ABOUT THIS.
BECAUSE HE'S GOT A JOB TO DO, DAMNIT. HE HAS TO REMOVE A SITTING PRESIDENT. AND IT HAS TO BE HIM--THE COUNTRY CAN'T AFFORD A BOB HELLER, OR ONE OF THESE NAMELESS FUCKS I SEE GHOSTING AROUND THE CON MAKING DEALS FOR A LEG UP...
WHATEVER YOU SAY. US NEW SCUM, WE KNOW OUR PLACE, MISS VITA.

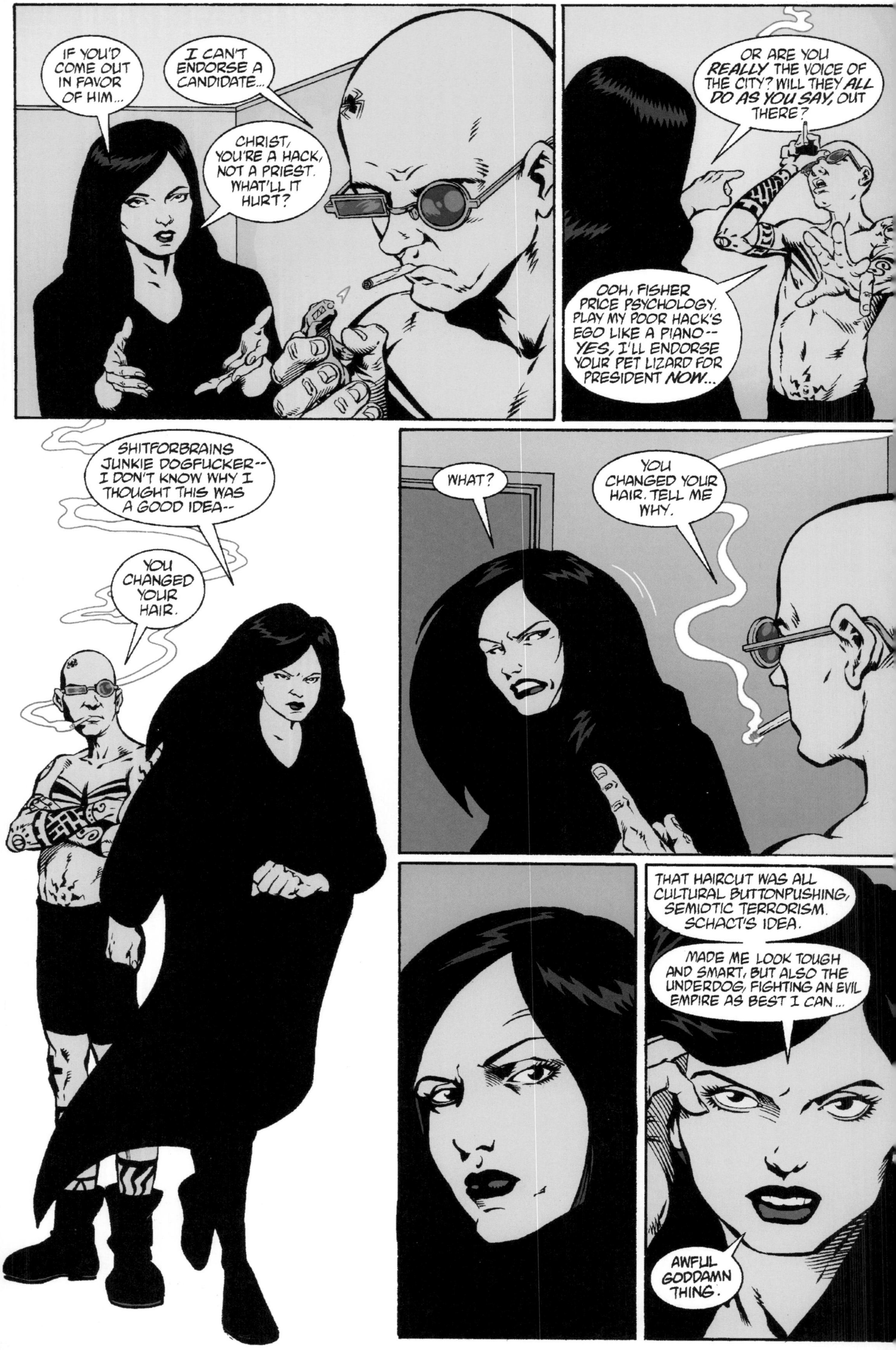
IF YOU'D COME OUT IN FAVOR OF HIM...
I CAN'T ENDORSE A CANDIDATE...
CHRIST, YOU'RE A HACK, NOT A PRIEST. WHAT'LL IT HURT?
OR ARE YOU REALLY THE VOICE OF THE CITY? WILL THEY ALL DO AS YOU SAY, OUT THERE?
OOH, FISHER PRICE PSYCHOLOGY. PLAY MY POOR HACK'S EGO LIKE A PIANO-- YES, I'LL ENDORSE YOUR PET LIZARD FOR PRESIDENT NOW...
SHITFORBRAINS JUNKIE DOGFUCKER-- I DON'T KNOW WHY I THOUGHT THIS WAS A GOOD IDEA--
YOU CHANGED YOUR HAIR.
WHAT?
YOU CHANGED YOUR HAIR. TELL ME WHY.
THAT HAIRCUT WAS ALL CULTURAL BUTTONPUSHING, SEMIOTIC TERRORISM. SCHACT'S IDEA.
MADE ME LOOK TOUGH AND SMART, BUT ALSO THE UNDERDOG, FIGHTING AN EVIL EMPIRE AS BEST I CAN...
AWFUL GODDAMN THING.

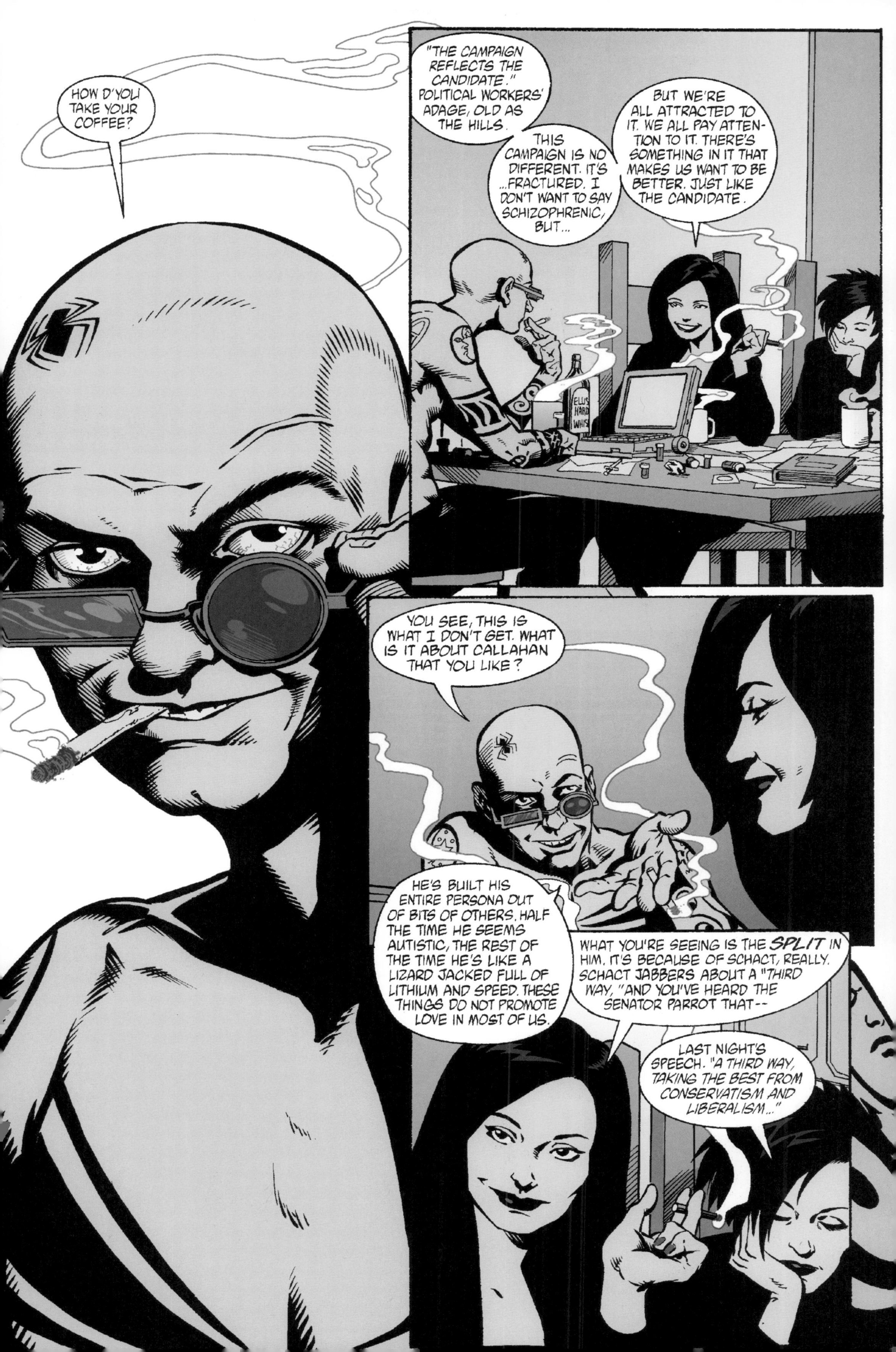
HOW D'YOU TAKE YOUR COFFEE?
"THE CAMPAIGN REFLECTS THE CANDIDATE." POLITICAL WORKERS' ADAGE, OLD AS THE HILLS.
THIS CAMPAIGN IS NO DIFFERENT. IT'S ...FRACTURED. I DON'T WANT TO SAY SCHIZOPHRENIC, BUT...
BUT WE'RE ALL ATTRACTED TO IT. WE ALL PAY ATTENTION TO IT. THERE'S SOMETHING IN IT THAT MAKES US WANT TO BE BETTER. JUST LIKE THE CANDIDATE.
YOU SEE, THIS IS WHAT I DON'T GET. WHAT IS IT ABOUT CALLAHAN THAT YOU LIKE?
HE'S BUILT HIS ENTIRE PERSONA OUT OF BITS OF OTHERS. HALF THE TIME HE SEEMS AUTISTIC, THE REST OF THE TIME HE'S LIKE A LIZARD JACKED FULL OF LITHIUM AND SPEED. THESE THINGS DO NOT PROMOTE LOVE IN MOST OF US.
WHAT YOU'RE SEEING IS THE *SPLIT* IN HIM. IT'S BECAUSE OF SCHACT, REALLY. SCHACT JABBERS ABOUT A "THIRD WAY," AND YOU'VE HEARD THE SENATOR PARROT THAT--
LAST NIGHT'S SPEECH. *"A THIRD WAY, TAKING THE BEST FROM CONSERVATISM AND LIBERALISM..."*

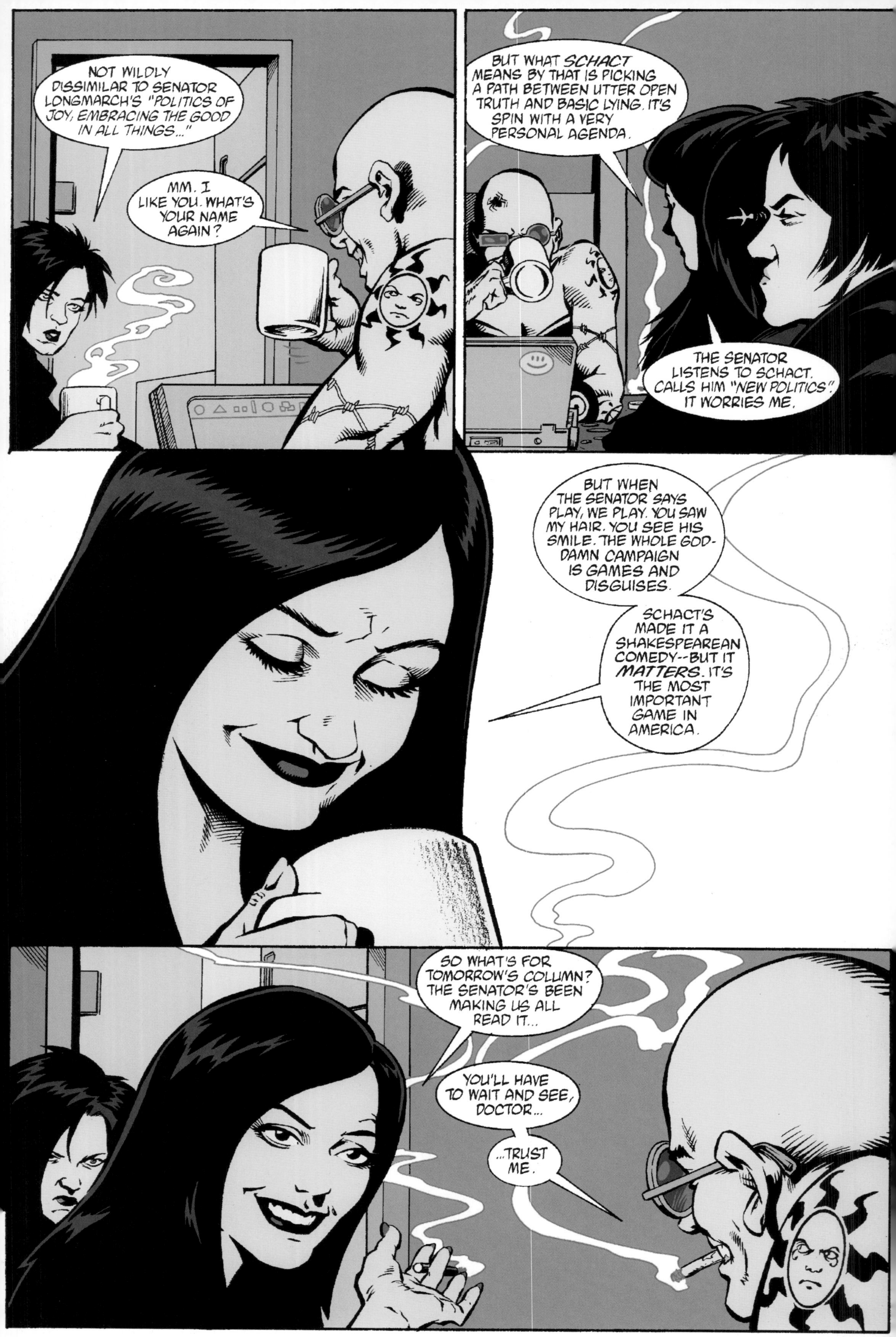
NOT WILDLY DISSIMILAR TO SENATOR LONGMARCH'S "POLITICS OF JOY, EMBRACING THE GOOD IN ALL THINGS..."
MM. I LIKE YOU. WHAT'S YOUR NAME AGAIN?
BUT WHAT SCHACT MEANS BY THAT IS PICKING A PATH BETWEEN UTTER OPEN TRUTH AND BASIC LYING. IT'S SPIN WITH A VERY PERSONAL AGENDA.
THE SENATOR LISTENS TO SCHACT. CALLS HIM "NEW POLITICS". IT WORRIES ME.
BUT WHEN THE SENATOR SAYS PLAY, WE PLAY. YOU SAW MY HAIR. YOU SEE HIS SMILE. THE WHOLE GOD-DAMN CAMPAIGN IS GAMES AND DISGUISES.
SCHACT'S MADE IT A SHAKESPEAREAN COMEDY--BUT IT MATTERS. IT'S THE MOST IMPORTANT GAME IN AMERICA.
SO WHAT'S FOR TOMORROW'S COLUMN? THE SENATOR'S BEEN MAKING US ALL READ IT...
YOU'LL HAVE TO WAIT AND SEE, DOCTOR...
...TRUST ME.

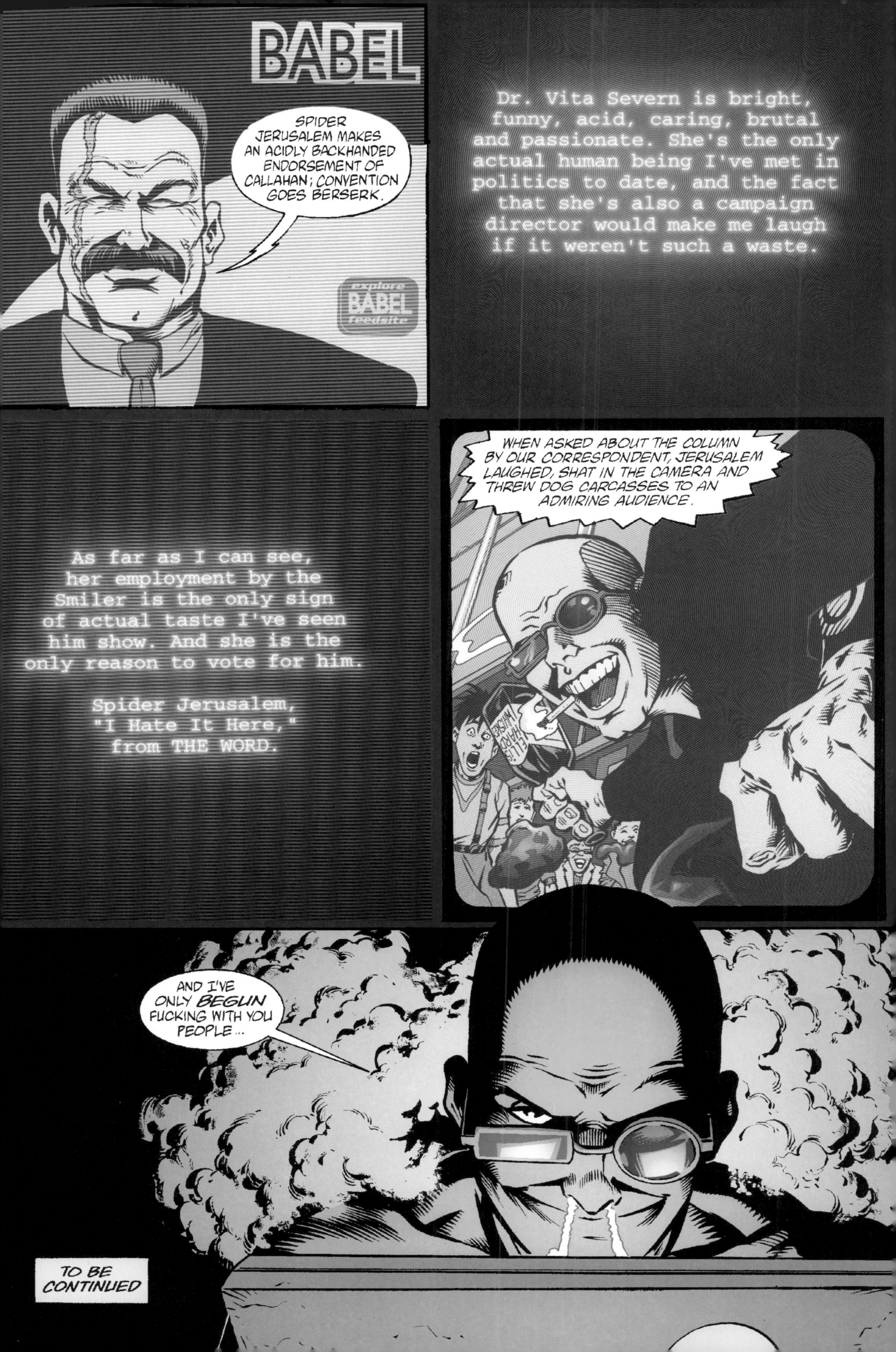
BABEL
SPIDER JERUSALEM MAKES AN ACIDLY BACKHANDED ENDORSEMENT OF CALLAHAN; CONVENTION GOES BERSERK.
explore BABEL feedsite
Dr. Vita Severn is bright, funny, acid, caring, brutal and passionate. She's the only actual human being I've met in politics to date, and the fact that she's also a campaign director would make me laugh if it weren't such a waste.
As far as I can see, her employment by the Smiler is the only sign of actual taste I've seen him show. And she is the only reason to vote for him.
Spider Jerusalem, "I Hate It Here," from THE WORD.
WHEN ASKED ABOUT THE COLUMN BY OUR CORRESPONDENT, JERUSALEM LAUGHED, SHAT IN THE CAMERA AND THREW DOG CARCASSES TO AN ADMIRING AUDIENCE.
AND I'VE ONLY BEGUN FUCKING WITH YOU PEOPLE...
TO BE CONTINUED

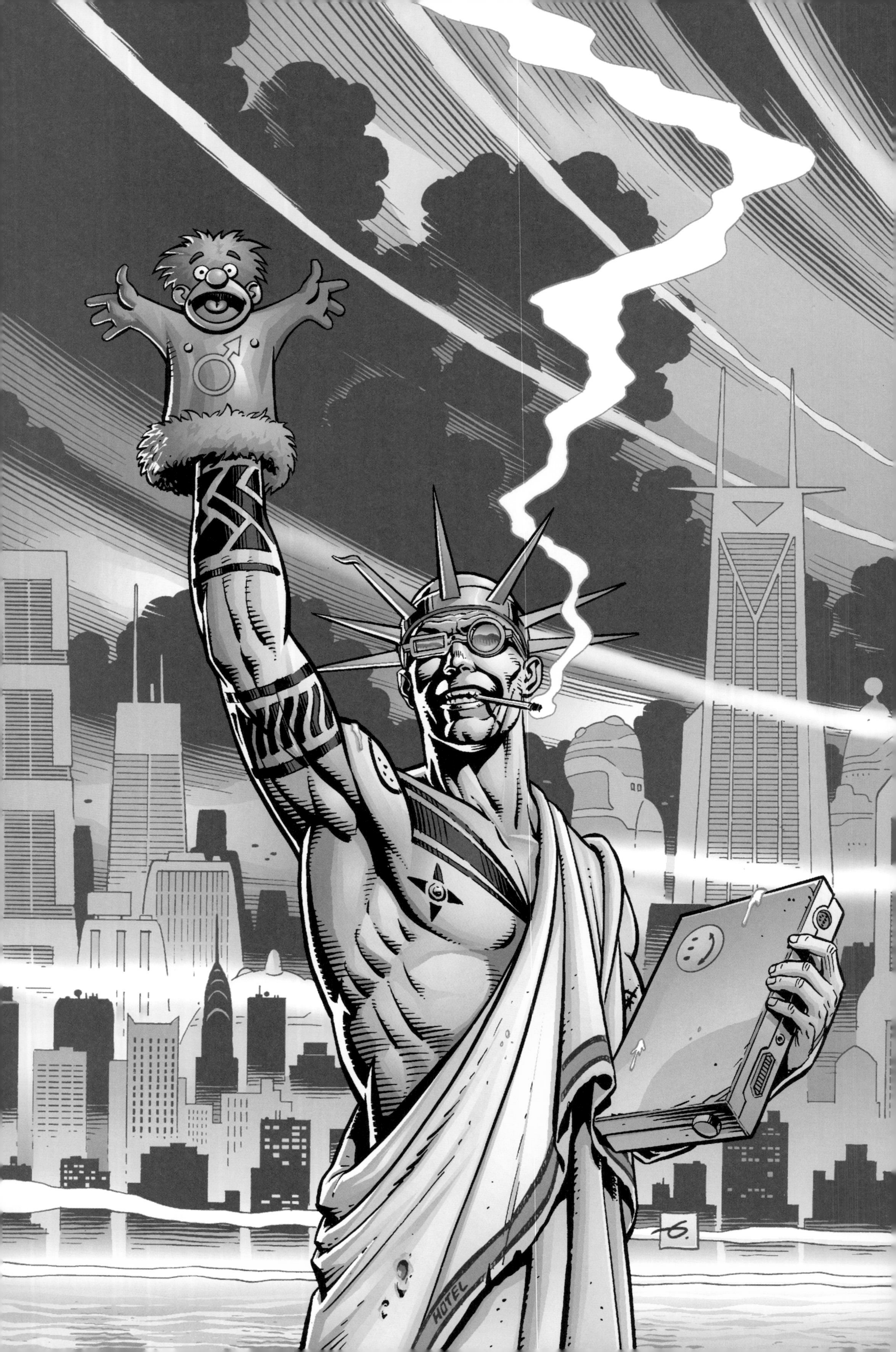
HOTEL

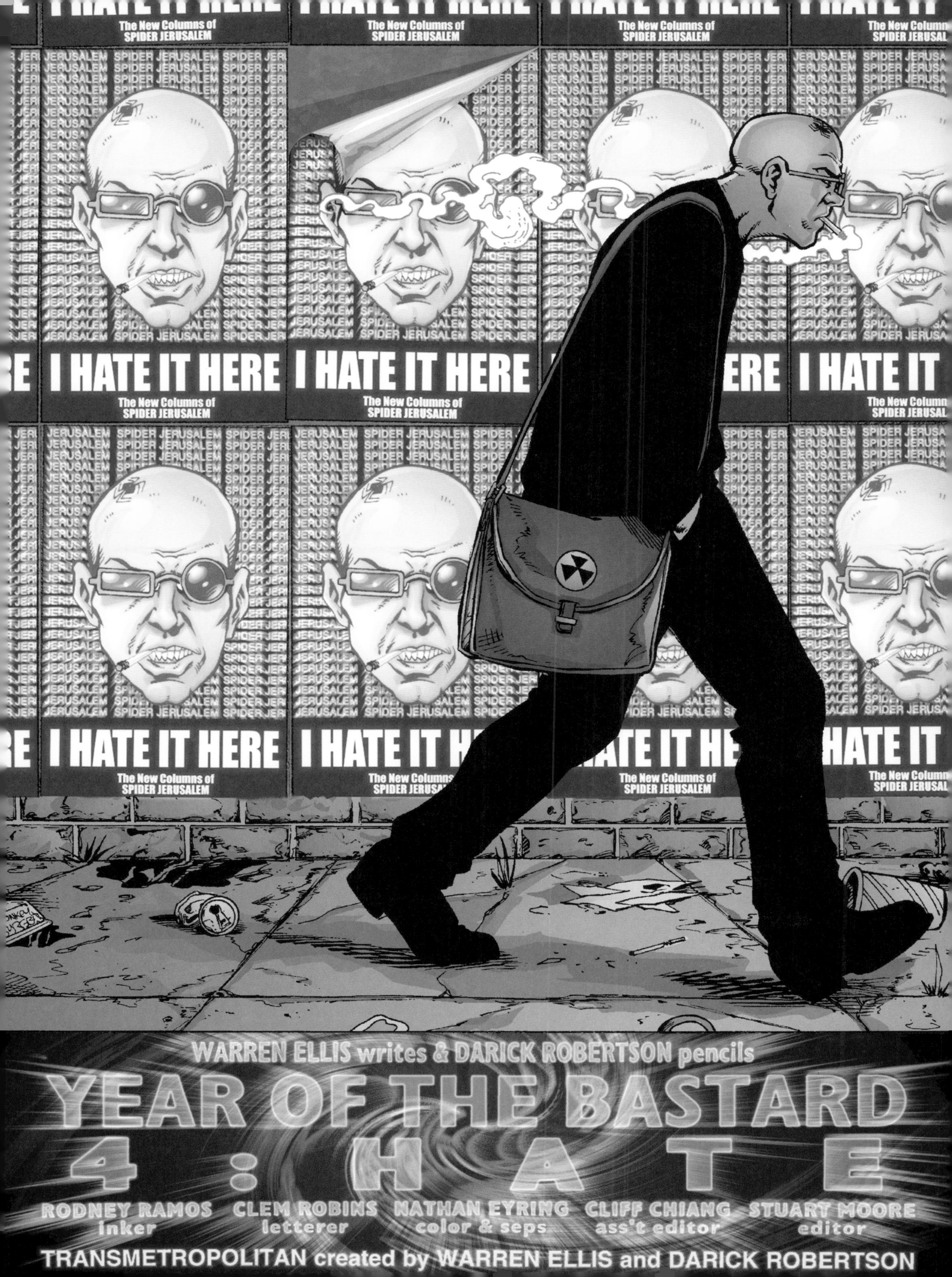
I HATE IT HERE
The New Columns of
SPIDER JERUSALEM

WARREN ELLIS writes & DARICK ROBERTSON pencils

# YEAR OF THE BASTARD
# 4 : HATE

RODNEY RAMOS inker
CLEM ROBINS letterer
NATHAN EYRING color & seps
CLIFF CHIANG ass't editor
STUART MOORE editor

TRANSMETROPOLITAN created by WARREN ELLIS and DARICK ROBERTSON

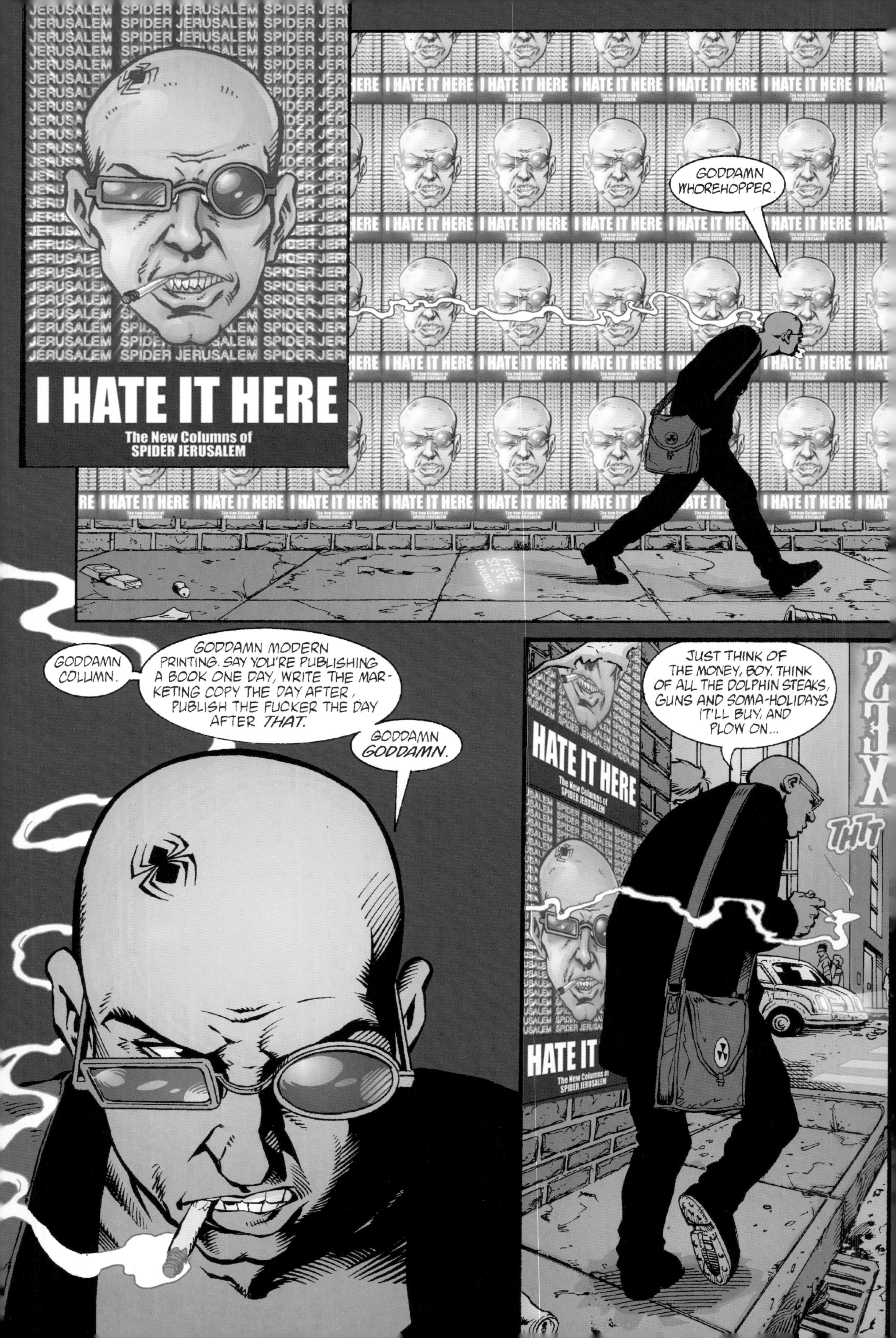
I HATE IT HERE
The New Columns of SPIDER JERUSALEM
GODDAMN WHOREHOPPER.
FREE STEVE CHUNG
GODDAMN COLUMN.
GODDAMN MODERN PRINTING. SAY YOU'RE PUBLISHING A BOOK ONE DAY, WRITE THE MARKETING COPY THE DAY AFTER, PUBLISH THE FUCKER THE DAY AFTER *THAT*.
GODDAMN *GODDAMN*.
JUST THINK OF THE MONEY, BOY. THINK OF ALL THE DOLPHIN STEAKS, GUNS AND SOMA-HOLIDAYS IT'LL BUY, AND PLOW ON...
HATE IT HERE
THTT

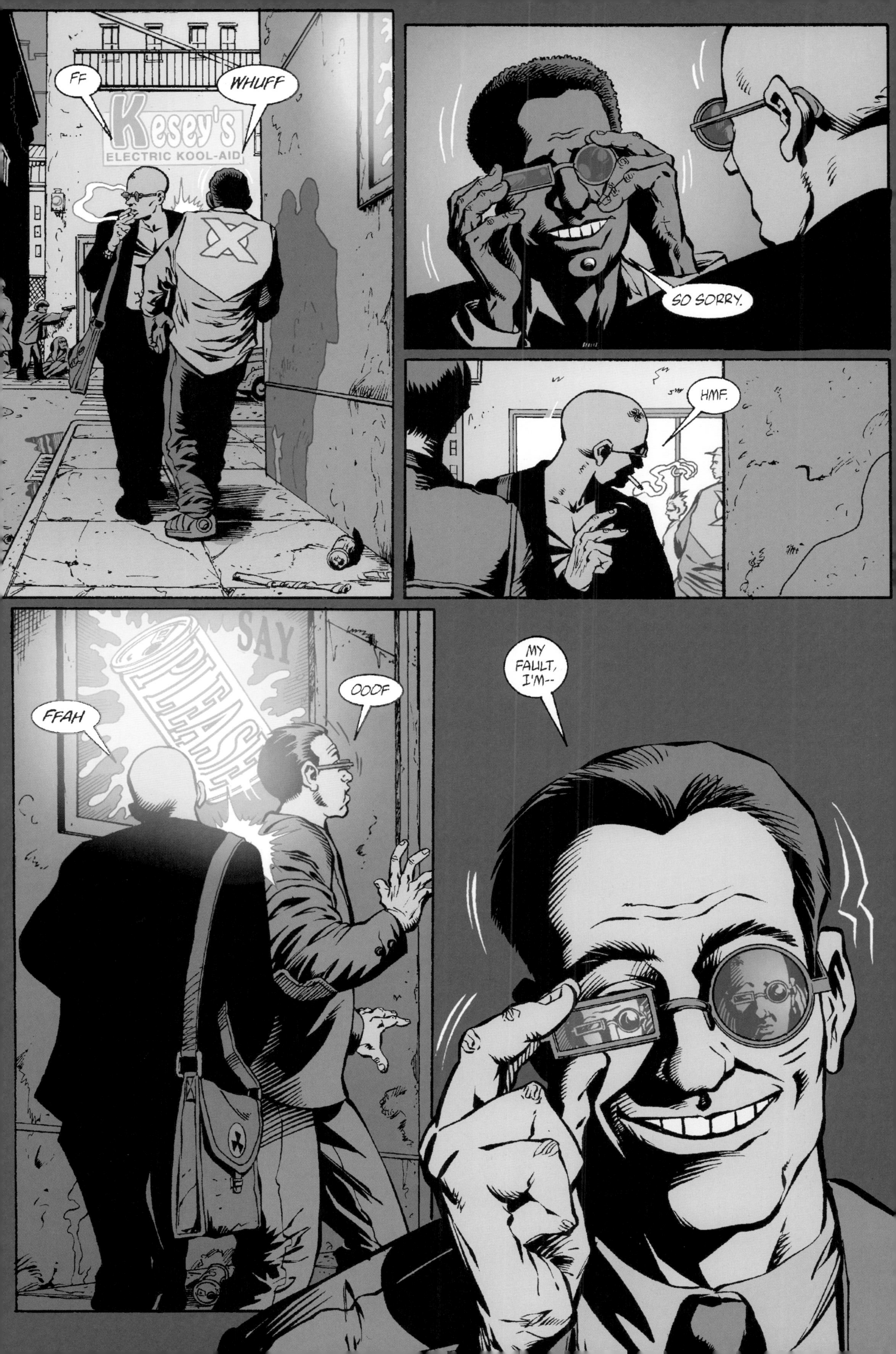
FF
WHUFF
Kesey's
ELECTRIC KOOL-AID
SO SORRY.
HMF.
SAY
PLEASE
FFAH
OOOF
MY FAULT, I'M--

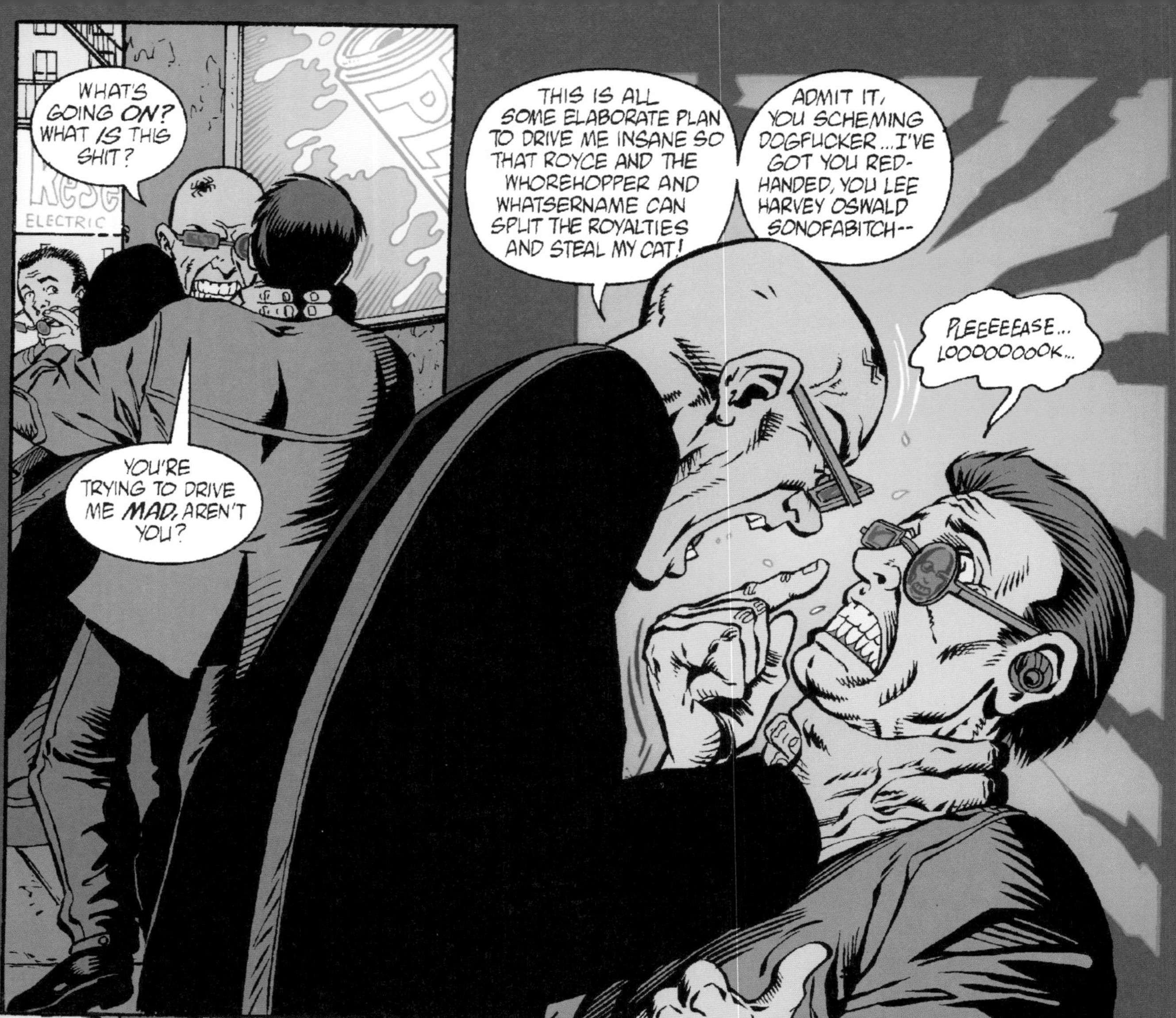
WHAT'S GOING ON? WHAT IS THIS SHIT?
ELECTRIC
YOU'RE TRYING TO DRIVE ME MAD, AREN'T YOU?
THIS IS ALL SOME ELABORATE PLAN TO DRIVE ME INSANE SO THAT ROYCE AND THE WHOREHOPPER AND WHATSERNAME CAN SPLIT THE ROYALTIES AND STEAL MY CAT!
ADMIT IT, YOU SCHEMING DOGFUCKER...I'VE GOT YOU RED-HANDED, YOU LEE HARVEY OSWALD SONOFABITCH--
PLEEEEEASE... LOOOOOOOOK...

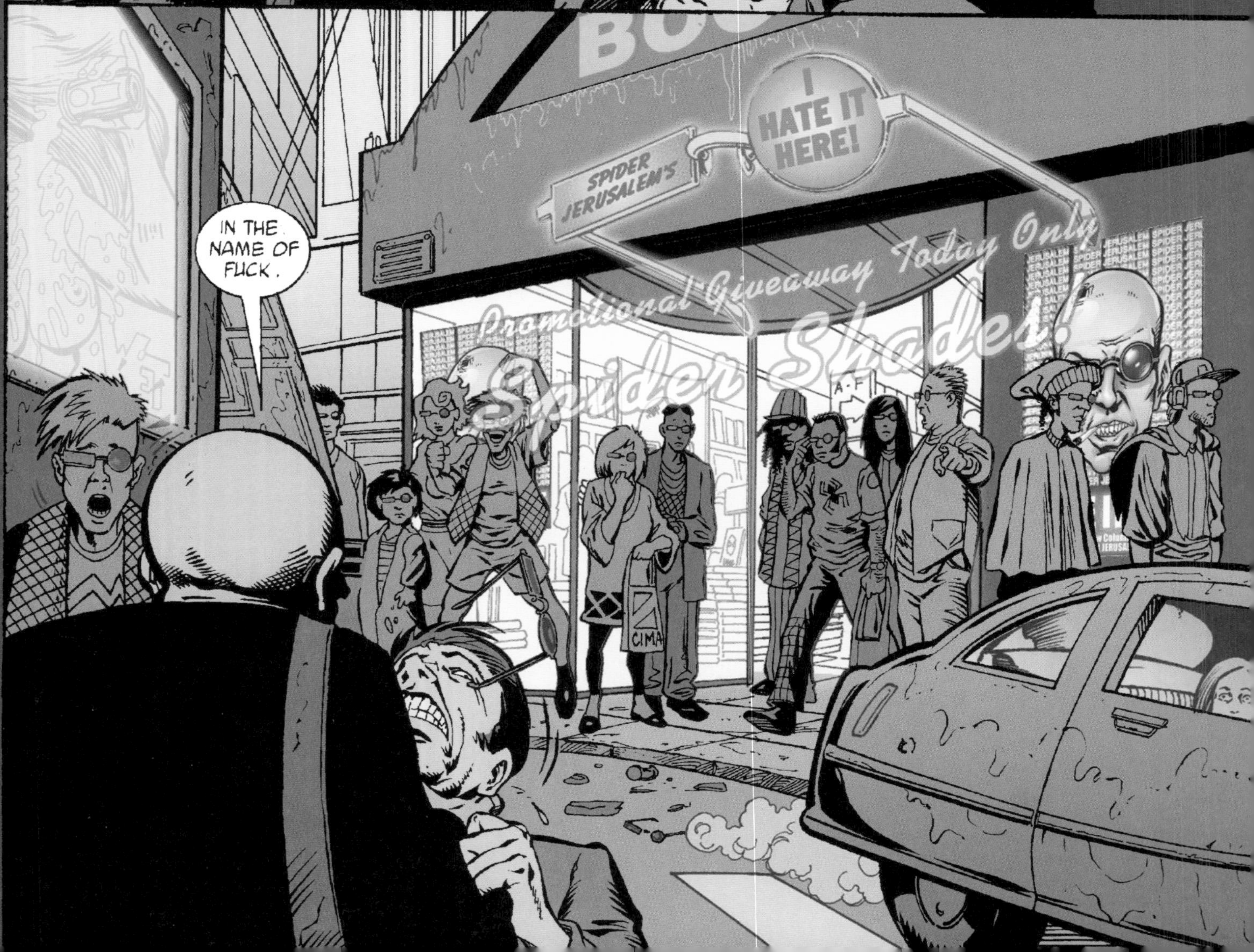
SPIDER JERUSALEM'S
I HATE IT HERE!
Promotional Giveaway Today Only
Spider Shades!
IN THE NAME OF FUCK.

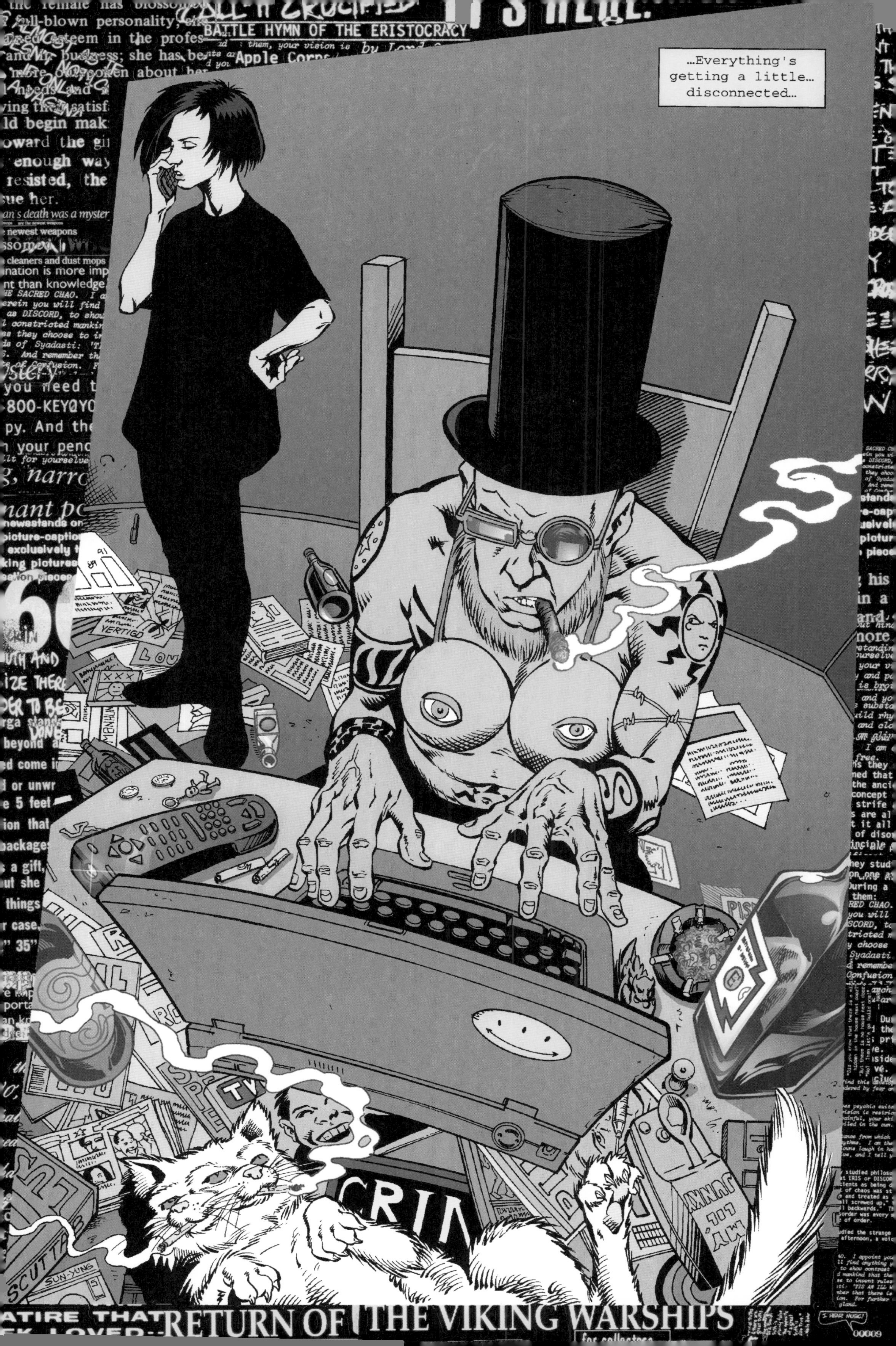

BATTLE HYMN OF THE ERISTOCRACY
Apple Corps
...Everything's getting a little... disconnected...
VERTIGO
RETURN OF THE VIKING WARSHIPS

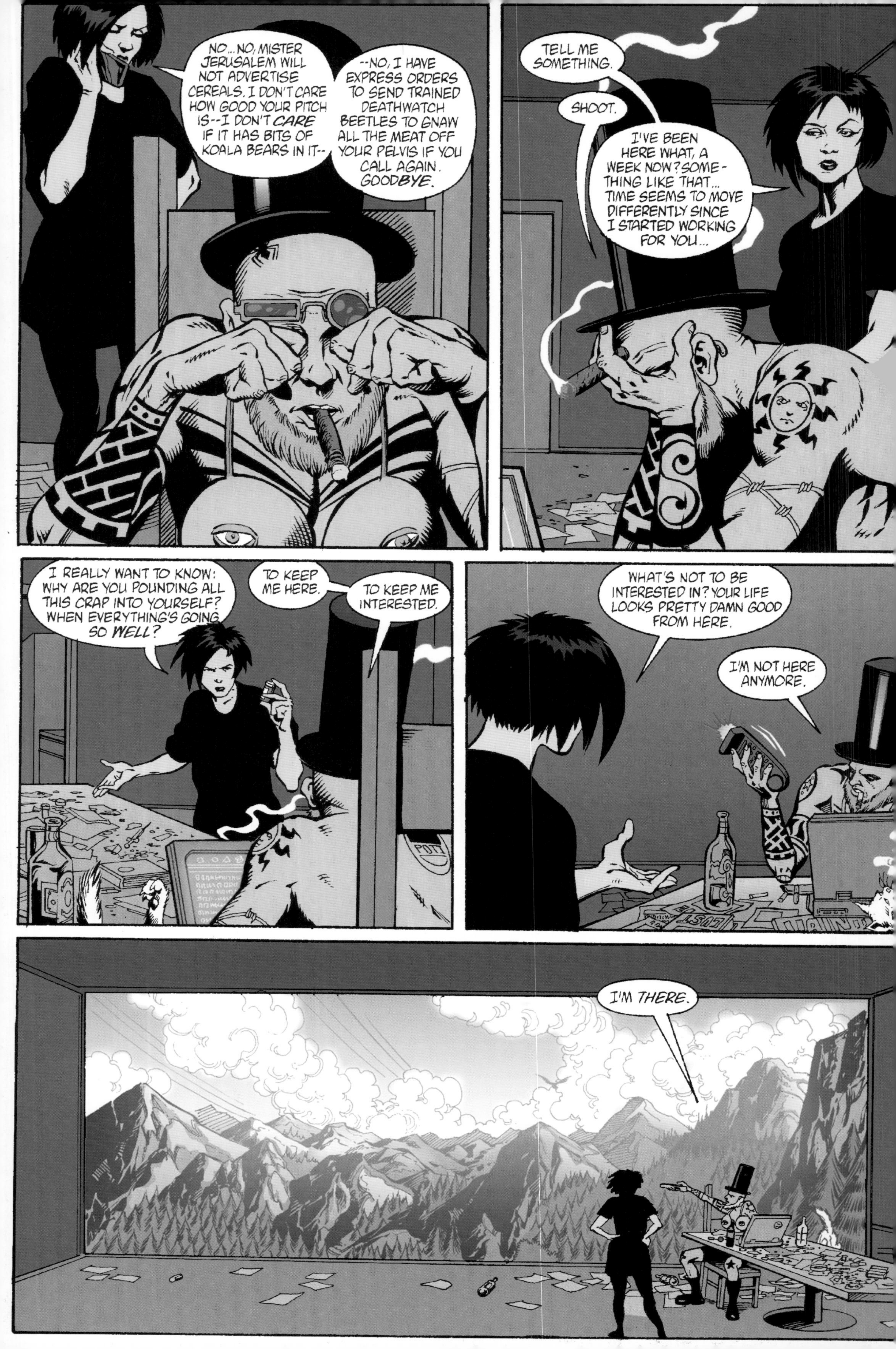
NO... NO, MISTER JERUSALEM WILL NOT ADVERTISE CEREALS. I DON'T CARE HOW GOOD YOUR PITCH IS--I DON'T CARE IF IT HAS BITS OF KOALA BEARS IN IT--
--NO, I HAVE EXPRESS ORDERS TO SEND TRAINED DEATHWATCH BEETLES TO GNAW ALL THE MEAT OFF YOUR PELVIS IF YOU CALL AGAIN. GOODBYE.
TELL ME SOMETHING.
SHOOT.
I'VE BEEN HERE WHAT, A WEEK NOW? SOMETHING LIKE THAT... TIME SEEMS TO MOVE DIFFERENTLY SINCE I STARTED WORKING FOR YOU...
I REALLY WANT TO KNOW: WHY ARE YOU POUNDING ALL THIS CRAP INTO YOURSELF? WHEN EVERYTHING'S GOING SO WELL?
TO KEEP ME HERE.
TO KEEP ME INTERESTED.
WHAT'S NOT TO BE INTERESTED IN? YOUR LIFE LOOKS PRETTY DAMN GOOD FROM HERE.
I'M NOT HERE ANYMORE.
I'M THERE.

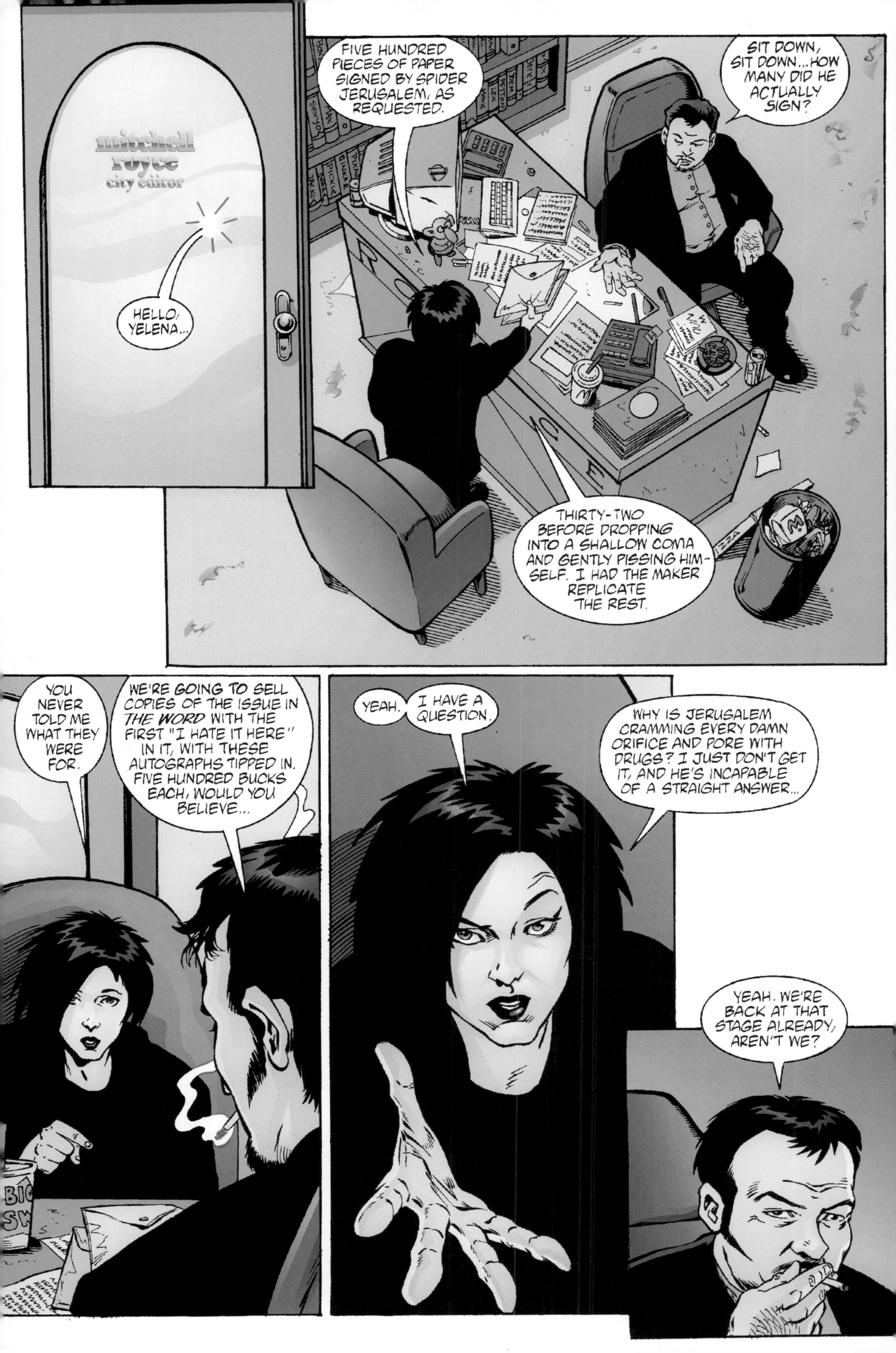
mitchell royce city editor
HELLO, YELENA...
FIVE HUNDRED PIECES OF PAPER SIGNED BY SPIDER JERUSALEM, AS REQUESTED.
SIT DOWN, SIT DOWN...HOW MANY DID HE ACTUALLY SIGN?
THIRTY-TWO BEFORE DROPPING INTO A SHALLOW COMA AND GENTLY PISSING HIMSELF. I HAD THE MAKER REPLICATE THE REST.
YOU NEVER TOLD ME WHAT THEY WERE FOR.
WE'RE GOING TO SELL COPIES OF THE ISSUE IN THE WORD WITH THE FIRST "I HATE IT HERE" IN IT, WITH THESE AUTOGRAPHS TIPPED IN. FIVE HUNDRED BUCKS EACH, WOULD YOU BELIEVE...
YEAH.
I HAVE A QUESTION.
WHY IS JERUSALEM CRAMMING EVERY DAMN ORIFICE AND PORE WITH DRUGS? I JUST DON'T GET IT, AND HE'S INCAPABLE OF A STRAIGHT ANSWER...
YEAH. WE'RE BACK AT THAT STAGE ALREADY, AREN'T WE?

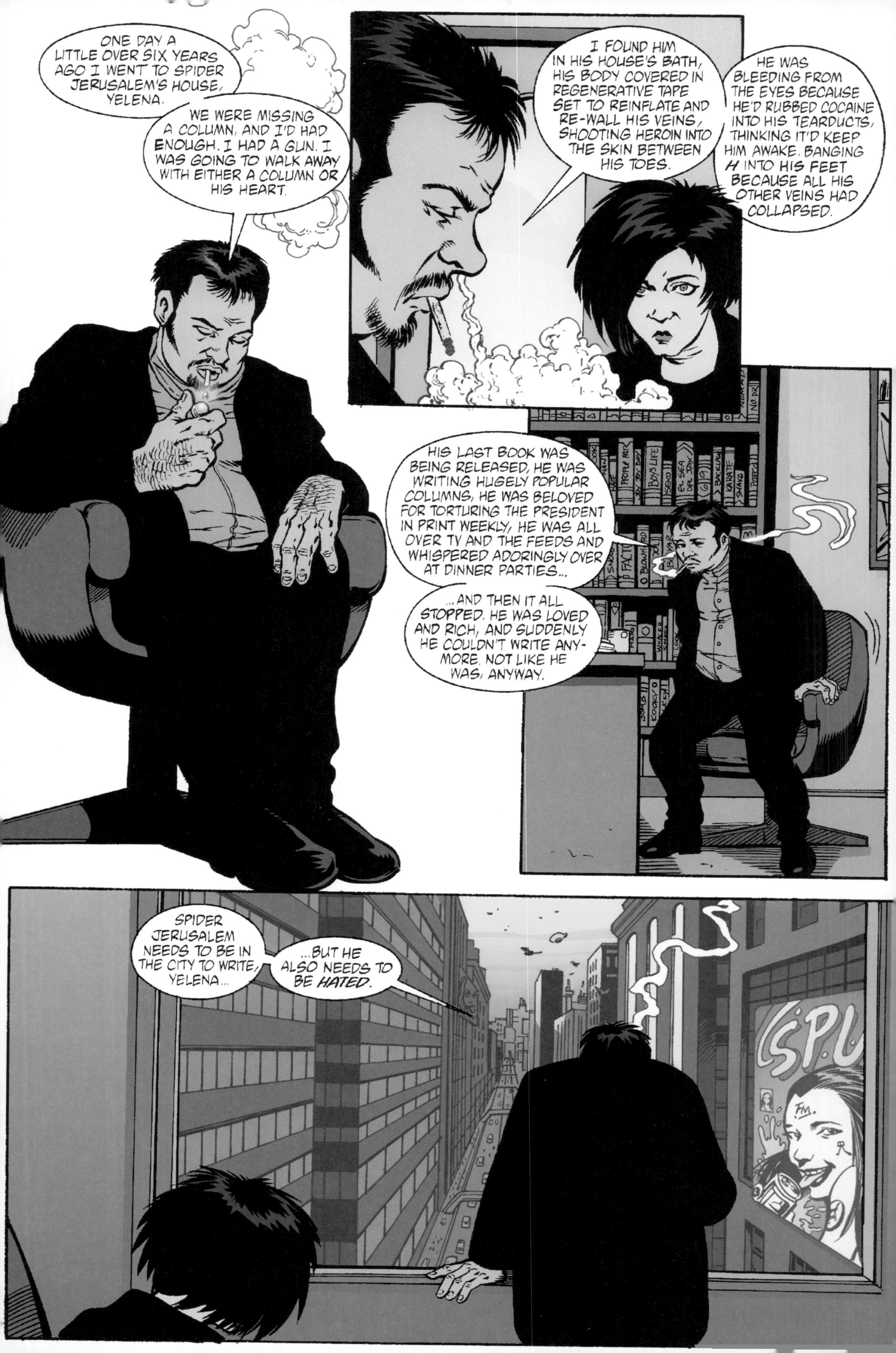
ONE DAY A LITTLE OVER SIX YEARS AGO I WENT TO SPIDER JERUSALEM'S HOUSE, YELENA.
WE WERE MISSING A COLUMN, AND I'D HAD ENOUGH. I HAD A GUN. I WAS GOING TO WALK AWAY WITH EITHER A COLUMN OR HIS HEART.
I FOUND HIM IN HIS HOUSE'S BATH, HIS BODY COVERED IN REGENERATIVE TAPE SET TO REINFLATE AND RE-WALL HIS VEINS, SHOOTING HEROIN INTO THE SKIN BETWEEN HIS TOES.
HE WAS BLEEDING FROM THE EYES BECAUSE HE'D RUBBED COCAINE INTO HIS TEARDUCTS, THINKING IT'D KEEP HIM AWAKE. BANGING H INTO HIS FEET BECAUSE ALL HIS OTHER VEINS HAD COLLAPSED.
HIS LAST BOOK WAS BEING RELEASED, HE WAS WRITING HUGELY POPULAR COLUMNS, HE WAS BELOVED FOR TORTURING THE PRESIDENT IN PRINT WEEKLY, HE WAS ALL OVER TV AND THE FEEDS AND WHISPERED ADORINGLY OVER AT DINNER PARTIES...
...AND THEN IT ALL STOPPED. HE WAS LOVED AND RICH, AND SUDDENLY HE COULDN'T WRITE ANYMORE. NOT LIKE HE WAS, ANYWAY.
SPIDER JERUSALEM NEEDS TO BE IN THE CITY TO WRITE, YELENA...
...BUT HE ALSO NEEDS TO BE HATED.

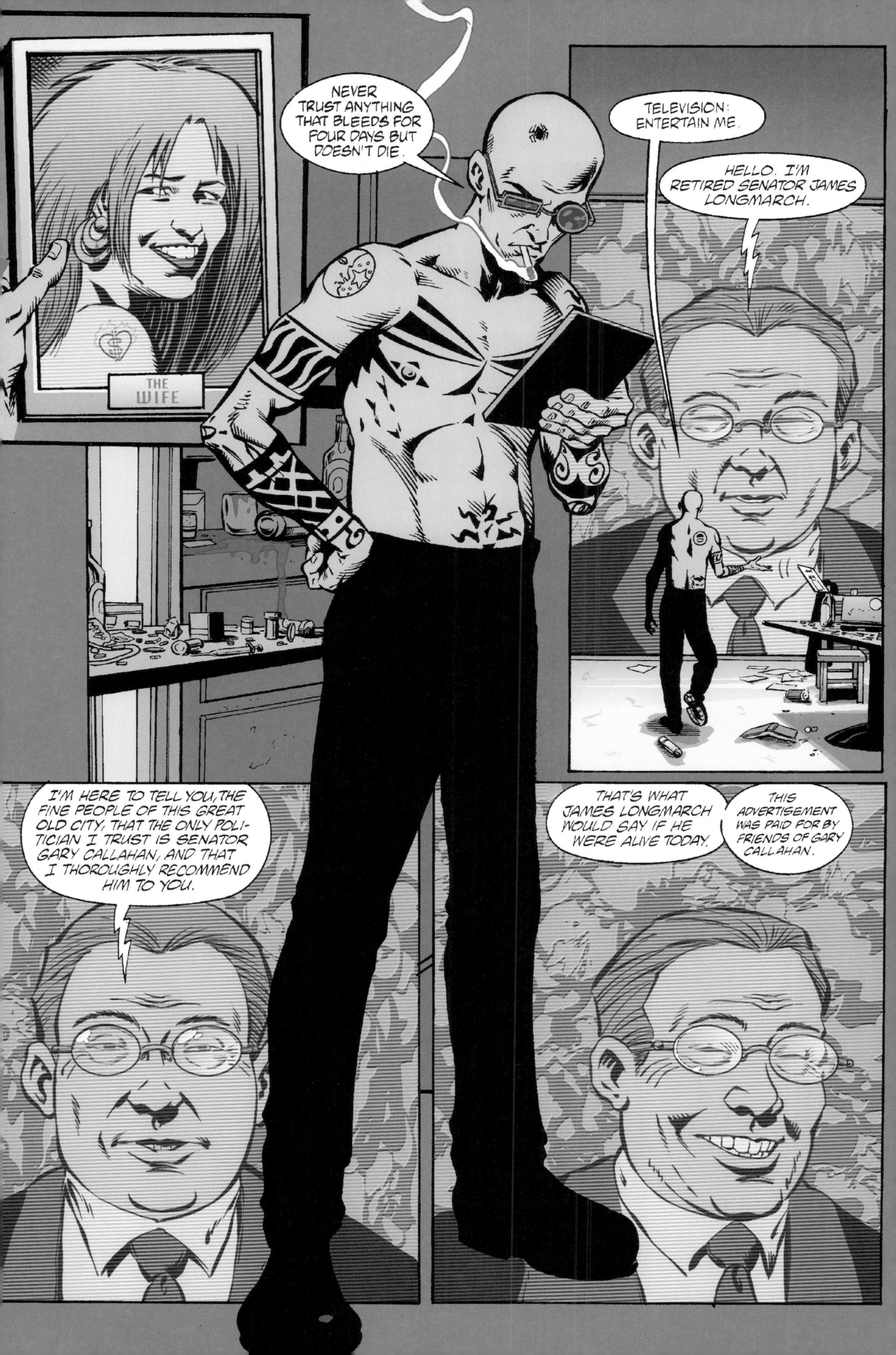
THE WIFE
NEVER TRUST ANYTHING THAT BLEEDS FOR FOUR DAYS BUT DOESN'T DIE.
TELEVISION: ENTERTAIN ME.
HELLO. I'M RETIRED SENATOR JAMES LONGMARCH.
I'M HERE TO TELL YOU, THE FINE PEOPLE OF THIS GREAT OLD CITY, THAT THE ONLY POLITICIAN I TRUST IS SENATOR GARY CALLAHAN, AND THAT I THOROUGHLY RECOMMEND HIM TO YOU.
THAT'S WHAT JAMES LONGMARCH WOULD SAY IF HE WERE ALIVE TODAY.
THIS ADVERTISEMENT WAS PAID FOR BY FRIENDS OF GARY CALLAHAN.

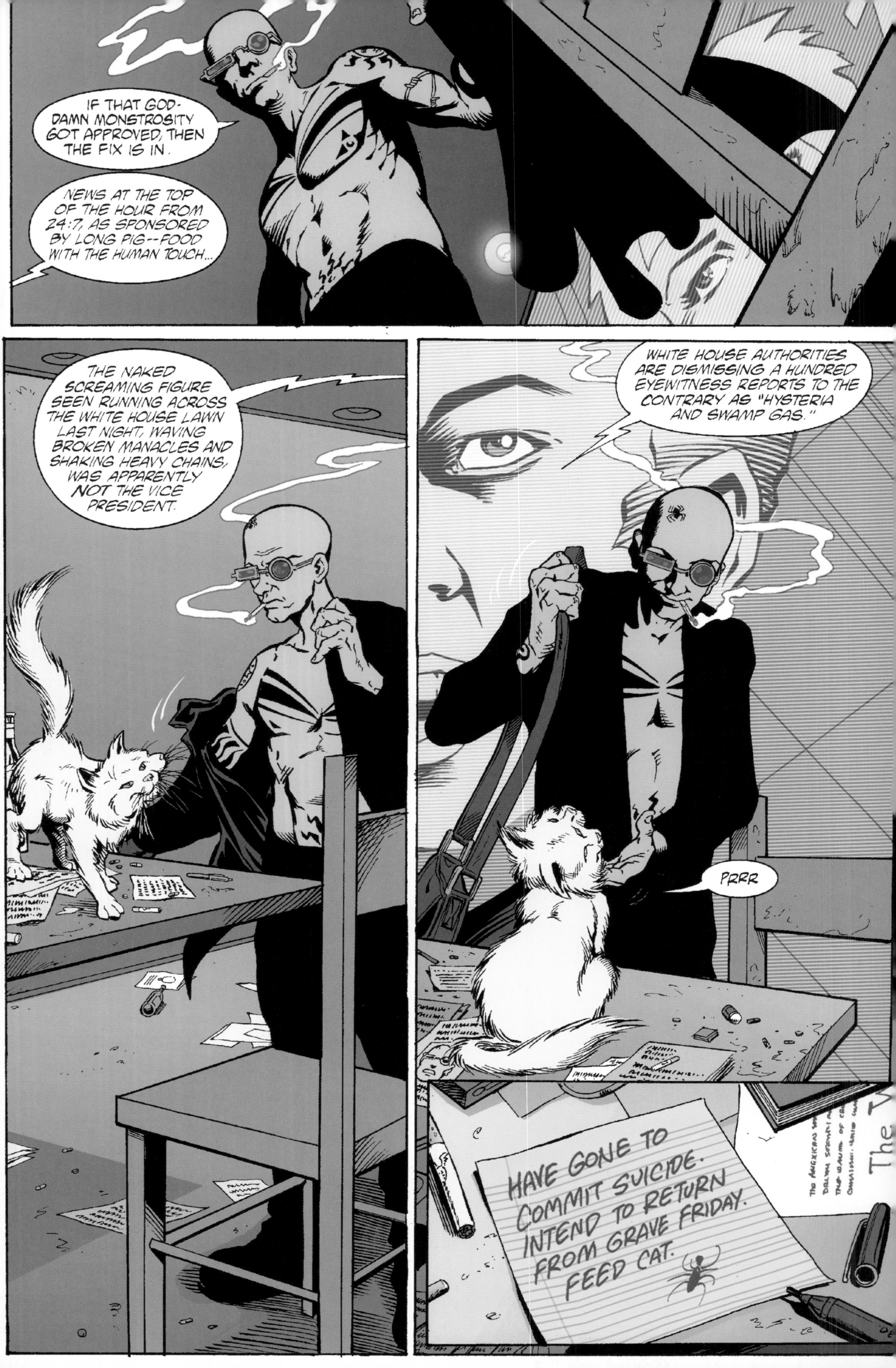
IF THAT GOD-DAMN MONSTROSITY GOT APPROVED, THEN THE FIX IS IN.
NEWS AT THE TOP OF THE HOUR FROM 24:7, AS SPONSORED BY LONG PIG--FOOD WITH THE HUMAN TOUCH...
THE NAKED SCREAMING FIGURE SEEN RUNNING ACROSS THE WHITE HOUSE LAWN LAST NIGHT, WAVING BROKEN MANACLES AND SHAKING HEAVY CHAINS, WAS APPARENTLY NOT THE VICE PRESIDENT.
WHITE HOUSE AUTHORITIES ARE DISMISSING A HUNDRED EYEWITNESS REPORTS TO THE CONTRARY AS "HYSTERIA AND SWAMP GAS."
PRRR
HAVE GONE TO COMMIT SUICIDE. INTEND TO RETURN FROM GRAVE FRIDAY. FEED CAT.

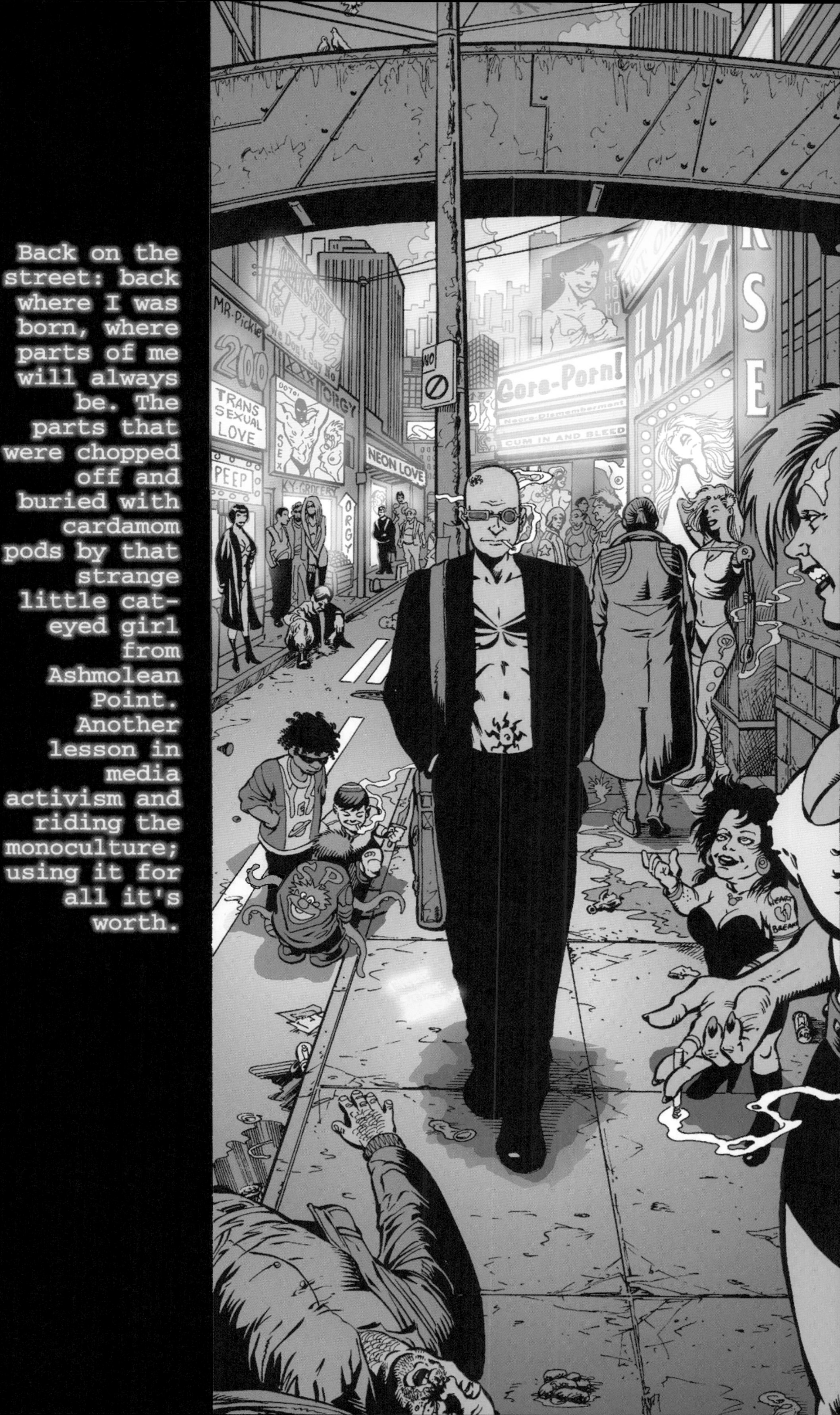
Back on the street: back where I was born, where parts of me will always be. The parts that were chopped off and buried with cardamom pods by that strange little cat-eyed girl from Ashmolean Point. Another lesson in media activism and riding the monoculture; using it for all it's worth.
MR. Pickle
200
We Don't Say No
XXX
ORGY
TRANS SEXUAL LOVE
PEEP
NEON LOVE
KY-GROCERY
ORGY
NO
Gore-Porn!
Necro-Dismemberment
CUM IN AND BLEED
HOLO STRIPPERS

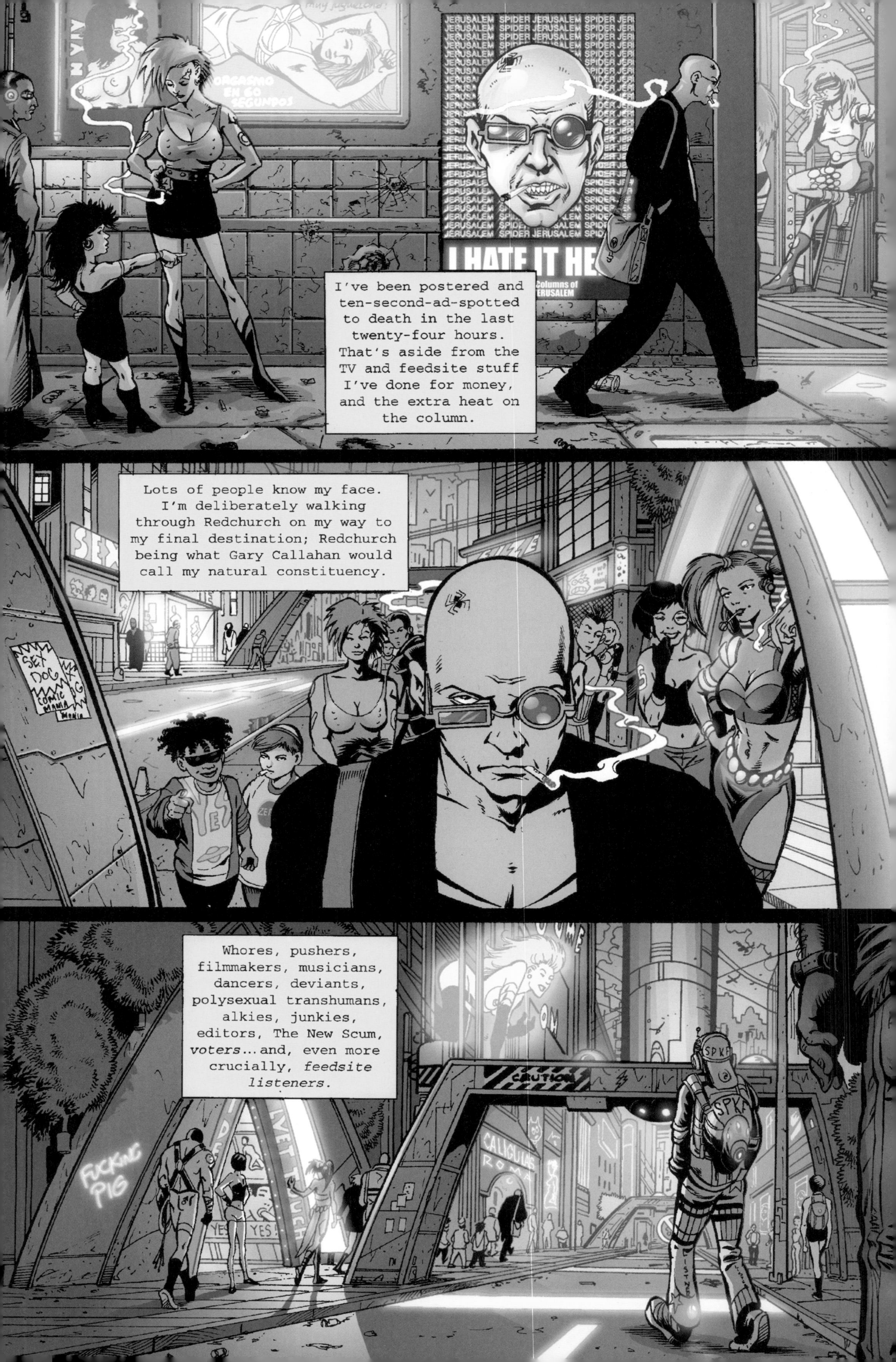
ORGASMO EN 60 SEGUNDOS
SPIDER JERUSALEM
I HATE IT HE
Columns of
JERUSALEM
I've been postered and ten-second-ad-spotted to death in the last twenty-four hours. That's aside from the TV and feedsite stuff I've done for money, and the extra heat on the column.
Lots of people know my face. I'm deliberately walking through Redchurch on my way to my final destination; Redchurch being what Gary Callahan would call my natural constituency.
SEX DOG
COMIC MANIA
Whores, pushers, filmmakers, musicians, dancers, deviants, polysexual transhumans, alkies, junkies, editors, The New Scum, *voters*... and, even more crucially, *feedsite listeners*.
CAUTION
FUCKING PIG
YES YES!
SPKA

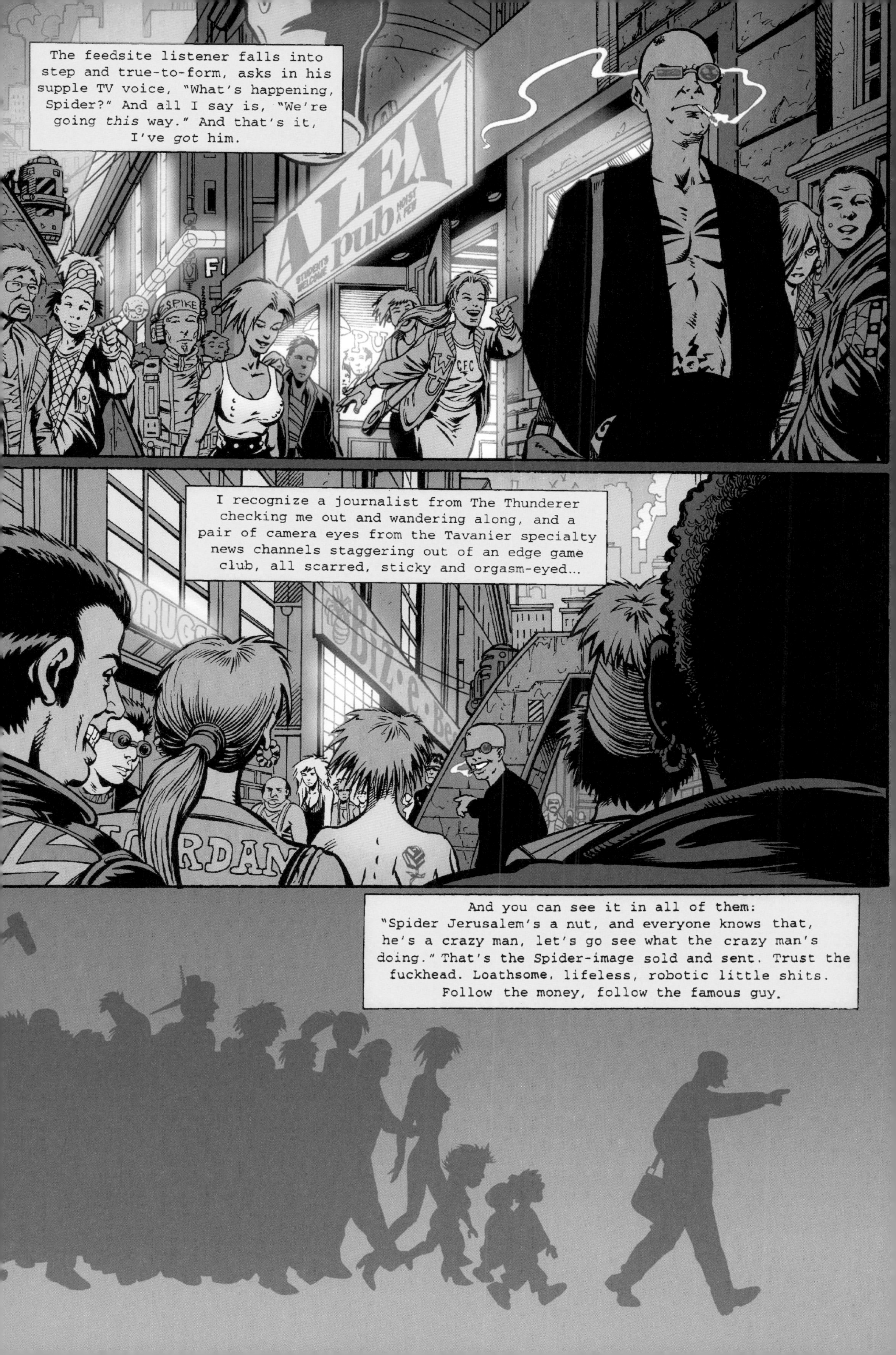

The feedsite listener falls into step and true-to-form, asks in his supple TV voice, "What's happening, Spider?" And all I say is, "We're going *this* way." And that's it, I've *got* him.
ALEX pub
STUDENTS WELCOME
HOIST A FEW
SPIKE
CFC
I recognize a journalist from The Thunderer checking me out and wandering along, and a pair of camera eyes from the Tavanier specialty news channels staggering out of an edge game club, all scarred, sticky and orgasm-eyed...
JORDAN
And you can see it in all of them: "Spider Jerusalem's a nut, and everyone knows that, he's a crazy man, let's go see what the crazy man's doing." That's the Spider-image sold and sent. Trust the fuckhead. Loathsome, lifeless, robotic little shits. Follow the money, follow the famous guy.

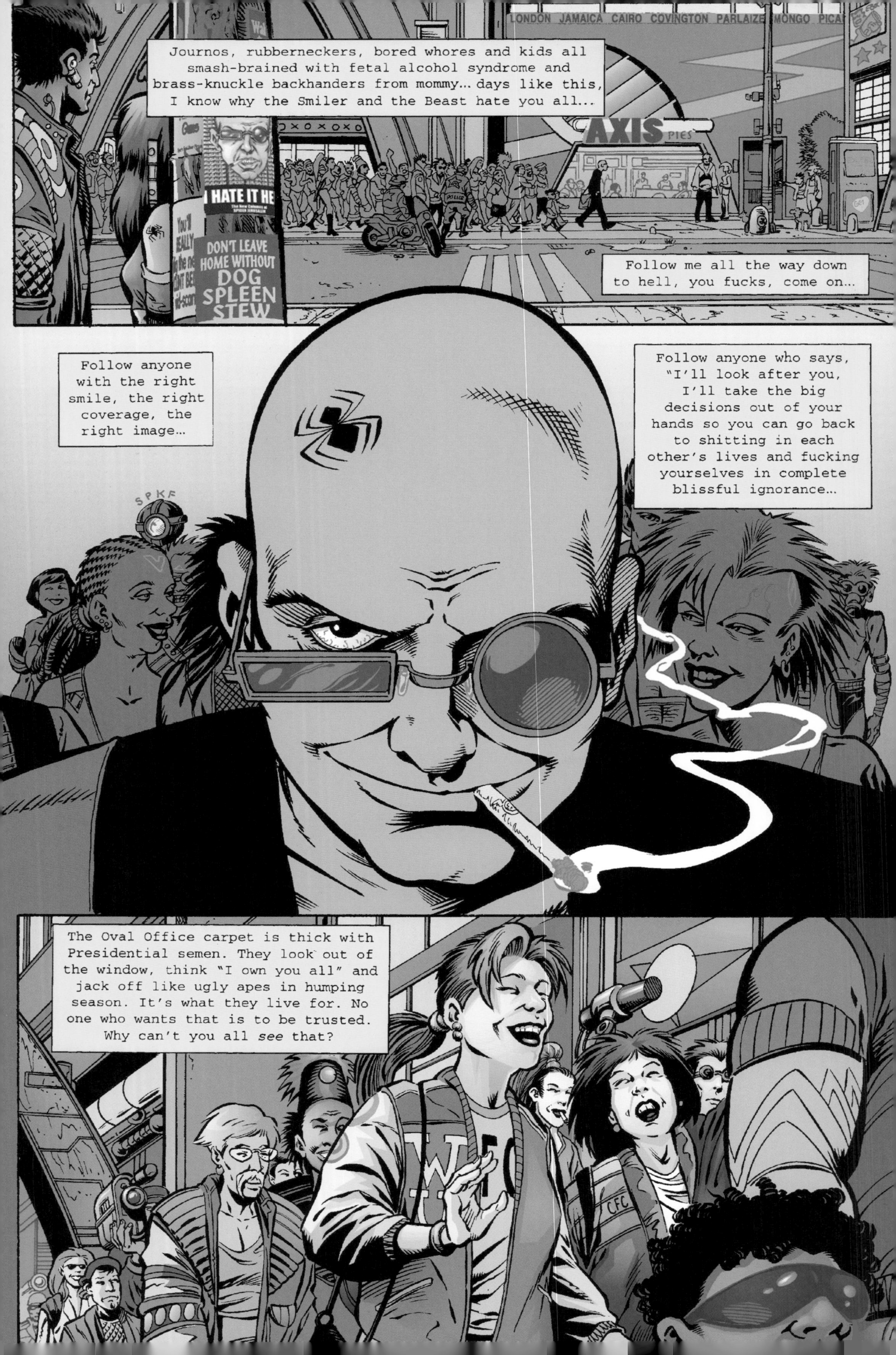
LONDON JAMAICA CAIRO COVINGTON PARLAIZE MONGO
Journos, rubberneckers, bored whores and kids all smash-brained with fetal alcohol syndrome and brass-knuckle backhanders from mommy… days like this, I know why the Smiler and the Beast hate you all…
AXIS PIES
DON'T LEAVE HOME WITHOUT DOG SPLEEN STEW
Follow me all the way down to hell, you fucks, come on…
Follow anyone with the right smile, the right coverage, the right image…
Follow anyone who says, "I'll look after you, I'll take the big decisions out of your hands so you can go back to shitting in each other's lives and fucking yourselves in complete blissful ignorance…
SPKF
The Oval Office carpet is thick with Presidential semen. They look out of the window, think "I own you all" and jack off like ugly apes in humping season. It's what they live for. No one who wants that is to be trusted. Why can't you all *see* that?
CFC

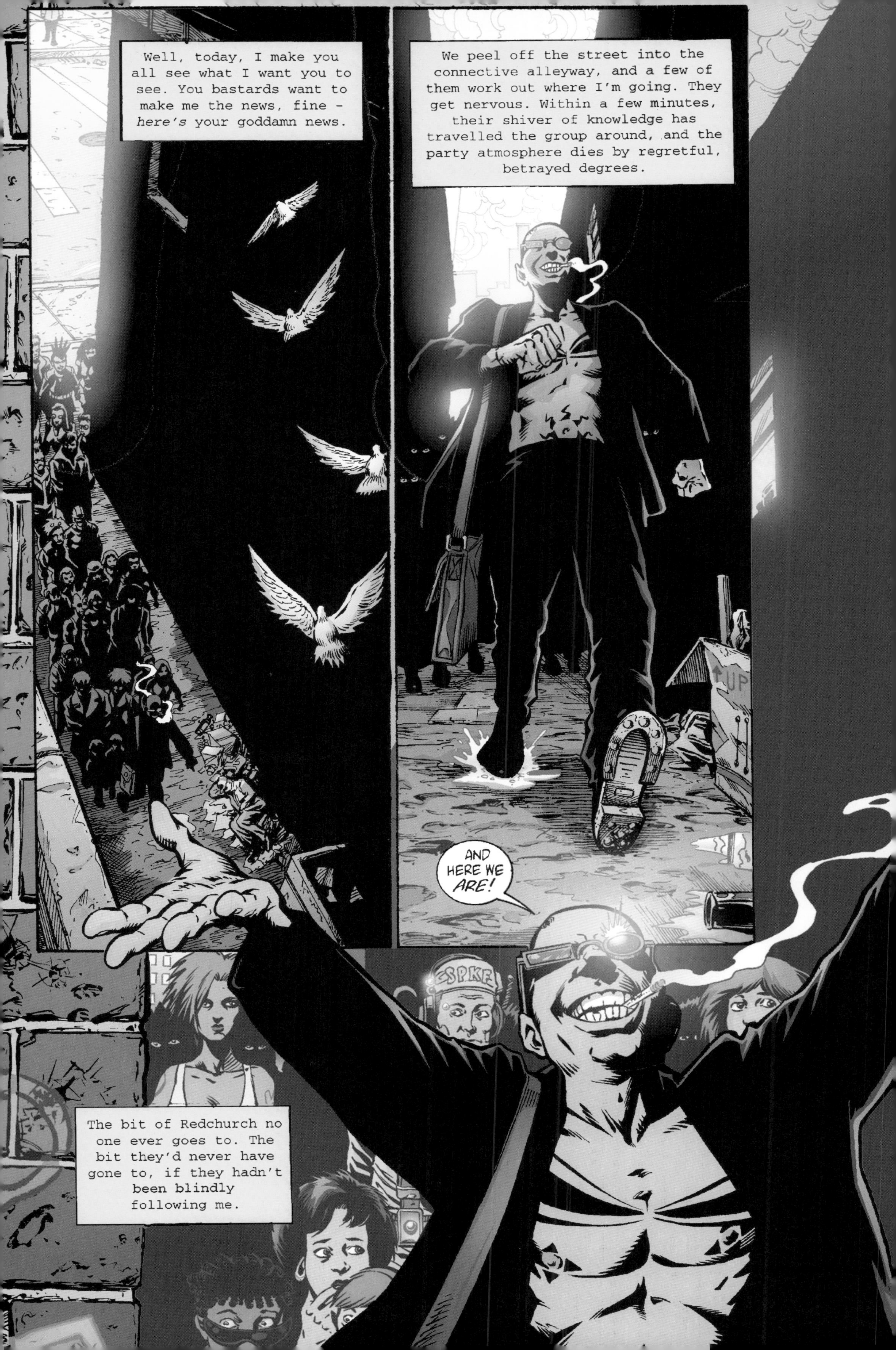

Well, today, I make you all see what I want you to see. You bastards want to make me the news, fine - *here's* your goddamn news.
We peel off the street into the connective alleyway, and a few of them work out where I'm going. They get nervous. Within a few minutes, their shiver of knowledge has travelled the group around, and the party atmosphere dies by regretful, betrayed degrees.
AND HERE WE *ARE!*
UP
SPKE
The bit of Redchurch no one ever goes to. The bit they'd never have gone to, if they hadn't been blindly following me.

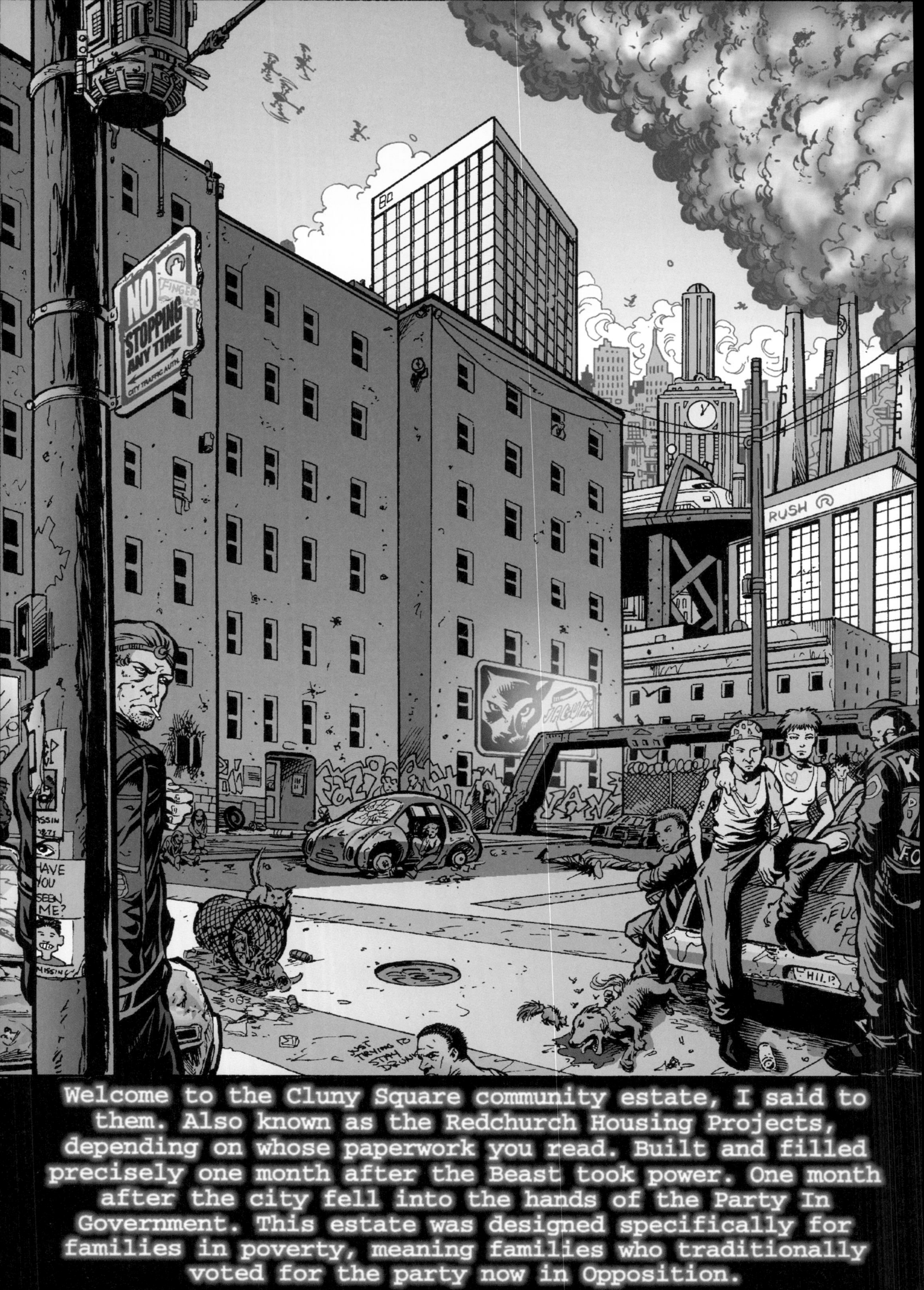
NO
STOPPING
ANY TIME
CITY TRAFFIC AUTH.
RUSH
HAVE YOU SEEN ME?

Welcome to the Cluny Square community estate, I said to them. Also known as the Redchurch Housing Projects, depending on whose paperwork you read. Built and filled precisely one month after the Beast took power. One month after the city fell into the hands of the Party In Government. This estate was designed specifically for families in poverty, meaning families who traditionally voted for the party now in Opposition.

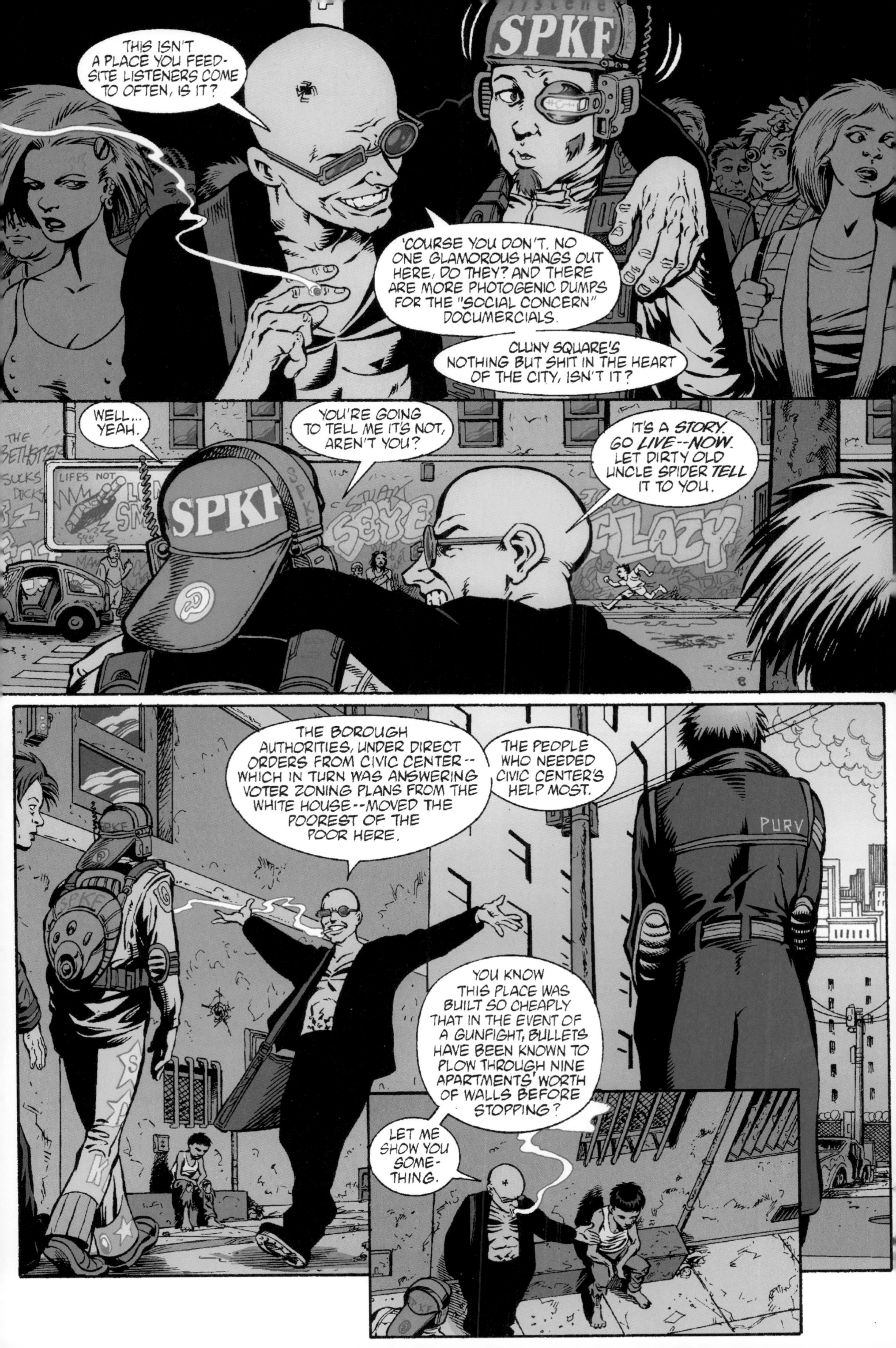
SPKF
THIS ISN'T A PLACE YOU FEED-SITE LISTENERS COME TO OFTEN, IS IT?
'COURSE YOU DON'T. NO ONE GLAMOROUS HANGS OUT HERE, DO THEY? AND THERE ARE MORE PHOTOGENIC DUMPS FOR THE "SOCIAL CONCERN" DOCUMERCIALS.
CLUNY SQUARE'S NOTHING BUT SHIT IN THE HEART OF THE CITY, ISN'T IT?
WELL... YEAH.
SPKF
YOU'RE GOING TO TELL ME IT'S NOT, AREN'T YOU?
IT'S A STORY. GO LIVE--NOW. LET DIRTY OLD UNCLE SPIDER TELL IT TO YOU.
THE BOROUGH AUTHORITIES, UNDER DIRECT ORDERS FROM CIVIC CENTER--WHICH IN TURN WAS ANSWERING VOTER ZONING PLANS FROM THE WHITE HOUSE--MOVED THE POOREST OF THE POOR HERE.
THE PEOPLE WHO NEEDED CIVIC CENTER'S HELP MOST.
PURV
YOU KNOW THIS PLACE WAS BUILT SO CHEAPLY THAT IN THE EVENT OF A GUNFIGHT, BULLETS HAVE BEEN KNOWN TO PLOW THROUGH NINE APARTMENTS' WORTH OF WALLS BEFORE STOPPING?
LET ME SHOW YOU SOME-THING.

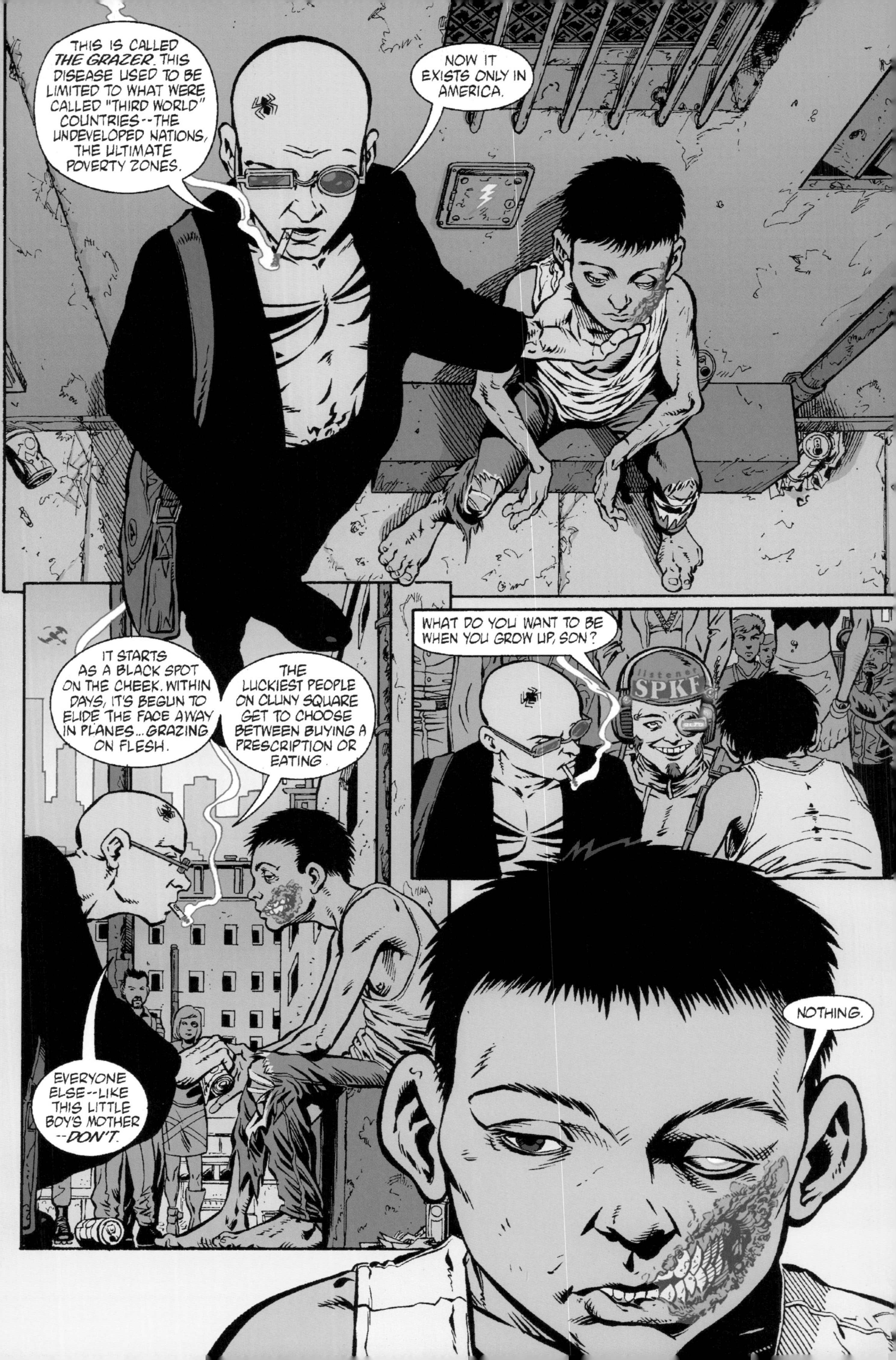
THIS IS CALLED THE GRAZER. THIS DISEASE USED TO BE LIMITED TO WHAT WERE CALLED "THIRD WORLD" COUNTRIES--THE UNDEVELOPED NATIONS, THE ULTIMATE POVERTY ZONES.
NOW IT EXISTS ONLY IN AMERICA.
IT STARTS AS A BLACK SPOT ON THE CHEEK. WITHIN DAYS, IT'S BEGUN TO ELIDE THE FACE AWAY IN PLANES...GRAZING ON FLESH.
THE LUCKIEST PEOPLE ON CLUNY SQUARE GET TO CHOOSE BETWEEN BUYING A PRESCRIPTION OR EATING.
EVERYONE ELSE--LIKE THIS LITTLE BOY'S MOTHER --DON'T.
WHAT DO YOU WANT TO BE WHEN YOU GROW UP, SON?
SPKF
NOTHING.

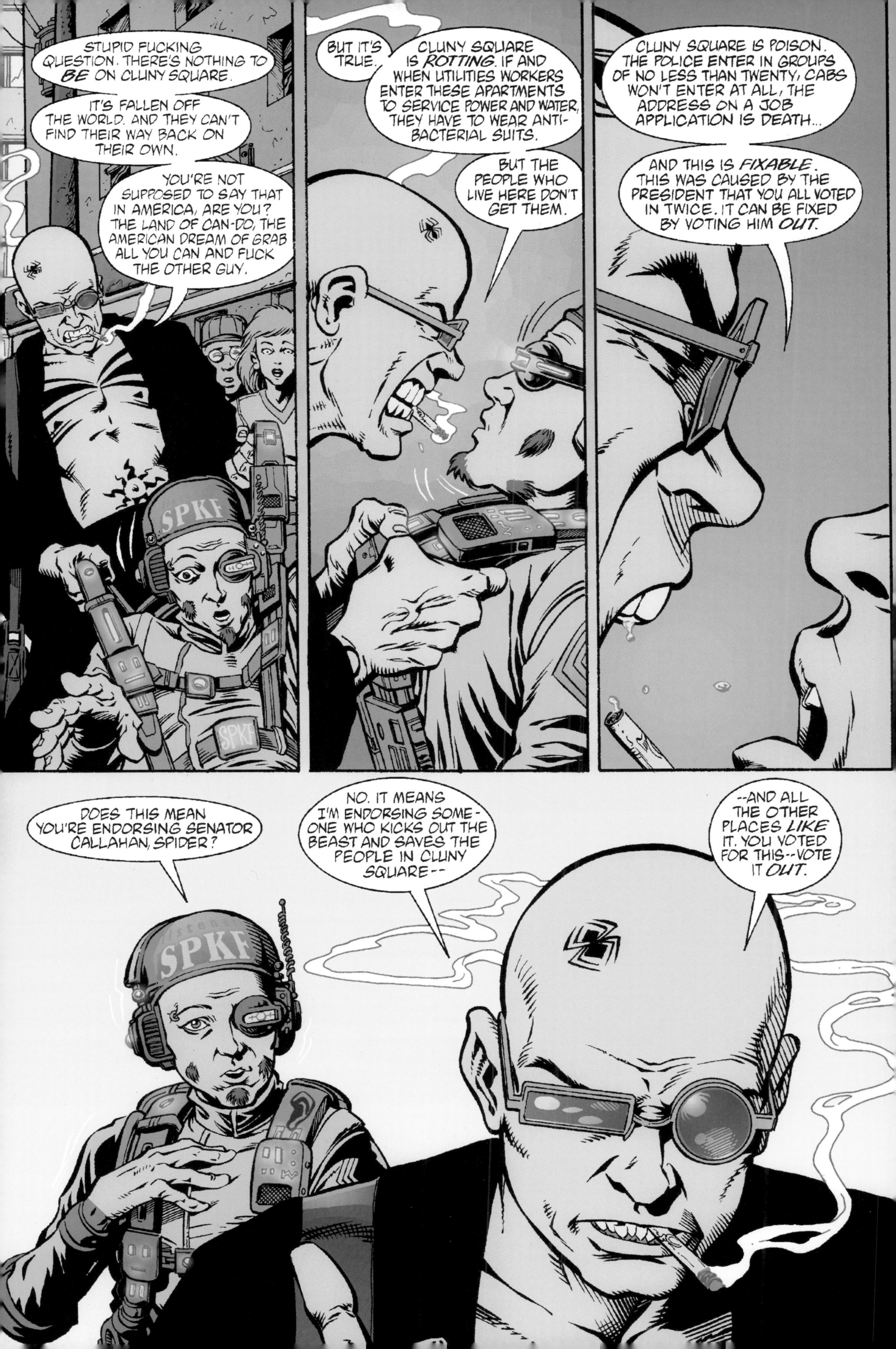
STUPID FUCKING QUESTION. THERE'S NOTHING TO BE ON CLUNY SQUARE.
IT'S FALLEN OFF THE WORLD. AND THEY CAN'T FIND THEIR WAY BACK ON THEIR OWN.
YOU'RE NOT SUPPOSED TO SAY THAT IN AMERICA, ARE YOU? THE LAND OF CAN-DO, THE AMERICAN DREAM OF GRAB ALL YOU CAN AND FUCK THE OTHER GUY.
SPKF
SPKF
BUT IT'S TRUE.
CLUNY SQUARE IS ROTTING. IF AND WHEN UTILITIES WORKERS ENTER THESE APARTMENTS TO SERVICE POWER AND WATER, THEY HAVE TO WEAR ANTI-BACTERIAL SUITS.
BUT THE PEOPLE WHO LIVE HERE DON'T GET THEM.
CLUNY SQUARE IS POISON. THE POLICE ENTER IN GROUPS OF NO LESS THAN TWENTY, CABS WON'T ENTER AT ALL, THE ADDRESS ON A JOB APPLICATION IS DEATH...
AND THIS IS FIXABLE. THIS WAS CAUSED BY THE PRESIDENT THAT YOU ALL VOTED IN TWICE. IT CAN BE FIXED BY VOTING HIM OUT.
DOES THIS MEAN YOU'RE ENDORSING SENATOR CALLAHAN, SPIDER?
NO. IT MEANS I'M ENDORSING SOME-ONE WHO KICKS OUT THE BEAST AND SAVES THE PEOPLE IN CLUNY SQUARE--
--AND ALL THE OTHER PLACES LIKE IT. YOU VOTED FOR THIS--VOTE IT OUT.
SPKF

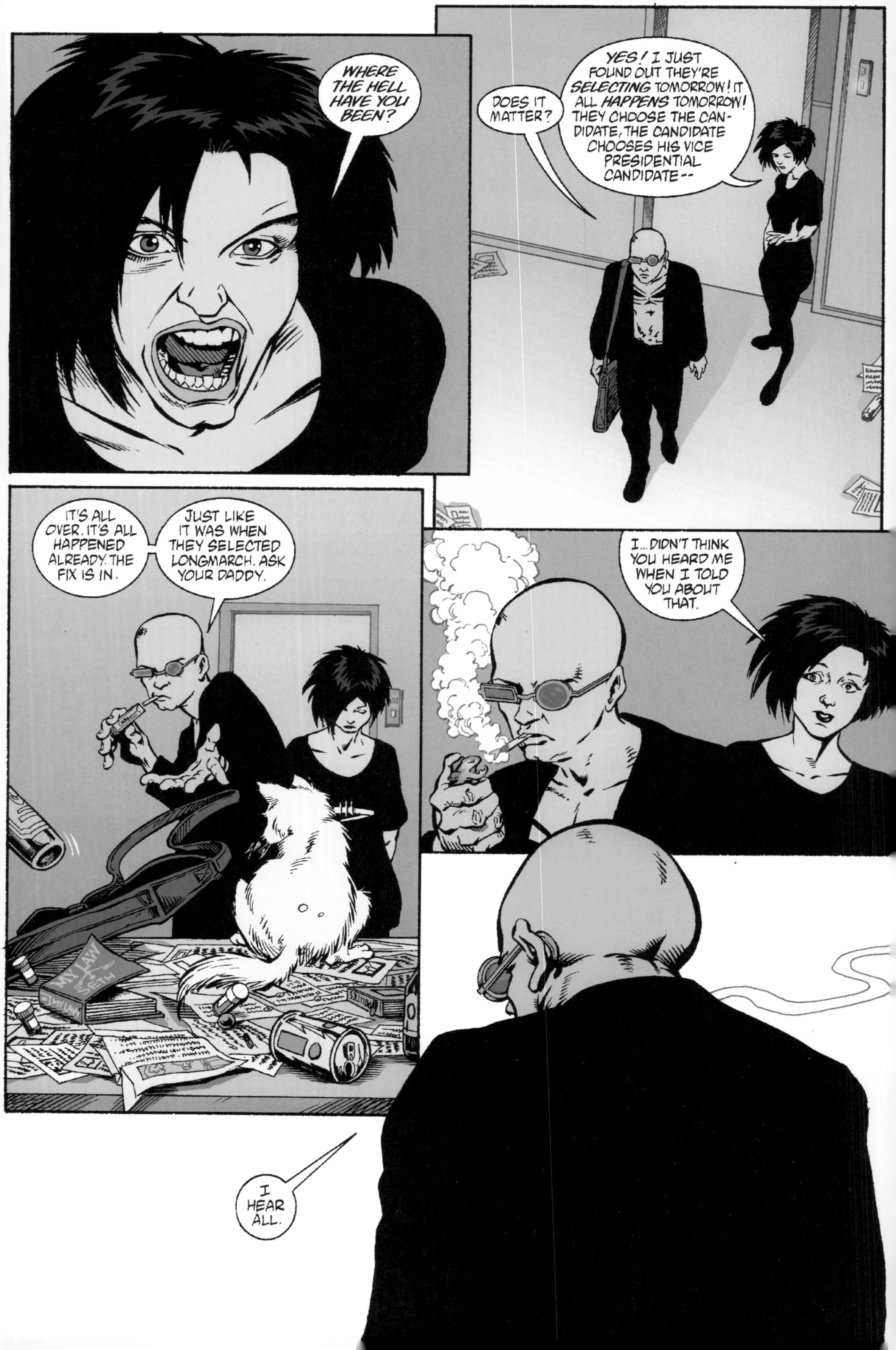
WHERE THE HELL HAVE YOU BEEN?
DOES IT MATTER?
YES! I JUST FOUND OUT THEY'RE SELECTING TOMORROW! IT ALL HAPPENS TOMORROW! THEY CHOOSE THE CAN-DIDATE, THE CANDIDATE CHOOSES HIS VICE PRESIDENTIAL CANDIDATE--
IT'S ALL OVER. IT'S ALL HAPPENED ALREADY. THE FIX IS IN.
JUST LIKE IT WAS WHEN THEY SELECTED LONGMARCH. ASK YOUR DADDY.
MY LAW
SETH
I...DIDN'T THINK YOU HEARD ME WHEN I TOLD YOU ABOUT THAT.
I HEAR ALL.

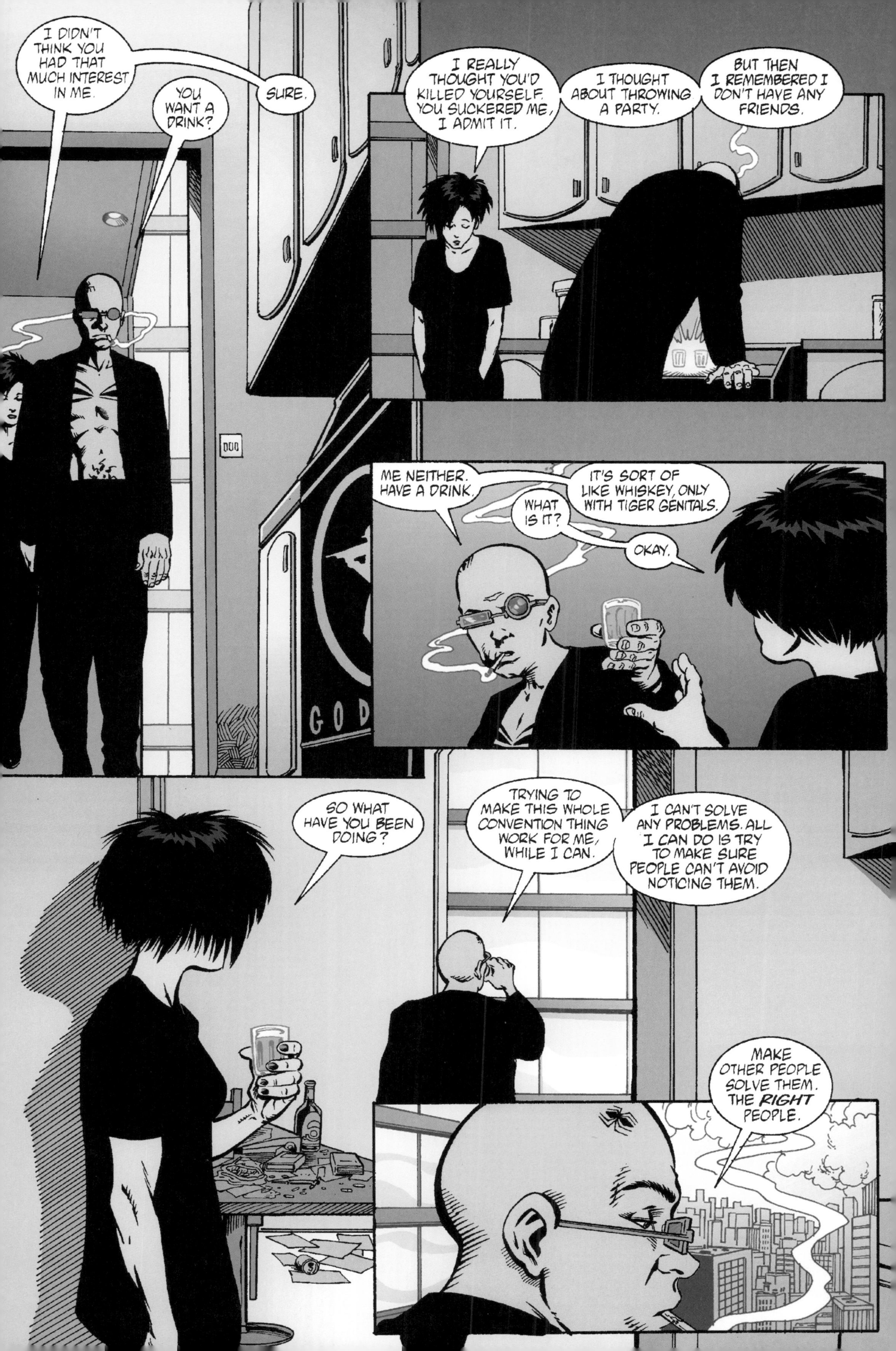
I DIDN'T THINK YOU HAD THAT MUCH INTEREST IN ME.
SURE.
YOU WANT A DRINK?
I REALLY THOUGHT YOU'D KILLED YOURSELF. YOU SUCKERED ME, I ADMIT IT.
I THOUGHT ABOUT THROWING A PARTY.
BUT THEN I REMEMBERED I DON'T HAVE ANY FRIENDS.
ME NEITHER. HAVE A DRINK.
WHAT IS IT?
IT'S SORT OF LIKE WHISKEY, ONLY WITH TIGER GENITALS.
OKAY.
GOD
SO WHAT HAVE YOU BEEN DOING?
TRYING TO MAKE THIS WHOLE CONVENTION THING WORK FOR ME, WHILE I CAN.
I CAN'T SOLVE ANY PROBLEMS. ALL I CAN DO IS TRY TO MAKE SURE PEOPLE CAN'T AVOID NOTICING THEM.
MAKE OTHER PEOPLE SOLVE THEM. THE *RIGHT* PEOPLE.

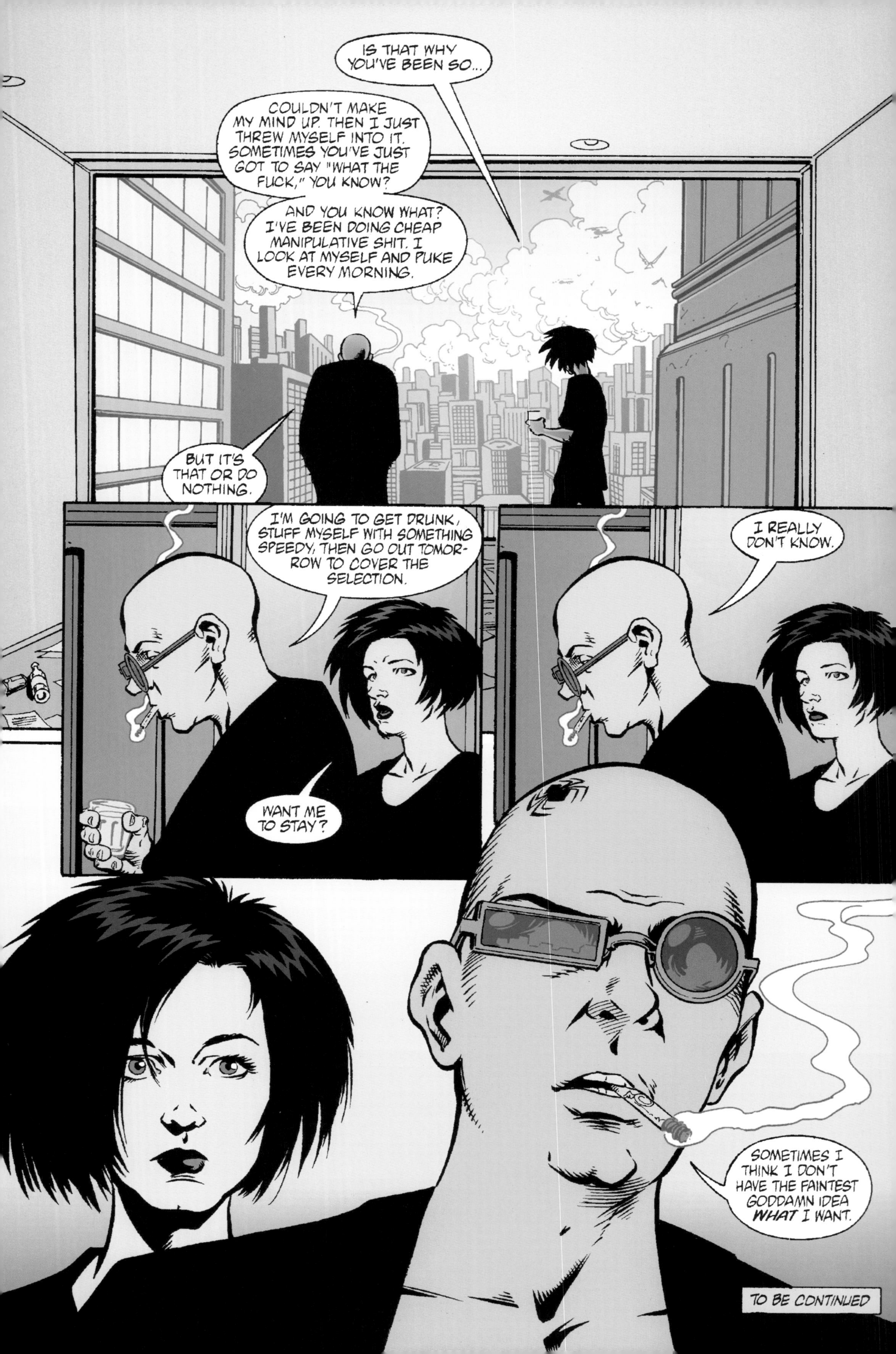
IS THAT WHY YOU'VE BEEN SO...
COULDN'T MAKE MY MIND UP. THEN I JUST THREW MYSELF INTO IT. SOMETIMES YOU'VE JUST GOT TO SAY "WHAT THE FUCK," YOU KNOW?
AND YOU KNOW WHAT? I'VE BEEN DOING CHEAP MANIPULATIVE SHIT. I LOOK AT MYSELF AND PUKE EVERY MORNING.
BUT IT'S THAT OR DO NOTHING.
I'M GOING TO GET DRUNK, STUFF MYSELF WITH SOMETHING SPEEDY, THEN GO OUT TOMORROW TO COVER THE SELECTION.
WANT ME TO STAY?
I REALLY DON'T KNOW.
SOMETIMES I THINK I DON'T HAVE THE FAINTEST GODDAMN IDEA *WHAT* I WANT.
TO BE CONTINUED

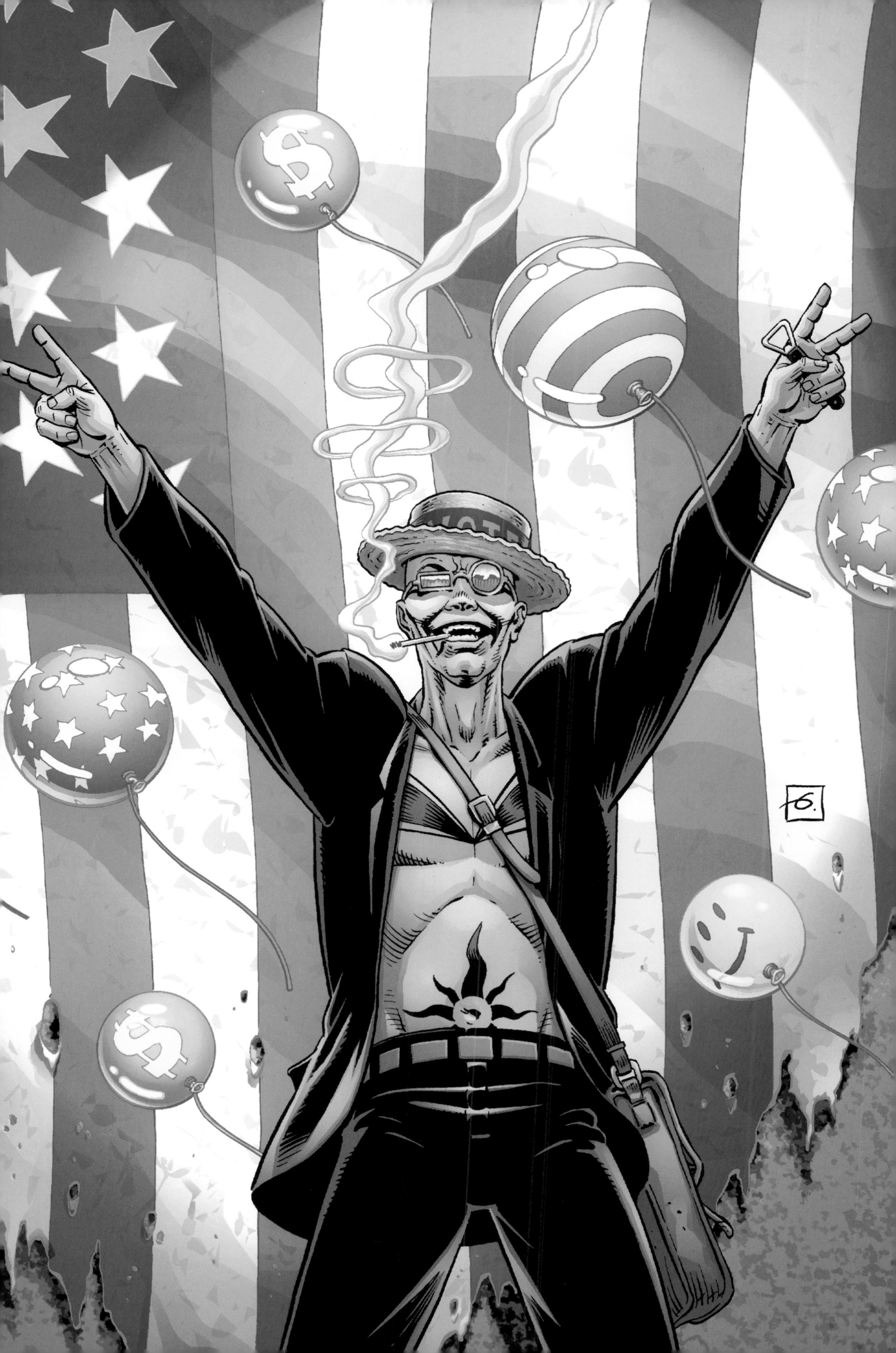

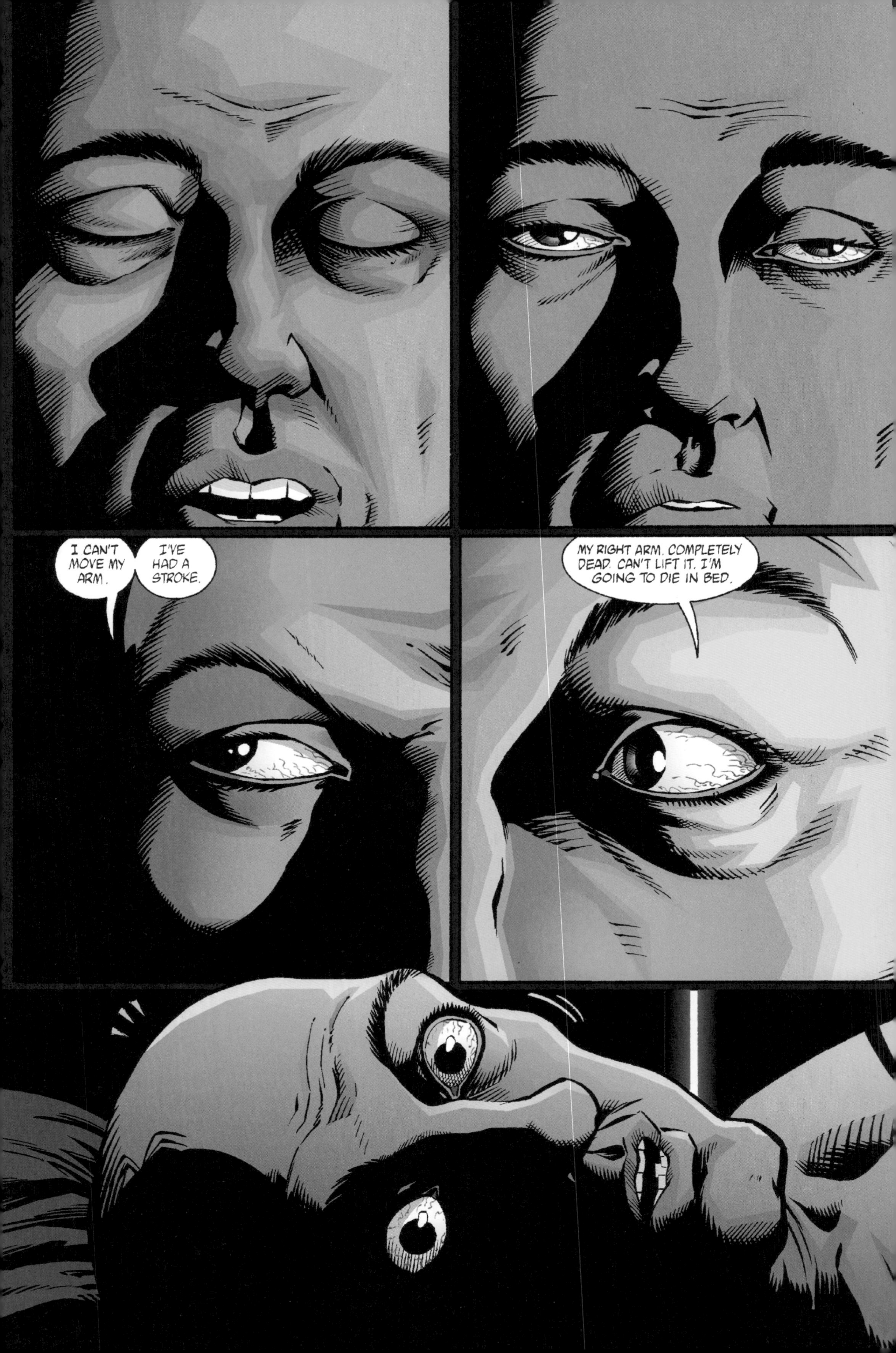

I CAN'T MOVE MY ARM.
I'VE HAD A STROKE.
MY RIGHT ARM. COMPLETELY DEAD. CAN'T LIFT IT. I'M GOING TO DIE IN BED.

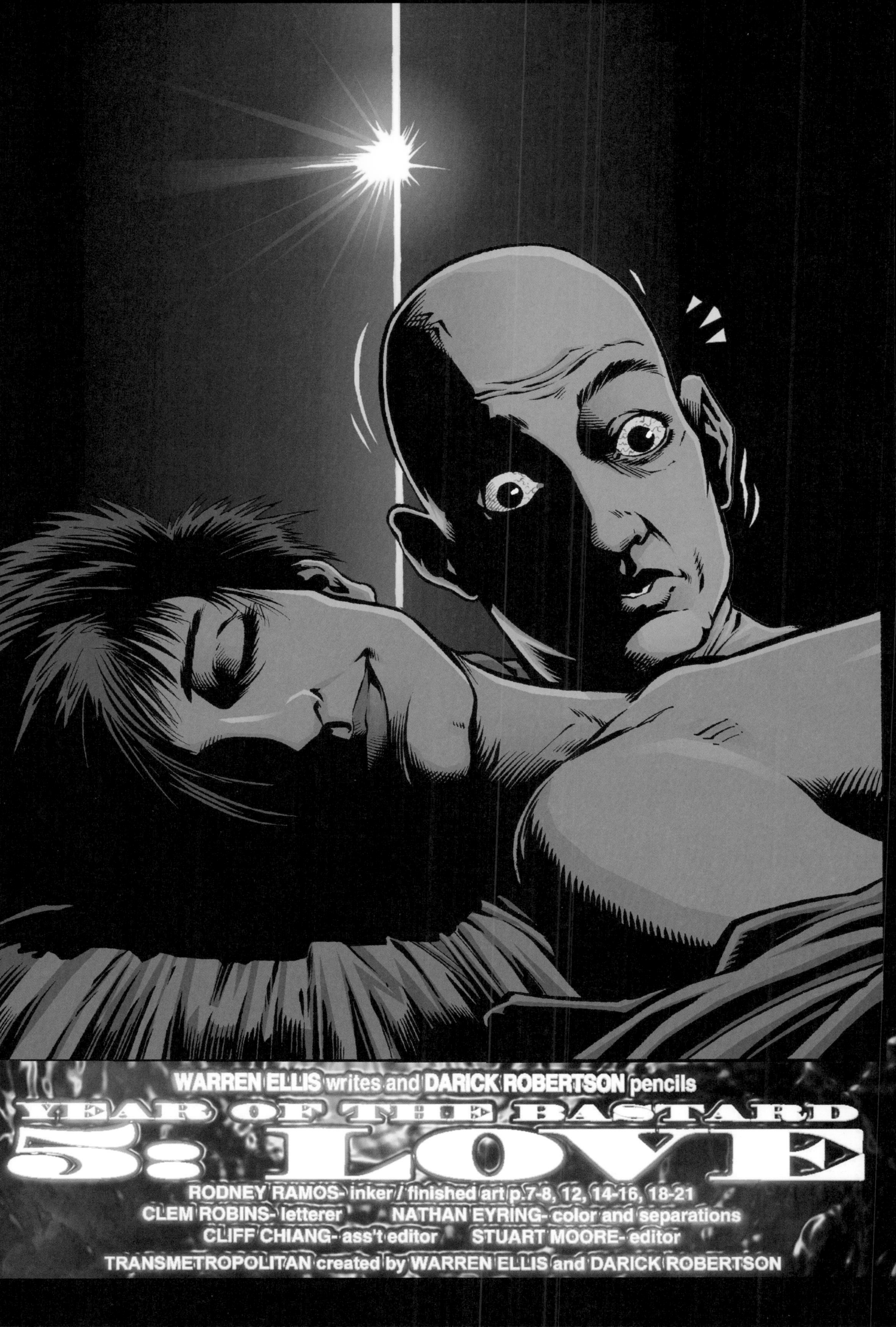

WARREN ELLIS writes and DARICK ROBERTSON pencils

# YEAR OF THE BASTARD
# 5: LOVE

RODNEY RAMOS- inker / finished art p.7-8, 12, 14-16, 18-21
CLEM ROBINS- letterer NATHAN EYRING- color and separations
CLIFF CHIANG- ass't editor STUART MOORE- editor
TRANSMETROPOLITAN created by WARREN ELLIS and DARICK ROBERTSON

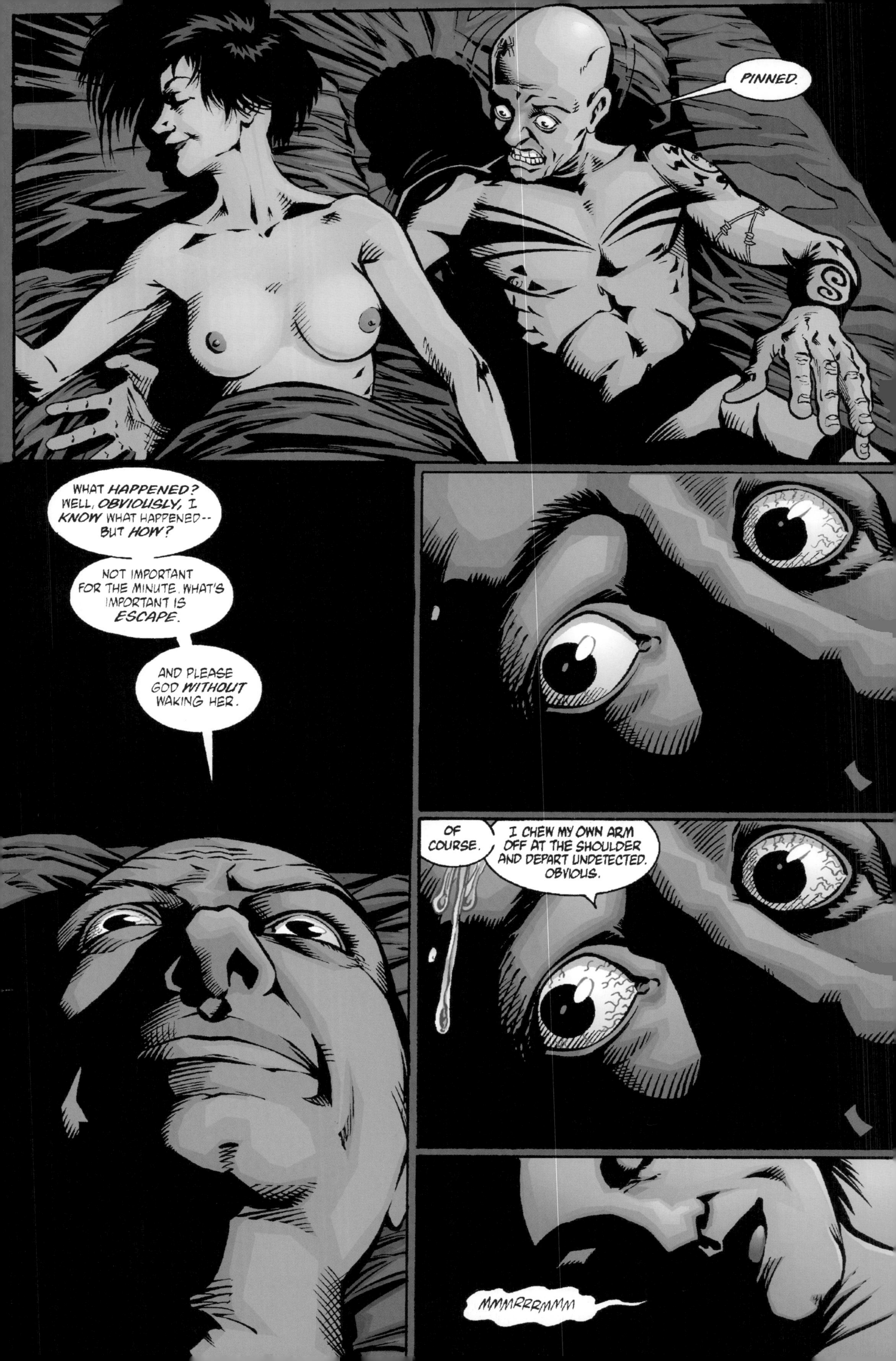
PINNED.
WHAT HAPPENED? WELL, OBVIOUSLY, I KNOW WHAT HAPPENED-- BUT HOW?
NOT IMPORTANT FOR THE MINUTE. WHAT'S IMPORTANT IS ESCAPE.
AND PLEASE GOD WITHOUT WAKING HER.
OF COURSE.
I CHEW MY OWN ARM OFF AT THE SHOULDER AND DEPART UNDETECTED. OBVIOUS.
MMMRRRMMM

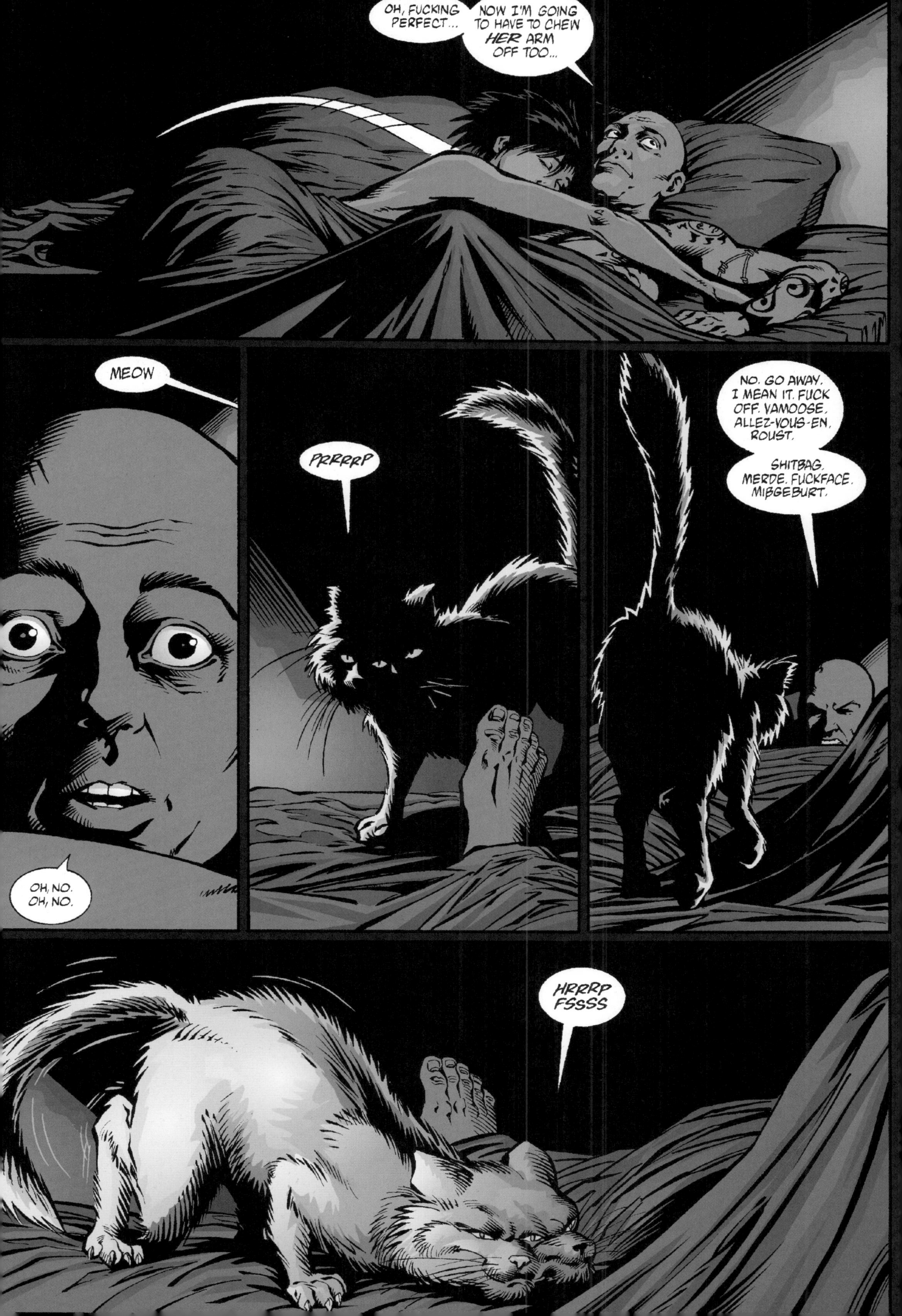
OH, FUCKING PERFECT...
NOW I'M GOING TO HAVE TO CHEW *HER* ARM OFF TOO...
MEOW
OH, NO. OH, NO.
PRRRRP
NO. GO AWAY. I MEAN IT. FUCK OFF. VAMOOSE. ALLEZ-VOUS-EN. ROUST.
SHITBAG. MERDE. FUCKFACE. MIßGEBURT.
HRRRP FSSSS

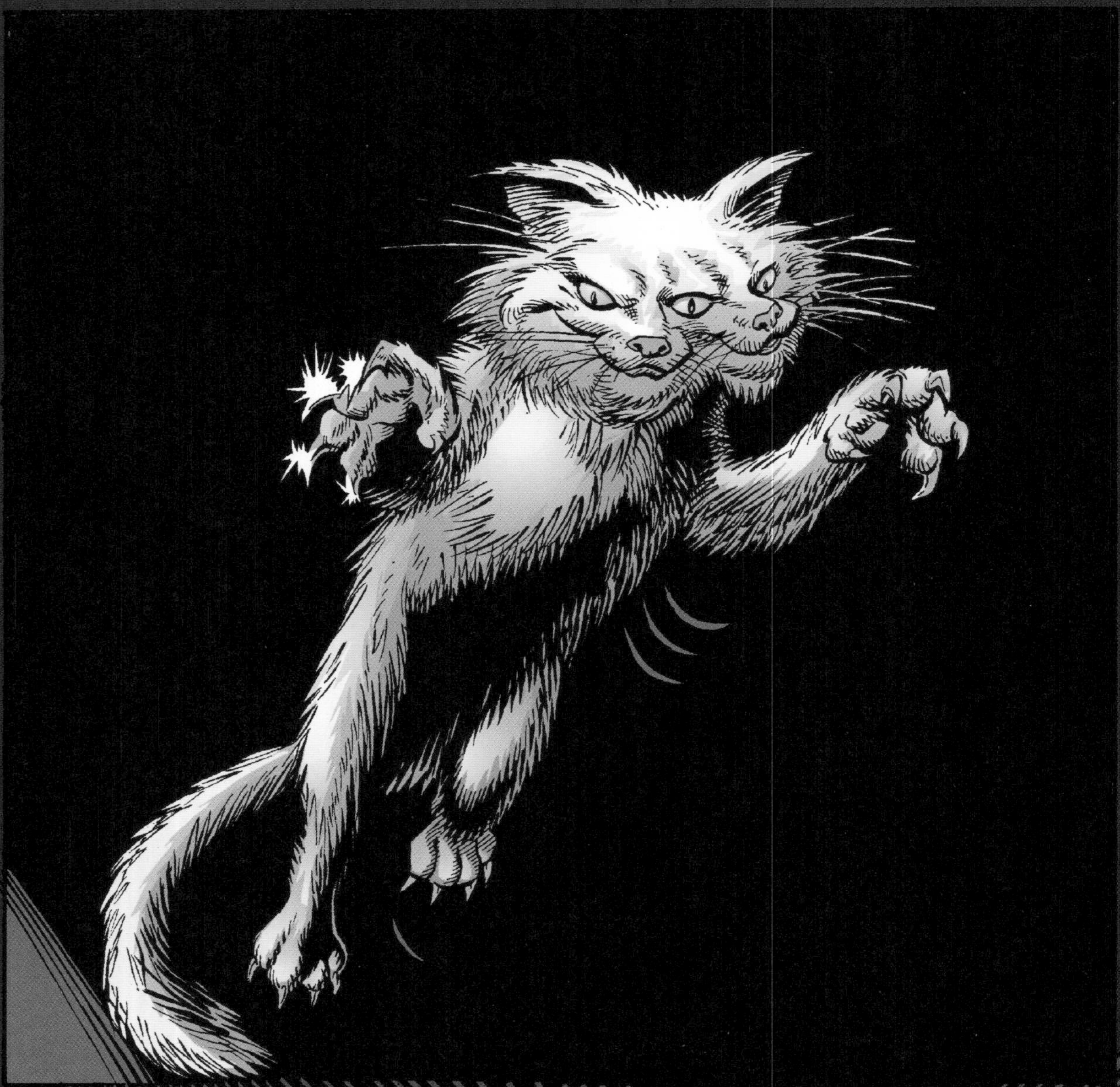

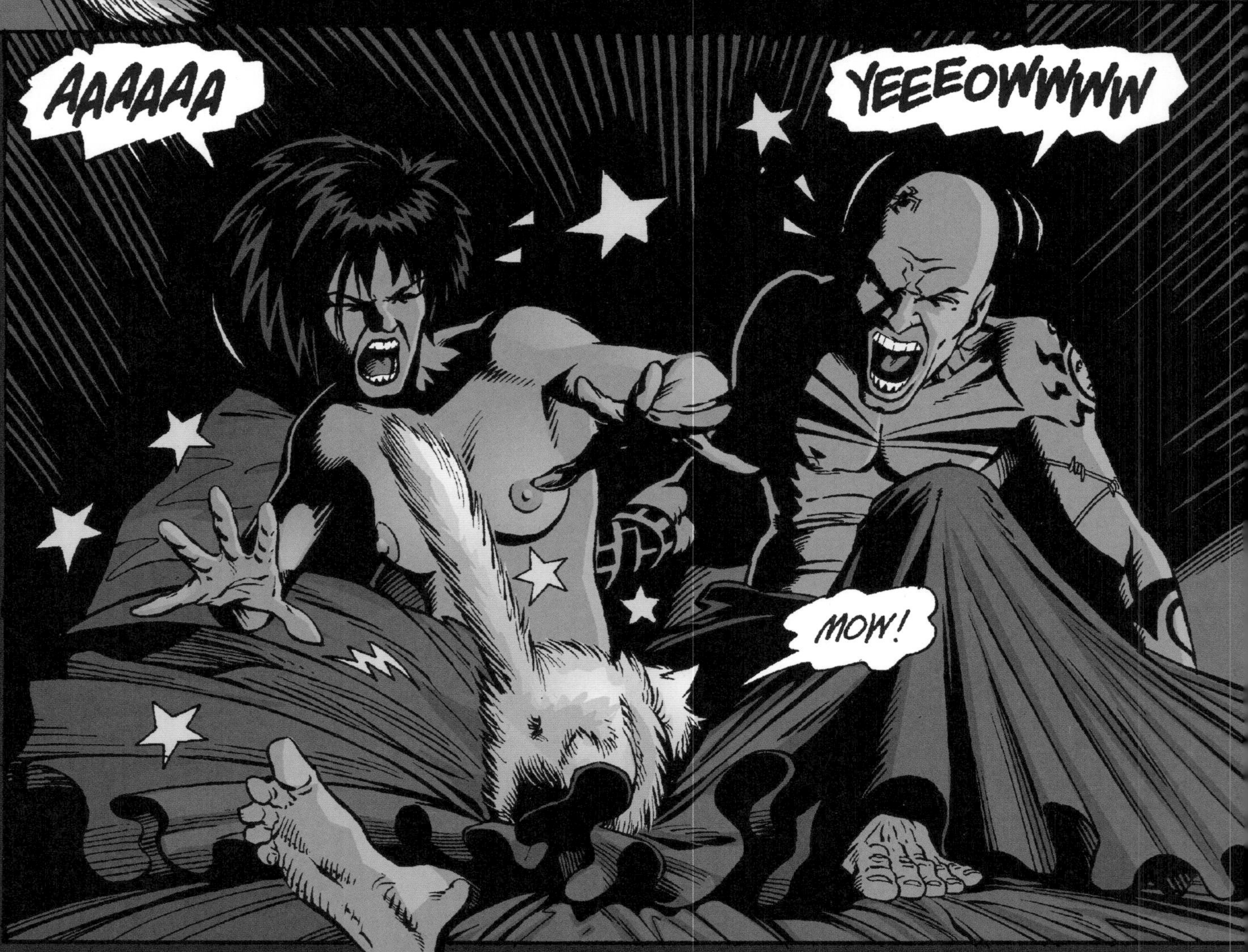
AAAAAA
YEEEOWWWW
MOW!

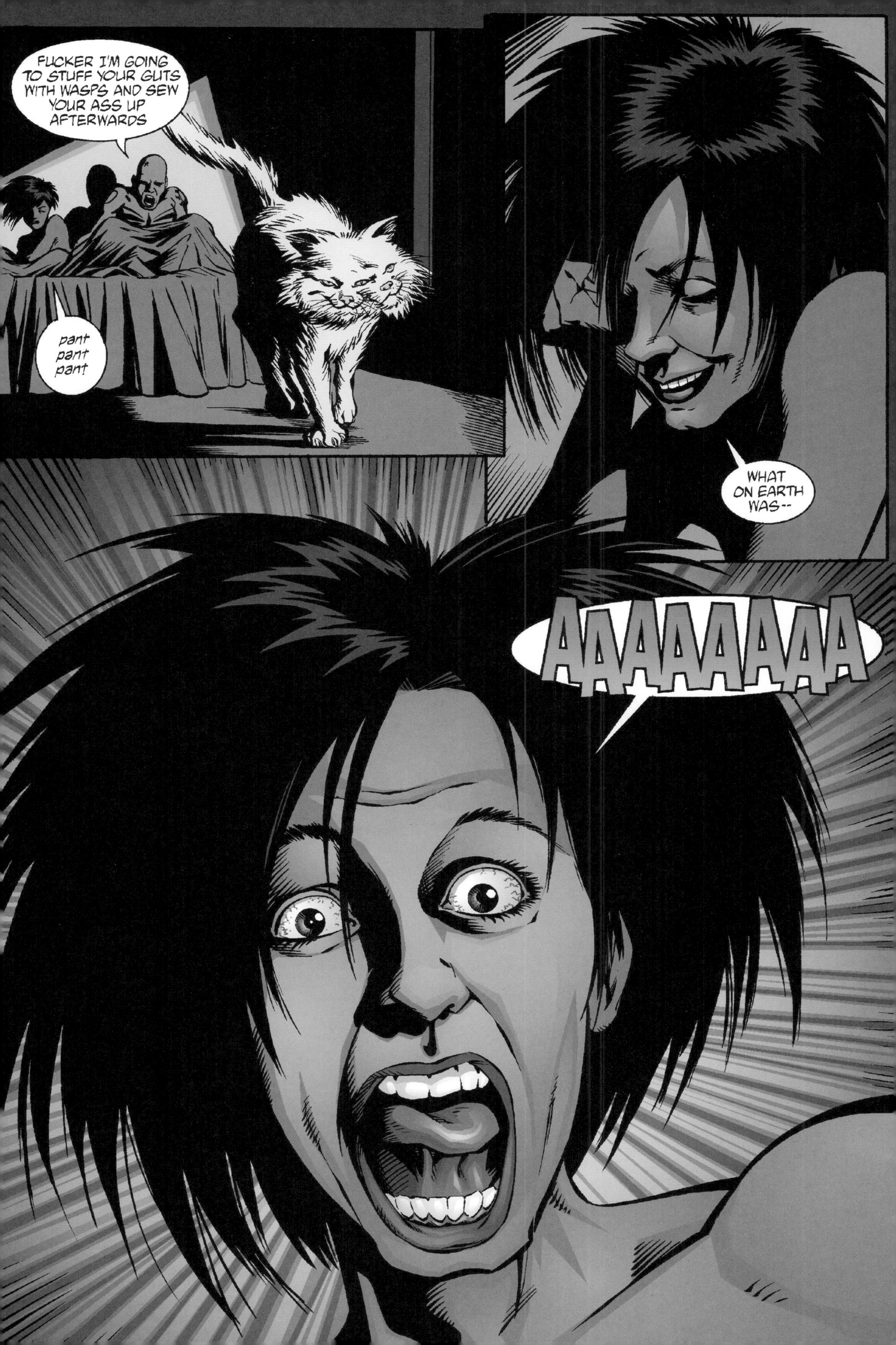
FUCKER I'M GOING TO STUFF YOUR GUTS WITH WASPS AND SEW YOUR ASS UP AFTERWARDS
pant pant pant
WHAT ON EARTH WAS--
AAAAAAAA

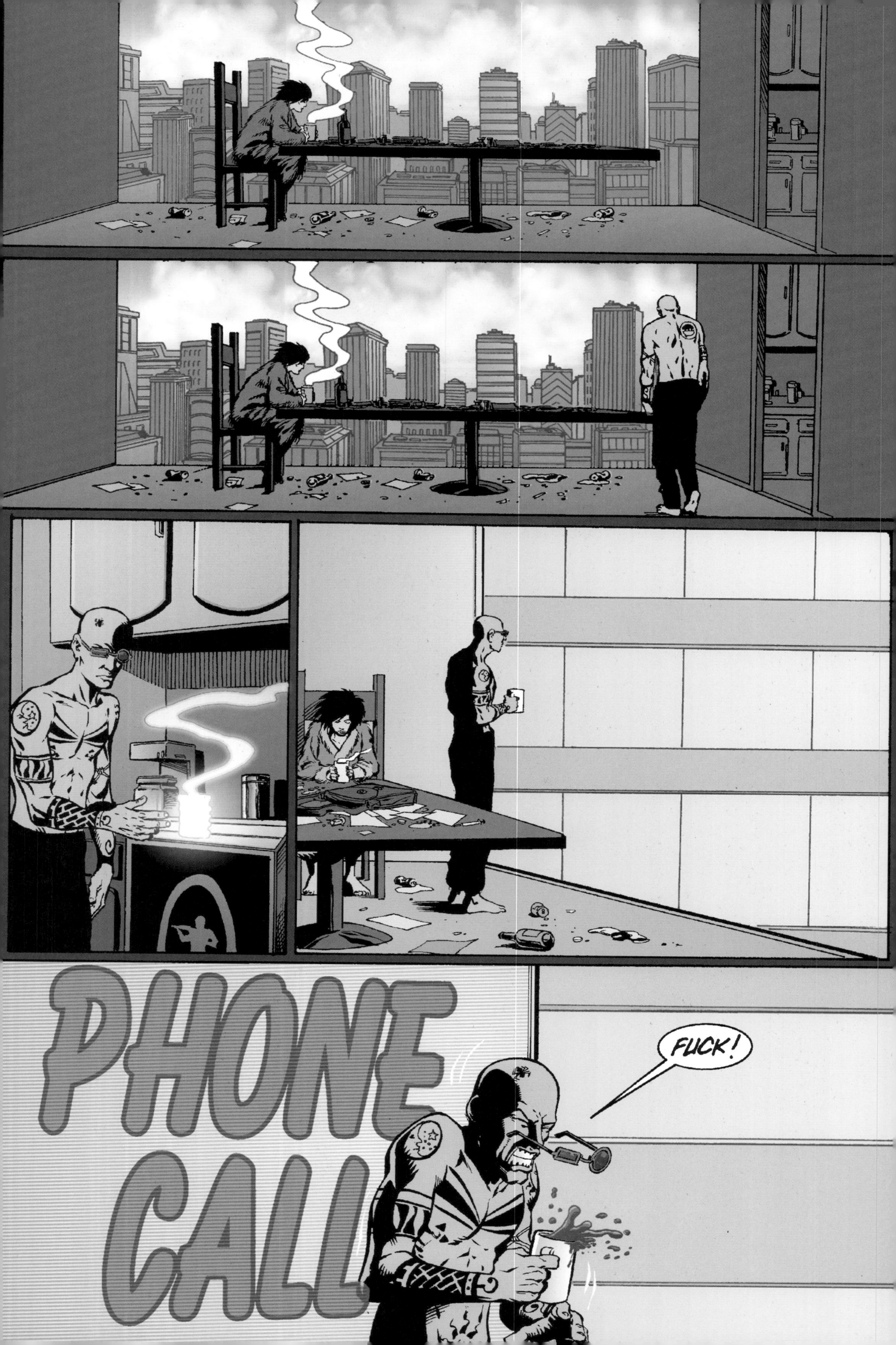
PHONE CALL
FUCK!

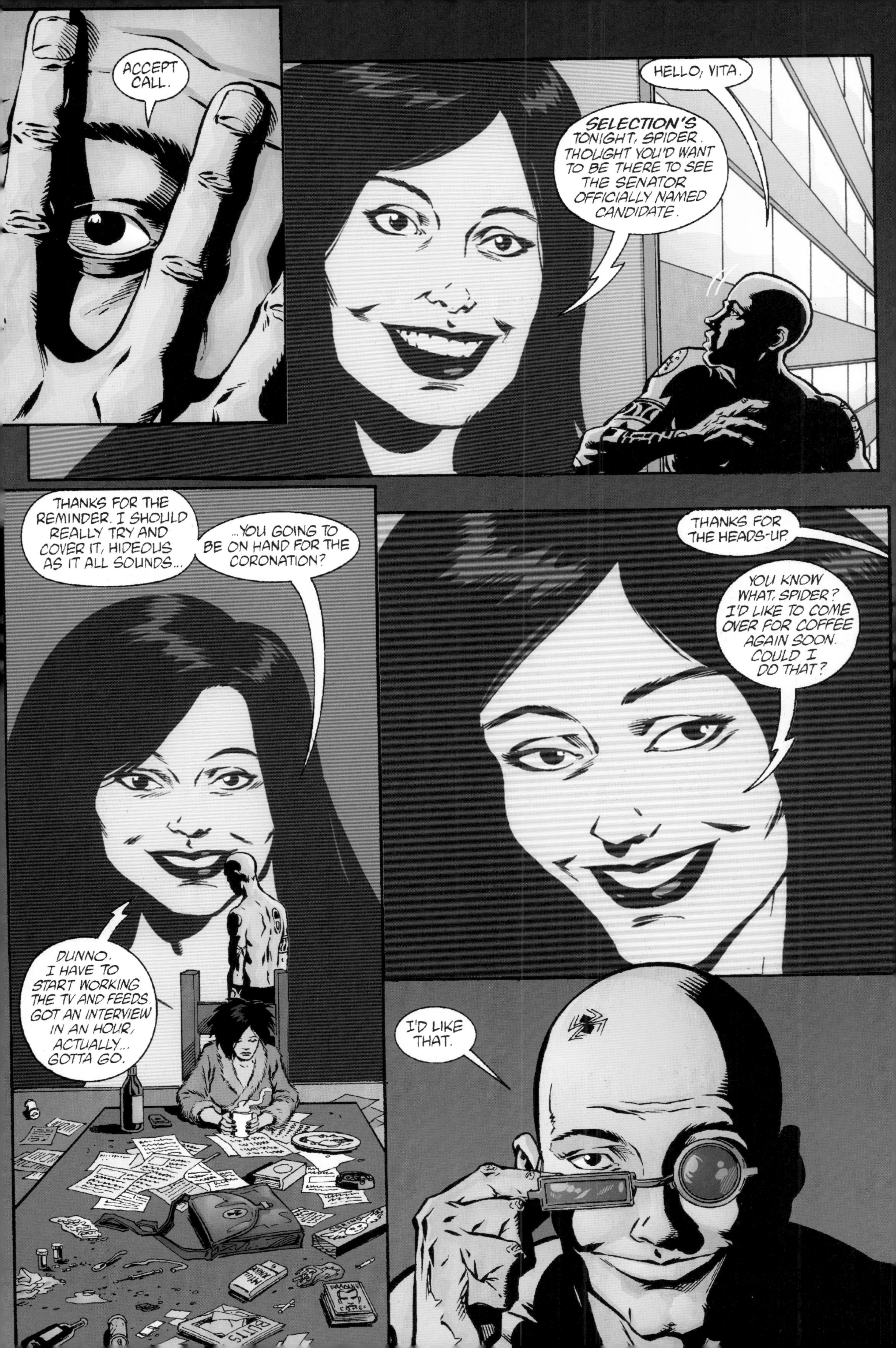
ACCEPT CALL.
HELLO, VITA.
SELECTION'S TONIGHT, SPIDER. THOUGHT YOU'D WANT TO BE THERE TO SEE THE SENATOR OFFICIALLY NAMED CANDIDATE.
THANKS FOR THE REMINDER. I SHOULD REALLY TRY AND COVER IT, HIDEOUS AS IT ALL SOUNDS...
...YOU GOING TO BE ON HAND FOR THE CORONATION?
DUNNO. I HAVE TO START WORKING THE TV AND FEEDS. GOT AN INTERVIEW IN AN HOUR, ACTUALLY... GOTTA GO.
THANKS FOR THE HEADS-UP.
YOU KNOW WHAT, SPIDER? I'D LIKE TO COME OVER FOR COFFEE AGAIN SOON. COULD I DO THAT?
I'D LIKE THAT.

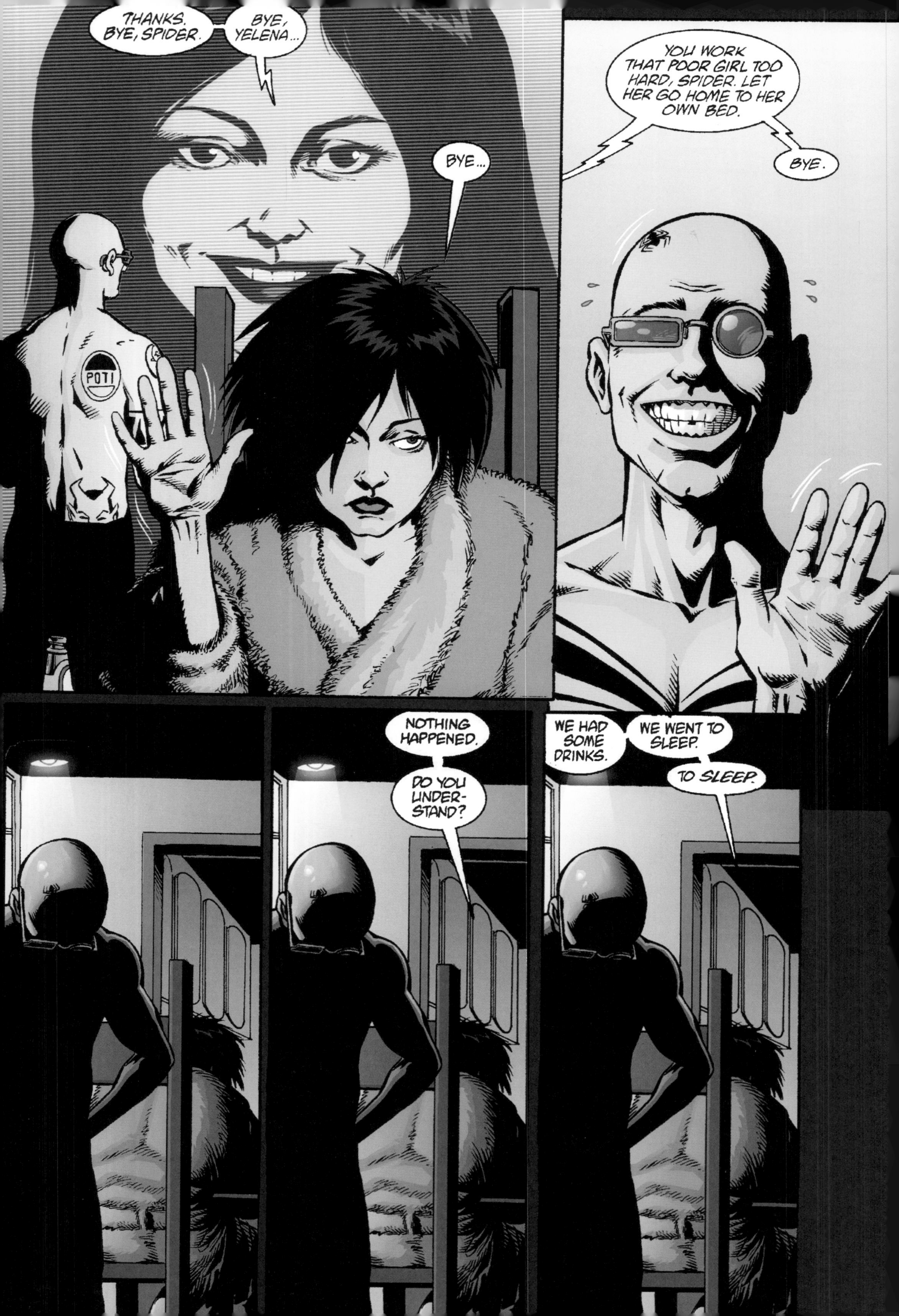
THANKS. BYE, SPIDER.
BYE, YELENA...
BYE...
YOU WORK THAT POOR GIRL TOO HARD, SPIDER. LET HER GO HOME TO HER OWN BED.
BYE.
NOTHING HAPPENED.
DO YOU UNDER-STAND?
WE HAD SOME DRINKS.
WE WENT TO SLEEP.
TO SLEEP.

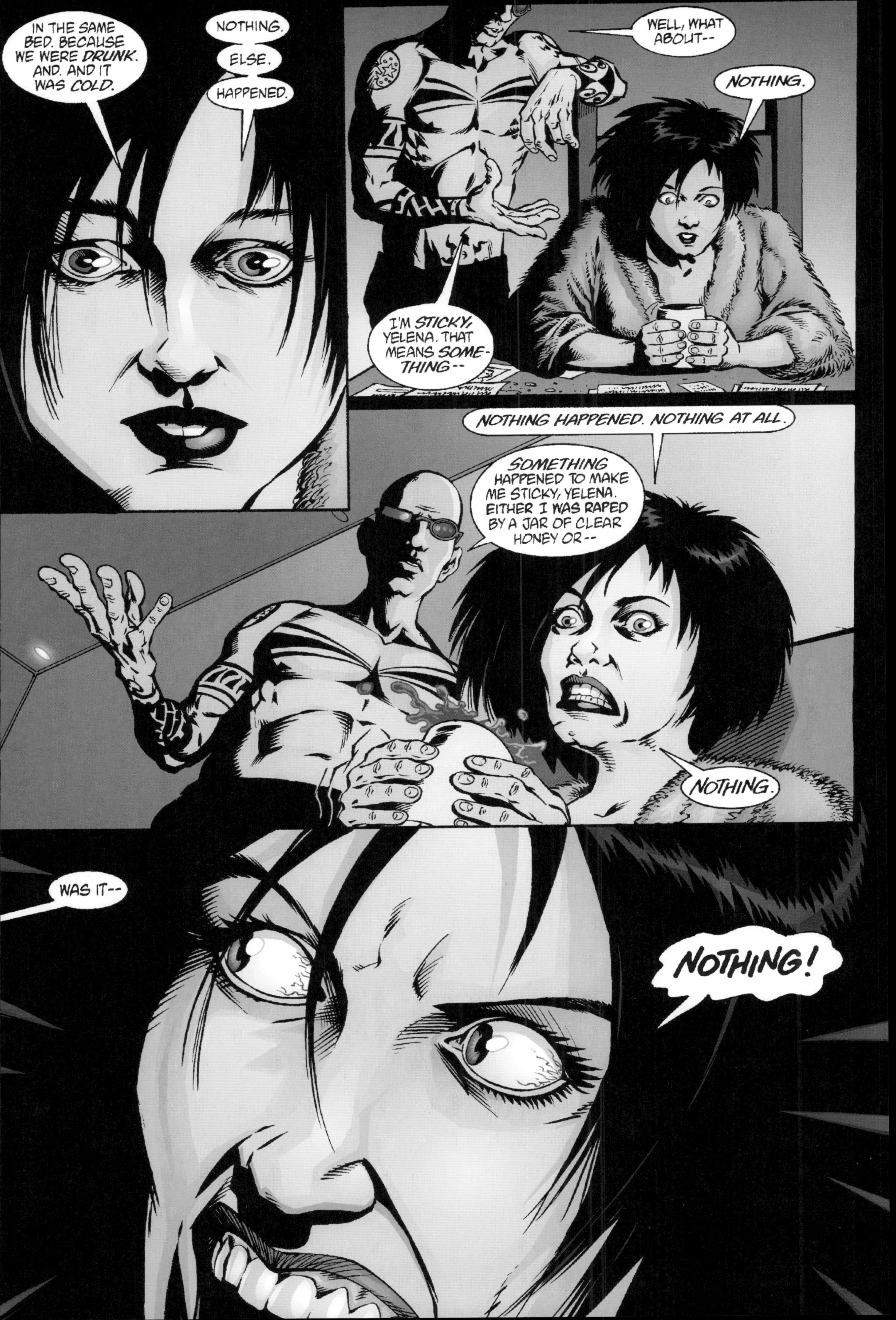
IN THE SAME BED. BECAUSE WE WERE DRUNK. AND. AND IT WAS COLD.
NOTHING.
ELSE.
HAPPENED.
WELL, WHAT ABOUT--
NOTHING.
I'M STICKY, YELENA. THAT MEANS SOMETHING--
NOTHING HAPPENED. NOTHING AT ALL.
SOMETHING HAPPENED TO MAKE ME STICKY, YELENA. EITHER I WAS RAPED BY A JAR OF CLEAR HONEY OR--
NOTHING.
WAS IT--
NOTHING!

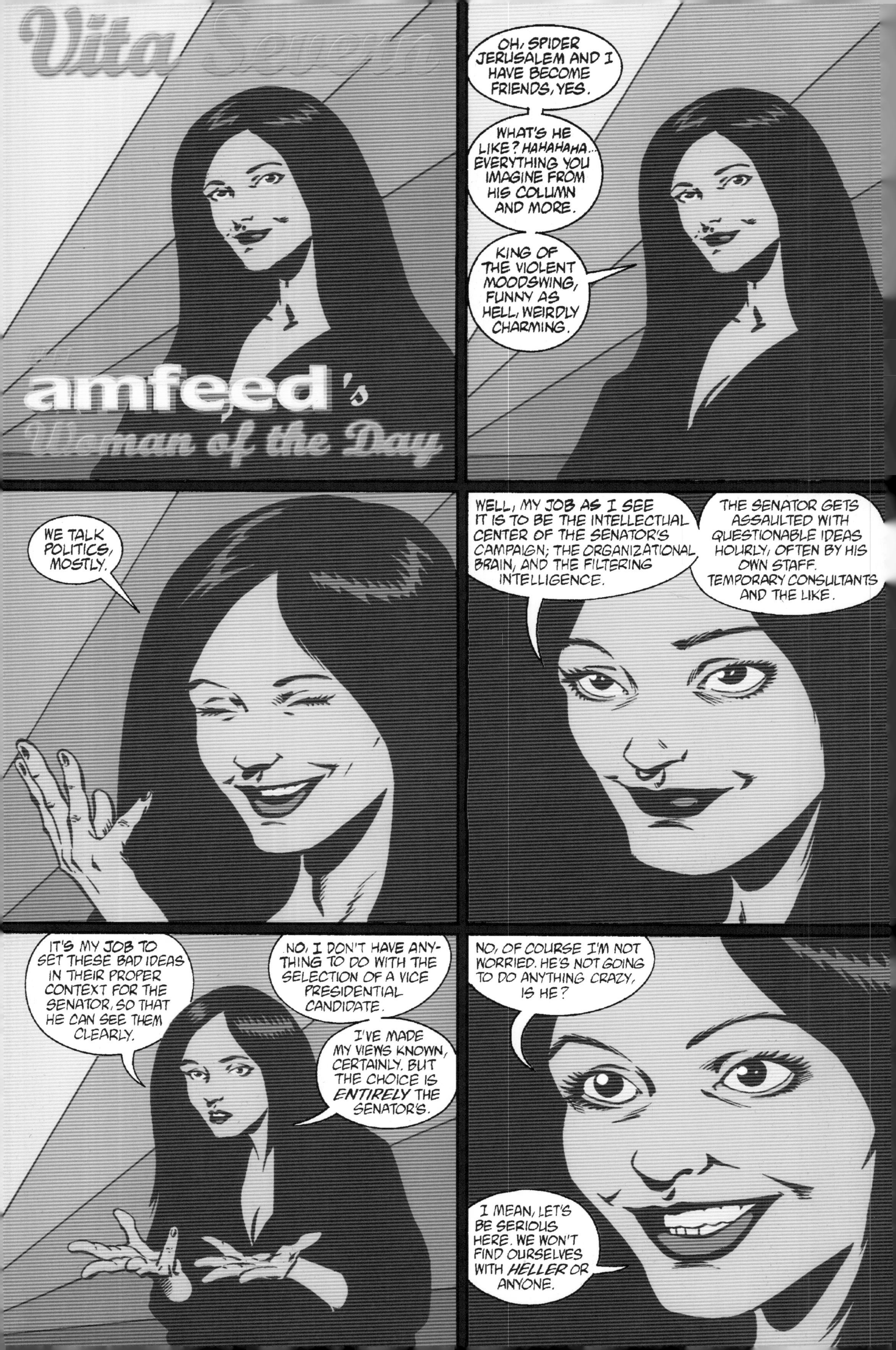
Vita Severn
amfeed's
Woman of the Day
OH, SPIDER JERUSALEM AND I HAVE BECOME FRIENDS, YES.
WHAT'S HE LIKE? HAHAHAHA... EVERYTHING YOU IMAGINE FROM HIS COLUMN AND MORE.
KING OF THE VIOLENT MOODSWING, FUNNY AS HELL, WEIRDLY CHARMING.
WE TALK POLITICS, MOSTLY.
WELL, MY JOB AS I SEE IT IS TO BE THE INTELLECTUAL CENTER OF THE SENATOR'S CAMPAIGN; THE ORGANIZATIONAL BRAIN, AND THE FILTERING INTELLIGENCE.
THE SENATOR GETS ASSAULTED WITH QUESTIONABLE IDEAS HOURLY, OFTEN BY HIS OWN STAFF. TEMPORARY CONSULTANTS AND THE LIKE.
IT'S MY JOB TO SET THESE BAD IDEAS IN THEIR PROPER CONTEXT FOR THE SENATOR, SO THAT HE CAN SEE THEM CLEARLY.
NO, I DON'T HAVE ANYTHING TO DO WITH THE SELECTION OF A VICE PRESIDENTIAL CANDIDATE.
I'VE MADE MY VIEWS KNOWN, CERTAINLY. BUT THE CHOICE IS *ENTIRELY* THE SENATOR'S.
NO, OF COURSE I'M NOT WORRIED. HE'S NOT GOING TO DO ANYTHING CRAZY, IS HE?
I MEAN, LET'S BE SERIOUS HERE. WE WON'T FIND OURSELVES WITH *HELLER* OR ANYONE.

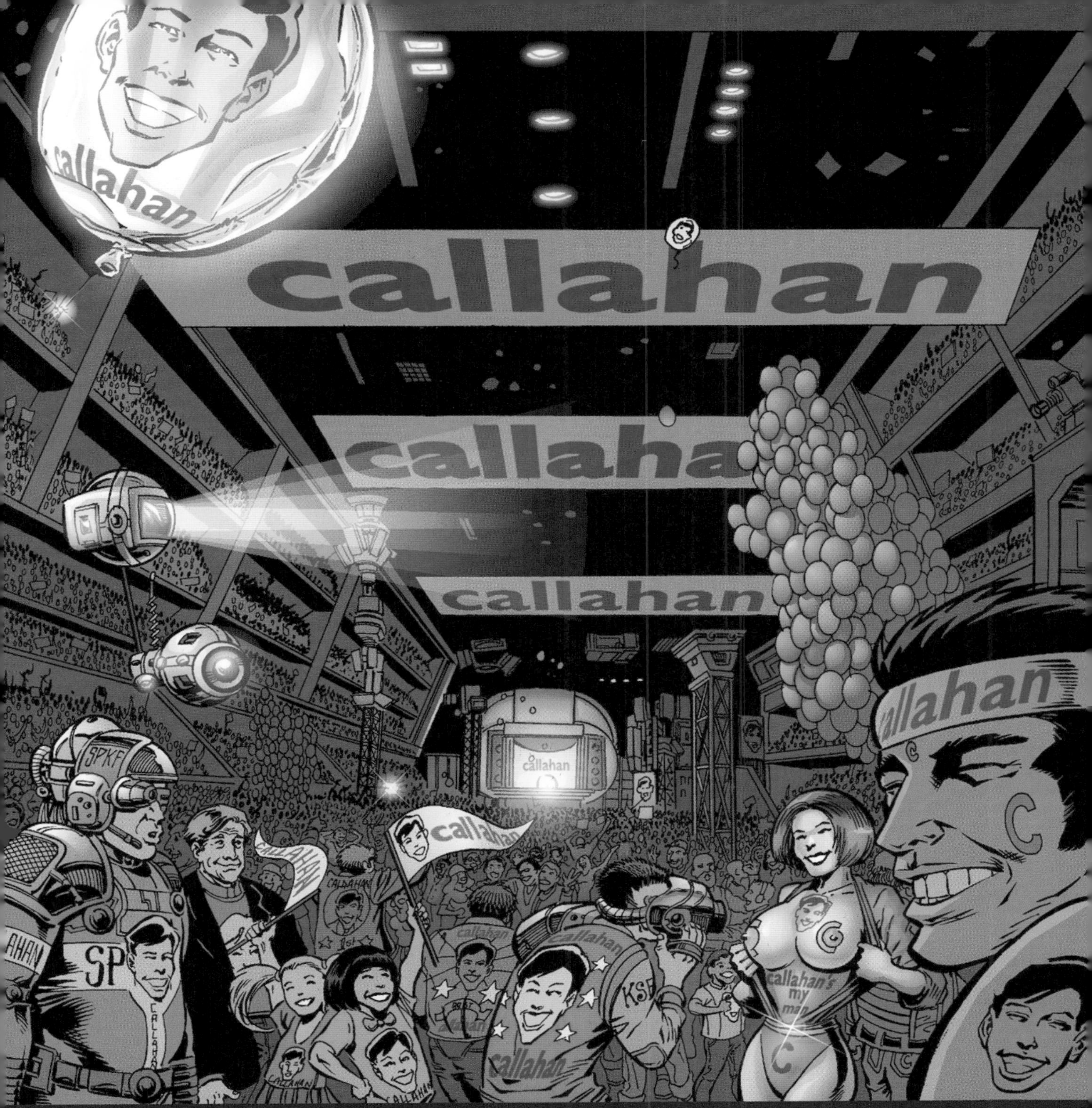
callahan
callahan
callahan
callahan
callahan
callahan
SPKF
callahan
callahan's my man
KSF

The fix is in. It remains only to see what it's been traded for. To get to this stage, anyone wanting to be Candidate has had to learn to enjoy the special flavor of pressure-group dick. The question is: will the Smiler stagger on stage with lungs half-full of steaming lobbyist semen? Or will he merely be licking his lips?

I so badly want to kill everyone in this room. Even the children.

*Especially* the children.

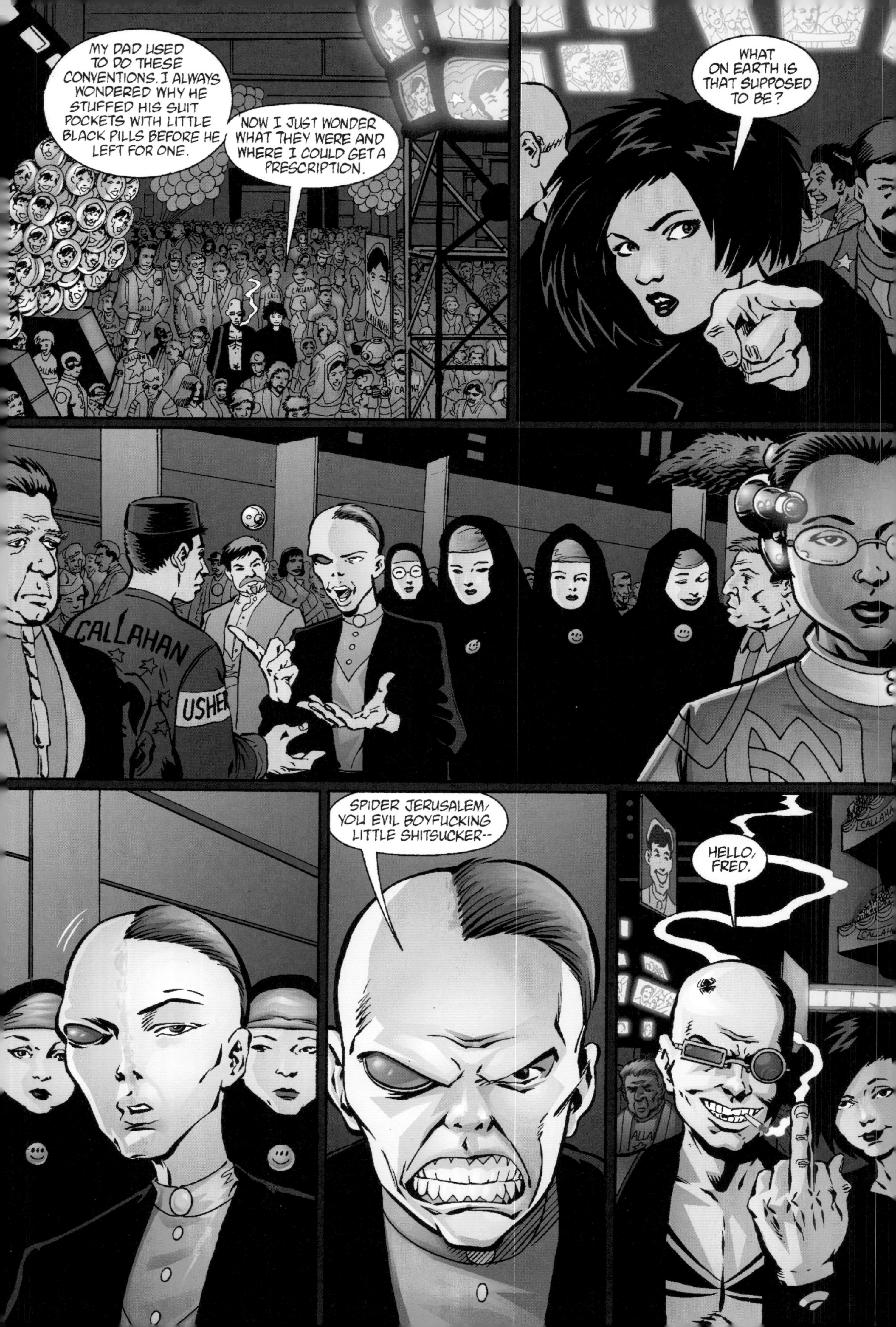
MY DAD USED TO DO THESE CONVENTIONS. I ALWAYS WONDERED WHY HE STUFFED HIS SUIT POCKETS WITH LITTLE BLACK PILLS BEFORE HE LEFT FOR ONE.
NOW I JUST WONDER WHAT THEY WERE AND WHERE I COULD GET A PRESCRIPTION.
WHAT ON EARTH IS THAT SUPPOSED TO BE?
CALLAHAN
USHER
SPIDER JERUSALEM, YOU EVIL BOYFUCKING LITTLE SHITSUCKER--
HELLO, FRED.

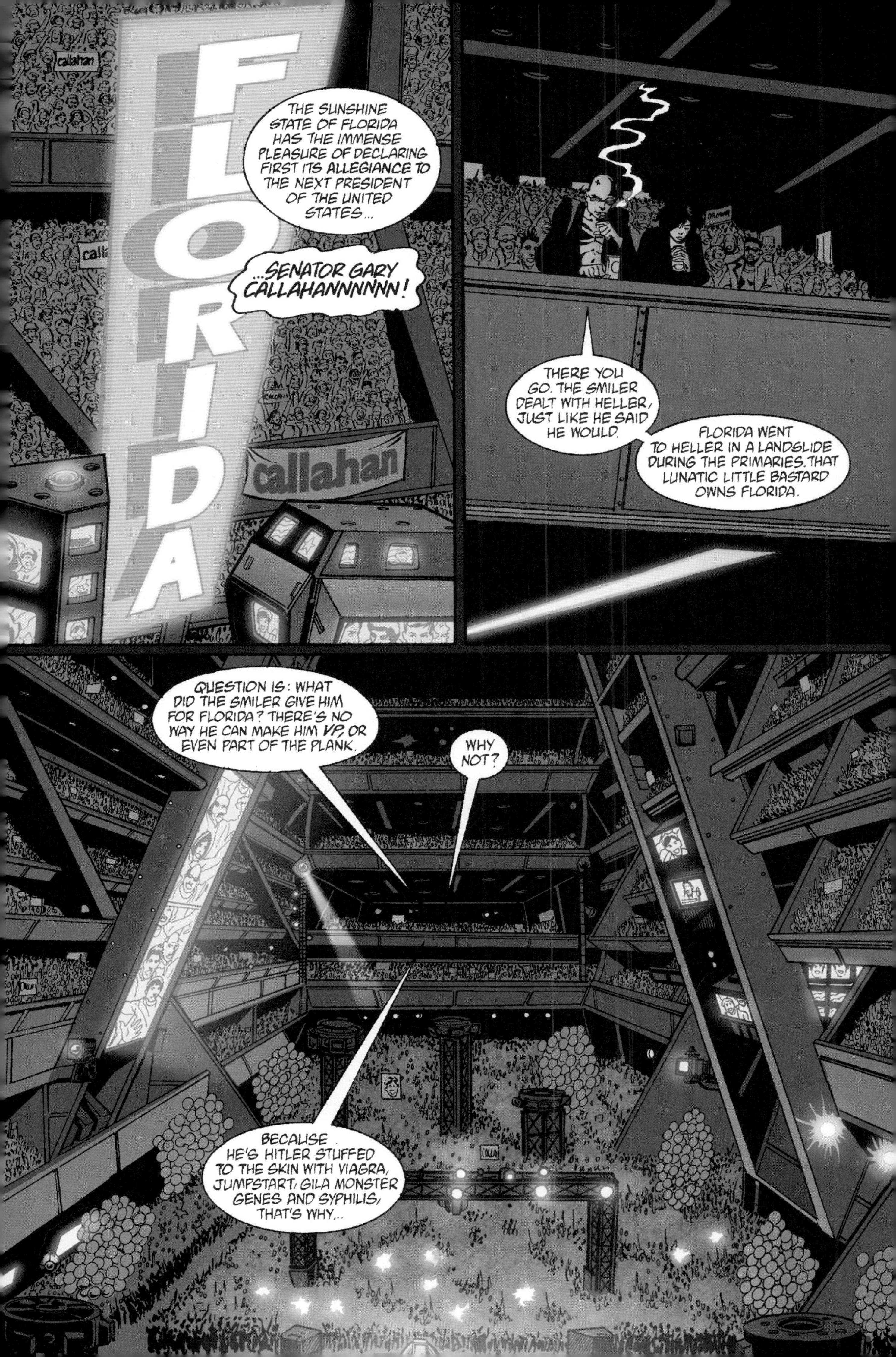
callahan
FLORIDA
THE SUNSHINE STATE OF FLORIDA HAS THE IMMENSE PLEASURE OF DECLARING FIRST ITS ALLEGIANCE TO THE NEXT PRESIDENT OF THE UNITED STATES...
...SENATOR GARY CALLAHANNNNNN!
callahan
THERE YOU GO. THE SMILER DEALT WITH HELLER, JUST LIKE HE SAID HE WOULD.
FLORIDA WENT TO HELLER IN A LANDSLIDE DURING THE PRIMARIES. THAT LUNATIC LITTLE BASTARD OWNS FLORIDA.
QUESTION IS: WHAT DID THE SMILER GIVE HIM FOR FLORIDA? THERE'S NO WAY HE CAN MAKE HIM VP, OR EVEN PART OF THE PLANK.
WHY NOT?
BECAUSE HE'S HITLER STUFFED TO THE SKIN WITH VIAGRA, JUMPSTART, GILA MONSTER GENES AND SYPHILIS, THAT'S WHY...

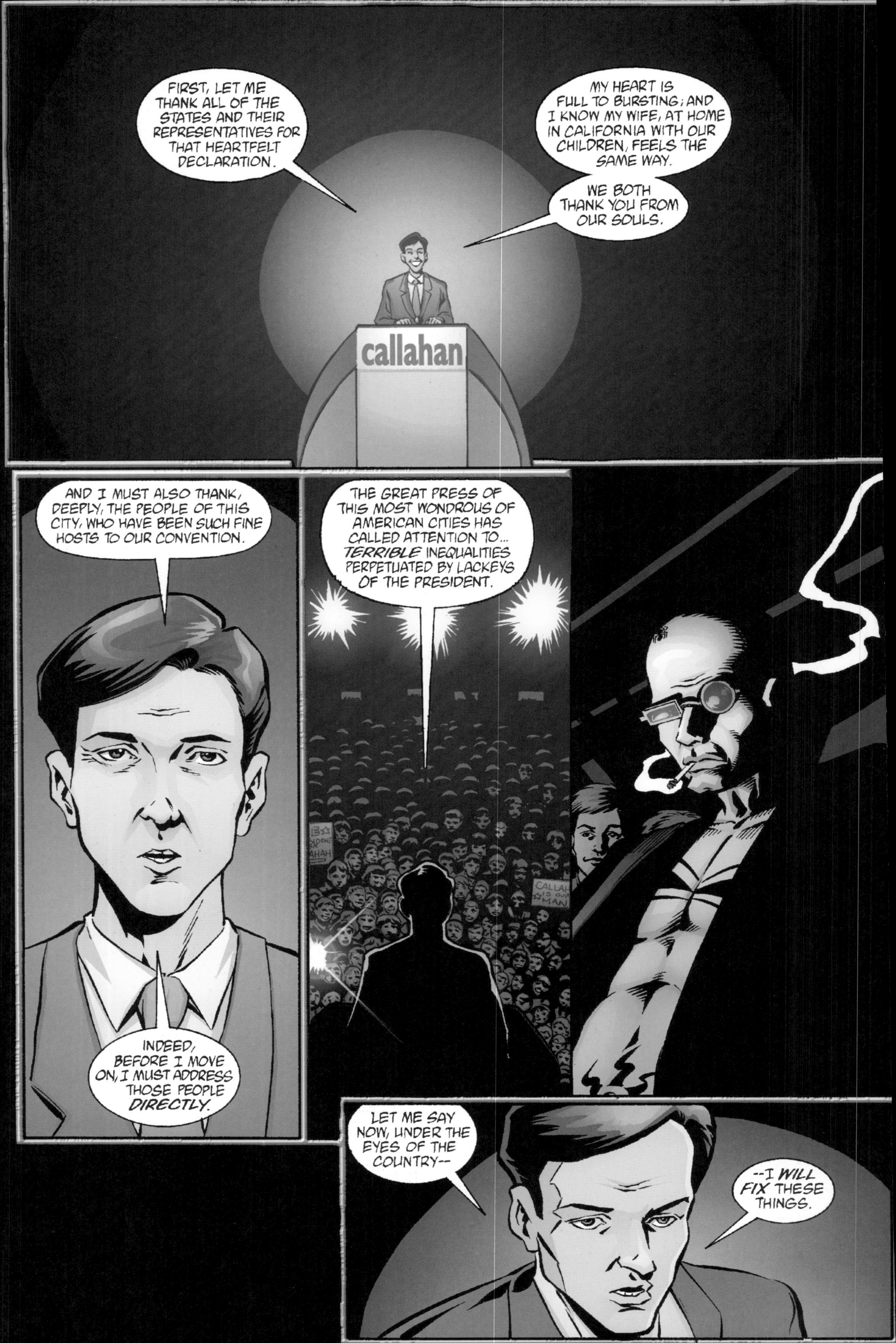

FIRST, LET ME THANK ALL OF THE STATES AND THEIR REPRESENTATIVES FOR THAT HEARTFELT DECLARATION.
MY HEART IS FULL TO BURSTING; AND I KNOW MY WIFE, AT HOME IN CALIFORNIA WITH OUR CHILDREN, FEELS THE SAME WAY.
WE BOTH THANK YOU FROM OUR SOULS.
callahan
AND I MUST ALSO THANK, DEEPLY, THE PEOPLE OF THIS CITY, WHO HAVE BEEN SUCH FINE HOSTS TO OUR CONVENTION.
INDEED, BEFORE I MOVE ON, I MUST ADDRESS THOSE PEOPLE *DIRECTLY*.
THE GREAT PRESS OF THIS MOST WONDROUS OF AMERICAN CITIES HAS CALLED ATTENTION TO... *TERRIBLE* INEQUALITIES PERPETUATED BY LACKEYS OF THE PRESIDENT.
LET ME SAY NOW, UNDER THE EYES OF THE COUNTRY--
--I ***WILL FIX*** THESE THINGS.

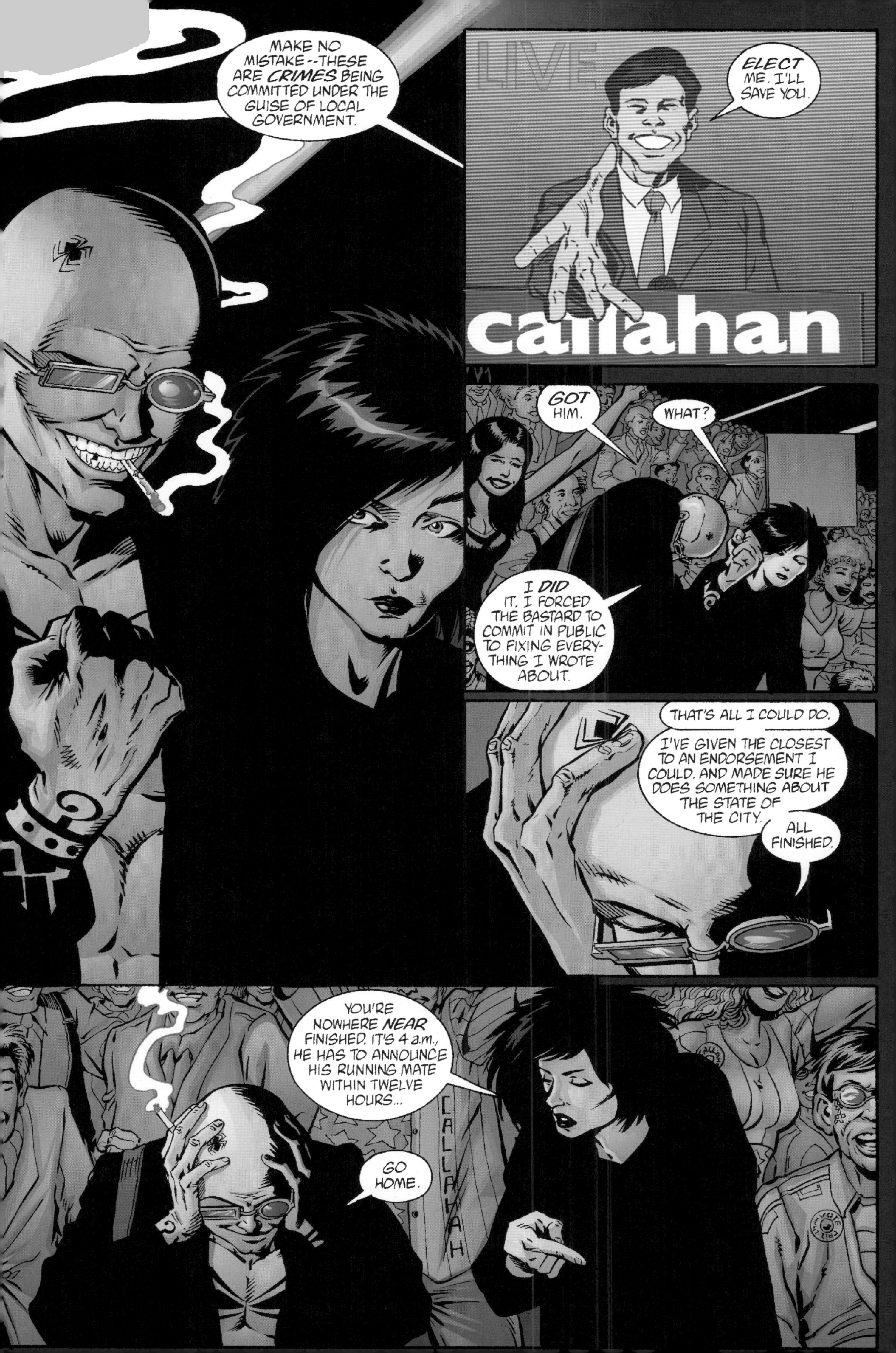
MAKE NO MISTAKE--THESE ARE CRIMES BEING COMMITTED UNDER THE GUISE OF LOCAL GOVERNMENT.
LIVE
ELECT ME. I'LL SAVE YOU.
callahan
GOT HIM.
WHAT?
I DID IT. I FORCED THE BASTARD TO COMMIT IN PUBLIC TO FIXING EVERYTHING I WROTE ABOUT.
THAT'S ALL I COULD DO.
I'VE GIVEN THE CLOSEST TO AN ENDORSEMENT I COULD. AND MADE SURE HE DOES SOMETHING ABOUT THE STATE OF THE CITY.
ALL FINISHED.
YOU'RE NOWHERE NEAR FINISHED. IT'S 4 a.m., HE HAS TO ANNOUNCE HIS RUNNING MATE WITHIN TWELVE HOURS...
CALLAHAH
GO HOME.

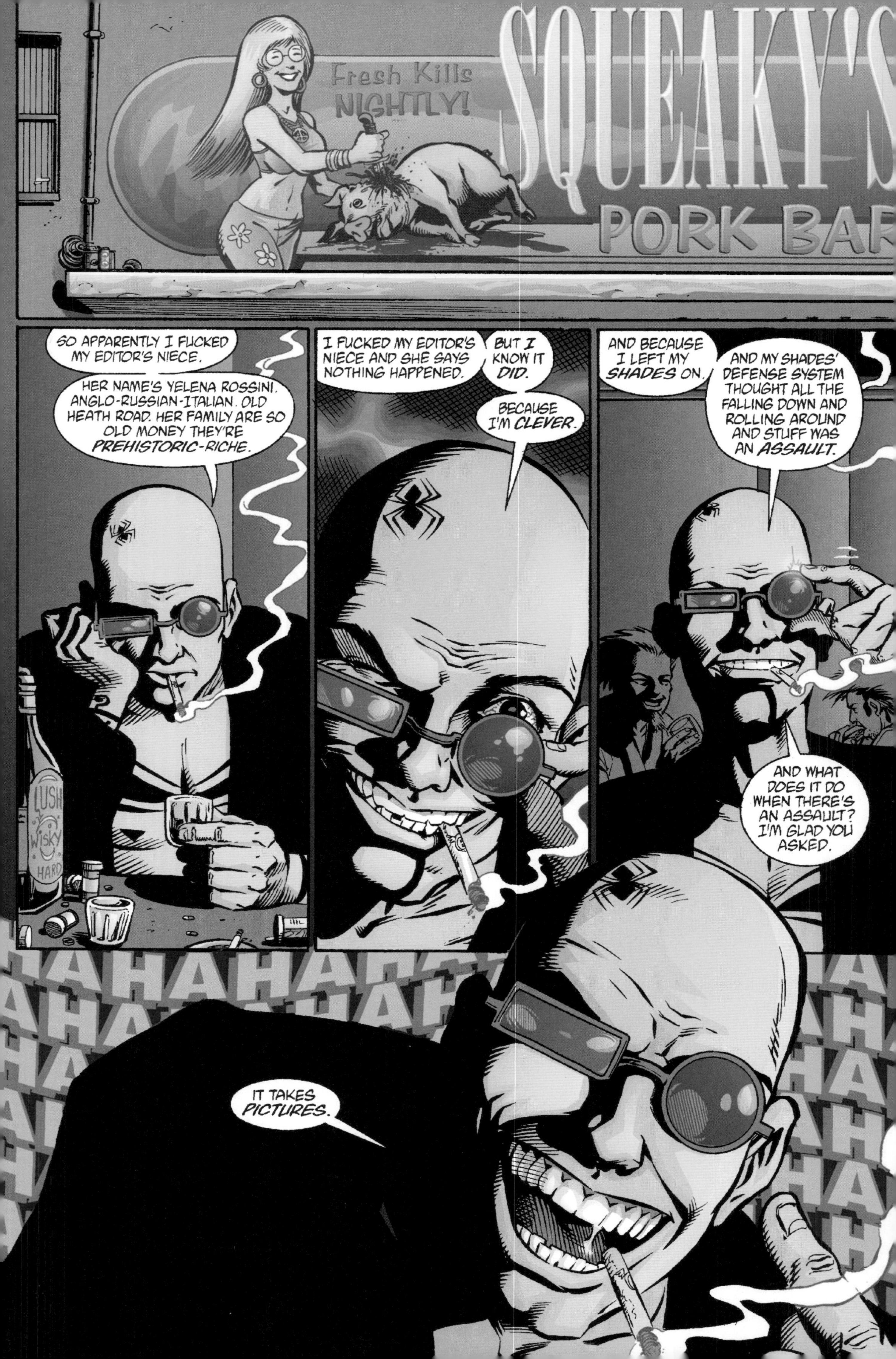

Fresh Kills NIGHTLY!
SQUEAKY'S
PORK BAR
SO APPARENTLY I FUCKED MY EDITOR'S NIECE.
HER NAME'S YELENA ROSSINI. ANGLO-RUSSIAN-ITALIAN. OLD HEATH ROAD. HER FAMILY ARE SO OLD MONEY THEY'RE PREHISTORIC-RICHE.
LUSH WISKY HARD
I FUCKED MY EDITOR'S NIECE AND SHE SAYS NOTHING HAPPENED.
BUT I KNOW IT DID.
BECAUSE I'M CLEVER.
AND BECAUSE I LEFT MY SHADES ON.
AND MY SHADES' DEFENSE SYSTEM THOUGHT ALL THE FALLING DOWN AND ROLLING AROUND AND STUFF WAS AN ASSAULT.
AND WHAT DOES IT DO WHEN THERE'S AN ASSAULT? I'M GLAD YOU ASKED.
HAHAHAHA
IT TAKES PICTURES.

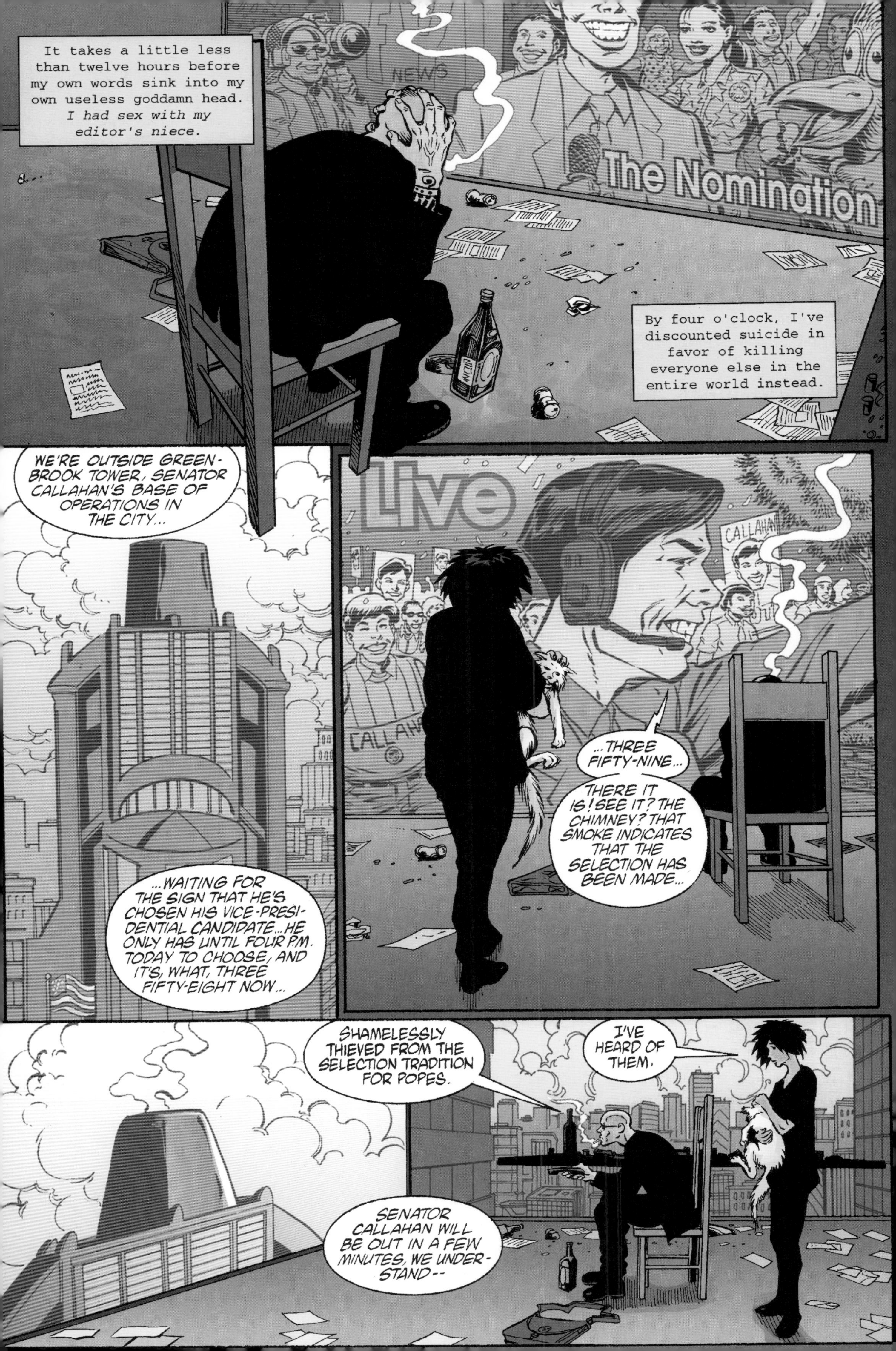
It takes a little less than twelve hours before my own words sink into my own useless goddamn head. *I had sex with my editor's niece.*
NEWS
The Nomination
By four o'clock, I've discounted suicide in favor of killing everyone else in the entire world instead.
WE'RE OUTSIDE GREEN-BROOK TOWER, SENATOR CALLAHAN'S BASE OF OPERATIONS IN THE CITY...
...WAITING FOR THE SIGN THAT HE'S CHOSEN HIS VICE-PRESIDENTIAL CANDIDATE...HE ONLY HAS UNTIL FOUR P.M. TODAY TO CHOOSE, AND IT'S, WHAT, THREE FIFTY-EIGHT NOW...
LIVE
CALLAHAN
...THREE FIFTY-NINE...
THERE IT IS! SEE IT? THE CHIMNEY? THAT SMOKE INDICATES THAT THE SELECTION HAS BEEN MADE...
SHAMELESSLY THIEVED FROM THE SELECTION TRADITION FOR POPES.
I'VE HEARD OF THEM.
SENATOR CALLAHAN WILL BE OUT IN A FEW MINUTES, WE UNDERSTAND--

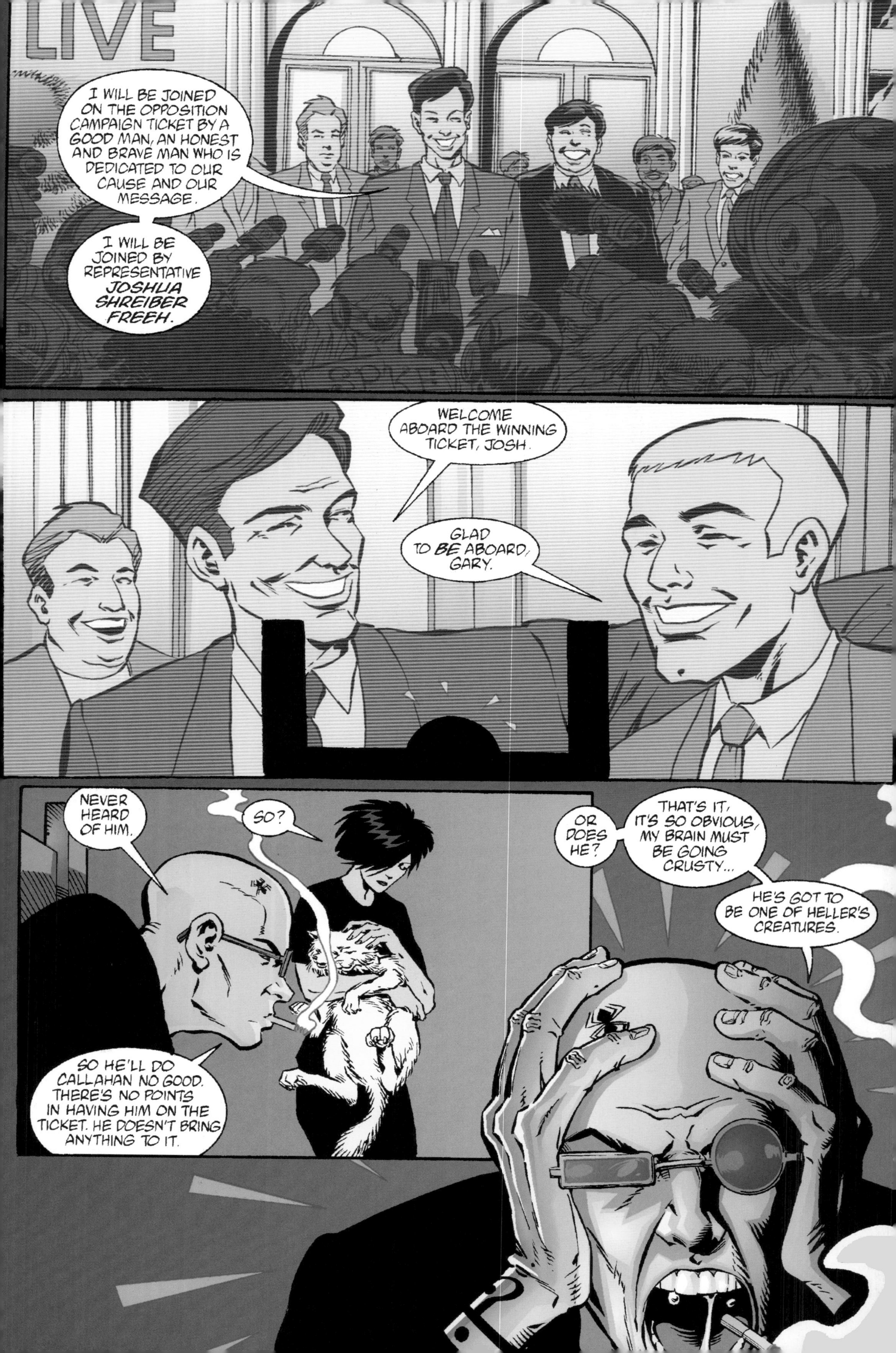
LIVE
I WILL BE JOINED ON THE OPPOSITION CAMPAIGN TICKET BY A GOOD MAN, AN HONEST AND BRAVE MAN WHO IS DEDICATED TO OUR CAUSE AND OUR MESSAGE.
I WILL BE JOINED BY REPRESENTATIVE JOSHUA SHREIBER FREEH.
WELCOME ABOARD THE WINNING TICKET, JOSH.
GLAD TO BE ABOARD, GARY.
NEVER HEARD OF HIM.
SO?
SO HE'LL DO CALLAHAN NO GOOD. THERE'S NO POINTS IN HAVING HIM ON THE TICKET. HE DOESN'T BRING ANYTHING TO IT.
OR DOES HE?
THAT'S IT, IT'S SO OBVIOUS, MY BRAIN MUST BE GOING CRUSTY...
HE'S GOT TO BE ONE OF HELLER'S CREATURES.

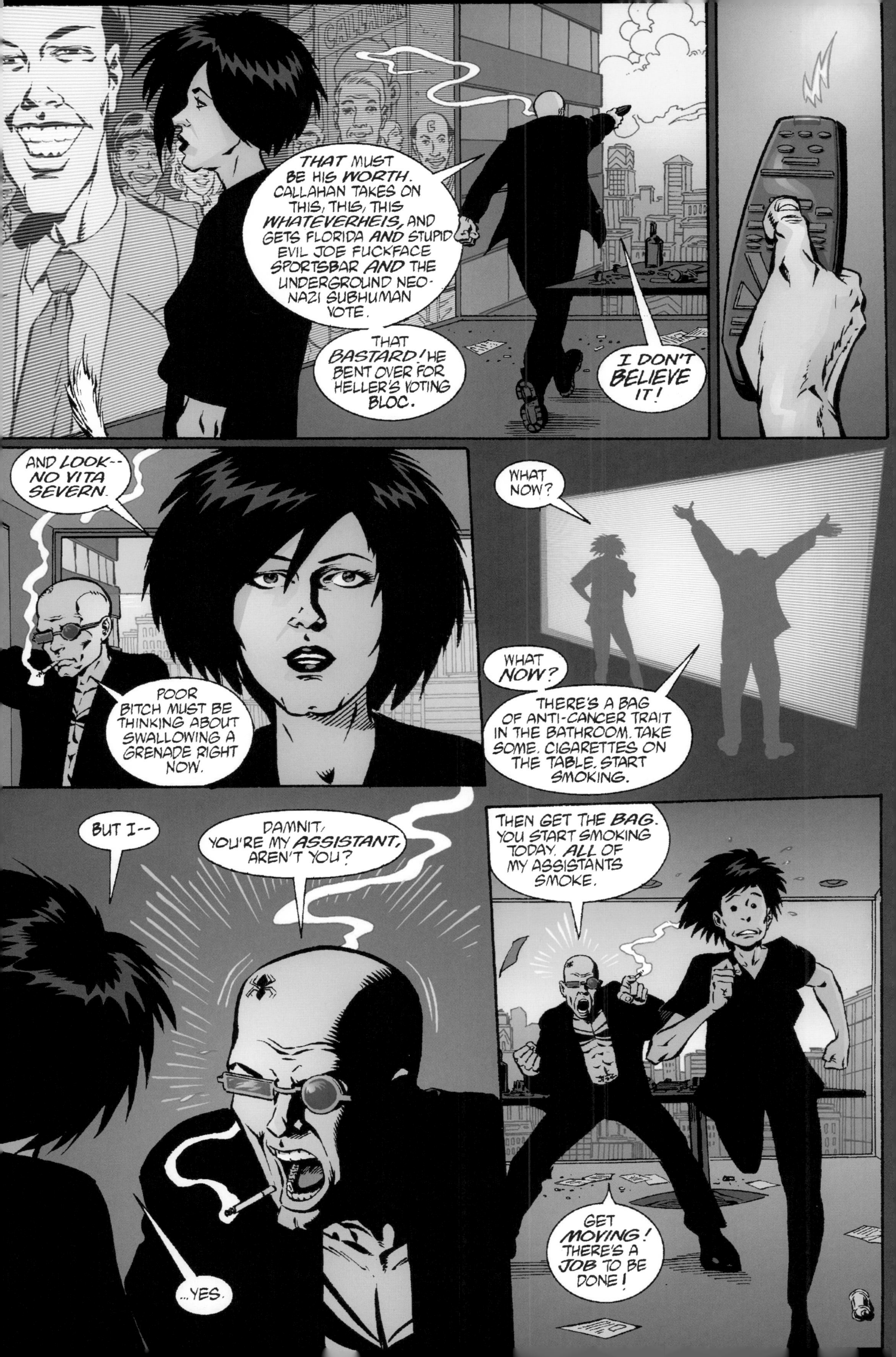
THAT MUST BE HIS WORTH. CALLAHAN TAKES ON THIS, THIS, THIS WHATEVERHEIS, AND GETS FLORIDA AND STUPID EVIL JOE FUCKFACE SPORTSBAR AND THE UNDERGROUND NEO-NAZI SUBHUMAN VOTE.
THAT BASTARD! HE BENT OVER FOR HELLER'S VOTING BLOC.
I DON'T BELIEVE IT!
AND LOOK-- NO VITA SEVERN.
POOR BITCH MUST BE THINKING ABOUT SWALLOWING A GRENADE RIGHT NOW.
WHAT NOW?
WHAT NOW?
THERE'S A BAG OF ANTI-CANCER TRAIT IN THE BATHROOM. TAKE SOME. CIGARETTES ON THE TABLE. START SMOKING.
BUT I--
DAMNIT, YOU'RE MY ASSISTANT, AREN'T YOU?
...YES.
THEN GET THE BAG. YOU START SMOKING TODAY. ALL OF MY ASSISTANTS SMOKE.
GET MOVING! THERE'S A JOB TO BE DONE!

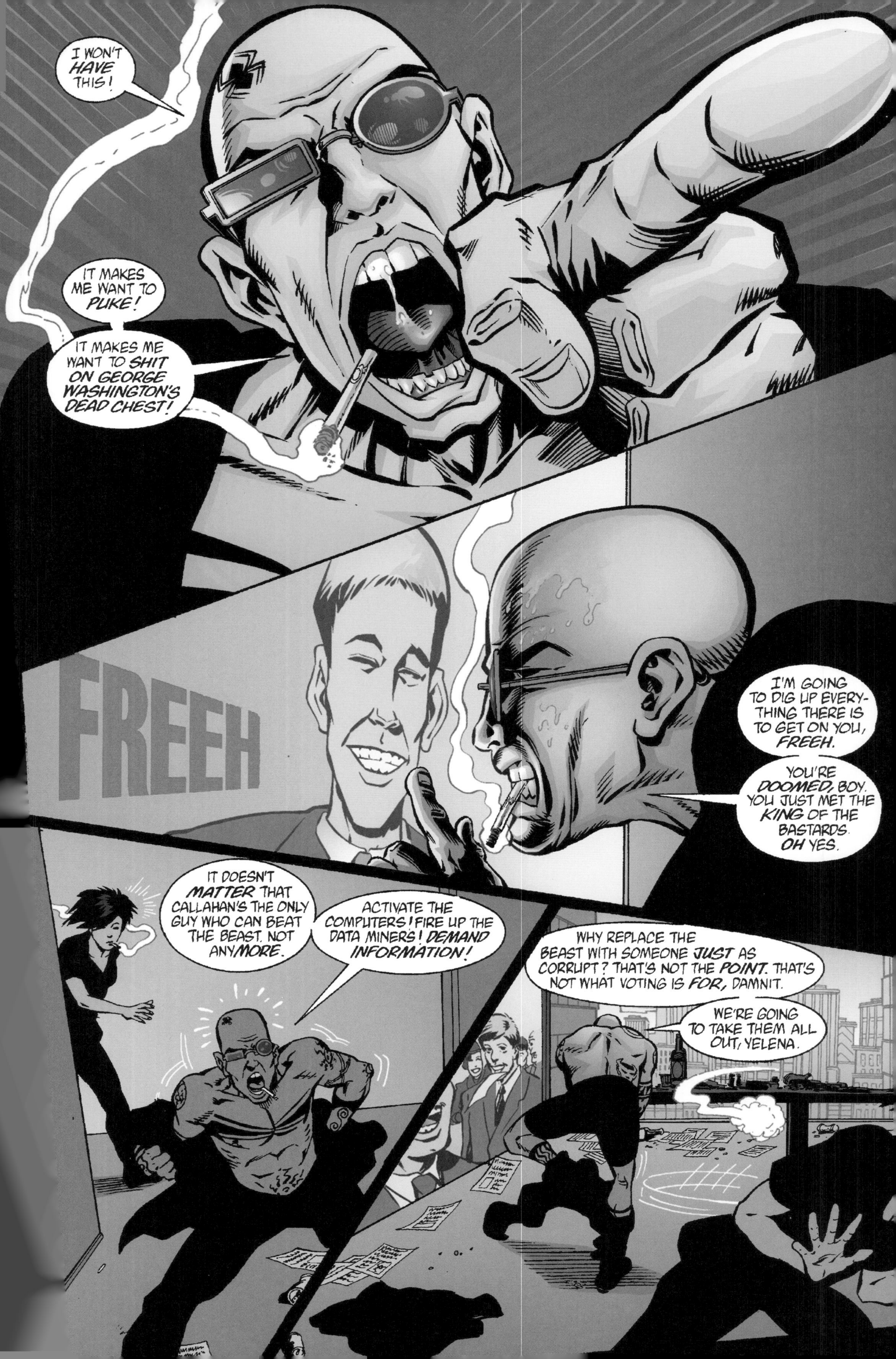
I WON'T HAVE THIS!
IT MAKES ME WANT TO PUKE!
IT MAKES ME WANT TO SHIT ON GEORGE WASHINGTON'S DEAD CHEST!
FREEH
I'M GOING TO DIG UP EVERYTHING THERE IS TO GET ON YOU, FREEH.
YOU'RE DOOMED, BOY. YOU JUST MET THE KING OF THE BASTARDS. OH YES.
IT DOESN'T MATTER THAT CALLAHAN'S THE ONLY GUY WHO CAN BEAT THE BEAST. NOT ANYMORE.
ACTIVATE THE COMPUTERS! FIRE UP THE DATA MINERS! DEMAND INFORMATION!
WHY REPLACE THE BEAST WITH SOMEONE JUST AS CORRUPT? THAT'S NOT THE POINT. THAT'S NOT WHAT VOTING IS FOR, DAMNIT.
WE'RE GOING TO TAKE THEM ALL OUT, YELENA.

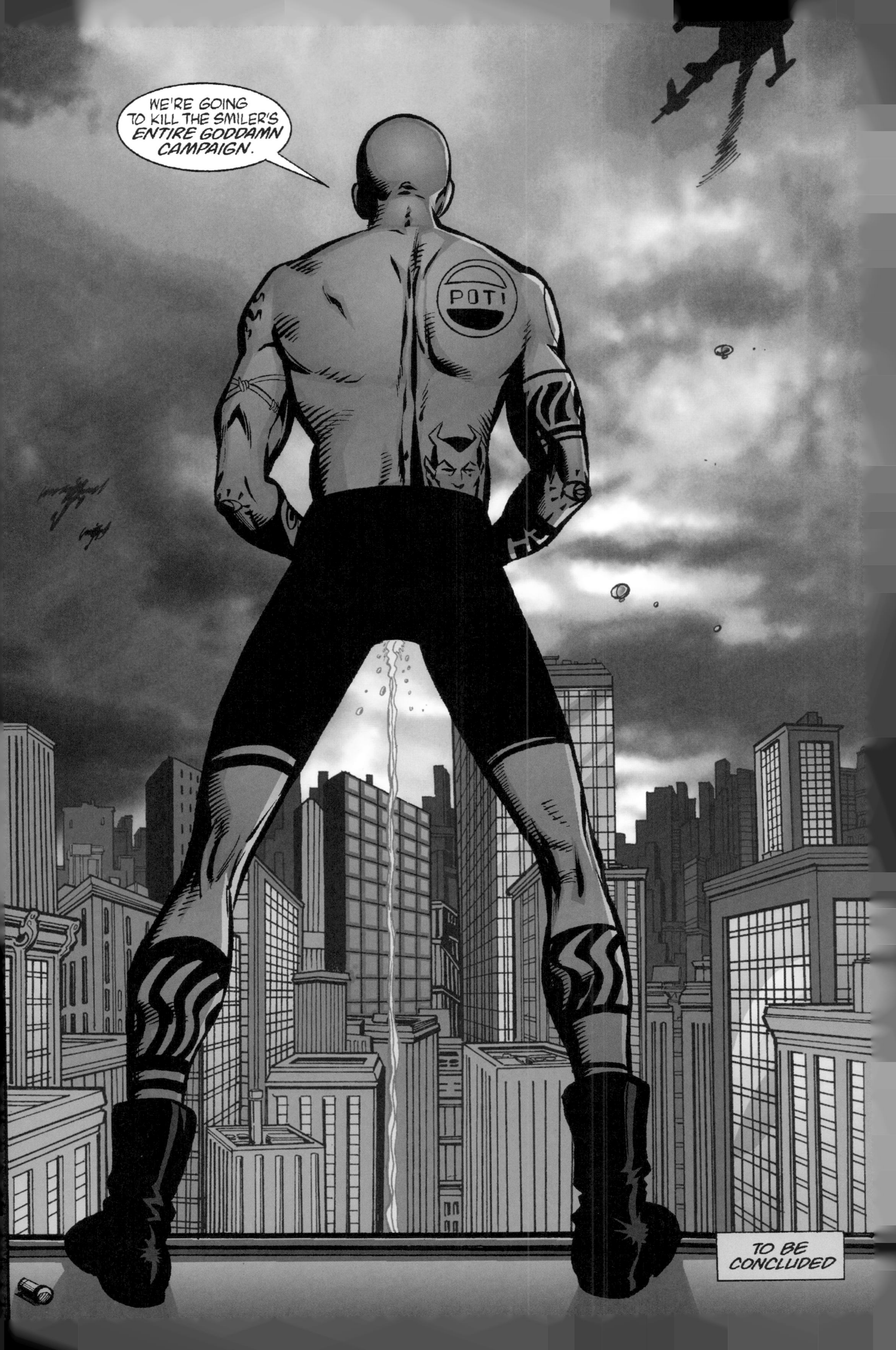
WE'RE GOING TO KILL THE SMILER'S ENTIRE GODDAMN CAMPAIGN.
POTI
TO BE CONCLUDED

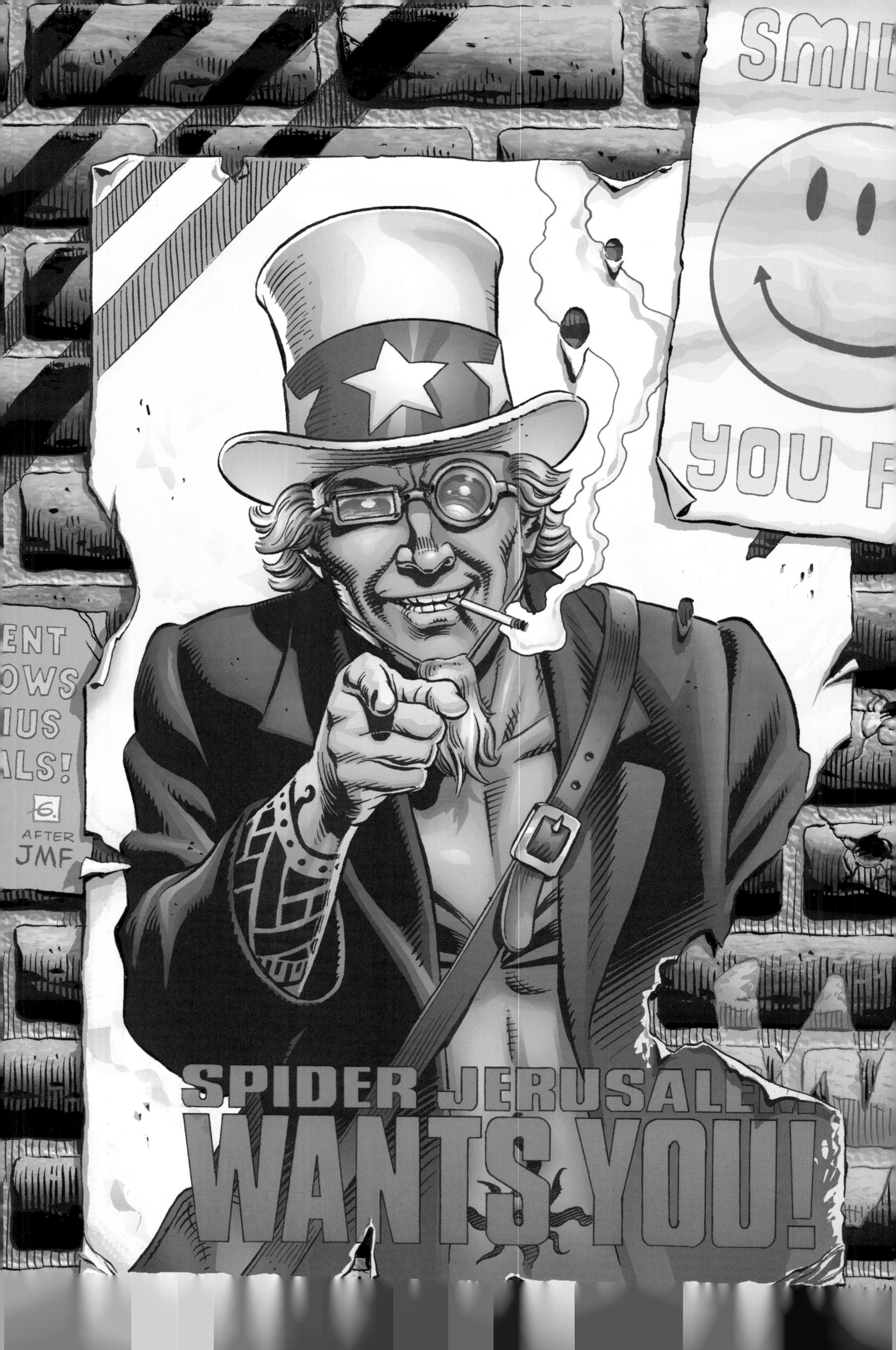

SPIDER JERUSALE
WANTS YOU!
G.
AFTER
JMF

Election Selection!

FREEH

TOP STORY

REPRESENTATIVE *JOSHUA SHREIBER FREEH* HAS COME FROM NOWHERE TO BE SELECTED AS SENATOR *GARY CALLAHAN'S* RUNNING MATE IN THIS YEAR'S PRESIDENTIAL ELECTION.

VOTED TO THE HOUSE OF REPRESENTATIVES BY THIS CITY ONLY TWO YEARS AGO, PARTICULARLY ACTIVE IN THE LAST YEAR ON DOMESTIC HUMAN RIGHTS, MR. FREEH IS A FRESH FACE IN NATIONAL POLITICS--AS MR. CALLAHAN SAYS, "JUST WHAT THE DOCTOR ORDERED."

WARREN ELLIS writes and DARICK ROBERTSON pencils

# YEAR OF THE BASTARD
# 6: BASTARD

| RODNEY RAMOS | NATHAN EYRING | CLEM ROBINS | CLIFF CHIANG | STUART MOORE |
|---|---|---|---|---|
| inker | color & separations | letterer | ass't editor | editor |

TRANSMETROPOLITAN created by WARREN ELLIS & DARICK ROBERTSON

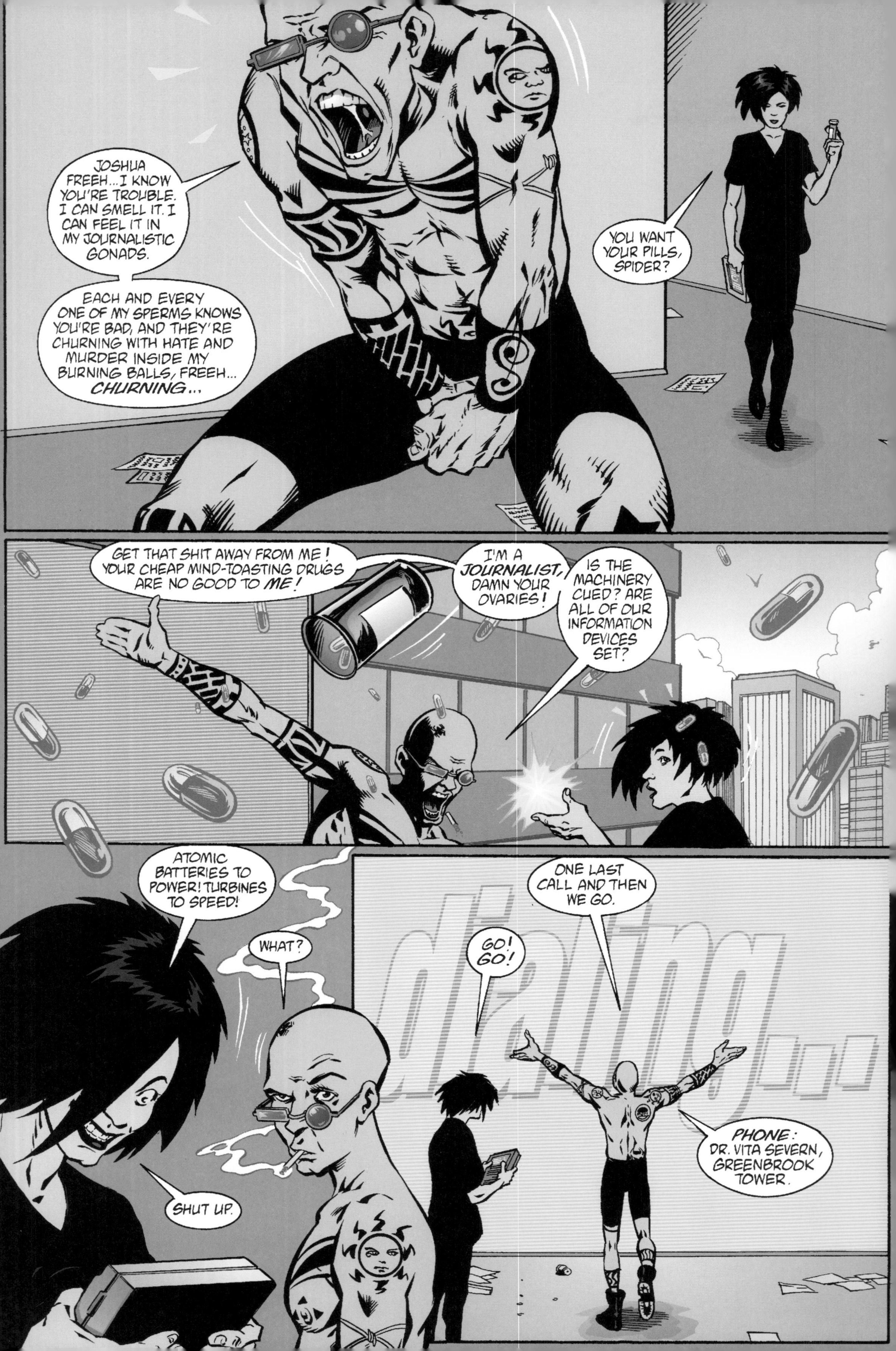
JOSHUA FREEH...I KNOW YOU'RE TROUBLE. I CAN SMELL IT. I CAN FEEL IT IN MY JOURNALISTIC GONADS.
EACH AND EVERY ONE OF MY SPERMS KNOWS YOU'RE BAD, AND THEY'RE CHURNING WITH HATE AND MURDER INSIDE MY BURNING BALLS, FREEH... CHURNING...
YOU WANT YOUR PILLS, SPIDER?
GET THAT SHIT AWAY FROM ME! YOUR CHEAP MIND-TOASTING DRUGS ARE NO GOOD TO ME!
I'M A JOURNALIST, DAMN YOUR OVARIES!
IS THE MACHINERY CUED? ARE ALL OF OUR INFORMATION DEVICES SET?
ATOMIC BATTERIES TO POWER! TURBINES TO SPEED!
WHAT?
SHUT UP.
dialing...
ONE LAST CALL AND THEN WE GO.
GO! GO!
PHONE: DR. VITA SEVERN, GREENBROOK TOWER.

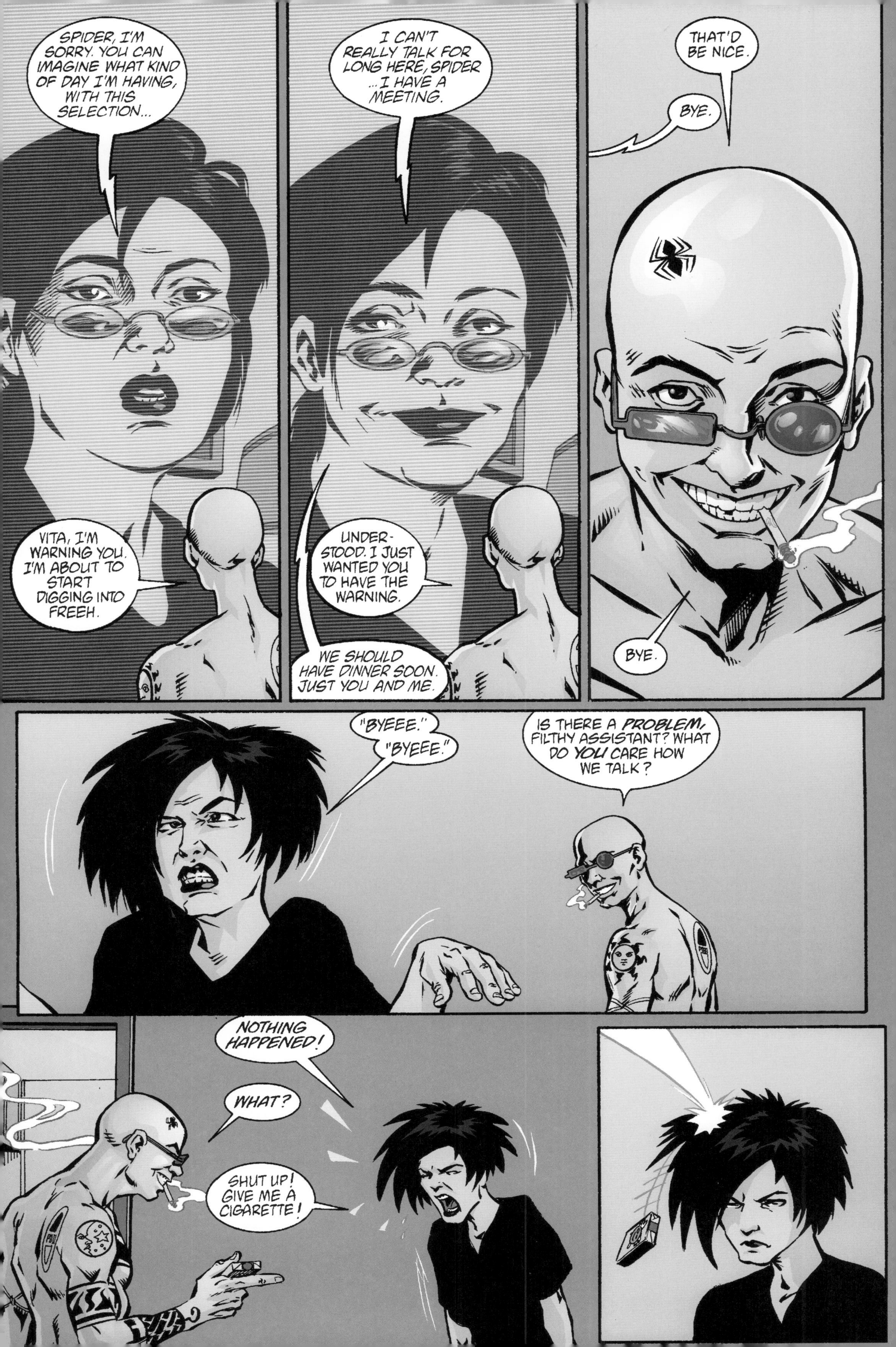
SPIDER, I'M SORRY. YOU CAN IMAGINE WHAT KIND OF DAY I'M HAVING, WITH THIS SELECTION...
VITA, I'M WARNING YOU. I'M ABOUT TO START DIGGING INTO FREEH.
I CAN'T REALLY TALK FOR LONG HERE, SPIDER ...I HAVE A MEETING.
UNDER-STOOD. I JUST WANTED YOU TO HAVE THE WARNING.
WE SHOULD HAVE DINNER SOON. JUST YOU AND ME.
THAT'D BE NICE.
BYE.
BYE.
"BYEEE."
"BYEEE."
IS THERE A PROBLEM, FILTHY ASSISTANT? WHAT DO YOU CARE HOW WE TALK?
NOTHING HAPPENED!
WHAT?
SHUT UP! GIVE ME A CIGARETTE!

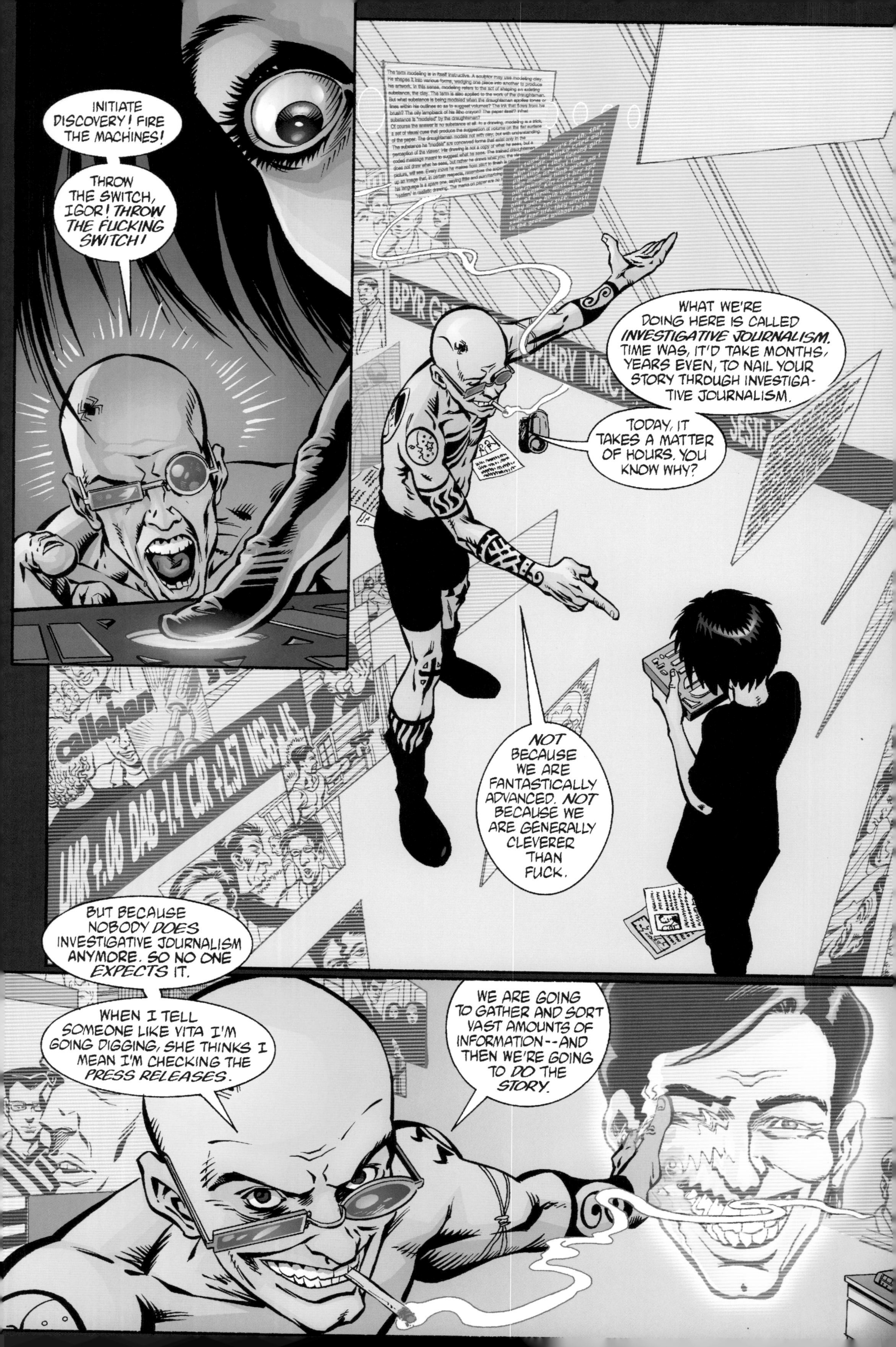
INITIATE DISCOVERY! FIRE THE MACHINES!
THROW THE SWITCH, IGOR! THROW THE FUCKING SWITCH!
WHAT WE'RE DOING HERE IS CALLED INVESTIGATIVE JOURNALISM. TIME WAS, IT'D TAKE MONTHS, YEARS EVEN, TO NAIL YOUR STORY THROUGH INVESTIGATIVE JOURNALISM.
TODAY, IT TAKES A MATTER OF HOURS. YOU KNOW WHY?
NOT BECAUSE WE ARE FANTASTICALLY ADVANCED. NOT BECAUSE WE ARE GENERALLY CLEVERER THAN FUCK.
BUT BECAUSE NOBODY DOES INVESTIGATIVE JOURNALISM ANYMORE. SO NO ONE EXPECTS IT.
WHEN I TELL SOMEONE LIKE VITA I'M GOING DIGGING, SHE THINKS I MEAN I'M CHECKING THE PRESS RELEASES.
WE ARE GOING TO GATHER AND SORT VAST AMOUNTS OF INFORMATION--AND THEN WE'RE GOING TO DO THE STORY.

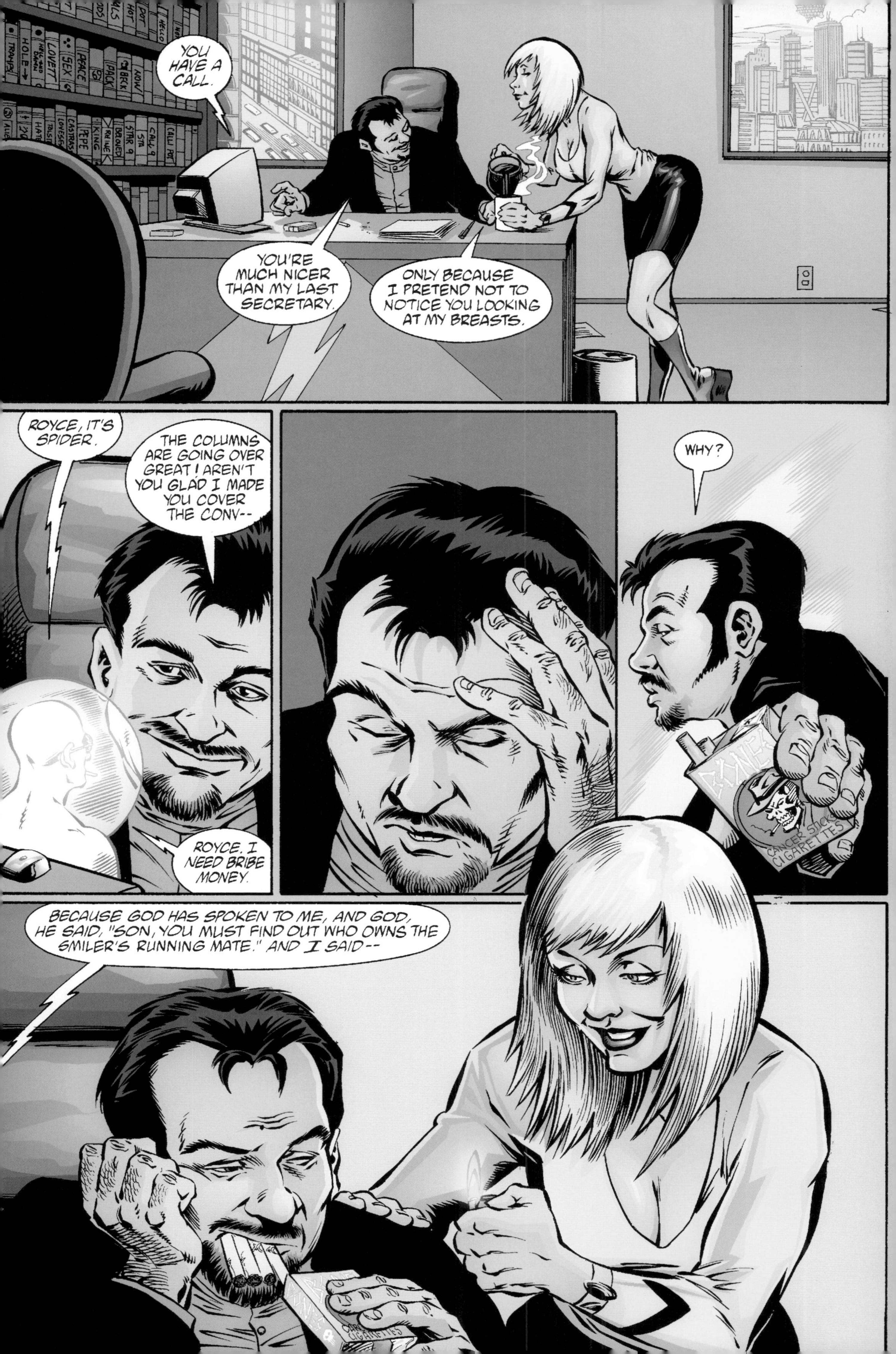
YOU HAVE A CALL.
YOU'RE MUCH NICER THAN MY LAST SECRETARY.
ONLY BECAUSE I PRETEND NOT TO NOTICE YOU LOOKING AT MY BREASTS.
ROYCE, IT'S SPIDER.
THE COLUMNS ARE GOING OVER GREAT! AREN'T YOU GLAD I MADE YOU COVER THE CONV--
ROYCE. I NEED BRIBE MONEY.
WHY?
CANCER STICKS CIGARETTES
BECAUSE GOD HAS SPOKEN TO ME, AND GOD, HE SAID, "SON, YOU MUST FIND OUT WHO OWNS THE SMILER'S RUNNING MATE." AND I SAID--

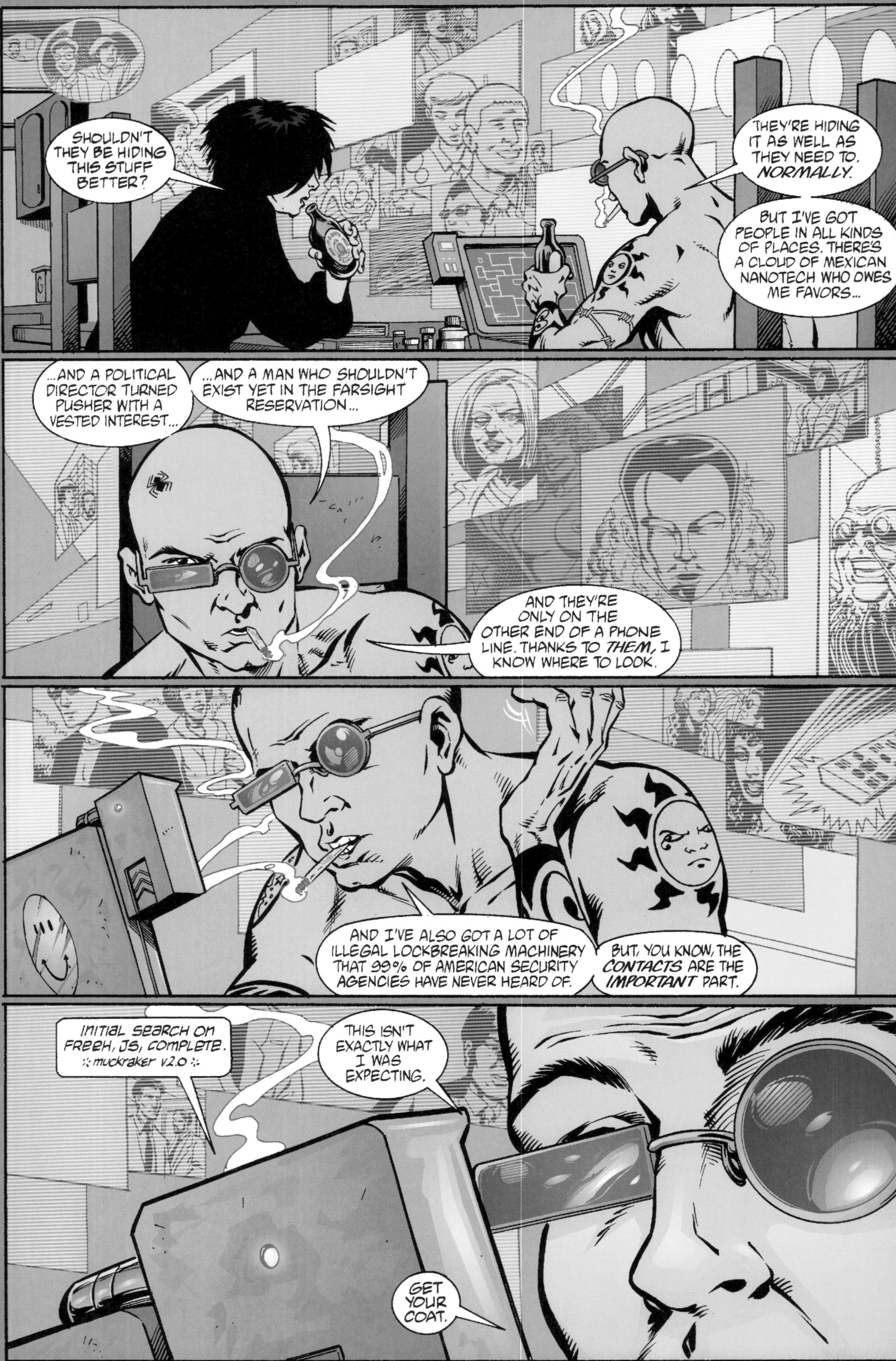
SHOULDN'T THEY BE HIDING THIS STUFF BETTER?
THEY'RE HIDING IT AS WELL AS THEY NEED TO. NORMALLY.
BUT I'VE GOT PEOPLE IN ALL KINDS OF PLACES. THERE'S A CLOUD OF MEXICAN NANOTECH WHO OWES ME FAVORS...
...AND A POLITICAL DIRECTOR TURNED PUSHER WITH A VESTED INTEREST...
...AND A MAN WHO SHOULDN'T EXIST YET IN THE FARSIGHT RESERVATION...
AND THEY'RE ONLY ON THE OTHER END OF A PHONE LINE. THANKS TO THEM, I KNOW WHERE TO LOOK.
AND I'VE ALSO GOT A LOT OF ILLEGAL LOCKBREAKING MACHINERY THAT 99% OF AMERICAN SECURITY AGENCIES HAVE NEVER HEARD OF.
BUT, YOU KNOW, THE CONTACTS ARE THE IMPORTANT PART.
Initial search on Freeh, JS, complete.
muckraker v2.0
THIS ISN'T EXACTLY WHAT I WAS EXPECTING.
GET YOUR COAT.

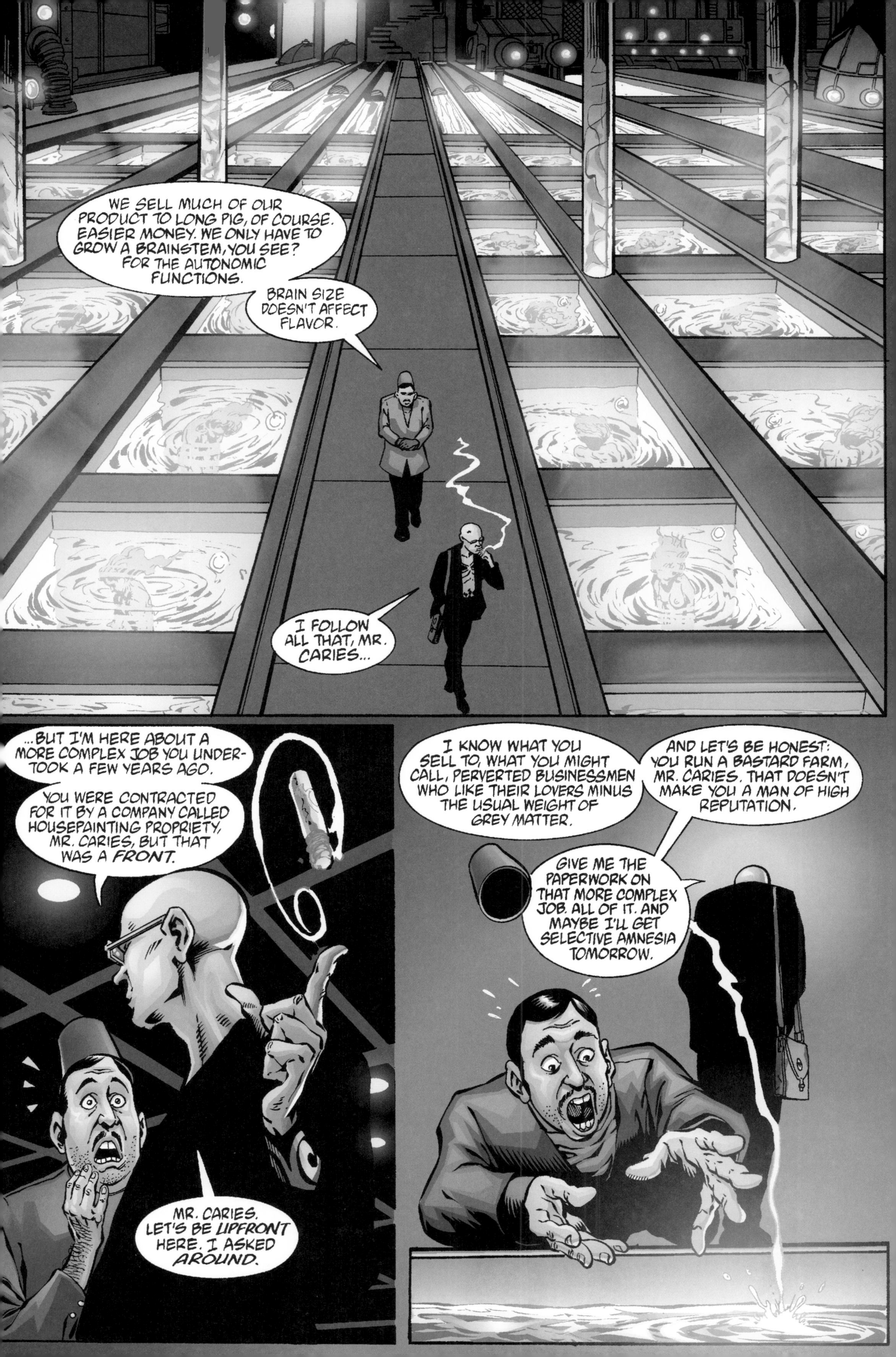
WE SELL MUCH OF OUR PRODUCT TO LONG PIG, OF COURSE. EASIER MONEY. WE ONLY HAVE TO GROW A BRAINSTEM, YOU SEE? FOR THE AUTONOMIC FUNCTIONS.
BRAIN SIZE DOESN'T AFFECT FLAVOR.
I FOLLOW ALL THAT, MR. CARIES...
...BUT I'M HERE ABOUT A MORE COMPLEX JOB YOU UNDER-TOOK A FEW YEARS AGO.
YOU WERE CONTRACTED FOR IT BY A COMPANY CALLED HOUSEPAINTING PROPRIETY, MR. CARIES, BUT THAT WAS A *FRONT*.
MR. CARIES. LET'S BE *UPFRONT* HERE. I ASKED *AROUND*.
I KNOW WHAT YOU SELL TO, WHAT YOU MIGHT CALL, PERVERTED BUSINESSMEN WHO LIKE THEIR LOVERS MINUS THE USUAL WEIGHT OF GREY MATTER.
AND LET'S BE HONEST: YOU RUN A BASTARD FARM, MR. CARIES. THAT DOESN'T MAKE YOU A MAN OF HIGH REPUTATION.
GIVE ME THE PAPERWORK ON THAT MORE COMPLEX JOB. ALL OF IT. AND MAYBE I'LL GET SELECTIVE AMNESIA TOMORROW.

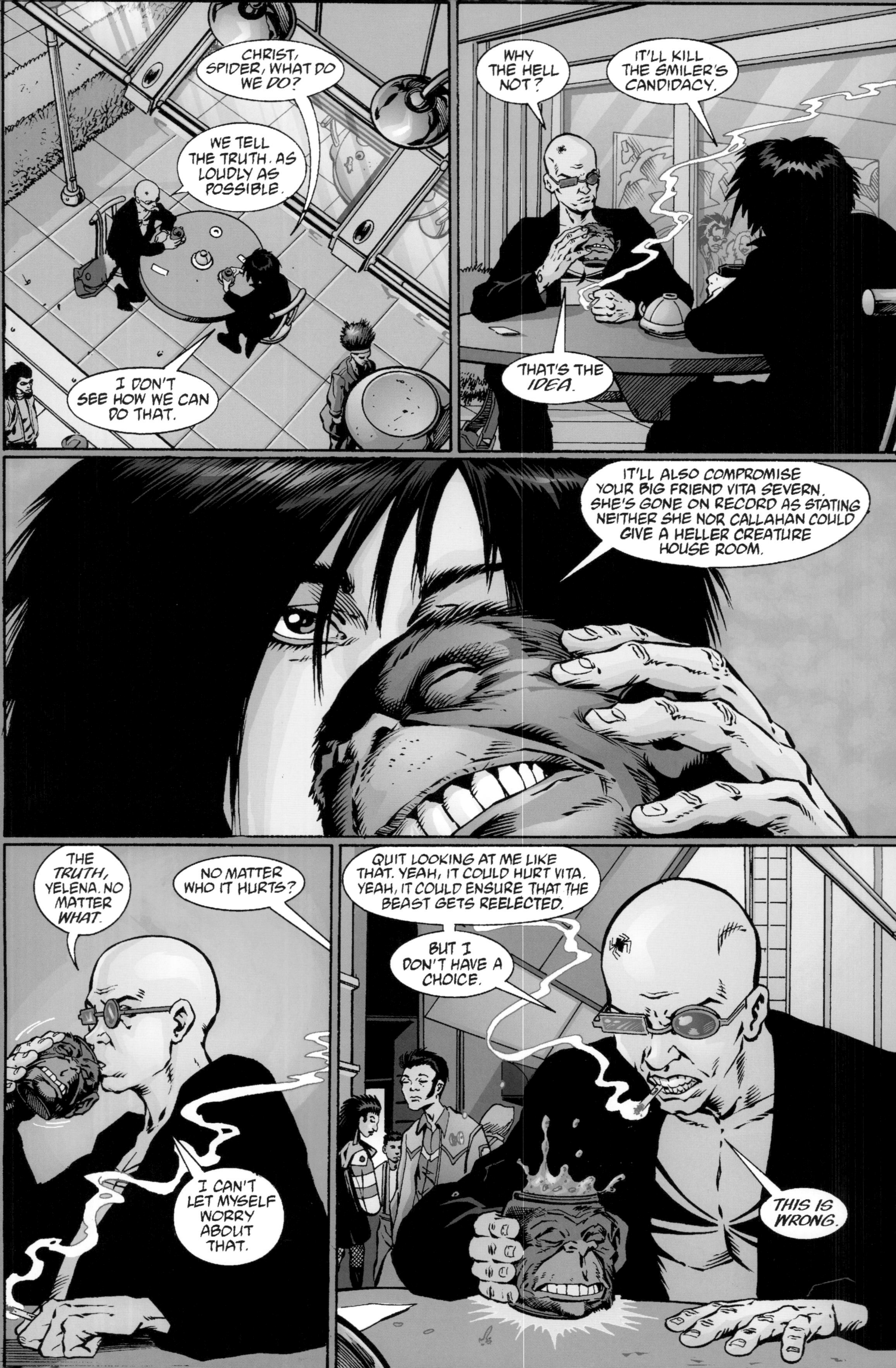
CHRIST, SPIDER, WHAT DO WE *DO*?
WE TELL THE TRUTH. AS LOUDLY AS POSSIBLE.
I DON'T SEE HOW WE CAN DO THAT.
WHY THE HELL NOT?
IT'LL KILL THE SMILER'S CANDIDACY.
THAT'S THE *IDEA*.
IT'LL ALSO COMPROMISE YOUR BIG FRIEND VITA SEVERN. SHE'S GONE ON RECORD AS STATING NEITHER SHE NOR CALLAHAN COULD GIVE A HELLER CREATURE HOUSE ROOM.
THE *TRUTH*, YELENA. NO MATTER *WHAT*.
NO MATTER WHO IT HURTS?
I CAN'T LET MYSELF WORRY ABOUT THAT.
QUIT LOOKING AT ME LIKE THAT. YEAH, IT COULD HURT VITA. YEAH, IT COULD ENSURE THAT THE BEAST GETS REELECTED.
BUT I DON'T HAVE A CHOICE.
*THIS IS WRONG*.

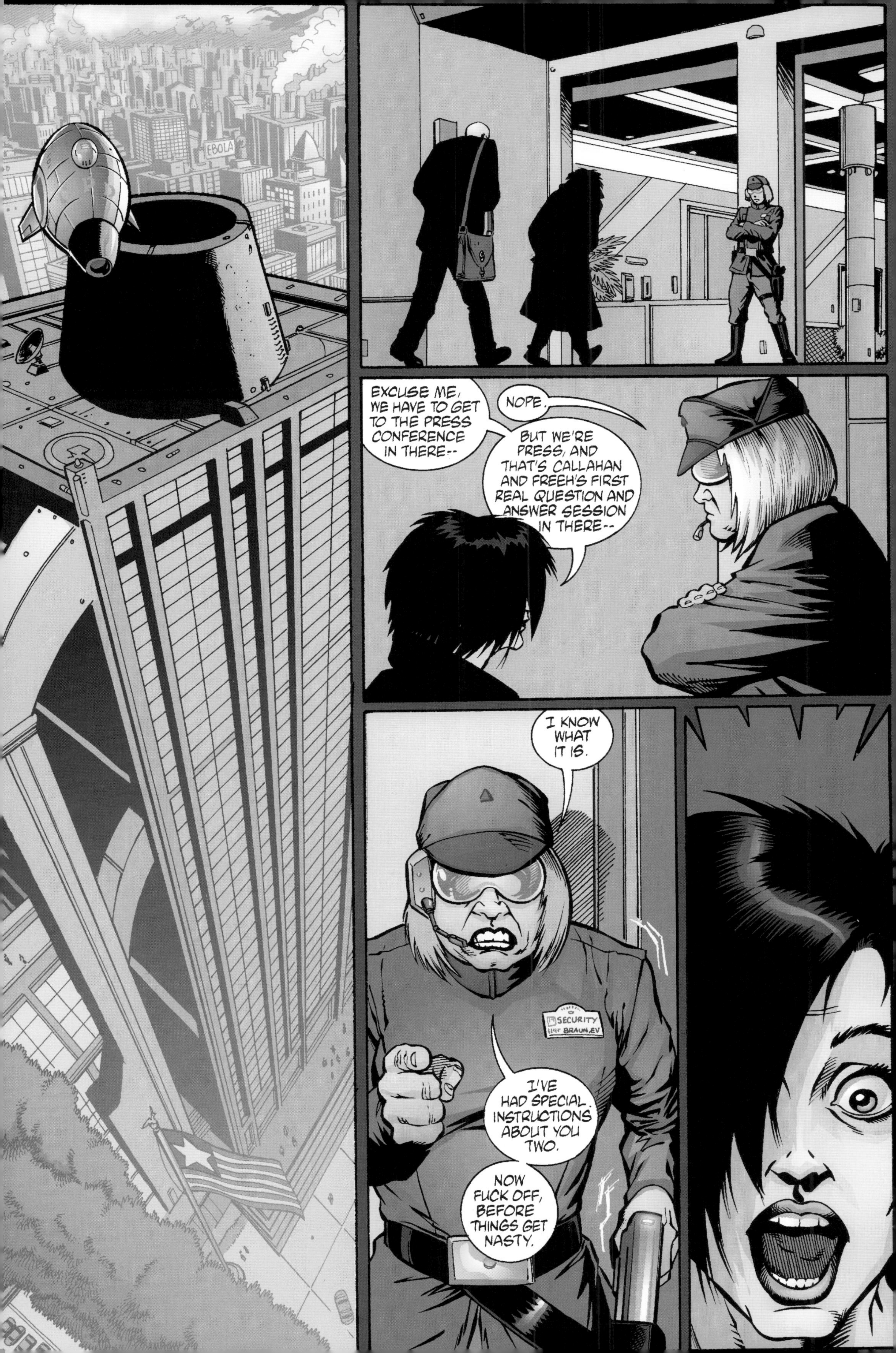
EBOLA
EXCUSE ME, WE HAVE TO GET TO THE PRESS CONFERENCE IN THERE--
NOPE.
BUT WE'RE PRESS, AND THAT'S CALLAHAN AND FREEH'S FIRST REAL QUESTION AND ANSWER SESSION IN THERE--
I KNOW WHAT IT IS.
SECURITY
BRAUN, EV
I'VE HAD SPECIAL INSTRUCTIONS ABOUT YOU TWO.
NOW FUCK OFF, BEFORE THINGS GET NASTY.

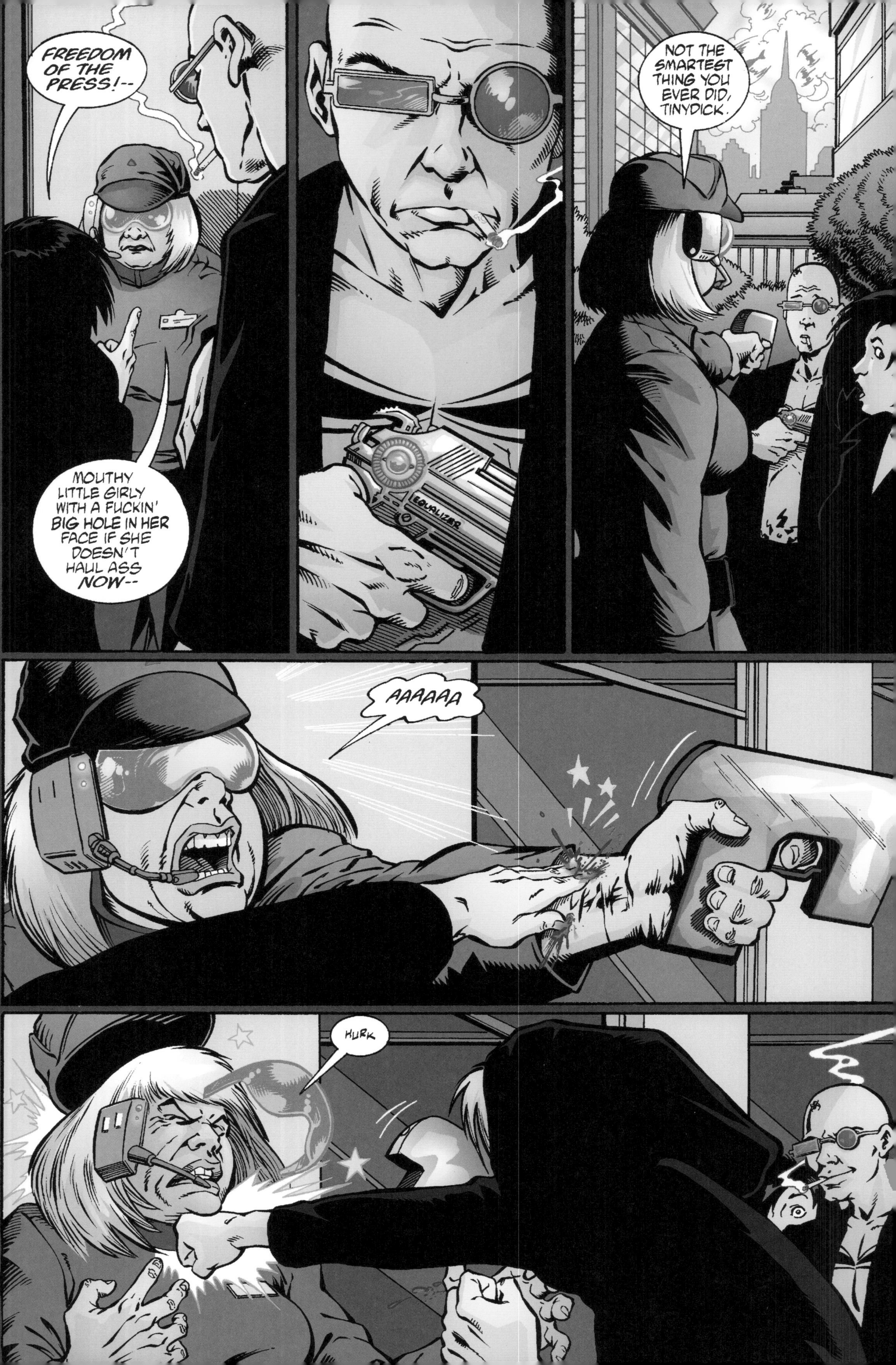
FREEDOM OF THE PRESS!--
MOUTHY LITTLE GIRLY WITH A FUCKIN' BIG HOLE IN HER FACE IF SHE DOESN'T HAUL ASS NOW--
EQUALIZER
NOT THE SMARTEST THING YOU EVER DID, TINYDICK.
AAAAAA
HURK

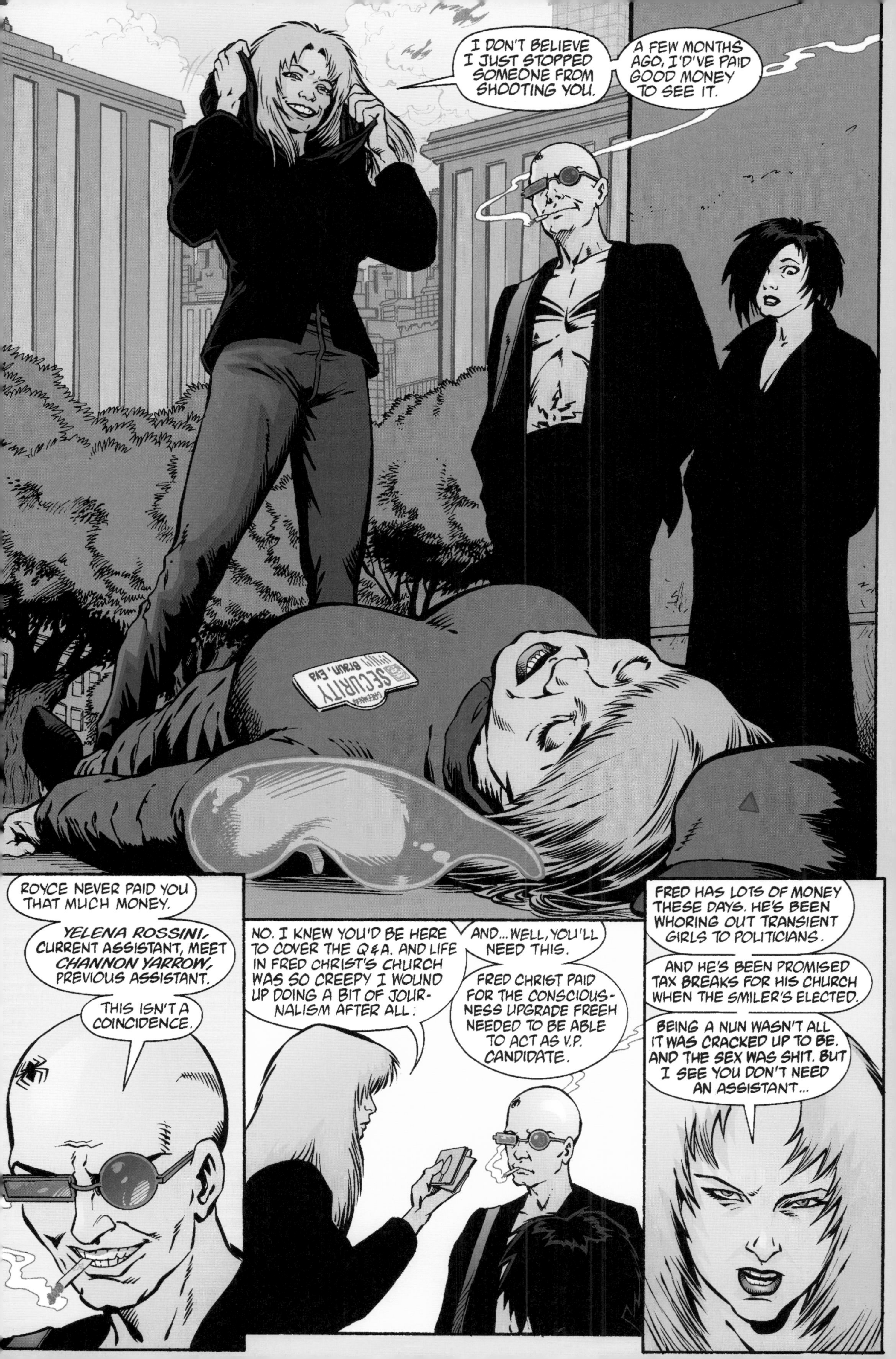

I DON'T BELIEVE I JUST STOPPED SOMEONE FROM SHOOTING YOU.
A FEW MONTHS AGO, I'D'VE PAID GOOD MONEY TO SEE IT.
SECURITY
Braun, Eva
ROYCE NEVER PAID YOU THAT MUCH MONEY.
*YELENA ROSSINI*, CURRENT ASSISTANT, MEET *CHANNON YARROW*, PREVIOUS ASSISTANT.
THIS ISN'T A COINCIDENCE.
NO. I KNEW YOU'D BE HERE TO COVER THE Q&A. AND LIFE IN FRED CHRIST'S CHURCH WAS SO CREEPY I WOUND UP DOING A BIT OF JOURNALISM AFTER ALL:
AND... WELL, YOU'LL NEED THIS.
FRED CHRIST PAID FOR THE CONSCIOUSNESS UPGRADE FREEH NEEDED TO BE ABLE TO ACT AS V.P. CANDIDATE.
FRED HAS LOTS OF MONEY THESE DAYS. HE'S BEEN WHORING OUT TRANSIENT GIRLS TO POLITICIANS.
AND HE'S BEEN PROMISED TAX BREAKS FOR HIS CHURCH WHEN THE SMILER'S ELECTED.
BEING A NUN WASN'T ALL IT WAS CRACKED UP TO BE. AND THE SEX WAS SHIT. BUT I SEE YOU DON'T NEED AN ASSISTANT...

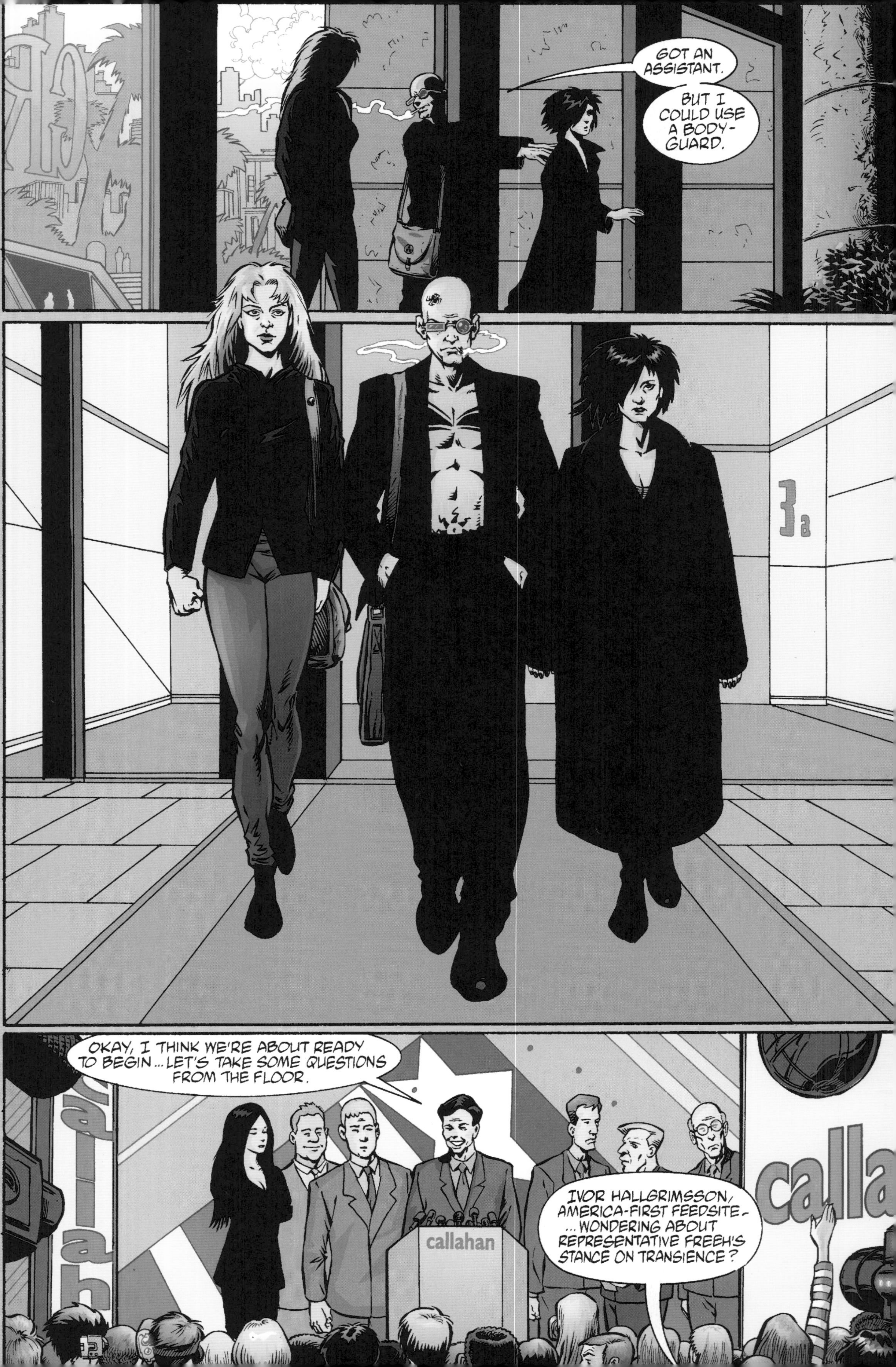
GOT AN ASSISTANT.
BUT I COULD USE A BODY-GUARD.
3a
OKAY, I THINK WE'RE ABOUT READY TO BEGIN... LET'S TAKE SOME QUESTIONS FROM THE FLOOR.
callahan
IVOR HALLGRIMSSON, AMERICA-FIRST FEEDSITE-... WONDERING ABOUT REPRESENTATIVE FREEH'S STANCE ON TRANSIENCE?

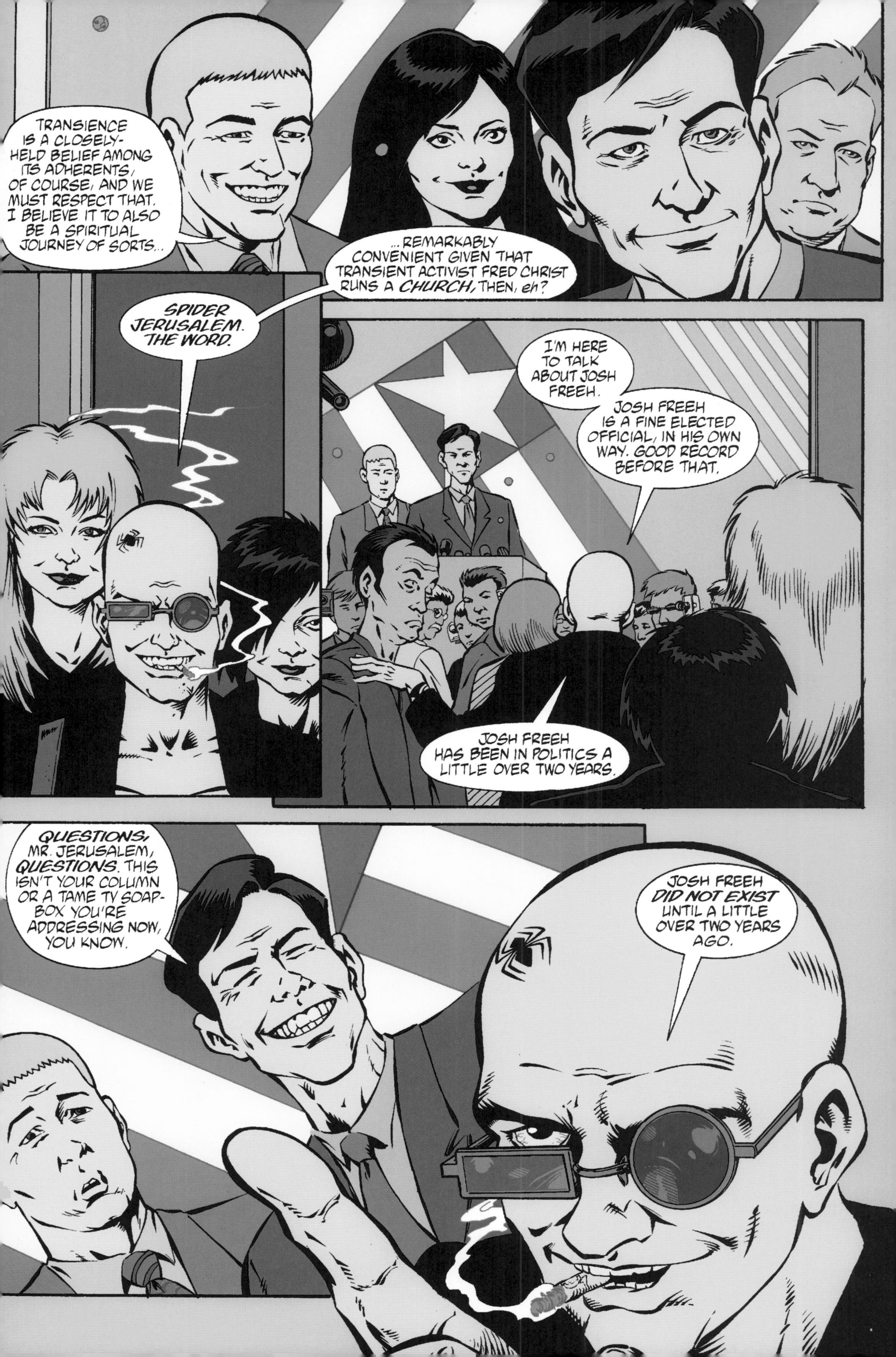
TRANSIENCE IS A CLOSELY-HELD BELIEF AMONG ITS ADHERENTS, OF COURSE, AND WE MUST RESPECT THAT. I BELIEVE IT TO ALSO BE A SPIRITUAL JOURNEY OF SORTS...
...REMARKABLY CONVENIENT GIVEN THAT TRANSIENT ACTIVIST FRED CHRIST RUNS A CHURCH, THEN, eh?
SPIDER JERUSALEM. THE WORD.
I'M HERE TO TALK ABOUT JOSH FREEH.
JOSH FREEH IS A FINE ELECTED OFFICIAL, IN HIS OWN WAY. GOOD RECORD BEFORE THAT.
JOSH FREEH HAS BEEN IN POLITICS A LITTLE OVER TWO YEARS.
QUESTIONS, MR. JERUSALEM, QUESTIONS. THIS ISN'T YOUR COLUMN OR A TAME TV SOAP-BOX YOU'RE ADDRESSING NOW, YOU KNOW.
JOSH FREEH DID NOT EXIST UNTIL A LITTLE OVER TWO YEARS AGO.

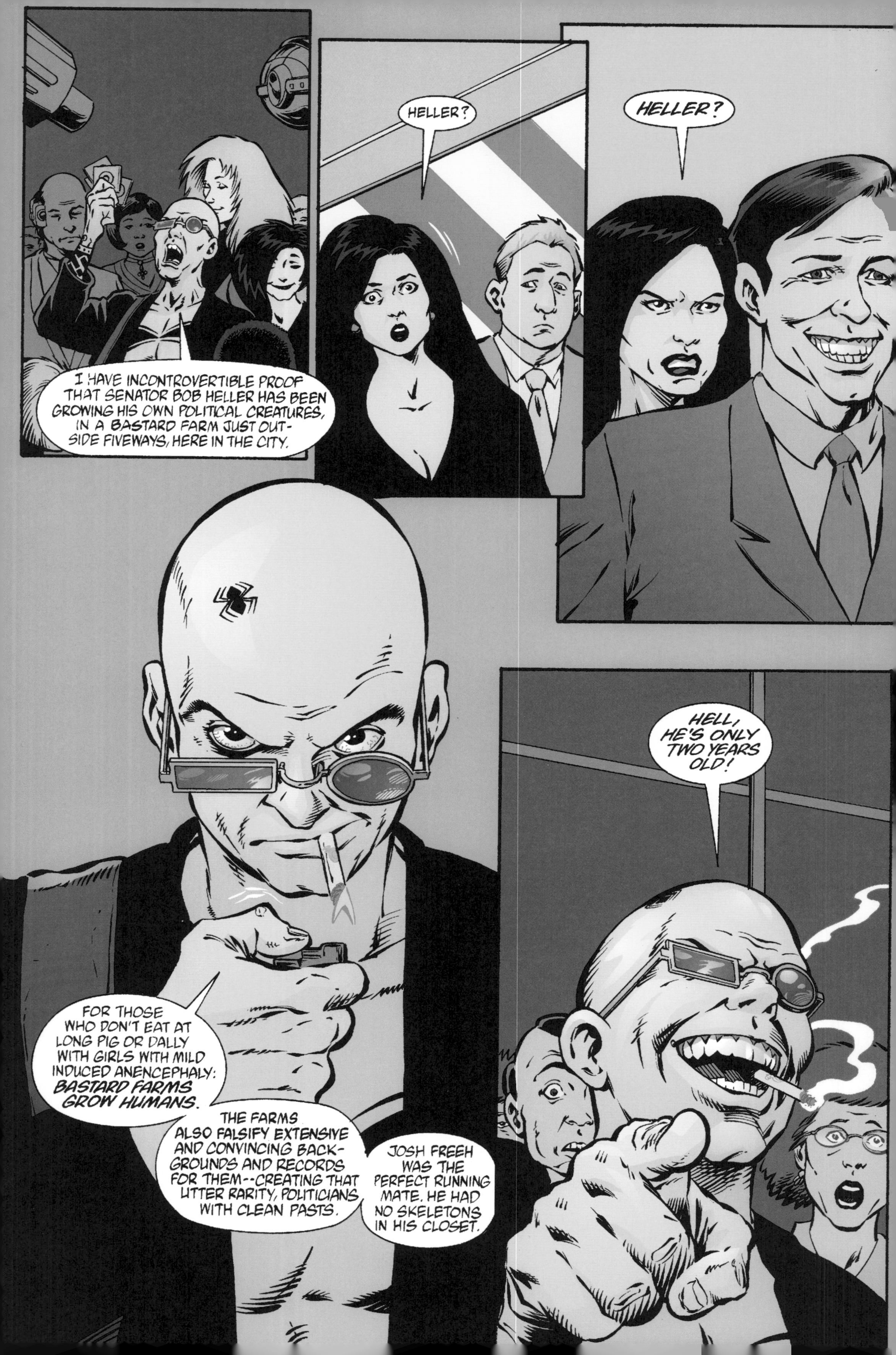
I HAVE INCONTROVERTIBLE PROOF THAT SENATOR BOB HELLER HAS BEEN GROWING HIS OWN POLITICAL CREATURES, IN A BASTARD FARM JUST OUTSIDE FIVEWAYS, HERE IN THE CITY.
HELLER?
HELLER?
FOR THOSE WHO DON'T EAT AT LONG PIG OR DALLY WITH GIRLS WITH MILD INDUCED ANENCEPHALY: BASTARD FARMS GROW HUMANS.
THE FARMS ALSO FALSIFY EXTENSIVE AND CONVINCING BACKGROUNDS AND RECORDS FOR THEM--CREATING THAT UTTER RARITY, POLITICIANS WITH CLEAN PASTS.
JOSH FREEH WAS THE PERFECT RUNNING MATE. HE HAD NO SKELETONS IN HIS CLOSET.
HELL, HE'S ONLY TWO YEARS OLD!

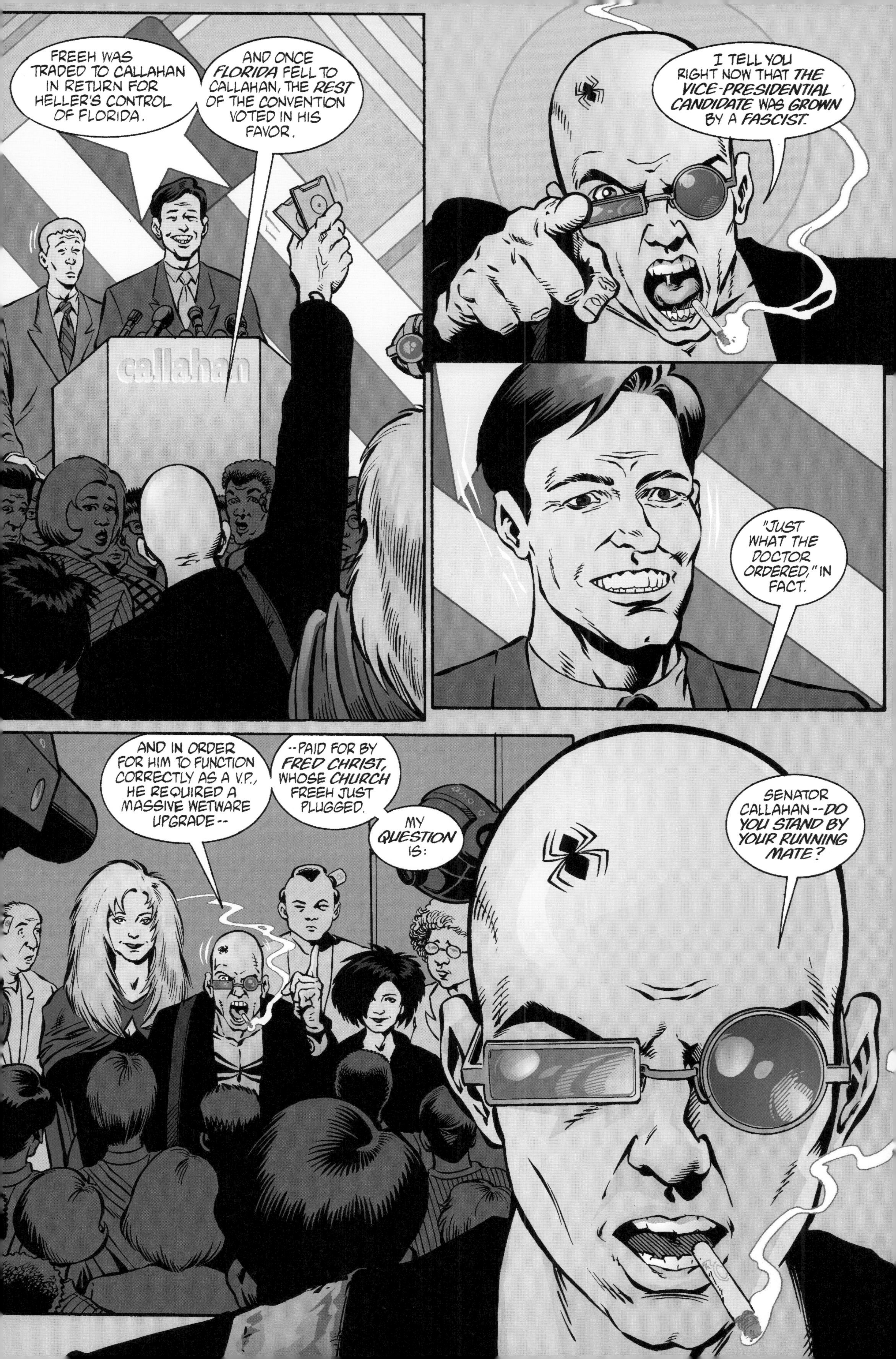
FREEH WAS TRADED TO CALLAHAN IN RETURN FOR HELLER'S CONTROL OF FLORIDA.
AND ONCE *FLORIDA* FELL TO CALLAHAN, THE *REST* OF THE CONVENTION VOTED IN HIS FAVOR.
callahan
I TELL YOU RIGHT NOW THAT *THE VICE-PRESIDENTIAL CANDIDATE* WAS *GROWN* BY A *FASCIST.*
"JUST WHAT THE DOCTOR ORDERED," IN FACT.
AND IN ORDER FOR HIM TO FUNCTION CORRECTLY AS A V.P., HE REQUIRED A MASSIVE WETWARE UPGRADE--
--PAID FOR BY *FRED CHRIST,* WHOSE *CHURCH* FREEH JUST PLUGGED.
MY *QUESTION* IS:
SENATOR CALLAHAN--*DO YOU STAND BY YOUR RUNNING MATE?*

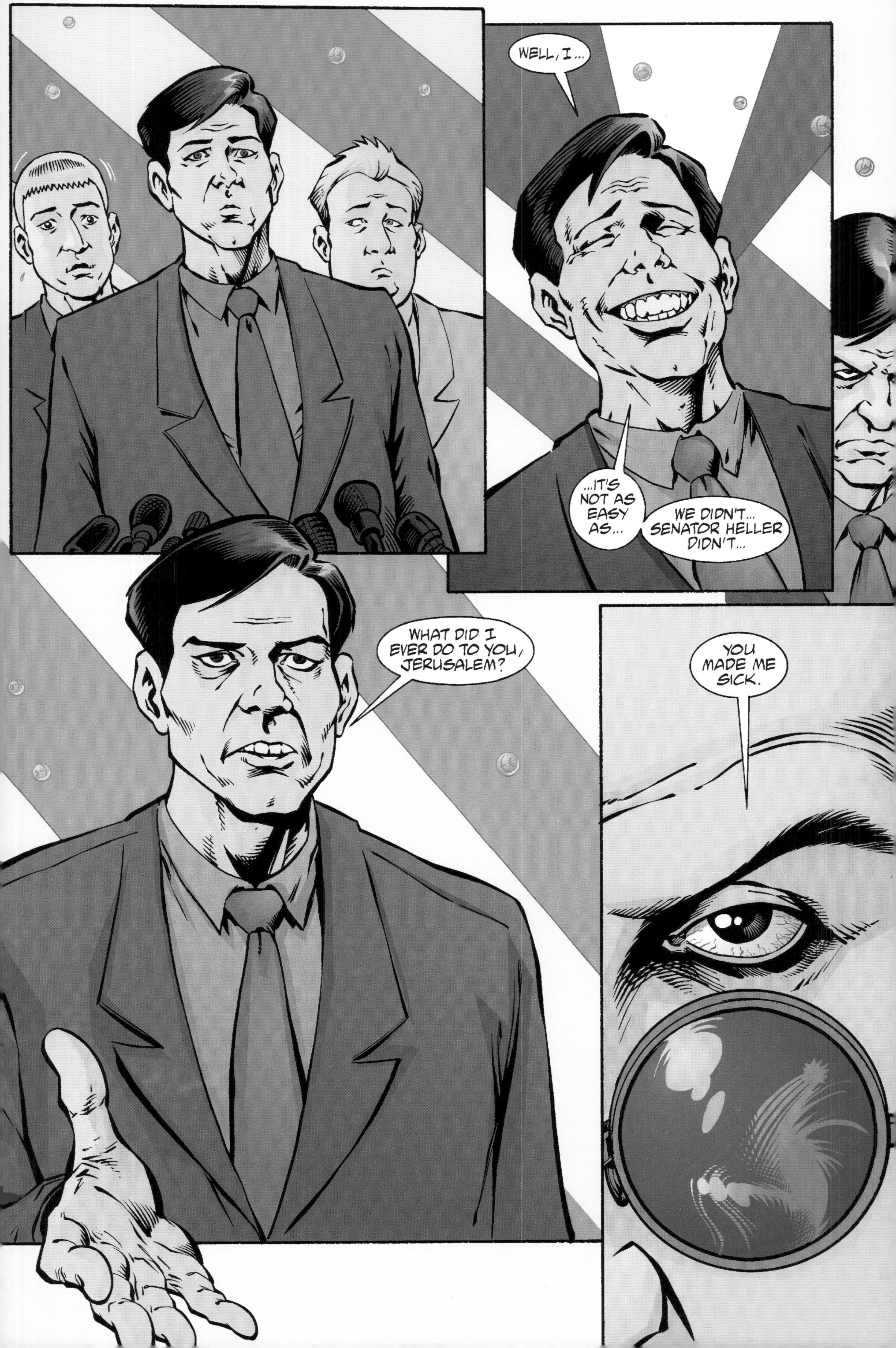
WELL, I...
...IT'S NOT AS EASY AS...
WE DIDN'T... SENATOR HELLER DIDN'T...
WHAT DID I EVER DO TO YOU, JERUSALEM?
YOU MADE ME SICK.

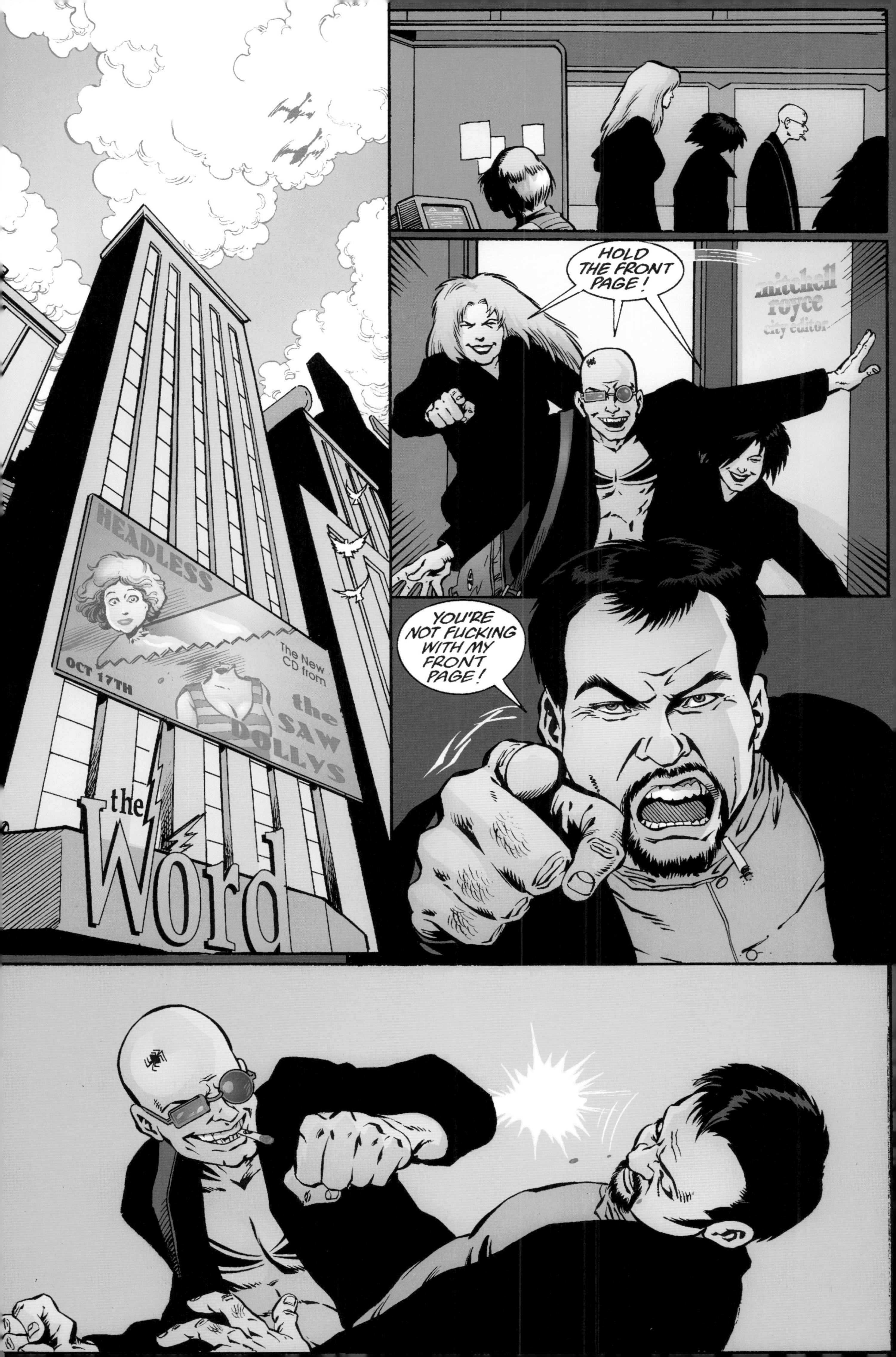
HEADLESS
OCT 17TH
The New CD from
the SAW DOLLYS
the Word
HOLD THE FRONT PAGE!
mitchell royce city editor
YOU'RE NOT FUCKING WITH MY FRONT PAGE!

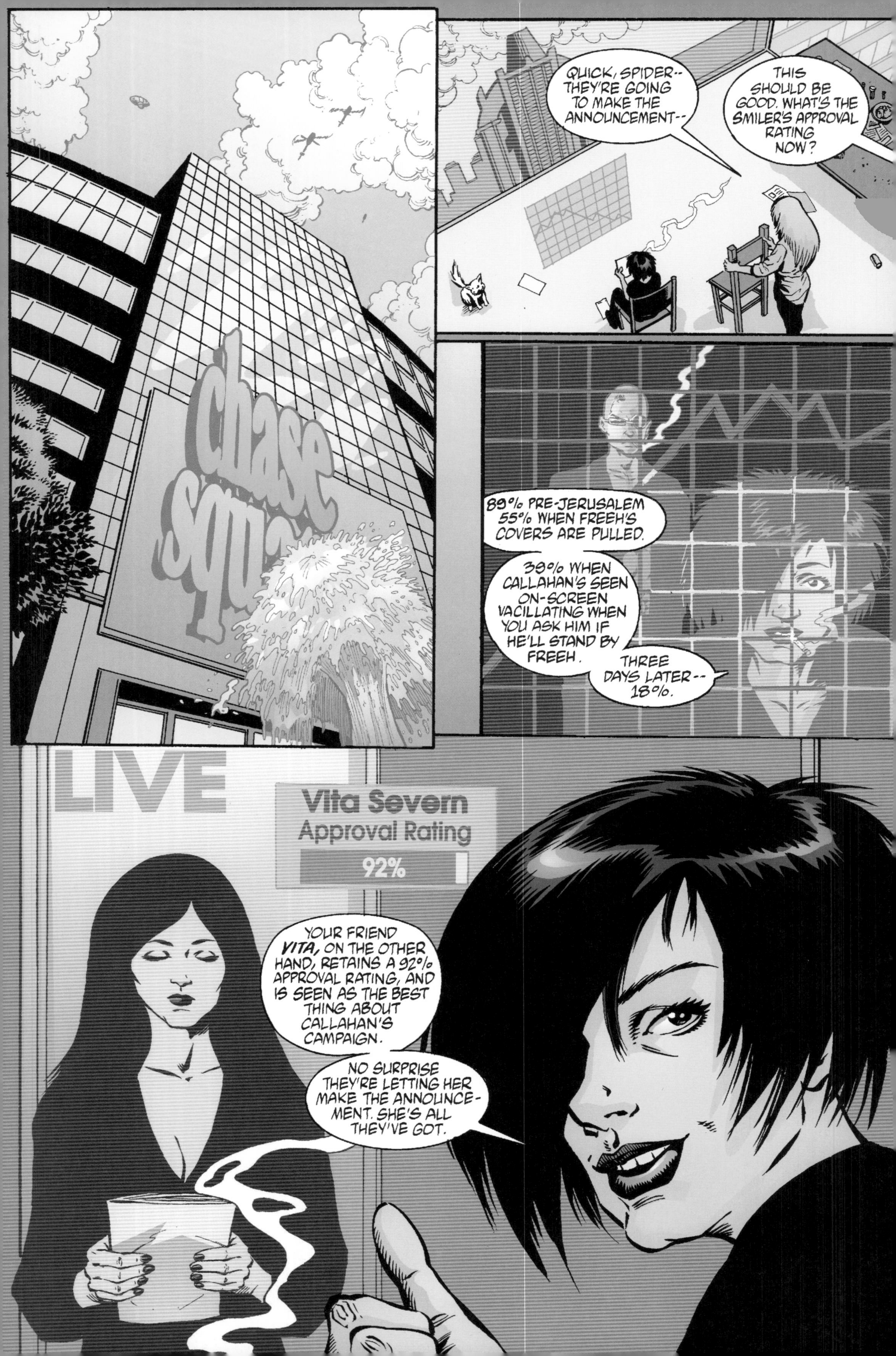
chase squ
QUICK, SPIDER-- THEY'RE GOING TO MAKE THE ANNOUNCEMENT--
THIS SHOULD BE GOOD. WHAT'S THE SMILER'S APPROVAL RATING NOW?
89% PRE-JERUSALEM 55% WHEN FREEH'S COVERS ARE PULLED.
39% WHEN CALLAHAN'S SEEN ON-SCREEN VACILLATING WHEN YOU ASK HIM IF HE'LL STAND BY FREEH.
THREE DAYS LATER-- 18%.
LIVE
Vita Severn
Approval Rating
92%
YOUR FRIEND VITA, ON THE OTHER HAND, RETAINS A 92% APPROVAL RATING, AND IS SEEN AS THE BEST THING ABOUT CALLAHAN'S CAMPAIGN.
NO SURPRISE THEY'RE LETTING HER MAKE THE ANNOUNCE-MENT. SHE'S ALL THEY'VE GOT.

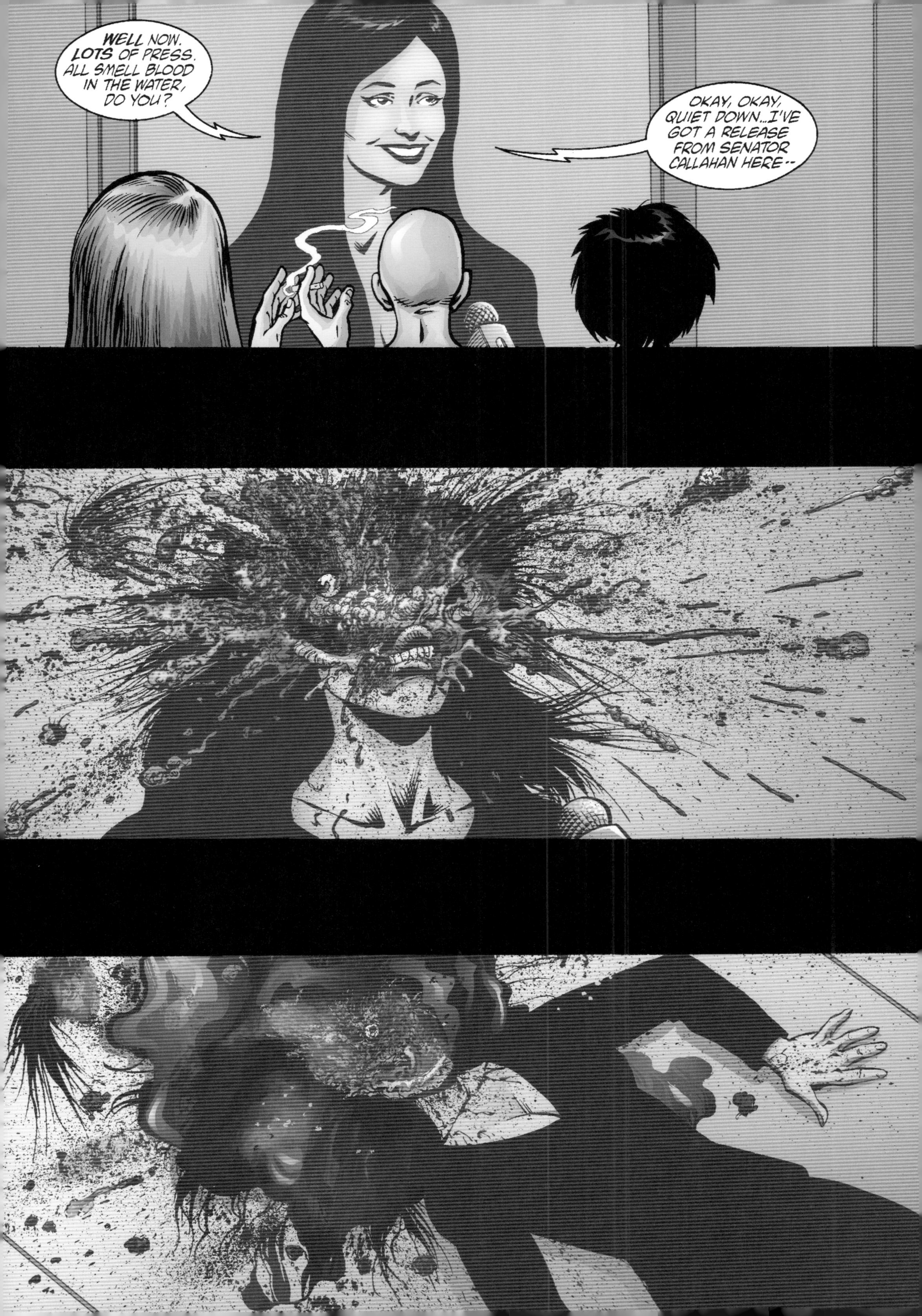
WELL NOW. LOTS OF PRESS. ALL SMELL BLOOD IN THE WATER, DO YOU?
OKAY, OKAY, QUIET DOWN...I'VE GOT A RELEASE FROM SENATOR CALLAHAN HERE--

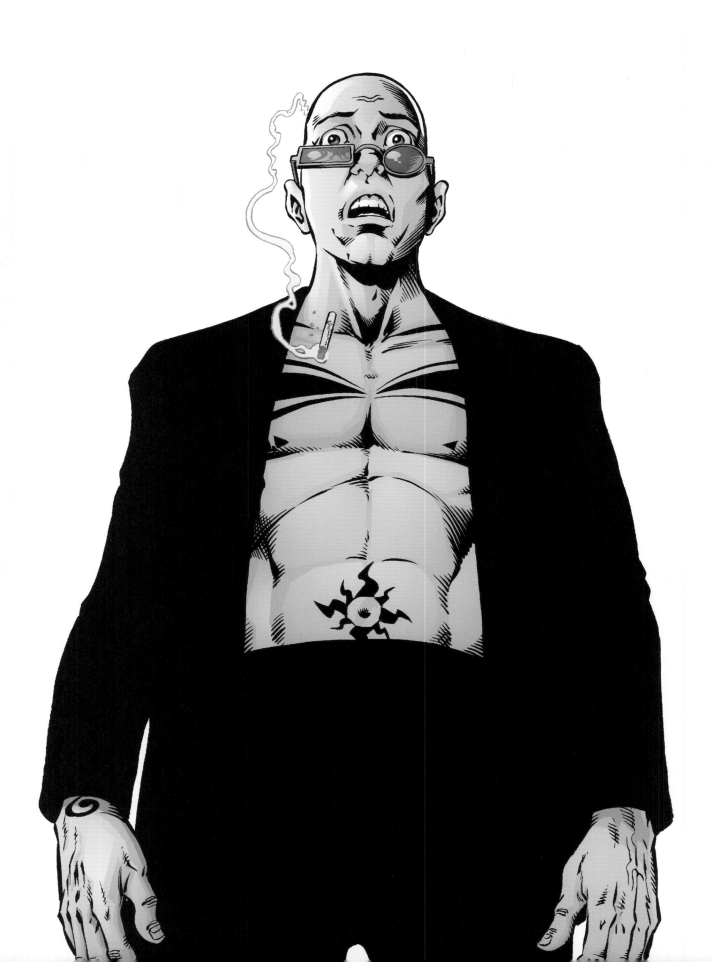

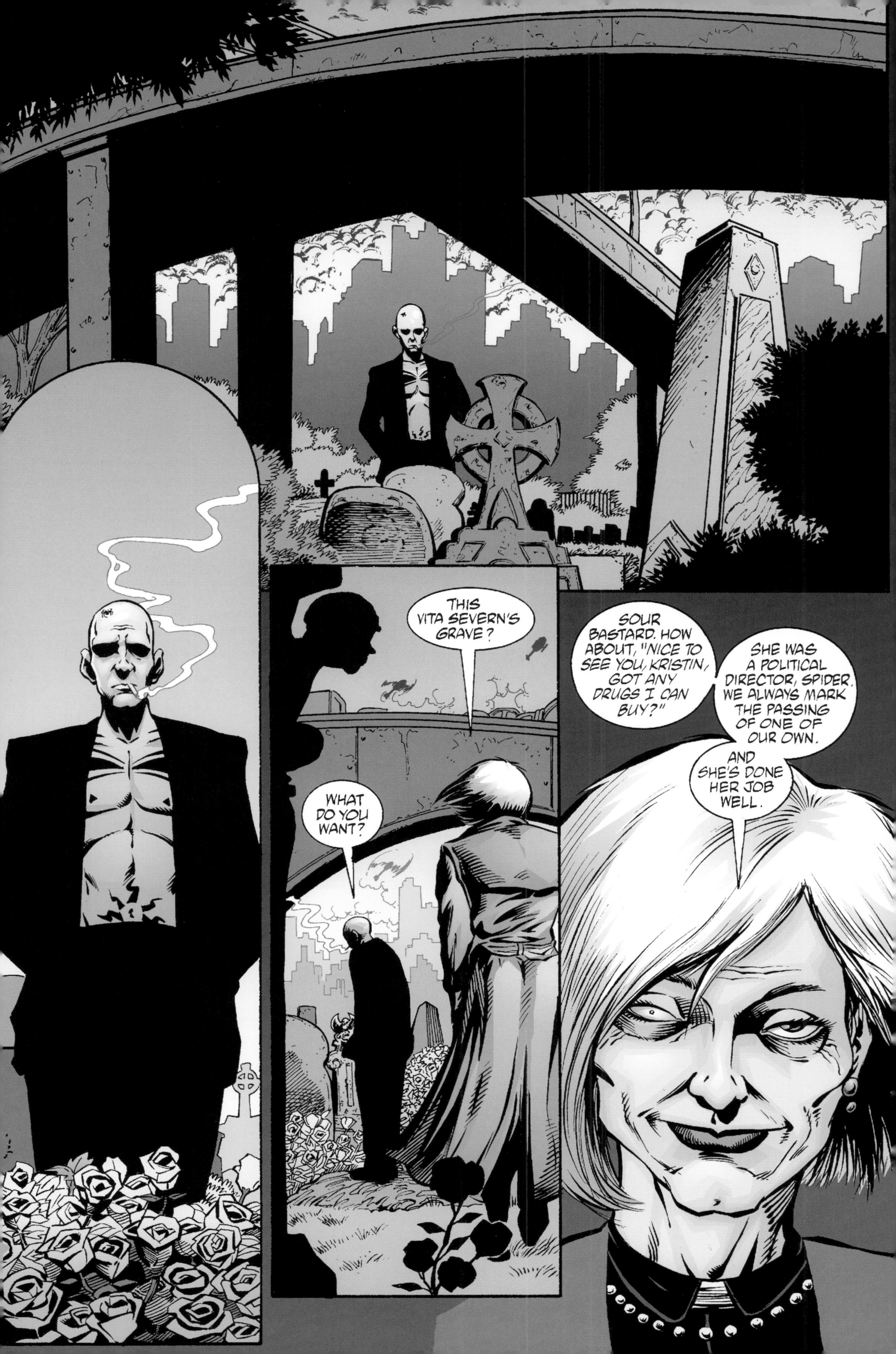
THIS VITA SEVERN'S GRAVE?
WHAT DO YOU WANT?
SOUR BASTARD. HOW ABOUT, "NICE TO SEE YOU, KRISTIN, GOT ANY DRUGS I CAN BUY?"
SHE WAS A POLITICAL DIRECTOR, SPIDER. WE ALWAYS MARK THE PASSING OF ONE OF OUR OWN.
AND SHE'S DONE HER JOB WELL.

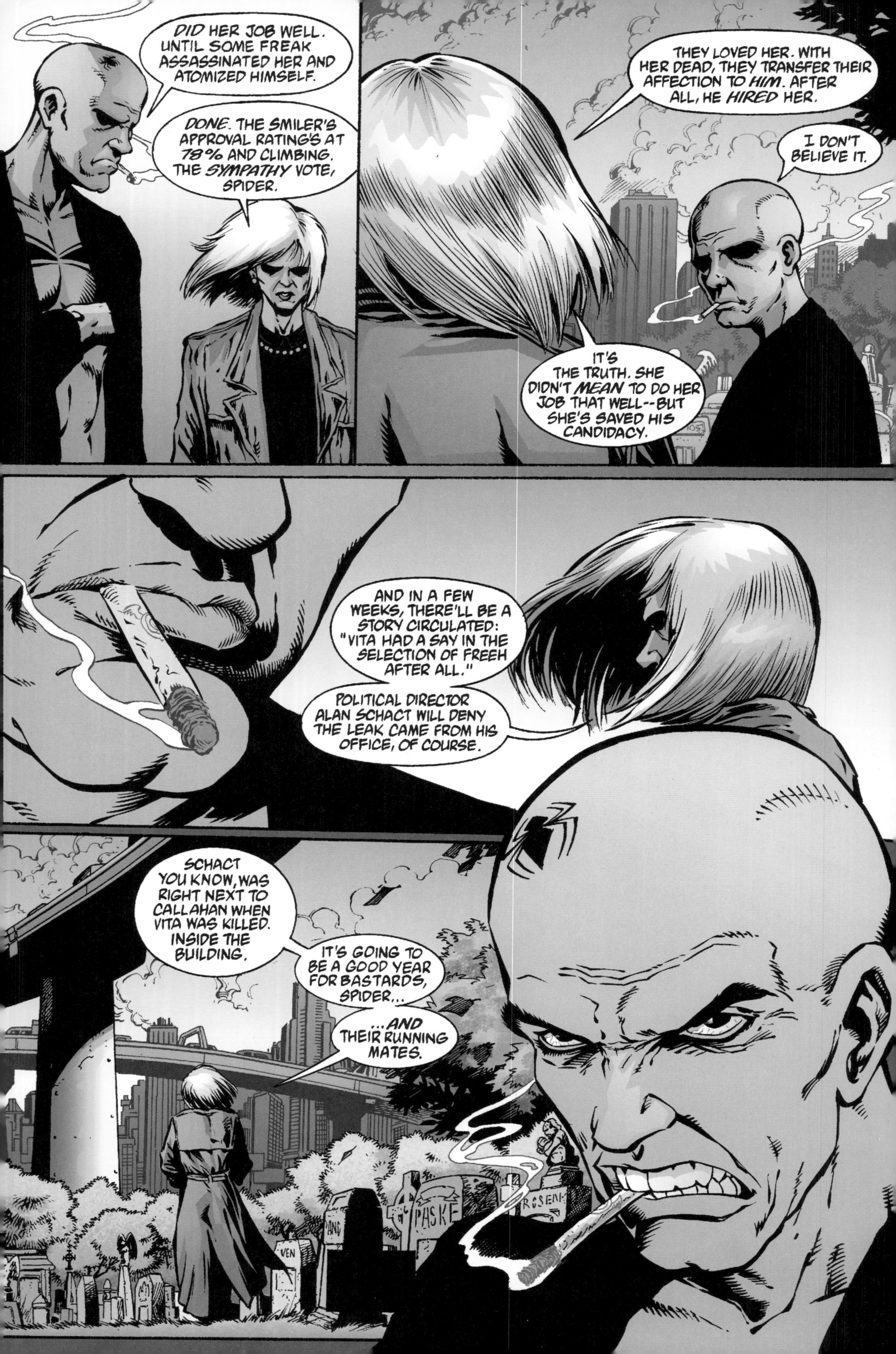
DID HER JOB WELL. UNTIL SOME FREAK ASSASSINATED HER AND ATOMIZED HIMSELF.
DONE. THE SMILER'S APPROVAL RATING'S AT 78% AND CLIMBING. THE SYMPATHY VOTE, SPIDER.
THEY LOVED HER. WITH HER DEAD, THEY TRANSFER THEIR AFFECTION TO HIM. AFTER ALL, HE HIRED HER.
I DON'T BELIEVE IT.
IT'S THE TRUTH. SHE DIDN'T MEAN TO DO HER JOB THAT WELL--BUT SHE'S SAVED HIS CANDIDACY.
AND IN A FEW WEEKS, THERE'LL BE A STORY CIRCULATED: "VITA HAD A SAY IN THE SELECTION OF FREEH AFTER ALL."
POLITICAL DIRECTOR ALAN SCHACT WILL DENY THE LEAK CAME FROM HIS OFFICE, OF COURSE.
SCHACT YOU KNOW, WAS RIGHT NEXT TO CALLAHAN WHEN VITA WAS KILLED. INSIDE THE BUILDING.
IT'S GOING TO BE A GOOD YEAR FOR BASTARDS, SPIDER...
...AND THEIR RUNNING MATES.

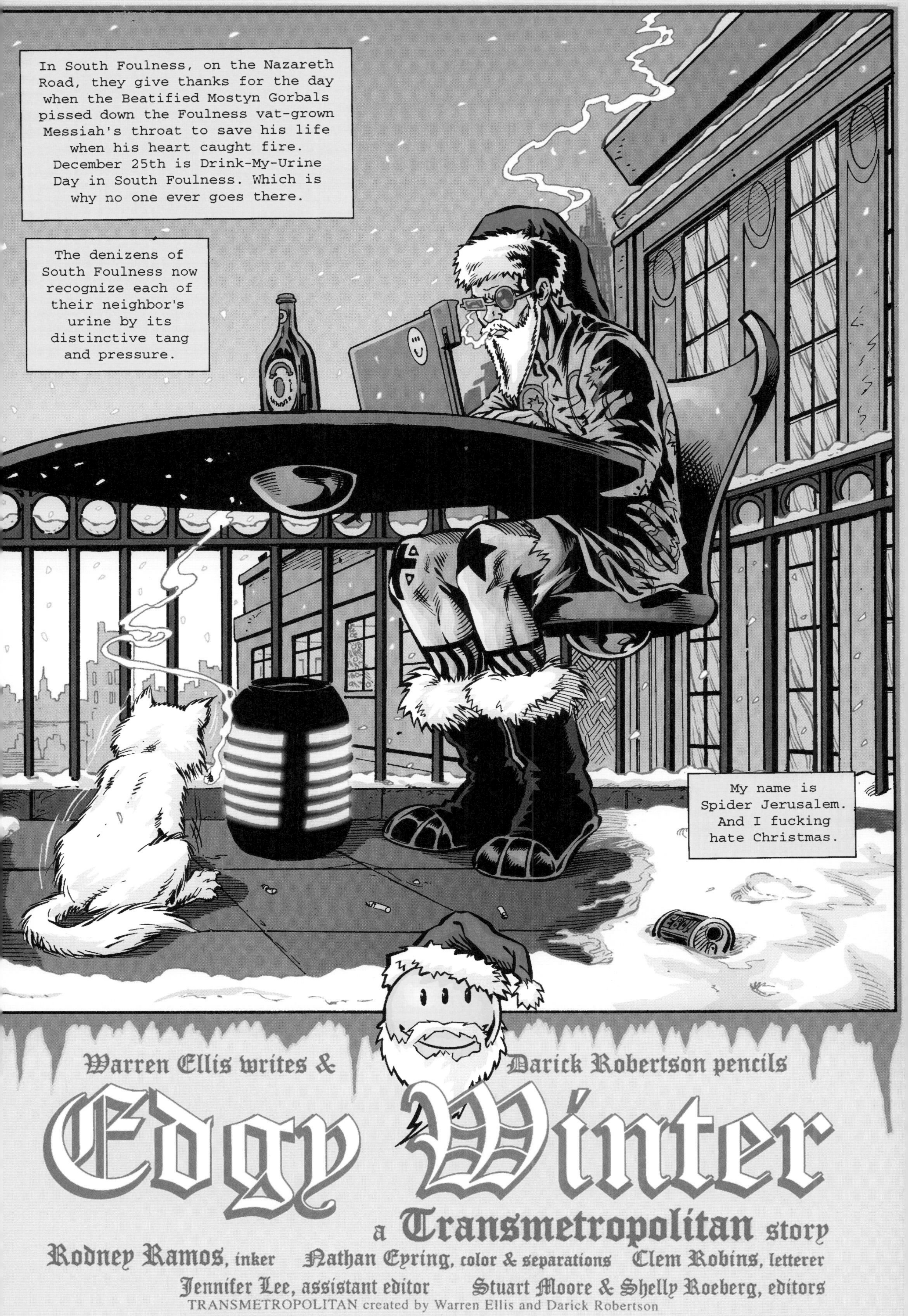
In South Foulness, on the Nazareth Road, they give thanks for the day when the Beatified Mostyn Gorbals pissed down the Foulness vat-grown Messiah's throat to save his life when his heart caught fire. December 25th is Drink-My-Urine Day in South Foulness. Which is why no one ever goes there.
The denizens of South Foulness now recognize each of their neighbor's urine by its distinctive tang and pressure.
My name is Spider Jerusalem. And I fucking hate Christmas.

Warren Ellis writes & Darick Robertson pencils

# Edgy Winter

a Transmetropolitan story

Rodney Ramos, inker Nathan Eyring, color & separations Clem Robins, letterer

Jennifer Lee, assistant editor Stuart Moore & Shelly Roeberg, editors

TRANSMETROPOLITAN created by Warren Ellis and Darick Robertson

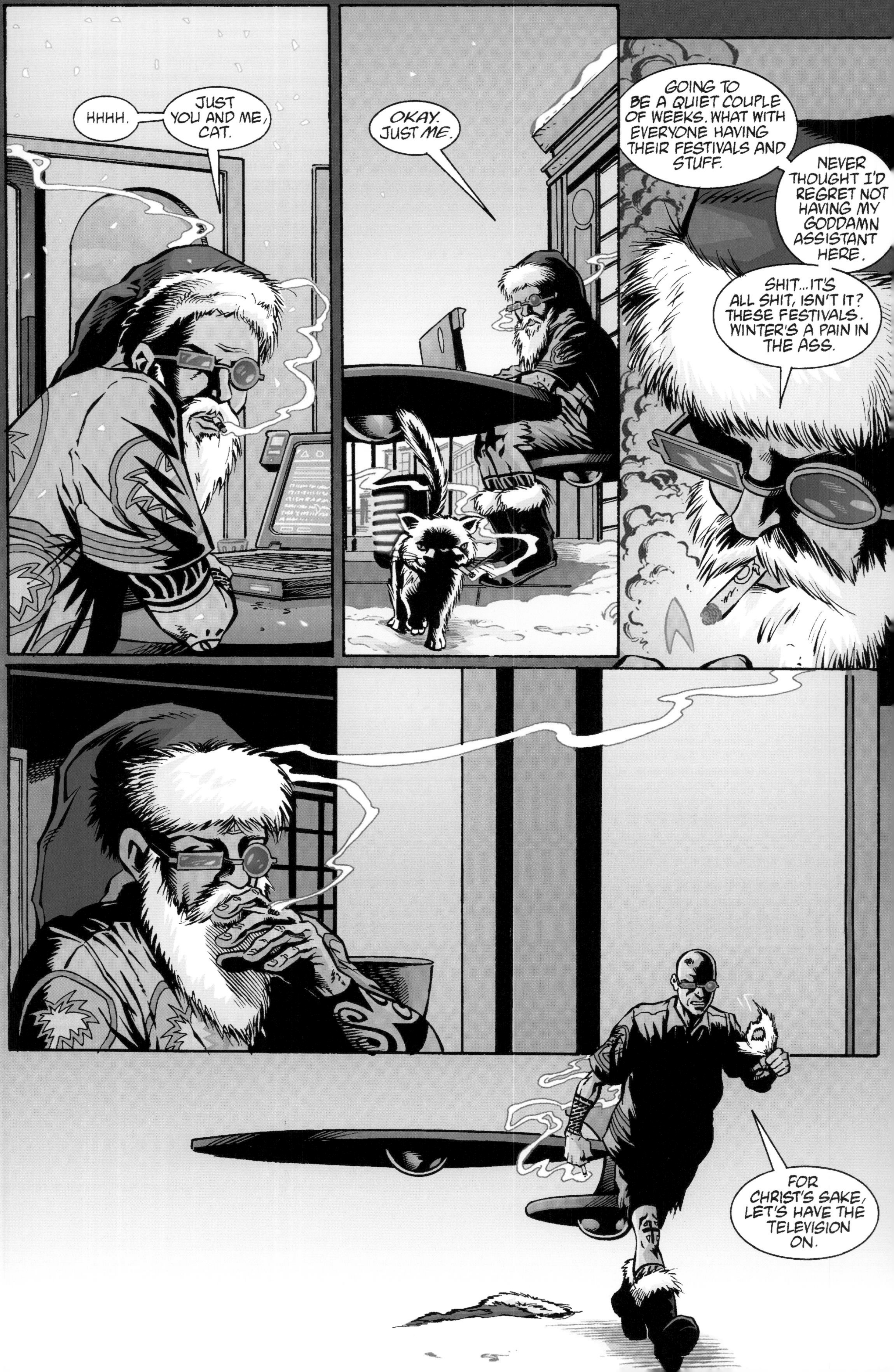
HHHH.
JUST YOU AND ME, CAT.
OKAY. JUST *ME*.
GOING TO BE A QUIET COUPLE OF WEEKS. WHAT WITH EVERYONE HAVING THEIR FESTIVALS AND STUFF.
NEVER THOUGHT I'D REGRET NOT HAVING MY GODDAMN ASSISTANT HERE.
SHIT...IT'S ALL SHIT, ISN'T IT? THESE FESTIVALS. WINTER'S A PAIN IN THE ASS.
FOR CHRIST'S SAKE, LET'S HAVE THE TELEVISION ON.

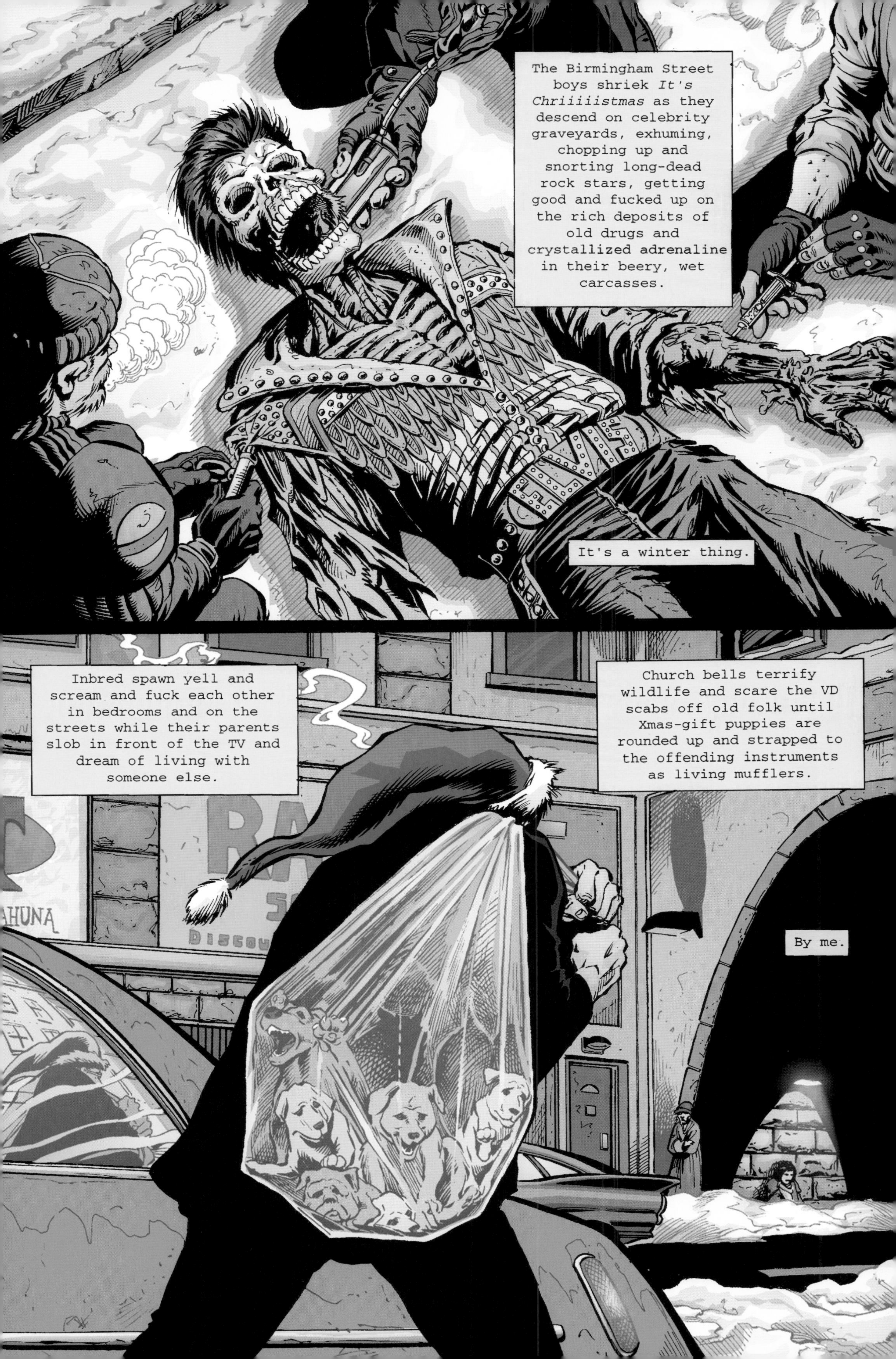
The Birmingham Street boys shriek *It's Chriiiiistmas* as they descend on celebrity graveyards, exhuming, chopping up and snorting long-dead rock stars, getting good and fucked up on the rich deposits of old drugs and crystallized adrenaline in their beery, wet carcasses.
It's a winter thing.
Inbred spawn yell and scream and fuck each other in bedrooms and on the streets while their parents slob in front of the TV and dream of living with someone else.
Church bells terrify wildlife and scare the VD scabs off old folk until Xmas-gift puppies are rounded up and strapped to the offending instruments as living mufflers.
By me.

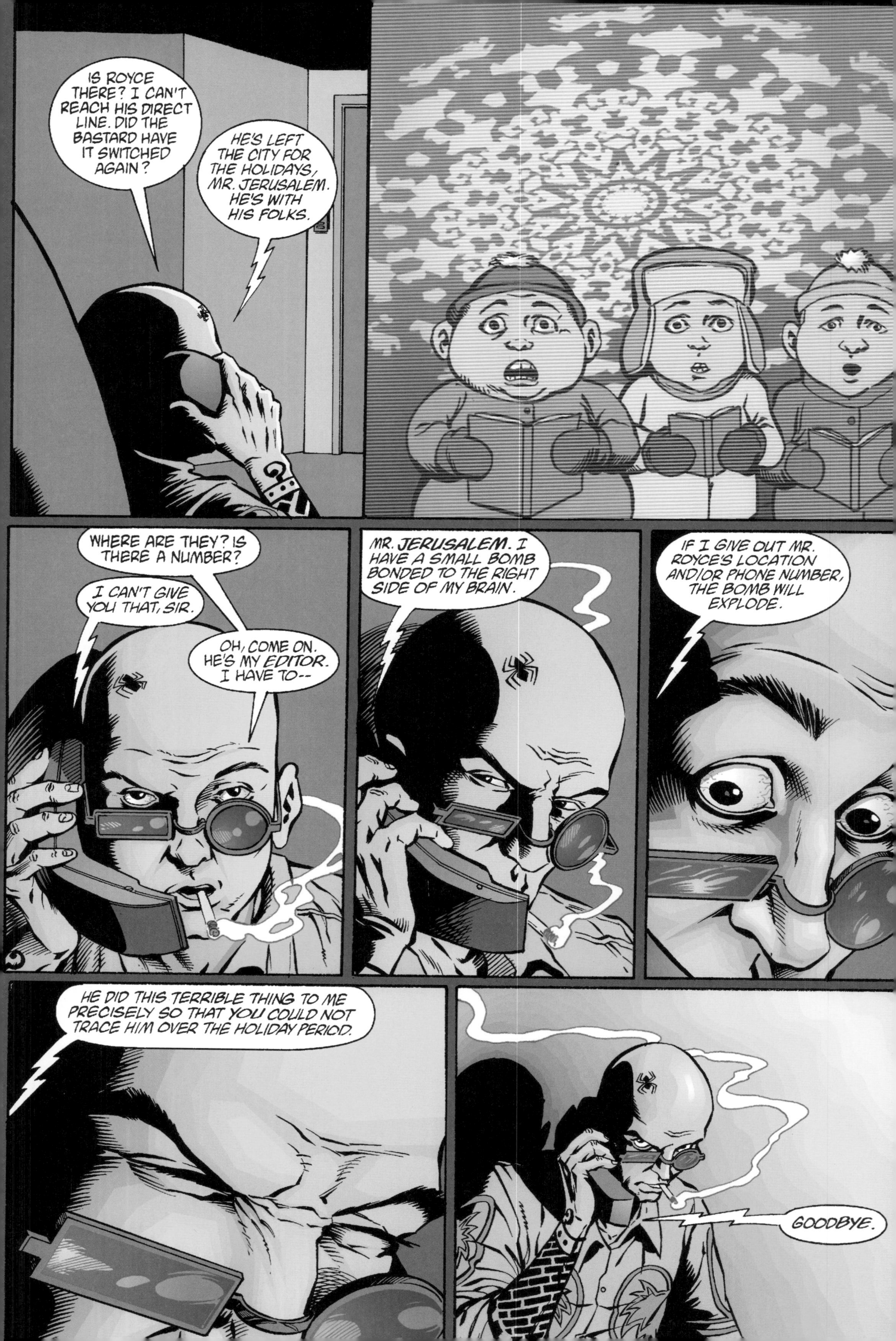
IS ROYCE THERE? I CAN'T REACH HIS DIRECT LINE. DID THE BASTARD HAVE IT SWITCHED AGAIN?
HE'S LEFT THE CITY FOR THE HOLIDAYS, MR. JERUSALEM. HE'S WITH HIS FOLKS.
WHERE ARE THEY? IS THERE A NUMBER?
I CAN'T GIVE YOU THAT, SIR.
OH, COME ON. HE'S MY EDITOR. I HAVE TO--
MR. JERUSALEM. I HAVE A SMALL BOMB BONDED TO THE RIGHT SIDE OF MY BRAIN.
IF I GIVE OUT MR. ROYCE'S LOCATION AND/OR PHONE NUMBER, THE BOMB WILL EXPLODE.
HE DID THIS TERRIBLE THING TO ME PRECISELY SO THAT YOU COULD NOT TRACE HIM OVER THE HOLIDAY PERIOD.
GOODBYE.

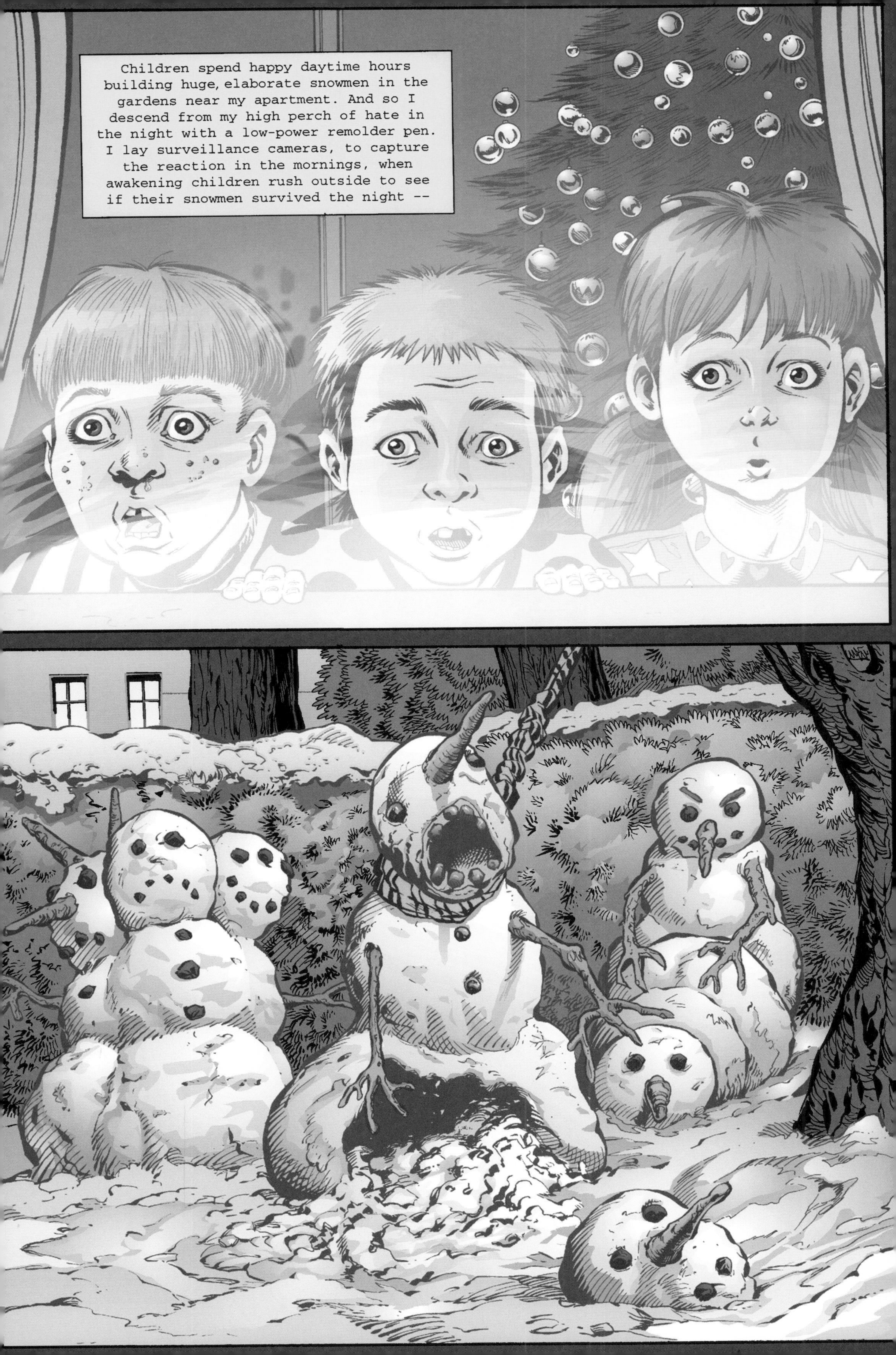
Children spend happy daytime hours building huge, elaborate snowmen in the gardens near my apartment. And so I descend from my high perch of hate in the night with a low-power remolder pen. I lay surveillance cameras, to capture the reaction in the mornings, when awakening children rush outside to see if their snowmen survived the night --

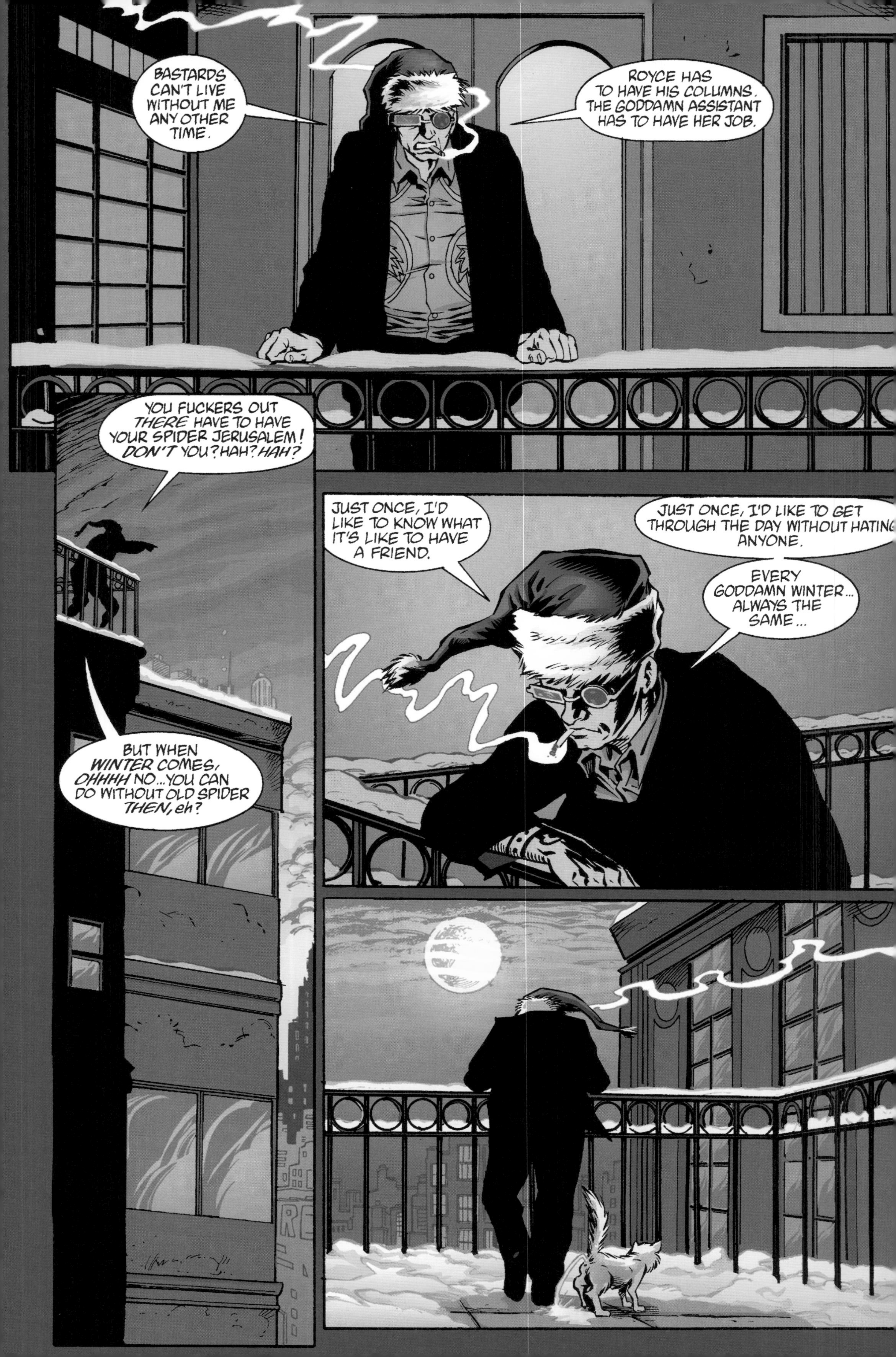
BASTARDS CAN'T LIVE WITHOUT ME ANY OTHER TIME.
ROYCE HAS TO HAVE HIS COLUMNS. THE GODDAMN ASSISTANT HAS TO HAVE HER JOB.
YOU FUCKERS OUT THERE HAVE TO HAVE YOUR SPIDER JERUSALEM! DON'T YOU? HAH? HAH?
BUT WHEN WINTER COMES, OHHHH NO...YOU CAN DO WITHOUT OLD SPIDER THEN, eh?
JUST ONCE, I'D LIKE TO KNOW WHAT IT'S LIKE TO HAVE A FRIEND.
JUST ONCE, I'D LIKE TO GET THROUGH THE DAY WITHOUT HATING ANYONE.
EVERY GODDAMN WINTER... ALWAYS THE SAME...

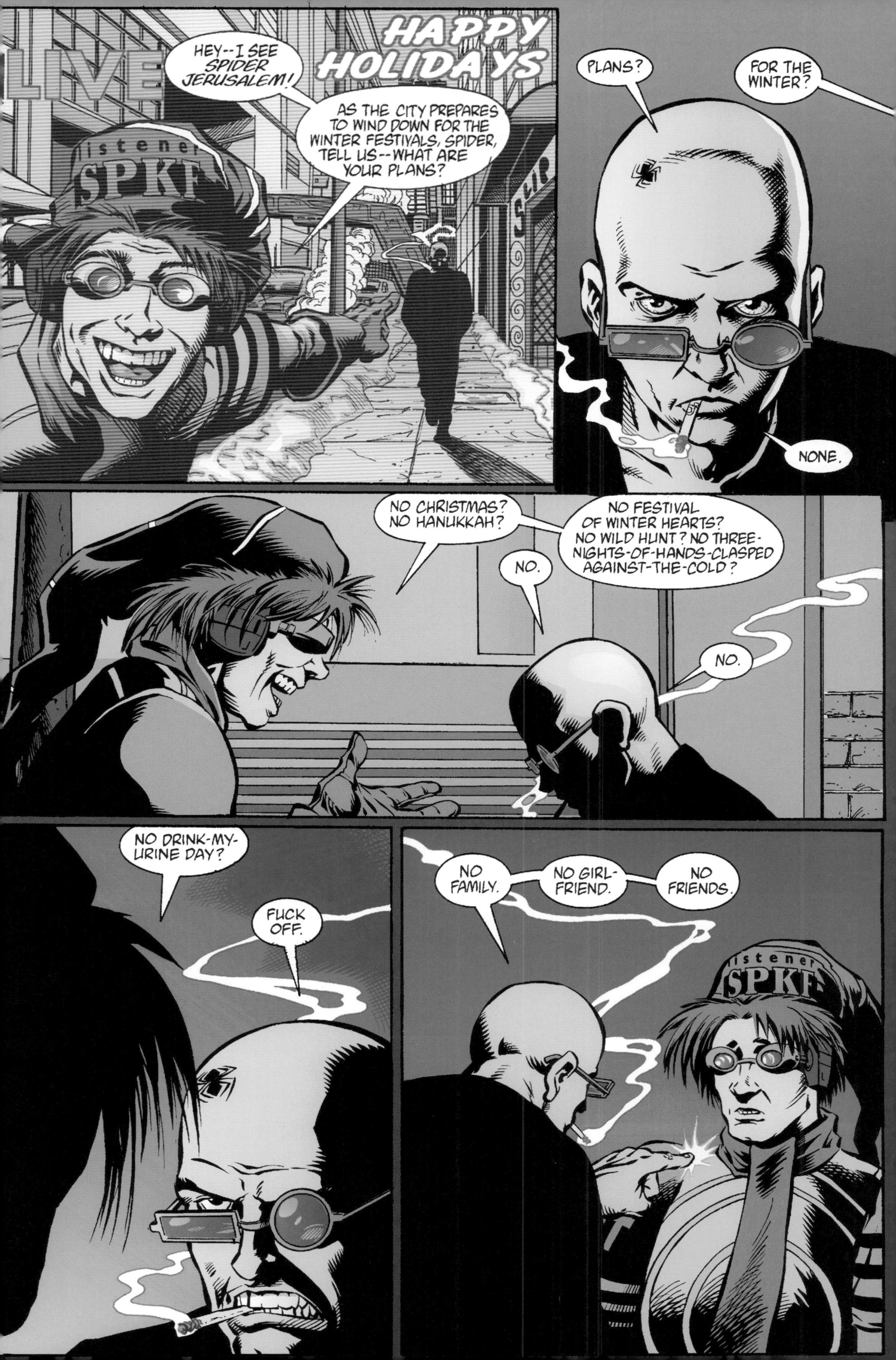
LIVE
HAPPY HOLIDAYS
HEY--I SEE SPIDER JERUSALEM!
listener SPKF
AS THE CITY PREPARES TO WIND DOWN FOR THE WINTER FESTIVALS, SPIDER, TELL US--WHAT ARE YOUR PLANS?
PLANS?
FOR THE WINTER?
NONE.
NO CHRISTMAS? NO HANUKKAH?
NO FESTIVAL OF WINTER HEARTS? NO WILD HUNT? NO THREE-NIGHTS-OF-HANDS-CLASPED AGAINST-THE-COLD?
NO.
NO.
NO DRINK-MY-URINE DAY?
FUCK OFF.
NO FAMILY.
NO GIRL-FRIEND.
NO FRIENDS.
listener SPKF

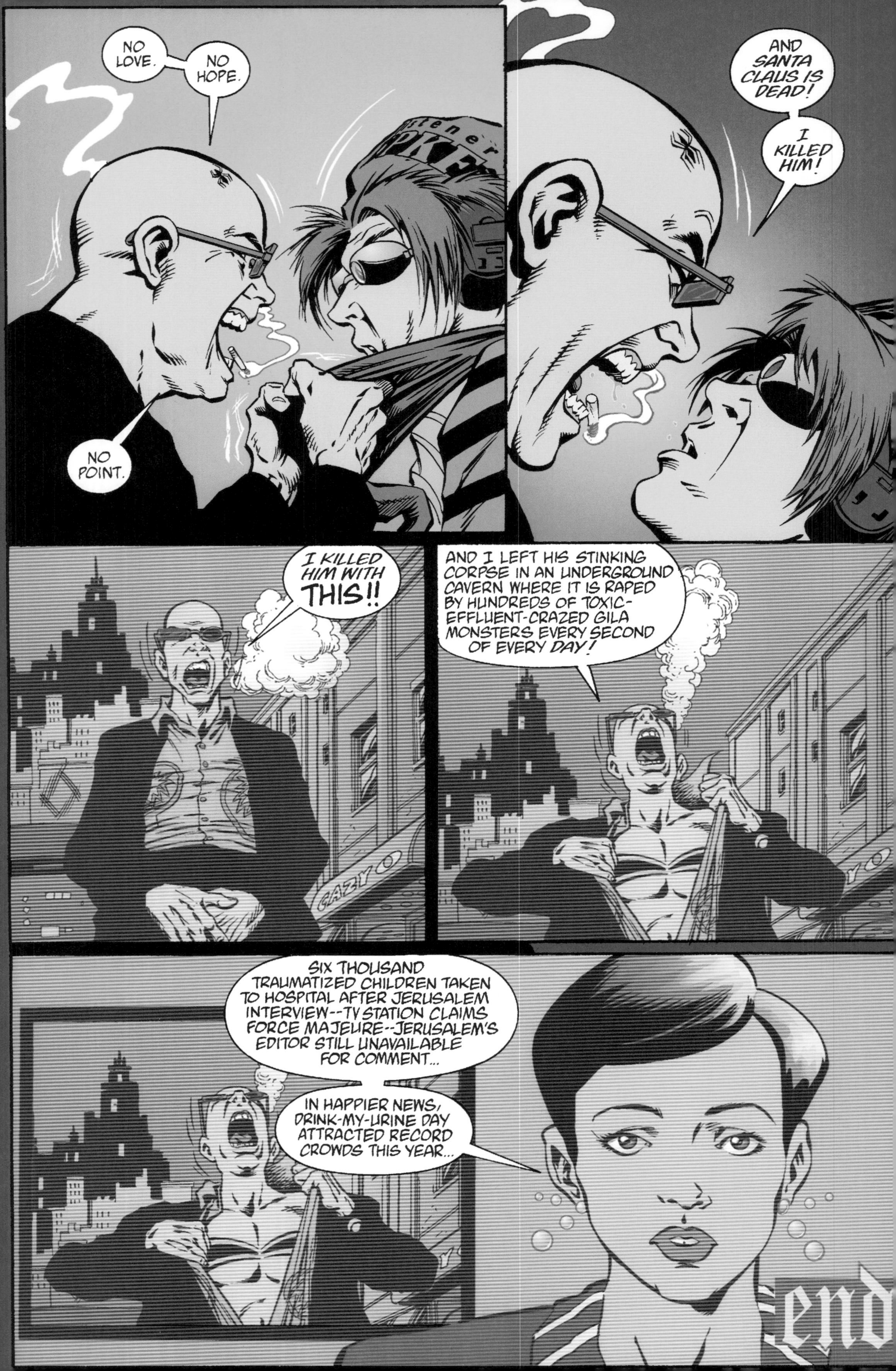
NO LOVE.
NO HOPE.
NO POINT.
AND SANTA CLAUS IS DEAD!
I KILLED HIM!
I KILLED HIM WITH THIS!!
AND I LEFT HIS STINKING CORPSE IN AN UNDERGROUND CAVERN WHERE IT IS RAPED BY HUNDREDS OF TOXIC-EFFLUENT-CRAZED GILA MONSTERS EVERY SECOND OF EVERY DAY!
SIX THOUSAND TRAUMATIZED CHILDREN TAKEN TO HOSPITAL AFTER JERUSALEM INTERVIEW--TV STATION CLAIMS FORCE MAJEURE--JERUSALEM'S EDITOR STILL UNAVAILABLE FOR COMMENT...
IN HAPPIER NEWS, DRINK-MY-URINE DAY ATTRACTED RECORD CROWDS THIS YEAR...
end

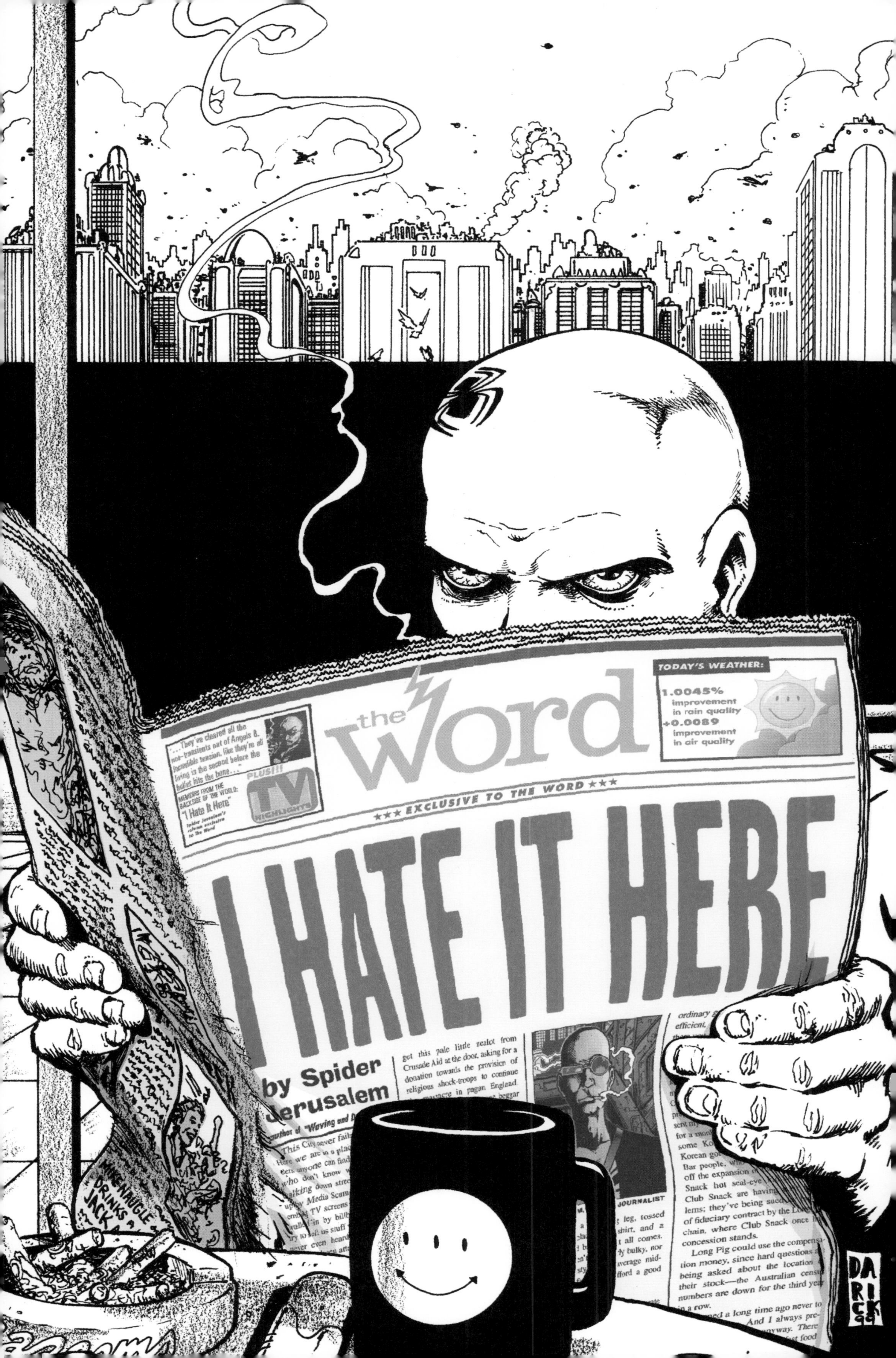

TODAY'S WEATHER:
1.0045% improvement in rain quality
+0.0089 improvement in air quality
the word
"... They've cleared all the non-transients out of Angels 8, incredible tension, like they're all living in the second before the bullet hits the bone..."
MEMOIRS FROM THE BACKSIDE OF THE WORLD: "I Hate It Here"
PLUS!!! TV HIGHLIGHTS
★★★ EXCLUSIVE TO THE WORD ★★★
I HATE IT HERE
by Spider Jerusalem
get this pale little zealot from Crusade Aid at the door, asking for a donation towards the provision of religious shock-troops to continue
JOURNALIST
concession stands.

# TRANSMETROPOLITAN
## I HATE IT HERE

Words by **Warren Ellis**          Colors by **Nathan Eyring**

## INTRODUCTION by SPIDER JERUSALEM

There's nothing more insulting than having to write the introduction to one of your own books.

I mean, the whole point of these things is that someone else comes in to make nice on you, to hype you up to the audience, to make you sound like you're worth listening to.

But no. Here we are at the hour before the book's shot down the wire to the printer -- and I mean we, I've got two editors, three assistants and a VP Publishing standing behind me as I write this -- and I'm having to write my own fucking introduction to what is essentially an excerpt from two and a half years of unremitting pain and horror.

What? You wanted something cuddly and welcoming? Well, you should have hired someone else to do it then, shouldn't you? I told you to get an actor or a singer or someone else with mental problems. Fuck all of you. Every day since I've been back in this endless shithole has been like being repeatedly hit over the head with a club hammer. Every single day. I wake up in the morning and I can feel my brain swelling, bulging up against the thin parts of my skull. If I look in the mirror really closely, I can see where my skin gets sucked in through the tiny cracks in my skull. One day, big chunks of my head are going to burst off and blood and poison will geyser out of my skull into your faces and you'll all choke on my bile and exploded brain-meat.

Before I am done here, you will all taste my brain-meat.

Get off me, you dogfuckers, I'm on a roll, no, don't take my inhaler away, you bastards

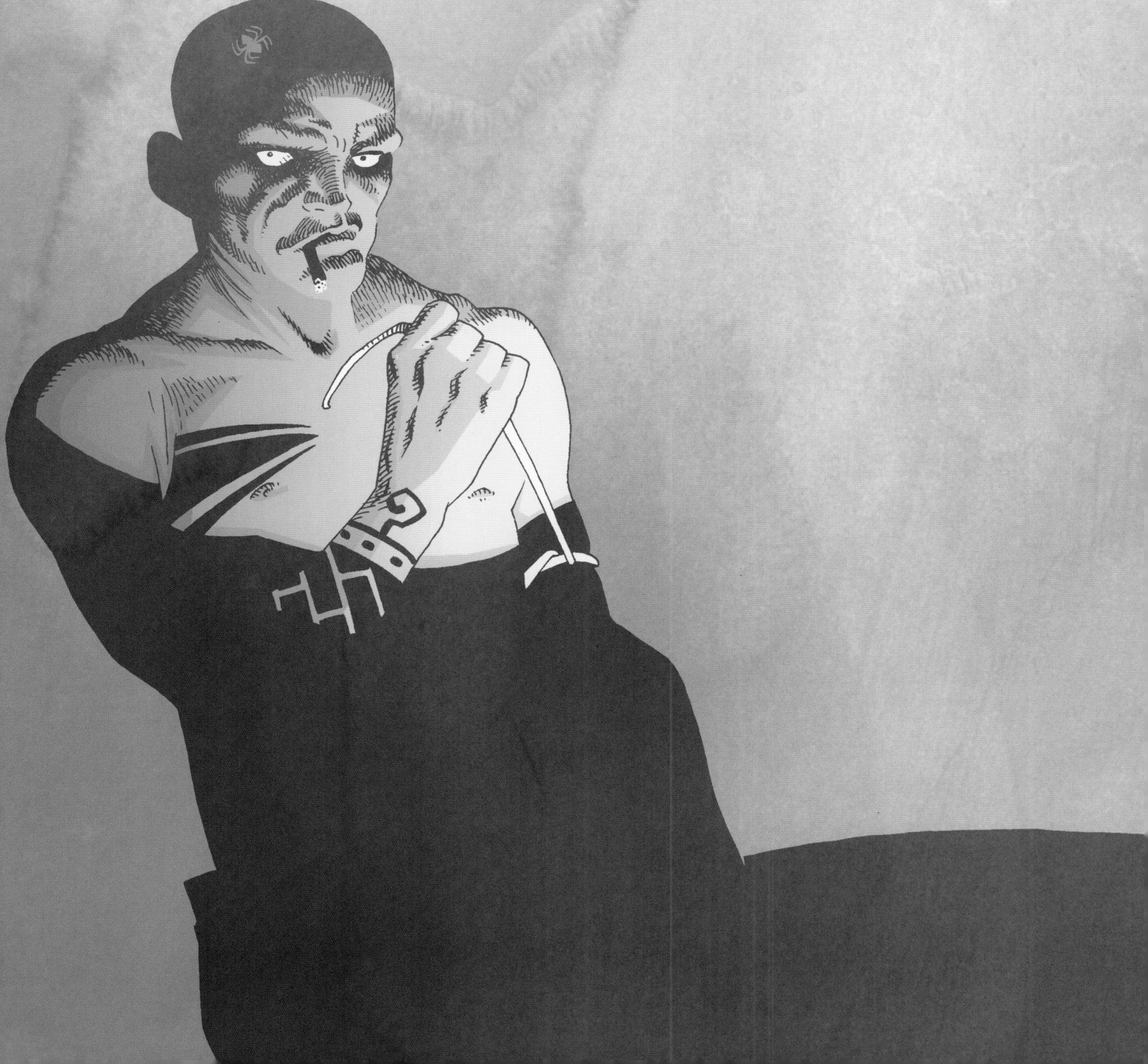

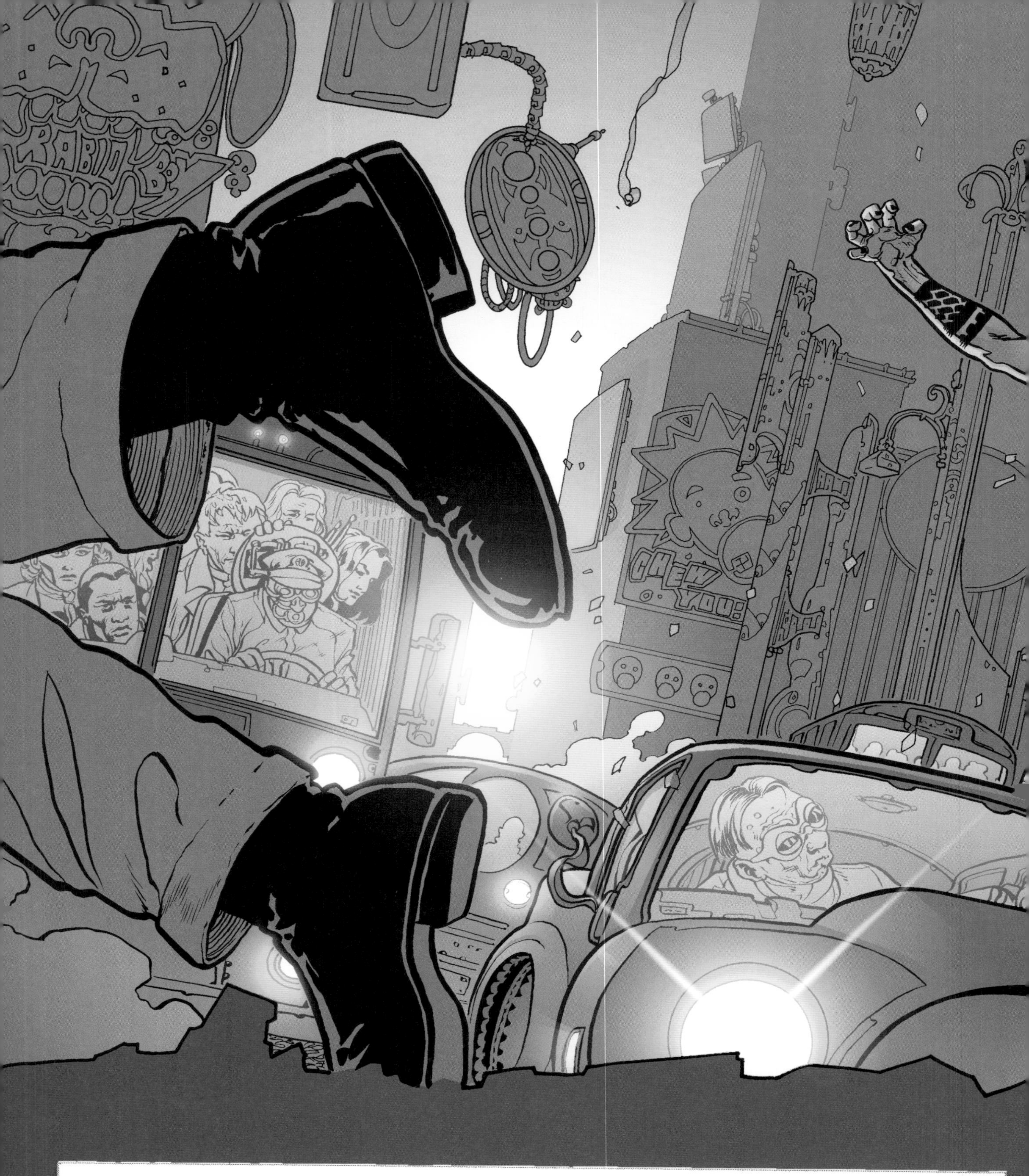
RABID BOY
CHEW YOU!

**I've been back in the City a week and things** are not going well.

You see, things have changed. I've only been away five years, and there are whole chunks of the ambient culture that I do not recognize. Yesterday, for instance. I bought some chewing gum called ALTER. Innocuous enough. Attempt to reduce the cigarette consumption a bit, you see -- all the goddamn additives in City cigarettes gave me a sore throat, so I thought I'd cut down a bit while I adjusted. Up in the mountains, there ain't nothing but tobacco, animal shit and ground glass in our smokes. Of course, you all know the gum brand in question, so you're laughing already. You know what happens next. No fucker told me that the gum induces mild temporary multiple personality disorder and comes pre-loaded with its own "alter."

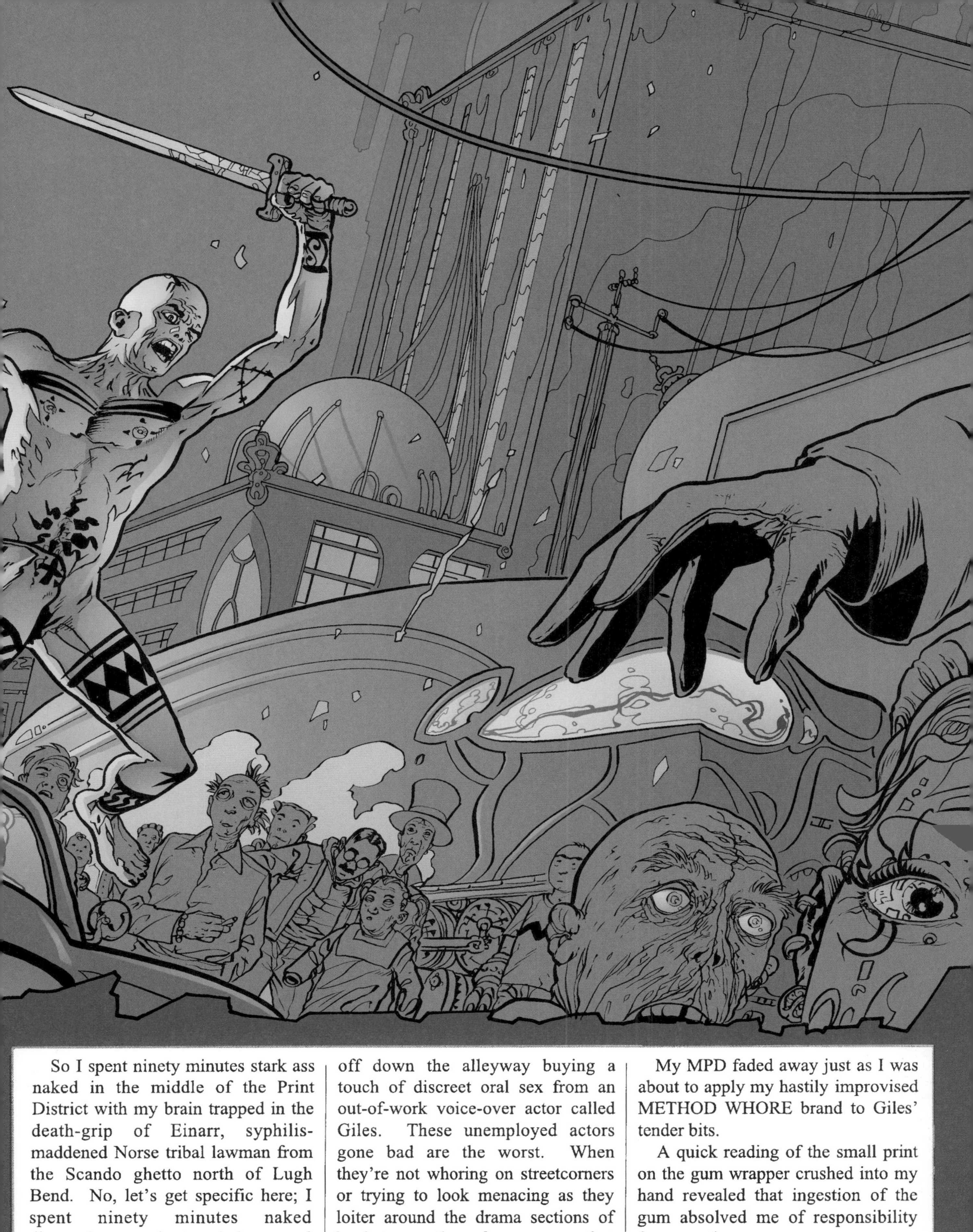

So I spent ninety minutes stark ass naked in the middle of the Print District with my brain trapped in the death-grip of Einarr, syphilis-maddened Norse tribal lawman from the Scando ghetto north of Lugh Bend. No, let's get specific here; I spent ninety minutes naked dispensing ancient wisdom and savage Law up and down the Print District, the alter only wearing off after I brutally beat a deeply unstable ten-year-old boy for pissing in his little sister's pram while mommy was off down the alleyway buying a touch of discreet oral sex from an out-of-work voice-over actor called Giles. These unemployed actors gone bad are the worst. When they're not whoring on streetcorners or trying to look menacing as they loiter around the drama sections of bookstores, they form gangs that relentlessly try to attach themselves to stylish homosexuals and break all the noise laws by bitching about pretty girls and people with talent. The bastards.

My MPD faded away just as I was about to apply my hastily improvised METHOD WHORE brand to Giles' tender bits.

A quick reading of the small print on the gum wrapper crushed into my hand revealed that ingestion of the gum absolved me of responsibility for my actions.

So I branded him and the woman, kicked the kid into passing traffic and had the baby rehomed.

You have no idea how much I hate it here.

**I want to travel back time and lop the** ddamn heads off all your innocent ɔmmies and daddies.

Come on. Tell me why you serve to live. I mean, I know I've en away, and things have changed, that. But there's absolutely no cuse for the behavior you've all en displaying since I came back.

I am talking specifically about the extensive shrines set up outside my apartment building. I am talking about the two people who attempted to have sex in my shadow to guarantee conception. I am talking about the Conclave who scrabbled through the bag of garbage I couldn't get my Maker to use. I am talking about the people who stole my bathwater and drank it.

This is *America.* I want *money* these things. I mean, I have so especially Holy underpants he shattered and ruined by unus stresses, and I can't let them go t good cause for anything less tha hundred...

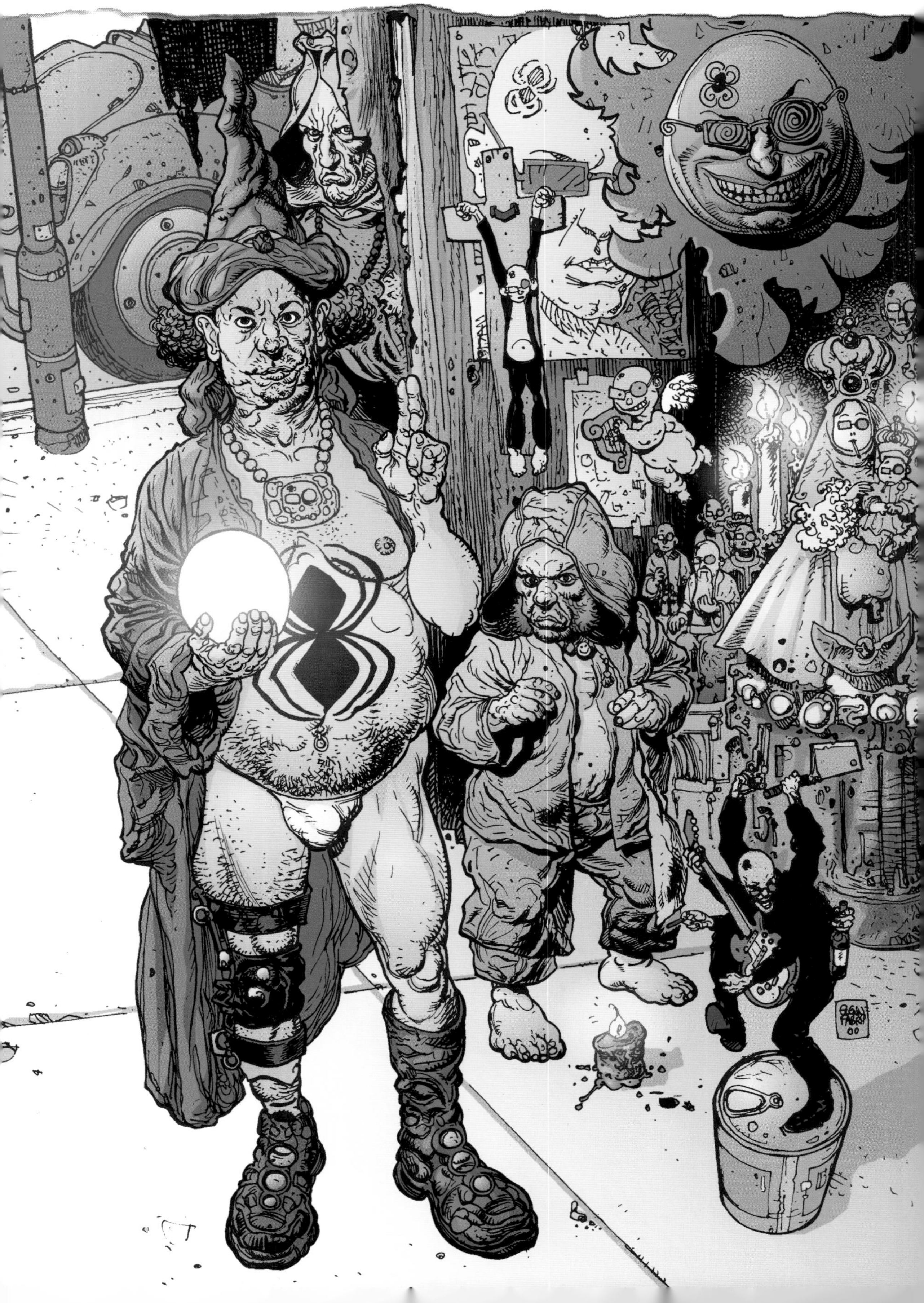

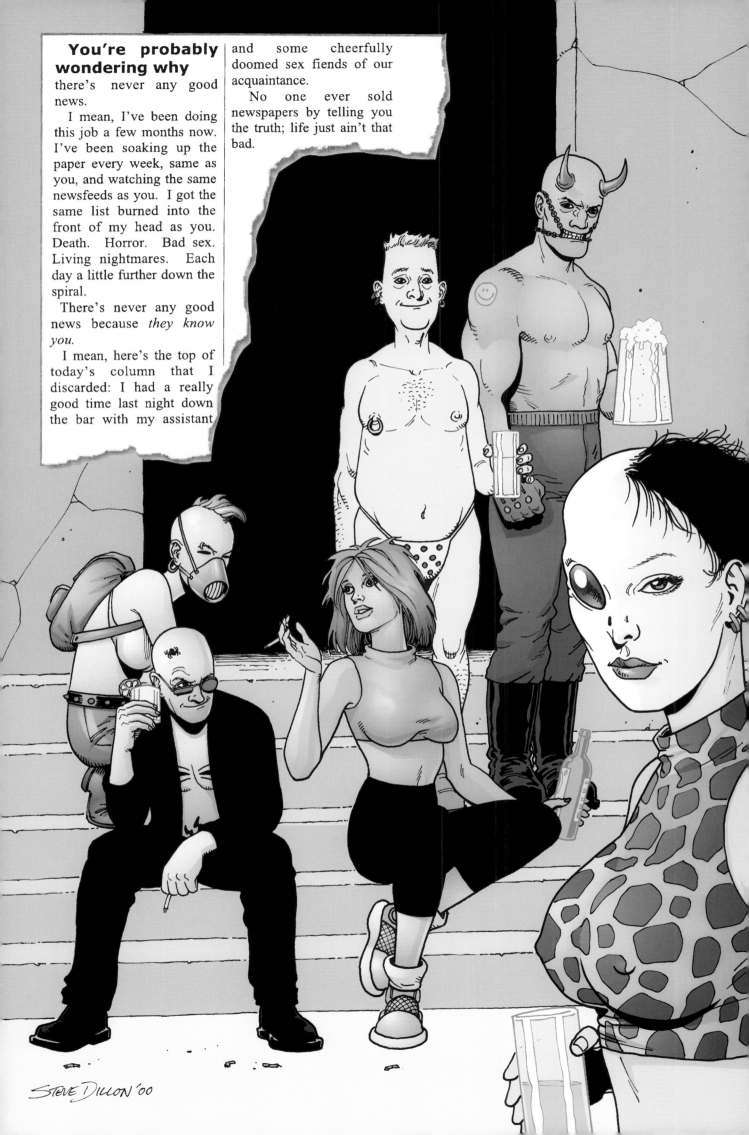

**You're probably wondering why** there's never any good news.

I mean, I've been doing this job a few months now. I've been soaking up the paper every week, same as you, and watching the same newsfeeds as you. I got the same list burned into the front of my head as you. Death. Horror. Bad sex. Living nightmares. Each day a little further down the spiral.

There's never any good news because *they know you.*

I mean, here's the top of today's column that I discarded: I had a really good time last night down the bar with my assistant and some cheerfully doomed sex fiends of our acquaintance.

No one ever sold newspapers by telling you the truth; life just ain't that bad.

STEVE DILLON '00

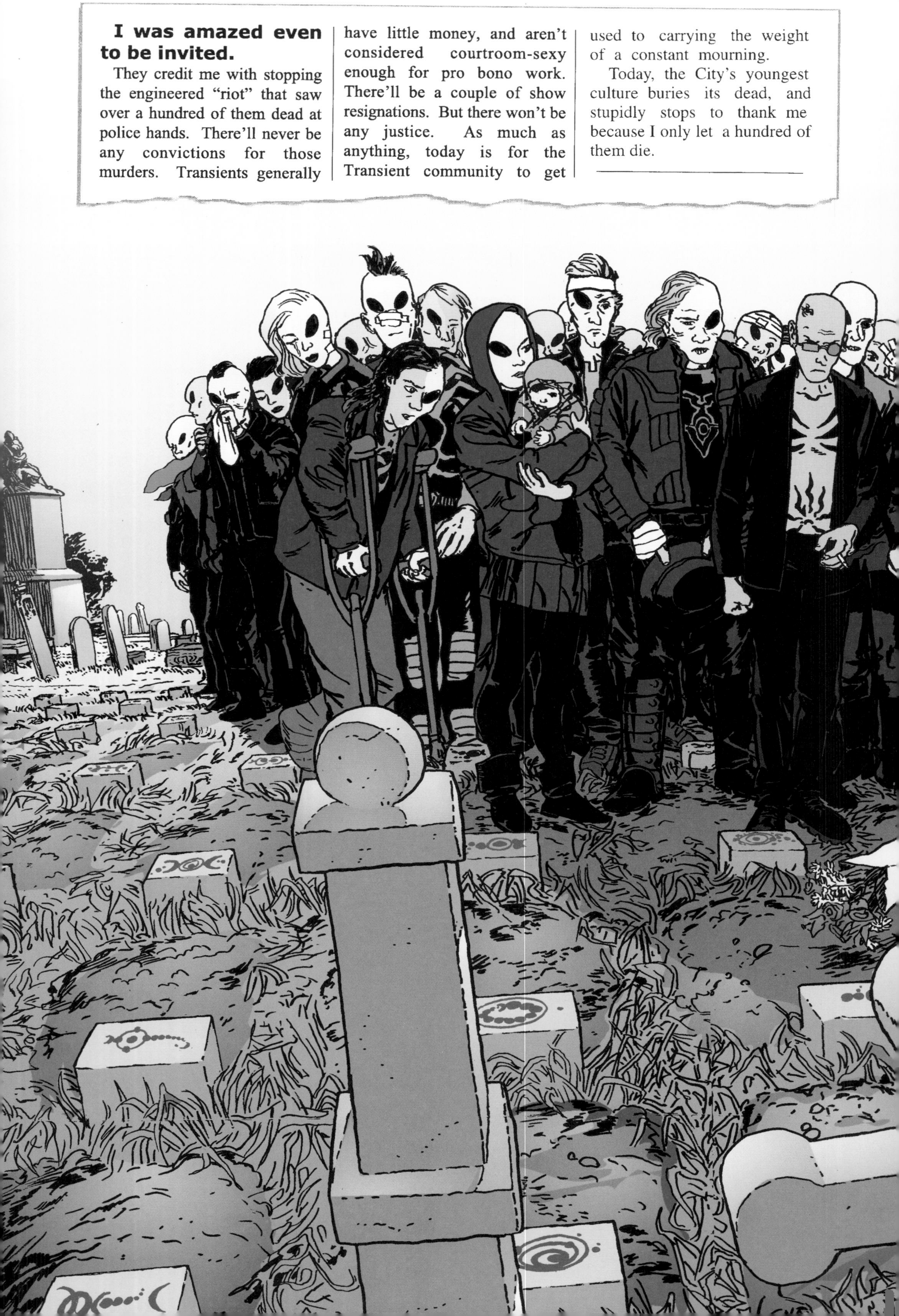
**I was amazed even to be invited.**
They credit me with stopping the engineered "riot" that saw over a hundred of them dead at police hands. There'll never be any convictions for those murders. Transients generally have little money, and aren't considered courtroom-sexy enough for pro bono work. There'll be a couple of show resignations. But there won't be any justice. As much as anything, today is for the Transient community to get used to carrying the weight of a constant mourning.
Today, the City's youngest culture buries its dead, and stupidly stops to thank me because I only let a hundred of them die.

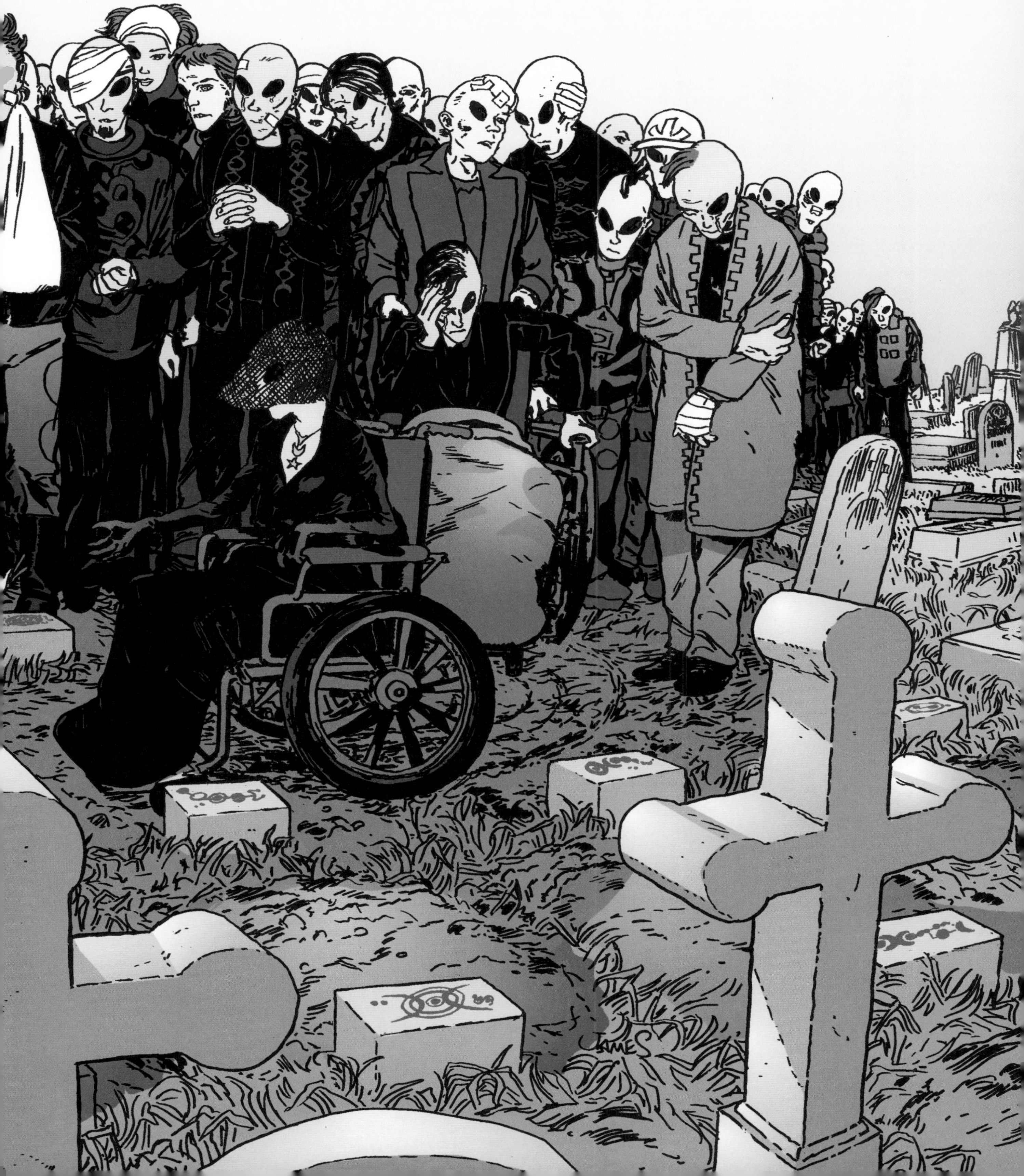
JAMES

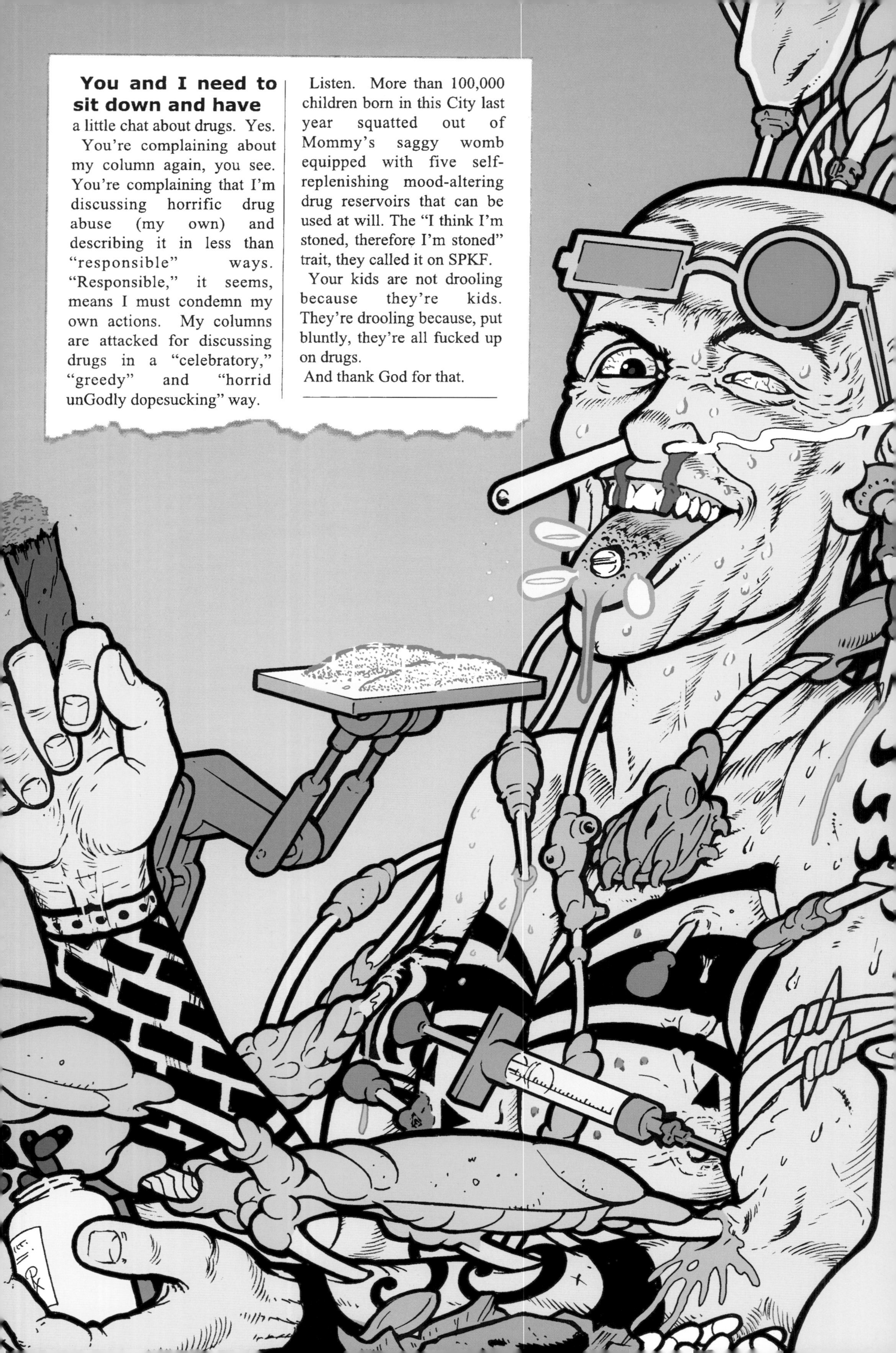
You and I need to sit down and have a little chat about drugs. Yes.
You're complaining about my column again, you see. You're complaining that I'm discussing horrific drug abuse (my own) and describing it in less than "responsible" ways. "Responsible," it seems, means I must condemn my own actions. My columns are attacked for discussing drugs in a "celebratory," "greedy" and "horrid unGodly dopesucking" way.
Listen. More than 100,000 children born in this City last year squatted out of Mommy's saggy womb equipped with five self-replenishing mood-altering drug reservoirs that can be used at will. The "I think I'm stoned, therefore I'm stoned" trait, they called it on SPKF.
Your kids are not drooling because they're kids. They're drooling because, put bluntly, they're all fucked up on drugs.
And thank God for that.

**I want to eat a swan. Is that wrong of me?**

I can't find anyone who'll sell me a swanburger.

I sent my assistant down to the African for a monkeyburger. I really fancied some Korean dog, but the local Korean got bought out by the Shark Bar people, who are trying to head off the expansion of those tiny Club Snack hot seal-eye kiosks. Mind, Club Snack are having their own problems; they're being sued for breach of fiduciary contract by the Long Pig chain, where Club Snack once had concession stands. Long Pig could use the compensation money, since hard questions are being asked about the location of their stock -- the New Zealand census numbers are down for the third year in a row. I learned a long time ago never to annoy an Incan. And I always preferred caribou eyes, anyway. There used to be loads of Eskimo fastfood stands around here. I wonder what happened to them?

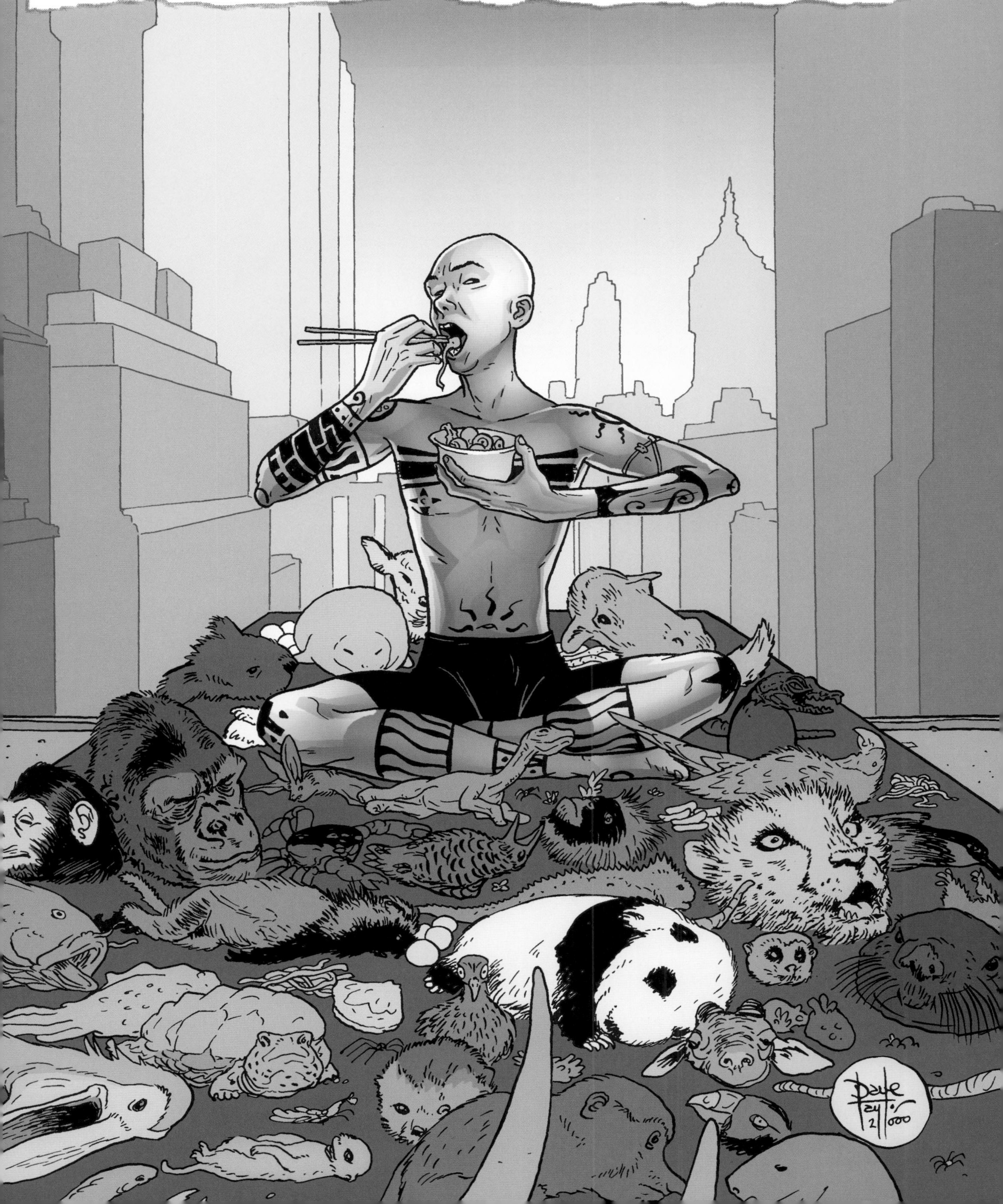

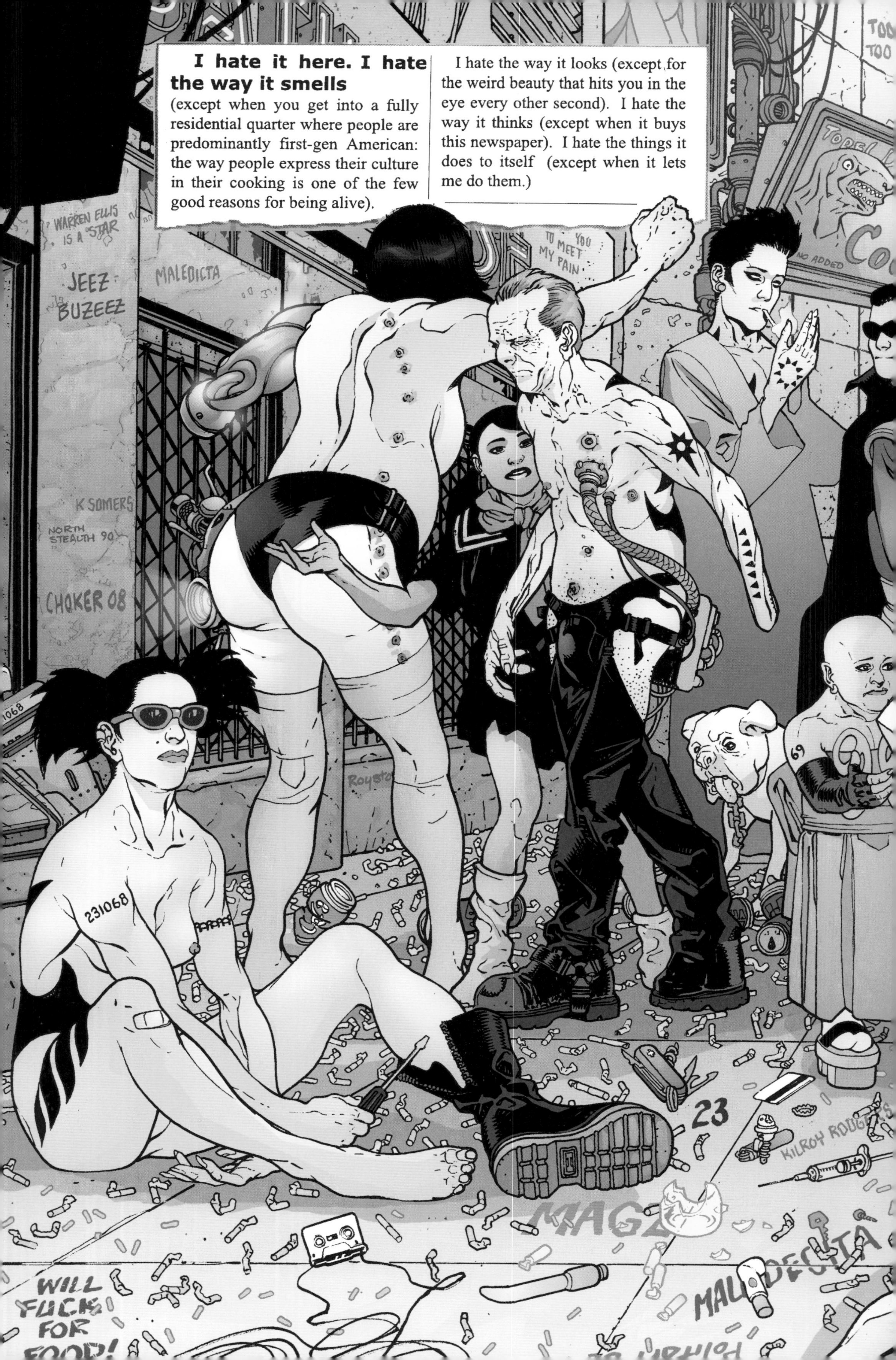
**I hate it here. I hate the way it smells**
(except when you get into a fully residential quarter where people are predominantly first-gen American: the way people express their culture in their cooking is one of the few good reasons for being alive).
I hate the way it looks (except for the weird beauty that hits you in the eye every other second). I hate the way it thinks (except when it buys this newspaper). I hate the things it does to itself (except when it lets me do them.)
WARREN ELLIS IS A STAR
JEEZ BUZEEZ
MALEDICTA
K SOMERS
NORTH STEALTH 90
CHOKER 08
231068
69
23
MALEDICTA
WILL FUCK FOR FOOD!

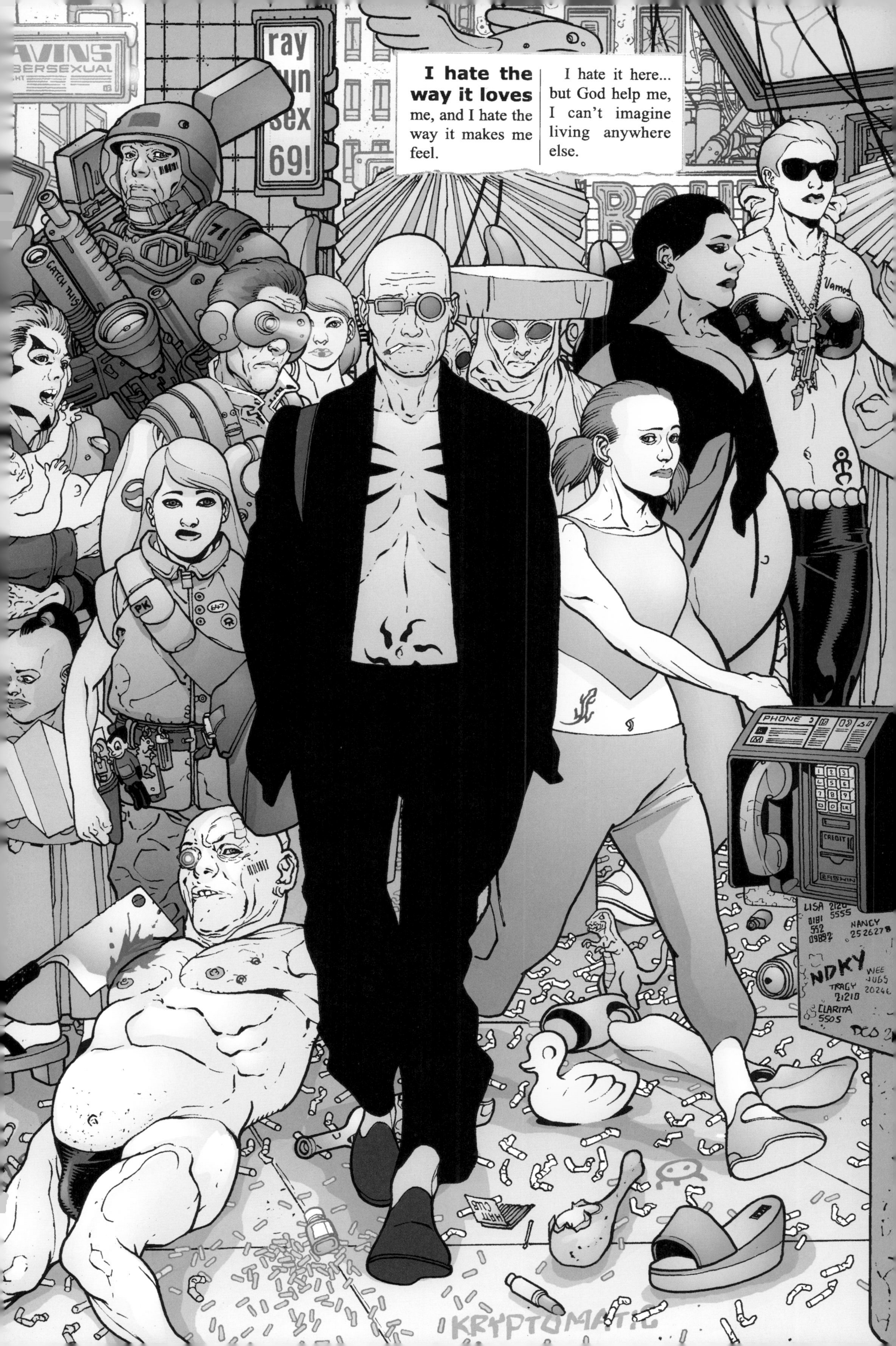

I hate the way it loves me, and I hate the way it makes me feel.
I hate it here... but God help me, I can't imagine living anywhere else.
ray
un
sex
69!
BERSEXUAL
CATCH THIS
Vamos
PK
PHONE
CREDIT
LISA
NANCY
NDKY
TRACY
CLARITA
5505
KRYPTOMATIC

**It was a horrific beating. Biblical** ferocity. The vengeful God of the Old Testament flowed in my veins, giving me power, Hate and an erection of uncommon savagery. What else could I do? I was left with no choice.

My journalist's insurance protected me from prosecution. The emergency services unscrewed my victim from the drain I'd attempted to finally dispose of him in. I'm told he'll walk again, with some time and some new legs. And new hips. And new eyes. And an unfried nervous system.

*No* fucker rewrites *me*.

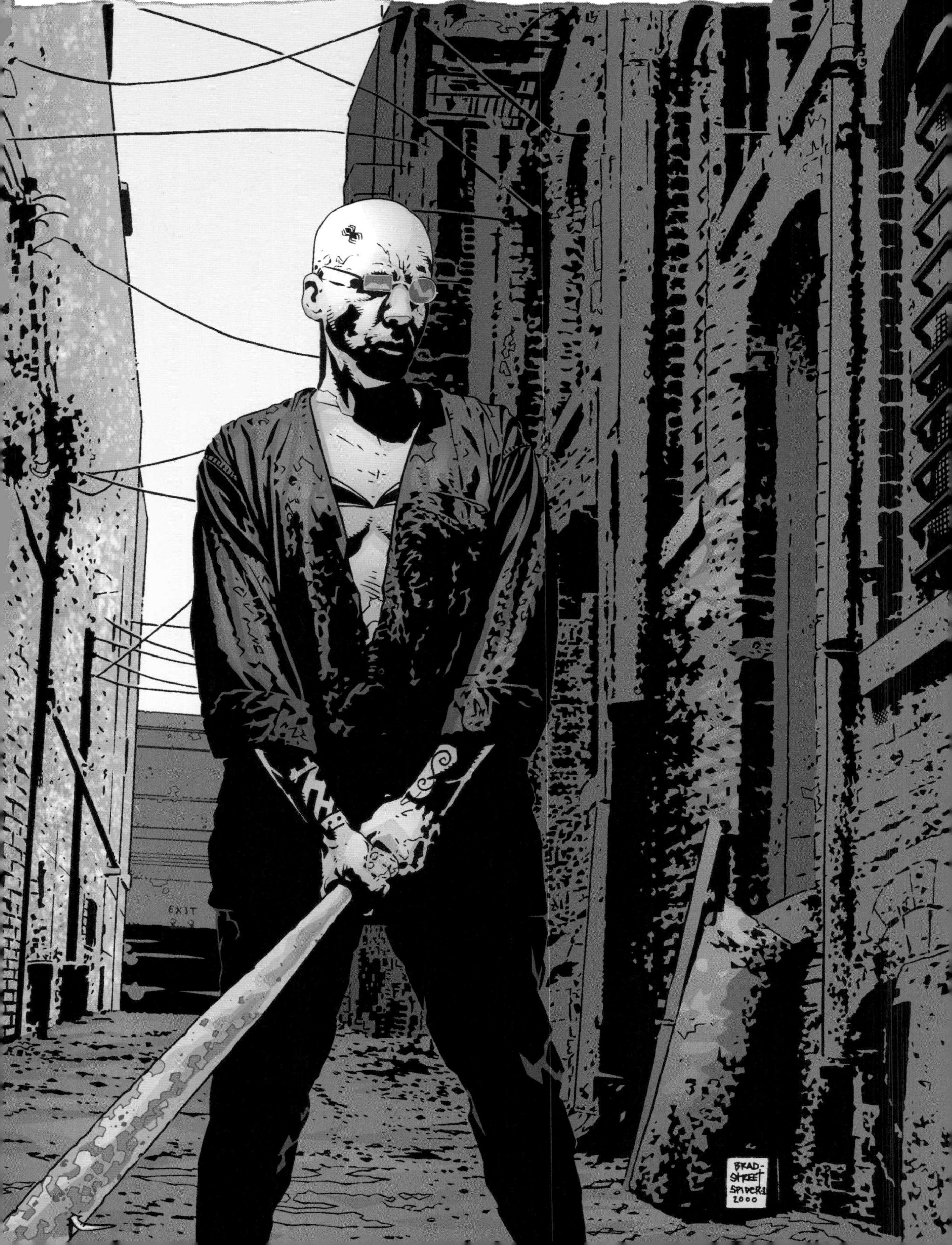
EXIT
BRAD-STREET SPIDER-1 2000

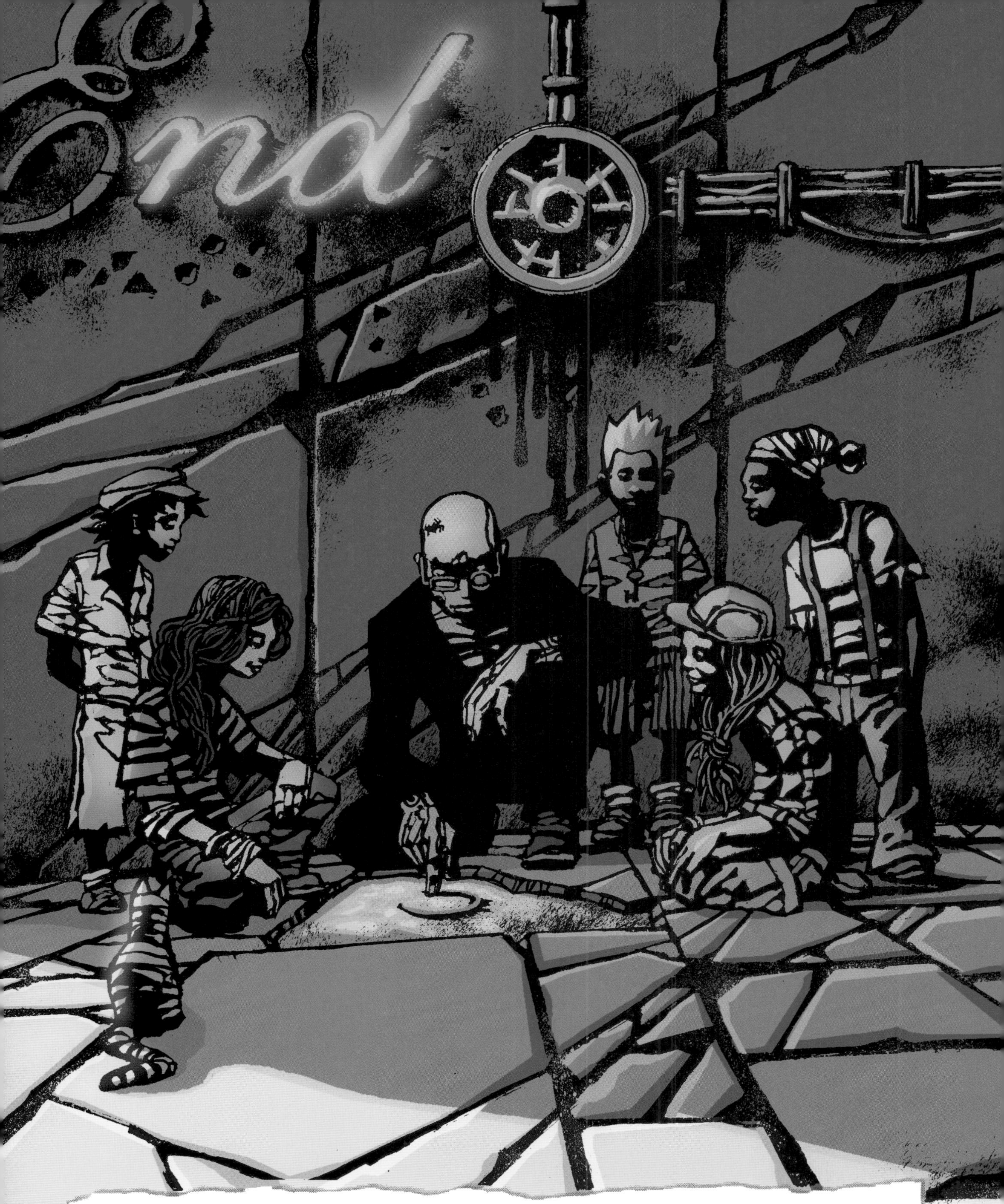

**You want to know how bad things have gotten? You people** spend all your time telling me I'm corrupting your damn children -- but your kids don't have the equipment to actually read what I'm writing.

The times when you could stop and point at California and say, "Well, our kids aren't as dumb as theirs" is long gone. Those kids aren't dumb anyway. They're just badly educated.

I spent some time with some kids today. First I hacked a sidewalk-screen and showed them a basic educational program -- the sort that you're supposed to show them, at home.

Once we established that they thought America was Russia "'cos it looks biggest," I got real primitive with them. You would have hated it.

I taught them something.

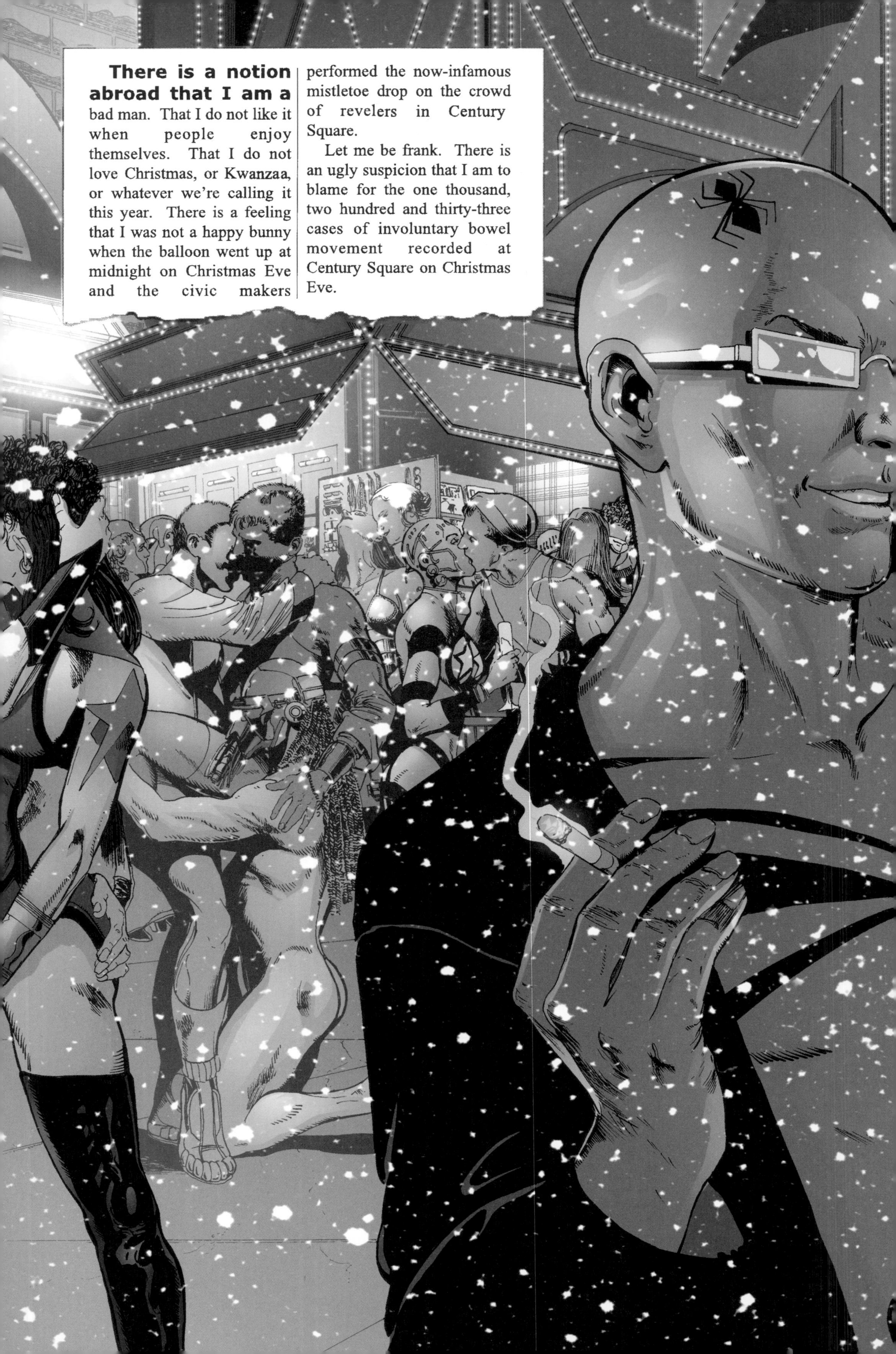
There is a notion abroad that I am a bad man. That I do not like it when people enjoy themselves. That I do not love Christmas, or Kwanzaa, or whatever we're calling it this year. There is a feeling that I was not a happy bunny when the balloon went up at midnight on Christmas Eve and the civic makers performed the now-infamous mistletoe drop on the crowd of revelers in Century Square.
Let me be frank. There is an ugly suspicion that I am to blame for the one thousand, two hundred and thirty-three cases of involuntary bowel movement recorded at Century Square on Christmas Eve.

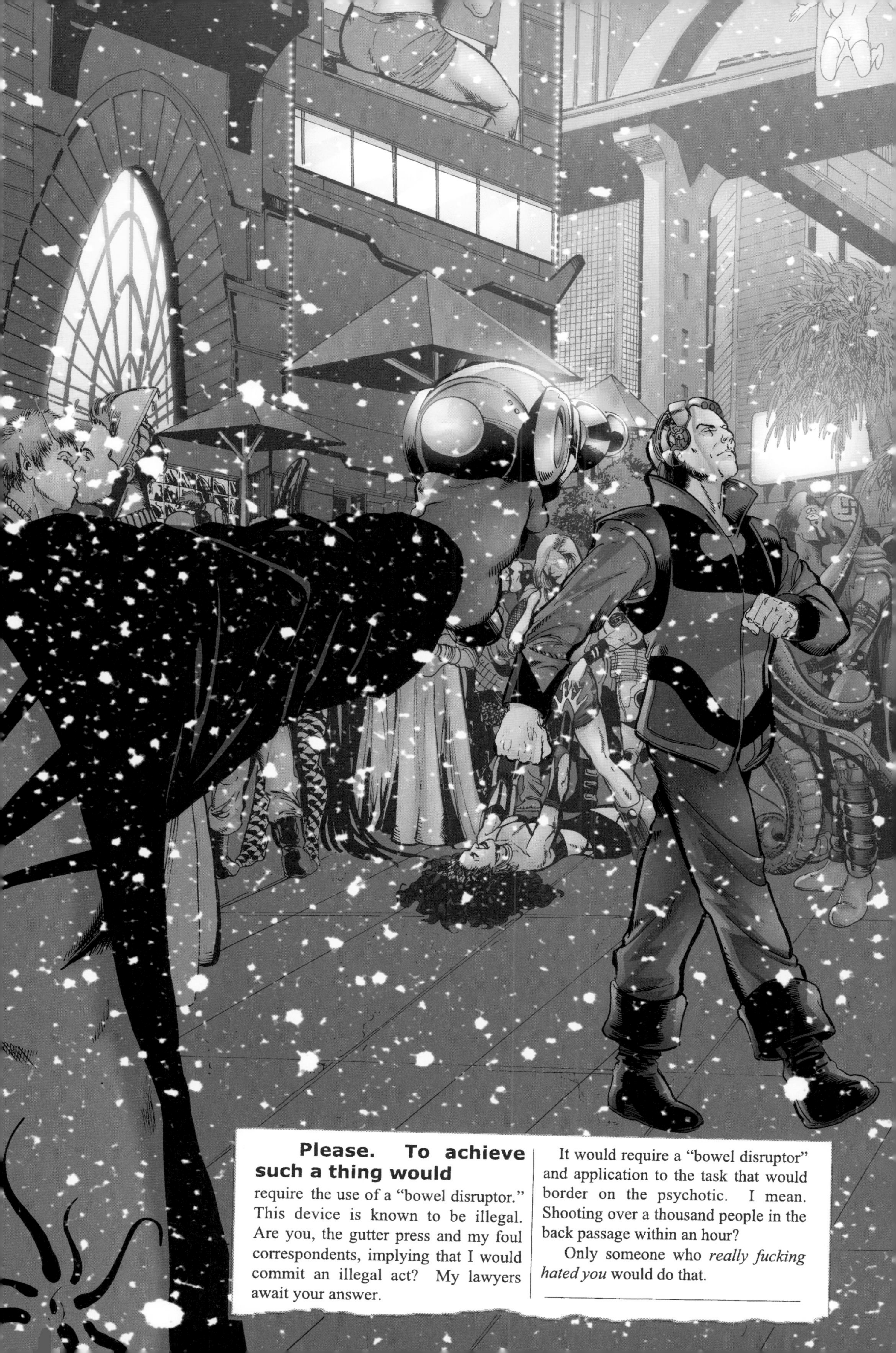
**Please. To achieve such a thing would** require the use of a "bowel disruptor." This device is known to be illegal. Are you, the gutter press and my foul correspondents, implying that I would commit an illegal act? My lawyers await your answer.
It would require a "bowel disruptor" and application to the task that would border on the psychotic. I mean. Shooting over a thousand people in the back passage within an hour?
Only someone who *really fucking hated you* would do that.

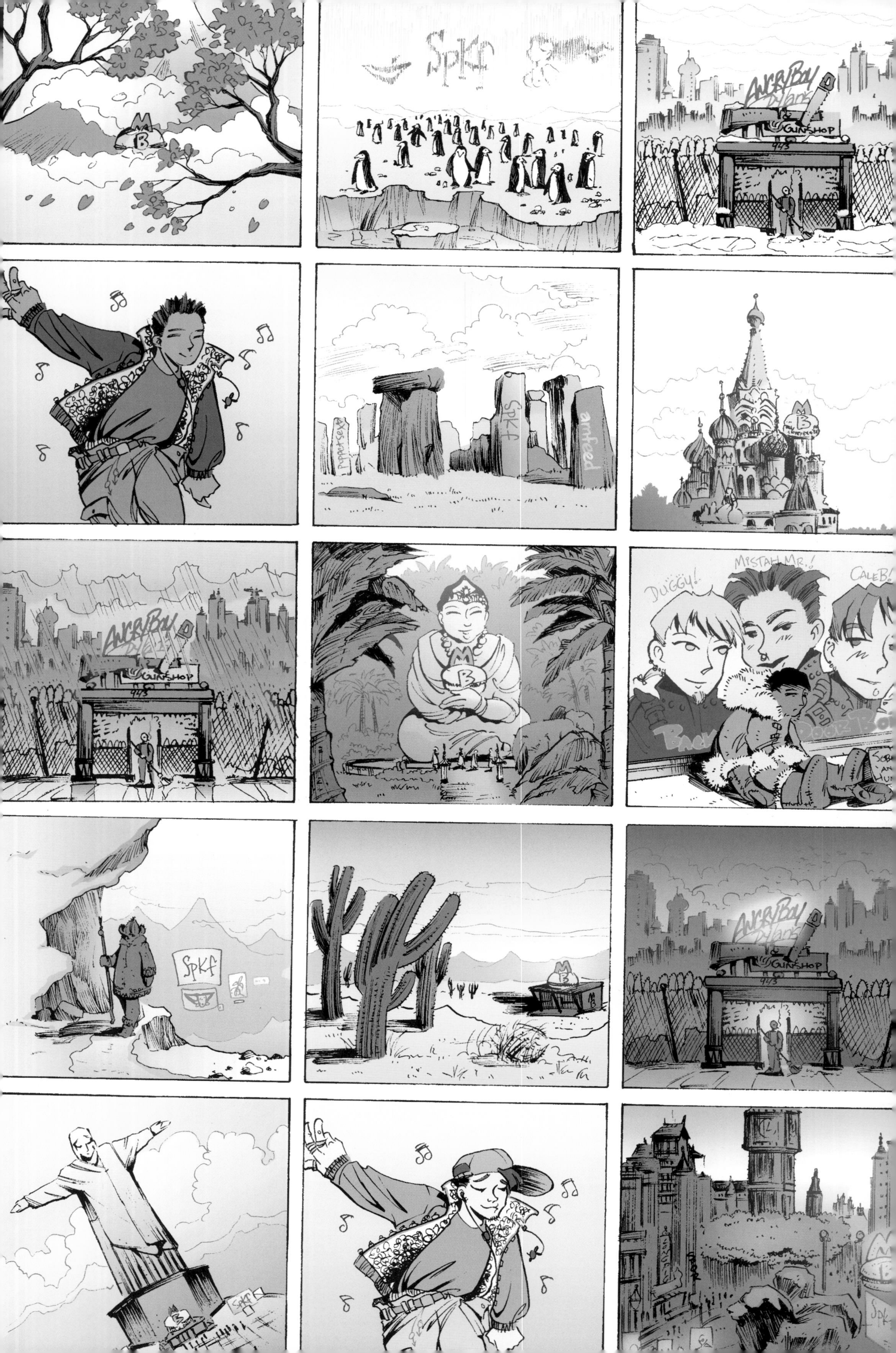

Spkf
GUNSHOP
943
puppetsex
SPKF
amfeed
DUGGY!
MISTAH MR.!
CALEB!
Spkf

MISTAH MR.!
CALEB!
SOBER "AND" HUNGRY
MISTAH MR.!
CALEB!
SOBER AND HUNGRY

**We live in a monoculture.**

What does that mean? Well, go out to your street corner. You'll probably see a Long Pig stand, SPKF on a screen somewhere, an Angry Boy Dylan's Gun Store. You'll go into a record store and see new recordings by the usual suspects, maybe a special Space Culture display rack.

Go out onto a streetcorner in London and you'll see the same thing. Same in Prague. Same in São Paulo. Same in Osaka, and Grozny, and Tehran, and Jo'burg, and Hobart.

That's what a monoculture is. It's everywhere, and it's all the same. And it takes up alien cultures and digests them and shits them out in a homogenous building-block shape that fits seamlessly into the vast blank wall of the monoculture.

This is the future. This is what we built. This is what we wanted. It must have been. Because we all had the fucking *choice*, didn't we? It is only our money that allows commercial culture to flower. If we didn't want to live like this, we could have changed it any time, by *not fucking paying for it.*

So let's celebrate by all going out and buying the same burger.

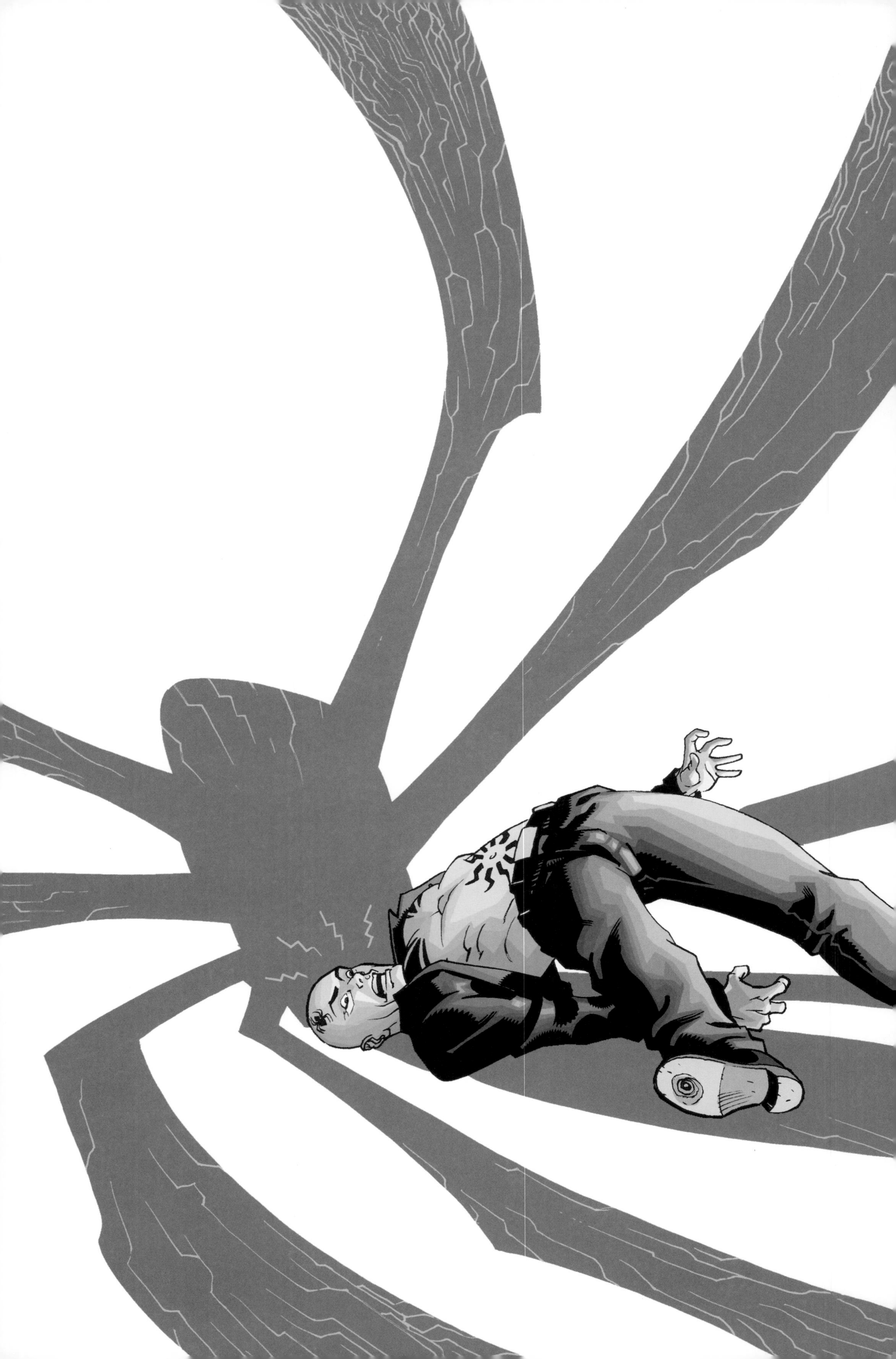

## Further to the debate about drug use

(mine and your children's): it's all over. You no longer have anything to worry about.

You know, when I was a kid, we listened to music that made our parents' eyes bleed and took drugs that made us want to dance and fuck and kill things. That is the way things are supposed to be.

It was, therefore, in the spirit of honest investigation that I internalized a heroic dose of Space, the new social drug enjoyed by the young folk of today as part of the youth culture referred to as Supermodernity.

Supermodernity, apparently, is the experience of being between places; that is, not being in a real place at all, but waiting in transit between one place and the other. This is why SM/Space Culture music appears to us to be utterly silent. You have to be on Space -- slowed down, across places, in the zone between ticks of the clock -- to be able to hear it.

This is what they do for fun, apparently: suck up appalling volumes of a drug that traps you in an airport waiting lounge of the mind and doesn't let you go for approximately two hundred years while someone plays an antique handheld electronic keyboard in your ear.

Mr. and Mrs. America, do not be afraid! Your children have finally found a drug that makes it impossible to dance, fuck or kill things. Youth culture has finally sterilized itself. Young America has finally achieved its terminal ambition -- fucking itself before anyone else could.

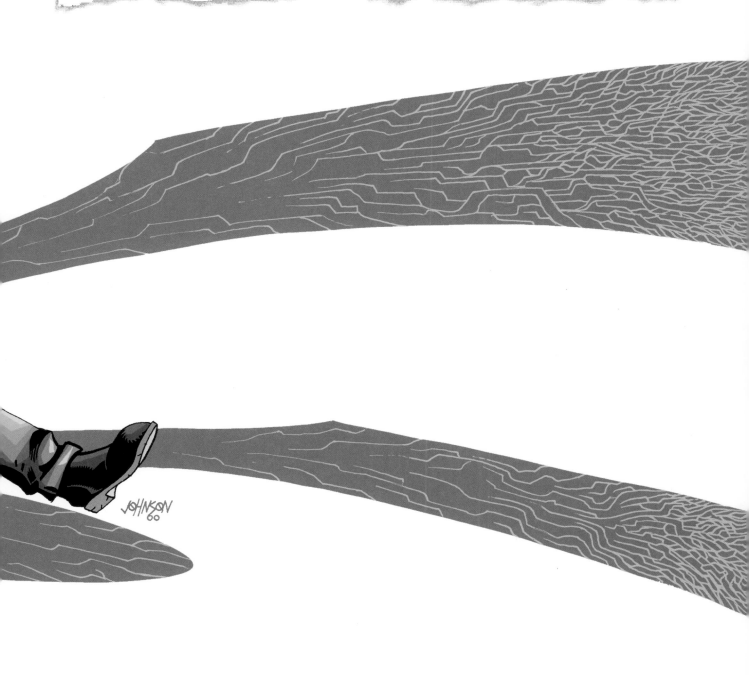

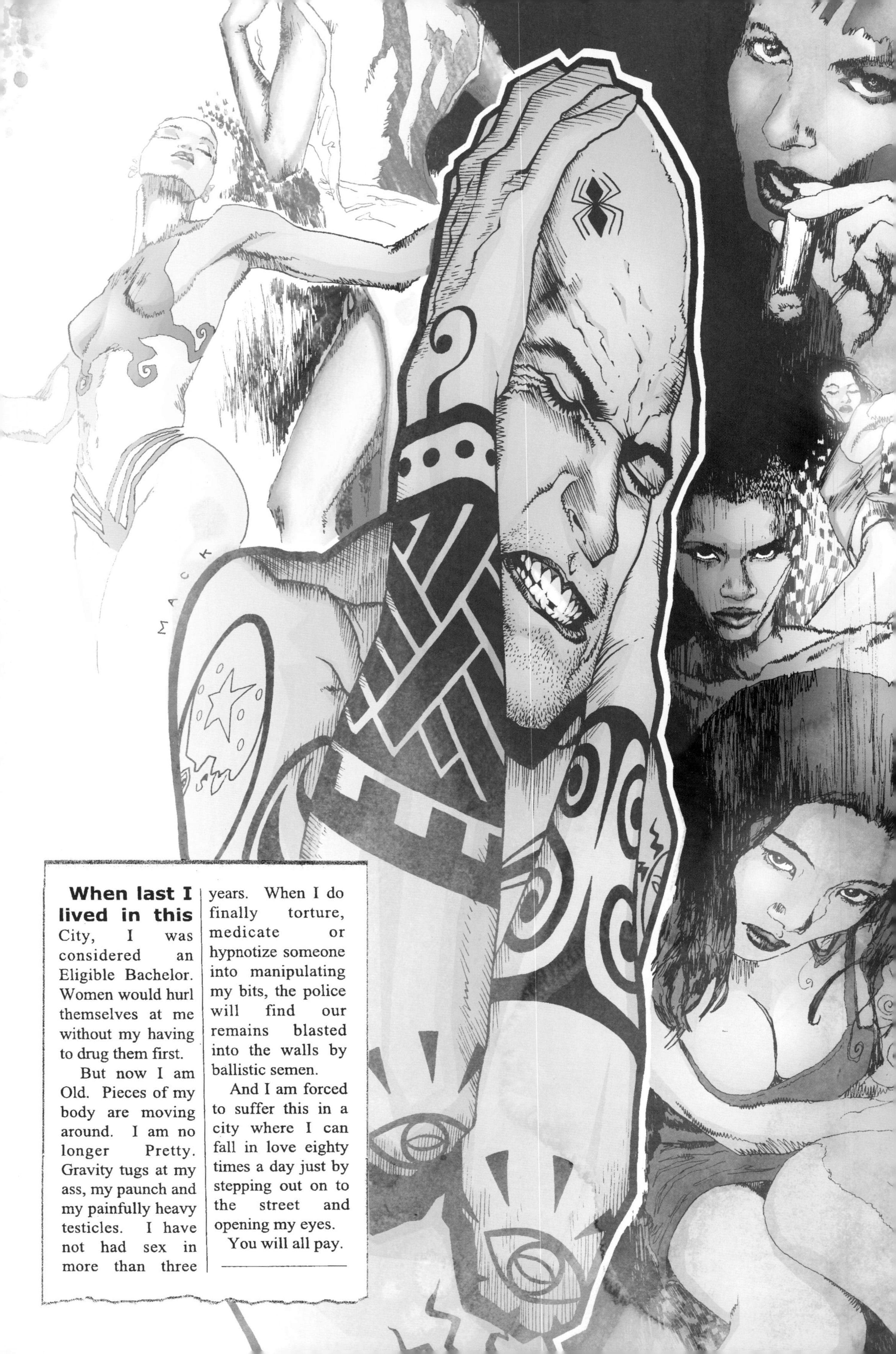
MACK

**When last I lived in this** City, I was considered an Eligible Bachelor. Women would hurl themselves at me without my having to drug them first.

But now I am Old. Pieces of my body are moving around. I am no longer Pretty. Gravity tugs at my ass, my paunch and my painfully heavy testicles. I have not had sex in more than three years. When I do finally torture, medicate or hypnotize someone into manipulating my bits, the police will find our remains blasted into the walls by ballistic semen.

And I am forced to suffer this in a city where I can fall in love eighty times a day just by stepping out on to the street and opening my eyes.

You will all pay.

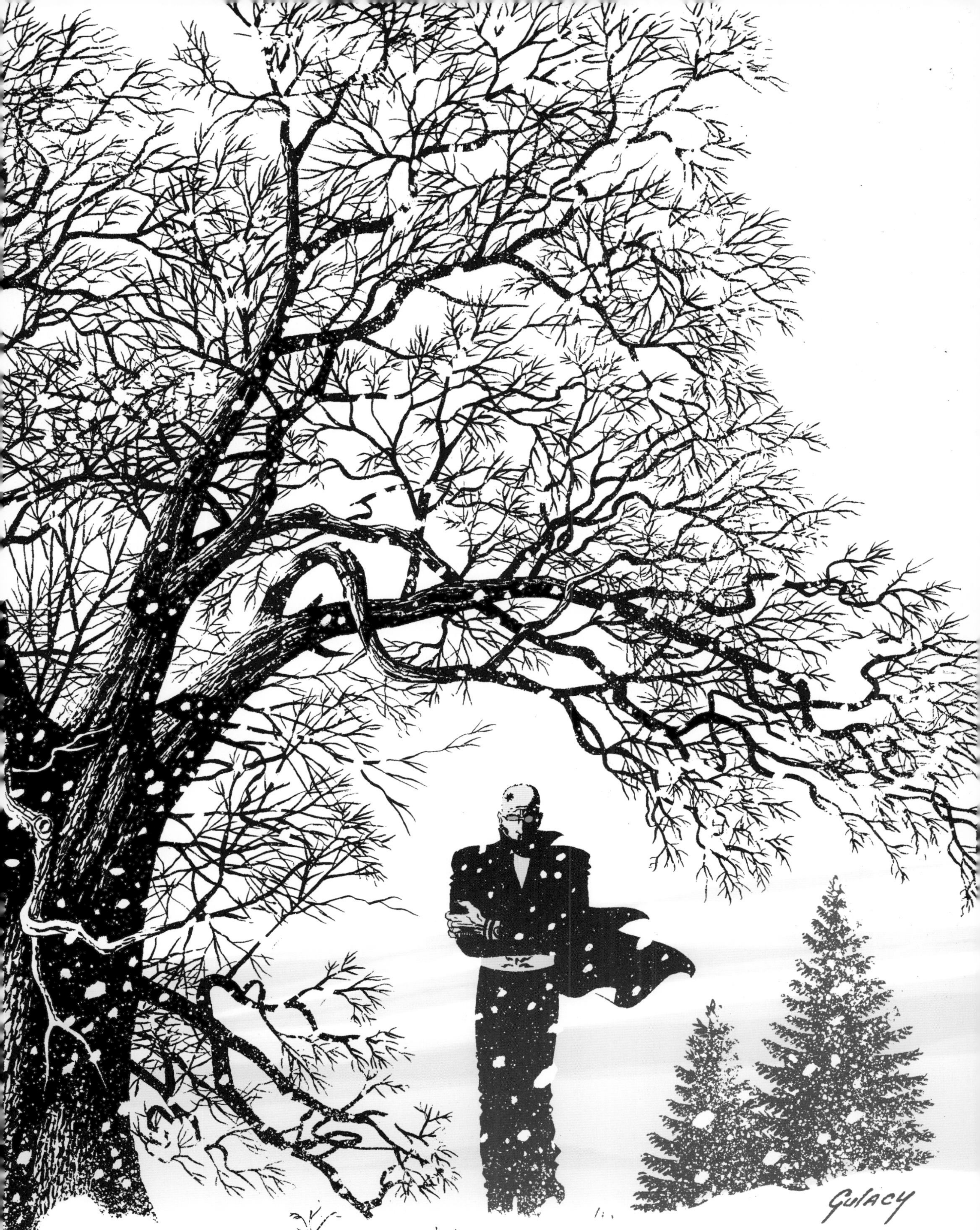
GULACY

**I came back down here from a place** where the snow would lay for miles, from first fall to thaw, with no mark on it other than the prints of birds, foxes and squirrels.

There's a Reservation under contruction, about ten miles south of Lugh Bend. No people in it yet, but the walls are up, creating the illusion of endless distance, and the environment and weather systems are running. I have friends there, who let me in from time to time.

Sometimes, I can do nothing but stand in constant winter, trying to remember what life is like without all of you.

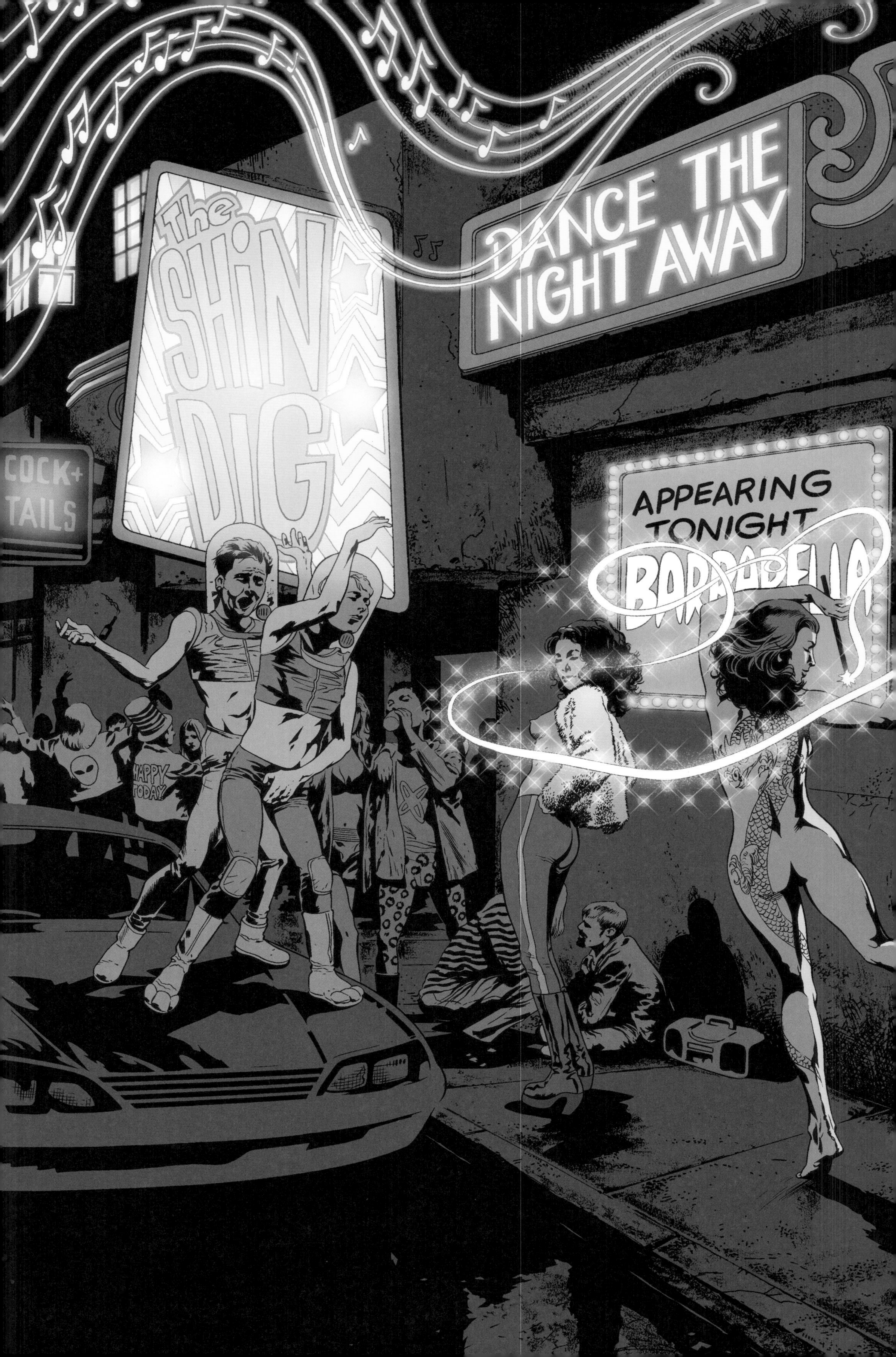
The SHINDIG
DANCE THE NIGHT AWAY
COCK+ TAILS
APPEARING TONIGHT
HAPPY TODAY

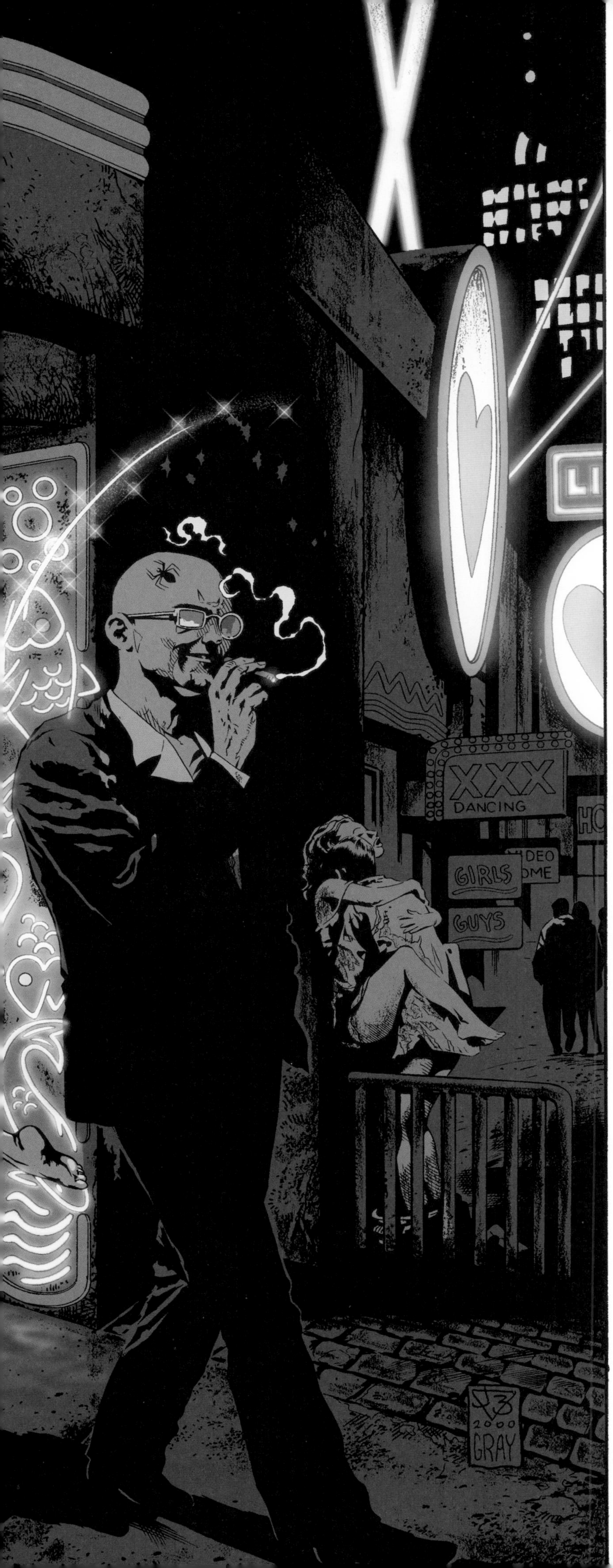
XXX
DANCING
GIRLS
GUYS
2000
GRAY

**And then the sun goes down and the** night comes up, and I remember why I lived here for so long.

I was born in this City, out on the docks, and as a child I'd see the glow come up in central City as the night fell down on us, and I'd sit there for hours, all happily stained by light pollution, wishing I could be there, dreaming of what I'd do. I built a thousand fantasies of night in the City, sitting there looking at the spotlights and lasers and light-snow and listening to ghost mixes of millions of different musics drifting over...

I had a thousand fantasies of what it was like here. I lived them all out in three months, and spent years coming up with new ones. It's that kind of place. The night brings out those kinds of people.

I hate this place, you know, because I can't let it go. But if you quote me I'll call you a liar.

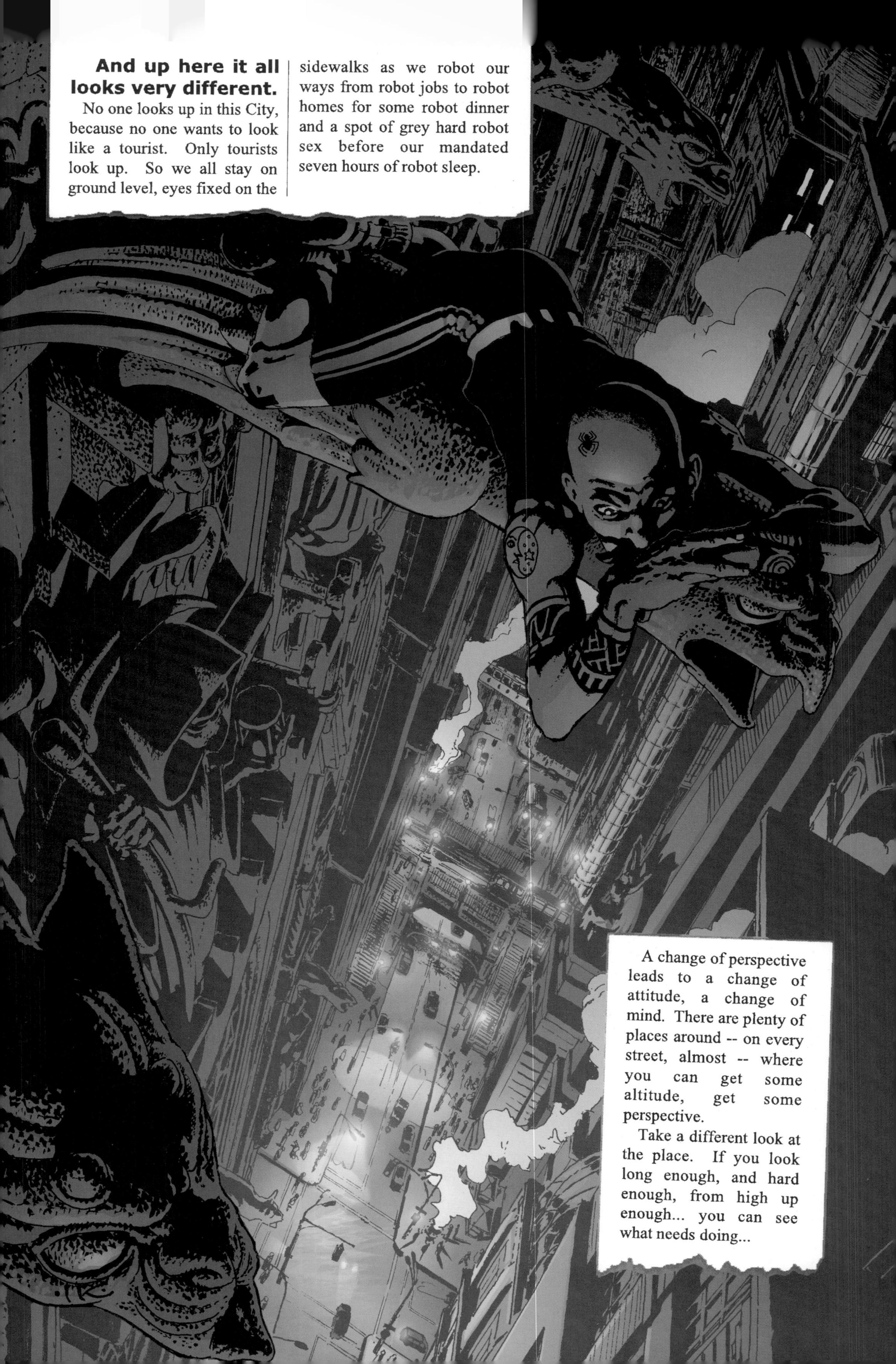
And up here it all looks very different.
No one looks up in this City, because no one wants to look like a tourist. Only tourists look up. So we all stay on ground level, eyes fixed on the sidewalks as we robot our ways from robot jobs to robot homes for some robot dinner and a spot of grey hard robot sex before our mandated seven hours of robot sleep.
A change of perspective leads to a change of attitude, a change of mind. There are plenty of places around -- on every street, almost -- where you can get some altitude, get some perspective.
Take a different look at the place. If you look long enough, and hard enough, from high up enough... you can see what needs doing...

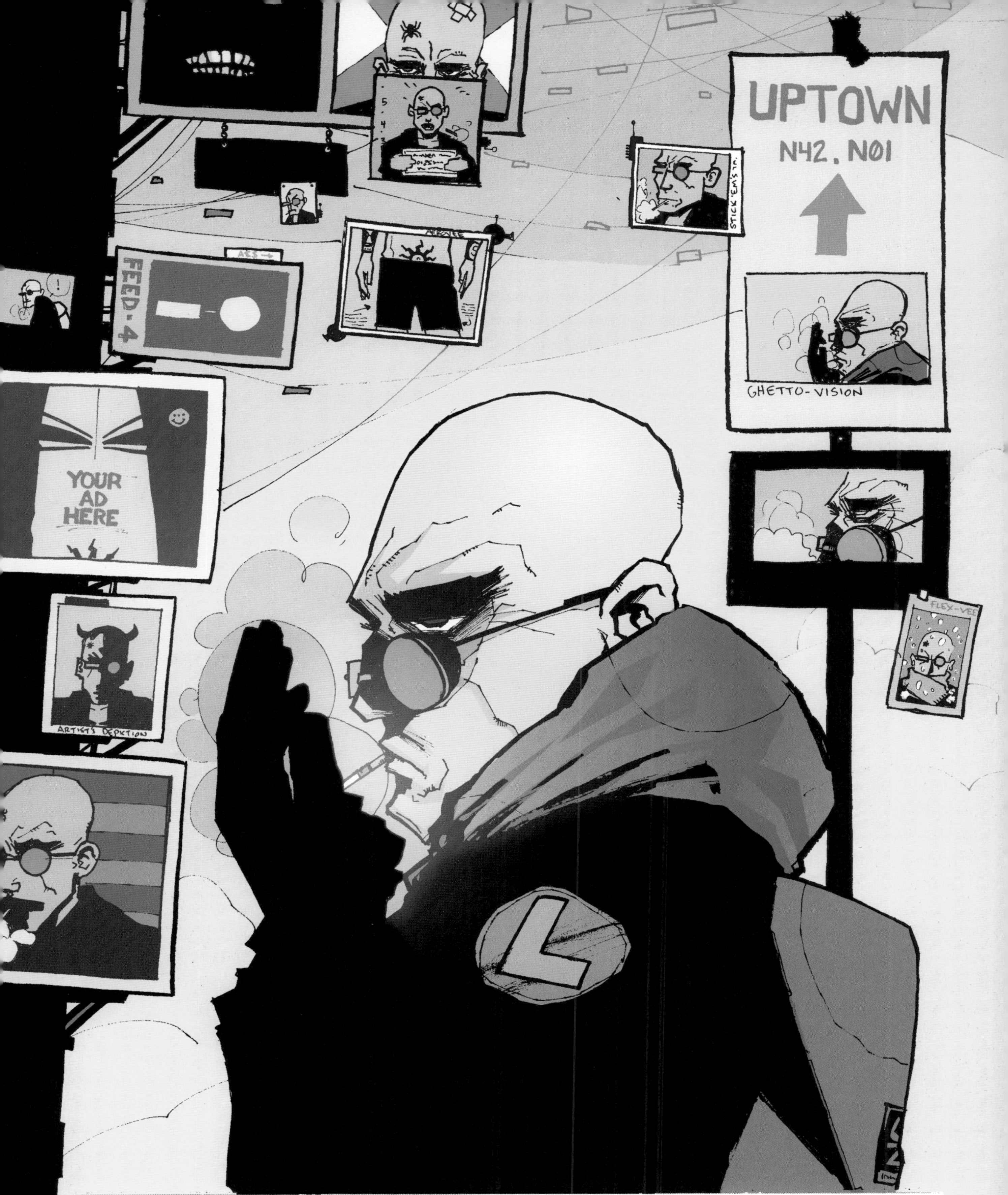
UPTOWN
N42. N01
GHETTO-VISION
YOUR AD HERE
FEED-4
ARTIST'S DEPICTION

**I am Famous again.**

This development does not please me. But I have found it useful. I have recorded a variety of spots discussing the important things in life. Voting. Truth. Horror. Loss. Being Fucked With Knives.

And now I am being Venerated. I have evidently Energized The Discourse and Made Politics Real Again. Children smile and laugh and rush to me in the street for comfort, singing my name. Old people clasp my hands for luck and to cheat death, and I am Beloved by the whores and the old people, who offer me all they have in return for my countenance, their cheap infected sex and blood products.

I'm back. I have a ragged army hanging on my every word. And I'm pissed off.

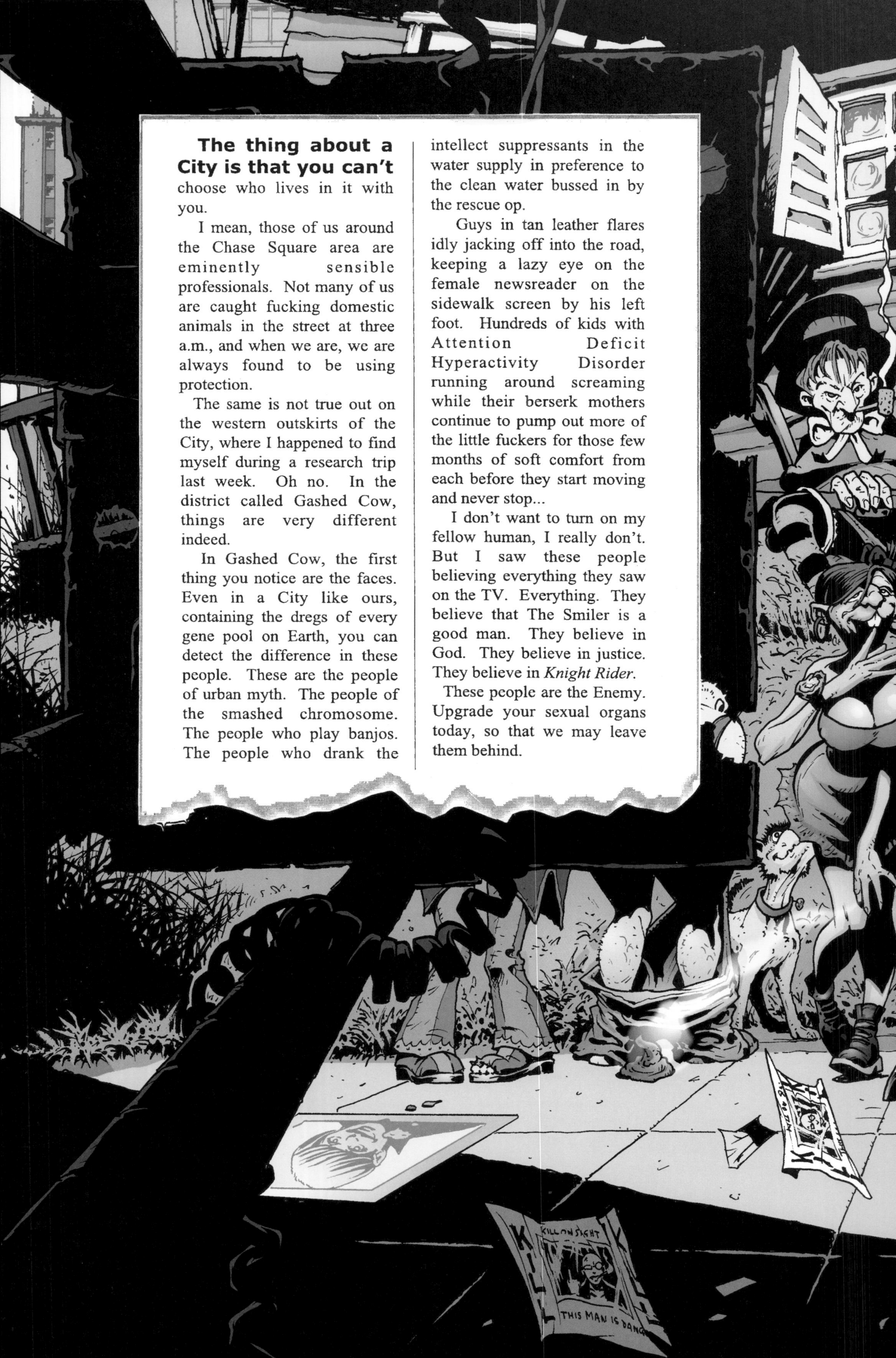
KILL ON SIGHT

**The thing about a City is that you can't** choose who lives in it with you.

I mean, those of us around the Chase Square area are eminently sensible professionals. Not many of us are caught fucking domestic animals in the street at three a.m., and when we are, we are always found to be using protection.

The same is not true out on the western outskirts of the City, where I happened to find myself during a research trip last week. Oh no. In the district called Gashed Cow, things are very different indeed.

In Gashed Cow, the first thing you notice are the faces. Even in a City like ours, containing the dregs of every gene pool on Earth, you can detect the difference in these people. These are the people of urban myth. The people of the smashed chromosome. The people who play banjos. The people who drank the intellect suppressants in the water supply in preference to the clean water bussed in by the rescue op.

Guys in tan leather flares idly jacking off into the road, keeping a lazy eye on the female newsreader on the sidewalk screen by his left foot. Hundreds of kids with Attention Deficit Hyperactivity Disorder running around screaming while their berserk mothers continue to pump out more of the little fuckers for those few months of soft comfort from each before they start moving and never stop...

I don't want to turn on my fellow human, I really don't. But I saw these people believing everything they saw on the TV. Everything. They believe that The Smiler is a good man. They believe in God. They believe in justice. They believe in *Knight Rider.*

These people are the Enemy. Upgrade your sexual organs today, so that we may leave them behind.

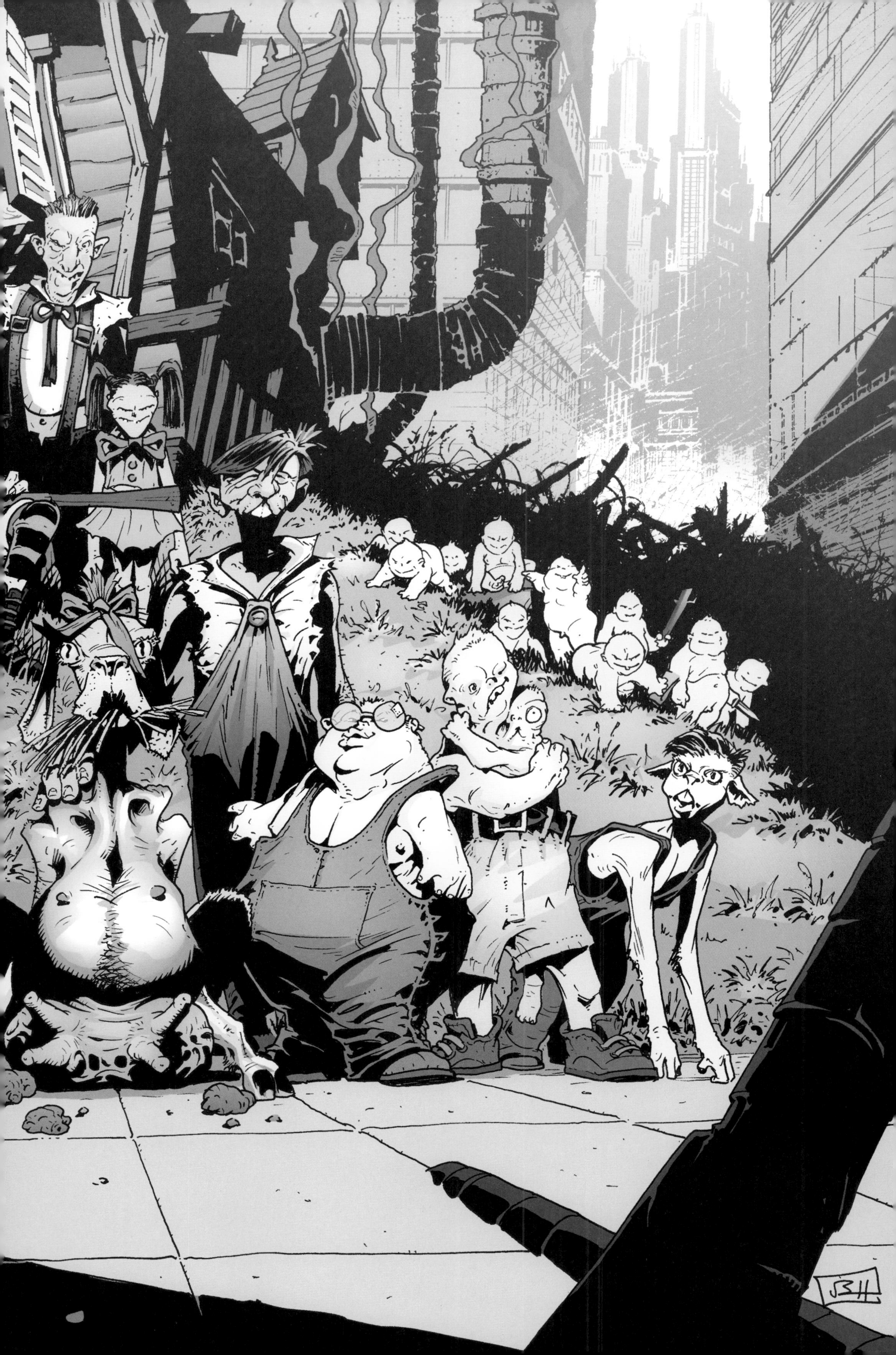

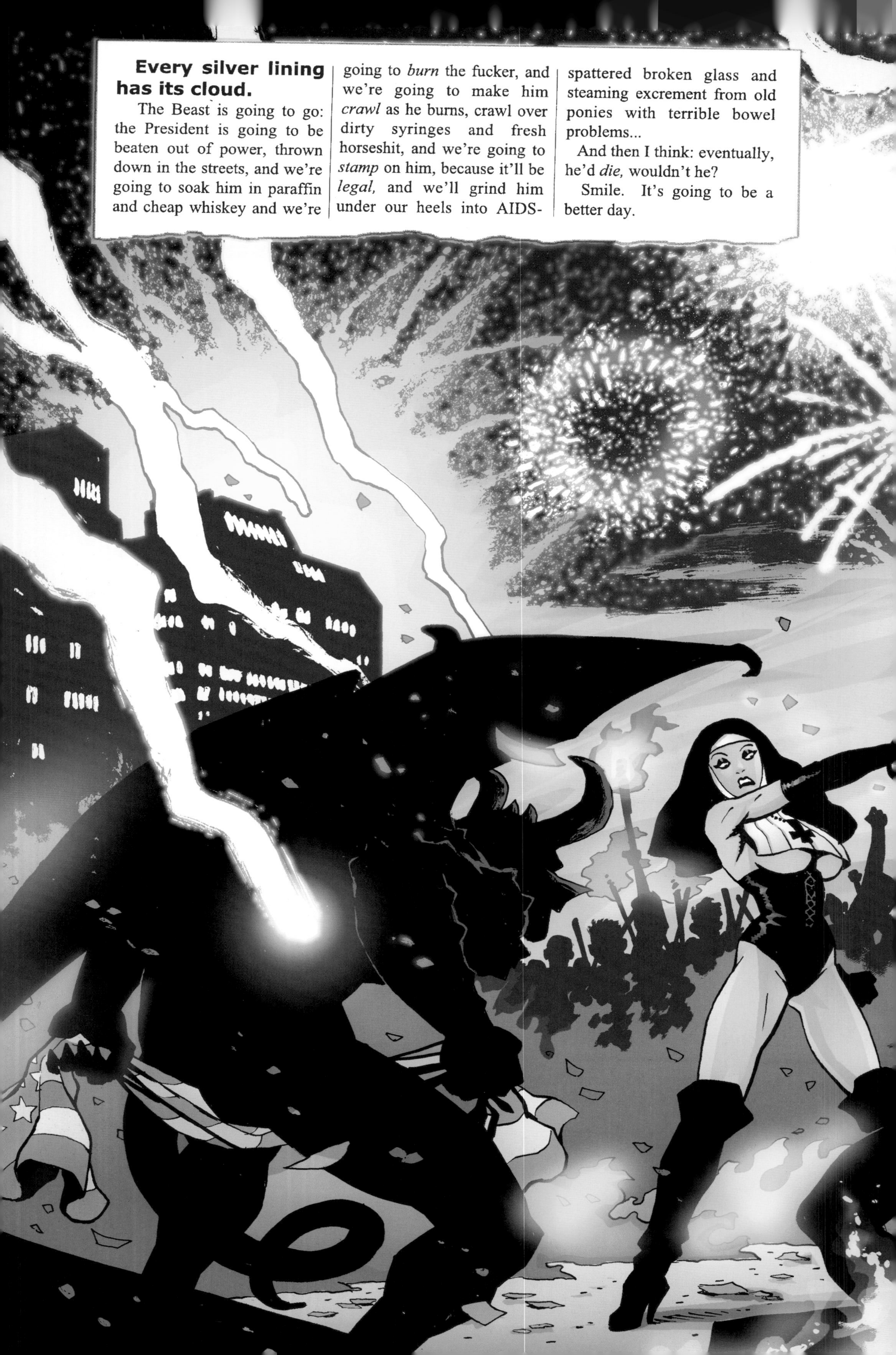
**Every silver lining has its cloud.**
The Beast is going to go: the President is going to be beaten out of power, thrown down in the streets, and we're going to soak him in paraffin and cheap whiskey and we're going to *burn* the fucker, and we're going to make him *crawl* as he burns, crawl over dirty syringes and fresh horseshit, and we're going to *stamp* on him, because it'll be *legal,* and we'll grind him under our heels into AIDS-spattered broken glass and steaming excrement from old ponies with terrible bowel problems...
And then I think: eventually, he'd *die,* wouldn't he?
Smile. It's going to be a better day.

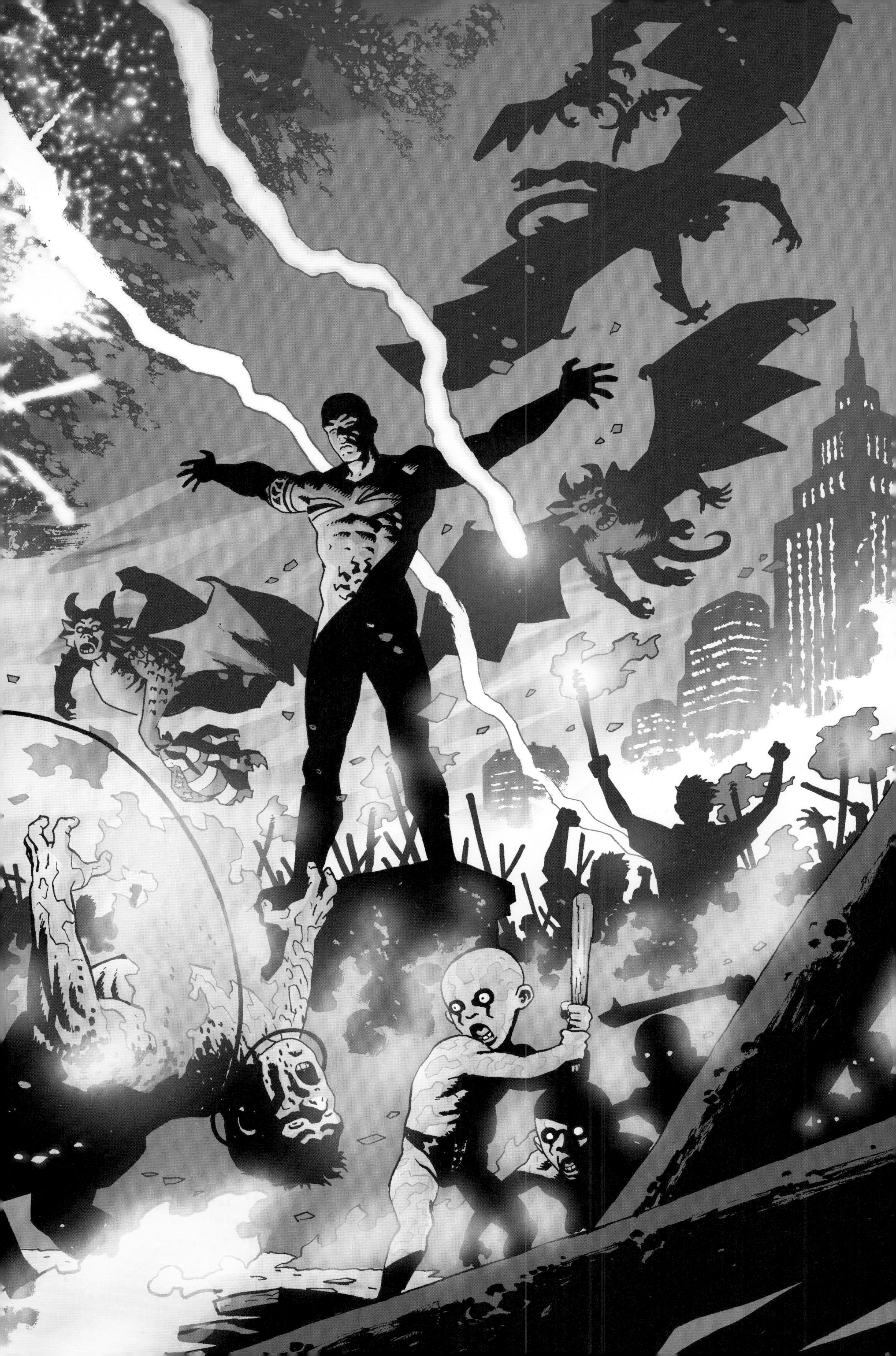

**I have developed a new assistant. This is** not, as far as she is concerned, a good thing. She hates me immediately. She is intelligent, and comes from a fascinating background. She is fairly quick on the uptake, and will be quicker when the studenty curves on her have been abraded into sharp edges. Frankly, she's far more intelligent than I am and has a genetic inheritance that leaves mine standing in the mire. Actually, now I think about it, my dad used to screw mire.

And she loathes me. No half measures here. She thinks I didn't notice the death trap she set outside my door, or the poison in the coffee.

Her name is Yelena Rossini, and she may well prove to be the best assistant I ever had. I'll tell you how she grows up. If you meet her, tell her none of this. You see, she refuses to read the column...

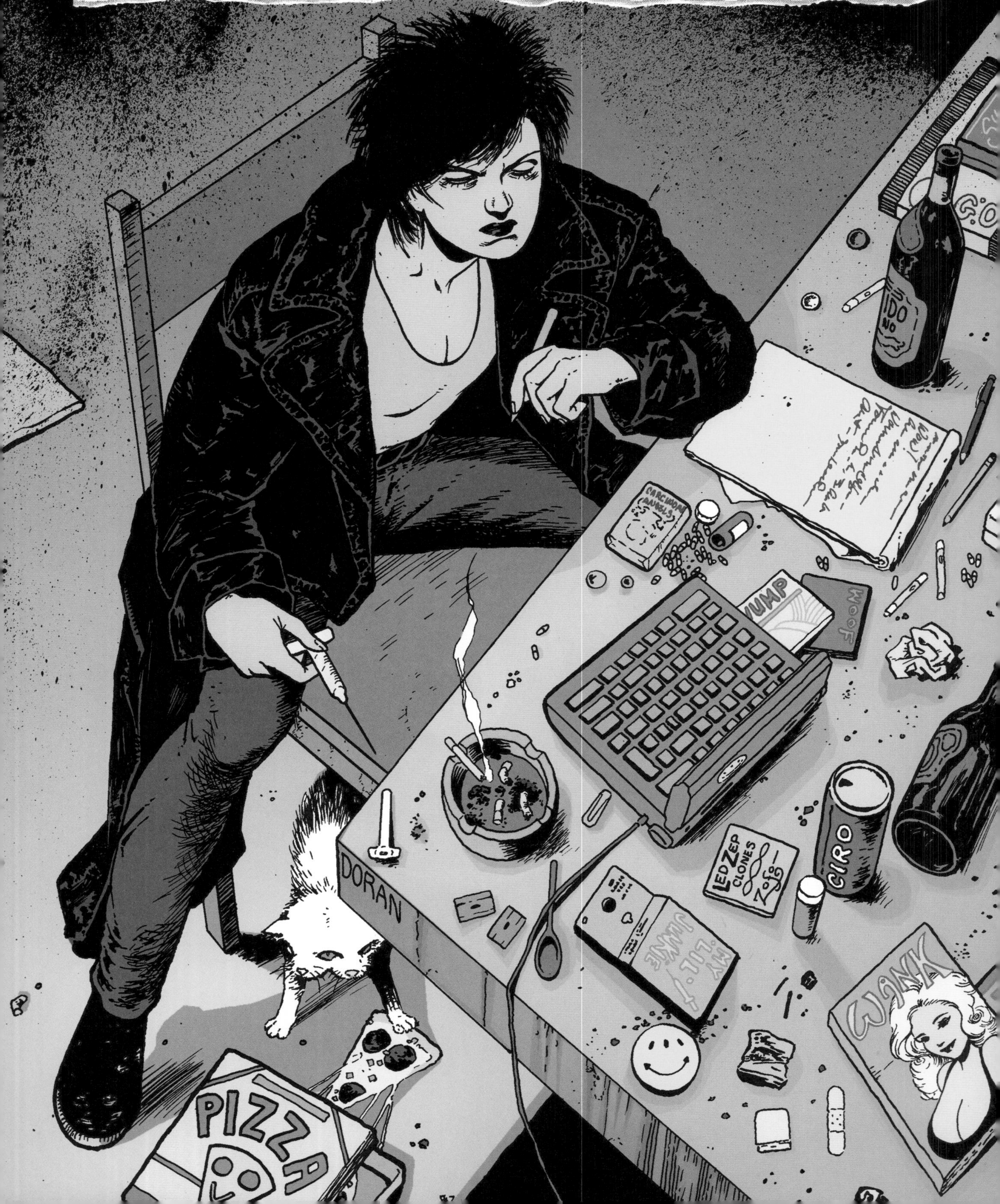
PIZZA
DORAN
CIRO
WOOF
LED ZEP CLONES
WANK

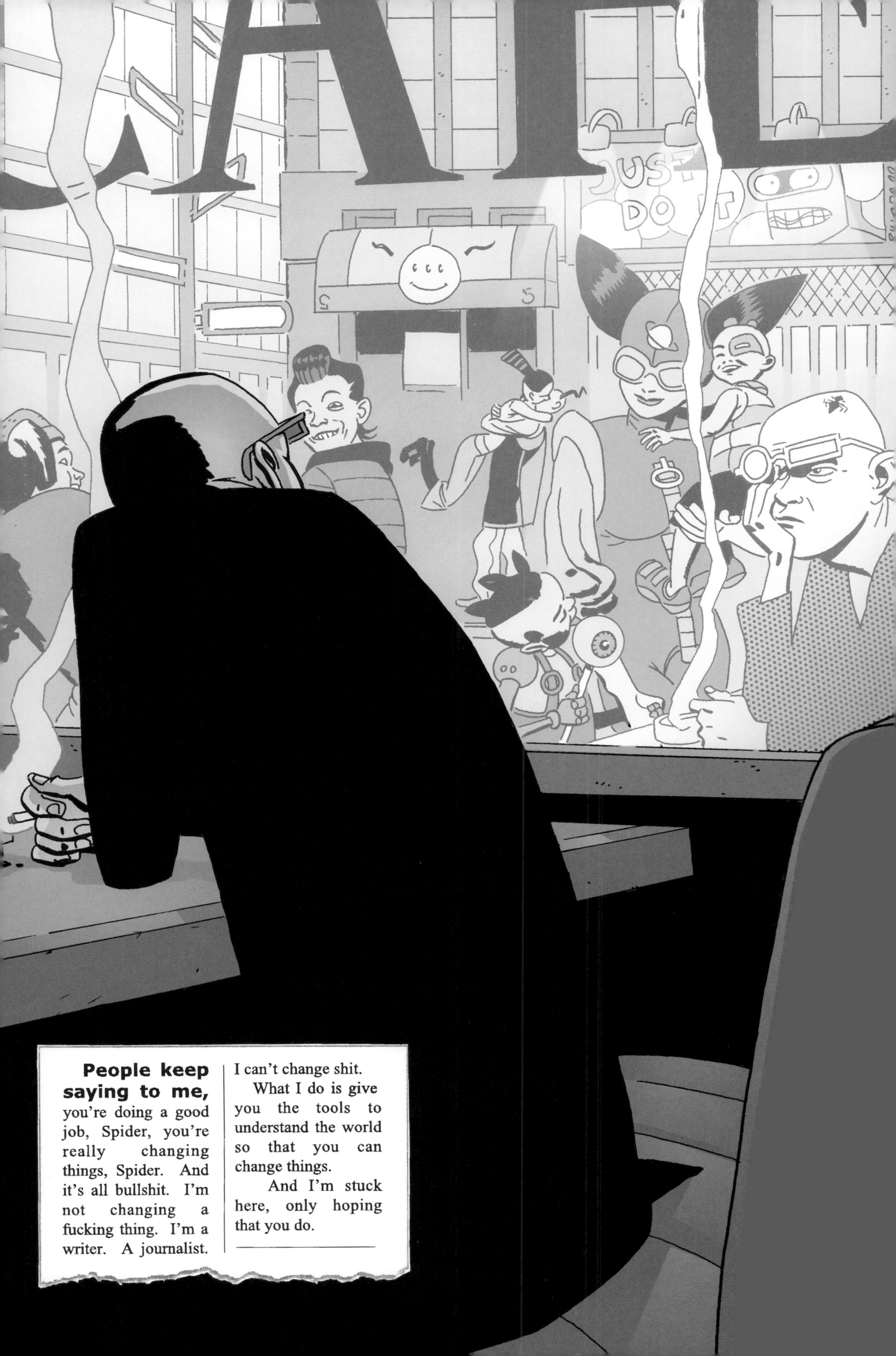
People keep saying to me, you're doing a good job, Spider, you're really changing things, Spider. And it's all bullshit. I'm not changing a fucking thing. I'm a writer. A journalist. I can't change shit.
What I do is give you the tools to understand the world so that you can change things.
And I'm stuck here, only hoping that you do.

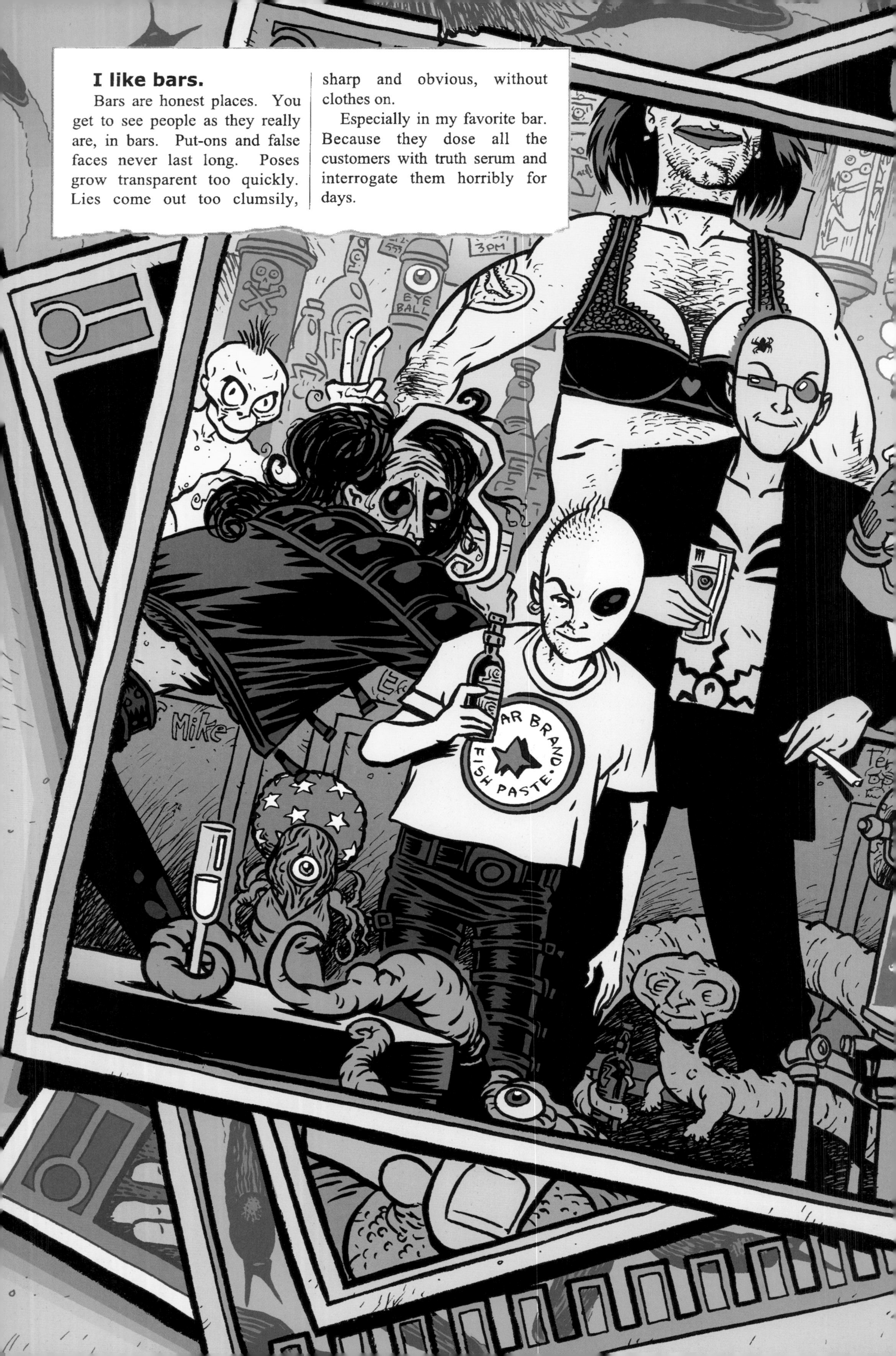
I like bars.
Bars are honest places. You get to see people as they really are, in bars. Put-ons and false faces never last long. Poses grow transparent too quickly. Lies come out too clumsily, sharp and obvious, without clothes on.
Especially in my favorite bar. Because they dose all the customers with truth serum and interrogate them horribly for days.
3PM
EYE BALL
AR BRAND FISH PASTE.
Mike

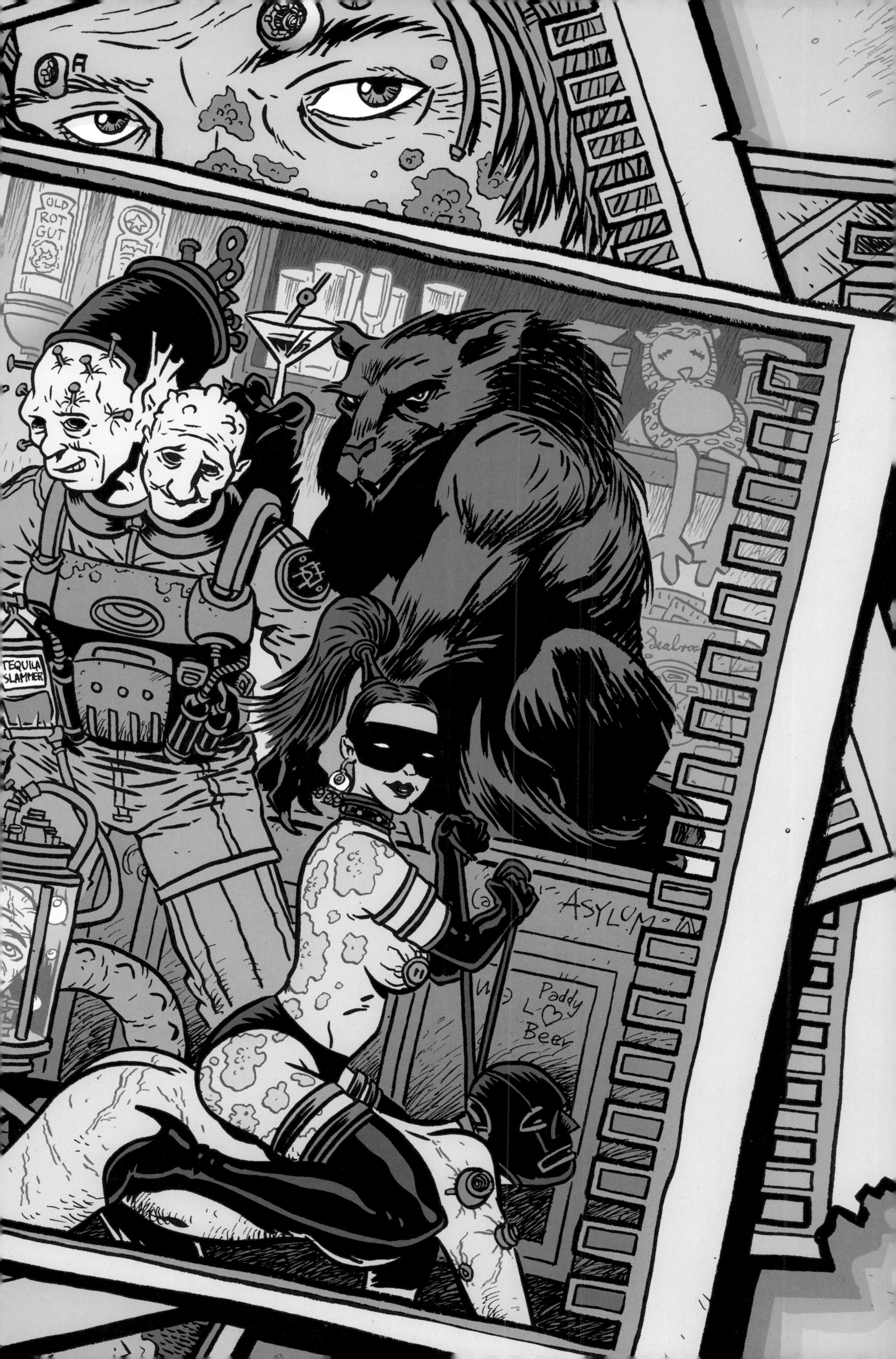
OLD
ROT
GUT
TEQUILA
SLAMMER
ASYLUM
Paddy
L♥
Beer

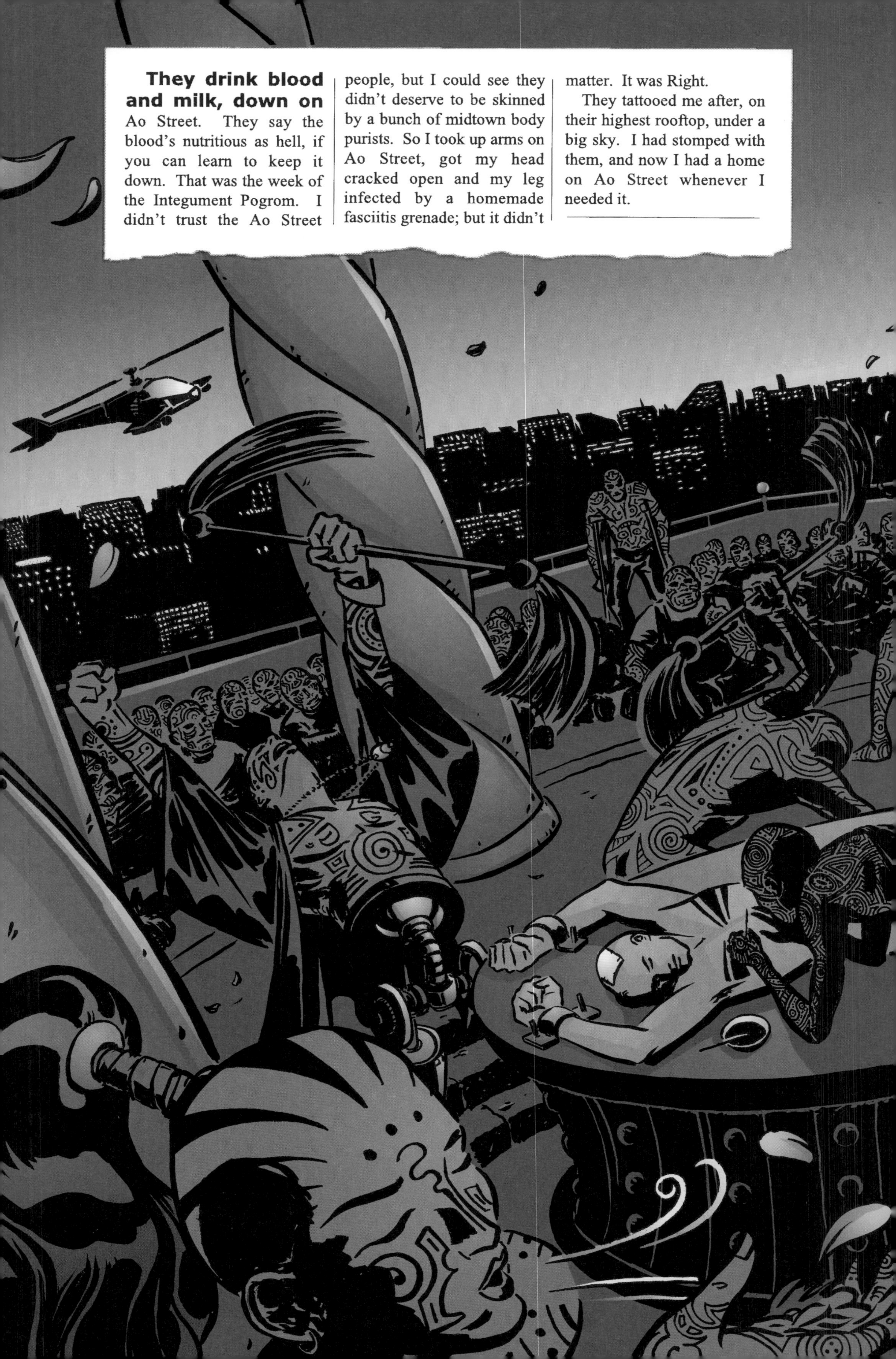
They drink blood and milk, down on Ao Street. They say the blood's nutritious as hell, if you can learn to keep it down. That was the week of the Integument Pogrom. I didn't trust the Ao Street people, but I could see they didn't deserve to be skinned by a bunch of midtown body purists. So I took up arms on Ao Street, got my head cracked open and my leg infected by a homemade fasciitis grenade; but it didn't matter. It was Right.
They tattooed me after, on their highest rooftop, under a big sky. I had stomped with them, and now I had a home on Ao Street whenever I needed it.

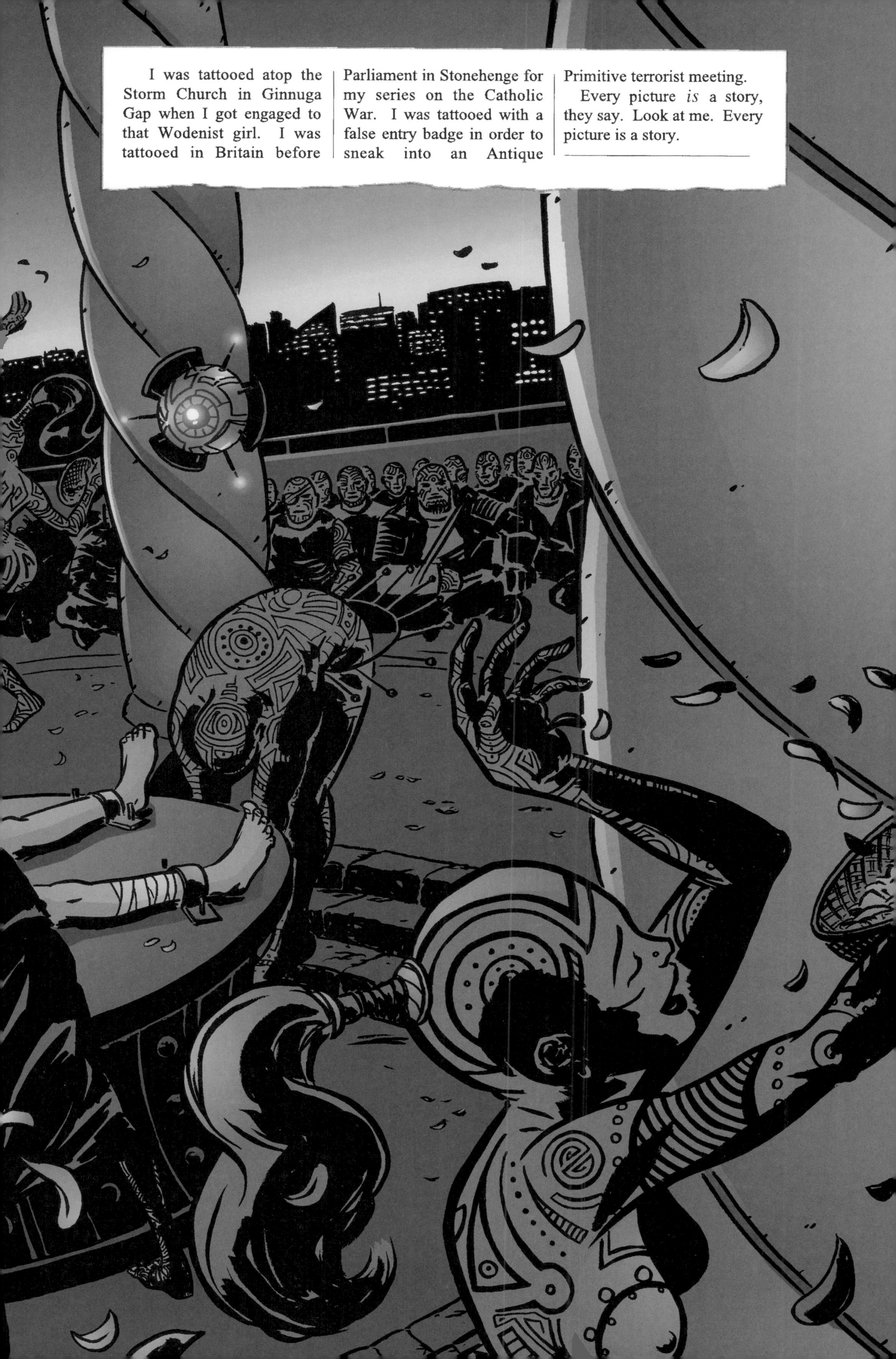
I was tattooed atop the Storm Church in Ginnuga Gap when I got engaged to that Wodenist girl. I was tattooed in Britain before Parliament in Stonehenge for my series on the Catholic War. I was tattooed with a false entry badge in order to sneak into an Antique Primitive terrorist meeting.
Every picture *is* a story, they say. Look at me. Every picture is a story.

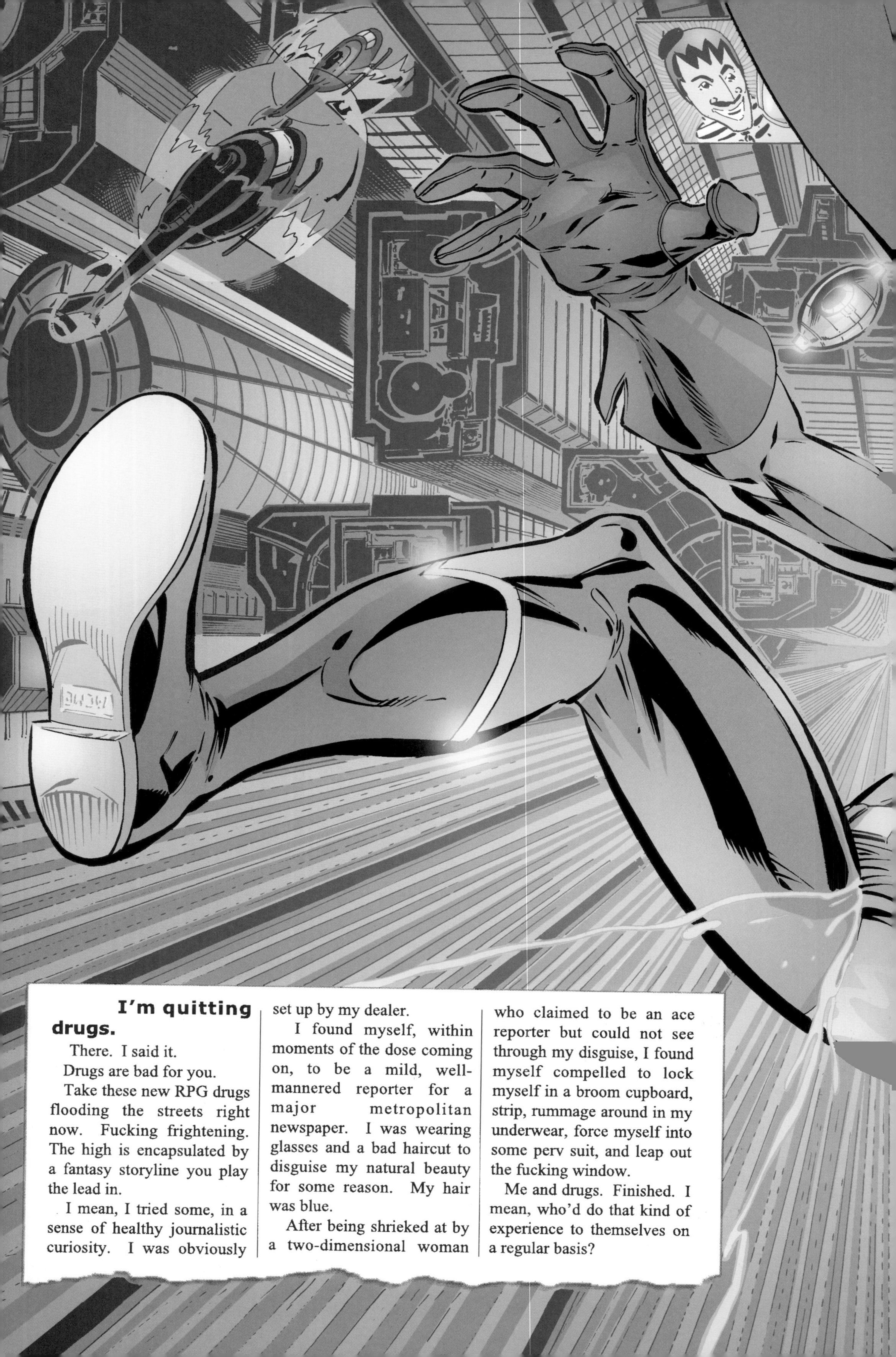

**I'm quitting drugs.**

There. I said it.

Drugs are bad for you.

Take these new RPG drugs flooding the streets right now. Fucking frightening. The high is encapsulated by a fantasy storyline you play the lead in.

I mean, I tried some, in a sense of healthy journalistic curiosity. I was obviously set up by my dealer.

I found myself, within moments of the dose coming on, to be a mild, well-mannered reporter for a major metropolitan newspaper. I was wearing glasses and a bad haircut to disguise my natural beauty for some reason. My hair was blue.

After being shrieked at by a two-dimensional woman who claimed to be an ace reporter but could not see through my disguise, I found myself compelled to lock myself in a broom cupboard, strip, rummage around in my underwear, force myself into some perv suit, and leap out the fucking window.

Me and drugs. Finished. I mean, who'd do that kind of experience to themselves on a regular basis?

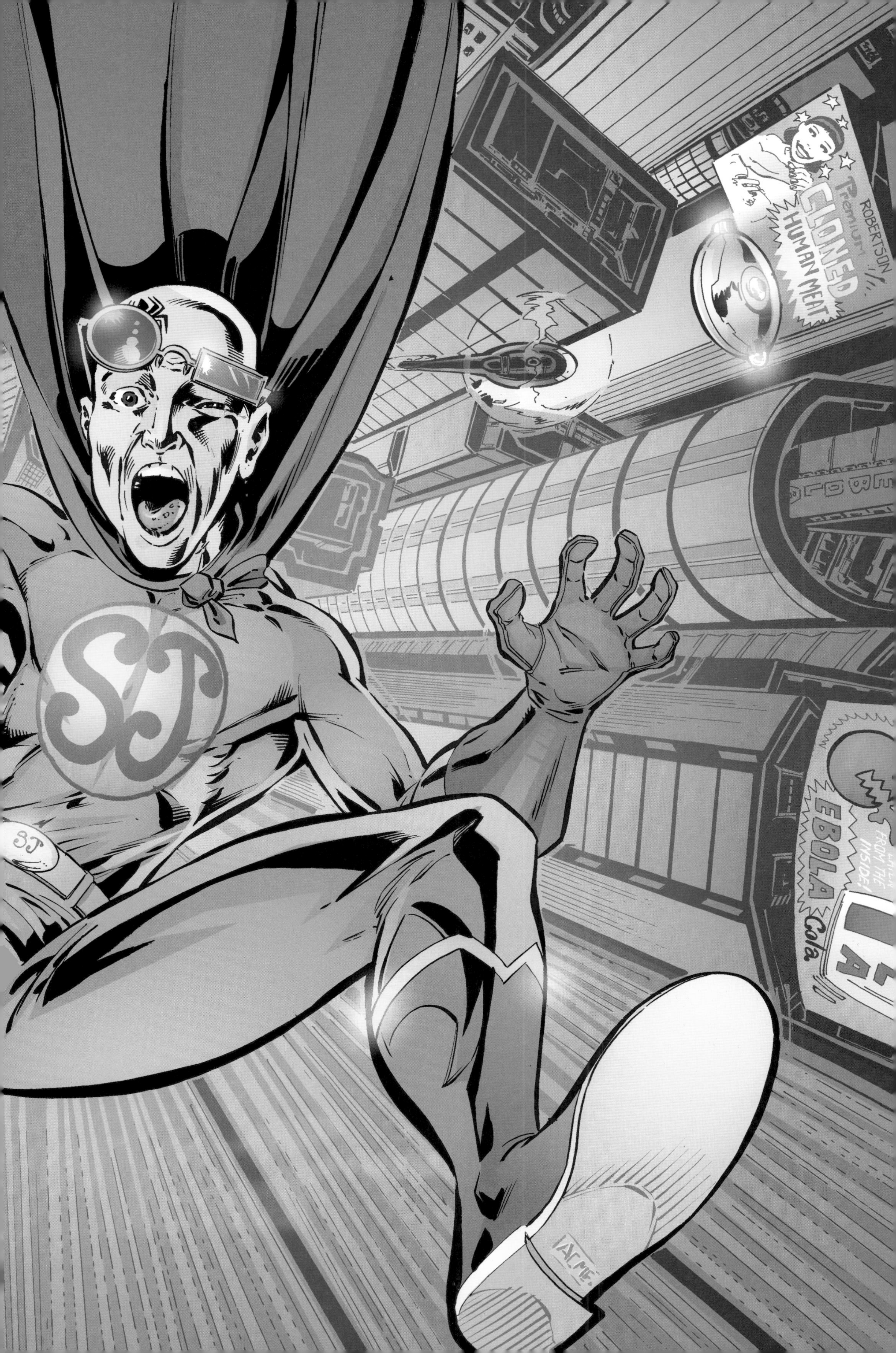

ROBERTSON
Premium
CLONED
HUMAN MEAT
EBOLA
FROM THE INSIDE!
EBOLA
Cola
SJ
SJ
ACME

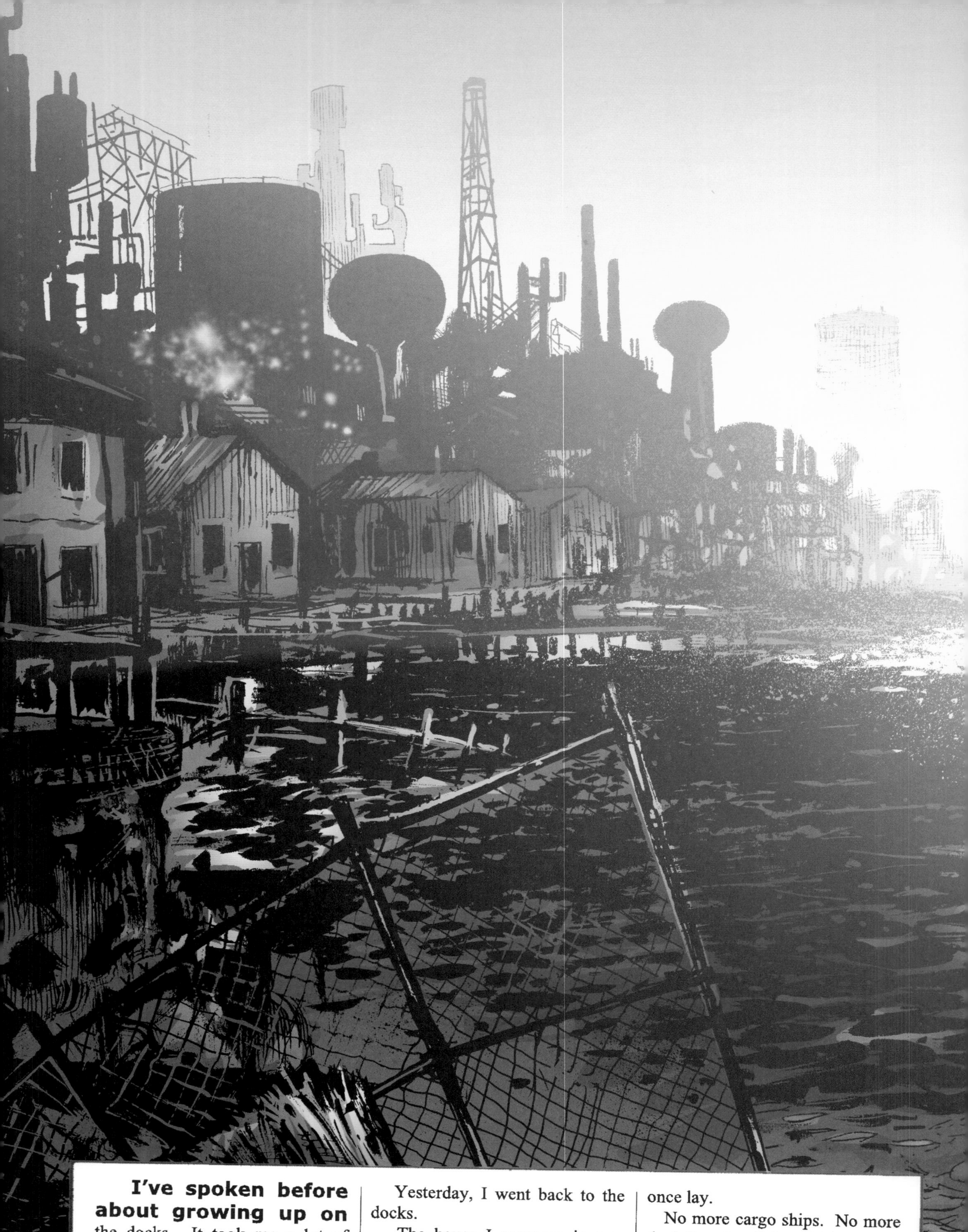

**I've spoken before about growing up on** the docks. It took me a lot of years to work up the escape velocity to launch out of here, and I've never been back. Never wanted to risk tumbling back down into that gravity well; never wanted to risk not being able to claw my way out again.

Yesterday, I went back to the docks.

The house I grew up in was burned out. You could clearly see a blackened little skeleton slumped in one corner, arranged in the student-sculpture of a melted aluminum bed, blobs of grey plastic sitting on its sooty bones where a disposable blanket once lay.

No more cargo ships. No more dock lizards. A few fishing boats. Spoiled catch rotting dockside. No one giving a shit. No one left alive here to tell the tale of how it was here. Except me.

Story of my life.

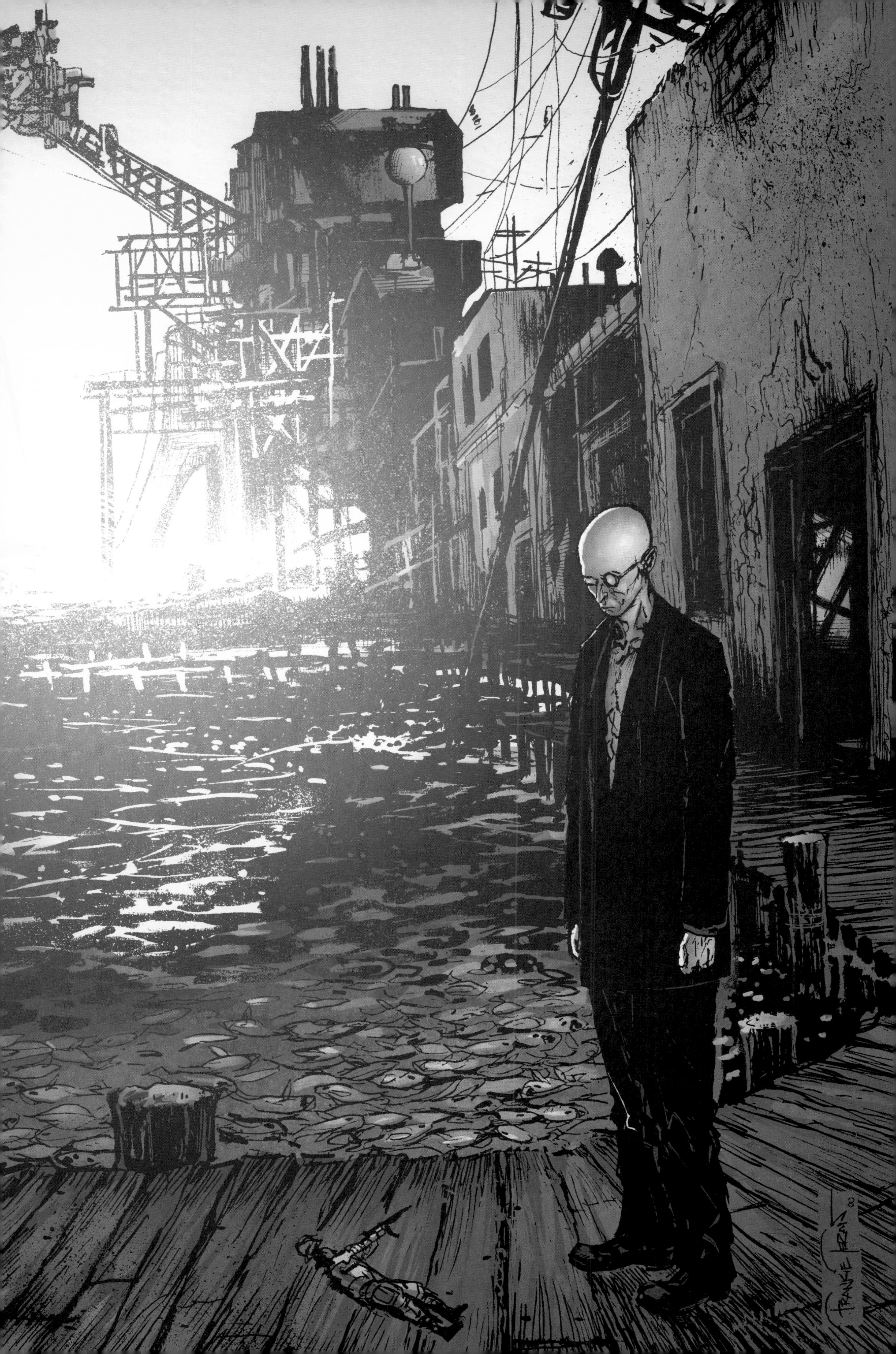

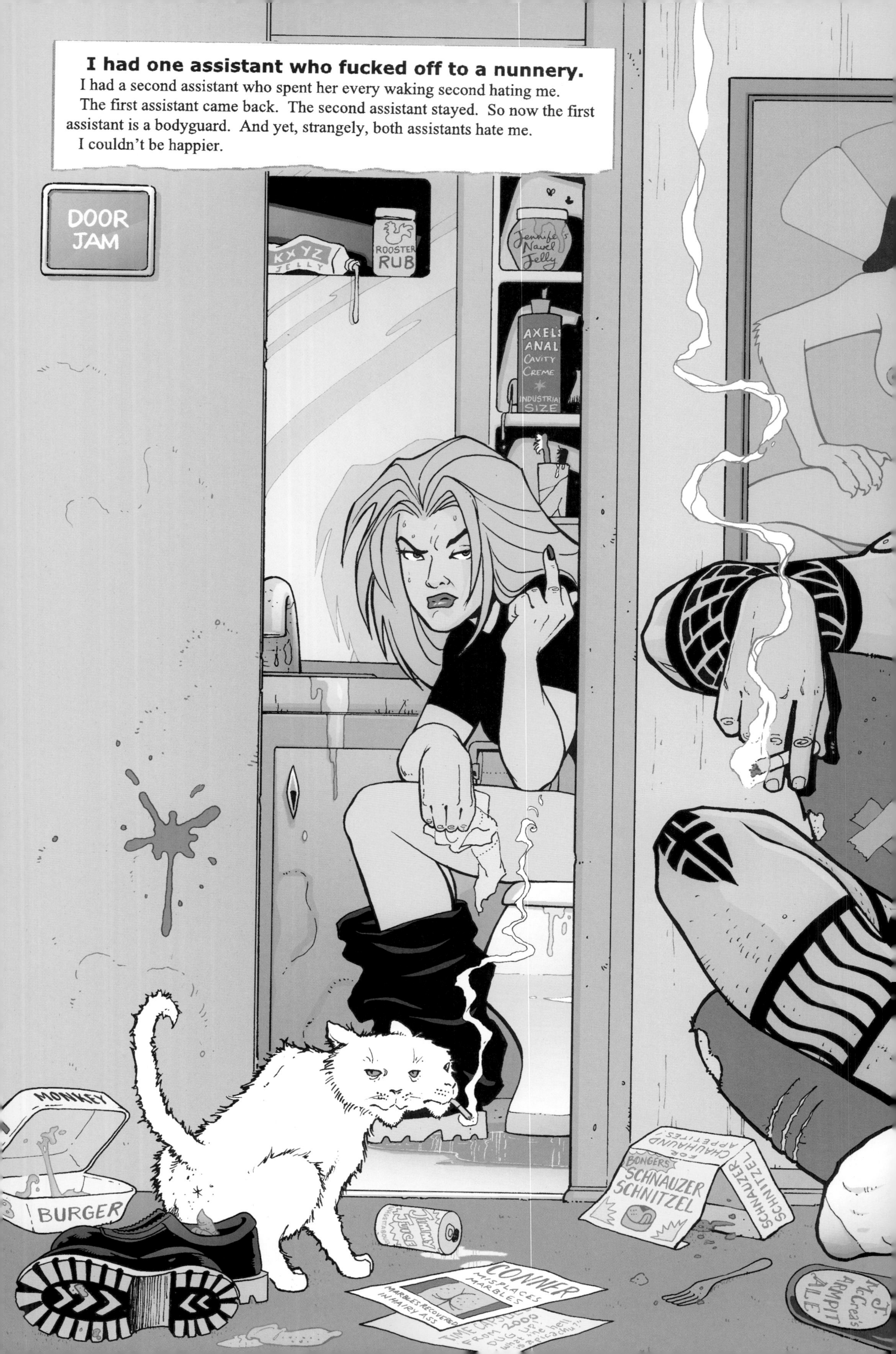
I had one assistant who fucked off to a nunnery.
I had a second assistant who spent her every waking second hating me.
The first assistant came back. The second assistant stayed. So now the first assistant is a bodyguard. And yet, strangely, both assistants hate me.
I couldn't be happier.
DOOR JAM
KXYZ JELLY
ROOSTER RUB
Jennifer's Navel Jelly
AXEL'S ANAL CAVITY CREME INDUSTRIAL SIZE
MONKEY
BURGER
Jimmy Juice
BONGERS SCHNAUZER SCHNITZEL
FOR CHAUHAUND APPETITES!
SCHNAUZER SCHNITZEL
CONNER MISPLACES MARBLES
MARBLES RECOVERED IN HAIRY ASS
TIME CAPSULE FROM 2000 DUG UP!
What the hell is a picachu?!
M.J. McCrea's ARMPIT ALE

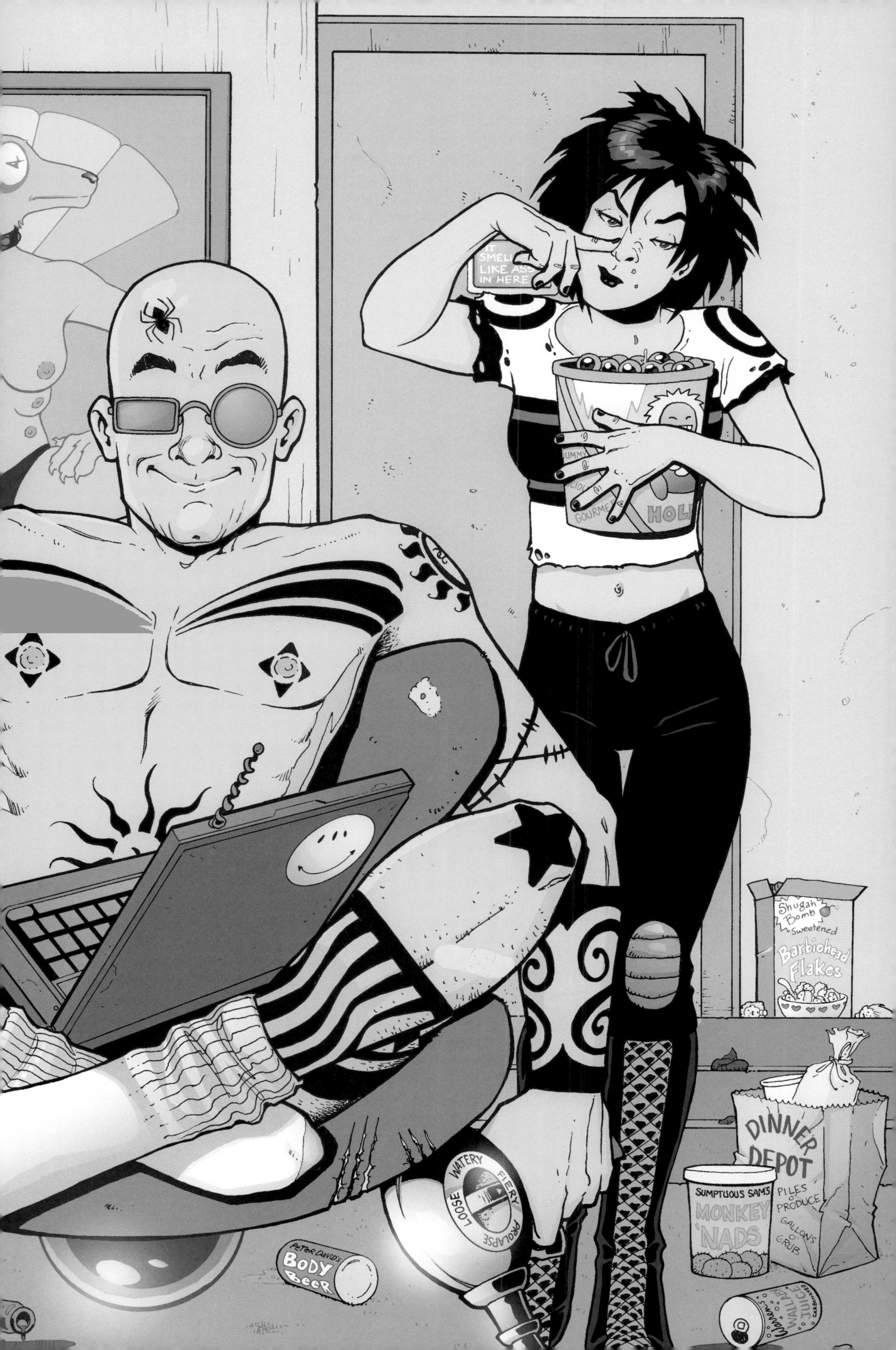
IT SMELL
LIKE ASS
IN HERE
Shugah Bomb
Sweetened
Barbiehead Flakes
DINNER DEPOT
PILES O' PRODUCE
GALLONS O' GRUB
SUMPTUOUS SAM'S
MONKEY NADS
PETER DAVID'S
BODY BEER
LOOSE WATERY FIERY PROLAPSE
WALLACE JUICE

**I've been on television again.** Taping a game show, no less. Now, before you start screaming Sellout and waving your pitchforks and torches in the air, hear me out. It's a game show produced by Pharmatopia. You'll have seen them in the news: the people attempting to bring back the dead by cloning them and reconstructing their electromagnetic auras. Well, they're partway there, and are funding the final big push via this game show. ZOMBIE GLADIATORS. Wherein celebrities engage in arena deathmatches with famous people from the past. So I'm not selling out. I'm helping fund the apotheosis of the human species while beating resurrected power-junkie fame-whores back into the grave.

Don't you wish you were me?

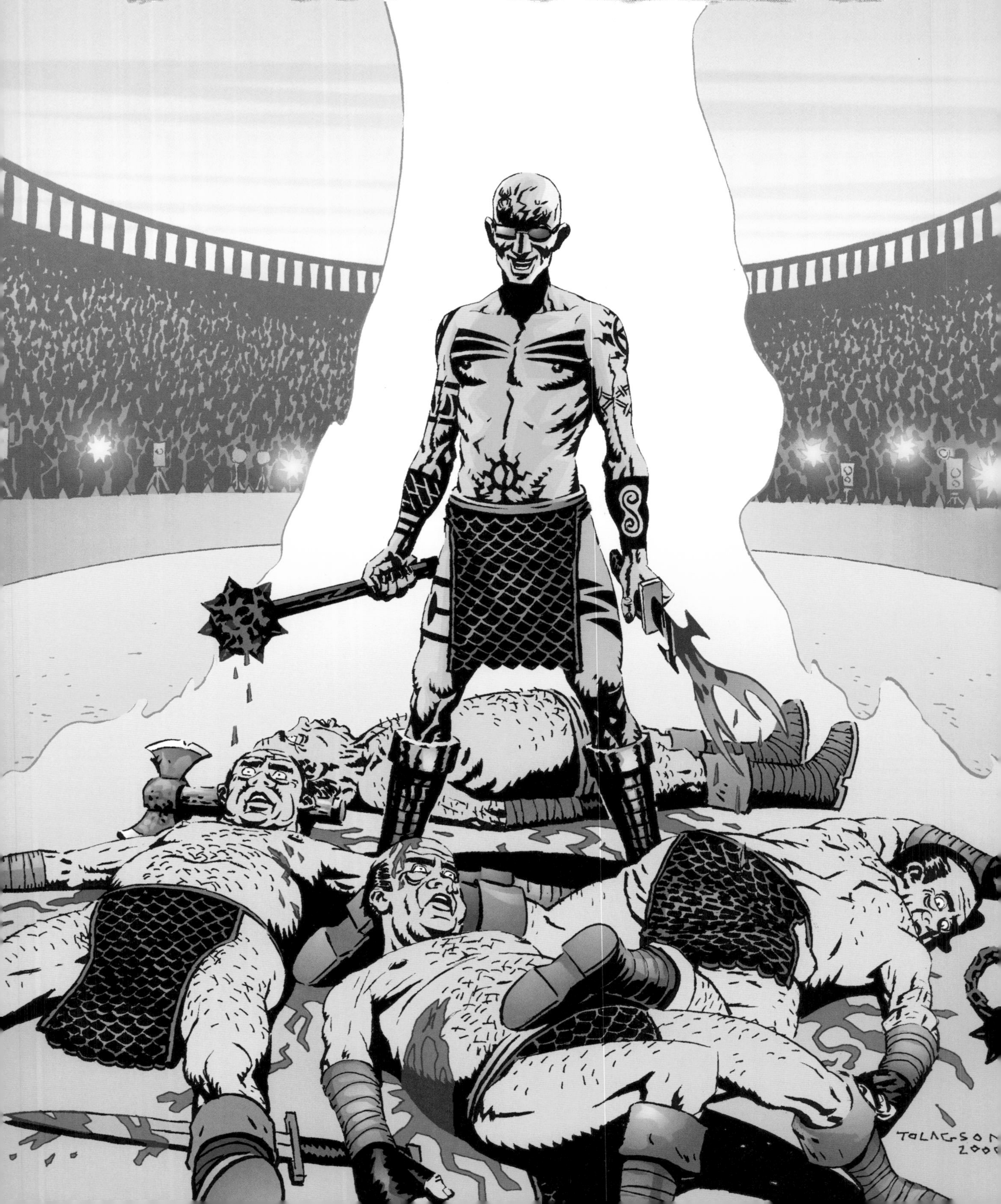
TOLAGSON

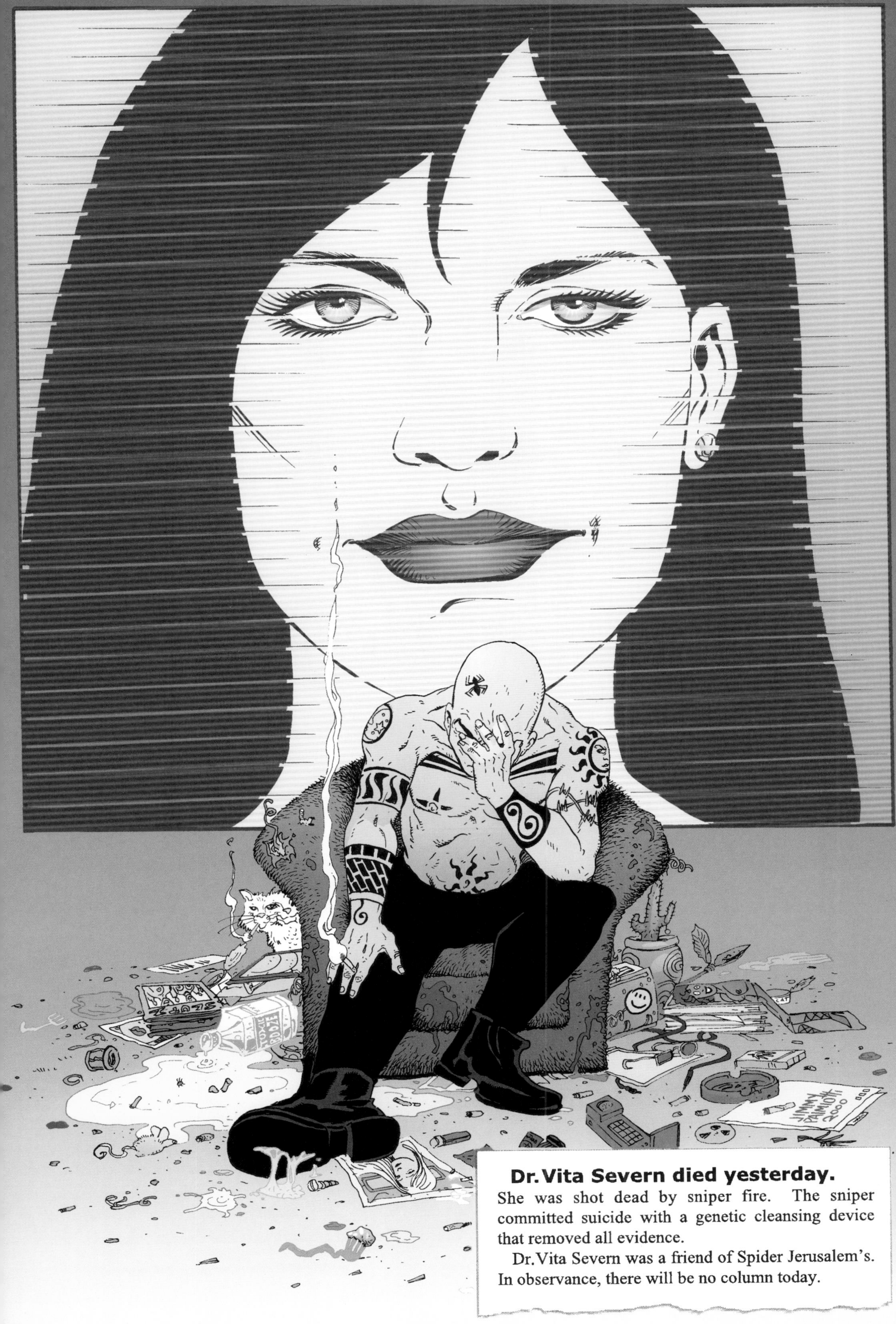
Dr. Vita Severn died yesterday.
She was shot dead by sniper fire. The sniper committed suicide with a genetic cleansing device that removed all evidence.
Dr. Vita Severn was a friend of Spider Jerusalem's. In observance, there will be no column today.

**This isn't Spider Jerusalem. I'm** Yelena Rossini, and I'm writing Mr. Jerusalem's column in his stead today, at his express invitation. Well. More like an order. He called it a "proclamation," in actual fact. This was during the afternoon he spent dressed as a pharaoh. Some of you may have seen that.

Rather more of you will have seen him two days ago, during what we are calling his "impromptu tour." Which brings me to the subject of this piece. I'd like to clear up a few misconceptions about Mr. Jerusalem's activities during the "tour."

For instance. At no time did Mr. Jerusalem mug anyone. The five elderly citizens who claim that a naked Mr. Jerusalem swooped down from the roof of their hut to lay about them with a large dried bull penis, pausing only to steal their wallets and real teeth before taking flight... well, we've had them checked out. They were all senile, dizzied by an extended session of The Biscuit Game, and confused by ionized swamp-like gas billowing off the nearby Second Canal.

Mr. Jerusalem's admittedly bizarre statements to various feedsite listeners during the two days are not connected to any possible or claimed drug use on his part. He was tired and emotional and suffering unusual brain chemistry due to the trauma of losing his TV remote control.

The bit about his standing on top of the big screen on Century Square and feigning sex with half a Doberman Pinscher is, however, entirely true, and we are in negotiation with the police at this time.

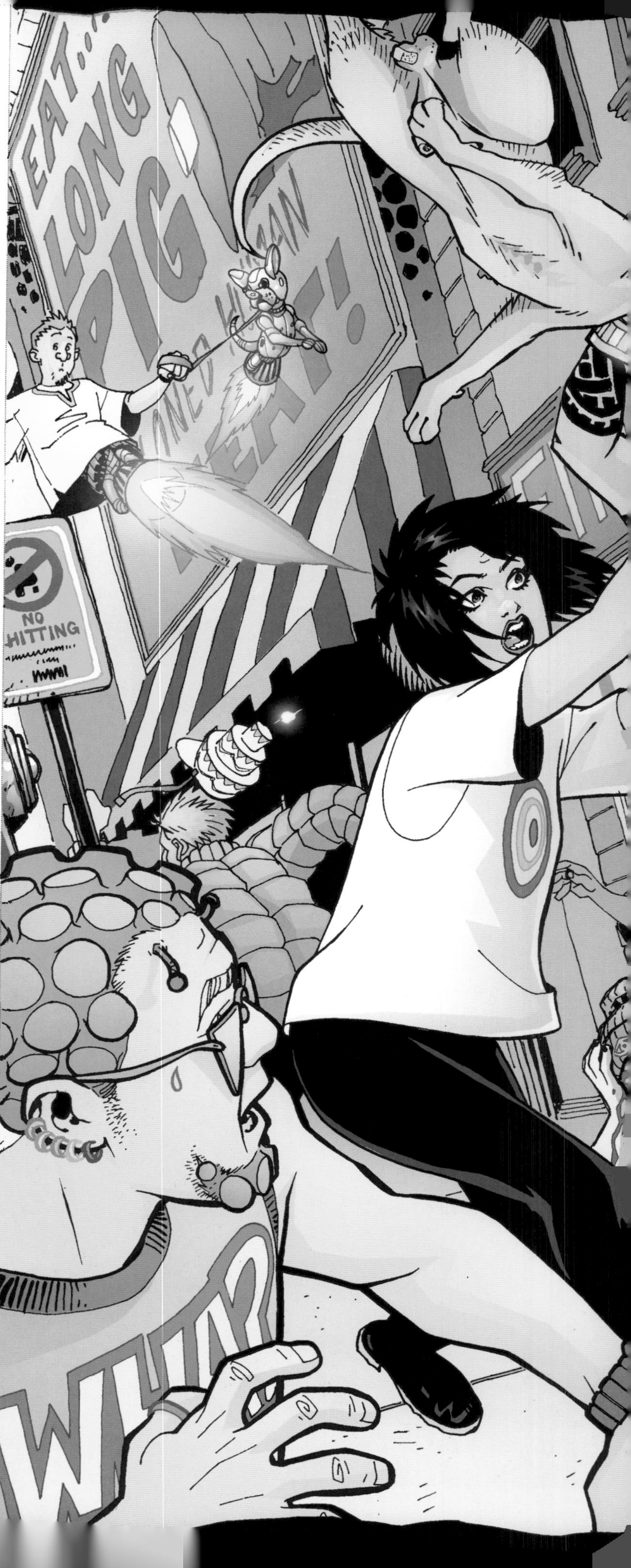
EAT LONG PIG
NO HITTING

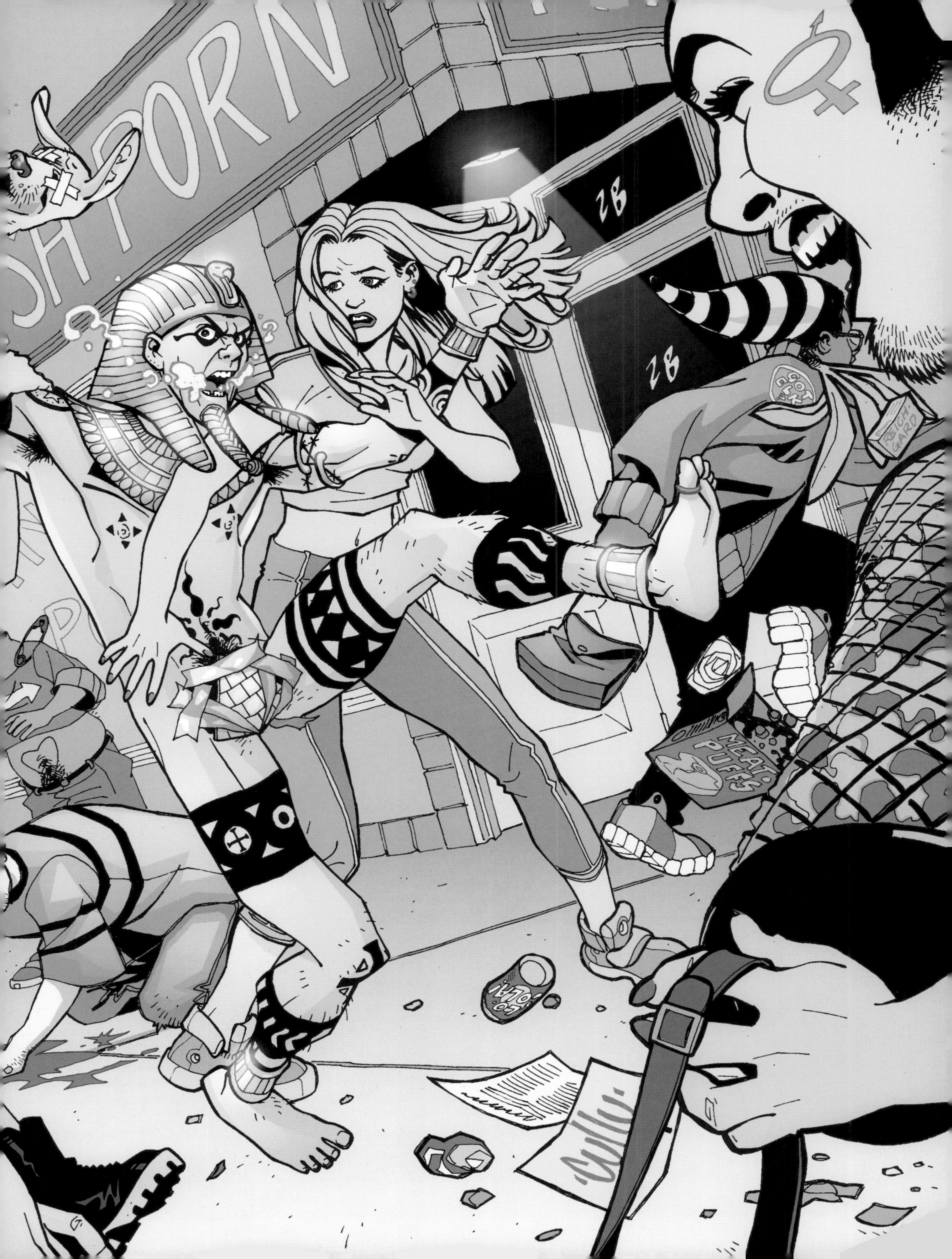
PORN
2B
2B
REICH-GARD
MEAT PUFFS

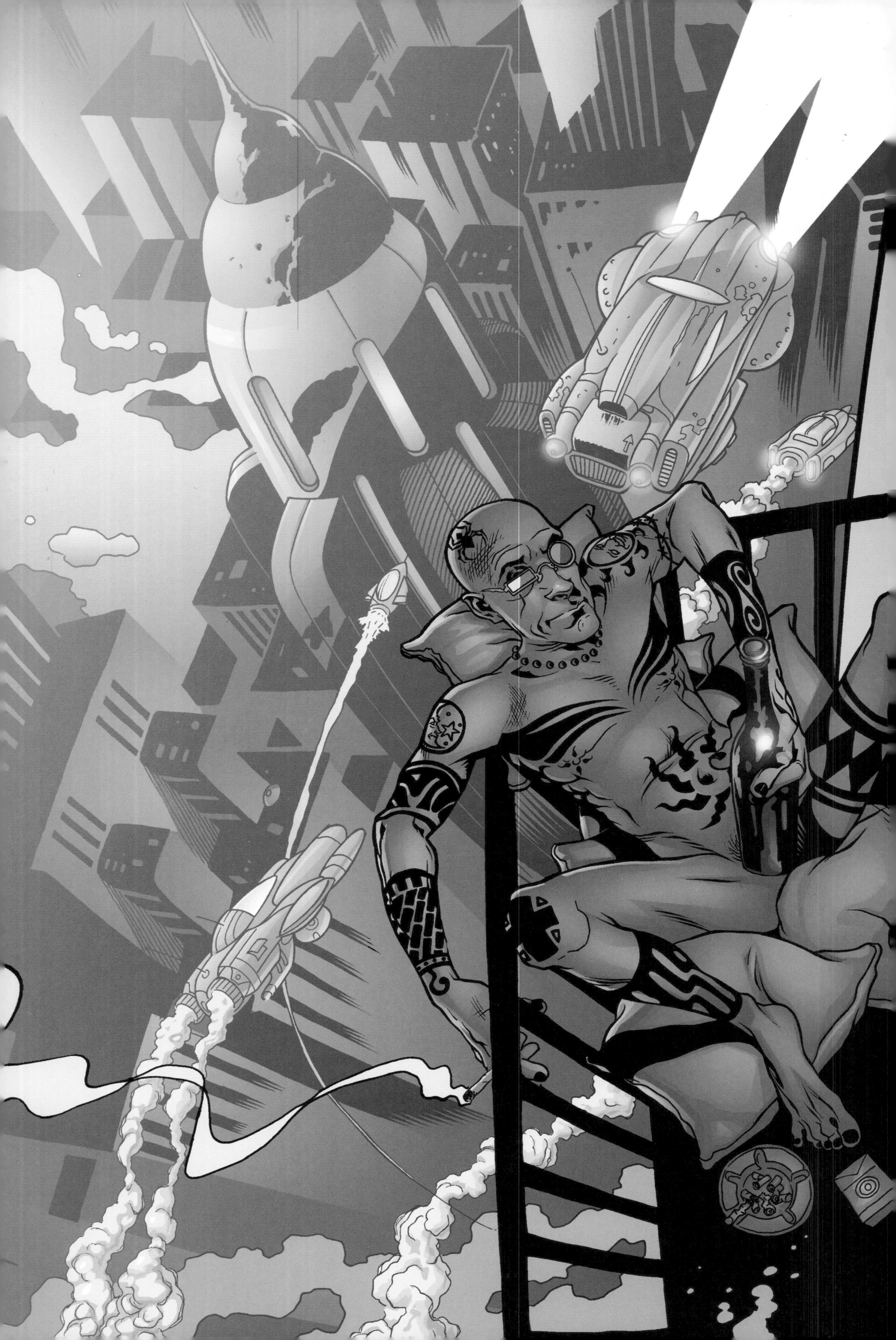

**Two years now. I've been back in** the City two years. It's been a loud, weird couple of years. White knuckle ride almost from the second I put my feet back on its streets. As I write this, I'm in a bubble of quiet. Suddenly, everything's gone quiet. I can hardly even hear the cars. There's occasional bars of nervous birdsong in the still air. Calm before the storm, maybe.

I hate it here. That's why I keep coming back.

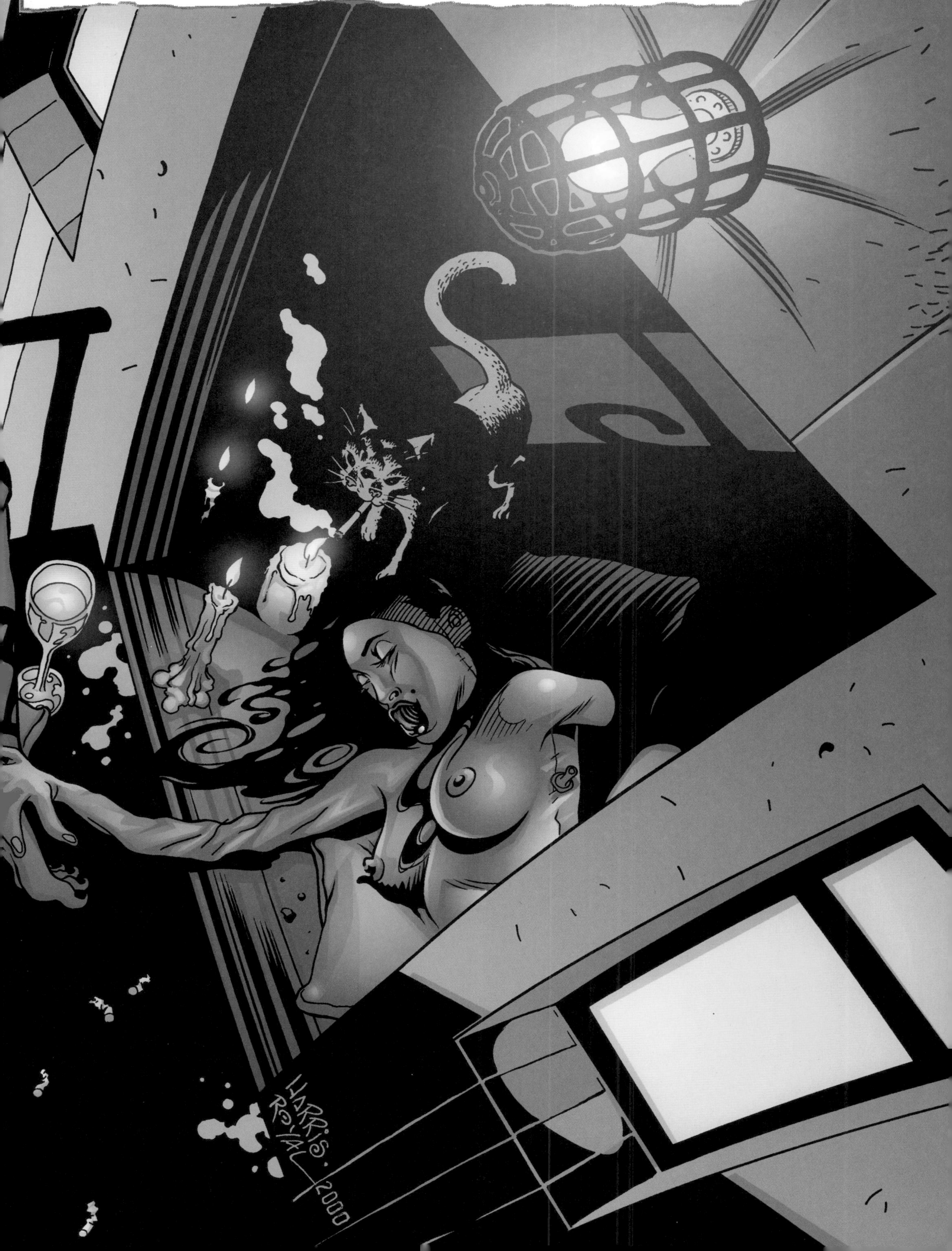
HARRIS ROYAL 2000

## AFTERWORD
## by
## MITCHELL ROYCE

I have been working with Spider Jerusalem for many years now. It was I who got him into France during the War of Verbals. I was with him in Prague, on The Terrible Night of the Telephone. I kept him alive in St. Lucia when the galloping cockrot threatened to clamber up his spinal column. I got his first column, the column that stopped The Transient Riots, on the major feedsites and public screens. I've known him longer than almost anyone else alive.

And I want you to know that I hate him and I wish he were dead. Now. I mean right fucking now. With harpoons in him. Big fucking harpoons.

Really fucking big ones.

***Mitchell Royce***
***City Editor***
***The Word***

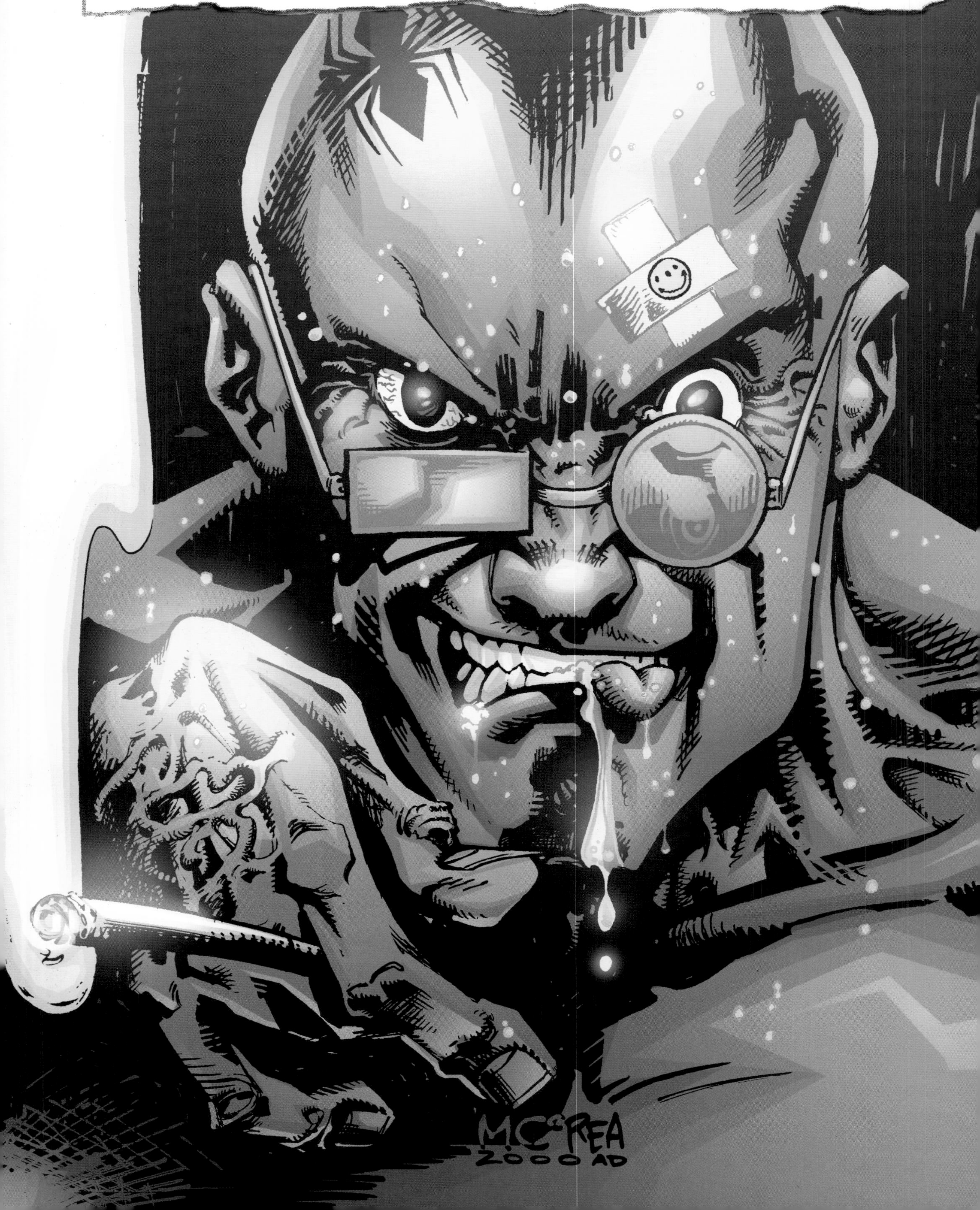
McCREA
2000 AD

Tonight on:

# LONELY CITY

**"NEXT WEEK'S DRUGS."**

**Following the FDA loophole that stops drugs being made illegal until they are actually discovered, our crack team of narcotic-munching investigative reporters tests a spread of fixes invented only hours previous to filming. Includes scenes of FDA troops capturing and taking stomach samples from our staff.**

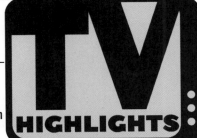

# TV HIGHLIGHTS

**8:00//78** (comedy)
***GOTCHA!*** Home videos of horrifically bloody and deeply disturbing domestic accidents.

**8:30//13.6** (children)
***SEX PUPPETS:*** Delightfully lighthearted educational show. Today, Darleen must decide which Puppet will live and which will die.

**9:30//45** (leisure)
***SLIDE:*** Mildly psychoactive visual wave effects combine with Kodo drum patterns and classified subliminal signals to gently chew holes in your frontal lobe.

**10:00//1002** (infomercial)
***GERIATRICIDE:*** Killing poverty-stricken old people for fun and profit. This week: arranging a good hard winter to thin the old toads out a bit.

**11:00//383** (news)
***SPKF:*** Patching to the Print District offices of the city's prime feedsite for a late-night news and event summary.

**11:30//78.4** (music)
***LOST:*** Featuring CFC performing pieces from their new disc, "Dirty Rain." Select interactive subchannel to have holographic simulations of dead, oil-drenched sea gulls tossed at you.

**12:00//3** (drama)
***CRIMINAL NATION:*** Adventures of City Police Department detectives. This week — a revived Ernest Hemingway in Sniper Alley! Captain Gacy eats a suspect!

**It's never too soon to start planning your holiday!**
**Hit the Peak at**

## *the Airy Aerie*

Shoot and kill your own food and neighbors!

*Weekend getaways available now!*
TV • TELEPHONE • MAKERS IN EVERY ROOM
*Paradise awaits you—just one hour from the City!*

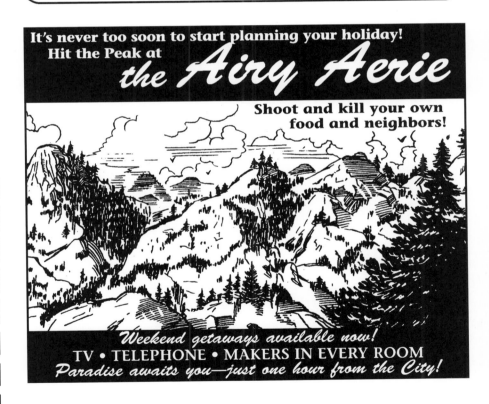

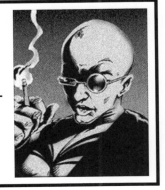

**"...They've cleared all the non-transients out of Angels 8. Incredible tension, like they're all living in the second before the bullet hits the bone..."**

***MEMOIRS FROM THE BACKSIDE OF THE WORLD:***
"I Hate It Here" *Spider Jerusalem's column exclusive to The Word : Every month in...*

LATE EDITION
**TRANSMETROPOLITAN**

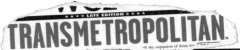

# TRANSVERSE SECTIONS

## Augmented Memories from Warren Ellis and Darick Robertson

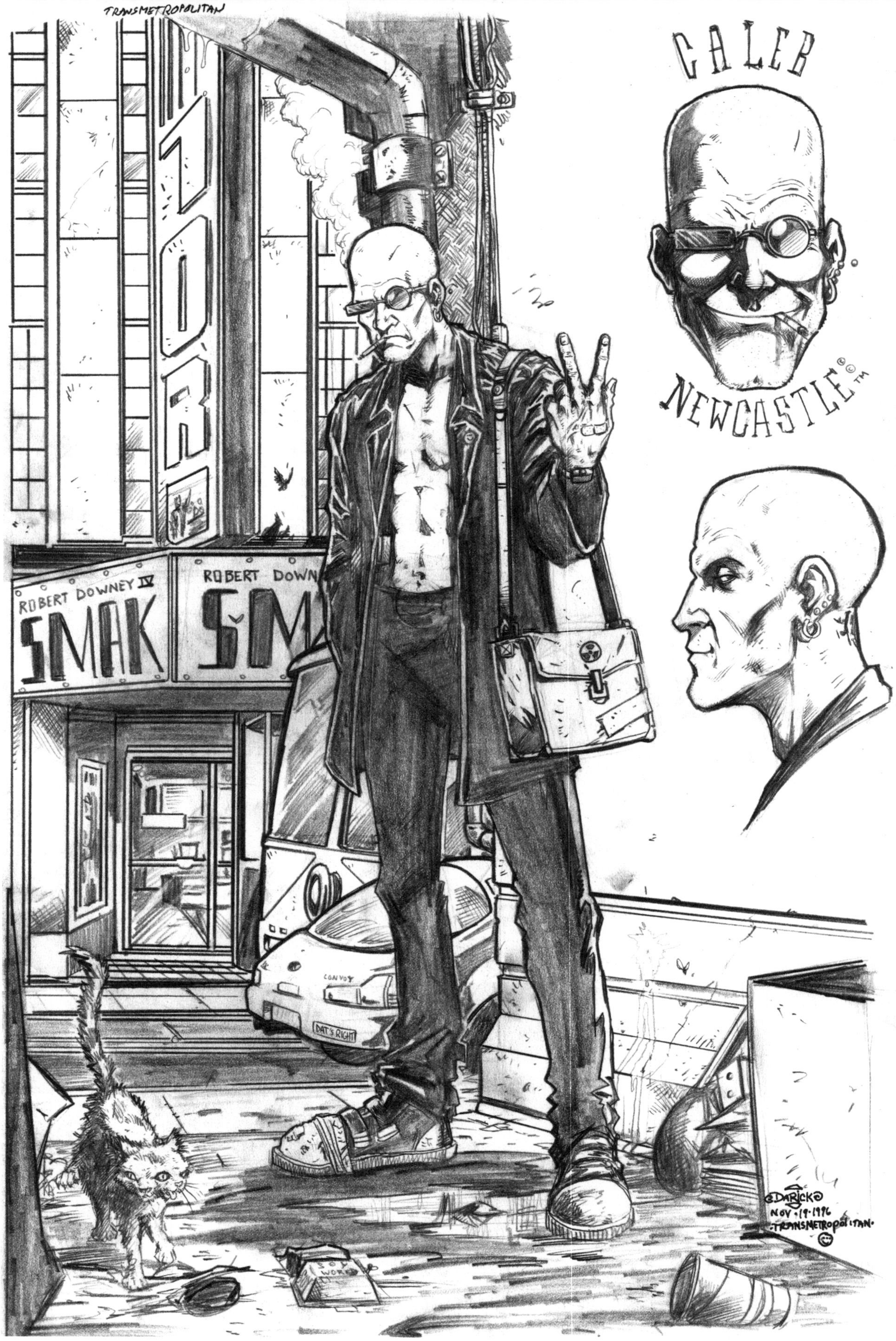
TRANSMETROPOLITAN
CALEB
NEWCASTLE
ROBERT DOWNEY IV
SMAK
ROBERT DOWN
SM
CONVOY
DAT'S RIGHT
DARICK
NOV·19·1996
·TRANSMETROPOLITAN·

Darick Robertson's first concept drawing of Spider Jerusalem, displaying the character's original name of Caleb Newcastle.

*For the first three issues of TRANSMETROPOLITAN, Warren Ellis provided original essays under the alternating titles of "Subway" and "I Hate It Here" which ran in the space that became the title's letter column. These uncensored textual biopsies are reprinted here for educational and cautionary purposes only.*

# ISSUE #1: SUBWAY

Shut up.

Norman Spinrad's *Bug Jack Barron* says "Crossing Fourteenth Street is like crossing the panel dividers between different style comic strips," and I love the shit out of it for that. And what if every street was like that? What if you erupted into eight, eighty, eight hundred different cultures, different speeds, different lights, in a tenner's-worth of cab ride?

*Blade Runner* says the city is dead, and so fuck it. Didn't have its eyes open. It doesn't allow for being in love in Covent Garden market while buying Kenyan sculpture and Tibetan religious artifacts and listening to a live band from Beijing, nor for tasting fifty different beers in fifty yards in Greenwich Village with the smell of dope and Thai curry wafting down the street. That ain't dead. There is a blaze of flowers on George Square in the middle of Glasgow.

So play blues for the city if you want to (and if you have to, I always liked Big Bill Broonzy's "I'm Moving to the Outskirts of Town"), but I'm not with you. That's not what my city sounds like. And for the record, my city doesn't suffer with The Sound of the city, because soul is the music of people killed by the city. It is weak music. In my city, I can hear the Kodo Drummers bashing out Ryogen-No-Hi, and My Bloody Valentine's gliding guitars, and Diamanda Galas shrieking in an alleyway, Buddhist chanting groups in a square, the creepy chime of Javanese court gamelan, the alien beat of The Prodigy and even the mutant bluegrass banjo nailed to the center of The Grid's "Swamp Thing"... Nick Cave and PJ Harvey crooning terrible things to each other, Lou Reed and Dick Dale, Portishead, and, yeah, Tuvan throat-singers... and John Lee Hooker is probably still alive...

I love cities. Always have done. I was born out in the sticks, down in South Essex where lazy childhoods smell of the burning of crop stubble and fresh horseshit in the roads. Big sky days of trying to chop lizards' tails off with spades, pissing in foxholes, beating up your friends in remote old tin air-raid shelters and culling the kids from the other side of the village with big heavy branches in the deep dark woods. There are worse ways to grow up. But it all faded into nothing on a drive into London. Watching the big fields slowly becoming infected with brick, the roads getting wider and blacker, the motorway becoming a canyon floor as the dirty glass and granite of tower blocks began to rise over our heads. Watching the city reach, surround, and take me inside...

It's an infection I'm stuck with. Getting Manhattan under my feet at three in the morning, watching the dawn come

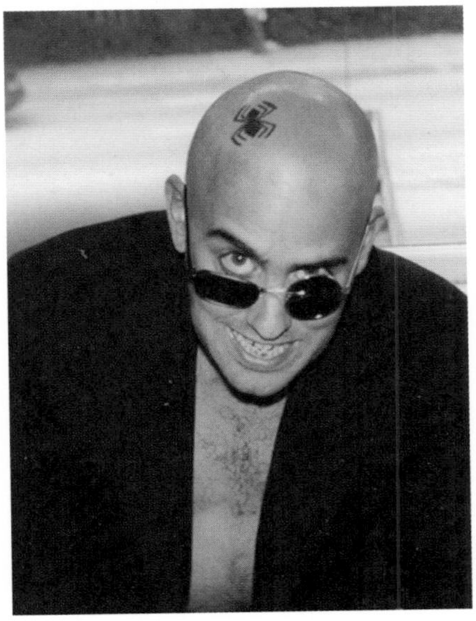

ABOVE: Darick Robertson's friend Andre Ricciardi modeling for Spider Jerusalem. (Photo by Darick Robertson.)

BELOW: An illustration by Darick Robertson created for a 2002 *Wired* magazine article on the series finale.

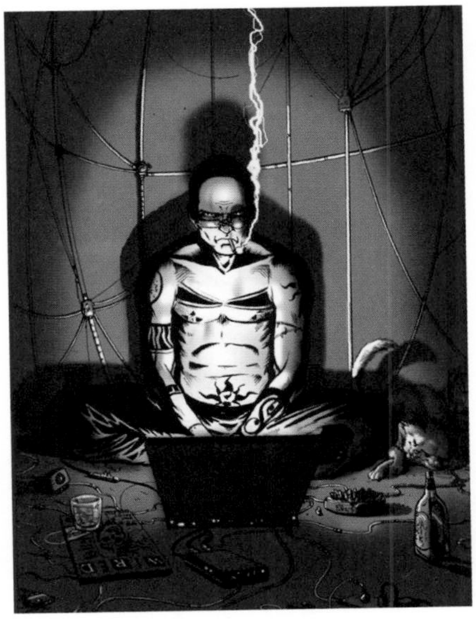

up in darkest inner London. In a smaller town, I'll still look for the concrete and electrics. Stick me in the country and I'll find a road to inhale exhaust fumes from.

Cities in science fiction have had a rough time. These days, the very phrase "cities in science fiction" conjures up Ridley Scott's rainy hellhole L.A. and its seven million knockoffs. It immediately suggests dystopian fiction and urban meltdown. Nobody sees past it. And I don't get it. Because cities don't give up. Cities are alive. And the bigger the cities get, the more cultures they encompass, the more alive they will become.

Shane McGowan rasps, "We'll burn this bloody city down in the summer of the year," and Spider Jerusalem is that firebomb, poor bastard. I've always had a love for journalism, unclean pursuit though it is. It's a job for meths men, chicken-stranglers, and perverts, people mad from language and discovery and indescribable hate. There's Hunter Thompson, of course, but that's not all that's in Spider. There's that vicious shitbag Mencken, the skip and soar of Tom Wolfe, the pure bloody magic of an obscure English music journalist called Chris Roberts, the ugly bloodthirst of Bob Woodward, the chilly gaze of Jean Stein and George Plimpton's *Edie*, the playful, brutal documentaries of Nick Broomfield and a dozen more. They deal in what has become a debased coin, a concept relativized almost out of existence: Truth. They look for the truth of a situation, any situation, and apply ruthless intellects to its excavation. And we ignore them, acting exactly as if we could live without Truth. We can survive it, sure. But we can't *live* without it.

Darick Robertson is not like the others. He likes the same things I do. Two-headed cats, and dogs embedded in motorcycles. He is my friend. We laugh a lot, terrible long laughs that unsettle our girlfriends and drive the neighbors to despair and suicide. He draws a place and it becomes real. This is an appalling skill that any sane society would outlaw. He is the perfect artist for TRANSMETROPOLITAN, and I'm damned glad to have him standing at my back. I came up with the place, but only he makes it live, and that's why he's called Co-creator. (Another way of looking at it, of course, is that he gets to take half the blame.) He lives in San Francisco, I live in southeast England, but we both live in the same City. The transatlantic phone cables are becoming frayed. Fuck 'em. If they break, we'll just grow lizardly telepathic organs in our guts and carry on as normal. We are professionals, after all.

This is our City. It doesn't have borders, it doesn't have a name, and nobody knows what year it is. And twenty-four pages' worth of comic hasn't even scratched the surface of what's in it. Come back next month. We've got some places we want to show you.

**– Warren Ellis**
Southend
April 1997

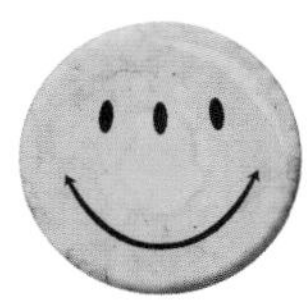

# ISSUE #2: I HATE IT HERE

This City never fails to amaze me. Here we are in a place with no borders anyone can find, full of people who don't know what year it is, walking down streets being ripped up by Media Scum so that they can embed TV screens in the sidewalks, walled in by billboards that either try to sell us stuff we don't need and never even heard of yesterday, or that have been attacked by ad terrorists so that they now project radio signals that cut little patterns on the surfaces of our brains...

... and yet it's *me* who gets arrested on a Temporarily Violently Insane charge.

It was like this. I keep getting beggars coming to my door. Small children with Boy Scout barcode stamps on their white little butts try to sell me poisoned cookies. Grinning dungheads from The Party in Government plead for me to give up some of my dollars for the Re-Election Fund. Wet-eyed professional compassion-mongers attempt to twist cash out of me for Help the Cryogenic Revivals. And just today, I get this pale little zealot from Crusade Aid at the door, asking for a donation towards the provision of religious shock-troops to continue the massacre in pagan England. What can I say? It was one beggar too many.

They found me in the kitchen with the zealot. I'd strung him up by his navel from the ceiling light and had beat him with wooden spoons until his nipples bled. His screams had woken up my landlord — which was a trick in itself, since his doctor had prescribed him a course of sloth genes to control his hypertension, and he hadn't moved from his branch since — who had called the police.

So now I'm under five days' house arrest, with seven fat ampoules of No-Chance stuck into my belly. If I step outside the front door, the ampoule's little brains notice and pump me full of some nasty police drug that makes me think I'm in a brig inside a Martian colony pylon with a heavily greased slave worker called Pththth who believes me

to be his pet rabbit. An interesting one-time experience for any healthily curious journalist, but nothing you'd ever want to repeat.

I hate it here.

\*\*\*

They've got dead eyes, like dolls. Shake them and the eyes swivel, lay them down and the eyes close, but they don't register anything. Not anymore. Blown lightbulbs of eyes, burned out by the cultural electricity of the City.

If they have a communal wish, it's to go back to sleep. To return to the cryogenic lock-tanks, curl up in that welcome winter and wait for the frost to rime their fingernails again. Because the eye-burning information-riot future they woke up in looked nothing like their chromed 20th-century dreams of tomorrow.

If they could only go back to sleep, the Revivals might wake up in the right future...

\*\*\*

It's raining tonight, the first rain we've seen in this district for months. From here, I can see right across to the Fourth Canal, a deep widescreen vista overlaid with the soft waterfall. My assistant's out on the balcony with her boyfriend, both stripped down to nothing, dancing like kids on Christmas morning, opening their mouths for a drink.

Couldn't do that when I was a kid. The rain was poison. We'd hide from it, cover our faces as if we were facing a firestorm. Now, I watch it running over her chin, making the wiring on his back glisten like ice... down on the street, phoneports are made new again by the water, and children lead wonderfully unbelieving old women by the hand into the rain...

\*\*\*

Makers are great. No argument. You turn to your maker and say, "Give me a roast dog leg, tossed salad, a black linen

shirt, and a taser," and bang, out it all comes. Makers aren't particularly bulky, nor power-thirsty, and an average middle class family can afford a good one.

But.

Makers are designed to operate with base blocks — superdense chunks of neutral matter which the maker breaks down and recombines into whatever you've requested. And base blocks are horrendously expensive. Out of a middle class family's price range. So the stores sell a converter that allows the maker to use ordinary garbage as the base. Not as efficient, and the mileage stinks, but there you go.

Which leads me to the City's new pest: middle class families raiding the backyards of the lower classes for garbage. Because if you've got a maker, you don't make garbage. Only those without makers buy prepackaged food and clothing.

\*\*\*

I sent my assistant down to the African for a monkeyburger. I really fancied some Korean dog, but the local Korean got bought out by the Shark Bar people, who are trying to head off an expansion of those tiny Club Snack hot seal-eye kiosks. Mind, Club Snack are having their problems; they're being sued for breach of fiduciary contract by the Long Pig chain, where Club Snack once had concession stands.

Long Pig could use the compensation money, since hard questions are being asked about the location of their stock — the Australian census numbers are down for the third year in a row. I learned a long time ago never to annoy an Incan. And I always preferred caribou eyes, anyway. There used to be loads of Eskimo fast food stands around here. I wonder what happened to them?

**– Spider Jerusalem**
Exclusive to *The Word*

# ISSUE #3: SUBWAY

Shut up.

British Telecom announces the possibility of a computer chip that could record your whole life's memories, from cradle to grave; every picture your eyes ever made for you, crackling inside a splinter of metal. A space exploration committee forwards a set of plans to put humans on Mars by 2005 for a tenth of the budget NASA's crippled, half-arsed Mars plans cost. NASA reads over the committee's plans — and announces that they're better than NASA's own.

Distinctly criminal attempts to shut down an experimental medical center flop dismally when they fail to disprove the center's central tenet: that "incurable" cancers can and have been put in full remission by non-invasive techniques free of side effects. There's a hand-held item called a "Communicator" on the market that is a fully mobile global satellite telephone, a fax machine, a short message service sender and receiver, an e-mail system and a World Wide Web browser. It doesn't quite pin to your

chest yet, but give it time. Cloning is now feasible, and the effort to map the human genome is well under way. We can write our names in atoms.

Now, you tell me: who *wouldn't* want to be writing speculative fiction today?

I read sf as a kid — hell, I read *everything* as a kid — but lost interest in the form in my teens, and didn't start reading it again with any real determination until after I put TRANSMET together. I followed much of the early cyberpunk stuff, which was so much of a

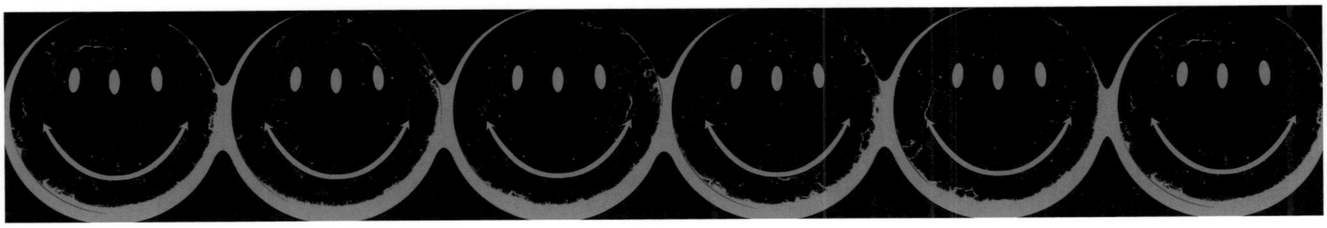

piece with the decade it generated; lots of light and noise and horror, very little real heat. As the eighties ran out of energy, so did the cyberpunk movement, and everyone went back to screaming in the privacy of their own little rooms again. Including me. I wrote my own cyberpunk-inspired work, the *Lazarus Churchyard* serial, on a commission at the end of the decade. (Comics get to everything last. It's like living in a country where the radio stations still play Abba and The Doobie Brothers.) Once the cyberpunk foci had been run through my own set of biases, the best stuff in the book came off like an sf treatment of the Decadent movement. We loved our misery, in the 1980s. And who can blame us?

I started reading sf again last year, out of curiosity and in the hope that the form had been taught some lessons by these strange years of the 1990s. In between times, the only sf I'd read was by the authors I consider important in any genre — J.G. Ballard, Philip K. Dick and the like — and the ones pivotal to the sf genre in specific, like Alfred Bester. (And, of course, the monstrously talented Iain Banks, who wanders across genre borders as if they didn't exist. Which, of course, is the only way to be.)

I've been largely disappointed. Something isn't taking. For every *Idoru* — and thank Christ William Gibson saw past his *Neuromancer* sequence and realized that it was the ongoing cultural mix that was important, not the boy's toys — there's a slew of New Space Opera turds that differ from those terrible antique *Lensmen* books only in the quality of their science and the bland Formica polish on their dismal prose. The scintillant intelligence and fine sociopolitical extrapolation of Kim Stanley Robinson's excellent Mars trilogy can't help but be clouded by the fogbank of dystopia-by-numbers let's-go-cosmic-at-the-end farts in paperback. They're missing something integral to our time.

The future's already *here*. We're *living* in it. Stop to notice. We're standing with our backs against The End of History, where everything happens simultaneously and time means nothing. In that sense, TRANSMETROPOLITAN is happening tomorrow. No one knows what year it is, or cares. It simply doesn't matter anymore. What matters is what's here, and what's happening. Does that sound screwed up to you? Well, the nineties are a fractured decade, and TRANSMET is a nineties work. What we're finding, in all forms of popular culture, is that we have reached a point, here on the edge of the end of history, where we can look back on history with sense. We're far enough away from an awful lot of things, now, that we can see them with a new clarity. And that's the unique energy of the 1990s.

I'm not making any claims for TRANSMET as High Science Fiction. But, in (strained) accordance with Ballard's dictum that the only alien planet is Earth, it seems to me that the only future worth exploring is the one we're living in. In a lot of ways, TRANSMET is a device with which I can lay open our world and conduct a laughing autopsy on the vital organs of our future.

**— Warren Ellis**
Southend
June 1997

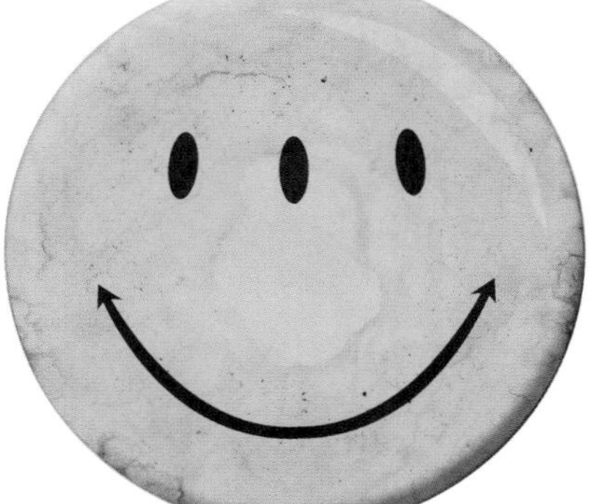

Darick Robertson's initial thumbnail and finished inks for the cover to issue #12.

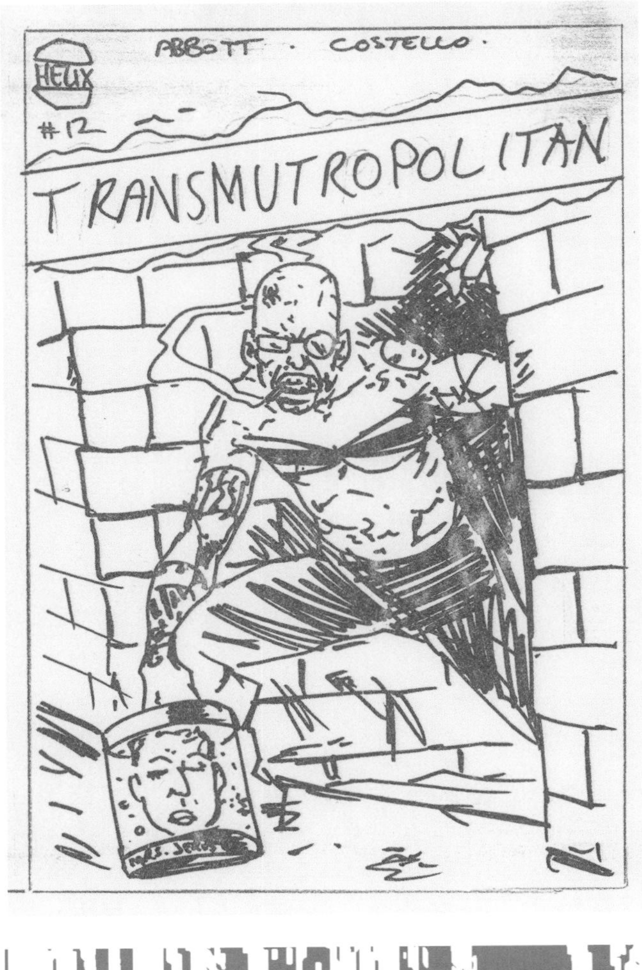
ABBOTT · COSTELLO ·
HELIX
#12
TRANSMUTROPOLITAN

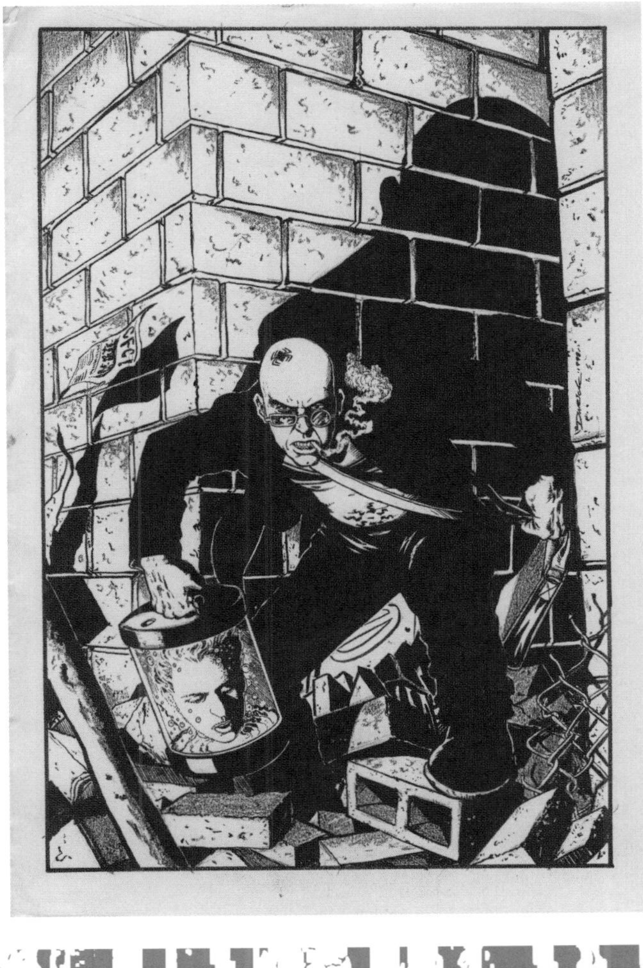

# TRANSMETROPOLITAN *NINE*

# "WILD IN THE COUNTRY"

## WARREN ELLIS

SPIDER discovers both The Reservations, where previous cultures are carefully maintained in stasis, and a place where people are trying to generate a brand new community, culture and language based around body modification...

## 22 PAGES

### PAGE ONE

**Pic 1:**
Full page panel.

**Spider Jerusalem** is in a desert. Big blue sky, blazing sun, dust and sand and a couple of scraggy trees in the background. Even further back in the background is the skyline of the City – somehow, this desert is located somewhere inside the City, an African territory locked in by streets and skyscrapers. But, right now, that doesn't matter to Spider – nor to the three or four Africans there with him. They're in authentic tribal garb, not wearing much, and they're dancing, kicking up sand in the unmistakable foot-sweeping arm-pumping motions of African dance.

And Spider, in his black linen suit, cigarette clamped in his mouth, is dancing with them. In a desert inside a city.

(He's not got his computer, by the way.)

| | |
|---|---|
| TYPED CAPTION: | SPIDER JERUSALEM/WORD/COLUMN #11 – POSS. LEADER PARAGRAPH |
| TYPED CAPTION: | When history looks down its weird evolved vestigial stump of a nose at us, it'll have a lot of very shitty things to say. |
| TYPED CAPTION: | But it will eventually have to admit that the Reservations justify our existence. |
| TYPED CAPTION: | We may have been crazed, strange and entirely too eager to find new things to have sex with – but we went out to preserve great chunks of this planet's cultures and we damned well did it with some *style*. |

TITLES AND CREDITS BLOCK:

WARREN ELLIS writes & DARICK ROBERTSON draws

# WILD IN THE COUNTRY

RODNEY RAMOS - inker CLEM ROBINS - letterer
NATHAN EYRING - color and separations
JULIE ROTTENBERG - asst editor STUART MOORE - editor

TRANSMETROPOLITAN created by WARREN ELLIS and DARICK ROBERTSON

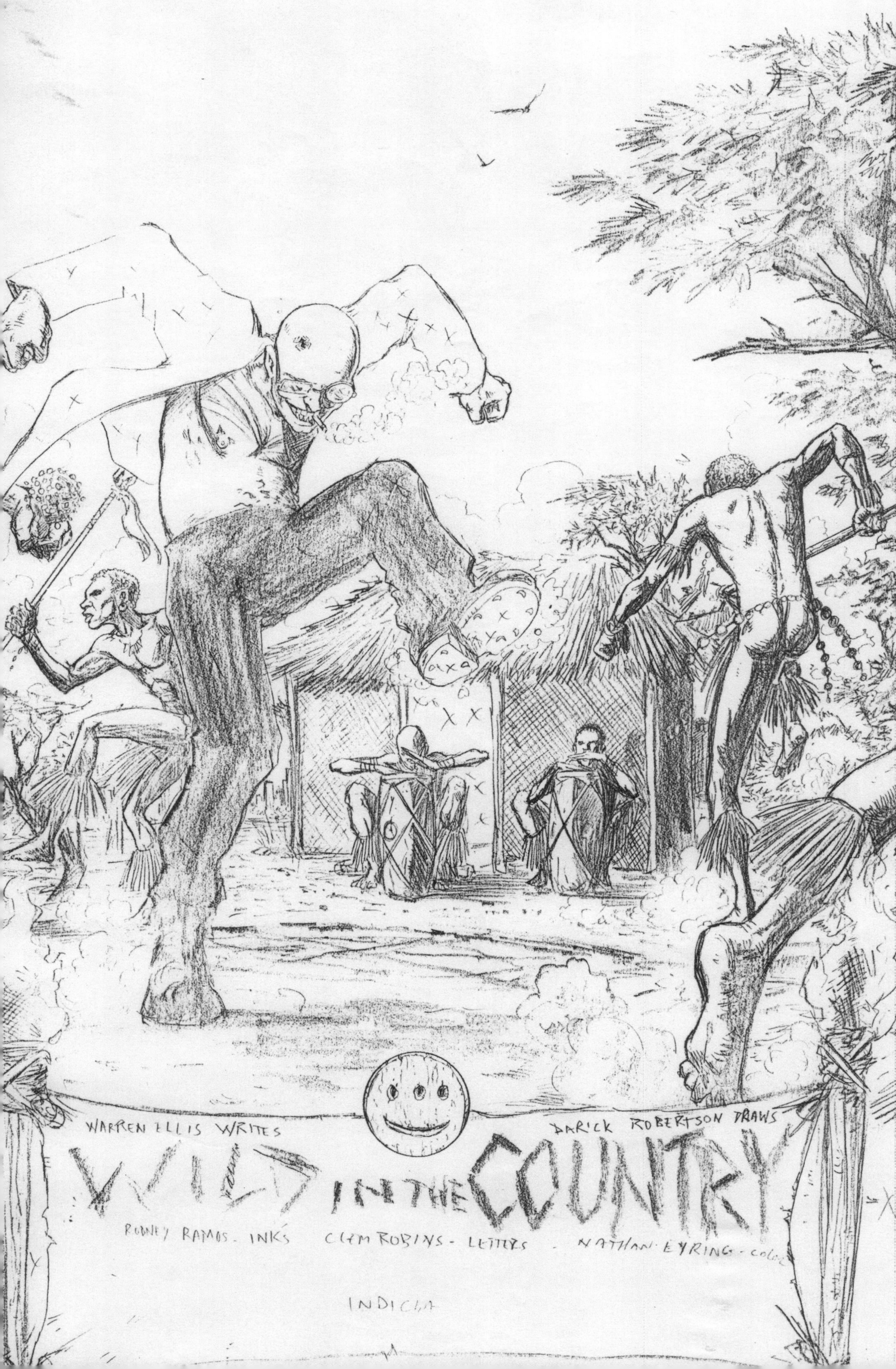
WARREN ELLIS WRITES
DARICK ROBERTSON DRAWS
WILD IN THE COUNTRY
RODNEY RAMOS - INKS
CLEM ROBINS - LETTERS
NATHAN EYRING - COLOR
INDICIA

**PAGE TWO**

**Pic 1:**
CUT: page-wide shot; sitting at a big wooden desk that looks like it's been hewn by native craftsmen of some kind (very primitive/ethnic) is an atttractive Chinese woman in her early forties, KISAKO. She wears a business suit, very elegant and professional-presentable. On the wall behind her are huge flat square images, constantly moving around on the curved wall – we'll discover in a while that the office we're in is round. The images are of different times, different places – African plains, ancient Japanese villages, tribesmen in furs on the Russian steppe, you get the idea. Snapshots of the world gone by. BUT – can we do this shot in MONOCHROME, please, guys.

TYPED CAPTION:                    INTERVIEW (1): KISAKO StEXUPERY,
                                  DIRECTOR, CULTURAL RESERVATION SYSTEMS

**Pic 2:**
And REPEAT PREVIOUS SHOT – but in FULL COLOR, now. As if the previous image was a photo or a freeze-frame, and now we're in full motion.

KISAKO:                           TO MY MIND, THE POINT IS TO PRESERVE
                                  CULTURES WITHOUT IMPOSING JUDGEMENT ON
                                  THEM.

KISAKO:                           FOR INSTANCE: ONE OR TWO OF THE OLDER
                                  CULTURES FROM THE MIDDLE EAST STILL
                                  PRACTISE THE CUTTING OF THE ROSE.

**Pic 3:**
And pull back, move round – to find SPIDER sitting in a chair on the other side of the desk from Kisako. We see now that the room is round. There is one window, the same size and dimensions as each of the big flat images, that looks out and down upon The City in morning.

SPIDER:                           EXCUSE ME?

KISAKO:                           EXTENSIVE FEMALE GENITAL MUTILATION,
                                  NORMALLY INVOLVING THE EXCISION OF THE
                                  CLITORIS.

SPIDER:                           CHRIST.

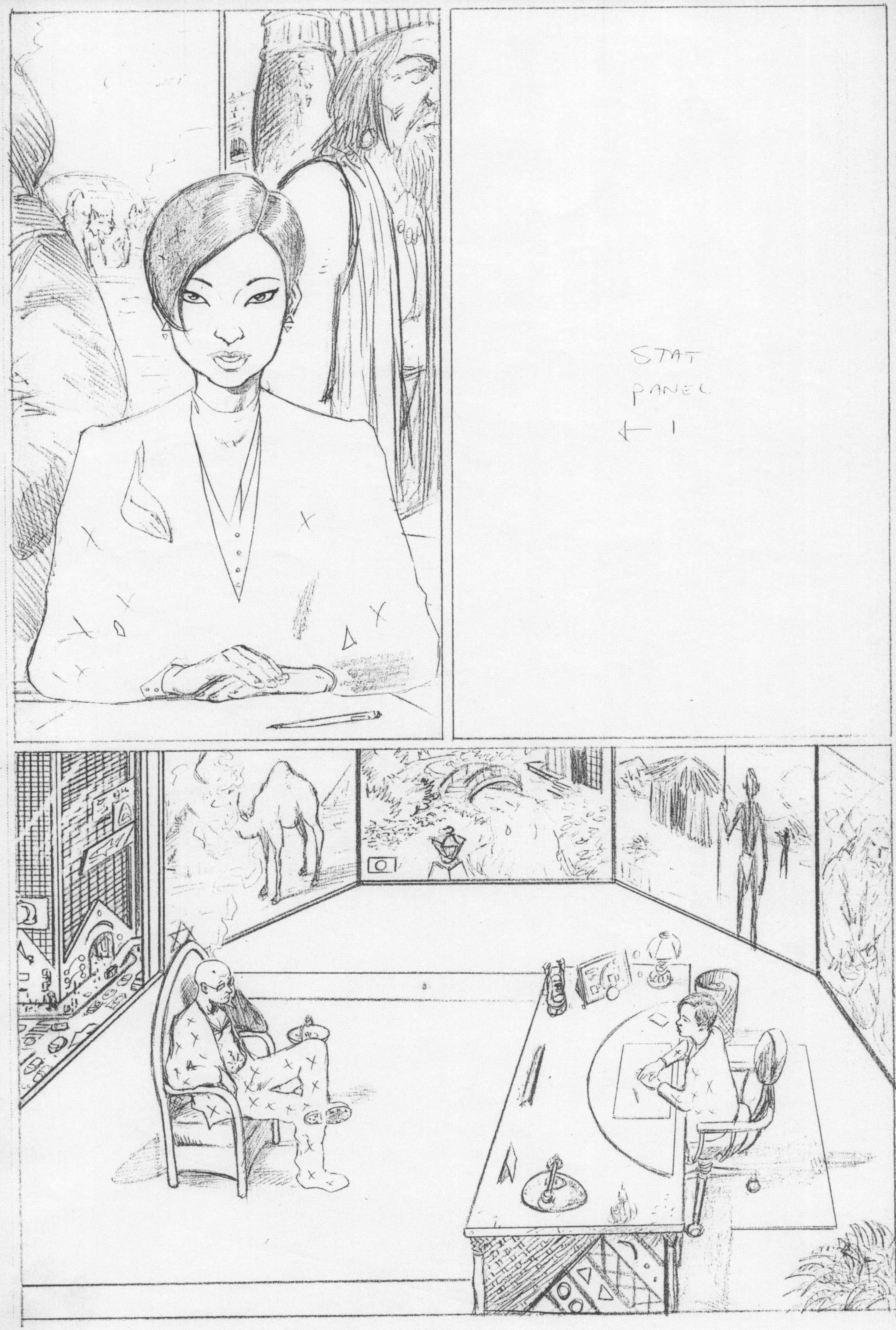
STAT
PANEL
← 1

**PAGE THREE**

**Pic 1:**
Kisako smiles, pulling a thin electric notepad towards her on the desk, looking up at Spider slyly. A woman he could get to like.

KISAKO:                                 MY REACTION EXACTLY. IN FACT, I IMAGINE MY REACTION IS A LITTLE MORE FORCEFUL THAN YOURS.

**Pic 2:**
She taps away at the pad a bit with a pen; Spider reaches a hand up to his shades and taps the top of one lens.

KISAKO:                                 IT'S DISGUSTING. IT VIOLATES MORE BASIC HUMAN RIGHTS THAN I HAVE TIME TO COUNT.

KISAKO:                                 BUT, IT'S A CENTRAL PART OF THE SEXUAL AND SOCIAL POLITICS OF THAT CULTURE. AND WE'RE DEDICATED TO PRESERVING PAST CULTURES HONESTLY.

SPIDER:                                 Picture.

**Pic 3:**
MONOCHROME – Kisako is caught in the act of looking up at us, gesturing at us with her pen, pressing a point home.

*(NO DIALOGUE)*

**Pic 4:**
REPEAT SHOT, in FULL COLOUR.

KISAKO:                                 TO SIT IN JUDGEMENT ON THAT, TO ERADICATE IT FROM THOSE CULTURES, WOULD BE TO SPOIL THE VERACITY OF THOSE RESERVATIONS.

**Pic 5:**
Spider arches an eyebrow at this last, recognising a kindred spirit of sorts.

SPIDER:                                 THE **TRUTH**, NO MATTER WHAT.

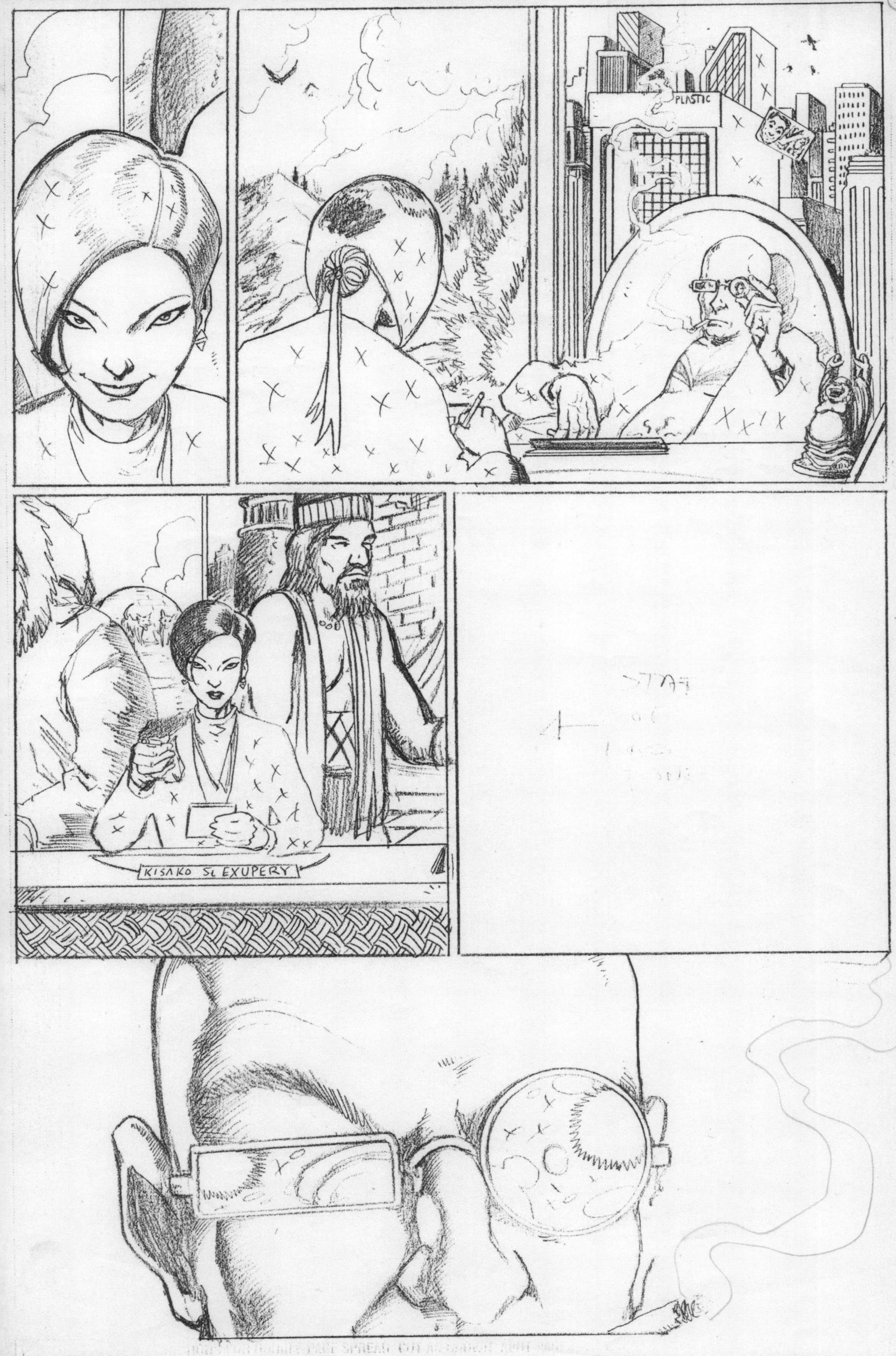
PLASTIC
KISAKO St EXUPERY

**PAGE FOUR**

**Pic 1:**
Kisako turns back to whatever she's tapping out on the pad. Spider, interested, leans forward unctuously in his chair. We're about to see a first — and how bad he is at it —

KISAKO:                          RIGHT.

SPIDER:                          YOU WANT TO COME OUT TO DINNER WITH ME
                                 SOME TIME?

**Pic 2:**
Kisako keeps her eyes on the pad — she gives it a final tap, and it starts to spit out a small business-card-sized strip of card, typed and stamped.

KISAKO:                          SORRY. GOT PLANS TONIGHT. AND, WELL, I PLAY
                                 ON THE OTHER TEAM, IF YOU SEE WHAT I MEAN.

**Pic 3:**
Spider sits back with his fist on his crotch, smiling his terrible painful fake smile.

SPIDER:                          OH, WELL.

**Pic 4:**
Same shot, same POV and all — except now we see Spider very carefully and surreptitiously punching himself in the cock.

*(NO DIALOGUE)*

**Pic 5:**
Kisako passes the card to him with a smooth professional smile, not quite as warm as before. Spider takes it, his fake smile on.

KISAKO:                          OKAY. I'VE DONE YOU A 24-HOUR PASS FOR ALL
                                 THE RESERVATIONS. HIT AS MANY AS YOU LIKE.

KISAKO:                          OH, AND A SPECIAL PASS FOR SOMETHING ELSE
                                 THAT FALLS UNDER OUR PURVIEW. MAKE THE EFFORT
                                 TO SEE IT. IT'S **DIFFERENT**.

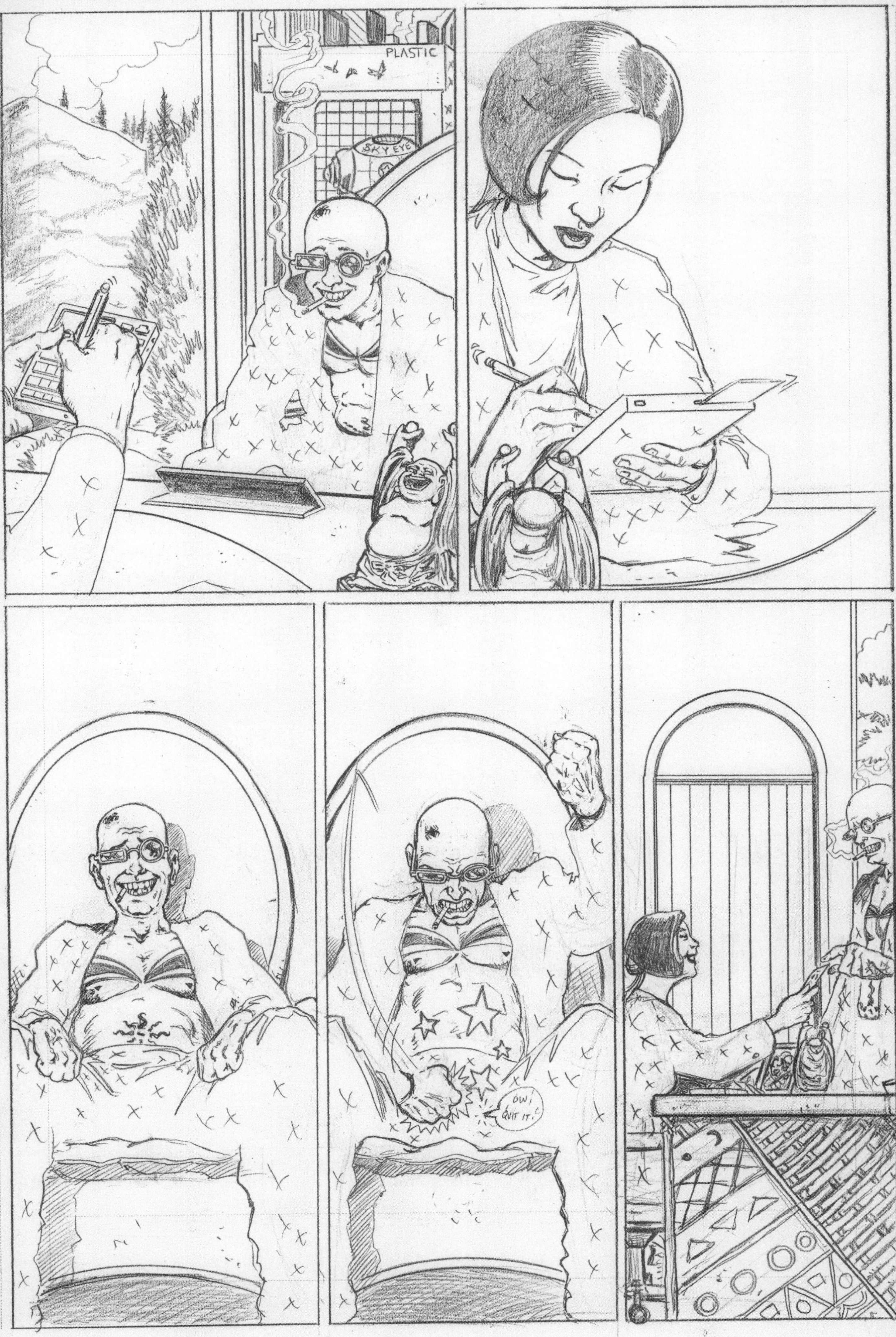
PLASTIC
SKY EYE
OW! QUIT IT!



#9

## PAGE FIVE

**Pic 1:**
Cut to: Spider in a bar, sitting at the counter, munching down a basket meal of some kind and watching the television mounted above and to one side of the bar. MONOCHROME.

TYPED CAPTION:                  **POSS. INSERT/ASIDE: TIME IN A BAR WITH THE MAN IN THE STREET (PICTURE FROM BAR AIRBORNE SECURICAM)**

**Pic 2:**
REPEAT SHOT in FULL COLOUR.

TV:                             TOP STORY ON THE AMFEED NEWS MORNING ROUND-UP: THE PARTY IN OPPOSITION CHOOSE THE CITY FOR THE ELECTION-YEAR CONVENTION!

TV:                             BUT FIRST, HERE ON USAC – CLASSIC TELEVISION TODAY – "REPUBLICAN PARTY RESERVATION COMPOUND"!

**Pic 3:**
Close on Spider as he looks up, looking utterly disgusted as he watches/listens to the television. Over his shoulder, we see there are two other men sharing the bar with him – big fat ugly Common Man bastards with eight kids each and lots of guns. One is **blond**, and we'll call him BERT – the other is **dark-haired, losing it fast**, and we'll call him ERNIE.

TV from off right:              IN LAST WEEK'S EPISODE: CHRISTIAN PRO-LIFE LOBBYIST HOWARD REESE –

SPIDER:                         MOTHER OF TWELVE BASTARDS.

TV from off right:              – HAS USED CURRENT-DAY MEDICAL TECH, ILLEGAL IN THE RESERVATION, TO FALL SECRETLY PREGNANT BY RONNIE, WHOSE ALZHEIMER'S IS BITING IN WITH A VENGEANCE...

**Pic 4:**
Bert and Ernie suddenly begin conversation over their beers; Spider looks over his shoulder at them.

BERT:                           YOU THINK IT'S REALLY LIKE THAT IN RESERVATIONS?

ERNIE:                          SURE. CAN'T BRING ANYTHING IN FROM OUTSIDE. SEALED OFF.

BERT:                           NO. I MEAN THE SEX. YOU THINK THEY'RE AT IT ALL THE TIME LIKE ON "REPUBLICAN PARTY RESERVATION COMPOUND"?

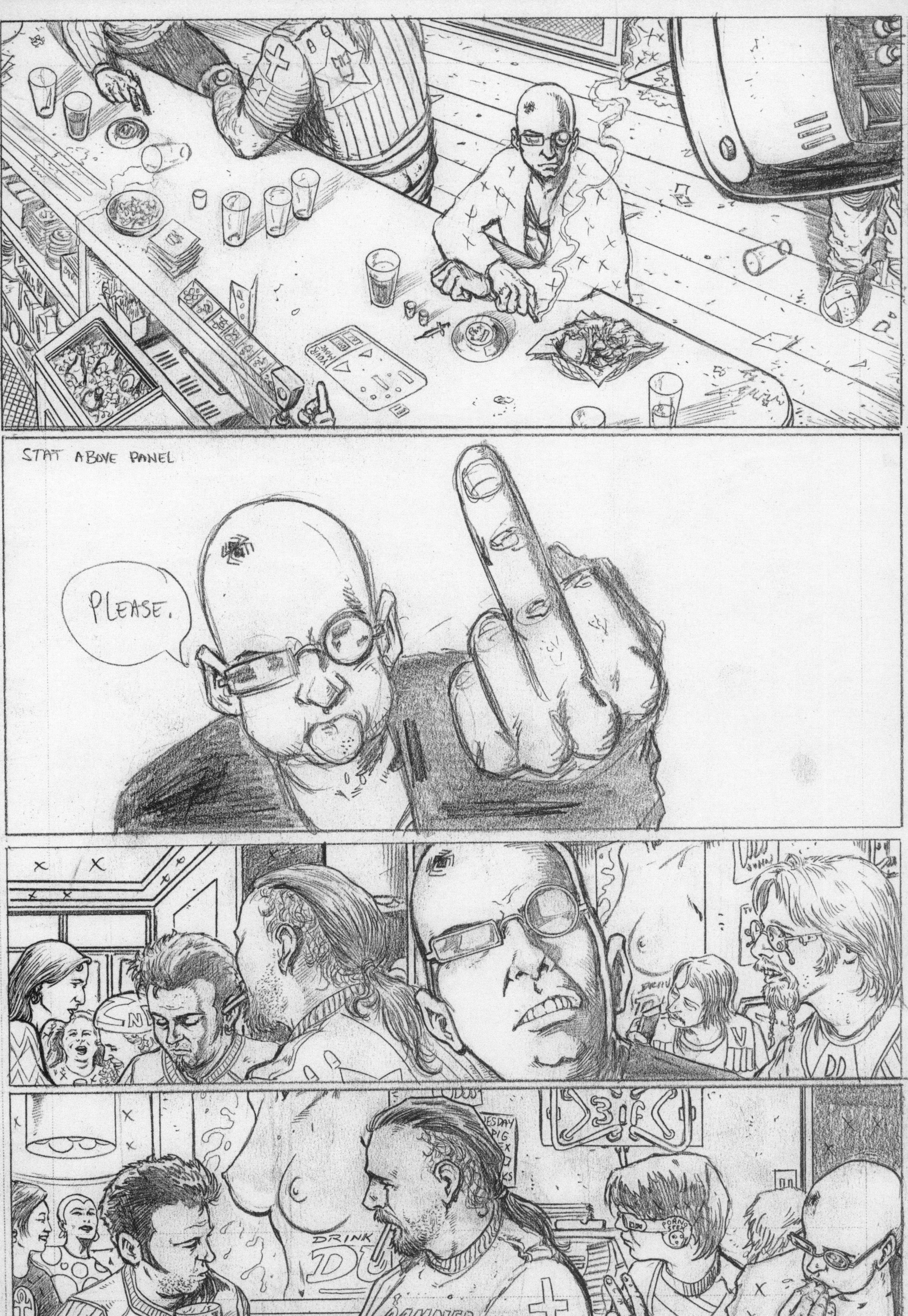
STAT ABOVE PANEL
PLEASE.
DRINK
DAMNED

ERNIE↑ BERT↑ #9 5

**PAGE SIX**

**Pic 1:**
Ernie takes a philosophical swig of his beer. Ernie is plainly the Man Who Knows Everything of the pair, as there often is amongst hardcore drunken barfly losers...

ERNIE:                                  SURE. HEARD BERLIN WALL RESERVATION IS
                                        FUCK CENTRAL.

ERNIE:                                  BUT YOU AND ME, WE COULDN'T GET LAID THERE.

BERT:                                   WHY NOT?

**Pic 2:**
Bert's slightly miffed that Ernie forgets the name of his pride and joy, his only son. You can see him getting bullish as Ernie warms to his topic, rotten with half-truth and arrogant ignorant though it may be...

ERNIE:                                  TOO MUCH DIFFERENT STUFF IN OUR SPERM. SEE,
                                        YOUR BOY, WHASSISNAME...

BERT:                                   **EICHMANN.**

ERNIE:                                  EICHMANN, RIGHT. HE GOT THE ANTI-CANCER
                                        TRAIT FROM YOUR SPERM, RIGHT?

**Pic 3:**
Spider is allowed into the shot, raising an eyebrow as he catches this snatch of conversation. It was probably the "designer warts" bit that did it. Bert's proud of his boy's designer warts, and forces it into the conversation.

BERT:                                   AND THE DESIGNER WARTS. DON'T FORGET THE
                                        DESIGNER WARTS.

ERNIE:                                  RIGHT, RIGHT. WELL, SEE, IN BERLIN WALL,
                                        THAT'D FUCK UP THE ECOSYSTEM, SEE? THEIR
                                        GUYS HAVE GOT, LIKE, REGULAR ISSUE SPERM.

**Pic 4:**
Bert looks down into his beer gloomily.

BERT:                                   SO THEY GOT INFERIOR SPERM, BUT THEY GET TO
                                        LIVE IN FUCK CENTRAL?

BERT:                                   THAT'S SICK.

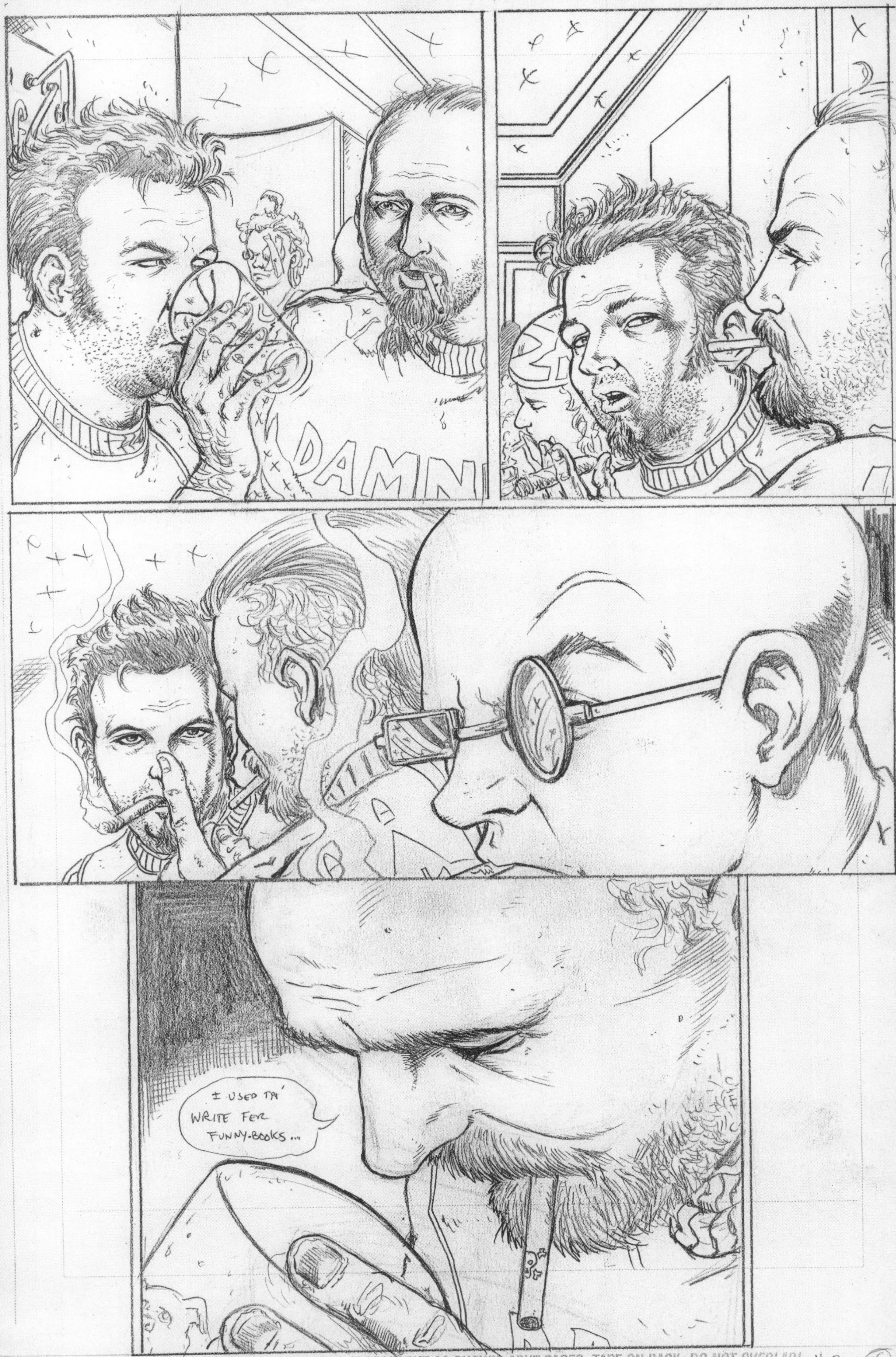
DAMN
I USED TA' WRITE FER FUNNY-BOOKS...

## PAGE SEVEN

**Pic 1:**
Bert looks across at Spider, and a faint glimmer of recognition sparks in his dinosaur brain. Spider looks down at his own drink quickly.

BERT:                                YOU'RE THAT WRITER GUY, AIN'CHA?

SPIDER:                           ... YEAH.

**Pic 2:**
Bert leans in, pointing one fat finger at Spider for emphasis. Spider finds his drink very interesting, and focusses his attention upon it exclusively.

BERT:                                  MY BOY'S GOT DESIGNER WARTS ALL OVER HIS
THING. HE GETS HARD, HE LOOKS LIKE A
GODDAMN SEX PORCUPINE.

BERT:                                  GIRLS LOVE HIM.

**Pic 3:**
Spider grunts down into his drink. Bert is not satisfied. He leans forward now, bringing his ugly face much closer to Spider, stabbing the air before Spider with that finger.

SPIDER:                           RIGHT.

BERT:                                  YOU DON'T **UNDERSTAND.** YOU **TELL** PEOPLE.
**GIRLS LOVE EICHMANN DOBBS.** WHAT THEY
**SAY** ABOUT HIM DON'T **MATTER.** THEY FUCKING
**LOVE** HIM.

**Pic 4:**
Bert leans away again, but keeps his eyes on Spider, keeps that finger raised, threatening, not certain if he's satisfied with Spider's response or lack thereof.

*(NO DIALOGUE)*

**Pic 5:**
Close on Spider as he lifts his drink and tries to drink it through gritted teeth, eyes flashing with hatred behind his shades.

TYPED CAPTION:                    `One day I'm going to drop a bomb on this`
`City.`

TYPED CAPTION:                    `A `*`contraceptive`*` bomb.`

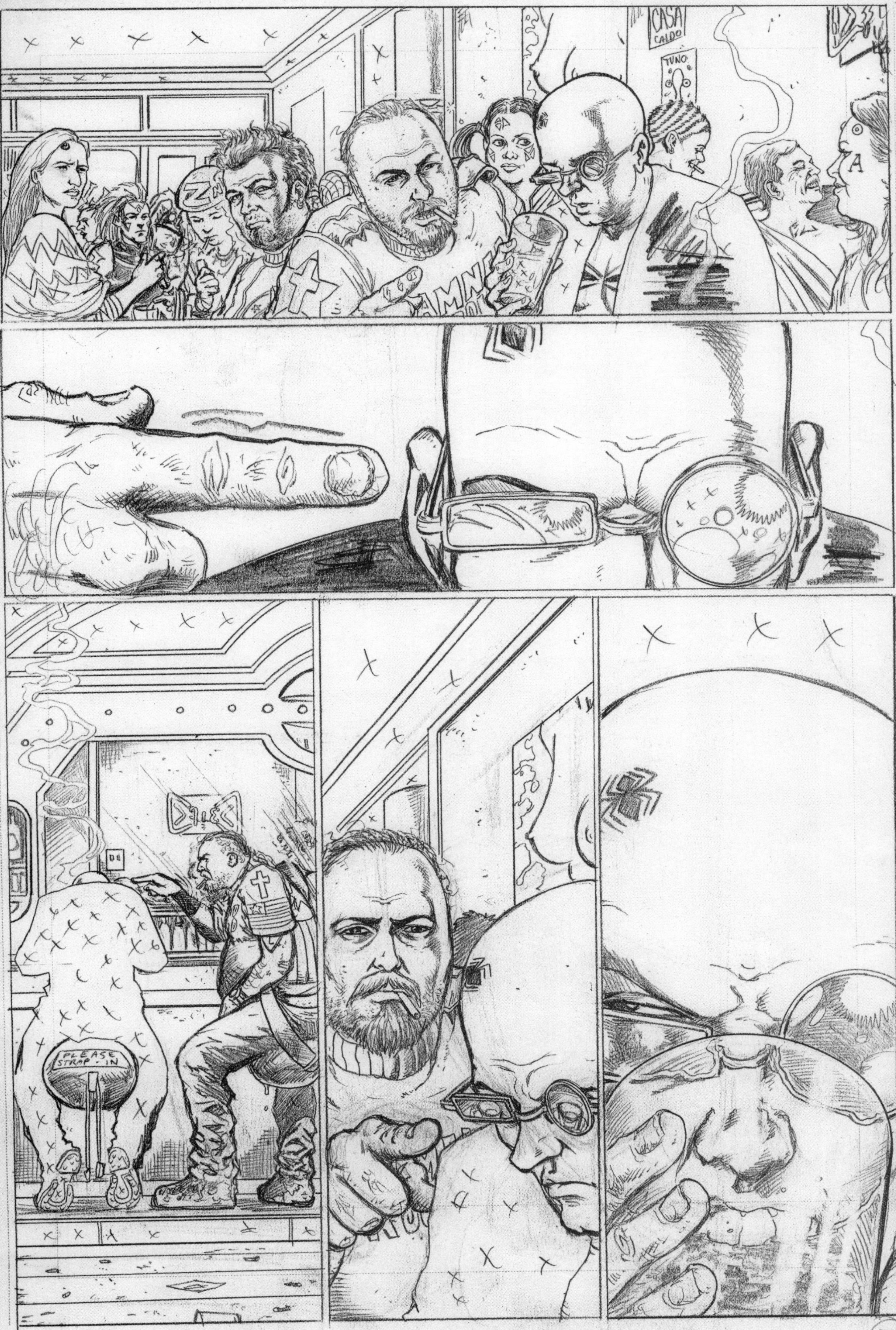
CASA CALDO
PLEASE STRAP-IN

## PAGE EIGHT

**Pic 1:**
ESTABLISH: The frontage of the **Caledonia Reservation.** A MONOCHROME shot – our POV, FYI, is Spider's – he's standing across the street from the place. That'll make for some subtle differences in the repeat image coming next... stick a few cars on the street between us and the building, a few pedestrians...

The Reservation frontage takes up the length of that side of the street – great high dull stone walls peppered with birdshit. Otherwise kind of unremarkable, not hinting at what it contains... other than the fact that we see very little City beyond that wall...

TYPED CAPTION:                          **RECORDED: ENTERING A RESERVATION**

**Pic 2:**
REPEAT IMAGE in FULL COLOUR – with just a few differences, Darick. Time's moved on, so there'll be different traffic on the street between us and the Reservation, different people walking past.

FROM INSIDE:                          OKAY, MISTER JERUSALEM, GET NAKED.

FROM INSIDE (JOINED):                          AND TAKE YOUR HANDS OFF **THAT** – WE'LL NEED
                                               TO EXAMINE IT.

**Pic 3:**
CUT: to Inside. We're in a lab-like room, whose only feature of interest is a big revolving door at one end. The door actually has a steel cylinder around it, with a man-sized hole cut in – one enters, and pushes the cylinder around until you're at the other end of the doorway, the entrance into the Reservation. The room is filled with weird equipment and several white-coated doctor-engineers. The one who does all the talking is a very pretty REDHEADed Asian girl, maybe twenty. They all move around him, poking him with probes, scanning him, taking Geiger counter readings, looking in all his crevices... Spider is stripped down, but for his shades, and baffled. **NATHAN**, could we consider a limited palette for this sequence (here to end of P. 10)? Page 11 is an explosion of color, so we could use the help beforehand...

REDHEAD:                          BASIC RULES: DON'T SPIT WHILE INSIDE THE
                                  RESERVATION.

REDHEAD:                          DON'T ALLOW ANYONE TO TASTE YOUR SWEAT.

REDHEAD:                          BURY YOUR FAECES WELL. URINATE INTO PITS
                                  AND OTHER LOW-ACCESS AREAS.

REDHEAD:                          IF YOU GET WOUNDED, DON'T LET ANYONE NEAR
                                  YOUR BLOOD.

**Pic 4:**
The Redhead looks up, a gun-like tool in her hand, and pokes Spider in the chest with it, making serious eye contact. Very professional.

REDHEAD:                          DO **NOT** – AND THAT'S NOT IN BIG-ASSED CAPITAL
                                  LETTERS – **NOT** HAVE SEXUAL INTERCOURSE
                                  WITH ANYONE OR ANYTHING INSIDE THE
                                  RESERVATION.

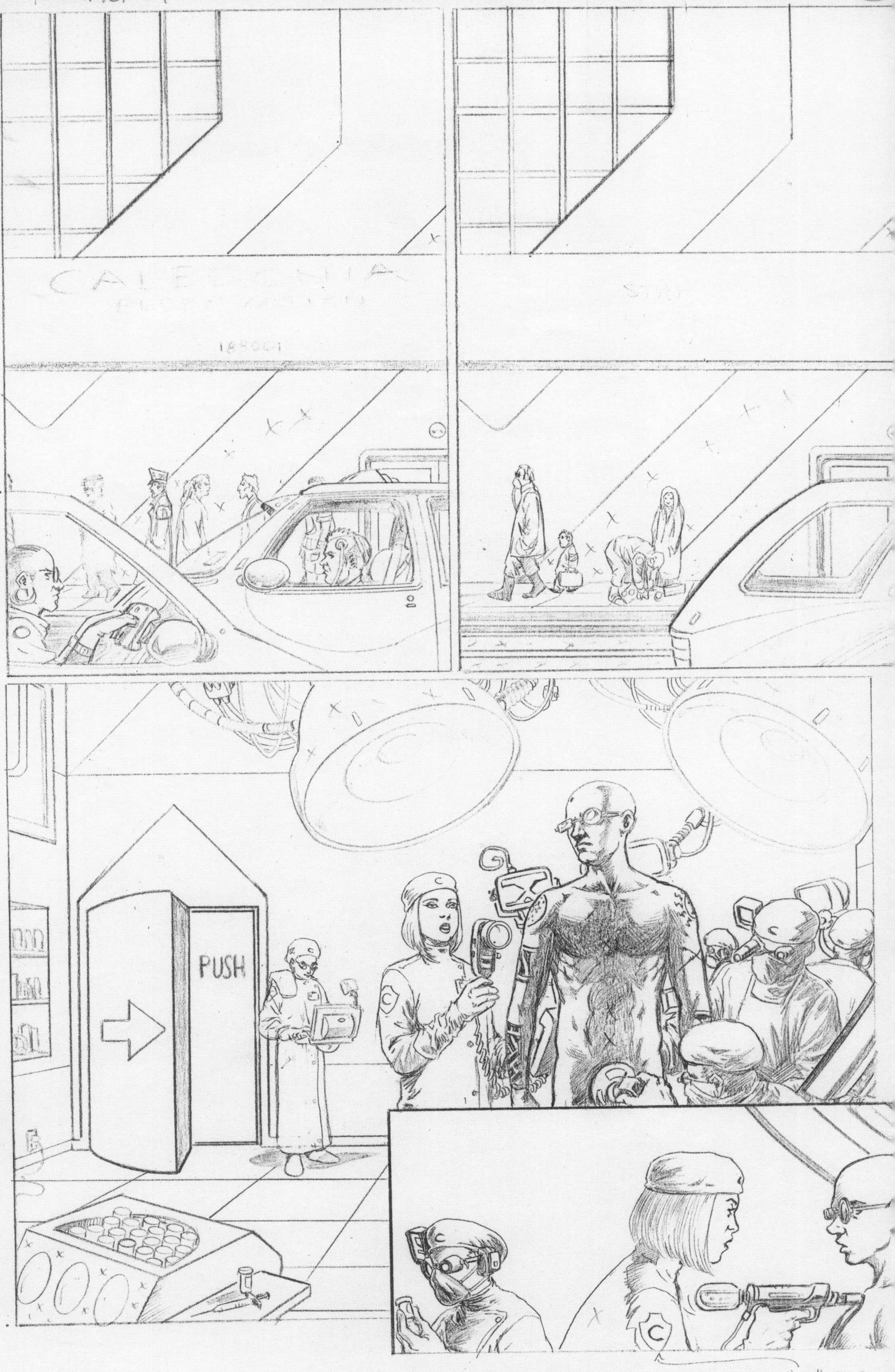
PUSH

RODNEY - NATHAN - THIS GUY IS LIKE A BLUR IN A PHOTO

CLEM - PLEASE DO A DISTINGUISHABLE "C" FOR TH
AND THE

**Pic 1:**
Spider looks down his shades at her. She smiles, efficiently jabbing the gun into his arm and firing it. It pisses smoke from vents in its barrel.

SPIDER:                          ANY**THING**? WHAT DO I LOOK LIKE TO YOU?

REDHEAD:                         A JOURNALIST. THIS IS A LOW-PAYLOAD
                                 DATASPIKE. IT'S GOT ENOUGH OF THE LOCAL
                                 LANGUAGE IN IT FOR YOU TO GET BY. GIVE IT
                                 FIVE MINUTES TO LOAD UP.

**Pic 2:**
She holds her other hand out like a surgeon — a doctor flashes past and deposits another tool in his upturned palm, anything you like, feel free to get silly...

REDHEAD:                         THIS IS AN EMISSION SUPPRESSOR. THE PEOPLE
                                 INSIDE HAVE BEEN CONFIGURED TO A TIME WHEN
                                 PEOPLE WERE A LOT LESS RADIOACTIVE.

REDHEAD:                         UNSUPPRESSED, YOUR VERY PRESENCE WOULD
                                 CONSTITUTE A NUCLEAR EXCURSION THE LIKES
                                 OF WHICH THEIR WORLD HAS NEVER SEEN.

**Pic 3:**
She applies the tool to his upper torso — hell, maybe it's a can of deodorant.

SPIDER:                          SURELY MY VERY PRESENCE FUCKS WITH THEIR
                                 WORLD ANYWAY.

REDHEAD:                         NAH. WE'VE GOT A TOGGLE ON THEIR MEMORIES.
                                 THEY'LL ACCEPT YOU WHEN THEY SEE YOU, AND
                                 FORGET ALL ABOUT YOU AND THE CITY ONCE
                                 YOU'RE GONE.

**Pic 4:**
Doctors gather to her, taking the tools away, placing new ones in her hand, These look identical — big fucking cylinders each with a circle of big needles at the end. Scary-looking.

REDHEAD:                         OKAY, YOUR MEDICAL LOADS: ONE TO REPEL THE
                                 DISGUSTING INFECTIONS THEY LIVE WITH DAILY,
                                 ONE TO KILL THE DISGUSTING INFECTIONS **YOU**
                                 LIVE WITH DAILY.

REDHEAD:                         LET'S NOT HAVE YOU KILLING EACH OTHER.

**Pic 5:**
Spider raises his arms as she jams each device into either side of his chest and fires them — they grind and spark and whir and look not very nice.

SPIDER:                          YOU KNOW, THIS IS A HELL OF A LOT OF WORK
                                 JUST FOR SOMEONE TO VISIT A RESERVATION.
                                 WHY DO YOU BOTHER LETTING PEOPLE IN?

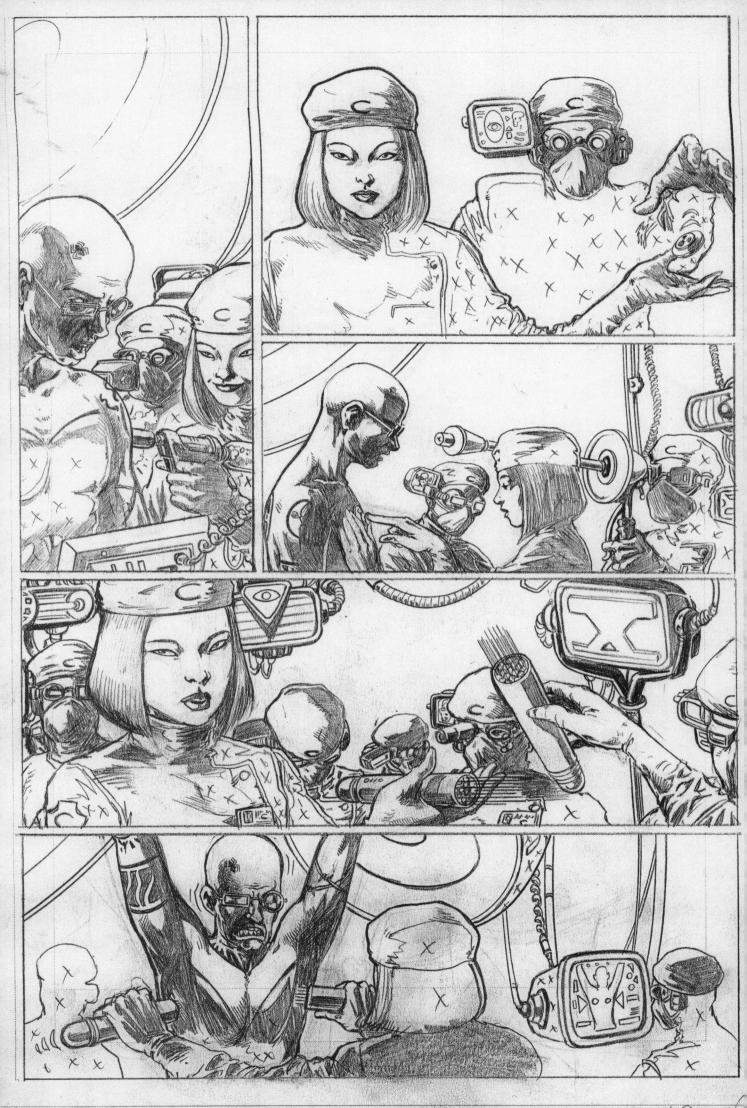

## PAGE TEN

**Pic 1:**
The doctors take away the cylinders, hand her a single long thing, like a car antenna.

REDHEAD:                              BECAUSE PEOPLE NEED TO SEE IT.

**Pic 2:**
She walks behind Spider, still chatting. Spider watches the other doctors scurry around, oblivious...

REDHEAD:                              YOU'LL UNDERSTAND BETTER ONCE YOU'RE IN.
                                      **FINALLY –**

**Pic 3:**
... and jumps a few inches off the ground as she plainly jams the antenna up his arsehole.

SPIDER:                               OWW!

REDHEAD:                              – **COMMUNICATOR**. PRESS THE BASE OF YOUR
                                      THUMB TO SEND. YOU'LL HEAR OUR VOICES
                                      INTERNALLY, THROUGH BONE RESONATION. YOU
                                      MIGHT FEEL A BIT NAUSEOUS AT FIRST, BUT IT
                                      PASSES.

**Pic 4:**
She comes back to him, smiling, as he ruefully rubs his bum.

SPIDER:                               YOU WANT TO GO OUT TO DINNER SOME TIME?

REDHEAD:                              SORRY. I DON'T EAT. I GOT THAT NEW TRAIT LAST
                                      MONTH, WHERE THEY REPLACE YOUR STOMACH
                                      WITH A STACK OF BACTERIA?

**Pic 5:**
Spider slumps off towards the door – hunched over, defeated. She shows him the way, pitying the old man a bit.

REDHEAD:                              WELL, MISTER JERUSALEM, I THINK WE'RE ABOUT
                                      SET. DOOR'S OVER THERE.

REDHEAD:                              SEND WHEN YOU'RE READY TO COME OUT AND
                                      WE'LL TRIGGER A MAP TO THE EXIT DOOR OVER
                                      YOUR RIGHT EYE – IT WAS IN THE LANGUAGE
                                      DATASPIKE.

**Pic 6:**
He goes into the doorway and starts pushing it through, disappearing from our sight. The redhead waves.

REDHEAD:                              HAVE FUN.

SPIDER:                               RIIIGHT.

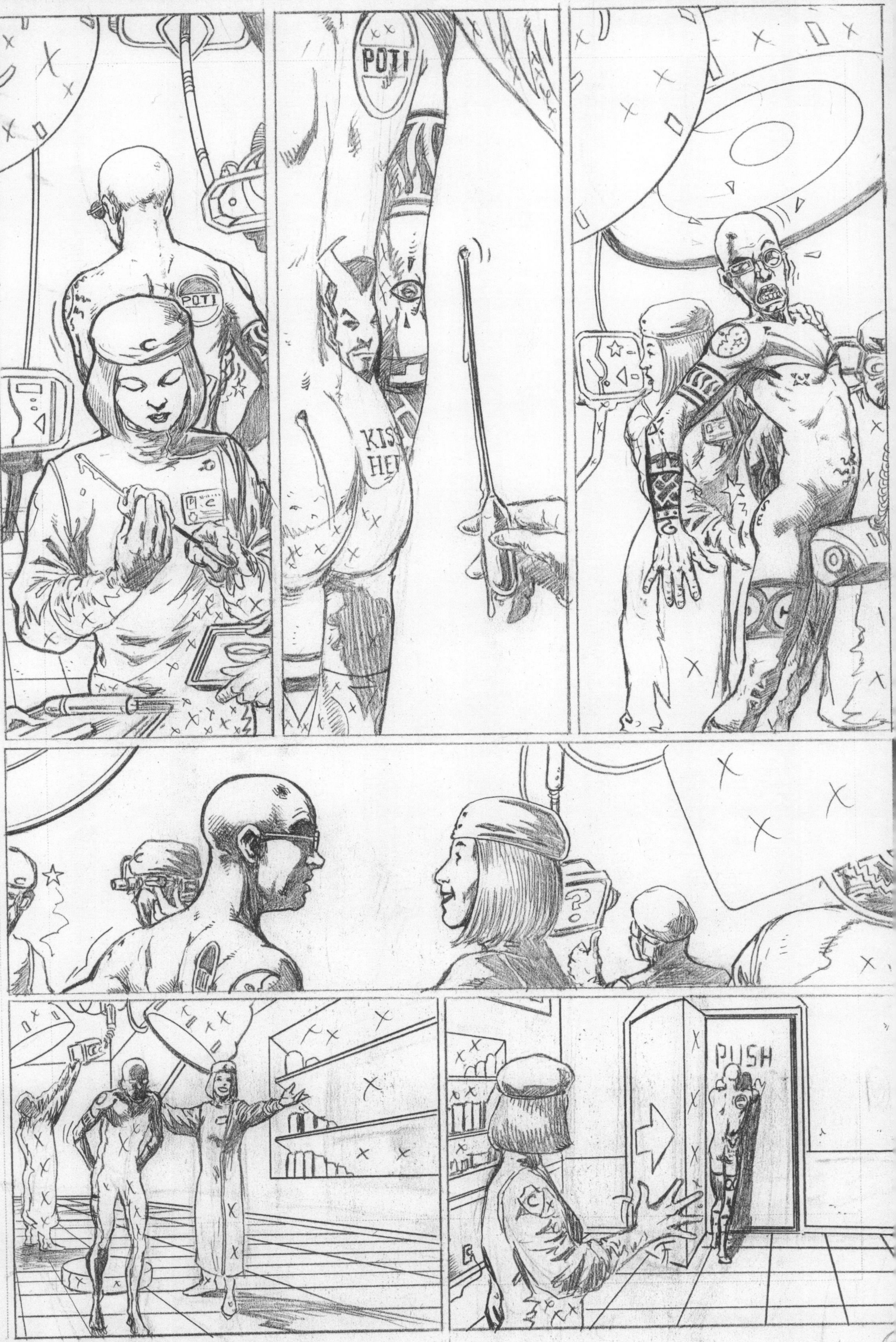
POTI
POTI
KISS HER
PUSH

#9

**PAGE ELEVEN**

**Pic 1:**
FULL PAGE PANEL.

We're looking down on unspoilt Scottish countryside. The door opened directly out onto the Reservation. Grass, trees, rocks, a river down that steep slope there... huge cold blue sky, birds, wild deer... utterly beautiful... and Spider, standing naked on the mountainside looking out at it all. An incredible, explosive difference from the City, from all of the sequences we've had so far. We haven't seen anything like this since the early pages of #1, and it should carry a huge punch just because of its natural simplicity...

TYPED CAPTION:                    THE CALEDONIA RESERVATION

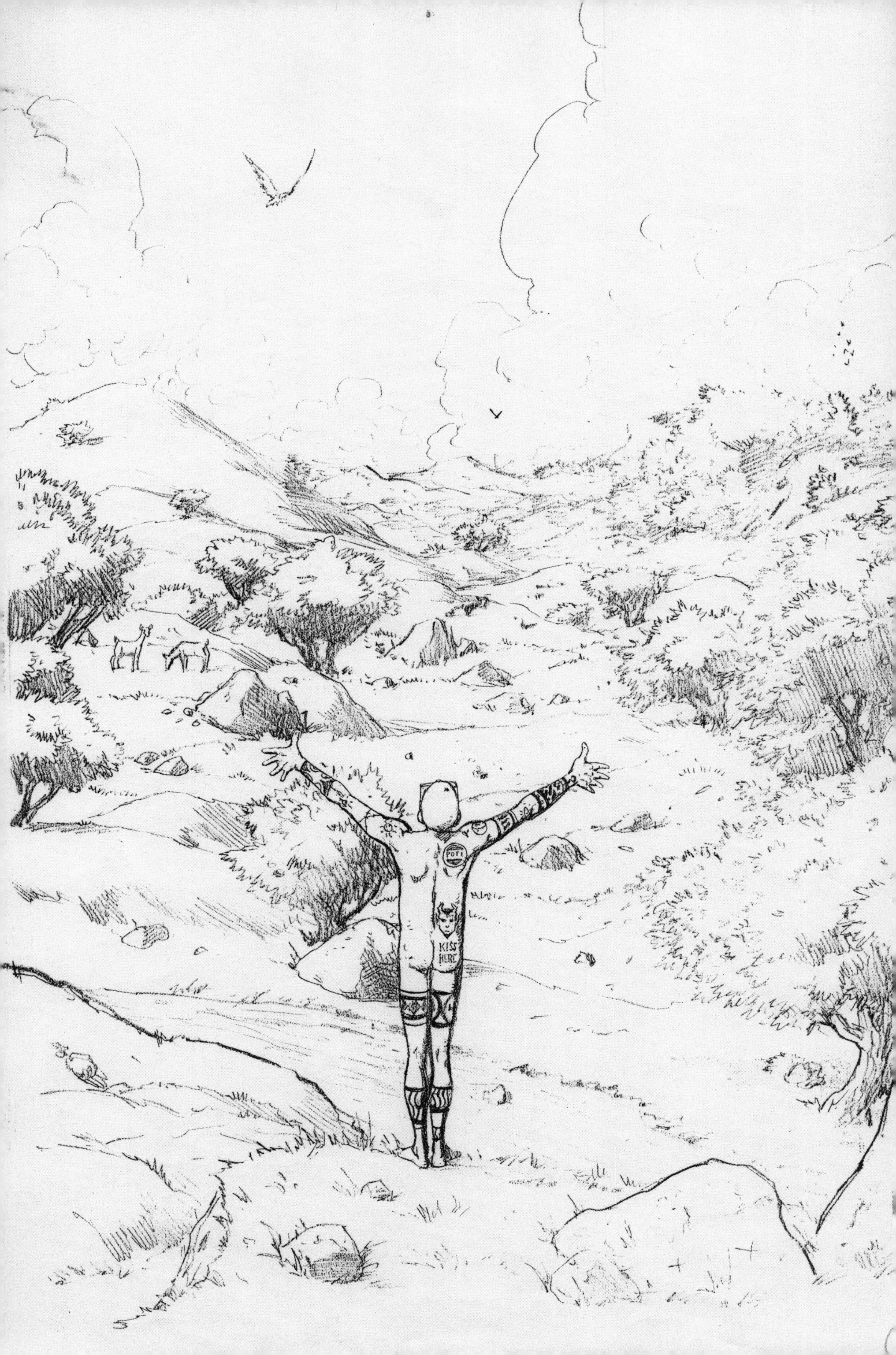
KISS HERE

## PAGE TWELVE

**Pic 1:**
CUT: for six panels of Spider screeching into a public telephone. No booth, but big weird speakers mounted on the pole that also holds the phone gear. We need an EFFECT here, a rippling heat-haze around Spider, with a blue tint to it, emanating from the speakers – they're anti-noise systems, obviating the need for a booth. Inside the eye of the silent hurricane blasting from the speakers, you can't hear anything but your own voice and that of whoever's on the phone. Stick a big obvious logo on the phone's pole, **TALKWEB**.

Do this on a grid, Darick, three rows of two. And this panel is frozen MONOCHROME.

TYPED CAPTION:

**TAPED PHONE CONVERSATION: SPIDER JERUSALEM AND MITCHELL ROYCE (CITY EDITOR, THE WORD NEWSPAPER)**

TYPED CAPTION:

**(PICTURE FROM TALKWEB TELECOM AMBIENT ANTI-VANDAL SURVEILLANCE BACTERICAM)**

**Pic 2:**
REPEAT SHOT in FULL COLOUR...

SPIDER:

IT'S LIKE THE MOUNTAIN... CHRIST, I DIDN'T THINK I WAS GOING TO SEE ANYTHING LIKE THIS FOR YEARS, IF EVER AGAIN...

**Pic 3:**
Spider sort of grimaces, an expression of irritated despair in Royce, whom we hear through the phone...

FROM PHONE:

YOU SOUND LIKE A FUCKING GARDENER. WHERE'S THE STORY, SPIDER?

**Pic 4:**
... and then fairly shrieks into the phone.

SPIDER:

THE STORY, YOU INCREDIBLE ASSHOLE, IS THAT THE CITY'S FULL OF RESERVATIONS AND NOBODY BOTHERS **GOING** TO THEM!

SPIDER:

CHRIST, PEOPLE GIVE UP THEIR **LIVES** TO MAKE THE RESERVATIONS RUN! WAKE **UP**! PAY **ATTENTION**! THERE WILL BE A **TEST**!

**Pic 5:**
Spider pauses to wipe his spittle, of which there is a lot, off the phone mouthpiece...

FROM PHONE:

ALL RIGHT, ALL RIGHT... YOU WANT TO DO A COLUMN ON THE RESERVATIONS, I'LL TRUST YOU. OKAY?

FROM PHONE:

WHERE'S YOUR ASSISTANT, BY THE WAY? I TRIED PHONING YOUR APARTMENT EARLIER.

**Pic 6:**
Spider lights himself up a cigarette, calming down... not knowing that these three pieces of dialogue activate next's issues plots and send him into a world of shit...

SPIDER:

OH, GOD KNOWS. SHE HASN'T BEEN RIGHT SINCE HER DICK BOYFRIEND WENT FOGLET. WHAT WERE YOU CALLING FOR?

FROM PHONE:

THAT ONCOGENE FARM YOU RIPPED INTO LAST WEEK? THEY'RE GOING NUTS, TALKING LAWSUIT –

SPIDER:

FUCK 'EM. CALL YOU LATER.

INSTRUCTIONS FOR DOUBLE-PAGE SPREAD: CUT AS SHOWN, ABUT PAGES, TAPE ON BACK. *DO NOT OVERLAP!* #9 12

**PAGE THIRTEEN**

**Pic 1:**
CUT: At a cabstand, queuing for a cab; Spider at the head of the queue, a very pretty, very slim African woman in white PVC next along the line. He's staring into space, she's peering at him as if she recognises him. Frozen shot, MONOCHROME.

TYPED CAPTION:                  **AT A CABSTAND (STAND #10191 — STILL FROM
FOOTAGE SHOT BY WHIPCABS DRIVER Y88759H)**

**Pic 2:**
REPEAT SHOT, full colour, action... perhaps you could make the previous shot a page-wide shot, actually, and this shot a cropped enlargement containing just Spider and the WOMAN...

WOMAN:                  YOU'RE SPIDER JERUSALEM, AREN'T YOU?

SPIDER:                  YEAH.

**Pic 3:**
Spider turns round to her, and realises that she really is very, very attractive...

WOMAN:                  I LIKE YOUR COLUMN.

SPIDER:                  THANKS.

**Pic 4:**
He asks her out. She shrugs, smiling.

SPIDER:                  YOU WANT TO GO OUT TO DINNER SOME TIME?

WOMAN:                  SORRY, NO. I'M BREATHARIAN.

**Pic 5:**
He asks her out again, desperation obvious in his face. She looks away, smiling...

SPIDER:                  HOW ABOUT GOING TO BED WITH ME INSTEAD?

WOMAN:                  I WENT NEUTER LAST YEAR. SORRY.

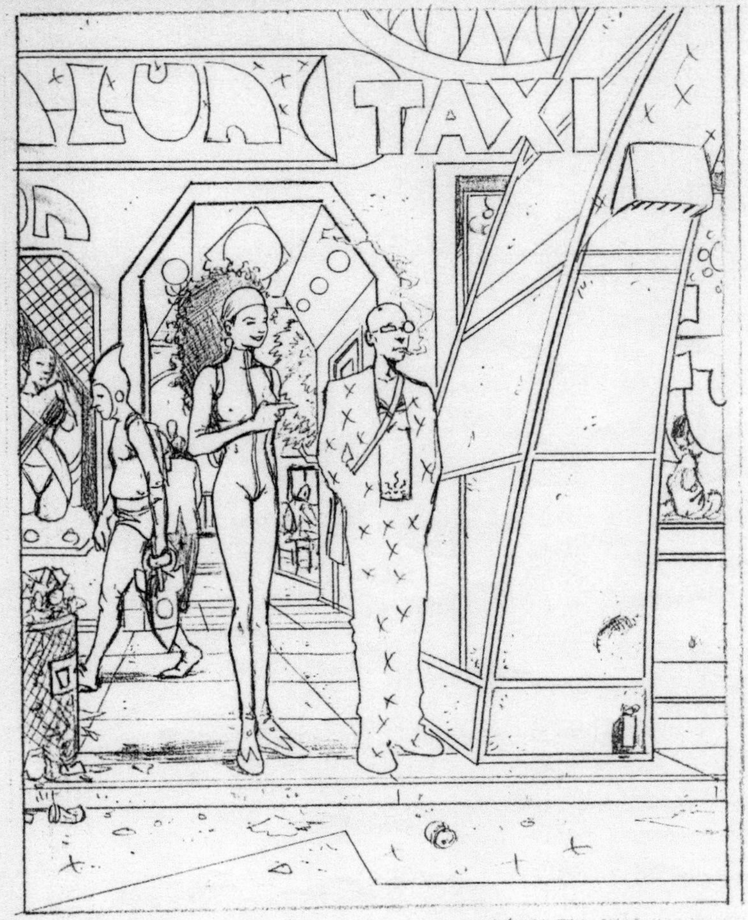
TAXI

STAT & ENLARGE
LAST PANEL
FOCUSING ON CHARACTERS

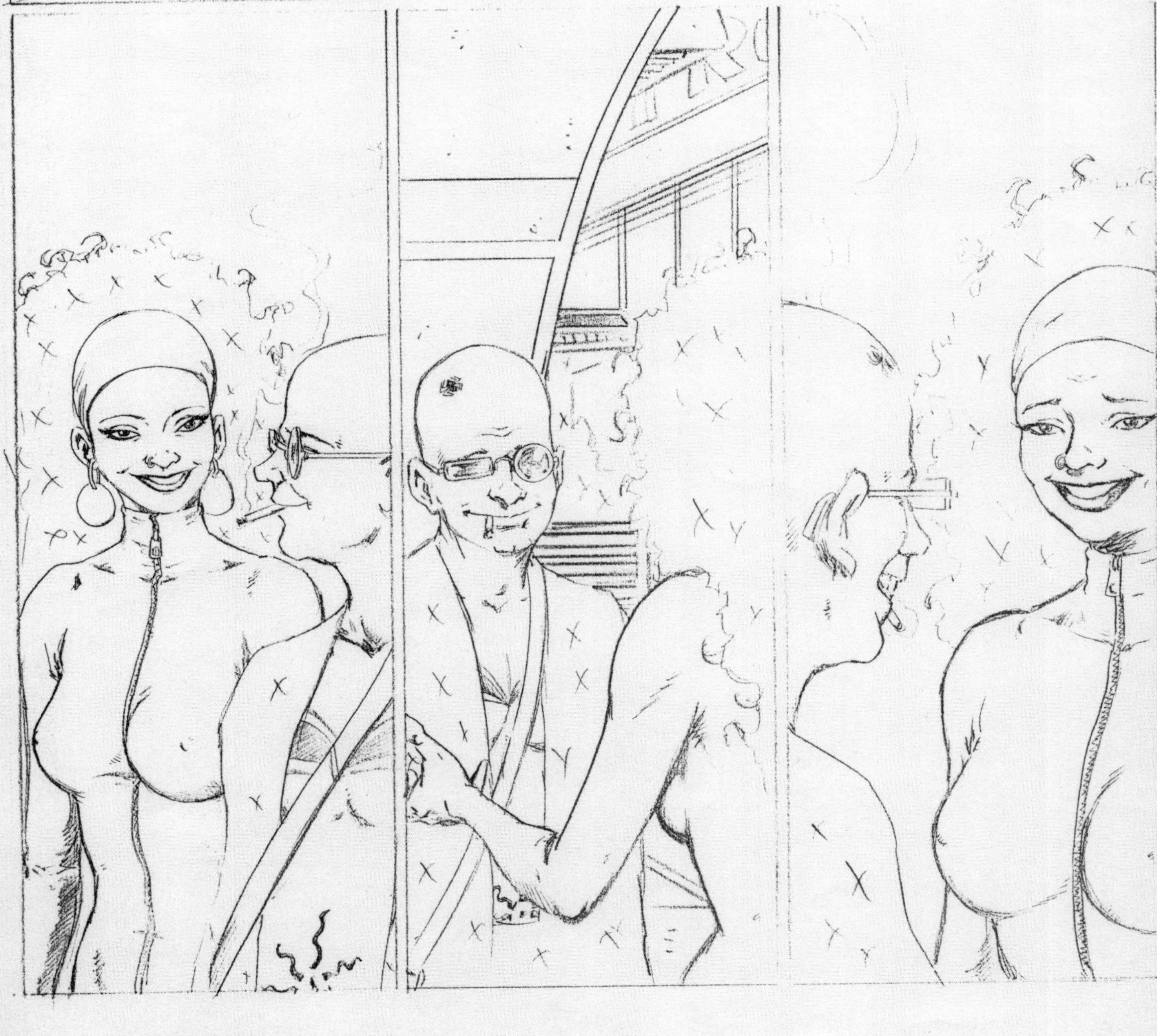

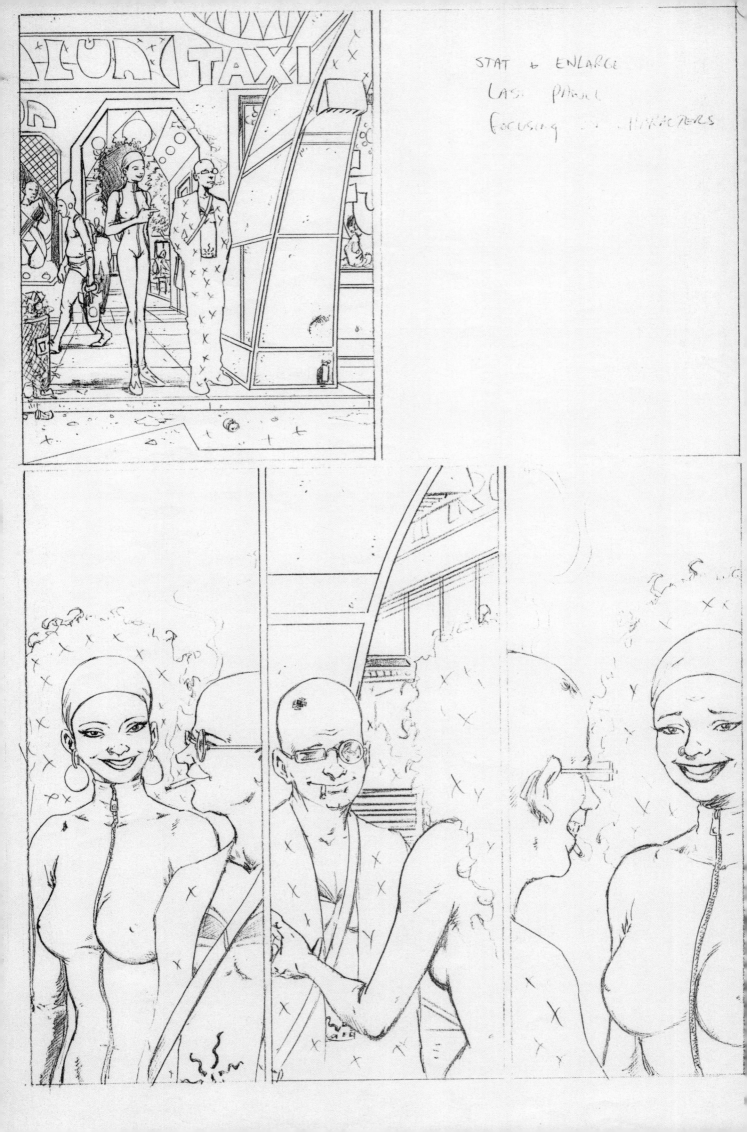

## PAGE FOURTEEN

**Pic 1:**
CUT: to an ancient and tiny Japanese village, surrounded on one side by forest, on the other side by a vast field of rushes... silent, still... Spider Jerusalem in his black suit, crouching at the forest's edge.

TYPED CAPTION:                    **THE AKITA PREFECTURE RESERVATION**

TYPED CAPTION:                    **VERBAL NOTES DICTATED INTO SUBDERMAL RECORDING INFECTION FOLLOW:**

CAPTION:                          FLUTES TALK TO EACH OTHER ACROSS THE FIELDS.

**Pic 2:**
Close on Spider, with birds alighting near him in the silence, a frog jumping across the wet ground in front of him...

CAPTION:                          HELL, I KNOW WHAT THOSE ARE. *SHINOBUE*. FLUTES HAND-CRAFTED FROM BAMBOO. SAW A DOCUMENTARY ON JAPANESE MUSIC.

**Pic 3:**
From over Spider's shoulder: we see a man before one of the little village huts, banging on one end of a long barrel drum...

CAPTION:                          FROM BEYOND THE PATH, I HEAR SOMEONE ELSE JOINING THE CONVERSATION. *TAIKO*, JAPANESE DRUMS.

**Pic 4:**
... and Japanese women emerging from the tall field of rushes with baskets full of harvested plants...

CAPTION:                          THIS IS HARVESTING MUSIC.

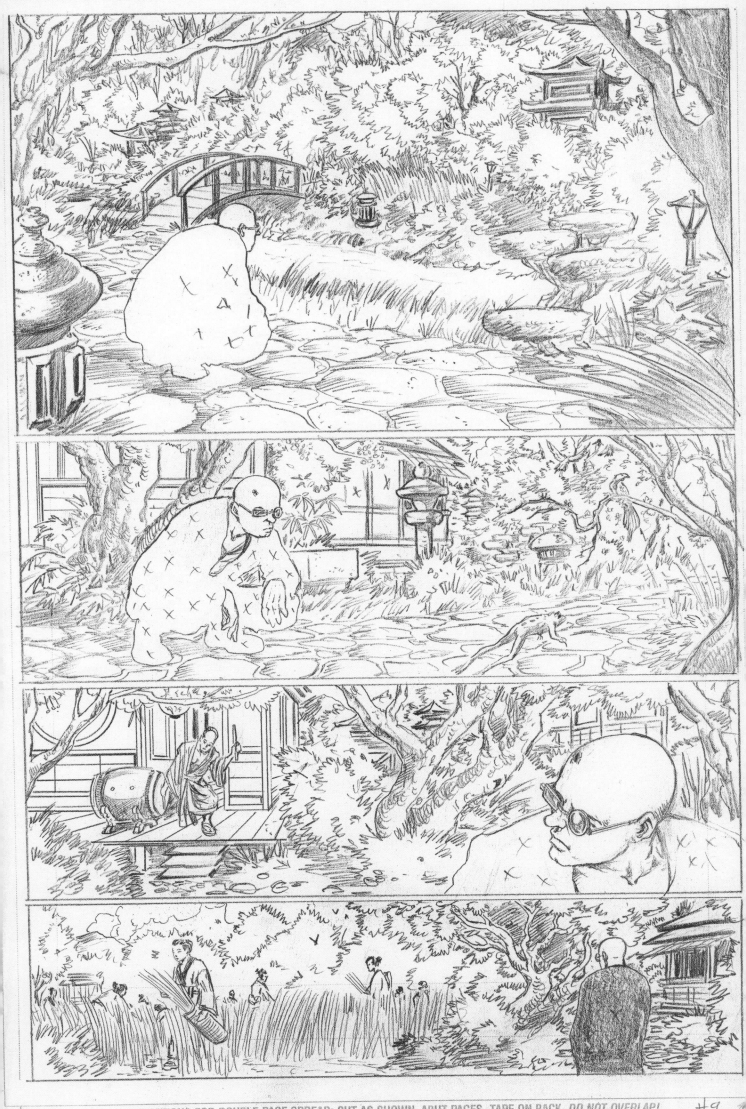

## PAGE FIFTEEN

**Pic 1:**
CUT: to a noisy, packed, chaotic City street, Spider walking away from us, hunched and smoking, just turning his head to one side as if someone from our POV were calling his name. frozen pic, MONOCHROME.

TYPED CAPTION:                    **ON LEBENSRAUM STREET, HEADED NORTH:**

TYPED CAPTION:                    **(IMAGE STOLEN FROM ARCHIVE OF HANNAH ENKIDU, SPKF FEEDSIDE LISTENER)**

**Pic 2:**
REPEAT PIC, unfrozen, FULL COLOR...

FROM OUR POV:                   HELLO? AREN'T YOU SPIDER JERUSALEM, COLUMNIST FOR THE WORD?

SPIDER:                          GRUNT.

FROM OUR POV:                   I'M HANNAH ENKIDU, FOR SPKF? I'M CURRENTLY LISTENING LIVE FOR THE STREETLIFE FEEDSITE?

**Pic 3:**
Move round, so we can see HANNAH: a drop-dead gorgeous young redhead in a tight red rubber feedsite listener's suit, studded all over with pickups (you did a listener in #1, remember? Listening to the Tuvan throat-signers?). Spider's interest is aroused once more...

SPIDER:                          LIVE?

HANNAH:                      THAT'S RIGHT. NOW, I LOVE "I HATE IT HERE", AND I WAS WONDERING EXACTLY WHAT YOU'RE DOING TODAY, SPIDER?

SPIDER:                          I'M DOING A TOUR OF THE CITY'S RESERVATIONS FOR THE COLUMN. YOU'LL READ ALL ABOUT IT FRIDAY.

**Pic 4:**
Spider rubs his hands together, cigarette jutting jauntily from his mouth... this fame has to be good for something...

SPIDER:                          YOU WANT TO GO OUT TO DINNER SOME TIME?

HANNAH:                      SORRY, NO. I'M NOT HUNGRY, MARRIED, INFECTED WITH SEVEN UNKNOWN DISEASES, GAY, PREGNANT WITH LIZARDS AND CLINICALLY DEAD.

**Pic 5:**
Spider is utterly deflated. His head goes down, shoulders go up. Hannah is businesslike, turning to leave, not even a smile...

SPIDER:                          "SORRY, NO" WOULD HAVE DONE ALL ON ITS OWN, YOU KNOW.

HANNAH:                      JUST MAKING SURE.

**Pic 6:**
Close on Spider, scowling, murder in his eyes...

TYPED CAPTION:                    **LATER NOTE: I didn't think she'd turn me down live on SPKF.**

TYPED CAPTION:                    **Have ordered crate of libido suppressant, a partial lobotomy, seventy nude pictures of Queen Victoria and a castration.**

CLEM. PLEASE IMPROVE MY SAD LETTERING ATTEMPTS, THANKS
KATY IS
THE SCHLAUMPE
PUH-LEEEEEASE
STAT DAT PANEL!
Listener
LISTENER
Listener
SCUTA DE MARE!
RODNEY: DON'T ADD PUPILS TO THE EYES, THE GIRL'S EYES LEAVE OPEN, KAY?

## PAGE SIXTEEN

**Pic 1:**
CUT: and open on – and this is going to be a bugger, I realise, go get the reference books out – a Mayan ziggurat temple. Brand spanking new, with Mayan people drifting around the grid-like streets and gardens laid before it. And Spider, mooching around.

TYPED CAPTION:                    THE TIKAL RESERVATION

TYPED CAPTION:                    I think what amazes me the most is that
                                  people volunteer to live here. Because
                                  once you're in a Reservation, you can
                                  never come back.

**Pic 2:**
Spider pauses at the foot of the ziggurat, wipes his brow – it's hot here, blazing sun and bone-dry air, desert floor beneath his feet. A Mayan woman holding a baby pauses next to him, looking up, ignoring Spider.

TYPED CAPTION:                    Your lifespan is dialled back to the
                                  natural average lifespan of the culture
                                  and time period.

TYPED CAPTION:                    Your immunities are stripped out, as are
                                  all the rest of your useful modern
                                  genetic traits.

**Pic 3:**
She holds the baby up, towards the ziggurat, showing him something important up at the summit. Spider looks up in that direction.

TYPED CAPTION:                    And your memories of being a modern-day
                                  human are locked off forever.

**Pic 4:**
The people at the top of the temple are silhouettes against the sun – we see a few figures up there, one apparently bringing a blade down –

TYPED CAPTION:                    You live as a person in that culture and
                                  timeframe, for as long as you can.

**Pic 5:**
– and a severed human head bounces down the steps of the ziggurat towards them, spurting blood from its stump.

TYPED CAPTION:                    And you die there.

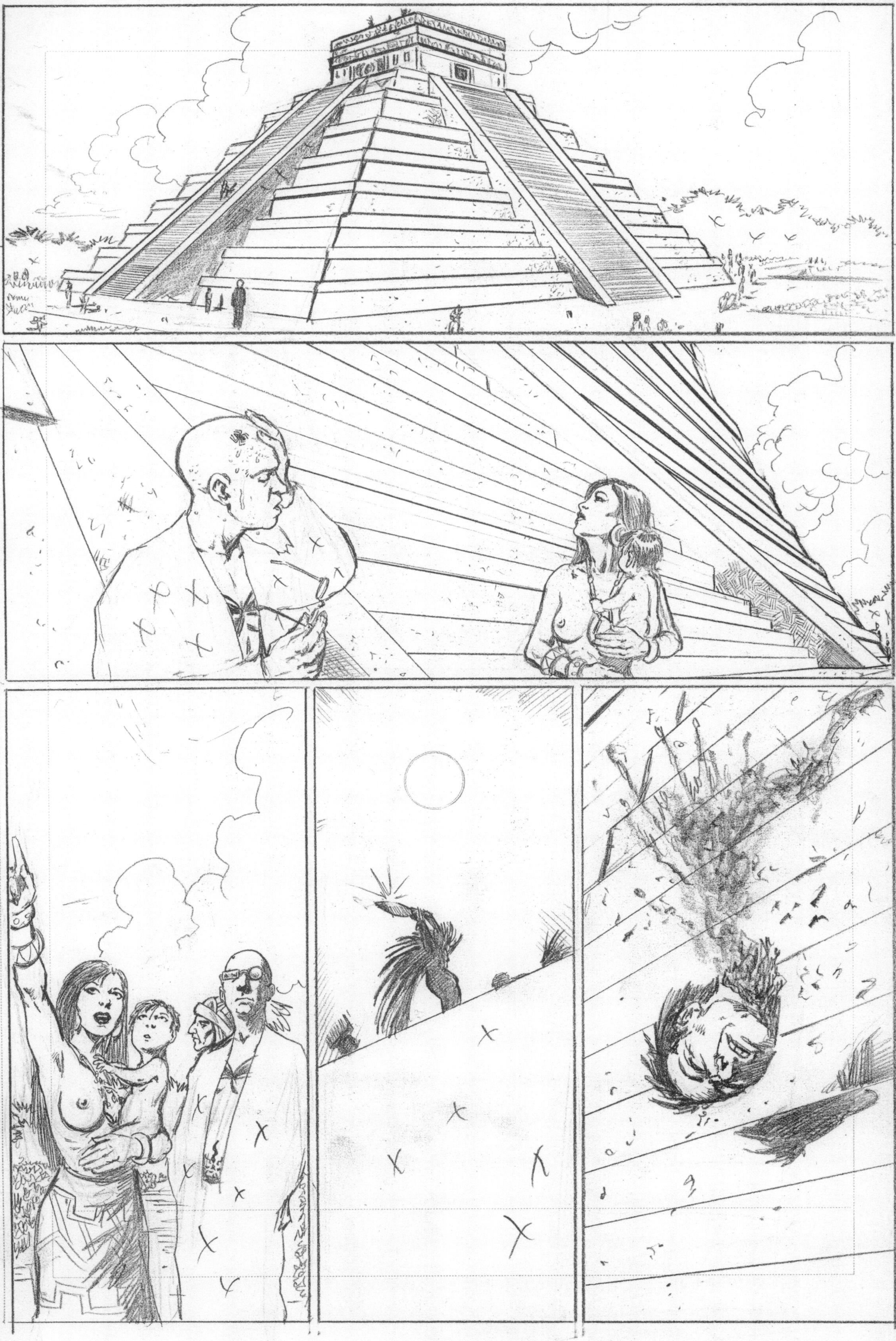

INSTRUCTIONS FOR DOUBLE-PAGE SPREAD: CUT AS SHOWN, ABUT PAGES, TAPE ON BACK. *DO NOT OVERLAP!*

#9

*ALL BLEED ART MUST EXTEND TO OUTERMOST SOLID LINE*

## PAGE SEVENTEEN

**Pic 1:**
The head stops at Spider's feet – he looks down at it with an expression of mild disgust, a tourist's lack of comfort with the customs of the natives.

TYPED CAPTION:                    The Tikal Reservation is due for shutdown
                                  in about ten years' time.

TYPED CAPTION:                    These heads are tossed into the waters
                                  adjoining the city, which are considered
                                  sacred.

**Pic 2:**
A Mayan man steps past Spider and scoops the head up, ignoring our man.

TYPED CAPTION:                    There's an awful lot of rotting heads in
                                  that water.

**Pic 3:**
Spider looks back at the woman and child; she hugs her child close, smiling quietly to herself, secure in her people's immortality and her child's shining future, glad to live in this marvellous city...

TYPED CAPTION:                    They drink from that water.

**Pic 4:**
Spider wanders off, hands jammed in pockets, looking sorry as more kids, older ones, run past, dirty, laughing, healthy and happy – for the moment – carrying another head that's had a few strips of fabric wrapped around it to serve as a football...

TYPED CAPTION:                    It may be sacred as all hell, but it's so
                                  full of disease right now that they could
                                  probably cut the water into blocks.

**Pic 5:**
He disappears off down a straight street flanked by blazes of flowers.

TYPED CAPTION:                    It'll kill them, just like it killed the
                                  original Mayan cities.

TYPED CAPTION:                    This is the fifth Tikal reservation.


TYPED CAPTION:                    People die to teach us lessons about
                                  religion and environment. We keep
                                  history close, to make damned sure we
                                  learn from it.

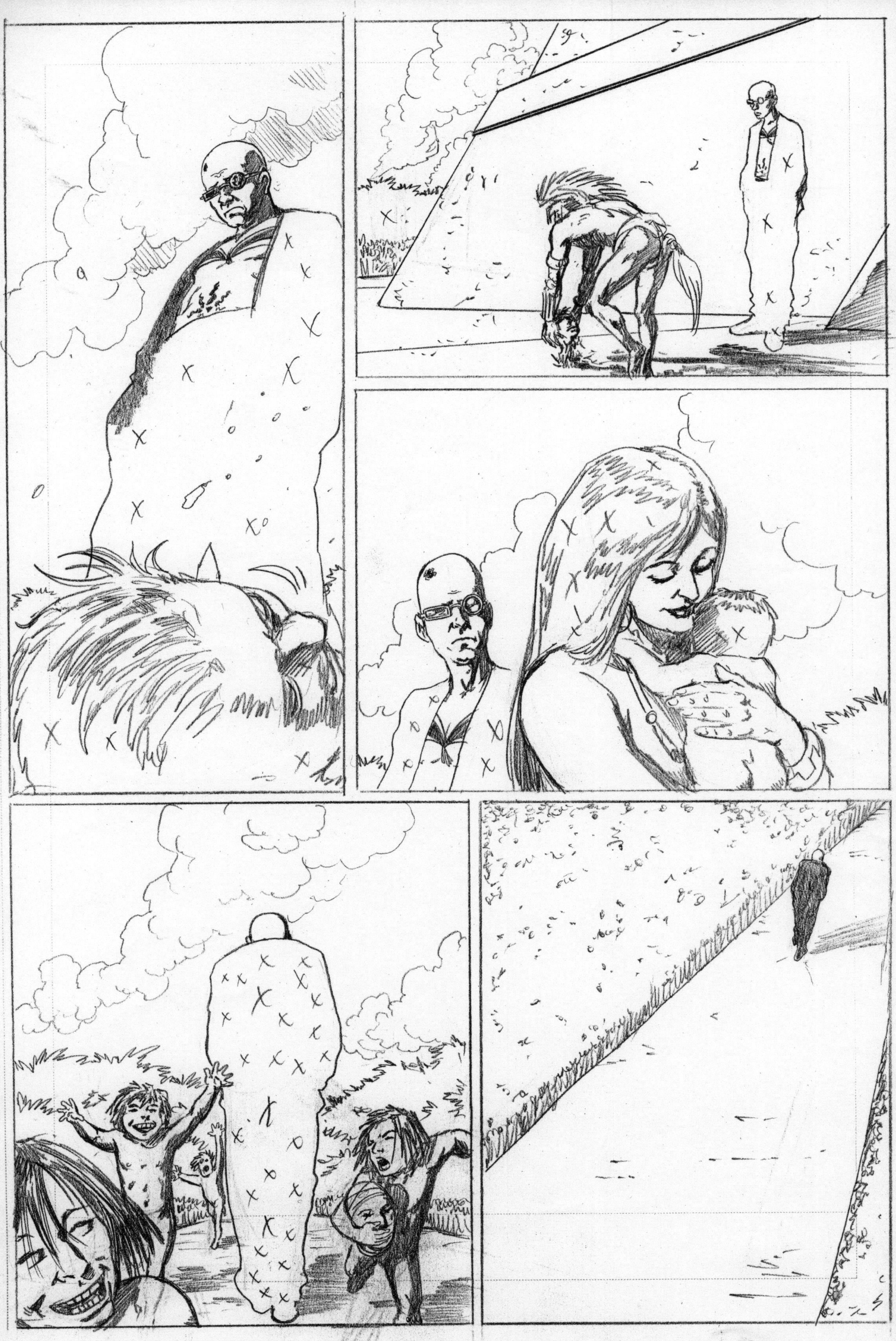

## PAGE EIGHTEEN

**Pic 1:**
CUT: to a City street. Two young men in Chairman Mao uniforms kiss passionately in the outside world. We did an image like this in #1, it was an element of a panel on Page Fourteen, I think, during Spider's walk up the Print District... City people mill past, anyway, most not taking any notice... MONOCHROME IT....

TYPED CAPTION:                              WILBUR DAIGH MILLS BOULEVARD, NEAR THE NO
                                            QUESTIONS ASKED™ REFUGE:

**Pic 2:**
Repeat image, in FULL COLOUR...

TYPED CAPTION:                              You see this more and more. Dissenters
                                            in Reservation communities who somehow
                                            find a way to go over the wall.

**Pic 3:**
The two men continue to embrace, just happy in each other... and on the street in the background, we see a man-drawn rickshaw pull up, Spider riding in the back.

TYPED CAPTION:                              Some of them were volunteers. They have
                                            no memory of the City.

TYPED CAPTION:                              Sympathizers will get them to a refuge,
                                            or to black-bag operations like the
                                            Toolbox Doctors who will remove their
                                            memory locks.

**Pic 4:**
With Spider: showing him looking on as the two men break it up, and hold hands, moving off...

TYPED CAPTION:                              The rest were born in Reservations, and
                                            have no knowledge of the City, locked or
                                            otherwise.

TYPED CAPTION:                              Some end up like Revivals, brain-shocked.

**Pic 5:**
... and the soft old bastard Spider Jerusalem allows himself a small smile.

TYPED CAPTION:                              Some are just happy to be able to be in
                                            love.

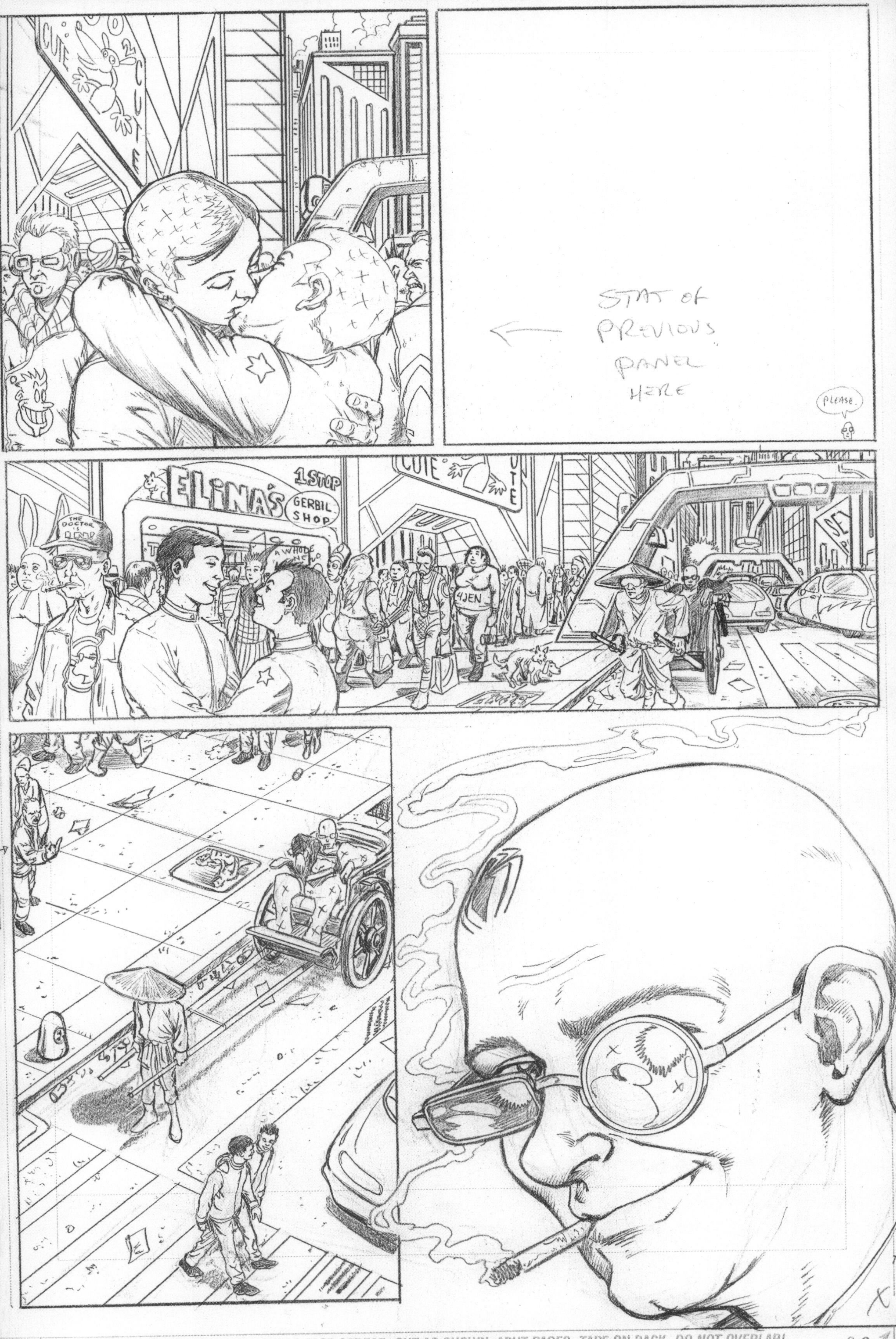
CUTE 2 CUTE
STAT OF PREVIOUS PANEL HERE
PLEASE.
ELiNA'S
1 STOP
GERBIL-SHOP
THE DOCTOR IS IN!
4JEN
CUTE

INSTRUCTIONS FOR DOUBLE-PAGE SPREAD: CUT AS SHOWN, ABUT PAGES, TAPE ON BACK. *DO NOT OVERLAP!*

#9

## PAGE NINETEEN

**Pic 1:**
CUT: to Spider walking through a vast field of metallic flowers. Some are taller than others, and bud chromed human internal organs off their branches like fruit. The sky behind him is reddish-orange, almost Martian in its pale alienness. He's smoking.

TYPED CAPTION:                    `THE FARSIGHT COMMUNITY`

**Pic 2:**
Fat, penile, steel bugs hover around the flowers, jamming their heads between the petals. Silver dust tumbles from the stamens like fairy dust. Spider stops, smokes his cigarette and watches.

TYPED CAPTION:                    `I went to the "special, different"`
`Reservation St.Exupery recommended to my`
`attention.`

**Pic 3:**
One fat metal dick-bug wobbles upward and away from a plant, towards Spider — it deploys several pairs of silver-leaf wings to get lift. He eyes it untrustingly...

TYPED CAPTION:                    `I don't know if it quite qualifies as a`
`Reservation. A Reservation preserves`
`past cultures.`

**Pic 4:**
... and it sprays him with sparkling dust from a wet-looking nozzle mounted on its belly. Spider tries to wave the stuff away with his hand...

TYPED CAPTION:                    `The Farsight Community is a culture yet`
`to happen.`

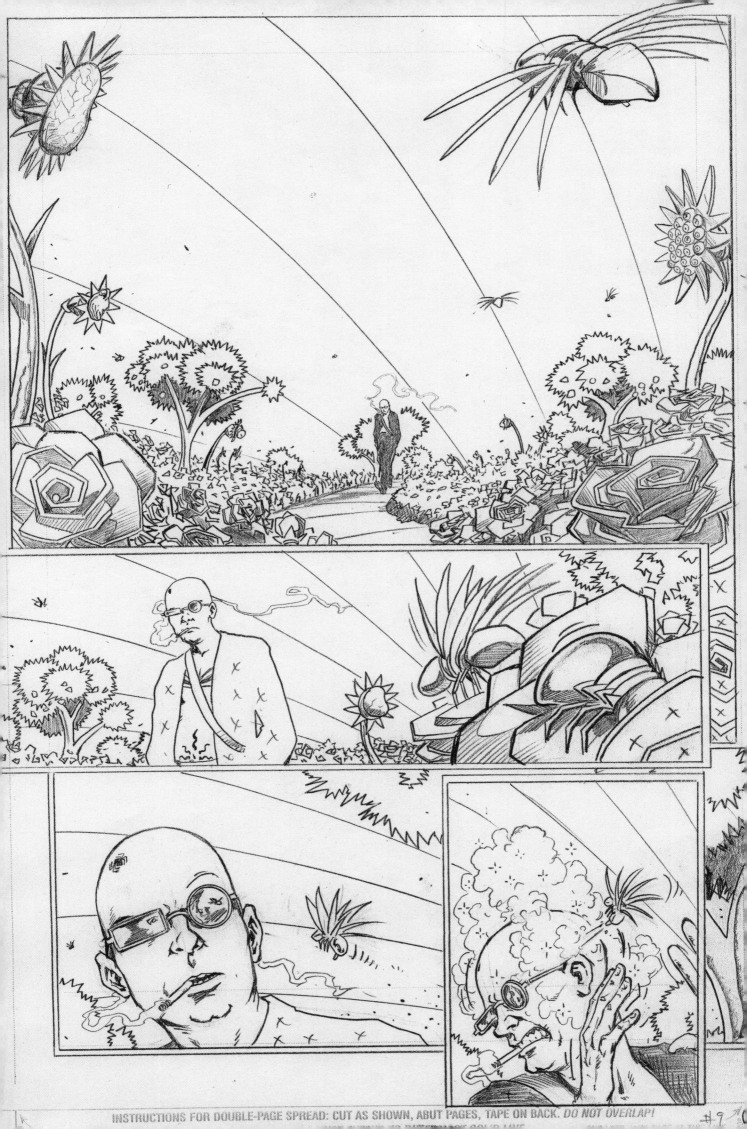

**Pic 1:**

... he takes his shades off, it's in his eyes, his mouth and nose, and he tries to wipe it off...

*(NO DIALOGUE)*

**Pic 2:**

And this panel is full of an EFFECT that Darick & Nathan had probably better plan out together.

A colorful mass of images, whose elements include childbirth, violence, steel crops, a weird organic spacecraft taking off, television screens, several weird looking chunks of technology... we'll see why we're seeing all this in a minute, and it'll give you a handle on how to play this...

*(NO DIALOGUE)*

**Pic 3:**

Find Spider sitting on his arse in the field, eyes wide, shocked and dizzy. A shadow falls across him from the left.

FROM LEFT:                    YOU OKAY?

SPIDER:                       I **THINK** SO. IT WAS LIKE WASHING DOWN A
                              BUCKET OF PEYOTE WITH A VATFUL OF
                              ABSINTHE... WHAT WAS IT?

**Pic 4:**

We pan round to see the figure standing over Spider. It's a man, just about. Naked, sexless, wearing plugged-in extra steel-like internal organs in a ring of bags around his stomach, all belted in. Nozzles cluster around his throat. One of his hands is a bush of thin extensions. The skin of his legs is rubber from the mid-shin down, contoured like a tyre. He smiles, revealing plastic teeth with no seperation between them – just hard sharp white bars. We'll call him JOHN, just because I can't think of anything else.

JOHN:                         THE NEWS.

JOHN:                         YOU JUST FOUND OUT WHAT'S HAPPENED IN
                              FARSIGHT OVER THE LAST MONTH.

JOHN:                         INFORMATIONAL POLLEN.

**Pic 5:**

Spider sits and scowls, drawing on his cigarette, unhappy.

SPIDER:                       I-POLLEN WAS BANNED TWENTY YEARS AGO.
                              THEY PROVED THE STUFF BUILT UP IN YOUR
                              SYNAPSE GAPS, BROUGHT ON AN ALZHEIMER'S-
                              LIKE EFFECT.

SPIDER:                       HAVE YOU DOOMED MY BRAIN, YOU WEIRD-
                              LOOKING FUCKER?

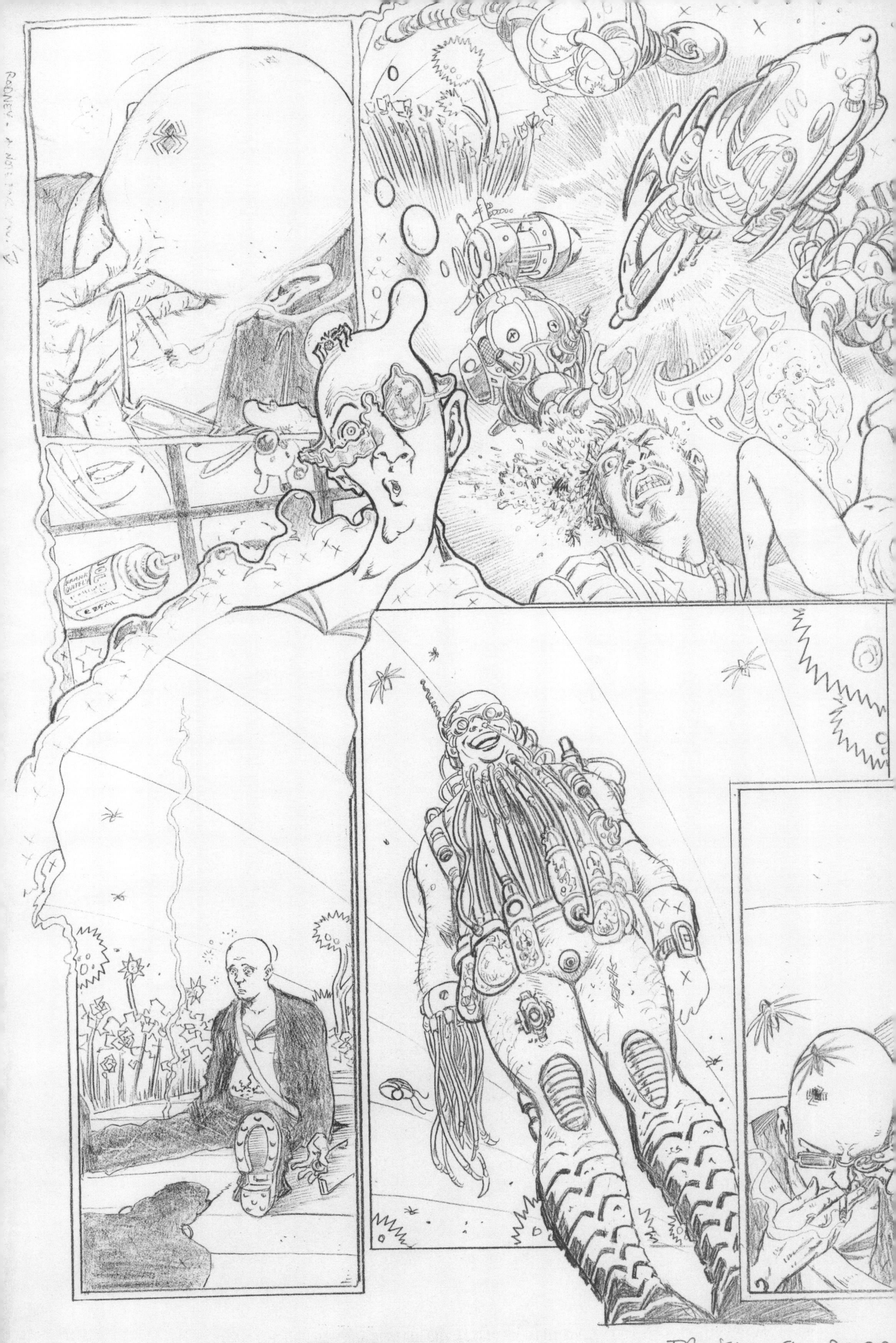

TRANSMET 9 PG 20

## PAGE TWENTY-ONE

**Pic 1:**
John shrugs, extending his real hand to pull Spider up. Spider complies, unhappily.

JOHN: IT'S NOT BANNED HERE. WE THINK WE LICKED THAT PROBLEM, ANYWAY.

JOHN: WE DON'T BAN TECHNOLOGY IN FARSIGHT. WE EXAMINE IT THROUGH USE.

**Pic 2:**
Spider, pulled up, makes a sick little joke. John shrugs this off too. Nothing seems to bother him much.

SPIDER: HEH. HOW'S THE DEATH RATE?

JOHN: PRETTY HIGH, ACTUALLY. BUT WE MANAGE.

SPIDER: I WAS JOKING.

**Pic 3:**
John turns the other way, pointing off panel towards the horizon there. While John's back is turned, Spider grabs one of the bugs out of the air and violently stubs his cigarette out on it.

JOHN: IT'S NOT A JOKE HERE. IT'S THE MEASURE OF OUR SUCCESS; AND, THEREFORE, THE SUCCESS OF THE HUMAN RACE AS A VIABLE SPECIES IN THE FUTURE.

JOHN: THIS IS THE TESTBED FOR HUMANS. WITHIN THESE WALLS, WE SEEK TO MAKE **HUMAN** WORK, WITHOUT ALL THE SHORT-CUTS AND GET-OUTS, LIKE GOING FOGLET.

JOHN: LOOK. IT'S MY **CHILDREN**.

**Pic 4:**
A couple of dozen feet over the surface of the field, three things float towards us. Children, maybe ten years old. Bloated guts, no legs, arms encrusted with chrome coral and gently-waving silver fronds. From the truncated ends of their torsos run undulating frameworks of thin metal, like live scaffolding, tapering off at their leisure into points, forming weird tails. They look like alien fish, sculling through the air...

TYPED CAPTION: They talk to each other using neutrino senders where their large intestine should be. They seal themselves against vacuum and have sex via bacteria.

TYPED CAPTION: They try to learn the lessons of the future before it arrives.

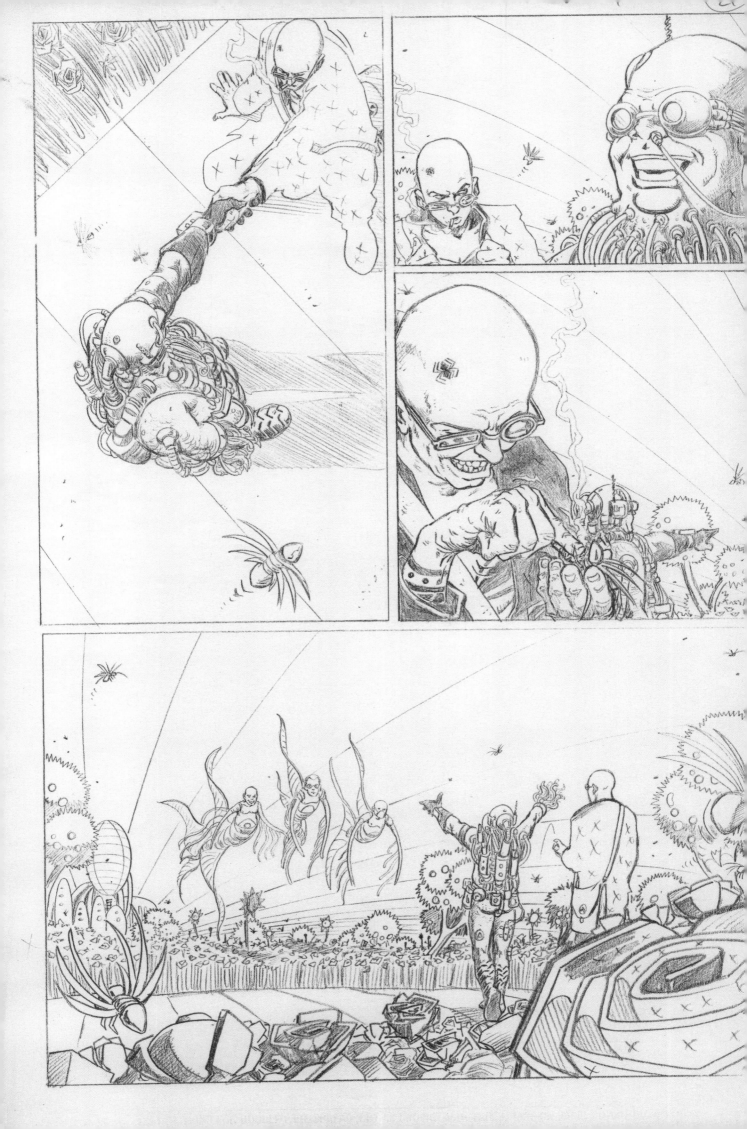

**PAGE TWENTY-TWO**

**Pic 1:**
The PUPIN GROVE signage and building...

FROM BUILDINGS:                         YOU DIDN'T ANSWER THE PHONE TO ROYCE
                                                       BECAUSE YOU'RE GOING TO JOIN A **NUNNERY**?

**Pic 2:**
Open on a miserable Channon, dressed in black, hair limp and eyes dead, lifelessly handing us a pamphlet. The back of it faces us – a picture of a nun and the tagline ARE YOU BEATEN? **GREAT!**

CHANNON:                                 I'VE HAD **ENOUGH**, SPIDER. I'M SICK OF BEING
                                                       YOUR ASSISTANT, I'M SICK OF DREAMING ABOUT
                                                       ZIANG EVERY NIGHT –

CHANNON:                                 – I'M SICK OF THIS FUCKING CITY AND THE WAY IT
                                                       JUMPS UP AND BITES YOU ON THE ASS EVERY FIVE
                                                       MINUTES.

**Pic 3:**
Spider yells at Channon, spittle flying over the pamphlet she just gave him – we see the front of the thing, he's got the back of it facing him – we can read the title, **Convent of Our Lady Of The Little Death.**

SPIDER:                                     OH, BULLSHIT! WHAT ABOUT YOUR FUTURE?
                                                       WHAT ABOUT BEER AND DRUGS? AND WHAT
                                                       ABOUT **SEX**, CHANNON? YOU'LL NEVER GET LAID
                                                       AGAIN!

**Pic 4:**
Channon hasn't got the strength to argue; she turns her back on his and wanders away, waving a hand in a gesture of So What?

CHANNON:                                 WHAT **ABOUT** SEX? IT'S A CONVENT. I'LL
                                                       BECOME A BRIDE OF CHRIST. I'LL GET PLENTY.

SPIDER:                                     THAT'S NOT WHAT "BRIDE OF CHRIST" MEANS AND
                                                       YOU **KNOW** IT –

**Pic 5:**
She pauses, looks over her shoulder at us weakly.

CHANNON:                                 BRIDE OF **CHRIST**, SPIDER.

CHANNON:                                 **FRED** CHRIST.

**Pic 6:**
Little black panel, containing the usual 3-eyed smiley at the bottom.

VOICE (NO TAIL):                      OH, NO.

**END**

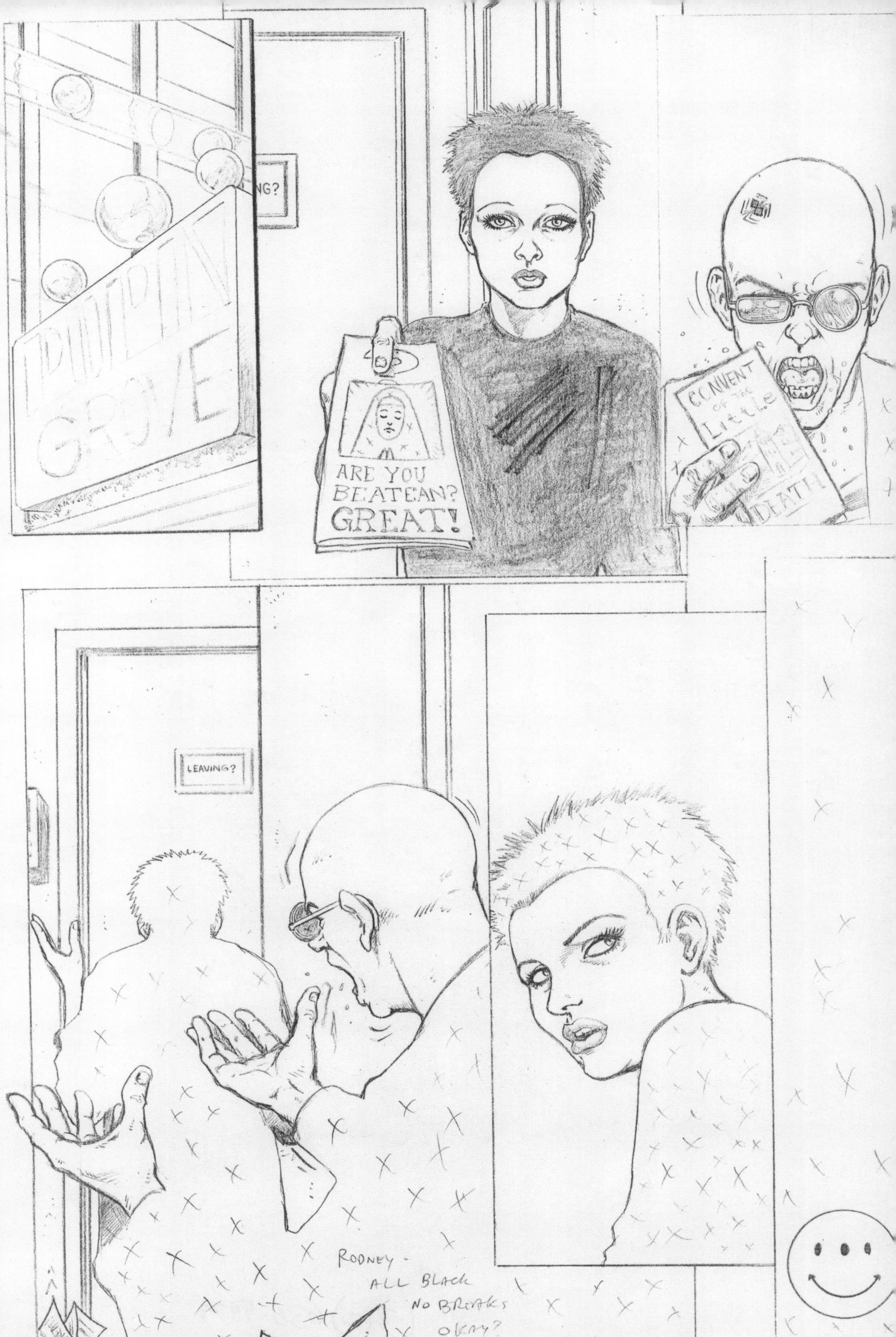

GROVE
NG?
ARE YOU BEATEAN? GREAT!
CONVENT of the Little
DEATH
LEAVING?
RODNEY - ALL BLACK NO BREAKS OKAY?

*The following pages showcase cover art created by Darick Robertson for the original trade paperback editions of TRANSMETROPOLITAN, which were released between 1998 and 2004. They include the covers from Volumes 2-10 – the first edition of Volume 1 used art from an interior story page as its cover image.*

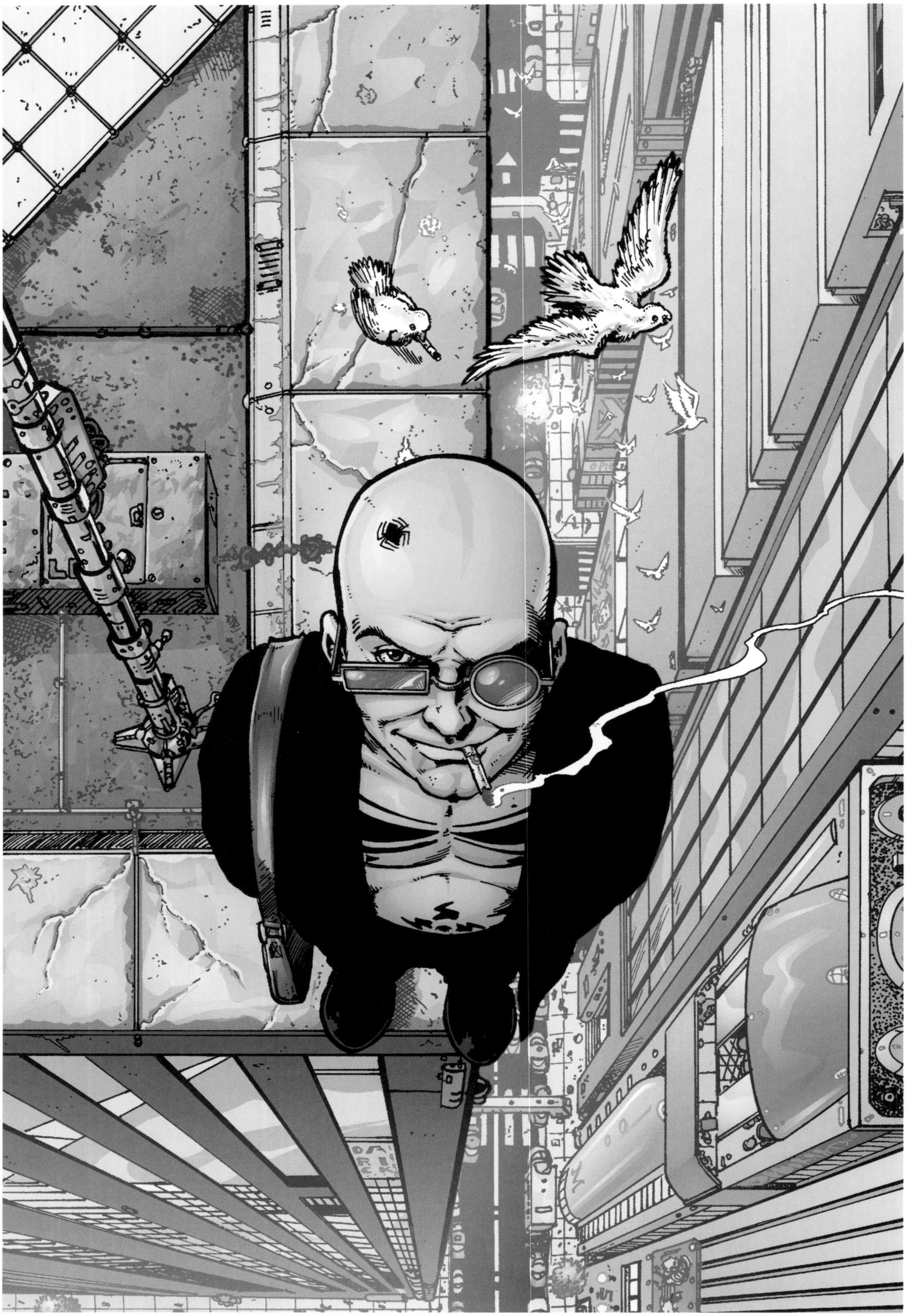

VOLUME 2: LUST FOR LIFE

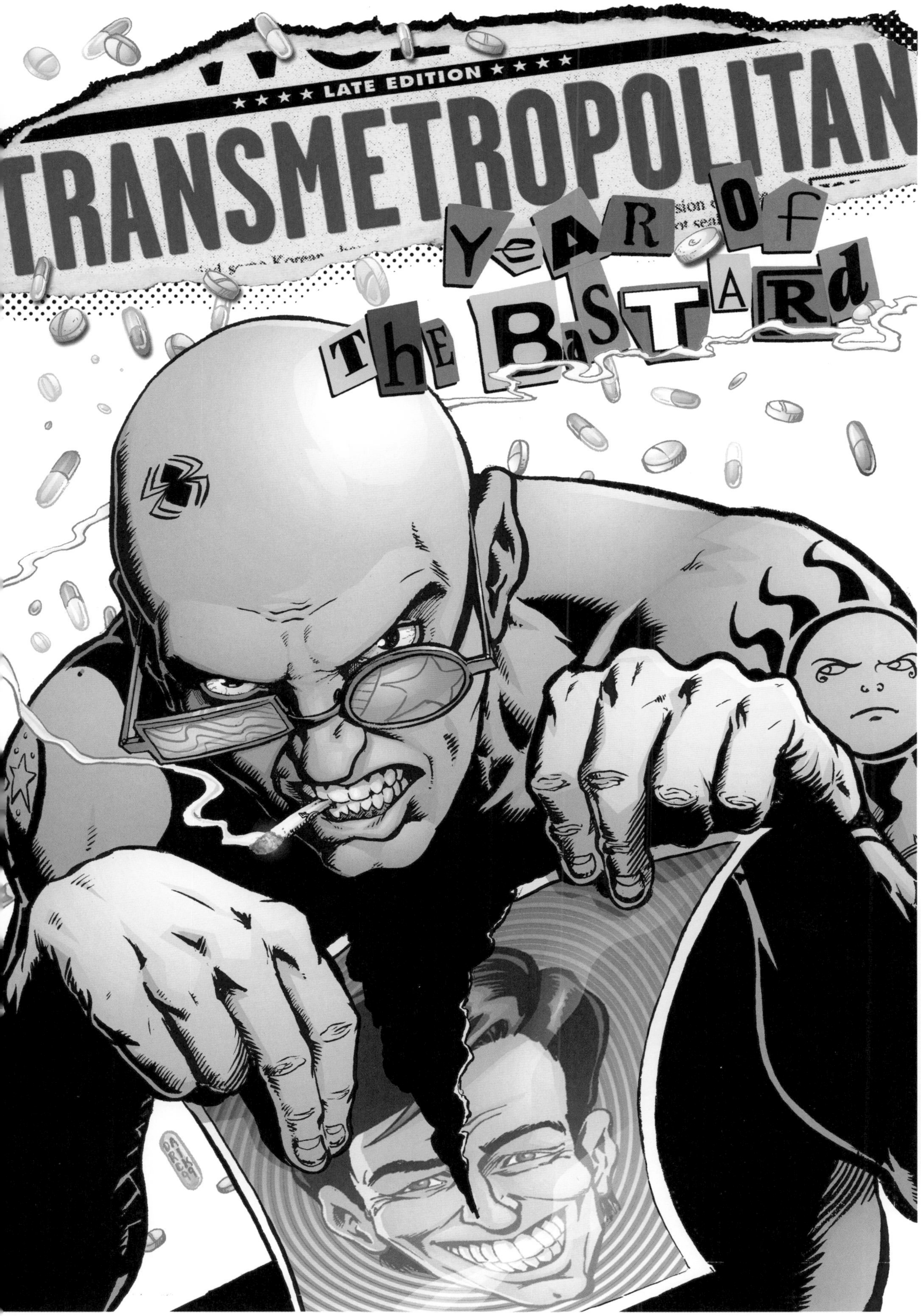
★ ★ ★ ★ LATE EDITION ★ ★ ★ ★
TRANSMETROPOLITAN
YEAR OF THE BASTARD

VOLUME 3: YEAR OF THE BASTARD

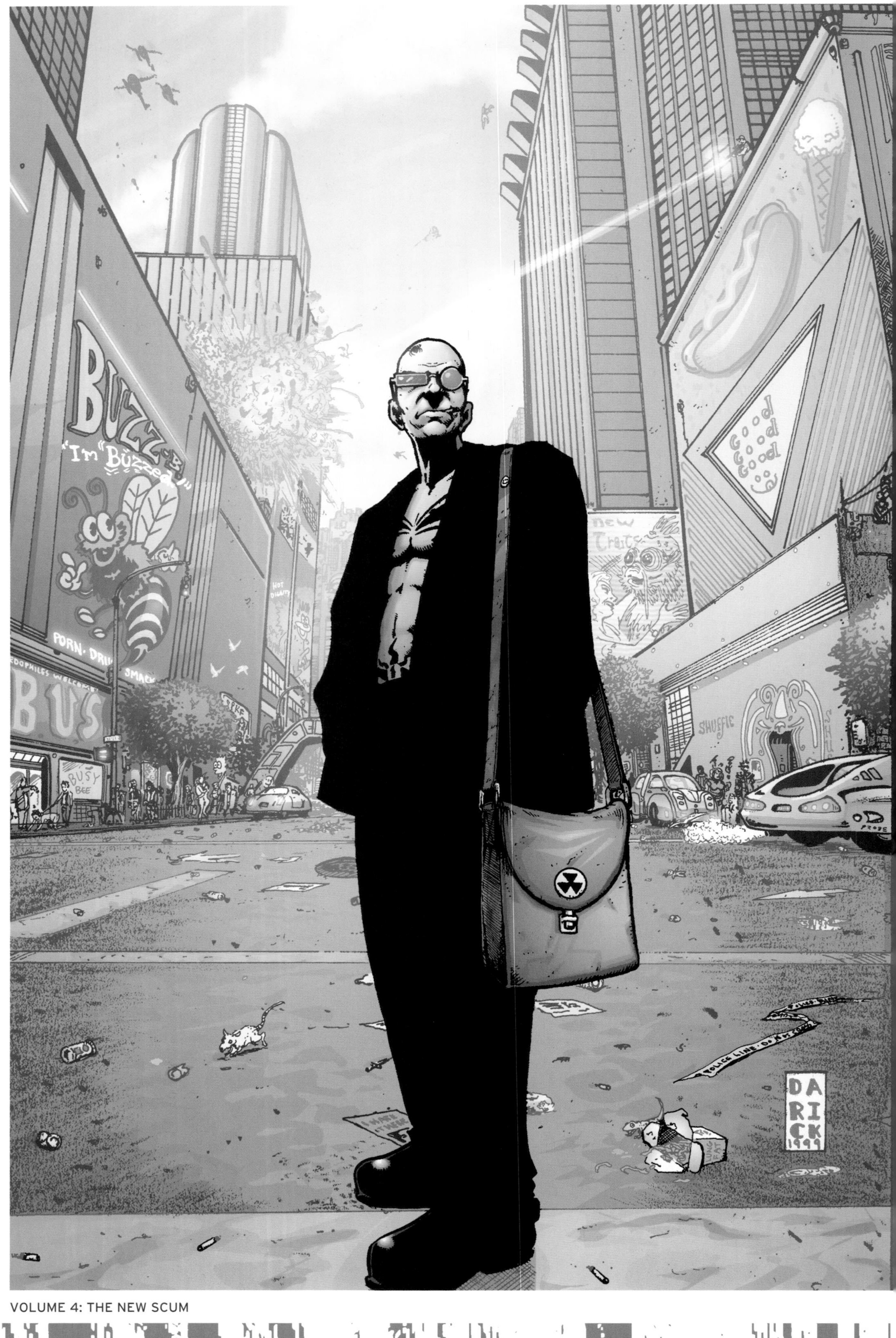

BUZZ
"I'm Buzzed"
BUSY BEE
Good
Good
Good!
DARICK 1999


VOLUME 4: THE NEW SCUM

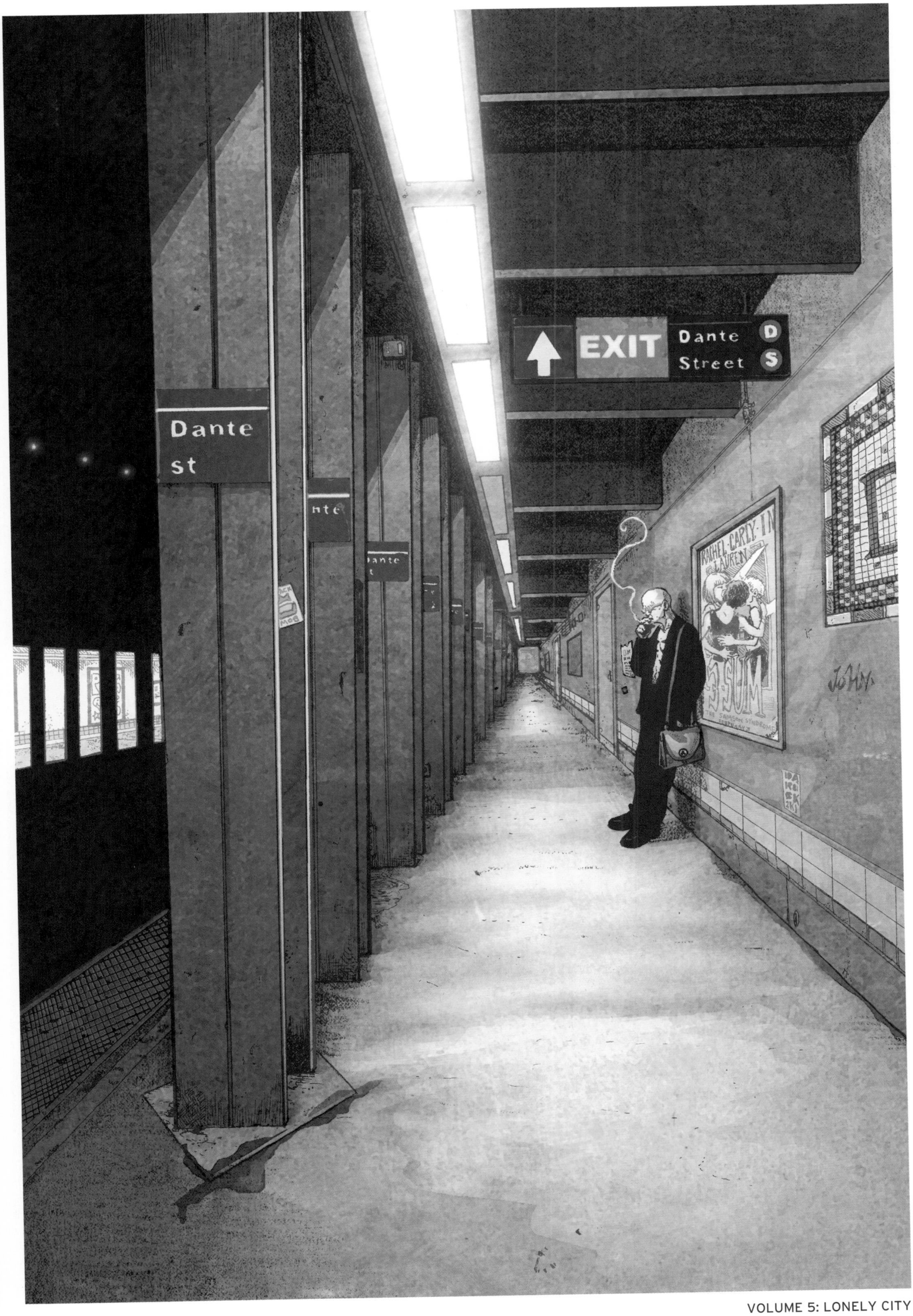

Dante
st
EXIT
Dante Street
D
S
RACHEL CARLY IN
LAUREN
3-SUM
THE SAMSON SYNDROME


VOLUME 5: LONELY CITY

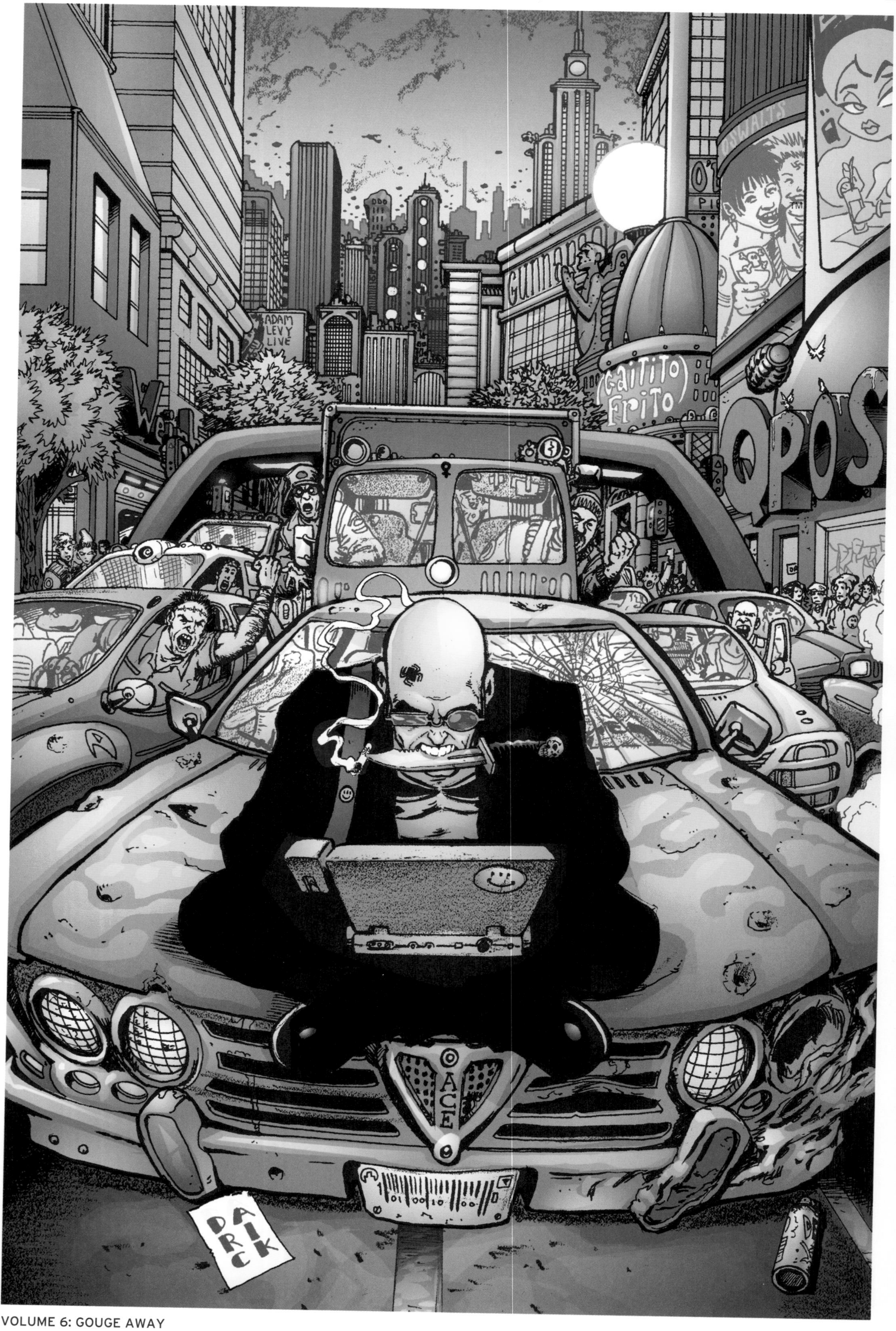
ADAM
LEVY
LIVE
ACE

VOLUME 6: GOUGE AWAY

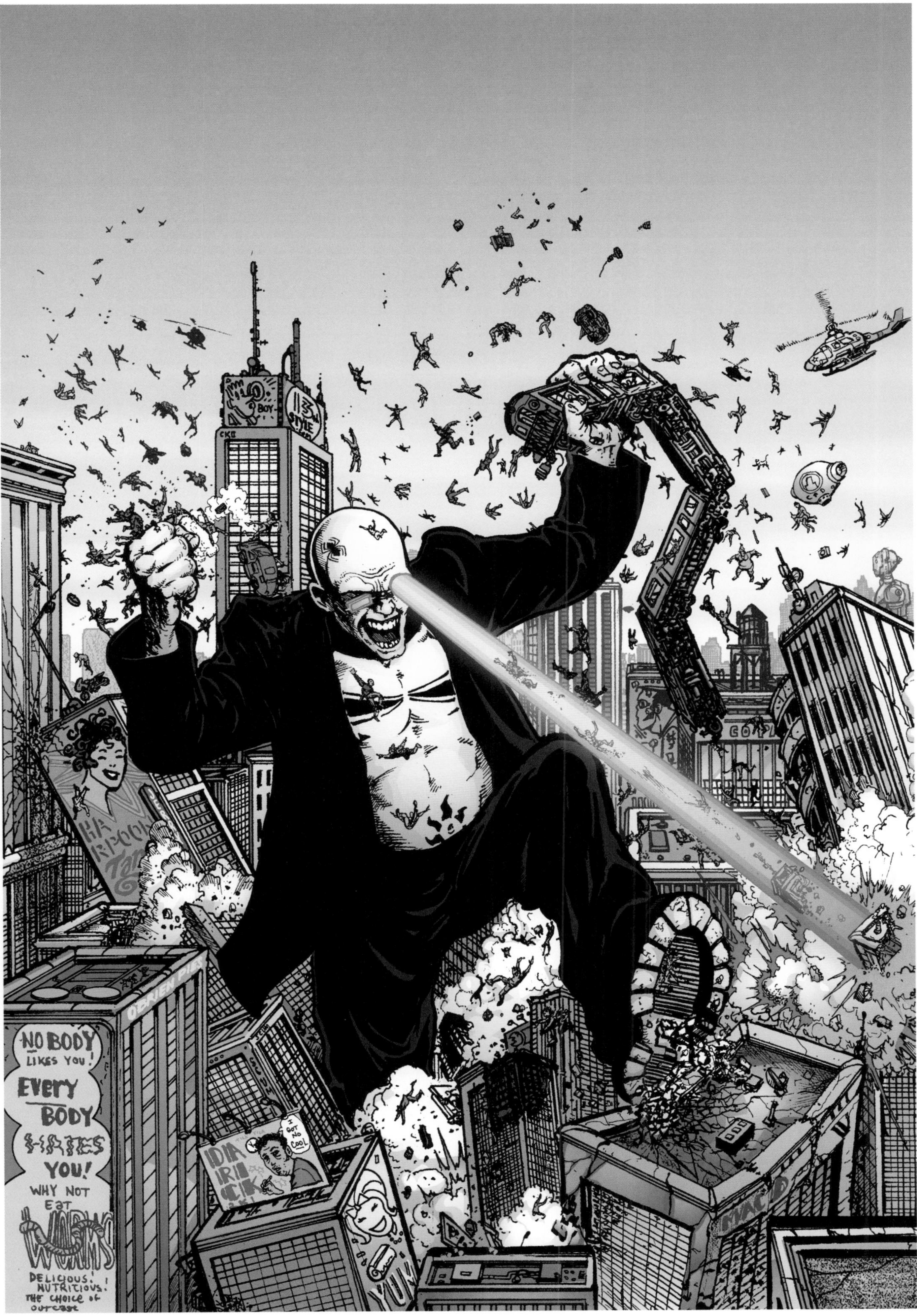
O'BRIEN PIES
NOBODY LIKES YOU!
EVERY BODY HATES YOU!
WHY NOT EAT WORMS
DELICIOUS! NUTRITIOUS!
THE CHOICE OF OUTCAST
I GOT NO COOL


VOLUME 7: SPIDER'S THRASH

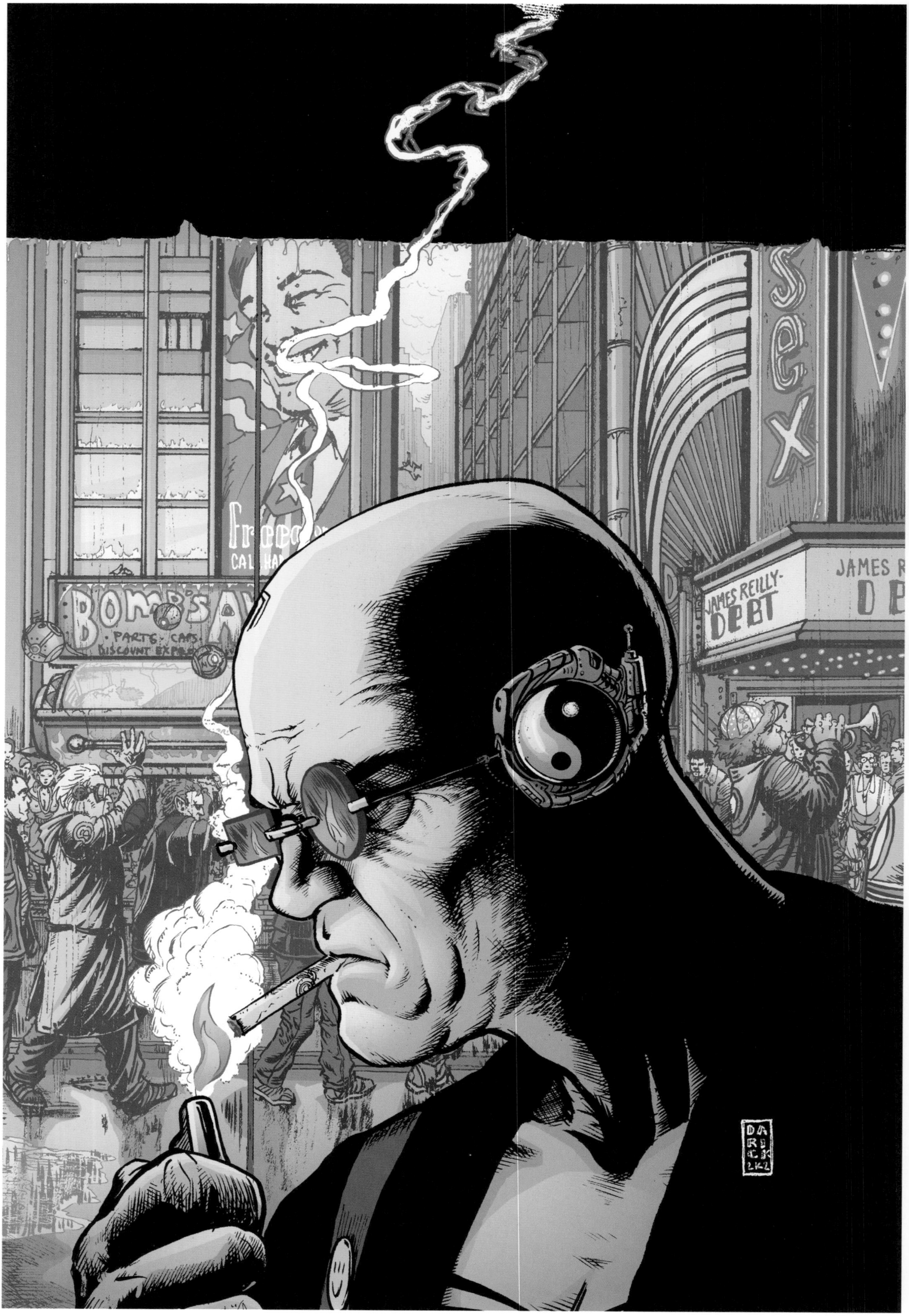
sex
JAMES REILLY-
DEBT
PARTS CARS

VOLUME 8: DIRGE

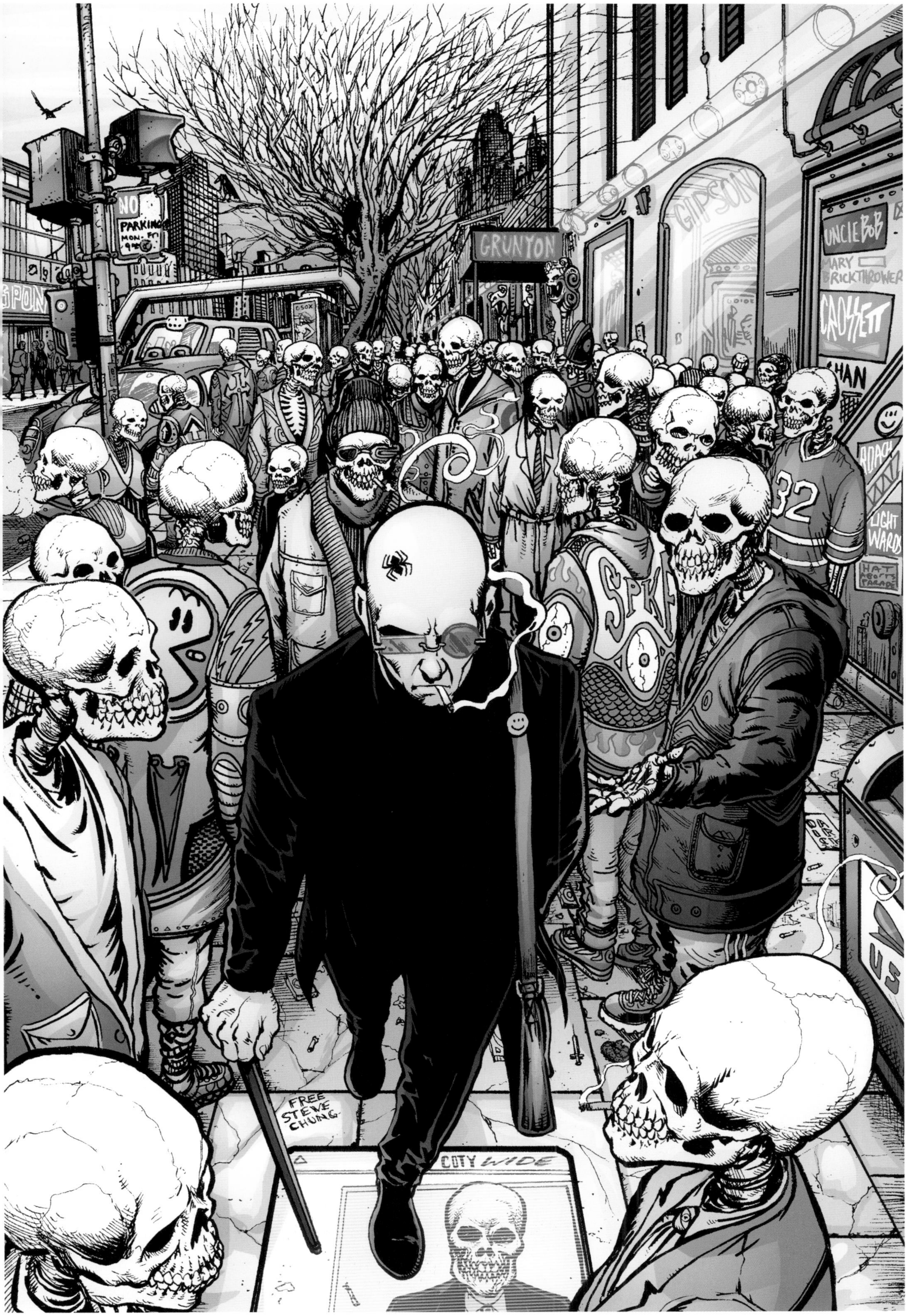
NO PARKING
GRUNYON
UNCLE BOB
MARY BRICKTHROWER
CROSSETT
CHAN
32
FREE STEVE CHUNG
CITY WIDE

VOLUME 9: THE CURE

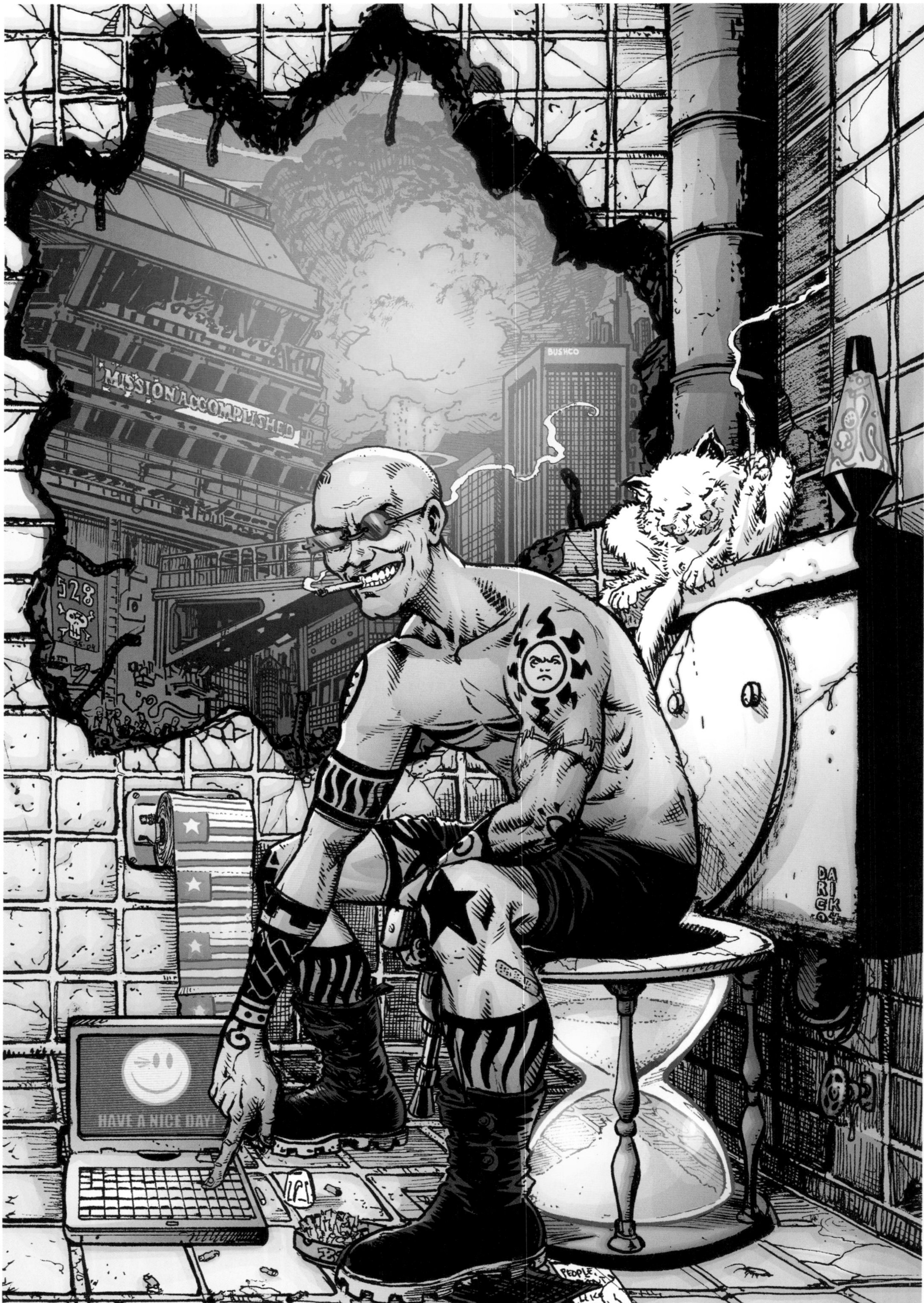
"MISSION ACCOMPLISHED"
BUSHCO
528
HAVE A NICE DAY!
DARICK O4
PEOPLE

VOLUME 10: ONE MORE TIME

**Warren Ellis** is the creator and writer of a host of critically acclaimed and award-winning graphic novels, including TRANSMETROPOLITAN, THE AUTHORITY, PLANETARY, RED, GLOBAL FREQUENCY, ORBITER, *Ultimate Fantastic Four*, *Ultimate Galactus*, *Ministry of Space*, *Gravel*, *FreakAngels* and *Fell*. Outside of comics he has also written screenplays, video games, nonfiction books, short stories and novels, and he maintains a nigh-ubiquitous online presence through every portal the Internet has to offer. His celebrated life and career are the subjects of several books as well as a documentary film entitled *Warren Ellis: Captured Ghosts*, released in 2012. He lives in southeast England with his girlfriend and daughter.

At the age of seventeen **Darick Robertson** wrote and drew eleven issues of his first comic book creation, *Space Beaver*, paving the way for assignments from more established publishers like Malibu, Innovation and DC. After a series of gigs at Marvel – including the miniseries *Spider-Man: The Power of Terror* and a lengthy run on *The New Warriors* – Robertson joined forces with writer Warren Ellis for Acclaim's 1997 *Solar, Man of the Atom* one-shot, which led directly to the pair's celebrated co-creation of TRANSMETROPOLITAN for DC/Helix/Vertigo. Robertson returned to Marvel in 2001 with the Garth Ennis-written Marvel Max miniseries *Fury*, and in 2002 he relaunched the company's flagship franchise *Wolverine* with writer Greg Rucka. Four years later he reunited with Ennis to bring the world *The Boys*, which originated at DC/WildStorm before finding its permanent home at Dynamite Entertainment. His newest work can be found in Black Mask Studio's *Ballistic* and Image Comics' *Oliver*, which he co-created with writers Adam Egypt Mortimer and Gary Whitta, respectively. Robertson lives in Napa, California, with his wife Meredith and their sons Owen and Andrew. When he's not drawing comics, which is almost all the time, he creates custom action figures, writes music, sings, and plays guitar.

**Rodney Ramos** has been a professional comic book illustrator for more than 25 years. His inks have graced over 500 issues of such titles as *The Amazing Spider-Man*, *X-Men Unlimited*, *Iron Man*, GREEN LANTERN, BATMAN, WONDER WOMAN, JUSTICE LEAGUE OF AMERICA, COUNTDOWN, 52, and the critically acclaimed TRANSMETROPOLITAN with Warren Ellis and Darick Robertson. Ramos began his career at Marvel Comics making art corrections under the direction of the legendary John Romita, Sr. as one of "Romita's Raiders." He contributed pencils to a wide variety of Marvel titles – including *Psi-Force*, *What If...?*, *Marvel Comics Presents*, *Thundercats*, and *Conan* – before moving more exclusively into inking. Over the years he has also drawn and inked for DC, Valiant, Malibu, Acclaim, Disney Publishing, and Neal Adams's Continuity Comics. His most recent work has been on Legendary Pictures Comics' *The Tower Chronicles: Geisthawk* with Matt Wagner and Simon Bisley.

**Keith Aiken** has worked as an inker for DC on TRANSMETROPOLITAN, THE INVISIBLES, TEMPEST, and various Superman and Green Lantern titles. His other comics credits include Marvel's Spider-Man titles, *The Uncanny X-Men*, *The Silver Surfer*, *The Fantastic Four*, *Ghost Rider*, *X-Men: Liberators*, and Mirage Studios' *Teenage Mutant Ninja Turtles*. A lifelong fan of Japanese monster movies, Aiken has provided audio commentaries and other content for several Godzilla/kaiju Blu-ray and DVD releases and has served as the co-editor of the website *SciFi Japan*. He has also worked as a storyboard and production artist for Sony Pictures and Activision.